PSYCHOLOGY
IN YOUR LIFE

THIRD EDITION

PSYCHOLOGY
IN YOUR LIFE

SARAH GRISON
Parkland College

MICHAEL S. GAZZANIGA
University of California, Santa Barbara

W. W. Norton & Company
NEW YORK · LONDON

W. W. Norton & Company has been independent since its founding in 1923, when William Warder Norton and Mary D. Herter Norton first published lectures delivered at the People's Institute, the adult education division of New York City's Cooper Union. The firm soon expanded its program beyond the Institute, publishing books by celebrated academics from America and abroad. By midcentury, the two major pillars of Norton's publishing program—trade books and college texts—were firmly established. In the 1950s, the Norton family transferred control of the company to its employees, and today—with a staff of four hundred and a comparable number of trade, college, and professional titles published each year—W. W. Norton & Company stands as the largest and oldest publishing house owned wholly by its employees.

Editor: Sheri L. Snavely
Electronic Media Editor: Kaitlin Coats
Developmental Editor and Project Editor: Kurt Wildermuth
Manuscript Editor: Ellen Lohman
Assistant Editor: Eve Sanoussi
Associate Media Editor: Victoria Reuter
Media Project Editor: Danielle Belfiore
Media Assistant: Allison Smith
Marketing Manager: Ashley Sherwood
Production Manager: Sean Mintus
Photo Editor/Researcher: Patricia Marx
Director of College Permissions: Megan Schindel
Permissions Associate: Elizabeth Trammell
Art Director: Lissi Sigillo
Design Director: Rubina Yeh
Designer: Faceout Studio
Composition: Six Red Marbles
Manufacturing: LSC Kendallville
Managing Editor, College: Marian Johnson
Managing Editor, College Digital Media: Kim Yi

Library of Congress Cataloging-in-Publication Data

Names: Grison, Sarah, author. | Gazzaniga, Michael S., author.
Title: Psychology in your life / Sarah Grison, Michael S. Gazzaniga.
Description: Third edition. | New York, NY : W. W. Norton & Company, [2019] |
Includes bibliographical references and index.
Identifiers: LCCN 2018026977 | ISBN 978-0-393-64447-0 (pbk.)
Subjects: LCSH: Developmental psychology. | Psychology.
Classification: LCC BF713 .G75 2019 | DDC 155—dc23 LC record available at https://lccn.loc.gov/
2018026977

W. W. Norton & Company, Inc., 500 Fifth Avenue, New York, N.Y. 10110
www.wwnorton.com

W. W. Norton & Company, Ltd., 15 Carlisle Street, London W1D 3BS

3 4 5 6 7 8 9 0

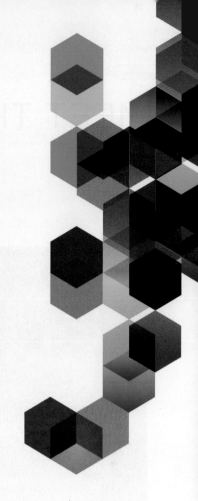

For all teachers who inspire
others, especially
Brian Dill, Ken Kotovsky, and Steve Tipper

With gratitude,
Lilli, Emmy, Garth, Dante,
Rebecca, and Leonardo

MEET THE AUTHORS

SARAH GRISON is an Associate Professor of Psychology at Parkland College and a Coordinator for the college's Center for Excellence in Teaching and Learning. She brings more than 20 years of psychology teaching experience to *Psychology in Your Life*. Sarah regularly teaches introductory psychology both face to face and online, as well as classes in human sexuality and in child and adolescent development. In addition, Sarah regularly teaches underprepared and first-semester college students in a First Year Experience course. Sarah uses psychological research as the basis of her own empirical classroom studies to examine students' attitudes, skills, performance, and learning. At the Center for Excellence in Teaching and Learning, Sarah provides courses and workshops for teachers in course design, pedagogy, and assessment, all aimed at helping students have excellent educational experiences. Sarah is a certified Teacher-Scholar who was recognized each year on the University of Illinois List of Excellent Teachers. She has won the University of Illinois Provost's Initiative for Teaching Advancement Award and the Association for Psychological Science Award for Teaching and Public Understanding of Psychological Science. She is a member of the American Psychological Association (Divisions 3 and 15); the Society for Teaching of Psychology; the Association for Psychological Science; the International Mind, Brain, and Education Society; the American Educational Research Association; the American Association of Community Colleges; the Illinois Community College Faculty Association. She is also an APA Community College Teacher Affiliate (PT@CC).

MICHAEL S. GAZZANIGA is Distinguished Professor and Director of the Sage Center for the Study of the Mind at the University of California, Santa Barbara. In his career, he has introduced thousands of students to psychology and cognitive neuroscience. He received a PhD from the California Institute of Technology, where he worked with Roger Sperry and had primary responsibility for initiating human split-brain research. He has carried out extensive studies on both subhuman primate and human behavior and cognition. He established centers for cognitive neuroscience at Cornell Medical School and Dartmouth College, and he established the Center for Neuroscience at UC Davis. He is the founding editor of the *Journal of Cognitive Neuroscience* and also a founder of the Cognitive Neuroscience Society. For 20 years he directed the Summer Institute in Cognitive Neuroscience, and he serves as editor in chief of the major reference text *The Cognitive Neurosciences*. He was a member of the President's Council on Bioethics from 2001 to 2009. He is a member of the American Academy of Arts and Sciences, the National Academy of Medicine, and the National Academy of Sciences. He has written many notable books, including, most recently, *Psychological Science*, 6e; *Cognitive Neuroscience*, 5e; and *The Consciousness Instinct: Unraveling the Mystery of How the Brain Makes the Mind*.

CONTENTS IN BRIEF

MISSION OF *PSYCHOLOGY IN YOUR LIFE*

Welcome to *Psychology in Your Life*! Whether you are a teacher or a student, this book will be a perfect fit for you. That's because, unlike any other introductory psychology textbook authors, we believe that teaching, learning, and improving are all interconnected. Because of this, we have created every aspect of the textbook, all of the teaching support tools, and the embedded assessments to ensure that they work together seamlessly to create great educational experiences. We achieve this goal for *Psychology in Your Life* by focusing on three ideas: 1. Helping both teachers and students achieve educational excellence; 2. Using empirical research to develop the best teaching and learning tools, and 3. Ensuring an inclusive approach to the text, teaching tools, and assessment materials to honor all teachers and students.

Helping Teachers and Students Achieve Educational Excellence

As teachers, we have learned that we cannot help our students learn when they do not actively participate in the learning process. And we have experienced how difficult it is to support our students when we did not receive the resources we needed to create excellent educational experiences. So if great teaching and great learning go hand in hand, then *Psychology in Your Life* must support both teachers and students in achieving their goals while also providing ways to show that students are learning.

Supporting Teachers To support teachers, we developed several resources related to the Learning Goals in the textbook. These resources can be found in the Interactive Instructor's Guide (IIG), an online repository of resources available for adopters. The teaching support tools in the IIG include Enhanced Lecture PowerPoints with Active Learning slides, which engage students in class; Student Demonstration Videos, which help students participate in class activities; and Concept Videos, which explain key concepts in

TEACHING
Flexible next-generation support tools in sync with the mission and message of the book

LEARNING
Text and ebook that give students strategies for successfully learning course topics

IMPROVING
Interactive study and homework questions that engage students and help instructors see how students are learning

Psychology in Your Life is based on the idea that teaching, learning, and improving are all interconnected to create great educational experiences.

fun animations. For every chapter, Teaching Videos describe challenging concepts and provide ways to make them interesting. All of these teaching tools are designed for use in face-to-face, online, or hybrid learning environments. Together, they help teachers support their students in the best ways possible.

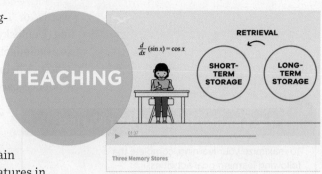

$$\frac{d}{dx}(\sin x) = \cos x$$

RETRIEVAL

SHORT-TERM STORAGE

LONG-TERM STORAGE

01:37

Three Memory Stores

Animated Concept Videos are just one of the best-practice teaching support tools that are an integral part of *Psychology in Your Life*.

Supporting Students   To support students, we designed the textbook and ebook to clearly state the Learning Goals. In addition, every chapter provides extra help through Learning Tips, which explain easy ways to think about and learn difficult concepts. Additional features in the textbook help students absorb the material by relating it to themselves: Has It Happened to You?, Try It Yourself, Using Psychology in Your Life, and Putting Psychology to Work. To check their mastery of the Learning Goals, students can answer the red Q questions throughout each chapter and the Self-Quizzes at the end of each chapter and check their answers in Appendix B.

Assessing Improvement   To ensure that students are learning, we provide many assessments related to the Learning Goals. For example, an adaptive online homework tool, InQuizitive, provides students and teachers with feedback about whether students have mastered the textbook concepts. We have also created several ways for teachers to get assessment data while in class, such as in-class videos in a learning management system, comprehension questions that can be used with a student response system, one-minute writing prompts, and topics for class discussions. Some of our assessment methods are particularly useful in online environments. When students view the Student Demonstration Videos or Concept Videos in a learning management system, they can answer our prepared quiz questions about what they saw. Finally, our team of trained teacher-researchers have written quiz and test questions that focus on whether students can remember and understand the concepts and also apply them to new situations. These questions are packaged into quizzes that teachers can give to students before class or after the material has been covered for a chapter. All of the quiz and test questions can be used either in class or online in a teacher's learning management system. When embedded into a teacher's class, these assessment tools provide well-rounded information that reveals whether students have mastered the material.

"The best aspects of *Psychology in Your Life* are the examples and real-life situations. They allowed me to relate different processes in psychology to my own life, which helped me learn better overall. Additionally, it was easy to read and understand, so the material itself was easier to understand."

—Gabrielle (Gabby) Wessels, introductory psychology student

Using Empirical Research to Develop the Best Teaching and Learning Tools

During our careers, we have seen vast growth in how much psychological research focuses on teaching and learning. As teachers and researchers, we realize how valuable this research is in creating tools that will work for teachers and students in face-to-face, online, and hybrid environments. Let's look at several specific ways that research has informed the creation of *Psychology in Your Life*. To learn more about these research-based strategies, and others, be sure to read the section below, Introducing the Third Edition, which describes our exciting, new *High-Impact Practices: A Teaching Guide for Psychology*.

Goal-Directed Active Reading Improves Learning   When we talk to college students about how they read textbooks, they often say "I don't," "I highlight key words," or "I reread." Yet research shows that these techniques do not support learning (Dunlosky et al., 2013). Unfortunately, students may never have been taught how to read effectively and may not have read textbooks in high school. So how can a textbook help students learn to read effectively? *Psychology in Your Life* uses several evidence-based approaches, including:

7.2 LEARNING GOAL ACTIVITIES

To maximize your learning, complete the following learning goal activities.

a. Understand all bold and italic terms by writing explanations of them in your own words.

b. Understand how attention affects memory by summarizing in your own words how selective attention influences the creation of a memory.

Learning Goal Activities at the start of each study unit are an evidence-based learning tool that supports reading *Psychology in Your Life*.

LEARNING

- Emphasizing goal-directed active learning (American Psychological Association, 2013) in each study unit and providing teachers with all the Learning Goals Activities so they can add their own goals.

- Embedding Learning Goal Activities in the textbook so students can write down their answers as they read (Nguyen & McDaniels, 2014) and supporting teachers in low-stakes grading of these writing assignments, which can help learning (Drabick, Weisberg, Paul, & Bubier, 2007; Elbow & Sorcinelli, 2005).

- Spreading questions across levels of Bloom's taxonomy of cognitive skills (Anderson et al., 2001; Pusateri, Halonen, Hill, & McCarthy, 2009) to improve students' ability to remember, understand, and apply material and clearly indicating these levels to teachers so they can add their own goals at different cognitive levels.

Active Engagement That Requires Deeper Processing Improves Learning
When we ask students what they do to learn material, they often reply, "I study." But when we press them on what they actually did, we often get blank stares. Luckily, learning is enhanced when students actively work with material and process information deeply (Bertsch & Pesta, 2014). In response, we designed *Psychology in Your Life* to entice students to work actively with materials through pedagogical features that encourage rich processing of information by:

"I have been teaching for over two decades, and this is the greatest textbook that I have ever used. I wish that I had used it sooner. But I guess you cannot appreciate filet mignon until you eat a lot of hamburger."

—Laura Scaletta, Niagara County Community College

- Asking students to relate new information to what they already know, that is, self-explanation (Dunlosky et al., 2013; Toukuhama-Espinosa, 2011), through textbook features—Has It Happened to You?, Try It Yourself, Using Psychology in Your Life, and Putting Psychology to Work—and providing teachers with Think-Pair-Share and Quick Write questions that relate to these features that can be used in class.

- Providing ways for students to explain particular concepts or phenomena, that is, elaborative interrogation (Dunlosky et al., 2013; Toukuhama-Espinosa, 2011), in the textbook's red Q questions, Evaluating Psychology in the Real World features, and The Methods of Psychology figures and providing teachers with materials to support in-class discussions about the research described in the text.

- Creating Student Demonstration Videos and Concept Videos that apply the material to new situations and that include embedded activities and questions for students, while also giving teachers engaging class materials in Enhanced Lecture PowerPoints with Active Learning slides to engage students in answering questions about these videos.

Practice Makes Perfect Most students want to get through studying as quickly as possible. In fact, most students think that studying is "one and done."

According to the research, however, students maximize their learning by distributing their studying over time (Cepeda et al., 2006). In addition, repeatedly practicing with material gives students multiple opportunities to learn it (Dunlosky et al., 2013). Indeed, reaccessing information during quizzes and tests enhances learning (Roediger & Karpicke, 2006; Pyc, Agarwal, & Roediger, 2014) and promotes transfer of the information to new involving the concepts (Carpenter, 2012). *Psychology in Your Life* uses all of these approaches to maximize learning by:

- Including low-stakes methods of repeatedly practicing with the material in the textbook, through red Q questions and Self-Quiz questions in each chapter, all of which have answers in Appendix B, so students can easily see what Learning Goals they have or have not mastered.
- Providing quiz questions, in the coursepack, related to features in the textbook and to the Student Demonstration Videos, which can be used either in class in a learning management system to reveal whether the concepts have been learned.
- Creating pre-lecture quizzes related to the Learning Goals, with learning benefits such as improved scores on later exams (Narloch, Garbin, & Turnage, 2006).
- Providing post-lecture quizzes and Test Bank items with multiple-choice and essay questions related to the Learning Goals, which can be used either in class or in a learning management system to provide repeated practice and show learning.

Interactive, Adaptive Online Homework Tools Are Beneficial to Students In these days of multimedia, it's no wonder that students get distracted easily and have a hard time paying attention when they study. Over and over again we have heard the same complaint: "Studying is boring!" Yet to learn, students must study actively over time. Luckily, adaptive online homework tools can help address these issues. In fact, students who get higher scores on online homework tools tend to also earn higher scores on exams (Regan, 2015). Because of these findings, we created InQuizitive to be an adaptive online homework tool that grabs attention and teaches effectively by:

- Designing it based on fun gaming techniques, because student interest is highly correlated with information retention (Naceur & Schiefele, 2005).
- Creating different types of interactive items—such as video questions, drag and drop, fill in the blank, and multiple choice—that require students to actively work with the concepts tied to specific Learning Goals (Bertsch & Pesta, 2014; Dunlosky et al., 2013).
- Ensuring InQuizitive supports learning through feedback provided to students (Pennebaker, Gosling, & Ferrell, 2013), where each student's mastery-based grade for a chapter can be imported automatically into a teacher's learning management system.
- Developing the most effective feedback for students by explaining how the student might be thinking incorrectly about the information and giving the textbook page numbers so students can review the concepts, all of which further enhances learning (Hattie & Yates, 2014).

"I would describe *Psychology in Your Life* as a first choice for an accessible and enjoyable introductory psychology text. The many inset features that essentially provide brief articles and applications deliver more tempting morsels for the reader than endless text. [This textbook] has made me consider more directed reading assignments for students than simply assigning chapters and the corresponding InQuizitive sections."

—James Sturges, California State Polytechnic University, Pomona

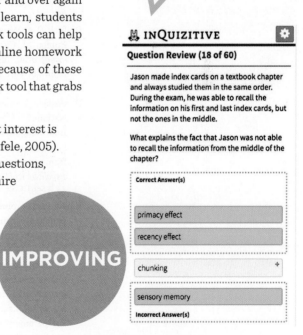

InQuizitive is one of the evidence-based tools for *Psychology in Your Life* that lets teachers and students see whether students are improving in learning the material.

- Providing easy-to-understand graphs of individual student performance over time, by specific concepts and by question type, which helps teachers check students' mastery of the material either before class, where difficult concepts can be discussed, or before quizzes and tests.

References

Anderson, L. W., Krathwohl, D. R., Airasian, R. W., Cruikshank, K. A., Mayer, R. E., Pintrich, P. R., …Wittrock, M. C. (2001). *A taxonomy for learning, teaching, and assessing: A revision of Bloom's taxonomy of educational objectives.* New York, NY: Addison Wesley Longman, Inc.

American Psychological Association. (2013). APA guidelines for the undergraduate psychology major: Version 2.0. Retrieved from http://www.apa.org/ed/precollege/undergrad/index.aspx

Bertsch, S., & Pesta, B. J. (2014). Generating active learning. In V. A. Benassi, C. E. Overson, & C. M. Hakala (Eds.), *Applying the science of learning in education: Infusing psychological science into the curriculum* (pp. 71–77). Retrieved from http://teachpsych.org/ebooks/asle2014/index.php

Carpenter, S. K. (2012). Testing enhances the transfer of learning. *Current Directions in Psychological Science, 21,* 279–283.

Cepeda, N. J., Pashler, H., Vul, E., Wixted, J. T., & Rohrer, D. (2006). Distributed practice in verbal recall tasks: A review and quantitative synthesis. *Psychological Bulletin, 132,* 354–380.

Drabick, D. A., Weisberg, R., Paul, L., & Bubier, J. L. (2007). Keeping it short and sweet: Brief, ungraded writing assignments facilitate learning. *Teaching of psychology (Columbia, Mo.), 34*(3), 172–176.

Dunlosky, J., Rawson, K. A., Marsh, E. J., Nathan, M. J., & Willingham, D. T. (2013). Improving students' learning with effective learning techniques: Promising directions from cognitive and educational psychology. *Psychological Science in the Public Interest, 14,* 4–58.

Elbow, P., & Sorcinelli, M. D. (2005). How to enhance learning by using high-stakes and low-stakes writing. In McKeachie, W. J., & Swinicki, M. (eds.), *McKeachie's Teaching Tips: Strategies, Research, and Theory for College and University Teachers* (12th ed., pp. 192–212). Retrieved from https://scholarworks.umass.edu/cgi/viewcontent.cgi?params=/context/peter_elbow/article/1004/type/native/&path_info=

Hattie, J. A. C., & Yates, G. C. R. (2014). Using feedback to promote learning. In V. A. Benassi, C. E. Overson, & C. M. Hakala (Eds.). *Applying the science of learning in education: Infusing psychological science into the curriculum* (pp. 45–58). Retrieved from http://teachpsych.org/ebooks/asle2014/index.php

Naceur, A., & Schiefele, U. (2005). Motivation and learning—the role of interest in construction and representation of text and long-term retention: Inter- and intraindividual analyses. *European Journal of Psychology of Education, 20*(2), 155–170.

Narloch R., Garbin, C. P., & Turnage K. D. (2006). Benefits of prelecture quizzes. *Teaching of Psychology, 33,* 109–112.

Nguyen, K., & McDaniels, M. A. (2014). Potent techniques to improve learning from the text. In V. A. Benassi, C. E. Overson, & C. M. Hakala (Eds.), *Applying the science of learning in education: Infusing psychological science into the curriculum* (pp. 104–117). Retrieved from http://teachpsych.org/ebooks/asle2014/index.php

Pennebaker, J. W., Gosling, S. D., & Ferrell, J. D. (2013). Daily online testing in large classes: Boosting college performance while reducing achievement gaps. *PLOS ONE 8*(11): e79774. doi:10.1371/journal.pone.0079774

Pusateri, T., Halonen, J., Hill, B., & McCarthy, M. (Eds.). (2009). The assessment cyberguide for learning goals and outcomes. Washington, D.C.: American Psychological Association.

Pyc, M., Agarwal, P. J., & Roediger, H. L. (2014). Test-enhanced learning. In V. A. Benassi, C. E. Overson, & C. M. Hakala (Eds.), *Applying the science of learning in education: Infusing psychological science into the curriculum* (pp. 78–90). Retrieved from http://teachpsych.org/ebooks/asle2014/index.php

Regan, R. A. R. (2015). Three investigations of the utility of textbook technology supplements. *Psychology Learning & Teaching, 14,* 26–35.

Roediger, H. L., III, & Karpicke, J. D. (2006). The power of testing memory: Basic research and implications for educational practice. *Psychological Science, 1,* 181–210.

Tokuhama-Espinosa, T. (2010). *Mind, brain, and education science: A comprehensive guide to the new brain-based teaching.* New York: Norton.

Ensuring an Inclusive Approach to the Text, Teaching Tools, and Assessment Materials to Honor All Teachers and Students

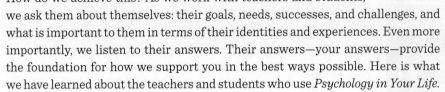

In our combined experience of nearly 80 years in higher education we have worked with teachers and students from all walks of life. If we have learned one thing, it is this: Teachers and students today are vibrant in their diverse identities, experiences, goals, and challenges. Because of this, a key aspect of our vision has been to develop *Psychology in Your Life* to reflect this diversity and be inclusive in all aspects of the textbook, teaching tools, and assessment materials. How do we achieve this? As we work with teachers and students, we ask them about themselves: their goals, needs, successes, and challenges, and what is important to them in terms of their identities and experiences. Even more importantly, we listen to their answers. Their answers—your answers—provide the foundation for how we support you in the best ways possible. Here is what we have learned about the teachers and students who use *Psychology in Your Life*.

"I liked the InQuizitive homework because if forced me to read about the material. I found that I usually could not do well on the homework until I read the textbook. Overall, though, I loved the way the InQuizitive homework was structured. It felt like a game rather than homework, so I was never reluctant to do it."

—Salman Khan, introductory psychology student

Teachers Face Significant Challenges in Supporting Their Students

Teaching is a difficult job, and in today's educational environment, teachers are increasingly being asked to do more. Teachers must teach more courses, even if they are outside their areas of expertise. Teachers now have greater numbers of students than ever before, including students with widely varying needs, and they must support more students who are underprepared for college. They are being asked to use innovative approaches they may be unfamiliar with and teach courses using formats that are new to them (such as online and hybrid). Many teachers are even being tasked with obtaining assessment data from their courses to give to institutions, even though they often have no training in this area. Yet even as the pressures of teaching increase, institutions provide less support, fewer professional development opportunities, fewer pedagogical resources, and less technical training. Part of our vision is to support teachers with the tools they need, in several ways:

- Because teachers have different learning goals for students, the Learning Goals in our textbook and the support materials, including quiz and Test Bank questions, focus on remembering, understanding, or applying the concepts. This approach lets teachers choose what goals to focus on and choose the appropriate materials to use with their students.

- Because teachers may want students to develop skills, we support reading and writing skills (through the Learning Goal Activities), study techniques (the Using Psychology in Your Life features), critical thinking (the Evaluating Psychology in the Real World features), scientific thinking (the Methods of Psychology figures), and career development (the Putting Psychology to Work features).

- For teachers just starting in the field or for those looking for refreshers, the IIG includes Teaching Videos for each chapter that explain difficult concepts and how to teach them and Teacher Versions of the Student Demonstration Videos that explain how to conduct specific in-class activities.

- For novice teachers who are looking to learn about pedagogies that increase active learning, or for experienced teachers who are excited to add to their pedagogical toolboxes, we have created the Enhanced Lecture PowerPoints with Active Learning slides, which include in-class activities and demonstrations as well as examples of different types of engaging activities, such as Think-Pair-Share, Quick Writes, and Did You Get It? comprehension questions.

- We have designed the new HIP Guide, or *High-Impact Practices: A Teaching Guide for Psychology* to support both novice teachers and experienced instructors who want to learn more about evidence-based pedagogies they can use in their classes as well as provide information about professional development opportunities.

- To help teachers develop excellent online and hybrid courses, we provide materials that can be used flexibly in those formats, such as the Concept Videos and the Student Demonstration Videos, and we ensure that all of these meet the current requirements for accessibility for all students.

- We have developed many ways for teachers to embed assessments into their courses, through InQuizitive, various quizzes (pre-lecture, post-lecture, and Student Demonstration Video quizzes), and through the Test Bank, so teachers can easily capture information about student performance and learning for their institutions.

- Lastly, teachers worry about keeping costs for their students as low as possible, so we provide several cost-effective textbook options: paperback, notebook, and ebook.

> "*Psychology in Your Life* is a great book. It has definitely helped me see psychology in my life and understand how psychology can help me in my future career as a teacher."
>
> —Thipachan (Mia) Radanavong, introductory psychology student

Students Face Challenges in Achieving Their Educational Goals Increasingly, students are underprepared for college and do not have the skills to read at their grade level, write competently, schedule their time, study effectively, or even focus their attention in class or when doing homework. At the same time, students are busier than ever, playing sports, participating in extracurricular activities, taking care of their families, and so on. Most of our students work, either part-time or full-time, even on overnight shifts in some jobs. Yet even if they are working, many students lack the basic necessities in life. Some students experience such extreme challenges that they find it extremely hard just to get to class or do homework, much less navigate the twists in their path to success in higher education. Part of our vision is to support students with the resources they need to succeed, such as by:

- Chunking information in the textbook into shorter, concise study units, with Learning Goal Activities to help students actively engage with and learn the concepts.

- Ensuring that students have a wide variety of effective active-learning tools at their disposal in the textbook and support materials so they can choose which methods they feel might be most interesting, motivating, or personally applicable.

- Providing examples and activities that are culturally sensitive and represent many diverse backgrounds.

- Creating quiz and test questions that use diverse names and situations that represent the students who use the textbook, while also avoiding scenarios and language that are culturally specific and might confuse students using these assessments.

- Choosing photos and developing graphics in the book that represent the diverse students who use the textbook so the students can see themselves in the images, by presenting people of varying genders, ethnicities, ages, body types, gender expressions, and sexual orientations.
- Using the most appropriate terms to describe people, situations, and phenomena, especially with respect to sex, gender, sexual orientation, psychological disorders, and intellectual abilities, among other topics.
- Supporting students' financial needs by providing them with the most effective textbook at the lowest cost as well as the least inexpensive, most evidence-based online homework tool, InQuizitive.

In summary, *Psychology in Your Life* is not just a textbook. Instead, we have developed an evidence-based pedagogical system with an integrated approach to teaching, learning, and improving that supports teachers and students from diverse backgrounds and with different identities and experiences. We hope that you will enjoy this newest edition of *Psychology in Your Life*, and the support materials, as much as the 100,000-plus other people who are using them.

Have fun. Learn things.

Sarah & Mike

Introducing the Third Edition

Psychology in Your Life has been developed based on evidence-based principles that help teachers support student learning. Because of this, the textbook and the integrated support materials are continuously updated to reflect new research findings and pedagogical input from introductory psychology teachers who are using the materials. Guided by the best practices in teaching, learning, and improving, the third edition of *Psychology in Your Life* has been updated in several important ways.

1. **Every chapter has been revised and updated.** Comments from reviewers, our teaching colleagues, and our students have helped us ensure that every chapter in the textbook is as accurate and compelling as possible. First, we added information on new topics that are becoming important in the field of psychology. Second, we cited the most recent psychological research for the topics discussed in each chapter. Third, we updated the references to popular culture to keep our discussions and images fresh. Fourth, we revised the support materials for teachers and students so they align perfectly with the changes in the textbook. As a result of these changes, this new edition of *Psychology in Your Life* provides teachers and students with the best, most up-to-date information on psychological research and current events related to psychology, along with excellent new interactive ways for students to engage with the material.

2. **Content has been organized into concise, goal-directed study units.** This new format supports the needs of underprepared readers by chunking text information into shorter sections that are linked with specific Learning Goals. For example, frequent pauses in the text provide opportunities for additional Learning Goals, so more concepts are covered by the Learning Goals. This also provides an opportunity for additional Learning Goal Activities, which support even stronger development of reading and writing skills.

3. **Opportunities for active learning have been increased in every chapter.** In the third edition, we have also increased active learning. We placed red Q questions throughout every chapter and placed Self-Quiz questions at the end of each chapter to increase likelihood students would use them. We also updated the active learning aspects of two of the book's pedagogical features, Evaluating Psychology in the Real World boxes and The Methods of Psychology figures, to include updated questions for students to think about and answer, either as homework or while in class. Finally, because our students have incredibly diverse reasons for being in college, we highlight how psychology can be useful in so many careers by adding a new feature, Putting Psychology to Work.

4. **Terms, examples, photos, graphics, and support materials have been revised to reflect the diversity of students and teachers.** Since the conception of *Psychology in Your Life*, we have ensured that examples, photos, graphics, and support materials are inclusive and reflect today's students in all their variety. In addition, terminology has been updated, such as in regard to sex, gender, and sexuality.

5. **InQuizitive has been updated with new active-learning questions.** Throughout InQuizitive, new questions provide students with opportunities for repeated practice online. These questions are aligned with the textbook's study units, such as in their use of terminology. In addition, InQuizitive includes questions about the Concept Videos.

"I would describe this book as very student centered and friendly. A lot of thought was given to making psychology relevant for students. There are lots of thought provoking questions to engage the student, the chapter summaries provide the important points, and there are lots of headings and subdivisions to help organize the information. This text actually positions students to be successful!"

—Krishna Stilianos, Oakland Community College, Highland Lakes Campus

6. **New evidence-based teacher support materials have been created.**
In addition to updating the existing teacher support tools, we have created the HIP Guide (*High-Impact Practices: A Teaching Guide for Psychology*), Concept Videos, Enhanced Lecture PowerPoints with Active Learning Slides, and quiz and test questions, especially at the application level.

Appreciation for Contributors and Reviewers

Like teaching and learning, writing a textbook and developing unique and integrated educational tools for teachers and students are joint efforts. Our work to support teachers and students in *Psychology in Your Life* has depended so much on the support that we received in the years we have been engrossed in this project. First, we wish to thank our families for their unwavering support. Our spouses and significant others have been incredibly understanding and generous when we repeatedly worked through family vacations. And our children and grandchildren have patiently waited for us to finish working on the days when they wanted to spend time with us. We are very grateful to each of you.

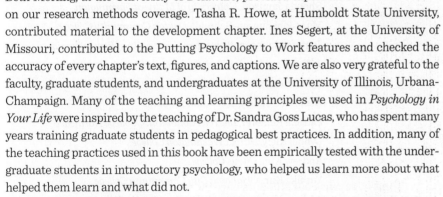

It has been our good fortune to have been joined by so many talented individuals during the process of developing and revising *Psychology in Your Life*. We are extremely grateful to our colleagues who lent their expertise in psychology to writing material for the textbook. Carrie V. Smith, at the University of Mississippi, wrote the Being a Critical Consumer features in the first and second editions. Beth Morling, at the University of Delaware, provided expert advice on our research methods coverage. Tasha R. Howe, at Humboldt State University, contributed material to the development chapter. Ines Segert, at the University of Missouri, contributed to the Putting Psychology to Work features and checked the accuracy of every chapter's text, figures, and captions. We are also very grateful to the faculty, graduate students, and undergraduates at the University of Illinois, Urbana-Champaign. Many of the teaching and learning principles we used in *Psychology in Your Life* were inspired by the teaching of Dr. Sandra Goss Lucas, who has spent many years training graduate students in pedagogical best practices. In addition, many of the teaching practices used in this book have been empirically tested with the undergraduate students in introductory psychology, who helped us learn more about what helped them learn and what did not.

Most importantly, we wish to thank the psychology teachers at Parkland College and the graduate student teachers and researchers, past and present, at the University of Illinois, Urbana-Champaign, for sharing with us their knowledge of psychological concepts and of evidence-based teaching and learning pedagogies. It is only with their expertise that we have been able to develop and update the materials to support teachers' skills in the Interactive Instructor's Guide and student learning in the Test Bank. In particular, Travis Sola, Crystal Carlson, Genevieve Henricks, Rachel Smallman, Angela Isaacs, and Lauren Bohn Gibson, we thank you. Your dedication to our mission, boundless energy, and drive for excellence are truly inspirational. Daniel Kolen, you are a fast learner about psychology, and your keen eye and production talent have perfected our video materials to support students and teachers. You are a true gem in your profession, and we are grateful to call you one of us—a member of "The Team."

> "*Psychology in Your Life* has excellent features that promote critical thinking and application. Moreover, the text excels when it comes to InQuizitive, supplemental materials such as the Interactive Instructor's Guide, and seamless integration with learning management systems in the form of a course pack."
>
> —Jon Skalski, College of Southern Nevada

Reviewers The chapters were thoroughly reviewed as they moved through the editorial and production process over three editions. Reviewers included star teachers who checked for issues such as level, detail, pacing, and readability, all of which support student comprehension. Reviewers also included experts who checked for scientific accuracy and helped us find the right balance of correctness, clarity, and conciseness. Our reviewers showed extraordinary attention to detail and understanding of the student experience. We are grateful to all the reviewers listed here. Their efforts reflect a deep commitment to excellence in psychology and in teaching students about the importance and applicability of our field.

Paul Abramson, *University of California, Los Angeles*

Carol Anderson, *Bellevue College*

Romina Angeleri, *University of New Mexico*

Sarah K. Angulo, *Texas State University*

Nicole Arduini–Van Hoose, *Hudson Valley Community College*

Michelle Bannoura, *Hudson Valley Community College*

Nicole Barbari, *Chaffey College*

Holly Beard, *Midlands Technical College*

Dan Bellack, *Trident Technical College*

Richard Bernstein, *Broward College*

John H. Bickford Jr., *University of Massachusetts Amherst*

David Biek, *Middle Georgia State University*

Phaer Bonner, *Jefferson State Community College*

Carol Borden, *Leech Lake Band of Ojibwe*

Allison Burton-Chase, *Albany College of Pharmacy and Health Sciences*

Pamela Case, *Richmond Community College*

Diana Ciesko, *Valencia Community College*

Scott Cohn, *Western State Colorado University*

Kevin Conner, *Liberty University*

Barbara Corbisier, *Blinn College*

Andrew Corr, *Kirkwood Community College, Iowa City Campus*

Jennifer E. Dale, *Community College of Aurora*

Jubilee Dickson, *Chicago State University*

Dale Doty, *Monroe Community College*

Gina Dow, *Denison College*

Michael Dudley, *Southern Illinois University, Edwardsville*

Sarah Estow, *Guilford College*

Laura Flewelling, *Johnston Community College*

Shannon Gadbois, *Brandon University*

Andrew C. Gallup, *SUNY, College at Oneonta*

Rebecca Gazzaniga, *University of California, Santa Barbara*

Ericka M. Goerling, *Portland Community College*

Gregg Gold, *Humboldt State University*

Jeffrey Green, *Virginia Commonwealth University*

Jerry Green, *Tarrant County College District*

Christine L. Grela, *McHenry County College*

Christine Harrington, *Middlesex County College*

Marissa A. Harrison, *Pennsylvania State University, Harrisburg*

Laura Hebert, *Angelina College*

Byron Heidenreich, *Illinois State University*

Carmon Hicks, *Ivy Tech Community College Northeast*

Jessica C. Hill, *Utah Valley University*

Debra A. Hope, *University of Nebraska-Lincoln*

David A. Houston, *University of Memphis*

Tasha Howe, *Humboldt State University*

Karin Hu, *City College of San Francisco*

Sandra Hunt, *College of Staten Island*

Malgorzata Ilkowska, *Georgia Institute of Technology*

Benetha Jackson, *Angelina College*

Mike James, *Ivy Tech Community College Northeast*

Rhonda Jamison, *University of Maine at Farmington*

Mary Johannesen-Schmidt, *Oakton Community College*

Jennifer Johnson, *Bloomsburg University of Pennsylvania*

Jeffrey Jourdan, *Ivy Tech Community College Northeast*

Tyson Keiger, *Utica College*

Deborah P. Kelley, *Tyler Junior College*

Patricia Kemerer, *Ivy Tech Community College Northeast*

Lynnel Kiely, *Harold Washington College*

Andrew Kim, *Citrus College*

Yuthika Kim, *Oklahoma City Community College*

Andrew Knapp, *Finger Lakes Community College*

Karen Kwan, *Salt Lake Community College*

Caleb W. Lack, *University of Central Oklahoma*

Marianne LaFrance, *Yale University*

Rachel L. Laimon, *Charles Stewart Mott Community College*

Sadie Leder-Elder, *High Point University*

Katie W. Lewis, *Pensacola State College*

Sheryl Leytham, *Grand View University*

Debbie Ma, *California State University, Northridge*

Pam Marek, *Kennesaw State University*

The Norton Team To realize a vision, you must take a first step. For *Psychology in Your Life*, the first step was a leap of faith, when W. W. Norton & Co. saw the possibilities of what this project could bring to teachers and students. As the oldest and largest independent publishing company, Norton has created some of the best-respected and iconic books in modern times. The excellence of these works makes Norton stand out as a beacon among publishers. Because the company is wholly owned by its employees, the employees are the heart and soul of this excellence.

Psychology in Your Life exists because of the extraordinary contributions of so many people at Norton. At the top of the list is Sheri Snavely, the editor of *Psychology in Your Life*. When Sarah and Sheri first discussed this project, many publishing companies were interested in taking a new approach to developing evidence-based educational products. While representatives from many companies wanted to hear about this project, Sheri wanted to learn about it through experience. She asked to sit in on Sarah's introductory psychology class. No one from another company had asked to do that, but Sheri needed to see if Sarah was a teacher who actually "walked the walk" of supporting student learning in class. That hands-on approach enabled Sheri to see the value in the vision. Sheri's leadership and guidance have provided a constant star to keep us oriented in the right direction. She has our utter gratitude, respect, and admiration. Assistant editor Eve Sanoussi managed the review program, created art manuscripts, and kept the project running smoothly. She also helped ensure that the book's illustration program is inclusive—reflecting today's students in all their variety.

One of our key goals for this textbook was providing appropriate, accurate, and engaging information about psychology while supporting students' abilities to understand the material. The developmental editor for the second and third editions, Kurt Wildermuth, helped us make the text accessible while maintaining the integrity of the content. He then patiently guided the chapters through the many stages from manuscript editing to publication.

The media for this third edition has benefitted tremendously from the expertise of media editor Kaitlin Coates. Kaitlin skillfully guided the new Concept Videos, Teaching Videos, and *High-Impact Practices: A Teaching Guide for Psychology* to completion, and we are grateful for her talent and hard work. Kaitlin and the excellent associate media editor, Victoria Reuter, worked tirelessly with us to design all aspects of the ebook; Integrated Instructor's Guide; InQuizitive online formative, adaptive homework tool; and Test Bank around the core learning goals in the textbook. The media editorial assistant, Allison Smith, ensured that the media processes went smoothly. The end result of these long hours of joint work is something remarkable: media that is part of an integrated package, connected to all aspects of *Psychology in Your Life*.

> "At several points in reviewing *Psychology in Your Life*, I thought to myself—Why is this not my textbook? It will be a top contender when we consider a new edition. That's how much I loved it."
>
> —Robin Musselman, Lehigh Carbon Community College

It has been a great joy to work with Ashley Sherwood, our energetic and creative marketing manager. Ashley has been a tireless champion, making sure people understand our mission to support teachers and students. She also is the source of our excellent swag: experiment buttons featuring the field's most pivotal studies, heart/PSYCH stickers that our children and grandchildren plaster on their laptops, and *Putting Psychology to Work* posters. Norton's sales managers, representatives, and specialists are truly invested in supporting teachers and students. Their expertise, insight, and mission focus make them extraordinary advocates for excellence in education.

Finally, we want to thank the teachers we have met at conferences and meetings, where we have exchanged ideas about challenges in teaching and how to address those challenges so that our students have great learning experiences. By contributing to the ideas behind *Psychology in Your Life*, those teachers have become part of the extended Norton family.

CONTENTS

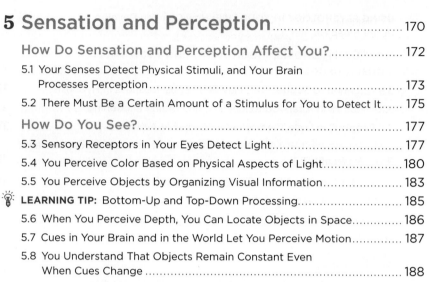

8 Thinking and Intelligence 292

9 Motivation and Emotion 334

11 Health and Well-Being 420

12 Social Psychology 462

13 Self and Personality 502

PSYCHOLOGY
IN YOUR LIFE

1 Introducing the World of Psychology

YOU'RE DRIVING DOWN THE STREET, talking on your cell phone as you negotiate the traffic, stop signs, and pedestrians. Then the driver in front of you stops suddenly. You frantically drop the phone and swerve, barely avoiding a collision. Your heart is pounding as you realize what could have happened.

BIG QUESTIONS

Why Is Psychology Important to You?

What Do Psychologists Investigate?

How Do Psychologists Conduct Research?

FIGURE 1.1

Psychology in Daily Life: The Dangers of Using a Cell Phone While Driving

Kelsey Raffaele took this photo of herself (photo courtesy of her mother, Bonnie Raffaele). Bonnie Raffaele helped get a law passed in their state that prevents novice drivers from using cell phones while driving. For more information on the dangers of using a cell phone while driving, please visit https://www.thekdrchallenge .com/kelsey-s-story.

Kelsey Raffaele, a 17-year-old high school senior in Michigan, wasn't so lucky (**Figure 1.1**). One day, Kelsey was driving through town after school and decided to pass a slower vehicle in front of her. When she saw an oncoming vehicle in the passing lane, she misjudged the distance and crashed. Kelsey spoke her last words on her cell phone as she talked with her best friend, Stacey Hough: "Oh [no], I'm going to crash."

If you are like most people in the United States, you have talked on a cell phone when you were driving. This habit is so common that many of us never think twice about it. That's exactly what Stacey Hough reported. She was driving behind Kelsey at the time of the accident. "[We] used our phones all the time behind the wheel. We never thought anything would come of it," said Stacey. "Until it happen[s], you don't think it could happen."

Statistics contradict people's intuition, their gut feeling, that they can drive safely when talking on the phone. The National Highway Traffic Safety Administration (n.d.) estimates that in 2015 about 391,000 people were injured and 3,477 people died in accidents due to distracted driving, including talking and texting on cell phones. Many people believe these accidents happen because the driver has only one hand on the wheel while holding the cell phone with the other. Because of this habit, by March 2016, 14 states had enacted laws that require the use of hands-free phones while driving (Pickrell & Li, 2017). But even when people have two hands on the steering wheel, can they really drive safely while talking on the phone?

According to one study, a driver's performance is still impaired when using a hands-free device (Strayer & Drews, 2007). This finding implies that the absence of one hand on the steering wheel is not the problem. Rather, diverting one's attention to the phone conversation and away from important visual and auditory cues is a key factor in car accidents. Having all the data gives us evidence so we can make informed decisions about what actions to take. In the case of cell phones and driving, banning the use of handheld cell phones while driving does not reduce accidents (Burger, Kaffine, & Yu, 2014). Instead, we must ban all cell phone use while driving. But how can public policies succeed in getting people not to use cell phones when driving, especially when drivers believe they are not at risk (Sanbonmatsu, Strayer, Behrends, Ward, & Watson, 2016)? Could manufacturers create cell phones and other in-car products that are less distracting when drivers use them? And how might we understand which drivers are most at risk and provide intervention for them? Psychological research is currently investigating these questions.

When you decided to take a psychology course, you probably did not think it would deal with issues such as why it is dangerous to use a cell phone while driving. But questions like these are at the forefront of psychological research. Unfortunately, we cannot use intuition or our personal beliefs to answer questions like this one. Why not? What seems to be obvious is rarely the whole story. Behind the "obvious" are mental processes that cause us to think and act in certain ways. Processes of this kind are one of the major subjects of psychology. This text introduces you to current topics such as this one, teaches you to think critically about them, and looks at how you can use psychology to improve your daily life. Just imagine what this knowledge might have done for Kelsey Raffaele—and for the thousands of other people like her who perish in distracted driving accidents every year.

Why Is Psychology Important to You?

Learning about psychology can affect you in critical ways. For example, psychology can help you understand why you should not talk on your cell phone while driving. It can also help you understand other people. Why are some people fascinated by celebrities and their lives, such as Beyoncé and Jay-Z, whereas many others try to ignore media coverage of celebrities (**Figure 1.2**)? Or think about the last time a friend or family member did something that really surprised you. You may have wanted to understand that person's motives, thoughts, desires, intentions, moods, actions, and so on.

All of us want to know whether other people are friends or enemies, leaders or followers, likely to reject us or fall in love with us. We also want to understand ourselves—why we love the people we do, why we get so angry when someone laughs at us, or why we made that "stupid mistake." Psychology can help us understand ourselves and other people. In turn, this understanding can help us have more success in our studies, be better parents, improve our friendships, work more effectively in groups, and succeed at our jobs. In short, psychology can help us improve our lives.

FIGURE 1.2

Understanding People

Psychology can help you understand yourself. It also provides insight into why some people find certain celebrities fascinating. The relationship between Beyoncé and Jay-Z has been the focus of intense interest by many people.

1.1 Psychology Explains Your Mental Activity and Behavior

1.1 LEARNING GOAL ACTIVITIES

To maximize your learning, complete the following learning goal activities:

a. Understand all bold and italic terms by writing explanations of them in your own words.

b. Apply psychology to your life by writing an example of your own mental activity and behavior in a situation.

As you saw in this chapter's opening story, people believe they can talk on a cell phone and still drive safely. This story is important because it shows that you cannot use your intuition or your personal beliefs to truly understand people or to predict behavior. By contrast, **psychology** is the scientific study of the mind and behavior, both of which depend on processing in the brain.

The mind is made up of all of the mental activity that lets you experience the world. That is, you use your senses—sight, smell, taste, hearing, and touch—to take in information from outside yourself. Through mental activity, you interpret that information. These processes of receiving and interpreting information are responsible for all of your memories, thoughts, and feelings. By contrast, the term "behavior" refers to all of the actions that result from sensing and interpreting information. It is important to remember that both mental activity and behavior are produced by the brain. In recent years, technology such as brain imaging has provided great insight into how the brain processes information to let you think about and respond to information in the world around you.

So psychology focuses on the scientific study of mental activity, behavior, and the brain processes that underlie them. The areas of investigation range from the simple to the complex. What are some of the topics of interest in psychology? Using the Try It Yourself feature on p. 6, see if you can figure out the answer.

psychology
The scientific study of mental activity and behavior, which are based on brain processes.

QUESTION: Which of these pictures show aspects of psychology?

These people are friends.

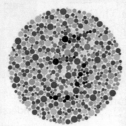

This is a color-blindness test—see the 5?

This woman is experiencing depression.

This couple enjoys the thrill of roller coaster rides.

The design of this door is confusing— push or pull?

Answer: All of these pictures reflect psychology because they suggest the presence of mental activity and behavior that depend on brain processes.

Are you getting the impression that every aspect of what you think and do relates to psychology? Then you are right. You might be surprised to know that as you sit reading this textbook, you are experiencing psychology. Your eyes move across the page so you can see the words and understand their meanings. But maybe you are also feeling hungry, so you are distracted by thoughts of food. Perhaps you are thinking about someone you just met whom you want to get to know better. Or maybe you are thinking about how to get a better job that relates more closely to your career interests. All these mental activities and actions relate to psychology, so psychology is a part of every moment of your life.

1.2 Psychology Teaches You to Think Critically

 1.2 LEARNING GOAL ACTIVITIES

To maximize your learning, complete the following learning goal activities:

a. Understand all bold and italic terms by writing explanations of them in your own words.

b. Apply critical thinking to real life by writing an example of each of the following: an intuition, a belief, an opinion, a pseudofact, and objective evidence.

Do you believe in astrology? Astrology is the idea that the positions of stars and of planets affect our lives. Many people know their star sign and even read their horoscope to discover what life may have in store for them. In fact, about 25 percent of Americans believe in astrology (Gallup, 2005). However, there is no compelling scientific support for astrology or for the accuracy of horoscopes. In fact, psychological research demonstrates that numerous factors other than a person's star sign better predict the individual's behavior and traits (Hartmann, Reuter, & Nyborg, 2006).

Before taking a psychology course, many students believe things about the brain, mental activity, and behavior without stopping to think about why they believe what they do. But a main goal of this textbook is to teach you to stop and investigate before you believe. In other words, in this textbook, you will learn to think critically to evaluate psychological information in the real world.

critical thinking
Systematically evaluating information to reach conclusions best supported by evidence.

STEPS IN CRITICAL THINKING   In **critical thinking,** we systematically evaluate information to reach conclusions based on the evidence that is presented. As shown in the Learning Tip below, three steps are involved in thinking critically about information in psychology, or on any other topic.

The first step in critical thinking is to ask, "What is the claim I am being asked to accept?" In other words, you have to identify the statement that you will then evaluate. Once you identify the claim, you must approach it with friendly skepticism. That is, keep an open mind about the new claim, but do not accept it at face value. This combination of openness and caution is important because it lets you receive new information but not absorb everything that comes your way. Ideally, you do not simply accept information because it fits with what you already believe.

The second step in critical thinking is to ask, "What evidence, if any, is provided to support the claim?" Evidence is the available information that is relevant to the

LEARNING TIP: Developing Critical Thinking Skills

Throughout this textbook, Evaluating Psychology in the Real World features will help you develop critical thinking skills. Each time you read one of these features, try to follow the steps in the diagram below to correctly evaluate the claim being made.

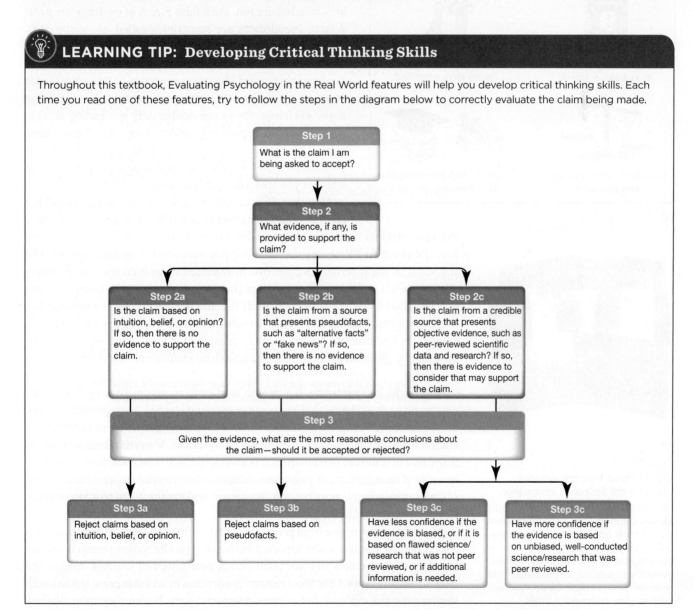

HOW TO SPOT FAKE NEWS

Figure out the source of the story. Is it reliable?

Don't just read the headline. What's the whole story?

Google the author. What's the person's background?

Click on links. Do they support the story?

Check the date. Is this story fresh or stale?

Look for humor. Is the story a put-on?

Look for bias—the story's and your own.

Confirm. Visit the library or a fact-checking Web site.

(a)

(b)

FIGURE 1.3

Good Critical Thinking Includes Knowing the Source of Information

(a) Sometimes pseudofacts are given as support for claims. Such fabrication occurs most often in fake news. Follow these tips to avoid accepting the claims you may see in fake news. **(b)** The best evidence to support claims comes from scientific and research-based sources such as peer-reviewed journals.

claim. People sometimes use the everyday word "fact" to describe evidence. Scientists avoid the word "fact" because nothing is ever really 100 percent certain and new evidence changes how we interpret any claim. Psychologists look for strong objective evidence to support a claim. Objective evidence means information that is not influenced by feelings or opinions. However, some claims are not based on solid evidence. Therefore, a key part of this step in critical thinking is recognizing when evidence is lacking to support a claim. Some claims reflect a person's *intuition*, which is an instinctive, gut feeling about something, not reflecting much thought. Other claims may reveal a person's *belief*, which is a long-held, bedrock thought about an issue. And yet other claims may reveal an *opinion*, which is a judgment about a topic, including a judgment about evidence. Intuitions, beliefs, and opinions are not credible evidence.

In addition, some claims are associated with "facts" that look true but are not. Such false pieces of evidence are *pseudofacts*. Pseudofacts are sometimes called *alternative facts*. Whatever they are called, these fake pieces of information are not meaningful evidence of any kind, because they are false. You may have heard about the existence of *fake news* (Lazer et al., 2018). Fake news is not news, because it is based on shaky evidence. These are deliberately misleading stories, with either no supporting evidence or false facts. These stories are made up for personal reasons, advertising, or political purposes. **Figure 1.3a** shows how you can determine whether you are looking at fake news.

However, it is one thing to know that some "facts" are fake. It is another thing to actually separate good evidence from pseudofacts. To do so, you must determine the source of the claim. Did you hear the claim on TV or on the radio? Did you read about it in a newspaper? Did you see it on the Internet? Did you overhear someone say it on the bus? Knowing the source of a claim helps you evaluate the support given for the claim. Was any support given? Was the support biased? A claim is based on biased information when the person making the claim twists the information to fit a personal or political agenda. For example, statistics can be presented in misleading ways. Or all the information given may support the claim, with no mention of support for competing claims.

You might be wondering: If a person is making an argument, why would that person present evidence that supports competing claims? An argument actually becomes stronger, more persuasive, when it acknowledges different perspectives and then shows the weaknesses in those perspectives. If a claim cannot stand up in the face of different perspectives, it is a weak claim. So when you hear about only one side of an argument, be suspicious. Employ your friendly skepticism. Ask yourself what's missing. If possible, ask the person making the claim to address other perspectives and fill in the gaps you noticed.

Now suppose you have been presented with information from a different source: a scientist. In science, well-supported evidence typically means research reports based on objective data that are published in peer-reviewed journals, such as the ones shown in **Figure 1.3b.** "Peer review" is a process by which other scientists with similar expertise evaluate and critique research reports before they are published.

Peer review ensures that published reports describe research studies that are well designed, are conducted ethically, and arrive at logical conclusions. Compared with information from other sources, evidence from peer-reviewed journals is most likely to be high-quality. As a result, you should feel more confident about accepting claims based on this type of evidence. Now, if a scientist says it, it must be true, right? On the contrary, you also must use critical thinking to evaluate claims that present evidence from scientific or research-based sources. These sources, like others mentioned above, may reflect bias.

The third and last step of critical thinking is to ask, "Given the evidence, what are the most reasonable conclusions about the claim—should it be accepted or rejected?" Suppose you have determined that no evidence has been presented to support the claim (as occurs when intuition, belief, or opinion is presented as support). Or suppose the claim is associated with pseudofacts (as occurs in fake news and with alternative facts). In these cases, you should reject the claim or at least be highly skeptical until you find better evidence. By contrast, if you decide that the evidence used to support the claim is based on scientific evidence and research, then you should be more likely to accept the claim. Yet even in this case you must use logic and reasoning to determine whether there are holes in the evidence (reasoning is discussed in study unit 8.4). Unfortunately, some peer-reviewed studies are published but still reflect flawed methods or analyses. After you have read this book, you will have a strong understanding of how scientific research is conducted and how claims can be safely made based on research findings. With that knowledge, you will be able to look at some scientific evidence and consider whether you need additional information to evaluate the claim being made. At the same time, you can think about whether there might be alternative explanations for the claim. You then can decide whether the evidence tends to support the claim.

The Learning Tip on p. 7 explains how this book will help you develop strong critical thinking skills. Throughout the book, you will practice using these three steps to evaluate real-world claims about psychology. Some of these claims may come from mainstream news. Others may come from social media. Everyone loves a good story, and people often jump on findings from psychological research. Unfortunately, as you will see, media reports can be distorted or even totally wrong. Because of this possibility, you should practice good critical thinking skills by being on the lookout for unreasonable claims.

Breaking News: Listening to Mozart Makes People Smarter

October 14, 1993

Recent research in psychology reveals that listening to Mozart increases intelligence. After reading about the power of the "Mozart effect," the governor of Georgia, Zell Miller, set aside a chunk of the state budget to provide classical music to every child born in the state each year.

According to Miller, the "Mozart effect"...

FIGURE 1.4

Thinking Critically About Psychology in the News

Media reports seek to grab attention. The claims can be based on psychological research, but they can also be hype. Consider what happened when research revealed small gains in one type of performance task after adult participants listened to a Mozart sonata for 10 minutes. The media dubbed these gains the Mozart effect and falsely reported that listening to Mozart could make people smarter.

EVALUATING PSYCHOLOGY IN THE NEWS One example of psychological research that was turned into an overblown news report concerns the so-called Mozart effect. According to the original research, adult research participants showed significant but temporary gains in performing one type of task after listening to a Mozart sonata for 10 minutes, compared with listening to relaxation instructions or silence (Rauscher, Shaw, & Ky, 1993).

News outlets quickly reported these results. However, the writers and editors either misunderstood the findings or misrepresented them with headlines that suggested that listening to Mozart was a way to increase intelligence (**Figure 1.4**). Even people surrounded by professional advisers can fall prey to such media reports.

In this case, the governor of Georgia, Zell Miller, set aside $105,000 of the state budget to provide classical music to each of the approximately 100,000 children born in the state each year. Though the babies and their parents may have enjoyed the music, there is no evidence that listening improved the infants' intelligence.

Thinking critically about claims in psychology will help you in your daily life. This ability will also help you study successfully in this and other classes. Indeed, one study found that students who use critical thinking skills complete an introductory psychology course with a more accurate understanding of the subject than do students who complete the same course without using critical thinking skills (Kowalski & Taylor, 2004).

1.3 Psychology Improves Your Life

 1.3 LEARNING GOAL ACTIVITIES

To maximize your learning, complete the following learning goal activities:

a. Understand all bold and italic terms by writing explanations of them in your own words.

b. Apply psychology to your life by writing one example each of how psychology can help you: do well in school, improve your personal life, and succeed at your job.

Apart from a good grade, what do you hope to get out of this class? Of course, you will learn many important psychology concepts and theories that guide psychological research. This information will be valuable especially if you become a psychology major or you eventually choose a career in psychology. However, even if this ends up being the only psychology course you ever take, studying psychology can pave the way for success in your schoolwork, personal life, and profession.

BETTER ACADEMIC SUCCESS IN YOUR CLASSES   What is the best way to read a textbook in order to really learn the material? If you are like most students, you might say that highlighting or rereading the text leads to the best learning. But psychological research reveals that this is not true; these are passive processes that do not require much thought (Dunlosky, Rawson, Marsh, Nathan, & Willingham, 2013). The more effort you put into studying actively over many days, the more you will learn. Every time you learn something, you create "memory traces" in your brain. And by working with the information, you strengthen the memory traces, so you will be more likely to recall the information in the future. As a result, merely highlighting or rereading textbook material is not as effective as using active mental processes to work with the information. The Using Psychology in Your Life feature on pp. 12–13 gives you a study checklist with specific steps on how to study actively in each chapter. If you follow this study checklist for each chapter, you will be using psychology to maximize your success in this class. If you also use a checklist like this for your other classes, you will improve your learning and performance in school overall.

Other chapters in this textbook also explain how psychology can help you succeed in your classes. For example, you will read about how sleep affects you and how to change your sleep patterns to improve learning (Chapter 3). You will also learn about your memory processes (Chapter 7), which will help you focus and remember material. Reducing stress in your life and avoiding test anxiety will also be important to your success in college and beyond (Chapter 11).

IMPROVING YOUR PERSONAL LIFE   Psychology can also enhance your personal life. For example, suppose your child's room is always a mess or a friend of yours sometimes acts unsupportively toward you. Chapter 6 of this book explains how people learn to change their behavior. You may be able to use the concepts in that chapter to help your child learn to clean up or help your friend learn to be more supportive.

Throughout this book, you will also discover information about yourself. Learning about your brain and how it processes information can help you understand yourself in ways you never imagined (Chapter 2). Knowledge about human interaction will help you develop and strengthen relationships (Chapter 12). Understanding the symptoms of mental health problems (Chapter 14) and how such problems can be treated (Chapter 15) may at some point apply to you or people you know.

(a)

SUCCESS IN YOUR PROFESSION   Psychology will also prepare you for success in your professional life. In terms of what you study and what career you pursue, psychological concepts can help you consider your options and make good decisions (Chapter 8). Motivation in achieving short-term and long-term goals is also an important area of study in psychology (Chapter 9).

To help inform and inspire your career choice, each chapter of this book includes a special feature, Putting Psychology to Work. In this series, you will read about applying the knowledge and skills of this field to various types of work. For example, teachers and education professionals need to understand how people's thinking, social abilities, and behaviors change over time (Chapter 4; **Figure 1.5a**). People employed in the food industry, including restaurants, need to know how human sensory systems process information from environments (Chapter 5). People in business, marketing, advertising, and sales need to know how attitudes are formed or changed and how well people's attitudes predict their behavior (Chapter 12; **Figure 1.5b**). Health care workers need to understand their patients' personalities and how to relate to their patients (Chapter 13; **Figure 1.5c**). In fact, in most fields it is vital to grasp the interconnections between the brain, mental activity, and behavior. Smart employers look for applicants who have knowledge and skills that come from training in psychology.

(b)

Some students become so fascinated by psychology that they decide to study the subject in college and even pursue a degree in it. Later in this chapter you will learn about exciting work you can do with an associate's, a bachelor's, or even a graduate degree in psychology. As you are about to discover, psychology is a dynamic field. Researchers around the globe are reporting new insights into issues that great scholars of the past tried to understand. These insights are helping to explain the very nature of what it means to be human.

(c)

FIGURE 1.5

Studying Psychology Develops Career Skills

Studying psychology helps people develop skills they can use in a wide range of careers. **(a)** Teachers need to understand how people learn. **(b)** To convince people to buy products, salespeople need to understand the relationship between motivation and emotion. **(c)** People in medical professions need to know how to gauge people's moods and their motivations to recover.

 Why Is Psychology Important to You?

To make sure you learned what you just read, write answers to the following questions and check your answers.

1.1   Explain the four parts of the definition of psychology.

1.2   Name and explain the three steps in critical thinking.

1.3   Explain why writing answers to the learning goal activities will help you learn the text information better than rereading or highlighting it.

See Appendix B for answers to the red Q questions.

The steps in this study checklist are based on psychological research (Putnam, Sungkhasettee, & Roediger, 2016). Following these steps will help you learn and improve your grades. Be sure to bookmark pp. 12–13. As you work through Chapter 1, check off each step here as you complete it. Through the rest of the book, refer back to this checklist to make sure you're on track.

☐ **STEP 1: Have a growth mindset.** Having a *growth mindset* means recognizing that doing well takes time, effort, and dedication (Yeager & Dweck, 2012). It also means understanding that making a mistake gives an opportunity to improve. Replace thoughts of "I'm no good at this" with thoughts of "I can work to get better." Then, gather all the resources that will help you. For example, read your teachers' syllabi, understand their rules, talk with them after class or during advising hours, and discuss what you should be doing to learn in their classes.

☐ **STEP 2: Make a schedule.** Knowing how much time you need to study and planning your time are critical to success. You can use a paper planner or an electronic tool, such as Google Calendar, Outlook, a calendar on your phone, or an app you download. You can discover many ways to create a schedule by doing an Internet search for "Ways to create a study schedule." Your schedule should be by the week, the day, and the hour. It should show your classes, homework sessions for each class, work, family commitments, and other obligations.

☐ **STEP 3: Read the textbook actively by completing the learning goal activities.** Each chapter of this book includes about 12 numbered sections. When you begin reading a section, look at the learning goal activities for that section. Then, as you read, write answers to the learning goal activities. This active process will force deeper thought about the material, which will lead to better learning (Dunlosky et al., 2013). Read only a few numbered

USING PSYCHOLOGY IN YOUR LIFE

How Can Psychology Help You Succeed in School?

What Do Psychologists Investigate?

For as long as people have been able to think, we have been trying to understand ourselves and others. The goal of understanding human mental processes and behavior actually originated in philosophy. In fact, ancient scholars asked some of the same important questions about humans that psychologists examine today. However, in the nineteenth century, scientists began to systematically investigate psychological processes. Since then, we have made incredible progress in understanding how people think and behave.

1.4 Psychology Originated in Philosophical Questions

 1.4 LEARNING GOAL ACTIVITIES

To maximize your learning, complete the following learning goal activities:

a. Understand all bold and italic terms by writing explanations of them in your own words.

b. Apply the nature/nurture debate to your own life by writing an example of how one of your traits might reflect the impact of both nature and nurture.

sections at a time because attention tends to fade quickly. Doing active reading over days also improves learning, because distributing studying over time improves memory for information (Putnam et al., 2016). As you get used to this process, you will get faster at it.

☐ **STEP 4: Check your learning by answering the red Q questions and taking the end-of-chapter self-quizzes.** Writing answers to the red **Q** questions throughout each chapter will encourage you to think actively about the material, which helps learning. Writing answers to the self-quizzes at the end of each chapter will make you aware of what you do and do not know. Go to Appendix B to check your answers to the red **Q** questions and the quizzes. Then go back to the chapter and relearn information related to items you got wrong.

☐ **STEP 5: Use the InQuizitive adaptive online homework tool.** Repeatedly practicing with concepts is a great way to learn (Roediger & Karpicke, 2006). InQuizitive provides a fun and easy way to practice in a game-style environment with a wide range of question types. The goal is to reach the number of points assigned by your teacher by getting items correct. Whenever you get an item wrong, click on the link to the section in the chapter that pertains to the question and relearn the material.

☐ **STEP 6: Attend class, participate actively, and take notes.** Recall from Step 3 that active processing improves learning (Dunlosky et al., 2013). Whether you are taking this course in the classroom or online, it is important to participate. Engage with your teacher by asking and answering questions. Work with your classmates during group activities. Take notes using one of several notetaking techniques, such as the Cornell Method. You can learn about the various ways to take notes by doing an Internet search for "Methods of taking notes." As you take notes, give examples of the concepts and apply them to yourself, because this makes the information more memorable.

☐ **STEP 7: Reduce stress when taking quizzes and tests.** Do you experience test anxiety? If your heart starts to race, your palms sweat, and your stomach churns when you take quizzes or tests, then the answer may be yes. When students experience test anxiety, they feel like the information they studied has flown out of their minds. To combat test anxiety, get to the test several minutes early. Breathe deeply and relax. Changing your thoughts about the quiz or test so you view it as a challenge that you can learn from, not as a threat, may help you improve performance (Seery, Weisbuch, Hetenyi, & Blascovich, 2010). Lastly, take a minute to write down why you are feeling anxious. This simple effort can improve test performance (Ramirez & Beilock, 2011).

☐ **STEP 8: Get feedback from your teacher and make changes.** At the end of each chapter, meet with your teacher to discuss your progress. Your teacher may have suggestions on how you can improve based on how the course is set up. On your own, take this opportunity to reflect on how well you have performed each step in this checklist. With a growth mindset, you always have a chance to improve, so decide what changes you need to make for the next chapter and start making improvements.

In ancient Greece, early philosophers, such as Aristotle and Plato, debated psychological issues. Was how a person thought and acted inborn—in other words, did mental activity and behavior result from a person's biological nature? Or were mental activity and behavior acquired through education, experience, and culture—for example, did they result from how a person was nurtured?

Psychologists have carried on this *nature/nurture debate* for as long as psychology has been a field of study. Psychologists now recognize that both nature and nurture influence psychological traits. Throughout this book, you will see many examples of how nature and nurture influence each other so much that they are hard to separate.

Another classic question in psychology is the *mind/body problem*. Are the mind and the body separate and distinct? Or is the mind simply a person's personal experience of the physical brain's activity? The ancient Greeks and Romans knew that the brain was essential for normal mental functioning. Their understanding came largely from their observations of people who had suffered blows to the head and then lost consciousness, or people who had experienced changes in certain mental abilities, or both. By contrast, at other points in history, scholars believed that the mind was separate from and in control of the body. This claim was partly based on the strong religious belief that humans have a divine and immortal soul. In this view, the soul is separate from the physical body and departs from the body upon death.

In the 1600s, the French philosopher René Descartes suggested the idea of *dualism*, that the mind and the body are separate yet intertwined (**Figure 1.6**). The body,

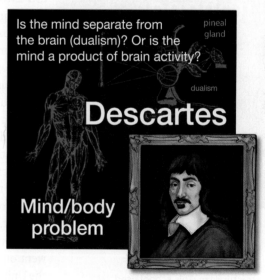

FIGURE 1.6

Descartes and the Mind/Body Problem: Dualism

According to the philosopher René Descartes, the mind and the body are separate yet intertwined. As discussed throughout this book, psychologists now reject this idea, called dualism. Instead, they view the mind as a product of brain processes.

FIGURE 1.7

Wundt's Experimental Psychology Laboratory

Wilhelm Wundt **(third from left)** established the first psychology laboratory in Germany in 1879. This event marked the beginning of modern experimental psychology.

Descartes argued, was nothing more than an organic machine governed by "reflex." In keeping with the prevailing religious beliefs, he concluded that the rational mind was divine and separate from the physical body. Today, psychologists reject dualism. The current view among psychologists is that the mind emerges from biological activity in the brain.

1.5 Psychologists Investigate the Conscious Mind and the Unconscious Mind

1.5 LEARNING GOAL ACTIVITIES

To maximize your learning, complete the following learning goal activities:

a. Understand all bold and italic terms by writing explanations of them in your own words.

b. Understand the three psychology schools of thought that investigated the conscious mind and the unconscious mind by using your own words to describe each school.

Historically, philosophers used thinking to answer the big questions about who we are. However, in the mid-1800s in Europe, psychology arose as a scientific field of study and then spread throughout the world. During this time, different ways of thinking about psychology emerged. After a school of thought emerged, it would dominate for a while. When the flaws of that approach became apparent, a new school of thought would emerge. Let's look at how several schools of thought have laid the foundation for the modern science of psychology (**Table 1.1**).

EXPERIMENTAL PSYCHOLOGY BEGINS Experimental psychology began in 1879, when Wilhelm Wundt established the first psychology laboratory (**Figure 1.7**). Wundt based his investigations on a realization: Psychological processes are the products of brain activity, so they must take time to occur. The time it takes to complete a psychological task is called *reaction time*. Wundt assumed that more-complex psychological tasks would require more brain activity and so would take longer than simple tasks. To this day, researchers use reaction time to study psychological processes, although their equipment is far more modern.

Wundt was not satisfied with studying mental reaction times. He developed a new method to measure people's conscious experiences. This method was called *introspection*. In using introspection, research participants had to reflect and report on their thoughts about their personal experiences of objects. For example, participants would experience a series of objects and say which one they found the most pleasant. Wundt's work investigating conscious experiences was critical to the development of psychology. He trained many of the great early psychologists who went on to establish psychological laboratories throughout Europe, Canada, and the United States.

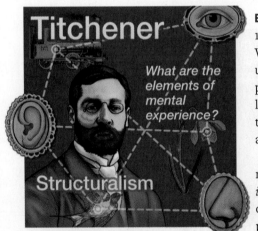

FIGURE 1.8

Edward Titchener

Edward Titchener founded structuralism. This school used introspection to investigate the basic parts of the conscious mind.

structuralism

An approach to psychology based on the idea that conscious experience can be broken down into its basic underlying components.

STRUCTURALISM: COMPONENTS OF THE CONSCIOUS MIND One of Wundt's students was Edward Titchener (**Figure 1.8**). Titchener pioneered a school of thought that became known as **structuralism**. This school is based on the idea that conscious experience can be broken down into underlying parts. Titchener believed that if psychologists could understand the basic elements of conscious experience, they would have a scientific basis for understanding the mind.

TABLE 1.1
Psychology's Schools of Thought

School of Thought and Influential Scientists	Goal
Structuralism (study unit 1.5) • Wilhelm Wundt • Edward Titchener • Margaret Floy Washburn	Identify the basic parts, or structures, of the conscious mind
Functionalism (study unit 1.5) • William James • Mary Whiton Calkins	Describe how the conscious mind aids adaptation to an environment
Psychoanalytic theory (study unit 1.5) • Sigmund Freud • Anna Freud	Understand how unconscious thoughts cause psychological disorders
Gestalt psychology (study unit 1.6) • Max Wertheimer • Wolfgang Köhler	Study individuals' personal perceptions as a unified whole
Behaviorism (study unit 1.6) • John B. Watson • B. F. Skinner	Describe behavior in response to environmental stimuli
Humanistic psychology (study unit 1.6) • Abraham Maslow • Carl Rogers	Investigate how people become happier and more fulfilled; focus on people's goodness
Cognitive psychology (study unit 1.6) • George Miller • Ulric Neisser	Explore internal mental processes that influence behavior

Suppose research participants were played a musical tone or shown an object, such as an apple. Through introspection, the participants would analyze their personal experiences of the stimulus. In this way, the researcher would identify the component parts of each participant's experience, such as the quality and intensity of the stimulus (**Figure 1.9**). Although Wundt ultimately rejected the use of introspection, Titchener relied on the method throughout his career.

The general problem with introspection is that it is unique to each person who is having the experience. In other words, each person brings to introspection a unique way of perceiving things. Researchers cannot determine whether participants in a study are using introspection in a similar way. Over time, psychologists largely abandoned introspection because it was not a reliable method for understanding psychological processes across different people. Even so, Wundt, Titchener, and other structuralists were important because they helped develop a science of psychology with its own vocabulary and set of rules.

Titchener was also important to the history of psychology because his first graduate student was female. Margaret Floy Washburn (**Figure 1.10a**) was the first woman to officially be granted a Ph.D. in psychology, in 1894, from Cornell University. Her work in understanding animal behavior led to the influential book *The Animal Mind: A Textbook of Comparative Psychology* (1908). In 1921, Washburn was elected the second female president of the American Psychological Association (APA).

"It's red. It's bright."

FIGURE 1.9

Structuralism and Introspection

In structuralism, a person would perform introspection about an object. For example, the person might report on the quality ("red") and intensity ("bright") of an apple. The person's verbal reports were thought to reveal the basic parts of the conscious mind.

(a)
(b)
(c)

FIGURE 1.10

The Early Women Pioneers of Psychology

(a) Margaret Floy Washburn was the first woman to be granted a Ph.D. in psychology. She investigated animal behavior and became the second female president of the APA. **(b)** Mary Whiton Calkins was one of the first female graduate students in psychology. Her influential research into memory helped her become the first female president of the APA. **(c)** Anna Freud received unofficial training in psychology from her father, Sigmund Freud. This background led to her becoming one of the most influential psychoanalytic theorists of her time.

FIGURE 1.11

William James

William James, the founder of functionalism, investigated the function of the conscious mind. He wanted to understand how the operations of the mind help people adapt to environmental demands.

functionalism
An early school of thought concerned with the adaptive purpose, or function, of mind and behavior.

natural selection
The basis of evolution; the idea that those who inherit characteristics that help them adapt to their particular environments have a selective advantage over those who do not.

FUNCTIONALISM: PURPOSE OF THE CONSCIOUS MIND One critic of structuralism was William James (**Figure 1.11**). James believed that structuralism failed to capture the most important aspects of mental experience. He argued that the mind was much more complex than its elements and could not be broken down into parts. Psychologists who used the structural approach, he said, were like people trying to understand a house by studying each of its bricks individually. More important to James was that the bricks together formed a house and that a house has a particular function. In short, the most important function of the mind is in how it is useful to people. This approach came to be known as **functionalism.**

According to functionalism, what is the purpose of the human mind? James felt that the answer was: to help preserve human life over time by helping people adapt to environmental demands. This key idea of functionalism was based on the work of the naturalist Charles Darwin, who observed that species change over generations. When these changes helped individuals of a species adapt to an environment, the individuals were more likely to survive and reproduce, and therefore to pass along those changes to their offspring. This process is called **natural selection,** and it is the basis of evolution. Included among the traits that are passed from parent to offspring is the functioning of the brain and mind. So natural selection explains how the human mind has evolved to help people adapt to their environments and bear children who are also more likely to survive.

James was not just a pioneer in developing the functionalist school of psychology. He also broke ground by admitting a woman, Mary Whiton Calkins (**Figure 1.10b**), to study in his graduate seminar at Harvard University in 1890. The rest of the students, all male, dropped out of the class in response, so James tutored Calkins individually. Although she completed the requirements to earn her Ph.D., Harvard refused to give her the degree because she was female. Regardless, Calkins continued her research on memory and became one of the most prominent psychologists of her time. In 1905, she was elected the first female president of the APA.

PSYCHOANALYTIC THEORY: UNCONSCIOUS CONFLICTS Twentieth-century psychology was profoundly influenced by one of its most famous thinkers,

Sigmund Freud (**Figure 1.12**). Freud was trained in medicine. At the beginning of his career, he worked with people who had nervous system disorders, such as paralysis of various body parts. He found that many of his patients had few medical reasons for their paralysis. Soon he came to believe that psychological factors were causing their conditions. To try to understand the connections between psychology and physical problems, Freud developed **psychoanalytic theory.**

Freud concluded that much of human behavior is determined by mental processes operating below the level of conscious awareness. He believed that these specific unconscious mental forces included both troubling childhood experiences blocked from memory and sexual urges that conflicted with acceptable behavior. By creating psychological blockages within the individual, these forces produced psychological discomfort and even mental disorders.

From his theories, Freud developed the practice of *psychoanalysis*. In this therapeutic approach, the therapist and the patient work together to bring the contents of the patient's unconscious into the patient's conscious awareness. Once the patient's unconscious conflicts are revealed, the therapist helps the patient deal with them constructively.

One of Freud's most famous patients was his daughter, Anna Freud (**Figure 1.10c**). Her experience with the process of psychoanalysis, and in hearing her father's conversations with influential thinkers of the time, had a more profound effect on her than her formal training as a teacher. In her most famous book, *The Ego and the Mechanisms of Defense* (1936), Freud detailed her psychoanalytic theory. Both Sigmund Freud and Anna Freud heavily influenced the public view of psychology. However, many of their ideas are difficult or impossible to test scientifically.

1.6 Psychologists Explore Behavior and Mental Activity

1.6 LEARNING GOAL ACTIVITIES

To maximize your learning, complete the following learning goal activities:

a. Understand all bold and italic terms by writing explanations of them in your own words.

b. Apply the four psychology schools of thought that investigated behavior and mental activity by writing an example of a topic that each school of thought would investigate.

In the early twentieth century, psychological researchers shifted away from studying the conscious and unconscious experiences of the mind. Some researchers, such as the Gestalt psychologists, believed that mental experience cannot be broken down into common underlying parts. Other researchers, such as the behaviorists, believed that the conscious mind and the unconscious mind were not appropriate topics for psychological investigation. The ideas of Gestalt psychology, behaviorism, and subsequent schools of thought (see Table 1.1) are the historical basis for modern psychological research on mental activity.

GESTALT PSYCHOLOGY: EXPERIENCING THE "WHOLE" Gestalt psychology developed in opposition to structuralism. This new school of thought sought to understand how people perceive information. The most prominent Gestalt psychologists included Max Wertheimer (**Figure 1.13**) and Wolfgang Köhler.

FIGURE 1.12

Sigmund Freud

Sigmund Freud founded psychoanalytic theory. Freud used psychoanalysis to treat unconscious mental forces that conflicted with acceptable behavior and that he believed produced psychological disorders.

psychoanalytic theory

The idea that our thoughts and actions are influenced by specific unconscious forces.

FIGURE 1.13

Max Wertheimer

Max Wertheimer was a founder of Gestalt psychology. According to this school of thought, people's experiences cannot be broken down into parts. Instead, perception is unique for each person and is affected by context.

FIGURE 1.14

John B. Watson

John Watson founded behaviorism, the scientific study of how observable environmental factors affect behavior.

Gestalt theory
The idea that the whole of personal experience is different from simply the sum of its parts.

behaviorism
A school of thought that emphasizes the role of environmental forces in producing behavior.

FIGURE 1.15

Carl Rogers

Carl Rogers was a founder of humanistic psychology. According to this school of thought, people are motivated to grow in ways that improve their lives.

Around 1912, the Gestalt psychologists began to explore how people experience sensory input. For example, why can two people view an object in very different ways? How can one person look at an object more than once and see it differently each time? Research into questions such as these led to the development of **Gestalt theory**. According to this set of ideas, the perception of objects is a personal experience. In other words—in direct contrast with structuralism—what a person experiences is different from all the parts of an object. The Gestalt perspective has influenced many areas of psychology, including the study of vision and our understanding of human personality.

BEHAVIORISM: STIMULI AND RESPONSES In 1913, the psychologist John B. Watson (**Figure 1.14**) challenged the focus on conscious and unconscious mental processes as being unscientific. He felt that if psychology were going to be a science, it had to stop trying to study mental events that could not be observed directly. Instead, Watson believed that animals—including humans—learned all behaviors through environmental factors. Specifically, Watson believed that psychologists needed to study the environmental stimuli, the behavioral triggers, in particular situations. By understanding the stimuli, people could predict the animals' behavioral responses in those situations. Watson developed the school of **behaviorism**, which investigates how observable stimuli in the environment affect behavior. Watson's views have been furthered by thousands of psychologists, including B. F. Skinner.

Behaviorism dominated psychological research well into the early 1960s. Behaviorists established many principles that are still viewed as critical to understanding behavior. For example, the use of rewards to teach children to clean their rooms is based on behaviorist principles. However, even researchers in the school of behaviorism, such as Edward Tolman, doubted that all psychological processes could be reduced to stimulus-response relationships. As you will learn in Chapter 6, Tolman's research with rats was among the first to reveal that animals have internal states that create a sense of purpose in their behavior. This work was among the first to indicate that psychology should not just focus on how stimuli affect behavior. Rather, psychology must also investigate internal mental processes, including feelings and thoughts.

HUMANISTIC PSYCHOLOGY: FOCUS ON POSITIVES In the 1950s, most schools of thought viewed behavior as resulting from events outside people's control. Freudians saw unconscious forces as guiding behavior, whereas behaviorists saw environmental factors as guiding behavior. Rejecting these views, psychologists such as Abraham Maslow and Carl Rogers (**Figure 1.15**) focused on how people are free to choose activities that make them feel happy and bring them fulfillment. This more positive perspective toward personal growth became known as **humanistic psychology**. This approach emphasized the basic goodness of people. It focused on how people should accept themselves, work on personal goals, and try to live up to their full potential as human beings. For example, humanistic psychologists might investigate why you are motivated to work hard to complete your education and how happy you feel when you achieve your goal.

Building on these earlier ideas, Martin Seligman launched the *positive psychology* movement (Seligman & Csikszentmihalyi, 2000). Seligman and others have encouraged the scientific study of how faith, values, creativity, courage, and hope affect us. Positive psychology emphasizes the quality of relationships and taking enjoyment from life's accomplishments. You will learn in Chapter 11 that there are many benefits to being positive in your outlook.

COGNITIVE PSYCHOLOGY: MENTAL ACTIVITY   In the second half of the twentieth century, researchers continued to gather evidence that learning was not as simple as the behaviorists believed. These findings suggested that mental functions were important for understanding behavior. In 1957, George A. Miller (**Figure 1.16**) and his colleagues, including Ulric Neisser, launched the cognitive revolution in psychology. Today, **cognitive psychology** is concerned with investigating mental functions such as intelligence, thinking, language, attention, learning, memory, problem solving, and decision making.

While some early cognitive psychologists focused exclusively on mental processes, others recognized that the brain was important to cognition. In the early 1980s, cognitive psychologists joined forces with computer scientists, philosophers, and researchers who studied the brain. The goal of this collaboration was to develop an integrated view of mind and brain. During the next decade, cognitive neuroscience emerged. The field of cognitive neuroscience studies the brain mechanisms that underlie thought, learning, and memory.

By now, you should understand how modern psychologists have come to focus on understanding mental activity, behavior, and the brain. As you will soon learn, this past work has laid the foundation for the development of many subfields in psychology. Each subfield investigates specific topics by using specific methods.

FIGURE 1.16

George Miller

George Miller was a founder of cognitive psychology. This modern school of psychology uses experimental methods to investigate how people think, remember, pay attention, make decisions, and solve problems.

1.7 Psychologists Today Investigate Many Different Topics

1.7 LEARNING GOAL ACTIVITIES

To maximize your learning, complete the following learning goal activities:

a. Understand all bold and italic terms by writing explanations of them in your own words.

b. Apply the subfields of psychology by choosing two subfields that interest you and explaining what research topic you would study in each subfield if you were a psychologist.

Through the history of psychology, the various schools of thought helped shape how psychologists viewed mental activity and behavior. Today, the schools are less important. Instead, psychologists understand that phenomena need to be examined from many different perspectives.

Table 1.2, on p. 20, shows the wide range of interests that modern psychologists have across the main subfields in the discipline. In many of these subfields, psychologists conduct research to help us understand the mind, behavior, and the brain processes underlying them. For example, a health psychologist might explore how having a pet influences heart rate and blood pressure to have positive health effects (**Figure 1.17a**). Or a social psychologist could explore how participating in sports helps teenagers develop leadership skills (**Figure 1.17b**). Yet other psychologists study **culture**. A culture is made up of beliefs, values, rules, norms, and customs that

humanistic psychology
A school of thought that investigates how people grow to become happier and more fulfilled; it focuses on the basic goodness of people.

cognitive psychology
A school of thought that studies how people think, learn, and remember.

culture
The beliefs, values, rules, and customs that exist within a group of people who share a common language and environment and that are transmitted through learning from one generation to the next.

TABLE 1.2
Subfields of Psychology

Subfield	Focus	Sample Questions
Evolutionary psychology	Explore how traits are selected to aid adaptation in an environment.	• How has evolution influenced the ability to do many tasks at once? • What evolutionary pressures affect selection of a romantic partner?
Biological psychology	Study how biological systems give rise to mental activity and behavior.	• How do chemicals in the brain influence sexual behavior? • How do brain cells change during learning?
Cognitive psychology/ Cognitive neuroscience	Investigate attention, perception, memory, problem solving, and language, often based on brain processes.	• What makes some problems harder to solve than others? • Do brain training programs increase attention and memory abilities?
Developmental psychology	Research how people change from infancy through old age.	• How do children learn to speak? • How can older adults maintain mental abilities as they age?
Health psychology	Examine how psychological factors affect health and well-being.	• How does feeling stressed affect the body? • How does viewing life optimistically improve health?
Personality psychology	Analyze enduring characteristics that people display over time and across circumstances.	• Why are some people shy? • How do biology, circumstances, and culture shape personality?
Social psychology	Explore how people are affected by others.	• When do people form impressions of others? • How do people form or dissolve intimate relationships?
Cultural psychology	Study how people are influenced by the societal rules that dictate behavior in their cultures.	• How does culture shape a person's sense of self? • Does culture create differences in perception?
Clinical psychology	Consider the factors that cause psychological disorders and the best methods to treat them.	• What factors lead people to feel depressed? • How does the brain change as a result of therapy for depression?
Educational psychology	Investigate effectiveness of techniques in teaching and learning.	• Do fidget spinners help students pay attention? • How can a teacher help students learn when watching videos?
Industrial/organizational psychology	Examine issues pertaining to industry and the workplace.	• How can increasing morale help motivate workers? • How can equipment be designed so workers can easily perform duties and avoid accidents?

FIGURE 1.17

The Work of Psychologists Influences Us Every Day

Psychologists today have a broad range of interests across many subfields, and their work affects our lives in many ways. **(a)** Health psychologists have found that having pets improves people's health. **(b)** Social psychologists have explained why people sometimes perform even better in a group than when they are alone. **(c)** Cultural psychologists might study why people in Korea love K-pop: modern pop music involving glossy production, electronic elements, and the visual dazzle of girl bands or boy bands, such as BTS. **(d)** Clinical psychologists use different techniques to help people overcome mental health problems to improve their lives.

people learn from one another when they share a common language or environment. A cultural psychologist might study why different cultures prefer different types of music (**Figure 1.17c**).

In other subfields, psychologists focus on providing services to individuals and groups. For example, clinical psychologists help people with mental health problems cope with challenges and crises in personal, professional, and academic domains (**Figure 1.17d**). In yet other subfields, such as educational psychology, professionals work in schools. For example, they help students with problems that interfere with learning, design age-appropriate curricula, and conduct aptitude achievement tests. In fact, as described in Has It Happened to You? on p. 22, your teacher for this class may be an educational psychologist.

Because psychologists today work in various subfields, they also work in diverse settings (**Figure 1.18**). Where they work depends on whether their primary focus is on research, teaching, clinical practice with patients, or applying scientific findings to improving the quality of daily living. Researchers who study the brain, the mind, and behavior may work in schools, businesses, universities, or clinics. Some practitioners apply the findings of psychological research to helping people in need of mental health treatment, designing safe and pleasant work environments, counseling people on career paths, or helping teachers design better educational experiences. The distinction between psychological research and clinical psychology can be fuzzy. Many researchers are also clinical practitioners, and many clinical psychologists study psychological disorders as well as treat them.

As you can see, psychology is remarkably diverse in its subfields of study and in the places where psychologists work. That's because psychologists are concerned with nearly every aspect of human life. Regardless of where they work and what

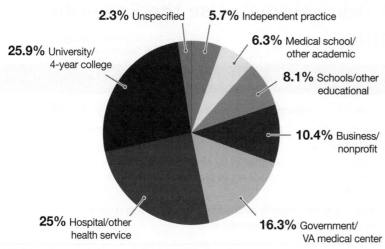

- **2.3%** Unspecified
- **5.7%** Independent practice
- **6.3%** Medical school/other academic
- **8.1%** Schools/other educational
- **10.4%** Business/nonprofit
- **16.3%** Government/VA medical center
- **25%** Hospital/other health service
- **25.9%** University/4-year college

FIGURE 1.18

Where Psychologists Work

This chart shows the type of settings where psychologists work, based on a survey of those obtaining their doctorates in psychology in 2009 (Michalski, Kohout, Wicherski, & Hart, 2011).

HAS IT HAPPENED TO YOU?

Have You Met a Psychologist?

Chances are good that you have met a psychologist. For example, if you have received counseling for a mental health problem, the professional providing that treatment may have been a psychologist. If you have received help with learning differences in school, the professional helping you succeed may have been a psychologist. Right now, the person teaching your psychology class is most likely a psychologist. In fact, your instructor may be an educational psychologist. Feel free to express interest in your instructor by politely asking, "Are you a psychologist?" If the answer is yes, follow up by asking, "What's your subfield?" and "How did you get interested in that?"

they do, psychologists are scientists. In seeking to understand the brain, the mind, and behavior, psychologists use the scientific method (discussed in study unit 1.8). Are you interested in pursuing a career in psychology? You can learn more about this career path in the Putting Psychology to Work feature on p. 42.

 What Do Psychologists Investigate?

To make sure you learned what you just read, write answers to the following questions and check your answers.

1.4 Explain why the nature/nurture and mind/body debates are appropriate topics for exploration in psychology.

1.5 Explain whether the theory of natural selection is related to structuralism or functionalism.

1.6 Name and explain what school of thought in psychology emphasizes the importance of choosing activities that bring personal fulfillment.

1.7 Name and explain which of the 11 subfields in psychology you might be working within if you conducted research on how using a cell phone affects the ability to pay attention when driving.

See Appendix B for answers to the red Q questions.

How Do Psychologists Conduct Research?

Are you a safe driver? If you are like most people, your gut reply is "Yes!" But as you saw in the chapter opener, even though people may believe they are good drivers, they sometimes use their cell phones while driving. The data show that this distraction can be deadly, but the question remains: Why does using a cell phone impair driving? Psychologists don't answer questions like this one based on intuition, beliefs, or even opinions. Instead, because psychology is a science, psychologists use specific goals and methods to learn about mental activity, behavior, and the brain processes that underlie them.

1.8 Psychologists Use the Scientific Method

 1.8 LEARNING GOAL ACTIVITIES

To maximize your learning, complete the following learning goal activities:

a. Understand all bold and italic terms by writing explanations of them in your own words.

b. Apply the four goals of science by writing how each one could be used to investigate students' use of active processes to learn material they read in a textbook.

c. Understand the scientific method by naming the five steps in this cycle and explaining each one in your own words.

SCIENCE HAS FOUR GOALS Science has four goals: *description*, *prediction*, *control*, and *explanation*. So the goals of psychological science are to describe *what* a particular phenomenon is, predict *when* it will occur, control *what* causes it to occur, and explain *why* it occurs. For example, consider the idea that using a cell phone interferes with driving. To understand how this interference happens, psychologists need to address each of the four goals of psychology. Different studies might examine any of these goals to better understand how cell phones affect driving.

First, psychologists describe the phenomenon that is happening. To pose a question that requires description, researchers might ask: How many people use their cell phones while driving? In addition, the researchers might describe whether people talk or text on the phone more while driving.

Second, psychologists predict when the phenomenon they have described happens. For example, they might examine how often using a cell phone is related to collisions. In this case, investigating an association between using a cell phone and crashing helps researchers predict that future cell phone use while driving might be associated with more crashes.

Third, psychologists may pursue the goal of control by changing one factor to influence another. For example, how do we know that using the cell phone is what negatively affects driving? Perhaps some other factor, such as the driver's personality, causes this outcome. After all, people who are more likely to take risks might drive dangerously, and they might be inclined to use cell phones more when driving. Controlling the conditions of their studies makes it possible for researchers to know that using the cell phone and not some other factor is responsible for the effects.

Finally, psychologists try to explain a phenomenon. In this case, researchers will have described and predicted cell phone use while driving, and they will have controlled the situation in which cell phone use leads to poor driving. Various additional studies are likely to be conducted to examine what aspects of cell phone use are responsible for its effects on driving. Is it because people use their hands to hold the phone, or that they take their eyes off the road to dial or to text, or that using the phone interferes with their mental ability to focus on driving? Careful research using the scientific method lets psychologists understand many aspects of using a cell phone while driving. This research lets psychologists develop good scientific explanations, or theories, for the behavior and its effects. Researchers might further examine why people continue to use their cell phones while driving despite the danger of doing so. Ultimately, the knowledge from psychological research may help scientists, technology developers, and policymakers create strategies to reduce this dangerous behavior.

Have you ever heard that talking on a cell phone impairs driving as much as being intoxicated? The Evaluating Psychology in the Real World feature on p. 24 will help you use the three steps in critical thinking to explore this claim and determine if you should accept it or not.

FIVE STEPS IN THE CYCLE OF THE SCIENTIFIC METHOD Because they are scientists, psychologists base their beliefs about behavior and mental processes on observing the world and measuring various aspects of it. This approach is called *empiricism*. To be confident about the conclusions drawn from their observations, psychologists conduct empirical research using the **scientific method.**

There are three key aspects of the scientific method. First, the scientific method requires that psychologists follow several carefully planned, systematic steps. Second, the processes that psychologists use in the scientific method must be objective—that is, free from bias. Third, the procedures must be reproducible. In other words, if other psychologists repeat the same procedures with similar research participants, they would expect to obtain the same results. This idea is called **replication**. Replication is an important part of the scientific method. It

scientific method
A systematic procedure of observing and measuring phenomena (observable things) to answer questions about *what* happens, *when* it happens, *what* causes it, and *why*. This process involves a dynamic interaction between theories, hypotheses, and research methods.

replication
Repetition of a research study to confirm or contradict the results.

Every day we come across claims in advertisements, on the news, and through the Internet that relate to topics in psychology. For example, recall the story at the start of this chapter about how thousands of people, such as Kelsey Raffaele, die in traffic accidents each year due to distracted driving. Why is distracted driving a psychological issue? The answer is that it is related to people's mental activity and behavior and the brain processes that underlie them.

Suppose that you want to learn more about this issue. On the Internet you find a story on the topic: https://www.livescience.com/872-cell-phones-drivers-bad-drunks.html. The article appears at a Web site called *LiveScience,* but does that mean you should you accept what it says? To answer this question, read the article (excerpted below) and answer the three steps in critical thinking:

ACTIVITY: To determine if you should accept the claim in this news article, review the Learning Tip on p. 7 and follow these steps:

Step 1 What is the claim I am being asked to accept?

Step 2 What evidence, if any, is provided to support the claim?

Step 3 Given the evidence, what are the most reasonable conclusions about the claim?

If you have rejected the claim or found the evidence lacking, why did you do so? If you have found that the evidence supports the claim, how might this information change how you think and act?

Cell Phones Make Drivers as Bad as Drunks

A study in which both the participants and the scientists got sloshed has shown that motorists who talk on cell phones while driving are as impaired as drunk drivers. . . .

"We found that people are as impaired when they drive and talk on a cell phone as they are when they drive intoxicated at the legal blood-alcohol limit," said [researcher] Frank Drews. . . .

The volunteers in the new study drove a virtual vehicle four times: once undistracted; once using a handheld cell phone in real conversations; then with a hands-free phone; and finally again after getting tipsy.

The volunteers, all self-labeled social drinkers who were used to three to five drinks a week, were paid $10 an hour.

The drinks—multiple rounds of vodka and orange juice—were on the house.

Blood tests and breathalyzers were used to measure alcohol levels of 0.08 percent—the minimum that defines illegal drunken driving in most U.S. states. Most European countries, recognizing this as quite a level of stupor, have reduced their legal threshold to 0.05.

Some of the participants were visibly out of control, Drews said. "When I saw them walking, I thought, 'Man, I don't want to come close to them when they're driving a car.'"

Those talking on either handheld or hands-free cell phones drove slightly slower, were 9 percent slower to hit the brakes when necessary, showed 24 percent more variation in following distance, and were 19 percent slower to resume normal speed after braking.

Three study participants rear-ended the virtual pace car while talking [on the phone]. . . . But nobody crashed while plastered. . . .

The study, announced today, is detailed in the summer 2006 issue of *Human Factors: The Journal of the Human Factors and Ergonomics Society.* It is the first peer-reviewed study on this topic to include drinking. The findings may well apply to in-car television, computers and other devices, the researchers write.

means that research is always continuing, and getting additional results from scientific studies increases our confidence in the findings (Goodman, Fanelli, & Ioannidis, 2016). The more researchers follow the scientific method, the more we can be confident that their empirical results provide a good understanding of mental activity and behavior.

The process of the scientific method includes the continuous cycle of five steps shown in **Figure 1.19**. To explore these steps, imagine you are doing research on using a cell phone while driving.

Psychologists study research questions they find interesting. For example, when they see a person behaving in a puzzling way, they may seek to understand that behavior. Think of using a cell phone while driving as a puzzling behavior. Research questions related to this particular puzzling behavior would revolve around why using a cell phone while driving is dangerous. To understand complex behavior, psychologists often start with a theory based on existing evidence. A **theory** is an explanation or a model of how some mental process or behavior occurs. The theory consists of interconnected ideas or concepts that are used to explain prior research findings and to make predictions about future events. Your theory might involve various mechanisms to explain the behavior, such as "distracted driving is a major cause of car crashes."

Formulating a theory is the first step in the scientific method (see Figure 1.19, Step 1). In formulating a theory, you need to learn about prior research related to the topic. As soon as possible, you should perform a *literature review*. A literature review explores the scientific articles related to your theory. There are many resources available to assist with literature reviews, including scientific research databases such as PsycINFO, Google Scholar, and PubMed. You can search these databases by keywords, such as "distraction and driving," or you might think of how people can be distracted while driving and then you would search for "cell phones and crashes." The results of your searches will reveal if and how other scientists have been testing the same idea or similar ones. For example, psychologists from various subfields may have investigated in different ways the topic of how using a cell phone disrupts driving. These researchers' findings may help you refine your theory, and they may guide the direction of your research.

A clearly stated theory is important because it is the basis for the next step of the scientific method: developing a **hypothesis** (see Figure 1.19, Step 2). A hypothesis is a specific, testable prediction about the theory. Any one theory is usually tested by several separate hypotheses. Each hypothesis tests a different aspect of the theory by targeting one of the goals of science (description, prediction, control, and explanation). For example, a hypothesis that is appropriate for your theory might have the goal of explaining why people drive worse when using a cell phone. A good hypothesis with this goal might be: "Research participants holding a conversation on a cell phone, whether handheld or hands-free, during a driving simulation task will perform more poorly than participants not holding a conversation on a cell phone."

1 Formulate a theory.

You develop a scientific explanation about a phenomenon. A literature review of existing studies informs your theory. In this example, your theory is that a major cause of car crashes is distracted driving.

2 Develop a testable hypothesis.

You create a specific, testable hypothesis related to the theory. In this example, a good testable prediction is that "Using a cell phone will interfere with driving because it is distracting."

3 Test with a research method.

You test your hypothesis by selecting the most appropriate research method (see study units 1.9–1.11). You then collect data to evaluate your hypothesis. For example, in an experiment you might have some participants talk on a handheld or hands-free cell phone in a driving simulator while other participants do not talk on a cell phone.

4 Analyze the data.

You analyze the data using appropriate statistical techniques and draw conclusions. If the data do not support your hypothesis, you either discard the theory or revise it (and make plans to test the revision). See, at the back of the book, Appendix A: How Do Psychologists Analyze Research Data?

5 Share the results and conduct more research.

You submit results to research journals and present them at conferences to share them with the scientific community. Then you continue the process by refining your theory, making further predictions, and testing hypotheses.

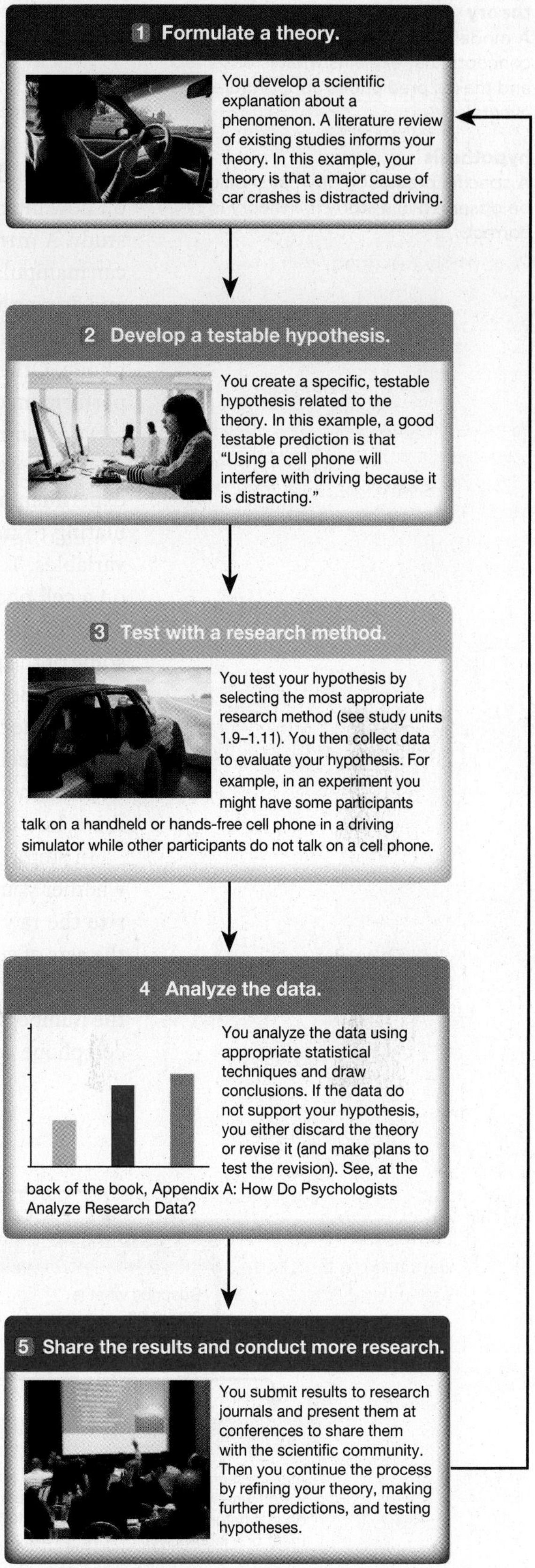

FIGURE 1.19

Five Steps in the Cycle of the Scientific Method

theory
A model of interconnected ideas or concepts that explains what is observed and makes predictions about future events.

hypothesis
A specific prediction of what should be observed in a study if a theory is correct.

Now you move to the third step in the scientific method: testing the hypothesis (see Figure 1.19, Step 3). The three main types of research methods you can use to test your research question are descriptive, correlational, and experimental (**Figure 1.20**). You will learn about all three of these research methods in study units 1.9–1.11. Which research method you use depends on the goal of your research and the hypothesis you have stated. What method you use also depends on how much control you need over manipulating and measuring factors in the study. A *variable* is something in the world that can vary and that the researcher can manipulate (change), measure (evaluate), or both. In a study of cell phone use and driving ability, some of the variables would be under the researcher's control, such as whether the people in the study held the phone or used a hands-free phone. Other variables are those that the researcher measures, such as driving performance.

For your research, because the goal is explanation and the hypothesis pertains to an explanation of how cell phone use interferes with driving, you must use an experimental method. In an experiment, you control the variables you are manipulating to investigate whether there is a cause/effect relationship between the variables. To test the hypothesis "Research participants holding a conversation on a cell phone during a driving simulation task will perform more poorly than participants not holding a conversation," you might create an experiment where some of the participants might just drive. Others would drive while carrying on a conversation on a cell phone. To rule out the possibility that it is not just simply holding the phone, you might include conditions in which people are talking while holding a cell phone and where they are talking using a hands-free cell phone. You could then observe people's driving in the simulator in terms of how quickly they drive, how carefully they drive, how many crashes they have, and so on.

In Step 4 of the scientific method, you analyze the data from your research to see whether your hypothesis is supported (see Figure 1.19, Step 4). First you summarize the raw data. Then you determine whether differences really exist between the sets of summarized data. Both of these forms of data analysis are described in Appendix A. In the current example, you could summarize the data by comparing the numbers of crashes people had when driving, while they were either holding a cell phone conversation, handheld or hands-free, or not using a cell phone. Then

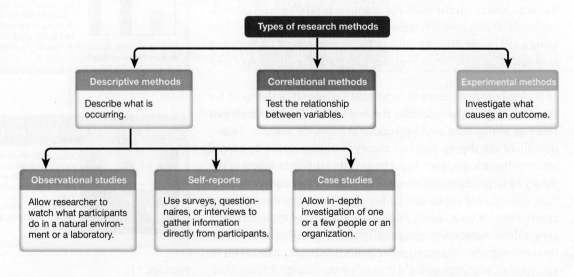

FIGURE 1.20
Three Main Types of Research Methods

you would decide whether any differences between these conditions were meaningful or whether they happened by chance. That is, you would determine whether you found a significant effect. If you have a significant effect, you can then examine whether your findings would be the same if you studied other groups of people. That is, you can consider whether your findings apply to people in general.

Lastly, you must report your research results (see Figure 1.19, Step 5). One way this can happen is at a scientific conference where attendees present their findings at talk or poster sessions. As described in Has It Happened to You?, you may have seen a psychology poster session at your own school. Another way of reporting research results is to publish them in a peer-reviewed scientific journal. Published articles are a more thorough means of presenting findings because they include all the background for the research, the full methodology for how the question was studied, the complete data analyses, and a discussion of what the results mean in relation to other research on the topic.

As part of the cycle of the scientific method, you or other researchers determine what issues related to the topic need additional investigation. Remember, no single study definitively answers any research question. A study shows only what happened in a particular set of circumstances. As a result, psychologists never say they have proved a theory. As mentioned in study unit 1.2, this is why scientists avoid the term "fact." However, you generally can feel more confident about research findings when two things have happened. First, the researchers have followed the scientific method in performing a particular study. Second, that study and its outcomes have been replicated by the same researchers or others. When the results from two or more studies are the same, or at least support the same conclusion, the findings are more likely to be trustworthy. In addition, with each new study that explores a related but slightly different aspect of the topic, more information becomes available. In psychology, the accumulated findings add to the understanding of mental activity and behavior.

1.9 Descriptive Methods Describe What Is Happening

1.9 LEARNING GOAL ACTIVITIES

To maximize your learning, complete the following learning goal activities:

a. Understand all bold and italic terms by writing explanations of them in your own words.

b. Apply the three descriptive methods by explaining how you could use each one to investigate a psychological topic you are interested in.

Now that you have learned the five steps of the scientific method, you are ready to look at the process in more detail. In this study unit, the focus is on the three main types of descriptive methods.

After you have stated your research hypothesis in Step 2, in Step 3 you must decide which research method is best suited for your study (see Figure 1.20). As you just learned, your choice of research method depends on the goal of your research. If the goal of your research is describing behavior, then you would use one of the **descriptive methods** to collect data that will test your hypothesis. Suppose your hypothesis is: "People use cell phones while driving." Because this hypothesis has the goal of describing behavior, you would use a descriptive method to investigate it.

So what are descriptive methods? Descriptive methods are a way of collecting data that provide a snapshot of what is occurring at a specific point in time. As

HAS IT HAPPENED TO YOU?

Have You Seen a Poster Session?

At the academic buildings of your school, are there sometimes research-related posters on the walls? Or do people—faculty members, students, or both—sometimes stand in groups, discussing the research posters? If you answered yes to either of these questions, then you may have witnessed one method of telling people about research results. At a poster session, researchers display large posters with information about their studies. The researchers stand by their posters and answer questions from those who are interested. Poster sessions are a great way to learn more about research in psychology. If you want to learn more about psychological research by attending a poster session, ask your teacher if you might have that opportunity.

descriptive methods
Research methods that provide a systematic and objective description of what is occurring.

a result, this technique is especially valuable in the early stages of research when researchers are trying to see whether a particular phenomenon exists. Let's look at three descriptive methods you might use: observational studies, self-reports, and case studies.

OBSERVATIONAL STUDIES   *Observational studies* are a specific type of descriptive method. They involve systematically assessing and coding observable behavior (**Figure 1.21**). By coding, we mean determining which previously defined category the behavior fits into. For example, researchers might record the types of foods that people eat in cafeterias, count the number and types of mating behaviors that penguins engage in during their mating season, or tally the number of times they see someone using a cell phone while driving. In observational studies, the investigator does not control the behavior being observed.

Observational studies are typically used in natural environments. Some researchers observe behavior at regular time intervals. These intervals may be as short as seconds or minutes, or they may be as long as years, entire lifetimes, and even across generations. By using intervals, the researchers can keep track of what research participants do at specific points in time.

In your research on using cell phones and driving, you might stand at a busy intersection and watch people driving. Every 5 minutes, you could record whether the drivers you see are talking on cell phones. In this case, you would be doing an observational study using a 5-minute interval.

Observational research is critical in showing what is happening so that future research can attempt to predict, control, and explain the phenomenon. However, it is often hard to observe a situation without seeing what you expect or want to see. Suppose that a person in a car alone is apparently engaged in a conversation but is not holding a phone. The person might be using a hands-free cell phone, thinking aloud, or singing along with the radio. You need to avoid assuming that all apparent speaking when alone is a cell phone conversation. To be most objective, you would

Observational studies are a descriptive method. They involve observing and classifying behavior, either with intervention by the observer or without intervention by the observer.

Advantages	Especially valuable in the early stages of research, when trying to determine whether a phenomenon exists. Can take place with intervention or without intervention.
Disadvantages	Errors in observation can occur because of an observer's expectations (*observer bias*). An observer's presence can change the behavior being witnessed (*reactivity*).

FIGURE 1.21

Observational Studies

(left) The evolutionary psychologist Lawrence Sugiyama, here hunting with a bow and arrow, has conducted observational research in Ecuadorian Amazonia among the Shiwiar, Achuar, Shuar, and Zaparo peoples. **(right)** The primatologist Jane Goodall observes a family of chimpanzees.

With intervention

Without intervention

use clear rules for identifying the behavior of interest. In this case, you might record the person as using a cell phone only when you observe an actual cell phone.

In conducting observational studies, researchers must guard against *observer bias*. Bias refers to errors in observation that occur because of the observer's expectations. Observer bias can especially be a problem if cultural norms favor behaving in certain ways. For instance, in many societies women are freer to express sadness than men are. As a result, in coding men's and women's facial expressions, an observer may be more likely to rate female expressions as indicating sadness. The observer may tend to rate men's expressions of sadness as reflecting annoyance or some other emotion.

Another problem with observational studies is that they can produce artificial behavior. Such behavior will not reflect how people naturally behave. For example, the presence of an observer might alter the behavior being observed. Suppose people want to make a positive impression on an observer. They may act differently when they believe they are being observed. A change in behavior as a result of being observed is called *reactivity*.

SELF-REPORTS   For some kinds of research, observational studies are not appropriate. A different descriptive method consists of obtaining *self-reports* from research participants (**Figure 1.22**).

Questionnaires or surveys can be used to gather data from a large number of people in a short time. These research tools are easy to administer as well as cost-efficient. With groups that cannot be studied through questionnaires or surveys (for example, young children), interviews can be used. Interviews are also helpful in getting more details about the respondents' opinions, experiences, and attitudes. That is, the answers during the interview may lead the researchers to ask questions they had not planned.

A problem common to all self-report methods is that people's answers can involve personal biases called *self-report bias*. Sometimes people may not reveal personal information that casts them in a negative light. If you are in your twenties, imagine having an interviewer around your parents' age ask you to describe intimate aspects of your sex life. If you are an older student, imagine a twentysomething interviewer asking the same question. How truthful would you be? Researchers

Self-reports are a descriptive method that involves asking questions of research participants. The participants then respond in any way they feel is appropriate or select from among a fixed number of options.

Advantages   Self-reports such as surveys and questionnaires can be used to gather data from a large number of people. They are easy to administer, cost-efficient, and a relatively fast way to collect data. Interviewing people face-to-face gives the researcher the opportunity to explore new lines of questioning.

Disadvantages   People can introduce biases into their answers (*self-report bias*). They may not recall information accurately.

Surveys and questionnaires

Interviews

FIGURE 1.22

Self-Reports

(left) Researchers can ask participants to complete surveys or questionnaires. **(right)** Alternatively, the researchers can interview the participants.

FIGURE 1.23

Case Studies

(left) In December 2012, a 20-year-old gunman went on a shooting spree at Sandy Hook Elementary School, in Newtown, Connecticut. The gunman killed 26 teachers and young students before killing himself. **(right)** The gunman's name was Adam Lanza. This photo shows Lanza as a seemingly happy and healthy young boy. The Sandy Hook shooting provides a case study of how an individual can become disturbed enough to commit a terrible act.

Case studies are a descriptive research method that involves intensive examination of one person or organization or a few individuals or organizations.

Advantages	Can provide a lot of data.
Disadvantages	Can be very subjective. If a researcher has a preexisting theory (for example, people who are socially awkward are dangerous), this theory can bias what is observed, investigated, and recorded. The results cannot be generalized from a single case study to the population.

have to consider whether their questions might lead a person to respond in a way that is most socially acceptable. Any distortion of the truth—whether it is meant to please or displease—will present a biased view. Psychologists therefore design self-reports so that people feel comfortable providing information. For example, the researchers make clear to the participant that all responses will be confidential.

CASE STUDIES   *Case studies* involve intensive examination of individuals. For example, a case study might try to understand the accident where Kelsey Raffaele was killed while driving (discussed in the chapter opener). Often, case studies focus on a few unique people or organizations (**Figure 1.23**). For example, case studies of people with brain injuries have provided a wealth of evidence about what parts of the brain are involved in various psychological processes. In one case, a man who was accidentally stabbed through the middle part of the brain with a fencing foil lost the ability to store new memories (Squire & Moore, 1979). This study was important for indicating which parts of the brain are involved in memory.

Case studies of people with psychological disorders are used frequently in psychology. The major problem with these clinical case studies is that it is difficult to know whether the researcher's theory about the cause of the psychological disorder is correct. The researcher has no control over the person's life and is forced to make assumptions about the effects of various life events.

1.10 Correlational Methods Study Relationships

 1.10 LEARNING GOAL ACTIVITIES

To maximize your learning, complete the following learning goal activities:

a. Understand all bold and italic terms by writing explanations of them in your own words.

b. Apply correlations by describing one example of a correlation in your life and explaining why the relationship is not causal.

Suppose now that you do not want to merely describe whether people use cell phones while driving. Instead, you want to study the relationship between using a cell phone and driving outcomes. To examine a naturally occurring relationship between two factors without attempting to alter them, researchers use **correlational methods** (**Figure 1.24**). How is this done? In correlational methods, researchers measure the two variables and then determine the degree of relationship between them. Various methods can be used to collect the data, including observational and self-reports methods. If there is a relationship, knowing one variable can help you predict what might happen with the other variable.

Suppose your hypothesis is "More frequent use of a cell phone while driving is related to having more crashes." You could use a correlational method to test this hypothesis. To do so, you might measure people's self-reported use of cell phones while driving and also their self-reported car crash history. These data would let you examine whether using a cell phone while driving and car crashes are related. If they are, then you can make predictions about how cell phone use is associated with car crashes. To learn more about what correlational research might reveal about the relationship between using a cell phone and driving performance, see Appendix A.

CORRELATION IS NOT CAUSALITY The data from your correlational study on cell phones do not show causation—they do not establish that using a cell phone while driving actually *causes* car crashes. Why not? A few potential problems prevent researchers from drawing causal conclusions from studies using correlational methods.

One problem with correlational methods is in not knowing the direction of the relationship between variables. That is, can you determine what causes what? This sort of ambiguity is known as the *directionality problem*. For example, suppose you survey a large group of people about their sleeping habits and their levels of stress. Those who report sleeping badly also report having a higher level of stress. Does lack of sleep increase stress levels, or does increased stress lead to shorter and worse sleep? The cause/effect relationship in this example could go in either direction. As shown in the Learning Tip on p. 32, both lack of sleep and more stress could be causes. But both of them also could be effects. In short, because of the directionality problem, correlational methods cannot tell you what causes a particular outcome.

correlational methods
Research methods that examine how variables are naturally related in the real world. The researcher makes no attempt to alter the variables or assign causation between them.

Correlational methods examine how variables are related, without intervention by the observer.

Advantages	Rely on naturally occurring relationships. May take place in a real-world setting.
Disadvantages	Cannot demonstrate causal relationships (that one thing happened because of the other). Cannot show the direction of the cause/effect relationship between variables (*directionality problem*). An unidentified variable may be involved (*third variable problem*).

FIGURE 1.24
Correlational Methods
Correlational methods help reveal whether two variables are related. A correlation may exist between the fitness level of parents and the fitness level of their children. A correlational study cannot demonstrate the cause of this relationship, which may include biological tendencies to gain weight or have a lean build, environmental factors such as access to nutritious food, or other factors.

The directionality problem and the third variable problem are the two main reasons that correlational methods prevent researchers from being able to state that changes in one variable actually cause changes in another. Failure to consider these problems may lead to wrong conclusions. Here is a way to visualize these problems in correlational methods.

The Directionality Problem

Lack of sleep (A) is correlated with greater stress (B). (A ↔ B)

- Does less sleep cause more stress? (A → B)

  or

- Does more stress cause less sleep? (B → A)

The Third Variable Problem

Using a cell phone while driving (A) is correlated with driving dangerously (B).

- Risk taking (C) may cause some people to use a cell phone while driving. (C → A)

  and

- Risk taking (C) may cause some people to drive dangerously. (C → B)

Another drawback of all correlational studies is the *third variable problem*. The Learning Tip above also explains why this problem prevents us from understanding what causes an outcome in a study using correlational methods. Say your theory is that using a cell phone while driving causes people to drive dangerously. What if some other variable, a third variable, causes both of those factors—using a cell phone while driving *and* dangerous driving? For example, people who are risk takers may be more likely to use a cell phone while driving. Risk takers might also tend to take dangerous chances when driving. Thus, the real cause of both using a cell phone when driving and dangerous driving might be the third variable, risk taking.

Many media reports of correlational studies make it sound as though one variable causes another (**Figure 1.25**). Failure to consider the directionality and third variable problems may lead people to make wrong conclusions about relationships. However, if you use the three steps in critical thinking (see the Learning Tip on p. 7), you can avoid making this mistake.

These examples may make it seem that you should simply disregard the results of correlational studies. On the contrary, correlational studies provide important information about the natural relationships between variables. That information lets researchers make valuable predictions. For example, correlational research has shown a strong relationship between depression and suicide. For this reason, clinical psychologists often assess symptoms of depression to determine suicide risk. In addition, researchers who conduct correlational studies use statistical procedures to rule out potential third variables and directionality problems. Once they have shown that a relationship between two variables holds even when potential third variables are taken into account, researchers can be more confident that the relationship is meaningful. In any case, to truly understand psychological findings, it is important to understand the difference between correlation and causation.

Eating Pizza Cuts Cancer Risk

Diet of Fish Can Prevent Teen Violence

Does Your Neighborhood Cause Schizophrenia?

Housework Cuts Breast Cancer Risk

FIGURE 1.25

Correlations in the News

When the media present results from correlational studies, the reports often suggest that one factor causes the other. In such cases, think critically and remember that just because two events are related to each other, you cannot know whether one causes the other.

1.11 Experimental Methods Test Causation

experimental methods
Research methods that test causal hypotheses by manipulating independent variables and measuring the effects on dependent variables.

1.11 LEARNING GOAL ACTIVITIES

To maximize your learning, complete the following learning goal activities:

a. Understand all bold and italic terms by writing explanations of them in your own words.

b. Apply experimental methods by explaining the control group, the experimental group(s), the independent variable(s), and the dependent variable(s) in a study exploring the effect of texting while driving on driving performance.

You have just learned that if a psychological researcher is using a correlational method, the study can uncover whether a relationship exists between variables. The resulting data will let the researcher predict how these variables are related in the future. However, the researcher will not have control over the situation and so cannot explain whether one variable causes the other. Therefore, if the goal of the research is to determine causation, the psychologist must use **experimental methods** to test the hypothesis (**Figure 1.26**). In this study unit, you will learn about experimental methods. Appendix A describes what experimental research might reveal about how using a cell phone affects driving performance.

VARIABLES IN AN EXPERIMENT To begin understanding experimental methods, return to the research example about whether using a cell phone while driving affects driving performance. You design an experiment in which you control whether people are using a cell phone and you measure driving performance. You could also add other conditions to try to understand why this effect occurs. Is it because of holding the phone or because talking on a cell phone is distracting? In this case, you might want to have two experimental conditions. In one condition, participants use a handheld phone. In the other, they use a hands-free phone. Your new hypothesis might be: "Using either hands-free or handheld cell phones impairs driving." How would you examine this hypothesis?

Experimental methods examine how one variable that is manipulated by researchers affects another variable.

Advantages	Provide control over the independent variable (which is manipulated), so can demonstrate that one thing causes another. Avoid the *directionality problem*.
Disadvantages	Varying something other than the independent variable (a *confound*) can affect the dependent variable (which is measured) and lead to inaccurate conclusions. Often take place in an artificial setting.

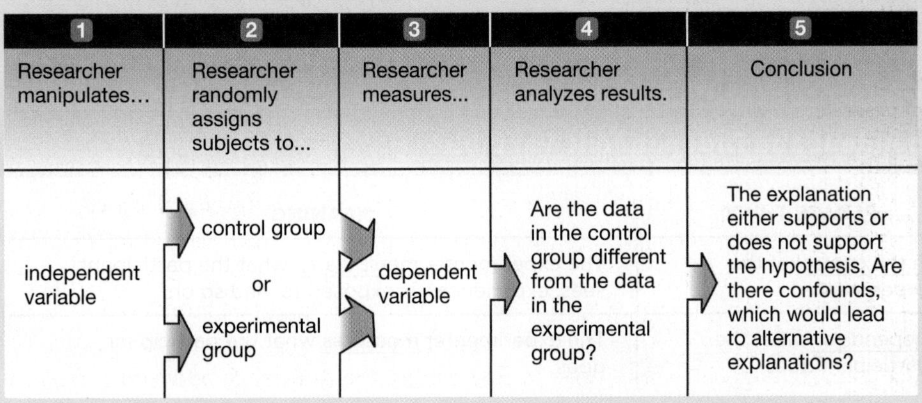

1	2	3	4	5
Researcher manipulates...	Researcher randomly assigns subjects to...	Researcher measures...	Researcher analyzes results.	Conclusion
independent variable	control group or experimental group	dependent variable	Are the data in the control group different from the data in the experimental group?	The explanation either supports or does not support the hypothesis. Are there confounds, which would lead to alternative explanations?

FIGURE 1.26

Experimental Methods

Experimental methods provide information about the causes of particular mental activities or behaviors.

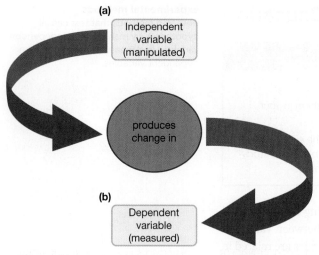

(a) Independent variable (manipulated)

produces change in

(b) Dependent variable (measured)

FIGURE 1.27

Independent and Dependent Variables

(a) The independent variable is under the control of the experimenter, and it is manipulated. **(b)** It may produce changes in the dependent variable, which is the outcome that is measured.

independent variable
In an experiment, the variable that the experimenter manipulates to examine its impact on the dependent variable.

dependent variable
In an experiment, the variable that is measured to determine how it was affected by the manipulation of the independent variable.

To perform an experiment that will test a hypothesis, the researcher manipulates one variable. This variable is called the **independent variable** (**Figure 1.27a**). In your experiment, the independent variable would be using a cell phone. You would manipulate how your research participants use or do not use their cell phones. After manipulating the independent variable, you would measure the effect that variable has on a second factor. The second variable is called the **dependent variable** (**Figure 1.27b**). In your experiment, the dependent variable is driving performance. Instead of letting your participants drive, you might measure their performance safely as they use a driving simulator or play a driving game on a computer (**Figure 1.28**). The Learning Tip below will help you remember the difference between independent variables and dependent variables.

OPERATIONAL DEFINITIONS OF VARIABLES To ensure that the research is objective and systematic, you have to define the variables more specifically. In other words, you must create *operational definitions* of the variables. Operational definitions *qualify* (describe) and *quantify* (measure) variables so they can be understood objectively. For example, how will you qualify cell phone use in the study? Do you mean holding the phone or using it hands-free? Do you mean talking, texting, reading content, or some combination of these activities? In addition, how will you quantify cell phone use? Will you count how many times a person uses the cell phone in an hour? Or perhaps how long a person uses it? Or even how many different activities the person engages in while using it? All these decisions need to be made before starting the research so you can be clear about how the independent variable is manipulated.

Just as you need to operationally define the independent variable, you also need to operationally define the dependent variable. In your experiment, the dependent variable is driving performance. How will you quantify and qualify driving performance so you can judge whether it is affected by cell phone use? Do you rely on people's self-reports of performance, or do you use observational methods? If the latter, will you record the speed of driving, the number of accidents, the closeness to cars up ahead, or the reaction time to red lights or road hazards? One option for the dependent variable might be to measure the amount of time it takes participants in the driving simulator to stop the car when an obstacle appears in the road. In this case, the operational definition of driving performance is in milliseconds of stopping time. But often, a single dependent variable can have many operational definitions. So another operational definition of driving performance, even in the same study, might be how many times the person playing the driving game crashes the virtual car. Deciding on clear operational definitions lets other researchers know

LEARNING TIP: Dependent and Independent Variables

WHEN YOU SEE	PLEASE THINK	MEANING
<u>In</u>dependent variable	<u>In the control</u> of the experimenter	The experimenter <u>manipulates</u> what the participant sees, experiences, is exposed to, and so on.
<u>Dependent</u> variable	<u>Depends on</u> what the participant does	The experimenter <u>measures</u> what the participant does.

how you measured your variables. Knowing your methods, other researchers can use identical methods to gather data that will build on your data, supporting or differing from your results. The use of operational definitions is therefore crucial for those trying to replicate the research findings.

GROUPS IN AN EXPERIMENT You now know that your experiment will test the hypothesis that the dependent variable (driving performance, as measured by the number of virtual crashes or how long it takes the driver to stop the car) is affected by the independent variable (specific ways of using the cell phone while driving in the simulator). But how will you know if the change in the dependent variable is really caused by your manipulation of the independent variable?

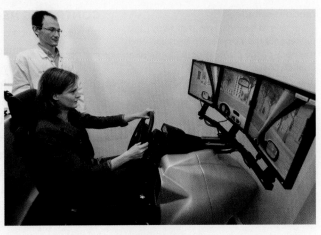

FIGURE 1.28

Participants in an Experiment with Simulated Driving

An experiment investigating how using a cell phone affects driving skills can be performed safely by having participants use a driving simulator or play a driving game. Information about the participants' driving performance would be recorded electronically.

To clarify the relationship between your variables, you assign some participants in the study to a **control group.** In this case, participants assigned to the control group would not use a cell phone while they are using the driving simulator. This is the baseline condition. The participants in the **experimental group** experience the manipulation you are interested in. These participants get the treatment in the experiment. In this particular experiment, you could use more than one experimental group so that each one is exposed to a condition that requires different use of the cell phone while driving. One experimental group might talk on a hands-free cell phone, whereas the other group might talk on a handheld cell phone while driving in the simulator. You will then compare the effects of driving without using a cell phone in the control group with the effects of using a cell phone in two different ways in the experimental groups.

In the experiment described so far, different people have been in the control and experimental groups. This type of experiment is called a *between-groups* design because different people receive different treatments. However, sometimes study participants serve as their own control group. In a *within-subject* design, the same people receive all treatments. For example, people would be tested in the driving simulator once without a cell phone, once when talking on a hands-free cell phone, and yet another time when talking on a handheld cell phone. In both between-groups and within-subject designs the goal is to determine whether differences in performance are caused by the different treatments.

A disadvantage of the within-subject design is that repeating the test means people experience the task multiple times. This repetition could influence performance. For example, people could improve in driving performance on the simulator each time regardless of whether they use the cell phone or how they use it. Such improvement would make it difficult to determine the exact relationship between cell phone use and driving performance. By contrast, in your experiment, a between-groups design enables you to draw clearer conclusions.

The benefit of using an experimental method is that the researcher can study the causal relationship between the two variables. Suppose the independent variable (how the cell phone is used) consistently influences the dependent variable (driving performance). The independent variable is then assumed to cause the change in the dependent variable. The experimenter always manipulates the independent variable and then measures the dependent variable. That is, manipulation of the independent variable (here, the way the cell phone is used) comes before the dependent measure (here, driving performance) is recorded. In this way, the experimenter solves the directionality problem that would occur in a correlational study. In the next subsection, you will learn about how experiments make it possible to rule out alternative explanations, such as third variables.

control group
In an experiment, a comparison group of participants that does not receive the experimental treatment.

experimental group
In an experiment, one or more treatment groups of participants that receive the manipulation of the independent variable being investigated.

random sample
A sample of participants that fairly represents the population because each member of the population had an equal chance of being included.

CONTROL IS NECESSARY TO DETERMINE CAUSALITY Only experimental methods let a researcher achieve the goals of control and explanation. Indeed, a properly performed experiment depends on rigorous control. Here, control means the steps taken by the researcher to minimize the possibility that anything other than the independent variable will affect the experiment's outcome. That is, when conducting an experiment, a researcher needs to ensure that the only thing that varies is the independent variable. That way, the researcher knows that the independent variable—nothing else—has affected the dependent variable. Anything that affects a dependent variable and that may unintentionally vary between the study's different experimental conditions is known as a *confound*. A confound can be a potential third variable in your study.

Consider a confound in your experiment on cell phone use and driving performance. Suppose that the driving simulator used by participants in the control group (who do not have a cell phone) has an automatic transmission. Now suppose a different driving simulator, one with a manual transmission (stick shift), is used by participants in the experimental conditions (where they are using a cell phone in different ways). If you're not familiar with both types of transmissions, you might think they're equal. However, driving a car with a manual transmission takes more skill than driving one with an automatic transmission. As a result, a change in driving performance might actually be caused by the type of car used in the driving simulator. In this example, the drivers' performance might be confounded with the type of transmission. The presence of a confound would make it impossible to determine the true effect of using a cell phone on driving performance.

The more confounds and thus alternative explanations that can be eliminated, the more confident a researcher can be that the change in the independent variable is causing the change in the dependent variable. Control represents the foundation of the experimental approach, because it allows the researcher to rule out alternative explanations for the observed data. As consumers of research, we all need to think about confounds that could be causing particular results that are reported in the news.

A RANDOM SAMPLE ALLOWS GENERALIZATION OF RESULTS At the start of research, experimenters need to consider the selection of participants. Psychologists typically want to know that their findings generalize. In other words, the results should apply to people beyond the participants in the study. When studying how using a cell phone affects driving skills, you want to know more than how the specific participants behaved. Ultimately, you want to discover how using a cell phone affects the driving performance of the average driver.

The general group you want to know about is your *population* (**Figure 1.29a**). For instance, you might want your results to generalize to college students, to students who belong to sororities and fraternities, to women, to men over the age of 45, and so on. To learn about the population, you study a subset, or a small number, from it. That subset, the people you actually study, is the *sample*. Sampling is the process you use to select people from the population to be in the study. The best way to represent the whole population is to take a **random sample** (**Figure 1.29b**). This method gives each member of the population an equal chance of being chosen to participate in the research. If you are trying to generalize to the entire human population, then random sampling from all humans is, of course, likely impossible.

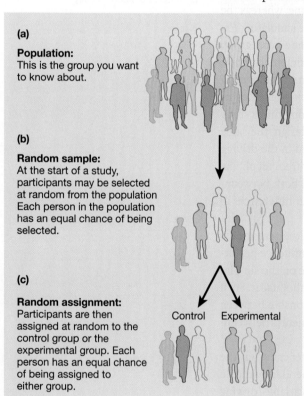

(a)

Population:
This is the group you want to know about.

(b)

Random sample:
At the start of a study, participants may be selected at random from the population Each person in the population has an equal chance of being selected.

(c)

Random assignment:
Participants are then assigned at random to the control group or the experimental group. Each person has an equal chance of being assigned to either group.

Control   Experimental

FIGURE 1.29

Random Sample and Random Assignment

In experiments, researchers use random sample of participants from a population of interest and then use random assignment of those people to the control group or experimental group.

Most of the time, researchers will use a sample consisting of people who are conveniently available for the study. This is called a *convenience sample*. Even if you wanted your results to generalize to all students in your country or in the world, you would probably use a sample from your own college or university. However, you would still try to collect a random sample from this convenience group. Even though a sample from your own college might not look like all students in the country, it seems reasonable to expect that the effect of using a cell phone on driving performance would be about the same no matter where you sampled the participants from. However, it is important for researchers to recognize that their results might not generalize to other samples that are quite different, such as people from other cultures (Henrich, Heine, & Norenzayan, 2010).

RANDOM ASSIGNMENT EQUATES GROUPS In experiments, one possible confound is that people in the experimental groups may differ in important ways. Suppose the people in the hands-free group have less experience driving than those in the handheld group. This difference could create a difference in driving performance that has nothing to do with the manipulation. One way that researchers try to make sure that experimental groups do not differ is to use **random assignment** to assign participants to the experimental and control groups (**Figure 1.29c**). Random assignment gives each potential research participant an equal chance of being assigned to the control or experimental groups. To randomly assign participants, you might have them draw numbers from a hat to determine who is assigned to the control group (not using a cell phone) and to both the experimental groups (talking on a hands-free phone or talking on a handheld phone).

Of course, there are always individual differences among participants. For example, each of your groups might include people with more or less experience using cell phones while driving and some people with excellent or weaker driving skills. If the control group happened to have many participants with less experience using cell phones or poorer driving skills, then any negative impact of driving while using a cell phone in the experimental groups might not be seen. But these differences will tend to average out when participants are randomly assigned to either the control group or the experimental group. This happens because the groups will be equivalent *on average* in terms of participants' use of cell phones and experience with driving. So, using random assignment to balance out known (and unknown) factors is important because it helps to reduce confounds that could limit the ability to say that a certain manipulation *caused* a certain outcome.

random assignment
Placing research participants into the conditions of an experiment in such a way that each participant has an equal chance of being assigned to any level of the independent variable.

1.12 Psychologists Today Follow Strict Ethical Guidelines

1.12 LEARNING GOAL ACTIVITIES

To maximize your learning, complete the following learning goal activities:

a. Understand all bold and italic terms by writing explanations of them in your own words.

b. Understand ethical issues in psychology by summarizing in your own words the four ethical guidelines that psychologists must address in their research.

Regardless of the research method that is used, psychologists must fully consider the ethical issues involved in their studies. Are the researchers asking the participants to do something unreasonable? Are the participants risking physical or emotional harm from the study? If there is any risk at all, are the objectives of the research important

institutional review boards (IRBs) Groups of people responsible for reviewing proposed research to ensure that it meets the accepted standards of science and provides for the physical and emotional well-being of research participants.

enough to justify asking people to accept those risks? To ensure the participants' well-being, all colleges, universities, and research institutes have strict guidelines in place regarding research. All researchers must follow those guidelines.

The guardians of the ethical guidelines at schools and other institutions where research is conducted are **institutional review boards (IRBs)**. These boards consist of administrators, legal advisers, trained scholars, and members of the community. The members review all proposed research to ensure that it meets scientific standards. For research to be ethical, four main issues must be addressed.

1. *Privacy*: Researchers must respect participants' privacy. For example, it is ethical to observe people without their knowledge in public, such as at an airport. It is not ethical to observe private behaviors without people's knowledge.

2. *Confidentiality*: Participants' information must be kept secret. It can be made available only to the few people who need to know it. This confidentiality prevents other people from linking the study's findings to the actual participants.

3. *Informed consent*: *Informed consent* means that people must be told about the research, and they can choose to participate or not. Usually, the participant gives consent in writing before the study begins. Sometimes, knowing a study's specific goals before the research starts could alter the participants' behavior. That alteration could make the results meaningless. In such a case, the researchers may use deception to mislead participants about the study. If deception is used, once the study is completed the researchers must inform the participants of the study's goals and explain why deception was necessary.

4. *Protection from harm*: Researchers cannot ask participants to endure unreasonable pain or discomfort. However, potential gains from research sometimes require asking participants to expose themselves to some risk to obtain important findings. The *risk/benefit ratio* is an analysis of whether the research is important enough to be worth placing participants at some risk.

FIGURE 1.30

Student Participants

When you volunteer to participate in psychological research, you will be protected by ethical guidelines as you learn about psychology and contribute to the field.

In fact, you can experience psychological research yourself if you volunteer to participate in studies (**Figure 1.30**). By participating in this research, you can learn more about psychology. And you can rest easy knowing that you will be protected by rigorous ethical guidelines. Importantly, you will also be contributing to the scientific research that shows how humans think, feel, and behave.

Q How Do Psychologists Conduct Research?

To make sure you learned what you just read, write answers to the following questions and check your answers.

1.8 In the scientific method, what do you call a specific, testable prediction?

1.9 What are two major limitations of case studies?

1.10 Suppose a study finds that hair length has a correlation with body weight: People with longer hair weigh less. Explain whether you should grow your hair in order to lose weight.

1.11 In a psychology experiment, what are the names of the two variables, the one that is manipulated and the one that is measured?

1.12 Name and explain which of the four ethical issues in psychological research is related to giving participants a choice about whether they want to be in a particular study.

See Appendix B for answers to the red Q questions.

BIG PICTURE

 Want to earn a better grade on your test? Go to **INQUIZITIVE** to practice actively with this chapter's content and get personalized feedback along the way.

Why Is Psychology Important to You?

1.1 Psychology Explains Your Mental Activity and Behavior

Review the learning goal activities on p. 5. You experience psychology every minute of your life, but you cannot understand it based on common sense alone. Psychology is the scientific study of the mind (mental activity), behavior (actions that result from sensing and interpreting information), and the brain processes underlying these.

1.2 Psychology Teaches You to Think Critically

Review the learning goal activities on p. 6. Studying psychology can improve critical thinking skills when you follow the three steps in critical thinking. Each step involves a question: (1) What is the claim I am being asked to accept?, (2) What

evidence, if any, is provided to support the claim?, and (3) Given the evidence, what are the most reasonable conclusions about the claim—should it be accepted or rejected?

1.3 Psychology Improves Your Life

Review the learning goal activities on p. 10. Learning about psychology helps develop academic skills. It also helps develop skills that can improve your personal life and help you be successful in your job.

KEY TERMS
psychology (p. 5)
critical thinking (p. 7)

What Do Psychologists Investigate?

1.4 Psychology Originated in Philosophical Questions

Review the learning goal activities on p. 12. The classic questions in psychology originated in philosophy. The nature/nurture debate contrasted whether psychological characteristics resulted from a person's biological nature or are acquired through education, experience, and culture. The mind/body problem was about whether the mind and body are separate and distinct or the mind is simply a person's personal experience of brain activity.

1.5 Psychologists Investigate the Conscious Mind and the Unconscious Mind

Review the learning goal activities on p. 14. Three historical schools of thought explored the conscious mind and the unconscious mind. Structuralism examined the basic elements of conscious experience. Functionalism examined the purpose of the conscious mind. Psychoanalytic theory focused on how unconscious forces affect us.

1.6 Psychologists Explore Behavior and Mental Activity

Review the learning goal activities on p. 17. Four historical schools of thought explored behavior and mental activity. Gestalt psychology focused on how people have a unique experience of a whole that is different from its parts. Behaviorism investigated how the environment affects behavior. Humanistic psychology

studied how people can increase positive aspects of their lives, focusing on how people are basically good. Cognitive psychology focused on studying mental functions.

1.7 Psychologists Today Investigate Many Different Topics

Review the learning goal activities on p. 19. Psychologists work across 11 psychology subfields to investigate mental activity and behavior or provide services to people: (1) evolutionary, (2) biological, (3) cognitive psychology/cognitive neuroscience, (4) developmental, (5) health, (6) personality, (7) social, (8) cultural, (9) clinical, (10) educational, and (11) industrial/organizational. In addition, psychologists work in many settings, such as at schools, colleges, and universities; in health care settings; for businesses; for the government; and in private practice.

KEY TERMS
structuralism (p. 14)
functionalism (p. 16)
natural selection (p. 16)
psychoanalytic theory (p. 17)
Gestalt theory (p. 18)
behaviorism (p. 18)
humanistic psychology (p. 18)
cognitive psychology (p. 19)
culture (p. 19)

How Do Psychologists Conduct Research?

1.8 Psychologists Use the Scientific Method

Review the learning goal activities on p. 22. Psychologists have four goals in their scientific research: (1) description, (2) prediction, (3) control, and (4) explanation. Psychologists use empiricism to achieve these goals by following the five steps of the scientific method: (1) Formulate a theory, (2) Develop a testable hypothesis, (3) Test with a research method, (4) Analyze the data, and (5) Share results and conduct more research.

1.9 Descriptive Methods Describe What Is Happening

Review the learning goal activities on p. 27. To achieve the scientific goal of describing a phenomenon, three descriptive methods of research can be used. Researchers use observational studies to describe naturally occurring behaviors. Self-reports use surveys, questionnaires, and interviews to directly ask people about their mental processes and behaviors. Case studies examine an unusual individual, a few individuals, or an organization.

1.10 Correlational Methods Study Relationships

Review the learning goal activities on p. 30. To achieve the scientific goal of predicting a phenomenon, correlational methods investigate a naturally occurring relationship between variables. However, due to the directionality problem and the third variable problem, correlational methods cannot determine the cause of a relationship (that is, which variable caused changes in another variable).

1.11 Experimental Methods Test Causation

Review the learning goal activities on p. 33. To achieve the scientific goals of control and explanation, experimental methods must be used. To do this, experimenters manipulate the independent variable and measure its effect on the dependent variable. Participants in the experimental groups experience the manipulation, whereas participants in the control group will reveal if the manipulation caused an effect. Researchers get a random sample of participants from the population they want to study. Then random assignment must be used to ensure all participants have an equal chance of being assigned to the control group or the experimental group. Random assignment controls for preexisting differences between the groups and helps reveal a cause/effect relationship between the variables.

1.12 Psychologists Today Follow Strict Ethical Guidelines

Review the learning goal activities on p. 37. Psychologists must adhere to rules governed by institutional review boards (IRBs). They also must show they are adhering to all four ethical guidelines when conducting scientific research: (1) privacy, (2) confidentiality, (3) informed consent, and (4) protection from harm.

KEY TERMS

scientific method (p. 23)
replication (p. 23)
theory (p. 25)
hypothesis (p. 25)
descriptive methods (p. 27)
correlational methods (p. 31)
experimental methods (p. 33)
independent variable (p. 34)
dependent variable (p. 34)
control group (p. 35)
experimental group (p. 35)
random sample (p. 36)
random assignment (p. 37)
institutional review boards (IRBs) (p. 38)

CHAPTER 1 SELF-QUIZ

To make sure you learned the information in this chapter, write answers to the following questions and check your answers. **See Appendix B for answers to the self-quiz.**

1. Linda is a psychologist. During her day at work, she is most likely to _____.
   a. investigate export policies
   b. study trends in foreign markets
   c. interpret a European burial site
   d. research thought processes

2. Harry has a different girlfriend every week. Jim's explanation for Harry's behavior is that Harry has a naturally high level of testosterone. Carolyn's explanation is that Harry's mother died when he was young. These explanations tell you that Jim likely believes that _____ influences who we are, whereas Carolyn believes that _____ influences who we are.
   a. nurture; nature
   b. structuralism; behaviorism
   c. nature; nurture
   d. behaviorism; structuralism

3. Monica believes that the human mind, like a piece of music, must be broken into component parts to be understood. Monica's beliefs best reflect the psychological school of thought called _____.
   a. structuralism
   b. functionalism
   c. psychoanalytic theory
   d. Gestalt theory

4. Carolina wants to investigate how mental processes, such as attention, affect the amount of time that a child will work on a difficult task. Carolina's research is most similar to the research approach taken by _____, who helped develop _____.
   a. Rogers; humanistic psychology
   b. Watson; behaviorism
   c. Miller; cognitive psychology
   d. Wertheimer; Gestalt theory

5. Frank is always polite and reserved. Elrico thinks that Frank's behavior can be explained by his shyness. Aidan thinks that Frank's behavior can be explained by his having been raised in rural Kentucky. Elrico's view of Frank's behavior most closely reflects the perspective of the subfield of _____ psychology, whereas Aidan's view most closely reflects the perspective of the subfield of _____ psychology.
   a. personality; cultural
   b. personality; developmental
   c. cognitive; cultural
   d. cognitive; developmental

6. Simon, a psychologist, studies whether people who watch a greater amount of TV are more likely to be good at memorizing visual information than those who watch less TV. To investigate this testable _____, Simon uses the number of remembered visually presented words as the _____ of amount of TV watching.
   a. theory; independent variable
   b. hypothesis; dependent variable
   c. theory; dependent variable
   d. hypothesis; independent variable

7. Jool wants to study whether children in public playgrounds tend to play with children of their own gender. To begin her study, Jool goes to the local playground, watches the kids for about 20 minutes, and takes notes about what she sees. Jool is conducting her research by using the descriptive method of a(n) _____.
   a. self-report
   b. case study
   c. experiment
   d. observational study

8. Keyshawn learns that, according to psychology research, students' active reading is related to their getting higher quiz scores. The research method used to get this data must have been _____.
   a. an observational study
   b. correlational
   c. a case study
   d. experimental

9. Dr. Chen designs an experiment to study the effect of facial expressions on dating preferences. His participants see photographs of people who have a neutral facial expression or who are smiling. Dr. Chen asks participants to rate the attractiveness of each photograph. In this experiment, the participants seeing the neutral faces are the _____, and the participants seeing the smiling faces are the _____.
   a. control group; experimental group
   b. dependent variable; independent variable
   c. experimental group; control group
   d. independent variable; dependent variable

10. Nancy is conducting a study on how couples communicate. However, she doesn't have the money to conduct laboratory tests, so she collects data in the field. To ensure that she does not violate the ethical rule of privacy, Nancy must _____.
    a. always keep the couples' personal information secret
    b. always obtain informed consent from the couples
    c. observe couples only in public settings
    d. observe couples only in their own homes

What Can You Do with a Degree in Psychology?

Now that you have read at least part of this chapter, do you find psychology to be intriguing enough to pursue a degree in it? If so, you might have some questions, such as "What can I do with a degree in psychology? Will I be able to get a job?" If you are thinking about a career specifically in psychology or a related field, there is good news.

According to the National Center for Education Statistics (NCES), the associate's degree in psychology is one of the fastest-growing associate's degrees in the United States (National Center for Education Statistics, 2017). In fact, in the decade before 2015, there was a 350 percent increase in the awarding of psychology associate's degrees, from 1,900 in 2004–05 to 8,700 in 2014–15. An associate's degree in psychology can prepare you for many jobs, as you will see in other Putting Psychology to Work features in this book.

The same report from NCES shows that the bachelor's degree in psychology is the fourth most popular in the United States, with 117,000 bachelor's degrees in psychology having been granted in 2015. Most of these psychology graduates get jobs, and their median starting salary in 2016 was about $45,000 (National Association of Colleges and Employers, 2016). According to 2014 data by the U.S. Census Bureau, shown in the figures below, people with psychology bachelor's degrees are employed in a wide variety of settings and fields. The largest concentrations are in social services, management, education, and health care. Other fields include computer technology, statistics, finance, arts and entertainment, and sales.

Even if you do not major in psychology, what you learn in this chapter will be useful for many types of occupations. Critical thinking is a valuable skill in any job that requires evaluating information, such as news reporting. Knowing the steps in scientific research is especially worthwhile in the health sciences, where strategies based on this method are used to treat and advise patients. Understanding research lets teachers apply findings in the classroom.

However, some students become so fascinated by psychology that they pursue graduate degrees in psychology to study mental activity, behavior, and the brain. According to the U.S. Department of Labor (U.S. Bureau of Labor Statistics, 2017), opportunities for people with graduate degrees in psychology to provide counseling services, investigate psychological disorders, or do research on other topics in psychology are expected to grow by about 19 percent by 2024. The outlook is equally positive in many other countries around the world. Developing countries, for example, are increasingly addressing the psychological well-being of their citizens. These data show that there are many opportunities for people trained in psychology to use their knowledge and skills to help improve the lives of people everywhere.

TAKEAWAY POINT: Will you be able to put psychology to work? If you earn a degree in psychology, the answer is clearly "Yes!" And as you will see in Putting Psychology to Work in future chapters, even if you take only this one psychology course, the concepts and skills that you learn now will help you in any career.

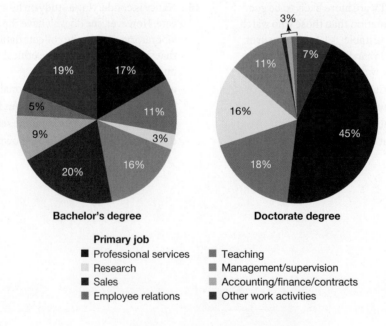

Bachelor's degree | **Doctorate degree**

Primary job
- ■ Professional services
- ☐ Research
- ■ Sales
- ■ Employee relations
- ■ Teaching
- ■ Management/supervision
- ■ Accounting/finance/contracts
- ■ Other work activities

 You can look up job descriptions, education requirements, salaries, and more at the Bureau of Labor Statistics: www.bls.gov. Visit the site and start putting psychology to work!

To learn about the use of statistics in research, see **Appendix A: How Do Psychologists Analyze Research Data?** There, you'll consider what the data from your hypothetical experiment—on how using a cell phone affects driving performance—reveal about people generally.

The Role
2 of Biology in Psychology

WHEN MICHAEL WAS A CHILD, it was clear that his brain worked differently from other people's brains. "Growing up," he recalls, "I was . . . constantly bouncing off the walls—I could never sit still" (Dowd, 2017). A doctor diagnosed Michael with attention-deficit/hyperactivity disorder (ADHD). The symptoms of this disorder include the inability to pay attention, impulsive behavior, and excessive levels of activity (American Psychiatric Association, 2013). Michael's symptoms were getting in the way of his success at school. One teacher told Michael that he would "never amount to anything."

But Michael's mother, Debbie, wanted "to prove everyone wrong. I knew that if I collaborated with Michael, he could achieve anything that he wanted to" (Dutton, 2007). Debbie worked with Michael's teachers to find ways to engage his attention. To get him to read, they gave him the sports section of the newspaper. To help him with math, they gave him questions such as "How

BIG QUESTIONS

How Does Your Nervous System Affect You?

How Do the Parts of Your Brain Function?

How Does Your Brain Communicate with Your Body?

How Do Nature and Nurture Affect Your Brain?

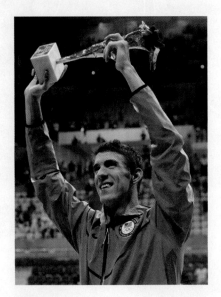

FIGURE 2.1

Michael Phelps and ADHD

Michael Phelps is just one of millions of people with attention-deficit/ hyperactivity disorder (ADHD). This psychological disorder is partially a result of how specific regions in the brain process information. Michael Phelps's story illustrates the good news about living with a brain that is not "typical": Most people's brains can be harnessed to let them succeed in life.

long would it take to swim 500 meters if you swam three meters per second?" Michael's extra energy was put to good use in sports, especially swimming, and these activities helped Michael compose himself and taught him self-discipline. When he felt ready to stop taking medication to reduce the symptoms of ADHD, Debbie cautiously agreed. It turned out that Michael's rigorous swimming schedule and motivation to succeed in swimming provided him with all the focus he needed. In 2016, Michael became the most decorated Olympic champion of all time. That's right, Michael Phelps, the Olympic swimmer with 28 medals—23 of them gold—has ADHD (**Figure 2.1**).

Chances are good that you know someone like Michael. In the United States, just over 7 percent of school-aged children have been diagnosed with ADHD (Thomas, Sanders, Doust, Beller, & Glasziou, 2015). Although the rates of ADHD vary by region, more boys than girls show symptoms of ADHD. But what is ADHD? It is a neurodevelopmental disorder. In other words, ADHD is related to how the brain functions—it is neurological. And it begins in childhood—it is developmental. As the symptoms of ADHD make clear, the nervous system is critical for development, mental activity, and behavior. The nervous system consists partly of nerve cells, also known as neurons. Throughout the nervous system, including the brain, these neurons work together to perform important functions. To determine what parts of the brain may be responsible for the symptoms of ADHD, scientists use tools that look at brain activity in real time to see how certain regions process information.

In this chapter, you will learn more about brain imaging techniques that help us understand ADHD. You will also learn more about parts of the brain that are involved in ADHD, including areas that regulate attention and cognitive control, alertness, and motivation (Nigg, 2005). Research into disorders and how biology contributes to them helps us understand the function of typical brains as well. To understand any mental activity or behavior, we need to understand the underlying biology. We also need to consider how both nature and nurture affect processing in the brain and body. Indeed, it is often true that as Michael Phelps puts it, "Your mind is the strongest medicine you can have. . . . You can overcome anything if you think you can and you want to" (Wedge, 2012).

How Does Your Nervous System Affect You?

Can you ride a bicycle? Are you afraid of spiders? What is your favorite flavor of ice cream? As you think about each of these questions, different parts of your nervous system are processing information to come up with responses. When (or if) you are actually riding a bicycle, feeling fear, or enjoying the taste of a double-dip vanilla cone, other parts of your nervous system are being activated. So to understand your psychology, you need to understand how your brain and body let you think and behave. Most of us have bodies and brains that process information in typical ways. But sometimes the processing is different from the norm, as happens in ADHD and other neurodevelopmental disorders. You will learn more about neurodevelopmental disorders in Chapters 14–15. One such disorder, dyslexia, is described in this chapter's Using Psychology in Your Life feature, on p. 48.

2.1 Your Nervous System Is the Basis of Your Mental Activity and Behavior

2.1 LEARNING GOAL ACTIVITIES

To maximize your learning, complete the following learning goal activities:

a. Understand all bold and italic terms by writing explanations of them in your own words.

b. Apply the nervous system to your life by describing the three functions of your nervous system during an experience you had recently.

nervous system
A network of billions of cells in the brain and the body, responsible for all aspects of what we think, feel, and do.

central nervous system (CNS)
The part of the nervous system that consists of the brain and the spinal cord.

peripheral nervous system (PNS)
The part of the nervous system that consists of all the nerve cells throughout the body except those in the brain and spinal cord.

The **nervous system** is a network of billions of cells in your brain and your body. This system is responsible for all aspects of what you think, feel, or do. The nervous system has three basic functions: (1) to receive sensory input from the world through vision, hearing, touch, taste, and smell; (2) to process this information in the brain by paying attention to it, perceiving it, and remembering it; and (3) to respond to the information by acting on it. To apply these functions to yourself, see Try It Yourself on p. 49.

These three functions are a result of processing in two divisions of the nervous system (**Figure 2.2**). The **central nervous system (CNS)** consists of the brain and the spinal cord, which both contain massive numbers of nerve cells. The **peripheral nervous system (PNS)** consists of the nerve cells outside of the brain and spinal cord. These two divisions are separate, but they interact

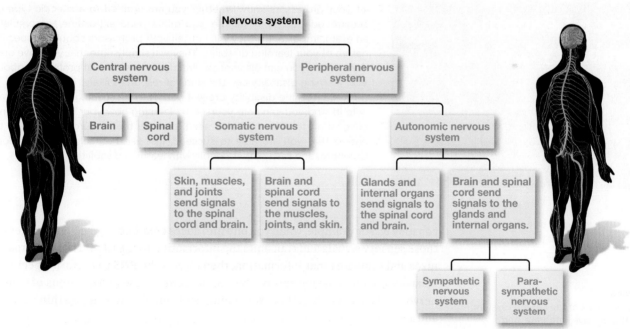

FIGURE 2.2

The Nervous System

The two main divisions of the nervous system are the central nervous system (CNS) and the peripheral nervous system (PNS). The CNS consists of the brain and the spinal cord. The PNS consists of the nerve cells in the rest of the body. Together with their subdivisions, which are described in detail across several sections in this chapter, these divisions of the nervous system (1) receive sensory input, (2) process it further, and (3) respond to it.

How Can You Succeed if You Have a Learning Disability?

Have you ever wondered if your brain functions differently from other people's brains? Although most brains are remarkably similar, how they work can vary from one person to another. Some people's brains work so differently that they may be diagnosed with a learning disability. According to the National Center for Learning Disabilities (Cortiella & Horowitz, 2014), a learning disability is a neurological disorder that affects the brain's ability to receive, process, store, or respond to information. Michael Phelps was diagnosed with the disorder ADHD, but he learned how to harness his mind and has been extraordinarily successful in life.

Another common neurodevelopmental disorder, dyslexia, is related to problems with processing symbols and sounds in the brain (Snowling & Melby-Lervåg, 2016). These processing problems can create great difficulties with reading, spelling, writing, and even doing math and telling time. But people with dyslexia can be creative problem solvers (Kapoula et al., 2016), with the ability to think "outside the box" in unique ways. And many people with learning disabilities such as dyslexia have experienced great success in their lives, including the actor Whoopi Goldberg, the entrepreneur Richard Branson, the basketball player Magic Johnson, and the celebrity chef Jamie Oliver.

If you have or suspect you might have a learning disability, then the new academic and organizational challenges of college might make the disability more apparent. In this case, the first thing to do is get in touch with your campus's disability support services or a member of student affairs (for example, the dean of students, a director of residential life, or a mental health counselor on your campus). Don't delay out of fear of embarrassment or shyness.

Schools must provide equal opportunity to the benefits of education for people with learning disabilities. If your learning disability is verified, support staff will work with you to help you understand how your brain functions and determine what is needed. Given your particular situation, some accommodations will help you maximize how your brain processes information, while others will not. Disability support services staff will let your professors know whether you are entitled to a specific type of accommodation. For example, you might need extra time to complete an exam. Importantly, they will not tell your professors about the specific nature of your learning disability. They will simply note that you have one. If you wish, you can also speak directly with individual professors about your learning disability and the kinds of resources likely to help you.

Will a learning disability prevent you from succeeding? Not if you can help it! And you can help yourself by learning how your brain works and advocating for the tools you need. Line up the resources you need to ensure that you are able to succeed, just like Michael Phelps, Whoopi Goldberg, and many other people with learning disabilities.

constantly. For example, when you bite into an ice cream cone, the PNS registers those sensory signals and transmits the information to the CNS. The CNS organizes and evaluates that information, then directs the PNS to perform specific behaviors, such as having another bite of the cone. These two divisions of your nervous system work together every moment of your life, letting you think, feel, and act.

NEURONS ARE THE BASIC UNITS OF YOUR NERVOUS SYSTEM In your body, as in the body of every person, both divisions of the nervous system are made up of smaller units. These units are the nerve cells, or **neurons** (**Figure 2.3**).

neurons
The basic units of the nervous system; cells that receive, integrate, and transmit information in the nervous system. Neurons operate through electrical impulses, communicate with other neurons through chemical signals, and form neural networks.

TRY IT YOURSELF: **Your Nervous System**

Your nervous system is responsible for how you experience things. To understand the three functions of your nervous system, describe the following: (1) What sensory input are you currently receiving? (2) How are you processing that information? In other words, what are you thinking about the sensory information you're receiving? (3) In what ways are you responding to the input? This exercise will help you understand how your nervous system is the core of all psychological experiences in your life.

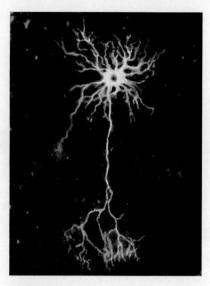

FIGURE 2.3
Human Nerve Cell
This is a nerve cell, also known as a neuron. Neurons are the basic units of the human nervous system.

Individual neurons receive, integrate, and transmit information in the nervous system. Each neuron communicates with tens of thousands of other neurons. But the neurons do not communicate randomly or by chance. Instead, they communicate selectively with other neurons. Through this selective communication, neurons form networks. The networks of billions of neurons sending and receiving signals make possible all the complex aspects of human mental activity and behavior. Through maturation and experience, the networks develop and strengthen. In other words, permanent connections form among groups of neurons. Those connections let the neurons process information efficiently.

You are able to think and act because neurons can communicate with each other. And neural communication is possible in part because of the neuron's structure and in part due to the neuron's electrical and chemical properties.

STRUCTURE OF NEURONS   Four parts of a neuron let it communicate with other neurons. These parts are the dendrites, cell body, axon, and terminal buttons (**Figure 2.4**).

The **dendrites** are short, branchlike extensions of the cell body. They receive signals from neighboring neurons. In the **cell body,** the information received from thousands of other neurons is collected and integrated (combined together). Once the incoming information has been integrated in the cell body, electrical impulses are transmitted along the **axon.** Axons vary tremendously in length. In fact, the longest axons stretch all the way from the spinal cord to each of the big toes. In everyday language, we commonly refer to neurons as nerves, as in the phrase "pinched nerve." In this context, a nerve is a bundle of axons that carry information between the brain and other specific locations in the body. At the end of the axon are knoblike structures called **terminal buttons.**

The site where communication occurs between neurons is called the **synapse.** In the synapse, the neurons do not actually touch each other. Instead, they communicate by releasing chemicals at the terminal buttons. These chemicals, called **neurotransmitters,** cross the tiny gap between the sending neuron and the dendrites of the receiving neurons. You will learn more about neurotransmitters in study unit 2.3.

dendrites
Branchlike extensions of the neuron's cell body with receptors that receive information from other neurons.

cell body
Part of the neuron where information from thousands of other neurons is collected and integrated.

axon
A long, narrow outgrowth of a neuron's cell body that lets the neuron transmit information to other neurons.

terminal buttons
Parts of the neuron, at the end of axons, that release chemical signals from the neuron into the synapse.

synapse
The space between neurons where communication takes place through neurotransmitters.

neurotransmitters
Chemical substances that carry signals from one neuron to another.

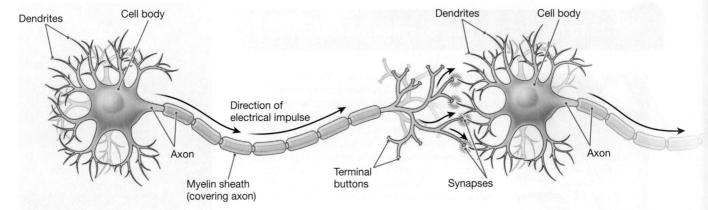

Dendrites   Cell body   Dendrites   Cell body

Direction of
electrical impulse

Axon   Axon

Myelin sheath
(covering axon)

Terminal
buttons   Synapses

FIGURE 2.4

Neuron Structure

Messages are received by the dendrites, processed in the cell body, transmitted along the axon, sent to other neurons via neurotransmitters released from the terminal buttons into the synapse, and then sent to the dendrites of the receiving neuron. The details of these processes are shown in Figures 2.6–2.7.

2.2 Neurons Communicate with Each Other in Your Nervous System

2.2 LEARNING GOAL ACTIVITIES

To maximize your learning, complete the following learning goal activities:

a. Understand all bold and italic terms by writing explanations of them in your own words.

b. Analyze how neurons communicate by organizing the three phases of neural communication into an illustrated short story for young children.

FIGURE 2.5

Jack Osbourne and MS

Jack Osbourne is one of the estimated 2.5 million people with multiple sclerosis (MS). This disease damages neurons in the nervous system and disrupts neural communication. The result causes sensory and motor impairment.

No matter what you are doing, at every moment of your life, your neurons are communicating with each other to let your nervous system receive information, process it, and respond to it. Without neural communication, you would not be able to smell a lily, think about your weekend plans, or hold the hand of someone you love. Some people experience a breakdown in this neural communication. This includes people with multiple sclerosis (MS), such as Jack Osbourne, the son of the rocker Ozzy Osbourne. Jack was diagnosed with MS at the age of 26 (**Figure 2.5**). After the birth of his daughter, Osbourne noticed he was having strange problems with his vision, such as black dots limiting his sight. Doctors determined that Jack was in the early stages of MS. MS is a disorder of the nervous system that is typically diagnosed in people between ages 20 and 40. This disorder affects the brain and the spinal cord, so that movements become jerky and people lose the ability to coordinate their actions. Gradually, for people with MS, the abilities to move, see, and think become severely impaired.

To understand how neurons communicate in most people, and how this process breaks down in disorders such as MS, you need to understand the three phases of neural communication (**Figure 2.6**). During the *transmission phase* of neural communication (Figure 2.6, Phase 1), electrical signals created in the cell body are passed along the axon and neurotransmitters are released from the terminal buttons. During the *reception phase* (Figure 2.6, Phase 2), the dendrites of neurons receive these signals from sending neurons. During the *integration phase* (Figure 2.6, Phase 3), neurons assess the incoming signals. Then this neural communication process repeats, with signals transmitted to yet more neurons, then received and integrated yet again.

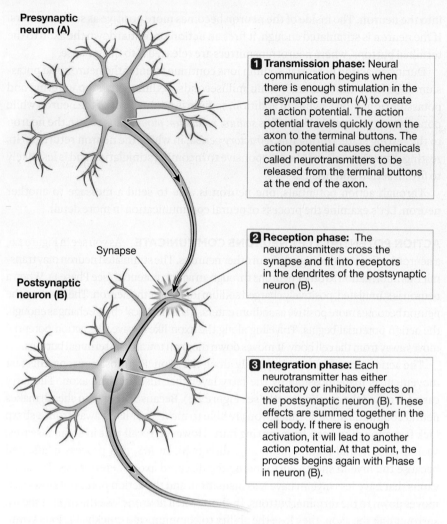

Presynaptic neuron (A)

Synapse

Postsynaptic neuron (B)

1 **Transmission phase:** Neural communication begins when there is enough stimulation in the presynaptic neuron (A) to create an action potential. The action potential travels quickly down the axon to the terminal buttons. The action potential causes chemicals called neurotransmitters to be released from the terminal buttons at the end of the axon.

2 **Reception phase:** The neurotransmitters cross the synapse and fit into receptors in the dendrites of the postsynaptic neuron (B).

3 **Integration phase:** Each neurotransmitter has either excitatory or inhibitory effects on the postsynaptic neuron (B). These effects are summed together in the cell body. If there is enough activation, it will lead to another action potential. At that point, the process begins again with Phase 1 in neuron (B).

FIGURE 2.6
Three Phases of Neural Communication
The three phases of neural communication are (1) the transmission phase, (2) the reception phase, and (3) the integration phase.

What determines whether a neuron will transmit the information it has received? In other words, what lets a neuron communicate? The answer to this question lies in the electrical properties of neurons and how neurons change when they are stimulated.

ELECTRICAL PROPERTIES OF NEURONS   Just as your body is covered with skin, the neuron is covered with a *membrane,* a thin covering. This barrier separates the inside of the neuron from the outside environment. The membrane is semi-permeable. In other words, some substances move through the membrane. These substances are electrically charged chemicals called *ions.* Ions, such as sodium and potassium, may move from outside the neuron to the inside or from inside the neuron to the outside. The movement of these ions across the membrane lets neurons communicate. The membrane contributes to neural communication by regulating the neuron's electrical activity.

It is important to know that the inside and the outside of a neuron have different electrical charges. The neuron begins in a *resting state*. During this state, the electrical charge inside the neuron is more negative than the electrical charge outside. This difference in electrical charge occurs because of the balance of various ions, charged molecules, inside and outside the neuron.

Now imagine the neuron receives stimulation from nearby neurons. This stimulation causes positively charged sodium ions to move through the membrane and

action potential
The neural impulse that travels along the axon and then causes the release of neurotransmitters into the synapse.

myelin sheath
A fatty material that covers and insulates some axons to allow for faster movement of electrical impulses along the axon.

into the neuron. The inside of the neuron becomes more positive as sodium enters. If the neuron is stimulated enough, it fires an **action potential** down the axon to the terminal buttons, where neurotransmitters are released into the synapse.

During an action potential, sodium ions continue to enter the neuron and potassium ions leave the neuron. Within milliseconds, sodium ions stop entering and potassium ions stop leaving. In addition, sodium is pumped out of the neuron while potassium is pumped back in. This *sodium potassium pump* helps return the neuron to the resting state. During this *refractory period,* in which the neuron returns to its resting state, the neuron is less responsive to incoming stimulation and is less likely to fire an action potential.

Through action potentials, one neuron is able to send a message to another neuron. Let's examine the process of neural communication in more detail.

ACTION POTENTIALS LET NEURONS COMMUNICATE   As you see in Figure 2.6, a neuron is stimulated by signals from other neurons. The stimulated neuron may transmit this information to other neurons through an action potential (see Phase 1). When a neuron is stimulated, positively charged sodium ions enter the neuron. The inside of the neuron becomes more positive as sodium enters. If the electrical charge changes enough, the action potential begins. Traveling along the axon like a wave, the action potential moves away from the cell body. It moves down the axon toward the terminal buttons.

The action potential travels quickly along the axon. For most neurons, this fast movement is made possible by the fatty layer that insulates the axon. The fatty casing is called the **myelin sheath** (see Figure 2.4). Because the myelin sheath makes neural communication so quick, you are able to move your hand away from a sharp tack fast enough to keep from getting hurt. However, recall that in some diseases, such as MS, neural communication is disrupted. In MS, this process is affected because the myelin sheath surrounding the diseased axons deteriorates. Diseased axons that have less myelin have less insulation, and the action potential slows as it moves down to the terminal buttons. In short, when neurons lose the myelin sheath surrounding the axon, they lose the ability to communicate quickly. Various symptoms result. Doctors determined that Jack Osbourne was in the early stages of MS when affected neurons disrupted his ability to process visual information.

To communicate, a neuron fires an action potential. A neuron cannot fire just a little bit: Either it fires or it does not. How often a neuron fires an action potential can change, though, depending on how much stimulation the neuron receives. To understand this idea, suppose you are playing a video game in which you fire missiles by pressing a button. Every time you press the button, a missile is launched at the same speed as the previous one. It makes no difference how hard you press the button. However, if you press faster, missiles will fire more rapidly one after another. Now suppose the missile launcher is a neuron in the visual system. The neuron receives information that a light is bright. The neuron might respond to that stimulation by firing more often than when it receives information that the light is dim. But whether the light is bright or dim, however many times the neuron fires, the strength of the action potential is the same every time.

NEUROTRANSMITTERS IN THE SYNAPSE   As you just learned, neurons communicate with each other by firing an action potential down to the terminal buttons. However, recall that neurons do not touch one another, because there is a gap between neurons called the synapse (see Figure 2.4). How can neurons communicate information from an action potential without touching each other? Neurons communicate with each other chemically, by sending information across

LEARNING TIP: Communication from Presynaptic Neuron to Postsynaptic Neuron

It will be easy to understand how neurons communicate with each other if you remember the following.

WHEN YOU SEE	PLEASE THINK	MEANING
Presynaptic	Before the synapse	Something that occurs in the sending neuron before the synapse (the gap between neurons)
Postsynaptic	After the synapse	Something that occurs in the receiving neuron after the synapse (the gap between neurons)

the synapse from one neuron to another. So in the first phase of neural communication, transmission, action potentials cause a neuron to release neurotransmitters (see Figure 2.6, Phase 1). In the reception phase, these chemicals travel across the synapse and connect to, or bind with, the receiving neuron's dendrites (see Figure 2.6, Phase 2). The neuron that sends the signal is called the *pre*synaptic neuron, and the one that receives the signal is called the *post*synaptic neuron. The Learning Tip above will help you remember these terms.

How do these chemical signals work (**Figure 2.7**)? When an action potential has arrived at the end of the axon, the terminal buttons release neurotransmitters, which are chemicals that carry information from one neuron to another. After neurotransmitters are released from the presynaptic neuron and spread across the synapse, they

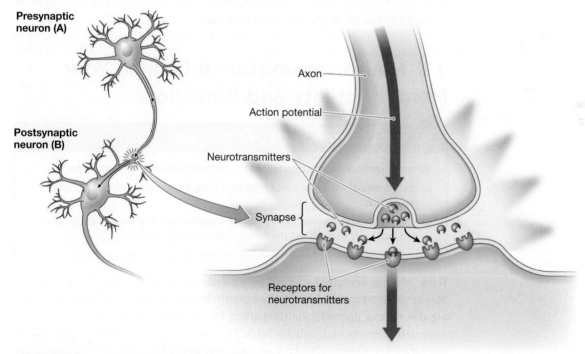

FIGURE 2.7

Neurotransmitters Move Across the Synapse

When the action potential in the presynaptic neuron reaches the terminal buttons, neurotransmitters are released into the synapse between the neurons. These neurotransmitters cross the synapse and attach (bind) to specific receptors on the dendrites of the postsynaptic neuron.

attach (bind) to receptors on the postsynaptic neuron. *Receptors* are specialized structures that respond to certain types of neurotransmitters. In much the same way as a lock opens only with the correct key, each receptor can be influenced by only one type of neurotransmitter.

Once neurotransmitters bind with specific receptors by attaching to them, they stimulate these receptors. This stimulation continues as long as the neurotransmitters are in the synapse. There are two major ways that neurotransmitters are removed from the synapse. The first way occurs when the neurotransmitters are reabsorbed by the presynaptic neuron in a process called *reuptake*. In the second way, enzymes destroy the neurotransmitters while they are in the synapse. Enzymes are special chemicals that break down other substances. Different enzymes break down different neurotransmitters in a process called *enzyme degradation*.

EXCITATORY AND INHIBITORY SIGNALS In the third phase of neural communication, integration, the postsynaptic neuron processes incoming signals (see Figure 2.6, Phase 3). The attaching, or binding, of neurotransmitters with their receptors on the postsynaptic neuron can produce signals of two types: excitatory or inhibitory. As the name indicates, excitatory signals excite the neuron—they increase the likelihood that it will fire an action potential. Inhibitory signals inhibit the neuron—they decrease the likelihood that it will fire an action potential. Any individual signal received by the neuron has little impact on whether the neuron fires. Instead, the thousands of excitatory and inhibitory signals that are received are added together within the cell body of the neuron. If the total amount of excitatory input goes past a certain threshold, the postsynaptic neuron fires an action potential. After firing, the neuron returns to its resting state. The process repeats hundreds of times per second. How do your neurotransmitters affect how you think and behave? You will learn the answer in the next study unit.

2.3 Neurotransmitters Influence Your Mental Activity and Behavior

2.3 LEARNING GOAL ACTIVITIES

To maximize your learning, complete the following learning goal activities:

a. Understand all bold and italic terms by writing explanations of them in your own words.

b. Apply neurotransmitters to your life by describing three experiences you have had that likely each reflect the function of a specific neurotransmitter.

Have you ever energized yourself with a caffeinated drink, such as coffee or tea? Maybe you start each day with a dose of caffeine. The energizing effects of caffeine are due to how neurotransmitters affect brain activity. There are many kinds of neurotransmitters. As detailed in **Table 2.1,** some neurotransmitters are particularly important in understanding how we think, feel, and behave. Much of our knowledge about neurotransmitters has come from research on how drugs, including caffeine, affect mental activity and behavior.

DRUGS ALTER HOW NEUROTRANSMITTERS FUNCTION Drugs that enhance the actions of neurotransmitters are called *agonists*. One example of an

TABLE 2.1
Common Neurotransmitters and Their Major Functions

Neurotransmitter	Functions
Acetylcholine	Motor control over muscles Attention, memory, learning, and sleeping
Norepinephrine	Arousal and alertness
Serotonin	Emotional states and impulse control Dreaming
Dopamine	Reward and motivation Motor control over voluntary movement
GABA (gamma-aminobutyric acid)	Inhibition of action potentials Anxiety reduction Intoxication (through alcohol)
Glutamate	Enhancement of action potentials Learning and memory
Endorphins	Pain reduction Reward

agonist is nicotine, a drug found in tobacco. Nicotine acts as an agonist to the neurotransmitter acetylcholine because it is chemically similar and so acetylcholine receptors cannot tell the difference between the two. What happens when a person ingests nicotine, such as by smoking a cigarette? The nicotine binds to acetylcholine receptors and causes effects that are typical of acetylcholine (see Table 2.1). So after smoking the cigarette, the person is more alert and may experience changes in motor coordination. The effect is short-lived, however.

By contrast, drugs that inhibit the actions of neurotransmitters are called *antagonists*. As discussed further in Chapter 3, in the United States an opioid abuse epidemic is leading to many deaths from overdose. Fortunately, the drug Naloxone is an antagonist that binds with endorphin receptors. Naloxone therefore blocks the ability of opioids to bind with the same receptors. When Naloxone is administered—for example, by a nasal spray—it can help prevent overdose (Wermeling, 2013). Every day, many people are helped by a scientific understanding of neurons and neural communication.

A neurotransmitter fits a receptor the way a key fits a lock. But receptors cannot sense the difference between the ingested drug and the real neurotransmitter released from a presynaptic neuron. The receptor can be affected by either a neurotransmitter or a drug that resembles the neurotransmitter. So addictive drugs, such as heroin and cocaine, and even nicotine and caffeine, have their effects because they are chemically similar to naturally occurring neurotransmitters. You will learn more about the addictive nature of drugs in Chapter 3.

To better understand how neurotransmitters affect behavior, researchers often inject agonists or antagonists into animals' brains. For instance, scientists may want to test the hypothesis that a certain neurotransmitter in a specific brain region leads to increased eating. Injecting an agonist into that brain region should increase an animal's eating. Injecting an antagonist should decrease its eating. Such studies help in the development of drug treatments for many psychological and medical disorders.

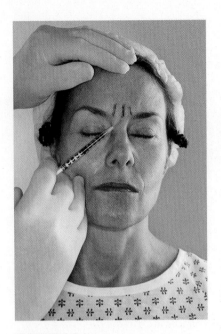

FIGURE 2.8

Acetylcholine and Botox

The neurotransmitter acetylcholine is responsible for motor control. Botox inhibits the release of acetylcholine, paralyzing muscles. Here, a woman gets a Botox injection to remove wrinkles in her forehead.

ACETYLCHOLINE   Maybe you have seen ads for Botox or known someone who received Botox injections to remove wrinkles. Botox treatments depend on the action of acetylcholine, the neurotransmitter responsible for motor control between nerves and muscles. After moving across the synapses, acetylcholine binds with receptors on muscle cells. This chemical binding makes the muscles contract.

Where does Botox come in? Botulism, a form of food poisoning, inhibits the release of acetylcholine. The resulting paralysis of muscles leads to difficulty in chewing, difficulty in breathing, and often death. In small, much less toxic doses, the botulism toxin (popularly known as Botox) paralyzes muscles that produce wrinkles in certain areas, such as the forehead (**Figure 2.8**). Because the effects of Botox wear off over time, a new dose of botulism toxin needs to be injected every 2 to 4 months. But Botox also paralyzes the facial muscles we use to express emotions, as in smiling and frowning. If too much Botox is injected, the result can be an expressionless face.

In addition to regulating motor control, acetylcholine is involved in some complex mental processes. For example, acetylcholine influences attention, memory, learning, and sleeping. Because acetylcholine plays a role in attention and memory, drugs that are acetylcholine antagonists can cause temporary amnesia. In a similar way, diminished acetylcholine functioning is associated with Alzheimer's disease, a condition characterized primarily by severe memory deficits (Koen & Yonelinas, 2014). Drugs that are acetylcholine agonists, such as nicotine, may enhance memory and decrease symptoms of Alzheimer's. So far, though, drug treatments for the disease have had only limited success (Cummings, Morstorf, & Zhong, 2014).

NOREPINEPHRINE   The neurotransmitter *norepinephrine* is involved in states of arousal and alertness. Norepinephrine is especially important for noticing what is going on around you. In your body, the same chemical is called *epinephrine.* Epinephrine, originally called adrenaline, can produce an adrenaline rush, that sudden burst of energy that seems to take over your whole body (see study unit 2.9). You may have experienced this effect as an adrenaline rush when doing something exciting or when confronted with a dangerous situation. The increased heart rate and perspiration of the adrenaline rush are part of a system called the fight-or-flight response, which prepares the body for dealing with threats from the environment. You will learn more about the fight-or-flight response in Chapter 11.

SEROTONIN   The neurotransmitter *serotonin* is involved in a wide range of psychological activities. It is especially important for emotional states, impulse control, and dreaming. A lack of serotonin is thought to contribute to sad and anxious moods, food cravings, and aggressive behavior. As you will learn in Chapter 15, one class of drugs that specifically target serotonin is prescribed widely to treat depression (Jakubovski, Varigonda, Freemantle, Taylor, & Bloch, 2016). These drugs, which include Prozac, are referred to as *selective serotonin reuptake inhibitors* (SSRIs). As you learned in study unit 2.2, reuptake is the process by which a neurotransmitter is reabsorbed by the presynaptic neuron. When this happens, the stimulation of postsynaptic receptors stops. SSRIs work to reduce the symptoms of depression in part by leaving more serotonin in synapses to bind with the receptors on postsynaptic neurons.

DOPAMINE   The neurotransmitter *dopamine* has many important brain functions. Its most important functions are motivation and reward. Consider that people eat when they're hungry, drink when they're thirsty, and have sex when they're aroused. What physiological system motivates these activities? Drives such as these activate the dopamine system, and the increased dopamine produces the desire to act. Unfortunately, as you will learn in Chapter 14, research suggests that too much dopamine is associated with psychological disorders, especially schizophrenia (Howes, McCutcheon, Owen, & Murray, 2015).

By contrast, a lack of dopamine may also be associated with specific problems. Severe loss of dopamine is connected to Parkinson's disease. First identified by the physician James Parkinson in 1917, Parkinson's is a degenerative and fatal neurological disorder. It affects about 1 in every 200 older adults and occurs in all known cultures. Most people with Parkinson's do not experience symptoms until after age 50, but the disease can occur earlier in life. For example, the boxer Muhammad Ali was diagnosed with Parkinson's disease at age 42, but he had been showing symptoms, such as slurred speech and shuffling walk, for many years. Before he died, Ali's toughest fight might have been with Parkinson's. He spent decades raising awareness about the disease and aiding others diagnosed with it, such as by helping to create the Muhammad Ali Parkinson Center (**Figure 2.9**).

FIGURE 2.9
Muhammad Ali and Parkinson's Disease
The neurotransmitter dopamine is depleted in Parkinson's disease, leading to impairments in motor abilities. After being diagnosed with Parkinson's, Muhammad Ali dedicated himself to supporting others with the disease.

With Parkinson's disease, the dopamine-producing neurons in the midbrain (see Figure 2.14) slowly die off. The resulting lack of dopamine causes disturbances in motor function: rigid muscles, tremors, and difficulty starting an action the person wants to perform. In the later stages of the disorder, people experience severe cognitive and mood disturbances. Injections of one of the chief chemical building blocks of dopamine, L-DOPA, help the surviving neurons produce more dopamine. When L-DOPA is used to treat Parkinson's disease, patients often have a remarkable, though temporary, recovery.

GABA AND GLUTAMATE The main inhibitory neurotransmitter is *GABA* (gamma-aminobutyric acid). It is more widely distributed throughout the brain than most other neurotransmitters. Without the inhibitory effect of GABA, the excitation of neurons might get out of control and spread through the brain chaotically. In fact, epileptic seizures may be caused by low levels of GABA (Shetty & Upadhya, 2016).

Drugs that are GABA agonists (for example, Xanax, Ativan) are widely used to treat anxiety disorders. The increased inhibitory effect provided by these drugs helps calm anxious people. Alcohol has similar effects on GABA receptors. As a result, people typically experience alcohol as relaxing. GABA reception may also be the primary mechanism that causes alcohol to interfere with motor coordination.

In contrast, glutamate is the main excitatory neurotransmitter. It is involved in fast-acting neural transmission throughout the brain. Glutamate receptors aid learning and memory by strengthening synaptic connections. Excessive glutamate release can lead to overexcitement of the brain, which can destroy neurons. For example, much of the damage inflicted to the brain following concussion is caused by the excessive release of glutamate that naturally occurs following brain injury (Cantu et al., 2015; concussion is discussed in Chapter 3).

ENDORPHINS You've no doubt heard about, or perhaps experienced, "runner's high." This psychological state results from a release of *endorphins*. In the early 1970s, researchers established that opioid drugs such as heroin and morphine bind to receptors in the brain, and this finding led to the discovery of naturally occurring substances in the body that bind to those sites (Pert & Snyder, 1973). Called endorphins (short for endogenous, or naturally occurring, morphine), these substances are a class of neurotransmitters involved in reward, such as runner's high, as well as in natural pain reduction. Pain is useful because it signals that you are hurt or in danger. That signal should then prompt you to try to escape or withdraw. If you

didn't experience pain when you touched a hot stove, you wouldn't know that you should pull your hand away to avoid being injured.

Pain can interfere with adaptive functioning, however. If pain prevents us from eating, competing, or mating, then we will fail to pass along our biological and psychological traits to offspring. Endorphins' painkilling, or analgesic, effects help us perform these behaviors even when we are in pain (for an example, see Has It Happened to You?). In people, drugs that bind with endorphin receptors (for example, morphine) reduce the subjective experience of pain. Apparently, morphine does not block the nerves that transmit pain signals. Instead, it alters the way pain is experienced. In other words, people still feel pain, but they report a sense of detachment that lets them not care about the pain.

Q How Does Your Nervous System Affect You?

To make sure you learned what you just read, write answers to the following questions and check your answers.

2.1 What are the four main parts of a neuron?

2.2 What happens when the axon of a neuron becomes sufficiently positively charged on the inside to cause the neuron to "fire"?

2.3 How do agonist drugs differ from antagonist drugs?

See Appendix B for answers to the red Q questions.

How Do the Parts of Your Brain Function?

As you learned in study unit 2.1, the nervous system has two main divisions: the peripheral nervous system (PNS) and the central nervous system (CNS; see Figure 2.2). The CNS consists of the brain and the spinal cord. Our basic biological processes—such as heartbeat, breathing, and reflexes—all depend on the spinal cord. But everything we are and do depends on the brain. To truly understand how we see, hear, remember, interact with others, and sometimes experience psychological disorders, we need to understand the main structures of the brain.

2.4 Understanding of the Brain Has Developed over Time

 2.4 LEARNING GOAL ACTIVITIES

To maximize your learning, complete the following learning goal activities:

a. Understand all bold and italic terms by writing explanations of them in your own words.

b. Understand the three modern approaches to brain research by describing the major advantage of each method.

An adult human brain—your brain—weighs about 3 pounds (1.4 kilograms). It may not be huge, but it is incredibly complex. Think of the brain as a collection of neurons that interact with each other in massive circuits. These neural circuits have developed throughout human evolution to help us survive in the environments where humans have lived. In adapting to those environments, the brain has evolved. As a result, specialized mechanisms in the brain regulate our breathing, food intake, sexual behavior, and body fluids. Likewise, because our ancestors had to protect themselves against dangers, sensory systems have evolved in the brain that aid our navigation and help us recognize friends and foes.

EARLY STUDIES OF THE BRAIN How do we know so much about the brain? By the beginning of the nineteenth century, early psychologists understood that the brain was the basis of mental activity. What's more, anatomists understood the brain's basic structure reasonably well. But debates raged over how the parts of the brain produced specific mental processes, such as memory and problem solving. Did different parts of the brain do different things? Or were all the parts equally important in all mental activities?

In the early nineteenth century, the neuroscientist Franz Gall and his assistant, the physician Johann Spurzheim, proposed their theory of phrenology. Gall and Spurzheim based their theory on the idea that different areas of the brain perform different functions (**Figure 2.10a**). Phrenology was the practice of assessing personality traits and mental abilities by measuring bumps on the human skull. Phrenology was popular until as late as the 1930s. At that time, a company made psychographs, which were devices used to analyze personality based on the locations and sizes of skull bumps (**Figure 2.10b**). The general public could even try these psychographs at fairs and amusement parks. People paid attention to phrenology because it was based on the seemingly scientific principle that brain functions had specific locations in the brain. In other words, people were not approaching this claim by using the critical thinking processes you learned about in study unit 1.2. At the time, the technology was not available to test the theory scientifically. Eventually, scientists found that bumps on the skull were not related to personality. But the idea of localization of brain function was an important insight.

The first strong evidence that brain regions perform specialized functions came from the work of the physician and anatomist Paul Broca (Finger, 1994). In 1861, Broca performed an autopsy on a patient who had been able to understand language but had lost the ability to say anything other than one word. When Broca examined the patient's brain, he found a large section of damaged tissue in the front left side (**Figure 2.11a**). Broca concluded that this particular region in the left hemisphere of the brain was important for speech. Broca's idea has survived the test of time. This left frontal region, now confirmed to be crucial for producing speech, is known as **Broca's area** (**Figure 2.11b**).

MODERN BRAIN RESEARCH For most of human history, theorists and researchers did not have methods for studying mental activity as it occurred in the working brain. Over the last century, scientists have developed various methods to study the brain in action.

The first method developed was a way to record the electrical activity of neurons firing in the brain. A researcher fits electrodes onto the participant's scalp. The electrodes act like small microphones, but they pick up the brain's electrical activity instead of sounds. The device that records this activity is called an *electroencephalograph* (EEG; **Figure 2.12a**). This measurement is useful because different behavioral states produce different and predictable EEG patterns. An EEG can reveal, for example, when someone is falling asleep. It has also shown that the brain is very active even when the body is at rest or asleep, especially during dreams.

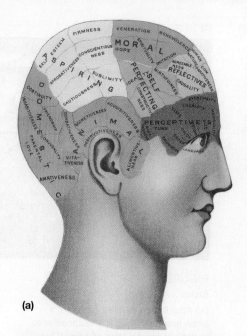

(a)

(b)

FIGURE 2.10

Phrenology and the Psychograph

(a) In phrenological maps, each region of the skull is associated with a different feature of personality to reflect processes occurring in the brain under the skull. **(b)** Psychographs were sold to the public and were claimed to "do the work of a psychoanalyst" by showing "your talents, abilities, strong and weak traits, without prejudice or flattery."

Broca's area
A small portion of the left frontal region of the brain; this area is crucial for producing speech.

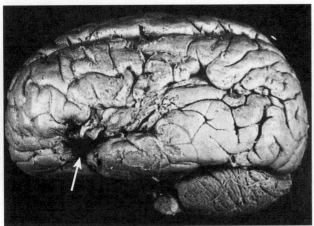

(a)

(b)

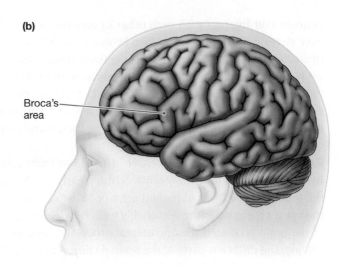

Broca's area

FIGURE 2.11

Broca's Area

(a) Paul Broca studied a patient's brain and identified the lesioned area in the left frontal lobe as crucial for producing speech. (b) This illustration shows the location of this region, called Broca's area.

(a)

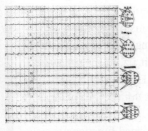

(b)

(c)

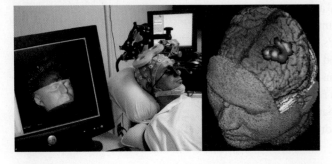

The brain's electrical activity is associated with changes in the flow of blood carrying oxygen and nutrients to the active brain regions. These changes can be measured with several different brain imaging methods.

The main brain imaging method used today in psychological research is *functional magnetic resonance imaging* (fMRI; **Figure 2.12b**). This technique measures changes in the blood's oxygen level. These changes let the researchers indirectly assess the brain's blood flow. Using this method, they are then able to map the working brain. For example, the participant performs a mental task (thinks about something), such as deciding whether a person is in a picture. During the task, the researchers scan the participant's brain. Next, the participant does a task that differs from the first in only one way, such as deciding whether a house is in a picture. The researchers then compare brain images to examine differences in activity between the two tasks.

How do researchers determine whether a brain region is important for a task? Ideally, they want to compare performances when that area is working effectively and when it is not. The method used for this purpose is *transcranial magnetic stimulation* (TMS; **Figure 2.12c**). This technique uses a very fast and powerful magnetic field to momentarily disrupt activity in a specific brain region. For example, placing the TMS coil over areas of the brain involved in language will disrupt a person's ability to

FIGURE 2.12

Measures of Brain Activity

There are several ways to measure how the brain responds to tasks or events. These methods give us insight into how mental activity and behavior depend on our biological processes. **(a)** An electroencephalograph (EEG) measures the brain's electrical activity. **(b)** Functional magnetic resonance imaging (fMRI) maps mental activity during a mental task by measuring the blood's oxygen level in the brain. **(c)** Transcranial magnetic stimulation (TMS) momentarily disrupts brain activity in a specific brain region.

speak. This technique has its limitations. In particular, it can be used only to examine brain areas close to the scalp. When used along with imaging, however, it is a powerful method for examining which brain regions are necessary for specific psychological functions. As you will learn in Chapter 15, TMS is also used as a treatment for certain psychological disorders.

Modern brain research using these methods has greatly advanced our understanding of the brain. Just how important is measuring brain activity? For researchers who want to understand the inner workings of the brain, imaging is equivalent to the telescope for astronomers. In the following study units, you will learn about the two parts of the CNS: the spinal cord and the brain. You will also learn how brain research reveals the three main divisions of the brain: the *hindbrain*, the *midbrain*, and the *forebrain*. Each of these divisions is associated with particular mental processes and particular behaviors (**Figure 2.13**; also see the Learning Tip below).

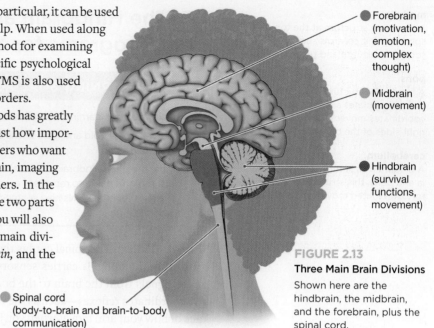

● Forebrain (motivation, emotion, complex thought)

● Midbrain (movement)

● Hindbrain (survival functions, movement)

● Spinal cord (body-to-brain and brain-to-body communication)

FIGURE 2.13

Three Main Brain Divisions
Shown here are the hindbrain, the midbrain, and the forebrain, plus the spinal cord.

💡 **LEARNING TIP:** **Processing in the Brain**

Use the table below to learn the three major regions of the brain and the most important structures in each part. If you think about how you use each structure in your life, or how they function in the brain of someone you know, it will help you remember them.

HINDBRAIN	**MEDULLA:** breathing, heart rate, other survival mechanisms
	PONS: sleep, arousal, left-right body movement coordination
	CEREBELLUM: motor learning, coordination, balance
MIDBRAIN	**SUBSTANTIA NIGRA:** initiation of voluntary motor activity
FOREBRAIN (SUBCORTICAL STRUCTURES)	**THALAMUS:** sensory information (except smell)
	HYPOTHALAMUS: regulation of body functions (for example, sleep, temperature) and motivation (for example, hunger, thirst, sex)
	HIPPOCAMPUS: formation of new memories
	AMYGDALA: association of emotions with experiences
FOREBRAIN (CORTICAL STRUCTURES)	**OCCIPITAL LOBES:** vision
	PARIETAL LOBES: touch, spatial information
	TEMPORAL LOBES: hearing, memory
	FRONTAL LOBES: planning, movement, complex thought

medulla
A hindbrain structure at the top of the spinal cord; it controls survival functions such as heart rate and breathing.

pons
A hindbrain structure above the medulla; it regulates sleep and arousal and coordinates movements of the left and right sides of the body.

cerebellum
A hindbrain structure behind the medulla and pons; this structure is essential for coordinated movement and balance.

FIGURE 2.14

The Hindbrain and the Midbrain

This drawing shows where the spinal cord meets the three hindbrain structures (medulla, pons, and cerebellum). It also shows the location of the midbrain (including the substantia nigra). The view shows the brain as though you could see inside to its middle.

2.5 The Hindbrain and Midbrain House Basic Programs for Your Survival

2.5 LEARNING GOAL ACTIVITIES

To maximize your learning, complete the following learning goal activities:

a. Understand all bold and italic terms by writing explanations of them in your own words.

b. Apply the three hindbrain and one midbrain regions by using the first letter of each region's name to represent a word. Together the four words should make up a new sentence. This new sentence can help you remember the names of these brain regions.

SPINAL CORD   The spinal cord is the gateway for information to travel into the brain from the body. It carries sensory information up to the brain and carries motor signals from the brain to the body parts to initiate action. The spinal cord also coordinates reflexes—such as the way your leg moves when a doctor taps your knee or how your arm moves when you jerk your hand away from a flame.

The spinal cord is composed of two distinct tissue types. One type is gray matter, which is dominated by the cell bodies of neurons. The other type is white matter, which consists mostly of axons and the myelin sheaths that surround them. These myelinated axons help neurons transmit messages over long distances, both in the spine and in the brain. It is the myelinated axons that are affected by MS, the disease diagnosed in Jack Osbourne. Indeed, the brain consists of both white matter and gray matter. Let's learn about the parts of the brain.

HINDBRAIN   At the base of the skull, the spinal cord thickens and becomes more complex. At this point, the spinal cord becomes the hindbrain. The hindbrain contains structures that control body functions that are essential for survival.

The hindbrain has three main structures (**Figure 2.14**). The first structure of the hindbrain is the **medulla**. The medulla controls the most basic functions of survival, including heart rate, breathing, swallowing, vomiting, urination, and orgasm. A significant blow directly to the medulla can even cause death. Have you ever gagged on something? If so, that was caused by the function of your medulla. Gagging is a reflex that prevents us from choking on something, so it is crucial for survival.

The second structure of the hindbrain, the **pons**, plays an important role in sleep and arousal and in coordinating movements between the left and right sides of the body (see Figure 2.14).

The third structure of the hindbrain is a large extension called the **cerebellum**. It is located behind the medulla and pons (see Figure 2.14). Its size and convoluted surface make it look like an extra brain. In fact, the name *cerebellum* comes from the Latin word for "little brain."

The cerebellum is essential for proper motor function. Damage to the different parts of the cerebellum produces

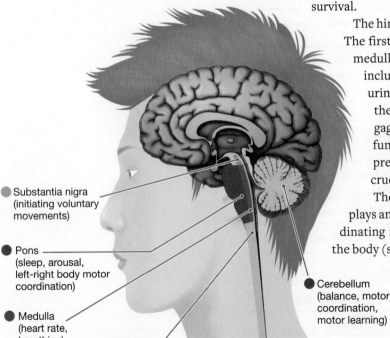

● Substantia nigra (initiating voluntary movements)

● Pons (sleep, arousal, left-right body motor coordination)

● Medulla (heart rate, breathing)

● Spinal cord (body-to-brain and brain-to-body communication)

● Cerebellum (balance, motor coordination, motor learning)

very different effects. Damage to the very bottom causes problems with head tilt and balance. Damage to the ridge that runs up the back of the cerebellum affects walking. Damage to the lobes on either side causes a loss of coordination in the limbs. For example, a person with this kind of damage could not reach out smoothly to pick up a pen.

The cerebellum is involved in motor learning and motor memory. For example, the cerebellum makes it possible for you to ride a bicycle effortlessly—and to do so while planning your next meal. In fact, the cerebellum may be involved in cognitive processes such as making plans, remembering events, using language, and experiencing emotion.

MIDBRAIN   The midbrain is located above the pons. It consists of several structures that are involved in the reflexive movement of the eyes and body. One structure in particular, the *substantia nigra*, is important for making voluntary movements and initiating movements (see Figure 2.14). This region is critical for the production of dopamine, the neurotransmitter that motivates behavior and controls normal motor function. Parkinson's disease (discussed in study unit 2.3) is caused by the death of substantia nigra cells and the resulting loss of dopamine produced by those cells. So the slurred speech and shuffling walk that Muhammad Ali experienced as symptoms of Parkinson's disease were a result of a loss of substantia nigra cells in his midbrain. If you know someone with Parkinson's disease, it might help you understand the changes you see by thinking about what is going on in this part of the person's brain.

2.6 Forebrain Subcortical Structures Control Your Motivations and Emotions

2.6 LEARNING GOAL ACTIVITIES

To maximize your learning, complete the following learning goal activities:

a. Understand all bold and italic terms by writing explanations of them in your own words.

b. Apply the four forebrain subcortical structures by using the first letter of each part's name to represent a word. Together the four words should make up a new sentence. This new sentence will help you remember the names of these brain parts.

Above the midbrain is the forebrain. The forebrain includes two main areas: the cerebral cortex and several subcortical structures (**Figure 2.15**). The cerebral cortex is the intricate surface that makes up the outermost part of the forebrain. The functions of the cerebral cortex are discussed in study unit 2.7. The name "subcortical" simply means that these structures are under (sub) the cortex (cortical). In this study unit, you will learn about four forebrain subcortical structures that are most important for psychological functions. You will read about these structures throughout this book, so learning them now will help you later.

These four subcortical structures are part of the *limbic system*: the thalamus, the hypothalamus, the hippocampus, and the amygdala. The word "limbic" comes from the Latin word for border. The limbic system serves as the border between the parts of the brain that evolved earliest (the hindbrain and the midbrain) and the part that evolved more recently (the cerebral cortex). This system is especially important for

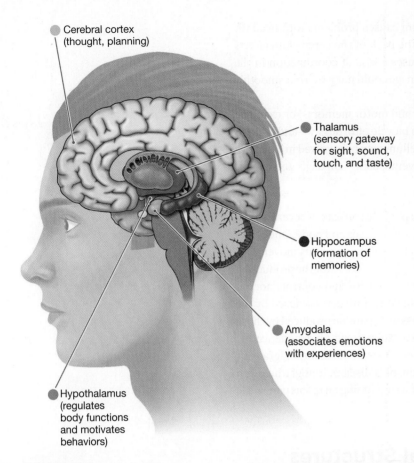

- Cerebral cortex (thought, planning)
- Thalamus (sensory gateway for sight, sound, touch, and taste)
- Hippocampus (formation of memories)
- Amygdala (associates emotions with experiences)
- Hypothalamus (regulates body functions and motivates behaviors)

FIGURE 2.15

The Forebrain

This drawing shows where the forebrain regions (the cerebral cortex and the four subcortical structures) are located. The view shows the brain as though you could see inside to its middle.

thalamus
A subcortical forebrain structure; the gateway to the brain for almost all incoming sensory information before that information reaches the cortex.

hypothalamus
A subcortical forebrain structure involved in regulating bodily functions. The hypothalamus also influences our basic motivated behaviors.

hippocampus
A subcortical forebrain structure; it is associated with the formation of new memories.

controlling motivated behaviors, such as eating and drinking. It is also important for controlling emotions and for forming memories.

THALAMUS Suppose you are served a platter of fajitas. You see the food and hear it sizzle. When you eat it, you feel it pass your lips and you taste it. The **thalamus** is critical in this process because it is the sensory gateway to the cortex (see Figure 2.15). It receives almost all incoming sensory information: sight, sound, touch, and taste. The thalamus also organizes this information and relays it to the cortex. But what about the smell of the fajitas? Smell is the oldest and most fundamental sense. Thus, smell has a direct route from the nerves in the nose to the cortex. So the smell of the fajitas would bypass your thalamus and be processed directly in your cortex. Another function of the thalamus is that, during sleep, it partially shuts out incoming sensations to help you stay asleep. You will learn more about how the thalamus processes sensory information in Chapter 5.

HYPOTHALAMUS The **hypothalamus** is the brain's master regulatory structure (see Figure 2.15). In other words, it keeps the body "in balance"—not too hot or cold, hungry or full, sleepy or awake. Because of this role, the hypothalamus is indispensable to the body's survival. "Hypo" means below, and the hypothalamus is located below the thalamus. It receives input from almost everywhere in the body, including other region of the brain, and it sends its influence to almost everywhere in the body and brain. The hypothalamus affects the functions of many internal organs, such as regulating blood pressure. It also regulates body rhythms such as sleeping and waking (see Chapter 3), body temperature and blood glucose (also known as blood sugar; see Chapter 9). It is also involved in the motivations for many behaviors, including drinking, eating, aggression, and sex (see Chapter 10).

HIPPOCAMPUS The **hippocampus** plays a critical role in the formation of new memories (see Figure 2.15). Its name comes from the Greek word for "sea horse," because of this structure's sea horse–like shape. The hippocampus seems to form new memories by creating new neural connections within the cerebral cortex for each new experience. New memories are not stored in the hippocampus itself; instead, permanent memories are stored in parts of the cortex (Eichenbaum, 2004). Do you know someone with Alzheimer's disease? You may have noticed that the person can remember events from the long past very well but cannot remember events from the recent past, such as what the person ate for breakfast or did last week. Alzheimer's disease affects the ability of the hippocampus to form new memories (Tate, Herbet, Moritz-Gasser, Tate, & Duffau, 2014).

The hippocampus helps you navigate in environments (Nadel, Hoscheidt, & Ryan, 2013). It may be particularly involved in how you remember the locations of both places and objects. For example, it may help you recall how streets are laid out in a city or how furniture is positioned in a room. An interesting study to support this theory focused on London taxi drivers. The researchers (Maguire et al., 2003) found that one region of the hippocampus was much larger in London taxi drivers' brains than in the brains of most other London drivers. London taxi drivers are well known for their knowledge of the city's streets, so this research suggested it is possible the hippocampus changes with experience to aid memory for locations. But as you learned in study unit 1.10, correlation does not prove causation. The Maguire study did not conclude that experience *causes* changes in the hippocampus.

AMYGDALA   The **amygdala** is located immediately in front of the hippocampus (see Figure 2.15). Its name comes from the Latin word for almond, because of the structure's almond-like shape.

One function of the amygdala is to increase memory processing during times of emotional arousal. As a result, the amygdala serves a vital role in how you learn to associate things in the world (such as a snake) with emotional responses (such as fear). For example, a frightening experience can be seared into your memory for life. Even if your memory of the event is not completely accurate (flaws in memory are discussed in Chapter 7), in your mind the event can still be associated with great anxiety.

The amygdala is also involved in learning about stimuli that are relevant for survival (Whalen et al., 2013), especially in responding to stimuli that cause fear. For example, this structure appears to be part of a system that automatically directs your visual attention to another person's eyes when you are evaluating that person's facial expression (Kennedy & Adolphs, 2010). Imaging studies have found that the amygdala activation is especially strong in response to a fearful face, especially to the large whites of the eyes that are seen in fearful expressions (Kim et al., 2016). People who are prone to anxiety show greater activation of the amygdala when viewing faces they haven't seen before (Schwartz, Wright, Shin, Kagan, & Rauch, 2003). You will learn more about how emotions are processed in the amygdala in Chapter 9, and you will learn about the amygdala's role in psychological disorders in Chapter 14.

amygdala
A subcortical forebrain structure; it serves a vital role in our learning to associate things with emotional responses and in processing emotional information.

2.7 The Cerebral Cortex of the Forebrain Processes Your Complex Mental Activity

2.7 LEARNING GOAL ACTIVITIES

To maximize your learning, complete the following learning goal activities:

a. Understand all bold and italic terms by writing explanations of them in your own words.

b. Apply the functions of the four lobes of the cerebral cortex and the six regions identified in this study unit by giving an example of how each processes information in your daily life.

Now that you understand how the four subcortical structures process information, it's time to learn about the wrinkly outer layer of your forebrain. This layer of tissue, the cerebral cortex, gives the brain its distinctive wrinkled appearance (**Figure 2.16**). *Cortex* is the Latin word for "bark." In reality, the cortex feels more like Jell-O than tree bark. In humans, the cerebral cortex is relatively large. If you could flatten it out, the cortex would be about the size of a large sheet of newspaper. However, because it

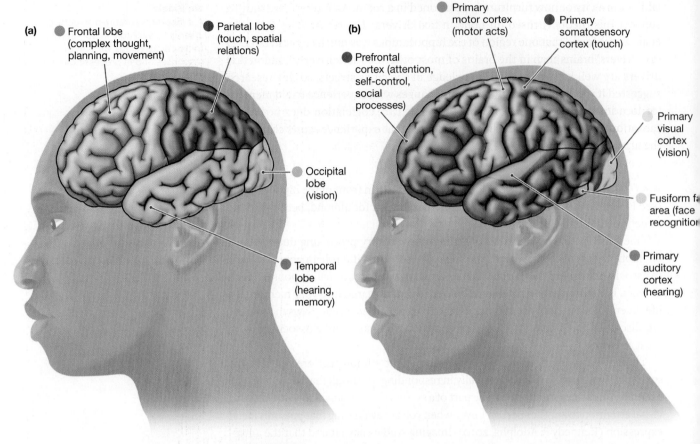

(a)
- Frontal lobe (complex thought, planning, movement)
- Parietal lobe (touch, spatial relations)
- Occipital lobe (vision)
- Temporal lobe (hearing, memory)

(b)
- Prefrontal cortex (attention, self-control, social processes)
- Primary motor cortex (motor acts)
- Primary somatosensory cortex (touch)
- Primary visual cortex (vision)
- Fusiform fa area (face recognitio
- Primary auditory cortex (hearing)

FIGURE 2.16

Lobes and Processing Centers of the Cerebral Cortex

(a) This diagram identifies the four lobes of the cerebral cortex. The same four lobes appear in each hemisphere of the cortex. **(b)** The colored areas in this diagram of the cerebral cortex mark six important regions within the lobes. Each region performs different functions.

is folded in against itself so many times, the cortex fits within the skull. It is the site of your thoughts, detailed perceptions, and complex behaviors. It lets you understand yourself, other people, and the outside world.

The cortex is divided into two halves. These halves are called the left hemisphere and the right hemisphere. Each cerebral hemisphere has four areas, which are called lobes: the occipital, parietal, temporal, and frontal lobes. Each lobe has specialized functions (see Figure 2.16a). In addition, areas within each lobe have specific functions (see Figure 2.16b). The hemispheres are connected by a structure called the *corpus callosum*. This massive bridge consists of millions of axons. It lets information flow between the left and the right hemispheres (**Figure 2.17**).

Do the left and right hemispheres process different information? In study unit 2.4, you learned about Broca's area and the relationship between the left hemisphere and language. For most people, the left hemisphere is responsible for logical thought and language. Being able to speak and write depends on the left hemisphere. By contrast, the right hemisphere is responsible for spatial relationships, such as understanding a map or locating objects that are around you. Recognizing faces, understanding emotional aspects of language, and abstract thinking involve more processing in the right hemisphere. Examining people who had damage to one side of the brain was the initial source of evidence for these patterns. In the 1960s, this book's coauthor Michael Gazzaniga, working with Nobel laureate Roger Sperry, conducted a series

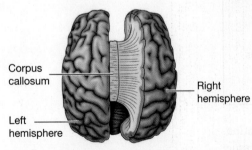

Corpus callosum

Left hemisphere

Right hemisphere

FIGURE 2.17

The Corpus Callosum

This fibrous structure connects the two hemispheres of the cerebral cortex (shown here from the top of the brain).

of studies on patients whose hemispheres had been separated as part of treatment for epilepsy. Studying these *split-brain* patients revealed important insights into how the left and right hemispheres are specialized for certain functions. In Chapter 3, you will read more about how information is processed in a split brain.

LOBES OF THE CEREBRAL CORTEX The **occipital lobes** are at the back portion of the head (see Figure 2.16a). These lobes are devoted almost exclusively to vision, and they include many distinct visual areas. By far the largest of these areas is the *primary visual cortex* (see Figure 2.16b). The primary visual cortex is an important processor of visual information.

The primary visual cortex is surrounded by a patchwork of secondary visual areas. These areas process various qualities of the visual input, such as its colors, forms, and motions.

Another portion of the cerebral cortex consists of the **parietal lobes** (see Figure 2.16a). If you enjoy getting a massage, you have your parietal lobes to thank, at least in part. The parietal lobes are devoted partially to touch. Their labor is divided between the left and right cerebral hemispheres. The information received by the hemispheres is actually reversed. The left hemisphere receives touch information from the right side of the body, and the right hemisphere receives touch information from the left side of the body. In each parietal lobe, this sensory information is directed to the *primary somatosensory cortex* (see Figure 2.16b). This area is a strip of brain matter in the front part of the lobe, running from the top of the brain down the sides.

In the primary somatosensory cortex, touch information from one body part registers in the cortex near regions where touch information is registered from nearby body parts (**Figure 2.18,** right side). For example, sensations on the fingers

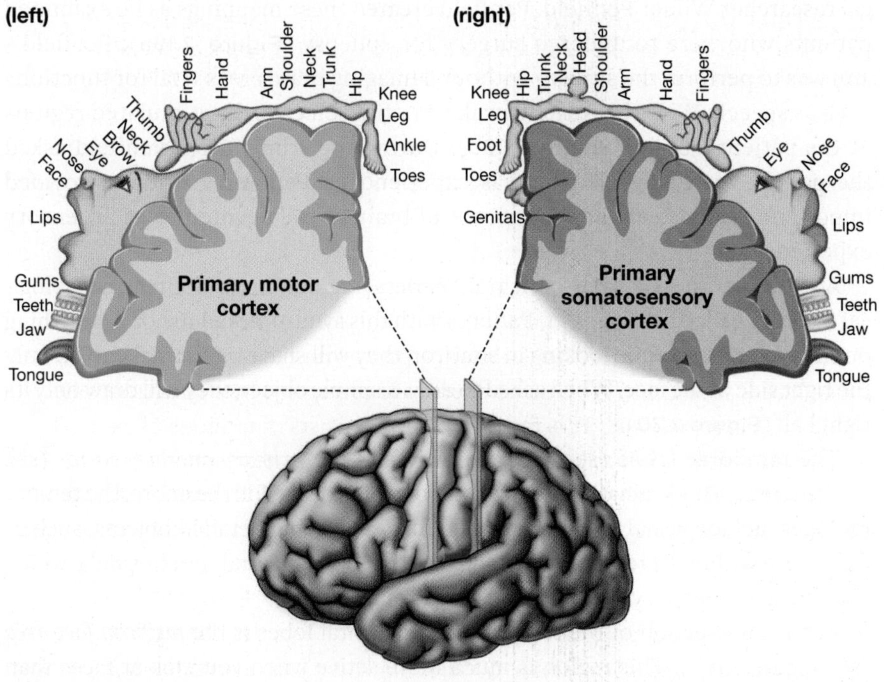

occipital lobes
Regions of the cerebral cortex at the back of the brain; these regions are important for vision.

parietal lobes
Regions of the cerebral cortex in front of the occipital lobes and behind the frontal lobes; these regions are important for the sense of touch and for picturing the layout of spaces in an environment.

FIGURE 2.18

The Primary Somatosensory and Motor "Homunculus"
The cortical representation of the body surface is organized in strips that run down the side of the brain. **(right)** Touch information is processed in the primary somatosensory cortex, part of the parietal lobe. **(left)** Motor information is processed in the primary motor cortex, part of the frontal lobe.

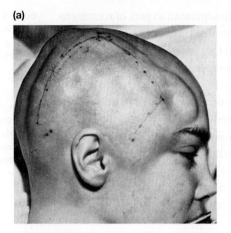

(a)

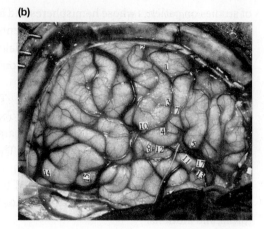

(b)

FIGURE 2.19

Mapping the Somatosensory Homunculus

(a) This photograph shows one of Wilder Penfield's patients immediately before direct stimulation of the brain. **(b)** Here, you can see the exposed surface of the patient's cortex. The numbered tags mark locations that were electrically stimulated.

register in the cortex near where sensations on the hand are registered. More cortical area is devoted to the body's more sensitive areas, such as the face and the fingers. Thus, the classic representation of the primary somatosensory area is like a distorted version of the entire body.

This representation of the somatosensory area is known as the somatosensory homunculus. (The word "homunculus" comes from the Greek for "little man.") The representation is based on mappings by the pioneering neurological researcher Wilder Penfield. Penfield created these mappings as he examined patients who were to undergo surgery for epilepsy (**Figure 2.19a**). Penfield's aim was to perform the surgery without damaging brain areas vital for functions such as speech. With the patient awake, Penfield electrically stimulated regions of the patient's brain (**Figure 2.19b**). During the stimulation, Penfield asked the patient to report what he was experiencing. Penfield's studies provided important evidence about the amount of brain tissue devoted to each sensory experience.

A stroke or other damage to the right parietal region can result in the neurological disorder called hemineglect. Patients with this syndrome fail to notice anything on their left sides. While looking in a mirror, they will shave or put makeup on only the right side of the face. When asked to draw a simple object, they will draw only its right half (**Figure 2.20**).

The **temporal lobes** (see Figure 2.16a) hold the *primary auditory cortex* (see Figure 2.16b). This brain region is responsible for hearing. Furthermore, the temporal lobes include visual areas specialized for recognizing detailed objects, such as faces. Also within the temporal lobes are the hippocampus and the amygdala, which are critical for memory (as discussed in study unit 2.6).

At the intersection of the temporal and occipital lobes is the *fusiform face area* (see Figure 2.16b). This region is much more active when you look at faces than when you look at other things. Other regions of the temporal lobe are more activated by objects, such as houses or cars, than by faces. If your fusiform face area were damaged, you would have no trouble recognizing objects, but you would have a very difficult time recognizing people's faces. Indeed, some people with this condition,

FIGURE 2.20

Hemineglect

This drawing was made by a patient with hemineglect who has damage to the parietal lobe in the right hemisphere. The patient did not draw much of the flower's left side.

called *prosopagnosia*, report that trying to tell one face from another is like trying to tell two rocks apart!

The **frontal lobes** are essential for complex thought, planning, and movement (see Figure 2.16a). The rear portion of the frontal lobes is the *primary motor cortex* (see Figure 2.16b). This structure includes neurons that send messages directly to the spinal cord to move the body's muscles. Like the primary somatosensory cortex, the motor cortex in one hemisphere controls the other side of body: The left hemisphere controls the right arm, for example, whereas the right hemisphere controls the left arm. So if you are right handed, you use the primary motor cortex in your left hemisphere to write. If you are left handed, the opposite is true. In addition, motor information for a body part is processed in cortical areas that are near regions that process motor acts for nearby body parts (see Figure 2.18, left side).

PREFRONTAL CORTEX The rest of the frontal lobes consists of the *prefrontal cortex* (see Figure 2.16b). In humans, this structure occupies about 30 percent of the brain. Scientists have long thought that our extraordinarily large prefrontal cortex makes humans unique in the animal kingdom. There is evidence, however, that what separates humans from other animals is not how much of the brain the prefrontal cortex occupies. Instead, the difference between the human brain and the brains of other animals is in the complexity and organization of these neural circuits (Bush & Allman, 2004; Schoenemann, Sheehan, & Glotzer, 2005).

The entire prefrontal cortex is critical for rational thought. It is also especially important for many aspects of human social life, such as the ability to follow social norms. It provides both our sense of self and our capacity to understand what other people are thinking, connect with them emotionally, empathize with them, and feel guilty about harming them. People with damage to this region do not typically have problems with memory or general knowledge. They often do have serious disturbances in their ability to get along with others.

Particular parts of the prefrontal cortex are also responsible for directing and maintaining attention, keeping ideas in mind while distractions bombard us from the outside world, and developing and acting on plans. People with attention-deficit/hyperactivity disorder (ADHD), such as Michael Phelps (see the chapter opener), experience abnormalities in the attention and self-regulation processes of the prefrontal cortex (Nigg, 2010). However, ADHD is very complex. People with ADHD also experience processing irregularities in several brain areas (Curatolo, D'Agati, & Moavero, 2010).

Over time, psychologists have learned much of what they know about how brain regions work by carefully studying people whose brains have been damaged by disease or injury. Perhaps the most famous historical example of brain damage is the case of Phineas Gage (**Figure 2.21a**). The first modern theories of the prefrontal cortex's role in both personality and self-control were based on Gage's case.

In 1848, Gage was a 25-year-old foreman on the construction of Vermont's Rutland and Burlington Railroad. One day, he dropped a tool called a tamping iron, which was over a yard long and an inch in diameter. The iron rod hit a rock, igniting some blasting powder. The resulting explosion drove the rod into his cheek, through his frontal lobes, and out through the top of his head (**Figure 2.21b**).

Physically, Gage recovered remarkably well. Unfortunately, the accident led to major personality changes. Whereas the old Gage had been regarded by his

temporal lobes
Regions of the cerebral cortex below the parietal lobes and in front of the occipital lobes; these regions are important for hearing and for recognizing objects, such as faces.

frontal lobes
Regions of the cerebral cortex at the front of the brain; these regions are important for movement and complex processes (rational thought, attention, social processes, etc.).

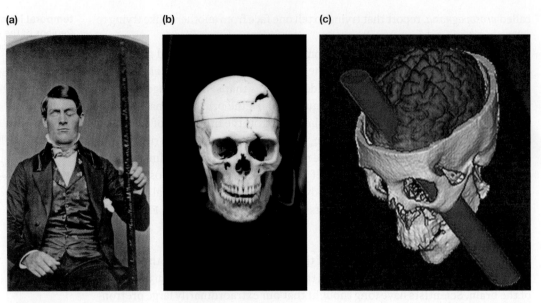

(a)   (b)   (c)

FIGURE 2.21

Phineas Gage

(a) This recently discovered photo shows Gage holding the rod that passed through his skull. **(b)** Here, you can see the hole in the top of Gage's skull. **(c)** This computer-generated image reconstructs the likely path of the rod through the skull.

employers as "the most efficient and capable" of workers, the new Gage was not. As one of his doctors later wrote,

> The equilibrium or balance, so to speak, between his intellectual faculties and animal propensities seems to have been destroyed. He is fitful, irreverent, indulging at times in the grossest profanity . . . impatient of restraint or advice when it conflicts with his desires. . . . A child in his intellectual capacity and manifestations, he has the animal passions of a strong man.

In other words, Gage was "no longer Gage." He could not get his foreman's job back. Instead, he exhibited himself in various New England towns and at the New York Museum (owned by the circus showman P. T. Barnum). After a decade, Gage's health began to decline, and in 1860 he started having epileptic seizures and died within a few months. At first, the medical community used Gage's recovery to argue that the entire brain works uniformly and that the healthy parts of Gage's brain had taken over the work of the damaged parts. However, Gage's severe psychological impairments eventually led to the recognition that some areas of the brain have specific functions. Reconstruction of Gage's injury clearly shows that the prefrontal cortex was the area most damaged by the tamping rod (Damasio, Grabowski, Frank, Galaburda, & Damasio, 1994; **Figure 2.21c**).

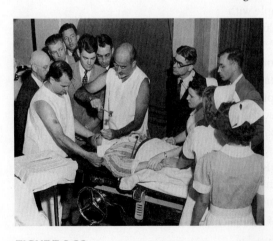

FIGURE 2.22

Lobotomy

This photo shows Dr. Walter Freeman performing a lobotomy in 1949.

In the late 1930s, mental health professionals developed a new treatment for many patients with psychological disorders—especially patients who could not control their emotions. The procedure was called a lobotomy, and it was a deliberate damaging of the prefrontal cortex (**Figure 2.22**). This form of brain surgery generally left patients lethargic and emotionally flat. Thus, the patients were much easier to manage in mental hospitals. But it also left them disconnected from their social surroundings, as Gage was. Most lobotomies were performed in the late 1940s and early 1950s. With the arrival of drugs to treat psychological disorders, the lobotomy was phased out.

How Do the Parts of Your Brain Function?

To make sure you learned what you just read, write answers to the following questions and check your answers.

2.4 How do EEG, fMRI, and TMS differ in terms of the brain activity they measure?

2.5 What part of your CNS sends information to and from your brain?

2.6 Which brain region is considered the gateway to the cortex?

2.7 Which region of the cerebral cortex most likely differs between humans and other animals?

See Appendix B for answers to the red Q questions.

How Does Your Brain Communicate with Your Body?

When you decide to move your arm, most of the time your arm moves. When you watch a sad movie, your eyes may produce tears. How do the parts of your body get the information from your brain that makes them respond the way they do?

Recall that the nervous system consists of the central nervous system (CNS; the brain and the spinal cord) and the peripheral nervous system (PNS; the nerves in the rest of the body). The PNS transmits a variety of information to the CNS. It also responds to messages from the CNS to perform specific behaviors or make bodily adjustments. The PNS has two primary subdivisions: the somatic nervous system and the autonomic nervous system (see Figure 2.2). In producing psychological activity, the nervous system also interacts with the hormones of the endocrine system. Let's examine how these various interactions affect mental activity and behavior.

2.8 Your Somatic Nervous System Detects Sensory Input and Responds

 2.8 LEARNING GOAL ACTIVITIES

To maximize your learning, complete the following learning goal activities:

a. Understand all bold and italic terms by writing explanations of them in your own words.

b. Analyze how the somatic nervous system processes information by describing how your somatic nervous system functions when you touch a hot pan.

The **somatic nervous system** is the part of the PNS that transmits signals to and from the CNS through nerves (see Figure 2.2). Specialized receptors in the skin, muscles, and joints send sensory information to the spinal cord, which relays it to the brain. In addition, the CNS sends signals through the somatic nervous system to muscles, joints, and skin to initiate or inhibit movement.

This process controls all voluntary movements you make. For instance, right now you should be actively reading this text by taking notes about the information. When you hold the pen, receptors in both your skin and your muscles send messages to your brain to help determine how much pressure is needed to hold the pen. You may contract and relax your hand muscles and finger muscles to adjust your fingers'

somatic nervous system
A subdivision of the PNS; it transmits sensory signals and motor signals back and forth between the CNS and the skin, muscles, and joints.

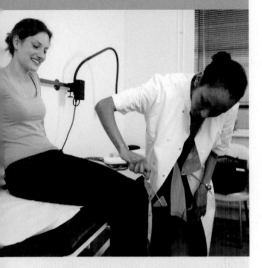

Have you ever had your knee-jerk reflex tested at the doctor's office? If so, you probably sat on a table. When the doctor used a tool to tap a spot just below your knee, your leg involuntarily jerked up. This procedure illustrates how your somatic nervous system makes reflexes possible: Nerves process information about the tap, and signals are processed through the spinal cord. This processing causes your leg to move. The communication happens in an instant because the signals never have to reach your brain. Instead, the reflex signals are processed only in the spinal cord.

autonomic nervous system
A subdivision of the PNS; it transmits sensory signals and motor signals back and forth between the CNS and the body's glands and internal organs.

pressure on the pen. When you want to use the pen, your brain sends messages to your finger muscles so they move in specific ways to let you take notes. This simple act of using a pen is a remarkable symphony of neural communication. Yet most of us employ motor control so easily that we rarely think about it.

As you learned in study unit 2.5, some movements can occur from spinal reflexes alone, without any processing in the brain. For each reflex action, a handful of neurons simply convert sensation into action based on processing only within the spinal cord. You have likely experienced reflexes yourself, such as the knee-jerk reflex discussed in Has It Happened to You?

2.9 Your Autonomic Nervous System Regulates the Body Automatically

2.9 LEARNING GOAL ACTIVITIES

To maximize your learning, complete the following learning goal activities:

a. Understand all bold and italic terms by writing explanations of them in your own words.

b. Apply the autonomic nervous system to your life by providing examples of two experiences you have had, one processed by the sympathetic system and one by the parasympathetic system.

The second major subdivision of the PNS is the **autonomic nervous system** (see Figure 2.2). As its name suggests, the autonomic nervous system automatically regulates the body's internal environment (see the Learning Tip below). It accomplishes this regulation by stimulating glands, such as sweat glands, and by maintaining internal organs, such as the heart. Nerves in the autonomic nervous system also carry signals from the glands and internal organs to the CNS. These signals provide information about, for example, the fullness of your stomach or how anxious you feel.

The autonomic nervous system has two further subdivisions: the *sympathetic nervous system* and the *parasympathetic nervous system* (see Figure 2.2). Both divisions control the activity of organs and glands. They do so by providing signals that travel from the CNS to the organs and glands and back again.

To understand these signals, imagine that you hear a fire alarm. In the second after you hear the alarm, signals go out to parts of your body that automatically prepare them for action (**Figure 2.23**, left side). As a result, blood flows to the muscles that move your skeleton. Epinephrine (also called adrenaline) is released, increasing your heart rate and blood sugar. Your lungs take in more oxygen. Your pupils dilate to maximize visual sensitivity. You perspire to keep from overheating. This preparation for action is prompted by the sympathetic nervous system. Now, if a fire really

LEARNING TIP: Remembering the Autonomic Nervous System

WHEN YOU SEE	PLEASE THINK	MEANING
<u>Auto</u>nomic nervous system	<u>Auto</u>matic processes	Processes that are out of a person's control, such as blood pressure, digestion, and respiration.

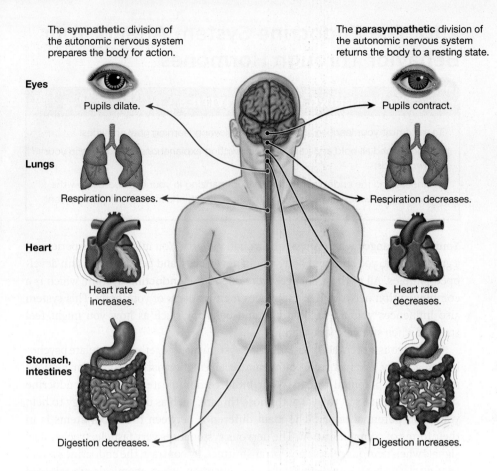

The **sympathetic** division of the autonomic nervous system prepares the body for action.

The **parasympathetic** division of the autonomic nervous system returns the body to a resting state.

Eyes — Pupils dilate. / Pupils contract.

Lungs — Respiration increases. / Respiration decreases.

Heart — Heart rate increases. / Heart rate decreases.

Stomach, intestines — Digestion decreases. / Digestion increases.

FIGURE 2.23

Sympathetic and Parasympathetic Divisions of the Autonomic Nervous System
The sympathetic and parasympathetic nervous systems in the autonomic portion of the PNS work together to keep the body in balance—not too aroused and not too calm.
(left) The sympathetic nervous system arouses the body and prepares it for action.
(right) The parasympathetic nervous system calms the body, letting it relax.

exists, you are physically prepared to flee. If the alarm turns out to be false, your body will return to a normal state (Figure 2.23, right side). Your heart will return to its normal steady beat, your breathing will slow, and you will stop perspiring. All the changes just described result from processing by the parasympathetic nervous system. Most of your internal organs are controlled by inputs from sympathetic and parasympathetic systems. The more aroused you are, the greater the sympathetic system's dominance.

It doesn't take a fire alarm to activate your sympathetic nervous system. Have you ever met someone whom you found attractive? You may have found that your heart beat quickly, your hands started to feel sweaty, your breathing got heavier, and your pupils dilated. These responses occur because sexual arousal has activated the sympathetic nervous system. The responses provide nonverbal cues during social interaction. The sympathetic nervous system is also activated by psychological states such as anxiety or unhappiness. If people worry a great deal or do not cope well with stress, their bodies are in a constant state of arousal. Important research in the 1930s and 1940s by Hans Selye demonstrated that chronic activation of the sympathetic nervous system is associated with medical problems such as heart disease and asthma. You will learn more about stress, stress responses, and coping mechanisms in Chapter 11.

2.10 The Endocrine System Affects Your Behavior Through Hormones

2.10 LEARNING GOAL ACTIVITIES

To maximize your learning, complete the following learning goal activities:

a. Understand all bold and italic terms by writing explanations of each one in your own words.

b. Understand the endocrine system by summarizing in your own words how the testes and ovaries secrete specific hormones that influence sexual development.

Your body changed when you went through puberty. You might have experienced a growth spurt, you sprouted body hair in new places, and perhaps your skin developed pimples. All of these changes were due to the **endocrine system,** which is a communication network that influences many aspects of your body. This system also influences your mental activity and behavior, such as how you might feel stressed when studying for exams.

The nervous system and the endocrine system work together to regulate psychological activity. For instance, your brain receives information from your nervous system about potential threats. Your brain communicates with your endocrine system to prepare you to deal with those threats, such as directing energy to help you avoid potential injury. The main difference between the two systems is in their forms of communication. The nervous system uses very fast electrochemical signals when neurons release neurotransmitters. By contrast, the endocrine system uses a relatively slower method of communication, when chemicals are released from glands.

Hormones are the chemical substances that are released into the bloodstream by endocrine glands (**Figure 2.24**). The endocrine glands include the pineal gland (see Chapter 3), the adrenal glands (see Chapter 11), the pituitary gland, the thyroid, and the testes or ovaries (see Figure 2.24 and Chapter 10). Once released, hormones travel through the bloodstream until they reach their target tissues. Because they travel through the bloodstream, hormones can take from seconds to hours to have an effect. Once hormones are in the bloodstream, their effects can last for a long time and affect multiple body regions.

HORMONES AND SEXUAL DEVELOPMENT   One example of hormonal influence is sexual development. The main endocrine glands influencing sexual behavior are the *gonads,* which are the sex glands used for reproduction. In males the gonads are the testes and in females the gonads are the ovaries (see Figure 2.24). Although people often talk about "male" and "female" hormones, males and females produce both of these hormones in the gonads. What differs is the quantity: *Androgens,* such as testosterone, tend to be greater in males. *Estrogens,* such as estradiol, tend to be greater in females. Gonadal hormones influence the development of secondary sex characteristics (for example, breast development in females, growth of facial hair in males). Gonadal hormones also influence adult sexual behavior. You will learn more about sexual development and how hormones are involved in the motivation to engage in sexual activity, or not, in Chapter 10.

HORMONES AND PHYSICAL GROWTH   Growth hormone (GH) prompts bone, cartilage, and muscle tissue to grow or helps them regenerate after injury.

endocrine system
A communication system that uses hormones to influence mental activity and behavior.

hormones
Chemical substances, released from endocrine glands, that travel through the bloodstream to targeted tissues; the tissues are later influenced by the hormones.

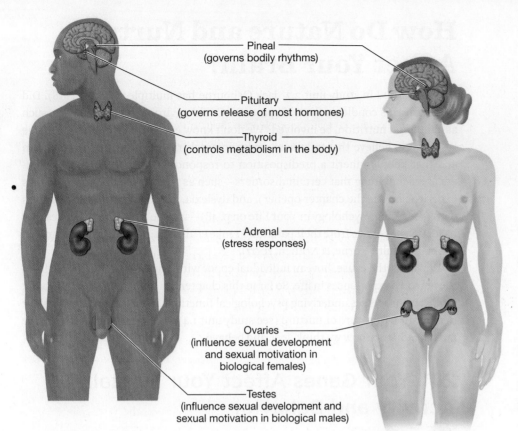

Pineal
(governs bodily rhythms)

Pituitary
(governs release of most hormones)

Thyroid
(controls metabolism in the body)

Adrenal
(stress responses)

Ovaries
(influence sexual development
and sexual motivation in
biological females)

Testes
(influence sexual development and
sexual motivation in biological males)

FIGURE 2.24

The Major Endocrine Glands

The glands in the endocrine system work with the nervous system by releasing chemicals that influence mental activity and behavior.

Since the 1930s, some people have used GH to increase body size and strength. Many athletes have sought a competitive advantage by using GH. For example, in early 2013 the legendary cyclist Lance Armstrong admitted to using GH and other hormones, including testosterone, to gain a competitive advantage. In an interview with Oprah Winfrey, Armstrong claimed it was impossible for any cyclist to win a major championship without doping (**Figure 2.25**). Sports and health are two of the major occupational fields that rely on an understanding of biological psychology, as explored in Putting Psychology to Work on p. 85.

FIGURE 2.25

Growth Hormone and Cycling

In January 2013, Lance Armstrong appeared on *The Oprah Winfrey Show* to admit using doping techniques to enhance his cycling performance.

Q How Does Your Brain Communicate with Your Body?

To make sure you learned what you just read, write answers to the following questions and check your answers.

2.8 When you stick your hand in running water, what part of your PNS detects the water temperature?

2.9 What division of your autonomic nervous system helps you calm down after taking a stressful exam?

2.10 Which glands are most important for releasing hormones that cause people to develop sexually?

See Appendix B for answers to the red Q questions.

How Do Nature and Nurture Affect Your Brain?

As you learned in study unit 2.2, Jack Osbourne has multiple sclerosis (MS). Did he inherit this condition from his parents? Could environmental influences, such as childhood nutrition, be involved? We don't know exactly what causes MS. Some researchers believe that unknown environmental triggers produce the condition and that people inherit a predisposition to respond to those triggers. Researchers are also finding that certain disorders—such as ADHD, which Michael Phelps experiences (see the chapter opener), and dyslexia, which Whoopi Goldberg lives with (see Using Psychology in Your Life on p. 48)—may be related to the genes that have been passed on from their parents (Franke et al., 2012; Schumacher, Hoffmann, Schmäl, Schulte-Körne, & Nöthen, 2007).

Whatever the cause, how an individual copes with a disorder depends partly on the person's experiences in life. So far in this chapter, you have read about the basic biological processes underlying psychological functions. Now it is time to consider the question of nature or nurture (see study unit 1.4), to explore how both of these factors influence how we think, feel, and behave.

2.11 Your Genes Affect Your Mental Activity and Behavior

2.11 LEARNING GOAL ACTIVITIES

To maximize your learning, complete the following learning goal activities:

a. Understand all bold and italic terms by writing explanations of them in your own words.

b. Apply the effects of genes in your life by describing one of your physical or psychological characteristics that was likely mostly influenced by genes.

Recall from study unit 1.4 that nature and nurture always work together to make you who you are. At the moment of conception, you inherited the **genes** you will possess for the rest of your life. But how much of who you are depends on your genes (nature)? And how much of who you are depends on environmental influences, such as the household and the culture you were raised in (nurture)?

We all know that genes control many of our physical characteristics, such as biological sex and eye color. Genes also influence our predispositions to particular diseases, including cancer and alcoholism. What about other factors, such as personality, intelligence, and athletic talent? There, too, genes have their influence.

Until fairly recently, genetic research focused almost entirely on whether people possessed certain types of genes. For example, did they have the genes for particular psychological disorders? It is important to discover the effects of individual genes. However, this approach misses the critical role of environmental factors in how genes work. Geneticists still study the inheritance of particular characteristics, but they also study gene expression. They examine the processes that turn genes "on" and "off." Their research reveals that your environment affects how your genes are expressed and therefore how they influence your brain, mental activity, and behavior.

genes
The units of heredity, which partially determine an organism's characteristics.

Increasingly, research indicates that genes lay the groundwork for many human traits. From this perspective, people are born essentially like undeveloped photographs: The image is already captured, but the way it eventually appears can vary based on the development process. All of your genes together make up your *genotype*. The genotype is set at the moment of conception and never changes. Your observable physical and psychological characteristics are called your *phenotype*. These factors are influenced in part by your genes. They are also affected by environmental factors. In other words, they can change. Your current height—part of your phenotype—is influenced by your genotype. It was also influenced by your environment, such as childhood diet.

Suppose you have inherited a predisposition to alcoholism (nature). If you were raised in a nondrinking environment and spend time with only moderate social drinkers (nurture), that predisposition may never be expressed. Psychologists study the ways that nature, nurture, and their combination affect psychological characteristics. In other words, they study the ways that genes are expressed in distinct environments.

2.12 Your Genes Interact with Your Environment to Influence You

2.12 LEARNING GOAL ACTIVITIES

To maximize your learning, complete the following learning goal activities:

a. Understand all bold and italic terms by writing explanations of them in your own words.

b. Understand how behavioral genetics studies the interaction of genes and environment by summarizing the results of twin studies and adoption studies in your own words.

"I'm so different from the rest of this family! I must be adopted!" Did you ever think that when you were a child? Most of us, at one time or another, have marveled at how different biological siblings can be. Even siblings raised around the same time and in the same household have their individual appearances, unique personalities, and so on. The differences are to be expected, however.

Biological siblings always share some genes and often share much of their environment. But most siblings do not have identical genes or identical life experiences. Within the household and outside it, environments differ subtly and not so subtly. Siblings have different birth orders. Their mother may have consumed different foods and other substances during the different pregnancies. The siblings may have different friends and teachers. Their parents may treat them differently. The study of how genes and environment interact to influence mental activity and behavior is known as *behavioral genetics*. Scientists in this field use two methods to assess the degree to which traits are inherited: twin studies and adoption studies.

BEHAVIORAL GENETICS Twin studies compare similarities between different types of twins to determine the genetic basis of specific traits. **Monozygotic twins** are identical. They result from one zygote (fertilized egg) dividing in two (**Figure 2.26a**). Because they come from the same fertilized egg, both twins have the same genetic makeup. **Dizygotic twins** are sometimes called fraternal twins. They result when two separately fertilized eggs develop in the mother's womb

monozygotic twins
Identical twins; these siblings result from one zygote splitting in two, so they share the same genes.

dizygotic twins
Fraternal twins; these siblings result from two separately fertilized eggs, so they are no more similar genetically than nontwin siblings are.

FIGURE 2.26

Genes Produce Two Types of Twins

(a) Monozygotic, or identical, twins result when one fertilized egg splits in two. Because of this, the twins are always the same biological sex. **(b)** Dizygotic, or fraternal, twins result when two separate eggs are fertilized at the same time. Thus, the twins may be the same biological sex or different sexes.

(a) Monozygotic (identical) twins

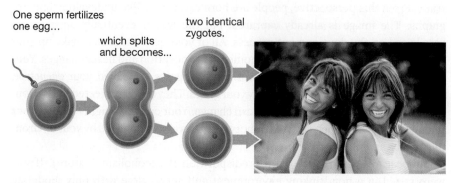

One sperm fertilizes one egg...

which splits and becomes...

two identical zygotes.

(b) Dizygotic (fraternal) twins

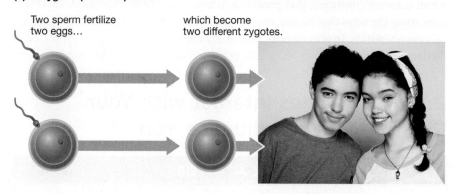

Two sperm fertilize two eggs...

which become two different zygotes.

simultaneously (**Figure 2.26b**). Because they come from two separately fertilized eggs, these twins are no more similar genetically than any other pair of siblings.

How do researchers use this information to judge genetic influence? They focus on a specific trait. They compare how similar monozygotic twins are in phenotypes (observable traits and characteristics) with how similar dizygotic twins are. The increased similarity in that trait for monozygotic twins is considered most likely due to genotypes (genetic influences).

By contrast, adoption studies compare the similarities between biological relatives and adoptive relatives. Adopted nonbiological siblings may share similar home environments, but they will have different genes. Therefore, researchers assume that similarities among adopted siblings who are not biologically related have more to do with environment than with genes. However, growing up in the same home turns out to have relatively little influence on many traits, such as personality.

One way to understand the importance of environment is to compare twins who have been raised together with twins who were raised apart in adoptive families. In a classic study, Thomas Bouchard and his colleagues at the University of Minnesota identified more than 100 pairs of identical and fraternal twins, some raised together and some raised apart (Bouchard, Lykken, McGue, Segal, & Tellegen, 1990). The researchers examined a variety of these twins' characteristics, including intelligence, personality, well-being, achievement, alienation, and aggression. The general finding from the Minnesota Twin Project was that identical twins, whether raised together or not, were likely to be similar (**Figure 2.27**).

The "Jim twins" were among the most famous case studies to emerge from this project. These twin brothers were separated at birth and raised by different

FIGURE 2.27

Identical Twins Raised Apart Are Also Similar

Identical twins Gerald Levey and Mark Newman, participants in Dr. Bouchard's study, were separated at birth. Reunited at age 31, they discovered they were both firefighters and had similar personality traits.

families. But in adulthood, they were strikingly similar. They were the same height and weight, chain-smoked the same brand of cigarettes, drank the same brand of beer, and were part-time law enforcement officers. The many similarities in the Jim twins' lives point to the possibility that strong genetic influences could have shaped their personalities and behavior.

Some critics have argued that most of the adopted twins in the Minnesota study were raised in relatively similar environments. Other critics feel that nothing more than coincidence is at work in these case studies. They argue that any two people of the same age would exhibit many surprising similarities just by coincidence, even though their lives differed in most other ways. Studies also fail to examine the many ways these twins differ on key traits. But twins and other relatives share similarities beyond coincidental attributes and behavior quirks. For instance, intelligence and personality traits such as shyness tend to run in families, indicating a strong genetic component.

EPIGENETICS An exciting new field of genetic study is *epigenetics* (Berger, Kouzarides, Shiekhattar, & Shilatifard, 2009; Holliday, 1987). This term literally means "on top of genetics." Here, environment is seen as layered over genes. Epigenetics researchers are looking closely at how environment affects gene expression. They have found that various environmental exposures do not alter the genes themselves but do alter how or when those genes are expressed. For example, living under stress or consuming a poor diet makes some genes more active and some less active.

According to recent research, these changes in how genes are expressed can be passed along to future generations (Daxinger & Whitelaw, 2012). For example, rats raised by stressed mothers are more likely to be stressed themselves (Zucchi et al., 2013). A simple way to think about epigenetic processes is that a parent's experiences create tags on genes that tell them when to express, and these tags are passed along with the genes. They may then be passed along to future generations.

2.13 Your Environment Changes Your Brain

2.13 LEARNING GOAL ACTIVITIES

To maximize your learning, complete the following learning goal activities:

a. Understand all bold and italic terms by writing explanations of them in your own words.

b. Apply the effects of environment to your life by describing one of the three ways in which your brain has been influenced by plasticity due to environment.

When Michelle Mack was a youngster, her parents realized that she was different from other children. They couldn't explain these differences. When Michelle was 27 years old, they learned that she was missing the left hemisphere of her brain (**Figure 2.28a**). Doctors suspected that Michelle's condition was the result of a stroke she experienced in the womb.

Without a left hemisphere, Michelle should have shown severe deficits in skills processed in that half of the brain. For example, the left hemisphere controls language, and it controls motor actions for the right side of the body. Losing a hemisphere as an adult would result in devastating loss of function. But Michelle's speech is only minimally affected. And she can move the right side of her body, although

(a)

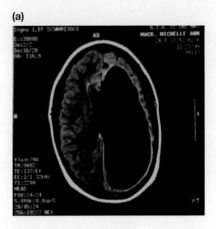

(b)

FIGURE 2.28

Michelle Mack and a Case of Extreme Plasticity

(a) While in her mother's womb, Michelle suffered a stroke that destroyed her left hemisphere (shown here as the black area on the right). **(b)** Over time, Michelle's right hemisphere took over the duties of the left hemisphere—language production and moving the right side of the body—to a surprising extent. Michelle's case shows the plasticity of the brain.

plasticity
A property of the brain that causes it to change through experience, drugs, or injury.

with some difficulty (**Figure 2.28b**). Michelle is able to lead a surprisingly independent life. She graduated from high school, has a job, pays her bills, and does chores. Where did her abilities come from? Her right hemisphere developed language and the ability to move the right side of her body, as well as functions that ordinarily occur across both hemispheres.

Michelle Mack's case shows that nurture can influence nature. Over time, Michelle interacted with the world. Her experiences let her brain reorganize itself. Her right hemisphere took over processing for the missing left hemisphere. In fact, despite the great precision and the specificity of its connections, the brain is extremely adaptable. Over the course of development, throughout our constant stream of experience, and after injury, the brain continually changes. This property is known as **plasticity**. It reflects the interactive nature of biological and environmental influences. Because of exposure to certain environments and experiences, the brain can change in three ways: growing new neurons, changing existing neural connections, and reorganizing.

GROWING NEW NEURONS   Brain plasticity decreases with age. Even into very old age, however, the brain can grow new connections among neurons and even grow new neurons. This rewiring and growth within the brain represents the biological basis of learning. That is, as you learn, your brain changes. Until about 30 years ago, scientists believed that adult brains produced no new brain cells. There is now evidence that new neurons are produced in some brain regions (Eriksson et al., 1998; Frisén, 2016). The production of new neurons is called *neurogenesis*. A fair amount of neurogenesis may occur in the hippocampus (Christian, Song, & Ming, 2014). As you learned in study unit 2.6, the hippocampus is involved in the storage of new memories. These memories are eventually transferred to the cortex as the hippocampus is continuously overwritten. Perhaps, without disrupting memory, neurons in the hippocampus can be lost and replaced. Further research might let us use neurogenesis to reverse the brain's natural loss of neurons. Curbing neuron loss could slow the mental decline that comes with aging. There is some controversy, however, as to whether neurogenesis occurs in adults (Sorrells, 2018; Boldrini et al., 2018).

CHANGING EXISTING NEURAL CONNECTIONS   Throughout life, you learn new things that you remember. Thanks to brain plasticity, all your memories are reflected in your brain's physical changes. Psychologists now believe that the changes are mainly in the strength of existing connections. One possibility is that when one neuron activates another, the connection between them strengthens. The strengthened connection then makes these neurons more likely to fire together in the future. This theory can be summarized by the psychologist Donald Hebb's catchphrase "neurons that fire together, wire together." By contrast, the connection between two neurons tends to get weaker if the neurons do not continue to communicate regularly. Early in life, overabundant connections form among the brain's neurons. Subsequently, life experiences help "prune" some of these connections to strengthen the rest, much as pruning weak or nonproductive branches will strengthen a fruit tree. Much of this *neural pruning* happens by the time you reach adolescence, and it results in a more efficient brain. You will learn more about this process in Chapter 4.

BRAIN REORGANIZATION   Sometimes the brain undergoes some reorganization, which is another example of brain plasticity. That is, entirely new connections develop between nearby brain regions. This new growth is a major factor in recovery from brain injury. Following an injury in the cortex, the surrounding gray matter assumes the function of the damaged area. Think of the healthy gray matter as a local business scrambling to pick up the customers of a newly closed competitor. The remapping seems to begin immediately, and it continues for years. Such plasticity involves all levels of the CNS, from the cortex down to the spinal cord.

Brain reorganization is much more common in children than in adults. As an extreme example, consider young children who have epilepsy so severe that it paralyzes one or more of their limbs. To control the epilepsy, surgeons may remove an entire cerebral hemisphere. Just as in the case of Michelle Mack, the remaining hemisphere eventually takes on many of the lost hemisphere's functions. The children regain almost complete use of their limbs. If this procedure were performed on adults, however, the lack of a cerebral hemisphere would result in severe deficits. With less chance of brain reorganization, the adults would lose all the functions of the missing hemisphere.

As you have seen in this chapter, this is an exciting time in psychology. Researchers are greatly increasing our understanding of how the brain works with the rest of the body to produce behavior and mental activity. The knowledge you have gained about biology's role in psychology will serve as a foundation for your learning in later chapters.

 How Do Nature and Nurture Affect Your Brain?

To make sure you learned what you just read, write answers to the following questions and check your answers.

2.11 What is the difference between genotype and phenotype?

2.12 What is behavioral genetics?

2.13 What are three ways that brain plasticity changes your brain?

See Appendix B for answers to the red Q questions.

BIG PICTURE

Want to earn a better grade on your test? Go to INQUIZITIVE to practice actively with this chapter's content and get personalized feedback along the way.

How Does Your Nervous System Affect You?

2.1 Your Nervous System Is the Basis of Your Mental Activity and Behavior

Review the learning goal activities on p. 47. The nervous system has three basic functions: (1) It receives sensory input, (2) it processes that information, and (3) it responds to that information by acting on it. There are two parts to the nervous system. The central nervous system (CNS) processes information in the brain and the spinal cord and sends signals to the peripheral nervous system (PNS) for action. The PNS processes information in the rest of the body and transmits information to the CNS. Neurons are the basic units of the nervous system. The four main parts of neurons are (1) dendrites, (2) cell body, (3) axons, and (4) terminal buttons.

2.2 Neurons Communicate with Each Other in Your Nervous System

Review the learning goal activities on p. 50. Neural communication is the basis of all mental activity and behavior. Neural communication occurs in three phases: (1) transmission, (2) reception, and (3) integration. In Phase 1, transmission, when the sending neuron is given sufficient stimulation, an action potential occurs. The action potential moves down the axon toward the terminal buttons, which causes the release of neurotransmitters across the synapse. Phase 2, reception, occurs when released neurotransmitters from the sending neuron bind with the receptors on the dendrites of receiving neurons. In Phase

3, integration, the neurotransmitters that bind with receptors produce signals that affect how that neuron will respond. Excitatory signals increase the likelihood that the new neuron will fire an action potential. Inhibitory signals decrease the likelihood that it will fire an action potential.

2.3 Neurotransmitters Influence Your Mental Activity and Behavior

Review the learning goal activities on p. 54. Neurons communicate through neurotransmitters, and this neural activity is the basis of all feelings, thoughts, and actions. Some drugs act as agonists, enhancing the actions of neurotransmitters. Other drugs act as antagonists, inhibiting the actions of neurotransmitters. Each neurotransmitter plays a different role in mental activity and behavior. Common neurotransmitters include acetylcholine, norepinephrine, serotonin, dopamine, GABA, glutamate, and endorphins.

KEY TERMS

nervous system (p. 47)	cell body (p. 49)
central nervous system (CNS) (p. 47)	axon (p. 49)
	terminal buttons (p. 49)
peripheral nervous system (PNS) (p. 47)	synapse (p. 49)
	neurotransmitters (p. 49)
neurons (p. 48)	action potential (p. 52)
dendrites (p. 49)	myelin sheath (p. 52)

How Do the Parts of Your Brain Function?

2.4 Understanding of the Brain Has Developed over Time

Review the learning goal activities on p. 58. The central nervous system (CNS) includes the brain and the spinal cord. Together, these structures make possible the complex processing that humans can do. The first case showing that a specific brain region processed certain information revealed that Broca's area produces normal speech. Modern methods let us study the brain in action. An electroencephalograph, or EEG, measures the brain's electrical activity. Functional magnetic resonance imaging (fMRI) maps brain activity during a mental task based indirectly on blood flow to different brain areas. Transcranial magnetic stimulation (TMS) disrupts brain activity in a specific brain region, letting researchers explore the brain processes involved in particular mental activity and behaviors.

2.5 The Hindbrain and Midbrain House Basic Programs for Your Survival

Review the learning goal activities on p. 62. The spinal cord carries sensory signals from the body to the brain and motor signals from the brain to the body. The spinal cord is also responsible for basic reflexes. The hindbrain is located at the top of the spinal cord. The hindbrain includes three main structures: (1) the medulla, which regulates basic survival functions; (2) the pons, which regulates sleep and arousal and coordinates body movements; and (3) the cerebellum, which is essential for movement and control of balance. The midbrain is located in the middle of the brain above the pons and includes the substantia nigra, which is responsible for initiating voluntary movements.

2.6 Forebrain Subcortical Structures Control Your Motivations and Emotions

Review the learning goal activities on p. 63. Beneath the cerebral cortex of the forebrain there are four subcortical forebrain structures that are part of the limbic system: the (1) thalamus, (2) hypothalamus, (3) hippocampus, and (4) amygdala. Together, these structures (1) process most sensory input, (2) regulate the basic functions of the body and control motivated behaviors, (3) form memories, and (4) control emotions.

2.7 The Cerebral Cortex of the Forebrain Processes Your Complex Mental Activity

Review the learning goal activities on p. 65. The wrinkly cerebral cortex processes the most complex information in the brain.

The two halves of the brain—the left and right hemispheres—are connected by a large band of fibers called the corpus callosum, which lets information flow between the sides of the brain. The cerebral cortex also has four structural areas: (1) occipital lobes, (2) parietal lobes, (3) temporal lobes, and (4) frontal lobes. Across the four lobes there are six regions that are specialized for processing certain information.

KEY TERMS

Broca's area (p. 59)	hippocampus (p. 64)
medulla (p. 62)	amygdala (p. 65)
pons (p. 62)	occipital lobes (p. 67)
cerebellum (p. 62)	parietal lobes (p. 67)
thalamus (p. 64)	temporal lobes (p. 68)
hypothalamus (p. 64)	frontal lobes (p. 69)

How Does Your Brain Communicate with Your Body?

2.8 Your Somatic Nervous System Detects Sensory Input and Responds

Review the learning goal activities on p. 71. The peripheral nervous system (PNS) includes the somatic nervous system and the autonomic nervous system. The first major subdivision of the PNS, the somatic nervous system, carries sensory information from the body to the CNS and carries signals from the CNS to the body to start or stop voluntary movement.

2.9 Your Autonomic Nervous System Regulates the Body Automatically

Review the learning goal activities on p. 72. The second major subdivision of the PNS, the autonomic nervous system, automatically regulates the body's internal environment by sending signals back and forth between the glands and internal organs and the brain. One division of the autonomic nervous system, the sympathetic nervous system, arouses the body and prepares it for action. The other division of the autonomic nervous system, the parasympathetic nervous system, calms the body and lets it relax.

2.10 The Endocrine System Affects Your Behavior Through Hormones

Review the learning goal activities on p. 74. The endocrine system works with the nervous system. The endocrine system includes glands that produce and release hormones, whose effects last from seconds to hours. The endocrine glands include the pineal gland, the adrenal glands, the pituitary gland, the thyroid, and the testes or ovaries. The hormones released from these glands travel through the bloodstream to organs and tissues to influence a variety of processes, including sexual development and human growth.

KEY TERMS

somatic nervous system (p. 71)
autonomic nervous system (p. 72)
endocrine system (p. 74)
hormones (p. 74)

How Do Nature and Nurture Affect Your Brain?

2.11 Your Genes Affect Your Mental Activity and Behavior

Review the learning goal activities on p. 76. The genes you inherit from your parents affect your physical characteristics and the ways you think, feel, and behave. Your genotype is your genes. It is determined at the moment of conception and never changes. Your phenotype is your observable physical characteristics and psychological characteristics. It is determined by your genes and then altered by the environment.

2.12 Your Genes Interact with Your Environment to Influence You

Review the learning goal activities on p. 77. Behavioral genetics explores how genes and environment interact to influence mental activity and behavior. Twin studies and adoption studies provide insight into how genes have important effects on

your mental activity and behavior. Research on epigenetics shows that the environment changes how certain genes are expressed.

2.13 Your Environment Changes Your Brain

Review the learning goal activities on p. 79. Your brain changes with experiences in different environments due to plasticity. Although brain plasticity decreases with age, your brain can rewire itself throughout life, affecting brain function and psychological characteristics. The three ways that plasticity occurs is through (1) growing new neurons, (2) strengthening or weakening neural connections, and (3) brain reorganization.

KEY TERMS

genes (p. 76)	dizygotic twins (p. 77)
monozygotic twins (p. 77)	plasticity (p. 80)

CHAPTER 2 SELF-QUIZ

To make sure you learned the information in this chapter, write answers to the following questions and check your answers. **See Appendix B for answers to the self-quiz.**

1. Marisol enjoys her first cup of coffee in the morning. Which of the following statements correctly describes the communication of Marisol's neurons in this situation?
   a. The axons of neurons receive neurotransmitters.
   b. The neurons fire stronger action potentials.
   c. The dendrites of neurons receive neurotransmitters.
   d. The neurons are in a resting state.

2. You participate in a medical study testing a drug that temporarily increases the function of the neurotransmitter glutamate. You correctly believe that the increased glutamate will _____.
   a. improve your ability to remember
   b. increase the number of hours you sleep
   c. make you feel more depressed
   d. make you feel less pain from a pin prick

3. Alyssa's grandmother had a stroke. Afterward, she experienced trouble keeping her balance and stumbled when she walked. Alyssa correctly believes that her grandmother's stroke affected a structure in her _____ called the _____.
   a. hindbrain; cerebellum
   b. forebrain; cerebellum
   c. hindbrain; substantia nigra
   d. forebrain; substantia nigra

4. Ever since he had a motorcycle accident, Cornelius has been unable to form new memories. Cornelius has most likely damaged his _____.
   a. hypothalamus
   b. amygdala
   c. hippocampus
   d. thalamus

5. Dane is looking at a photo that his friend emailed him. During this task, the part of Dane's brain that processes his ability to see the information in the photo is most active. This part of his brain is in the _____ lobes.
   a. frontal
   b. temporal
   c. parietal
   d. occipital

6. George touches a baby lamb at the local petting zoo. George says the lamb feels "soft." The softness of the fur is a result of how the feel of the lamb was processed in George's _____ system.
   a. autonomic nervous
   b. endocrine
   c. parasympathetic nervous
   d. somatic nervous

7. While walking through the woods one day, Ricardo sees a large bear. His sympathetic nervous system will most likely _____.
   a. cause his heart to beat faster as he prepares to run away
   b. allow him to notice how smooth his can of bear spray feels against his hand
   c. cause a reflexive reaction in his spinal cord that lets him run away
   d. allow his breathing to slow as he relaxes and thinks about what to do next

8. Corbin, a 13-year-old, asks his brother if hormones are responsible for Corbin's sudden growth of facial hair. His brother responds, "Yes, it's because hormones called _____ are being released into your bloodstream, where they affect the organs in your body through the _____ system."
   a. androgens; endocrine
   b. estrogens; central nervous
   c. estrogens; endocrine
   d. androgens; central nervous

9. Dr. Rieker does research in the field of behavioral genetics. He wants to investigate associations between different siblings' grades in school. To study the role of "nature" in siblings' grades, he should conduct _____. By contrast, to study the role of "nurture" in siblings' grades, he should conduct _____.
   a. an experiment on genotypes; an experiment on phenotypes
   b. a twin study; an adoption study
   c. an experiment on phenotypes; an experiment on genotypes
   d. an adoption study; a twin study

10. Louisa had a stroke that damaged the motor cortex in her right hemisphere, making it impossible for her to walk. However, over time and with practice, Louisa started walking again because different, undamaged parts of her brain took over control of this ability. Louisa was able to walk again most likely because of the influence of _____ on her brain.
    a. genotypes
    b. plasticity
    c. the sympathetic nervous system
    d. the parasympathetic nervous system

How Can Understanding Biological Psychology Help You in Your Job?

For many occupations, having a strong understanding of the body and brain is vital. One of the largest and fastest-growing areas of employment is health care. As life spans increase and populations age, more and more people need medical assessments and treatments. As people get older, they often have to take many medications. If you work in a pharmacy, you need to understand how neurotransmitters work. Knowing that different drugs might have their effects through the same neurotransmitters will help you explain to patients why they need to be careful if they are taking multiple medications. For example, you can say why they should avoid mixing alcohol with other drugs that have their effects through activation of GABA receptors. In pharmaceutical sales, knowledge from this chapter can help you explain why a particular drug is a better choice for your clients. Consider, too, other people who work in health-related areas.

For example, specialists in the new field of neuroprosthetics collaborate with medical professionals to develop technologies that help people with neurological disorders and limb differences regain function (Leuthardt, Roland, & Ray, 2014; see also www.lukehand.org). If you are an occupational therapist, knowing about the functions of different brain regions will help you understand the problems that a client with damage to a specific brain area is likely to experience. Neuromarketers use EEG and fMRI recordings to predict consumer behavior in response to particular advertisements and products. This neuroscientific approach has been somewhat successful, with fMRI activity of brain reward regions predicting actual consumer behavior (Venkatraman et al., 2015).

Even if you are not drawing directly on biology in the workplace, knowledge about the body and brain can help you deal with job stress. Since you now understand the effects of hormones and stress on behaviors, you can learn relaxation techniques and seek to maintain balance in yourself.

TAKEAWAY POINT: Health care, business, and occupational therapy are some of the fields in which a knowledge of biological psychology is vital or important. Whatever job you have, a knowledge of mind and body can help you maintain your mental activity and behavior on the job.

 You can look up job descriptions, education requirements, salaries, and more at the Bureau of Labor Statistics: www.bls.gov. Visit the site and start putting psychology to work!

3 Consciousness

"IRON MIKE" WEBSTER WAS A WORKHORSE. As the center for the Pittsburgh Steelers football team from 1974 to 1988, he anchored the offensive line (**Figure 3.1a**). Webster played in 150 consecutive games during a career that spanned more than 200 games (Varley, 2016). Webster played through pain and injuries, including multiple concussions where blows to his head caused his brain to bounce inside his skull. The former Steelers quarterback Terry Bradshaw called Webster "the best [center] to ever play the game." Webster was inducted into the Professional Football Hall

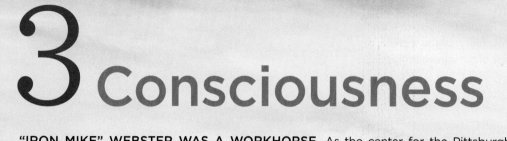

BIG QUESTIONS

What Does It Mean to Be Conscious?

How Does Sleep Affect Consciousness?

How Do Hypnosis, Meditation, and Flow Alter Consciousness?

How Do Drugs Alter Consciousness?

(a)

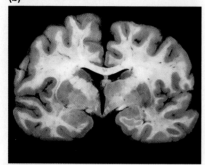

(b)

FIGURE 3.1

"Iron Mike" Webster and Chronic Traumatic Encephalopathy

Football player Mike Webster's tragic story illustrates how repeated concussions affect consciousness and cause brain injury. **(a)** This is Mike Webster, number 52, at the peak of his career with the Pittsburgh Steelers. **(b)** After Webster's death, an examination of his brain revealed chronic traumatic encephalopathy (CTE) from repeated concussions, which caused extreme long-term changes in consciousness. Here, a typical brain **(left)** is contrasted with a brain that shows the devastating structural changes associated with CTE **(right)**.

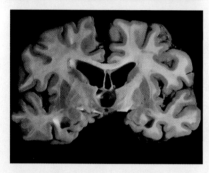

of Fame in 1997. Then, five years later, he was dead. What happened to this extraordinary athlete?

Long before his death, Webster showed a steep decline in family relations and finances. Webster's mental state also deteriorated. He was quick to anger, abused substances, engaged in self-harm, experienced depression, and had trouble concentrating and thinking. According to Webster's wife, Pam, "He couldn't hold a sentence. . . . He compared [communicating] to tangled fishing wire. When fishing wire gets tangled you can't untangle it. . . . And that's how his thought process was" (Kirk, Wiser, Fainaru, & Fainaru-Wada, 2013). After Webster's death in 2002, the cause of his decline was revealed. In the movie *Concussion* (2015), Will Smith plays the pathologist Bennet Omalu, who conducted an autopsy on Webster and discovered massive brain damage.

Up to that point, people knew that a concussion had a negative effect, but they did not know the severity of that effect. Dr. Omalu's research changed this. We now know that concussions and their associated brain damage can create short-term changes in consciousness, including headaches, dizziness, mental confusion, an inability to focus, difficulty reading, memory problems, extreme mood swings, and even anxiety and depression. The most serious concussions lead to unconsciousness.

Dr. Omalu's research showed that repeated concussions caused massive brain damage, leading to chronic traumatic encephalopathy (CTE; **Figure 3.1b**). This degenerative disease had tragic effects on Webster's consciousness by impairing his awareness of both his inner mental activity and the outer world. Clearly, concussions can have large long-term consequences. One study that investigated the brains of 202 deceased football players, some of whom had played only in high school, found that 87 percent of the brains showed evidence of concussion-related CTE (Mez et al., 2017).

The question of consciousness is clearly not just theoretical: Consciousness reflects health—in the brain, in mental activity, and in behavior. Changes in consciousness can reflect severe trauma that can ultimately be life-threatening. Trying to answer the question "What is consciousness?" is one of the most fundamental issues in psychology. This chapter explores what it means to be conscious, what happens when consciousness changes, and how consciousness results from brain activity.

What Does It Mean to Be Conscious?

Consciousness can change in an instant. One moment a football player is being tackled. Seconds later, that player is on the ground, out cold. Within a minute, the player might be up and walking but feeling dazed. A change in consciousness can also last longer—in a positive way, such as when a person meditates, or in a negative way, such as when a person is in a coma. To begin understanding the relationship between consciousness and brain activity, you need to consider different experiences of consciousness.

3.1 Consciousness Is Your Subjective Experience

3.1 LEARNING GOAL ACTIVITIES

To maximize your learning, complete the following learning goal activities.

a. Understand all bold and italic terms by writing explanations of them in your own words.

b. Apply consciousness to your life by naming one level of consciousness and one state of consciousness and giving an example of how you have experienced each of these.

consciousness
The combination of a person's subjective experience of the external world and the person's internal mental activity; this combination results from brain activity.

conscious
A level of consciousness that reflects awareness of the external world and inner mental activity.

unconscious
A level of consciousness that reflects a lack of awareness of the external world and inner mental activity.

Consciousness is your moment-by-moment awareness of your experiences, both of the world around you and of your thoughts, feelings, and actions. Because your experiences are subjective, your awareness of them is also personal and unique. The Learning Tip below explains how the word "subjective" differs from the word "objective." Listening to music is an example of a conscious experience that is subjective. A volume that seems low to you might seem loud to other people. Thinking about the songs you hear and what they mean to you is another conscious experience that is subjective. You know you are conscious because you are experiencing the outside world through your senses. You also know that you are conscious because you are aware of your mental activity.

YOUR EXPERIENCE OF CONSCIOUSNESS VARIES As you are reading these words, are you hearing any noises around you? For example, are people talking, or are the lights humming? Before you were asked the question, were you aware of this background noise? Now take a minute, and try to remember what you ate for lunch yesterday. If you were able to do this, you went from being unaware of this information to recalling details of the experience, including your subjective experience of whether the lunch was delicious (**Figure 3.2**).

Both of these examples show that one way to understand consciousness is based on the *level* of your awareness. At any particular moment, you might be **conscious**—that is, aware of stimuli around you and aware of your thoughts. At any other moment, you might be less aware, or **unconscious**, of this same information. In fact, within any particular moment you might be conscious of some things

FIGURE 3.2

Experiencing the Levels of Consciousness

Experiencing a shift in consciousness can be as simple as recalling what you ate for lunch yesterday. At first you are unconscious of the information. But as you think about lunch and become aware of what you ate, you become conscious of that information.

LEARNING TIP: Understanding Objectivity and Subjectivity

The words "objective" and "subjective" are important in psychology. The information in this chart will help you remember the difference between them.

WHEN YOU SEE	PLEASE THINK	MEANING
Objective	This is when you consider information as an <u>object</u> that exists apart from your opinion of it.	You can experience information for itself, by being unbiased and free of thoughts or feelings about the information. Others experience this information the same way.
Subjective	This is when you consider information as <u>subject</u> to your opinion of it.	You can experience information from an individual perspective, which may be biased by thoughts and feelings about the information. Each person has a unique experience of the information.

TABLE 3.1
Altered States of Consciousness

Created by disease or brain injury	Occurring normally	Self-induced
Concussion (study unit 3.2) Traumatic brain injury (study unit 3.2) Coma (minimally conscious state and unresponsive wakefulness syndrome; study unit 3.2)	Daydreaming (study unit 3.3) Falling asleep (study unit 3.5) Dreaming (study unit 3.6) Watching television (study unit 3.11)	Hypnosis (study unit 3.9) Meditation (study unit 3.10) Flow (study unit 3.11) Use of drugs and alcohol (study units 3.12–3.13)

normal waking state of consciousness
A state of consciousness that reflects a clear awareness of the external world and inner mental activity.

altered state of consciousness
A state that deviates from a normal waking state of consciousness. It may reflect either a more vivid awareness of the external world and inner mental activity or a less clear awareness of them.

(a)

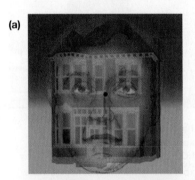

(b)

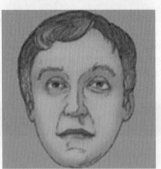

(c)

and unconscious of others. Your experience of consciousness varies because your awareness changes.

Another way to understand consciousness is in terms of the *state* of your awareness. Let's say you are wide awake, reading this chapter easily and thinking about it clearly. If so, then you are likely in a state of awareness called **normal waking state of consciousness,** where the external world and your inner thoughts and feelings are clear to you, which is how people feel most of the time. By contrast, if you have a cold and have taken some medicine for it, then you might be struggling to read and think. In this case, you might be in an **altered state of consciousness.** Any deviation from a normal waking state of consciousness can be considered an altered state. In one altered state, the outer world and your internal mental activity may be fuzzy, indistinct, or less clear to you. But in another type of altered state, external stimuli may be more vivid and your thoughts more organized. Throughout our lives, we experience many altered states of consciousness. Some of these altered states result from physical problems. Other altered states occur on a nearly daily basis (**Table 3.1**).

3.2 Consciousness Results from Brain Activity

 3.2 LEARNING GOAL ACTIVITIES

To maximize your learning, complete the following learning goal activities.

a. Understand all bold and italic terms by writing explanations of them in your own words.

b. Apply the global workspace model by providing examples from your life of how each of the five mentioned regions of your brain process your awareness of specific information.

Philosophers have long debated the nature of consciousness. One aspect of this debate is the mind/body problem, which you learned about in study unit 1.4. In the 1600s, the philosopher René Descartes stated one view on this question. He said that the mind is separate from the brain and the rest of the body. This view is called *dualism.* Most psychologists reject dualism for another view on the mind/body problem. This second view is called *materialism.* Materialism is the modern idea

FIGURE 3.3

The Relationship Between Consciousness and Brain Activity

(a) In a 1998 study by Tong and colleagues, participants were shown images with houses superimposed on faces. Participants were asked to report whether they saw **(b)** a face or **(c)** a house. Researchers used fMRI to measure neural responses in participants' brains when the participants reported seeing a house or a face.

that the brain and the mind are inseparable. In other words, the processing of information in the brain creates the experiences of the mind. According to materialism, the activity of neurons in the brain produces consciousness. Neurons produce, for example, consciousness of the sight of a familiar face or consciousness of the sweet smell of a rose. More specifically, for each experience—each sight, each smell, each memory—there is an associated pattern of brain activity. The activation of particular groups of neurons in certain parts of the brain gives rise to particular conscious experiences. The following subsections in this study unit discuss important parts of the brain that contribute to the experience of consciousness. Then they explore how brain damage can affect consciousness.

global workspace model
Consciousness is a product of activity in specific brain regions.

THE GLOBAL WORKSPACE MODEL   Despite what you might see in some movies, scientists cannot—yet—read your intimate thoughts by looking at your brain activity. However, psychologists now examine, even measure, consciousness and other mental states that once were considered too subjective to be studied. For example, Frank Tong and colleagues (Tong, Nakayama, Vaughan, & Kanwisher, 1998) studied the relationship between consciousness and neural responses in the brain. Participants were shown images of houses that were superimposed on faces (**Figure 3.3a**). Participants were then asked if they saw a face (**Figure 3.3b**) or a house (**Figure 3.3c**). When participants reported seeing a face, neural activity increased within the brain regions associated with face recognition—the fusiform face area. When participants reported seeing a house, neural activity increased within brain regions associated with object recognition. This finding suggests that different types of sensory information are processed by different areas in the brain. Importantly, these specific neural processes are associated with awareness of particular information. Additional research in this area has revealed brain activity patterns that show whether you are looking at faces or bodies (Norman, Polyn, Detre, & Haxby, 2006; O'Toole et al., 2014), which emotions you are experiencing (Kragel & LeBar, 2016), or whether you are thinking of yourself or a close friend (Chavez, Heatherton, & Wagner, 2017).

The **global workspace model** is a psychological theory that is based on this brain activity research. According to the global workspace model, consciousness depends on which brain circuits are active (Baars, 1988; Dehaene, Changeux, Naccache, Sackur, & Sergent, 2006). To put it another way: You experience your brain regions' activity as conscious awareness of specific information. For instance, when you listen to music, your conscious experience results from activation in particular brain regions. Those regions are processing the sound of the music, the meaning of the lyrics, perhaps your memories of hearing the song in the past, and the emotional states those memories produce. Your total experience results from the simultaneous activity of all the different brain regions supporting these psychological processes.

The key idea of the global workspace model is that no one area of the brain is responsible for general "awareness." Instead, specific areas of the brain process certain types of information. The processing in these brain areas produces conscious experience of the information (**Figure 3.4**). Unfortunately, the flip side of this perspective is that damage to specific brain regions negatively affects consciousness.

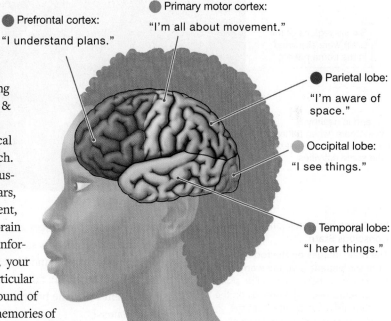

Prefrontal cortex:
"I understand plans."

Primary motor cortex:
"I'm all about movement."

Parietal lobe:
"I'm aware of space."

Occipital lobe:
"I see things."

Temporal lobe:
"I hear things."

FIGURE 3.4
Global Workspace Model
The global workspace model states that conscious awareness of different aspects of the world is associated with processing in different parts of the brain. This simplified diagram indicates major cortical regions where processing leads to awareness.

TRAUMATIC BRAIN INJURY Football players who experience extreme hits are sometimes described as having their "bell rung." In fact, a hard hit to the head can produce the sensation of a ringing sound. However, as discussed in the chapter opener, concussions affect consciousness in part because they cause brain damage. In other words, severe concussions cause *traumatic brain injury (TBI)*.

TBIs occur when an external trauma causes changes in consciousness as well as physical damage to the brain. TBIs range from mild to severe, and severe TBIs are responsible for about 30 percent of all injury deaths (Faul, Xu, Wald, & Coronado, 2010). The greater the severity of the injury, the more likely a TBI is to cause negative effects on consciousness with respect to thinking, memory, emotions, and even personality that can last for many years or be permanent. In study unit 2.7, you learned about the TBI experienced by Phineas Gage, when a rod blew through his frontal lobe and changed his personality from that point on.

As noted in the chapter opener, a concussion used to be thought of as a mild TBI. After all, most people recover from a concussion within one to two weeks (Baldwin, Breiding, & Sleet, 2016). However, numerous studies have documented the long-term effects of concussions (Bailes et al., 2013), including an increased risk of multiple sclerosis later in life for adolescents who suffer concussions (Montgomery et al., 2017; multiple sclerosis is discussed in study units 2.2 and 2.11). Each concussion a person experiences can lead to more-serious symptoms that are longer lasting (Baugh et al., 2012; Zetterberg, Smith, & Blennow, 2013). And the repeated effects of TBIs from severe concussions are associated with the deaths of many athletes, including Mike Webster, the Canadian wrestler Chris Benoit, the BMX racer Dave Mirra, and many others. Females may be even more prone to getting concussions (Comstock, Currie, Pierpoint, Grubenhoff, & Fields, 2015), but the long-term effects of repeated concussions in females are less well documented. For this reason, professional soccer player Brandi Chastain has donated her brain to science so that it can be studied after her death for evidence of concussion-related CTE. Taken together, these findings have led to guidelines for reducing the occurrence of such injuries (Harmon et al., 2013).

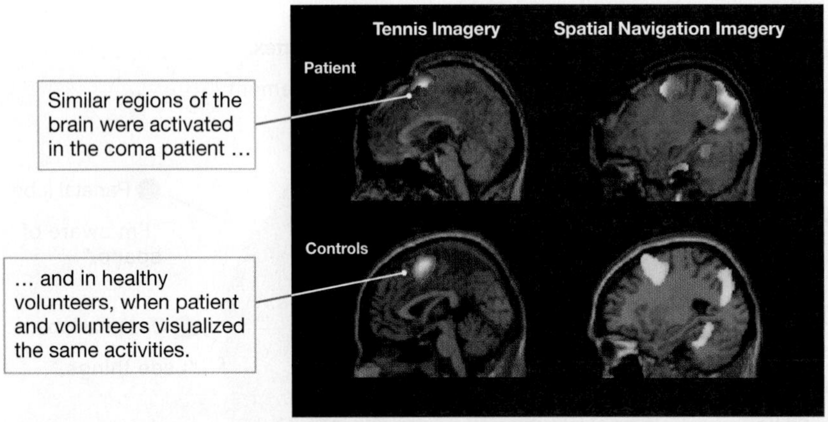

Similar regions of the brain were activated in the coma patient …

… and in healthy volunteers, when patient and volunteers visualized the same activities.

FIGURE 3.5

In a Coma but Conscious: Minimally Conscious State

The brain images on the top are from the patient, a young woman in a coma who showed no visible signs of consciousness. The images on the bottom are a composite from the control group, which consisted of healthy volunteers. Both the patient and the control group were told to visualize playing tennis **(left)** and walking around **(right)**. Right after the directions were given, the patient's neural activity appeared similar to the control group's neural activity. This similarity suggests that the coma patient was in a minimally conscious state, where she actually was conscious.

COMA Medical advances are helping a greater number of people survive TBIs. For example, doctors now save the lives of many people who previously would have died from injuries sustained in car accidents or on battlefields. However, many of those who sustain TBIs fall into comas or are induced into coma as part of medical treatment to let the brain rest. What exactly is the relation between coma and consciousness?

People in comas have sleep/wake cycles—they open their eyes and appear to be awake, close their eyes and appear to be asleep—but they generally do not respond to their surroundings. Because of this activity and inactivity, it is hard to know what level of consciousness they have. However, brain imaging has shown that some people in comas are aware but unable to respond. A 23-year-old woman in a coma was asked to imagine playing tennis or walking through her house (Owen et al., 2006). This woman's pattern of brain activity became quite similar to the patterns of control subjects who also imagined playing tennis

(**Figure 3.5**, left) or walking through a house (Figure 3.5, right). The woman could not give outward signs of awareness, but researchers believe she was able to understand language and respond to the experimenters' requests. The implications of this finding are extraordinary. This research team has now evaluated 54 coma patients and found 5 who could willfully control brain activity to communicate (Monti et al., 2010). These advances add up to one astonishing fact: Some people in comas are conscious! But because these coma patients cannot make their bodies respond, observers think they are unconscious. This situation is referred to as a *minimally conscious state*.

Most people come out of a coma within a few days. For others, it may take weeks. Some people never emerge from the coma. When a coma lasts for more than a month, the person is said to have *unresponsive wakefulness syndrome* (Laureys et al., 2010). This unresponsive state is not associated with consciousness. Normal brain activity does not occur when a person is in this state, in part because much of the person's brain may be damaged beyond recovery. The longer the unresponsive wakefulness state lasts, the less likely it is that the person will ever recover consciousness or show normal brain activity. Terri Schiavo, a woman living in Florida, spent more than 15 years with unresponsive wakefulness syndrome. Eventually, her husband wanted to terminate her life support, but her parents wanted to continue it. Both sides waged a legal battle. A court ruled in the husband's favor, and life support was terminated. After Schiavo's death, an autopsy revealed substantial and irreversible damage throughout her brain (**Figure 3.6**, left). Schiavo had been unconscious because the cortical areas of her brain that create conscious awareness had been completely destroyed.

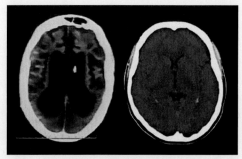

FIGURE 3.6

In a Coma and Unconscious: Unresponsive Wakefulness Syndrome

Before Terri Schiavo was taken off life support, her parents and their supporters believed she showed some awareness. But the dark areas of her brain scan **(left)** indicate that her cortex had deteriorated beyond recovery (an undamaged brain is shown on the **right**). There could not have been activity in these areas.

3.3 Consciousness Involves Attention

3.3 LEARNING GOAL ACTIVITIES

To maximize your learning, complete the following learning goal activities.

a. Understand all bold and italic terms by writing explanations of them in your own words.

b. Apply attention to your life by describing one type of information that you use automatic processing for (and have less awareness of) and one type of information that you use controlled processing for (and have more awareness of).

As you read this chapter, are you finding it easy to focus? Or are you getting distracted and daydreaming? If you realize you have no idea of what you just read, perhaps you should go back and reread the material but pay closer attention. What does it mean to pay attention to something? **Attention** is the focusing of mental resources on specific information to become consciously aware of it. For example, when you are reading, attention lets you be aware of what you read. In addition, you can choose where to direct attention, such as when you return to material you didn't understand when you first read it.

ATTENTION AND CONSCIOUSNESS IN THE TWO-TRACK MIND   In his book *Thinking, Fast and Slow* (2011), Daniel Kahneman discusses the relationship between attention and awareness. Kahneman explains that we have a "two-track mind." Each track involves a different level of attention to produce awareness of particular information. The low mental road uses *automatic processing*. The high

attention
The focusing of mental resources on specific information to become consciously aware of that information.

FIGURE 3.7

Attention and Consciousness During Automatic and Controlled Processing

(a) An experienced driver can rely on automatic processing while performing this task. Automatic processing requires less attention, but it is associated with less awareness of external stimuli and inner mental activity. **(b)** During bad driving conditions, an experienced driver must use controlled processing. This type of processing requires more attention, but it is associated with greater awareness of external stimuli and increased inner mental activity.

change blindness
A failure to be aware of visual information when one's attention is directed elsewhere.

mental road uses *controlled processing*. To understand how these two forms of processing work, think of them in terms of driving a car.

If you have known how to drive for many years, it may seem as if you can drive effortlessly. All of us can perform well-learned and easy tasks, such as driving or reading, by using automatic processing (**Figure 3.7a**). Automatic processing is fast and does not require a lot of mental resources. In other words, it doesn't require much attention. However, a side effect of paying less attention to the information is that we are not fully conscious of engaging in such tasks, so we won't be as aware of the details of the experiences. Suppose, for instance, you drive to a familiar place on autopilot. You probably won't be aware of what vehicles you pass, how many traffic lights you stop at, or your thoughts about driving.

However, some tasks require much greater effort. If you drive in difficult conditions, such as terrible rain or a snowstorm, you most likely have to use controlled processing to stay focused on hazards (**Figure 3.7b**). Controlled processing is slow and requires more mental resources in terms of attention given to the task. In turn, the additional attention makes you very aware of your experiences and mental activity. After driving in difficult conditions, you might remember, for example, passing certain cars that slid off the road or how you felt anxious about driving in bad conditions.

LIMITED ATTENTION AFFECTS CONSCIOUSNESS Having two mental tracks does not mean having unlimited mental resources. There is a limit to how many things the mind can be consciously aware of at the same time. Even though multitasking is now a way of life, we almost never successfully complete tasks that require even automatic processing, such as reading or driving, while doing other things. This is a simple psychological fact: We have only so much attention available to consciously experience and respond to information. This is why it is so dangerous to talk on a cell phone or text while driving, as discussed throughout Chapter 1. These activities distract the driver's attention.

You experience the limits of attention daily without knowing it. If the person you were talking to suddenly changed into another person, would you notice? The answer seems obvious: Of course you would. But according to research by Simons and Levin (1998), we can be "blind" to some visual information in our environment. This phenomenon is known as **change blindness**.

In this research, shown in The Methods of Psychology on p. 95, participants were approached by a stranger, who asked for directions. Then the stranger was momentarily blocked from the participants' view by a large object and replaced with another person of the same sex and race. Surprisingly, half of the people giving directions never noticed that they were talking to a different person. The reason for this failure to notice is that attention is limited. When giving directions to a stranger, we normally do not pay attention to the distinctive features of the stranger's face or clothing. Without paying attention to that information, we do not become consciously aware of it.

The surprising fact is that large discrepancies exist between what most of us believe we can pay attention to and what we actually attend to. As a result, our perceptions of the world are often inaccurate. We simply do not know how much information we miss in the world around us. But every time we fail to pay attention, we most likely will not create a memory of the information. You will learn more about the critical relationship between attention and memory in Chapter 7.

Hypothesis: People can be "blind" to visual information that they are not consciously aware of.

Research Method:

1 A participant is approached by a stranger asking for directions.

2 The stranger is momentarily blocked by a larger object.

3 While being blocked, the original stranger is replaced by another person.

Results: Half the participants giving directions never noticed they were talking to a different person (as long as the replacement was of the same race and sex as the original stranger).

Conclusion: Change blindness results from not paying attention to certain visual information and results in a lack of conscious awareness about that information.

QUESTION: What does change blindness tell us about how much attention we pay to strangers?

ANSWER: This phenomenon reveals that we pay attention to only the characteristics of a stranger that are easy to see, such as age, gender, and race.

Source: Photos from Simons, D. J., & Levin, D. T. (1998). Failure to detect changes to people during a real-world interaction. *Psychonomic Bulletin and Review*, 5, 644–649. © 1998 Psychonomic Society, Inc. Figure courtesy of Daniel J. Simons.

3.4 Unconscious Processing Sometimes Affects Behavior

3.4 LEARNING GOAL ACTIVITIES

To maximize your learning, complete the following learning goal activities.

a. Understand all bold and italic terms by writing explanations of them in your own words.

b. Understand consciousness in a person with a split brain by describing how that person experiences visual information presented to each hemisphere and how that person can (or cannot) verbally report the information.

Have you ever had a slip of the tongue, when you were thinking one thing and said another? Most people have, at some point, made this classic mistake. It is called a Freudian slip—where we express an unconscious thought at an inappropriate time or in an inappropriate social context. As we try to overcome our blunder, we wonder why it happened. There is much evidence that people are affected by thoughts, stimuli, and events they are not aware of (Schooler, Mrazek, Baird, & Winkielman, 2015).

UNCONSCIOUS PROCESSING IN SUBLIMINAL PERCEPTION Subliminal perception happens when our sensory systems process stimuli, but because the

subliminal perception
The processing of information by sensory systems without a person's conscious awareness.

stimuli last only a short time or are subtle, we are generally not aware of them. Over the last several decades, many researchers have explored different ways that unconscious processing during subliminal perception can influence thinking and behavior. For example, in a classic experiment by Richard Nisbett and Timothy Wilson (1977), participants were asked to examine pairs of obviously associated words, such as *ocean* and *moon*. Then they were asked to view single words, such as *detergent*, and merely state what other words came to mind. Nisbett and Wilson wanted to find out if viewing the word pairs would influence which words came to mind when participants viewed single words. And if so, would the participants be conscious of this influence?

Indeed, the researchers found that when given the word pair *ocean–moon*, followed by the word *detergent*, participants typically said the word *tide*. Because the moon affects the ocean and the tides, it is not surprising that participants chose the word *tide* with the word pair. What is surprising is that when the participants were asked why they said "tide," they usually gave reasons pertaining to the detergent's brand name, such as "My mom used Tide when I was a kid." This response shows that participants were not aware that the word pair had influenced them. In other words, unconscious processing of the information affected their thoughts and behavior. Considerable evidence indicates that how we think is influenced by many factors, many of which we don't notice (Bargh, 2017).

Though material presented subliminally can influence how people process information, it has little or no effect on complex thinking and actions (Kihlstrom, 2016a). For example, advertisers have long been accused of using subliminal cues to influence people's attitudes or get people to buy their products. However, buying a product is a result of many cognitive processes, and the evidence suggests that subliminal messages have quite small effects on purchasing behavior (Greenwald, 1992). For a further look at subliminal perception in advertising, see Try It Yourself below.

UNCONSCIOUS PROCESSING IN THE SPLIT BRAIN   Another way researchers have gained a better understanding of the conscious mind—and the unconscious mind—is by studying people who have had brain surgery. As you learned in study units 2.4 and 2.7, the brain has a right hemisphere and a left hemisphere. The major connection between the hemispheres is the corpus callosum, a massive bundle of neural fibers (see Figure 2.17). When people have severe epilepsy that does not respond to medication, the corpus callosum can be severed, so that the two halves

 TRY IT YOURSELF: **Subliminal Perception in Advertising**

During the 2000 U.S. presidential election, a television advertisement critical of Democratic candidate Al Gore's Medicare plan contained a hidden word for about one-thirtieth of a second. The ad was aired in 17 states, reaching over 30 million viewers (Stewart, 2008). Some people felt that this ad was an attempt to use subliminal perception to persuade people not to vote for Gore. In response, Gore's opponent, George W. Bush, stated that "the idea of putting subliminal messages into ads is ridiculous" (Bruni, 2000, A19). The video is now widely available on the Internet. Before you continue reading, search for the clip and watch it. Imagine yourself as undecided about the candidates in that long-ago election.

Did you see a hidden word? Did you feel any shift in your attitudes based on the video and the word that you may or may not have seen? Just before the phrase "BUREAUCRATS DECIDE" appeared, the word *RATS* stretched across the screen. But as discussed in this study unit, there is no evidence that subliminal perception of messages like this one change complex attitudes or behaviors, including voting choices.

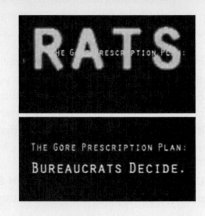

of the brain are almost completely isolated from each other. After the procedure, a seizure that begins in one hemisphere is less likely to spread throughout the cortex. The resulting condition, called **split brain,** has provided many important insights into the specialized functions of each brain hemisphere.

The hemispheres normally work together. Images from the left visual field (left half of what you are looking at) are processed by the right hemisphere. Images from the right visual field are processed by the left hemisphere (**Figure 3.8**). The left hemisphere also controls movements by the right side of the body, and the right hemisphere controls movements by the left side of the body. In addition, the left hemisphere also controls language processes (see Figure 2.11). In a healthy person, the corpus callosum lets the hemispheres communicate so that the right brain knows what the left is doing and vice versa, and it also allows a person to speak about information processed in either hemisphere.

By contrast, in split-brain patients, the hemispheres are separated, so information cannot be transferred from one hemisphere to another. Each hemisphere works on its own. This split lets psychologists test the functions of the two hemispheres

split brain
A condition in which the corpus callosum is surgically cut and the two hemispheres of the brain do not receive information directly from each other.

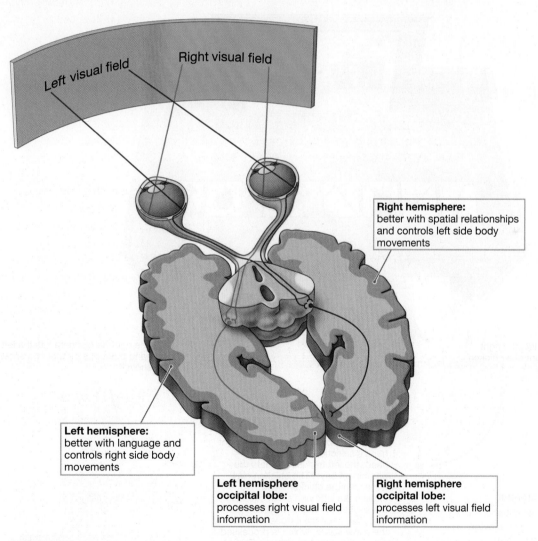

FIGURE 3.8

The Brain's Hemispheres Work Together

Each hemisphere of the brain processes distinct information, but the hemispheres work together to process all the information.

separately. In tests on the first people with split brains, Michael Gazzaniga and Roger Sperry (1967; Gazzaniga, 2015) came up with a stunning result: Just as the brain had been split in two, so had the conscious mind!

In one experiment (Gazzaniga & LeDoux, 1978), a split-brain patient saw two pictures flashed on a screen briefly at the same time. One image, a chicken foot, was shown to the right visual field. The other image, a snow-covered house, was shown to the left visual field (**Figure 3.9a**). The patient was asked to respond to what was shown. To do so, the patient had to point each hand at the most related image from a row of items below the screen (**Figure 3.9b**). The left hemisphere, having processed the chicken foot, made the right hand point at a picture of a chicken head (**Figure 3.9c**). The right hemisphere, having processed the snowy house, made the left hand point at a picture of a snow shovel (**Figure 3.9d**).

Then the patient was asked to verbally explain these responses. Recall that the left hemisphere (or "left brain") processes language. Therefore, the patient had no trouble explaining why his right hand pointed to the picture of the chicken head. The left hemisphere had processed the picture from the right visual field (the chicken claw), and so the patient could state that "the chicken claw goes with the chicken."

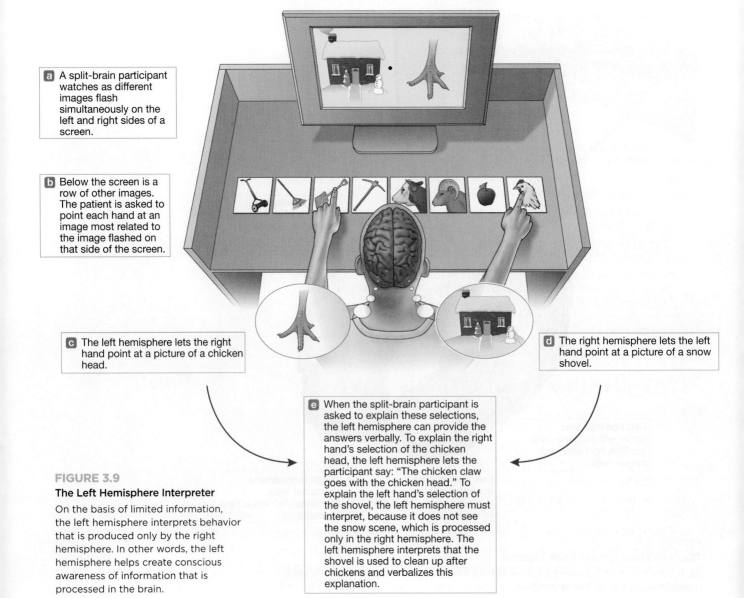

a A split-brain participant watches as different images flash simultaneously on the left and right sides of a screen.

b Below the screen is a row of other images. The patient is asked to point each hand at an image most related to the image flashed on that side of the screen.

c The left hemisphere lets the right hand point at a picture of a chicken head.

d The right hemisphere lets the left hand point at a picture of a snow shovel.

e When the split-brain participant is asked to explain these selections, the left hemisphere can provide the answers verbally. To explain the right hand's selection of the chicken head, the left hemisphere lets the participant say: "The chicken claw goes with the chicken head." To explain the left hand's selection of the shovel, the left hemisphere must interpret, because it does not see the snow scene, which is processed only in the right hemisphere. The left hemisphere interprets that the shovel is used to clean up after chickens and verbalizes this explanation.

FIGURE 3.9

The Left Hemisphere Interpreter

On the basis of limited information, the left hemisphere interprets behavior that is produced only by the right hemisphere. In other words, the left hemisphere helps create conscious awareness of information that is processed in the brain.

What about the action of the patient's left hand? Because the patient's brain had been split, the right hemisphere had no access to language production. The left hemisphere had access to language but no information about the left hand's actions, which it tried to make sense of. So the patient's answer to why his left hand had pointed to the shovel was that "you need a shovel to clean out the chicken shed" (**Figure 3.9e**). The left brain could not verbalize the relationship between the shovel and the snowy house because the snow scene was processed only in the right hemisphere. Instead, the left hemisphere interpreted the left hand's pointing to the shovel in a way that was consistent with the only knowledge available to the left brain: the chicken claw.

In other words, even with a split brain, the brain's hemispheres work together to reconstruct our conscious experiences. This happens because the left hemisphere tends to construct a world that makes sense. The sense-constructing activity in the left hemisphere is called the *interpreter*. This term means that the left hemisphere is interpreting or explaining the left hand's action, which had been performed by the independent right hemisphere in the split-brain patient (Gazzaniga, 2000). The left hemisphere's explanation, however, was unrelated to the right hemisphere's real reason for commanding that action. Yet to the split-brain patient, the movement seemed perfectly logical once the action had been interpreted.

Experiencing consciousness with a split brain is extremely rare, of course. Nearly all people have two hemispheres that communicate and cooperate on the tasks of daily living and being aware of experiences.

What Does It Mean to Be Conscious?

To make sure you learned what you just read, write answers to the following questions and check your answers.

3.1 What is the difference between a person's level of consciousness and that person's state of consciousness?

3.2 How does the global workspace model support materialism, not dualism, as the current view of consciousness?

3.3 What is the difference between automatic processing and controlled processing of information?

3.4 Viewing pictures of delicious food, even at too fast a rate for you to state what you saw, can have a later effect on how much food you eat. What is this influence an example of?

See Appendix B for answers to the red Q questions.

How Does Sleep Affect Consciousness?

It's midnight, and you've finally gotten into bed. But you're so nervous about a job interview in the morning that you're sure you'll be up all night worrying. The next thing you know, the alarm is going off at 7:00 AM. Once again, your brain did that mysterious thing, and you fell asleep. What was your brain doing during those seven hours?

People commonly think that the brain shuts itself down during sleep. In fact, many brain regions are more active when we are asleep than when we are awake. And evidence indicates that some complex thinking, such as working on difficult problems, occurs in the brain even when we are sleeping (Walker & Stickgold,

2006). Given that brain activity is the basis for consciousness, how conscious are we during sleep? How does our consciousness change during dreaming? To answer these questions, let's consider how aware we are of the outer world and our mental processes when we sleep.

3.5 Consciousness Changes During Sleep

3.5 LEARNING GOAL ACTIVITIES

To maximize your learning, complete the following learning goal activities.

a. Understand all bold and italic terms by writing explanations of them in your own words.

b. Understand the four stages of sleep by naming each one, explaining the brain activity during that stage, and describing the consciousness during it.

Whether you are a night owl or an early bird, most days there will be a time when you feel sleepy and ready for bed. Like clockwork, that sleepy feeling will most likely occur around the same hour each day. This happens because your body has an internal "clock" that regulates your sleeping and waking.

SLEEP IS PART OF THE NORMAL RHYTHM OF LIFE   Brain activity and other physiological processes are regulated into daily patterns known as **circadian rhythms** (*circadian* roughly translates to "about a day"). Sleep/wake cycles operate according to circadian rhythms, as do body temperature and hormone levels. Circadian rhythms are influenced by the cycles of light and dark. Even when removed from light cues, however, we (and nonhuman animals) continue to show these rhythms.

Multiple brain regions are involved in producing and maintaining circadian rhythms and our sleep/wake cycle. For instance, information about light detected by the eyes is sent to a small region of the hypothalamus called the suprachiasmatic nucleus (**Figure 3.10**). This region then sends signals to a tiny structure in the endocrine system called the pineal gland (see study unit 2.10 and Figure 2.24). The pineal gland influences the release of **melatonin**, a hormone that travels through the bloodstream and affects various receptors in the body, including some receptors in the brain. Bright light reduces the production of melatonin, whereas darkness triggers its release. It is believed that melatonin helps regulate the accuracy of our biological clock. Taking melatonin as a dietary supplement can help people cope with jet lag and shift work, both of which interfere with circadian rhythms. Taking melatonin also appears to help people fall asleep, although it is unclear why this happens.

Individuals differ tremendously in how much they sleep. Infants sleep much of the day. As adults, we spend about one-third of our time sleeping, an average of around 8 hours per night. Some adults report needing 9 or 10 hours of sleep a night to feel rested, whereas others report needing only a few hours. People tend to sleep less as they age. However, researchers were skeptical when a 70-year-old retired nurse, Miss M., reported sleeping only about an hour a night—that is, until she agreed to participate in a study. On her first two nights in a research laboratory, Miss M. was unable to sleep, apparently because of the excitement. But on her

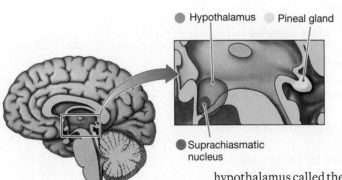

FIGURE 3.10

Pineal Gland and Sleep/Wake Cycles

Changes in light register in the suprachiasmatic nucleus of the hypothalamus. The hypothalamus then signals the pineal gland. The pineal gland releases melatonin, which signals the body that it is time to sleep or wake up.

circadian rhythms
The regulation of biological cycles into regular, daily patterns.

melatonin
A hormone that aids regulation of circadian rhythms; bright light reduces production and darkness increases production.

third night, she slept for only 99 minutes, then awoke refreshed, cheerful, and full of energy (Meddis, 1977). You might like the idea of sleeping so little and having all those extra hours of spare time. But bear in mind that most of us do not function well on so little sleep.

FOUR STAGES OF HEALTHY SLEEP   How is being awake different from being asleep? The difference has as much to do with conscious experience as with biological processes. When you sleep, your conscious experience of the outside world is largely turned off. To some extent, however, you remain aware of your surroundings and your brain still processes certain information. Your mind analyzes potential dangers, controls body movements, and shifts body parts to maximize comfort. This is why people who sleep next to children or pets tend not to roll over onto them and why, after infancy, most people do not fall out of bed while sleeping.

Before the development of objective methods to assess brain activity, most people believed the brain went to sleep along with the rest of the body. As you learned in study unit 2.4, the invention of the electroencephalograph (EEG) let researchers measure the brain's electrical activity. When you are awake and fully conscious in a normal waking state, you experience many different sources of sensory activity. As a result, the neurons in your brain are extremely active. An EEG shows this brain activity as short, frequent, irregular electrical signals called beta waves (shown in **Figure 3.11a**). When you really focus your attention on something, or when you close your eyes and relax, brain activity slows and becomes more regular, producing the electrical pattern known as alpha waves (**Figure 3.11b**).

As EEG readings indicate, sleep typically occurs in four stages (**Figure 3.11c–f**). These stages are marked by changes in consciousness. When you start to drift off, you enter **stage 1 sleep,** shown on an EEG as theta waves (see Figure 3.11c). Your awareness of both the outer world and your inner mental activity starts to decline. You can easily be aroused from stage 1 sleep. If awakened, you probably won't be aware that you were drifting off. In this stage before true sleep, you might see fantastical images or geometric shapes. Or you might have the sensation of falling or that your limbs are jerking (see Has It Happened to You? on p. 102).

As you progress to **stage 2 sleep,** your breathing becomes more regular, and you become even less aware of the outside world and your inner mental activity. In this stage, you are truly asleep. Now the EEG shows large waves called *K-complexes* and occasional bursts of activity called *sleep spindles* (see Figure 3.11d). Abrupt noises can trigger K-complexes, which may be signals from brain mechanisms involved with shutting out the external world and keeping people asleep (Halász, 2016). As people age and sleep more lightly, their EEGs show fewer sleep spindles, which may be associated with the development of long-term memories (Fogel & Smith, 2011).

The progression to deep sleep occurs through stages 3 and 4 sleep, which are seen as one stage because the brain activity is nearly identical (Silber et al., 2007). This period is marked by large, regular delta waves, and it is often referred to as **slow-wave sleep** (see Figure 3.11e). People in slow-wave sleep are very hard to wake and are often disoriented when they do wake up. People still process some outside information in slow-wave sleep, however, because the mind continues to evaluate the environment for potential

stage 1 sleep
First stage of sleep, where a person is drifting off; EEGs show slower theta waves, and conscious awareness of both the external world and inner mental activity starts to decline.

stage 2 sleep
Second stage of sleep, where a person is truly asleep; EEGs show K-complexes and sleep spindles, and there is much less conscious awareness of both the external world and inner mental activity.

slow-wave sleep
Stages 3 and 4 of deep sleep, where a person is substantially less conscious and is hard to awaken; EEGs reveal large, regular delta waves.

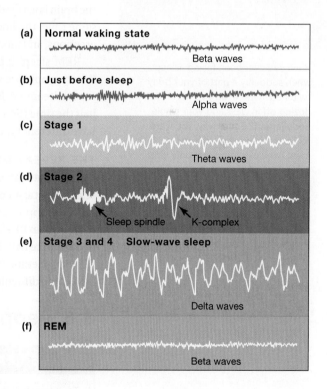

FIGURE 3.11

Brain Activity Before and During Sleep
These EEG patterns are examples of electrical brain activity before sleep **(a–b)** and during the four stages of healthy sleep **(c–f)**.

FIGURE 3.12

Stages of Sleep

This chart shows how the four stages of sleep progress over the course of a night's sleep.

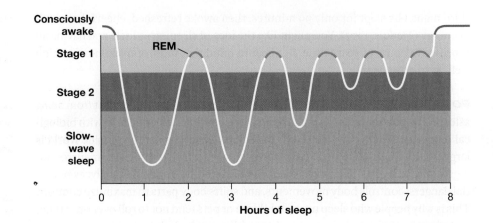

REM sleep

The stage of sleep where a person experiences rapid eye movements, dreaming, and paralysis of motor systems; EEGs show beta wave activity, which is also associated with an awake, conscious mind.

HAS IT HAPPENED TO YOU?

The Hypnic Jerk

Have you ever been falling asleep when suddenly a part of your body twitched? Or maybe you were dozing off in class and your whole body jerked? Either way, you were most likely aware of your movement, which is called a hypnic jerk. Experts don't know exactly what causes hypnic jerks, but many agree that they come from the muscles' responding to brain activity that occurs in stage 1 sleep. Because these jerks shift us briefly out of stage 1 sleep, we become aware that we just moved. This conscious awareness usually does not last long, though. It fades when we slip back into sleep for the night, or at least for the class period.

danger. For example, parents in slow-wave sleep can be aroused by their children's cries. Yet they can blissfully sleep through the sounds of sirens or traffic noise, which are louder than the crying children but are not necessarily relevant.

After about 90 minutes of sleep, the sleep cycle reverses, returning to stage 1 sleep. At this point, the EEG suddenly shows a flurry of beta wave activity that usually represents an awake, alert mind. The eyes dart back and forth beneath closed eyelids. Because of these rapid eye movements, this stage is called **REM sleep** (see Figure 3.11f). It is sometimes called paradoxical sleep because of the paradox of a sleeping body with an active brain. Indeed, some regions of the brain are more active during REM sleep than during a normal waking state of consciousness. But although the brain is active during REM sleep, most of the body's muscles are paralyzed. At the same time, the body shows signs of genital arousal: Most males of all ages develop erections, and most females of all ages experience engorgement of the clitoris.

REM sleep is psychologically significant because of its relation to dreaming. When people are awakened during REM sleep, about 80 percent of the time they report dreaming. By contrast, they report dreaming during non-REM sleep less than half the time (Solms, 2000). What's more, as you will see in the next study unit, you have different types of dreams in these two types of sleep.

THE REPEATING SLEEP CYCLE   Over the course of a typical night, you cycle through the four stages of sleep about five times. As shown in **Figure 3.12,** you progress from stage 1 sleep to stage 2 sleep and slow-wave sleep, then to REM sleep. As morning approaches, the sleep cycle becomes shorter, and you spend relatively more time in REM sleep. You may say you slept like a log all night long, but it's probably not quite true. People briefly awaken many times during the night, although they do not remember these awakenings in the morning. As people age, they sometimes have more difficulty going back to sleep after awakening.

3.6 People Dream While Sleeping

3.6 LEARNING GOAL ACTIVITIES

To maximize your learning, complete the following learning goal activities.

a. Understand all bold and italic terms by writing explanations of them in your own words.

b. Apply the two types of altered consciousness during REM and non-REM dreams by giving an example of each from your life.

Dreams are one of life's great mysteries. Why do our minds create images, fantasies, stories that make little sense, and scenes that ignore physical laws and rules of both time and space? Why does the mind confuse these creations with reality? Although they sometimes incorporate external sounds or other sensory experiences that happen while we sleep, dreams are the products of our consciousness. Some people claim they do not dream, or never remember their dreams, but everyone dreams unless a brain injury or medication interferes with it. In fact, the average person spends 6 years of the person's life dreaming. Yet no one knows if dreaming serves any biological function.

dreams
Products of consciousness during sleep in which a person confuses images and fantasies with reality.

REM DREAMS AND NON-REM DREAMS   You dream during both REM and non-REM sleep. But in the two types of sleep, the content of your dreams differs. REM dreams are more likely to be bizarre. They may involve intense emotions, visual and auditory hallucinations (but rarely taste, smell, or pain), and an uncritical acceptance of illogical events. You fly, are chased by monsters, or tunnel through the center of the Earth. Non-REM dreams feel normal, like everyday life. They may concern ordinary activities such as deciding what clothes to wear or going to the grocery store.

The activity of different brain regions during REM and non-REM sleep may be responsible for the different types of dreams and your experiences of them. During non-REM sleep, many brain regions are generally deactivated. In contrast, during REM sleep, some areas of the brain show increased activity, whereas others show decreased activity (Hobson, 2009; **Figure 3.13**). The content of REM dreams results from the activation of brain structures associated with motivation, reward, and emotion (for example, the amygdala). The visual association areas,

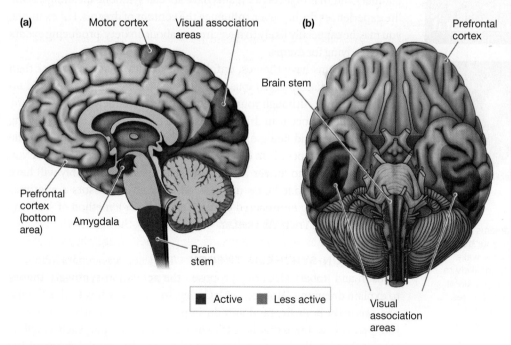

FIGURE 3.13

Brain Activity During REM Sleep

These two views of the brain show the regions that are more active (red) and less active (blue) during REM sleep. **(a)** As seen here from the side, the motor cortex, the brain stem, and visual association areas are active. So is the amygdala, which is involved in emotion. The prefrontal cortex is less active. **(b)** This view from beneath the brain shows other visual association areas and the brain stem, which are active. This view also reveals the bottom of the prefrontal cortex, which is less active.

FIGURE 3.14

Sigmund Freud's Theory of Dreams
Freud interpreted dreams as disguised fulfillment for the wishes of the unconscious mind. An image such as this in a dream might be interpreted as a person fleeing from a real-world problem.

TRY IT YOURSELF
Keeping a Dream Journal

Do you want to remember your dreams better? Just keep a pen and paper next to your bed so you can record your dreams as you wake up. If you wait to record them, you are likely to forget most of them. Keeping a dream journal can help you see repeating patterns (images, themes, people) in your dreams, and these patterns might reveal issues you are thinking about.

activation-synthesis theory
The idea that dreams are the result of the brain's attempts to make sense of random brain activity by combining the activity with stored memories.

motor cortex, and brain stem are also activated. At the same time, the prefrontal cortex becomes less activated (Schwartz & Maquet, 2002). As discussed in study unit 2.7, the prefrontal cortex is necessary for processing self-awareness, reflective thought, and conscious input from the external world. Because this brain region is less active during REM dreams, the brain's emotion centers and visual association areas interact without rational thought. The separation between one's feelings and logic contributes to the wilder images in REM dreams.

WHAT DO DREAMS MEAN? Perhaps we should ask, do dreams mean anything? One of the first major theories of dreams was proposed by Sigmund Freud. As you learned in study unit 1.5, Freud founded psychoanalytic theory. In his classic book *The Interpretation of Dreams* (1900), Freud claimed that dreams contain hidden content. That content represents wish fulfillment of unconscious desires in the mind of the dreamer. The *manifest content* is the way visual information is seen (manifested) in the dream and remembered by the dreamer. For example, in your dream you might fly through the air (**Figure 3.14**). The *latent content* is the meaning behind the visual manifestation. Your dream of flight might mean that you are trying to get away from someone, such as a bad relationship. Some theorists believe that the manifest content disguises the latent content to protect the dreamer from directly confronting an unconscious conflict.

Virtually no support exists for Freud's ideas that dreams represent hidden conflicts and that objects in dreams have special symbolic meanings. Daily life experiences do, however, influence the content of dreams. For example, you may be especially likely to have dreams about anxiety-producing events while studying for exams.

Some dreams have themes, unfolding as events or stories rather than as jumbles of disconnected images. Still, such themes apparently hold no secret meanings. Although your dreams may seem uniquely your own, many common themes occur in dreams. Have you ever dreamed about showing up for an exam and being unprepared or finding that you are taking the wrong test? Many people in college have dreams like these. Even after you finish school and no longer take exams routinely, you probably will have similar dreams about being unprepared. Retired professors sometimes dream about being unprepared to teach classes. For a method of studying your dreams, see Try It Yourself.

ACTIVATION-SYNTHESIS THEORY The sleep researchers John Alan Hobson and Robert McCarley proposed the **activation-synthesis theory** to explain dreaming (Hobson & McCarley, 1977). According to this theory, neurons in the brain fire randomly during sleep. This random firing can activate parts of the brain that normally process sensory input, such as sights, sounds, and smells. The sleeping mind tries to make sense of the resulting sensory activity by combining it with stored memories, and the result is our experience of having a dream. From this perspective, dreams are simply the side effects of mental processes produced by random neural firing.

In 2000, Hobson and his colleagues revised the activation-synthesis theory. They wanted to take into account recent findings in cognitive neuroscience. For instance, they suggested that activation of the limbic regions of the brain (such as the amygdala), which are associated with emotion and motivation, is the source of the emotional content of dreams. They also proposed that the deactivation of the prefrontal cortices contributes to the delusional and illogical aspects of dreams. Critics of Hobson's theory argue that dreams are rarely as chaotic as we might expect if they were based on random brain activity (Domhoff, 2003). Indeed, most dreams are fairly similar to waking life—they just have some strange features. Psychologists are still not sure what causes us to dream, and they continue to conduct research on the topic.

3.7 Sleep Is an Adaptive Behavior

3.7 LEARNING GOAL ACTIVITIES

To maximize your learning, complete the following learning goal activities.

a. Understand all bold and italic terms by writing explanations of them in your own words.

b. Apply the three reasons people need to sleep by giving, for each reason, one example from your own life of why you need to sleep.

As you learned in study unit 1.5, certain traits are adaptive for a species. That is, each species has traits that help it to survive and reproduce in a changing environment. At first glance, sleep hardly seems adaptive. Tuning out the external world for periods of time can be a threat to survival if a predator pounces or you drive your car into a tree. But we cannot avoid the need to sleep. Eventually our bodies shut down, and we sleep whether we want to or not.

But why do we sleep? Most animals sleep, even if they have peculiar sleeping styles. For instance, in some dolphin species the left and right cerebral hemispheres take turns sleeping. So sleep must serve an important biological purpose. In other words, it must help us adapt and respond in our environment. Researchers have proposed three reasons that sleeping is adaptive and beneficial to us: restoration of the body, preservation from harm, and support for memory and learning.

THREE BENEFITS OF SLEEP Sometimes we sleep longer than usual. Why? Think about the last time you engaged in demanding physical activity—maybe spending the day helping a friend move or running a long race. Most likely you needed extra sleep afterward. According to the *restorative theory*, sleep lets the body, including the brain, rest and repair itself. Growth hormone, released from the endocrine system (see study unit 2.10) during deep sleep, helps bring about the repair of damaged tissue. Sleep apparently lets the brain replenish energy stores and also strengthens the immune system (Hobson, 1999). Consider that after a traumatic brain injury (TBI), people need more sleep. One study found that people who had experienced any type of TBI slept about an hour longer per night, and this increased sleepiness lasted at least 18 months (Imbach et al., 2016).

According to the *circadian rhythm theory*, sleep has evolved to preserve animals, including humans, from harm. Sleep keeps creatures quiet and inactive when the danger of attack is greatest—usually when it is dark. Each day, animals need only a limited amount of time to accomplish the necessities of survival, such as getting food. As a result, it is adaptive for animals to spend the rest of the time inactive, preferably hidden. So an animal's typical amount of sleep depends on how much time that animal needs to obtain food, how easily it can hide, and how vulnerable it is to attack. Small animals tend to sleep a lot. Large animals that are vulnerable to attack, such as

FIGURE 3.15
Sleeping Predator
After a fresh kill, a lion may sleep for days.

FIGURE 3.16
Sleep Deprivation
Students may try to avoid sleep. But sleep will catch up with them!

cows and deer, sleep little. Large predatory animals, which are generally not vulnerable, sleep a lot (**Figure 3.15**). We humans depend greatly on vision for survival. We are adapted to sleeping at night because our early ancestors were more at risk in the dark.

Scientists have also proposed that sleep is important because it is involved in strengthening neural connections that serve as the basis of learning. The general idea of this *consolidation theory* is that circuits wired together during the waking period are consolidated, or strengthened, during sleep (Wilson & McNaughton, 1994). When research participants in one study slept after learning word lists, their recall was better than in control conditions where participants remained awake after learning the lists (Drosopoulos, Schulze, Fischer, & Born, 2007).

Both slow-wave sleep and REM sleep appear to be important for learning to take place, but people may be especially likely to perform better if they dream about the task while sleeping. In one study, participants learned how to run a complex maze. Those who then slept for 90 minutes went on to perform better on the maze than participants who hadn't slept. Those who dreamed about the maze performed the best of all (Wamsley, Tucker, Payne, Benavides, & Stickgold, 2010).

In addition, students may experience more REM sleep during exam periods, when they might be consolidating a great deal of information (Smith & Lapp, 1991). Changes in sleep patterns over the life cycle also support the argument that sleep, especially REM sleep, promotes the development of brain circuits for learning. Infants and the very young, who learn an enormous amount in a few years, sleep the most and also spend the most time in REM sleep.

SLEEP DEPRIVATION CAN IMPAIR FUNCTION We've all gone through periods when we didn't get enough sleep. Does the occasional lack of sleep harm us? Many laboratory studies have examined the effects of temporary sleep deprivation on physical and mental abilities. Surprisingly, most studies find that two or three days of sleep deprivation have little effect on strength, athletic ability, or the performance of complex tasks. If you find yourself nodding off over your textbook after a night without sleep, however, you're not alone (**Figure 3.16**). When deprived of sleep, people find it difficult to perform quiet tasks, such as reading, and nearly impossible to perform boring or mundane tasks.

By contrast, a long period of sleep deprivation decreases mental abilities. People who suffer from chronic sleep deprivation may experience attention lapses and reduced short-term memory. Studies with rats have found that extended sleep deprivation compromises the immune system and leads to death. Sleep deprivation is also dangerous and potentially disastrous because it makes people prone to microsleeps, in which they fall asleep during the day for a few seconds or even a minute (Coren, 1996).

If your main style of studying is the all-nighter, then findings that link sleep to learning should make you think twice. In one study, students who were sleep deprived for just one night showed reduced activity the next day in the hippocampus, a brain area essential for memory (Yoo, Hu, Gujar, Jolesz, & Walker, 2007; see study unit 2.6). These sleep-deprived students also showed poorer memory during later testing. The researchers found substantial evidence that sleep does more than consolidate memories. Sleep also seems to prepare the brain for its memory needs for the next day. The best advice for preparing for exams is to study, sleep, and then study again (Mazza et al., 2016). To do well on exams, get your sleep!

Sleep deprivation also interferes with the body's hunger signals, contributing to overeating and weight gain (late-night pizza run, anyone?). It impairs motor abilities, contributing to accidents and injuries. Sleep deprivation also increases anxiety, depression, and distress. And—to add insult to injury—others perceive us as less attractive when we are sleep deprived, compared with when we are well rested (Axelsson et al., 2010).

When you finally do sleep after a long period of deprivation, you will enter the REM stage more quickly and will have more REM dreams than usual. This *REM rebound* after deprivation implies that REM sleep is a particularly important part of the sleep process (Suchecki, Tiba, & Machado, 2012).

3.8 Sleep Disorders Are Relatively Common Throughout Life

3.8 LEARNING GOAL ACTIVITIES

To maximize your learning, complete the following learning goal activities.

a. Understand all bold and italic terms by writing explanations of them in your own words.

b. Understand the five sleep disorders by describing each one in your own words.

Nearly everyone occasionally has trouble falling asleep or going back to sleep after waking up during the night. When repeated problems with sleep cause significant difficulty in daily life, the problems have reached the point of being a sleep disorder. Five sleep disorders that can cause disruption are insomnia, sleep apnea, narcolepsy, REM behavior disorder, and sleepwalking.

INSOMNIA It's 3:00 AM, and you're turning over in bed for what seems like the 500th time. You're exhausted, but your brain refuses to turn off, and you're beginning to feel desperate. Now and then, each of us has a hard time sleeping. If you experience this problem often, you might have a sleep disorder. **Insomnia** is a sleep disorder in which a person's mental health and ability to function are reduced by the repeated inability to sleep. Indeed, insomnia is associated with reduced psychological well-being, including feelings of depression (Bootzin & Epstein, 2011; Hamilton et al., 2007).

Researchers estimate that between 12 percent and 20 percent of adults have insomnia; it is more common in women than in men and in older adults than in younger adults (Espie, 2002; Ram, Seirawan, Kumar, & Clark, 2010). It is hard to estimate how many people truly have insomnia, however. One reason is that many people who believe they are poor sleepers overestimate how long it takes them to fall asleep and often underestimate how much sleep they get in a typical night. Some people even experience pseudoinsomnia, in which they basically dream they are not sleeping. Their EEGs would show they were sleeping, but if you woke them, they would claim they had been awake. Ironically, a major cause of insomnia is worrying about sleep. When you experience this kind of insomnia, you may be tired enough to sleep. As you try to fall asleep, however, you worry about whether you will get to sleep and may even panic about how a lack of sleep will affect you. This anxiety leads to increased arousal, which interferes with normal sleep patterns. It's a vicious cycle.

If you look at the many TV ads and pharmacy shelves filled with both prescription pills and over-the-counter sleep aids, it would seem that medication is a simple way to deal with insomnia. Sleeping pills may work in the short run, but they can cause

insomnia
A disorder characterized by a repeated inability to sleep.

sleep apnea
A disorder in which a person, while asleep, stops breathing because the throat closes; the condition results in frequent awakenings during the night.

narcolepsy
A disorder in which a person experiences excessive sleepiness during normal waking hours, sometimes going limp and collapsing.

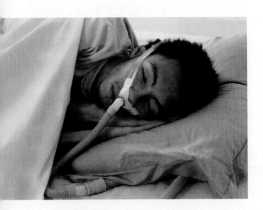

FIGURE 3.17
Sleep Apnea
This man has sleep apnea. While he sleeps, a continuous positive airway pressure (CPAP) device blows air into his nose or mouth to keep his throat open.

significant problems down the road. People may come to depend on the pills to help them sleep. Then if they try to stop taking the pills, they may lie awake wondering whether they can get to sleep on their own.

According to research, the most successful treatment for insomnia combines drug therapy with cognitive-behavioral therapy (CBT, which is discussed in Chapter 15). CBT helps people overcome their worries about sleep and relieves the need for the drugs, which they should stop taking before the therapy ends (Morin et al., 2009). For improving the quality of sleep, CBT is even better than prescription medication, such as antidepressants (Carney et al., 2017).

Other factors that contribute to insomnia include poor sleeping habits, so you might try preventing or even curing insomnia by changing your habits. You can read about some techniques in Using Psychology in Your Life on p. 109.

SLEEP APNEA   Another fairly common sleep disorder is **sleep apnea**. While asleep, a person with this disorder stops breathing for short periods because the throat closes. In struggling to breathe, the person briefly awakens and gasps for air.

Sleep apnea is most common among middle-aged men and is often associated with obesity, although it is unclear if obesity causes sleep apnea or sleep apnea contributes to obesity (Pack & Pien, 2011; Spurr, Graven, & Gilbert, 2008). Sleep apnea causes people to sleep poorly, feel tired in the daytime, and even have problems such as an inability to concentrate while driving. What's more, sleep apnea is associated with cardiovascular problems and stroke.

Because they do not remember awakening frequently during the night, people with sleep apnea are typically unaware of their condition. The main symptom that may bring it to their attention is loud snoring that disturbs a partner. For serious cases, physicians often prescribe a device that blows air into the nose or mouth while the person sleeps (**Figure 3.17**).

NARCOLEPSY   A student who falls asleep during class is likely sleep deprived, but a professor who falls asleep while lecturing could be experiencing an episode of **narcolepsy**. In this rare disorder, extreme sleepiness occurs during normal waking hours. During an episode of narcolepsy, a person may experience the muscle paralysis that accompanies REM sleep, perhaps causing the person to go limp and collapse. Obviously, people with narcolepsy have to be very careful about the activities they engage in. Unexpectedly falling asleep can be dangerous or fatal, depending on the situation. Evidence suggests that narcolepsy is a genetic condition that affects transmission of a specific neurotransmitter in the hypothalamus (Chabas, Taheri, Renier, & Mignot, 2003; Nishino, 2007). The most widely used treatments for this condition are drugs that act as stimulants.

REM BEHAVIOR DISORDER AND SLEEPWALKING   *REM behavior disorder* is roughly the opposite of narcolepsy. In this condition, the normal paralysis that accompanies REM sleep is disabled. People who experience REM behavior disorder act out their dreams while sleeping. Often, in acting out dreams, they strike their sleeping partners. No treatment exists for this rare sleep disorder. The condition is caused by a neurological deficit and is most often seen in elderly males.

By contrast, sleepwalking is most common among young children. Technically called *somnambulism*, this relatively common behavior occurs during slow-wave sleep, typically within the first hour or two after falling asleep. But it is not a person acting out a dream. During an episode, the person is glassy-eyed and seems disconnected from other people and/or the surroundings. Contrary to popular belief, no

USING PSYCHOLOGY IN YOUR LIFE

How Can You Develop Better Sleep Habits?

An Example of What Not to Do

An Example of What to Do

If you don't get enough sleep, you are setting yourself up for poor mental health, poor physical health, and academic difficulties. You probably know this from personal experience as well as from what you've read. But even though you may have the best intentions, sleep may sometimes play hard to get. Anxiety, excitement, getting too tired, or having bad sleep habits may leave you lying in bed, dog-tired, but wide awake. Here are some strategies that can help you develop better sleep habits:

1. **Establish a routine to help set your biological clock.** Every day, go to bed at the same time and wake up at the same time. Changing the time you go to bed or wake up each day alters your regular nightly sleep cycle and can disrupt other physiological systems.

2. **Avoid alcohol and caffeine in the evening.** Alcohol might help you get to sleep more quickly, but it will interfere with your sleep cycle and most likely make you wake up early the next day. Caffeine is a stimulant, so it will prevent you from falling asleep.

3. **Avoid electronic devices late at night.** Most electronic devices emit blue light, which can signal the brain to remain awake, making it more difficult to fall asleep. So if possible, you should put your phone, tablet, or both away early. You can also install programs on most devices that will cause the device to emit a red frequency rather than blue. Red light has the opposite effect of blue light and can signal the body to begin winding down.

4. **Exercise regularly.** Regular exercise will help maintain your sleep cycle. In fact, exercising during the day promotes slow-wave sleep at night, which helps you feel rejuvenated in the morning (Youngstedt & Kline, 2006).

5. **Remember, your bed is for sleeping.** Most of us do not sleep in our kitchens. We also should not eat in our beds. Or watch TV. Or study. Your mind needs to associate your bed with sleeping. The best way to make that association is to use your bed only for sleeping. And maybe a little cuddling.

6. **Relax.** Do not worry about the future (easier said than done, right?). Write down things to do or worries on a notepad and then put them aside until the next day. Have a warm bath or listen to soothing music. Download a couple of meditation and relaxation podcasts, and use the techniques to help you deal with stress and guide you to restfulness.

7. **Get up.** When you cannot fall asleep, get up and do something else. Do not lie there trying to force sleep (we all know how well that works, or rather does not work). If you start feeling sleepy a bit later, go back to bed and give sleep another chance.

8. **Let bygones be bygones.** When you have trouble falling asleep on a particular night, do not try to make up for the lost sleep by sleeping late the next morning or napping during the day. Those zzzz's are gone. You want to be sleepy when you go to bed the next night. Sleeping late, napping, or both will make the next night's sleep more difficult.

The sleep attitudes and habits you establish during college will be with you for the rest of your life. Set yourself up for academic success, and for good physical and mental health, by making good sleep a priority and taking charge of your sleep.

For additional resources, visit the National Sleep Foundation's Web site at https://sleepfoundation.org.

harm is done if the sleepwalker is awakened during the episode. Being gently walked back to bed is safer for the sleepwalker than being left to wander around and potentially get hurt.

Q How Does Sleep Affect Consciousness?

To make sure you learned what you just read, write answers to the following questions and check your answers.

3.5 Which one of the four stages of sleep represents the beginning of full sleep, with less conscious awareness of both the outer world and mental processes? What does an EEG reveal during this stage?

3.6 Imagine that you dream about folding and putting away laundry. Did you most likely have a REM dream or a non-REM dream?

3.7 Suppose you run a marathon and sleep a lot afterward. Which theory of sleep best explains this behavior, and why?

3.8 What time should you go to bed if you want to establish good sleeping habits?

See Appendix B for answers to the red Q questions.

How Do Hypnosis, Meditation, and Flow Alter Consciousness?

When you hear the phrase "altered state of consciousness," you might think of science fiction. But while consciousness can be altered in extreme ways, this section considers three common methods a person can use to achieve an altered state of consciousness: hypnosis, meditation, and immersion in an enjoyable activity. Through such methods, a person's awareness of both the outer world and the person's mental activity can be made fuzzy or clearer.

3.9 Attention to Suggestions May Alter Consciousness in Hypnosis

3.9 LEARNING GOAL ACTIVITIES

To maximize your learning, complete the following learning goal activities.

a. Understand all bold and italic terms by writing explanations of them in your own words.

b. Understand how hypnosis affects consciousness by summarizing the two theories of how hypnosis may or may not alter awareness.

In June 2012, Maxime Nadeau, a young hypnotist-in-training, hypnotized a group of 13- and 14-year-old girls during a performance at a school in Quebec, Canada. But Nadeau could not bring several of the girls out of hypnosis. He had to call on his mentor, Richard Whitbread, to break the spell. Whitbread did so and later said, "There were a couple of students who had their heads lying on the table, and there were [others] who, you could tell, were in trance. . . . The eyes were open and there was nobody home" (CBC News, 2012). What does it mean that "nobody was home"? Can a hypnotist produce a real change in mental state, or is hypnosis just good theater? What exactly is hypnosis?

POSTHYPNOTIC SUGGESTION   In **hypnosis**, a person, responding to suggestions, experiences changes in memory, perception, and/or voluntary action (Kihlstrom, 2016b; Kihlstrom & Eich, 1994). Psychologists generally agree that hypnosis affects some people, but they do not agree on whether hypnotists can produce a genuinely altered state of consciousness (Jamieson, 2007).

A hypnotist may work with one or more people at a time. To begin the hypnosis, the hypnotist makes a series of suggestions, such as "You are becoming sleepy. . . . Your eyelids are drooping. . . . Your arms and legs feel very heavy." As the listener falls more deeply into the hypnotic state, the hypnotist makes more suggestions. "You cannot move your right arm," "You feel warm," and so on. If everything goes according to plan, the listener follows all the suggestions as though they are true, until the hypnotist ends the session (**Figure 3.18**).

Sometimes the hypnotist suggests that, after the hypnosis session, the listener will experience some change. Such a posthypnotic suggestion is usually accompanied by the instruction to not remember the suggestion. For example, a hypnotist might suggest, "When I say the word 'dog,' you will stand up and bark like a dog. You will not remember this suggestion." And, to the delight of the audience, later on the person stands up and barks like a dog.

Therapists sometimes hypnotize patients and give them *posthypnotic suggestions* to help them lose weight or quit smoking. But evidence suggests that hypnosis has quite modest effects on these behaviors. There is clear evidence, however, that some posthypnotic suggestions can at least subtly influence behaviors.

To the extent that hypnosis works, it relies more on the person being hypnotized than on the skill of the hypnotist. Indeed, tests for hypnotic suggestibility show that hypnosis works primarily for people who are highly suggestible (Kallio & Revonsuo, 2003). Researchers cannot precisely identify the personality characteristics of people who can or cannot be hypnotized, but suggestibility is related to getting absorbed in activities easily, not being distracted easily, and having a rich imagination (Balthazard & Woody, 1992; Crawford, Corby, & Kopell, 1996; Silva & Kirsch, 1992). Furthermore, a person who dislikes the idea of being hypnotized or finds it frightening would probably not be hypnotized easily. To be hypnotized, a person must go along with the hypnotist's suggestions willingly. There is no reliable evidence that people will do things under hypnosis that they would normally object to.

TWO THEORIES OF HYPNOSIS   Some psychologists believe that a person under hypnosis doesn't experience an altered state of consciousness. The person is not faking, but acts the part of a hypnotized person as if in a play, aware of and willing to perform actions called for by the "director," the hypnotist. According to this **sociocognitive theory of hypnosis**, hypnotized people behave as they expect hypnotized people to behave, even if those expectations are faulty (Kirsch & Lynn, 1995; Spanos & Coe, 1992).

An alternative theory, the **dissociation theory of hypnosis**, acknowledges the importance of social context, but views hypnosis as a truly altered state of consciousness. According to this theory, hypnosis is a trancelike state in which conscious awareness is separated, or dissociated, from other aspects of consciousness (Gruzelier, 2000). In support of this theory, many brain imaging studies have found alterations in the brain activity of a hypnotized person (Rainville, Hofbauer, Bushnell, Duncan, & Price, 2002). One of the earliest such studies (Kosslyn, Thompson, Constantine-Ferrando, Alpert, & Spiegel, 2000) demonstrated that when hypnotized participants were asked to imagine black-and-white objects

hypnosis
A social interaction during which a person, responding to suggestions, experiences changes in memory, perception, and/or voluntary action.

sociocognitive theory of hypnosis
Theory that hypnotized people are not in an altered state of consciousness, but they behave in a way that is expected in that situation.

dissociation theory of hypnosis
The idea that hypnotized people are in an altered state of consciousness where their awareness is separated from other aspects of consciousness.

FIGURE 3.18
Hypnotized
Hypnosis uses suggestions to create altered memories, perceptions, and behaviors. Hypnotized people may be in an altered state of consciousness, or they may just be playing a part suggested to them by the hypnotist.

as having color, they showed activity in visual cortex regions involved in color perception. Hypnotized participants asked to drain color from colored images showed diminished activity in those same brain regions. This activity pattern did not occur when participants were not hypnotized. These results indicate that hypnotic suggestion may indeed change brain function. And if brain function is changed during hypnosis, then maybe hypnosis really does alter consciousness. After all, it seems unlikely that people could alter their brain activity to please hypnotists, even if the hypnotists are psychological researchers.

HYPNOSIS FOR PAIN   One of the best-supported uses of hypnosis is *hypnotic analgesia,* a form of pain reduction (**Figure 3.19**). Laboratory research has demonstrated that this technique works reliably (Hilgard & Hilgard, 1975; Nash & Barnier, 2008). For instance, a woman who plunges her arm into extremely cold water will feel great pain, and the pain will intensify over time. On average, a person can keep the arm in the water for only about 30 seconds, but a person experiencing hypnotic analgesia can hold out longer. As you might expect, people high in suggestibility who experience hypnotic analgesia can tolerate the cold water the longest (Montgomery, DuHamel, & Redd, 2000).

In clinical settings, hypnosis has been effective in treating acute pain (for example, during surgery and dental work) and chronic pain (for example, from arthritis, cancer, or diabetes; Patterson & Jensen, 2003). A patient can also be taught self-hypnosis to improve recovery from surgery.

Hypnotic analgesia may work by changing the patient's interpretation of pain rather than by diminishing pain. That is, the patient feels the sensations associated with pain, but feels detached from those sensations (Price, Harkins, & Baker, 1987). An imaging study confirmed this pattern by showing that although hypnosis does not affect the sensory processing of pain, it reduces brain activity in regions that process the emotional aspects of pain (Rainville, Duncan, Price, Carrier, & Bushnell, 1997).

Findings such as these provide considerable support for the dissociation theory of hypnosis. It seems unlikely that either expectations about hypnosis or social pressure to not feel pain could explain how people experiencing hypnotic analgesia are able to undergo painful surgery and not feel it. Nor is it likely that expectations or social pressure could result in the altered brain activity seen during hypnotic analgesia.

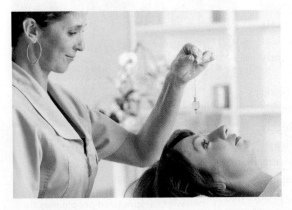

FIGURE 3.19

Hypnotic Analgesia Changes the Perception of Pain

Hypnosis can help people feel detached from their pain.

3.10 Meditation Alters Consciousness and Brain Functioning

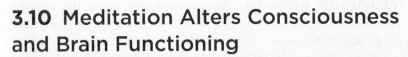

3.10 LEARNING GOAL ACTIVITIES

To maximize your learning, complete the following learning goal activities.

a. Understand all bold and italic terms by writing explanations of them in your own words.

b. Understand that meditation can alter consciousness by describing in your own words the similarities and differences between the three forms of meditation.

With a growing awareness of different cultural and religious practices and alternative approaches to medicine, people in the West have become more interested in examining Eastern techniques of creating an altered state of consciousness. One such technique is **meditation**. Different forms of meditation are central to many Eastern religions, including Hinduism, Buddhism, and Sikhism. These religious forms of meditation are meant to bring spiritual enlightenment.

Most forms of meditation popular in the West are not necessarily religious. They are meant primarily to expand the mind, bring about feelings of inner peace, and help people deal with the tensions and stresses in their lives (**Figure 3.20**).

There are three main forms of meditation. In *concentrative meditation,* you focus your attention on one thing, such as your breathing pattern, a mental image, or a specific phrase (sometimes called a mantra). In *mindfulness meditation,* you let your thoughts flow freely, paying attention to them but not examining their meaning or reacting to them in any way. The meditation practice perhaps best known in the West is *transcendental meditation (TM)*. This form involves meditating with great concentration for 20 minutes twice a day.

In a 2006 study, a large number of heart patients were randomly assigned to TM or an educational program. After 16 weeks, the patients practicing TM improved more than the control group on a number of health measures, such as blood pressure, levels of fatty acid and cholesterol, and signs of diabetes (Paul-Labrador et al., 2006). Unfortunately, this study does not show which aspects of TM produced the health benefits. Was it simply relaxing, or was it an altered state of consciousness?

Psychologists also study how meditation affects cognitive processing and brain function (Cahn & Polich, 2006). One such study found that participants who completed meditation training showed greater stress reduction and more significant improvement in attention than a group that received simple relaxation training (Tang et al., 2007). When participants in another study were made to feel sad, those who had received meditation training felt less sad than those in a control group who did not receive meditation training (Farb et al., 2010; **Figure 3.21**).

Some researchers argue that long-term meditation brings about structural changes in the brain that help maintain brain function over the life span. For instance, although the volume of gray matter typically diminishes with age, one study found that this volume did not diminish in older adults who practiced meditation (Pagnoni & Cekic, 2007). This finding suggests that meditation might help preserve cognitive functioning as people age. However, as you learned in study unit 1.10, correlation does not prove causation. People who meditate may differ greatly from people who do not, especially regarding lifestyle choices such as diet and taking care of their health. Careful empirical research should contribute significantly to our understanding of meditation's effects. To begin assessing the results of such research, see Evaluating Psychology in the Real World on p. 115.

FIGURE 3.20

Meditation Increases Tranquility
Some people meditate to achieve an altered state of consciousness that produces a sense of calm.

meditation
A practice in which intense contemplation leads to a deep sense of calmness that has been described as an altered state of consciousness.

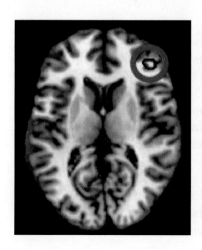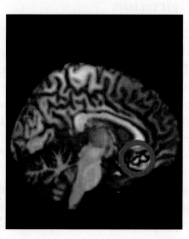

FIGURE 3.21

The Brain on Meditation
In these fMRI scans, the circles indicate brain areas that typically show less activity when people are sad. After control subjects watched sad clips from movies, these areas of their brains were less active. In other words, as expected, they felt sad. However, in the brains of participants who had received eight weeks of meditation training, these areas remained active, which may explain why participants felt less sadness even after viewing the sad clips.

3.11 People Can Lose Themselves in Enjoyable Activities

3.11 LEARNING GOAL ACTIVITIES

To maximize your learning, complete the following learning goal activities.

a. Understand all bold and italic terms by writing explanations of them in your own words.

b. Apply flow to your own life by describing a flow experience you have had and how you experienced an altered state of consciousness.

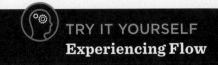

FIGURE 3.22

Religious Ecstasy

This woman appears to be overcome with religious ecstasy during a ceremony in an African-Christian church in Nigeria. In such cases, people experience an altered state of consciousness when their attention is directed away from themselves and onto spiritual awareness.

flow

A highly focused, altered state of consciousness, when awareness of self and time diminishes due to being completely engrossed in an enjoyable activity.

TRY IT YOURSELF

Experiencing Flow

You can experience flow by immersing yourself in a favorite activity. Pick something that engages and satisfies you, perhaps letting you lose track of time as you pursue a goal. A few possibilities for producing this altered state of consciousness are painting, gardening, listening to music, writing, or exercising.

Hypnosis and meditation are activities specifically intended to alter a person's state of consciousness. But participation in a rigorous sport or an intense religious ceremony can also lead to an altered state of consciousness.

Here's a situation you've likely heard about or even experienced yourself: A marathon runner goes from feeling pain and fatigue to being euphoric and feeling a glorious release of energy. Commonly known as runner's high, this state is partially caused by physiological processes (especially endorphin release; see study unit 2.3). It also occurs due to a shift in the person's state of consciousness. Religious ceremonies can create similar alterations in consciousness. Indeed, such rituals often involve chanting, dancing, or other behaviors as a way for people to lose themselves in religious ecstasy. Like meditation, religious ecstasy directs attention away from the self and allows the practitioners to focus on their spiritual awareness (**Figure 3.22**).

One psychological theory about such peak experiences is based on the concept of **flow**, "a particular kind of experience that is so engrossing and enjoyable [that it is] worth doing for its own sake even though it may have no consequence outside itself" (Csikszentmihalyi, 1999, p. 824). Flow is an altered state of consciousness in that you lose track of time, forget about your problems, and fail to notice other things going on (Csikszentmihalyi, 1990). Flow experiences have been reported during many activities, including playing music (O'Neil, 1999), playing a moderately challenging version of the computer game *Tetris* (Keller & Bless, 2008), participating in sports (Jackson, Thomas, Marsh, & Smethurst, 2001), and simply doing satisfying jobs (Demerouti, 2006). Flow experiences may bring personal fulfillment and make life worth living (Csikszentmihalyi, 2014). To see if you can experience the positive effects of flow, see Try It Yourself.

ESCAPING THE SELF Our conscious thoughts can be dominated by worries, frustrations, and feelings of personal failure. Sometimes people get tired of dealing with life's problems and try to make themselves feel better through activities that let them "escape" life. Potential flow activities such as sports or work may help people escape thinking about their problems, but people engage in such activities mainly to feel fulfilled. The difference is between escaping and engaging. Sometimes people choose to escape the self rather than engage with life. To forget their troubles, they drink alcohol, take drugs, play video games, watch television, surf the Web, text, and so on. The selective appeal of escapist entertainment is that it distracts people from reflecting on their problems or their failures. That distraction helps people avoid feeling bad about themselves.

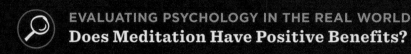

EVALUATING PSYCHOLOGY IN THE REAL WORLD
Does Meditation Have Positive Benefits?

If you are like most students, at some point you will feel some stress and worry, whether it is about school, work, family, friends, or a health situation. Suppose that you want to learn about reducing stress and worry. If you search on the Internet, you will find many possible approaches, including this one on how meditation may alter consciousness in ways that can reduce anxiety (http://www.npr.org/sections/health-shots/2014/01/07/260470831/mindfulness-meditation-can-help-relieve-anxiety-and-depression).

The National Public Radio Web site is a reliable news source, right? Should you accept what the article says? Read the version excerpted below.

ACTIVITY: To determine if you should accept the claim in this news article, review the Learning Tip on p. 7 and follow these steps:

Step 1 What is the claim I am being asked to accept?

Step 2 What evidence, if any, is provided to support the claim?

Step 3 Given the evidence, what are the most reasonable conclusions about the claim?

If you have rejected the claim or found the evidence lacking, why did you do so? If you have found that the evidence supports the claim, how might this information change how you think and act?

Mindfulness Meditation Can Help Relieve Anxiety and Depression

People are increasingly turning to mindfulness meditation to manage health issues, and meditation classes are being offered through schools and hospitals.

But doctors have questioned whether this ancient Eastern practice really offers measurable health benefits. A fresh review of the evidence should help sort that out.

Meditation does help manage anxiety, depression and pain, according to the 47 studies analyzed in *JAMA Internal Medicine*. . . , but does not appear to help with other problems, including substance abuse, sleep and weight.

"We have moderate confidence that mindfulness practices have a beneficial effect," wrote the author of the paper, Dr. Madhav Goyal of Johns Hopkins School of Medicine. . . . He says the positive effects on anxiety, depression and pain can be modest, but are seen across multiple studies.

"It was surprising to see that with so little training [about 2.5 hours of meditation practice per week] we were still seeing consistent effects," Goyal wrote.

One type of mindfulness training that was used in many of the research studies is called Mindfulness-Based Stress Reduction (or MBSR). It's typically taught in eight sessions.

Think of it as Buddhist meditation "but without the Buddhism," says Jon Kabat-Zinn, the father of MBSR. It's completely secular.

The focus of mindfulness meditation is to train the brain to stay in the moment. To do this, practitioners are taught to let go of the regrets of the past as well as anxieties about the future....

In one breast cancer study, researchers enrolled 163 women with stage 1 or stage 2 breast cancer. The women were randomized to either an

8-week mindfulness-based stress reduction class or to other kinds of more standard supportive care.

Techniques taught during the meditation class included visualizations to help shift attention away from thoughts that cause anxiety.

One technique is called the body scan. This is where you lie back on a mat and the teacher has you check in with each part of your body

You're told to relax all the tension in your jaws, then your neck, your shoulders, and so on, down the body.

The point is to stop the mind from wandering off and to connect with your body. Do your toes feel colder than the rest of your body? Are you feeling resistance in any part of the body? The teacher guides participants to tune in.

After four months, the women who meditated experienced significant improvements in what the researchers called quality of life and coping outcomes, compared to the women in other groups....

In addition, the meta-analysis found little evidence that meditation programs could help treat substance abuse, sleep or weight issues.

But the researchers concluded that meditation has no harmful side effects. And it's free and something people can easily do at home....

FIGURE 3.23

Escapist Activities

Simple entertainment can shift toward obsession when a person continually tries to escape from problems.

Some escapist activities—such as running or reading—tend to have positive effects. Others tend to be relatively harmless distractions. Still others tend to come at great personal expense (**Figure 3.23**). For example, people obsessively playing online games such as *World of Warcraft* have lost their jobs and even their marriages. In South Korea in 2010, Kim Jae-beom and his common-law wife, Kim Yun-jeong, reportedly spent every night raising a virtual daughter as part of a role-playing game. At the same time, they neglected their 3-month-old daughter to the point that she died of starvation. Some ways of escaping the self can also be associated with self-destructive behaviors, such as binge eating, unsafe sex, and, at the extreme, suicide. According to the social psychologist Roy Baumeister (1991), people engage in such behaviors because they want to escape their problems by reducing self-awareness. The state of being in lowered self-awareness may reduce long-term planning, reduce meaningful thinking, and help bring about uninhibited actions. The next section of this chapter looks at a common way people try to escape their problems—namely, using drugs or alcohol to create an altered state of consciousness.

 How Do Hypnosis, Meditation, and Flow Affect Consciousness?

To make sure you learned what you just read, write answers to the following questions and check your answers.

3.9 Can anyone be hypnotized?

3.10 Suppose a person who is meditating focuses on thoughts of waves rolling onto a beautiful beach. Is the person practicing concentrative meditation or mindfulness meditation?

3.11 What is flow?

See Appendix B for answers to the red Q questions.

How Do Drugs Alter Consciousness?

Throughout history and across all cultures, people have discovered that ingesting certain substances can alter their mental states. Some of those altered states of consciousness can be similar to the flow experience described in study unit 3.11. Others can be very pleasant for a brief period. However, some of those mental states, especially over the long term, can have negative consequences, including addiction, injury, or death. According to the United Nations Office on Drugs and Crime (2013a), upward of 317 million people around the globe use illicit drugs each year. This section looks at the effects of drug use from the perspective of psychology.

3.12 Psychoactive Drugs Affect the Brain

 3.12 LEARNING GOAL ACTIVITIES

To maximize your learning, complete the following learning goal activities.

a. Understand all bold and italic terms by writing explanations of them in your own words.

b. Understand psychoactive drugs by naming the four classes of psychoactive drugs and explaining how each class creates an altered state of consciousness.

If you drank coffee, tea, or a caffeinated soda within the past few hours, you may be reading under the influence of a drug. When people think of drugs, they often think of illegal ones. But psychoactive drugs are any mind-altering substances that change the brain's neurochemistry by activating neurotransmitter systems. So even caffeinated beverages are psychoactive drugs. To consider the effects of everyday psychoactive drugs, see Has It Happened to You? on p. 116.

There are four main classes of drugs that create altered states of consciousness (Table 3.2). Some of these drugs have legitimate medical uses, but all of them are commonly abused outside of treatment. **Stimulants** increase behavior and mental activity. By contrast, **depressants** decrease behavior and mental activity. **Opioids** reduce pain, but also provide pleasure. **Hallucinogens** change perceptions, thoughts, and emotions. They may also increase or decrease behavior or mental activity. This section considers a few common psychoactive drugs and describes how the effects of a particular drug on a user depend on which neurotransmitter systems it activates.

STIMULANTS Stimulants activate the sympathetic nervous system, increasing heart rate and blood pressure. They improve mood, but they also make people restless, and they disrupt sleep. Many substances act as stimulants, even though the effects are often mild. For instance, coffee, soda, and energy drinks often contain moderate doses of the stimulant caffeine, but those doses can add up if someone has several drinks in a day. Drinking these beverages at night commonly interferes with sleep. Chocolate contains a chemical similar to caffeine that produces stimulating effects. The drug nicotine, found in cigarettes (and e-cigarettes), is also a stimulant. More-powerful stimulants include cocaine and amphetamines. Amphetamines are found in some drugs used to treat attention-deficit/hyperactivity disorder (ADHD; discussed at the start of Chapter 2; in study units 2.1, 2.7, and 2.11; and extensively in Chapter 15). Students sometimes take amphetamines, such as Adderall, to help them study. The majority of college students report knowing someone who has used a nonprescribed stimulant as a study aid (Weyandt et al., 2013).

stimulants
Psychoactive drugs that result in an altered state of consciousness by increasing behavior and mental activity.

depressants
Psychoactive drugs that cause an altered state of consciousness by decreasing behavior and mental activity.

opioids
Psychoactive drugs that create an altered state of consciousness by reducing pain and producing pleasure.

hallucinogens
Psychoactive drugs that create an altered state of consciousness by affecting perceptual experiences and evoking sensory images even without sensory input.

TABLE 3.2
Four Classes of Psychoactive Drugs

Class of Drug	Examples of Specific Drugs	Psychological Effect(s)	Neurotransmitter System(s)
Stimulants	Amphetamines, methamphetamine (meth), cocaine, nicotine, caffeine	Increase behavior and mental activity	Dopamine, norepinephrine, acetylcholine (nicotine), adenosine (caffeine)
Depressants	Anti-anxiety drugs (such as benzodiazepines), alcohol	Decrease behavior and mental activity	GABA
Opioids	Heroin, morphine, codeine	Reduce pain and bring pleasure	Endorphins
Hallucinogens	LSD, PCP, peyote, psilocybin mushrooms	Change perceptions, thoughts, and emotions	Serotonin (LSD, peyote, psilocybin), glutamate (PCP)
	MDMA (also acts as a stimulant)	MDMA may also increase behavior and mental activity	Serotonin, dopamine, norepinephrine (MDMA)
	Marijuana (also can be a stimulant or depressant)	Marijuana may also increase or decrease behavior and mental activity	Cannabinoid (marijuana)

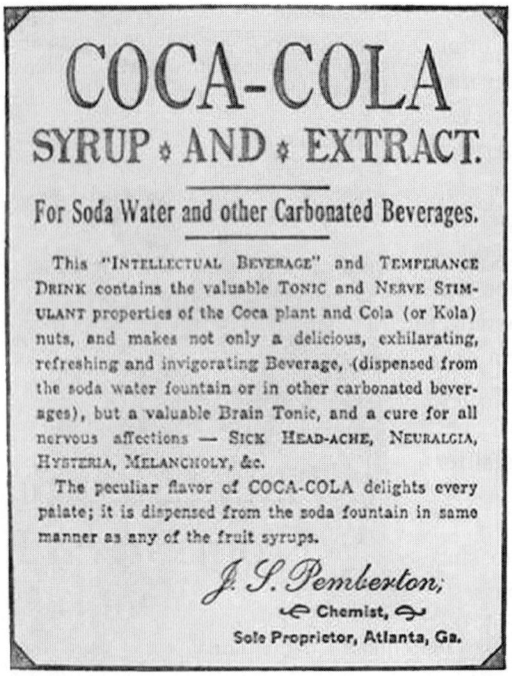

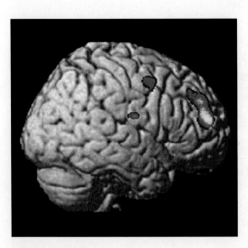

COCA-COLA
SYRUP ⚬ AND ⚬ EXTRACT.

For Soda Water and other Carbonated Beverages.

This "INTELLECTUAL BEVERAGE" and TEMPERANCE DRINK contains the valuable TONIC and NERVE STIMULANT properties of the Coca plant and Cola (or Kola) nuts, and makes not only a delicious, exhilarating, refreshing and invigorating Beverage, (dispensed from the soda water fountain or in other carbonated beverages), but a valuable Brain Tonic, and a cure for all nervous affections — SICK HEAD-ACHE, NEURALGIA, HYSTERIA, MELANCHOLY, &c.

The peculiar flavor of COCA-COLA delights every palate; it is dispensed from the soda fountain in same manner as any of the fruit syrups.

J. S. Pemberton;
⚬ Chemist, ⚬
Sole Proprietor, Atlanta, Ga.

FIGURE 3.24
Early Coke Ad
This advertisement's claim that Coca-Cola is "a valuable Brain Tonic" may have been made because the company included cocaine in the drink before 1906.

FIGURE 3.25
Methamphetamine's Effects on the Brain
This image is a combination of the brain scans from 29 methamphetamine addicts. The red and yellow areas represent the brain damage that typically occurs in the frontal lobes because of methamphetamine abuse (Kim et al., 2006). Such damage may explain the cognitive problems that occur with methamphetamine use.

Most stimulants work by letting the neurotransmitter dopamine (see study unit 2.3) remain in synapses longer, which prolongs the impact of the dopamine. However, sometimes stimulants also increase the release of dopamine by neurons (Fibiger, 1993). Dopamine seems to be involved in drug use in two ways. First, the increased dopamine is associated with greater reward, or increased liking (Volkow, Wang, & Baler, 2011). Second, the increased dopamine leads to a greater desire to take a drug, even if that drug does not produce pleasure. Thus, sometimes addicts *want* a drug even if they do not *like* the effects of the drug (Kringelbach & Berridge, 2009). Available evidence suggests that dopamine is particularly important for the wanting aspect of addiction.

Cocaine is a stimulant derived from the leaves of the coca bush, which grows primarily in South America. Cocaine has a long history of legal use in America. John Pemberton, a pharmacist from Georgia, was impressed with cocaine's effects. In 1886, he added the drug to soda water for easy ingestion, creating Coca-Cola (**Figure 3.24**). In 1906, the U.S. government outlawed cocaine, so it was removed from the drink. To this day, coca leaves are still used in the making of Coke, but the active ingredient has been removed. Illegal use of cocaine occurs when the drug is inhaled (snorted) as a powder or smoked in the form of crack cocaine. Users experience a wave of confidence and feel good, alert, energetic, sociable, and wide awake. Cocaine produces its stimulating effects by increasing the concentration of dopamine in synapses. These short-term effects are especially intense for crack cocaine users. But habitual use of cocaine in large quantities can lead to paranoia, psychotic behavior, and violence (Ottieger, Tressel, Inciardi, & Rosales, 1992).

Methamphetamine (meth) is also a stimulant, as it breaks down into amphetamine in the body. Meth is the world's second most commonly used illicit drug, after marijuana (Barr et al., 2006). However, the use of meth may be declining (Gonzales, Mooney, & Rawson, 2010). This drug was first developed in the early twentieth century as a nasal decongestant, but its recreational use became popular in the 1980s. The National Institute of Drug Abuse (2014) estimates that around 4 percent of the U.S. population has tried methamphetamine. One factor that has encouraged use of this drug and may explain its popularity is how easy it is to make using common over-the-counter drugs and simple lab methods. By blocking the reuptake of dopamine and increasing its release, methamphetamine yields much higher levels of dopamine in the synapse. Methamphetamine stays in the body and brain much longer than, say, cocaine, so its effects are prolonged. Over time, methamphetamine damages various brain structures—including the frontal lobes, where complex thought is processed (**Figure 3.25**). The drug's effects on the temporal lobes and the limbic system may explain the harm done to memory and emotion in long-term users (Kim et al., 2006; Thompson et al., 2004). Methamphetamine also causes considerable damage to the rest of the body (**Figure 3.26**).

DEPRESSANTS In contrast to stimulants, depressants reduce behavioral and mental activity by slowing down the central nervous system. Anti-anxiety drugs, such as benzodiazepines, commonly given to calm people and to reduce worry, are depressants. In large doses, depressants can cause sleep, which is why they are sometimes referred to as sedatives. (Chapter 15 discusses the use of anti-anxiety drugs to treat psychological disorders.)

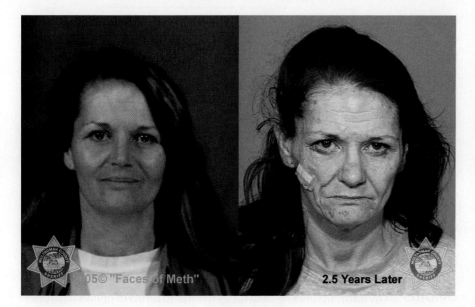

2005© "Faces of Meth"   2.5 Years Later

Methamphetamine's Effects on the Person
These before-and-after photos dramatically illustrate physical damage from methamphetamine. When the photo on the left was taken, Theresa Baxter was 42 and not a methamphetamine addict. The photo on the right was taken less than 3 years later, after Baxter was arrested for crimes she committed to support her addiction.

Depressants produce their effects by activating GABA receptors. As you learned in study unit 2.3, GABA is the primary inhibitory neurotransmitter in the brain. Through their effects on GABA receptors, depressants inhibit neural activity, which may be why they are experienced as relaxing. Alcohol is the most widely used depressant—in fact, it is the most widely used and abused drug.

Perhaps you know someone who drank a lot of alcohol, experienced a blackout, and can't remember the details. Alcohol is a depressant that, like other addictive drugs, may offer its rewards by activating dopamine receptors. But it also interferes with the neurochemical processes involved in memory, and memory loss can follow extreme alcohol intake. Heavy long-term alcohol intake can cause extensive brain damage. Korsakoff's syndrome, a disorder sometimes caused by alcoholism, is characterized by both severe memory loss and mental decline.

Many societies have a love/hate relationship with alcohol. On the one hand, moderate drinking is an accepted part of social interaction and may even be good for health. On the other hand, alcohol is a major contributor to many societal problems, such as spousal abuse and other forms of violence. Although the percentage of traffic fatalities due to alcohol is dropping, alcohol is a factor in more than one-third of fatal accidents (Mayhew, Brown, & Simpson, 2002). One study found that approximately one-third of college students reported having had sex during a drinking binge, and the heaviest drinkers were likely to have had sex with a new or casual partner (Leigh & Schafer, 1993), thus increasing their risk for exposure to sexually transmitted diseases. The overall cost of problem drinking in the United States—including lost productivity due to employee absence, health care expenses, and so on—is estimated to be more than $100 billion each year.

In every region of the world, men drink a lot more alcohol than women across a wide variety of measures (for example, drinking versus not drinking, heavy drinking versus occasional drinking, and alcohol-related disorders). Men are twice as likely to report binge drinking (having five or more drinks in one evening), chronic drinking, and recent alcohol intoxication (Patrick et al., 2013). Gender gaps in binge drinking may be smaller among university students (Swendsen et al., 2012).

Alan Marlatt is a leading researcher on substance abuse. Marlatt (1999) has noted that in many cultures, people view alcohol as the "magic elixir," capable of increasing social skills, sexual pleasure, confidence, and power. They anticipate that alcohol will have positive effects on their emotions and behavior. For example, people tend to think that alcohol reduces anxiety, so both light and heavy drinkers turn to alcohol after a difficult day. Alcohol *can* interfere with the way the brain processes suggestions of threats, so anxiety-provoking events may be less troubling when people are intoxicated. However, this effect occurs only if people drink *before* the anxiety-provoking events. In fact, according to the research, drinking after a hard day can increase people's focus on and obsession with their problems (Sayette, 1993). What's more, although moderate doses of alcohol are associated with more-positive moods, larger doses are associated with more-negative moods.

Expectations about alcohol's effects are learned very early in life, through observation. Children may see that people who drink seem to have a lot of fun and that drinking is an important part of many celebrations. Teenagers may view drinkers as sociable and grown up, two things they desperately want to be. Studies have shown that children who have very positive expectations about alcohol are more likely to start drinking and become heavy drinkers than children who do not share those expectations (Leigh & Stacy, 2004).

OPIOIDS The term "opioids" is used today to refer to forms of opium regardless of whether they are natural (for example, heroin, morphine, and codeine) or synthetic (for example, fentanyl and Vicodin). All of these opioid drugs produce feelings of relaxation, insensitivity to pain, and euphoria. Heroin provides a rush of intense pleasure that most addicts describe as similar to sexual orgasm. The rush evolves into a pleasant, relaxed stupor. Heroin and morphine are highly addictive, perhaps because they have dual physical effects. Specifically, they increase pleasure by binding with opiate receptors, and they increase wanting of the drug by indirectly activating dopamine receptors (Kuhn, Swartzwelder, & Wilson, 2003). As a result, people enjoy the experience and want to use the drug again (Berridge & Kringelbach, 2013).

Opioids have been used to relieve pain for hundreds of years. Indeed, before the twentieth century, heroin was widely available without a prescription and was marketed by Bayer, the aspirin company (**Figure 3.27**). The benefits of short-term opioid use to relieve severe pain seem clear. But long-term opioid use to relieve chronic pain is much more likely to lead to abuse or addiction than is short-term use (Ballantyne & LaForge, 2007). In addition, long-term use of opioids is associated with a number of neurological and cognitive deficits, such as attention and memory problems (Gruber, Silveri, & Yurgelun-Todd, 2007). In fact, as noted in study unit 2.3, during the past few decades an epidemic of opioid abuse has been growing. Most experts view the epidemic as resulting from the greater use of prescription opioids, such as Vicodin, for chronic pain (Compton, Jones, & Baldwin, 2016).

Many first responders now carry naloxone, an opioid antagonist, which can reverse opioid effects and help people survive an overdose. In 2015, the Federal Drug Administration (FDA) approved Narcan, a nasal spray containing naloxone that is easy to administer. Narcan is now available without prescription in a growing number of states. Unfortunately, some opioid users might be increasing their risky drug use because of the widespread availability of Narcan (Doleac & Mukherjee, 2018). The FDA is also establishing new guidelines for the safe and effective use of pain medications for the 9–12 million Americans who suffer chronic pain (Califf, Woodcock, & Ostroff, 2016). Clinicians need to be cautious in prescribing opioids, especially when the drugs will be used for long periods.

HALLUCINOGENS Hallucinogens alter sensation and perception, changing how users experience the world around them. One well-known hallucinogen is

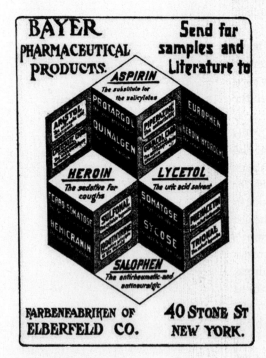

FIGURE 3.27

Early Heroin Ad

Before 1904, Bayer advertised heroin as "the sedative for coughs."

lysergic acid diethylamide (LSD). LSD was discovered in 1938 and is made from a chemical found in certain types of fungus, called ergot, that grow on rye and other wheats. It is usually taken orally, and the drug experience, informally referred to as a "trip," lasts for about 12 hours. LSD changes sensory experiences and can produce extreme hallucinations, which can be pleasurable or unpleasurable. People using LSD also have a distorted sense of time. Many other substances, such as certain plants and fungi, have psychedelic properties. For example, eating the top part of the peyote cactus or certain types of mushrooms, such as psilocybin mushrooms, produces hallucinogenic effects. These psychedelic substances have been used in various religious rites throughout history.

The most commonly used drugs with hallucinogenic effects are MDMA and marijuana. MDMA produces an energizing effect similar to that of stimulants, but it also causes slight hallucinations. The street version of MDMA is sold as pills named ecstasy or Molly, but these pills often contain other chemicals in addition to MDMA. The drug first became popular in the 1990s among young adults in nightclubs and at all-night parties known as raves. According to the National Institute of Drug Abuse (2014), ecstasy use by high school students increased from 3.7 percent to 4.7 percent between 2009 and 2010.

Compared with amphetamines, MDMA is associated with less dopamine activity and more serotonin activity. The serotonin release may explain ecstasy's hallucinogenic properties. Research on animals has shown that MDMA can cause damage to a number of brain regions, particularly the prefrontal cortex and the hippocampus (Halpin, Collins, & Yamamoto, 2014). Studies with humans show evidence of a range of impairments from long-term ecstasy use, especially memory problems and a diminished ability to perform complex tasks (Parrott, 2013). Of course, any drug can be toxic in large doses or when taken for long periods. Currently, controversy exists over whether occasional recreational use of ecstasy by itself causes long-term damage. Some ecstasy users take very high doses or regularly use other drugs, such as methamphetamine, that are known to be neurotoxic (Gallagher et al., 2014). Growing evidence suggests that MDMA may have potential benefits for use in the treatment of posttraumatic stress disorder (Doblin et al., 2014; you will learn more about this disorder in Chapter 14). The drug promotes feelings of compassion and trust and reduces the negative emotions that people have about their traumatic experiences even after the drug wears off (Mithoefer et al., 2013). When used as part of treatment, MDMA does not have negative effects on health or cognition (White, 2014).

One concern is that many pills being sold as ecstasy or Molly contain other dangerous chemicals, such as drugs used to anaesthetize animals. Even when they contain MDMA, the doses vary widely, increasing the likelihood of overdose (Morefield, Keane, Felgate, White, & Irvine, 2011; Wood et al., 2011). Since the early 2000s, many concertgoers have died after consuming what they believed to be ecstasy or Molly (**Figure 3.28**).

Marijuana consists of the dried leaves and flower buds of one type of cannabis plant. It is the most widely used illicit drug in the world. Marijuana is unique because it can be categorized as a stimulant (for example, by increasing appetite), a depressant (when it makes people feel mellow and tired), or a hallucinogen. The psychoactive ingredient in marijuana is tetrahydrocannabinol (THC). This chemical produces a relaxed mental state, an uplifted or contented mood, and some perceptual and cognitive distortions. Marijuana users report that THC creates an altered state of consciousness because it makes perceptions more vivid, and some say it especially affects taste. However, most first-time marijuana users do not experience the "high" felt by more experienced users. Novice smokers might use inefficient techniques, they might have

FIGURE 3.28

Deaths from MDMA

Concertgoers are shown at Electric Zoo 2013, a Labor Day weekend of electronic dance music in New York City. Two attendees died after taking MDMA sold as Molly, and the festival was ended a day early.

addiction
Compulsive drug craving and use, despite the negative consequences of using the drug.

tolerance
A physical aspect of addiction that occurs when a person needs to take larger doses of a drug to experience its effect.

withdrawal
A physical and psychological aspect of addiction that occurs when a person experiences anxiety, tension, and cravings after stopping use of an addictive drug.

trouble inhaling, or both. Users apparently must learn how to appreciate the drug's effects (Kuhn, Swartzwelder, & Wilson, 2003). In this way, marijuana differs from most other drugs. Generally, the first time someone uses a drug other than marijuana, the effects are very strong, and in later uses the person has to use more of the drug to get the same effect.

Marijuana is also used for its medicinal properties. For instance, cancer patients undergoing chemotherapy report that marijuana is effective for overcoming nausea. Nearly 1 in 4 AIDS patients reports using marijuana to relieve nausea and pain (Prentiss, Power, Balmas, Tzuang, & Israelski, 2004). The medical use of marijuana is controversial due to the possibility that chronic use can cause health problems or lead to abuse of the drug. Some countries and American states have concluded that such risks are offset by a reduction in the problems created by criminal activity associated with illegal drug use. The majority of states allow medical use of marijuana, and many states have legalized recreational use.

3.13 Addiction Has Physical and Psychological Aspects

 3.13 LEARNING GOAL ACTIVITIES

To maximize your learning, complete the following learning goal activities.

a. Understand all bold and italic terms by writing explanations of them in your own words.

b. Analyze the physical and psychological aspects of addiction by explaining tolerance (physical) and withdrawal (physical and psychological) in your own words.

Drugs are a mixed blessing. If they are the right ones, taken under the right circumstances, they can relieve severe pain or a moderate headache. They can help people suffering from depression lead more satisfying lives. But many of these same drugs can be used for "recreational" purposes: to alter physical sensations, consciousness, thoughts, moods, and behaviors in ways that users believe are desirable. This recreational use can sometimes have negative consequences, including addiction and even death. More Americans are now killed by drug overdoses than by traffic accidents (**Figure 3.29**), and the majority of those overdoses result from opioid addiction (Rudd, Aleshire, Zibbell, & Gladden, 2016). We see these negative effects in the news and our own communities.

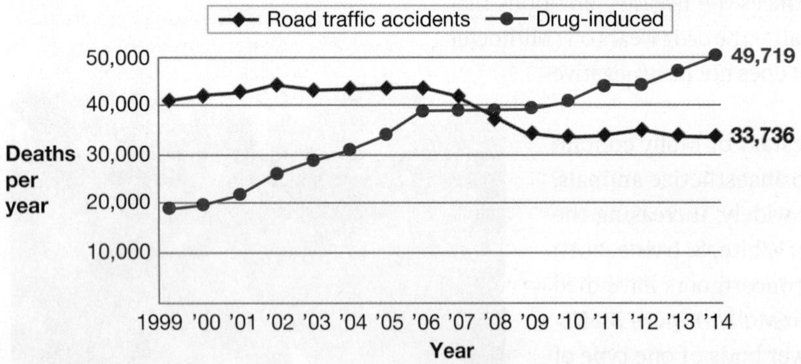

FIGURE 3.29

Fatal Overdoses

In the United States, the number of annual deaths due to drug use has increased dramatically since 1999 and has become greater than the number of deaths due to traffic accidents.

Deaths per year

—◆— Road traffic accidents   —●— Drug-induced

50,000 — 49,719
40,000
30,000 — 33,736
20,000
10,000

1999 '00 '01 '02 '03 '04 '05 '06 '07 '08 '09 '10 '11 '12 '13 '14
Year

PHYSICAL AND PSYCHOLOGICAL ASPECTS OF ADDICTION Addiction is behavior that remains compulsive despite its negative consequences. Drug addiction has physical and psychological factors. In physical dependence, a user develops **tolerance** to the drug. The person then needs to consume more of that drug to achieve the same subjective effect (**Figure 3.30a**). If the user fails to ingest the drug, that person will experience symptoms of **withdrawal**. This physical and psychological state is characterized by anxiety, tension, and craving for the drug.

The physical symptoms of withdrawal vary widely from drug to drug and from individual to individual. The symptoms commonly include nausea, chills, body aches, and tremors. A person can be psychologically dependent, however, without showing tolerance or withdrawal. Though the focus here is on addiction to substances that create an altered state of consciousness, people can also become psychologically dependent on behaviors, such as shopping or gambling (**Figure 3.30b**).

How do people become addicted? One central factor appears to be dopamine activity in the limbic system (see study units 2.3 and 2.6, respectively), which underlies the rewarding properties of taking drugs (Baler & Volkow, 2006). Because dopamine is a powerful reinforcer, any behavior that increases dopamine activity is likely to be repeated. Activating dopamine receptors leads to pleasure and the desire to take more of the drug.

It is possible that genes predispose some people to be more responsive to the reinforcing properties of drugs, making them more vulnerable to addiction. While there is some evidence for genetic components of addiction, especially alcoholism, there is little direct evidence for a single "addiction" or "alcoholism" gene. Instead, people inherit a cluster of characteristics. Inherited factors such as risk-taking and impulsivity, a reduced concern about personal harm, or a predisposition to finding chemical substances pleasurable may make some people more likely to explore drugs and enjoy them.

WHO IS LIKELY TO BECOME ADDICTED?   Only about 5–10 percent of people who use drugs become addicted. Indeed, more than 90 million Americans have experimented with illicit drugs, yet most of them use drugs only occasionally or try them for a while and then stop. Further, Jonathan Shedler and Jack Block (1990) found that people who had experimented with drugs as adolescents were better adjusted in adulthood than people who had never tried them and people who were heavy users. This finding does not suggest, however, that everyone should try drugs or that parents should encourage their kids to experiment with drugs. We cannot know in advance how an individual will react to a drug.

Though we can't predict who will become addicted, we can identify some adolescents who are especially likely to experiment with illegal drugs and to abuse alcohol. Children who are attracted to novelty and risk-taking and have poor relationships with their parents are more likely to associate with troublemaking peers, smoke, and use drugs, including alcohol (Wills, DuHamel, & Vaccaro, 1995). It is also possible that an inherited predisposition to seeking out strong sensations may predict behaviors, such as associating with drug users, that increase the possibility of substance abuse.

Does the family or social environment determine drug use? Social learning theorists have emphasized the roles of parents, the mass media, and peers, including self-identification with high-risk groups (for example, "stoners" or "druggies"). Teenagers want to fit in somewhere, even with groups that society perceives as deviant. Children also imitate the behavior of role models, especially those they admire or identify with. Consider children who, during their preschool and elementary school years, have seen their parents drinking alcohol routinely. These children tend to have positive attitudes about alcohol and to begin drinking early (Sher, Grekin, & Williams, 2005). Understanding the psychology of addiction is important in many aspects of life, as discussed in Putting Psychology to Work on p. 127.

FIGURE 3.30

Physical Dependence Versus Psychological Dependence

In addiction, both types of dependence can force people to go to extremes. **(a)** In physical dependence, a person develops a tolerance to the effects of a drug. As a result, the person must consume more of the drug to prevent the adverse physical side effects of withdrawal. Someone addicted to alcohol might even abuse products that contain alcohol, such as cough syrup. **(b)** Casinos encourage a psychological dependence on gambling. People suffering from this dependence spend increasing amounts of time and money gambling, to the point where their lives are seriously disrupted.

How Do Drugs Alter Consciousness?

To make sure you learned what you just read, write answers to the following questions and check your answers.

3.12 Caffeine, nicotine, amphetamines, meth, and cocaine are examples of what class of psychoactive drug and have what effects on consciousness?

3.13 What are the two physical aspects of addiction?

See Appendix B for answers to the red Q questions.

BIG PICTURE

Want to earn a better grade on your test? Go to **INQUIZITIVE** to practice actively with this chapter's content and get personalized feedback along the way.

What Does It Mean to Be Conscious?

3.1 Consciousness Is Your Subjective Experience

Review the learning goal activities on p. 89. Consciousness is how the brain lets you be aware of and experience the external world and your internal mental activity. Your level of consciousness reflects the amount of your awareness, which can range from conscious to unconscious. Your state of consciousness reflects the clarity of your awareness, which can range from a normal waking state of consciousness to an altered state of consciousness, which can be either very vivid or quite fuzzy.

3.2 Consciousness Results from Brain Activity

Review the learning goal activities on p. 90. Most psychologists reject dualism, the idea that the mind and the brain are separate. Instead they accept materialism, the idea that consciousness results from brain activity. According to the global workspace model, conscious experiences of specific types of information are a result of activity in five regions of the brain: (1) prefrontal cortex, (2) primary motor cortex, (3) parietal lobes, (4) occipital lobes, and (5) temporal lobes. Brain damage to one or more of these regions will affect consciousness, as seen in traumatic brain injuries (TBIs) and comas.

3.3 Consciousness Involves Attention

Review the learning goal activities on p. 93. Attention is the focusing of mental resources on specific information needed to perform a task, which allows us to be aware of the information.

Easy and well-learned tasks can be performed using automatic processing, which does not require much attention. New or difficult tasks require controlled processing, which requires more attention. However, some information escapes our awareness, as happens with change blindness.

3.4 Unconscious Processing Sometimes Affects Behavior

Review the learning goal activities on p. 95. Subliminal perception is the processing of stimuli without conscious awareness. Such processing can influence basic thinking and behavior for only short periods of time. Research on people with split brains shows that the consciousness of each hemisphere can be assessed separately. A left hemisphere interpreter tries to make sense of actions produced by the right hemisphere.

KEY TERMS

consciousness (p. 89)
conscious (p. 89)
unconscious (p. 89)
normal waking state of consciousness (p. 90)
altered state of consciousness (p. 90)
global workspace model (p. 91)
attention (p. 93)
change blindness (p. 94)
subliminal perception (p. 95)
split brain (p. 97)

How Does Sleep Affect Consciousness?

3.5 Consciousness Changes During Sleep

Review the learning goal activities on p. 100. Sleep/wake cycles operate according to circadian rhythms, which are produced and maintained by multiple brain regions. Sleep has four stages: (1) stage 1 sleep, (2) stage 2 sleep, (3) slow-wave sleep, and (4) REM sleep. Each stage is characterized by brain activity that is the basis for how the sleeper experiences that stage. During sleep, a sleeper's consciousness changes, becoming less aware of thoughts and the external world, then regaining awareness. Even in slow-wave sleep, the sleeper remains somewhat aware and able to respond to stimuli when necessary.

3.6 People Dream While Sleeping

Review the learning goal activities on p. 102. Because REM dreams and non-REM dreams each affect the activation of different brain regions, dreams are different during REM sleep than during non-REM sleep. Sigmund Freud believed that dreams represent unconscious attempts to fulfill certain wishes the dreamer has. Evidence does not support this view. According to activation-synthesis theory, dreams result from the brain's attempts to make sense of random brain activity during sleep.

3.7 Sleep Is an Adaptive Behavior

Review the learning goal activities on p. 105. Three reasons have been proposed to explain why sleeping is adaptive and beneficial. (1) According to restorative theory, sleep lets the body, including the brain, rest and restore itself. (2) According to circadian rhythm theory, sleep protects animals from harm at times of the day when they are most susceptible to danger. (3) According to consolidation theory, sleep facilitates learning through the strengthening of neural connections. Over time, losing sleep impairs thoughts and behavior.

3.8 Sleep Disorders Are Relatively Common Throughout Life

Review the learning goal activities on p. 107. Five sleep disorders are (1) insomnia (an inability to sleep that causes significant problems in daily living), (2) sleep apnea (stopping breathing during sleep), (3) narcolepsy (extreme tiredness and falling asleep at inappropriate times), (4) REM behavior disorder (REM sleep without paralysis so people act out dreams), and (5) sleepwalking (somnambulism).

KEY TERMS

circadian rhythms (p. 100)
melatonin (p. 100)
stage 1 sleep (p. 101)
stage 2 sleep (p. 101)
slow-wave sleep (p. 101)
REM sleep (p. 102)
dreams (p. 103)
activation-synthesis theory (p. 104)
insomnia (p. 107)
sleep apnea (p. 108)
narcolepsy (p. 108)

How Do Hypnosis, Meditation, and Flow Alter Consciousness?

3.9 Attention to Suggestions May Alter Consciousness in Hypnosis

Review the learning goal activities on p. 110. Scientists debate whether hypnotized people merely play the role they are expected to play (sociocognitive theory of hypnosis) or truly experience an altered state of consciousness (dissociation theory of hypnosis). Patterns of brain activity suggest that people who have been hypnotized experience a shift to an altered state of consciousness and are not simply faking it. The existence of hypnotic analgesia, reduced pain perception during hypnosis, also suggests hypnosis creates an altered state of consciousness.

3.10 Meditation Alters Consciousness and Brain Functioning

Review the learning goal activities on p. 112. The goal of meditation is to bring about a state of deep calmness. An altered state of consciousness may be achieved through three forms of meditation: (1) concentrative, (2) mindfulness, and (3) transcendental. Meditation appears to have many benefits for physical and mental health.

3.11 People Can Lose Themselves in Enjoyable Activities

Review the learning goal activities on p. 114. When people engage in an enjoyable activity to the point of becoming completely absorbed, they are experiencing an altered state of consciousness called flow. Flow is experienced as a positive state. In contrast to activities that generate flow, activities used to escape the self or reduce self-awareness can have harmful consequences.

KEY TERMS

hypnosis (p. 111)
sociocognitive theory of hypnosis (p. 111)
dissociation theory of hypnosis (p. 111)
meditation (p. 113)
flow (p. 114)

How Do Drugs Alter Consciousness?

3.12 Psychoactive Drugs Affect the Brain

Review the learning goal activities on p. 116. People can create altered states of consciousness by using psychoactive drugs that change the way they think, feel, and act. Psychoactive drugs can be divided into four categories based on their psychological effects. (1) Stimulants—including caffeine, nicotine, cocaine, amphetamines, and meth—increase behavior and mental activity. (2) Depressants—including anti-anxiety drugs and alcohol—decrease behavior and mental activity. (3) Opioids—including heroin, morphine, codeine, fentanyl, and Vicodin—produce relaxation, pain reduction, and pleasure. (4) Hallucinogens—such as LSD, peyote, psilocybin mushrooms, MDMA (ecstasy or Molly), and marijuana—change perceptions, thoughts, and emotions, but may also increase or decrease behavior and mental activity.

3.13 Addiction Has Physical and Psychological Aspects

Review the learning goal activities on p. 122. Excessive drug use can lead to addiction and even death, as seen in the current opioid epidemic. Addiction is characterized by physical dependence (involving tolerance and withdrawal) and by psychological dependence (which can involve withdrawal). Addiction is influenced by personality factors, such as sensation seeking. Environment, or the context in which drug use occurs, also influences addiction.

KEY TERMS

stimulants (p. 117)
depressants (p. 117)
opioids (p. 117)
hallucinogens (p. 117)
addiction (p. 122)
tolerance (p. 122)
withdrawal (p. 122)

CHAPTER 3 SELF-QUIZ

To make sure you learned the information in this chapter, write answers to the following questions and check your answers. **See Appendix B for answers to the self-quiz.**

1. Matilda's boyfriend just sent her a beautiful teddy bear as a gift. According to the global workspace model, Matilda's awareness of how the teddy bear looks is most likely due to _____.
   a. brain activity in her occipital lobe
   b. the fact that her corpus callosum has been cut
   c. the amount of REM sleep she got last night
   d. her being in an altered state of consciousness

2. When Fiona was a child, her grandmother taught her to make lasagna. Now, when Nicholas asks Fiona for her lasagna recipe, she realizes she doesn't know the measurements for the ingredients because she always "just makes it." Fiona's ability to cook lasagna without being aware of measuring the ingredients is best described as an example of _____.
   a. controlled processing
   b. the global workspace model
   c. automatic processing
   d. subliminal perception

3. Clark's corpus callosum was surgically cut to reduce epilepsy. When a picture of his dog is shown only to Clark's left hemisphere, he will be _____ to name the object as "dog" and will be _____ to use his left hand to pick up a toy dog out of a group of objects.
   a. able; able
   b. able; unable
   c. unable; unable
   d. unable; able

4. Leo is participating in a sleep study. During his sleep, his brain shows delta wave activity. At that point, the researchers wake him up, and he is very disoriented. When the researchers wake Leo up, he is most likely in _____ sleep.
   a. stage 2
   b. REM
   c. stage 1
   d. slow-wave

5. For spring break, you spend ten days with friends, going dancing late every night and not getting enough sleep. According to the consolidation theory of sleep, afterward you will _____.
   a. have trouble remembering things you did during spring break
   b. secrete more growth hormone to restore your body
   c. have fewer dreams for a while because of the REM rebound effect
   d. sleep less during the night for a while because your circadian rhythms have shifted

6. While sleeping, Kevin dreamed about being in a dancing competition. As he dreamed about doing dance moves, he kicked his foot against the wall. The kick was most likely due to _____.
   a. sleep apnea
   b. narcolepsy
   c. somnambulism
   d. REM behavior disorder

7. Steven goes to a hypnotism show with his friend Missy and is chosen to be brought on stage to be hypnotized. Missy believes in the dissociation theory of hypnosis, so she thinks that when Steven is hypnotized he will _____.
   a. only pretend to act how a hypnotized person should act
   b. NOT be able to experience hypnotic analgesia
   c. actually be in a trancelike state where he can't access his conscious awareness
   d. experience flow

8. Remy likes to go home after a hard day at work and relax in a chair, watching the fire roar in his fireplace. In these situations, he often feels "zoned out." His thoughts and the world around him seem very fuzzy and indistinct. Remy is most likely experiencing _____.
   a. withdrawal
   b. REM sleep
   c. an altered state of consciousness
   d. a posthypnotic suggestion

9. Vivian is under the influence of a psychoactive drug. She is experiencing changes in her emotions and perceptions. In particular, she sees in "Technicolor" because everything looks so vivid. Vivian is most likely experiencing an altered state of consciousness due to the effects of _____.
   a. stimulants
   b. hallucinogens
   c. depressants
   d. opioids

10. When Jerry began college, he rarely drank coffee, so it didn't take much coffee to get enough caffeine to make him feel energetic. But now Jerry must drink much more coffee to get enough caffeine to experience the same energy level. However, he experiences no negative side effects from drinking so much coffee. Taken together, this information most likely indicates that Jerry _____.

    a. has developed a tolerance for caffeine
    b. is experiencing flow when he drinks caffeine
    c. has become addicted to caffeine
    d. is experiencing caffeine withdrawal

PUTTING PSYCHOLOGY TO WORK

How Can Understanding Consciousness Help You in Your Job?

The death of the musician Prince, in 2016, was a high-profile example of opioid abuse (described in study unit 3.12). Prince reportedly used fentanyl and prescription medicine to relieve chronic pain. Other people use and abuse drugs for various reasons: stimulants to increase attention and endurance, alcohol to relax in social settings, or marijuana to alter mood or consciousness.

Although most people who report using recreational drugs can avoid becoming addicted, more than 22 million people are estimated to require treatment for drug and alcohol abuse (Substance Abuse and Mental Health Services Administration [SAMHSA], 2014). Because of this increasing need, job prospects for occupations involved in treating and preventing substance abuse are projected to grow by up to 20 percent in 2016–2026 (U.S. Bureau of Labor Statistics, 2017b).

Knowing how particular drugs affect consciousness and why some people become addicted can lead to a wide range of careers in substance abuse counseling and prevention. This material will give you insights into peoples' lives, such as the reasons they seek out and use particular drugs. If you are a psychiatric aide, for instance, you can use this information to improve the lives of addicts you work with, such as helping them in daily living skills and monitoring their treatment progress. Indeed, knowledge about addiction is valuable in many mental health settings, such as treatment clinics and community mental health centers, as well as at schools and prisons. Counselors in these settings evaluate the symptoms of an individual's drug addiction, create a treatment plan, and help the person develop the skills needed for recovery.

The material in this chapter is also useful in other jobs. For instance, if you work with athletes you need to understand how concussions harm the brain and negatively affect mental activity and behavior. You will know which signs indicate that further medical evaluation or treatment is important. Another theme in this chapter is how people are influenced by material that

captures their attention. This knowledge is useful in many kinds of design work. For example, roadways need to be designed so that drivers are not distracted and can attend to potential dangers. Web sites need to be designed to direct users' attention to various features.

Understanding circadian cycles and sleep patterns is useful in the travel or hospitality industry. For example, such information would help you set up hotel rooms to encourage sound sleeping. And in any job that involves shift work, understanding circadian cycles can help ease the burden of changing shifts. In the airline industry, such as at a job where you cross time zones, understanding sleep is valuable.

TAKEAWAY POINT: Understanding how changes in consciousness affect people is useful for many jobs. From being able to support and counsel addicts, to designing safe roadways and cozy hotel rooms, to knowing about circadian cycles so you can better schedule work shifts, employees can benefit from understanding the conscious (and less conscious) mind.

 You can look up job descriptions, education requirements, salaries, and more at the Bureau of Labor Statistics: www.bls.gov. Visit the site and start putting psychology to work!

4 Development Across the Life Span

WHO ARE YOU RIGHT NOW? Are you the same person you were at 13, and 8, and 3? Almost certainly the answer is no. As virtually all people do, you have changed in many ways over the years.

Now look at **Figure 4.1.** How old do you think the infant was? Her name was Brooke Greenberg, and in this photo she was 19 years old. She was being held by her younger sister, 16-year-old Carly. In 1993, Brooke was born prematurely. At first, she seemed to develop normally. But at about the age of 19 months, after various medical problems, Brooke stopped growing. Her brain also seemed to stop changing developmentally. In lots of ways, Brooke seemed to be "frozen" as a toddler.

BIG QUESTIONS

How Does Development Happen in the Womb?

How Do Infants and Children Develop?

How Do Adolescents Develop?

How Do Adults Develop?

FIGURE 4.1

Brooke Greenberg: The Infant Who Didn't Change

Brooke Greenberg was 19 years old here and was being held by her younger sister. In most ways, Brooke looked and acted like a toddler. The fact that Brooke did not grow or change may provide insight into "normal" human development.

Brooke was happy and laughed a lot. She enjoyed music and shopping trips to the mall, but she refused to engage in activities she didn't like. At such times, Brooke's family thought of her as a typically rebellious teenager. However, she couldn't speak, so she expressed herself with sounds like those an infant would make. She couldn't walk, so she traveled in a stroller. She had the bone development of a 10-year-old, but she still had all of her baby teeth. She wore diapers. Her family took care of Brooke her entire life. When she died, in 2013, she was 20 years old but still looked like a toddler.

Brooke's stalled development in many, but not all, areas baffled doctors over the years. They named the unknown cause of Brooke's disjointed development *Syndrome X.* Her condition was extremely rare, but by working to understand why Brooke did not develop and age, scientists may have begun to better understand the changes that occur throughout all of our lives.

How Does Development Happen in the Womb?

Brooke Greenberg gave us a rare opportunity to learn about how humans develop. Unlike Brooke, people normally change, but many of these changes happen so slowly that we don't notice them in ourselves or in people around us. The 2014 movie *Boyhood* gives us a fascinating opportunity to see what happens over 12 years in the lives of fictional characters: Mason Evans Jr.; his older sister, Samantha; and his parents, Olivia and Mason Sr. What's special about the movie is that it was actually filmed over 12 years, so we also see how the actors in the movie changed in real life. For example, the actor who played Mason Jr., Ellar Coltrane, began filming the movie at age 6 and ended at age 18 (**Figure 4.2**). According to Coltrane, the director of the movie, Richard Linklater, "would ask me about similar experiences that I had had to what Mason might be going through, and the different dynamics between me and friends, girlfriends or family members" (Bennett, 2014). In *Boyhood,* Linklater created a movie that truly shows how people change over time.

FIGURE 4.2

***Boyhood* Reveals 12 Years of Human Development**

In 2014, the movie *Boyhood* depicted how the members of one family developed physically, socio-emotionally, and cognitively, as it filmed the actors over 12 years of their lives. The main character was the son, Mason Jr., played by Ellar Coltrane. **(a)** Here is Mason Jr./ Ellar at age 6, when filming began. **(b)** And here he is at age 18, when filming ended.

(a)

(b)

4.1 Humans Develop Across Three Domains

developmental psychology
The scientific study of how humans change over the life span, from conception until death.

🖉 4.1 LEARNING GOAL ACTIVITIES

To maximize your learning, complete the following learning goal activities.

a. Understand all bold and italic terms by writing explanations of them in your own words.

b. Apply the three domains of development to yourself by describing how you are changing in the physical, socio-emotional, and cognitive domains.

Developmental psychology explores how all of us grow across the phases of our lives, through infancy, childhood, adolescence, and adulthood. These changes are a result of both nature (our genetics and biology) and nurture (the environment around us). Together, nature and nurture influence growth in three developmental domains: physical, socio-emotional, and cognitive (**Figure 4.3**).

Changes in the *physical domain* revolve around changes in levels of hormones and growth of the body, including the brain. For example, in *Boyhood*, we see how Mason develops physically from a chubby-faced young boy into a tall, muscular teenager, while his sister blooms into a curvaceous young woman. Changes in the *socio-emotional domain* include how we understand ourselves, interact with others, and experience and regulate emotions. In the movie, we see socio-emotional development in Mason and his parents as they struggle to find who they are, improve themselves, or make strong emotional connections with others. Lastly, changes in the *cognitive domain* relate to how we think, reason, and communicate. In *Boyhood*, Mason grows cognitively from thinking about concrete ideas, such as how to sharpen rocks, to abstract thoughts about how to create art.

Physical:
growth of the body and changes in the brain, sensory and motor skills, and levels of hormones

Cognitive:
how our mental processes and abilities to think and communicate change over time

Socio-emotional:
changes in how we understand ourselves, interact with others, and experience and regulate emotions

FIGURE 4.3

Interactions Between Three Developmental Domains and the Environmental Context
Humans develop in three domains: physically, socio-emotionally, and cognitively. Change in each area affects and is affected by change in other areas.

Throughout life, nature and nurture both influence our development in these three domains. The interaction of nature and nurture begins at the very start of life, in the womb.

4.2 Prenatal Development Includes Three Periods of Physical Growth

4.2 LEARNING GOAL ACTIVITIES

To maximize your learning, complete the following learning goal activities.

a. Understand all bold and italic terms by writing explanations of them in your own words.

b. Understand the three prenatal periods by summarizing in your own words the physical changes that occur in each period.

This fact might surprise you, but who you are right now has been influenced by development in your mother's womb (that is, her uterus). You began life as just one cell, and about 40 weeks later you were born. This critical time is called *prenatal development*. It includes three major periods of physical growth: the germinal period, the embryonic period, and the fetal period (**Figure 4.4**).

GERMINAL PERIOD The **germinal period** begins with conception, when the sperm from the male unites with the egg from the female (**Figure 4.4a**). This union creates the *zygote*, the first cell of a new life. The zygote begins to divide rapidly into two cells, then four cells, then eight cells, and so on (**Figure 4.5a**). Just seven or eight days after fertilization, implantation occurs in the wall of the uterus, and the placenta begins to form in order to nourish the developing human. If any abnormalities occur during this earliest stage of development, the result is usually a miscarriage before the woman even knows she is pregnant. However, if development continues in a typical way, then at the end of two weeks the next stage of prenatal development begins.

EMBRYONIC PERIOD From about the start of week 3 to the end of week 8, the developing human is known as an embryo (**Figure 4.4b**). The **embryonic period** is the most important time for physical development of the spinal cord, brain, and all internal organs, including the heart, lungs, liver, kidneys, and sex organs (**Figure 4.5b**). This stage is considered to be the critical time for organ formation. If development goes wrong, the organ(s) will develop improperly,

germinal period
The period in prenatal development from conception to two weeks after conception, when the zygote divides rapidly and implants in the uterine wall.

embryonic period
The period in prenatal development from three through eight weeks after conception, when the brain, spine, major organs, and bodily structures begin to form in the embryo.

fetal period
The period in prenatal development from nine weeks after conception until birth, when the brain continues developing, bodily structures are refined, and the fetus grows in length and weight and accumulates fat in preparation for birth.

FIGURE 4.4

Prenatal Development

(a) In the germinal period, the union of egg and sperm forms a zygote that implants in the wall of the uterus by the end of two weeks. **(b)** In the embryonic period, from the start of week 3 through week 8, the organs develop in the embryo. **(c)** The fetal period, from the start of week 9 until birth, is a time of tremendous physical growth and brain development that prepares the baby to survive outside the womb.

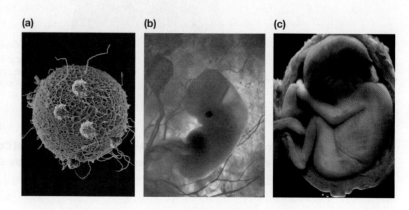

(a) (b) (c)

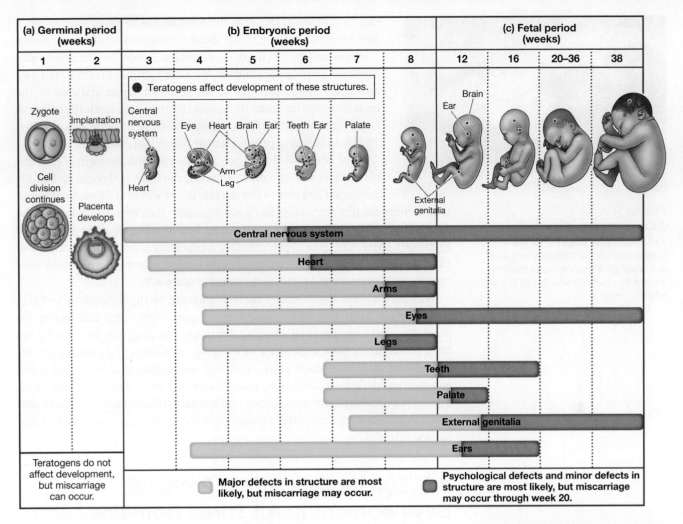

(a) Germinal period (weeks)	(b) Embryonic period (weeks)	(c) Fetal period (weeks)

● Teratogens affect development of these structures.

Teratogens do not affect development, but miscarriage can occur.

■ Major defects in structure are most likely, but miscarriage may occur.

■ Psychological defects and minor defects in structure are most likely, but miscarriage may occur through week 20.

FIGURE 4.5

Physical Changes in the Three Prenatal Periods

(a) The germinal period starts when the sperm meets the egg. Problems encountered during this period usually result in miscarriage. **(b)** The internal organs develop during the embryonic period. In the embryonic period, differences in development may result in major defects in structures, psychological deficits, or minor physical defects in structures. **(c)** In the fetal period, the organs start to function. Developmental differences in the fetal period are primarily related to psychological deficits, minor physical defects in structures, or both.

which most commonly results in birth defects (though miscarriage remains a threat). For example, if the mother has not consumed enough of the nutrient folic acid during the first month of prenatal development, the embryo's spinal cord and brain may not develop properly. If the embryo then survives, the baby may be born with serious birth defects (such as spina bifida, which includes an abnormally formed spine). For this reason, women who want to become pregnant are encouraged to eat foods such as spinach, broccoli, citrus fruits, beans, and avocado, which contain folic acid, or to take prenatal vitamins containing folic acid (**Figure 4.6**).

FETAL PERIOD From the start of week 9 until birth, the growing human is called a fetus (**Figure 4.4c**). During this **fetal period,** no new structures develop, but birth defects remain possible (and miscarriage remains a threat through week 20). The whole body continues to change physically (**Figure 4.5c**). For

FIGURE 4.6

The Importance of Folic Acid

Nutritional deficiencies can cause serious birth defects. This mom-to-be is doing the right thing. Eating dark leafy greens, such as spinach, can help her baby's spine and brain develop.

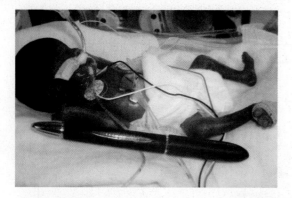

FIGURE 4.7

A Case of Extreme Prematurity

At birth, Amillia Sonja Taylor was a little longer than a ballpoint pen, and she weighed 10 ounces—less than the weight of a can of soda. Today she is a healthy child.

example, at about 16 weeks the fetus begins to move its muscles. A first-time mother might feel these movements by about 20 weeks. The eyes and eyelids finish developing at 6 months. The organs also finish developing, so the infant, once it is born, can breathe on its own and digest food it eats. In the last 12 weeks of prenatal growth, the fetus develops fat under its skin and increases dramatically in length and weight. While the fetus is growing larger, its brain also matures. The brain begins to process sensory input and motor output.

Most healthy full-term pregnancies end with the birth of the baby between 38 and 42 weeks. However, the fetus is thought to be fully developed and able to live outside of the womb at 28 weeks of gestation. Modern medical technology has made it possible for a fetus to live outside the womb much earlier in its development. About half of infants born at 25 weeks of gestation survive, and up to 10 percent of fetuses born at 22 weeks of gestation now survive outside the womb. For example, Amillia Sonja Taylor was born in 2006, after spending just 21 weeks and 6 days in the womb (**Figure 4.7**).

We don't always know what causes premature birth, although it is likely that genetics, nutrition, and environment all play roles. Clear risk factors for premature birth are parental smoking, drinking, and drug use. Babies who are born prematurely have a greater risk of dying as infants. They also may have disabilities, such as cerebral palsy, breathing and feeding problems, and vision and hearing deficits. In addition, prematurity can have long-term effects on intellectual development and school performance (Nomura et al., 2009). But this is not always the case. After a rough start, baby Amillia is now a healthy and successful child.

4.3 Substances Affect Prenatal Development in All Three Domains

4.3 LEARNING GOAL ACTIVITIES

To maximize your learning, complete the following learning goal activities.

a. Understand all bold and italic terms by writing explanations of them in your own words.

b. Understand information about teratogens by describing the effects of alcohol, opiates, and Zika virus during prenatal development.

Smoking, drugs, alcohol, and pollutants are just some of the substances that can make us sick. But a developing human can also be harmed by these substances. The same placenta that provides oxygen and nutrients to the baby helps protect it from harmful stimuli. Even so, some substances can pass through the placenta and sometimes have terrible consequences.

teratogens
Environmental substances that can harm prenatal development.

TERATOGENS Teratogens (from the Greek word *tera*, which means "monster") are substances that can harm prenatal development. As shown in the Learning Tip on p. 135, there are several classes of teratogens. The impact of each one depends on when exposure occurs, the amount of exposure, and how long it lasts during prenatal development. The physical impact of some teratogens can be obvious at birth. However, some teratogens have effects that are not apparent until the child is much older, including disorders involving language, reasoning, attention, social behavior, and/or emotions.

This table will help you understand the various classes of teratogens and their effects on prenatal development.

LEGAL DRUGS	**Alcohol:** fetal alcohol syndrome, facial malformations, intellectual disabilities, learning difficulties
	Nicotine: miscarriage, still birth, low birth weight, intellectual disabilities, learning difficulties
	Caffeine: miscarriage, low birth weight
RECREATIONAL DRUGS	**Cocaine:** low birth weight, breathing problems, seizures, learning difficulties, irritability
	Marijuana: irritability, nervousness, tremors
INFECTIONS	**German measles (rubella):** blindness, deafness, heart defects, brain damage
	Syphilis: intellectual disabilities, deafness, meningitis
	Zika: brain abnormalities, microcephaly (abnormally small head)
ENVIRONMENTAL FACTORS	**Radiation (X-rays):** higher incidence of cancer, physical deformities
	Mercury: intellectual disabilities, blindness

There are no standards about how much exposure to any teratogen is safe for normal development. Even small exposure to some teratogens can have terrible effects.

DRUGS, INCLUDING ALCOHOL, ARE COMMON TERATOGENS The use of recreational drugs—such as cocaine, marijuana, or opioids—during pregnancy can affect the mother and the developing human. Such substances can also affect long-term development during childhood and beyond. Unfortunately, recent surveys in the United States show that about 4.4 percent of pregnant women aged 15–44 years use recreational drugs (Behnke & Smith, 2013).

Premature birth and other complications have been associated with the use of these drugs during pregnancy (Gillogley, Evans, Hansen, Samuels, & Batra, 1990; Sherwood, Keating, Kavvadia, Greenough, & Peters, 1999). Among infants exposed to opioids in the womb, 40–80 percent show withdrawal symptoms as newborns (Yazdy, Desai, & Brogly, 2015). These symptoms include irritability, high-pitched crying, tremors, vomiting, diarrhea, and rapid breathing. The current opioid epidemic (discussed in study unit 3.12) is associated with nearly three times as many infants born with this condition (Volkow, 2016). Babies of women taking opioids, particularly methadone, have five to ten times greater risk for SIDS (Ali, Ahmed, & Greenough, 2012).

While a woman's behavior before or during pregnancy can affect her baby, mothers are only half the story when it comes to prenatal development. Potential fathers, as well as mothers, must be cautious about their diets, exposure to toxins, and use of substances. Less research has been done on how men's health and lifestyles relate to prenatal development. However, there is evidence that fathers' behaviors—including diet, toxin exposure, and amount of stress experienced—can affect prenatal development (Schagdarsurengin & Steger, 2016; Siklenka et al., 2015). For example, paternal smoking may be related to infant hydrocephalus (a dangerous excess of fluid in the brain), and paternal alcohol use is related to infant heart defects (Savitz, Schwingle, & Keels, 1991).

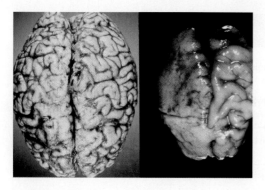

FIGURE 4.8

Alcohol Is a Teratogen

Compare **(left)** the brain of a normal 6-week-old baby with **(right)** the seriously deformed brain of a baby of the same age with fetal alcohol syndrome (FAS).

FIGURE 4.9

Zika Virus Is a Teratogen

Prenatal exposure to Zika virus can produce major birth defects, such as microcephaly.

The take-home message here is that, as you learned in study unit 2.12, life experiences and environmental circumstances can be passed along in sperm as epigenetic information (Chen, Yan, & Duan, 2016). These effects may then be passed along to subsequent generations.

Both women and men can impair prenatal development with the most commonly used teratogen: alcohol. Women who drink alcohol when pregnant are gambling with their baby's development, because alcohol can lead to various defects. The most severe disorder is *fetal alcohol syndrome (FAS)*, which results in abnormalities such as a small head, malformations of the face and limbs, heart defects, and abnormal brain development, and evidence of impairment, as indicated by behavioral or cognitive problems or low IQ (Hoyme et al., 2016; **Figure 4.8**). Besides these physical impairments, FAS babies often have a low birth weight, slight intellectual disabilities, and behavioral and cognitive problems (Guerri, 2002). In the United States, about 1 in 8 unborn babies is exposed to alcohol and the risks associated with it (Olson et al., 2009). For this reason, many health workers recommend that women completely avoid drinking any alcohol when they are pregnant or trying to become pregnant (Mukherjee, Hollins, Abou-Saleh, & Turk, 2005). Men might want to follow the same advice before and during efforts to conceive.

ZIKA VIRUS IS A NEW TERATOGEN In 2015, health experts raised concerns that Zika virus was causing birth defects throughout the Americas. Zika is spread mainly by infected mosquitoes, but it can also be transmitted via sexual activity. A pregnant woman may pass the virus on to her fetus, which can experience serious birth defects such as brain abnormalities and microcephaly, an abnormally small head often due to limited brain development (Rasmussen, Jamieson, Honein, & Petersen, 2016; **Figure 4.9**). Such defects are quite rare in normally developing babies. However, 6 percent of infants exposed to Zika have virus-related defects, particularly if they are exposed during the first trimester, when the brain is forming (Honein et al., 2017).

Q How Does Development Happen in the Womb?

To make sure you learned what you just read, write answers to the following questions and check your answers.

4.1 How do you think a person's ability to intentionally smile reflects growth in all three developmental domains?

4.2 When a woman is 16 weeks pregnant, what prenatal period of development is the baby now in?

4.3 Why should men and women avoid drinking alcohol when they are trying to conceive a child?

See Appendix B for answers to the red Q questions.

How Do Infants and Children Develop?

Have you ever seen a newborn baby? Do they seem completely helpless? In fact, babies arrive in the world with basic abilities that aid their survival. In *infancy*, beginning at birth and lasting between 18 and 24 months, babies can suck for nourishment and see the face of a caregiver who feeds them. They can cry when hungry, which makes parents want to feed them. Infants also smile and bond with caregivers, which develops attachments that aid their survival. And they can remember and learn. These abilities aid infants' survival until *childhood*, which lasts from age 2 until about ages 11–14. Both infancy and childhood are times of great change across all three developmental domains: physical, cognitive, and socio-emotional.

4.4 Infants and Children Change Physically

4.4 LEARNING GOAL ACTIVITIES

To maximize your learning, complete the following learning goal activities.

a. Understand all bold and italic terms by writing explanations of them in your own words.

b. Understand physical development in an infant by summarizing in your own words the motor and sensory changes involved.

As infants and children develop, the brain changes in two critical ways. The first critical change is that myelinated axons form synapses with other neurons. As you learned in study unit 2.2, myelin ensures efficient communication between neurons by functioning like the plastic that insulates electrical wires. The synaptic connections between neurons let regions of the brain communicate to process information. By age 4, the human brain has grown to about 80 percent of the adult size. This size increase is due to myelination and to new synaptic connections among neurons, particularly in the frontal lobes (Paredes et al., 2016). More of these connections develop than a brain will ever use, but this growth gives every brain the chance to adapt well to any environment. The second critical change to the brain is that over time and with experience, the synaptic connections change. Connections that are not used will decay and disappear, which (as noted in study unit 2.13) is called neural pruning. The loss of connections might seem like a bad thing, but it lets the brain process information more efficiently. Indeed, the brain continues to develop and mature through adolescence and beyond (Matsui et al., 2016).

Unfortunately, sometimes infants and young children are raised in environments that do not stimulate their brains (**Figure 4.10a**). In these cases, fewer synaptic connections are made. As a result, these understimulated brains will be less able to process complex information, solve problems, or allow the children to develop advanced language skills (Perry, 2002; **Figure 4.10b**, left side). But the reverse is also true: When infants and young children are able to explore the external world, and when they have ample opportunities to move, talk, and read, their brains are stimulated (**Figure 4.10c**). In short, when the brain is stimulated, the brain is encouraged to develop (**Figure 4.10b**, right side). Consider that a program designed to enhance parental support for those living in poverty—in other words, to help parents stimulate their children's brains—reduced the effects of poverty on brain development (Brody et al., 2017). And when the brain develops, it can support the individual's rich physical, socio-emotional, and cognitive development.

INBORN REFLEXES Babies come into the world hardwired with basic motor reflexes that aid survival. For example, infants must eat in order to grow, and they are born with innate, unlearned reflexes that help them find food. When infants are

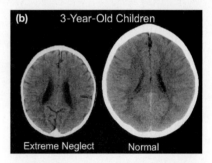

FIGURE 4.10

Environmental Stimulation and Brain Development

(a) Some infants and children are raised in environments that provide little stimulation or comfort. **(b)** These images illustrate the impact of neglect on the developing brain. The brain scan on the left is from a 3-year-old child with minimal exposure to language, touch, and social interaction, who has a significantly smaller head. The brain scan on the right is from a healthy 3-year-old child with an average head size. **(c)** The best brain development takes place in environments with rich stimulation and comforting contact with caregivers.

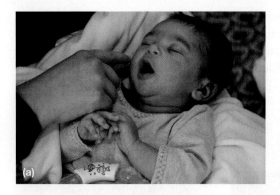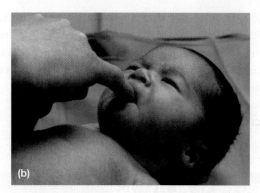

FIGURE 4.11
Infant Reflexes
Infants are born with innate abilities that help them survive, including the **(a)** rooting reflex, **(b)** sucking reflex, and **(c)** grasping reflex.

stroked at a corner of the mouth, they will show the *rooting reflex* (**Figure 4.11a**). That is, they turn and open the mouth in anticipation of food. If they find a nipple where they have turned, the infants will show the *sucking reflex* (**Figure 4.11b**). Automatically closing the mouth on the nipple, they will begin to suck to eat.

Another inborn reflex that aids survival is the *grasping reflex* (**Figure 4.11c**). If you stroke infants' palms, they automatically curl their fingers around the stroked areas. Some scholars believe that this survival mechanism persists from our prehistoric ancestors. Young primates need to be carried from place to place, so grasping their mothers is an adaptive reflex. Though such inborn reflexes help infants survive in the first months of life, being able to move on purpose is another matter entirely. Babies have to learn these *motor skills*.

MOTOR SKILLS   Have you ever watched infants trying to lift their heads to look around? At first, the infants' heads wobble on weak neck muscles. (This is why it is so important to cradle a baby's head in your hand, so you can help control the head until the baby learns to do so.) It takes a lot of practice for infants to learn to move their heads—for example, to turn toward a voice they recognize.

In the first years of life, children progress from moving their heads to sitting up, standing, and walking. The process of developing these motor skills is a sequence of steps that usually occur within a predictable range of ages. The process is called **maturation** (**Figure 4.12**). Maturation was originally thought to be determined only by nature, not by nurture. For an example of nature's effects on development, consider that Brooke Greenberg (discussed in the chapter opener) could not walk primarily because of her biological deficits. But then, even in cases of normal brain development, occasionally an infant skips a step in maturation. The fact that not all babies crawl is an example of how nurture also affects maturation.

When infants sleep on their backs, they often skip the crawling phase. Perhaps infants who sleep on their backs do not develop the stomach muscles needed to crawl. In any case, pediatricians strongly recommend that infants sleep on their backs. Why? Since the mid-1980s, research has shown that placing infants on their backs for sleeping reduces the incidence of sudden infant death syndrome (SIDS). Preventing SIDS is far more important than making sure that babies crawl before walking. And skipping the crawling phase does not affect long-term motor development! So some differences in maturation, caused by how an individual is nurtured, can be perfectly natural. You have to consider the circumstances.

maturation
Physical development of the brain and body that prepares an infant for voluntary movement, such as rolling over, sitting, and walking.

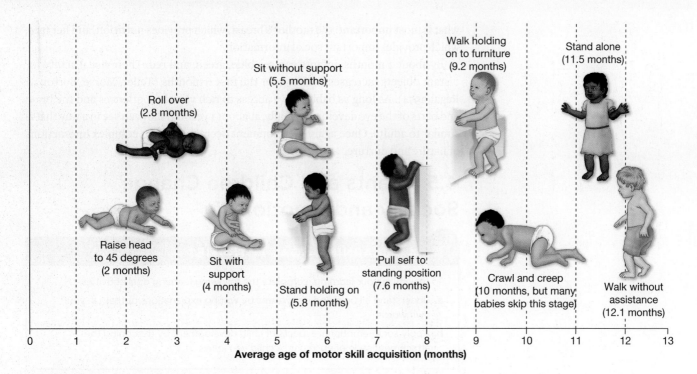

FIGURE 4.12

Physical Maturation and Learning to Walk

Usually, a human baby learns to walk without formal teaching, in a sequence that is typical of most humans. However, the age when a child develops a certain skill varies a lot, so the average age of acquisition is shown here. A child might deviate from this sequence—for example, by skipping the crawling phase—yet still develop normal walking abilities.

SENSORY DEVELOPMENT   To learn, infants need information. They get information from the world by hearing, seeing, smelling, tasting, and perceiving touch. Some of these sensory abilities are more fully developed at birth than others. The earliest fully developed sensory abilities are directly connected with the infant's survival. For instance, 2-hour-old infants prefer sweet tastes to all other tastes (Mennella, Bobowski, & Reed, 2016). This preference makes sense because breast milk is sweet, so infants are born with a built-in mechanism that makes them want to drink this nutritious milk. Infants also have a good sense of smell, especially for scents associated with feeding. In a number of studies, infants turned their heads toward a pad containing their own mother's milk but not toward pads containing milk from other breast-feeding mothers (for example, Marin, Rapisardi, & Tani, 2015; Winberg & Porter, 1998).

When infants are born, they can also hear quite well. They startle at loud sounds and turn their heads in the direction of everyday sounds. Infants even hear well enough to prefer specific sounds. For instance, a newborn can change her sucking pattern in order to hear her mother's voice (DeCasper & Fifer, 1980). The newborn's ability to recognize and discriminate her mother's voice makes sense because a fetus starts hearing that voice inside the womb at 4½ months. Infants' abilities to recognize and locate sounds improve as they gain experience with objects and people and as the auditory cortex develops further. By the age of 6 months, babies hear nearly as well as adults (DeCasper & Spence, 1986).

By contrast, newborns have quite poor vision. Initially they can see only about 8–12 inches from their heads and cannot make out differences between colors. They can see high-contrast patterns better than they see patches of gray (Fantz, 1966; **Figure 4.13**). These visual abilities are adaptive, because they let the infant focus on

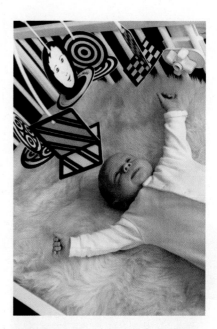

FIGURE 4.13

Babies Are Born Able to See High Contrast

The innate ability to see large blocks of black and white helps a baby survive. It lets the baby locate the mother's nipple, which contrasts in color with the surrounding tissue, in order to eat.

what is most important: the mother's breast, which provides nutrition, and her face, which provides important social information.

By about 2 months, infants can see blue, green, and red. Their visual acuity for distant objects increases rapidly over the first 6 months (Teller, Morse, Borton, & Regal, 1974). As long as babies have access to rich visual experiences and the brain and parts of the eye develop normally, at about 1 year old they can see in a way that is similar to adults. Once again, development occurs thanks to complex interactions of nature and nurture.

4.5 Infants and Children Change Socially and Emotionally

4.5 LEARNING GOAL ACTIVITIES

To maximize your learning, complete the following learning goal activities.

a. Understand all bold and italic terms by writing explanations of them in your own words.

b. Apply socio-emotional aspects of child development by describing the attachment style of an infant or child you know.

Humans are social animals. We spend a good part of our lives getting along with other people, or trying to. How do we learn how to do it? Infants and children develop socially and emotionally by interacting with others. Our early experiences with our primary caregivers—such as a mother, a father, a grandparent, a day care teacher—are critical for developing the bonds that are essential for socio-emotional development.

EARLY ATTACHMENT Infants—even those with brain damage and disabilities, such as Brooke Greenberg (see the chapter opener)—have a fundamental need to form strong connections with caretakers. These connections help aid the infants' survival. In order to develop these connections, infants innately behave in ways that motivate adults to care for them over time and across situations (Bowlby, 1982).

For example, an infant can cry immediately after birth. The crying causes caregivers to respond, typically by offering the newborn comfort, food, or both. In virtually every culture studied, men, women, and children raise the pitch of their voices when talking to babies. This high-pitched tone is referred to as "mother-ese." People know intuitively that babies can hear and will pay attention to high-pitched voices. In turn, the babies maintain eye contact with these people (Fernald, 1989; Vallabha, McClelland, Pons, Werker, & Amano, 2007). Eventually, between 4 and 6 weeks of age, infants display a first social smile, which creates powerful feelings of love in caregivers (**Figure 4.14**). When babies' inborn behaviors create these connections, how do caregivers care for them?

During the late 1950s, psychologists believed infants mainly needed care in the form of food from their mothers. However, the psychologist Harry Harlow wondered if care was really about providing food or about something else (Harlow & Harlow, 1966). To investigate this question, as you can see in The Methods of Psychology on p. 141, Harlow placed infant rhesus monkeys in a cage with two surrogate "mothers." One mother was made of wire and provided milk through a bottle. The second mother was made of soft terrycloth, but did not give milk. Harlow found that the monkeys approached the wire mother, the mother with food, only when they were hungry. The rest of the day, they clung to the cloth mother. To these monkeys,

FIGURE 4.14

Infant Attachment Behaviors
When newborns smile, it makes their caretakers want to care for them.

Hypothesis: Infant monkeys will form an attachment to a surrogate mother that provides comfort.

Research Method: Infant rhesus monkeys were put in a cage with two different "mothers":

1 One mother was made of cloth, but could not give milk.

2 The other was made of wire, but could give milk.

Results: The monkeys clung to the cloth mother and went to it for comfort in times of threat. The monkeys approached the wire mother only when they were hungry.

Conclusion: Infant monkeys will prefer and form an attachment to a surrogate mother that provides comfort over a wire surrogate mother that provides milk.

Note: Photographs are not available from the original experiments. These images are from the CBS television show *Carousel,* which filmed Harlow simulating versions of his experiments in 1962. He deliberately manipulated the faces for another experiment.

QUESTION: Do these findings imply that children can become attached to their mothers even if they are regularly bottle-fed by others? Why or why not?

ANSWER: Yes, because the children can be comforted by contact with their mothers (and fathers) even if not fed by them.

Source: Harlow, H. F., & Harlow, M. (1966). Learning to love. *American Scientist, 54,* 244–272.

caring was really about having comforting contact, so they became attached to the soft, cloth mothers.

To test this attachment, Harlow put a scary metal robot with flashing eyes and large teeth in the cage. Upon seeing the robot, the infants always ran to the cloth mother, never to the mother with food. Harlow repeatedly found that the infants were calmer, braver, and better adjusted overall when near the cloth mother. The mother-as-food theory of attachment was shown to be wrong. Harlow's findings showed that comforting touch is critical in the socio-emotional development of infants.

VARIATIONS IN ATTACHMENT Clearly, infants need physical closeness with and comfort from caregivers to develop socio-emotional bonds. At about 8 to 12 months, however, the infants begin to crawl or toddle and start to move away

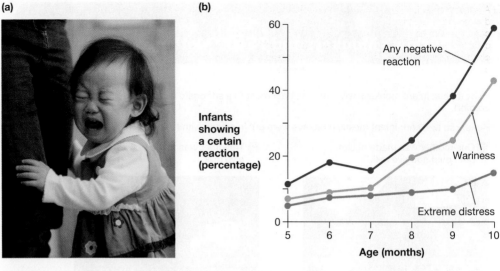

(a)

(b)

Infants showing a certain reaction (percentage)

Any negative reaction

Wariness

Extreme distress

Age (months)

FIGURE 4.15

Separation Anxiety

(a) Beginning at about 8-12 months of age, infants show distress when separated from caregivers.
(b) This separation anxiety increases dramatically as the infants approach their first year of life.

from caregivers. When they cannot see their attachment figures or are left with babysitters or strangers they don't know, they often show signs of distress (Waters, Matas, & Sroufe, 1975; **Figure 4.15a**). This phenomenon, *separation anxiety,* occurs in all human cultures and increases up to age 1 (**Figure 4.15b**). You've probably seen babies displaying separation anxiety. You can read about two typical situations in Has It Happened to You? on p. 143.

To study variations in infant attachment, the developmental psychologist Mary D. Salter Ainsworth created the *strange-situation test.* In a playroom, an infant, a caregiver, and a friendly but unfamiliar adult participate in a series of separations and reunions between the infant and each adult. The researchers observe the test through a one-way mirror in the laboratory and record the infant's responses to the caregiver and the stranger. The strange-situation test has revealed the three attachment styles infants might have (Ainsworth, Blehar, Waters, & Wall, 1978).

In **secure attachment**, the infant is happy to play alone and is friendly to the stranger as long as the caregiver is present. When the caregiver leaves the playroom, leaving the infant with the stranger, the infant is distressed, whines or cries, and looks for the caregiver. When the caregiver returns, the infant usually reaches out to be picked up and is quickly comforted by the caregiver (**Figure 4.16a**). The infant then feels secure enough to return to playing. Just as in Harlow's findings, the caregiver is a source of security in times of distress. Approximately 60–65 percent of infants show secure attachment (Van Ijzendoorn & Kroonenberg, 1988).

The remaining 35–40 percent of infants display one of the types of insecure attachment. Those with **avoidant attachment** do not get upset or cry at all when the caregiver leaves. They may even prefer to play with the stranger rather than the caregiver during their time in the playroom. They may also avoid the caregiver upon the caregiver's return (**Figure 4.16b**). Those with **ambivalent attachment** may cry a great deal when the caregiver leaves the room, yet both seek and reject caring contact when the caregiver returns and tries to calm them down (**Figure 4.16c**). Insecurely attached infants have learned that their caregiver is not available, or only inconsistently available, to soothe them when they are distressed. These infants may be emotionally neglected or actively rejected by the people who take care of them.

(a) A **secure** child is distressed when the caregiver leaves. The child is also quickly comforted when the caregiver returns.

(b) An **avoidant** child is not distressed when the caregiver leaves. The child also avoids the caregiver when the caregiver returns.

(c) An **ambivalent** child is inconsolably upset when the caregiver leaves. The child will also both seek and reject caring contact when the caregiver returns.

FIGURE 4.16

The Strange-Situation Test

This test is a method of exploring the attachment style of infants or young children. Attachment style is based on (1) how infants respond when caregivers leave them with strangers, and (2) how infants respond when caregivers return. Shown here are **(a)** secure, **(b)** avoidant, and **(c)** ambivalent attachment styles.

Decades of research show that secure attachment is related to better socio-emotional functioning in childhood, better peer relations, and successful adjustment at school (for example, Bohlin, Hagekull, & Rydell, 2000; Granot & Mayseless, 2001). In contrast, insecure attachments have been linked to poor outcomes later in life, such as depression and behavioral problems (for example, Munson, McMahon, & Spieker, 2001). In cases of insecure attachment, interventions may help the caregivers learn the skills that increase the likelihood of forming secure attachments.

4.6 Infants and Children Change Cognitively

4.6 LEARNING GOAL ACTIVITIES

To maximize your learning, complete the following learning goal activities.

a. Understand all bold and italic terms by writing explanations of them in your own words.

b. Understand the four stages of cognitive development in children by summarizing in your own words the main aspects of development in each stage.

Two-year-old Rowen is in her car seat looking at a book. She asks her father, who is driving the car, "What's this?" Her father replies, "Sorry, I am looking at the road. I can't see what you see there in the backseat." But Rowen doesn't understand, so she keeps asking the same question. Young children cannot put themselves in another person's shoes to understand what that person senses, thinks, or feels. However, through exchanges such as this one, children begin to learn about the world around them. Rowen, like most children, will eventually realize that other people's perspectives are different from her own. In other words, she will develop cognitively.

DEVELOPING THEORY OF MIND Infants take a big step in cognitive development when they begin to understand who they are. We know infants have this ability if they recognize themselves in a mirror. If there are infants in your life, you can follow the steps in Try It Yourself on p. 144 to see if they have developed this cognitive ability.

Once infants become self-aware enough to recognize themselves in a mirror, they can learn that their thoughts are different from those of other people (Gergely & Csibra, 2003; Sommerville & Woodward, 2005). The ability to understand that other

HAS IT HAPPENED TO YOU?

Separation Anxiety

Have you ever been in a room with babies when their parents left for a minute? Or have you seen infants left with babysitters they didn't know? How did the infants react in these situations? If they were 8–12 months old, they probably started to cry. The infants may have been experiencing separation anxiety, a condition of great distress when the caregiver is out of sight. It is a completely normal reaction for infants at this age. The infants were most likely fine as soon as loved ones comforted them. In fact, you were probably left more shaken by these experiences than the infants were!

To determine whether infants you know have developed the cognitive ability to recognize themselves, gently place a red dot about the size of a dime on their noses, using red lipstick or face paint. Then, carefully, hold the infants in front of a mirror. If the infants can recognize themselves, they will stare at the dot, touch it, or try to remove it. If the infants cannot recognize themselves, they will not notice the red dot as unusual, so they won't focus on it at all. If the infants do not show self-recognition, do this task again every few weeks. At a certain point, the infants will suddenly show this cognitive ability.

assimilation
The process we use to incorporate new information into existing schemas (mental representations).

accommodation
The process we use to create new schemas (mental representations) or drastically alter existing ones to incorporate new information that otherwise would not fit.

people have minds and intentions is called *theory of mind* (Baldwin & Baird, 2001). In one study demonstrating theory of mind in infants, an adult begins handing a toy to an infant, but then stops. On some trials, the adult acts unwilling to hand over the toy, teasing the infant with the toy or playing with it. On other trials, the adult becomes unable to hand it over, "accidentally" dropping it or being distracted by a ringing telephone. Infants older than 9 months showed greater signs of impatience—for example, reaching for the toy—when the adult was unwilling than when the adult was unable (Behne, Carpenter, Call, & Tomasello, 2005).

This and other studies (for example, Onishi & Baillargeon, 2005) provide strong evidence that infants begin to read the intentions of other people in the first year of life. By the end of the second year, perhaps even by 13–15 months of age, young children become very good at reading intentions (Baillargeon, Scott, & Bian, 2016). And as infants and children acquire theory of mind, they develop the ability to think in increasingly sophisticated ways.

PIAGET'S THEORY OF COGNITIVE DEVELOPMENT As the movie *Boyhood* opens, the mother of 6-year-old Mason is scolding him. He ruined his teacher's pencil sharpener by putting rocks in it. Mason's mother can't understand what he was thinking. "What were you going to do with sharpened rocks?" she asks. "I was trying to make arrowheads for my rock collection," he explains. If you have ever spent time with a child, you may recognize this explanation as an example of "child logic." This kind of logic makes no sense to an adult, but to a child it makes perfect sense.

The developmental psychologist Jean Piaget investigated how children's thinking changes as they develop. By exploring the mental abilities of his own three children and many others, Piaget discovered that children's minds truly do work in a different way than those of adults.

Specifically, Piaget proposed that we change how we think as we form new *schemas,* or ways of thinking about how the world works. Piaget described two ways that we develop a schema, which are shown in the Learning Tip on p. 146. During **assimilation,** we place a new experience into an existing schema, which is a mental representation about that information. For example, a 2-year-old might see a butterfly for the first time and shout, "Bird!" After all, a butterfly has wings and flies just like birds. The child is trying to assimilate the idea of butterfly into the existing schema of birds. But the toddler's parent says, "No, honey, that's a butterfly! See, it doesn't have a beak!" During **accommodation,** we create a new schema, or dramatically alter an existing one to include new information that otherwise would not fit into the existing schema. So now the child must accommodate this new information about beaks into the existing schema about birds. And the child must also accommodate by creating a new schema about flying animals that can include "butterfly." The constant repetition of assimilation and accommodation allows a child to develop increasingly complex schemas over time. These schemas allow the child to think in more-sophisticated ways. Piaget's research became the basis for his influential theory that children go through four progressively complex stages of cognitive development, which are summarized in **Figure 4.17.**

Stage	Characteristics	
1 Sensorimotor (birth–2 years)	• Starts to mentally represent information acquired through the senses and motor exploration. • Begins to act intentionally—for example, pulls a string to set a mobile in motion or shakes a rattle to make a noise. • Achieves object permanence by realizing that things continue to exist even when no longer present to the senses. 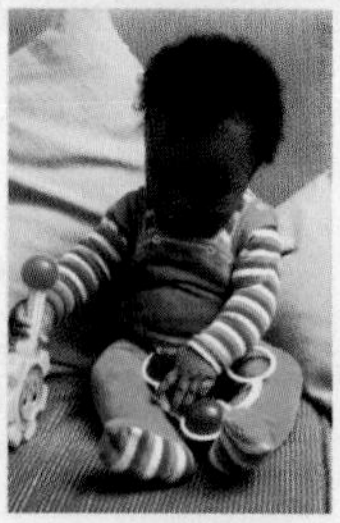	
2 Preoperational (2–7 years)	• Learns to use language and to represent objects by images and words. • Thinking is egocentric, where the child has difficulty taking the viewpoint of others. • Can think intuitively, not logically. • Classifies objects by a single feature—for example, groups blocks by color regardless of their shape. 	
3 Concrete operational (7–12 years)	• Can think logically about concrete objects and events. • Achieves conservation of number, volume, mass, and weight. • Flexibly classifies objects by several features and can order them in a series along a single dimension, such as size. 	
4 Formal operational (12 years and up)	• Can think logically about abstract propositions and test hypotheses systematically. • Becomes concerned with hypothetical issues, the future, and ideological problems. 	

FIGURE 4.17

Piaget's Four Stages of Cognitive Development

Piaget described how children's thinking abilities are characterized across four stages of cognitive development.

SENSORIMOTOR STAGE: BIRTH TO 2 YEARS According to Piaget, children from birth until about age 2 are in the **sensorimotor stage** of cognitive development. During this period, they acquire information primarily through their senses and motor exploration. For example, they first learn reflexively, by sucking on a nipple, grasping a finger, or seeing a face.

As infants begin to control their motor movements, they develop their first schemas. These mental representations contain information about actions that can be performed on certain kinds of objects. For instance, the sucking reflex lets the infants realize they can suck other things, such as a bottle, a finger, a toy, or a blanket. Piaget described sucking other objects as an example of assimilation to the schema of sucking. But sucking a toy or a blanket does not result in the same experience as the reflexive sucking of a nipple. The difference between these experiences leads the infants to alter the sucking schema to include new experiences and information. For example, while sucking a blanket, they may create a new schema that includes using less force than sucking on a bottle. They use the process of accommodation to create this new schema.

sensorimotor stage
The first stage in Piaget's theory of cognitive development; during this stage, infants acquire information about the world through their senses and motor skills.

Use this graphic to help you understand the difference between the two ways that thinking develops as described by Jean Piaget.

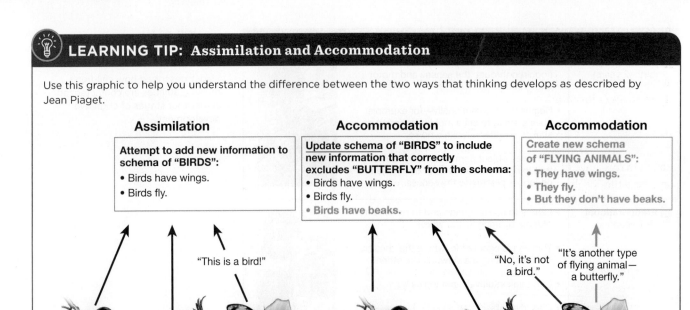

Assimilation

Attempt to add new information to schema of "BIRDS":
• Birds have wings.
• Birds fly.

"This is a bird!"

Accommodation

Update schema of "BIRDS" to include new information that correctly excludes "BUTTERFLY" from the schema:
• Birds have wings.
• Birds fly.
• Birds have beaks.

"No, it's not a bird."

Accommodation

Create new schema of "FLYING ANIMALS":
• They have wings.
• They fly.
• But they don't have beaks.

"It's another type of flying animal— a butterfly."

preoperational stage
The second stage in Piaget's theory of cognitive development; during this stage, children think symbolically about objects, but they reason based on intuition and superficial appearances rather than logic.

FIGURE 4.18

Egocentrism

This toddler is playing hide-and-seek with her mother. Because the toddler's head is in the box and she cannot see the mother, she believes that the mother also cannot see her. She is definitely in the preoperational stage.

According to Piaget, one important cognitive concept developed in this stage is *object permanence*—the understanding that an object continues to exist even when it is hidden from view. Piaget noted that until 9 months of age, most infants will not search for objects they have seen being hidden under a blanket. At around 9 months, they will look for the hidden object by picking up the blanket. A child's full comprehension of object permanence was, for Piaget, one key accomplishment of the sensorimotor period.

PREOPERATIONAL STAGE: 2 TO 7 YEARS According to Piaget, children from about 2 to 7 years of age can begin to think about objects not in their immediate view. They have developed mental representations of objects that are not in view. During this **preoperational stage**, children begin to think symbolically. For example, they can pretend that a stick is a sword or a wand. However, Piaget believed that children at this stage cannot think operationally—in other words, they cannot imagine the logical outcomes of performing certain actions on certain objects. Instead, they use intuitive reasoning based on superficial appearances. For example, if preoperational children are in a moving car with the sun shining in their eyes, they might complain that the sun is following them.

Statements of this kind reveal a key cognitive limitation of this stage: *centration*. That is, the children cannot think about more than one aspect of a problem at a time. They center on one detail of a situation, so their ability to think logically is limited.

Another cognitive characteristic of the preoperational period is *egocentrism*. Preoperational thinkers generally view the world through their own experiences. They can understand how others feel, and they are able to care about others, but their thought processes tend to revolve around their own perspectives. For example, 2-year-olds may play hide-and-seek by placing boxes over their heads, believing that if they cannot see other people, other people cannot see them (**Figure 4.18**). Instead of viewing this egocentric thinking as a limitation, modern scholars agree with Piaget that such "immature" skills prepare children to take special note of their immediate surroundings and learn as much as they can about how their own minds and bodies interact with the world. A clear egocentric focus prevents them from trying to expand their schemas too much before they understand how they think about and understand their own experiences (Bjorklund, 2007).

CONCRETE OPERATIONAL STAGE: 7 TO 12 YEARS At about 7 years of age, according to Piaget, children enter the **concrete operational stage.** They remain in this stage until adolescence. Piaget believed that humans do not develop logic until they begin to think about and understand operations. A classic operation is an action that can be undone: A light can be turned on and off, a stick can be moved across the table and then moved back, and so on. According to Piaget, when children are able to understand that an action is reversible, they can begin to understand concepts such as conservation. Children in this stage are not fooled by superficial transformations, such as how the volume of liquid can look different in glasses of varying size. Instead, they can reason logically about problems.

For instance, children at this stage understand the *law of conservation.* This law states that even if the appearance of a substance changes in one dimension, the properties of that substance remain unchanged. For example, if you pour a short, wide glass of water into a tall, narrow glass, the amount of water does not change. So, if you ask children in the concrete operational stage which glass contains more, they will correctly say that both glasses have the same amount of liquid (**Figure 4.19**). By contrast, children in the preoperational stage would pick the tall, narrow glass because the water is at a higher level. Preoperational children will make this error even when they have seen someone pour the same amount of water into each glass or when they pour the liquid themselves. They cannot understand that it is the narrower diameter of the taller glass that makes the water level higher.

Although using operations is the beginning of logical thinking in the concrete operational stage, Piaget believed that children at this stage reason only about concrete things. That is, they reason about objects they can act on in the world. They are not yet able to reason abstractly, or hypothetically, about what might be possible. Because they cannot do operations "in their heads," children in first, second, and third grades often use objects to do math. They use their fingers to add and subtract, and they group objects, such as tokens, to multiply and divide. By using concrete information, children in this stage can think in much more logical ways than children in the preoperational stage. However, according to Piaget, they cannot truly engage in sophisticated abstract thinking until they reach adolescence.

FORMAL OPERATIONAL STAGE: 12 YEARS TO ADULTHOOD Piaget's final stage of cognitive development is the **formal operational stage.** Here, people can reason in sophisticated, abstract ways. Formal operations involve critical thinking, such as the ability to form a hypothesis about something and test the hypothesis through logic. Critical thinking also involves using information to systematically find answers to problems. To study this ability, Piaget gave teenagers and younger children four flasks of colorless liquid and one flask of colored liquid. He then explained that the colored liquid could be obtained by combining two of

concrete operational stage
The third stage in Piaget's theory of cognitive development; during this stage, children begin to think about and understand logical operations, and they are no longer fooled by appearances.

formal operational stage
The final stage in Piaget's theory of cognitive development; during this stage, people can think abstractly, and they can formulate and test hypotheses through logic.

1 A child in the concrete operational stage understands that two identical short glasses contain the same amount of water.

2 Here, the child observes the water from one of the short glasses poured into the tall, narrower glass.

3 When asked which one contains more water, the child will know that both glasses hold the same amount of water.

FIGURE 4.19

Conservation Task Based on Volume

In the concrete operational stage, according to Piaget, children reason logically, not intuitively as they did in the preoperational stage. As a result, these children can now understand the concept of conservation, which is shown here in a task focusing on the volume of a liquid.

FIGURE 4.20

Trends in Cognitive Development

Modern interpretations view Piaget's theory in terms of trends, not rigid stages. Children shift gradually in their thinking over a wider range of ages than previously thought, and they can demonstrate thinking skills of more than one stage at a time.

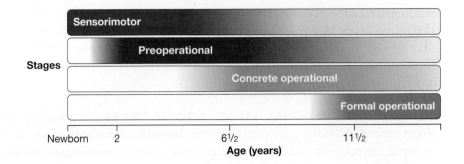

the colorless liquids. Adolescents, he found, systematically try different combinations to obtain the correct result. Younger children just randomly combine liquids. Adolescents are also able to consider abstract notions and think about many viewpoints at once. Lastly, this kind of thinking is characterized by an ability to envision the future and predict the consequences of certain actions.

OTHER WAYS OF THINKING ABOUT COGNITIVE DEVELOPMENT Piaget's theory revolutionized the understanding of cognitive development. And he was right about many things. For example, infants do learn about the world through sensorimotor exploration. Also, people do move from intuitive, illogical thinking to a more logical understanding of the world. However, modern research has revealed that we have to consider Piaget's theory more flexibly.

For example, we now know that Piaget underestimated the ages at which certain skills develop. In his various studies, Piaget may have confused infants' cognitive abilities with their physical capabilities. Because of this, he may have underestimated the age at which some thinking skills develop. For example, infants may not be able to grasp a hidden object, but they may still understand that it exists. When contemporary researchers use age-appropriate methods, they find that object permanence develops in the first few months of life, rather than at 8 or 9 months of age, as Piaget thought (Baillargeon, 1987). Similarly, numerous studies have indicated that infants even have a primitive understanding of some of the basic laws of physics (Spelke, 2016).

In addition, psychologists now think of cognitive development in terms of trends rather than strict stages. People gradually shift from one or more ways of thinking to other ways of thinking, so they may exhibit skills from different stages simultaneously (**Figure 4.20**). For example, while particular children might not understand the conservation of volume (see Figure 4.19), they may be able to perform a conservation task based on number (**Figure 4.21**). This view of cognitive development is consistent with our understanding of brain development. Cognitive development may not necessarily follow strict and uniform stages, because different areas of the brain are responsible for different skills (Bidell & Fischer, 1995; Case, 1992; Fischer, 1980).

1 A 4-year-old is shown two rows of marbles. Each row has the same number of marbles, but one row is spread out. When asked which row has more marbles, the 4-year-old says the longer row. In this case, he fails to show conservation of number.

2 However, when asked to count the marbles in each row, the 4-year-old counts correctly and states that the two rows have the same number of marbles. Now he does show conservation of number.

FIGURE 4.21

Conservation Task Based on Number

When a task is performed in an age-appropriate manner, children are able to show conservation of number at a much younger age than they can show conservation of volume (see Figure 4.19).

Finally, some approaches to understanding cognitive development focus on how social and cultural contexts affect the development of cognition and language. According to Lev Vygotsky, a contemporary of Piaget, humans are unique because they use symbols and psychological tools, such as speech, writing, maps, and art. Through these tools, people create culture. Culture, in turn, dictates what people need to learn and the sorts of skills they need to develop. For example, some cultures value science and rational thinking. Other cultures emphasize supernatural and mystical forces. These cultural values shape how people think about the world around them and relate to it. People respond to the world in terms of both elementary mental functions (such as innate sensory experiences) and higher mental functions (such as language, perception, abstraction, and memory). As children develop, their elementary capacities are gradually shaped by social and cultural contexts (Vygotsky, 1978). In addition, the ability to speak about their thoughts aids children's cognitive development.

4.7 Language Develops in an Orderly Way

4.7 LEARNING GOAL ACTIVITIES

To maximize your learning, complete the following learning goal activities.

a. Understand all bold and italic terms by writing explanations of them in your own words.

b. Analyze the five stages of language development in childhood by stating the typical age of children at each stage and giving an example of what they might say at that stage.

As you learned in the chapter opener, Brooke Greenberg's physical and mental development stopped when she was a toddler. At age 19, Brooke could communicate only by making infant-like sounds. The ability to speak in sentences develops as the brain changes and as cognitive abilities become more sophisticated. As children develop social skills, they also improve their language abilities. Thanks to language, we can live in complex societies where our ability to communicate helps us learn the history, rules, and values of our culture. Language also helps us communicate across cultures and learn much more than other animals can. How do we develop our remarkable ability to use language?

FROM ZERO TO 60,000 Language is a system of using sounds and symbols according to grammatical rules. It can be viewed as a hierarchical structure. Sentences can be broken down into smaller units, called phrases, and phrases can be broken down into words (**Figure 4.22a**). Each word consists of one or more *morphemes* (the smallest units that have meaning, including suffixes and prefixes). Each morpheme consists of one or more *phonemes* (basic sounds; **Figure 4.22b**). For example, the word *asked* has two morphemes ("ask" and "ed") and four phonemes (the sounds you make when you say the word: /a/s/k/t/). *Syntax* is the system of rules about how words are combined into phrases and how phrases are combined to make sentences. For example, English syntax dictates that we say *Stephanie asked for some milk*, not *Stephanie some milk for asked*.

FIVE STAGES OF LANGUAGE DEVELOPMENT Infants are born ready to learn language. In fact, the language or languages that mothers speak during pregnancy influence the listening preferences of newborns.

(a)

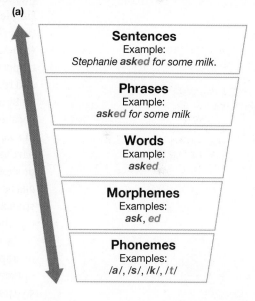

(b)

FIGURE 4.22

Organization of Language

(a) Language is organized hierarchically. Sentences and phrases are created from words, words are created from morphemes, and morphemes are created from phonemes. **(b)** In learning to read, these children are combining phonemes into morphemes.

babbling
Intentional vocalization, often by an infant, that does not have a specific meaning.

telegraphic speech
The tendency for toddlers to speak by combining basic words in a logical syntax, but not a complete sentence, to convey a wealth of meaning.

overregularization
The tendency for young children to incorrectly use a regular grammar rule where they should use an exception to the rule.

For instance, Canadian newborns whose mothers spoke only English during pregnancy showed a strong preference for sentences in English as compared with sentences in Tagalog, a major language of the Philippines. Newborns of mothers who spoke both Tagalog and English during pregnancy paid attention to both languages (Byers-Heinlein, Burns, & Werker, 2010). Further, up to 6 months of age, a baby can discriminate all the speech sounds that occur in all languages, even if the sounds do not occur in the language spoken in the baby's home (Kuhl, 2006; Kuhl et al., 2006; Kuhl, Tsao, & Liu, 2003).

From hearing sounds immediately after birth and then learning the sounds of their own languages, babies develop the ability to speak. Without working very hard at it, humans appear to go from babbling as babies to employing a full vocabulary of about 60,000 words as adults. Learning to speak follows a distinct path. During the first months of life, newborns' actions—crying, fussing, eating, and breathing—generate all their sounds. In other words, in the first stage of language development, babies' first verbal sounds are cries, gurgles, grunts, and breaths. During this stage, from 3 to 5 months, they begin to coo and laugh. In the second stage, they begin **babbling**. Between 5 and 7 months their babbling includes using single consonants and vowels. From 7 to 8 months, they babble in syllables (*ba-ba-ba, dee-dee-dee*).

Between the ages of 8 and 18 months, but usually by the end of their first year, infants around the world are usually saying their first words. During this third stage in language development, the *one-word stage*, toddlers typically combine phonemes into morphemes to label items in their environment (*kitty, milk*), simple action words (*go, up, sit*), quantifiers (*all gone! more!*), qualities or adjectives (*hot*), socially interactive words (*bye, hello, yes, no*), and even internal states (*boo-boo* after being hurt; Pinker, 1984). Thus even very young children use words to perform a wide range of communicative functions. They name, comment, and request.

By about 18 to 24 months, in the fourth stage of language development, children's vocabularies start to grow rapidly. They put words together and form basic sentences of roughly two words. Though these mini-sentences are missing some words, they have what is known as syntax. Typically, the word order indicates what has happened or should happen: For example, "Throw ball. All gone" translates as *I threw the ball, and now it's gone*. The psychologist Roger Brown called these utterances **telegraphic speech** because the children speak as if they are sending a telegram. They put together bare-bones words according to correct syntax (Brown, 1973).

As children use language in increasingly sophisticated ways, they sometimes overapply regular grammar rules. This tendency, in the fifth stage of language development, is called **overregularization** and is seen between the ages of about 3 and 5 years. For example, when children learn that adding -*ed* makes a verb past tense, they add -*ed* to every verb, even verbs that do not follow that rule. Thus they may say "runned" or "holded" even though they may have said "ran" or "held" at a younger age. This trend usually lasts through the early elementary school years, when children begin to master irregular forms of words. Such overregularizations reflect an important aspect of language acquisition: Children are not simply repeating what they have heard others say. After all, they most likely have not heard anyone say "runned." Instead, these errors occur because children recognize patterns in spoken grammar and then apply the patterns to new sentences they never heard before (Marcus, 1996; Marcus et al., 1992). Of course, as children gain experience using language with other people, they usually learn to correct these mistakes. By about age 6, children use language nearly as well as most adults. Their vocabulary will continue to grow throughout their lives.

How Do Infants and Children Develop?

To make sure you learned what you just read, write answers to the following questions and check your answers.

4.4 Why are many toys for young infants black-and-white?

4.5 An infant cries when the caregiver leaves the room, but is quickly comforted when the caregiver returns. What style of attachment is the infant displaying?

4.6 An 8-month-old is crying while trying to reach a toy, then stops crying when a caregiver places a towel over the toy. How would Piaget explain this behavior?

4.7 Before about 24 months of age, how does a toddler typically speak?

See Appendix B for answers to the red Q questions.

How Do Adolescents Develop?

Do you remember when you began to go through *adolescence*? We all go through this stage, unless there is some problem with our physical development (as was the case with Brooke Greenberg, discussed in the chapter opener). This period starts at the end of childhood, about age 11 through 14, and lasts until about age 18 or 21. Your adolescent body was changing in major ways, growing larger and sometimes doing things beyond your control. Your emotions may have seemed uncontrollable as well. And you suddenly may have felt wildly attracted to people you never thought about before.

As children approach adolescence, all aspects of the self are changing. Physical changes occur, socio-emotional changes emerge as part of evolving relationships with parents and peers, and cognitive changes arise as part of the potential emergence of critical and analytical thinking. Taken together, changes in these three domains lay the foundation for the development of a sense of personal identity.

4.8 Adolescents Develop Physically

4.8 LEARNING GOAL ACTIVITIES

To maximize your learning, complete the following learning goal activities.

a. Understand all bold and italic terms by writing explanations of them in your own words.

b. Understand the physical changes in puberty by summarizing in your own words the changes in secondary and primary sex characteristics and when they occur in girls and in boys.

Physically, adolescence is characterized by the onset of sexual maturity and the ability to reproduce. **Puberty,** a roughly two-year developmental period, marks the beginning of adolescence. The first signs of puberty typically begin at about age 8 for girls and at about age 9 or 10 for boys. Most girls complete pubertal development by age 16 (Ge, Natsuaki, Neiderhiser, & Reiss, 2007; Herman-Giddens, Wang, & Koch, 2001; Sun et al., 2005), and boys finish by the age of 18 (Lee, 1980).

PUBERTY When you were around 10 or 12 years old, did you seem to grow overnight? This adolescent growth spurt—a rapid, hormonally driven increase in height and weight—is an obvious dividing line between childhood and puberty. During puberty, hormone levels increase throughout the body, stimulating many physical changes that allow us to develop into sexually mature adults.

puberty
The physical changes in the body that are a part of sexual development.

secondary sex characteristics
Physical changes during puberty that are not directly related to reproduction but that indicate the differences between the sexes.

primary sex characteristics
Physical development during puberty that results in sexually mature reproductive organs and genitals.

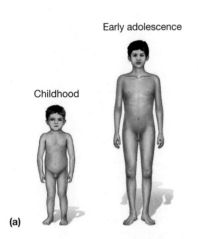

Early adolescence

Childhood

(a)

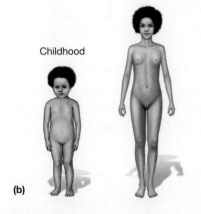

Early adolescence

Childhood

(b)

FIGURE 4.23

Physical Development During Adolescence

These graphics show how adolescents develop secondary sex characteristics during puberty that change them from looking like children to looking like adults. **(a)** Boys develop darker and thicker body hair on the legs, in the armpits, in the pubic area, and on the face and chest. They grow taller and gain muscle mass. Their jaw becomes more angular. **(b)** Girls develop darker and thicker body hair on the legs, in the armpits, and in the pubic area. They become taller, they grow breasts, their waists become more defined, and they gain more fat on their hips.

The first changes that occur are the **secondary sex characteristics** (**Figure 4.23**). Boys and girls start to experience greater growth of body hair, first as darker and thicker hair on the legs, then under the arms, then as pubic hair (Marshall & Tanner, 1970), then in other places. Boys' muscle mass increases, their voices deepen, and their jaws become more angular. Girls lose baby fat on their bellies as their waists become more defined, and they also develop fat deposits on the hips and breasts (Lee, 1980). You will learn more about puberty, and how these changes affect the sexual desires of adolescents, in Chapter 10.

Puberty also brings the development of the **primary sex characteristics**. That is, the male and female external genitals and internal sex organs mature, menstruation begins in girls, and sperm develops in boys. These physical changes result in adolescents' becoming sexually mature and able to reproduce.

Puberty may seem to be purely physical, but it is affected by environment. For example, a girl who lives in a stressful environment or has insecure attachments to caregivers is likely to begin menstruating earlier than a girl in a peaceful, secure environment (Wierson, Long, & Forehand, 1993). This finding suggests that a girl's body responds to stress as a threat. Because the body feels threatened, it speeds up the ability to reproduce in order to continue the girl's gene pool. Thus, environmental forces trigger hormonal changes, which send the girl into puberty (Belsky, Houts, & Fearon, 2010). Because boys do not have an easily identifiable pubertal event like menstruation in girls, we know less about the effects of environment on puberty in boys. Boys and girls experience similar changes in brain development during adolescence, however, so researchers are able to identify a few key characteristics of the teenage brain.

BRAIN CHANGES DURING ADOLESCENCE While teenagers are experiencing pubertal changes, their brains also are in an important phase of reorganization. Synaptic connections are being refined, and gray matter is increasing. However, the frontal cortex of the brain is not fully developed until the early 20s. An adolescent's limbic system—the motivational and emotional center of the brain—tends to be more active than the frontal cortex. As a result, although teenagers are *able* to think critically, they often have a difficult time doing so. Instead, they are more likely to act irrationally and engage in risky behaviors than adults are (Blakemore & Choudhury, 2006; Casey, Jones, & Somerville, 2011). Because teenagers have the ability to understand behavioral consequences, it is important to help them learn about the consequences of their own actions. If parents, teachers, community members, and other adults are supportive and provide the proper guidance and discipline, adolescents will know that people who care about them will help them develop good decision-making skills (Steinberg & Sheffield, 2001).

4.9 Adolescents Develop Socially and Emotionally

4.9 LEARNING GOAL ACTIVITIES

To maximize your learning, complete the following learning goal activities.

a. Understand all bold and italic terms by writing explanations of them in your own words.

b. Apply socio-emotional aspects of development to your own adolescence by describing the development of your sense of identity, including your ethnic identity and how you relate to family and friends.

Adolescents may be physically able to reproduce, but they are still developing socially and emotionally. Typically, they are focused less on family at this age and more on themselves as they develop friendships and try to answer the question "Who am I?" The search for who each of us is as a person is at the core of socio-emotional development for every adolescent (**Figure 4.24**).

How we define ourselves is influenced by many factors, including the culture in which we are raised and our beliefs about personal characteristics such as race, ethnicity, gender, and sexual orientation. The quest for identity is an important challenge during development, especially in Western cultures, where individuality is valued. As adolescents seek to understand how they fit into the world and to imagine what kind of person they will become later in life, they build on the preceding developmental stages.

DEVELOPING A UNIQUE IDENTITY   The psychologist Erik Erikson (1959) proposed a theory of human development based on the psychological challenges we face at different ages in our lives and how these challenges affect our social relationships. Erikson thought of psychosocial development as having eight stages, starting from an infant's first year of life to old age (**Table 4.1**). Because it recognizes the importance of the entire life span, Erikson's theory has been extremely influential in developmental psychology. However, a theory is only as good as the evidence that supports it (see study unit 1.8), and few researchers have tested Erikson's theory directly.

Erikson thought of each life stage as having a major developmental "crisis." The individual reaches a challenge to be confronted. All of these crises are present throughout life, but each takes on special importance at a particular stage. Although each crisis

FIGURE 4.24

Development of Identity in a Teen
Who are you? What do you love? How do you see yourself? All adolescents face such questions as part of their socio-emotional development.

TABLE 4.1
Erikson's Eight Stages of Psychosocial Development

Stage	Age	Major Psychosocial Crisis	Successful Resolution of Crisis
1. Infancy	0–2	Trust versus mistrust	Children learn that the world is safe and that people are loving and reliable.
2. Toddler	2–3	Autonomy versus shame and doubt	Encouraged to explore the environment, children gain feelings of independence and positive self-esteem.
3. Preschool	4–6	Initiative versus guilt	Children develop a sense of purpose by taking on responsibilities, but they also develop the capacity to feel guilty for misdeeds.
4. Childhood	7–12	Industry versus inferiority	By working successfully with others and assessing how others view them, children learn to feel competent.
5. Adolescence	13–19	Identity versus role confusion	By exploring different social roles, adolescents develop a sense of identity.
6. Young adulthood	20s	Intimacy versus isolation	Young adults gain the ability to commit to long-term relationships.
7. Middle adulthood	30s to 50s	Generativity versus stagnation	Adults gain a sense that they are leaving behind a positive legacy and caring for future generations.
8. Old age	60s and beyond	Integrity versus despair	Older adults feel a sense of satisfaction that they have lived a good life and developed wisdom.

Source: Erikson, E. H. (1959). *Identity and the Life Cycle*. New York: International Universities Press.

identity versus role confusion
Fifth stage of Erikson's theory of psychosocial development, where adolescents face the challenge of figuring out who they are.

provides an opportunity for psychological development, a lack of progress may impair further psychosocial development (Erikson, 1980). However, if the crisis is successfully resolved, the challenge provides skills and attitudes that the individual will need to face the next challenge. Successful resolution of the early challenges depends on the supportive nature of the child's environment as well as the child's active search for information about what the child is skilled at. According to Erikson's theory, adolescents face perhaps the most fundamental challenge: how to develop an adult identity. This crisis of **identity versus role confusion** includes addressing questions about who the person is. Some of these questions concern gender and sexual orientation, which are discussed fully in Chapter 10. Other questions within the adolescent's search for identity concern culture, ethnicity, parents, and peers.

CULTURE AND ETHNICITY Culture shapes much of who we are as we develop a full sense of identity during adolescence. Culture also determines whether each person's identity will be accepted or rejected. In a multiracial country such as the United States, questions of racial or ethnic identity can be complicated. Forming an ethnic identity can be a particular challenge for adolescents of color.

Children entering middle childhood have some awareness of their ethnic identities. They know the labels and attributes that the dominant culture applies to their ethnic group. During middle childhood and adolescence, children in ethnic minority groups often engage in additional processes aimed at forming an ethnic identity (Phinney, 1990). The factors that influence these processes vary widely among individuals and groups.

For instance, a child of Mexican immigrants may struggle to live successfully in both a traditional Mexican household and a Westernized American neighborhood and school. The child may have to serve as a "cultural broker" for the family, perhaps translating materials sent home from school, calling government agencies or insurance companies, and handling more adultlike responsibilities than other children the same age. In helping the family adjust to the stress of life as immigrants in a foreign country, the child may feel additional pressures, but may also develop important skills in communication, negotiation, and caregiving (Cooper, Denner, & Lopez, 1999). And by successfully negotiating these tasks, a child can develop a *bicultural identity*. That is, the child strongly identifies with two cultures and seamlessly combines a sense of identity with both groups (Vargas-Reighley, 2005). A child in this situation who develops a bicultural identity is likely to be happier, be better adjusted, and have fewer problems in adult social and economic roles.

FIGURE 4.25
Peers and Cliques

(a) Adolescents develop strong friendships with peers who share similar interests and values. **(b)** Outside observers might tend to place the young men in this peer group into a single clique, "punks," and would tend to react to all of them in similar ways. Each adolescent, however, might view himself as an individual.

PARENTS AND PEERS If you were asked for one adjective that best describes "teenager," what would you say? The odds are high that it would be *rebellious*. Recall from the chapter opener that even 19-year-old Brooke Greenberg, who was frozen in the body of a 19-month-old toddler, displayed this rebellious nature by refusing to do things she did not like. Throughout the world, it seems that as adolescents develop their own identities, they come into more conflict with their parents.

For most families, this conflict leads only to minor annoyances. It can actually help adolescents develop important skills, including negotiation, critical thinking, communication, and empathy (Holmbeck, 1996). According to Erikson's theory, negotiating a pathway to a stable identity requires breaking away from childhood beliefs by questioning and challenging parental and societal ideas (Erikson, 1968). But even though adolescents and their parents may disagree and sometimes argue, across cultures parents have a great deal of direct influence on their children's behaviors, values, and independence (Feldman & Rosenthal, 1991). Parents also indirectly affect social development by influencing children's choices about friends (Brown, Mounts, Lamborn, & Steinberg, 1993; Cairns & Cairns, 1994).

Peers play a crucial role in identity development. Peer groups are created when teenagers form friendships with others who have similar values and worldviews (**Figure 4.25a**). Observers outside the peer groups tend to place teenagers who dress or act a certain way into groupings, called *cliques* (**Figure 4.25b**). The observers often see members of cliques as virtually interchangeable, and community members may respond to all youths from that group in similar ways (Urberg, Değirmencioğlu, Tolson, & Halliday-Scher, 1995). The teenagers, however, often see themselves as unique and individual, or as connected to a small subset of close friends, not just as members of a certain clique. The friendships created in these peer groups provide an important sense of belonging, social support, and acceptance. By contrast, being bullied can make adolescents feel socially excluded, which can have many negative effects.

4.10 Adolescents Develop Cognitively

4.10 LEARNING GOAL ACTIVITIES

To maximize your learning, complete the following learning goal activities.

a. Understand all bold and italic terms by writing explanations of them in your own words.

b. Analyze one aspect of cognitive development by describing three ways you could reason morally about a dilemma in your life based on Kohlberg's theory.

Teenagers may be rebellious, but we still expect them to make good decisions based on the rules of the culture they live in. Moral choices, large ones and small ones alike, affect other people. Ideally, the ability to consider questions about morality develops during childhood and continues into adulthood.

MORAL REASONING AND MORAL EMOTIONS Moral development is the way people learn to decide between behaviors with competing social outcomes. In other words, when is it acceptable to take an action that may harm others or that may break a stated or unstated social contract? Theorists typically divide morality into two factors: moral reasoning, which depends on cognitive processes, and moral emotions.

Moral emotions—such as pride, embarrassment, and shame—are considered self-conscious emotions. They are called self-conscious because they involve how people think about themselves. For example, the emotional experience of sadness might become the self-conscious emotional experience of shame when you feel sad about yourself. Even though moral reasoning and moral emotions may be studied separately, moral emotions affect moral reasoning (Moll & de Oliveira-Souza, 2007). In fact, the development of moral emotions is vital to acting morally. Cognition and emotions are intertwined. If people lack adequate cognitive abilities, their moral emotions may not translate into moral behaviors (Tangney, Stuewig, & Mashek, 2007).

preconventional level
Lowest level of moral reasoning; at this level, self-interest and event outcomes determine what is moral.

conventional level
Middle level of moral reasoning; at this level, strict adherence to societal laws and the approval of others determine what is moral.

postconventional level
Highest level of moral reasoning; at this level, decisions about morality depend on abstract principles and the value of all life.

Psychologists who study the cognitive processes of moral behavior have focused largely on Lawrence Kohlberg's stage theory. Kohlberg (1984) tested moral-reasoning skills by asking people to respond to hypothetical situations in which someone was faced with a moral dilemma. For example, should a person steal a drug to save his dying wife because he could not afford the drug? Kohlberg was most concerned with the reasons people provided for their answers, not just the answers themselves. He devised a theory of moral judgment that involved three main levels of moral reasoning.

At the **preconventional level** of moral reasoning, people solve the moral dilemma in terms of self-interest. For example, a person at this level might say, "He should steal the drug because he could get away with it." Or "He should not steal the drug because he will be punished." At the **conventional level** of moral reasoning, people's responses conform to rules of law and order or focus on others' approval or disapproval. For example, a person at this level might say, "He should take the drug because everyone will think he is a bad person if he lets his wife die." Or "He should not take the drug because that's against the law." At the **postconventional level,** the highest level of moral reasoning, people's responses center on complex reasoning. This reasoning concerns abstract principles that transcend laws and social expectations. For example, a person at this level might say, "He should steal the drug. Sometimes people have to break the law if the law is unjust." Or "He should not steal the drug. If people always did what they wanted, it would be anarchy. Society would break down." As you can see, Kohlberg believed that advanced moral reasoning includes considering the greater good for all people and giving less thought to personal wishes or fear of punishment.

Not all psychologists agree with moral-reasoning theories such as Kohlberg's. To begin with, Kohlberg's initial research examined only American males (Gilligan, 1977). Does his theory also apply to females or to those raised in different cultures (Snarey, 1985)? In addition, moral-reasoning theories emphasize the cognitive aspects of morality and neglect emotional issues that influence moral judgments, such as shame, pride, or embarrassment. But think about moral actions in daily life, such as helping others in need. Aren't they influenced as much by emotions as by cognitive processes?

Finally, not everyone progresses through the stages of moral development at the same rate or in the same order. How can a parent, guardian, or other authority figure help guide a younger person's moral development? There is great value in showing the general consequence of a specific behavior. Saying "You made Chris cry. It's not nice to hit, because it hurts people" is more effective than saying simply "Don't hit people." Such explanation promotes children's sympathetic attitudes, appropriate feelings of guilt, and awareness of other people's feelings. The resulting attitudes, feelings, and awareness then influence the children's moral reasoning and behavioral choices, which also help instill moral values that guide behavior throughout life. This cycle of moral development can be readily seen in cases of bullying, as discussed in Using Psychology in Your Life on p. 157.

 How Do Adolescents Develop?

To make sure you learned what you just read, write answers to the following questions and check your answers.

4.8 What is the likely relationship between brain development and adolescent risk taking?

4.9 According to Erikson, which of the eight crises in psychosocial development do adolescents need to resolve in order to develop socio-emotionally?

4.10 Why do bullies tend not to feel bad about their behavior?

See Appendix B for answers to the red Q questions.

Bullying

Have you ever been the victim of bullying? Have you seen children or adolescents being bullied? Have you ever bullied someone? Bullying is when a person repeatedly uses physical power or control over another person, behaving aggressively in a way that is unwanted (Espelage & Holt, 2012). There are many types of bullying:

- **Physical:** physical contact that hurts a person (for example, hitting, kicking, punching, taking away an item and destroying it), physical intimidation (for example, threatening someone, frightening the person into doing what the bully wants).

- **Verbal:** name-calling; making offensive remarks; joking about a person's appearance, religion, gender, ethnicity, sexual orientation; verbal intimidation.

- **Social:** spreading rumors or stories about someone, excluding someone from a group on purpose, or making fun of someone by pointing out the person's differences.

- **Cyber:** sending aggressive, threatening, and/or intimidating messages, pictures, or information using social media, e-mail, instant messaging, text messaging, or voicemail.

Cyberbullying became an issue in recent years, with the rise of social networking sites. Estimates of its prevalence vary, with 3–72 percent of adolescents reporting being victims across separate studies (Selkie, Fales, & Moreno, 2016).

All bullying, including cyberbullying, is a complex behavior with many contributing factors. Experts tend to agree that bullies might not strongly feel the moral emotions of guilt and shame (Hymel, Rocke-Henderson, & Bonanno, 2005). Bullies also often show increased moral disengagement, such as indifference or pride, when explaining their behavior and more-positive attitudes about using bullying to respond to difficult social situations. Because bullying tends to get people what they want and society traditionally turns a blind eye to it, bullying goes on. However, both kids who are bullied and those who bully kids can have serious, lasting problems. For example, being bullied during childhood is associated with psychological disorders such as anxiety disorders and depression (Copeland, Wolke, Angold, & Costello, 2013).

What can you do if you see a child or adolescent being bullied? Here are three steps to take:

1. **Stop the bullying on the spot:** Intervene in a calm and respectful manner, separate the children, make sure they are safe, and get any needed medical help.

2. **Find out what happened:** Once you have separated the kids, ask for their views on what happened. Seek evidence from other people who witnessed the act. Do not jump to conclusions or place blame.

3. **Support the kids involved:** Assure the person being bullied that the situation is not that person's fault, and work to resolve the situation. Also work with the person doing the bullying: help that person to realize the behavior is wrong, to understand the motivation for it, and to reduce or put an end to it.

By modeling good moral reasoning and good moral behavior, and reducing the rewards associated with bullying, you can help children and adolescents develop appropriate moral values. Even other kids can learn to be more than bystanders and help reduce bullying. For more information on how to respond to bullying and prevent it, visit www.stopbullying.gov.

How Do Adults Develop?

We've all seen adults who still act like adolescents. Watching them can be funny or make us feel uncomfortable. But what does it really mean to be an adult? For many years, developmental psychologists focused on childhood and adolescence, as if most important aspects of development occurred by age 20 and then people did not change anymore. In recent decades, researchers working in a wide range of fields have demonstrated that throughout adulthood, important changes occur physically, socio-emotionally, and cognitively. Therefore, many contemporary psychologists consider development from the perspective of the entire life span. Their goal is to understand how mental activity and social relations change over the entire course of life. *Adulthood*, then, becomes an important topic for study. Beginning at the end of adolescence, lasting through old age and concluding with death, adulthood makes up most of our life span. The developmental changes during adulthood vary from stage to stage.

4.11 Bodies Change in Adulthood

4.11 LEARNING GOAL ACTIVITIES

To maximize your learning, complete the following learning goal activities.

a. Understand all bold and italic terms by writing explanations of them in your own words.

b. Understand physical development as we age by describing in your own words how people change physically across the two main stages of adulthood.

Our bodies are ready to reproduce when we reach our teens. We peak in fitness during our 20s. So, evolutionarily speaking, a 40-year-old is quite old. In fact, for most of our history, humans lived only a few decades. As recently as the beginning of the twentieth century, the average life expectancy in the United States was only 47 years. After 1900, through modern medicine and improvements in hygiene and in food availability, the average life expectancy in the United States increased by more than 30 years (Organization for Economic Cooperation and Development, 2013). However, in 2015, for the first time in decades, life expectancy in the United States dropped (Xu, Murphy, Kochanek, & Arias, 2016). As described in Chapter 11, the world is currently facing an obesity epidemic, where people today may be the first to live shorter life spans than their parents' generations did. Many people may be living longer, but are most people getting healthier?

EARLY TO MIDDLE ADULTHOOD It's the prime of life! Really? Between the ages of 20 and 40, we actually experience a steady decline in muscle mass, bone density, eyesight, and hearing (Shephard, 1997). As we approach middle age, we start to notice that we can no longer drink as much alcohol, eat as much junk food, or get by on as little sleep as we could in our 20s. That "middle-age spread," the accumulation of fat around the belly, becomes harder and harder to work off.

FIGURE 4.26

Staying Healthy in Adulthood

Good nutrition and exercise in early adulthood help keep us physically fit and psychologically healthy. Exercise also helps us live longer.

How can we respond to such natural changes? A healthy lifestyle, including good nutrition and exercise, in early adulthood can improve health through the rest of life. In addition, exercise during early adulthood is associated with a longer life (**Figure 4.26**). Study participants who walked briskly 15 minutes per day (Wen et al., 2011) or ran 5–10 minutes per day (Lee et al., 2014) lived an average of 3 years longer than participants who did not exercise.

TRANSITION TO OLD AGE   In Western societies—despite the 2015 drop in life expectancy in the United States—people are living much longer. The number of people over age 85 is growing dramatically. Indeed, it is becoming commonplace for people to live beyond 100. By 2030, more than 1 in 5 Americans will be over age 65, and these older people will be ethnically diverse, well educated, and physically fit (National Research Council, 2006). With this "graying" of the population in Western societies, much greater research attention has been paid to the lives of people over age 60.

Our view of the elderly is changing a lot. The baby boom generation, the one born just after World War II, is reaching old age. Many older adults work productively well past their 70s. For instance, nearly 40 percent of U.S. federal judges are over 65 (Markon, 2001; **Figure 4.27a**). Popular entertainers such as Samuel L. Jackson and the Rolling Stones are performing into their 70s and beyond, defying common stereotypes of older people (**Figure 4.27b–c**).

Nevertheless, the body and mind start deteriorating more rapidly at about age 50. The cosmetics and plastic surgery industries are booming as we try to cover up superficial physical changes such as the graying of hair and the wrinkling of skin. But some of the most serious changes affect the brain, whose frontal lobes shrink proportionally more than other brain regions (Cowell et al., 1994). Scientists once believed that cognitive problems such as confusion and memory loss were a normal, inevitable part of aging. They now recognize that most older adults remain alert. Older adults just do some things more slowly.

4.12 Adults Develop Lifelong Social and Emotional Bonds

4.12 LEARNING GOAL ACTIVITIES

To maximize your learning, complete the following learning goal activities.

a. Understand all bold and italic terms by writing explanations of them in your own words.

b. Evaluate socio-emotional development in adulthood by explaining why overcoming the three psychosocial challenges in adulthood can make this one of the happiest and most satisfying times of life.

Despite its sometimes rocky road, adolescence can be an exciting and gratifying time. Ideally, during this period we meet new friends, learn new ideas, and consolidate our emerging sense of identity. Successfully meeting the challenges of adolescence prepares us to face the challenges of adulthood. This new set of challenges is based on the need to find meaning in our lives.

PSYCHOSOCIAL CHALLENGES   Think back to Erikson's theory that we develop psychosocially through eight life stages (see Table 4.1, on p. 153). According to Erikson, successful adult development includes having intimate relationships with friends

FIGURE 4.27

Changing Views of the Elderly

(a) The Supreme Court justice Ruth Bader Ginsburg is in her 80s. **(b)** The actor Samuel L. Jackson is in his early 70s. **(c)** The Rolling Stones, now in their 70s, are still making music after nearly six decades.

and partners, giving back to society, and viewing life in a generally positive light, even through the many ups and downs or tragedies.

Young adulthood is the time of Erikson's sixth stage. The psychosocial challenge during this stage, **intimacy versus isolation**, is about forming and maintaining committed friendships and romantic relationships. The key idea is that as young adults we are finding people to share life with in intimate ways. We are moving outward from ourselves rather than being socially isolated. Erikson emphasized the Western value of merging with others while not losing our own sense of identity. For Erikson, building a strong sense of identity in adolescence is crucial for being able to form truly intimate relationships with others in adulthood. He argued that if a person has no sense of self, it is more difficult to engage in honest, open, emotionally close relationships with others (Erikson, 1980).

Erikson's seventh-stage challenge, **generativity versus stagnation**, takes place during middle age. This stage focuses on making improvements for future generations. Caring for children, being productive in a career, having regard for others, and being concerned about the future are positive psychosocial actions of this stage. Some adults, for example, achieve generativity by choosing careers that use their knowledge of psychology to educate children, as described in Putting Psychology to Work on p. 169.

If we have had children and they turned out well, and if we have contributed to our communities, we are more likely to leave middle age with a sense of generativity, or leaving a positive legacy. The opposite of generativity, stagnation, includes a feeling that life is going nowhere or that we are very materialistic and self-centered. Contemporary research indicates that people who are high in generativity have a more positive outlook on life (McAdams & Olson, 2010).

In old age, we reach Erikson's last challenge, **integrity versus despair**. Integrity refers to a sense of honesty about ourselves and a feeling that our lives have been well lived, so that facing death is neither scary nor depressing. For Erikson, the psychosocial challenge of late adulthood involves how we view our lives, not whether those lives were easy or trauma free. The crisis at this stage can be triggered by events that highlight the mortal nature of human life, such as the death of a spouse or close friend. The crisis also can be triggered by changing social and occupational roles, such as retirement. Resolving the final challenge lets us come to terms with the reality of death. If we have many regrets, lack close relationships, or are angry about getting older, we may resolve the psychosocial conflict with a sense of despair instead of integrity. Although Erikson's theory paints a rather mixed view of old age, a great deal of evidence suggests that older adults are much more satisfied with their lives than was traditionally believed. One recent study of older adults between ages 65 and 92 found that life satisfaction generally increased over an 8-year period (Gana, Bailly, Saada, Joulain, & Alaphilippe, 2013).

MARRIAGE In adulthood, people devote a great deal of effort to having satisfying relationships. One way to do this is through marriage. Around the world, the vast majority of people marry at some point in their lives or form some type of permanent bond with a relationship partner (**Figure 4.28**). As marriage equality increases globally, more same-sex couples are also marrying. However, the percentage of people who marry is declining slowly in most industrialized countries, and people today marry later in life than did those in the past (Grossman, 2005).

Most research done to date shows that marriage has psychological benefits for heterosexual couples. For example, married people generally live longer than people who were never married, were divorced, or were widowed (Waite, 1995). When people's income rises (as by combining two salaries through marriage), they are able to live in safer neighborhoods, have better health care, eat better, and so on. Compared with those who are unmarried, married people typically experience greater happiness and joy and are at less risk for psychological disorders such as depression (Robles & Kiecolt-Glaser, 2003). These benefits also exist for same-sex married people (Herek, 2006).

Since same-sex marriage was legalized in many countries around the world, including the United States in 2015, more studies have explored the benefits of marriage for same-sex couples. The few studies conducted so far have found that marriage also provides significant physical and mental health benefits for lesbian, gay, or bisexual individuals (Wight, LeBlanc, & Badgett, 2013). In addition, the benefits of being in a relationship also extend to cohabiting same-sex couples compared with those in a relationship who are living on their own (Williams & Fredriksen-Goldsen, 2014).

Overall, the research with heterosexual couples indicates that the benefits of marriage are more significant for men than for women (House, Landis, & Umberson, 1988; Umberson, 1992). Studies suggest that men may benefit from marriage because their wives make sure they smoke less, eat more healthily, and go to the doctor (Ross, Mirowsky, & Goldsteen, 1990). Women serve as the primary social support for their husbands. Married men report higher sexual and relationship satisfaction than do cohabiting and single men (Hughes & Waite, 2009). By contrast, married women report more emotional satisfaction than do cohabiting or single women (Christopher & Sprecher, 2000), but they report no difference in sexual or relationship satisfaction. You will read more about the sexual lives of older adults in Chapter 10.

Despite its advantages, marriage is not a cure-all. Unhappily married people are at greater risk for poor health and even mortality than happily married people. In general, people who are in unhappy marriages, are separated, or are divorced have many physical and psychological struggles, ranging from depression to physical illness to violent behavior (Carrère, Buehlman, Gottman, Coan, & Ruckstuhl, 2000). Note, though, that these studies are largely correlational. It could be that happy, well-adjusted people are more likely to get married and not that marriage causes good outcomes for people. Or perhaps unhappy, negative people have both health problems and strained marriages.

The good news is that according to national surveys, at any given time the vast majority of married people report satisfaction with their marriages. Those reporting the most satisfaction tend to have sufficient economic resources, share decision making, and together hold the view that marriage should be a lifelong commitment (Amato, Johnson, Booth, & Rogers, 2003). Having a successful marriage contributes to a sense of generativity in middle adulthood, as does having children.

HAVING CHILDREN   The birth of a first child is a profound event for most couples. In fact, this arrival changes their lives in almost every respect. Seeing a baby's first social smile, watching the first few steps, and hearing the child's first words are powerful rewards for parents. Being a parent is central to the identity of many adults. They often become immersed in their children's lives, making sure their children have playmates, exposing them to new experiences, and seeking ways to make them happy and healthy. Having children can provide meaning in life and many moments of joy (Nelson, Kushlev, English, Dunn, & Lyubomirsky, 2013; **Figure 4.29a**).

Children can strain a couple's relationship, however, especially when time and money are tight. For example, Philip and Carolyn Cowan, a married couple who are also marriage researchers, have found that couples with children, especially those with adolescent children, consistently report less marital satisfaction than those who are childless (Belsky, 1990; Cowan & Cowan, 1988; Hansen, 2012). Most couples feel their love will be enough to make the birth of a baby a blissful time. These couples often receive a rude awakening when they are sleep deprived,

(a)

(b)

(c)

FIGURE 4.28
Marriage

Across cultures, marriage remains a building block of society. If the statistics hold true, **(a)** this Sami couple in Norway, **(b)** this English couple in the London Borough of Islington, and **(c)** this Hani couple in China will report being happy in their marriages.

(a)

(b)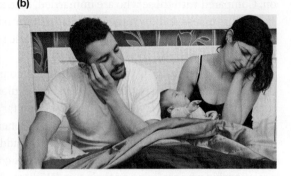

FIGURE 4.29
Having Children Is Both a Joy and a Strain on a Couple's Relationship
(a) Having children is a key part of socio-emotional development for most adults because it provides an amazing opportunity to experience the joy of a parent-child emotional bond. **(b)** But having children can also create conflict within a couple's relationship. Such conflict has to be managed in a positive way to ensure success for the family.

agitated, and less than skilled at caring for their new bundle of joy, especially during the first months (Cowan & Cowan, 1988; **Figure 4.29b**).

However, researchers are also trying to find ways to prepare parents for parenthood so the transition does not put such a strain on the relationship. The Cowans (1988) have found that many couples do not discuss their roles and responsibilities before they have a child. This failure to communicate leads to misunderstandings and feelings of resentment after the child's birth. The Cowans recommend that couples have serious and detailed conversations about all aspects of their lives and how they will approach each task after the baby is born.

Partners who report their early married life as chaotic or negative are more likely to find that having a baby does not bring them closer together or solve their problems. Instead, raising the child increases the existing strain. Teaching newlyweds or young partners how to communicate and understand each other's needs may prevent divorce, and it may also let the couple enjoy parenting when their children are young as well as when the couple grows older and the children eventually leave home (Shapiro, Gottman, & Carrère, 2000).

However, after studying millions of people around the world, Deaton and Stone (2014) have concluded, "If parents choose to be parents, and nonparents choose to be nonparents, there is no reason to expect that one group will be better or worse off than the other one" (p. 1328). In other words, if you choose the parenting status that makes sense for you as an individual, the decision to have kids (or not) will not make or break your happiness. The important thing is to consider the consequences before you make your decision.

FINDING MEANING IN LATER LIFE   People of all ages want to find meaning in life. But meaning often becomes a preoccupation for the elderly. As people grow older, they perceive time to be limited, so they adjust their priorities to emphasize emotionally meaningful events, experiences, and goals (Carstensen, 1995; Fung & Carstensen, 2004). For instance, they may choose to spend more time with a smaller group of close friends and avoid new people. They may spend an increasing amount of time reflecting on their lives and sharing memories with family members and friends. Indeed, they report shorter and fewer negative emotional experiences in their daily lives (Charles, Mogle, Urban, & Almeida, 2016).

The message here is that older adults want to savor their final years by putting their time and effort into meaningful and rewarding experiences. To the extent that they consider their time well spent, older adults are satisfied and can live their final years gracefully. This result is especially likely if throughout their lives they have worked hard to maintain their physical health, their social ties, and their cognitive capacities.

4.13 The Mental Abilities of Adults Begin to Decline

4.13 LEARNING GOAL ACTIVITIES

To maximize your learning, complete the following learning goal activities.

a. Understand all bold and italic terms by writing explanations of them in your own words.

b. Apply the cognitive aspects of development in adulthood by providing a description of how the mental abilities of someone you know have changed as the person has aged.

As you learned in study unit 4.11, the baby boom generation is filling a large percentage of judgeships and providing us with some still-favorite entertainers. That generation has also brought us the common phrase *a senior moment*—the inability to remember something we knew a moment before. In that moment, we know we're just not as sharp as we once were.

Although we may not notice until later adulthood, our cognitive abilities actually begin declining much earlier in our lives. It's difficult to pinpoint exactly what causes the decline. The frontal lobes, which play an important role in certain types of memory and many other cognitive skills, typically shrink as people grow older. One of the most consistent and identifiable cognitive changes is a slowing of mental processing speed. As early as the mid-20s, it takes us longer to process a sensory input and react with a motor response, and the response time becomes greater as we age (Era, Jokela, & Heikkinen, 1986).

Some of the observed decline may result from sensory-perceptual changes that occur with age. For instance, our sensitivity to visual contrast decreases, so activities such as climbing stairs or driving at night may become more difficult and more dangerous. Sensitivity to sound also decreases with age, especially the ability to tune out background noise. This change may make older people seem confused or forgetful when they simply are not able to hear well enough. And unfortunately, aging also affects memory and intelligence.

INTELLIGENCE, LEARNING, AND MEMORY   For 7 years, the Seattle Longitudinal Study tracked participants between the ages of 25 and 81 to address questions of intelligence during aging (Schaie, 1990). By testing cognitive abilities such as verbal and mathematical skills, the researchers found that intellectual decline does not occur until people are in their 60s or 70s. Further, they found that people who were healthy and stayed mentally active demonstrated less decline.

Older adults do take longer to learn new information. But once they learn it, they use that information as efficiently as young adults do. For example, in one study, providing specific and meaningful cues—triggers for memories—allowed older adults to remember just as many personal details about their lives as young adults did (Aizpurua & Koutstaal, 2015). Moreover, older adults have accumulated a great deal of knowledge over their lives and therefore tend to know more than younger adults. Perhaps for this reason, we often view older adults as wise.

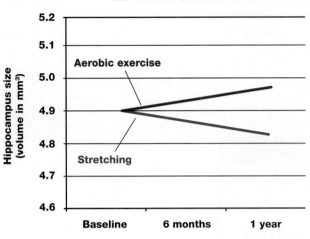

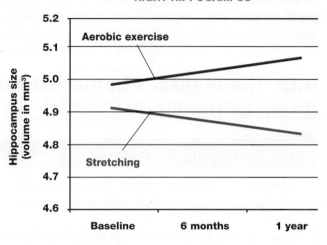

FIGURE 4.30

Aerobic Exercise May Improve Memory Abilities Even as We Age

Participants in this study engaged in either vigorous aerobic exercise or gentle stretching activities. A year later, the results showed an increase in the size of the left and right hippocampi and improvements in memory, but only in the group who did aerobic exercise.

dementia
Severe impairment in intellectual capacity and personality, often due to damage to the brain.

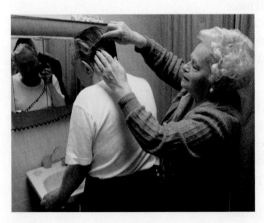

FIGURE 4.31

Impairments from Alzheimer's Disease

A woman helps her husband, who has Alzheimer's disease. This brain condition, which is the major cause of dementia, occurs in the elderly.

Older people tend to have difficulty with memory tasks that require juggling multiple pieces of information at the same time. Tasks that call for them to do several things at once, such as driving while listening to the radio, also prove difficult. Although memory and the speed of processing may decline, the continued ability to learn new information may offset those losses in terms of daily functioning. For example, decades of research show that when people challenge their brains by learning new tasks, working puzzles, reading, remaining socially active, and maintaining physical exercise at least three days per week, their risk of dementia declines significantly (Fratiglioni, Paillard-Borg, & Winblad, 2004; Larson et al., 2006). Older adults can improve their memories if they do aerobic exercise in particular (Erickson et al., 2011; Prakash, Voss, Erickson, & Kramer, 2015). This benefit seems to come because vigorous exercise that increases the heart rate increases the size of the hippocampus (**Figure 4.30**). And as you learned in study unit 2.6, the hippocampus is important for creating memories, so these findings make sense.

DEMENTIA Older adults who experience dramatic losses in mental ability may be experiencing **dementia**. This brain condition causes declines in thinking, memory, and behavior. Dementia has many causes, including excessive alcohol intake and HIV. But for older adults, the major causes are Alzheimer's disease and small strokes that affect the brain's blood supply. After age 70, the risk of dementia increases with each year of life. Approximately 5 percent of people will develop Alzheimer's disease by age 70–75, and 6.5 percent will develop the disease after age 85 (Kawas, Gray, Brookmeyer, Fozard, & Zonderman, 2000).

The initial symptoms of Alzheimer's are typically minor memory impairments, but the disease eventually progresses to more serious difficulties, such as forgetting daily routines (**Figure 4.31**). It takes about 4 years for people to progress from mild cognitive impairment to a diagnosis of Alzheimer's (Villemagne et al., 2013). Eventually, the person loses all mental capacities, including memory and language. Many people with Alzheimer's also experience profound personality changes. While we do not know the exact cause of Alzheimer's, some people seem to have a genetic predisposition to its development (Sala Frigerio & De Strooper, 2016).

WELL-BEING IN OLDER ADULTS The picture for older adults may seem grim, but predispositions for Alzheimer's or other kinds of dementia are not hopeless cases. Environment also has an impact on older adults' development. As people age, playing active roles in their own development may help ease adulthood transitions. Some of those transitions may become nonthreatening, even deeply rewarding experiences.

Except for dementia, older adults have fewer mental health problems, including depression, than younger adults (Jorm, 2000). Indeed, some individuals thrive in old age, especially those with adequate financial resources and good health (Crosnoe & Elder, 2002). Most older adults report being just as satisfied with life, if not more so, as younger adults are (Mroczek & Kolarz, 1998).

Despite the physical, social, and emotional challenges of aging, most older adults are healthy and happy (**Figure 4.32**).

Thus this chapter ends where it began, with a reminder that all aspects of human development result from a complex interplay of influences. These influences include genes, hormones, family, social ties, culture, and each individual's motivations and actions. We all play active roles in our own development. We are not passively absorbing our environments, nor are we solely ruled by our genes. How we experience each phase of the life span depends on our own perceptions, the social support we receive, and the choreographed dance between nature and nurture.

FIGURE 4.32

Maintaining Health and Happiness
Most older adults report being very happy. Activities that stimulate the brain (such as doing crossword puzzles) and the body (such as swimming and walking) are associated with staying healthy and happy for as long as possible.

 How Do Adults Develop?

To make sure you learned what you just read, write answers to the following questions and check your answers.

4.11 What are the two main ways of sustaining physical and psychological health in adulthood?

4.12 In heterosexual marriage, why might husbands generally receive more benefit than wives do?

4.13 What is dementia?

See Appendix B for answers to the red Q questions.

BIG PICTURE

Want to earn a better grade on your test? Go to **INQUIZITIVE** to practice actively with this chapter's content and get personalized feedback along the way.

How Does Development Happen in the Womb?

4.1 Humans Develop Across Three Domains

Review the learning goal activities on p. 131. Developmental psychology explores growth in terms of how nature and nurture affect human development. Human development occurs in three interacting domains: (1) physical, (2) socio-emotional, and (3) cognitive.

4.2 Prenatal Development Includes Three Periods of Physical Growth

Review the learning goal activities on p. 132. Prenatal physical development occurs in three periods: (1) The germinal period is from conception to the end of week 2. It includes conception, cell division, implantation in the womb, and development of the placenta to nourish the zygote. Abnormalities occurring at this stage usually result in miscarriage. (2) The embryonic period is from week 3 through week 8. During this critical time, all the organs are formed. Developmental differences occurring in this period primarily cause major physical defects, but also psychological deficits and minor physical defects. (3) The fetal period is from week 9 to birth, usually about week 40. During this time, organ development is finalized, the organs begin to function, and the fetus prepares for birth. Developmental differences in this period primarily result in psychological deficits and physical defects.

4.3 Substances Affect Prenatal Development in All Three Domains

Review the learning goal activities on p. 134. Teratogens are substances that can harm prenatal development. They may have long-term effects on physical, cognitive, and/or socio-emotional development. Teratogens can include legal drugs, recreational drugs, infections, and environmental factors.

KEY TERMS
developmental psychology   (p. 131)
germinal period   (p. 132)
embryonic period   (p. 132)
fetal period   (p. 133)
teratogens   (p. 134)

How Do Infants and Children Develop?

4.4 Infants and Children Change Physically

Review the learning goal activities on p. 137. In the first years of life, infants and children experience two major changes in the brain: (1) More myelinated axons form synapses with other neurons, (2) and then unneeded synapses are eliminated through neural pruning. Infants are born with innate survival abilities, including the rooting, sucking, and grasping reflexes. They also develop physically in consistent stages, called maturation. Maturation, together with experience, allows infants to learn how to move voluntarily to roll over, sit up, and walk. Early feeding and social bonding are encouraged through infants' taste preferences and sensory abilities in vision, hearing, and smell.

4.5 Infants and Children Change Socially and Emotionally

Review the learning goal activities on p. 140. An attachment is an enduring emotional connection that can motivate care, protection, and social support. Forming strong attachments with caregivers helps infants develop appropriate social interactions and emotion regulation. According to Harlow's research, attachments form due to receiving comfort and warmth, not food. Indeed, when infants are apart from caregivers they show signs of distress, called separation anxiety. The strange-situation test reveals that infants have three types of attachment: (1) secure, (2) avoidant, and (3) ambivalent.

4.6 Infants and Children Change Cognitively

Review the learning goal activities on p. 143. Cognitive development is related to theory of mind. This ability—to understand that other people have minds and intentions—develops by about 13–15 months of age. Infants' and children's cognitive abilities also become more advanced with time and experience as they use what Piaget described as assimilation and accommodation to create and adjust mental schemas about objects and experiences. These schemas form the basis of Piaget's theory of four stages of children's cognitive development: (1) sensorimotor (0–2 years), (2) preoperational (2–7 years), (3) concrete operational (7–12 years), and (4) formal operational (12 years–adulthood). While Piaget's theory correctly describes much of cognitive development, it seems to underestimate early cognitive abilities. Theories such as Vygotsky's emphasize that cognitive development is guided by cultural and social experiences and that development of language further promotes higher thinking.

4.7 Language Develops in an Orderly Way

Review the learning goal activities on p. 149. Language is made up of sounds: phonemes (basic sounds) and morphemes (the smallest units of speech that have meaning). Sounds make up words that are combined into phrases and sentences based on rules called syntax. Children develop language in five stages: (1) cooing (3–5 months), (2) babbling (5–8 months), (3) one-word (8–18 months), (4) telegraphic speech (18–24 months), (5) overregularization (3–5 years).

KEY TERMS

maturation (p. 138)
secure attachment (p. 142)
avoidant attachment (p. 142)
ambivalent attachment (p. 142)
assimilation (p. 144)
accommodation (p. 144)
sensorimotor stage (p. 145)

preoperational stage (p. 146)
concrete operational stage (p. 147)
formal operational stage (p. 147)
babbling (p. 150)
telegraphic speech (p. 150)
overregularization (p. 150)

How Do Adolescents Develop?

4.8 Adolescents Develop Physically

Review the learning goal activities on p. 151. Adolescence begins with puberty, when physical changes turn children into young adults. Pubertal changes start with the development of secondary sex characteristics (such as pubic hair), which are not directly related to reproduction. Puberty then continues with the development of primary sex characteristics (such as mature genitals and internal sex organs, menstruation in females, and sperm production in males), which directly allow sexual reproduction. Pubertal changes also occur in the brain, where the frontal lobes mature more slowly than emotional processing in the amygdala and brain reward systems, so adolescents may tend to act impulsively and take risks.

4.9 Adolescents Develop Socially and Emotionally

Review the learning goal activities on p. 152. During adolescence, teens develop socio-emotionally. According to Erikson's theory of psychosocial development, people must overcome a series of challenges from birth through old age. The challenge during adolescence is to develop an adult identity or risk role confusion. The factors involved in developing an identity in adolescence include understanding one's gender, sexual orientation, culture, ethnicity, and relationships with parents and peers.

4.10 Adolescents Develop Cognitively.

Review the learning goal activities on p. 155. During adolescence, cognitive development leads to more-sophisticated moral reasoning and moral emotions. According to Kohlberg, this development occurs in three stages. (1) In the preconventional stage, a person makes moral decisions based on self-interest. (2) In the conventional stage, a person makes moral decisions based on following rules or laws or trying to gain social approval from others. (3) In the postconventional stage, a person makes moral decisions based on complex reasoning, the value of life, and the greater good for all people. Theories of moral reasoning have been criticized for being gender-biased and culture-biased and for ignoring emotional aspects of moral decisions.

KEY TERMS

puberty (p. 151)
secondary sex characteristics (p. 152)
primary sex characteristics (p. 152)
identity versus role confusion (p. 154)

preconventional level (p. 156)
conventional level (p. 156)
postconventional level (p. 156)

How Do Adults Develop?

4.11 Bodies Change in Adulthood

Review the learning goal activities on p. 158. Between ages 20 and 40, we experience physical decline. A healthy lifestyle, especially during early adulthood, can help maintain physical and psychological health through adulthood. At about age 50, the body and mind, especially the frontal lobes of the brain, deteriorate more rapidly.

4.12 Adults Develop Lifelong Social and Emotional Bonds

Review the learning goal activities on p. 159. In adulthood, we experience several psychosocial challenges: in young adulthood,

intimacy versus isolation; in middle age, generativity versus stagnation; in old age, integrity versus despair. Adults work to resolve these challenges by developing long-term relationships, having children and rewarding careers, and feeling satisfied. In general, married people, both heterosexual and same-sex couples, are healthier and happier than those who are single or cohabitating. This advantage is more pronounced in heterosexual men. Couples with children report less marital satisfaction than couples without children, but raising children can enhance life. Whether to become a parent is best considered a matter of individual choice. In old age, people often become preoccupied with the meaning of life.

4.13 The Mental Abilities of Adults Begin to Decline

Review the learning goal activities on p. 163. Despite natural cognitive declines for people after age 60 or 70, older adults generally maintain their intelligence, knowledge, and memory for long-past events into very old age. Most older adults remain healthy, alert, and vital. Only some older adults experience dementia. Staying active mentally and physically can help maintain cognitive abilities. Older people are often more satisfied with their lives than younger adults are.

KEY TERMS

intimacy versus isolation   (p. 160)
generativity versus stagnation   (p. 160)
integrity versus despair   (p. 160)
dementia   (p. 164)

CHAPTER 4 SELF-QUIZ

To make sure you learned the information in this chapter, write answers to the following questions and check your answers. **See Appendix B for answers to the self-quiz.**

1. Latonia is pregnant. Her doctor told her that the baby has developed enough that it can now live outside of the womb. Right now, Latonia is most likely in the _____ period of pregnancy.
   a. fetal
   b. teratogen
   c. embryonic
   d. germinal

2. Reagan is 3 weeks pregnant, but doesn't know it yet. She drinks a few glasses of wine two or three days each week. In this case, alcohol is a _____ that may put her baby at risk for _____.
   a. teratogen; irritability and high-pitched crying
   b. germinal; irritability and high-pitched crying
   c. germinal; malformation of the face and limbs and intellectual disabilities
   d. teratogen; malformation of the face and limbs and intellectual disabilities

3. Dr. Cortez, a pediatrician, focuses on the biological factors that influence physical development. In his view, children learn to walk only after they can stand and crawl. His wife reminds him that their children learned to walk at somewhat different ages, depending on how often each child was willing to practice walking with her. From this information, you might assume that Dr. Cortez believes that physical development is primarily influenced by _____ and his wife believes that it is mainly affected by _____.
   a. maturation; nature
   b. maturation; nurture
   c. assimilation; nature
   d. assimilation; nurture

4. Peter is 2 years old, and his mother takes him to see a new dentist. When Peter's mother leaves him alone with the dentist for a few minutes, Peter begins to cry and cannot be calmed down. When his mother returns, Peter lets her pick him up, then pushes her away. This scenario suggests that Peter has most likely formed a(n) _____ attachment with his mother.
   a. ambivalent
   b. avoidant
   c. secure
   d. mature

5. Shay's parents pay attention to the new thinking skills that Shay acquires. They realize he has passed out of Piaget's preoperational stage into the next stage of cognitive development when he _____.
   a. plans his next several chess moves in his head when playing chess with his dad
   b. tells them his "truck is happy" because it got a bath in the washing machine
   c. found his favorite pacifier hiding under the blanket in his crib
   d. correctly answered the question "What is 8 minus 2?" with the help of his fingers

6. Mary and her younger brother, Eric, are playing in the front yard. Eric has mastered correct grammar in English, but he displays overregularization when he says, _____
   a. "Ball me pass to play!"
   b. "Water now!"
   c. "Mary! I forgetted to feed my pet worms!"
   d. "We need to play outside and not watch TV!"

7. Eva was 9 years old when she started to develop breasts, which is a _____. Then, at age 12, Eva began menstruation, which is a _____.
   a. sign of maturation; sign of puberty
   b. sign of puberty; sign of maturation
   c. primary sex characteristic; secondary sex characteristic
   d. secondary sex characteristic; primary sex characteristic

8. Kurt's friend Friedrich steals an iPad from another student in their dorm. Kurt decides to tell the police what Friedrich did because Kurt thinks that stealing the iPad was against the law. This reasoning reveals that Kurt is most likely in the _____ stage of moral development.
   a. preconventional
   b. postconventional
   c. unconventional
   d. conventional

9. Zach, a 42-year-old, very much wants to have children, but he has never found the right person to have them with. He decides to adopt a child because he wants to make a positive contribution to the future. Zach's decision to adopt and raise a child most likely reflects that he is successfully dealing with the psychosocial challenge of _____.

   a. trust
   b. generativity
   c. integrity
   d. intimacy

10. Tanya is 78 years old and has stayed physically and mentally active, so she is experiencing only the normal cognitive decline of a person her age. As a result, Tanya is least likely to have trouble with _____.
    a. thinking and reacting quickly to road signs when she is driving
    b. trying to keep in mind a list of items to buy at the store while also talking to a friend she sees in the store
    c. remembering what she learned long ago, such as the names of the state capitals
    d. quickly learning the names of several new people that she meets at a party

How Does Knowledge of Human Development Help in Educational Settings?

In April 2017, Mayor Bill de Blasio announced a plan to provide free, full-time preschool for all New York City 3-year-olds. This program, known as 3-K for All, extends the early education programs already in place for 4-year-olds and will be the largest program of its kind in the United States. As you learned in study units 4.5–4.7, ages 3–5 are a critical time for the development of children's cognitive and socio-emotional abilities. Not surprisingly, preschool and daycare programs are being implemented throughout the country, particularly for high-need groups. As the number of such programs increases, so does the need for highly qualified teachers, daycare providers, and administrators.

With an associate's degree and proper certification, you can become a skilled childcare worker in a daycare center. This position involves tending to children's basic needs, such as feeding and cleaning. It may also involve supporting their socio-emotional development through nurturing and promoting cognitive development through enriching and engaging activities. Knowing how children learn language will help you understand the stages that children go through and the typical mistakes they make as they learn to talk.

What makes a preschool teacher "highly qualified"? The Institute of Medicine and National Research Council (2015, p. 328) recommends that early childhood teachers and directors hold at least a bachelor's degree, with expertise in "developmental science that underlies important domains of early learning and child development." This recommendation is, of course, good news for psychology students who are interested in working with children. Preschool teachers who are familiar with the cognitive and socio-emotional needs of very young children will be better able to design and implement age-appropriate programs, improving the likelihood of long-term benefits.

Beyond daycare and preschool, teachers and administrators with knowledge of human development can help elementary and secondary school students. Supporting student learning in a developmentally suitable fashion can involve positive daily interactions and designing learning programs. To improve academic, mental, and behavioral outcomes, a psychology graduate can pursue a master's degree to become a school psychologist. And because people remain students throughout their lives, understanding the development of adults is important in any aspect of life, including the workplace.

TAKEAWAY POINT: An understanding of how children develop physically, socio-emotionally, and cognitively has many applications in the education job sector. Examples include daycare worker, teacher, and administrator, from the preschool level to elementary and secondary school levels.

 You can look up job descriptions, education requirements, salaries, and more at the Bureau of Labor Statistics: www.bls.gov. Visit the site and start putting psychology to work!

5 Sensation and Perception

WHAT DO YOU EXPERIENCE when you see the color red or eat chocolate? If you are like most people, you experience red as a visual phenomenon. You may associate this color with stoplights or stop signs. You experience eating chocolate as a sweet taste. You may associate this taste with pleasure. Every moment of your life, you are processing information from your senses, consciously or unconsciously. But some people have pretty strange descriptions for their experiences.

William hates driving because, to him, the sight of road signs tastes like a gross mixture of pistachio ice cream and earwax (McNeil, 2006). For Michael, any personal name has a specific taste—for

BIG QUESTIONS

How Do Sensation and Perception Affect You?

How Do You See?

How Do You Hear?

How Are You Able to Taste and Smell?

How Do You Feel Touch and Pain?

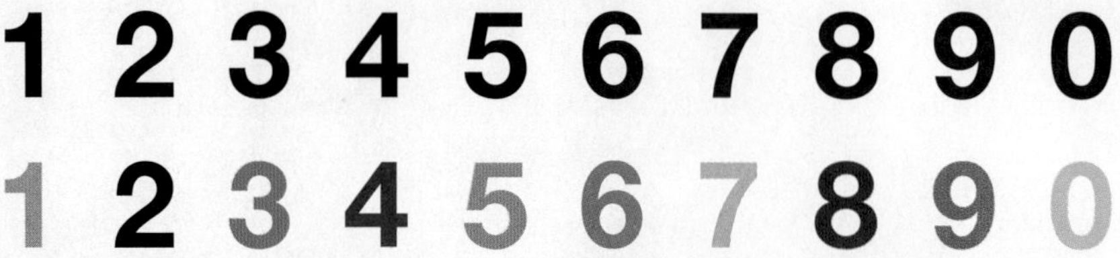

1 2 3 4 5 6 7 8 9 0
1 2 3 4 5 6 7 8 9 0

FIGURE 5.1

Synesthesia Shows Unusual Relationships Between Sensation and Perception
In synesthesia, sensory input in one form triggers an additional experience in another form. For example, in color-number synesthesia, each number printed in black ink is perceived as a particular color.

example, the name "John" tastes like corn bread (Simner et al., 2006). Another person experiences each day of the week, or month of the year, as a particular color—Monday is red, Tuesday is indigo, December is yellow, and so on (Ramachandran & Hubbard, 2003). Other people experience colors as smells, sights as sounds, or sounds as colors and shapes.

This condition, where sensory input in one form triggers an additional experience in another form, is called synesthesia. If you have never experienced synesthesia, it is almost impossible to imagine. Indeed, each person who has synesthesia experiences it in a very personal and consistent way. For example, a certain number printed in black ink may always appear to be one particular color (Ramachandran, 2003; **Figure 5.1**). Estimates of the percentage of the population that reports these cross-sensory experiences range from 1 in 2,000 to 1 in 200. And reports of people with synesthesia date as far back as ancient Greece (Ferry, 2002).

Research into synesthesia can give us insight into how people process sensory input as well as how our brains help us perceive sensory information in our own unique ways. The perceptual system is stunningly intelligent in its ability to guide us around. For example, right this minute your brain is making millions of calculations to produce a unified experience of your environment. Your abilities to see, hear, taste, smell, and touch emerge from these brain processes.

How Do Sensation and Perception Affect You?

Imagine you take half a grapefruit out of the refrigerator and dig into it with a spoon. Some juice splashes out of the fruit and hits your nose and mouth. What do your senses tell you? You smell some strong fragrance. You feel something cold on your skin. You taste something sharp on your tongue. So far, your experience consists of raw sensation. Your sensory systems have detected features of the juice.

But even when people experience the exact same sensory input, they experience that input differently. If you like grapefruit, you might experience this splash as at least partly pleasant. But suppose you dislike grapefruit—maybe your father has insisted that you eat it. In this case, you might experience the splash as totally unpleasant.

In every second of your life, you are bombarded with input from the world around you. All of this information is processed into sights, sounds, smells, tastes, and touches that you experience in your own unique way.

5.1 Your Senses Detect Physical Stimuli, and Your Brain Processes Perception

5.1 LEARNING GOAL ACTIVITIES

To maximize your learning, complete the following learning goal activities:

a. Understand all bold and italic terms by writing explanations of them in your own words.

b. Apply the four steps from sensation to perception to your life, using a sensory input you have experienced.

sensation
The sense organs' detection of external physical stimulus and the transmission of information about this stimulus to the brain.

perception
The processing, organization, and interpretation of sensory signals in the brain; these processes result in an internal neural representation of the physical stimulus.

Sensation is the detection of physical stimuli from the world around you and the sending of that information to your brain. Physical stimuli can be light waves, sound waves, food molecules, odor molecules, temperature changes, or pressure changes on the skin. When you detect a splash of grapefruit juice, you are sensing food molecules, odor molecules, slight temperature changes, and slight pressure changes on your skin.

Perception is the brain's further processing of sensory information. This processing results in your conscious experience of the world. The essence of perception is interpreting sensation. That is, your perceptual systems (as opposed to your sensory systems) translate sensation into information that is meaningful and useful. In the grapefruit juice example, perception is your interpretation of the sensory stimuli of cold droplets, a strong smell, and a sharp taste as qualities of grapefruit. To help you understand the differences between sensation and perception, see Try It Yourself below.

FROM SENSATION TO PERCEPTION   Suppose you are driving, and the traffic signal changes from red to green. Believe it or not, there is actually no red or green color in the signal or in the light you see. Instead, your eyes and brain work together so that you see the redness or greenness of the light. Objects in the physical world don't actually have color. Each object reflects light waves of particular lengths. Our visual systems interpret those waves as different colors.

TRY IT YOURSELF: Sensation and Perception

If you and your friends look at the same car, will you all agree on the color? Check it out with this example:

1. Look only at the picture of the car. Decide what color the car is, and write down the name of the color. Then look at the color bar and decide which color sample is most similar to how you see the color of the car. Write down the number.

2. Now ask a few other people to do the things in Step 1.

3. Most likely, some people have labeled the car color the same way you did. Some people have chosen different labels. However, the label a person chooses for the color doesn't tell us what that person has actually perceived.

4. But even people who labeled the car the same way you did might have chosen a different color sample from the one that you chose. This result suggests you had different perceptions of the same color.

What does this demonstration show? The sensory input, the sensation, is the same for people. Yet each person has a unique perception of that input. Taken together, sensation and perception make up all of our individual experiences with the world.

1 Physical stimulus:
A traffic light turns green. Light waves are the physical stimulus.

2 Sensation:
The light waves are detected by sensory receptors in the driver's eyes.

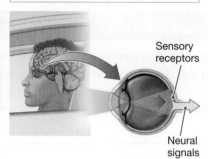

3 Transduction:
The sensory receptors translate the physical stimulus into signals. Those signals will become neural signals.

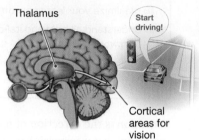

4 Perception:
The neural signals travel along nerve fibers to the thalamus. Then cortical areas in the brain process the signals and construct a representation of a green light. The brain interprets the light as indicating "*Start driving!*"

Sensory receptors

Thalamus

Start driving!

Neural signals

Cortical areas for vision

FIGURE 5.2

From Sensation to Perception

Here is a summary of the four steps in the process of changing sensory input into a personal experience. The example is for sensation and perception of vision, but the steps in general also apply to hearing, taste, smell, and touch. However, information about smell is not processed through the thalamus.

sensory receptors
Sensory organs that detect physical stimulation from the external world and change that stimulation into information that can be processed by the brain.

transduction
A process by which sensory receptors change physical stimuli into signals that are eventually sent to the brain.

So how do light waves get changed into information that the brain can process? Special cells in our eyes respond to these different wavelengths and change that physical signal into information that the brain can interpret. If you are driving and your brain receives information about a green traffic light, your brain most likely will interpret that light as meaning "Go."

To understand more clearly both sensation and perception, imagine that you drive up to a traffic signal as it turns green. The green light is actually the physical stimulus in the form of light waves (**Figure 5.2**, Step 1). That stimulus is detected by specialized cells called **sensory receptors.** The receptors' detection of the stimulus is sensation (see Figure 5.2, Step 2).

In a process called **transduction,** the sensory receptors change the stimulus input to signals that the brain can understand (see Figure 5.2, Step 3). In some cases, such as taste, transduction directly results in neurons firing action potentials (to review the firing of action potentials, see study unit 2.2). For vision, more processing must happen before the information is coded as action potentials. When the brain does process the action potentials, you will interpret them as green light. You will also register the meaning of that traffic signal as "Go." This further processing of the information following transduction is perception (see Figure 5.2, Step 4).

This example demonstrates the general processes of sensation and perception. However, the details are slightly different for each sense. In this chapter, you will

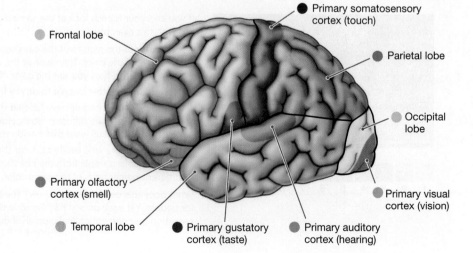

FIGURE 5.3

The Brain's Primary Sensory Areas

Except for smell, all sensory input travels to the thalamus and then on to cortical regions that process information about touch, vision, hearing, taste, and smell.

Primary somatosensory cortex (touch)

Frontal lobe

Parietal lobe

Occipital lobe

Primary olfactory cortex (smell)

Primary visual cortex (vision)

Temporal lobe

Primary gustatory cortex (taste)

Primary auditory cortex (hearing)

learn about the four steps of sensation and perception for each major sensory system. In each case, a physical stimulus is detected, specialized sensory receptors transduce the stimulus information, and neurons fire action potentials. These action potentials are the sensory information that is sent through the thalamus (except for information about smell) to specific regions of the brain for interpretation (**Figure 5.3**).

The sum of this activity, across all of your senses, is your huge range of perceptions. And your perceptions add up to your experience of the world. If you get splashed with grapefruit juice or see the color of a traffic light, your sensations and perceptions let you interpret the information and respond appropriately. For example, you decide the juice is delicious or you accelerate the car.

5.2 There Must Be a Certain Amount of a Stimulus for You to Detect It

5.2 LEARNING GOAL ACTIVITIES

To maximize your learning, complete the following learning goal activities:

a. Understand all bold and italic terms by writing explanations of them in your own words.

b. Understand absolute threshold and difference threshold by comparing their similarities and differences in your own words.

Stop reading for a moment and listen carefully. What do you hear? Suppose you hear voices in the next room or music down the hall. Now imagine looking out a nearby window. You can see people across the street talking, but you can't hear them. Why are you able to hear some sounds and not others? How much physical stimulus is required for your sense organs to detect sensory information? How much change in the physical stimulus is required before you notice that change in the sensory information?

THRESHOLD TO DETECT SENSORY INFORMATION An enormous amount of physical stimulation from the world around you reaches your sensory receptors. Even so, you do not notice much of it. Physical stimulation has to go beyond some level before you experience a sensation. The **absolute threshold** is the minimum amount of physical stimuli required before you detect the sensory input (**Figure 5.4**). You can also think of the absolute threshold as the smallest amount of a stimulus a

absolute threshold
The smallest amount of physical stimulation required to detect a sensory input half of the time it is present.

FIGURE 5.4

Absolute Threshold

(a) Can this man detect a soft sound, such as a whisper? **(b)** This graph shows the relationship between the intensity of stimulus input and a person's ability to correctly detect the input. The absolute threshold is the point of stimulus intensity that a person can correctly detect half the time.

(a)

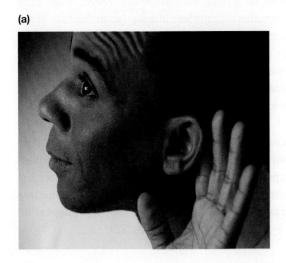

(b)

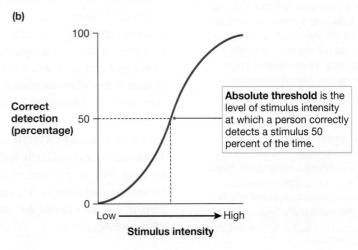

Absolute threshold is the level of stimulus intensity at which a person correctly detects a stimulus 50 percent of the time.

TABLE 5.1

Absolute Threshold to Detect Stimulus Input for Each Sense

Sense	Minimum Sensory Input Required for Detection
Taste	1 teaspoon of sugar in 2 gallons of water
Smell	1 drop of perfume diffused into the entire volume of six rooms
Touch	A fly's wing falling on your cheek from a distance of 0.04 inch
Hearing	The tick of a clock at 20 feet under quiet conditions
Vision	A candle flame 30 miles away on a dark, clear night

Source: Galanter (1962).

difference threshold
The minimum difference in physical stimulation required to detect a difference between sensory inputs.

sensory adaptation
A decrease in sensitivity to a constant level of stimulation.

HAS IT HAPPENED TO YOU?

Difference Threshold

Have you ever been in a car and had to keep turning up the music so that you could hear it above the wind or road noise? You may have turned it up a bit but heard no difference in loudness. So you turned it up a bit more. And maybe even louder still, until you could finally hear the music. This example illustrates the difference threshold. You could not detect small changes in loudness because the music was already so loud. But later on, when you entered the car under quieter conditions, you were probably shocked at how loud the music really was.

person can detect half of the time the stimulus is present. For instance, how loudly must someone in the next room whisper for you to hear it? In this case, the absolute threshold is the quietest whisper you could hear half the time. **Table 5.1** lists some approximate minimum amounts of physical stimuli that are required to detect sensory input for each sense.

A **difference threshold** is the smallest difference that you can notice between two pieces of sensory input. In other words, it is the minimum amount of change in the physical stimulus required to detect a difference between one sensory experience and another. Suppose your friend is watching a television show. You are reading and not paying attention to what's on the screen. If a commercial comes on that is louder than the show, you might look up, noticing that something has changed. In this case, the difference threshold is the minimum change in volume required for you to detect a difference.

The difference threshold increases as the stimulus becomes more intense. Say you pick up a 1-ounce jar of spice and a 2-ounce jar of spice. You will easily detect the difference of 1 ounce. Now pick up a 5-pound package of flour and a package that weighs 5 pounds and 1 ounce. The same difference of 1 ounce between these two will be harder to detect, maybe even impossible to detect.

The principle at work here is called *Weber's law*. This law is based on the work of the nineteenth-century psychologist Ernst Weber. The law states that the *just-noticeable difference* between two sensory inputs is based on a proportion of the original sensory input rather than on a fixed amount of difference. What does that mean? Assume the overall stimulus input is less intense (as in the case of the 1-ounce container). A specific change in input (say, 1 ounce) can easily be detected by a person. But now assume the original stimulus is more intense (as in the case of the 5-pound package). That same change in input (1 ounce) is much harder to detect. Weber's law may sound complex. But as shown in Has It Happened to You?, we experience difference thresholds all the time.

SENSORY ADAPTATION   Our sensory systems are tuned to notice changes in our surroundings. It is important for us to be able to notice such changes because they might require responses. It is less important to keep responding to unchanging stimuli. This tendency for our sensory systems to become less sensitive to processing a constant level of input is called **sensory adaptation** (**Figure 5.5**).

Imagine you are studying and work begins at a nearby construction site. When the loud equipment starts, the sounds might startle you. It makes sense for your sensory systems to process these noises because they could signal danger in your environment. But after a few minutes, the noises seem to fade into the background. Again, it makes sense that if stimuli are presented continuously, your sensory system responses will tend to diminish over time. Once the stimuli continue long enough, they do not seem to indicate danger that you need to respond to.

FIGURE 5.5
Sensory Adaptation
Because of sensory adaptation, people tend to get used to a sensory input over time when it does not require a response.

 How Do Sensation and Perception Affect You?

To make sure you learned what you just read, write answers to the following questions and check your answers.

5.1 What is transduction?

5.2 Is the just-noticeable difference related to the absolute threshold, the difference threshold, or sensory adaptation?

See Appendix B for answers to the red Q questions.

How Do You See?

Does a place look safe or dangerous? Does a person look friendly or hostile? We acquire information through our senses, and vision is an extremely important source of knowledge. Yet sight seems so effortless, so automatic, that most of us take it for granted. But every time you open your eyes, nearly half of your brain springs into action. Your brain is racing to make sense of the light waves arriving in your eyes. Of course, your brain can do this only based on sensory signals from your eyes.

5.3 Sensory Receptors in Your Eyes Detect Light

 5.3 LEARNING GOAL ACTIVITIES

To maximize your learning, complete the following learning goal activities:

a. Understand all bold and italic terms by writing explanations of them in your own words.

b. Understand the four steps in visual sensation and perception by summarizing each step in your own words.

FOCUSING LIGHT IN THE EYE Intricate processes in your eyes are required for you to see as familiar an image as the face of a friend. What is the first step in this process? Believe it or not, light bounces off that object. That light enters your eyes in the form of light waves (**Figure 5.6**). The waves pass through the *cornea* of your eye. The cornea is the eye's thick, transparent outer layer (see Figure 5.6, Step 1).

The light then passes through the *pupil*. This feature is the small opening that looks like a dark circle at the center of the eye. The *iris*, a circular muscle, gives eyes

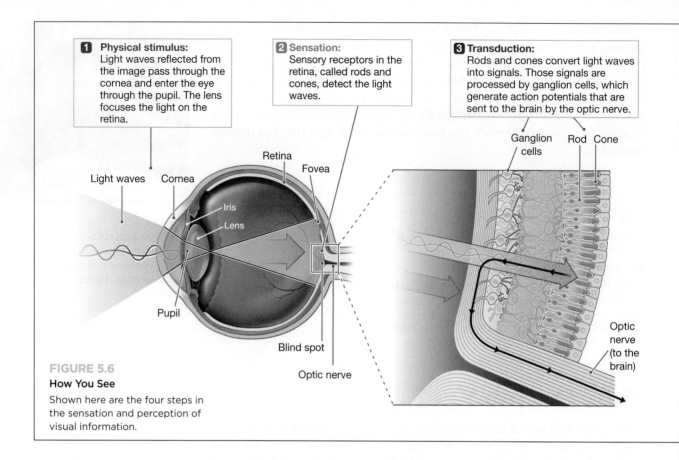

1 Physical stimulus:
Light waves reflected from the image pass through the cornea and enter the eye through the pupil. The lens focuses the light on the retina.

2 Sensation:
Sensory receptors in the retina, called rods and cones, detect the light waves.

3 Transduction:
Rods and cones convert light waves into signals. Those signals are processed by ganglion cells, which generate action potentials that are sent to the brain by the optic nerve.

Light waves   Cornea   Retina   Fovea

Iris
Lens

Pupil

Blind spot

Optic nerve

Ganglion cells   Rod   Cone

Optic nerve (to the brain)

FIGURE 5.6

How You See

Shown here are the four steps in the sensation and perception of visual information.

lens

The adjustable, transparent structure behind the pupil; this structure focuses light on the retina, resulting in a crisp visual image.

retina

The thin inner surface of the back of the eyeball; this surface contains the sensory receptors.

rods

Sensory receptors in the retina that detect light waves and transduce them into signals that are processed in the brain as vision. Rods respond best to low levels of illumination, and therefore they do not support color vision or seeing fine detail.

cones

Sensory receptors in the retina that detect light waves and transduce them into signals that are processed in the brain as vision. Cones respond best to higher levels of illumination, and therefore they are responsible for seeing color and fine detail.

their color and controls the pupil's size to determine how much light enters the eye. In dim lighting, the iris allows the opening of the pupil to become larger to let more light into the eye. The iris also increases the size of the pupil when you see something you like, such as a beautiful painting or a cute baby (Lick, Cortland, & Johnson, 2016).

Behind the iris, muscles change the shape of the **lens.** If you look at something far from you, your lenses will flatten. This flattening lets you focus on something in the distance. If you look at something close to you, your lenses will thicken so you can focus. If you look at something too close to you, your eyes will feel uncomfortable. They are straining because the muscles cannot make the lenses any fatter. At that point, you have to back away a bit to see the object.

Together, the cornea and lens focus light so you see objects accurately. Light is actually focused more by the cornea than by the lens. Because the lens is adjustable, it fine-tunes how the light is bent. Glasses and contact lenses provide clear, focused vision by helping the lens bend the light. As we get older, the muscles of the lens lose their ability to change the shape of the lens. As a result, it becomes hard to focus on near objects. After about age 50, most of us have to hold our menus far away from us to be able to read them, or we need to get reading glasses to bend the light more than our lenses can.

RODS AND CONES   The cornea and the lens work to focus light on the **retina,** the thin inner surface of the back of the eye (see Figure 5.6, Step 2). The retina contains the **rods** and **cones,** which allow sensation of the light waves. The rods and cones are the sensory receptors in the eye that transduce light waves into signals (see Figure 5.6, Step 3). The name of each type of visual sensory receptor cell comes from its distinctive shape.

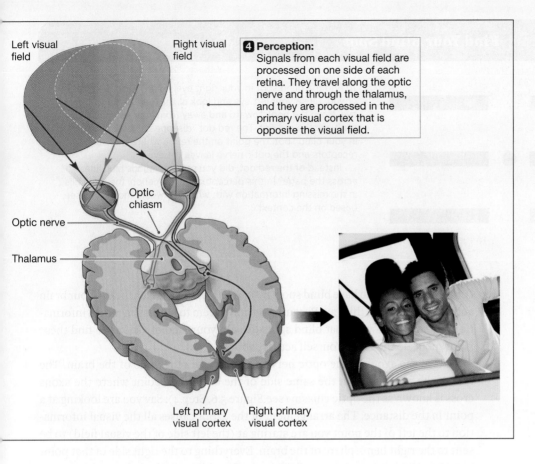

Left visual field

Right visual field

④ Perception: Signals from each visual field are processed on one side of each retina. They travel along the optic nerve and through the thalamus, and they are processed in the primary visual cortex that is opposite the visual field.

Optic chiasm

Optic nerve

Thalamus

Left primary visual cortex

Right primary visual cortex

Each retina holds approximately 120 million rods and 6 million cones. Near the center of the retina is a small region called the *fovea*. Here, cones are densely packed. Cones are spread throughout the rest of the retina (except in the blind spot, as you will see shortly). However, they become increasingly scarce near the outside edge. Cones are responsible primarily for vision under bright conditions and for seeing color and detail. When you look at the faces in Figure 5.6, do you see them clearly? If so, your cones are processing the small features of each face and the colors of the clothes.

Unlike cones, the rods are concentrated at the retina's edges. None are in the fovea. Also unlike cones, rods respond well at extremely low levels of light. Rods are responsible primarily for night vision. They do not support color vision, and they are poor at providing information about fine details. For these reasons, on a moonless night, objects appear in shades of gray. If you look directly at a very dim star on a moonless night, the star will appear to vanish because its light will fall on the fovea, where there are no rods. If you look just to the side of the star, the star will be visible, because its light will fall just outside the fovea, where there are rods.

FROM THE EYE TO THE BRAIN Our ability to perceive objects means that this initial visual stimulation must be processed in our brains. Rods and cones are the visual sensory receptors that detect the light waves and turn them into messages that are modified by other support cells in the retina. But finally, the information about what the eye has sensed is delivered to the *ganglion cells* (see Figure 5.6, Step 3). Ganglion cells are the first true neurons in the visual system in that they fire action potentials.

The axons of each ganglion cell are gathered into a bundle. This bundle is called the *optic nerve*. The optic nerve exits the eye at the back of the retina (see Figure 5.6, Step 4). At the point where the optic nerve exits the retina, there are no rods or

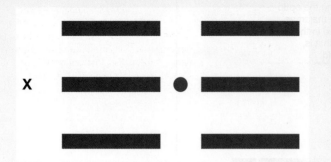

To find the blind spot in your right eye, hold this book in front of you. Close your left eye and look at the X with your right eye. Move the book toward and away from your face until you can't see the red dot. The red dot "disappears" because it is in your blind spot, the point on the retina where there are no receptors and the optic nerve leaves the eye.

Instead of the red dot, did you see continuous blue lines across the page? In this perceptual phenomenon, the brain fills in the missing information with what you would most likely see, based on the context.

cones. As a result, you have blind spots in your left and right visual fields. Your brain automatically fills in this gap. Because you don't seem to be missing visual information, you are not aware that blind spots exist in your field of vision. To find these blind spots, do the Try It Yourself activity above.

Half of the axons in the optic nerves cross to the other side of the brain. The rest of the axons stay on the same side of the brain. The point where the axons cross is known as the optic chiasm (see Figure 5.6, Step 4). Say you are looking at a point in the distance. The arrangement of the axons causes all the visual information to the left of the point you are staring at (the left side of the visual field) to be sent to the right hemisphere of the brain. Everything to the right side of that point is sent to the left hemisphere of the brain. In each case, the information passes through the thalamus and travels to the *primary visual cortex* in the occipital lobes (see Figure 5.6, Step 4). This region of the brain provides basic information about what is seen. Basic information includes the orientation, size, and movement of objects in the visual field. However, more-complex information is processed later in other specialized brain regions.

5.4 You Perceive Color Based on Physical Aspects of Light

5.4 LEARNING GOAL ACTIVITIES

To maximize your learning, complete the following learning goal activities:

a. Understand all bold and italic terms by writing explanations of them in your own words.

b. Analyze the two theories of color perception by differentiating between trichromatic theory and opponent-process theory.

When you look at Figure 5.6, how do you know what colors the clothes are? An object appears to be a particular color because of two factors: the wavelengths of light that the object reflects and how the receptors in the eye process the light. Because of these two factors, we can identify millions of different shades of color.

PHYSICAL EXPERIENCE OF COLOR For humans, visible light consists of electromagnetic waves ranging in length from about 400 to 700 nanometers (abbreviated

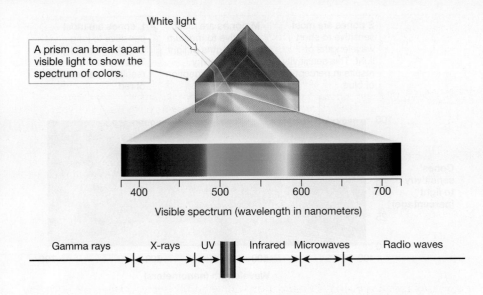

A prism can break apart visible light to show the spectrum of colors.

White light

Visible spectrum (wavelength in nanometers)

400   500   600   700

Gamma rays   X-rays   UV   Infrared   Microwaves   Radio waves

FIGURE 5.7

Visible Light

When white light shines through a prism, the spectrum of color that is visible to humans is revealed. As shown here, the visible color spectrum is only a small part of the electromagnetic spectrum. It consists of electromagnetic wavelengths from just under 400 nm (perceived as the color violet) to just over 700 nm (perceived as the color red).

nm; this length is about one billionth of a meter; **Figure 5.7**). The physical qualities of this light correspond to the perception of color in different ways. One physical quality of light is the *amplitude* (**Figure 5.8a**). The amplitude is the height of the light wave from base to peak. Psychologically, people experience this quality as *brightness.* So a lower-amplitude waveform creates a perception of a darker color, and a higher-amplitude waveform makes us perceive a brighter color. For example, brightness is the difference between a bright blue and a dark blue of the same shade.

The *wavelength* of the light wave is the distance from peak to peak (**Figure 5.8b**). This distance affects your perception of hue. *Hue* refers to the distinctive characteristics that place a particular color in the spectrum. As shown in Figure 5.7, longer

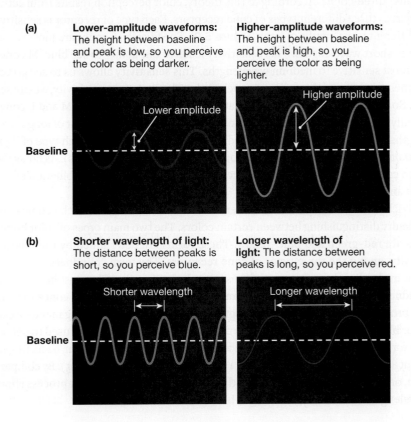

(a) **Lower-amplitude waveforms:** The height between baseline and peak is low, so you perceive the color as being darker.

Higher-amplitude waveforms: The height between baseline and peak is high, so you perceive the color as being lighter.

Lower amplitude

Higher amplitude

Baseline

(b) **Shorter wavelength of light:** The distance between peaks is short, so you perceive blue.

Longer wavelength of light: The distance between peaks is long, so you perceive red.

Shorter wavelength

Longer wavelength

Baseline

FIGURE 5.8

Physical Aspects of Light Relate to Perception of Brightness and of Hue

The amplitude and wavelength—physical aspects of visible light—are processed into the perceptual experiences. **(a)** The amplitude of a light wave is experienced as the brightness of a color. **(b)** The wavelength of a light wave is experienced as the hue of a color.

FIGURE 5.9

Trichromatic Theory Explains Color Perception

Our perception of hue is determined by the wavelength of the visible light that reaches the eye. This graph shows how each type of cone best absorbs light of different wavelengths.

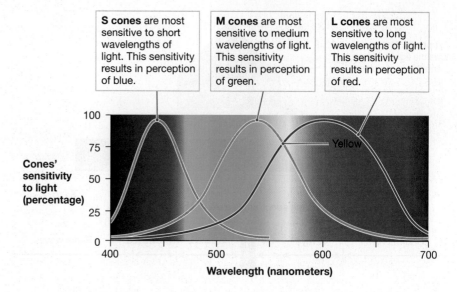

S cones are most sensitive to short wavelengths of light. This sensitivity results in perception of blue.

M cones are most sensitive to medium wavelengths of light. This sensitivity results in perception of green.

L cones are most sensitive to long wavelengths of light. This sensitivity results in perception of red.

Yellow

Cones' sensitivity to light (percentage)

Wavelength (nanometers)

trichromatic theory
The idea that three types of cone receptor cells in the retina are responsible for color perception. Each type responds optimally to different, but overlapping, ranges of wavelengths.

(a)

(b)

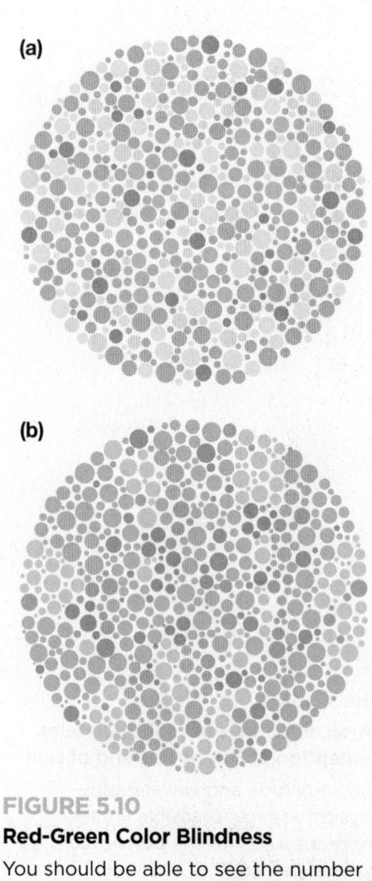

FIGURE 5.10

Red-Green Color Blindness

You should be able to see the number 45 in one of these circles. **(a)** If you are not red–green color-blind, you will see 45 here. **(b)** If you are red–green color-blind, you will see 45 here.

wavelengths of light tend to yield perception of hues that are red, whereas shorter wavelengths of light create perceptions of hues that are violet or blue. Wavelengths also mix to create colors. For example, a green hue might look more blue-green or more yellow-green, depending primarily on the light's dominant wavelength when it reaches the eye.

TRICHROMATIC THEORY   Most of us would have no problem saying that a certain flower is yellow rather than blue. But how do we know that? How do the physical aspects of light become the colors we perceive? Here our cone receptors come into play.

The **trichromatic theory** relates color perception to cone receptors. *Trichromatic* means "three-color." According to this theory, color perception results from activity across three different types of cone receptors. Each type of receptor is sensitive to different wavelengths of light (**Figure 5.9**). Specifically, S cones are most sensitive to short wavelengths. This sensitivity leads to our ability to see blue. M cones are most sensitive to medium wavelengths. This sensitivity allows us to see green. L cones are most sensitive to long wavelengths. Thanks to this sensitivity, we can see red. So because wavelengths of light at about 570 nm stimulate the M and L cones equally, we perceive yellow. In fact, we can perceive yellow when light of long wavelengths is combined with light of medium wavelengths, because each type of light stimulates the corresponding cone population (L cones and M cones). As far as the brain can tell, there is no difference between yellow light and a combination of red light and green light!

Trichromatic theory helps us understand color blindness, in which people have difficulty distinguishing between certain colors. The two main types of color blindness are red–green and blue–yellow. These forms are determined by the relative activity among the three types of cone receptors. The term "blindness" is somewhat misleading, because most of these people do see color. They just have partial blindness for certain colors. For example, people may have M or L cones that do not process medium or long wavelengths in the typical way, resulting in red–green color blindness. Simple tests, such as the ones in **Figure 5.10**, can be used to detect this form of color blindness (Wong, 2011). This form is quite common, occurring in about 8 percent of males but less than 1 percent of females (Deeb, 2005). By comparison, only a very small percentage of the population has S cones that process short wavelengths abnormally, resulting in blue–yellow color blindness.

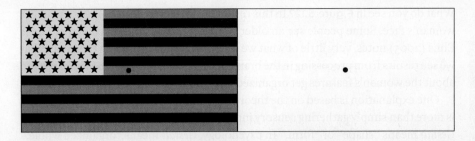

FIGURE 5.11

Afterimages Reveal Color Opposites

Focus on the dot in the middle of the flag and stare at the flag for at least 30 seconds. Then look at the dot to the right, on the white background. What do you see? You should see a red, white, and blue American flag. This result occurs due to processing in the ganglion cells.

OPPONENT-PROCESS THEORY Some aspects of color vision cannot be explained by the responses of our cone receptors. For example, we have trouble visualizing certain color mixtures. It is easier to imagine reddish yellow or bluish green, say, than reddish green or bluish yellow. Moreover, the trichromatic theory does not explain certain perceptual experiences. For instance, some colors appear to be opposites (**Figure 5.11**). When we stare at a red image for some time, we see a green afterimage when we look away. When we stare at a green image, we see a red afterimage when we look away. Likewise, when we stare at a blue image for some time, we see a yellow afterimage when we look away. When we stare at a yellow image, we see a blue afterimage. These perceptual afterimage effects are better explained by **opponent-process theory.**

To understand color opposites, we move to the next stage in visual processing. Remember that cones are receptors that detect wavelengths of light. The cones process that sensory input, and that processing ultimately leads to our perception of colors. Cones send the information to ganglion cells. The ganglion cells fire action potentials to send visual information to the brain. Some types of ganglion cells make it seem that red and green are opposites, whereas other types make it seem that yellow and blue are opposites. The ways that these different ganglion cells respond to cone input explain why we see colors as opposites.

Ultimately, how the brain converts light waves to the experience of color is quite complex. On the one hand, it can be understood by considering the response of cones to different wavelengths. On the other hand, processing by the ganglion cells leads to seeing colors as opposites. But what about people with number-color synesthesia (see Figure 5.1)? When these people look at numbers printed in ink that most of us perceive as black, they perceive each number to be a unique color even in the absence of those wavelengths of light. This phenomenon reveals how each person's perception of color, and other aspects of visual perception, are based on how that person's own, unique brain processes information. Most synesthetes never know—until they test their perceptions—that their perceptions are different from other people's.

opponent-process theory
The idea that ganglion cells in the retina receive excitatory input from one type of cone and inhibitory input from another type of cone, creating the perception that some colors are opposites.

5.5 You Perceive Objects by Organizing Visual Information

5.5 LEARNING GOAL ACTIVITIES

To maximize your learning, complete the following learning goal activities:

a. Understand all bold and italic terms by writing explanations of them in your own words.

b. Understand the three principles of object perception by organizing a table that summarizes each category in your own words.

FIGURE 5.12

Reversible Figure

What do you see when you look at this figure? Some see the face of a younger woman (her ear, her jawline, and a black necklace). Other people see the face of an older woman (an eye, a nose, and a black, open mouth).

grouping

The visual system's organization of features and regions to create the perception of a whole, unified object.

FIGURE 5.13

Gestalt Principles of Grouping

Gestalt psychology describes several principles of grouping that explain how we perceive features of the visual field as a unified, whole object.

What do you see in **Figure 5.12?** In this reversible image, some people see a younger woman's face. Some people see an older woman's face. As the psychologist James Enns (2005) notes, very little of what we call "seeing" takes place in the eyes. What we see results from processing in the brain. In this case, then, how does information about the woman's features get organized into our individual visual experiences?

One explanation is based on the theory of Gestalt psychologists that perception is more than simply gathering sensory input (see study unit 1.6). The German word *Gestalt* means "shape" or "form." In psychology, *Gestalt* means "organized whole." The founders of Gestalt psychology proposed a series of laws to explain how our brains group the perceived features of a visual scene into organized wholes. Gestalt psychology holds that our brains use a number of built-in principles to organize sensory information. These principles explain why we perceive, say, "a car" as opposed to metal, tires, glass, hubcaps, fenders, and so on. For us, an object exists as a unit, not as a collection of separate features. Let's consider these principles of object perception.

FIGURE AND GROUND　One of the visual perception system's most basic principles is organizing visual features into an object. In discussions of Gestalt principles, an object is a figure that is distinct from the background. The background is referred to as the ground. In identifying any figure, the brain assigns the rest of the scene to the ground. A classic illustration of this principle is the reversible figure (again, see Figure 5.12). Here, you can go back and forth in perceiving two possible figures—the younger woman's face or the older woman's—but you cannot perceive them both at the same time. The "correct" assignment of figure and ground is ambiguous. Sometimes you perceive the relationship one way, and sometimes you perceive it the other way. This illusion demonstrates how visual perception of figure and ground is dynamic and ongoing.

GROUPING　Whether the object is a reversible figure or an "ordinary" object in the world, your visual system seeks to form a coherent image of what you are seeing. To form that image, the system must determine what parts "go together." This process is called **grouping**. The Gestalt psychologists identified several principles that explain how visual grouping works (**Figure 5.13**).

Have you ever seen many geese together in one area? We tend to visually put the individual geese into one large group, a flock, because they look alike and they stay close together. This example shows how we group visual information based on the *proximity* of parts and by the *similarity* of parts. By clustering visual elements based on proximity and similarity, we are able to consider the scene as a whole rather than as the individual parts.

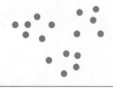

a Proximity:
Close figures are grouped as an object. So we see these 16 dots as three groups of objects.

b Similarity:
Similar figures are grouped in an object. So we see this rectangle as having two locked pieces.

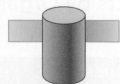

c Continuity:
Intersecting lines are interpreted as continuous. So we see the green bar as one piece that continues behind the purple cylinder.

d Closure:
Figures with gaps are interpreted as complete. So we see the figure as one whole triangle.

e Illusory contours:
Contours are perceived even when they do not exist. So we see the contours of a square here.

Now think about a common experience: You see a person, but the person is partially obscured by a table. Why didn't you perceive the person and the table as parts of the same object? Clearly, we can determine what parts of visual input go together to make coherent forms. We can make out the person and the table, not the person-table. Three additional Gestalt principles are at work here: the *continuity* of a line, *closure* of gaps, and the creation of *illusory contours*.

BOTTOM-UP AND TOP-DOWN PROCESSING   How do we assemble information about parts into a perception of a whole object? According to most models, perceptual organization is hierarchical. Specifically, perception of objects and patterns occurs through **bottom-up processing**. This term means that processing begins with the external world and the sensory input, which is detected by sensory receptors. Then the information is processed from these basic, lower levels to higher, more conceptual levels within the brain.

Perception also includes **top-down processing**. This term means that information at higher levels of conceptual processing can influence object perception at lower, more basic levels in the processing hierarchy. Information at higher levels includes our prior experiences and our expectations. For help remembering the difference between bottom-up and top-down processing, see the Learning Tip below.

Unfortunately, faulty expectations can lead to faulty perceptions. On November 28, 1979, Air New Zealand Flight 901 crashed into the slopes of Mount Erebus, on Ross Island in Antarctica. The crash killed 237 passengers and 20 crew members. The pilots believed they were flying over the Ross Ice Shelf, where there are no mountains, so they reduced altitude to give the passengers a better view of the spectacular Antarctic landscape (**Figure 5.14a**). However, the plane was actually far off course. Given the whiteout conditions and the pilots' expectations, the flight crew failed to notice the 12,000-foot volcano looming in front of them (**Figure 5.14b**). In this case, top-down expectations influenced bottom-up processing of the visual information the pilots were seeing, and the consequences were tragic.

Top-down processing is an important feature of everyday perception. It helps you interpret and make sense of incoming sensory experiences, even when they sometimes fail to make sense. For instance, Y0U C4N R3AD TH15 PR377Y W3LL even though it is nonsensical. The ability to make sense of "incorrect" stimuli through top-down processing is why proofreading our own writing can be so difficult.

bottom-up processing
Perception based on the physical features of the stimulus.

top-down processing
Perception based on knowledge, expectations, or past experiences, which affect the interpretation of sensory information.

(a)

(b)

FIGURE 5.14

Ross Ice Shelf and Mount Erebus

(a) The pilots on Air New Zealand Flight 901 expected to see the flat terrain of the Ross Ice Shelf in Antarctica. **(b)** This expectation led to tragic consequences when the pilots failed to see Mount Erebus, a 12,000-foot-high volcano, directly in their flight path.

 LEARNING TIP: Bottom-Up and Top-Down Processing

To remember what it means to process information from the bottom up or the top down, just remember this tip.

WHEN YOU SEE	PLEASE THINK	MEANING
<u>Bottom</u>-up	Processing based on information about the <u>basic</u> stimulus properties	The processing of information that is based on the properties of the stimulus in the world
<u>Top</u>-down	Processing based on information in your brain, at the <u>top</u> of your body	The processing of information that is based on your knowledge, personal experiences, and expectations

binocular depth cues
Cues of depth perception that arise because people have two eyes.

monocular depth cues
Cues of depth perception that are available to each eye alone.

5.6 When You Perceive Depth, You Can Locate Objects in Space

5.6 LEARNING GOAL ACTIVITIES

To maximize your learning, complete the following learning goal activities:

a. Understand all bold and italic terms by writing explanations of them in your own words.

b. Apply depth perception by providing one example from your life of each of the two types of depth perception.

Look up from this book and reach for something in front of you, perhaps a pen or a coffee cup. To accomplish this simple task, you need to perceive the object coherently. You also have to know where the object is in space. Without this spatial ability, it would be very difficult to navigate in the world and interact with things and people. In fact, your brain uses two types of cues to help you perceive depth. **Binocular depth cues** are based on input from both eyes together. **Monocular depth cues** are based on input from one eye alone.

BINOCULAR DEPTH PERCEPTION   Look at the objects around you. You see them as three-dimensional. Indeed, they are three-dimensional. Yet inside your eyes, once the light reflected from the images hits your retinas, all of the depth information is lost. The information is represented on the retinas in two dimensions only, just as it would be in a photograph. How can you perceive depth in the world if it is processed on the flat retinas in two dimensions?

To understand the process, look at something very close up. Hold your hand or your book up to your face. Repeatedly blink your left eye and then your right eye. When you do this, does whatever you are looking at quickly change positions from the left to the right and back again? This perception of "jumping" occurs because the retina of each eye has a slightly different view. Together, the different views on the retina are called *binocular disparity*. This phenomenon is one way you perceive depth.

Because each eye has a slightly different view, the brain has access to two different, though overlapping, retinal images. The brain uses the disparity between these two retinal images to compute distances to nearby objects. By computing distances, the brain lets us perceive depth (**Figure 5.15**). But binocular disparity is an important cue for depth perception only when the objects are relatively close to you. And it requires using both eyes. So another set of cues also helps you perceive depth.

MONOCULAR DEPTH PERCEPTION   Photographs, movies, videos, and television images are flat. Flat images have no depth, yet you perceive depth in them. What's more, you perceive this three-dimensionality in two-dimensional images just by using one eye. For this reason, another set of visual cues are called monocular depth cues. Artists routinely use these cues to create a sense of depth, so monocular depth cues are also called *pictorial depth cues*. For example, when you look at **Figure 5.16,** you can see depth in the picture in several ways. The Renaissance

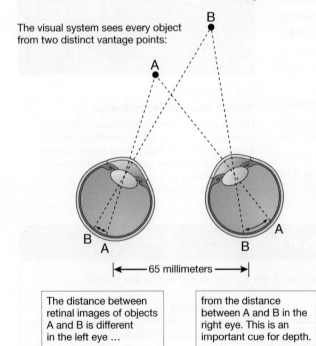

The visual system sees every object from two distinct vantage points:

← 65 millimeters →

The distance between retinal images of objects A and B is different in the left eye …

from the distance between A and B in the right eye. This is an important cue for depth.

FIGURE 5.15

Binocular Disparity

You use both eyes to perceive depth through binocular disparity, where each retina has a slightly different view of the world.

a **Occlusion:** A near object (woman's head) blocks an object that is farther away (the building).

b **Height in field:** Objects that are lower in the visual field (woman) are seen as nearer than objects that are higher in the visual field (man on the sidewalk at [c]).

c **Relative size:** Objects that are farther away (man on the sidewalk) project a smaller retinal image than close objects of a similar size (man on the street next to [b]).

d **Familiar size:** We know how large familiar objects are (car), so we can estimate how far away they are by the size of their retinal images.

e **Linear perspective:** Seemingly parallel lines (sidewalk) appear to converge in the distance.

f **Texture gradient:** As a uniformly textured surface recedes, its texture continuously becomes denser (pattern on the pavement).

FIGURE 5.16

Pictorial Depth Cues

You can perceive depth with just one eye. In this image, six monocular depth cues create the illusion of distance. Monocular depth cues are also called pictorial depth cues.

painter, sculptor, architect, and engineer Leonardo da Vinci first identified many of these cues, which include *occlusion*, *height in field*, *relative size*, *familiar size*, *linear perspective*, and *texture gradient*.

5.7 Cues in Your Brain and in the World Let You Perceive Motion

5.7 LEARNING GOAL ACTIVITIES

To maximize your learning, complete the following learning goal activities:

a. Understand all bold and italic terms by writing explanations of them in your own words.

b. Apply motion perception by providing one example from your life of each of the two types of motion perception.

You see something move—a person walks by, or a car whizzes past. You are aware of all this motion because you are sensing changes in illumination on your retinas. Changes in illumination, together with object recognition processes, enable you to perceive that an object is in motion, changing locations. Two phenomena offer insights into how the visual system perceives motion: motion aftereffects and stroboscopic motion.

MOTION AFTEREFFECTS *Motion aftereffects* may occur when you gaze at a moving image for a long time and then look at a stationary scene. You experience a momentary impression that the new scene is moving in the opposite direction from the moving image. This illusion is also called the *waterfall effect*, because if you stare at a waterfall and then turn away, the scenery you are now looking at will seem to move upward for a moment.

FIGURE 5.17

How Moving Pictures Work

This static series would appear transformed if you spun the wheel. With the slightly different images presented in rapid succession, the stroboscopic movement would tell your brain that you are watching a moving zebra.

Motion aftereffects are strong evidence that motion-sensitive neurons exist in the brain. According to the theory that explains this illusion, the visual cortex has neurons that respond to movement in a given direction. When you stare at a moving sensory input long enough, these direction-specific neurons start adapting to the motion. That is, they become fatigued and so are less sensitive. If the sensory input is suddenly removed, the motion detectors that respond to all the other directions are more active than the fatigued motion detectors. Thus you see the new scene moving in the other direction.

STROBOSCOPIC MOTION Motion pictures are called movies because they seem to be moving. Actually, though, movies are made up of still images. Each image is slightly different from the one before it. When the series is presented fast enough, you perceive the illusion of motion pictures. This perceptual illusion is called *stroboscopic motion* (**Figure 5.17**).

In 1912, the Gestalt psychologist Max Wertheimer conducted experiments on stroboscopic motion. Wertheimer flashed, at different intervals, two vertical lines placed close together. When the interval was less than 30 milliseconds, observers thought the two lines were flashing simultaneously. When the interval was greater than 200 milliseconds, they saw two lines being flashed at different times. Between those times, movement illusions occurred: When the interval was about 60 milliseconds, the line appeared to jump from one place to another. At slightly longer intervals, the line appeared to move continuously. This phenomenon has brought us to productions such as *Black Panther* and *Avengers: Infinity War*. In other words, all the special effects, fancy camera work, and fast editing you see in today's movies are ways of manipulating a very simple perceptual trick.

5.8 You Understand That Objects Remain Constant Even When Cues Change

5.8 LEARNING GOAL ACTIVITIES

To maximize your learning, complete the following learning goal activities:

a. Understand all bold and italic terms by writing explanations of them in your own words.

b. Apply object constancy to the real world by explaining how we know that snow is white and a tire is black, even when the snow at night or a tire in bright light sends the same visual input to our eyes.

As you walk around each day, you come closer to some objects and go farther from others. You see things from different angles. You also encounter changing environments, such as when a cloud changes the light on a sunny day. The sensory information you receive is affected by such cues. Consider your image in a mirror. What you see in the mirror might look like it is your actual size, but the image is much smaller than the parts of you being reflected. (If you doubt this claim, try tracing around the

image of your face in a steamy bathroom mirror.) Now consider another person, who approaches you from down the block. How is it that you have a constant sense of the person's height even though your retinal image of the person changes based on the person's distance from you? The answer is **object constancy.** Despite sensory input that could mislead perception, object constancy lets you correctly perceive objects as remaining the same in their size, shape, color, and lightness.

For the most part, changing an object's angle, distance, or illumination does not change your perception of that object's size, shape, color, and lightness (**Figure 5.18**). To perceive any of these four constancies, you need to understand the relationship between the object and at least one other factor. For *size constancy*, you need to know how far away the object is from you. For *shape constancy*, you need to know what angle or angles you are seeing the object from. For *color constancy*, you need to compare the wavelengths of light reflected from the object with those reflected from its background. Likewise, for *brightness constancy*, you need to know how much light is being reflected from the object and from its background. In each case, your brain computes the relative magnitude rather than relying on each sensation's absolute magnitude. For example, parts of the visual cortex quickly process different views of a certain shape so you perceive the object as the same (Li & DiCarlo, 2008). Through such processes, the perceptual system can judge relationships between objects and other factors. These judgments let the system maintain constancy across changing situations.

By studying how illusions work, many perceptual psychologists have come to believe that the brain has built-in assumptions that influence perceptions. The vast majority of visual illusions appear to be beyond our conscious control—we cannot make ourselves not see illusions, even when we know they are not true representations of objects or events. If you find this hard to believe, take a quick look at **Figure 5.19** and decide whether the tables are the same size or different. Believe it or not, they are the same. Go ahead and trace one and place it over the other. Object constancy allows you to see both a stable world and perceptual illusions that you cannot control.

Q How Do You See?

To make sure you learned what you just read, write answers to the following questions and check your answers.

5.3 Does the fovea have more rods or cones?

5.4 Explain whether afterimages are best explained by trichromatic theory or opponent-process theory.

5.5 How do the Gestalt principles of proximity and similarity help explain our visual perceptions of crowds?

5.6 What is the main difference between seeing depth based on binocular depth cues and seeing depth based on monocular depth cues?

5.7 The holiday lights on a house blink one after another, so they appear to be continuously "running" in a line along the side of the house. What aspect of motion perception explains this?

5.8 What are the four different types of object constancy?

See Appendix B for answers to the red Q questions.

FIGURE 5.18
Object Constancy
The image on the retina is vastly different for these four drawings of a car. Because you know how large a car normally is, knowing how far away the car is from you lets you maintain size constancy. Knowing the angles you are seeing the car from enables you to maintain shape constancy. The shadows help maintain color and brightness constancy because they suggest the angle of lighting and you know that light makes colors brighter.

object constancy
Correctly perceiving objects as staying the same in their size, shape, color, and lightness, across viewing conditions that yield different physical input to the eyes.

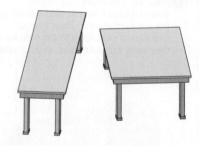

FIGURE 5.19
The Tabletop Illusion
Created by the psychologist Roger Shepard, this illusion demonstrates the brain's automatic perceptual processes. Even when we know the two tabletops are the same size and shape—even if we have traced one image and placed it on top of the other—perspective cues make us see them as different.

How Do You Hear?

Like seeing, hearing is an important source of information about the world. Suppose you are driving along a crowded, curving street. You can't see all the vehicles behind you. Suddenly you hear a siren coming toward you from back there. The siren lets you know that you should pull over to let an emergency vehicle pass.

Hearing is also called *audition*. It provides a way to receive spoken language. It brings pleasure, such as through music. This section first discusses how sound waves are transduced in the auditory system, then how sound information is perceived in the brain.

5.9 Receptors in Your Ears Detect Sound Waves

5.9 LEARNING GOAL ACTIVITIES

To maximize your learning, complete the following learning goal activities:

a. Understand all bold and italic terms by writing explanations of them in your own words.

b. Understand the four steps in auditory sensation and perception by summarizing each step in your own words.

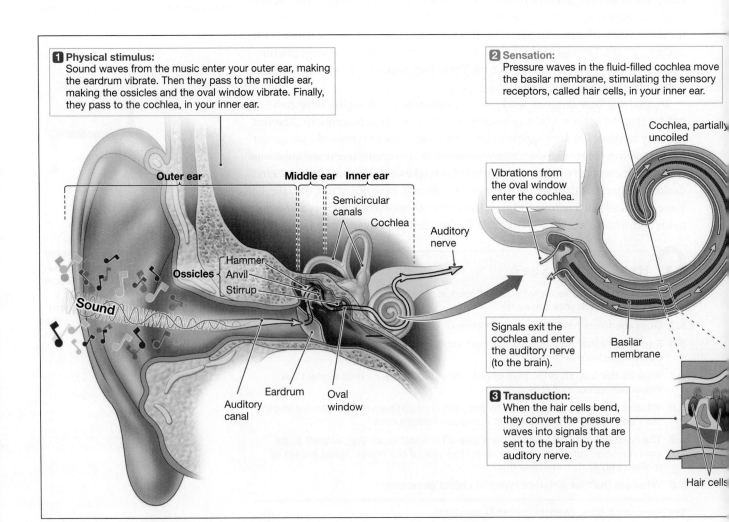

1 Physical stimulus:
Sound waves from the music enter your outer ear, making the eardrum vibrate. Then they pass to the middle ear, making the ossicles and the oval window vibrate. Finally, they pass to the cochlea, in your inner ear.

2 Sensation:
Pressure waves in the fluid-filled cochlea move the basilar membrane, stimulating the sensory receptors, called hair cells, in your inner ear.

Cochlea, partially uncoiled

Vibrations from the oval window enter the cochlea.

Signals exit the cochlea and enter the auditory nerve (to the brain).

Basilar membrane

3 Transduction:
When the hair cells bend, they convert the pressure waves into signals that are sent to the brain by the auditory nerve.

Hair cells

Outer ear   Middle ear   Inner ear

Semicircular canals

Cochlea

Auditory nerve

Hammer
Anvil
Stirrup

Ossicles

Sound

Eardrum   Oval window

Auditory canal

The world is full of sound. A song plays, a person speaks, the TV drones, an overhead light hums. But everything you hear is merely changes in air pressure produced within your hearing distance. Just as objects in the world have no essential color, these changes in air pressure have no sound. Instead, your ability to hear is based on the intricate interactions of various regions of the ear and on processing in the brain.

An age-old question asks, "If a tree falls in the woods and no one is there to hear it, does it make a sound?" The answer is no. The falling of the tree makes vibrations in the air. Ears and brains process the vibrations in the air, creating the perception of sound.

FROM THE EAR TO THE BRAIN   Suppose you hear music, such as the sound of a saxophone. The sound waves from the music are the sensory input (**Figure 5.20**). The process of hearing begins when sound waves arrive at the shell-shaped structure of your *outer ear* (see Figure 5.20, Step 1). The odd shape of the outer ear actually is functional. That is, the shell shape increases the ear's ability to capture sound waves and then funnel the waves down the auditory canal. When you have trouble hearing something, it helps to cup or bend your outer ear because you funnel even more sound waves into the auditory canal.

Next, the sound waves from the music travel down the auditory canal to the **eardrum.** The eardrum is a membrane stretched tightly across the canal. This membrane marks the beginning of the *middle ear*. When the sound waves hit the

eardrum
A thin membrane that marks the beginning of the middle ear; sound waves cause the eardrum to vibrate.

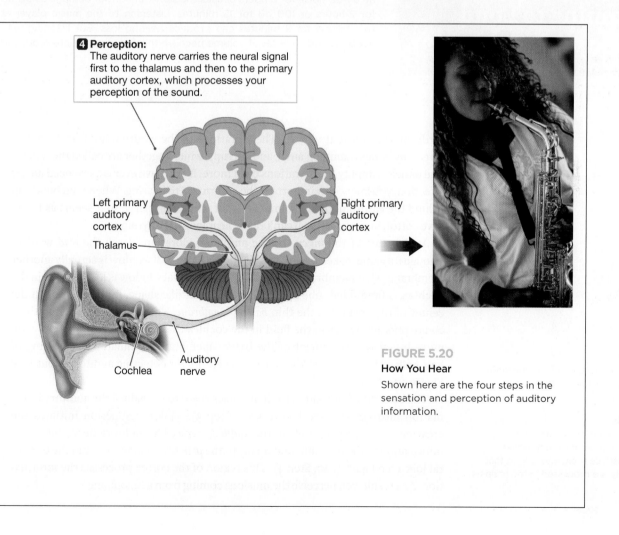

4 Perception:
The auditory nerve carries the neural signal first to the thalamus and then to the primary auditory cortex, which processes your perception of the sound.

Left primary auditory cortex

Right primary auditory cortex

Thalamus

Cochlea

Auditory nerve

FIGURE 5.20

How You Hear

Shown here are the four steps in the sensation and perception of auditory information.

Hearing Deficiencies from Listening to Loud Music with Ear Buds

You see it all the time: young adults, teenagers, and increasingly even young children using ear buds to listen to music on portable devices. The music is often so loud that people around them can hear it too. It may surprise you to learn that this common activity has been linked with noise-induced hearing loss (NIHL) in nearly 13 percent of American children between the ages of 6 and 19—affecting more than 5 million young people (Centers for Disease Control and Prevention, 2013a). Furthermore, research suggests that some people in their 20s have hearing loss to a degree that has traditionally been seen in 50-year-olds. But the good news is that you don't have to give up listening to music on the go. If you know a little bit about how your body processes sound waves to hear music, then you can prevent hearing loss in these situations.

Any loud noise can damage hearing. People who work in noisy environments, such as factories, often experience hearing loss, especially if they don't wear ear protection. This hearing loss occurs because loud sounds produce sound waves with higher amplitudes. These waves stimulate hair receptors in the basilar membrane much more than do soft sounds, which produce sound waves with lower amplitudes. When hair cells in the basilar membrane of the cochlea are repeatedly overstimulated, they lose the ability to transduce sound waves.

One cause of damage to the hair cells is the volume, or loudness, of the sound, which is measured in decibels (dB). The measured volume of some sounds may surprise you—in the following table, for example, you can see that a portable music player at maximum volume can be louder than a rock concert! But volume is not the only source of damage. The length of exposure to the noise is also important. For example, hearing an 85-dB noise for 8 hours causes the same amount of damage as 90 dB for 2 hours or 100 dB for 15 minutes. Listening to the music player at top volume for 2 minutes can produce hearing loss. But listening with ear buds adds 6–9 dB of volume because the sound waves are produced

cochlea
A coiled, bony, fluid-filled tube in the inner ear that houses the sensory receptors.

hair cells
Sensory receptors located in the cochlea that detect sound waves and transduce them into signals that ultimately are processed in the brain as sound.

eardrum, they make it vibrate. The vibrations of the eardrum are transferred to three tiny bones (hammer, anvil, and stirrup), which together are called the *ossicles*. The ossicles amplify the vibrations even more. If you have ever experienced an ear infection, you know how important the eardrum is to hearing. When fluid builds up behind the eardrum, the membrane cannot vibrate properly, so it seems as if you have cotton in your ears. You can't really hear much of anything.

At the start of the *inner ear*, the amplified vibrations reach the *oval window*. Though its name makes it seem like an opening, the oval window is actually another membrane. That membrane vibrates in turn. The oval window is located within the **cochlea**, a fluid-filled tube that curls into a snail-like shape. Running through the center of the cochlea is the thin *basilar membrane*. The oval window's vibrations create pressure waves in the fluid in the cochlea that make the basilar membrane move in a wave. Movement of the basilar membrane stimulates the bending of **hair cells**. These cells are the sensory receptors for detecting auditory input (see Figure 5.20, Step 2).

The bending of the hair cells then causes them to transduce the auditory information into signals (see Figure 5.20, Step 3). This transduction initiates the creation of action potentials in the *auditory nerve*. The auditory nerve sends the information to the thalamus and finally to the *primary auditory cortex* in the temporal lobe (see Figure 5.20, Step 4). This region of the cortex processes the information. As a result, you perceive the music as coming from a saxophone.

inside the auditory canal, close to the eardrum. In this situation, just 15 seconds of exposure can cause hearing loss. The result is similar to the effect of listening to the noise from jet engines.

So how can you enjoy your music and avoid hearing loss? Just follow these simple rules.

1. **Use the 60/60 rule.** Listen to your portable music device for 60 minutes at 60 percent of the maximum volume. If you can't tell what 60 percent of maximum volume is, just use a volume where you can still understand someone speaking to you in a normal voice from an arm's length away. After 60 minutes, give your ears a break for a while. This recovery time significantly reduces the chance of damaging your hearing.

2. **Don't use ear buds.** Instead, use headphones that go over your ears. Noise dampening or canceling headphones are even better. These headphones reduce the noise that you hear around you, so you don't feel the need to increase the volume on your music player.

3. **Ringing ears are sending a warning.** If your ears are ringing, buzzing, or roaring, or sounds seem muffled or distorted 24 hours after you've been exposed to loud noise, have your hearing checked by a doctor. Hearing loss can be temporary and decrease over time, and your doctor can help you avoid further, more permanent damage.

Noise in the Environment	Loudness in Decibels (approximate)	Listening Time Until Damage to Hair Cells (approximate)
Whisper	20	
Normal conversation	40–60	Safe for any length of time
Vacuum cleaner	70	
Vehicle traffic	85	8 hours
Gas lawnmower	90	2 hours
Average rock concert	100	15 minutes
Portable music player at max volume (depending on model)	110	2 minutes
When using ear buds	*116-19*	*15 seconds*
Jet engine	140	
Gunshot	165	Immediate damage occurs
Rocket launch	180	

5.10 You Perceive Sound Based on Physical Aspects of Sound Waves

5.10 LEARNING GOAL ACTIVITIES

To maximize your learning, complete the following learning goal activities:

a. Understand all bold and italic terms by writing explanations of them in your own words.

b. Apply pitch perception to your own life by describing how temporal coding and place coding allow you to perceive sounds of different pitches.

In October 2017, at New York City's Metropolitan Opera, the soprano Audrey Luna sang a higher note than had ever been sung before in the Met's 137-year history (Woolfe, 2017). Although very few singers can manage to hit a high C, Luna was the first to nail a high A. Genes, great vocal cords, and practice let her produce this sound. But how was the audience able to hear that Luna's special note was different from any other note?

LOUDNESS AND PITCH OF SOUNDS   Recall that what you eventually hear begins with changes in air pressure. The pattern of changes in air pressure over a period of time

FIGURE 5.21

Physical Aspects of Sound Waves Relate to Perception of Loudness and Pitch

The amplitude and wavelength—physical aspects of sound waves—are processed into perceptual experiences. **(a)** The amplitude of a sound wave is experienced as the loudness of a sound. **(b)** A sound wave has a wavelength. The time between the wavelength peaks is the frequency, which is experienced as the pitch of a sound.

(a)

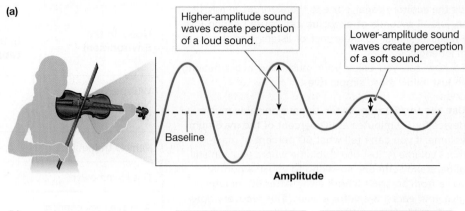

Higher-amplitude sound waves create perception of a loud sound.

Lower-amplitude sound waves create perception of a soft sound.

Baseline

Amplitude

(b)

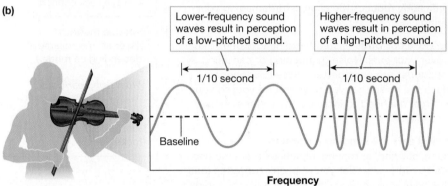

Lower-frequency sound waves result in perception of a low-pitched sound.

Higher-frequency sound waves result in perception of a high-pitched sound.

1/10 second

1/10 second

Baseline

Frequency

is a sound wave. The height of the sound waves is called the amplitude (**Figure 5.21a**). The amplitude determines your perception of loudness: You hear sound waves with higher amplitudes as louder sounds and sound waves with lower amplitudes as softer sounds. You can tell the difference between these when someone is yelling in your ear versus when they are whispering to you. To see how high-amplitude sound waves can damage your hearing, see Using Psychology in Your Life on pp. 192–93.

The distance between peaks of sound waves is the wavelength, and the *frequency* of a sound wave is the time between one peak and the next in the sound wave (**Figure 5.21b**). The frequency of a sound wave is measured in vibrations per second, called *hertz* (abbreviated Hz). The *frequency* of the sound waves determines the pitch of the sound, which is how high or low the sound is. You hear a lower-frequency sound wave as a lower-pitched sound and a higher-frequency sound wave as a higher-pitched sound. Most humans can detect sound waves with frequencies from about 20 Hz to about 20,000 Hz, at least in the lab. The most important sounds we hear in everyday life range from about 300 Hz to about 5,000 Hz. Our ability to hear sounds above 15,000 Hz drops off rapidly early in adulthood.

TEMPORAL AND PLACE CODING   Most of the sounds we hear, from conversations to concerts, are made up of many frequencies of sound waves. Those frequencies activate a broad range of hair cells. How does the auditory system signal different frequencies of sound, such as high notes and low notes in a song? In other words, how is pitch coded by the auditory system? There are two mechanisms for encoding the frequency of a sound wave. Both of these mechanisms operate at the same time in the basilar membrane.

Temporal coding is the process of encoding relatively low frequencies. This type of coding is called "temporal" because the sound waves are coded by matching the frequency of the waves with the speed—the timing—of firing of the auditory nerve. For example, when you hear a tuba, temporal coding is involved. A 40-Hz tone from

temporal coding
The perception of lower-pitched sounds that results from the timing of firing of the auditory nerve when the basilar membrane vibrates from sound waves of lower frequencies.

a tuba makes the basilar membrane vibrate 40 times per second. This vibration causes the hair cells in the basilar membrane to send impulses to the auditory nerve at the same rate, so that the auditory nerve also fires at 40 times per second. This strict matching between the frequency of auditory stimulation and the firing rate of the auditory nerve occurs up to about 4,000 Hz. At higher frequencies, temporal coding can be maintained only if hair cells fire in volleys. That is, different groups of hair cells in the basilar membrane take turns firing, so that the overall temporal pattern matches the sound frequency. Think of one group of soldiers firing their weapons together while another group reloads. Then that second group fires while another group reloads. Then that third group fires . . . and so on.

The second mechanism for encoding frequency is **place coding**. This type of coding is called "place" because different frequencies are encoded by hair cells in different locations—different places—on the basilar membrane. This membrane responds to sound waves like a reed from a woodwind instrument, vibrating in resonance with the sound. For example, a piccolo producing a very high frequency of 4,000 Hz causes the basilar membrane to move at the base, by the oval window, and so it stimulates hair cells in that location. Sounds of somewhat lower frequencies—such as from an upright bass, which may be about 200 Hz—cause the basilar membrane to move farther down by its tip, causing hair cells in that location to fire. In short, the frequency of a sound wave is encoded by the hair cells on the area of the basilar membrane that moves the most.

After the hair cells and auditory nerve have fired based on the frequency of a sound wave, processing in the brain allows you to perceive that pitch. The processing of pitch takes place in the primary auditory cortex. Auditory neurons in the thalamus extend their axons to the primary auditory cortex. There, other neurons code the frequency of the auditory stimuli. The neurons toward the rear of the auditory cortex respond best to sounds at higher frequencies. The neurons toward the front of the auditory cortex respond best to sounds at lower frequencies.

LOCALIZATION   Suppose you hear a siren while driving, but you can't tell which direction the sound is coming from. Locating the origin of a sound is called localization. This ability is an important part of auditory perception. However, the hair cells cannot code where events occur. Instead, your brain integrates the different sensory information coming from each of your ears.

Much of our understanding of auditory localization has come from research with barn owls. These nocturnal birds have finely tuned hearing, which helps them locate their prey. In fact, in a dark laboratory, a barn owl can locate a mouse through hearing alone.

The owl uses two cues to locate a sound (**Figure 5.22**). The first cue is the time when the sound arrives in each ear. The second cue is the amplitude, or intensity, of the sound wave in each ear. Unless the sound comes from exactly in front or in back of the owl, the sound will reach one ear first. Whichever side it comes from, it will sound softer on the other side because the owl's head acts as a barrier. These differences in timing and intensity are minute, but they are not too small for the owl's brain to detect and act on. Although a human's ears are not as finely tuned to the locations of sounds as an owl's ears are, the human brain uses information from the two ears in a similar way to localize sounds.

place coding
The perception of higher-pitched sounds that is a result of the location on the basilar membrane where hair cells are stimulated by sound waves of varying higher frequencies.

(a)

(b)

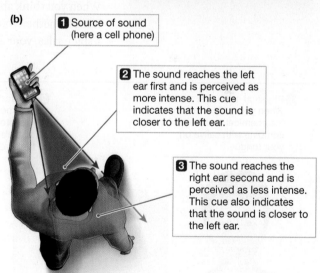

1 Source of sound (here a cell phone)

2 The sound reaches the left ear first and is perceived as more intense. This cue indicates that the sound is closer to the left ear.

3 The sound reaches the right ear second and is perceived as less intense. This cue also indicates that the sound is closer to the left ear.

FIGURE 5.22

Perceiving Location and Loudness of Sound

(a) Both barn owls and **(b)** humans draw on the intensity and timing of sounds to locate where sounds are coming from.

FIGURE 5.23

The Vestibular Sense Helps Maintain Balance

The vestibular sense is an internal sense that lets you maintain balance. It uses structures in the inner ear.

VESTIBULAR SENSE   Unlike vision, hearing, taste, smell, and touch, some sensory systems process stimuli that are inside the body. The *vestibular sense* is one such internal sensory system. It lets you maintain your balance. Thanks to balance, you are able to perform activities such as riding a bike or walking on a balance beam (**Figure 5.23**).

Unlike the other senses, which detect external stimuli, the vestibular sense uses information from receptors in structures of the inner ear called the semicircular canals. These canals contain a liquid that moves when the head moves, bending hair cells in the canals. The bending generates signals that inform you of your head's rotation, and this information affects your sense of balance.

If an inner-ear infection or standing up quickly has made you dizzy, you have experienced a disturbance in your vestibular sense. And the experience of being seasick or carsick results in part from conflicting signals arriving from the visual system and the vestibular system.

 How Do You Hear?

To make sure you learned what you just read, write answers to the following questions and check your answers.

5.9 How do loud sounds lead to hearing loss?

5.10 What type of sounds can you hear due to temporal coding: low pitches or high pitches?

See Appendix B for answers to the red Q questions.

How Are You Able to Taste and Smell?

When you think about your favorite foods, you can almost taste them. But regardless of whether you swoon over a grilled steak, chow mein with mustard greens, or a spicy salsa, your appreciation of a certain food depends on more than taste alone.

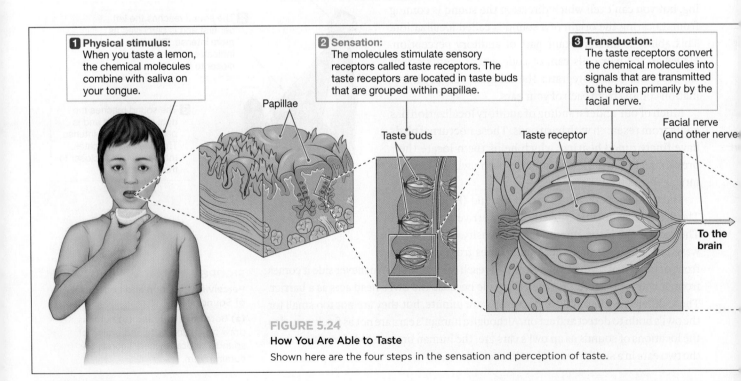

1 Physical stimulus:
When you taste a lemon, the chemical molecules combine with saliva on your tongue.

2 Sensation:
The molecules stimulate sensory receptors called taste receptors. The taste receptors are located in taste buds that are grouped within papillae.

3 Transduction:
The taste receptors convert the chemical molecules into signals that are transmitted to the brain primarily by the facial nerve.

Papillae

Taste buds

Taste receptor

Facial nerve (and other nerve

To the brain

FIGURE 5.24

How You Are Able to Taste

Shown here are the four steps in the sensation and perception of taste.

As you likely know from having had a cold, food seems tasteless when your nose is really stuffed up. This lack of perception happens because your sense of taste relies heavily on your sense of smell. Together, taste and smell produce the experience of *flavor*. In fact, flavor is based more on smell than on taste. This perceptual experience does not take place in your mouth and nose, however. Like seeing and hearing, experiencing flavor occurs in your brain.

5.11 Receptors in Your Taste Buds Detect Chemical Molecules

5.11 LEARNING GOAL ACTIVITIES

To maximize your learning, complete the following learning goal activities:

a. Understand all bold and italic terms by writing explanations of them in your own words.

b. Apply the four steps in taste sensation and perception to your life by imagining that you are tasting something, then describing each step of the process.

The sense of taste is also called *gustation*. Gustation has an adaptive function. In other words, taste is related to survival. If something you eat tastes really bad, you are likely to spit it out. This response is adaptive, because the job of taste is to keep poisons out of the digestive system while allowing good food in.

FROM THE MOUTH TO THE BRAIN Suppose you taste a lemon (**Figure 5.24**). The physical stimulus that causes you to taste this food consists of chemical molecules that dissolve in saliva (see Figure 5.24, Step 1). The *taste receptors* are the sensory receptors that detect the chemical molecules. They are located in the **taste buds** (see Figure 5.24, Step 2). On the tongue, the taste buds reside in tiny, mushroom-shaped structures called **papillae**. But the taste buds are also spread

taste buds
Structures, located in papillae on the tongue, that contain the sensory receptors called taste receptors.

papillae
Structures on the tongue that contain groupings of taste buds.

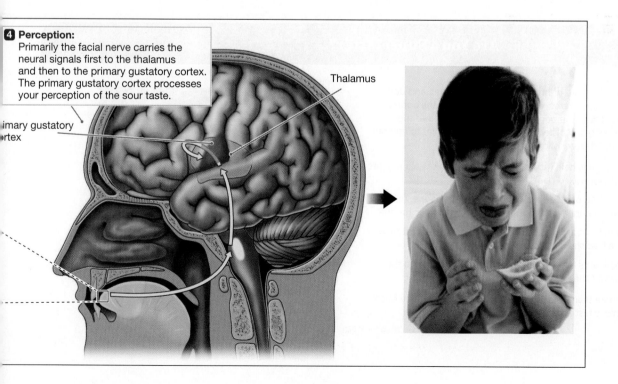

4 Perception:
Primarily the facial nerve carries the neural signals first to the thalamus and then to the primary gustatory cortex. The primary gustatory cortex processes your perception of the sour taste.

Thalamus

imary gustatory
rtex

throughout the mouth and throat. Most individuals have approximately 8,000 to 10,000 taste buds.

Food, fluid, or any other substance—for example, dirt—will stimulate the taste buds. At that point, the taste receptors transduce the sensory input into action potentials (see Figure 5.24, Step 3). The taste information is sent to other brain regions through a set of nerves, primarily the *facial nerve* (see Figure 5.24, Step 4). After processing by the thalamus, the information is further processed in the *primary gustatory cortex.*

FIVE MAIN TASTES   Like the other senses, taste involves a nearly infinite variety of perceptions. These perceptions arise from the activation of unique combinations of receptors. Every taste experience is composed of a mixture of five basic qualities: sweet, sour, salty, bitter, and umami (Japanese for "savory" or "yummy"; pronounced "oo-MOM-ee"; Barretto et al., 2015). Umami is the most recently recognized taste sensation. If you have eaten foods such as meat, mushrooms, or soy sauce, you may have noticed how they seem to be bursting with flavor. If so, you have experienced umami. Researchers are still investigating how the cells in the taste buds lead to perception of all five of these taste qualities and where these cells are located on the tongue. In addition, the experience of taste can be affected by other aspects of food, such as its spiciness or the amount of fat in it.

Some people experience taste sensations intensely. This trait is determined largely by genetics. These individuals, known as supertasters, are highly aware of flavors and textures and are more likely than others to feel pain when eating very spicy foods (Bartoshuk, 2000). Supertasters have nearly six times as many taste buds as normal tasters. The more taste buds you have, the more intense your taste experiences will be.

Although it might sound enjoyable to experience intense tastes, many supertasters are especially picky eaters because particular tastes can overwhelm them. When it comes to sensation, more is not necessarily better. Being a supertaster may

---

TRY IT YOURSELF: **Are You a Supertaster?**

Do you dislike the taste of broccoli, coffee, grapefruit, and dark chocolate? If you answered yes, you may be part of the approximately 25 percent of the population that is several times more sensitive to strong and bitter tastes than other people. To find out if you are a supertaster, follow these simple steps.

1. Punch a small hole (about 7 millimeters or ¼ of an inch) into a square of waxed paper.

2. Place a drop of blue food coloring on your tongue, then put the waxed paper with the hole in it on top of your tongue.

3. Use a magnifying glass and a mirror to view the part of your tongue that shows through the hole.

4. The pink dots are the papillae, which do not take up the dye. Count the number of papillae visible in the hole.

If you have more than 30 papillae, you also have more taste buds. If you have more taste buds, you may be a supertaster.

Hypothesis: Taste preferences in newborns are influenced by their mothers' food preferences during the months immediately before and after birth.

Research Method: Pregnant women were assigned at random to one of four groups. They were instructed to drink a certain beverage every day for two months before the baby's birth and two months after the baby's birth:

	Before birth	After birth
Group 1:	carrot juice	water
Group 2:	carrot juice	carrot juice
Group 3:	water	carrot juice
Group 4:	water	water

Results: Babies whose mothers were in Groups 1, 2, or 3 preferred the taste of carrot juice more than did babies whose mothers were in Group 4 and did not drink carrot juice.

Conclusion: Babies become familiar with the taste of foods their mothers consume around the time of their birth, and they prefer familiar tastes.

QUESTION: How might the findings of this study account for cultural differences in food preferences?

ANSWER: What pregnant women eat influences the food preferences their offspring develop in the womb. Cultural preferences shape what pregnant mothers eat. Therefore cultural preferences influence newborns' food preferences and presumably people's food preferences later in life.

Source: Mennella, J. A., Jagnow, C. P., & Beauchamp, G. K. (2001). Prenatal and postnatal flavor learning by human infants. *Pediatrics, 107,* e88.

also affect health. Supertasters tend to avoid bitter-tasting foods, which they find extremely distasteful. This avoidance may put the supertasters at risk for some cancers that bitter foods may protect against (Basson et al., 2005). The upside is that supertasters also dislike the taste of fatty, sugary foods, so they tend to be thin and may have a lower risk of cardiovascular disease. To see if you are a supertaster, take the test in Try It Yourself on p. 198.

TASTE PREFERENCE   Do you love or hate anchovies? Each of us has individual taste preferences. These preferences come partly from our different numbers of taste receptors. The same food can actually taste different to different people, because the sensation associated with that food differs in their mouths. The texture of food also affects taste preferences: Whether a food is soft or crunchy, creamy or granular, tender or tough affects perception of the sensory experience. Another factor is whether the food causes discomfort, as can happen with spicy chilies. And as discussed in this chapter's Putting Psychology to Work feature, on p. 211, the visual presentation of food affects people's perception of taste.

Cultural factors influence taste preferences as well. In fact, cultural influences on food preferences begin in the womb. One study of infant food preferences found that, through their own eating behaviors before and immediately following birth, mothers apparently pass their eating preferences on to their offspring (Mennella, Jagnow, & Beauchamp, 2001). The details of this study are summarized in The Methods of Psychology on p. 199. Once again, as noted throughout this book, the effects of nature and of nurture are very difficult to separate.

5.12 Your Olfactory Receptors Detect Odorants

5.12 LEARNING GOAL ACTIVITIES

To maximize your learning, complete the following learning goal activities:

a. Understand all bold and italic terms by writing explanations of them in your own words.

b. Understand why we have evolved the senses of taste and smell by describing in your own words how these senses are important to the survival of humans.

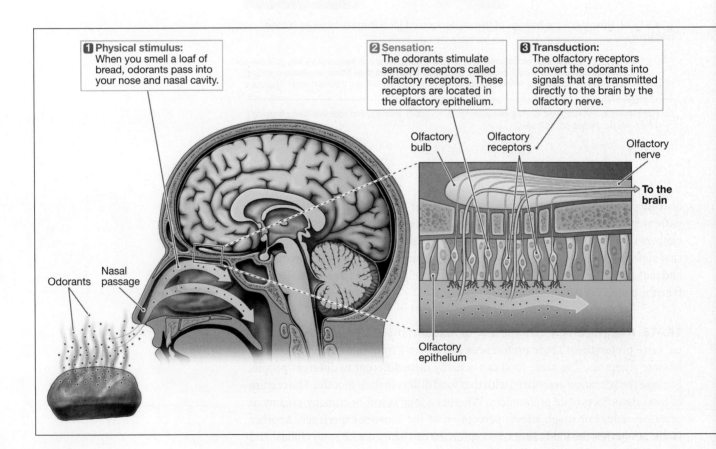

1 Physical stimulus: When you smell a loaf of bread, odorants pass into your nose and nasal cavity.

2 Sensation: The odorants stimulate sensory receptors called olfactory receptors. These receptors are located in the olfactory epithelium.

3 Transduction: The olfactory receptors convert the odorants into signals that are transmitted directly to the brain by the olfactory nerve.

Olfactory bulb

Olfactory receptors

Olfactory nerve

To the brain

Odorants

Nasal passage

Olfactory epithelium

When a dog is out for a walk, why does it sniff virtually every object and creature it encounters? The sense of smell, which is also called *olfaction,* is the dog's main way of perceiving the world. Our sense of smell is much weaker than that of dogs, and in fact of many animals. For example, dogs have 40 times more olfactory receptors than humans do and are 100,000 to 1 million times more sensitive to odors. Our less developed sense of smell comes from our ancestors' reliance on vision. Yet the importance of smell to us in our daily lives is made clear, at least in Western cultures, by the vast sums of money we spend on fragrances, deodorants, and mouthwash.

FROM THE NOSE TO THE BRAIN   Of all the senses, olfaction has the most direct route to the brain. But it may be the sense we understand the least. Like taste, smell begins when you sense chemical molecules that come from outside your body. The chemical molecules are called *odorants.* Say you smell a fresh loaf of bread (**Figure 5.25**). The odorants pass into your nose and through the upper and back portions of the nasal cavity (see Figure 5.25, Step 1). In the nose and the nasal cavity, a warm, moist environment helps the sensory receptors, called *olfactory receptors,* detect the odorant molecules. The olfactory receptors are embedded within the **olfactory epithelium.** This layer of tissue, as thin as a dime, is located deep in the nasal cavity (see Figure 5.25, Step 2).

The olfactory receptors transduce the odorants into signals that the brain will ultimately process (see Figure 5.25, Step 3). These signals are processed in the **olfactory bulb,** the brain center for smell. From the olfactory bulb, which is just below the frontal lobes, the *olfactory nerve* transmits smell information to various brain

olfactory epithelium
A thin layer of tissue, deep within the nasal cavity, containing the olfactory receptors; these sensory receptors produce information that is processed in the brain as smell.

olfactory bulb
A brain structure above the olfactory epithelium in the nasal cavity; from this structure, the olfactory nerve carries information about smell to the brain.

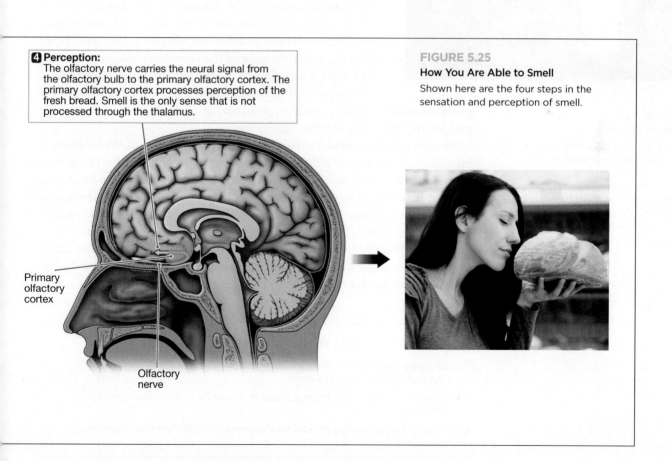

4 Perception:
The olfactory nerve carries the neural signal from the olfactory bulb to the primary olfactory cortex. The primary olfactory cortex processes perception of the fresh bread. Smell is the only sense that is not processed through the thalamus.

Primary olfactory cortex

Olfactory nerve

FIGURE 5.25

How You Are Able to Smell

Shown here are the four steps in the sensation and perception of smell.

(a)

(b)

FIGURE 5.26

A World of Smells

Humans' ability to experience an enormous variety of smells—such as **(a)** this herb, rosemary, and **(b)** peaches—most likely results from a combination of 350 different odor receptors. Stimulation of receptors and then the pattern of activity across the receptors determine the resulting smell.

regions, including the *primary olfactory cortex* (see Figure 5.25, Step 4). Unlike all other forms of sensory information, smell signals bypass the thalamus, the early relay station in the brain.

VARIETY OF SMELLS There are thousands of olfactory receptors in the olfactory epithelium, but there are only about 350 types of odor receptors (Miller, 2004). Each receptor responds to different odorants. It remains unclear exactly how these receptors encode distinct smells. One possibility is that each type of receptor is uniquely associated with a specific odor. For example, one type would encode only the scent of roses, and another would encode the smell of baked bread. This explanation is unlikely, however, given the huge number of scents we can detect. According to a recent estimate, humans can distinguish more than a trillion odorants (Bushdid, Magnasco, Vosshall, & Keller, 2014). Thus, a more likely possibility is that each odorant stimulates several types of receptors and the pattern of activity across these receptors determines the olfactory perception (Lledo, Gheusi, & Vincent, 2005; Zou, Li, & Buck, 2005; **Figure 5.26**). Remember that in all sensory systems, sensation and perception result from both the specificity of receptors and the larger pattern of receptor responses.

SMELL PERCEPTION Information about whether a smell is pleasant or unpleasant is processed in the brain's prefrontal cortex. The smell's intensity is processed in the amygdala, a brain area involved in emotion and memory (Anderson, Christoff, et al., 2003). Because of the amygdala's role in processing smell, it is not surprising that olfactory stimuli can evoke feelings and memories. For example, many people find that the aromas of certain holiday foods, the smell of bread baking, or the fragrances of particular perfumes generate fond childhood memories.

We can readily say whether an odor is pleasant or offensive to us. We can discriminate among thousands of different odors. However, according to the researchers Yaara Yeshurun and Noam Sobel (2010), most people are pretty bad at identifying odors by name. Try asking people to name the smells of odorous items from your refrigerator. You will probably find that people are unable to name the smell at least half the time (de Wijk, Schab, & Cain, 1995). Women, though, are generally better than men at identifying odors (Bromley & Doty, 1995; Ohla & Lundström, 2013). This difference may indicate that women have more cells in the olfactory bulb than men do (Oliveira-Pinto et al., 2014).

 How Are You Able to Taste and Smell?

To make sure you learned what you just read, write answers to the following questions and check your answers.

5.11 What are the five basic taste qualities that have been confirmed through research?

5.12 How is the processing of olfactory information different from the other senses?

See Appendix B for answers to the red Q questions.

How Do You Feel Touch and Pain?

When you see, hear, taste, or smell something, receptors in just one small part of your body have been stimulated. But for the sense of touch, receptors exist all over your body. In fact, your skin is your largest organ for sensory reception. It's no wonder that touches can feel so good.

5.13 Receptors in Your Skin Detect Temperature and Pressure

5.13 LEARNING GOAL ACTIVITIES

To maximize your learning, complete the following learning goal activities:

a. Understand all bold and italic terms by writing explanations of them in your own words.

b. Understand the four steps in touch sensation and perception by summarizing each step in your own words.

Suppose you are splashed with cold water. That water, like anything else that makes contact with your skin, provides tactile stimulation (**Figure 5.27,** Step 1). Tactile stimulation produces the experience of touch. Touch conveys sensations of temperature, of pressure, and of pain.

FROM THE SKIN TO THE BRAIN Specialized receptors detect temperature and pressure (see Figure 5.27, Step 2). These sensory receptors are embedded within the skin. For sensing temperature, there are **warm receptors** and **cold receptors**. Intense hot or cold stimuli can trigger both warm and cold receptors, however. Such simultaneous activation can produce strange sensory experiences, such as a false feeling of wetness. In addition, there are five types of **pressure receptors**. Some of these receptors are nerve fibers at the base of hair follicles. These receptors respond to movement of the hair. Four other types of pressure receptors are capsules in the skin. These receptors respond to continued vibration; to light, fast pressure; to light, slow pressure; or to stretching and steady pressure.

With tactile stimulation, such as being splashed with cold water, these receptors transduce the information into signals that will be sent to the brain (see Figure 5.27, Step 3). When skin is touched above the neck, the information is sent directly into the brain through *cranial nerves* (those that connect directly to the brain; see Figure 5.27, Step 4). When the touch is below the neck, the information is sent to the spinal cord and then *spinal nerves* transmit that information to the brain. In both cases, touch information travels first through the thalamus and then to the *primary somatosensory cortex*. In the primary somatosensory cortex, the information is processed.

PERCEPTION OF TOUCH How do you know where on your body you're being touched? In the 1940s, the neurosurgeon Wilder Penfield studied patients undergoing brain surgery. Penfield discovered that electrical stimulation of the

warm receptors
Sensory receptors in the skin that detect the temperature of stimuli and transduce it into information processed in the brain as warmth.

cold receptors
Sensory receptors in the skin that detect the temperature of stimuli and transduce it into information processed in the brain as cold.

pressure receptors
Sensory receptors in the skin that detect tactile stimulation and transduce it into information processed in the brain as different types of pressure on the skin.

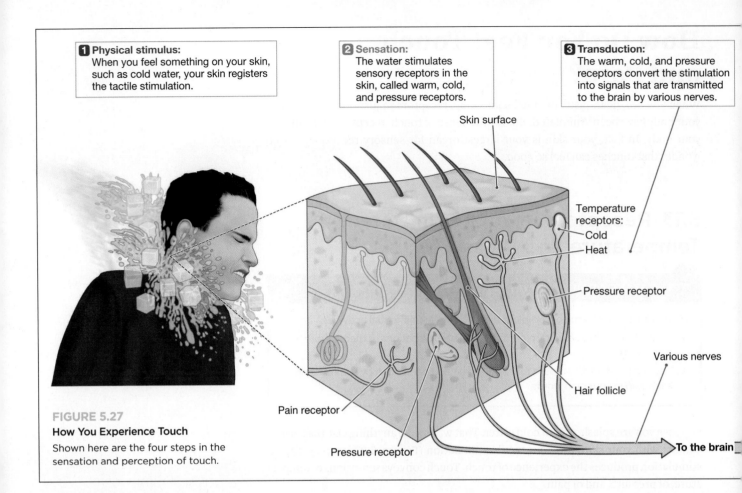

1 Physical stimulus:
When you feel something on your skin, such as cold water, your skin registers the tactile stimulation.

2 Sensation:
The water stimulates sensory receptors in the skin, called warm, cold, and pressure receptors.

3 Transduction:
The warm, cold, and pressure receptors convert the stimulation into signals that are transmitted to the brain by various nerves.

Skin surface

Temperature receptors:
- Cold
- Heat

Pressure receptor

Various nerves

Hair follicle

To the brain

Pain receptor

Pressure receptor

FIGURE 5.27

How You Experience Touch

Shown here are the four steps in the sensation and perception of touch.

FIGURE 5.28

The Kinesthetic Sense Reveals Where Your Limbs Are in Space

The kinesthetic sense is an internal sense that tells you how your body and limbs are positioned in space.

primary somatosensory cortex could evoke the perception of touch in different regions of the body (Penfield & Jasper, 1954). Parts of the body that are located near each other, such as the hand and arm, are processed in adjacent brain areas in the somatosensory cortex. You saw this processing mapped in the homunculus of Figure 2.18 (right side).

For the most sensitive regions of the body, such as lips and fingers, a great deal of cortex is dedicated to processing touch. For less sensitive areas, such as the back and the calves, very little cortex is dedicated to processing touch. Caressing certain parts of the body feels so good because more of your brain processes that information.

KINESTHETIC SENSE While your sense of touch is a sensory system that processes stimuli from the external world, you also have an internal sensory system that lets you feel where the parts of your body are in space. This internal sense, related to touch, is called the *kinesthetic sense*. Kinesthetic information comes from receptors inside of the muscles, in tendons, and in joints. This information lets you coordinate voluntary movement and is invaluable in avoiding injury. You experience your kinesthetic sense every day. For example, you can pinpoint your position in space. You register the movements of your body and your limbs. Without these abilities, you would be unable to perform activities such as yoga (**Figure 5.28**).

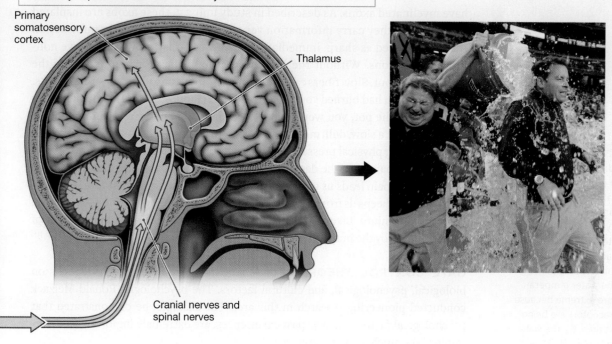

4 Perception:
For touches above the neck, cranial nerves send neural signals to the brain. But for touches below the neck, neural signals are sent to the spinal cord, and spinal nerves transmit them to the brain. Signals travel to the thalamus and then to the area of the primary somatosensory cortex that processes the body part that was touched. This processing makes you perceive the cold water on your neck.

Primary somatosensory cortex

Thalamus

Cranial nerves and spinal nerves

5.14 You Detect Pain in Your Skin and Throughout Your Body

5.14 LEARNING GOAL ACTIVITIES

To maximize your learning, complete the following learning goal activities:

a. Understand all bold and italic terms by writing explanations of them in your own words.

b. Apply pain perception to your life by imagining that you bang your knee on the corner of a table, then naming the pain receptors involved and explaining how they would process the information.

Ouch! You reach for a pan on the stove, not knowing that the handle is really hot. You pull your hand away quickly before you get badly burned. Just as taste can prevent you from eating something harmful, pain is part of a warning system that stops you from continuing activities that may harm you (see Has It Happened to You? on p. 206). Children born with a rare genetic disorder that leaves them insensitive to pain usually die young, no matter how carefully they are supervised. They simply do not know how to avoid activities that harm them or to report when they are ill (Melzack & Wall, 1982).

fast fibers
Sensory receptors in skin, muscles, organs, and membranes around both bones and joints; these myelinated fibers quickly convey intense sensory input to the brain, where it is perceived as sharp, immediate pain.

slow fibers
Sensory receptors in skin, muscles, organs, and membranes around both bones and joints; these unmyelinated fibers slowly convey intense sensory input to the brain, where it is perceived as chronic, dull, steady pain.

TWO TYPES OF PAIN RECEPTORS   Most experiences of pain result when damage to the skin triggers pain receptors. The nerves that carry pain information are thinner than those for temperature and for pressure. These thinner nerves are found in all body tissues that sense pain: skin, muscles, membranes around both bones and joints, organs, and so on.

Two kinds of nerve fibers carry pain information to the brain. **Fast fibers** have myelinated axons. As described in study unit 2.2, these axons are insulated by myelin, so they carry information very quickly. Fast fibers carry information that is perceived as sharp, immediate pains. By contrast, **slow fibers** have non-myelinated axons. Without the insulation around these "wires," some of the signal "leaks" out. Slow fibers carry information about chronic, dull, steady pains.

Suppose you had burned yourself on a hot pot (**Figure 5.29**). The moment your skin touched the pot, you would have felt a sharp, fast, localized pain. Then you would have felt a slow, dull, more diffuse pain. In this case, the fast fibers were activated by strong physical pressure and temperature extremes. The slow fibers were activated by changes in the damaged skin tissue. Both fast pain and slow pain are adaptive. Fast pain leads us to recoil from harmful objects and therefore is protective. Slow pain keeps us from using the affected body parts and therefore helps them recover from injury. Like all other sensory experiences, the actual perception of pain is created by the brain.

GATE CONTROL THEORY   Pain is a complex experience that depends on biological, psychological, and cultural factors. The psychologist Ronald Melzack conducted pioneering research in this area. For example, he demonstrated that psychological factors, such as past experiences, are extremely important in determining how much pain a person feels.

With his collaborator Patrick Wall, Melzack formulated the *gate control theory of pain*. According to this theory, we experience pain when pain receptors are activated and a neural "gate" in the spinal cord allows the signals through to the brain (Melzack & Wall, 1982). These ideas were radical in that they viewed pain as a perceptual experience within the brain rather than simply a response to nerve stimulation. The theory states that pain signals are transmitted by thin nerve fibers. These fibers can be blocked at the spinal cord (prevented from reaching the brain) by the firing of larger sensory nerve fibers involved in the perception of touch. Thus, sensory nerve fibers can "close a gate" and reduce the perception of pain. This is why scratching an itch is so satisfying, why rubbing an aching muscle helps reduce the ache, and why vigorously rubbing the skin where an injection is about to be given reduces the needle's sting.

CONTROLLING PAIN   When you are in pain, does the pain feel worse when you're wide awake and active or when you're trying to sleep? Most of us have taken over-the-counter drugs, usually ibuprofen or acetaminophen, to reduce pain perception. If you have ever suffered from a severe toothache or needed surgery, you have probably experienced the benefits of pain medication. When a dentist administers Novocain to sensory neurons in the mouth, pain messages are not transmitted to the brain, so the mouth feels numb.

Distraction can also reduce your perception of pain. When ready for sleep, you generally try to remove distractions. As a result, the pain probably feels more intense. Without distractions, you might focus on or worry about the pain, thus increasing your pain perception. So as you prepare for a painful procedure or suffer after one, try to distract yourself. Don't focus on or worry about the pain. Watching an entertaining movie can help reduce pain perception, especially if it is funny enough to elevate your mood. And Swedish researchers found that listening to music was an extremely effective means of reducing postoperative pain, perhaps because it helps patients relax (Engwall & Duppils, 2009).

Keep in mind, however, that severe pain is a warning that something in the body is seriously wrong. If you experience severe pain, you should be treated by a medical professional.

 How Do You Feel Touch and Pain?

To make sure you learned what you just read, write answers to the following questions and check your answers.

5.13 When someone shakes your hand, what receptors are activated, and what part of the cortex processes the touch?

5.14 Why do people often rub parts of their bodies that are injured?

See Appendix B for answers to the red Q questions.

FIGURE 5.29

Types of Pain

A painful touch, such as a burn, creates two types of pain. Activation of fast fibers leads to perception of intense pain. Activation of slow fibers leads to the perception of duller, throbbing pain.

BIG PICTURE

 Want to earn a better grade on your test? Go to **INQUIZITIVE** to practice actively with this chapter's content and get personalized feedback along the way.

How Do Sensation and Perception Affect You?

5.1 Your Senses Detect Physical Stimuli, and Your Brain Processes Perception

Review the learning goal activities on p. 173. Sensation is the detection of physical stimuli from an environment and the transmission of that information to your brain. Sensory receptors allow the transduction of sensory input into neural activity, which the brain can process. Except for smell, this neural activity is sent to the thalamus and relevant parts of the cortex for further processing. Perception is how various parts of the brain interpret this information to let you experience what you see, hear, smell, taste, and touch.

KEY TERMS

sensation (p. 173)

perception (p. 173)

sensory receptors (p. 174)

transduction (p. 174)

5.2 There Must Be a Certain Amount of a Stimulus for You to Detect It

Review the learning goal activities on p. 175. Physical stimulation needs to be greater than some amount before you experience a sensation. Absolute threshold is the minimum amount of physical stimuli needed to detect a sensory input. Difference threshold is the minimum difference in physical stimuli required to detect a difference between sensory inputs. Sensory adaptation is a decrease in sensitivity to a constant level of stimulation.

absolute threshold (p. 175)

difference threshold (p. 176)

sensory adaptation (p. 176)

How Do You See?

5.3 Sensory Receptors in Your Eyes Detect Light

Review the learning goal activities on p. 177. In visual sensation, rods and cones are the sensory receptors that transduce light waves into signals. Ganglion cells then fire action potentials, and these neural signals are sent to the brain. This information first passes through the thalamus, and then it is sent to the primary visual cortex for perceptual processing.

5.4 You Perceive Color Based on Physical Aspects of Light

Review the learning goal activities on p. 180. You perceive the brightness of a color based on the amplitude of light waves. You perceive the hue and saturation of color based on the wavelengths of light waves. Trichromatic theory explains how color perception is based on the stimulation of three sets of cones. S cones respond best to short wavelengths of light, M cones to medium wavelengths, and L cones to long wavelengths. Trichromatic theory explains how color blindness is based on atypical processing in one or more of the three types of cones. Opponent-process theory also explains how color perception, especially in afterimages, is based on the function of the ganglion cells.

5.5 You Perceive Objects by Organizing Visual Information

Review the learning goal activities on p. 183. You perceive objects through three main pieces of information: (1) by determining figure and ground, (2) by using grouping principles (such as proximity, similarity, continuity, closure, and illusory contours) to organize information into wholes, and (3) through bottom-up and top-down processing.

5.6 When You Perceive Depth, You Can Locate Objects in Space

Review the learning goal activities on p. 186. You perceive depth from a two-dimensional image on the retina based on binocular cues, especially binocular disparity, which is how the brain processes the unique information on each of the two retinas. You also perceive depth due to six monocular cues: (1) occlusion, (2) height in field, (3) relative size, (4) familiar size, (5) linear perspective, and (6) texture gradient.

5.7 Cues in Your Brain and in the World Let You Perceive Motion

Review the learning goal activities on p. 187. Two phenomena give insight into how we perceive motion: (1) motion aftereffects (stationary scene seems to move) and (2) stroboscopic motion (movies).

5.8 You Understand That Objects Remain Constant Even When Cues Change

Review the learning goal activities on p. 188. Object constancy refers to how the brain accurately perceives images even with minimal or changing stimulus cues. The four types of object constancy are (1) size, (2) shape, (3) color, and (4) lightness.

How Do You Hear?

5.9 Receptors in Your Ears Detect Sound Waves

Review the learning goal activities on p. 190. In auditory sensation, hair cells detect sound waves, then transduce them into auditory information. The auditory nerve sends this information to the thalamus and finally to the primary auditory cortex for perceptual processing.

5.10 You Perceive Sound Based on Physical Aspects of Sound Waves

Review the learning goal activities on p. 193. You perceive the loudness of a sound based on the amplitude of sound waves. You perceive pitch based on temporal coding and place coding of the frequencies of the wavelengths of sound waves. You perceive the location of a sound when the brain compares the time and the intensity of a sound as it arrives at each ear. The vestibular sense is an internal sense that uses the semicircular canals in the inner ear to let you maintain balance by judging direction and intensity of head movements.

How Are You Able to Taste and Smell?

5.11 Receptors in Your Taste Buds Detect Chemical Molecules

Review the learning goal activities on p. 197. In taste sensation, taste receptors transduce chemical molecules into taste information. The facial nerve sends this information to the thalamus and primary gustatory cortex for perceptual processing. Research has confirmed the detection of five basic taste sensations: (1) sweet, (2) sour, (3) salty, (4) bitter, and (5) umami (savory).

5.12 Your Olfactory Receptors Detect Odorants

Review the learning goal activities on p. 200. In the sense of smell, olfactory receptors transduce odorants and send smell information to the olfactory bulb. The olfactory nerve then transmits the signals directly to the primary olfactory cortex for perceptual processing. Humans can perceive and discriminate a huge variety of smells, but are generally poor at naming odors.

How Do You Feel Touch and Pain?

5.13 Receptors in Your Skin Detect Temperature and Pressure

Review the learning goal activities on p. 203. In touch, sensory receptors in the skin transduce information about temperature (warm and cold receptors) and pressure (pressure receptors). Cranial nerves and spinal nerves then send this information to the thalamus and somatosensory cortex for perception. The kinesthetic sense, an internal sense related to touch, lets you judge where your body and limbs are in space.

5.14 You Detect Pain in Your Skin and Throughout Your Body

Review the learning goal activities on p. 205. For pain, fast fibers transduce information about immediate, sharp pain. Slow fibers transduce information about chronic, dull pain. According to the gate control theory, the perception of pain can be reduced if other information is processed simultaneously. Activities such as rubbing the area around the painful skin, distracting yourself, or thinking happy thoughts can decrease the perception of pain.

CHAPTER 5 SELF-QUIZ

To make sure you learned the information in this chapter, write answers to the following questions and check your answers. **See Appendix B for answers to the self-quiz.**

1. Mia is taking a hearing test. The technician instructs her to tell him when she hears a sound. The test moves from louder to softer sounds, until Mia can hear a sound of a certain volume only half the time it is given. The technician is determining Mia's _____ auditory stimuli.
   a. difference threshold for
   b. absolute threshold for
   c. transduction of
   d. sensory adaptation to

2. McKayla and Ben are walking at night and looking at the stars. They are able to detect the dim light of the stars due to the process of _____, which occurs in their _____.
   a. perception; cones
   b. perception; rods
   c. sensation; cones
   d. sensation; rods

3. Luis stares at Marigold's green dress, then looks at a white wall. On the wall, he sees a red afterimage of the dress. The fact that Luis sees a red afterimage is best explained by _____.
   a. opponent-process theory
   b. trichromatic theory
   c. top-down processing
   d. bottom-up processing

4. Benjamin injured one of his eyes and needs to wear an eye patch over it for the next 6 weeks. He finds it difficult to reach out and grab things, such as the buttons on his shirt, because with the use of only one eye he lacks the depth cue of _____.
   a. relative size
   b. occlusion
   c. binocular disparity
   d. linear perspective

5. In a science fiction movie, the villain wants to cause deafness in people by preventing auditory transduction. The villain tries to achieve this goal by _____ in her victims.
   a. removing the thalamus
   b. destroying all the hair cells
   c. fusing the ossicles
   d. damaging the auditory nerve

6. Kai has been attending loud rock concerts for several years. Recently, she has been having problems hearing high-pitched sounds. This loss is most likely due to impaired _____ coding in her _____.
   a. temporal; cochlea
   b. temporal; semicircular canals
   c. place; cochlea
   d. place; semicircular canals

7. Roberto has strong taste sensations and is very sensitive to spiciness. Hot spices are almost physically painful to him. To find out if Roberto is a supertaster, you would determine if he has _____.
   a. many papillae, because papillae contain taste receptors
   b. the unusual ability to detect umami
   c. a very responsive olfactory epithelium
   d. a highly active gustatory cortex

8. Cosette is experiencing a decline in her sense of smell. The doctor correctly tells her that the problem could be with any one of the following structures EXCEPT for her _____.
   a. olfactory cortex
   b. olfactory bulb
   c. olfactory nerve
   d. thalamus

9. Jase's phone is on vibrate. Jase feels the vibration due to processing by his _____.
   a. hot receptors
   b. fast and slow fibers
   c. pressure receptors
   d. cold receptors

10. While playing soccer, Viveca was kicked in her thigh. She felt sharp pain due to _____ fibers. The immediacy of this sensation was due to the _____ of myelin on the axons of these fibers.
    a. fast; absence
    b. fast; presence
    c. slow; absence
    d. slow; presence

How Can Understanding Sensation and Perception Help You in Your Career?

Have you ever wondered how the appearance of food affects your taste experience? Or how food companies come up with so many new tasty flavors and pleasing smells? As you are learning in this chapter, the perception of stimuli is a psychological process. Qualities such as appearance, taste, and smell are actively constructed in the brain after physical stimuli reach sensory receptors. Understanding how perceptual experiences are created and influenced by psychological factors can be applied in the workplace in many ways.

In the restaurant industry, presentation of food is key to success. For example, arranging food attractively or plating it artfully leads people to rate the food as tasting better (Zellner et al., 2011; Michel, Velasco, Gatti, & Spence, 2014). Even sounds affect desire for food. The restaurant Chili's has found that when servers come out of the kitchen with sizzling plates of fajitas, other patrons respond to those sounds and sights by ordering more fajitas (Beckerman & Gray, 2014). Even background music can influence people's perception of food (Spence, 2012). If you are interested in a restaurant career, an associate's degree can help you become, for example, a food service manager. Knowledge of sensation and perception will let you improve the experiences of restaurant-goers and even increase sales.

Understanding sensation and perception can also be applied to the development of food products. In his book *Salt, Sugar, Fat* (2014), Michael Moss describes how companies such as Pillsbury, General Mills, and Schweppes employ food scientists to develop products that appeal to consumers. For example, food scientists work to find the perfect level of sugar in a soft drink or ice cream, or the perfect level of salt in a chip. This ideal combination of tastes is known as the "bliss point," and it encourages continued eating of the food.

What about the other forms of sensation and perception—sight, hearing, and the feeling of touch? Understanding visual perception is vital in fields such as advertising, marketing, architecture, engineering, design, and the fine arts. Understanding hearing can lead to a career in audiology (hearing therapy) and spoken-language pathology (speech therapy). Knowledge of pain processing can aid health care workers, including doctors, nurses, and physical therapists. Because the processes of sensation and perception are so important to human life, you may find yourself employing this knowledge in any career.

TAKEAWAY POINT: Understanding how sensation and perception operate can be very useful in the food industry, both in the serving of food at restaurants and in the development of products at food companies. Applications of sensation and perception can also extend to many fields in business, the arts, and health care.

 You can look up job descriptions, education requirements, salaries, and more at the Bureau of Labor Statistics: www.bls.gov. Visit the site and start putting psychology to work!

6 Learning

THE PARTY WAS GREAT. The DJ was entertaining, and the food was terrific—especially the shrimp, and you ate a lot of them. But almost immediately something didn't feel right, and you ended up having a night that you would like to forget. Even now, a year later, the sight, the smell, and the thought of shrimp make you feel ill. You never eat them anymore.

Sound familiar? Have you ever responded this way to a food after becoming sick? If so, you have experienced conditioned taste aversion. This particular form of learning is not limited to humans. You can see a striking example of conditioned taste aversion in the way wolves have learned not to prey on domestic livestock.

BIG QUESTIONS

How Do You Learn?

How Do You Learn Through Classical Conditioning?

How Do You Learn Through Operant Conditioning?

How Do You Learn by Watching Others?

FIGURE 6.1
Wolves Experiencing Conditioned Taste Aversion
Conditioned taste aversion helps train wolves not to eat sheep when wolves are reintroduced to areas in the United States.

Gray wolves of the Northern Rocky Mountain region were native to Yellowstone National Park when the park was created in 1872. By the 1970s, however, all the wolves in the park had been killed as part of a predator control plan. Some gray wolves remained in the lower 48 states, but in 1974 the species was listed as endangered. In 1987, the U.S. Fish and Wildlife Service announced a recovery plan to reintroduce wolves to Yellowstone Park. At the same time, some conservation groups were proposing to reintroduce other subspecies of wolves, such as the Mexican wolf, to other parts of the United States. In all of these regions, the local farmers and ranchers were afraid the wolves would prey on their sheep. An important part of all the reintroduction plans, therefore, was gaining the support of the farmers and ranchers by finding creative ways to limit the killing of sheep by wolves. Here is where the psychology behind conditioned taste aversion came into play.

The bodies of sheep were treated with nonlethal doses of poison. Then they were placed where wolves would find them (**Figure 6.1**). After eating the meat, the wolves immediately vomited. Just as you now avoid food that made you sick in the past, the wolves soon learned to associate eating sheep with becoming ill. So they avoided preying on sheep. As a result, many ranchers stopped opposing reintroduction of wolves. Thus conditioned taste aversion for the flavor of sheep's meat has allowed the wolves to flourish in regions where agriculturists would normally kill them. Today, in several regions of the United States, wolves have been taken off the endangered species list.

Using conditioned taste aversion to help wolves learn not to eat sheep is an example of how psychology can be put to work in "the real world." The principles behind the wolves' learning are also the basis for some of the ways that humans learn. This chapter examines how learning takes place. This material represents some of psychology's major contributions to our understanding of behavior. Learning theories have been used to improve quality of life and to train humans as well as nonhuman animals to learn new tasks.

How Do You Learn?

Learning is central to almost all areas of human existence. It makes possible our basic abilities (such as walking and speaking) and our complex ones (such as flying airplanes, performing surgery, or maintaining intimate relationships). What music you listen to, how you choose to dress, social rules about how close you stand to someone else, cultural values about whether you harm or preserve the environment—learning affects these and many other aspects of daily life. To understand how you develop new behaviors over time, you must first understand what learning is and how it happens.

6.1 You Learn from Experience

6.1 LEARNING GOAL ACTIVITIES

To maximize your learning, complete the following learning goal activities.

a. Understand all bold and italic terms by writing explanations of them in your own words.

b. Apply learning to your life by describing an example of how your behavior changed because of your experiences.

Learning is a change in behavior, resulting from experience. While that definition is simple, the processes of learning have been debated for centuries. Formal theories about learning arose in the early twentieth century. These were developed partly because some psychologists were not satisfied with the ideas of Freud that had been at the heart of psychological theorizing. As you learned in study unit 1.5, Freud and his followers used psychoanalysis. Through this method, they worked with patients to reveal unconscious mental processes that they believed caused behavior. But other psychologists argued that Freud's theory was unscientific and ultimately meaningless, and they developed theories of behavior and learning that were based on observable events.

John Watson, in particular, rejected any psychological approach that did *not* focus on what could be observed directly (Watson, 1924). According to Watson, observable behavior was the only valid indicator of psychological activity. As you learned in study unit 1.6, this idea was the basis for behaviorism. In formulating his ideas on behaviorism, Watson was influenced by the seventeenth-century philosopher John Locke. An infant, Locke argued, is a *tabula rasa* (Latin for "blank slate"). Born knowing nothing, the infant develops over time by acquiring all of its knowledge through sensory experiences. Watson built on this foundation by stating that learning was determined completely by environment and its effects on animals, including humans.

Behaviorism was also the basis for B. F. Skinner's groundbreaking studies of animals, often using pigeons or rats. Skinner designed these experiments to discover the basic rules of learning. He found that by giving an animal food for doing particular actions, he could radically change that animal's behavior.

Modern psychologists agree that learning results from an individual's experience. Learning occurs when an animal, including a human, benefits from experience so that the animal's behavior is better adapted to the environment. Indeed, the ability to learn is crucial for all creatures. To survive, all creatures need to learn things such as which sounds indicate potential dangers, what foods are dangerous, and when it is safe to sleep. Furthermore, learning is critical to success in any job, and understanding learning can help you train animals, including humans, as a career (see Putting Psychology to Work on p. 249). But according to psychological research, all forms of learning are not the same. The following study unit looks at the three different ways you learn.

learning
A change in behavior, resulting from experience.

6.2 You Learn in Three Ways

6.2 LEARNING GOAL ACTIVITIES

To maximize your learning, complete the following learning goal activities.

a. Understand all bold and italic terms by writing explanations of them in your own words.

b. Understand the three main types of learning by describing each one in your own words.

What would you do if you heard a loud crashing sound right now? You would probably look around for what had happened or even get up to investigate. You would do this because you have learned in the past that a loud crashing sound is something to respond to. Is this type of learning the same as learning to be afraid when you hear creepy music in a horror movie? Or learning to do your homework to earn a good grade? Or learning how to cook a particular dish by watching someone do it? Psychologists have divided learning into three main types: non-associative learning,

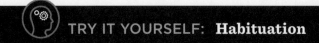

LEARNING TIP: Types of Learning

This graphic will help you understand the relationship between the three main types of learning and all of the subtypes.

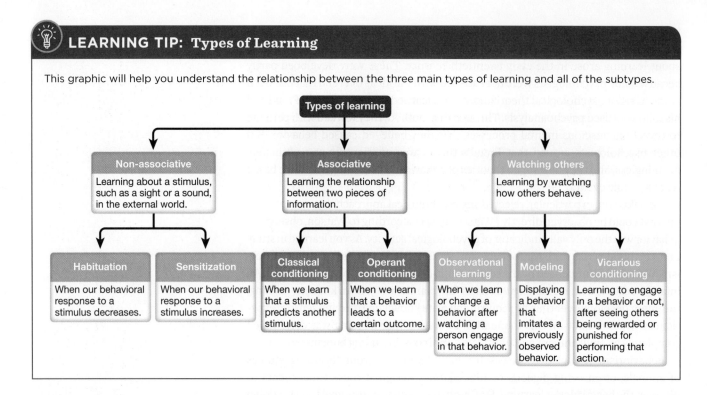

habituation
A decrease in behavioral response after lengthy or repeated exposure to a stimulus.

sensitization
An increase in behavioral response after lengthy or repeated exposure to a stimulus.

associative learning, and learning by watching others. These three main types of learning are summarized in the Learning Tip above.

One main type of learning is *non-associative learning*. In non-associative learning, a person learns about one stimulus, which is information in the external world. A stimulus could be a sight, smell, or sound, for example. One important form of non-associative learning is **habituation,** where an individual is exposed to a stimulus for a long time, or repeatedly. Eventually, the individual's behavioral response to that stimulus decreases (**Figure 6.2a**). Habituation happens particularly if the stimulus is neither harmful nor rewarding. For example, if an animal experiences a new stimulus, such as hearing a sound, it will pay attention for a while, because the sound might indicate a potential danger. If the sound does not result in a threat, the animal soon learns to ignore it. In your everyday life, you also constantly habituate to meaningless events around you (see Try It Yourself).

Sensitization is a second form of non-associative learning. It takes place when an individual is exposed to a stimulus for a long time, or many times, and then has an increased behavioral response. In general, sensitization leads to heightened preparation to respond in an important situation where there is some potential harm or reward (**Figure 6.2b**). For instance, suppose that while you are studying, you smell something burning. You probably will not habituate to this smell, because it is an important stimulus. You might focus even greater attention on the smell to determine whether it is just a candle, someone burning dinner, or something potentially dangerous.

A second main type of learning is *associative learning*. Unlike non-associative learning, associative learning requires understanding how two or more pieces of information are related to each other. Associations develop through two forms of conditioning. The first form, classical conditioning, occurs when you learn that two stimuli go together. For example, if you

TRY IT YOURSELF: Habituation

Right now, you can experience learning about a stimulus through habituation. Sit back and listen to the background sounds wherever you are. Perhaps you can hear the hum of a light, a computer fan whirring, or music playing nearby. But did you notice this noise before it was pointed out to you? No, because you habituated to it. And in a few minutes, because of habituation, you will probably stop noticing the noise again.

always hear a certain kind of music during scary scenes in a movie, you learn to feel anxious whenever you hear that music. The second form, operant conditioning, occurs when you learn that a behavior leads to a particular outcome. For example, you learn that studying leads to better grades.

The third main type of learning, *learning by watching others,* is just what it sounds like. Animals (including humans) can learn by watching others, such as through observational learning, modeling, and vicarious conditioning. For example, you might have learned the latest popular dance by watching a YouTube video.

Later sections of this chapter consider associative learning and learning by watching others in more detail. The following study unit looks briefly at what happens in the brain during all three types of learning.

(a)

6.3 Your Brain Changes During Learning

(b)

6.3 LEARNING GOAL ACTIVITIES

To maximize your learning, complete the following learning goal activities.

a. Understand all bold and italic terms by writing explanations of them in your own words.

b. Understand how the brain changes during learning by summarizing in your own words how long-term potentiation works.

All of the types of learning just described result from experience. But what happens in the brain during learning? Exposure to environmental events actually causes changes in the brain that let learning occur. As you learned in study unit 2.13, when one neuron repeatedly activates another neuron, the connection between them strengthens. The strengthened connection then makes these neurons more likely to fire together in the future. The neuropsychologist Donald Hebb proposed this theory (Hebb, 1949), referred to as *Hebbian learning,* which is easily remembered by the catchphrase "neurons that fire together, wire together."

To understand how learning occurs in the brain, researchers have investigated the enhanced activity that results from the strengthening of synaptic connections between neurons. This phenomenon is known as *long-term potentiation (LTP)*. This term is easy to remember if you know that the word *potent* suggests something is strong. So potentiation indicates the strengthening of synaptic connections that make learning possible. A lot of evidence supports the idea that long-term potentiation is involved in learning and memory (Cooke & Bliss, 2006; Herring & Nicoll, 2016). For instance, LTP effects are most easily observed in brain sites known to be active in learning and memory, such as the hippocampus. What's more, the same drugs that improve learning also lead to increased LTP, and those that block learning also block LTP.

FIGURE 6.2

Two Forms of Non-Associative Learning

(a) Habituation: Suppose you live or work in a noisy environment. You learn to ignore the constant noise, because you do not need to respond to it.
(b) Sensitization: Suppose you're sitting with your brother. He keeps annoying you, until finally you react.

How Do You Learn?

To make sure you learned what you just read, write answers to the following questions and check your answers.

6.1 What is learning?

6.2 What is the primary difference between habituation and sensitization?

6.3 What is the basis of learning in the brain?

See Appendix B for answers to the red Q questions.

classical conditioning
A type of learned response in which a neutral object comes to elicit a response when it is associated with a stimulus that already produces a response.

How Do You Learn Through Classical Conditioning?

It's only a movie, but when the music starts to play, you feel tense as you watch the woman descend into the dark basement in the middle of the night. The music helps make the situation scary. You just know that something bad is about to happen to her. But how do you know this? You know it because you have learned the association between the presence of certain music and bad things happening to the characters in the movie. It makes sense, then, that this type of learning is called associative learning. After all, you are learning to associate, or link, two things together. Learning in this way is so familiar because it has happened to all of us (see Has It Happened to You?). We even describe it with a familiar phrase: acting like Pavlov's dog. But what was Pavlov's dog, and what does it have to do with learning?

6.4 Through Classical Conditioning, You Learn That Stimuli Are Related

 6.4 LEARNING GOAL ACTIVITIES

To maximize your learning, complete the following learning goal activities.

a. Understand all bold and italic terms by writing explanations of them in your own words.

b. Apply the four steps of classical conditioning by describing how to train a horse to run at the sound of a bell. Hint: Horses naturally run when hit on the rump.

Ivan Pavlov was a Russian physiologist. In 1904, he won a Nobel Prize for his research on the digestive system. Pavlov was interested in the salivary reflex, which is an automatic and unlearned response that occurs when food is presented to a hungry animal or human (**Figure 6.3a**). To investigate the digestive system, Pavlov created an apparatus that measured how various types of food placed into a dog's mouth resulted in different amounts of saliva (**Figure 6.3b**).

Like so many major scientific advances, Pavlov's contribution to psychology started with a simple observation. One day, he realized that the dogs he was studying were salivating before they actually tasted their food. In fact, the dogs began to salivate the moment they saw the bowls that contained the food or whenever the lab technician who usually delivered the food walked into the room. Pavlov's genius was in recognizing that this behavioral response was a window into the working mind. Unlike innate reflexes, such as salivating when actually tasting the food, salivating at the sight of a bowl or of a person is not automatic. Therefore, that response must have been acquired through experience by associating two stimuli with each other. In other words, the dogs showed learning by **classical conditioning** (review the Learning Tip in study unit 6.2, on p. 216). This insight led Pavlov to devote the rest of his life to studying the basic principles of learning.

PAVLOV'S EXPERIMENTS REVEAL FOUR STEPS IN CLASSICAL CONDITIONING The Methods of Psychology on p. 220 describes classical conditioning as revealed by Pavlov's research. In addition, the Learning Tip on p. 219 will help you learn the four main terms associated with classical conditioning.

Classical conditioning always begins with a stimulus that naturally elicits a response. In other words, the stimulus produces the response, much like a reflex. In

1 The dog was presented with a bowl that contained meat.

2 A tube carried the dog's saliva to a container.

3 The container was connected to a device that measured the amount of saliva.

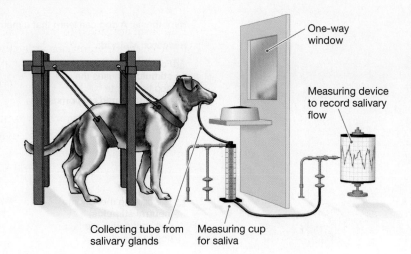

One-way window

Measuring device to record salivary flow

Collecting tube from salivary glands

Measuring cup for saliva

FIGURE 6.3

Pavlov's Apparatus and Classical Conditioning

(a) Ivan Pavlov, the white-haired man pictured here with his colleagues and one of his canine subjects, conducted groundbreaking work on classical conditioning. **(b)** Pavlov's apparatus collected and measured a dog's saliva.

the case of Pavlov's research, the presentation of food causes the salivary reflex, and no learning is required to produce the salivation. As shown in Step 1 of The Methods of Psychology on p. 220, Pavlov called the food the **unconditioned stimulus (US)**, because nothing is learned about the stimulus. Pavlov called the salivation elicited by food the **unconditioned response (UR)**. The response is "unconditioned" because it is an unlearned behavior, like any simple reflex.

In Step 2, a *neutral stimulus* is presented. The neutral stimulus can be anything that the dog can see or hear, but it must not be associated with the UR. Pavlov used a metronome as the neutral stimulus. A metronome is a device that helps musicians keep time to music by making rhythmic clicking sounds, but it does not cause salivation.

Step 3 of the process is the conditioning trials. Now the neutral stimulus is presented along with the unconditioned stimulus that reliably produces the unconditioned response. Recall that the unconditioned stimulus here was the food, and the neutral stimulus was the clicking of a metronome. This is when the dog begins to

unconditioned stimulus (US)
A stimulus that elicits a response that is innate and does not require any prior learning.

unconditioned response (UR)
A response that does not have to be learned, such as a reflex.

💡 **LEARNING TIP: Understanding Classical Conditioning**

In classical conditioning, the word "conditioned" simply means "learned," as shown below.

WHEN YOU SEE	PLEASE THINK	MEANING
Unconditioned stimulus	Stimulus that is not learned	Something that instinctively (innately) prompts a reaction
Unconditioned response	Response that is not learned	Reaction that is elicited instinctively (innately)
Conditioned stimulus	Stimulus that is learned	Something that prompts a reaction only after learning has occurred
Conditioned response	Response that is learned	Reaction that is elicited only after learning has occurred

Hypothesis: A dog can learn that a metronome predicts food.

Research Method:

Before conditioning

1 Food (**unconditioned stimulus**) causes the dog to salivate (**unconditioned response**).

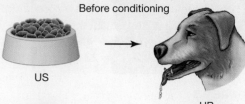

US

UR

2 The clicking metronome (**neutral stimulus**) does not cause the dog to salivate.

Neutral stimulus

No response

3 During conditioning trials, the clicking metronome is presented to a dog just before the food.

Conditioning

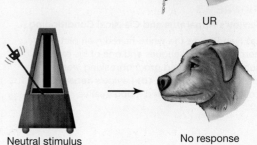

Neutral stimulus   +   US

After conditioning

4 During critical trials, the clicking metronome (**conditioned stimulus**) is presented without the food, and the dog salivates (**conditioned response**).

CS

CR

Result: After conditioning, the metronome causes the dog to salivate (**conditioned response**).

Conclusion: The dog was conditioned to learn the association between the metronome and food.

QUESTION: In this example, what is the unconditioned stimulus, and why is it considered unconditioned?

ANSWER: Food is the unconditioned stimulus because it causes salivation without learning.

Source: Pavlov, I. P. (1927). Conditioned reflexes: *An investigation of the physiological activity of the cerebral cortex.* (Translated and edited by G. V. Anrep). London: Oxford University Press; Humphrey Milford.

associate the two stimuli, the clicking metronome and the appearance of food, and we say the animal is learning.

In Step 4, the critical trials, we see evidence that the dog has learned the association between the food and the metronome. This is because presenting the clicking metronome alone, without the presence of the food, makes the dog salivate. We now say that the animal has been classically conditioned. At this point, the metronome is called the **conditioned stimulus (CS)**, because its clicking sound causes the dog to salivate only after the dog has gone through the process of conditioning. In our example, the dog has learned the relationship between the metronome and the food. Similarly, the salivation elicited by the metronome is now called the **conditioned response (CR)**, because it is a behavior that occurs only after conditioning. In this case, both the unconditioned and the conditioned responses are salivation, but they are not identical. The conditioned response usually is weaker than the unconditioned response. Thus the metronome sound alone produces less saliva than the food does.

Now think back to the scenario at the beginning of this section. As you watch the movie and see the woman descending into the basement in the middle of the night, you have a natural feeling of fear about this scary situation. In this case, the stimulus and your response to it are unconditioned. Imagine music begins to play in the movie. You first heard that music earlier in the movie, but you did not notice it very much. When it repeats, you realize that it comes on just before something bad happens to a character in the movie. As the movie progresses, you will probably start to feel tense as soon as you hear the music. You have learned that the music, the conditioned stimulus, predicts scenes where terrible things happen to the characters. This learning makes you feel tense as you watch the movie, because that feeling is the conditioned response (**Figure 6.4**).

Just as Pavlov's studies revealed, the conditioned stimulus (music) produces a somewhat weaker, or slightly different, response than does the unconditioned stimulus (the scary scene). Because this association is learned, the conditioned response may be more a feeling of tension or anxiety than one of fear. But suppose you later hear this music in a different setting, such as on the radio. Again you will feel tense, even though you are not watching the movie. You have been classically conditioned to feel anxious when you hear the music.

conditioned stimulus (CS)
A stimulus that elicits a response only after learning has taken place.

conditioned response (CR)
A response to a conditioned stimulus; a response that has been learned.

FIGURE 6.4

Classical Conditioning in Horror Movies

In many suspenseful or scary movies, the soundtrack music becomes intense just before something exciting or terrible happens. The classic 1975 movie *Jaws* uses this classical conditioning technique to make you feel afraid, as the "duh-duh, duh-duh" theme music always plays just before the shark attacks.

6.5 Learning Varies in Classical Conditioning

6.5 LEARNING GOAL ACTIVITIES

To maximize your learning, complete the following learning goal activities.

a. Understand all bold and italic terms by writing explanations of them in your own words.

b. Apply the six concepts of acquisition, extinction, spontaneous recovery, generalization, discrimination, and second-order conditioning to the classical conditioning situation you described in Learning Goal Activity 6.4b.

Like many other scientists of his time and in the decades since, Pavlov believed that conditioning is how animals adapt to their environments. That is, animals learn to predict what objects bring pleasure or pain, such as when they learn that the clicking of a metronome predicts the appearance of food. By making such associations, animals learn new adaptive behaviors.

ACQUISITION The gradual formation of a learned association between a conditioned stimulus (here, a metronome) and an unconditioned stimulus (here, food)

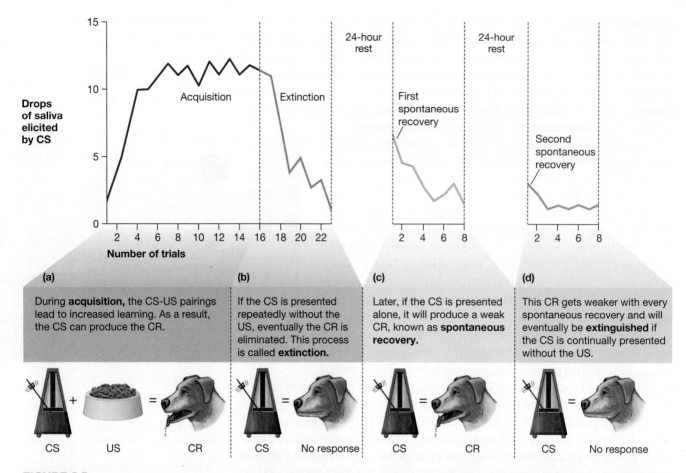

FIGURE 6.5

Acquisition, Extinction, and Spontaneous Recovery

Classical conditioning varies in strength and persistence, as shown by these three conditioning processes.

(a) During **acquisition,** the CS-US pairings lead to increased learning. As a result, the CS can produce the CR.

(b) If the CS is presented repeatedly without the US, eventually the CR is eliminated. This process is called **extinction.**

(c) Later, if the CS is presented alone, it will produce a weak CR, known as **spontaneous recovery.**

(d) This CR gets weaker with every spontaneous recovery and will eventually be **extinguished** if the CS is continually presented without the US.

acquisition
The gradual formation of an association between conditioned and unconditioned stimuli.

to produce the conditioned response (here, salivation) is known as **acquisition** (**Figure 6.5a**).

From his research, Pavlov concluded that for an animal to acquire a learned association, the two stimuli must occur at the same time. But later research has shown that the strongest conditioning occurs when the conditioned stimulus is presented slightly before the unconditioned stimulus. Thus, in the case of Pavlov's dogs, if the metronome (CS) comes just *before* the food (US), this will produce a stronger acquisition of a salivation response (CR) than if the metronome comes at the same time as, or after, the food. The metronome's role in predicting the food is an important part of classical conditioning because it alerts the dog that food is coming. This process is even easier to understand in the movie example, where the music is setting you up to feel anxious just before you watch the woman go into the basement. The next time you watch a horror movie, pay attention to the way the music gets louder just before a scary part begins, and notice how it makes you feel. And if you have not seen *Jaws* yet, now might be a good time, because you will really understand how that music works to make you feel anxious, or even scared, about what will happen in the movie.

EXTINCTION But what happens in this example if the food is never again presented with the metronome? In other words, once the salivation behavior (CR) is acquired, how long does it continue even without presentation of the food (US)? Animals sometimes have to learn when associations are no longer adaptive. Normally, after standard classical conditioning, the metronome (CS) leads to salivation (CR) because the animal learns to associate the metronome with the food (US). If the metronome is presented many times and food does not arrive, the animal learns that the metronome is no longer a good predictor of food. Because of this new learning, the animal's conditioned salivary response to the metronome gradually disappears. This process is known as **extinction**. The conditioned response is extinguished when the conditioned stimulus is no longer paired with the arrival of the unconditioned stimulus (**Figure 6.5b**). Extinction is actually a form of learning that takes the place of the previous association. Through extinction, the animal learns that the original association is no longer true (Bouton, 1994; Bouton, Trask, & Carranza-Jasso, 2016). Although extinction reduces the strength of the associative bond, it does not completely eliminate that bond.

SPONTANEOUS RECOVERY Imagine that a long time after extinction, the sound of the metronome is again presented. In this case, the most adaptive response by the dog is to see if the metronome will once again predict the arrival of food. When this occurs, the extinguished conditioned response of salivation is reactivated in a process called **spontaneous recovery** (**Figure 6.5c**). This recovery will fade quickly and lead to extinction once again, however, unless the CS is paired with the US again. Even a single presentation of the CS with the US will reestablish the CR, but the response will get weaker again if CS-US pairings do not continue (**Figure 6.5d**).

GENERALIZATION, DISCRIMINATION, AND SECOND-ORDER CONDITIONING In any learning situation, hundreds of possible stimuli can be associated with the unconditioned stimulus to produce the conditioned response. How does the brain determine which stimulus is worth responding to? For instance, suppose we classically condition a dog so that it salivates (CR) when it hears a 1,000-hertz (Hz) tone (CS) that is paired with food (US). After the CR is established, the dog will also salivate when it hears tones close to 1,000 Hz. The farther the tones are from 1,000 Hz, the less the dog will salivate. **Stimulus generalization** occurs when stimuli that are similar, but not identical, to the CS produce the CR. Generalization is adaptive, because in nature animals seldom repeatedly experience the CS in an identical way. Slight differences in background noise, temperature, lighting, and so on lead to slightly different perceptions of the CS. Thanks to these different perceptions, animals learn to respond to variations in the CS (**Figure 6.6a–b**).

Of course, generalization has limits. Sometimes it is important for animals to distinguish among similar stimuli. For instance, two plant species might look similar, but one of them might be poisonous. In **stimulus discrimination**, an animal learns to differentiate between two similar stimuli if one is consistently associated with the US and the other is not (**Figure 6.6a,c**). Pavlov and his students demonstrated that dogs could learn to make very fine distinctions between similar stimuli. You may have used stimulus discrimination to learn which ringtone or phone music belongs to which of your friends.

FIGURE 6.6

Stimulus Generalization and Stimulus Discrimination
Stimulus generalization and stimulus discrimination help us learn about objects in the environment. **(a)** When people touch poison ivy and get an itchy rash, they learn to fear this three-leafed plant, and so they avoid it. **(b)** People may then experience stimulus generalization if they fear and avoid similar three-leafed plants—even nonpoisonous ones, such as fragrant sumac. **(c)** People may also experience stimulus discrimination related to poison ivy. They do not fear or avoid dissimilar plants—such as Virginia creeper, which has five leaves and is nonpoisonous.

Now consider what might happen if another stimulus is added to the situation. You know that in one of Pavlov's early studies, a dog learned to associate a tone (CS) and food (US) so that the tone (CS) led to salivation (CR). In a second training session, a black square was repeatedly presented at the same time as the tone (CS). The dog salivated (CR) even though no food (US) was presented. After a few trials, the black square was presented alone, and again the dog salivated (CR). In such cases, the first conditioned stimulus (the tone) became associated with another stimulus (the black square), which was then indirectly associated with the US (food). Effectively, the black square became the second conditioned stimulus (CS-2), which elicited the conditioned response of salivation even when presented alone, without the US or the original CS. This phenomenon is known as *second-order conditioning*.

6.6 You Can Learn Fear Responses Through Classical Conditioning

 6.6 LEARNING GOAL ACTIVITIES

To maximize your learning, complete the following learning goal activities.

a. Understand all bold and italic terms by writing explanations of them in your own words.

b. Analyze how classical conditioning can explain a phobia by identifying how a phobia of snakes can be acquired through classical conditioning and reduced through counterconditioning.

Many people are afraid of certain things, but some people's fears can get in the way of their daily functioning. For example, people can be so afraid of spiders that they feel panicky when they even look at a picture of one. Such extreme fear reactions, or phobias, may result from classical conditioning. A *phobia* is an acquired fear that is exaggerated in comparison to the real threat of an object or of a situation. Common phobias include the fear of heights, enclosed places, insects, snakes, or the dark. According to classical-conditioning theory, one way that phobias can develop is through generalization of a fear experience, as when a person stung by a wasp develops a fear of all flying insects. (Phobias are discussed further in Chapter 14.)

THE CASE OF LITTLE ALBERT John Watson is known as the father of behaviorism. He was one of the first researchers to demonstrate the role of classical conditioning in the learning of phobias. In 1919, Watson asked a wet nurse at the Johns Hopkins clinic to let him use her son in what became a classic study. The study began when the boy, who became known as "Little Albert," was 9 months old. Watson and his lab assistant presented Little Albert with various neutral objects, including a white rat, a rabbit, a dog, a monkey, costume masks, and a ball of white wool. Albert showed a natural curiosity about these items, but he displayed no apparent emotional responses.

When Albert was 11 months old, the conditioning trials began. This time, as they presented the white rat and Albert reached for it, Watson smashed a hammer into an iron bar, producing a loud clanging sound (**Figure 6.7**). The sound scared the child, who immediately withdrew and hid his face. Watson did this a few more times, at intervals of five days, until Albert would whimper and cringe when the rat was presented alone. Thus the US (loud sound) led to a UR (fear). Eventually, the pairing of the CS (rat) with the US (loud sound) led to the rat alone producing a CR (fear). The fear response generalized to other stimuli that Watson had presented along with the rat at the initial meeting. Over time, Albert became frightened of

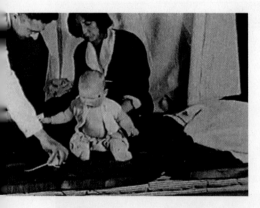

FIGURE 6.7

Case Study of "Little Albert" Reveals Phobias Can Be Learned Through Classical Conditioning

Little Albert learned to associate a white rat with a loud sound that made Albert feel afraid. Eventually Albert showed the conditioned fear response when he saw the white rat. This case study revealed that phobias could be learned through classical conditioning.

them all, including the rabbit and the ball of wool. Even a Santa Claus with a white beard produced a fear response. Thus Watson demonstrated that phobias could be brought about by classical conditioning.

Though Albert was emotionally stable when the study began, and Watson believed the study would cause him little harm, Watson's conditioning of Albert has long been criticized as unethical. Today an ethics committee probably would not approve such a study. Watson had planned a series of trials where he would continually present the feared items to Albert paired with more pleasant things, but Albert's mother removed the child from the study before Watson could conduct the trials. Watson did not keep track of Albert, but various researchers have sought to identify him over the years (Griggs, 2015). According to the best available evidence, he was William Albert Barger, who died in 2007 at age 87 (Powell, Digdon, Harris, & Smithson, 2014; **Figure 6.8**). His relatives described him as easygoing, so he does not seem to have suffered long-term problems from being in the study. However, Barger was described as disliking animals, especially dogs, throughout his life and would cover his ears when he heard barking.

COUNTERCONDITIONING A colleague of Watson's—the behavioral pioneer Mary Cover Jones—did use this method successfully to reduce phobias. Jones eliminated the fear of rabbits in a 3-year-old by bringing a rabbit closer as she provided the child with a favorite food (Jones, 1924). Such classical-conditioning techniques have since proved valuable in developing very effective behavioral therapies to treat phobias. In the example above, where a person has a phobia of spiders, a clinician might expose the client to spiders while having the client engage in an enjoyable task. This technique, called *counterconditioning,* may help the client overcome the phobia.

The behavioral therapist Joseph Wolpe has developed a formal treatment based on counterconditioning (Wolpe, 1997). If you were undergoing Wolpe's treatment, called *systematic desensitization,* first you would be taught how to relax your muscles. Then you would be asked to imagine the feared object or situation while you continued to use the relaxation exercises. Eventually, you would be exposed to the feared stimulus while relaxing. The general idea is that the $CS \rightarrow CR_1$ (fear) connection can be broken by developing a $CS \rightarrow CR_2$ (relaxation) connection. Psychologists now believe that in breaking such a fear connection, repeated exposure to the feared stimulus is more important than relaxation (as you will read about in Chapter 15).

6.7 Adaptation and Cognition Influence Classical Conditioning

6.7 LEARNING GOAL ACTIVITIES

To maximize your learning, complete the following learning goal activities.

a. Understand all bold and italic terms by writing explanations of them in your own words.

b. Understand how some stimuli are more likely to produce conditioned responses by describing, in your own words, the influences of evolution and cognition on conditioning.

Pavlov's original explanation for classical conditioning was that any two events presented together would produce a learned association. In other words, any object or phenomenon could be converted to a conditioned stimulus when associated with any unconditioned stimulus. Pavlov and his followers believed that the strength of the association was determined by factors such as the intensity of the conditioned and unconditioned stimuli. For example, a louder metronome or a larger piece of meat would produce stronger associations than a quieter metronome or a smaller piece of meat. In the mid-1960s, a number of challenges to Pavlov's theory suggested that some conditioned stimuli were more likely to produce learning than others.

EVOLUTIONARY INFLUENCES Return for a moment to the situation that opened this chapter: your response to shrimp after your bad experience with it at the party. Such conditioned taste aversion is the result of classical conditioning. Conditioned taste aversion also stopped the gray wolves of the Northern Rocky Mountain region from preying on sheep, after the wolves became ill from eating poisoned sheep meat. In the case of the wolves, when the sheep meat (CS) was paired with the poison (US), the wolves that ate the meat vomited. They associated feeling sick (CR) with the sheep, so it was adaptive for them to stop preying on the sheep. However, certain pairings of stimuli are more likely to become associated than others (Garcia & Koelling, 1966). For instance, new foods are especially likely to produce learned aversions (Lin, Arthurs, & Reilly, 2017).

Conditioned taste aversions like these are easy to produce with smell or taste, but they are very difficult to produce with light or sound. This difference makes sense, because smell and taste are the main cues that guide an animal's eating behavior. From an evolutionary viewpoint, animals that quickly associate a certain flavor with illness, and therefore avoid that flavor, will be better adapted. That is, they will be more likely to survive and pass along their genes.

However, auditory and visual stimuli may have survival value for particular animals in particular environments. Thus animals may learn adaptive responses that are related to the potential dangers associated with the stimuli. For example, monkeys can more easily be conditioned to fear snakes than to fear objects such as flowers or rabbits (Cook & Mineka, 1989). The psychologist Martin Seligman (1970) has argued that animals are genetically programmed, or biologically prepared, to fear specific objects. Preparedness helps explain why animals, including humans, tend to fear potentially dangerous things (for example, snakes, fire, heights) rather than objects that pose little threat (for example, flowers, shoes, babies). Indeed, when people view photos of snakes and flowers, the snakes tend to grab the viewers' attention (Hayakawa, Kawai, & Masataka, 2011; **Figure 6.9**).

COGNITIVE INFLUENCES Until the 1970s, most learning theorists were behaviorists. They were concerned only with observable stimuli and observable responses. Since then, there has been more emphasis on trying to understand the mental processes that are the basis of conditioning. An important principle has emerged from this work: Classical conditioning is a way that animals, including humans, come to *predict* the occurrence of events.

The psychologist Robert Rescorla (1966) conducted one of the first studies that highlighted the role of cognition in learning. He argued that for learning to take place, the conditioned stimulus must accurately predict the unconditioned stimulus. For instance, a stimulus that occurs *before* the US is more easily conditioned than one

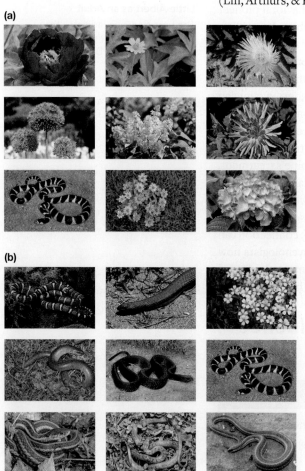

(a)

(b)

FIGURE 6.9

Fearing Dangerous Things Is a Helpful Adaptive Response

Animals, including humans, have evolved to be able to detect threats. Thus, **(a)** you will quickly see the snake in this group of images, and **(b)** you will have a harder time detecting the flowers in this group.

that comes *after* it. Even though both are close to the US in time, the stimulus that comes before the US is more easily learned because it predicts the US. You saw this effect in the example of creepy music before scary scenes in movies.

The cognitive model of classical learning states that animals (including humans) learn to expect that some predictors (potential CSs) are better than others. According to this model, the strength of the CS-US association is determined by how unexpected or surprising the US is. When animals encounter a new stimulus, they pay attention to this US. The more surprising the US, the harder they try to understand how it happened. Figuring out the US helps them predict when it will happen again. The result of this effort is greater classical conditioning of the new event (CS) that predicted the US.

Suppose you always use an electric can opener to open a can of dog food. Your dog associates the sound of the can opener (CS) with the appearance of food (US). The dog has the conditioned response (CR) of wagging its tail when it hears that sound (**Figure 6.10**, Step 1). Now say the electric can opener breaks, and you replace it with a manual one. According to the cognitive model of learning, the unexpected appearance of the food (US) without the electric can opener sound (CS) will cause your dog to pay attention to events in the environment that might have produced the food (Figure 6.10, Step 2). Soon the dog will learn to associate being fed with use of the new can opener and will again show the CR of tail wagging (new CS; Figure 6.10, Step 3).

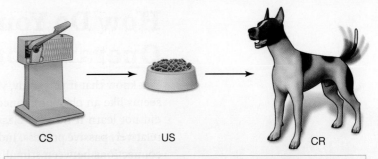

CS   US   CR

1 A dog learns to associate an electric can opener (**conditioned stimulus**) with the arrival of food (**unconditioned stimulus**). This association causes the dog's tail to wag (**conditioned response**).

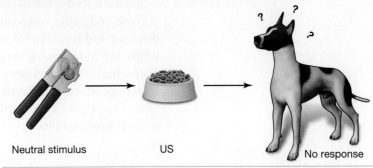

Neutral stimulus   US   No response

2 The dog is surprised when a manual can opener (*neutral stimulus*) replaces the electric one. Because it is surprised, the dog does not show the conditioned response.

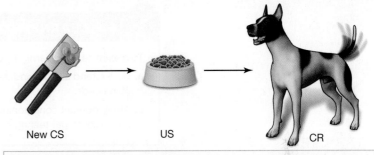

New CS   US   CR

3 The dog now pays attention to the environment and so comes to associate the new can opener (**new conditioned stimulus**) with the arrival of food (**unconditioned stimulus**). Now the manual can opener (new conditioned stimulus) becomes the better predictor of the expected event: food. As a result, the manual can opener elicits the **conditioned response**.

FIGURE 6.10

The Role of Cognition in Learning
The cognitive model of learning emphasizes the role of prediction and expectation in learning.

Q How Do You Learn Through Classical Conditioning?

To make sure you learned what you just read, write answers to the following questions and check your answers.

6.4 In Pavlov's classic research on classical conditioning, what type of stimulus was food?

6.5 When you are taking a gardening class, what learning process helps you tell the difference between the various species of flowers?

6.6 How does counterconditioning explain why a child who is afraid of dogs might become less afraid if slowly exposed to dogs and taught to relax at the same time?

6.7 Is a person more likely to learn a conditioned taste aversion when feeling nausea before eating a particular food or after eating a particular food?

See Appendix B for answers to the red Q questions.

How Do You Learn Through Operant Conditioning?

You know that if you study, you're likely to get a better grade on an exam. That seems like an obvious connection, but how did you learn this association? You did not learn it through classical conditioning. That form of conditioning is a relatively passive process. Indeed, in classical conditioning, you learn predictive connections between stimuli, no matter how you behave. So in classical conditioning, the particular behavior doesn't affect the learning of the link between two stimuli.

But consider that behaviors are often instrumental—meaning they are done for a purpose. You study to get good grades, you eat your favorite dessert because it tastes delicious, and so on. You learn that behaving in certain ways leads to good things happening and behaving in other ways results in bad things happening. In other words, you learn to associate a behavior with the consequences of the behavior. This knowledge affects your future actions. The following study unit explores how this form of associative learning, where you learn the consequences of an action, changes your behavior over time.

6.8 Through Operant Conditioning, You Learn the Consequences of Your Actions

6.8 LEARNING GOAL ACTIVITIES

To maximize your learning, complete the following learning goal activities.

a. Understand all bold and italic terms by writing explanations of them in your own words.

b. Apply operant conditioning by describing how you would use an operant and a reinforcer to get teenagers to clean their bedrooms.

Learning the relationship between a behavior and its consequences, and having the relationship affect future actions, is called **operant conditioning** (review the Learning Tip in study unit 6.2, on p. 216). Research on such learning in animals began in the late nineteenth century, at Harvard University. A young graduate student, Edward Thorndike, was working with the psychologist William James. Thorndike performed the first reported carefully controlled experiments in comparative animal psychology. Specifically, he studied whether nonhuman animals showed signs of intelligence.

THORNDIKE'S EXPERIMENTS REVEAL THE EFFECTS OF ACTION   To conduct his research, Thorndike built a puzzle box—a small cage with a trapdoor (**Figure 6.11a**). The trapdoor would open if the animal inside performed a specific action, such as pulling a string. Thorndike placed food-deprived animals, at first chickens but later cats, inside the puzzle box to see if they could figure out how to escape.

To motivate the cats, Thorndike placed food just outside the box (**Figure 6.11b**, Step 1). When first placed in the box, the cat usually made several unsuccessful

operant conditioning
A learning process in which an action's consequences determine how likely an action is to be performed in the future.

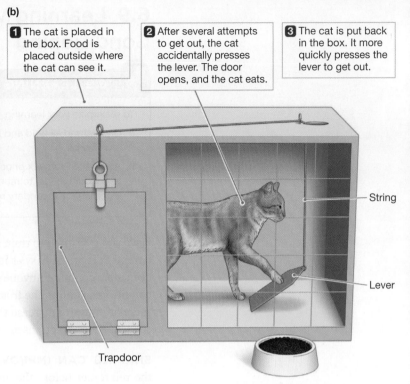

(a)

(b)

1 The cat is placed in the box. Food is placed outside where the cat can see it.

2 After several attempts to get out, the cat accidentally presses the lever. The door opens, and the cat eats.

3 The cat is put back in the box. It more quickly presses the lever to get out.

String

Lever

Trapdoor

FIGURE 6.11

Thorndike's Puzzle Box

(a) Thorndike's experiments used puzzle boxes, like the one shown here. **(b)** The box was designed to assess learning in animals, and Thorndike used it in developing the law of effect. Because stepping on the lever to pull the string led to the satisfying state where the cat could escape from the box, the cat stepped on the lever more quickly the next time it was in the box.

attempts to escape. After 5–10 minutes of struggling, the cat would accidentally step on the lever that pulled the string, and the door would open (Figure 6.11b, Step 2). Thorndike would then return the cat to the box and repeat the trial. During each of the following trials, the cat more and more quickly pushed the lever. Soon it learned to escape from the puzzle box within seconds (Figure 6.11b, Step 3). Thorndike's research led him to develop a general theory of learning. According to this *law of effect,* any behavior that leads to a "satisfying state of affairs" is likely to occur again. Any behavior that leads to an "annoying state of affairs" is less likely to occur again.

B. F. Skinner later developed a more formal learning theory based on the law of effect. Skinner, the psychologist most closely associated with operant conditioning, chose the term **operant** to express the idea that animals *operate* on their environments to produce effects. Skinner also coined the term **reinforcer** to describe a stimulus that occurs after a response and increases the likelihood that the response will be repeated. Skinner believed that behavior—studying, eating, driving on the correct side of the road, and so on—occurs because it has been reinforced.

To test his theory, Skinner developed a simple device that is now known as a Skinner box. Inside the box, a lever that can be pressed is connected to a food supply. An animal, usually a rat or pigeon, is placed in the Skinner box. In this case, pressing the lever is the operant, and receiving food is the reinforcer. Through operant conditioning, the animal learns that pressing the lever results in food and so is more likely to press the bar in the future (**Figure 6.12**).

Lever

Food tray

FIGURE 6.12

Skinner Box

In B. F. Skinner's research, pressing a lever (pressing is the operant) results in getting food (food is the reinforcer). Getting the food made the animal more likely to repeatedly press the bar. Learning a response in this way is called operant conditioning.

operant
An action that is performed on an environment and has consequences.

reinforcer
A consequence of an action that affects the likelihood of the action being repeated, or not, in the future.

6.9 Learning Varies in Operant Conditioning

Have you ever tried to train an animal to do a specific behavior, such as sitting for a treat? It is not as easy as it sounds! Trying to modify a person's behavior can be even more complex. Anyone who has ever tried to discipline a child through operant conditioning knows the frustration of a child who won't sit in time out. However, there are ways to increase the likelihood that the animal or person will learn the consequences of actions in a way that will affect future behavior.

SHAPING CAN IMPROVE LEARNING In operant conditioning, providing the reinforcer before the animal displays the appropriate behavior usually does not lead to learning. Inside a Skinner box, an animal eventually makes the correct response spontaneously by chance. Outside a Skinner box, however, the same animal might be distracted and take longer to perform the action you are looking for. Rather than wait for the animal to spontaneously perform the action, you can use an operant-conditioning technique to teach the animal to do so. This powerful process, called *shaping,* consists of reinforcing behaviors that are increasingly similar to the desired behavior.

For example, suppose you are trying to teach your dog to roll over. At first, you give a treat to the dog or praise it for any behavior that even slightly resembles rolling over, such as lying down. Once this behavior is established, you selectively reinforce it. That is, you praise the dog each time it gets closer to performing the behavior you want. For instance, you might praise the dog for rolling onto one side. Next you might praise it for lying on its back. This system eventually produces the desired behavior as the animal learns what behavior is being reinforced. Indeed, shaping has been used to condition animals to perform amazing feats: pigeons playing table tennis, dogs playing the piano, pigs doing housework such as picking up clothes and vacuuming, and so on (**Figure 6.13**).

FIGURE 6.13

Shaping

The operant conditioning technique of shaping consists of reinforcing behaviors that are increasingly similar to the desired behavior. Shaping can be used to train animals to perform unusual behaviors.

1 If you are trying to teach your dog to surf, you first reward the dog for approaching the surfboard.

2 Then you reward the dog for getting on the surfboard and standing there.

3 Then you reward the dog for continuing to stand on the board as the waves move it.

4 As the dog learns what behavior is being reinforced, it eventually learns to produce the desired behavior: surfing!

Shaping has also been used to teach people. People with psychological disorders can learn appropriate social skills, children with autism spectrum disorder can learn language, and individuals with differences in developmental abilities can learn life skills. More generally, parents and educators often use shaping to encourage appropriate behavior in children. For example, they praise children for their first, often unreadable, attempts at handwriting.

REINFORCERS IMPROVE LEARNING   The most obvious reinforcers are those necessary for survival, such as food or water. Because they satisfy biological needs, they are called *primary reinforcers*. From an evolutionary standpoint, the learning value of primary reinforcers makes a great deal of sense: Animals that repeatedly perform behaviors that are reinforced by food or water are more likely to survive and pass along their genes.

Many apparent reinforcers do not directly satisfy biological needs, however. Receiving a grade of A on your term paper, a compliment on your art project, or a raise at work can all be reinforcing. Events or objects that serve as reinforcers but do not satisfy biological needs are called *secondary reinforcers*. These reinforcers are established through classical conditioning. You learn to associate a neutral stimulus, such as money, with a primary reinforcer such as food (US). Money is really only pieces of metal or slips of paper, but these and other neutral objects become meaningful conditioned stimuli (CS) thanks to their associations with unconditioned stimuli.

REINFORCERS CAN BE MORE POWERFUL OR LESS POWERFUL   Some reinforcers are more powerful than others. The psychologist David Premack (1959; Holstein & Premack, 1965) theorized about how a reinforcer's value could be determined. The key is the amount of time an animal, when free to do anything, engages in a specific behavior associated with the reinforcer. For instance, given freedom of choice, children more often eat ice cream than spinach. Ice cream is therefore more reinforcing for children than spinach is. One great advantage of Premack's theory is that it can account for differences in individual people's values. For people who eat ice cream more often than spinach, ice cream serves as a stronger reinforcer.

A logical application of Premack's theory, called the *Premack principle*, is that a more valued activity can be used to reinforce the performance of a less valued activity. When parents tell their children, "Eat your spinach and then you'll get dessert," they're using the Premack principle. You've probably used it on yourself a few times: "After I finish reading this chapter, I'll watch that YouTube clip" (**Figure 6.14**).

FIGURE 6.14

The Premack Principle in Our Daily Lives

When you were younger, did you have to eat your dinner before you got your dessert? If so, then you experienced the Premack principle firsthand. In this case, you had to accept the less desired food in order to receive the food you really wanted.

6.10 Both Reinforcement and Punishment Influence Operant Conditioning

6.10 LEARNING GOAL ACTIVITIES

To maximize your learning, complete the following learning goal activities.

a. Understand all bold and italic terms by writing explanations of them in your own words.

b. Understand the four types of reinforcement and punishment in operant conditioning by summarizing in your own words the four ways that reinforcement and punishment affect behavior.

LEARNING TIP: Four Types of Reinforcement and Punishment

It's easy to remember the difference between the four types of reinforcement and punishment: positive reinforcement, negative reinforcement, positive punishment, and negative punishment. Ask these two questions to get it right:

1. Is a stimulus added or taken away?
   - If a stimulus is <u>added</u>, then this is "positive."
   - If a stimulus is <u>taken away</u>, then this is "negative."
2. After adding or taking away a stimulus, does the behavior increase or decrease?
   - If the behavior <u>increases</u>, then this is "reinforcement."
   - If the behavior <u>decreases</u>, then this is "punishment."

If you put together the two words from your answers to Questions 1 and 2, you will know which of the four types of reinforcement and punishment is being used.

positive reinforcement
The addition of a stimulus to increase the probability that a behavior will be repeated.

negative reinforcement
The removal of a stimulus to increase the probability that a behavior will be repeated.

Reinforcement and punishment have opposite effects on behavior. Reinforcement makes a behavior more likely to be repeated, and punishment makes that behavior less likely to occur again. Furthermore, in both positive reinforcement and positive punishment, a stimulus is added. But in negative reinforcement or negative punishment, a stimulus is removed. The operant conditioning terminology can be confusing, so let's look at each of these concepts next. **Figure 6.15** also gives an overview of all these situations, and the Learning Tip on this page will help you remember the terms correctly.

POSITIVE AND NEGATIVE REINFORCEMENT Both positive and negative reinforcement increase the likelihood of a certain behavior. **Positive reinforcement** is the addition of a stimulus that increases the probability that a behavior will be repeated. Positive reinforcement is often called reward, and when behaviors are rewarded, the actions increase in frequency. For example, feeding a rat after it presses a lever will increase the probability that the rat will press the lever again (see Figure 6.15a). Similarly, when you receive praise from your boss or an increase in pay, your response is to work harder. In contrast, **negative reinforcement** increases behavior by removing a stimulus. Negative reinforcement occurs when a rat presses a lever to turn off a painful electric shock. The rat will be more likely to press the lever again in the future (see Figure 6.15b). However, be aware that negative reinforcement is not the same as punishment.

Negative reinforcement is common in everyday life. You take a pill to get rid of a headache. You close your door to shut out noise. You change the channel to avoid watching an awful show. You pick up a crying baby. In each case, you are trying to stop a stimulus. If the action you take successfully reduces the stimulus, then the next time you have a headache, hear noise in your room, see an awful program, or are with a crying baby, the more likely you are to repeat the behavior that reduced the stimulus. Your behavior has been negatively reinforced.

	POSITIVE (Add stimulus)	NEGATIVE (Remove stimulus)
REINFORCEMENT (Increases behavior)	**(a) Positive reinforcement:** When the lever is pressed, food is given.	**(b) Negative reinforcement:** When the lever is pressed, a shock is removed.
PUNISHMENT (Decreases behavior)	**(c) Positive punishment:** When the lever is pressed, a shock is given.	**(d) Negative punishment:** When the lever is pressed, food is removed.

FIGURE 6.15

Reinforcement and Punishment

This graphic will help you understand the four types of reinforcement and punishment: **(a)** positive reinforcement, **(b)** negative reinforcement, **(c)** positive punishment, and **(d)** negative punishment.

Note, however, that while picking up the crying infant is negatively reinforcing for you, it positively reinforces the infant for crying! The infant learns that crying increases the likelihood of being picked up and comforted. Likewise, a parent who gives a child candy to stop a tantrum is negatively reinforced (the tantrum stops), but the child is positively reinforced to have more tantrums in the future.

POSITIVE AND NEGATIVE PUNISHMENT By contrast, both positive and negative punishment reduce the likelihood that a behavior will be repeated. **Positive punishment** is when the addition of a stimulus decreases the probability of a behavior being repeated. This happens when a rat receives an electric shock for pressing a lever, which makes it less likely to press the lever again (see Figure 6.15c). If a teenager gets a speeding ticket, then she has experienced positive punishment, which should make her less likely to speed in the future. However, by removing a stimulus, **negative punishment** decreases the likelihood a behavior will be repeated. For example, when a rat presses a lever and food is removed, the rat is not likely to press the lever again (see Figure 6.15d). And when a teenager loses driving privileges for speeding, he has received negative punishment that should prevent speeding in the future. As these examples show, negative and positive forms of punishment should produce the same result: The teen will be less likely to speed the next time he or she gets behind the wheel.

SCHEDULES OF PARTIAL REINFORCEMENT How often should a reinforcer be given? To produce fast learning, behavior might be reinforced each time it occurs. This process is known as *continuous reinforcement*. In the real world, behavior is seldom reinforced continuously. Animals do not find food each time they look for it, and people do not receive praise each time they behave acceptably. Instead, occasional reinforcement of behavior is more common. This is called *partial reinforcement*.

The effect of partial reinforcement on conditioning depends on the reinforcement schedule. Partial reinforcement can be given on a predictable basis, which is called a fixed schedule, or on an unpredictable basis, called a variable schedule. Partial reinforcement can also be given based on either the passage of time, called an interval schedule, or the number of behavioral responses, called a ratio schedule. Crossing how reinforcement is given with how consistently it is given provides the four most common schedules of reinforcement, as shown in **Figure 6.16** and in the Learning Tip on p. 234.

positive punishment
The addition of a stimulus to decrease the probability that a behavior will recur.

negative punishment
The removal of a stimulus to decrease the probability that a behavior will recur.

FIGURE 6.16

Effect of Reinforcement Schedules on Behavior

The curves show cumulative responses over time for four different schedules of reinforcement: **(a)** fixed interval, **(b)** variable interval, **(c)** fixed ratio, and **(d)** variable ratio. Notice that the steeper the line, the greater the response rate.

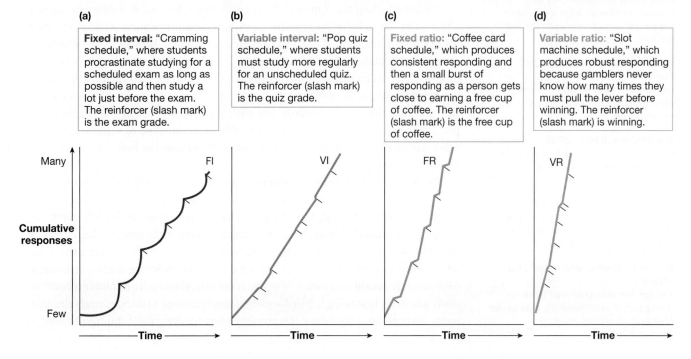

(a) **Fixed interval:** "Cramming schedule," where students procrastinate studying for a scheduled exam as long as possible and then study a lot just before the exam. The reinforcer (slash mark) is the exam grade.

(b) **Variable interval:** "Pop quiz schedule," where students must study more regularly for an unscheduled quiz. The reinforcer (slash mark) is the quiz grade.

(c) **Fixed ratio:** "Coffee card schedule," which produces consistent responding and then a small burst of responding as a person gets close to earning a free cup of coffee. The reinforcer (slash mark) is the free cup of coffee.

(d) **Variable ratio:** "Slot machine schedule," which produces robust responding because gamblers never know how many times they must pull the lever before winning. The reinforcer (slash mark) is winning.

LEARNING TIP: Four Schedules of Reinforcement

It's easy to remember the difference between the four schedules of reinforcement: fixed interval, variable interval, fixed ratio, and variable ratio. Ask these two questions to get it right:

1. Is the schedule predictable, or does it change?
   - If the schedule is predictable, then it is "fixed."
   - If the schedule changes, it is "variable."
2. Does the schedule refer to the amount of time that has passed or the number of responses that have occurred?
   - If the schedule refers to the passage of time, then it is "interval."
   - If the schedule refers to the number of responses, then it is "ratio."

Put together the two words from your answers to Questions 1 and 2, and you will know which of the four types of reinforcement schedules is being used.

fixed interval schedule (FI)
Reinforcing the occurrence of a particular behavior after a predetermined amount of time since the last reinforcement.

variable interval schedule (VI)
Reinforcing the occurrence of a particular behavior after an unpredictable and varying amount of time since the last reinforcement.

fixed ratio schedule (FR)
Reinforcing a particular behavior after that behavior has occurred a predetermined number of times.

variable ratio schedule (VR)
Reinforcing a particular behavior after the behavior has occurred an unpredictable and varying number of times.

partial-reinforcement extinction effect
The greater persistence of behavior under partial reinforcement than under continuous reinforcement.

On a **fixed interval schedule (FI)**, reinforcement is given after a fixed amount of time has passed. For example, many jobs pay employees at the end of each pay period. One feature of fixed interval schedules is a scalloping pattern. "Scalloping" refers to a series of circle segments that look like the edge of a scallop shell. The rises in this pattern mean that behavior continually increases just before the opportunity for reinforcement, and then behavior drops off after reinforcement (see Figure 6.16a). You're probably familiar with this pattern in your courses that have regularly scheduled examinations. Students often slack off a bit after an exam and then "cram" their studying into the time just before the next exam.

A **variable interval schedule (VI)** provides reinforcement after an unpredictable amount of time has passed. A good example of a variable interval schedule is the pop quiz schedule, in which students know that they could face a quiz at any time (see Figure 6.16b). As you might guess, variable interval schedules lead to more consistent response rates than FI schedules. In a class with pop quizzes, you cannot slack off in studying, because you need to be ready for a quiz at any time.

By contrast, in a **fixed ratio schedule (FR)**, reinforcement is given after a fixed number of responses. For instance, a factory might pay its workers by the piece, or a coffee shop might give regular customers a free cup of coffee after they buy 10 cups (see Figure 6.16c). Fixed ratio schedules often elicit more robust responding than FI schedules. For example, factory workers paid by the piece are usually more productive than those paid by the hour, especially if the workers receive incentives for higher productivity.

A **variable ratio schedule (VR)** provides reinforcement after an unpredictable number of responses. One example is slot machines. These games may pay out a consistent amount over the long term, but you never know which pull of the handle will result in winning money (see Figure 6.16d).

Besides affecting the number of responses, the schedule of reinforcement also affects how long a behavior persists. Continuous reinforcement is highly effective for teaching a behavior. If the reinforcement is stopped, however, the behavior is quickly extinguished. For instance, normally when you put money in a vending machine, it gives you a product in return. If it fails to do so, you quickly stop putting your money into it. By contrast, at a casino you might drop a lot of money into a slot machine that rarely rewards you with a jackpot. Psychologists explain this persistent behavior as the effect of a variable ratio schedule of reinforcement. In other words, people put money in slot machines because the machines sometimes provide monetary rewards.

The **partial-reinforcement extinction effect** says that behavior goes on longer under partial reinforcement than it does under continuous reinforcement. During continuous reinforcement, the learner easily can detect when reinforcement has stopped. But when the behavior is reinforced only some of the time, the learner needs to keep repeating the behavior over time to notice the absence of reinforcement. Thus, when reinforcement is less frequent during training, the behavior is more resistant to extinction. To condition a behavior so that it persists, you need to reinforce it continuously when it is first being learned and then slowly change to using partial reinforcement. Parents naturally follow this strategy when teaching their children behaviors, for example, during toilet training. While the parent may initially provide continuous reinforcement each time a toddler uses a toilet, the reinforcement naturally becomes less frequent as the toddler starts to use the toilet more frequently. The use of partial reinforcement is what helps the toddler finally master consistent use of the toilet.

The persistence of partially reinforced behaviors also provides an important lesson for trying to extinguish unwanted behaviors. For instance, suppose your cat meows when demanding to be fed. You try to ignore it, because you don't want to reinforce the behavior. But once in a while, you break down and feed the cat. You've just made it even harder to extinguish the behavior. The longer you take to break down, the more persistent the cat will be. To extinguish the behavior, you have to consistently withhold reinforcement. The same is true for a child who demands a candy bar at the grocery store. To stop the child from making demands, you refuse to buy the candy bar. Then, any other time the child demands that you buy an item, you refuse again and again.

6.11 Operant Conditioning Affects Your Life

6.11 LEARNING GOAL ACTIVITIES

To maximize your learning, complete the following learning goal activities.

a. Understand all bold and italic terms by writing explanations of them in your own words.

b. Understand why punishment is often an ineffective means of learning by explaining the three main complications with positive punishment.

Imagine that a child demands a candy bar at a grocery store. The parent says no, and the child throws a temper tantrum. The exasperated parent yells, "If you don't stop screaming, you're going to get a smacked bottom!" Will this approach produce the desired behavior?

POSITIVE PUNISHMENT IS OFTEN INEFFECTIVE   To make their children behave, parents sometimes use positive punishment as a means of discipline. Remember that the word "positive" here does not mean "good." Instead, it means the addition of something, such as a spanking, meant to punish and therefore to decrease a particular behavior. Many contemporary psychologists believe that positive punishment is often applied ineffectively, and that it may have unintended and unwanted consequences. Research has shown that for positive punishment to be effective, it must be reasonable, unpleasant, and applied immediately so that the relationship between the unwanted behavior and the punishment is clear (Goodall, 1984; O'Leary, 1995). Obviously, there is considerable potential for confusion.

Sometimes positive punishment is wrongly applied after a behavior that is actually desirable. For example, if a student is given a failing grade after admitting to cheating on an exam, he may then associate the punishment with being honest rather than with the original offense. As a result, the student learns not to tell the truth. As Skinner once pointed out, one thing people learn from punishment is how to avoid it. Rather than learning how to behave appropriately, they may learn not to get caught.

Positive punishment can also lead to negative emotions, such as fear and anxiety. Through classical conditioning, these emotions may become associated with

FIGURE 6.17

Parents Should Avoid the Use of Positive Punishment

Spank Out Day recognizes what research has shown to be true. In general, using reinforcement to improve children's behavior is more effective than using positive punishment, such as spanking. In reinforcing children's behavior, it is especially important to say what they should be doing instead of what they should not be doing.

(a)

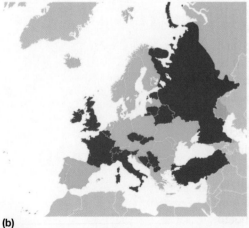

(b)

■ Spanking prohibited in schools and the home
■ Spanking prohibited in schools only
■ Spanking not prohibited

the person who administers the punishment. If a parent spanks a child for misbehaving, the child may learn to fear the parent, and the long-term relationship between child and parent may be damaged (Gershoff, 2002).

In addition, positive punishment often fails to offset the reinforcing aspects of the undesired behavior. In real life, any behavior can be reinforced in multiple ways. For instance, thumb sucking may be reinforced because it makes a child feel good, because it provides relief from negative emotions, and because it eases hunger. Punishment may not be enough to offset such reinforcement, and it may reinforce the child's secrecy about thumb sucking.

For these and other reasons, most psychologists agree with Skinner's recommendation that reinforcement is a better way than positive punishment to teach desirable behavior (**Figure 6.17**). A child complimented for being a good student is likely to perform better academically than one punished for doing poorly. After all, reinforcing good behavior tells the child what to do. Punishing the child for bad behavior does not tell the child how to improve.

One form of positive punishment that most psychologists believe is especially ineffective is physical punishment, such as spanking. Even so, spanking is very common in the United States (**Figure 6.18a**). Nearly three-quarters of American parents spank their children and apparently believe it is effective (Gallup, 1995; Lansford et al., 2010). As noted by Alan Kazdin and Corina Benjet (2003), beliefs about the appropriateness of spanking are related to religious beliefs, cultural views, and legal issues. Many countries—for example, Austria, Denmark, Israel, Sweden, and Italy—have banned physical punishment in homes or schools (**Figure 6.18b**). Even the United Nations has passed resolutions discouraging it.

A recent meta-analysis involving more than 160,000 children found that spanking was not effective in improving children's behavior (Gershoff & Grogan-Kaylor, 2016). Indeed, spanking was associated with many negative outcomes, including more aggression and antisocial behavior, more mental health problems, lower self-esteem, and negative relationships with parents. One concern is that physical punishment teaches the child that violence is an appropriate behavior for adults. Study unit 6.13 discusses such imitative behavior as a form of learning by watching others.

How often do mild forms of spanking cause problems? That question is open to debate (Baumrind, Larzelere, & Cowan, 2002). However, other forms of punishment, especially negative punishment, such as taking away cell phone or Internet access, seem to be more effective for decreasing unwanted behaviors (Kazdin & Benjet, 2003). Many psychologists believe that any form of punishment, positive or negative, is less effective than using positive reinforcement to increase the likelihood of engaging in "better" behaviors. By rewarding the behaviors they wish to see, parents are able to increase those behaviors while building more positive bonds with their children.

FIGURE 6.18

Legality of Spanking

These maps compare **(a)** the United States and **(b)** Europe in terms of the legality of spanking children.

BEHAVIOR MODIFICATION CAN REPLACE UNWANTED BEHAVIORS

Behavior modification is the use of operant-conditioning techniques to eliminate unwanted behaviors and replace them with desirable ones. The general reasoning behind behavior modification is that most unwanted behaviors can be unlearned. Conditioning strategies are widely used, for example, to teach people to be more productive at work, to save energy, and to drive more safely. Children with severe learning disabilities can be trained to communicate and to interact. As you will learn in Chapter 15, operant conditioning techniques are also effective for treating many psychological conditions. You can even modify your own behavior to exercise more (see Using Psychology in Your Life on pp. 238–39).

One widespread behavior modification method draws on secondary reinforcement. Chimpanzees can be trained to perform tasks in exchange for tokens, which they can later trade for food. The tokens thus reinforce behavior, and the chimps work as hard to obtain the tokens as they work to obtain food. Prisons, mental hospitals, schools, and classrooms often use *token economies,* in which people earn tokens for completing tasks and lose tokens for behaving badly. The people can later trade their tokens for objects or privileges (**Figure 6.19**). Here, the rewards not only reinforce good behavior but also give participants a sense of control over their environment.

6.12 Biology and Cognition Influence Operant Conditioning

6.12 LEARNING GOAL ACTIVITIES

To maximize your learning, complete the following learning goal activities.

a. Understand all bold and italic terms by writing explanations of them in your own words.

b. Apply the three cognitive aspects of conditioning by describing an example from your own life of learning via a cognitive map, latent learning, and insight learning.

Behaviorists such as B. F. Skinner believed that all behavior could be explained by straightforward conditioning principles. In reality, as described in this study unit, reinforcement explains only certain human behaviors. On the one hand, biological factors can either increase the effects of reinforcers or limit their effects on learning. On the other hand, reinforcement does not always have to be present for learning to take place.

DOPAMINE ACTIVITY AFFECTS REINFORCEMENT As you learned in study unit 1.6, Skinner and other traditional behaviorists were interested only in observable behavior, not in any mental processes associated with a behavior. Because of this focus, they defined reinforcement strictly in terms of whether it did or did not increase behavior. They were uninterested in *why* reinforcement changed behavior—whether any personal feelings might be involved, for instance. After all, they believed that mental states were impossible to study empirically.

Studies of learning have made it clear, however, that positive reinforcement works in two ways. Positive reinforcement provides the subjective experience of pleasure, and it increases the desire for the object or event that produced the pleasure. If you behave in a way that produces a favorable outcome—for instance, studying for an exam and then getting an A—the experience creates responses in the brain that support studying for exams again.

FIGURE 6.19

Token Economies Change Behavior

Many teachers give tokens (or stickers or pencils) for obeying class rules, turning in homework on time, and helping others. At some future point, the tokens can be exchanged for rewards, such as fun activities or extra recess time.

Can Behavior Modification Help You Exercise Regularly?

The Centers for Disease Control and Prevention (CDC) report that less than half of adults meet the goal of exercising 30 minutes a day, 5 days per week (United States Department of Health and Human Services, 2008). Maybe you intend to exercise daily, but then struggle to find the time to get to the gym. Or maybe you make working out a priority for a few weeks and then stop. How can psychology help you stick with your exercise program?

Just as psychologists use operant conditioning to change the behaviors of animals, including humans, you can condition yourself to perform healthful behaviors. Consider these steps:

STEP 1: Identify a behavior you wish to change. First, you need to decide what behavior you wish to modify. In this case, you want to increase your level of physical activity.

STEP 2: Set goals. Set goals that are realistic, specific, and measurable. If your current exercise program consists of a daily race to beat the closing elevator door, setting a goal to run 10 miles per day every day this month is not realistic. A goal of "exercise more" is too vague. Instead, set a goal that you can accomplish in a relatively short time, and one you can measure objectively. For example: Walk up the three flights of stairs at work at least four days this week; or attend three yoga sessions this week; or walk at least 10,000 steps each day this week. Setting goals you can meet quickly allows for more opportunities for reinforcement. If your ultimate goal is to have 30 minutes of moderate exercise 5 days per week, you need to set small, incremental subgoals that you can reinforce along the way.

Both the liking and the wanting involved in positive reinforcement result from biological factors, particularly the neurotransmitter dopamine (Gershman & Daw, 2017; Schultz, 2016). When hungry rats are given food, they experience increased dopamine release in the regions of the brain that process reward information: the greater the hunger, the greater the dopamine release (Rolls, Burton, & Mora, 1980). Food tastes better when you are hungry, and water is more rewarding when you are thirsty, because more dopamine is released when you have been deprived. In addition to dopamine, endorphins are also important for the liking aspect of reinforcement (Berridge & Kringelbach, 2015).

In operant conditioning, dopamine has a biological influence on how reinforcing something is. Drugs that block dopamine's effects disrupt operant conditioning. On the other hand, drugs that enhance dopamine activation, such as cocaine and amphetamines, increase the reinforcing value of stimuli. As you learned in study unit 3.12, this effect helps explain why dopamine is involved in addictive behavior, especially in terms of increased desire for the addictive substance.

BIOLOGY CONSTRAINS REINFORCEMENT Though behavior can be shaped through reinforcement, animals have a hard time learning behaviors that run counter to their evolutionary adaptation. A good example of such biological constraints comes from the experience of Marian and Keller Breland. These psychologists used operant-conditioning techniques to train animals for commercials (Breland & Breland, 1961). Many of their animals refused to perform certain tasks they had been taught. For instance, a raccoon learned to place coins in a piggy bank, but eventually it refused to perform this task. Instead, the raccoon stood over the piggy bank and

cognitive map
A visuospatial mental representation of an environment.

STEP 3: Monitor your behavior. Monitor your behavior for a week before you begin your new physical activity regimen. This will likely move you toward your goal, since you will be more conscious of your behavior. It will also give you a baseline against which you can measure your progress. Record your observations. If you have a smartphone, you might download an app for recording physical activity. Or you can register at an exercise-tracking Web site. Or just use a paper notebook.

STEP 4: Select a reinforcer and decide on a reinforcement schedule. When you choose a reinforcer, pick something attainable that you genuinely find enjoyable. For example, perhaps for every yoga class you attend, you will earn one song from iTunes. Or you could give yourself a penny for every hundred steps you take each day. Later, when the money adds up, you can use it to buy something you do not normally spend money on.

STEP 5: Reinforce the desired behavior. To bring about the behavior change you want to see, you need to reinforce the desired behavior whenever it occurs. Be consistent. Suppose that if you work out at the gym three times this week, you treat yourself to a movie. This is important: If you do not work out at the gym three times this week, do not go to the movie. You may be tempted to go anyway, but if you want the behavior modification to work, you have to resist. If you do not behave appropriately, you do not receive the reinforcer. Allow yourself no exceptions. However, you may be more likely to hit your exercise goals if you have a friend or family member give out the reinforcer. That way, you won't make the critical mistake of rewarding yourself before you have earned it.

STEP 6: Modify your goals, reinforcements, or reinforcement schedules, as needed. Once you begin consistently hitting your stated goals, make the goals more challenging. Add more days of exercise per week, more minutes, or more reps per workout. If you find yourself getting bored with a reinforcer, mix it up a bit. If you need a new person to provide the reinforcement, then make that change. Select a reinforcer that is genuinely appealing, and don't let the person giving the reinforcer reward you prematurely. And change the reinforcement schedule so you have to work harder to get the reward—for example, delay the reinforcement until you've completed two workouts rather than one.

Of course, you can use these principles to address other behaviors, such as procrastinating on your studies, neglecting to call your family, spending too much time on Facebook, and so on. For now, just pick one behavior you want to modify and try following the steps described. Once you get the hang of it, see if you can translate these steps to other areas of your life. You might amaze yourself with the power of behavior modification.

---

briskly rubbed the coins in its paws. This rubbing behavior was not reinforced. In fact, the rubbing delayed reinforcement. One explanation for the raccoon's behavior is that the task it was supposed to perform was incompatible with its innate, biologically determined, adaptive behaviors. The raccoon associated the coin with food and treated it the way it would have treated food. Rubbing food between the paws is hardwired for raccoons (**Figure 6.20**).

Conditioning is most effective when the association between the response and the reinforcement is consistent with the animal's built-in biological predispositions. For instance, the psychologist Robert Bolles has argued that animals have built-in defense reactions to threatening stimuli (Bolles, 1970). Pigeons can be trained to peck at keys to obtain food or secondary reinforcers, but it is difficult to train them to peck at keys to avoid electric shock. They can learn to avoid shock by flapping their wings, however, because wing flapping is their natural means of escape.

LEARNING WITHOUT REINFORCEMENT Another challenge to the idea that reinforcement is responsible for all behavior is the fact that learning can take place without reinforcement. Edward Tolman, an early cognitive theorist, argued that reinforcement has more impact on performance than on acquisition of knowledge through learning.

Tolman's research investigated the answer to this question. In his experiments, rats had to learn to run through complex mazes to obtain food. Tolman believed that each rat developed a **cognitive map.** That is, during an experiment, each rat held in its brain a representation of the particular maze. That representation was based on

FIGURE 6.20
Biology Constrains Learning Through Operant Conditioning

Animals have a hard time learning behaviors that go against their biological predispositions. For example, raccoons are hardwired to rub food between their paws, as this raccoon is doing. They have trouble learning *not* to rub objects.

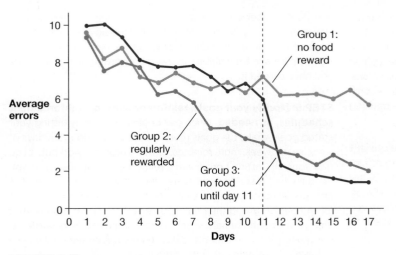

FIGURE 6.21

Tolman's Study of Latent Learning

Rats that were regularly reinforced for correctly running through a maze (Group 2) showed improved performance over time compared with rats that did not receive reinforcement (Group 1). Rats that were not reinforced for the first 10 trials but were reinforced thereafter showed an immediate change in performance (Group 3). Note that between days 11 and 12 Group 3's average number of errors decreased dramatically.

latent learning
Learning that takes place in the absence of reinforcement.

insight learning
A sudden understanding of how to solve a problem after a period of either inaction or thinking about the problem.

the things and spaces the rat had seen inside the maze. The rat used this knowledge of the environment to help it find the food quickly.

To test his theory, Tolman and his students studied three groups of rats (**Figure 6.21**). The rats in Group 1 traveled through the maze but received no reinforcement. That is, they reached the "goal box" but found no food in the box. On later trials, rats continued to wander through the maze slowly, making many "wrong turns" on the way to the goal box. The rats in Group 2 received reinforcement on every trial because there was food in the goal box. On each of the following trials, these rats found the box faster and with fewer errors. The rats in Group 3 started receiving reinforcement only after the first 10 trials. For the first 10 days, they performed as slowly and incorrectly as the unrewarded rats in Group 1. But the rats in Group 3 showed something amazing when they received their first reward on day 11. Suddenly, these rats very quickly and accurately navigated the maze to get to the goal box. In fact, they performed even better than rats in Group 2 that had been rewarded regularly (Tolman & Honzik, 1930).

Tolman's results suggest that the third group of rats had learned a cognitive map of the maze all along. However, based on their performance once the reinforcement began, the Group 3 rats did not use that map to reveal their learning until they started being rewarded. In other words, they were learning even without reinforcement, a situation Tolman termed **latent learning**. The reinforcement led to demonstration of this learning over time through improved performance.

Another form of learning that takes place without reinforcement is **insight learning**. In this form of problem solving, a solution suddenly emerges after a delay—a period of either inaction or thinking through the problem. You probably have had this sort of experience. After mulling over a problem for a while and seeming to get nowhere, suddenly you know the answer.

 How Do You Learn Through Operant Conditioning?

To make sure you learned what you just read, write answers to the following questions and check your answers.

6.8 Studying an extra hour per day for the exam led to a grade of A on the exam. What was the operant, and what was the reinforcer?

6.9 When a boss gives a cash bonus to the salesperson with the most sales, is the boss giving a primary or secondary reinforcer?

6.10 What is the basic difference between positive reinforcement and negative reinforcement?

6.11 What is it called when elementary-school students earn points for good behavior that they can trade for items they want from the school store?

6.12 Why does latent learning challenge traditional operant conditioning theory?

See Appendix B for answers to the red Q questions.

How Do You Learn by Watching Others?

Suppose you were teaching someone to fly an airplane. How might you apply the learning principles discussed in this chapter to accomplish your goal? Obviously, if you were training a beginning pilot, just waiting until your student did something right and then reinforcing that behavior would be disastrous. Similarly, though with less serious consequences, teaching someone to play football, eat with chopsticks, or perform complex dance steps requires more than simple reinforcement. We learn many behaviors not by doing them, but by watching others do them. This is true not only for mechanical skills, because we learn social etiquette by watching others. We sometimes learn to be anxious in particular situations by seeing that other people are anxious. We often get our attitudes about politics and religion from parents, peers, teachers, and the media. In general, we learn by watching others in these three ways: observational learning, modeling, and vicarious conditioning (Bandura, 1977b).

6.13 There Are Three Ways You Learn by Watching Others

6.13 LEARNING GOAL ACTIVITIES

To maximize your learning, complete the following learning goal activities.

a. Understand all bold and italic terms by writing explanations of them in your own words.

b. Apply learning by watching others by providing an example from your own life of each of the three types of learning by watching others.

Observational learning occurs when an individual either acquires or changes a behavior after viewing at least one performance of that behavior (review the Learning Tip in study unit 6.2, on p. 216). This kind of learning is a powerful adaptive tool. Offspring can learn basic skills by watching adults perform those skills. They can learn which things are safe to eat by watching what adults eat, and they can learn to fear dangerous objects and situations by watching adults avoid them. Young children are sponges, absorbing everything that goes on around them (**Figure 6.22**). This behavior can be a bad thing too. When a young child starts to curse, you know the child learned that behavior from an adult, a sibling, or a peer.

BANDURA'S RESEARCH REVEALS LEARNING THROUGH OBSERVATION
In the 1960s, the psychologist Albert Bandura conducted the most thorough work on observational learning (**Figure 6.23**). In a now-classic series of studies, Bandura divided preschool children into two groups. One group watched a film of an adult playing quietly with a large inflatable doll called Bobo. The other group watched a film of the adult attacking Bobo furiously: whacking the doll with a mallet, punching it in the nose, and kicking it around the room. When the children were later allowed to play with numerous toys, including the Bobo doll, those who had seen the more aggressive display were more than twice as likely to act aggressively toward the doll (Bandura, Ross, & Ross, 1961).

observational learning
The acquisition or modification of a behavior after exposure to at least one performance of that behavior.

FIGURE 6.22
Observational Learning
This boy is not just watching his grandfather woodworking. Through observational learning, he is acquiring the skills to do woodworking himself.

Bandura's Bobo Doll Studies

In Bandura's studies, some preschool children saw an adult attack an inflatable Bobo doll (**top row**). When children were allowed to play with the doll later, both males (**middle row**) and females (**bottom row**) who had watched the adult attack the doll were more likely to act in an aggressive way toward the doll.

modeling
Demonstrating a behavior to imitate a behavior that was previously observed.

FIGURE 6.24
Early Modeling

Babies frequently show learning by watching and then imitating behaviors and expressions.

Bandura's results suggest not only that people learn through observation, but that exposing children to violence is associated with acting aggressively. But is that correct? This question comes up frequently in relation to the violent TV shows, movies, and video games that are common in our culture. If you had children, would you let them watch violent TV shows or play violent video games? To help you answer that question, see Evaluating Psychology in the Real World on p. 243.

LEARNING THROUGH MODELING Can you remember learning to tie your shoes? It probably happened as you watched your parents using slow and exaggerated motions, repeated many times. After your parents demonstrated how to tie shoes, you would have tried it yourself, making an effort to imitate them. Because humans can learn through observation, they readily imitate the actions of others and learn new things. Demonstrating a behavior that you saw someone else engage in is commonly called **modeling** (review the Learning Tip in study unit 6.2, on p. 216).

Within a few days (or even hours) of birth, human newborns will model actions seen in others, such as sticking out the tongue and making facial expressions. And infants will continue to model gestures and other actions as they develop (**Figure 6.24**). Animals may also be imitators. Indeed, one study found that infant macaque monkeys imitate facial expressions when they are 3 days old (Ferrari et al., 2006). However, research is unclear on whether animals engage in imitation in the same way that humans do.

Modeling in humans is influenced by many factors. Generally, we are more likely to imitate the actions of models who are attractive, have high status, and are somewhat similar to ourselves. In addition, modeling is effective only if the observer is physically capable of imitating the behavior. Simply watching Michael Phelps blast through the water in the 100-meter butterfly does not mean we could do that if we jumped in the pool.

Adolescent smoking is a particularly striking example of modeling. For example, adolescents whose favorite actors smoke in movies are much more likely to smoke (Tickle, Sargent, Dalton, Beach, & Heatherton, 2001). In addition, the more smoking that adolescents observe in movies, the more positive their attitudes about smoking become, and the more likely they are to begin smoking (Sargent et al., 2005;

Does Playing Violent Video Games Cause Children to Become More Violent?

As discussed in this chapter and Chapter 4, learning hugely affects the developing mind. Therefore it is vital for children to have the best learning experiences possible. However, some learning experiences can have negative effects. As articles such as the one excerpted below illustrate, people debate how watching violent media and playing violent video games may affect children. (The full article is available at https://www.livescience.com/44325-video-games-aggression-debate.html.)

What is the article's point, and how well does it make that point? Should you accept the claim being made here? To answer this question, use the three steps in critical thinking:

ACTIVITY: To determine if you should accept the claims in this article, please review the Learning Tip on p. 7 and follow these steps:

Step 1 What is the claim I am being asked to accept?

Step 2 What evidence, if any, is provided to support the claim?

Step 3 Given the evidence, what are the most reasonable conclusions about the claim?

QUESTION: If you have rejected the claim or found the evidence lacking, why did you choose to do so? If you have found that the evidence supports the claim, how might this information change how you think and act?

Do Violent Games Boost Aggression? Study Adds Fire to Debate

Children who play violent video games may experience an increase in aggressive thoughts, which in turn could boost their aggressive behavior, a controversial new study conducted in Singapore suggests.

In the study, children ages 8 to 17 who played a lot of violent video games showed an increase in aggressive behavior—such as hitting, shoving, and pushing—three years later, compared to their behavior at the study start.

Meanwhile, those who decreased the amount of time they spent playing violent video games saw a decrease in aggressive behavior, the researchers said.

The reason for the increase in aggressive behavior was that children who played a lot of violent video games had an increase in aggressive thoughts: for instance, they were more likely to interpret an ambiguous act, like someone bumping into them, as hostile, said study researcher Craig Anderson, a psychologist and professor at Iowa State University. They were also more likely to see aggressive behavior as an appropriate way to respond to provocation, Anderson said.

"Children and adolescents who play a lot of [violent] games change over time, they start to see aggressive solutions as being more reasonable," ways to respond to conflict or frustration, Anderson told Live Science.

However, experts not involved with the study say that the research has flaws, and does not add anything meaningful to the debate over whether violent video games increase aggression, which has been a contentious issue. They also say that other researchers should be allowed to analyze the data, to see if they find the same result.

Study criticism

Studies on whether violent video games lead to aggression in children have been mixed: some

studies have found a strong connection, while others find no link.

Christopher Ferguson, an associate professor of psychology at Stentson University in DeLand, Fla., who was not involved in the new study, said that data used in the new study has been used in the past to make connections between violent video games and aggression, but that such work has been previously criticized.

"Given that this data has been out there already, and that there's so many problems, I don't think that much is here for parents or policy makers to take away from it," Ferguson said.

One issue is that the study asked only the children themselves to rate the violence of their video games, which could bias the results, Ferguson said.

Ferguson noted that despite increases in violent games, movies, and television programs in recent decades, youth violence has not increased. "If video games really did have this direct, linear affect, we would be able to see it in society, and we're not," he said. . . .

FIGURE 6.25

Modeling and Smoking

Eye-catching movie images such as this one, from the 2012 James Bond movie *Skyfall*, contribute to viewers' sense that smoking is a mature, cool, sexy behavior. Because people learn to model what they see, they readily imitate the actions of people they admire, including movie stars who smoke.

vicarious conditioning

Learning the consequences of an action by watching others being reinforced or punished for performing the action.

Figure 6.25). Surprisingly, these effects are strongest among children whose parents do not smoke. Why would this be so? Movies tend to glamorize the habit, often presenting images of smokers as mature, cool, sexy—things adolescents want to be, and different from how they see their parents. Adolescents do not generally decide to smoke after watching one movie that makes smoking seem glamorous. But repeated demonstrations shape their attitudes about smoking and subsequently lead to imitation. As adolescent viewers learn to associate smoking with people they admire, even fictional movie characters, they incorporate the general message that smoking is desirable.

LEARNING THROUGH VICARIOUS CONDITIONING

Another factor that determines whether a person imitates a model is whether the person observes the model being rewarded for performing the behavior. In the study mentioned earlier, Bandura and colleagues showed children a film of an adult aggressively playing with a Bobo doll (Bandura et al., 1961). However, in a different study the film ended in one of three different ways (Bandura, Ross, & Ross, 1963). In the first version, the control condition, the adult experienced no consequences for the aggressive behavior. In the second version, the adult was rewarded for the aggressive behavior with candy and praise. In the third version, the adult was punished for the behavior by being both spanked and verbally reprimanded.

When the children were subsequently allowed to play with the Bobo doll, those who observed the model being rewarded for aggressive behavior were much more likely to be aggressive toward the doll than were the children who watched the control condition of the film. In contrast, those who saw the model being punished were less likely to be aggressive than were those in the control group. Through **vicarious conditioning**, people learn about the consequences of an action by watching others being reinforced or punished for performing the action (review the Learning Tip in study unit 6.2, on p. 216). This learning then affects people's own likelihood to engage in that behavior at a later time (**Figure 6.26**).

These findings do not mean that the children who did not show aggression did not learn the behavior. Later, the children were offered small gifts to perform the model's actions, and all—even those who had watched the model being punished—performed the aggressive actions reliably. As noted earlier in the discussion of latent learning, a key distinction in learning is between the *acquisition* of a behavior and its *performance*. In this case, all the children acquired the behavior. In other words, they learned it. But only those who saw the model being rewarded performed the behavior. That is, not until the children themselves were actually rewarded for acting in that way did they all perform the behavior. Direct rewards prompted the children in the control group to reveal the behavior they had acquired.

FIGURE 6.26

Learning Through Vicarious Conditioning

When a person observes someone else being reinforced or punished for a particular behavior, the observer may learn to do, or not do, the same thing. This type of learning happens all the time with siblings. Because this boy is watching his sister get a "talking to" after behaving badly, he will probably learn to not make the same mistake that she made.

6.14 Biology Influences Observational Learning

6.14 LEARNING GOAL ACTIVITIES

To maximize your learning, complete the following learning goal activities.

a. Understand all bold and italic terms by writing explanations of them in your own words.

b. Understand what happens in the brain during observational learning by summarizing how mirror neurons may be the brain mechanism responsible for observational learning.

Suppose you're watching somebody handle a piece of paper and that person gets a paper cut. You might find yourself flinching as if you received the cut (**Figure 6.27**). Why do you experience this empathy, the emotional response of feeling what someone else is experiencing?

During observational learning, when you watch someone performing an action, *mirror neurons* in your brain become activated (Iacoboni, 2009). Mirror neurons are especially likely to become activated when you observe someone making a movement that has some goal, such as reaching for a glass of water. Your mirror neurons are not activated when you see just the water glass or when you see a person just sitting. But these same mirror neurons become activated when you reach for a glass of water. Every time you watch another person engaging in an action, similar neural circuits are firing in your brain and in the other person's brain.

Scientists are debating the function of mirror neurons. This system may support observational learning (McGregor, Cashaback, & Gribble, 2016). However, the firing of mirror neurons in the observer's brain does not always lead that person to actually imitate the behavior being observed. Therefore, some theorists think that mirror neurons may help us explain and predict the behavior of others. In other words, mirror neurons may let us step into the shoes of people we observe so that we empathize with them and better understand those people's actions.

FIGURE 6.27

Activation of Mirror Neurons in Observational Learning May Underlie Empathy

We sometimes "feel the pain" when we watch someone experiencing an injury. This response may be due to the fact that our mirror neurons are activated when we see someone else getting injured, so that we ourselves "feel" the pain too.

 How Do You Learn by Watching Others?

To make sure you learned what you just read, write answers to the following questions and check your answers.

6.13 Why are you less likely to cheat if you see another student suspended for cheating?

6.14 What are mirror neurons?

See Appendix B for answers to the red Q questions.

BIG PICTURE

 Want to earn a better grade on your test? Go to **INQUIZITIVE** to practice actively with this chapter's content and get personalized feedback along the way.

How Do You Learn?

6.1 You Learn from Experience

Review the learning goal activities on p. 214. Learning is a change in behavior, resulting from experience. Because learning lets animals (including humans) better adapt to the environment, it aids the survival of species.

6.2 You Learn in Three Ways

Review the learning goal activities on p. 215. There are three main types of learning: (1) non-associative, (2) associative, and (3) learning by watching others. Non-associative learning about a stimulus happens through habituation or through sensitization. Associative learning about relationships occurs through classical conditioning and operant conditioning. Learning by watching others occurs through observational learning, modeling, and vicarious conditioning.

6.3 Your Brain Changes During Learning

Review the learning goal activities on p. 217. According to the theory of Hebbian learning, neurons that fire together develop synaptic connections that make them likely to fire together in the future. Learning occurs when these synaptic connections in the brain become stronger over time through long-term potentiation (LTP). The hippocampus, where memories are formed, is one part of the brain where LTP is seen during learning.

KEY TERMS
learning (p. 215)
habituation (p. 216)
sensitization (p. 216)

How Do You Learn Through Classical Conditioning?

6.4 Through Classical Conditioning, You Learn That Stimuli Are Related

Review the learning goal activities on p. 218. In classical conditioning, an association between two stimuli is learned, which changes future behavior. First, an unconditioned stimulus (food) automatically elicits an unconditioned response (salivating). Then a neutral stimulus (sound) is repeatedly associated with the unconditioned stimulus. The animal or human learns that the conditioned stimulus (sound) predicts the unconditioned stimulus (food). Finally, this learned pairing produces a new, conditioned response (salivation to the sound). Eventually the animal or human learns to respond to the first stimulus, the sound, even without the second, the food.

6.5 Learning Varies in Classical Conditioning

Review the learning goal activities on p. 221. Six factors affect the strength and persistence of learning from classical conditioning: (1) acquisition, (2) extinction, (3) spontaneous recovery, (4) generalization, (5) discrimination, and (6) second-order conditioning.

6.6 You Can Learn Fear Responses Through Classical Conditioning

Review the learning goal activities on p. 224. Phobias are learned fear associations. Phobias, such as of snakes, may develop when classical conditioning makes a fear experience generalize to new situations. Techniques based on classical conditioning, such as counterconditioning, can be used to treat phobias by breaking the link between the stimulus and the learned fear response.

6.7 Adaptation and Cognition Influence Classical Conditioning

Review the learning goal activities on p. 225. Some stimuli are stronger than others in creating classical conditioning. Humans are biologically prepared to fear stimuli that are potentially dangerous, which helps them avoid danger and improves the chances of survival. The cognitive model says that the amount of conditioning that occurs depends on how unexpected or surprising the unconditioned stimulus is.

KEY TERMS
classical conditioning (p. 218)
unconditioned stimulus (US) (p. 219)
unconditioned response (UR) (p. 219)
conditioned stimulus (CS) (p. 221)
conditioned response (CR) (p. 221)
acquisition (p. 222)
extinction (p. 223)
spontaneous recovery (p. 223)
stimulus generalization (p. 223)
stimulus discrimination (p. 223)

How Do You Learn Through Operant Conditioning?

6.8 Through Operant Conditioning, You Learn the Consequences of Your Actions

Review the learning goal activities on p. 228. Operant conditioning involves learning the association between a behavior and its consequences, which changes future behavior. An operant is an action that is performed on an environment (such as doing homework) and that has consequences. A reinforcer is a consequence of an action (such as getting an A on the homework) that affects whether the action is repeated, or not, in the future.

6.9 Learning Varies in Operant Conditioning

Review the learning goal activities on p. 230. Operant conditioning can be performed through shaping, where behaviors are reinforced that are increasingly similar to the desired behavior. Primary reinforcers, such as food and water, aid survival by satisfying biological needs. Secondary reinforcers, such as money, do not satisfy biological needs, but their importance is learned. According to the Premack principle, a highly valued activity (such as eating ice cream) can be used to reinforce a less valued activity (such as doing homework).

6.10 Both Reinforcement and Punishment Influence Operant Conditioning

Review the learning goal activities on p. 231. Reinforcement increases the likelihood that a behavior will be repeated. Punishment reduces the likelihood that a behavior will be repeated. Positive reinforcement and positive punishment change behavior by adding a stimulus. Negative reinforcement and negative punishment change behavior by removing a stimulus. Behavior is rarely reinforced continuously. There are four schedules of partial reinforcement: (1) fixed interval, (2) variable interval, (3) fixed ratio, and (4) variable ratio. Each schedule of partial reinforcement has a different impact on behavior.

6.11 Operant Conditioning Affects Your Life

Review the learning goal activities on p. 235. Positive punishment is often ineffective because it is applied after desired behaviors, can lead to negative emotional responses, and is not strong enough to overcome the reinforcement of an undesired behavior. Using reinforcement tends to have better outcomes for learning. For example, behavior modification using token economies is one successful means of replacing undesired behavior.

6.12 Biology and Cognition Influence Operant Conditioning

Review the learning goal activities on p. 237. Biological factors influence learning. Rewards are associated with dopamine activity in the brain. In addition, innate biological constraints affect what is likely to be learned or not learned. Cognitive maps, latent learning, and insight learning all reveal that learning can occur as a result of cognitive processes in the brain that may not be observed in outward behavior.

KEY TERMS

operant conditioning (p. 228)
operant (p. 229)
reinforcer (p. 229)
positive reinforcement (p. 232)
negative reinforcement (p. 232)
positive punishment (p. 233)
negative punishment (p. 233)
fixed interval schedule (FI) (p. 234)

variable interval schedule (VI) (p. 234)
fixed ratio schedule (FR) (p. 234)
variable ratio schedule (VR) (p. 234)
partial-reinforcement extinction effect (p. 234)
cognitive map (p. 239)
latent learning (p. 240)
insight learning (p. 240)

How Do You Learn by Watching Others?

6.13 There Are Three Ways You Learn by Watching Others

Review the learning goal activities on p. 241. Humans learn basic and complex skills, beliefs, attitudes, habits, and emotional responses by watching others. Three types of learning by watching are (1) observational learning (learning by watching the behavior of others), (2) modeling (imitation of an observed behavior), and (3) vicarious conditioning (learning about an action's consequences by observing others being rewarded or punished for their behavior).

6.14 Biology Influences Observational Learning

Review the learning goal activities on p. 245. Mirror neurons become active when you observe someone performing an action, especially a goal-directed behavior. So the processing of mirror neurons may be a neural basis of observational learning. Mirror neurons may also be the basis of empathy, the emotional response of feeling what others are experiencing.

KEY TERMS

observational learning (p. 241)
modeling (p. 242)
vicarious conditioning (p. 244)

CHAPTER 6 SELF-QUIZ

To make sure you learned the information in this chapter, write answers to the following questions and check your answers. **See Appendix B for answers to the self-quiz.**

1. Sanjay's roommate has a habit of chewing gum very loudly. At first, Sanjay found the noise really disruptive when he was studying. After a week, however, the noise stopped bothering him. Sanjay's adjustment resulted from a type of learning called _____.
   a. habituation
   b. sensitization
   c. conditioning
   d. modeling

2. Whenever Erin first sees her boyfriend, her heart beats fast. And whenever her boyfriend comes to her dorm room and the door is closed, he knocks five times before entering the room. After a while, Erin's heart jumps with excitement whenever she hears five knocks. The knocking is a(n) _____ for Erin.
   a. unconditioned stimulus
   b. unconditioned response
   c. conditioned stimulus
   d. conditioned response

3. Christopher used to drink water from a drinking fountain just before physics class. One time, he felt nauseated right after drinking the water. After that, to avoid the risk of nausea, he stopped drinking at the fountain. Christopher learned a connection between the water fountain and feeling nauseated because he experienced _____.
   a. acquisition
   b. extinction
   c. spontaneous recovery
   d. counterconditioning

4. Lola's new dog, Hoss, is afraid of loud noises. Every time her cell phone rings, Hoss starts barking out of fear. After a while, Hoss also starts barking when a phone rings on a television show. The fact that Hoss now barks when he hears a telephone ring on TV is most likely due to _____.
   a. stimulus discrimination
   b. stimulus generalization
   c. spontaneous recovery
   d. second-order conditioning

5. Rosie wants her cat to meow when the doorbell rings. Each time a visitor rings the bell and the cat meows, Rosie gives him a treat. Soon the cat always meows when the doorbell rings. Rosie's cat is demonstrating _____.
   a. non-associative learning
   b. classical conditioning
   c. vicarious conditioning
   d. operant conditioning

6. Ajeet's younger sister is always bugging him. One day, Ajeet lets her play his video game, and she stops bugging him for several hours. Ajeet now lets her play his video game more and more, because doing so stops her from bugging him. Ajeet's learning in this situation is best explained by _____.
   a. positive reinforcement
   b. negative reinforcement
   c. positive punishment
   d. negative punishment

7. Glen and Lynda are hired to rake leaves. Glen is paid $3 for each bag of leaves he rakes. Lynda is paid $7 for each hour she works. Glen is paid according to a _____ schedule of reinforcement. Lynda is paid according to a _____ schedule.
   a. variable ratio; variable interval
   b. fixed ratio; fixed interval
   c. variable ratio; fixed interval
   d. fixed ratio; variable interval

8. Dante often shopped at the same grocery store. One day, another customer asked Dante if he knew where the plastic storage containers were located in the store. Dante immediately gave directions to the correct aisle, even though he had never bought plastic storage containers from that store. The fact that Dante knew the location of the containers is best explained by _____.
   a. insight learning
   b. vicarious conditioning
   c. latent learning
   d. continuous reinforcement

9. Three-year-old Sam watches as his 5-year-old sister, Mindy, draws on her bedroom wall with crayons. Their mother enters the room, but doesn't yell at Mindy. Instead, as Sam watches, their mother gets cleaning supplies and scrubs the wall clean. The next day, Sam displays modeling when he _____.
   a. stops himself from drawing on the walls to avoid punishment
   b. thinks about where they have a coloring book he can color in
   c. yells at Mindy for drawing on the walls
   d. gets his markers and colors on the laundry room wall

10. During a spelling test, Jung's friend is caught cheating and gets suspended from school for three days. Jung decides not to cheat because she does not want to get suspended for cheating. In this example, Jung is most likely displaying learning that is due to _____.
    a. modeling
    b. observational learning
    c. insight learning
    d. vicarious conditioning

How Can Understanding the Principles of Learning Help You Work with Animals?

Learning is such an important part of daily life that it's hard to imagine a job that does not include some kind of learning. At a new job, you need to learn how to perform your duties. You may need to teach other people at your company. So understanding how learning happens is bound to help you in your career.

For example, if you love animals, you can use your knowledge of learning to work with animals in many fields. Perhaps you want to be an animal care worker. In this position, you may take part in feeding, exercising, and grooming animals in many settings, including adoption centers, kennels, farms, stables, zoos, and aquariums, or as a veterinarian assistant at veterinary clinics. Or you can work as an animal trainer. You may teach pets to obey their owners, prepare horses to accept riders, train livestock and zoo animals to allow health exams and grooming, and train service animals to help people with disabilities.

Knowledge about the principles of learning provides the tools to help shape animal behavior through the application of specific methods from operant conditioning. For example, you know from this chapter that positive reinforcement is much more effective than punishment at producing desired behaviors. And you also understand that the schedule of reinforcement is crucial to maintain the behaviors you have produced. You will know when it is better to reward every response or to only reward occasional responses in order to make the behavioral change more long-lasting.

Behavioral principles are also important in shaping consumer behavior. As mentioned in the chapter, retail stores or coffee shops can bolster customer loyalty, and increase spending, through reward programs. Video game designers incorporate just the right level of rewards and challenges in their games, at the optimal schedule, in order to keep players engaged. It is also useful for Web developers to understand what drives behaviors so as to increase the number of clicks generated on digital platforms, thereby increasing revenue. As you may now appreciate, there are widespread employment opportunities in the business sector for people who are able to apply learning principles. According to the Bureau of Labor Statistics, the projected employment growth in 2014–24 for marketing analysts (19 percent) and Web and software developers (27 percent) is much stronger than average. Jobs for human resources managers are also projected to grow in the same period.

TAKEAWAY POINT: Understanding the psychological processes behind learning can help you learn or teach others at any job. You can put knowledge about learning to work in many jobs that relate to the care and training of animals as well as businesses in which employee behavior can be shaped by learning principles.

Ψ You can look up job descriptions, education requirements, salaries, and more at the Bureau of Labor Statistics: www.bls.gov. Visit the site and start putting psychology to work!

7 Memory

AUSTIN ROGERS DOESN'T COME ACROSS AS A SERIOUS PERSON, but in 2017 he was a serious competitor on the game show *Jeopardy!* (Van Luling, 2017; **Figure 7.1a**). Rogers tended bar in New York City, but he had also held various other jobs, such as doing stand-up comedy and hosting a quiz show in a bar for many years (**Figure 7.1b**). On *Jeopardy!* he clowned for the camera and told funny stories, but he also won 12 shows in a row. When Rogers's winning streak ended, he had earned $411,000 and tied as the fifth most-winning *Jeopardy!* champion of all time. How did he do it?

BIG QUESTIONS

How Do You Create Memories?

How Do You Maintain Memories over Time?

What Are Your Different Long-Term Storage Systems?

How Do You Retrieve Memories?

FIGURE 7.1

Austin Rogers's *Jeopardy!* Success Reveals How Memory Works

(a) In 2017, bartender Austin Rogers became one of the top *Jeopardy!* champions. **(b)** Rogers's success comes down to actively learning information over long periods of time so that he would remember it later. For example, he worked with facts while hosting a quiz show in a bar.

According to Rogers, he does not have a photographic memory or use any particular memory tricks to learn the vast amount of information necessary to become a *Jeopardy!* champion. Instead, his success is due to many hours of working to learn information over the years. As a child, Rogers watched *Jeopardy!* nightly with his family, so that over time he began to see patterns in the questions. For example, Rogers discovered that any time a question was about a famous painter from Iowa, the answer was Grant Wood. In addition, as the host of a quiz show in a bar, Rogers had "written tens and tens of thousands of questions, I mean, 60 questions a week over nine years or whatever—several times questions I've written have come up [on *Jeopardy!*]. And it helped me, literally like, I would not have known *this* had I not written *that* question three months ago."

Rogers's success reveals four facts about how memory works. First, creating memories is an active process, which means that you must focus on information to remember it. Rogers clearly did this when he watched *Jeopardy!* and when he researched information for trivia questions. Second, working with information and manipulating it at a deep level, as Rogers did by writing his own trivia questions, makes information more memorable. Third, processing information repeatedly over time, and accessing it repeatedly, improves your ability to remember it. Fourth, using cues, as Rogers did when he remembered the cue of "a famous painter from Iowa," can help you remember other information associated with it, in this case the name Grant Wood.

In short, Austin Rogers's experience provides an inspiring message: You can improve your memory by using several simple techniques. The better your memory, the greater your chances of succeeding at school, at work, and in your personal life. In this chapter, you will learn about the tools that helped Rogers succeed, as you explore what memory is and how it works.

How Do You Create Memories?

Since the late 1960s, most psychologists have viewed memory as a form of information processing. This view means that a memory is formed when information from the external world is processed into a code that can be recognized by the brain, and then that code is stored for some time so that it can be accessed later. This process is similar to computer processing. A computer receives information through the keyboard or modem, and software determines how the information is processed. The information may be stored in some altered format on the hard drive. Later, the information may be retrieved when it is needed. The processing of information into a memory is also similar to computer processing because both forms of processing include three phases. However, the comparison ends here. In the brain, the processing of information into memories is much more complex, personal, and imperfect than computer processing.

7.1 You Create Memories by Processing Information

7.1 LEARNING GOAL ACTIVITIES

To maximize your learning, complete the following learning goal activities.

a. Understand all bold and italic terms by writing explanations of them in your own words.

b. Apply the three phases of information processing to describe how you encoded, stored, and retrieved a specific memory that you have.

Memory is the nervous system's ability to obtain and retain information and skills. Austin Rogers demonstrated this capacity over many years, as he learned information he later used to answer *Jeopardy!* questions. The creation of memories occurs in three processing phases: (1) during encoding, you take in information from experiences, (2) you hold the information in storage for some period of time, and (3) you access the information later through retrieval (**Figure 7.2**). To understand the three processing phases of memory, consider that right now you are reading the information in this textbook. What is actually occurring as you read the words on this page?

DURING ENCODING YOU TAKE IN INFORMATION   As you go through your life, you have certain experiences. Often, it will benefit you to remember those experiences and learn from them. Reading the words on this page and remembering them for quizzes and tests later is an excellent example of this process. In the first phase of creating a memory, called **encoding**, your brain changes information into a meaningful neural code that it can use (**Figure 7.2**, Phase 1). For example, as you are reading this textbook, the words and pictures you see on this page are encoded into patterns of neural activity in your brain. However, without some system of maintaining that information in your brain, all of your experiences would be lost. For this reason, you need to also store your experiences.

memory
The nervous system's ability to obtain and retain information and skills for later retrieval.

encoding
The processing of information so it can be stored in the brain.

1 Encoding: changing information into a neural code the brain can use. Here the reader is encoding the visual input—the words and pictures on the page—to be stored.

2 Storage: maintaining information for some time. Here the reader is storing the encoded information. He is strengthening storage by taking notes.

3 Retrieval: accessing the information for use. If the reader encodes and stores well, he will later be able to retrieve the information and use it, such as on an exam.

FIGURE 7.2

Three Phases of Information Processing in Memory

The creation of a memory involves three phases of information processing: (1) encoding of external information into a neural code, (2) storage of the information for a period of time, and (3) retrieval of the information to access it later.

DURING STORAGE YOU MAINTAIN INFORMATION   In the second phase of creating a memory, the newly created neural codes are maintained for a period of time. For example, in reading this textbook you retain the information about the words and the pictures for use later. The **storage** phase lets you maintain the information in your brain (**Figure 7.2**, Phase 2). Storage can last a fraction of a second or as long as a lifetime. Think of this phase as maintaining the text material from when you read it until you take the test, or even longer.

DURING RETRIEVAL YOU ACCESS INFORMATION LATER   The third phase of memory creation, called **retrieval**, is the process of accessing the information later (**Figure 7.2**, Phase 3). Think of this phase as bringing to your mind a previously encoded and stored memory when it is needed, such as for answering a question on a psychology quiz. If the first two phases of creating a memory go well, then often the retrieval phase should also be successful.

7.2 Your Memories Are Unique

7.2 LEARNING GOAL ACTIVITIES

To maximize your learning, complete the following learning goal activities.

a. Understand all bold and italic terms by writing explanations of them in your own words.

b. Understand how attention affects memory by summarizing in your own words how selective attention influences the creation of a memory.

Humans always process information into memories through the three phases of encoding, storage, and retrieval. Computers store information through the same three phases, so it is tempting to think human memory works just like computers.

However, have you ever had a disagreement with someone about how a shared experience "really happened"? If so, then you know that human memory is not perfect like computer memory. This is because human brains are more complex, unique, and imperfect than computers. In short, the processing of information into memories is affected by these traits of human brains.

HUMANS DON'T CREATE MEMORIES THE WAY COMPUTERS STORE INFORMATION   Comparing human memory to computer processing is not perfect for three main reasons. First, as you learned in Chapter 2, your brain is complex. In fact, it is much more complicated than a computer. Some researchers suggest that the human brain is best thought of as a complex system of neurons and synapses that dynamically change over time (Gazzaniga, Doron, & Funk, 2009).

Second, your brain is unique. Every PC or Mac should store information like every other PC or Mac, but how each person processes experiences leads to individuals' having their own memories. Each of us remembers information that is relevant to ourselves and filters memories through our own perceptions and knowledge of related events. In other words, memories are not "truth," but a person's perception of what occurred based on what the person processed and what seemed meaningful to that person. Furthermore, this perception is altered during the processes of creating, maintaining, and accessing the memories. As a result, different people have different memories of the same information.

Third, human memory sometimes fails. If memory were perfect, you would never get an exam question wrong. But unlike computers or digital recorders, brains

storage
The retention of information in the brain over time.

retrieval
The act of accessing stored information when it is needed.

selective attention
The ability to direct mental resources to relevant information in order to process that information further, while also ignoring irrelevant information.

do not remember all information equally. Some experiences leave no lasting memories. Others are remembered but later forgotten. Still others remain for a lifetime. As you will learn in this chapter, human memory involves multiple systems, and each memory system has its own "rules." Failure to follow the "rules" can lead to memory problems.

All three of these reasons why human memory differs from computer processing can be connected. What unites them is the role of attention in how memories are created.

LIMITED ATTENTION IMPAIRS CREATION OF MEMORIES   Starting when you were very young, your parents and teachers have probably told you to pay attention. As you learned in study unit 3.3, attention is the focusing of mental resources on information to allow further processing. Attention is essential for conscious awareness of information. In addition, attention is critical for memory creation.

Think about the difference between the words "look" and "see," and between "listen" and "hear." "Look" and "listen" refer to directing attention to some information. You do so at the cost of paying less attention to other information. In fact, the word "pay" implies that costs are associated with attending to some information but not to others. That is, attention is limited. When it is divided among too many tasks or the tasks are difficult, your performance on each task suffers. In short, if you do not pay attention to look or listen, then you cannot even process sensory input to see or hear. In this case, you will not have a memory of that information.

Do you ever have problems remembering information? Perhaps you can't remember the material covered in class or in your textbook. These problems may have nothing to do with the way your brain creates memories. Instead, like everyone, you have limited attention resources. And sometimes you do not pay attention when you are supposed to be learning. So you must decide what to pay attention to and what to ignore.

It might seem unfortunate to have a limited ability to pay attention to information. However, this limitation actually helps you function in the world. A task as simple as listening to your instructor during class requires attention. If a classmate's hair was recently dyed purple, that change might capture your attention and make it difficult to follow what the instructor is saying. Or if the lecture is somewhat boring, you might start daydreaming. In short, your attention can be distracted by external stimuli or your own thoughts (Chun, Golomb, & Turk-Browne, 2011). Because distraction can make it hard to succeed at a given task, imagine what your life would be like if you could not block out the irrelevant information that comes at you all the time. For advice about improving your ability to pay attention in the classroom, see Has It Happened to You?

SELECTIVE ATTENTION IMPROVES CREATION OF MEMORIES   Paying attention to your teacher in class, instead of to a student with a distracting new hair color, shows that in most cases you can choose where to direct your attention. **Selective attention** is the ability to direct mental resources to relevant information in order to process that information further, while also ignoring irrelevant information.

Selective-listening research examines what we do with information that is not attended to. Some studies by Edward Cherry (1953) used a shadowing task where participants wore headphones that delivered a message to one ear and a different message to the other ear. Each person was asked to attend to one message

and repeat the message aloud (in other words, "shadow" it; **Figure 7.3**). Later on, participants often had no conscious awareness of the content of the unattended message. In 1958, the psychologist Donald Broadbent developed *filter theory* to explain this effect, where we selectively attend to the most important information in a message. In this model, attention is like a filter. Important information is allowed through the filter, but irrelevant information is prevented from getting through the filter.

However, certain information can pass through this attentional filter to be processed at least to some extent. For example, consider the cocktail party phenomenon. The psychologist Cherry (1953) described the process this way: You can focus on a single conversation at a chaotic cocktail party, such as talking to the person next to you. However, a particularly prominent stimulus—such as hearing your name mentioned in another conversation or hearing a juicy piece of gossip—can capture your attention. Because your attention is now divided, what you can understand of that conversation is less than if you had been giving it your full attention. Also, you may lose the thread of the conversation you were having with the person next to you because you were no longer paying attention to it.

In addition to your own name, other things you see, smell, taste, or touch can grab your attention, such as the person with purple hair. Suppose you are searching for a friend who you know is wearing a red coat. That person will "pop out" among a group of people wearing black coats but will be harder to spot if many other people are wearing red coats (Treisman & Gelade, 1980). Stimuli that cause emotional reactions are especially likely to capture your attention because they provide important information about potential threats in your environment (Phelps, Ling, & Carrasco, 2006). Faces are a good example of stimuli that are allowed through the filter because they provide important social information. For example, a face indicates whether someone is a potential mate (that is, has an attractive face) or may intend to cause physical harm (that is, has an angry face). Indeed, a series of studies found that the attentional system prioritizes faces, especially when they appear threatening, over less meaningful stimuli (West, Anderson, & Pratt, 2009).

The fact that selective attention is a demanding and imperfect process is critical to understanding how you create memories. To increase your ability to use selective attention, and other strategies, to remember information for exams, read Using Psychology in Your Life on pp. 258–59.

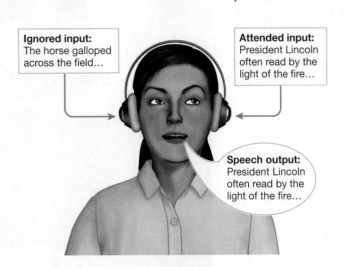

FIGURE 7.3

Selective Attention in a Listening Task

In this shadowing task, the participant receives a different auditory message in each ear and must repeat, or "shadow," just one of the messages. Typically, the person has no awareness of the unattended message.

Ignored input:
The horse galloped across the field...

Attended input:
President Lincoln often read by the light of the fire...

Speech output:
President Lincoln often read by the light of the fire...

Q How Do You Create Memories?

To make sure you learned what you just read, write answers to the following questions and check your answers.

7.1 What are the three phases of information processing in memory?

7.2 If one student, Darren, uses selective attention to focus on his teacher's lesson better than another student, Luisa, then how will this difference affect each of their abilities to create new memories about the class material?

See Appendix B for answers to the red Q questions.

How Do You Maintain Memories over Time?

Have you been paying attention to what you are reading in this chapter? If you have, then you should be able to answer this question: What is the first phase of processing involved in creating a memory? Did you remember that the first phase is encoding of information so it can be processed by the brain (see Figure 7.2, Phase 1)? The study units in this section explore the second key phase, in which memories are stored so that the information can be used later.

7.3 You Maintain Information in Three Memory Stores

7.3 LEARNING GOAL ACTIVITIES

To maximize your learning, complete the following learning goal activities.

a. Understand all bold and italic terms by writing explanations of them in your own words.

b. Understand the three memory stores by naming each one and describing why each one exists.

Who were your favorite teachers in elementary school? Most likely, you were able to remember at least one name. This ability means that you stored the information many years ago. But how is information maintained in storage, even for many years? In 1968, the psychologists Richard Atkinson and Richard Shiffrin proposed that we have three different types of memory stores: sensory storage, short-term storage, and long-term storage (**Figure 7.4**).

Each of these three memory stores is unique in four ways (**Table 7.1,** on p. 258). First, each memory store exists to serve a different function. Second, each store retains information that has been encoded in ways specific to itself. Third, each

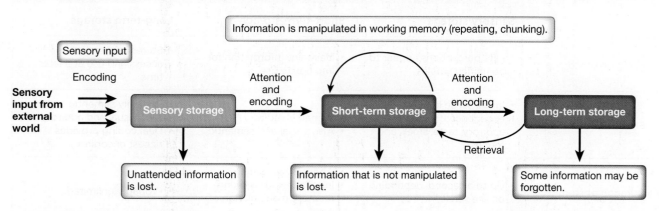

FIGURE 7.4

Three-Part Model of Memory Storage

This model proposes three different memory stores: (1) sensory storage, (2) short-term storage, and (3) long-term storage. Each memory store is unique in four ways (see Table 7.1, on p. 258). In addition, this model suggests that four different processes are needed in order to move information from one memory store to another: (1) encoding, (2) attention, (3) working memory, and (4) retrieval.

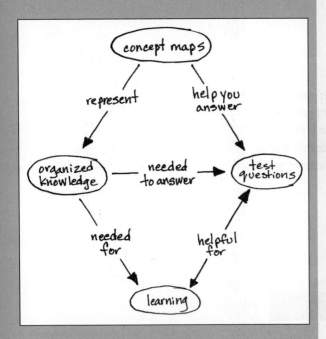

How Can You Remember Information for Exams?

What part of the college experience do most students particularly dislike? There's a good chance you said "exams." Psychology can't make exams go away, but it can help you be more successful at them. As you have already learned in this chapter, remembering information takes time and effort. But just as Austin Rogers used memory creation to become a *Jeopardy!* champion, you can use evidence-based strategies to study effectively and remember information more easily (Putnam, Sungkhasettee, & Roediger, 2016).

1. **Read actively.** When your instructor assigns reading, do the assignment. However, it is important to read actively. Many students read material, highlight what they think is important, then reread the highlighted passages for hours the night before an exam. Despite the popularity of this method, it is not associated with effective learning or good grades (Blasiman, Dunlosky, & Rawson, 2017). In addition, speed reading does not work, no matter how much you practice it. There is a trade-off between speed and accuracy (Rayner, Schotter, Masson, Potter, & Treiman, 2016). Instead of these approaches, use selective attention to process what you read thoroughly. For example, you can take notes on the information using your own words, write answers to the Learning Goal Activities in this book, or turn the headings of sections into questions and write answers to those.

2. **Attend class and participate actively.** You cannot get by with just reading the text and looking at online lecture notes. In class, your instructor may tie together ideas across lectures, present new ways of thinking about the material, or mention information not found in the textbook. As advised in the Has It Happened to You? feature on p. 255, unless otherwise instructed, leave your laptop at home to reduce distractions and use your selective attention to focus on the teacher and take notes by hand. Writing by hand and writing ideas in your own words will help you understand the material more thoroughly.

3. **Distribute learning.** Though pulling an all-nighter is a college cliché, cramming does not work. You can't focus your attention for that long!

TABLE 7.1

Four Functions of the Three Memory Stores

	Sensory storage	Short-term storage	Long-term storage
Function of storage	• Lets perceptions appear to be unified wholes	• Maintains information for immediate use	• Stores information for access and use at a later time
Encoding for storage	• In the sense it is experienced: visual, auditory, taste, smell, and touch	• Primarily auditory • Also visual and semantic	• Primarily semantic • Also visual and auditory • Dual coding provides richest encoding
Duration of storage	• Up to a second, depending on the sense	• About 20 seconds • Indefinite with working memory manipulation of items	• Probably unlimited
Capacity of storage	• Vast due to huge amount of sensory input	• About 7 items, plus or minus 2 • Using working memory aids capacity	• Probably unlimited

Six sessions of 1 hour each, spread over days or weeks, are much better for learning than one 6-hour marathon because you will retain information better (Cepeda, Pashler, Vul, Wixted, & Rohrer, 2006). Spacing out your study sessions requires you to begin earlier in the term rather than waiting until the night before exams, but distributing your time is perhaps the best way to learn the information and do well on exams.

4. **Process deeply.** When you are learning something new, do not just read, copy, or repeat the material. This type of shallow processing won't help your memory. Instead, focus your attention on the material to put the ideas into your own words, think about the meaning of the material, consider how the concepts are related to each other, and apply your learning to your own life to make it personally relevant. Using such deeper processing methods is an especially good way to remember information easily.

5. **Retrieve information repeatedly.** To make your memories more durable, you need to practice retrieving the information you are trying to learn. In fact, repeated testing is a more effective memory-building strategy than spending the same amount of time rereading or reviewing information you have already read (Roediger & Karpicke, 2006). Answering practice questions after you read a section of the textbook and doing homework about the material will help you remember the information during exams. Practicing retrieval also protects memories from the negative effects of stress (Smith, Floerke, & Thomas, 2016).

6. **Overlearn.** With material in front of you, you may be overly confident that you "know" the information and believe you will remember it later. But seeing an answer and knowing it is right is much easier than coming up with the answer from memory with no help. As a result, information in a book might not be as accessible when the book is closed and you have to answer questions about what you read. If you want to be able to retrieve information, you need to put in extra effort when processing the material. Even after you think you have learned it, test yourself by trying to access the material a few hours and a few days after studying. Keep doing this until you can retrieve the material easily.

7. **Create visuals.** Creating a visual is an especially good way to remember something. Visual imagery strategies include making a sketch to help you link ideas to images, creating a flowchart to show how some process unfolds over time, or drawing a concept map that shows the relationships between ideas. The picture in this feature is a concept map that presents some ideas about—you guessed it—concept maps. When you need to visualize the relationships between different ideas about any subject, you can adapt this model. The ovals represent main ideas. The arrows indicate connections between ideas.

8. **Make mnemonics.** Whatever their goals for remembering, people employ many types of mnemonics. For example, how many days are there in September? In the Western world, at least, most people can readily answer this question thanks to the old jingle that begins "Thirty days has September." Another common type of mnemonic is the acronym, such as HOMES to remember the great lakes (Huron, Ontario, Michigan, Erie, and Superior).

To use these strategies, you need to remember them. As a first step toward improving your study skills, use the first letter of each strategy's name to represent a word that makes up a new sentence. This new sentence can help you remember the names of these strategies.

store is able to hold information for a particular length of time. Fourth, each store has the ability to maintain a particular amount of information.

The three-part model of memory storage reveals the importance of how information is processed when it is being transferred from one type of memory store to another. Four processes that are critical in the model are encoding, attention, working memory, and retrieval (see Figure 7.4). The following study units look at how these processes help you move information from one memory store to another.

7.4 Sensory Storage Lets You Maintain Information Very Briefly

 7.4 LEARNING GOAL ACTIVITIES

To maximize your learning, complete the following learning goal activities.

a. Understand all bold and italic terms by writing explanations of them in your own words.

b. Understand sensory storage by explaining in your own words how visual sensory storage and auditory sensory storage let you experience perceptions as unified wholes.

sensory storage
A memory storage system that very briefly holds a vast amount of information from the five senses in close to their original sensory formats.

FIGURE 7.5

Sensory Storage

You could see the word "LOVE" spelled by a sparkler because the visual input would be maintained briefly in sensory storage.

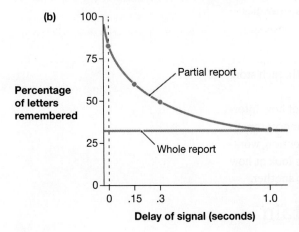

(a)

Rows of letters	Tone signaling which row to report
GTFB	High tone
QZCR	Medium tone
KPSN	Low tone

(b)

Percentage of letters remembered

Partial report

Whole report

Delay of signal (seconds)

FIGURE 7.6

Duration and Capacity of Sensory Storage

A clever experiment investigated visual sensory storage. **(a)** Twelve letters were flashed. In the whole report condition, participants had to name all 12 letters. In the partial report condition, they heard a tone that signaled which row of 4 letters to report. **(b)** According to the results of the partial report condition, many of the 12 letters are maintained in sensory storage for about one-third of a second.

"You're not paying attention to me." Like most of us, you have probably heard this complaint at some point. In that situation, even if you were thinking about something else, you may have been relieved to find that you could repeat the last few words the other person spoke. Sensory storage is the reason you can do this.

FIVE TYPES OF SENSORY STORES As you learned in Chapter 5, you receive all your information about the world through your senses: vision, hearing, taste, smell, and touch. This sensory information is the basis for your memories. When you see someone twirling a sparkler, for instance, the visual input to your eyes is transduced into a neural signal that is processed in your brain. One way this sensory input is processed is through encoding into sensory storage. Here, the sensory input—the sparkler—leaves a visual trace in the nervous system for just a fraction of a second. In this way, **sensory storage** is a very brief maintenance system for sensory information. In this case, the sensory storage lets you see the trail of light left by the sparkler just long enough to see the message written in the sparkler's light (**Figure 7.5**).

In the same way that one type of sensory storage very briefly maintains visual input, four other types of sensory stores maintain all the other sensory input: auditory, smell, taste, and touch. These kinds of input are not what we usually think of as memory, because each sensory store is so brief that we are unaware it is operating. However, sensory storage of all this vast amount of input is important because it lets us have a unified experience of the world around us.

DURATION AND CAPACITY OF SENSORY STORAGE How long can information be maintained in sensory storage? And how much information can be maintained? In a classic 1960 study, the cognitive psychologist George Sperling performed a now-classic study that provided the initial answers to these questions for visual sensory storage.

Three rows of four letters were flashed on a screen for one-twentieth of a second (**Figure 7.6a**). Then participants were asked to recall all 12 of the letters (that is, provide a whole report). Most people could name only three or four letters (**Figure 7.6b**, blue line). But they stated that they believed they had seen all the letters. Perhaps participants actually had a very brief memory for all 12 of the items. But in the time it took them to name the first 3 or 4 letters, they forgot the other 8 or 9 letters.

To test this interpretation, Sperling repeated the study, but he asked participants to report just one of the three rows of letters (that is, partial report). They knew which row they had to report based only on hearing a high-pitched, medium-pitched, or low-pitched sound (see Figure 7.6a). When the sound occurred immediately after the letters disappeared, the participants correctly remembered almost all the letters in the signaled row. But when there was a longer delay between the disappearance of the letters and the sound, participants recalled fewer letters in the signaled row. Based on this result, Sperling concluded that participants maintained many of the 12 items in sensory storage for about one-third of a second (see Figure 7.6b, green line). After that very brief period, the trace of the memory in sensory storage faded progressively until it was no longer accessible.

By maintaining a large amount of information for a fraction of a second, sensory storage lets you experience the world as a continuous stream of information rather than as discrete sensations (see Table 7.1, on p. 258). You can see this for yourself in Has It Happened to You? Also thanks to visual sensory storage, you can enjoy a movie. A movie is actually a series of still pictures that follow each other very closely in time. But your sensory storage retains information just long enough for you to connect one image with the next in a smooth way so that the images look like continuous action.

7.5 Working Memory Lets You Actively Maintain Information in Short-Term Storage

7.5 LEARNING GOAL ACTIVITIES

To maximize your learning, complete the following learning goal activities.

a. Understand all bold and italic terms by writing explanations of them in your own words.

b. Understand the relationship between short-term storage and working memory by summarizing how using working memory to chunk information increases the duration and capacity of short-term storage.

What do you do when you need to remember a phone number, such as 463-5456, for a few seconds? If you are like most people, you probably repeat the numbers silently in your head until you can write them down or call them. Some people may remember the number temporarily by visualizing the numbers. Your ability to maintain the numbers by repeating or visualizing them for a time shows the important role of short-term storage in maintaining information.

Researchers initially saw **short-term storage** as simply a buffer or holding place. A small amount of information could be encoded. This coding was primarily based on auditory information but also based on visual information, and it was maintained for only a short time. According to this view, you could remember a phone number for a few seconds, but there was no mechanism to actively manipulate information in short-term storage. Newer research has revealed that short-term storage includes the important process of **working memory**. As the name implies, working memory lets you work on the information you have in short-term storage (Baddeley, 2002; Baddeley & Hitch, 1974). For example, this mechanism lets you repeat a phone number so that you can maintain more of the digits in short-term storage for a longer period of time.

To better understand the relationship between short-term storage and working memory, it helps to think about the duration and capacity of short-term storage (see Table 7.1, on p. 258). As the following two subsections explain, working memory can increase these qualities.

DURATION OF SHORT-TERM STORAGE   To investigate how long information is maintained in short-term storage, researchers gave participants a string of three meaningless letters to remember, such as X C J (Peterson & Peterson, 1959). Then participants had to count backward by threes from 100 for a period of time before being asked to recall the letters. As shown in **Figure 7.7**, if the participants did no backward counting, then they recalled about eight letter strings. However, after only six seconds of backward counting, participants recalled fewer than four letter strings. By 18 seconds of counting, most people could not recall any of the letter strings. So in the best case, people can remember about eight items

short-term storage
A memory storage system that briefly holds a limited amount of information in awareness.

working memory
An active processing system that allows manipulation of different types of information to keep it available for current use.

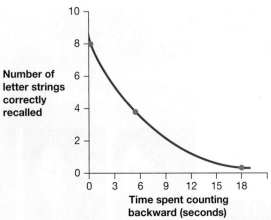

Number of letter strings correctly recalled

Time spent counting backward (seconds)

FIGURE 7.7

Duration and Capacity of Short-Term Storage

In an experiment that explored short-term storage, researchers found that about 8 items can be maintained for about 20 seconds when a person is prevented from using working memory processes.

TRY IT YOURSELF
Digit Span Task

1. Have a friend read the first row of numbers to you at the rate of one per second.

2. When the person is done reading, write down the numbers in the order you heard them.

3. Repeat the process with each row until you reach a row where you fail to recall the numbers in the correct order.

4. Whichever row your memory failed on, go to the row above it and count the number of digits that you were correctly able to recall in that row. This number is your short-term storage digit span. For example, if you made a mistake on the row 19223530, but recalled all the numbers in row 0401473, then your memory span is 7 items.

925
8642
37654
627418
0401473
19223530
486854332
2531971768
85129619450
918546942937

in short-term storage. In addition, short-term storage lasts up to 20 seconds when people don't use working memory processes to actively maintain the information they want to remember.

By contrast, if people are allowed to use working memory to manipulate the letters by repeating them over and over, then the information can be maintained for at least as long as the person continues to pay attention to repeating the letters. This research indicates that although short-term storage may be a "location" for maintaining memories, working memory allows manipulation of sounds, images, and ideas to keep information longer in short-term storage (Baddeley, 2002; Baddeley & Hitch, 1974).

CAPACITY OF SHORT-TERM STORAGE Completing the backward-counting task in the example just described makes it impossible to repeat the letters using working memory. This effect shows that without working memory, you can hold only a limited amount of information in short-term storage at a time. The cognitive psychologist George Miller noted that the capacity limit of short-term storage is generally seven items (plus or minus two), which is referred to as the *memory span* (Miller, 1956). Notice that this memory span is consistent with the research findings in Figure 7.7, where participants remembered eight letter strings. Even so, Miller's estimate may be too high, as some research suggests that short-term storage may be limited to as few as four items (Cowan, 2010). However, some individuals have a smaller or larger memory span. In addition, the capacity of short-term storage increases as children develop (Garon, Bryson, & Smith, 2008) and decreases with advanced aging (McCabe, Roediger, McDaniel, Balota, & Hambrick, 2010). Researchers continue to explore the capacity of short-term storage. You can do the activity in Try It Yourself to check your own memory span.

Because short-term storage is limited in capacity, you might expect people to have great difficulty remembering a string of letters such as NHTSACAFBIMSCIAILDEA. These 20 letters would tax even the largest memory span. But what if we organized the information into smaller, meaningful units? For instance, NH TSA CA FBI MS CIA IL DEA. Here the letters are shown grouped together to produce abbreviations for states and acronyms for U.S. federal government agencies. This process of using working memory to organize information into meaningful groups or units is known as **chunking**. The more efficiently you chunk information, the more you can remember.

Chunking makes information much easier to recall for two reasons. First, by using working memory, we can reduce the 20 items to be recalled into 7 chunks, and 7 items are within the capacity of our memory span. Second, meaningful units are easier to remember than nonsense units. Meaningful units are easier to remember because they draw on information that we already know. In short, chunking shows how working memory can increase the capacity of short-term storage, just as repetition can extend the duration of short-term storage.

Master chess players use this memory tool when they glance at a scenario on a chessboard, even for a few seconds, and later reproduce the exact arrangement of pieces (Chase & Simon, 1973). They instantly chunk the board into a number of meaningful units based on their prior experience with the game. If the pieces are arranged on the board in ways that make no sense in terms of chess, however, experts are no better than novices at reproducing the board. In general, the greater your expertise with the material, the more efficiently you can chunk information. As a result, you will be able to transfer more information into long-term storage, and you will be able to access and use that information later when you need it.

7.6 Long-Term Storage Lets You Maintain Memories Relatively Permanently

7.6 LEARNING GOAL ACTIVITIES

To maximize your learning, complete the following learning goal activities.

a. Understand all bold and italic terms by writing explanations of them in your own words.

b. Apply encoding processes in long-term storage to your life by providing a description of how you have used maintenance rehearsal and elaborative rehearsal to store two long-term memories.

Do you remember the phone number that was given at the beginning of the section on short-term storage? Unless you really paid attention and repeated the number, it's unlikely that you remember it. You might have maintained the information in short-term storage for a few seconds, but it was probably not processed into long-term storage.

When people talk about memory, they usually are referring to this relatively permanent type of memory. To envision **long-term storage,** try to imagine everything you know and everything you are likely to know in your lifetime. It is hard to imagine how much information that might be, because you can always learn more. Unlike the other two memory stores, long-term storage has nearly limitless capacity and duration (see Table 7.1, on p. 258). This type of storage enables you to remember nursery rhymes from childhood, the meanings and spellings of words you rarely use (such as "aardvark"), what you had for lunch yesterday, and so on.

However, given the billions of sensory experiences and thoughts you have each day, some type of filtering system must limit what goes into long-term storage. So what gets prioritized for encoding into long-term storage? Generally, information that helps you adapt to your environment is likely to be transformed into a memory held in long-term storage. According to evolutionary theory, memory lets you use information in ways that assist in reproduction and survival. For example, remembering which objects are edible, which people are friends and which ones are enemies, and how to get home are all critical for survival. The key is that this information, and anything you want to remember for a long time, must be deeply encoded into long-term storage for you to remember it.

DEEP ENCODING FOR LONG-TERM STORAGE Paying attention to information lets it be encoded into short-term storage. For information to be stored more permanently, attentional processing must be used to encode that information into long-term storage. According to the *levels of processing model,* the more deeply an item is processed during encoding, the more meaning it has and the better it is remembered (Craik & Lockhart, 1972).

Encoding can be achieved through two types of rehearsal. **Maintenance rehearsal,** simply repeating the item over and over, provides shallow encoding of information. This rehearsal is based on how the item sounds (auditory information). **Elaborative rehearsal** encodes the information more deeply. This rehearsal is based on

chunking
Using working memory to organize information into meaningful units to make it easier to remember.

long-term storage
A memory storage system that allows relatively permanent storage, probably of an unlimited amount of information.

maintenance rehearsal
Using working memory processes to repeat information based on how it sounds (auditory information); provides only shallow encoding of information and less successful long-term storage.

elaborative rehearsal
Using working memory processes to think about how new information relates to yourself or your prior knowledge (semantic information); provides deeper encoding of information for more successful long-term storage.

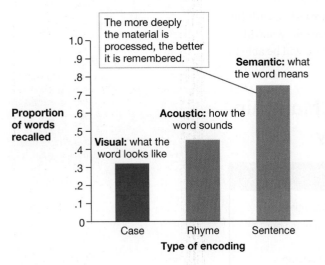

FIGURE 7.8

Deeper Encoding Aids Long-Term Storage

If participants are asked to remember a list of words based on how the words look (case), how they sound (rhyme), or what they mean (semantics), they usually have better recall after processing the meaning of the information. This result suggests that deeper encoding of semantic information aids long-term storage.

meaning (semantic information). In other words, information is encoded more deeply when it is meaningful to you, especially when it refers to you, and when you can link it to knowledge already in your long-term storage.

You have also experienced this effect yourself. Do you remember the phone number mentioned earlier? If you used maintenance rehearsal to repeat the phone number to yourself, you probably did not remember it. This failure to store the phone number in long-term storage shows how attention and memory function hand in hand: You attend just enough to complete the current task and lose information that seems irrelevant to you or insignificant. However, if you use elaborative rehearsal you might remember that phone number better. Suppose that the number, 463-5456, is the phone number of a potter, and the last four digits correspond to the letters KILN. A kiln is an oven used in pottery making. Your ability to remember the number is increased because you are encoding the information more richly based on semantic information. In fact, you may even use a combination of both visual and semantic encoding, called *dual coding*, which is a very successful method of transferring the information into long-term storage.

Research on the levels of processing model supports the idea that information that is deeply encoded is more memorable (Craik & Tulving, 1975). When participants are shown a list of words, they are then asked to do one of three things: (1) make simple visual judgments, such as whether each word is printed in capital or lowercase letters; (2) judge the sound of each word, such as whether the word rhymes with "boat"; or (3) decide whether a word's meaning fits into a sentence, such as "They had to cross the _____ to reach the castle." When participants complete the task, they must remember as many words as possible. The results show that words processed based on semantics are remembered the best (**Figure 7.8**). Brain imaging studies have shown that deep encoding based on semantics activates more brain regions than shallow encoding and that this greater brain activity is associated with better memory (Kapur et al., 1994). Together, these findings suggest that deeper encoding improves the likelihood of long-term storage, which then improves the likelihood of remembering.

LONG-TERM STORAGE VERSUS SHORT-TERM STORAGE By now it should be clear that long-term storage differs from short-term storage in several ways. Long-term storage lasts longer and has a far greater capacity, and it depends on deep encoding of information. But is long-term storage truly a different type of memory than short-term storage?

Some evidence that short-term storage and long-term storage are separate systems comes from research that required people to recall a long list of words. The ability to recall items from the list depended on the order of presentation. That is, people remembered items presented early or late in the list better than items in the middle of the list. The *primacy effect* refers to the better memory people have for items presented at the beginning of the list. The *recency effect* refers to the better memory people have for the most recent items, the ones at the end of the list (**Figure 7.9**).

One explanation for the primacy and recency effects relies on a distinction between short-term storage and long-term storage. When research participants study a long list of words, they rehearse the earliest items the most. As a result, that information is transferred into long-term storage. By contrast, the last few items

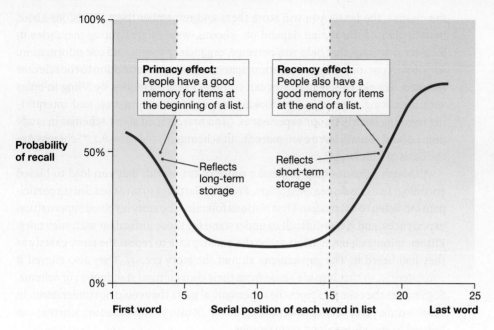

FIGURE 7.9
Primacy and Recency Effects
This graph illustrates the primacy effect: People have better memory for items at the beginning of a list because those items are in long-term storage. The graph also illustrates the recency effect: People have better recall for items at the end of a list because those items are still in short-term storage. These effects indicate that there is a difference between short-term storage and long-term storage.

are still in short-term storage when the participants have to recall the words immediately after reading them. This research suggests that primacy effects are due to retrieving information from long-term storage, whereas recency effects are due to retrieving information from short-term storage.

7.7 Your Long-Term Storage Is Organized Based on Meaning

7.7 LEARNING GOAL ACTIVITIES

To maximize your learning, complete the following learning goal activities.

a. Understand all bold and italic terms by writing explanations of them in your own words.

b. Understand how long-term storage is organized based on semantic meaning by describing an association network that you have about two related ideas.

In 2017, when Austin Rogers wrote down "What is sepia?" he became the fifth most-winning *Jeopardy!* champion of all time. How many of us would know that "sepia" is the answer to the *Jeopardy!* question "A Latin word for a sea creature; in photography this is a color that conveys nostalgia." How did Rogers store that piece of information so he could retrieve it later?

Imagine if a library put each of its books wherever there was empty space on a shelf. To find a particular book, a librarian would have to look through the entire inventory book by book. This type of random storage would not work well for libraries, and it would not work well for memories. When an event or some information is important enough, you want to be able to retrieve it later. So to make retrieval possible, long-term storage is based on the meaning of the information being stored.

SCHEMAS If you maintain memories in long-term storage according to their meaning, how do you determine the meanings of particular memories? Chunking is a good way to encode groups of items for long-term storage. The more meaningful the chunks, the better you will store them and remember them. Decisions about how to chunk information depend on *schemas,* ways of structuring memories in long-term storage that help you perceive, organize, process, and use information. As you sort out incoming information, schemas guide your attention to the relevant features. Thanks to schemas, you can construct new memories by filling in holes within existing memories, overlooking inconsistent information and interpreting meaning based on your experiences. (You first learned about schemas in study unit 4.6, and you will learn even more about schemas in study unit 8.2, "Schemas Are the Basis of Thinking.")

Although schemas help you make sense of the world, they can lead to biased encoding. In a classic demonstration, Frederic Bartlett (1932) asked British participants to listen to a Canadian First Nations folktale. The story involved supernatural experiences, and it was difficult to understand for those unfamiliar with such tales. Fifteen minutes later, Bartlett asked the participants to repeat the story exactly as they had heard it. The participants altered the story greatly. They also altered it consistently, so that it made sense from their own cultural standpoint, or schema. Sometimes they simply forgot the supernatural parts they could not understand. In other words, pieces of information that do not fit into your preexisting schemas can be hard to encode into long-term storage.

In addition, schemas also affect your ability to retrieve information from long-term storage. Read the following paragraph carefully:

> The procedure is actually quite simple. First arrange things into different bundles depending on makeup. Don't do too much at once. In the short run this may not seem important, however, complications easily arise. A mistake can be costly. Next, find facilities. Some people must go elsewhere for them. Manipulation of appropriate mechanisms should be self-explanatory. Remember to include all other necessary supplies. Initially the routine will overwhelm you, but soon it will become just another facet of life. Finally, rearrange everything into their initial groups. Return these to their usual places. Eventually they will be used again. Then the whole cycle will have to be repeated. (Bransford & Johnson, 1972, p. 722)

Now, can you say what this paragraph was specifically about? You probably cannot say exactly. If you can't say what it was about, do you think you will remember it well or be able to answer questions about it? What if you know that the paragraph is describing washing clothes? Go back and reread the paragraph with that information in mind. Notice how your schema for doing laundry can help you understand and remember how the words and sentences are connected to one another. In a research setting, college students who read this paragraph knowing that it was about washing clothes found it easy to understand and relatively straightforward to recall. In short, having a schema about information can help you remember it later on.

ASSOCIATION NETWORKS Another way that the meaning of information is organized in long-term storage is based on *networks of associations.* In a network model proposed by Allan Collins and Elizabeth Loftus (1975), an item's distinctive features are linked in a way that identifies the item. Each unit of information in the network is a node. Each node is connected to many other nodes. The resulting network is like the linked neurons in your brain, but the nodes are simply bits of information, not physical objects (**Figure 7.10**). For example, when you look at a fire engine, all the nodes that represent a fire engine's features, such as the color red, are activated. The resulting activation pattern across nodes gives rise to the knowledge that the object is a fire engine rather than, say, a car, a vacuum cleaner, or a cat.

An important feature of network models is that activating one node increases the likelihood that closely associated nodes in the same category will also be activated. As shown in Figure 7.10, the closer the nodes, the stronger the association between them and therefore the more likely it is that activating one node will activate the other. Seeing a fire engine activates linked nodes, so you will quickly recognize other vehicles, such as an ambulance. In fact, you will recognize vehicles more quickly than you will recognize items in other categories, such as an apple, which is a fruit.

The main idea here is that activating one node increases the likelihood that closely linked nodes will become active. This idea is central to *spreading activation models* of memory. According to these models, information that is heard or seen activates specific nodes for memories in long-term storage. This activation increases the ease of access of stored information to linked material. Easier access of stored information means easier retrieval.

Think about the huge amount of material in your memory. It is amazing how quickly you can search through that long-term storage and obtain the memories you need. Each time you hear a sentence, you have to remember what all the words mean. You also have to recall all the relevant information that helps you understand the sentence's overall meaning. For this process to occur, the information needs to be organized logically. Imagine trying to find a specific file on a full 600-gigabyte hard disk by opening one file at a time. Searching that way would be hopelessly slow. Instead, most computer disks are organized into folders, within each folder are more-specialized folders, and so on. Associative networks in the brain work similarly. The network is organized by category. Because the categories are structured in a hierarchy, they provide a clear and explicit blueprint for where to find needed information quickly.

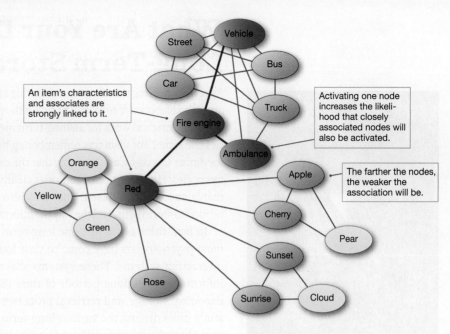

An item's characteristics and associates are strongly linked to it.

Activating one node increases the likelihood that closely associated nodes will also be activated.

The farther the nodes, the weaker the association will be.

FIGURE 7.10

A Network of Associations

Memories are organized in long-term storage based on the meaning of information. Concepts are connected through their associations. The closer the concepts are to each other, the stronger the association between them. Activation of a concept (fire engine) spreads to close associates and activates them (dark lines). But far associates become only weakly activated (lighter lines).

 ## How Do You Maintain Memories over Time?

To make sure you learned what you just read, write answers to the following questions and check your answers.

7.3 In the three memory stores model, what is the name of the first memory store that information can pass into?

7.4 What is the function of sensory memory?

7.5 What active processes can be used in short-term storage to keep information available for current use?

7.6 If you want to retain information in long-term storage, which type of rehearsal should you use?

7.7 What is the main idea behind spreading activation models of memory?

See Appendix B for answers to the red Q questions.

What Are Your Different Long-Term Storage Systems?

As you are reading this chapter and writing answers to the Learning Goal Activities, you are using elaborative rehearsal to retain the information in long-term storage. But does this same method work for all long-term memories? Are all kinds of long-term memories the same? For instance, remembering how to ride a bicycle, recalling what you ate for dinner last night, and knowing that the capital of Canada is Ottawa are all long-term memories. However, these memories clearly differ in terms of the type of information that is encoded and stored. They may also differ in how much deliberate effort was needed to store them. And the way the information is accessed later on can differ as well.

In fact, there is not just one long-term memory store. In the past few decades, most psychologists have come to view long-term memory as composed of several interacting systems. These systems share a common function: to retain and use information over long periods of time (Schacter & Tulving, 1994). However, the encoding, storage, and retrieval processes may function differently. The following study units discuss the various long-term storage systems so that you can understand how they work together to let you remember everything from your first-grade teacher to the main ideas in this chapter.

7.8 Amnesia Reveals Different Long-Term Stores

7.8 LEARNING GOAL ACTIVITIES

To maximize your learning, complete the following learning goal activities.

a. Understand all bold and italic terms by writing explanations of them in your own words.

b. Understand the two types of amnesia by naming and explaining each one in your own words.

How do psychology researchers study memory? Sometimes they work with participants who process memories in atypical ways. Henry Molaison was one of the most famous participants in memory research (**Figure 7.11**). Molaison was born in 1926 and died in 2008. However, in vital ways, his world stopped in 1953, when he was 27 years old. As a young man, Molaison suffered from severe epilepsy, which caused seizures that made it impossible for him to lead a normal life. Molaison's seizures originated in the temporal lobes of his brain and spread from there to other parts of the brain. Because the medications available at that time could not control his seizures, surgery was the only choice for treatment. The reasoning behind this surgery was that if the seizure-causing portions of his brain were removed, he would stop having seizures.

So in September 1953, Molaison's doctors removed parts of his medial temporal lobes, the area in the middle of the temporal lobes, including the hippocampus (**Figure 7.12**). The surgery quieted Molaison's seizures, but it had an unexpected and very unfortunate side effect: He lost the ability to store most types of new information in long-term storage. This condition, called amnesia, includes two basic types.

FIGURE 7.11

Henry Molaison (H.M.)

Known to the world only by his initials, Molaison became one of the most famous people in memory research by participating in countless experiments. He died at a nursing home on December 2, 2008.

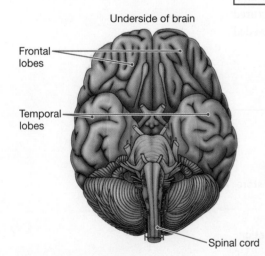

Underside of brain

Frontal lobes

Temporal lobes

Spinal cord

FIGURE 7.12

Surgery on H.M.'s Brain

The blue regions are the parts of the medial temporal lobes that were removed from H.M.'s brain.

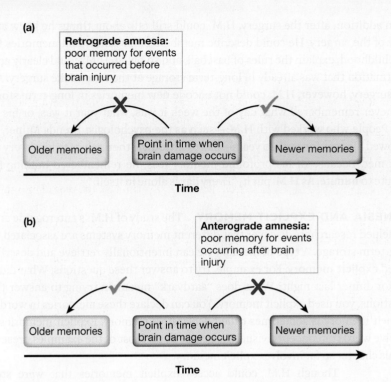

(a)

Retrograde amnesia: poor memory for events that occurred before brain injury

| Older memories | Point in time when brain damage occurs | Newer memories |

Time

(b)

Anterograde amnesia: poor memory for events occurring after brain injury

| Older memories | Point in time when brain damage occurs | Newer memories |

Time

FIGURE 7.13

Retrograde and Anterograde Amnesia

Amnesia involves two forms of memory loss. **(a)** Retrograde amnesia is an inability to access memories that were created before the brain damage (see red X). **(b)** Anterograde amnesia is an inability to create new memories after the brain damage (see red X).

TWO TYPES OF AMNESIA In **retrograde amnesia,** people lose memories for past events, facts, people, and even personal information (**Figure 7.13a**). By contrast, in **anterograde amnesia,** people lose the ability to form new memories (**Figure 7.13b**). After his surgery, Molaison experienced anterograde amnesia. Until his death, the larger world did not know Molaison's real name or what he looked like. His privacy was guarded by the researchers who studied how anterograde amnesia affected his memory abilities. But the knowledge provided by this research with Molaison (known as H.M.) is the basis for what we know about the types of memories in long-term storage. In the following study units, you will learn more about these long-term memory stores.

retrograde amnesia
A condition in which people lose the ability to access memories they had before a brain injury.

anterograde amnesia
A condition in which people lose the ability to form new memories after experiencing a brain injury.

7.9 Your Explicit Memories Involve Conscious Effort

7.9 LEARNING GOAL ACTIVITIES

To maximize your learning, complete the following learning goal activities.

a. Understand all bold and italic terms by writing explanations of them in your own words.

b. Apply explicit memory to your life by providing an example of an episodic memory and a semantic memory you have, and explain whether you would recall them if you developed retrograde amnesia today.

According to the psychologists who tested H.M., his IQ was slightly above average. His thinking abilities remained intact after his surgery. He could hold a normal conversation as long as he was not distracted, though he forgot the conversation in a minute or less. H.M.'s ability to hold a conversation showed that he was still able to remember things for short periods. After all, to grasp the meaning of spoken language, a person needs to remember the words recently spoken, such as the beginning and end of a sentence. So his short-term storage was intact.

In addition, after the surgery, H.M. could still talk about things he knew at the time of the surgery. He could describe members of his family and memories from his childhood, explain the rules of baseball, and so on. So H.M. could clearly access information that was already in long-term storage at the time of the surgery. After the surgery, however, H.M. could not encode new memories in long-term storage. He never remembered what day of the week it was, what year it was, or his own age. People who worked with H.M.—such as the psychologist Brenda Milner, who followed his case for over 40 years—had to introduce themselves to him every time they met. Because of his profound memory loss, he remembered nothing from minute to minute. As H.M. put it, "Every day is alone in itself."

AMNESIA AND EXPLICIT MEMORY The study of H.M.'s anterograde amnesia helped researchers discover that different memory systems are associated with long-term storage. A type of memory we can intentionally retrieve and describe is called **explicit memory**. For example, try to answer these questions: What did you eat for dinner last night? What does "aardvark" mean? In trying to answer these questions, you used explicit memory. You can declare these memories in words, so explicit memory is sometimes called declarative memory. Explicit memories can involve words or concepts, visual images, or both. Most of the examples presented in this chapter so far involve explicit memory.

Though H.M. could access explicit memories that were stored before his surgery, he could not store any new explicit memories after the surgery. The fact that his anterograde amnesia affected this ability suggests that regions in the medial temporal lobes that were removed during the surgery are critical for forming new explicit memories. Further research has shown that there are actually two main types of explicit memories: episodic and semantic.

EPISODIC AND SEMANTIC MEMORY In 1972, Endel Tulving observed that people have two types of explicit memory: episodic memory and semantic memory. **Episodic memory** refers to our personal experiences and includes information about the time and place each experience occurred (**Figure 7.14a**). Memories of where you were and what you did on your sixteenth birthday, for example, are part of your episodic memory. **Semantic memory** is our knowledge of facts independent of personal experience. We might not remember where or when we learned a fact, but we know it (**Figure 7.14b**). For instance, most people know what Jell-O is. They know the capitals of places they have never visited. Even people who have never played baseball know that three strikes mean the batter is out.

Scientists have learned a great deal about memory by studying people like H.M. and others who have impaired memory. Evidence that episodic and semantic systems of explicit memory are separate can be found in cases of brain injury in which a person's semantic memory is intact even though episodic memory is impaired. Researchers found this pattern in three British people who had experienced brain damage as children (Vargha-Khadem et al., 1997). Each of the three developed poor memory for episodic information. As children, they had trouble reporting what they had for lunch, what they had watched on television 5 minutes earlier, or what they did during summer vacation. Their parents reported that the children had to be constantly monitored to make sure they remembered things as basic as going to school. Remarkably, these three children attended mainstream schools and did reasonably well. Moreover, when tested as young adults,

FIGURE 7.14

Two Types of Explicit Memory

(a) One type of explicit memory is episodic memory. Episodic memory enables people to recall and describe their prior experiences, as these veterans are doing. **(b)** Another type of explicit memory is semantic memory, a person's knowledge of facts. Game shows such as trivia contests test semantic memory.

their IQs fell within the normal range. They learned to speak and read, and they could remember many facts. For instance, one of the three, at age 19, was asked, "Who is Martin Luther King Jr.?" The person answered, "An American; fought for Black rights, Black rights leader in the 1970s; got assassinated." In other words, despite their brain damage, these people were able to encode and retrieve semantic memories from long-term storage. But they could not remember their own personal experiences.

7.10 Your Implicit Memories Function Without Conscious Effort

7.10 LEARNING GOAL ACTIVITIES

To maximize your learning, complete the following learning goal activities.

a. Understand all bold and italic terms by writing explanations of them in your own words.

b. Understand implicit memory by describing it in your own words and explaining whether a person with anterograde amnesia could or could not learn a new motor task, such as riding a bicycle.

As you learned in study units 7.8–7.9, after his surgery H.M. could not form new explicit memories. However, H.M.'s memory abilities revealed the existence of a second form of memory: implicit memory.

H.M. was able to learn some new things after his surgery, such as motor tasks. But he could not state that he had learned these things. In one series of tests, he was asked to trace the outline of a star while watching his hand in a mirror (**Figure 7.15**). Most people do poorly the first few times they try this difficult task. On each of three consecutive days, H.M. was asked to trace the star 10 times. His performance improved over the three days. This finding indicated that he had retained some information about the task. Given his deficits in explicit memory, H.M. could not recall ever performing the task. Nevertheless, his ability to learn new motor skills let him work at a factory, where he mounted cigarette lighters on cardboard cases.

IMPLICIT MEMORY AND AMNESIA   Although H.M. could not form explicit memories after his surgery, he was able to retain implicit memories in long-term storage. **Implicit memory** refers to memories that you are not conscious of. Because you cannot declare implicit memories in words, this system is sometimes called nondeclarative memory. Implicit memory influences your life in subtle ways. For example, advertisers rely on implicit memory to influence your purchasing decisions. Constant exposure to brand names makes you more likely to think of them when you buy products. If you find yourself wanting a particular brand, you might be unconsciously remembering advertisements for that brand, even if you cannot recall the specifics.

H.M.'s ability to form new implicit memories after the surgery suggests that parts of the medial temporal lobe that were removed are not necessary for storing these types of memories. This idea further suggests that implicit memory is a second unique long-term storage system. Furthermore, there are two main types of implicit memory: classical conditioning and procedural memory.

FIGURE 7.15

H.M.'s Performance in Mirror Drawing

When H.M. got better at mirror drawing over time, he showed that he could form new implicit memories (procedural) after his surgery. When he could not remember doing the mirror drawing task, H.M. showed that he could not form new explicit memories (episodic) after his surgery. These findings are evidence for the existence of multiple memory systems in long-term storage.

implicit memory
The system for long-term storage of unconscious memories that cannot be verbally described.

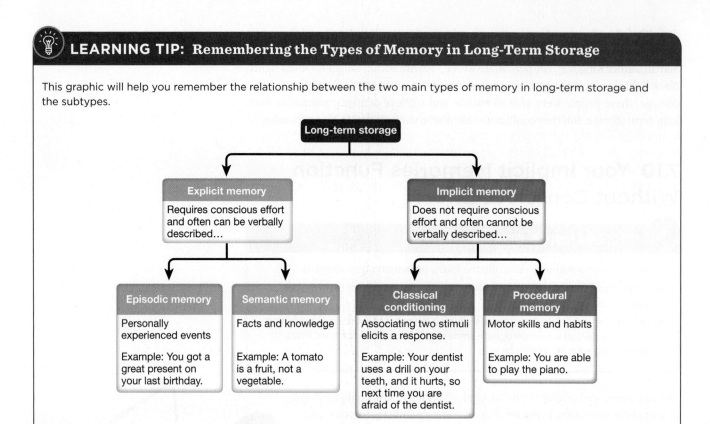

LEARNING TIP: Remembering the Types of Memory in Long-Term Storage

This graphic will help you remember the relationship between the two main types of memory in long-term storage and the subtypes.

Long-term storage

Explicit memory
Requires conscious effort and often can be verbally described…

Implicit memory
Does not require conscious effort and often cannot be verbally described…

Episodic memory
Personally experienced events

Example: You got a great present on your last birthday.

Semantic memory
Facts and knowledge

Example: A tomato is a fruit, not a vegetable.

Classical conditioning
Associating two stimuli elicits a response.

Example: Your dentist uses a drill on your teeth, and it hurts, so next time you are afraid of the dentist.

Procedural memory
Motor skills and habits

Example: You are able to play the piano.

FIGURE 7.16

Two Types of Implicit Memory

(a) One type of implicit memory is classical conditioning. For example, you may learn to associate a stimulus, such as a spider, with a certain response, such as fear. **(b)** A second type of implicit memory is procedural memory, or motor memory. One example is the muscle coordination that lets you ride a bicycle.

procedural memory
A type of implicit memory that involves motor skills and behavioral habits.

CLASSICAL CONDITIONING AND PROCEDURAL MEMORY Implicit memories do not require conscious attention. They are formed automatically, without deliberate effort. There are two main types of implicit memory. Classical conditioning, which you learned about in study units 6.4–6.7, employs implicit memory (**Figure 7.16a**). For example, if you always experience fear at the sight of a person in a white lab coat, you might have past associations between a person in a white lab coat and pain. This memory is implicit.

Now suppose you are driving. Suddenly, you realize you have been daydreaming and have no episodic memory of the past few minutes. During that time, you employed implicit memories of how to drive and where you were going. Because you drew on that information, you did not crash the car or go in the wrong direction. This type of implicit memory is called **procedural memory** (**Figure 7.16b**). Also called motor memory, it involves motor skills, habits, and other behaviors employed to achieve goals. For example, this type of memory lets you coordinate muscle movements to ride a bicycle, to play the piano, or to follow the rules of the road while driving.

Procedural memories are generally so unconscious that most people find that consciously thinking about automatic behaviors interferes with the smooth production of those behaviors. The next time you are riding a bicycle, try to think about each step involved in the process. How does that conscious effort affect the action?

Procedural memories tend to last a long time. Once you learn to ride a bike, you most likely will always be able to ride one. It would take brain damage to a specific region of the hindbrain for you to lose that skill.

The two main types of long-term memory stores, along with their subtypes, are shown in the Learning Tip. As we know from the research H.M. participated in, brain damage to the hippocampus can affect explicit memories that you purposely retrieve and describe (see the orange boxes in the Learning Tip on p. 272). However, brain damage to the hippocampus may not affect implicit memories that you display through behavior, such as mirror drawing and how to ride a bike (see the blue boxes in the Learning Tip). You will learn more about the brain regions associated with different types of memories in study unit 7.12.

7.11 Prospective Memory Lets You Remember to Do Something

7.11 LEARNING GOAL ACTIVITIES

To maximize your learning, complete the following learning goal activities.

a. Understand all bold and italic terms by writing explanations of them in your own words.

b. Apply prospective memory to your life by explaining one method you use to successfully remember information for the future.

"When you see Juan, remind him that we're watching *Stranger Things* tonight at 8. And don't forget to bring the popcorn!" Unlike the other types of memory we have discussed so far, **prospective memory** is future oriented and helps you remember to do something at some future time (Graf & Uttl, 2001).

Prospective memory comes with a cost. Recall that the cognitive effort involved in paying attention to certain information makes us unable to attend closely to other information. In the same way, remembering to do something takes up valuable cognitive resources. This type of memory reduces either the number of items we can deal with in short-term storage or the number of things we can attend to and process in working memory (Einstein & McDaniel, 2005).

In a study of prospective memory, participants had to learn a list of words (Cook, Marsh, Clark-Foos, & Meeks, 2007). In one condition, the participants also had to remember to do something. For example, they had to press a key when they saw a certain word. That group—the participants who had to remember to do something—took longer to learn the list than the control group that learned the same list of words but did not have to remember to do something.

Cues can help prospective memory. For example, seeing Juan might automatically trigger your memory. You would then effortlessly remember to give Juan the message. But particular environments do not always have obvious cues for certain prospective memories. So you might not encounter a cue for remembering to bring the popcorn. Prospective memory for events without cues is the reason sticky notes are so popular (**Figure 7.17a**). In this case, you might stick a note that says "Bring popcorn" on the steering wheel of your car. By jogging your memory, the note saves you the effort of remembering. For an even more urgent reminder, you might set your cell phone alarm or use an electronic calendar (**Figure 7.17b**) For tips on improving your prospective memory for doing homework, see Try It Yourself on p. 274.

prospective memory
Remembering to do something at some future time.

(a)

(b)

FIGURE 7.17
Prospective Memory
People use several tools to help with prospective memory. **(a)** You might use sticky notes to remind you to do things. **(b)** You might use a device, such as a smartphone, to remember appointments and deadlines.

TRY IT YOURSELF: Improving Your Prospective Memory for Doing Homework

Have you ever forgotten to do a homework assignment? You can improve your prospective memory by using a calendar to plan what days and times to do your homework for each class. The particular tool you use could be a printed journal, an electronic calendar, or a scheduling app. For each day of the week, include entries for your classes, scheduled homework time, your job if you have one, and personal activities, such as exercise and family time. A three-credit-hour class usually requires about six hours per week of homework, so schedule those hours and spread them across at least three days in the week. Lastly, set alarms on your cell phone a little before you are supposed to start each study session to help you remember to get started!

7.12 Memory Is Processed by Several Regions of Your Brain

7.12 LEARNING GOAL ACTIVITIES

To maximize your learning, complete the following learning goal activities.

a. Understand all bold and italic terms by writing explanations of them in your own words.

b. Understand how the brain processes memories by summarizing in your own words the brain areas that contribute to explicit memory and implicit memory.

Over the past twenty years, memory researchers have made tremendous progress in understanding what happens in the brain when we encode, store, and retrieve memories. The research on people with memory disorders clearly reveals that there are separate long-term storage systems. Moreover, distinct brain regions are involved in processing information related to different long-term stores.

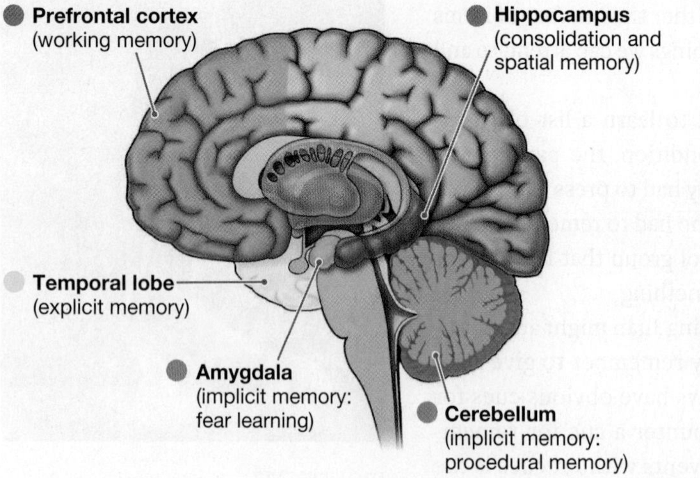

MEMORY'S PHYSICAL LOCATIONS Not all brain areas are equally involved in memory. A great deal of specialization occurs. In fact, different brain regions are responsible for storing different aspects of information (**Figure 7.18**).

Recall that H.M.'s anterograde amnesia left him unable to create new explicit memories. However, he remained able to create new implicit memories. H.M.'s surgery removed regions within the temporal lobes, such as the hippocampus. Clearly, this area is important for the ability to form new explicit memories. However, the temporal lobes are less important for implicit memories, such as classical conditioning and procedural memory.

By contrast, the cerebellum plays a role in implicit memory. It is especially involved in procedural memory for learning motor actions. The amygdala is especially important for another type of implicit memory. Recall that in classical conditioning, an animal may unconsciously learn to be afraid of something. But an animal without an amygdala cannot learn to fear objects that signal danger.

- **Prefrontal cortex** (working memory)
- **Hippocampus** (consolidation and spatial memory)
- **Temporal lobe** (explicit memory)
- **Amygdala** (implicit memory: fear learning)
- **Cerebellum** (implicit memory: procedural memory)

FIGURE 7.18

Brain Regions Associated with Memory

There are several different memory systems for long-term storage. Specific brain regions process information for each long-term store.

The take-home message here is that memory does not "live" in one part of the brain. Memory is distributed among different brain regions. So if you lose one particular brain cell, you will not lose a memory. To consider "brain training" products that claim to improve memory, see Evaluating Psychology in the Real World on p. 276.

CONSOLIDATION OF MEMORIES   Your brain is different than it was before you began reading this chapter. Reading the chapter is making some of your neural connections stronger and creating new neural connections—especially in your hippocampus (Miller, 2005). This process is known as **consolidation**. Through consolidation, your experiences become your lasting memories.

The medial temporal lobes are responsible for coordinating and strengthening the connections among neurons when we learn something. This region, including the hippocampus, is particularly important for the formation of new memories. The actual storage of memories, however, occurs in the particular brain regions engaged during the perception, processing, and analysis of the material being learned. For instance, visual information is stored in the cortical areas involved in visual perception. Sound is stored in the areas involved in auditory perception. Now think about memories of those sensory experiences. Remembering something we have seen or heard involves reactivating the same cortical circuits that were involved when we first saw or heard the information (**Figure 7.19**). It is almost as if the brain is reexperiencing what we saw or heard. This reexperience occurs even though the original stimulus is no longer in front of us.

The medial temporal lobes are important for coordinating the storage of information between the different cortical sites and also are involved in strengthening the connections between these sites (Squire, Stark, & Clark, 2004). Think about what Google does for the Internet. Google doesn't store all the information on the Internet, but it provides links to where that information is stored. That's what the medial temporal lobes do for memories. Once the connections between different brain sites are strengthened sufficiently, the medial temporal lobes become less important for memory. H.M.'s surgery removed parts of his medial temporal lobes. Without those

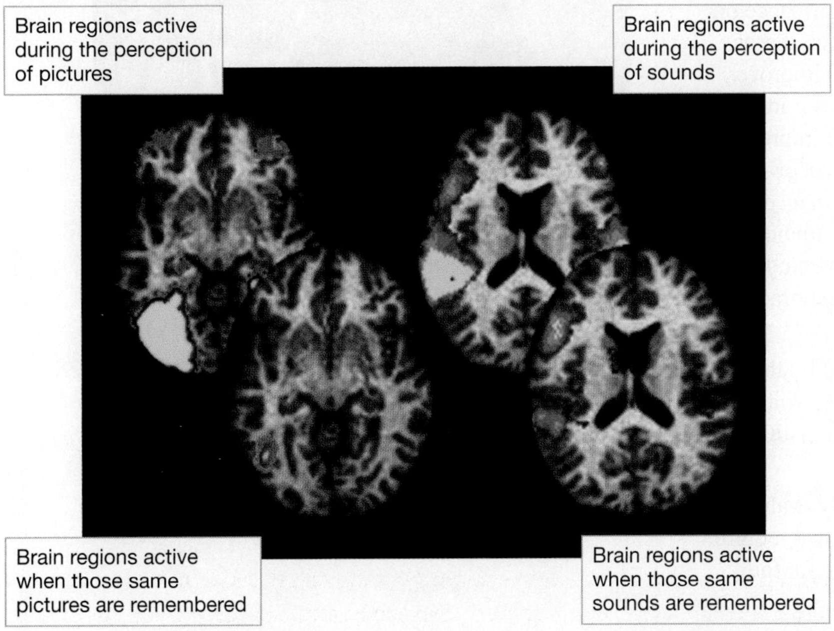

consolidation
A process where immediate memories become lasting memories when new neural connections are created and prior neural connections get stronger.

Brain regions active during the perception of pictures

Brain regions active during the perception of sounds

Brain regions active when those same pictures are remembered

Brain regions active when those same sounds are remembered

FIGURE 7.19

Brain Activation During Perception and Remembering

These four horizontally sliced brain images were created using magnetic resonance imaging. In each pair, the top image shows the brain activity for sensory-specific perception. The bottom image shows the regions of the sensory cortex that are activated when that sensory-specific information is remembered. Notice that the perceptions and the memories both activate similar cortical areas.

The promoters of brain training programs claim that their products can improve your performance on everyday tasks. You might be excited about an opportunity to boost your attention and memory—even if it did cost you $15 per month. But do brain training tools actually do what they claim? A quick Internet search reveals many articles investigating the claims of companies offering brain training. One such article is by the psychologist Daniel J. Simons and colleagues (2016). The Association for Psychological Science reviews this article at https://www.psychologicalscience.org/publications/brain-training.html, and that review is excerpted below.

Based on this review, should you accept the claim being made here? To answer this question, use the three steps in critical thinking:

ACTIVITY: To determine if you should accept the claim in this article, review the Learning Tip on p. 7 and follow these steps:

Step 1 What is the claim I am being asked to accept?

Step 2 What evidence, if any, is provided to support the claim?

Step 3 Given the evidence, what are the most reasonable conclusions about the claim?

If you have rejected the claim or found the evidence lacking, why did you do so? If you have found that the evidence supports the claim, how might this information change how you think and act?

Do "Brain-Training" Programs Work?

The brain-training industry is a multibillion-dollar enterprise that has risen based on the promise that playing simple cognitive games can improve a wide variety of cognitive skills used in daily life. In the current issue of *Psychological Science in the Public Interest* (Volume 17, Number 3), psychological scientist Daniel J. Simons and colleagues review research that calls into question these claims. . . .

Their review of the literature found that brain-training tasks seem to improve performance on the trained tasks themselves; however, there is less evidence that cognitive training improves performance on closely related–but not identical–tasks, and very little evidence that it improves performance on distantly related tasks or improves everyday cognitive performance. In reviewing the literature, the authors found that many of the studies suffered from methodological problems and did not conform to best practices for research. . . .

Many of those who are most enticed by the claims of brain-training companies are those who are the most vulnerable: children and adults with cognitive deficits. . . .

Policymakers need to more critically evaluate the claims of brain-training companies and require more rigorous standards of evidence for the benefits of these programs. . . .

The public needs to be skeptical of brain-training programs and consider the quality of the science behind companies' claims. . . .

Unfortunately for the many people interested in popular traditional brain-training programs, this review shows that these programs generally fall short of their advertised effectiveness and that people may profit more from adopting better-supported alternatives for improving cognitive performance.

parts, he could not make new memories (at least ones he could talk about). He still was able to retrieve old memories.

To understand the basic consolidation process, consider this example. While reading this chapter, you have come to understand that "medial" means "in the middle." Now that you have gained this information, you need to think about it over time so that it will be consolidated in your memory. A good night's sleep might also help this process. As you learned in study unit 3.7, there is compelling evidence that sleep helps with the consolidation of memories and that disturbing sleep interferes with learning.

RECONSOLIDATION OF MEMORIES   All of us have probably wished we could forget some things that are particularly embarrassing or painful. Could we actually do that?

A theory developed by Karim Nader and Joseph LeDoux proposes that once memories are activated, they need to be consolidated again for long-term storage (Alberini & LeDoux, 2013; Nader & Einarsson, 2010). This process is known as *reconsolidation* (**Figure 7.20**). When memories for past events are retrieved, those memories can be affected by new circumstances, so reconsolidated memories may differ from their original versions (Nader, Schafe, & LeDoux, 2000). In other words, our memories begin as versions of what we have experienced, but they might change when we use them.

To understand how reconsolidation works, think of a student working with a textbook. After each study session, the student returns the book to its place on a bookshelf for later reference. While working, the student turns down the edges of pages used most frequently. When the student retrieves the book later, it might naturally open to those pages. What if some pages become damaged to the point of falling out? If the student looks for those pages later, they won't be available. The idea here is that the book placed back on the shelf is now different from the one the student started with. The dog-eared pages make some information easier to access, and the damaged pages make other information impossible to access. Reconsolidation actually changes your memories every time you access them.

According to this theory, reconsolidation occurs each time a memory is activated and placed back in storage. This process may explain why your memories for events can change over time. Think about another intriguing possibility: Could bad memories be erased by activating them and then interfering with reconsolidation of them (Kroes, Schiller, LeDoux, & Phelps, 2016)? More research is needed to know whether reconsolidation is a viable method for erasing or modifying bad memories (Treanor, Brown, Rissman, & Craske, 2017).

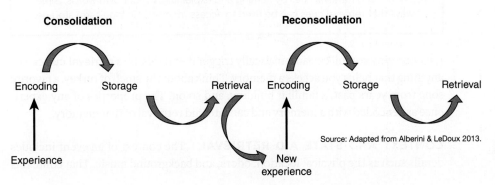

Source: Adapted from Alberini & LeDoux 2013.

FIGURE 7.20
Reconsolidation
Reconsolidation is the idea that memories can change each time they are retrieved. Each memory is of the previous retrieval, not the original experience, because new information becomes paired with the retrieved memory to create a new, reconsolidated memory.

Q What Are Your Different Long-Term Storage Systems?

To make sure you learned what you just read, write answers to the following questions and check your answers.

7.8 If you have a car crash and can't remember anything from the week before the crash, what form of amnesia are you experiencing?

7.9 When you recall your last vacation, are you retrieving an implicit memory or an explicit memory?

7.10 Practicing a dance routine requires what type of implicit memory?

7.11 What type of memory lets you remember to do something in the future?

7.12 What is the main difference between consolidation of a memory and reconsolidation?

See Appendix B for answers to the red Q questions.

How Do You Retrieve Memories?

Austin Rogers and other *Jeopardy!* champions are able to store large amounts of information in their brains by using various processing techniques. But when it comes time to compete, how do they actually remember the information? How do they get the information out of storage?

Up to this point, you have learned primarily about two phases of information processing. In the first phase, memories are created through encoding. In the second phase, memories are stored in one of three systems. The third phase of processing information is to access the stored memories at a later date to use that information in some way. Four processes affect the ability to access stored memories, as shown in the Learning Tip on p. 279.

7.13 Retrieval Cues Help You Access Your Memories

7.13 LEARNING GOAL ACTIVITIES

To maximize your learning, complete the following learning goal activities.

a. Understand all bold and italic terms by writing explanations of them in your own words.

b. Understand retrieval cues by naming and explaining, in your own words, three ways that retrieval cues can be used to access memories in long-term storage.

Encountering stimuli can automatically trigger memories. So a **retrieval cue** can be anything that helps you access a memory. Think about the smell of turkey, a favorite song from years past, a familiar building, and so on. The properties of any experience are encoded with a memory and can later aid retrieval of that memory.

CONTEXT AND STATE AID RETRIEVAL The context of an event includes details such as the physical location, odors, and background music. That context is

retrieval cue
Anything that helps a person access information in long-term storage.

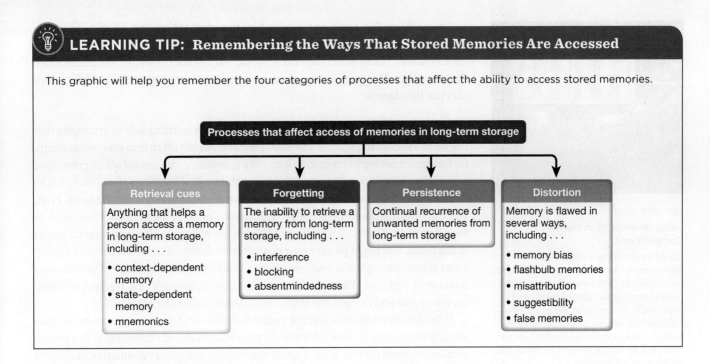

This graphic will help you remember the four categories of processes that affect the ability to access stored memories.

Processes that affect access of memories in long-term storage

Retrieval cues	Forgetting	Persistence	Distortion
Anything that helps a person access a memory in long-term storage, including . . . • context-dependent memory • state-dependent memory • mnemonics	The inability to retrieve a memory from long-term storage, including . . . • interference • blocking • absentmindedness	Continual recurrence of unwanted memories from long-term storage	Memory is flawed in several ways, including . . . • memory bias • flashbulb memories • misattribution • suggestibility • false memories

encoded along with the memory. As a result, the context produces a sense of familiarity that helps us retrieve the memory (Hockley, 2008).

In a dramatic research demonstration of this *context-dependent memory* effect, two groups of scuba divers learned lists of words. Some divers learned the words on land. Other divers learned the words underwater (Godden & Baddeley, 1975; **Figure 7.21a**). Later, both groups recalled the words better when they were in the same environment where they had learned them (**Figure 7.21b**). That is, when divers learned information on land, they recalled that information better on land than underwater. When divers learned the words underwater, they recalled them better underwater than on land. This study confirms that when the person is in the same context where information was learned, the environment where learning took place provides a cue that aids access to the information.

Like physical context, internal cues—such as mood and physiological states— are also encoded with a memory. When our internal states are the same during both encoding and retrieval, the situation can provide a retrieval cue that enhances access to a memory. This effect is known as *state-dependent memory*.

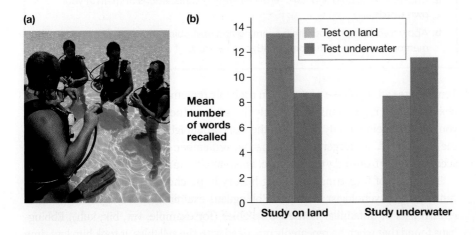

(a)

(b)

Mean number of words recalled

Test on land
Test underwater

Study on land   Study underwater

FIGURE 7.21

Context-Dependent Memory

A unique study showed that the context of a memory can help retrieve that memory. **(a)** People learned lists of words either on land or underwater. **(b)** Later, they remembered more words if they were tested in the same environment where they had learned the words.

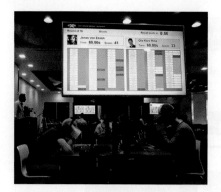

FIGURE 7.22
Using Mnemonics in Memory Competitions
Contestants in the Extreme Memory Tournament—as shown here at the 2015 meet, held at Dart NeuroScience in San Diego—memorize names, faces, and even decks of cards. To aid retrieval of information, almost all participants in such memory contests use elaborative rehearsal to create mnemonics that aid retrieval of information.

Research on this topic was inspired by the observation that people experiencing alcoholism often can't find important objects, such as paychecks. They store the objects in safe places while they are drinking, but cannot remember the places when they are sober. The next time they are drinking, however, they may remember where they put the objects.

MNEMONICS AID RETRIEVAL   *Mnemonics* are learning aids or strategies that use retrieval cues to improve access to memory. People often find mnemonics helpful for remembering items in long lists. One mnemonic, the *method of loci*, consists of associating items you want to remember with physical locations you already know. Suppose you want to remember a grocery list of items to buy from the store. First, you might visualize parts of the physical layout of some familiar location, such as your bedroom. Then you would associate the list of items to buy with certain places in the room. You might picture your open dresser drawer filled to the top with apples, a loaf of bread snuggled in your bed under a comforter, and a waterfall of milk flowing down your curtains. When you later need to remember the items, you would visualize your room and retrieve the information associated with each location.

Why do mnemonics such as the method of loci work? As you may remember from study unit 7.6, linking new information with what is already meaningful to a person is called elaborative rehearsal. This deeper form of encoding information during the use of mnemonics is what makes this strategy so successful at helping retrieval.

Contestants in extreme memory competitions also use elaborative rehearsal to create mnemonics (**Figure 7.22**). For example, they may memorize a sequence of playing cards by linking each card with a person, an action, or an object that they know. A string of three or more associations makes a very memorable sentence. For Edward Cooke, a grand master from England, a three of clubs, a nine of hearts, and a nine of spades trigger a visual image of "Brazilian lingerie model Adriana Lima in a Biggles biplane shooting at [Cooke's] old public-school headmaster in a suit of armor" (Foer, 2005). While the technique may sound silly, using this mnemonic requires elaborative rehearsal, and this deep encoding creates a meaningful and vivid image that is easy to retrieve later.

7.14 You Forget Some of Your Memories

7.14 LEARNING GOAL ACTIVITIES

To maximize your learning, complete the following learning goal activities.

a. Understand all bold and italic terms by writing explanations of them in your own words.

b. Apply forgetting to your life by naming and describing three ways to forget memories in long-term storage with one example of each from your own life.

forgetting
The inability to access a memory from long-term storage.

retroactive interference
When access to older memories is impaired by newer memories.

proactive interference
When access to newer memories is impaired by older memories.

Ten minutes after you see a movie, you probably remember plenty of the details. The next week, you might remember mostly the plot and the main characters. Years later, you might remember only the gist of the story. You might not remember having seen the movie at all. We forget far more than we remember. **Forgetting** is the inability to access memory from long-term storage. This inability is a normal, everyday experience.

The study of forgetting has a long history in psychology. In the late nineteenth century, the psychologist Hermann Ebbinghaus examined how long it took him to relearn lists of unfamiliar nonsense syllables (for example, vut, bik, kuh). Ebbinghaus found that when he repeatedly practiced with the syllables, it took him less time to relearn them the next day. In other words, the more time he spent learning material, the less he forgot. His results are shown in a forgetting curve (**Figure 7.23**). Luckily, most of us do not need to memorize nonsense syllables. But Ebbinghaus's general findings apply to meaningful material as well. You may remember very little of the Spanish or calculus you took in high school, but relearning these subjects would take you less time and effort than it took to learn them the first time. This finding is great news for students: When you spend more time actively working with material to learn it, you will forget less of the material.

Most people feel bad about forgetting. They wish they could better recall the material they study for exams, the names of childhood friends, the names of all seven dwarfs who lived with Snow White, what have you. But imagine what life would be like if you could not forget. Imagine, for example, walking up to your locker. You want to recall its combination. Instead, you recall the 10 or 20 combinations for all the locks you have ever used. A Russian newspaper reporter had nearly perfect memory. If someone read him a tremendously long list of items and he visualized the items for a few moments, he could recite the list, even many years later. But his memory was so cluttered with information that he had great difficulty functioning in normal society. This condition tortured him to the point that he eventually was institutionalized (Luria, 1968).

Not being able to forget is as maladaptive as not being able to remember. In this way, forgetting is a desirable and useful aspect of human memory. Forgetting may even be necessary for survival. Normal forgetting helps us remember and use important information. There are three main ways that we forget: interference, blocking, and absent-mindedness.

INTERFERENCE When Ebbinghaus studied nonsense syllables, he observed forgetting over time. Many early theorists argued that such forgetting results from the decay of the particular memory trace in a person's brain. Some evidence does indicate that unused memories are forgotten. However, research over the last few decades has established that most forgetting occurs because of interference from other related information. There are two types of interference.

In **retroactive interference,** access to older memories is impaired by newer memories. Say you're about to take a psychology test. You study the psychology material, and then you study some related biology material. Your performance on the psychology test might suffer because the psychology material you studied first is harder to access due to interference from the biology material you studied second (**Figure 7.24a**). By contrast, in **proactive interference,** access to newer memories is impaired by older memories. In this case, say you're about to take a history test. But before you study the history material, you study some similar political science material. When you take your history test, your performance on that test might suffer because you recall the older information that you studied first, the political science material, not the newer information you studied second, the history material (**Figure 7.24b**).

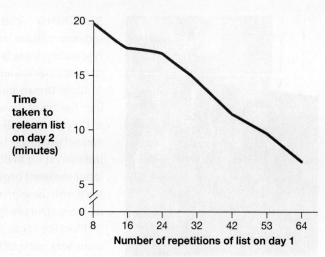

FIGURE 7.23

Forgetting Curve

Research shows that when people repeatedly practice with nonsense syllables, it takes them less time to relearn the syllables later.

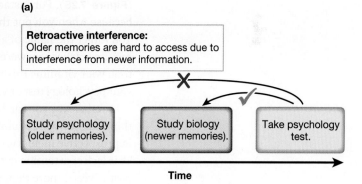

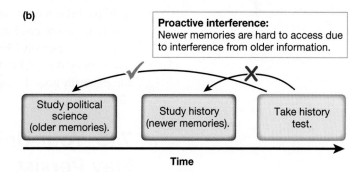

FIGURE 7.24

Retroactive and Proactive Interference

(a) Retroactive interference occurs when retrieving old memories (here, psychology material) is hard due to interference from new memories (here, history material). **(b)** Proactive interference occurs when retrieving new memories (history material) is hard due to interference from old memories (psychology material).

FIGURE 7.25

Absentmindedness

The celebrated musician Yo-Yo Ma is pictured here with his $2.5 million eighteenth-century cello. This instrument was returned to Yo-Yo Ma after he absentmindedly left it in a cab.

BLOCKING   You can't recall the name of a favorite song. You forget the name of someone you are introducing. You "blank" on some lines when acting in a play. This type of forgetting is called *blocking*. Blocking occurs when we are temporarily unable to remember something. It is frustrating but common.

Roger Brown and David McNeill (1966) described another good example of blocking: the *tip-of-the-tongue phenomenon*. Here, people experience great frustration as they try to recall specific words. For instance, when asked to provide a word that means "patronage bestowed on a relative, in business or politics" or "an astronomical instrument for finding position," people often struggle. Sometimes they know which letter the word begins with, how many syllables it has, and even what it sounds like. Even with these partial retrieval cues, they cannot pull the precise word into working memory. (Did you know the words were "nepotism" and "sextant"?)

Blocking often occurs because of interference from words that are similar in some way, such as in sound or meaning, and that are repeatedly experienced. For example, you might repeatedly call an acquaintance Margaret although her name is Melanie. The tip-of-the-tongue phenomenon increases with age, perhaps because older people have more memories that might interfere.

ABSENTMINDEDNESS   *Absentmindedness* is the inattentive or shallow encoding of events. The major cause of absentmindedness is failing to use selective attention to pay attention to relevant information and ignore irrelevant information (**Figure 7.25**). For instance, you absentmindedly forget where you left your keys because when you put them down, you were also reaching to answer your phone. You forget the name of a person you are talking with because when you met him 5 minutes earlier, you were wondering where your keys went. You forget whether you took your vitamins this morning because you were deciding whether to study for your psychology test or your history test.

Another way you can be absentminded is when you fail to remember to do something that you were planning to do. This form of absentmindedness, which is a failure in prospective memory, often occurs because you are caught up in another activity. This lack of attention can have serious consequences. In the United States over the past 15 years, more than 600 children have died because they were left unattended in hot cars and 39 died in 2016 alone (Null, 2016). In many cases, the parent forgot to drop off the child at day care on the way to work. It is easy to imagine forgetting your lunch in the car, but your child? Fortunately, such incidents are rare, but they seem to be especially likely when the parent's typical routine does not include day care drop-off duty. While the parent is driving, his or her brain shifts to autopilot and automatically goes through the process of driving to the workplace instead of stopping at day care first.

7.15 Your Unwanted Memories May Persist

7.15 LEARNING GOAL ACTIVITIES

To maximize your learning, complete the following learning goal activities.

a. Understand all bold and italic terms by writing explanations of them in your own words.

b. Understand memory persistence by explaining in your own words the main way that memory persistence differs from forgetting and distortion.

Do you have a memory that you wish you could forget? Sometimes people do want to forget something but have difficulty doing so. **Persistence** occurs when unwanted memories recur despite the desire not to have them. Some unwanted memories can be so traumatic that they can have terrible effects on the life of the person who suffers from them. One prominent example of persistence occurs in posttraumatic stress disorder (PTSD).

PERSISTENCE IS RELATED TO PTSD   PTSD occurs when a person who has had a traumatic experience suffers extreme distress because of the inability to forget the trauma. In fact, during a PTSD episode, the person mentally relives the traumatic experience. PTSD is a serious mental health problem, affecting 7 percent of people in the United States alone (Kessler, Demler, et al., 2005). The most common causes of PTSD include events that threaten people or those close to them. For example, the unexpected death of a loved one, a physical or sexual assault, military combat, a car crash, a natural disaster, or seeing someone badly injured or killed can lead to PTSD.

A team of Canadian memory researchers studied PTSD by focusing on a traumatic airline flight. On August 24, 2001, a plane flying from Toronto to Portugal ran out of fuel while over the Atlantic Ocean. The nearly 300 passengers were told to prepare for the plane to ditch at sea (**Figure 7.26**). As you might expect, there was considerable panic as the aircraft lost power, cabin lights, and cabin pressure. Fortunately, the pilots located a remote military landing strip and were able to glide the large jet for 75 miles before coming to an extremely rough landing. Mercifully, those on board suffered only minor injuries, most of which were caused by evacuating the plane. One passenger was the researcher Margaret McKinnon. She and her colleagues studied a sample of the survivors.

About half of these research participants developed PTSD. Compared with their recollections of another highly negative event—the September 11, 2001, terrorist attacks—the participants showed enhanced memory for many details of their experiences on the flight (McKinnon et al., 2015). Indeed, a brain imaging study showed heightened amygdala activity when survivors were remembering events from the doomed flight (Palombo et al., 2016). The point here is that a highly emotional experience and heightened amygdala activity produce very powerful and vivid memories. In addition, the release of hormones associated with emotional states strengthens memory consolidation and thereby enhances memories (McGaugh, 2015).

persistence
The continual recurrence of unwanted memories from long-term storage.

FIGURE 7.26

Persistent Memories of Passengers on Air Transat Flight 236

The life-threatening landing of this aircraft left many survivors with PTSD. As a result, they suffered from powerful and vivid memories of their traumatic experience.

7.16 Your Memories Can Be Distorted

7.16 LEARNING GOAL ACTIVITIES

To maximize your learning, complete the following learning goal activities.

a. Understand all bold and italic terms by writing explanations of them in your own words.

b. Understand memory distortion by naming and comparing the five ways that memories in long-term storage can become distorted.

You may think that you remember everything about your senior prom just as it happened. But research has shown that human memory provides less-than-accurate

distortion
Human memory is not a perfectly accurate representation of the past, but is flawed.

portrayals of past events. In fact, human memory is really quite flawed. In general, **distortion** occurs in memory in five ways: memory bias, flashbulb memories, misattribution, suggestibility, and false memories.

MEMORY BIAS *Memory bias* is the changing of your memories over time so that they become consistent with your current beliefs or attitudes. As one of psychology's greatest thinkers, Leon Festinger (1987), put it: "I prefer to rely on my memory. I have lived with that memory a long time, I am used to it, and if I have rearranged or distorted anything, surely that was done for my own benefit" (p. 1).

If you are like most people, you tend to recall your past beliefs and past attitudes as being consistent with your current ones. For example, you may tend to revise your memories when they contradict your attitudes and beliefs. You may also tend to remember events as casting you in prominent roles or favorable lights. You are also likely to exaggerate your contributions to group efforts. You may also take credit for successes and blame failures on others. And you are likely to remember your successes more than your failures.

(a)

FLASHBULB MEMORIES Do you remember where you were when you first heard about the Boston Marathon bombings (**Figure 7.27a**)? Some events lead to what Roger Brown and James Kulik (1977) termed *flashbulb memories*. These vivid memories seem like a flash photo, capturing the circumstances in which you first learned of a surprising and consequential or emotionally arousing event. Flashbulb memories are an example of episodic memory. They are not like the problem of persistence, however. They are not recurring unwanted memories.

An obvious problem affects research into the accuracy of flashbulb memories. Researchers have to conduct a study immediately after an event occurs so they can compare the memories of people at different times.

(b)

Three years after the terrorist attacks on September 11, 2001 (**Figure 7.27b**), a follow-up study was conducted of more than 3,000 people in various cities across the United States (Hirst et al., 2009). Participants were initially surveyed one week after the attacks. Memories related to 9/11—such as where the people first heard about the attacks, what they were doing at the time, and whom they were talking to—declined during the first year, but memory remained stable after that. As might be expected, people who were living in New York City on 9/11 had the most accurate memories of the objective details of the World Trade Center attacks, but they experienced the same level of forgetting for their personal memories of the day as did others across the country. After ten years, people recalled the experience pretty much the same way they did after the first year, even though several aspects of those reports were inconsistent with their initial reports (Hirst et al., 2015). This pattern appears to be generally true of flashbulb memories. Although normal forgetting takes place, people tend to repeat the same story over time, and this repetition bolsters their confidence of their memory (Hirst & Phelps, 2016).

So people are more confident about their flashbulb memories than they are about their ordinary memories (Talarico & Rubin, 2003). In reality, flashbulb memories are imperfect, but they are at least as accurate as memory for ordinary events. Any event that produces a strong emotional response is likely to produce

FIGURE 7.27

Flashbulb Memories
Surprising and consequential or emotionally arousing events can produce flashbulb memories. Well-known examples include **(a)** the Boston Marathon bombings, in 2013, and **(b)** the attacks on the World Trade Center, in 2001.

a vivid, although not necessarily accurate, memory (Christianson, 1992). Or a distinctive event might simply be recalled more easily than a trivial event, however inaccurate the result.

MISATTRIBUTION *Misattribution* occurs when you misremember the time, place, person, or circumstances involved with a memory. Source amnesia is a form of misattribution that occurs when you have a memory for an event but cannot remember where you encountered the information. Consider your earliest childhood memory. How vivid is it? Are you actually recalling the event? How do you know you are not remembering either something you saw in a photograph or a story related to you by family members? Most people cannot remember specific memories from before age 3. The absence of early memories may be due to the early lack of language as well as to frontal lobes that are not fully developed.

An intriguing example of source misattribution is *cryptomnesia*. Here, you think you have come up with a new idea, but really you have retrieved an old idea from memory and failed to attribute the idea to its proper source (Macrae, Bodenhausen, & Calvini, 1999; **Figure 7.28**). Consider students who take verbatim notes while conducting library research. Sometimes these students experience the illusion that they have composed the sentences themselves. This mistake can later lead to an accusation of plagiarism. (Be especially vigilant about recording the source of verbatim notes while you are taking them.)

George Harrison, the late Beatle, was sued because his 1970 song "My Sweet Lord" is strikingly similar to the song "He's So Fine," recorded in 1962 by the Chiffons. Harrison acknowledged having known "He's So Fine," but vigorously denied having plagiarized it. He argued that with a limited number of musical notes available to all musicians, and an even smaller number of chord sequences appropriate for rock and roll, some compositional overlap is inevitable. In a controversial verdict, the judge ruled against Harrison.

SUGGESTIBILITY During the early 1970s, a series of important studies conducted by Elizabeth Loftus and colleagues demonstrated that when people are given misleading information, this information affects their memory for an event. In one experiment, a group of participants viewed a videotape of a car—a red Datsun—approaching a stop sign (Loftus, Miller, & Burns, 1978; **Figure 7.29a**). A second group viewed a videotape of that same scene but with a yield sign instead of a stop sign (**Figure 7.29b**). Each group was then asked, "Did another car pass the red Datsun while it was stopped at the stop sign?" Some participants in the second group claimed to have seen the red Datsun stop at the stop sign, even though they had seen it approaching a yield sign.

In another experiment, Loftus and John Palmer (1974) showed participants a videotape of a car accident. When participants heard the word "smashed" applied to the tape, they estimated the cars to be traveling faster than when they heard "contacted," "hit," "bumped," or "collided." One week later, they were asked if they had seen broken glass on the ground in the video. No glass broke in the video, but nearly one-third of those who heard "smashed" falsely recalled having seen broken glass. Very few of those who heard "hit" recalled broken glass. The way that the question was asked apparently influenced their memory for the information. This research reveals the *suggestibility* of memories in long-term storage.

The suggestibility of memories in long-term storage creates problems for one of the most powerful forms of evidence in our justice system: the eyewitness account. Research has demonstrated that very few jurors are willing to convict an accused

FIGURE 7.28

Cryptomnesia

The 2006 novel *How Opal Mehta Got Kissed, Got Wild, and Got a Life* turned into a possible case of cryptomnesia. The author was a student at Harvard University named Kaavya Viswanathan. Viswanathan admitted that several passages in the work were taken from books that she read in high school. As a result, *How Opal Mehta Got Kissed* had to be recalled from bookstores. Perhaps Viswanathan, thinking she had come up with new material, had retrieved other people's writing from memory.

(a)

(b)

FIGURE 7.29

Suggestibility

In a classic series of studies on suggestibility, participants viewed a video showing **(a)** a stop sign or **(b)** a yield sign. When later asked whether another car passed the car at a stop sign, those who saw the video with a yield sign falsely reported seeing a stop sign.

FIGURE 7.30

Eyewitness Accounts Can Be Unreliable

William Jackson **(top)** served five years in prison because he was wrongly convicted of a crime based on the testimony of two eyewitnesses. Note the similarities and differences between Jackson and the real perpetrator **(bottom)**.

individual on the basis of circumstantial evidence alone. But if just one person says, "That's the one!" then conviction becomes much more likely. This effect occurs even if it is shown that the witness had poor eyesight or some other condition that raises questions about the testimony's accuracy. The power of eyewitness testimony is troubling because witnesses are so often in error. Gary Wells and his colleagues (1998) studied 40 cases in which DNA evidence indicated that a person had been falsely convicted of a crime. They found that in 36 of these cases, the person had been misidentified by at least one eyewitness (**Figure 7.30**). Why is eyewitness testimony so prone to error?

First, recall the phenomenon of change blindness, which you learned about in study unit 3.3. Research on this error showed that people fail to notice that the stranger they are talking with has been replaced with a new stranger (see The Methods of Psychology on p. 95). Eyewitness testimony depends critically on paying sufficient attention to an incident when it happens, rather than after it happens. If we are not attending to the information, it won't be encoded and stored in a way that is accurate. Ultimately, then, the testimony is prone to error because often the eyewitness is not paying attention to the right details when the event happens. To learn how understanding memory can help you in many jobs, including those related to criminal justice and law, read Putting Psychology to Work on p. 291.

FALSE MEMORIES How easily can people develop *false memories*? To consider this question, read aloud the following list: sour, candy, sugar, bitter, good, taste, tooth, nice, honey, soda, chocolate, heart, cake, tart, pie. Now put aside your book and write down as many of the words as you remember.

Researchers have devised tests such as this for studying whether people can be misled into recalling or recognizing events that did not happen (Roediger & McDermott, 1995). For instance, without looking back at the list, answer this question: Which of the following words did you recall—"candy," "honey," "tooth," "sweet," "pie"?

If you recalled "sweet" or think you did, you have experienced a false memory, because "sweet" was not on the original list. All the words on that list are related to sweetness, though. This basic procedure produces false memories reliably. It occurs because each word activates semantic knowledge of related words as explained by spreading activation models, discussed in study unit 7.7. This semantic activation leads to potential confusion about which of the related words were actually read. A brain imaging study showed that related words produce overlapping patterns of brain activity in the front part of the temporal lobe, where semantic information is processed (Chadwick et al., 2016). As a result, even though the memories are false, people are often extremely confident in saying they have seen or heard the words they recollect falsely.

Now think back to when you were 5 years old. Do you remember getting lost in a mall and being found by a kind old man who returned you to your family? No? Well, what if your family told you about this incident, including how upset your parents were when they could not find you? According to research by Elizabeth Loftus, you might then remember the incident, even if it did not happen.

In an initial study, a 14-year-old named Chris was told by his older brother Jim, who was part of the study, about the "lost in the mall" incident, in which Chris was lost and then found by an older adult. Jim told Chris the story while they were playing a game called "Remember when." All the other events described by Jim were true. Two days later, when asked if he had ever been lost in a mall, Chris began reporting memories of how he felt during the mall episode. Within two weeks, he reported the following:

> I was with you guys for a second and I think I went over to look at the toy store, the Kay-bee toy and uh, we got lost and I was looking around and I thought, "Uh-oh. I'm in trouble now." You know. And then I . . . I thought I was never going to see my family again. I was really scared you know. And then this old man, I think he was wearing a blue flannel shirt, came up to me. . . . [H]e was kind of old. He was kind of bald on top. . . . [H]e had like a ring of gray hair . . . and he had glasses. (Loftus, 1993, p. 532)

You might wonder if there was something special about Chris that made him susceptible to developing false memories. In a later study, however, Loftus and her colleagues used the same method to see whether they could create false memories in 24 participants. Seven of the participants falsely remembered events that had been told to them by family members who were part of the study. How could this be?

When you imagine an event happening, you form a mental image of the event. You might later confuse that mental image with a real memory. Essentially, you have a problem figuring out the source of the image. To Chris, the memory of being lost in the mall became as real as other events in childhood.

Children are especially likely to develop false memories. The take-home message is that although most times your memory system works well, there are occasions when your memories can be distorted or flat-out wrong.

How Do You Retrieve Memories?

To make sure you learned what you just read, write answers to the following questions and check your answers.

7.13 Your math teacher wants to hold the final exam in a different classroom than your normal room. Explain to her why that's not a good idea based on what research reveals about retrieval cues.

7.14 During childhood, you called your best friend Katie. As an adult, she wants to be called Kathleen. Why do you have a hard time remembering to call her Kathleen now?

7.15 Explain why you might remember more information from an exciting speech than from a dull one.

7.16 What is the major reason that eyewitness testimony is so often wrong?

See Appendix B for answers to the red Q questions.

BIG PICTURE

 Want to earn a better grade on your test? Go to INQUIZITIVE to practice actively with this chapter's content and get personalized feedback along the way.

How Do You Create Memories?

7.1 You Create Memories by Processing Information

Review the learning goal activities on p. 253. Memories are created during three phases of information processing, which are similar to how a computer processes information. First, information from sensory input is changed into a neural code during encoding. Second, encoded information is maintained for some time during storage. Third, during retrieval the previously encoded and stored information is accessed to be used in some way.

7.2 Your Memories Are Unique

Review the learning goal activities on p. 254. Memory creation is unlike computer information processing in three ways. First,

the brain is complex. Second, the process of making memories is individualized. Third, memory can fail. The way your brain functions and the way you use attention to focus on processing relevant information and ignore irrelevant information lead to your unique memories. Selective attention allows you to direct mental resources to whatever information needs it most so that you can successfully remember it later.

KEY TERMS

memory (p. 253)   retrieval (p. 254)
encoding (p. 253)   selective attention (p. 255)
storage (p. 254)

How Do You Maintain Memories over Time?

7.3 You Maintain Information in Three Memory Stores

Review the learning goal activities on p. 257. According to the three-part model of memory storage, you maintain information in: (1) sensory storage, (2) short-term storage, and (3) long-term storage. Each of these stores has a different function, encodes information in a specific way, maintains a particular amount of information, and retains that information for a particular length of time.

7.4 Sensory Storage Lets You Maintain Information Very Briefly

Review the learning goal activities on p. 259. Sensory input from environmental information is encoded through the sense it is received in. This encoded input is held in sensory storage for each of the five senses for less than 1 second. A huge amount of visual, auditory, taste, smell, and touch information is maintained in sensory storage to ensure continuous sensory experiences.

7.5 Working Memory Lets You Actively Maintain Information in Short-Term Storage

Review the learning goal activities on p. 261. Information is usually encoded into short-term storage in an auditory format. Short-term storage keeps about five to nine encoded items available for up to 20 seconds so that it can be used right now. However, active processing in working memory through chunking or making information meaningful increases both the capacity and the duration of short-term storage.

7.6 Long-Term Storage Lets You Maintain Memories Relatively Permanently

Review the learning goal activities on p. 263. Long-term storage of memories is achieved when semantic encoding or dual coding is used. Long-term storage is relatively permanent and virtually limitless for deeply encoded information. This allows accessing of information over very long periods of time. According to the levels of processing model, deep encoding enhances memory. Maintenance rehearsal—repeating an item over and over—leads to shallow encoding and poorer memory at a later time. Elaborative rehearsal, using working memory processes to link new information with what a person already knows (semantic information), will lead to deeper encoding and better memory later.

7.7 Your Long-Term Storage Is Organized Based on Meaning

Review the learning goal activities on p. 265. Information in long-term storage is organized based on meaning through schemas and association networks. Schemas are cognitive structures that aid in the perception, organization, processing, and use of information. According to association network models, information in memory is stored in nodes, and nodes are connected via networks to many other nodes. Activating one node results in spreading activation of all associated nodes within the network.

KEY TERMS

sensory storage (p. 260)   working memory (p. 261)   long-term storage (p. 263)   elaborative rehearsal (p. 263)
short-term storage (p. 261)   chunking (p. 262)   maintenance rehearsal (p. 263)

What Are Your Different Long-Term Storage Systems?

7.8 Amnesia Reveals Different Long-Term Stores

Review the learning goal activities on p. 268. Research suggests that multiple long-term storage systems encode, store, and retrieve information differently. These multiple memory systems are revealed by two forms of amnesia: (1) retrograde amnesia, the loss of memories for events experienced before a brain injury; and (2) anterograde amnesia, the loss of the ability to create new memories for events experienced after a brain injury.

7.9 Your Explicit Memories Involve Conscious Effort

Review the learning goal activities on p. 269. People with anterograde amnesia, like patient H.M., have problems creating new explicit memories after their brain injuries. Explicit memories, which are consciously remembered, include episodic memory for personally experienced events and semantic memory of facts independent of personal experience.

7.10 Your Implicit Memories Function Without Conscious Effort

Review the learning goal activities on p. 271. Some people, like H.M., can still form implicit memories even after they experience brain damage. Implicit memories are processed without conscious effort and include classical conditioning and procedural memories of motor skills.

7.11 Prospective Memory Lets You Remember to Do Something

Review the learning goal activities on p. 273. Prospective memory is remembering to do something in the future. It has costs in terms of reducing attentional resources and impairing short-term storage and working memory processing.

7.12 Memory Is Processed by Several Regions of Your Brain

Review the learning goal activities on p. 274. Consolidation is the process of making memories lasting. Consolidation of explicit memories occurs in the medial temporal lobes and especially the hippocampus. By contrast, sensory information is stored in the cortical areas that process the individual senses. The process of consolidation explains why the removal of H.M.'s hippocampi meant he could no longer store new memories. H.M. could still learn new motor information because implicit memories, such as procedural memories, tend to be processed through the cerebellum. Memories may be altered through reconsolidation, where retrieval of information changes a memory before it is stored again.

KEY TERMS

retrograde amnesia (p. 269)

anterograde amnesia (p. 269)

explicit memory (p. 270)

episodic memory (p. 270)

semantic memory (p. 270)

implicit memory (p. 271)

procedural memory (p. 272)

prospective memory (p. 273)

consolidation (p. 275)

How Do You Retrieve Memories?

7.13 Retrieval Cues Help You Access Your Memories

Review the learning goal activities on p. 278. Retrieval cues can help us access information in long-term storage by providing information about: (1) the context in which the information was encoded (context-dependent memory), (2) the internal moods or physiological states, associated with the memory (state-dependent memory), or (3) mnemonics.

7.14 You Forget Some of Your Memories

Review the learning goal activities on p. 280. Forgetting prevents the access of information from long-term storage due to (1) interference, (2) blocking, or (3) absentmindedness. Retroactive interference is a difficulty retrieving old information due to interference from new information. By contrast, proactive interference is a difficulty retrieving new information due to interference from old information.

7.15 Your Unwanted Memories May Persist

Review the learning goal activities on p. 282. Persistence is the recurrence of unwanted memories. It is common among individuals with posttraumatic stress disorder, most likely due to activation of the amygdala and because emotional events increase consolidation of memories.

7.16 Your Memories Can Be Distorted

Review the learning goal activities on p. 283. Memories can become distorted in five ways, through: (1) memory bias, (2) flashbulb memories, (3) misattribution, (4) suggestibility, and (5) false memories.

KEY TERMS

retrieval cue (p. 278)

forgetting (p. 280)

retroactive interference (p. 281)

proactive interference (p. 281)

persistence (p. 283)

distortion (p. 284)

CHAPTER 7 SELF-QUIZ

To make sure you learned the information in this chapter, write answers to the following questions and check your answers. **See Appendix B for answers to the self-quiz.**

1. Johanna was asked to remember a string of letters. She heard x during the presentation of the letters. In her brain, this input was changed into the neural code s. Later, when she was asked to recall the letters, Johanna included s, not x, in her list. Johanna most likely made this error on the recall test due to an error in the _____ phase of memory.
   a. encoding
   b. retrieval
   c. creation
   d. storage

2. Demetra's husband is watching a football game on television. When Demetra asks if he will pick up their daughter, Zoe, from day care the next day, he doesn't reply. When Demetra asks, "Did you hear me?" her husband replies, "Yes, I heard you. I'll pick up Zoe tomorrow." However, the next day, her husband comes home without Zoe. He claims to have no memory of being asked to pick her up. The fact that he did not have the information about picking up Zoe from day care in _____ storage was most likely due to his _____.
   a. short-term; never having that information in sensory memory
   b. short-term; not paying attention to the request
   c. long-term; never having that information in sensory memory
   d. long-term; not paying attention to the request

3. Lily gets a new debit card and must memorize her PIN, vt0806. To remember this sequence, she thinks of vt as representing Vermont. She thinks of 0806 as representing August 6th, her husband's birthday. With this combination in mind, Lily remembers the PIN easily. She has used _____.
   a. maintenance rehearsal to encode information into long-term storage
   b. the primacy effect
   c. the working memory strategy of chunking
   d. the recency effect

4. To do his math homework, Brandon looked at the formulas and solved the problems by keeping track of the variables that he manipulated in his mind. However, when Brandon took a math test, he could not recall the formulas. Brandon's problem during the test reveals that he most likely did not retain the information in his _____.
   a. sensory storage
   b. working memory
   c. long-term storage
   d. short-term storage

5. When someone says the word "doctor," 13-year-old Vanessa remembers her most recent medical visit. She also thinks of objects related to the concept of a doctor, such as an examination room, a stethoscope, and an X-ray machine. The fact that a word brings up memories about many related ideas is best explained by _____.
   a. the primacy effect
   b. spreading activation models of memory
   c. the recency effect
   d. level of processing model of memory

6. Professor Linsmeier was recently in a motorcycle accident that left him with brain damage. He has no trouble teaching his economics course, which he has taught for 15 years. However, Professor Linsmeier has lost the ability to remember new information, such as the names of his students. He is most likely experiencing _____.
   a. retrograde amnesia
   b. proactive interference
   c. anterograde amnesia
   d. retroactive interference

7. Nathaniel's friend asks him what he ate for breakfast this morning. When Nathaniel remembers that he ate eggs, toast, and bacon, this recall is an example of _____ memory. When Nathaniel tells his friend what he ate, his ability to verbalize that information is an example of _____ memory.
   a. episodic; explicit
   b. episodic; implicit
   c. semantic; explicit
   d. semantic; implicit

8. Louis recovers from a severe illness. While he used to be a good piano player, now he cannot remember what finger movements to make to play his favorite pieces. Louis most likely has damage in his _____.
   a. amygdala
   b. temporal lobe
   c. hippocampus
   d. cerebellum

9. Cadence, a teacher, is currently frustrated with a coworker. She wants to write a recommendation for one of her students, Jamie, who has many talents and is a hard worker. However, as she writes the letter, the only memories that come to mind are times when she was frustrated with Jamie. Cadence's experience of remembering only situations where Jamie frustrated her is best explained by _____.
   a. context-dependent memory
   b. state-dependent memory
   c. retroactive interference
   d. proactive interference

10. When Russell was growing up, he thought his grandma Betty was a hoarder because she had so much junk that you could hardly walk around her house. Now that Russell is an adult, he obsessively buys old board games and action figures that remind him of his youth. He has so many boxes lying around, he can barely make a pathway from his bedroom to his kitchen. Russell claims that he learned to collect from his grandma Betty, whose house he loved visiting because she "always collected really cool, meaningful stuff." The fact that Russell's memory about his grandmother is currently positive can best be described by _____.
   a. forgetting
   b. misattribution
   c. memory bias
   d. suggestibility

How Can Understanding Memory Help You Succeed at Your Job?

Do you enjoy crime shows such as *Law & Order*? If so, then you may have already considered a criminal justice career, either in law enforcement or in the legal system. Fans of crime shows know the importance of understanding human memory when solving crimes. However, as discussed in this chapter, victims and eyewitnesses may not remember information from a crime very well. This inaccuracy can make it much harder for detectives to catch perpetrators, for prosecutors to help convict defendants, or for defense attorneys to make good cases for their clients. Understanding human memory is crucial for succeeding in a criminal justice career.

Perhaps the most relevant information you learned in this chapter is that people do not create memories the ways computers store information. How people remember events depends on how much they were paying attention at the time and how relevant the events were to them personally. And people may be unaware of how unreliable memories can be. If you are a detective questioning potential witnesses, you will be more effective if you understand that asking questions certain ways can lead to faulty descriptions because people are suggestible. Even asking people about events the wrong ways may lead them to develop false memories. When attorneys question crime victims in court, it will help the attorneys to know that emotions affect how memories are stored. Events that produce a lot of emotion are associated with more vivid, lasting memories.

Of course, knowing about memory will help you in any job that requires remembering things. If you work as a barista, you have to remember the ingredients for many different types of drinks, along with the unusual names people might use to order them. Knowing how you can use special techniques to better retrieve information from long-term memory, such as mnemonics, will help you stay at the top of your game.

By contrast, restaurant servers need to know how to keep memories active for shorter periods, such as between when people place their orders and when those orders are communicated to the kitchen staff. Keeping information available in working memory, such as through chunking, helps make sure that everyone around the table gets the food they ordered. Remembering the order correctly and delivering it to the right people helps maximize tips.

TAKEAWAY POINT: Understanding psychology in general, and memory in particular, is critical to a criminal justice career, either in law enforcement or in the legal system. This knowledge is beneficial for any job, including for those working in restaurants. After all, knowing how memory works can help you improve your own ability to remember facts and develop skills, which is valuable no matter what you do.

Ψ You can look up job descriptions, education requirements, salaries, and more at the Bureau of Labor Statistics: www.bls.gov. Visit the site and start putting psychology to work!

8 Thinking and Intelligence

IN 2014, 3-YEAR-OLD ALEXIS MARTIN, from Arizona, did something unusual. She was accepted to Mensa, the international society for people with extremely high intelligence (**Figure 8.1a**). Her parents reported that at 1 year of age, Alexis had often recited the bedtime story from the night before word for word. When her father would try to pitch in, she would correct him. If he said, "Oh, yeah, and then the elephant was the one that was sharing," she would say, "No, Dad, it was the kangaroo that was sharing" (KABC-TV, 2014). By age 2, Alexis could read and had taught herself Spanish using her parents' iPad. "Anytime she learns a word," her father explained, "and just picks it up through anything, she never ever uses it in the incorrect context" (Schwartz, 2014). How was a child able to become so smart in only three years?

BIG QUESTIONS

What Is Thinking?

How Do You Use Thinking?

What Is Intelligence?

How Is Intelligence Measured?

FIGURE 8.1

Extraordinary Intelligence and Thinking

(a) At age 3, Alexis Martin was accepted to Mensa, the international society for people with extremely high intelligence. **(b)** At age 15, Phiona Mutesi **(front left)** used her excellent thinking skills in reasoning, solving problems, and decision making to become the youngest African chess champion ever.

Now consider Phiona Mutesi, a young woman who grew up in very different circumstances (**Figure 8.1b**). Phiona was raised in an extremely poor neighborhood in Kampala, the capital of Uganda. In 2005, unable to read or write, sleeping on the streets, and desperate for food, the 9-year-old Phiona traveled with her brother to meet a missionary who promised a bowl of porridge to any child who would try chess. Phiona developed a love for the game. She also discovered that she was very good at it. Indeed, at age 15 Phiona became her country's chess champion and the youngest African chess champion ever (Crothers, 2012). Chess requires reasoning about possible moves, solving tactical problems, and making good decisions. How was Phiona, a child with no education, able to think so skillfully and become a master at this difficult game?

Because Alexis is thought to be highly intelligent and Phiona shows excellent thinking skills, you might get the idea that intelligence and thinking are two different things. But actually they are connected, because a person's ability to show intelligence is linked to having excellent thinking skills. The important point is that you can always improve your thinking. Thinking helps you act intelligently. And by acting intelligently, you can improve your personal life, your academic work, and your professional career. This chapter explores aspects of thinking, such as decision making and problem solving. It also explores how thinking relates to intelligence.

What Is Thinking?

The chapter opener described Phiona Mutesi's extraordinary thinking skills in playing chess. But thinking does not have to be extraordinary—you are thinking throughout your daily life. In fact, you are thinking right now. Are you thinking about Phiona's skills, the game of chess, or how she has risen above the circumstances she was born in? This chapter considers the nature of thought: how you represent ideas in your mind and how you use these ideas to engage in reasoning, decision making, and problem solving.

8.1 Thinking Is the Mental Manipulation of Representations

 8.1 LEARNING GOAL ACTIVITIES

To maximize your learning, complete the following learning goal activities.

a. Understand all bold and italic terms by writing explanations of them in your own words.

b. Apply representations to your life by providing one example each of analogical and symbolic representations that you have used.

Representations of the external world are all around you. For example, a road map represents streets. A menu represents food options. A photograph represents a particular part of the world.

As you learned in Chapter 5, representations are created when sensory input is changed into signals the brain can process. When you look at a chair, for instance, your eyes transduce the light into signals, and your brain processes the signals into an image that you call "chair." In other words, patterns of brain activity provide meaningful information about objects you encounter in environments. **Thinking** is the mental manipulation of these representations.

Cognitive psychologists study thought and the understanding that results from thinking. For these scientists, the challenge is to understand the nature of our internal, mental representations of information around us. For example, when are the internal representations in our minds like maps or pictures? And when are they more abstract, like language?

ANALOGICAL AND SYMBOLIC REPRESENTATIONS When you think about information, you use two basic types of internal representations: analogical and symbolic. **Analogical representations** usually correspond to images. They have some characteristics of actual objects. Therefore, they are "analogous" to actual objects. For example, maps correspond to geographical layouts. Family trees depict branching relationships between relatives. A clock corresponds directly to the passage of time. **Figure 8.2a** is a drawing of a violin from a particular perspective. This drawing is an analogical representation.

In your mind's eye, you often form images without trying. For example, think about a lemon. Did your "lemon" thought take the form of an image that resembled an actual lemon? Did you see the lemon's yellow, waxy, dimpled skin? Did your mouth water (a different sort of mental image)?

Of course, no "picture" exists inside your head. And the mental image is not perfectly accurate. Instead, it generally matches the physical object it represents. By using mental images, you can answer questions about objects that are not in your presence. For example, what color is a lemon? Manipulating mental images also lets you think about your environment in novel and creative ways. Novel and creative thinking can help you solve problems.

By contrast, **symbolic representations** are abstract. These representations usually consist of words or ideas. They do not have relationships to physical qualities of objects in the world. The word "hamburger" is a symbolic representation that usually represents a cooked patty of beef served on a bun. The word "violin" stands for a musical instrument (**Figure 8.2b**). There are no correspondences between what a violin looks like, what it sounds like, and the letters or sounds that make up the word "violin." The individual characters that make up the word stand for what a violin is, but the letters are arbitrary. You cannot "see" any part of a violin in the shape of the letters *v-i-o-l-i-n*.

Together, both analogical and symbolic representations form the basis of human thought, intelligence, and the ability to solve the complex problems of everyday life or of special challenges. For instance, recall Phiona from the chapter opener. Like most expert chess players, Phiona probably has rich images in her mind of where the pieces will be on the chessboard many moves in the future (analogical representations). What's more, she likely uses information about specific chess strategies that she has read about (symbolic representations). Taken together, Phiona's rich and accurate mental representations and her ability to manipulate them skillfully are the main reason for her success in chess.

thinking
The mental manipulation of representations of information we encounter in our environments.

analogical representations
Mental representations that have some of the physical characteristics of objects.

symbolic representations
Abstract mental representations that consist of words or ideas.

(a)   (b)

FIGURE 8.2

Analogical and Symbolic Representations

(a) Analogical representations, such as this picture of a violin, have some characteristics of the objects they represent. **(b)** Symbolic representations, such as the word "violin," are abstract and do not have relationships to the physical qualities of objects.

FIGURE 8.3

Mental Maps May Not Represent Information Accurately

In a mental map, you cannot represent all analogical and symbolic information with perfect accuracy. As a result, mental maps sometimes lead to incorrect thinking. For example, San Diego is actually farther east than Reno.

schemas
Mental structures—collections of ideas, prior knowledge, and experiences—that help organize information and guide thought and behavior.

MENTAL MAPS You can probably pull up a visual image of Africa's contours even if you have never seen the actual contours with your own eyes. Such mental maps include a combination of analogical and symbolic representations. But how accurate are mental maps?

Consider this question: Which is farther east, San Diego, California, or Reno, Nevada? If you are like most Americans, you answered that Reno is farther east than San Diego. But as you can see from the map in **Figure 8.3**, the reverse is true. Even if you formed an analogical representation of a map of the western United States, your symbolic knowledge might have told you that a city on the Pacific Coast is farther west than a city in a state that does not border the Pacific Ocean. In this case, a symbolic representation yielded a wrong answer.

Mental maps can sometimes lead to errors because you can represent only a limited range of knowledge. Although your general knowledge is correct, it does not take into account the way Nevada extends to the west and the Pacific Coast near Mexico slants to the east. Regularizing irregular shapes is a shortcut you use unconsciously for organizing and representing information in memory. Such shortcuts are generally useful, but they can lead to errors.

8.2 Schemas Are the Basis of Thinking

 8.2 LEARNING GOAL ACTIVITIES

To maximize your learning, complete the following learning goal activities.

a. Understand all bold and italic terms by writing explanations of them in your own words.

b. Apply schemas and concepts to your life by describing a schema that you have and one concept that is part of that schema.

Much of your thinking, such as the idea of where San Diego and Reno are, reflects visual and verbal representations of objects in the world. It also reflects what you know about the world. Say that you are shown a drawing of a small yellow object and asked to identify it. Your brain forms a mental image (analogical representation) of a lemon and provides you with the word "lemon" (symbolic representation). So far, so good.

But picturing a lemon and knowing its name do not tell you what you can do with a lemon. You also know that certain parts of a lemon are edible and that lemon juice usually tastes strong and sour. This additional information helps you know that you can make lemonade by diluting the juice with water and adding sugar. In short, what you know about a lemon and how you think about it influence what you do with a lemon. How do you organize representations of objects so that you can think about them—and interact with them—effectively and efficiently?

SCHEMAS ALLOW CATEGORIZATION OF CONCEPTS As you learned in study unit 7.7, your long-term memories are organized based on schemas. **Schemas** are mental structures—collections of ideas, prior knowledge, and experiences—that help you organize information and guide your thought and behavior. Schemas are also related to your mental organization of analogical and symbolic representations.

To understand the relationship between schemas and these representations, consider two musical situations: a country music dance (**Figure 8.4a**) and a symphony orchestra performance (**Figure 8.4b**).

First, schemas are useful because many of the most commonly encountered situations have consistent attributes. For example, you might expect to see guitars and fiddles at a country music dance, but you probably don't expect to see them in an orchestral concert. There, you might expect to see violins and trumpets instead. Second, schemas are useful because people have specific roles within the context of a situation. Your country music schema would include people dancing, but your orchestral schema would not include dancing. Finally, schemas are useful because they allow you to think efficiently about objects by categorizing them.

When you use a schema to group things based on shared properties, you create a *category* about the information. For example, based on the schema for Types of Music, you can create these two categories: Country Music Instruments and Orchestral Music Instruments (**Figure 8.5a**). Some instruments might exist in just one category or the other (the guitar is used in country bands, and the trumpet is used in orchestras). However, other instruments belong in both categories. For example, the violin, which is used in orchestras, is the same thing as a fiddle, which is used in country music.

Besides creating a category with several things together, you also create a *concept*, a single mental representation of an object or event, to store unique knowledge about each specific member of a category (**Figure 8.5b**). For example, your concept of a guitar might include the knowledge that it "usually has six strings and is played by plucking." Your concept of a trumpet may be based on knowing that "it is made of brass tubing and is played by blowing into it." A concept can include knowledge about a relation between items (such as "violins are smaller than guitars" or "watermelons are heavier than lemons"). Or it can consist of information about certain dimensions of each item (such as pitch or sweetness).

The bottom line is that a schema is a common theme. You use that theme to group information by categorizing concepts together based on their similarities and differences. This grouping method is a very efficient way to organize information in your mind, because it means that you do not have to store every instance of an object, relationship, or dimension individually. Instead, you store concepts

FIGURE 8.4

Schemas About Types of Music Events

Your experiences with music create memories that are organized into schemas. **(a)** Because of your schemas about country music concerts, you might expect to see guitars and fiddles and people dancing. **(b)** Because of your schemas about orchestral music concerts, you might expect to see violins and trumpets and people sitting still while listening.

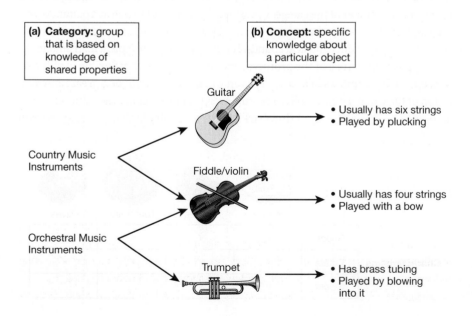

(a) Category: group that is based on knowledge of shared properties

(b) Concept: specific knowledge about a particular object

Guitar
• Usually has six strings
• Played by plucking

Country Music Instruments

Fiddle/violin
• Usually has four strings
• Played with a bow

Orchestral Music Instruments

Trumpet
• Has brass tubing
• Played by blowing into it

FIGURE 8.5

The Schema for Types of Music Includes Categories and Concepts

(a) Schemas let you group objects into categories based on shared properties. For example, you might have two categories for instruments. **(b)** In turn, categories are made up of concepts, which are stored information about each unique object. The category of Country Music Instruments might include the concept "guitar." The category of Orchestral Music Instruments might include the concept "trumpet." One concept can be stored in more than one category. For example, "fiddle/violin" is used in both country music and orchestral music.

TABLE 8.1

Models of Organizing Concepts into Categories

Model	Ways of categorizing concepts	Examples for the category of Sports
Prototype model	• Concepts are organized in hierarchical categories. • The prototype is the concept that is the "most typical" category member. • Other concepts are categorized as similar or different from the prototype based on how many characteristics they share with the prototype.	• In the category of Sports, the prototype might be "baseball." • Characteristics of "baseball" might include that the game uses a ball. • Sports with shared characteristics ("basketball") are similar to the prototype. • Sports with dissimilar characteristics ("surfing") are different from the prototype.
Exemplar model	• Concepts are not organized hierarchically. • No single concept is the best member of a category. • All examples, or exemplars, of concepts in a category equally represent the category.	• The category of Sports is equally represented by all exemplars in the category (including "baseball," "basketball," "surfing," etc.).

prototype model
A way of thinking about concepts: Within each category, there is a best example—a prototype—for that category.

exemplar model
A way of thinking about concepts: All concepts in a category are examples (exemplars); together, they form the category.

based on the properties shared by certain items, or particular ideas. As described in **Table 8.1,** two models explain how you organize concepts into categories.

PROTOTYPE MODEL OF CATEGORIZATION One model of concept organization is the **prototype model.** According to this model, concepts are organized based on the "most typical" member of a category. The most typical member, called the *prototype,* has certain characteristics. We decide whether an item belongs in the category by comparing its characteristics with those of the prototype.

For example, many people consider an orange to be the prototypical concept for the category of Fruit. Oranges have seeds, are edible, and taste sweet, so items that share most or all of these characteristics are also considered members of the category Fruit (**Figure 8.6**). Concepts that don't share some of these traits are not thought of as members of that category. Thus most people do not think of tomatoes and olives as fruits, even though they are. The same idea applies to the category of Musical Instruments. Consider the instruments used in the musical *Stomp.* The performers make music with many unconventional objects, such as trash cans and broomsticks (**Figure 8.7**). A trash can has few traits in common with what might be thought of as a prototypical member of the category of Musical Instruments, such as a guitar. Nevertheless, *Stomp* shows us that a trash can might be considered a musical instrument, because it does produce musical sounds. It is just a non-prototypical instrument.

One positive feature of the prototype model is that it is very flexible in allowing concepts to be members of a category even when they may not be a great representation of the category. So an olive is a fruit even though it seems very different from an orange (see Figure 8.6). A drawback of this flexibility is that a specific person

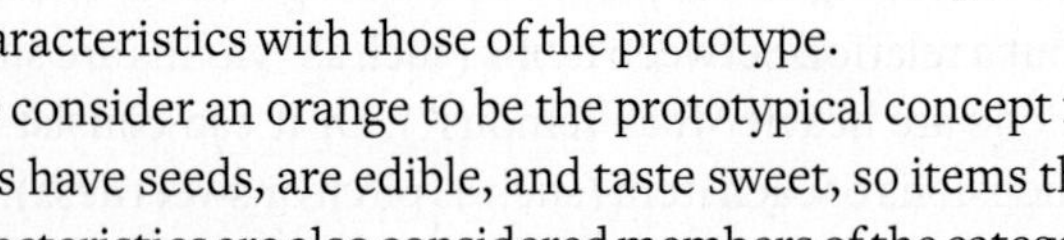

FIGURE 8.6

The Prototype Model of Categorization

According to the prototype model, some concepts in a category are prototypes. That is, they are more representative of that category than are other concepts in the category. For this reason, an orange seems to be the prototype of the category Fruit. By contrast, olives do not seem to be very representative of the category.

	Oranges	Grapes	Tomatoes	Olives
Seeds	✓	✓	✓	✓
Edible	✓	✓	✓	✓
Sweet	✓	✓		

Characteristics

may choose a prototype as the best representation of a category for many different reasons. For example, an orange may be considered as the prototype of fruit because it is the most common member of that category. Or it may be because it represents a combination of the typical attributes in the category. Unfortunately, the prototype model cannot distinguish between these possibilities.

EXEMPLAR MODEL OF CATEGORIZATION The **exemplar model** addresses this flexibility concern in the prototype model by suggesting that a category has no single concept as its best representation. Instead, you form a fuzzy representation based on your experiences. That is, all the concepts in a category form the basis for the category. The concepts are called *exemplars*. And the exemplar model accounts for the observation that some category members are more prototypical than others: The prototypes are simply concepts that you have encountered more often.

For instance, your representation of cats is made up of all the cats you have encountered in your life. If you see an animal in a house, you compare this animal with your memories of other animals you have encountered. If it more closely resembles the dogs you have encountered (as opposed to the cats, squirrels, rabbits, and other animals), you conclude it is a dog (**Figure 8.8**). Similarly, according to this model, all types of instruments, including trash cans, are equally good exemplars of the category Musical Instruments.

FIGURE 8.7

The Non-Prototypical Musical Instruments in *Stomp*

The musical *Stomp* demonstrates that we can use unusual objects, such as trash cans and broomsticks, to make music.

8.3 Schemas Are the Basis of Stereotypes

8.3 LEARNING GOAL ACTIVITIES

To maximize your learning, complete the following learning goal activities.

a. Understand all bold and italic terms by writing explanations of them in your own words.

b. Apply stereotypes to your life by explaining how a schema you have has caused you to develop either a positive or negative stereotype.

FIGURE 8.8

The Exemplar Model of Categorization

Quick—what animal are you looking at? Is it a dog or a sheep or a pig? How does it match your exemplar for each of these animals? It is actually a Mangalitsa pig.

The prototype and exemplar models explain how you use schemas to categorize concepts and how you represent these concepts in your mind. In your daily life, what is the effect of having these mental representations and classifications?

SCHEMAS ALLOW DEVELOPMENT OF STEREOTYPES As you move through various real-world settings, you act appropriately by drawing on knowledge of what objects, behaviors, and events apply to each setting. For example, in your classes, it is appropriate to squeeze in at a desk that is between people already sitting at other desks. In a restaurant, it might be very rude to squeeze into a chair at a table where people are already dining together. Knowledge of how to behave in each setting relies on schemas.

You can use schemas for two reasons. First, common situations have consistent rules (for example, students in classrooms generally sit at desks). Second, people have specific roles within situational contexts (for example, students in classrooms behave differently than diners in restaurants do). Unfortunately, schemas sometimes have unintended consequences, such as reinforcing beliefs about people in particular groups. These generalizations are called **stereotypes**.

stereotypes

Schemas that allow for easy, fast processing of information about people, events, or objects, based on their membership in particular groups.

FIGURE 8.9

Stereotypes Affect Thoughts and Behaviors Toward Others

(a) As shown in this photo of the New York Philharmonic in 1960, the stereotype that women were worse musicians often led to the formation of all-male orchestras. **(b)** Changes in attitudes and in audition procedures have contributed to the diversification of talent in contemporary orchestras.

To demonstrate the tendency to stereotype, think back to the example of the country music dance and the orchestral concert. When you first looked at each of the pictures in Figure 8.4, did any particular thoughts enter your mind about one or the other? For example, maybe you thought that only wealthy people listen to orchestral music. Or maybe you thought about how country music is uplifting and easy to dance to. This demonstration makes it clear that although your schemas let you think efficiently about related concepts, they can lead to generalizations about people, events, or objects. As shown in The Methods of Psychology on p. 301, schemas cause people to begin developing stereotyped thinking at a very young age.

Stereotypes can limit people's opportunities. In the past, orchestra conductors always chose men for principal positions because the conductors believed that women did not play as well as men. The schema of women as inferior musicians interfered with the conductors' ability to rate auditioners objectively when the conductors knew the names and sexes of the musicians. After recognizing this bias, the top North American orchestras began holding auditions with the musicians hidden behind screens and their names withheld from the conductors. Since these methods were instituted, the number of women in orchestras has increased considerably (Goldin & Rouse, 2000; **Figure 8.9**). So while thinking in schemas is natural and efficient, you must actively work to overcome how you stereotype others as an accidental negative side effect of your schemas. In Chapters 10 and 12, you will learn that stereotypes influence how people think about and behave toward others.

Q What Is Thinking?

To make sure you learned what you just read, write answers to the following questions and check your answers.

8.1 When an architect produces a blueprint for a new house, is this an analogical or symbolic representation?

8.2 How does the prototype model of categorization differ from the exemplar model?

8.3 What is the relationship between schemas and stereotypes?

See Appendix B for answers to the red Q questions.

Preschoolers' Stereotypes About Adult Drinking and Smoking

Hypothesis: Preschoolers' behaviors will reveal stereotyped thinking based on schemas about how adults use alcohol and tobacco.

Research Method: Children used props and dolls to act out a social evening for adults. As part of the role play, each child selected items from a miniature grocery store stocked with 73 different products. The items on the shelves included beer, wine, and cigarettes.

Results: Out of 120 children, 34 (28 percent) "bought" cigarettes, and 74 (62 percent) "bought" alcohol. Children were more likely to buy cigarettes if their parents smoked. They were more likely to buy beer or wine if their parents drank alcohol at least monthly or if they viewed PG-13 or R-rated movies in which adults were pictured drinking.

Conclusion: Children's play behavior suggests they are highly attentive to the use and enjoyment of alcohol and tobacco and have well-established expectations about how cigarettes and alcohol fit into social situations. Observation of adult behavior, especially parental behavior, may influence preschool children to develop schemas where smoking and drinking are "normal" adult behaviors. Adopting this stereotype early in life might be related to adopting certain attitudes and behaviors later in life.

QUESTION: Why might children of parents who smoke be more likely to choose cigarettes?

ANSWER: Because these children likely observe their parents smoking, they are more likely to form schemas that stereotype smoking as a "typical adult behavior."

Source: Dalton, M. A., Bernhardt, A. M., Gibson, J. J., Sargent, J. D., Beach, M. L., Adachi-Mejia, A. M., Titus-Ernstoff, L. T., & Heatherton, T. F. (2005). "Honey, have some smokes." Preschoolers use cigarettes and alcohol while role playing as adults. *Archives of Pediatrics & Adolescent Medicine, 159,* 854–859.

How Do You Use Thinking?

What to eat for breakfast, what to wear, what time to leave for work or class—these choices may not be life changing, but they are examples of the many decisions you make throughout every day. You also solve problems, such as figuring out how to organize the paper you're writing or how to break bad news to someone. The previous section looked at how thinking lets you represent and organize your knowledge about the world. How do you use that knowledge to guide your daily actions? Thinking serves many purposes, and three of the most important are the skills of reasoning, decision making, and problem solving.

8.4 You Use Thinking in Three Ways

8.4 LEARNING GOAL ACTIVITIES

To maximize your learning, complete the following learning goal activities.

a. Understand all bold and italic terms by writing explanations of them in your own words.

b. Apply the two types of reasoning by describing one example of each from your life.

Sometimes the terms "reasoning," "decision making," and "problem solving" are used interchangeably, but they are not really the same thing. In **reasoning**, you determine if a conclusion is valid (**Figure 8.10a**). To do so, you use information that you believe is true. Suppose your friend announces that Kendrick Lamar is the greatest rapper of all time. What information would you consider in judging whether that conclusion is valid? To judge this claim, you would probably use *informal reasoning*. For example, you might consider other people's opinions, hearsay, your familiarity with his music, and your knowledge of rap. By contrast, psychologists engage in *formal reasoning* by using the standardized and objective procedures of the scientific method to collect empirical evidence and test hypotheses to see if they are valid (for a refresher on the terms "empiricism" and "hypothesis," see study unit 1.8). For formal reasoning, the opinions of others, hearsay, and information from personal experience are not relevant.

You see this contrast between informal and formal reasoning quite often in your daily life. You might choose a spot for a vacation based on the opinions of

(a)

You use **reasoning** to determine if a conclusion is valid. In the 2016 presidential campaign, candidate Jeb Bush stated that psychology majors needed to "realize, you're going to be working at Chick-fil-A." To show this statement was not valid, many people provided evidence. They posted signs showing what they do with their psychology degrees.

(b)

You use **decision making** to select between options. In 2008, a 9-month-old girl's uncle had to decide whether to carry her through a burning apartment building or drop her several stories into the arms of a police officer waiting below. The uncle said, "I looked into his eyes and saw that he would catch her. Then I let her go."

(c)

You use **problem solving** to overcome obstacles. For example, how did this man solve the problem of getting out of the corner he painted himself into?

FIGURE 8.10

Three Forms of Thinking

You experience three forms of thinking in your daily life: **(a)** reasoning, **(b)** decision making, and **(c)** problem solving.

your friends (informal reasoning) or based on research that you do to find out the temperature, cost, and available activities (formal reasoning). People often reject weight-loss programs and medical therapies that are supported by science, but they readily accept ones supported by personal testimonials of friends and family (Diotallevi, 2008).

Decision making is another form of thinking. In this case, you select among choices (**Figure 8.10b**). Usually, you identify important criteria and determine how well each alternative satisfies these criteria. For example, say you need to choose between taking a course in psychology and taking a course in another topic. What criteria would you use in making this decision?

Problem solving is yet another form of thinking. In general, you have a problem when a barrier or a gap exists between where you are and where you want to be. To solve the problem, you overcome obstacles to move from your present state to your desired goal state (**Figure 8.10c**). If you decide to enroll in the psychology class but it conflicts with another course in your schedule, you have a problem that you must solve, perhaps by dropping the conflicting class.

The following study unit explores in more detail how thinking about information is related to decision making.

decision making
Attempting to select the best alternative among several options.

problem solving
Finding a way around an obstacle to reach a goal.

8.5 How You Think Biases Decision Making

8.5 LEARNING GOAL ACTIVITIES

To maximize your learning, complete the following learning goal activities.

a. Understand all bold and italic terms by writing explanations of them in your own words.

b. Understand the three main biases in decision making by explaining in your own words how heuristics, framing, and the paradox of choice can lead to faulty decision making.

In the 1970s, Amos Tversky and Daniel Kahneman spearheaded research to identify the ways that people make everyday decisions. In particular, they investigated why people's decisions are not based on perfect logic. Instead, many decisions are based on processes that speed up the decision making. That is, the decision maker takes shortcuts instead of taking time to consider all the possible pros and cons. In recognition of this important research, Kahneman received the 2002 Nobel Prize in Economic Sciences. (Tversky was deceased when the prize was awarded.)

Consider a typical everyday decision. Imagine that you have a round pool and you want a cover for it. How can you decide what size of pool cover to buy? One rational way to answer this question is by thinking about the area of the circle that is the pool's opening. For example, you could multiply pi (3.1416) by the radius of the pool squared. This formula, which you may remember from geometry, is an algorithm for calculating the area of a circle. An *algorithm* is a set of procedures to follow when thinking and making a decision. When followed correctly, the algorithm will always yield the correct result. In this case, the area of the circle you're looking to find is the opening of the pool. But would you actually use this algorithm to decide on the pool cover size?

Instead, you might note whether the pool is small, medium, or large. You would then choose a cover by matching what is available at the store to what you think the

heuristic
A shortcut (rule of thumb or informal guideline) used to reduce the amount of thinking that is needed to make decisions.

size of your pool is. This approach is not completely rational, nor is it guaranteed to produce the correct result. But as Kahneman and Tversky revealed, this type of thinking leads you to make "rule of thumb" decisions that are generally fine—good enough in your daily life.

HEURISTICS When you use a rule of thumb as an informal way to make a decision, you are using what is known as a **heuristic.** You may not even be aware of taking these mental shortcuts, because heuristic thinking often occurs unconsciously. But heuristics are useful because they require minimal cognitive resources. They let you focus your attention on other things. Heuristic thinking is also adaptive, because sometimes survival depends on quick decisions that don't require weighing all the evidence. Three of the heuristics most commonly used in your daily life are the availability, representativeness, and affective heuristics.

The *availability heuristic* is the tendency to make a decision based on information that comes to mind. In other words, you tend to rely on information that is easy to retrieve from memory (**Figure 8.11a**). Consider this question: In most industrialized countries, are there more farmers or more librarians? If you live in an agricultural area, you probably said farmers. If you live in an urban area, you probably said librarians. Most people who answer this question think of the librarians they know about and the farmers they know about. If they can retrieve many more instances in one category, they assume it is the larger category. In fact, most industrialized countries have many more farmers than librarians. Because people who live in cities and suburbs tend not to meet many farmers, they are likely to believe there are more librarians.

The *representativeness heuristic* is the tendency to place people or objects in a category if they are similar to the concept that is the prototype. You use this heuristic when you base a decision on how closely each option matches what you already believe (**Figure 8.11b**). For example, say that Helena is intelligent, ambitious, and scientifically minded. She enjoys working on mathematical puzzles, talking with other people, reading, and gardening. Would you guess that she is a cognitive psychologist or a postal worker? Most people, employing the representativeness heuristic, would guess that Helena is a cognitive psychologist because her characteristics better match their prototype of psychologists.

The representativeness heuristic can lead to faulty reasoning if you fail to take other information into account. One very important bit of information is the *base rate*, which is how frequently an event occurs. For example, there are many more postal workers than cognitive psychologists, so the base rate for postal workers is higher than that for cognitive psychologists. Therefore, any given person, including

(a)

(b)

(c)

FIGURE 8.11

Three Heuristics Influence Decision Making

(a) Availability heuristic: In 2012, Hurricane Sandy damaged parts of New Jersey. Most people remembered the news footage of devastation, so tourists decided to vacation elsewhere. Atlantic City had to launch an advertising campaign to show that the boardwalk was repaired and the casinos were open for business. Only then did tourists stop relying on their outdated heuristic and start returning to the city. **(b) Representativeness heuristic:** If you're familiar with Mayim Bialik's work on television, you might automatically place her in the category of actress. When you learn that she holds a Ph.D. in neuroscience, you might be surprised that she belongs to a second category: scientist. **(c) Affective heuristic:** Fans of teams that win major championships are often less happy one week later than they expected to be, whereas fans of losing teams are happier than they expected to be.

Helena, is much more likely to be a postal worker. People generally do not pay much attention to base rates in reasoning, focusing instead on whether the information is more representative of one prototype or another. Although Helena's traits may be more representative of cognitive psychologists overall, they also likely apply to a large number of postal workers.

Now consider another question: Would you prefer to go out dancing in a night-club or go to a poetry reading in a quiet café? In considering this question, did you think rationally about all the implications of either choice? Or did you flash on how you would feel in either situation? If you considered only how you would feel, then you most likely used the *affective heuristic* to make your decision. The word "affective" refers to emotions (**Figure 8.11c**). Emotions influence decision making in several ways (Lerner, Valdesolo, & Kassam, 2015). People often decide to do things they believe will make them happy, whereas they avoid doing things they believe they will regret. Unfortunately, people are poor at affective forecasting—predicting how they will feel about things in the future (Gilbert & Wilson, 2007). People overestimate how happy they will be for positive events, such as getting married, having children, or having their candidate win an election or their team win a championship (Dolan & Metcalfe, 2010). Likewise, they overestimate the extent to which negative events—such as breaking up with a romantic partner, losing a job, or being diagnosed with a serious medical illness—will affect them in the future (Gilbert, Pinel, Wilson, Blumberg, & Wheatley, 1998; Wilson & Gilbert, 2003). Unfortunately, because of these biases, people tend to make decisions based on assumptions about their future emotions that may be inaccurate.

As Tversky and Kahneman demonstrated, these three heuristics result in biases, and biases may lead to errors. Consider the commonly believed heuristic that a high price equals high quality. Although laboratory studies show that one type of soap is basically as good as any other, many consumers believe that "fancy" soaps are superior. Unfortunately, we cannot be aware of every heuristic we rely on. But we can be aware of frequently used ones, such as the availability and representativeness heuristics. Once we know that such shortcuts can lead us to make faulty judgments, we can use heuristics more carefully as we seek to make rational decisions.

FRAMING If you are completely rational in making decisions, then you should consider the possible alternatives and choose the one with the most value. For example, would you be more likely to buy a package of ground beef if it were described as "75 percent lean" or if it were described as "25 percent fat"? If you are like many people, you find the first description much more appealing, and so you would be likely to purchase that meat (Sanford, Fay, Stewart, & Moxey, 2002). But in reality, the information on each label is the same—it is just presented in a different way. (In other words, "75 percent lean" means "25 percent fat.") So you should choose each alternative equally. But you might not, which shows that you do not always make decisions rationally. Instead, the way information is presented can alter how you perceive it and make decisions about it. This effect is known as **framing**. Framing can significantly influence decision making in various situations (**Figure 8.12**).

THE PARADOX OF CHOICE Five hundred cable channels! Fifty choices at a restaurant buffet! Thirty different styles of running shoes to choose from! What more could you ask for? If you are like most people in Western cultures, not being able to choose violates your sense of freedom. But when too many options

framing
How information is presented affects how that information is perceived and influences decisions.

FIGURE 8.12

The Impact of Framing on Decision Making

The framing of the gas prices makes it seem very attractive to pay in cash in order to get the discount. What if the sign at a competing gas station stated that if you used a credit card to pay for the gas, there would be an additional charge of five cents per gallon? Which gas station would you buy gas from?

FIGURE 8.13

Too Much Choice

As part of Iyengar and Lepper's study, **(a)** one display presented 24 jams, and **(b)** the other display presented 6 jams. The results indicated that having many possibilities led to fewer sales of jam.

are available, especially when all of them are attractive, you may experience conflict and indecision.

Although some choice is better than none, too much choice can be frustrating and unsatisfying, and ultimately it can impair your thinking (Schwartz, 2004). This effect was demonstrated in a study where shoppers at a grocery store were presented with a display of either 24 or 6 varieties of jam to sample (Iyengar & Lepper, 2000). The shoppers also received a discount coupon for any variety of jam. The greater variety attracted more shoppers, but it failed to produce more sales. Only 3 percent of shoppers at the display with many choices bought jam (**Figure 8.13a**). By contrast, 30 percent of the shoppers at the display with limited choices bought jam (**Figure 8.13b**). In a later study, the same investigators found that people choosing among a small number of chocolates were more satisfied with the products they selected than were people who chose from a wider variety. Why might this happen? Because people take different approaches to decision making.

Two approaches to decision making are "maximizing" and "satisficing." Maximizers try to make the perfect choice among their options, whereas satisficers seek to find a "good enough" choice that meets their minimum requirements (Schwartz et al., 2002). It turns out that maximizers, compared to satisficers, tend to choose the objectively best option, but those choices bring them less happiness. For example, college graduates who are maximizers land jobs with much higher salaries than their satisficing counterparts, but in the long run they are also less satisfied with their career choices (Iyengar, Wells, & Schwartz, 2006).

Are you a maximizer? Try It Yourself will help you find out. Read Using Psychology in Your Life on p. 307 to learn how to be more satisfied with your decisions.

 TRY IT YOURSELF: **Are You a Maximizer?**

To find out if you are a maximizer, complete this maximization scale. For each item on this list, award yourself anywhere from 1 point (for "completely disagree") to 7 points (for "completely agree").

1. No matter how satisfied I am with my job, it's only right for me to be on the lookout for better opportunities.
2. When I am in the car listening to the radio, I often check other stations to see if something better is playing, even if I am relatively satisfied with what I'm listening to.
3. When I watch TV, I channel surf, often scanning through the available options even while attempting to watch one program.
4. I treat relationships like clothing: I expect to try a lot on before finding the perfect fit.
5. I often find it difficult to shop for a gift for a friend.
6. Renting videos is really difficult. I'm always struggling to pick the best one.
7. When shopping, I have a hard time finding clothing that I really love.
8. I'm a big fan of lists that attempt to rank things (the best movies, the best singers, the best athletes, the best novels, etc.).
9. I find that writing is very difficult, even if it's just writing a letter to a friend, because it's so hard to word things just right. I often do several drafts of even simple things.
10. I never settle for second best.
11. Whenever I'm faced with a choice, I try to imagine what all the other possibilities are, even ones that aren't present at the moment.
12. I often fantasize about living in ways that are quite different from my actual life.
13. No matter what I do, I have the highest standards for myself.

Scoring:

Add up your points. People who get high scores on this scale are considered maximizers.

How Can You Be Satisfied with Big Decisions?

Making your own decisions is one of the luxuries of adulthood. The flip side is that making important life decisions can be stressful. What if you make the wrong decision? What if your decision has unexpected consequences? Cognitive psychologists study how people make small and big decisions. Some cognitive researchers are particularly interested in college students' thinking about important academic decisions, such as choosing what they will study in college.

Jennifer Kay Leach and Erika A. Patall (2013) wanted to know if the "maximizing" and "satisficing" approaches to decision making were related to college students' tendency to second-guess their chosen majors as well as their satisfaction with their choices. The researchers surveyed 378 juniors and seniors, all of whom had declared a major. Maximizers spent more time thinking about how things might have turned out better if they made different decisions than did satisficers. For example, the maximizers in this study more strongly agreed with self-report items such as "I often consider how other majors would have allowed me more career opportunities/options." This kind of thinking was related to lower satisfaction with the chosen major. Many studies point to the same general pattern: Maximizers go through a lot of effort to make the best choice, but they end up being unhappy with the choices they make.

If you are a maximizer, are you doomed to always second-guess your decisions? Will you always be unhappy? Not necessarily. Ultimately, you get to decide how you will feel about your decision making.

The psychologist Barry Schwartz has conducted many studies on maximizers. In his book *The Paradox of Choice* (2004), Schwartz offers advice on making choices. Here are some of his ideas applied to the decision of whether to choose to pursue a certificate, an associate's degree, a transfer program, or a bachelor's degree in college:

1. **Approach the decision thinking like a satisficer.** Try to identify your minimum requirements for what is a good course of study. You might, for instance, want a degree that allows you to learn about people from different cultures and that also helps you develop business skills. You do not need to find the single best option for achieving these goals. You need to choose a course of study that will set you on the right path by helping at least somewhat with both goals.

2. **Promise yourself that you will stick with your decision.** You may tend to be less satisfied with your decisions if you know you can change them. Know that you picked your course of study for a good reason and accept that decision. Schwartz notes, "The only way to find happiness and stability in the presence of seemingly attractive and tempting options is to say, 'I'm simply not going there. I've made my decision. . . . I'm not in the market—end of story'" (p. 299). Once you have decided, quit thinking about other options you might have chosen.

3. **Have realistic expectations.** Sure, you will probably have to take some classes that you do not enjoy. A couple of your professors might even be boring. Tests and other requirements may challenge your limits. But such drawbacks will be true of any course of study. As with any decision, you will experience occasional dips in satisfaction.

4. **Practice an attitude of gratitude.** Think about the good that has come from your decisions instead of lingering on the bad. Each term, as you get ready to register for the next term's classes, list 5–10 things you are grateful for related to your course of study: something surprising you learned, an eye-opening experience you had because of a class, an interesting conversation you had with a good teacher, a new friend you met in class, and so on.

Finally, whether you are choosing what to study in college or making another major decision, keep in mind that there are many perfectly fine options. Thinking carefully about your choices and making a "good enough" decision might help free your mind and give you time to do other worthwhile things.

8.6 You Solve Problems to Achieve Goals

How do you get into your car when you have locked the keys inside? How can you make enough money to spend your spring break somewhere nice? What do you have to do to get a grade of A in this course? Your thoughts are often focused on your goals and how to achieve them. Even so, there aren't always simple and direct means of attaining a particular goal. You must use knowledge to determine how to move from your current state to the goal state, and you must use good strategies to overcome obstacles. How you think about the problem and use problem solving strategies can help or hinder your ability to find effective solutions. The four most common problem solving strategies are subgoals, working backward, analogy, and insight.

SUBGOALS   Once you have identified a goal, how do you get to it? How do you proceed from one step to the next to the next, what errors might you typically make in negotiating tricky or difficult steps, and how do you decide on more efficient (or, in some cases, less efficient) solutions? In many cases, solving the problem requires breaking the task into *subgoals*. Reaching each subgoal will result in achieving the main goal of solving the problem. You can see a classic example of a problem that must be solved using subgoals in **Figure 8.14a**. Try to solve it yourself before looking at the solution (**Figure 8.14b**).

Using subgoals is important for many problems. Suppose a high school student would like to become a doctor. To achieve this goal, the student needs first to attain the more immediate subgoal of being admitted to college. Getting into college means meeting another subgoal: earning good grades in high school. This subgoal requires developing good study skills and paying attention in class. Breaking down a problem into subgoals is an important component of problem solving. When you are facing a complex problem, identifying the appropriate subgoals and their order can be challenging. The following subsections consider some approaches you can follow instead.

WORKING BACKWARD   When the appropriate steps for solving a problem are not clear, proceeding from the goal state to the initial state can help yield a solution.

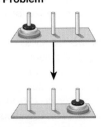

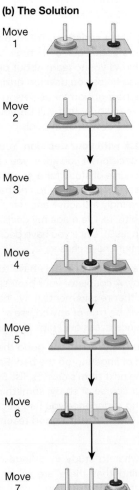

(a) The Problem

(b) The Solution

Move 1

Move 2

Move 3

Move 4

Move 5

Move 6

Move 7

FIGURE 8.14

Using Subgoals to Solve Problems

The Tower of Hanoi is a problem that requires using subgoals to solve. Try solving it yourself here. You can use a quarter, a nickle, and a penny, and a sheet with three dots on it to represent the three pegs. **(a)** Move the disks to the peg on the other end. You can move only one disk at a time. You cannot place a larger disk on top of a smaller disk. **(b)** Break the task down into subgoals. The first subgoal is to move the largest disk to the farthest peg. This requires four moves. The next subgoal is to move the middle disk to the farthest peg. The smallest disk is moved to the first peg. This requires two moves. Finally, to reach the main goal, the smallest disk is moved to the farthest peg in one move.

This process is called *working backward*. Consider the water lily problem (Fixx, 1978, p. 50):

> Water lilies double in area every 24 hours. On the first day of summer there is only one water lily on the lake. It takes 60 days for the lake to be completely covered in water lilies. How many days does it take for half of the lake to be covered in water lilies?

One way to solve this problem is to work from the initial state to the goal state: You figure that on day 1 there is one water lily, on day 2 there are two water lilies, on day 3 there are four water lilies, and so on, until you discover how many water lilies there are on day 60 and you see which day had half that many. It will take you quite a while to solve the problem this way. But consider what happens if you work backward, from the goal state to the initial state. If on day 60 the lake is covered in water lilies and water lilies double every 24 hours, then half the lake must have been covered in water lilies on day 59. In this case, working backward helps you solve the problem more quickly and easily.

ANALOGY Imagine that a surgeon needs to use a laser at high intensity to destroy a patient's tumor. The surgeon must aim the laser very precisely to avoid destroying healthy surrounding tissue. This example poses a very difficult problem. The problem cannot be solved by using subgoals or working backward. Instead, an analogy can help solve the problem (**Figure 8.15a**).

The surgeon remembers reading a story about a general who wanted to capture a fortress. The general needed to move a large number of soldiers up to the fortress, but all the roads to the fortress were planted with mines. A large group of soldiers would have set off the mines, but small groups could travel safely. So the general divided the soldiers into small groups and had each group take a different road to the fortress, where the groups converged and attacked together.

Because the surgeon's problem has restrictions that are analogous (that is, similar) to the general's problem, she gets the idea to aim several lasers at the tumor from different angles. By itself, each laser will be weak enough to avoid destroying the living tissue in its path. But the combined intensity of all the converging lasers will be enough to destroy the tumor (**Figure 8.15b**).

Finding an appropriate *analogy* for a problem can help you achieve your goals, the way it did for the surgeon (Reeves & Weisberg, 1994). Analogous solutions work, however, only if you recognize the similarities between the problem you face now and ones that have been solved before (Keane, 1987; Reeves & Weisberg, 1994).

INSIGHT You may not recognize that something is a problem until it seems unsolvable and you feel stuck. For example, it is only when you spot the keys in the ignition of your locked car that you know you have a problem. As you stand there pondering the problem for a period of time, a solution may pop into your head. *Insight* is the metaphorical lightbulb that goes on in your head when you suddenly realize the solution to a problem. Unlike the other three problem solving strategies, insight happens only when you stop actively thinking about a problem.

In 1925, the Gestalt psychologist Wolfgang Köhler conducted one of psychology's most famous studies on insight. Convinced that some nonhuman animals could behave intelligently, Köhler studied whether chimpanzees could solve problems. He placed bananas beyond a chimp's reach and provided objects that the chimp could use to reach the bananas. Could the chimp figure it out?

First the chimp just jumped at the bananas. That didn't work. Then the chimp began a period of repeatedly looking at the bananas and walking around to the objects

(a) The Problem

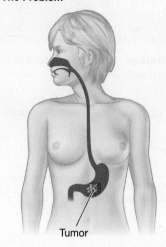

Tumor

(b) The Solution

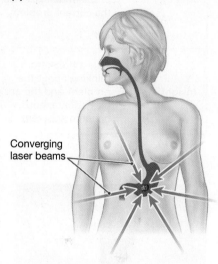

Converging laser beams

FIGURE 8.15

Using Analogies to Solve Problems
The "tumor problem" is best solved through an analogy. Can you solve the problem? **(a)** A surgeon must use a laser at high intensity to destroy a tumor deep inside a patient's body without destroying healthy surrounding tissue. **(b)** To solve the tumor problem, it may help you to return to the main text and read the paragraph that discusses the "fortress problem." The surgeon knows the answer to the fortress problem. So she uses it as an analogy to solve her problem, by employing several laser beams at a lower intensity but aiming them all in one area to destroy the tumor.

TABLE 8.2
Problem Solving Strategies

Strategy	Characteristics	Sample Problem	Solution
Subgoals	Identify the goal state and several subgoals to be achieved.	You want to repair your car muffler, but you don't have enough money to pay for repairs.	To reach the goal of having enough money for repairs, you research the best price, cut spending for a month, and work more.
Working backward	Begin from the goal state and work backward to the current state.	You want to graduate in 2 years, but you aren't sure what courses you need to take.	You identify the credits needed to graduate, then the credits needed per term, then the credits needed this term, and finally the classes that provide the needed credits for this term.
Analogy	Identify a previously solved problem that is similar to the current problem.	You cook beef with broccoli, but the broccoli ends up soggy.	You think about how, when you put an iced coffee in your lunch bag, your sandwich got damp. Similarly, moisture from the beef ruins the broccoli. Next time, you cook the beef and broccoli separately, then combine them.
Insight	Take a break from actively thinking about the problem, and the answer may spontaneously become apparent.	You have a hard time solving a difficult calculus homework problem.	You put the problem away. After a while, the solution pops into your mind, and you write the answer in your homework.

FIGURE 8.16

Chimpanzees Use Insight to Solve Problems

Chimpanzees try to solve problems, such as reaching bananas that are too high. They seem to suddenly come to realize a solution and then implement it. As shown here, the chimp in Köhler's study suddenly stacked several boxes on top of each other and stood up on them to reach the bananas. This behavior suggested that the chimp solved the problem through insight.

in the enclosure. Finally, the chimp began to use the objects to get at the food. Eventually, the chimp was able to stack up several boxes and stand on them to reach the bananas. Köhler argued that these actions were examples of insight (**Figure 8.16**). Having solved the problem, the chimp transferred the solution to new, similar problems and solved them quickly. These additional solutions confirmed that the chimp's behavior had resulted from insight (to review insight learning, see study unit 6.12).

Table 8.2 summarizes how subgoals, working backward, analogy, and insight can help solve many problems. But some problems are harder to solve than others. One way to solve difficult problems, "thinking outside the box," has become a cliché (at least in Western cultures). The next study unit looks at what this approach actually involves.

8.7 You Overcome Obstacles to Solve Problems

 8.7 LEARNING GOAL ACTIVITIES

To maximize your learning, complete the following learning goal activities.

a. Understand all bold and italic terms by writing explanations of them in your own words.

b. Understand obstacles in problem solving by summarizing in your own words the three ways that changing representations helps overcome obstacles in problem solving.

"Have you heard about the new restaurant that opened on the moon? It has great food but no atmosphere!" The point of this joke is that "atmosphere" means one thing in the restaurant but something else on the moon. Humor often violates an expectation, such as the meaning of "atmosphere." To get the joke, you have to rethink some common representation. You can think of getting a joke as a kind of problem solving. In problem solving, you often need to revise a mental representation to overcome an obstacle to thinking successfully. Three common strategies for revising mental representations are restructuring, overcoming mental sets, and overcoming functional fixedness.

RESTRUCTURING   One strategy that problem solvers commonly use to overcome obstacles is **restructuring** the problem. This strategy consists of mentally representing the problem in a novel way. Ideally, the new mental view reveals a solution that was not visible under the old problem structure. The revelation leads to the sudden "Aha!" moment that is characteristic of insight.

In one now-famous study, Scheerer (1963) gave each participant a sheet of paper that had a square of nine dots on it. The task was to connect all nine dots, using at most four straight lines, without lifting the pencil off the page (**Figure 8.17a**). Can you solve this problem? As shown in **Figure 8.17b,** one solution is to literally think outside the box: to realize that keeping the lines within the box is not a requirement. People don't usually realize this. Instead, they tend to think that the lines must stay within the box, even though that restriction is never stated. Solving the problem requires restructuring the representation, to remove restrictions that aren't actually part of the problem.

OVERCOMING MENTAL SETS   In trying to solve a problem, you probably think back to how you have solved similar problems. You may tend to persist with previous strategies. These established ways of thinking are known as **mental sets.** Mental sets are often useful because they may save the time and effort of searching for new types of solutions. But sometimes they make it difficult to find the best solution. Consider this question: What happens once in June, once in July, and twice in August? If you are like most people, you are probably trying to think of various summertime activities or events that happen more in August than in June or July. But the correct answer is "the letter *u*." Thinking about things that happen during summer months leads you to expect the question to be about events, not the letters that make up the words. If this happened to you, then you have just experienced the effects of a mental set.

OVERCOMING FUNCTIONAL FIXEDNESS   In a 1945 study, Karl Duncker gave participants a candle, a pack of matches, a box of tacks, and the following challenge: Using only these objects, attach the candle to the wall in such a way that the candle can be lit and burn properly (**Figure 8.18a**). Can you think of how this might be done?

If you are like most people, you had difficulty in coming up with a good solution. You may have struggled because you have mental representations about the typical functions of particular objects. This kind of obstacle is called **functional fixedness.** To overcome functional fixedness, you need to reinterpret the objects' potential functions (**Figure 8.18b**). If the participants in Duncker's study reinterpret the function of the tack box, a solution emerges: The side of the box can be tacked to the wall so that it creates a stand. The candle is then placed in the box and lit. In general, participants have difficulty viewing the box as a possible stand when it is being used

restructuring
Thinking about a problem in a new way in order to solve it.

mental sets
A tendency to approach a problem in the same way that has worked in the past, which may make it harder to solve a problem.

functional fixedness
A tendency to think of things based on their usual functions, which may make it harder to solve a problem.

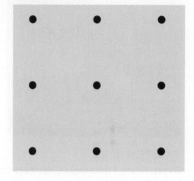

(a) The Problem

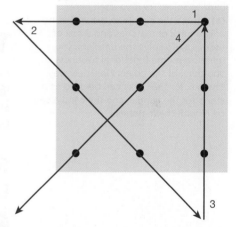

(b) The Solution

FIGURE 8.17

Using Restructuring to Solve Problems
The nine-dot problem is hard to solve unless you use restructuring to think of the problem in a new way. Can you solve this problem? **(a)** Without lifting your pencil from the page, connect the dots by using at most four straight lines. Most participants consider only solutions that fit within the square formed by the dots. **(b)** One way to solve the problem is to use restructuring to represent the problem in a new way. In this case, think of how the lines can extend beyond the boundary lines formed by the dots.

(a) The Problem

(b) The Solution

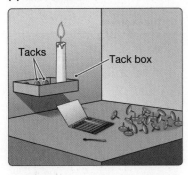

Tacks

Tack box

FIGURE 8.18

Overcoming Functional Fixedness to Solve Problems

The Duncker candle problem is very hard to solve. Try it yourself here. **(a)** Attach the candle to the wall using only a pack of matches and a box of tacks. **(b)** To solve the problem, you must overcome functional fixedness and think of the objects in a new way. The box for the tacks can be used as a stand for the candle, and the candle can be lit with the matches.

intelligence
The ability to use knowledge to reason, make decisions, make sense of events, solve problems, understand complex ideas, learn quickly, and adapt to environmental challenges.

as a container for the tacks. When participants are shown representations of this problem with an empty box and the tacks on the table next to the box, they solve the problem somewhat more easily.

In general, people who have excellent thinking skills can demonstrate the abilities to create, change, and manipulate internal representations to make decisions and solve problems. These abilities are just one reason that Phiona Mutesi, discussed in the chapter opener, excels at playing chess. However, do Phiona's thinking skills mean that she is intelligent? So far, this chapter has considered the use of knowledge in thinking. The following section considers what it means to think intelligently.

How Do You Use Thinking?

To make sure you learned what you just read, write answers to the following questions and check your answers.

8.4 Your friend says that all of the upgrades on the newest iPhone justify its expensive price. If you decide that this statement is valid without doing any research, then what thinking process have you engaged in?

8.5 You are planning to visit Puerto Rico. If you cancel your trip because you remember a news article about how devastated the island was by Hurricane Maria, which heuristic has influenced your decision making?

8.6 How is insight different from the three other problem solving strategies of subgoals, working backward, and analogy?

8.7 Your uncle uses a dial-up modem to connect to the Internet because it always works. How does the idea of a mental set explain why your uncle has not upgraded to more modern technology?

See Appendix B for answers to the red Q questions.

What Is Intelligence?

Look at the people in **Figure 8.19**. Which of these people do you believe are intelligent? You may believe that only some of the people are intelligent, or that they are all intelligent but in different ways. How did you make your decision about who is intelligent?

8.8 One General Factor May Underlie Intelligence

✎ **8.8 LEARNING GOAL ACTIVITIES**

To maximize your learning, complete the following learning goal activities.

a. Understand all bold and italic terms by writing explanations of them in your own words.

b. Understand general intelligence by explaining in your own words how general intelligence is based on the single-factor model as revealed by IQ scores.

Sometimes thinking leads to great ideas and creative discoveries. At other times thinking leads to bad decisions and regret. Some people seem to be better at thinking about and using knowledge than others, and we often say those people are intelligent. We say this because **intelligence** is the ability to use knowledge to reason,

(a)

Albert Einstein developed the general theory of relativity. He is considered by many to be the father of modern physics.

(b)

Ananya Vinay won the 2017 Scripps National Spelling Bee by spelling the word "marocain."

(c)

According to the Guinness Book of World Records, the rapper, songwriter, producer, and actor Eminem holds the record for most words in a song.

(d)

In 2014, the Google executive Alan Eustace broke the world record for freefalls. He used a parachute to fall from the stratosphere, a drop of 135,890 feet.

(e)

The influential talk-show host, media mogul, and philanthropist Oprah Winfrey was the first African American billionaire.

FIGURE 8.19
Who Is Intelligent?
Which of these people are intelligent? Why do you think so?

make decisions, make sense of events, solve problems, understand complex ideas, learn quickly, and adapt to environmental challenges.

Clearly, intelligence has many aspects. But suppose you are especially talented in some areas but weak in others. Maybe you can't solve difficult calculus problems, but you write brilliant poems. Are you intelligent? Does intelligence reflect one overall talent or many individual ones?

IQ SCORES REVEAL INTELLIGENCE If you have ever taken an intelligence test, you no doubt noticed that it included many different types of questions concerning math, English, and other knowledge and skills. As a result of your performance on the test, you were given one overall score. This score is called an **intelligence quotient (IQ)**. In the next section of this chapter, you will learn about modern intelligence tests. These tests are all based on the first assessment of intelligence. This test was developed in the early 1900s by the psychologist Alfred Binet and his collaborator Theodore Simon (**Figure 8.20**).

The French government encouraged Binet to identify children in the French school system who needed extra attention and special instruction. Binet proposed that intelligence is best understood as a collection of high-level mental processes. Accordingly, Binet and Simon developed a test for measuring each child's vocabulary, memory, skill with numbers, and other mental abilities. The result was the Binet-Simon Intelligence Scale.

One assumption underlying the test was that children might do better on some components by chance, but how children performed on average across the different components would indicate their overall level of intelligence. Indeed, Binet found

intelligence quotient (IQ)
A mathematical measure of intelligence (originally computed by dividing a child's estimated mental age by the child's chronological age, then multiplying this number by 100).

FIGURE 8.20
Alfred Binet
Binet launched the approach of assessing intelligence by using the intelligence quotient.

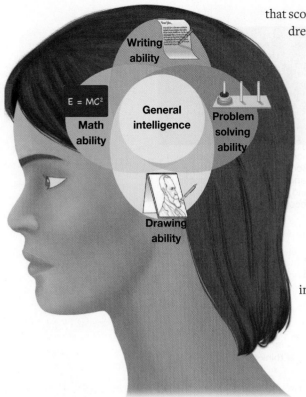

Writing ability

$E = MC^2$

Math ability

General intelligence

Problem solving ability

Drawing ability

FIGURE 8.21

General Intelligence: A Single Factor of Intelligence

As depicted in this cluster of overlapping ovals and circle, Spearman viewed general intelligence as the single factor of intelligence. This underlying factor influences an individual's specific abilities related to intelligence, such as writing and math.

general intelligence
The theory that one common factor underlies intelligence.

fluid intelligence
Intelligence that reflects the ability to process information, particularly in novel or complex circumstances.

crystallized intelligence
Intelligence that reflects both knowledge gained through experience and the ability to use that knowledge.

that scores on his tests were consistent with teachers' beliefs about the children's abilities. They were also consistent with the children's grades.

The result was an intelligence test with many different types of questions that yielded a single IQ score. This type of test reflects the theory that one general factor underlies intelligence.

GENERAL INTELLIGENCE Charles Spearman (1904) used statistical methods to investigate scores on the various types of questions in intelligence tests. Spearman found that people who scored high on one type of item also tended to score high on other types of items. In general, people who are very good at a specific ability, such as math, are also good at other abilities, such as writing, problem solving, and other mental challenges. Spearman viewed **general intelligence** as the single, common factor that contributes to performance on any intellectual task (**Figure 8.21**). In his view, general intelligence tends to yield higher IQ scores on intelligence tests.

Over the past century, research has shown that general intelligence influences important life outcomes. For example, things that are affected by general intelligence, such as performance in school and at work, can influence everything from socioeconomic status to health. Indeed, general intelligence may directly affect health. Why? As medical knowledge rapidly advances and becomes more complex, trying to keep up with and process all this new information is a challenge. People who are higher in general intelligence have an advantage in meeting that challenge. Those with higher scores on intelligence tests may be more literate about health issues, accumulate greater health knowledge, follow medical advice, and understand the link between behavior and health (Gottfredson, 2004). This provocative idea warrants further investigation because it could have important implications for the medical system and the way doctors communicate medical advice.

8.9 There May Be Multiple Aspects of Intelligence

 8.9 LEARNING GOAL ACTIVITIES

To maximize your learning, complete the following learning goal activities.

a. Understand all bold and italic terms by writing explanations of them in your own words.

b. Apply the four theories of multiple intelligences to your life by providing four examples of intelligence in people you know, basing each example on a different theory of multiple intelligences.

Most psychologists agree that some form of general intelligence exists. But researchers also recognize that intelligence can be characterized in alternative ways—that it has multiple aspects. **Table 8.3** presents some of these theories of intelligence and how they compare with the theory of general intelligence.

FLUID AND CRYSTALLIZED INTELLIGENCE Raymond Cattell (1971) proposed that general intelligence actually consists of two specific types of intelligence

TABLE 8.3
Theories of Intelligence

Theory	Key Characteristics	Example
General intelligence	• There is a single factor underlying intelligence. • This factor tends to yield higher IQ scores.	• Your high IQ score reveals that you have high general intelligence.
Fluid and crystallized intelligence	• General intelligence is made up of fluid and crystallized intelligence. • Fluid intelligence: thinking quickly and flexibly in novel, complex situations. • Crystallized intelligence: knowledge from experience that is used to solve problems.	• You show fluid intelligence when you quickly and calmly think of another way to present your data after your laptop dies. • Your strong crystallized intelligence helps you know the answers to crossword puzzles.
Multiple intelligences	• Many intelligences are not measurable by IQ tests. • These intelligences include musical, bodily-kinesthetic, linguistic, mathematical/logical, spatial, intrapersonal, and interpersonal.	• You can play any tune on your guitar after hearing it once. You are probably high in musical intelligence. • You show high intrapersonal intelligence when you create a study plan based on your study habits.
Triarchic theory	• There are three aspects of intelligence. • Analytical intelligence: skill in solving problems and puzzles. • Creative intelligence: ability to think in new and interesting ways. • Practical intelligence: skill in dealing with everyday tasks.	• You show strong analytical intelligence by playing chess strategically. • You show creative intelligence by being able to survive anywhere on just a few dollars. • You may be low in practical intelligence if you constantly lose your car keys.
Emotional intelligence	• Emotional intelligence: skills in managing emotions and recognizing them in other people.	• When you feel yourself getting angry with your boss, you take a walk to calm down. You likely have high emotional intelligence.

(**Figure 8.22**). **Fluid intelligence** involves information processing, especially in novel or complex circumstances, such as reasoning, drawing analogies, and thinking quickly and flexibly. In contrast, **crystallized intelligence** involves knowledge gained through experience, such as vocabulary and spelling and cultural information, and the ability to use this knowledge to solve problems (Horn, 1968; Horn & McArdle, 2007). Fluid intelligence is somewhat analogous to working memory, whereas crystallized intelligence is somewhat analogous to long-term memory. Because both fluid and crystallized intelligence are components of general intelligence, people who score high on one factor also tend to score high on the other. This finding suggests that strong crystallized intelligence is likely aided by strong fluid intelligence.

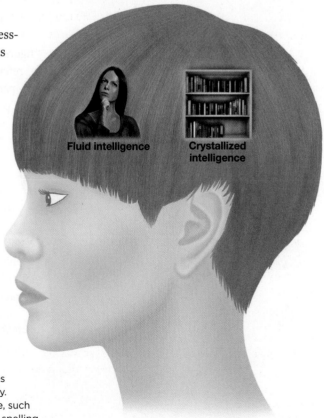

Fluid intelligence   Crystallized intelligence

FIGURE 8.22

Multiple Intelligences: Fluid and Crystallized Intelligence

Cattell saw general intelligence as made up of two types of intelligence. Fluid intelligence represents working memory processes and information processing that allow us to think quickly and flexibly. Crystallized intelligence pertains to information in long-term storage, such as knowledge gained through experience, including vocabulary and spelling.

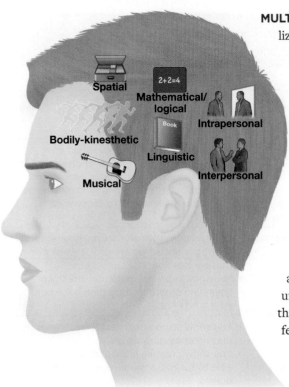

FIGURE 8.23

Multiple Intelligences: Gardner's Theory of Multiple Intelligences

Howard Gardner has theorized that people have many types of intelligence that are independent of each other.

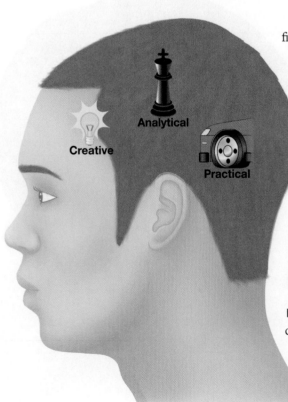

MULTIPLE INTELLIGENCES Whereas Cattell argued that fluid and crystallized intelligence both contribute to general intelligence, Howard Gardner (1983) proposed a theory of **multiple intelligences.** Gardner identified several different types of intellectual talents that are independent of one another (**Figure 8.23**). For example, he proposed that musical intelligence enables some people to discriminate subtle variations in pitch or in timbre and therefore to have above average musical abilities. Among the other intelligences Gardner proposed are mathematical/logical (the ability to calculate and think sequentially), intrapersonal (self-understanding), interpersonal (social understanding), linguistic (excellent verbal skills), spatial (thinking in terms of images and pictures), and bodily-kinesthetic (the ability of athletes and dancers to control their motions with exquisite skill).

Gardner's theory is important partly because it recognizes that people can be average or even deficient in some aspects of intelligence and outstanding in others. According to Gardner, each person has a unique pattern of intelligences. No one should be viewed as "smarter" than others, just differently talented. Some psychologists find this is a feel-good philosophy with little basis in fact. These critics have questioned whether being able to control body movements or compose music is truly a form of intelligence or should instead be considered a specialized talent. Does clumsiness or tone deafness indicate a lack of intelligence? Moreover, there are no standardized ways to assess many of Gardner's intelligences.

Another psychologist who proposed that there are different types of intelligence is Robert Sternberg. Sternberg theorized (1999) that people have three types of intelligence, which he described in his **triarchic theory** (**Figure 8.24**). Analytical intelligence is similar to that measured by standard intelligence tests—being good at problem solving, completing analogies, figuring out puzzles, and similar challenges. Practical intelligence refers to dealing with everyday tasks, such as knowing whether a parking space is large enough for your vehicle, being a good judge of people, being an effective leader, and so on. Creative intelligence involves the ability to gain insight and solve novel problems—to think in new and interesting ways.

Evidence for the existence of multiple intelligences is that many phenomenally successful public figures did not excel academically. For example, Oprah Winfrey was born in poverty, became a teen mother, and has no college degree. Nevertheless, she has become one of the most influential women in the world as a media proprietor, talk-show host, actress, producer, and philanthropist. Arguably, her vast accomplishments are a result of intelligence in several domains, including analytical, creative, and practical intelligence.

EMOTIONAL INTELLIGENCE *Emotional intelligence* (EI) was conceived by the psychologists Peter Salovey and John Mayer and

FIGURE 8.24

Multiple Intelligences: Sternberg's Triarchic Theory
Robert Sternberg has theorized that intelligence can take three forms: analytical, practical, and creative.

subsequently popularized by the science writer Daniel Goleman. This form of intelligence consists of four abilities: managing your emotions, using your emotions to guide your thoughts and actions, recognizing other people's emotions, and understanding emotional language (Salovey & Grewel, 2005; Salovey & Mayer, 1990). People high in EI are good at understanding emotional experiences in themselves and others, then responding to those emotions productively. Regulating your moods, resisting impulses and temptations, and controlling your behaviors are all important components of EI.

Emotional intelligence is correlated with the quality of people's personal relationships (Reis et al., 2007). The idea of emotional intelligence has had a large impact in schools and industry, and programs have been designed to increase students' and workers' emotional intelligence. These efforts may be valuable, since emotional intelligence is a good predictor of high school grades (Hogan et al., 2010). In addition, people high in emotional intelligence cope best with the challenges of college exams (Austin, Saklofske, & Mastoras, 2010).

At the same time, some critics have questioned whether EI really is a type of intelligence or whether it stretches the definition of intelligence too far. Whether or not EI is a type of intelligence, the concept highlights the idea that many human qualities are important and advantageous for those who have them.

8.10 Intelligence Is a Result of Genes and Environment

8.10 LEARNING GOAL ACTIVITIES

To maximize your learning, complete the following learning goal activities.

a. Understand all bold and italic terms by writing explanations of them in your own words.

b. Analyze how nature and nurture influence intelligence by identifying one way that your intelligence has been influenced by nature and one way that it has been influenced by nurture.

Think back to Alexis Martin, the young Mensa member discussed in the chapter opener. Does showing exceptional intelligence very early in her life mean that Alexis was born with a certain amount of intelligence? Is everyone born with particular intelligence, or is intelligence a product of how you are raised and the environment you are in? To understand intelligence, you must once again return to questions of nature and nurture. You need to consider how genes and environment influence intelligence.

Here's one example: Humans have a genetic capacity for having a large vocabulary, but every word in a person's vocabulary is learned in a particular environment (Neisser et al., 1996). Moreover, the specific words a person learns are affected by the person's culture, amount of schooling, and social context. Thus even if intelligence has a genetic component, the expression of intelligence is affected by circumstances. Instead of seeking to demonstrate whether nature or nurture is the more important factor, psychologists try to identify how each crucial factor contributes to intelligence.

BEHAVIORAL GENETICS As you learned in study unit 2.12, behavioral geneticists study the genetic basis of behaviors and traits such as intelligence. Many twin and adoption studies have made it clear that genes help determine

multiple intelligences
The idea that people have many different types of intelligence that are independent of one another.

triarchic theory
The idea that people have three types of intelligence: analytical, creative, and practical.

FIGURE 8.25

Genes and Intelligence

This graph represents average IQ correlations obtained from family, adoption, and twin studies. Siblings raised together show more similarity than siblings raised apart or siblings who are adopted and raised together. However, as shown by the red and blue bars on the right, the highest correlations are found among identical twins, whether they are raised in the same household or not. Overall, the greater the degree of genetic relation, the greater the correlation in intelligence.

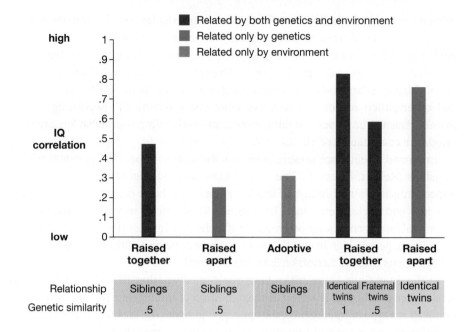

- ■ Related by both genetics and environment
- ■ Related only by genetics
- ■ Related only by environment

	Raised together	Raised apart	Adoptive	Raised together		Raised apart
Relationship	Siblings	Siblings	Siblings	Identical twins	Fraternal twins	Identical twins
Genetic similarity	.5	.5	0	1	.5	1

(a)

(b)

FIGURE 8.26

Optimal Environments Help Develop Intelligence

Parents can provide an enriched environment that will support the development of intelligence in their children. Good practices include (a) reading books to children and (b) providing children with intellectual opportunities from a young age.

intelligence (**Figure 8.25**). For example, studies show that twins raised apart are highly similar in intelligence. Though this finding seems to support the importance of genetics in the development of intelligence, it fails to consider the ways people interact with and alter their environments. Even when raised apart, twins might have similar experiences (Flynn, 2007). Suppose the twins have inherited a higher than average verbal ability. Adults who notice this ability might read to the twins more often and give them more books. The "intelligence gene" has eluded researchers, probably because thousands of genes contribute to intelligence and each one of them has only a small effect (Plomin & Spinath, 2004).

ENVIRONMENTAL FACTORS As you learned in study units 4.1–4.7, various factors influence human development in the womb, then through infancy and childhood. These factors also affect the development of intelligence. For example, poor nutrition can affect brain development and result in lower intelligence (Noble, Korgaonkar, Grieve, & Brickman, 2013; von Stumm & Plomin, 2015). Other environmental influences that can lead to lower intelligence include prenatal factors (for example, the parents' intake of drugs and alcohol) and postnatal factors (for example, family, social class, education, cultural beliefs, drug and alcohol use). On the positive side, an enriched environment can aid in the development of intelligence in many ways (**Figure 8.26**).

For instance, breast-feeding during infancy is related to higher IQs later in childhood. Two large studies—following more than 3,000 people from birth to age 18 or 27—found that breast-feeding for more than 6 months was associated with a 5-point to 7-point difference in IQ (Mortensen, Michaelsen, Sanders, & Reinisch, 2002). There is also an apparent relation between birth weight and intelligence later in life (Shenkin, Starr, & Deary, 2004; **Figure 8.27**).

Not surprisingly, the intellectual opportunities a child receives affect intelligence. For instance, schooling encourages the development of children's brains and cognitive capacities. As Stephen Ceci (1999) notes, the more years that children remain in school, the higher their IQs will be. And students who start school at a younger age because of where their birth dates fall on the calendar have higher test scores than their same-age peers who start school a year later. Schooling not only builds knowledge. Schooling also teaches critical thinking skills, such as being able to think abstractly and learn strategies for solving problems (Neisser et al., 1996). Overall, the evidence is considerable that environmental factors contribute to intelligence. To look at the relationship between one environmental factor and intelligence, see Evaluating Psychology in the Real World on p. 321.

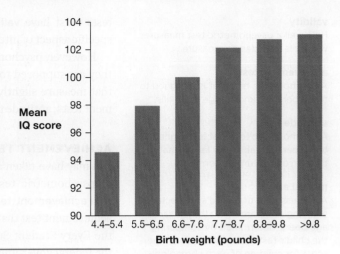

FIGURE 8.27

Birth Weight and Intelligence

For children whose birth weight is within the normal range, IQ scores increase along with birth weight.

Q What Is Intelligence?

To make sure you learned what you just read, write answers to the following questions and check your answers.

8.8 What is the difference between IQ and general intelligence?

8.9 Is knowing the answers to trivia questions related to fluid intelligence or crystallized intelligence?

8.10 How do genes and environment together influence intelligence?

See Appendix B for answers to the red Q questions.

How Is Intelligence Measured?

As you learned in study unit 8.8, Binet and Simon pioneered the measurement of intelligence, in the early 1900s. Since then, Binet and Simon's work has been the basis for psychometric tests that assess intelligence. However, you have also learned that there are many ways to think about intelligence. Psychometric tests are only one way to measure intelligence.

8.11 Intelligence Is Assessed with Psychometric Tests

8.11 LEARNING GOAL ACTIVITIES

To maximize your learning, complete the following learning goal activities.

a. Understand all bold and italic terms by writing explanations of them in your own words.

b. Analyze the three common types of psychometric tests of intelligence by distinguishing how they are similar and different.

All *psychometric tests* have some features in common. They are standardized tests, designed to be given consistently, with uniform procedures for objective scoring (**Figure 8.28**). In other words, psychometric tests must have **reliability**: People's results should be similar each time they take the test. In addition, psychometric

FIGURE 8.28

Standardized Procedures in Psychometric Testing

All psychometric tests—including achievement tests, aptitude tests, and intelligence tests—are standardized tests. They are administered consistently and scored objectively. These students are taking one psychometric test: the SAT for college applications.

reliability
How consistently a psychometric test produces similar results each time it is used.

validity
How well a psychometric test measures what it is intended to measure.

achievement test
A psychometric test that is designed to test a person's knowledge and skills.

aptitude test
A psychometric test that is designed to test a person's ability to learn—that is, the person's future performance.

mental age
An assessment of a child's intellectual standing compared with that of same-age peers; determined by comparing the child's test score with the average score for children of each chronological age.

tests must have **validity:** They should measure what they claim to measure—a specific aspect of intelligence.

However, psychometric tests differ based on the specific aspect of intelligence they are supposed to measure. Psychometric tests fall into three main categories that measure slightly different, but overlapping, aspects of intelligence: achievement tests, aptitude tests, and intelligence tests.

ACHIEVEMENT TESTS AND APTITUDE TESTS   To be admitted to college, you may have taken a test such as the ACT or the SAT. These two different types of psychometric tests measure different aspects of intelligence. A standardized **achievement test** assesses your current skills and knowledge. The ACT is an achievement test that measures the knowledge you acquired in high school. Under the Every Student Succeeds Act, which was signed in 2015 by President Obama, the federal government encourages the states to give achievement tests to school-children to determine their success in learning the core class material.

By contrast, the SAT is a standardized **aptitude test** that measures your ability to learn in the future. Various aptitude tests are also used to predict what tasks you will perform with skill. Employers sometimes use aptitude tests to determine whether a prospective employee will be successful in a certain position. For both achievement and aptitude tests, the stakes can be high because your performance can greatly affect your life.

MODERN INTELLIGENCE TESTS   In 1919, the psychologist Lewis Terman, at Stanford University, modified the Binet-Simon test and established normative scores (average scores for each age) for American children. This test is commonly known as the Stanford-Binet test. It remains among the most widely used intelligence tests for children in the United States. In 2003, the test was revised for the fifth time.

In 1939, the psychologist David Wechsler developed an intelligence test for use with adults. This test is called the Wechsler Adult Intelligence Scale (WAIS). The most current version, the WAIS-IV, was released in 2008. As illustrated in Try It Yourself on p. 322, the WAIS-IV has two parts, and each part consists of several tasks. The verbal part measures aspects such as reading comprehension, vocabulary, and general knowledge. The performance part involves nonverbal tasks, such as arranging pictures in proper order, assembling parts to make a whole object, and identifying a picture's missing features.

INTELLIGENCE QUOTIENT   An intelligence score is based on how many questions people answer correctly on intelligence tests. Binet's original test assessed a child compared with same-age peers. Binet introduced the important concept of **mental age.** This measure is determined by comparing a child's test score with the average score for children of each chronological age.

Suppose an 8-year-old gets right most of the test questions that other 8-year-olds get right but does not correctly answer questions that a 9-year-old gets right. Binet would characterize that child as having a mental age of 8. If the 8-year-old can correctly answer most of the questions an average 10-year-old would get right, the 8-year-old would have a mental age of 10. When a child's mental age equals the child's chronological age, the child's intelligence is typical of children in that particular age group.

The psychologist Wilhelm Stern refined Binet's scoring system by developing the intelligence quotient. A child's IQ is computed by dividing the child's mental age by the child's chronological age and multiplying the result by 100 (**Figure 8.29**).

$$\frac{\text{MENTAL AGE}}{\text{CHRONOLOGICAL AGE}} \times 100 = \text{IQ}$$

FIGURE 8.29

Calculating Intelligence Quotient (IQ)

IQ is determined by dividing a person's mental age by the person's chronological age and multiplying by 100.

People judge the intelligence of others all the time. The people being judged may hear such comments and come to believe them. But do our beliefs about our own intelligence affect us? An Internet search reveals many articles on this topic. For example, this article, from National Public Radio, discusses how children's beliefs about their own intelligence affect their school performance: www.npr.org/templates /story/story.php?storyId=7406521.

What does this article (excerpted below) suggest to you about intelligence? In other words, should you accept the claim being made here? To answer this question, use the three steps in critical thinking:

ACTIVITY: To determine if you should accept the claim in this article, review the Learning Tip on p. 7 and follow these steps:

Step 1 What is the claim I am being asked to accept?

Step 2 What evidence, if any, is provided to support the claim?

Step 3 Given the evidence, what are the most reasonable conclusions about the claim?

If you have rejected the claim or found the evidence lacking, why did you do so? If you have found that the evidence supports the claim, how might this information change how you think and act?

Students' View of Intelligence Can Help Grades

A new study in the scientific journal *Child Development* shows that if you teach students that their intelligence can grow and increase, they do better in school.

All children develop a belief about their own intelligence, according to research psychologist Carol Dweck from Stanford University.

"Some students start thinking of their intelligence as something fixed, as carved in stone," Dweck says. "They worry about, 'Do I have enough? Don't I have enough?'"

Dweck calls this a "fixed mindset" of intelligence. "Other children think intelligence is something you can develop your whole life," she says. "You can learn. You can stretch. You can keep mastering new things."

She calls this a "growth mindset" of intelligence.

Dweck wondered whether a child's belief about intelligence has anything to do with academic success. So, first, she looked at several hundred students going into seventh grade, and assessed which students believed their intelligence was unchangeable, and which children believed their intelligence could grow. Then she looked at their math grades over the next two years.

"We saw among those with the growth mindset steadily increasing math grades over the two years," she says. But that wasn't the case for those with the so-called "fixed mindset." They showed a decrease in their math grades.

This led Dweck and her colleague, Lisa Blackwell, from Columbia University to ask another question.

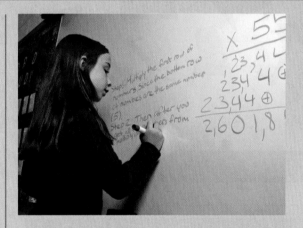

"If we gave students a growth mindset, if we taught them how to think about their intelligence, would that benefit their grades?" Dweck wondered.

So, about 100 seventh graders, all doing poorly in math, were randomly assigned to workshops on good study skills. One workshop gave lessons on how to study well. The other taught about the expanding nature of intelligence and the brain.

The students in the latter group "learned that the brain actually forms new connections every time you learn something new, and that over time, this makes you smarter."

Basically, the students were given a mini-neuroscience course on how the brain works. By the end of the semester, the group of kids who had been taught that the brain can grow smarter had significantly better math grades than the other group. . . .

You can experience questions from an IQ test yourself by answering the example items below (similar to those used in the WAIS III).

1. The verbal portion of IQ tests contains questions about knowledge and language.
   a. General Knowledge: What day of the year is Independence Day in the United States?
   b. Vocabulary: What does "corrupt" mean?
   c. Comprehension: Why do people buy home insurance?
2. The performance portion of IQ tests includes nonverbal tasks.
   a. Picture Arrangement: The pictures below tell a story. Put them in the right order to tell the story.

   b. Object Assembly: If these pieces are put together correctly, they make something. Put them together as fast as you can.

   c. Digit-Symbol Substitution: Using the code below, fill in the missing information in the test picture.

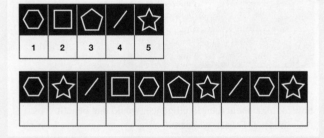

To calculate the IQ of the 8-year-old with a mental age of 10, for instance, you would calculate (10/8) × 100. The result is 125, a very high IQ.

The formula breaks down when used with adults, however. Therefore, the IQs of adults are measured in comparison with the average adult and not with adults at different ages. Today, the average IQ is set at 100. Across large groups of people, the distribution of IQ scores forms a bell curve. The bell curve is also known as a *normal distribution*. Most people are close to the average. Fewer and fewer people score at the tails of the distribution (**Figure 8.30**).

VALIDITY AND RELIABILITY   How do we know that intelligence tests are actually good indicators of intelligence? As noted at the start of this study unit, for

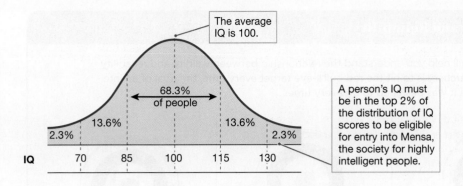

The average IQ is 100.

68.3% of people

13.6%   13.6%

2.3%   2.3%

IQ   70   85   100   115   130

A person's IQ must be in the top 2% of the distribution of IQ scores to be eligible for entry into Mensa, the society for highly intelligent people.

FIGURE 8.30
The Distribution of IQ Scores
IQ is a score on a normed test of intelligence. That is, each person's score is relative to the scores of the large number of people who already took the test. The average, or mean, score on intelligence tests is 100. As shown in this bell curve, approximately 68 percent of people have an IQ score between 85 and 115.

psychometric tests to be useful, they must have three characteristics: They must be standardized, they must have reliability, and they must have validity.

What do we mean when we say that intelligence tests should be valid? We are saying that they should really measure what they claim to measure (**Figure 8.31a**). To explore the validity of intelligence tests, researchers analyzed data from 127 different studies. As part of these 127 studies, more than 20,000 participants took the Miller Analogy Test. This test is widely used for admission to graduate school as well as for hiring decisions in many work settings. It requires test takers to complete analogies such as "Fingers are to hands as toes are to ____." The researchers found that scores on the Miller Analogy Test predicted not only graduate students' academic performance but also individuals' productivity, creativity, and job performance in the workplace (Kuncel, Hezlett, & Ones, 2004).

By contrast, if an intelligence test has reliability, the results for a person will be stable and consistent over time. That is, someone who takes the same intelligence test multiple times should have a similar score each time (**Figure 8.31b**). Reliability is tied to validity. If a test is valid, then it is also likely to be reliable. But even when a test is reliable, it is not necessarily valid. You can get the same score on a test over many trials, whether or not the test actually measures what it is supposed to measure. The relationship between reliability and validity is summarized in the Learning Tip on p. 324.

Even when an IQ test is a valid, reliable measurement of general intelligence, it is not always an accurate predictor of success in school or work. In fact, additional factors contribute to life success (Neisser et al., 1996). For example, people from privileged backgrounds tend to have higher IQs. However, they also tend to have other advantages, such as family contacts, access to internships, and acceptance to schools that can cater to their needs. Even if two people have more or less equal IQ and social backgrounds, the person working twice as many hours per week may have a better chance of accomplishing personal goals (Lubinski, 2004). Another study found that children's self-control was much better than IQ in predicting final grades (Duckworth & Seligman, 2005). In other words, IQ may be important, but it is only one of the factors contributing to success in the classroom, the workplace, and life generally.

CULTURAL BIAS One important early criticism of intelligence tests was that they may penalize people who belong or don't belong to particular cultures or

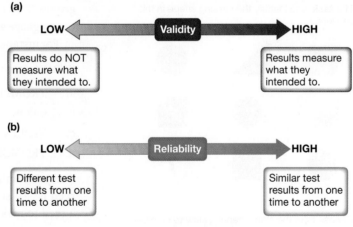

(a)

LOW ◄————— Validity ————► HIGH

Results do NOT measure what they intended to.

Results measure what they intended to.

(b)

LOW ◄————— Reliability ————► HIGH

Different test results from one time to another

Similar test results from one time to another

FIGURE 8.31
Validity and Reliability
In addition to being standardized, an intelligence test that is a good indicator of intelligence has two key aspects.
(a) Good intelligence tests must have validity. That is, they should measure what they intend to: intelligence.
(b) Good intelligence tests must also have reliability. In other words, people should score similarly each time they take the test.

This graphic provides an analogy that will help you understand the relationship between validity and reliability in intelligence tests. Just as the goal in archery is to hit the red bull's-eye target every time, the goal of an intelligence test is to measure intelligence as it was designed to do every time.

ARCHERY ANALOGY	**Valid:** The shots <u>did hit</u> the intended target. **Reliable:** Repeated shots <u>did result</u> in very similar outcomes.	**Not valid:** The shots <u>did not hit</u> the intended target. **Reliable:** Repeated shots <u>did result</u> in very similar outcomes.	**Not valid:** The shots <u>did not hit</u> the intended target. **Not reliable:** Repeated shots <u>did not result</u> in very similar outcomes.
TRANSFER TO INTELLIGENCE TESTS	**Valid:** The test <u>did measure</u> intelligence as it was designed to do. **Reliable:** Repeated testing <u>did result</u> in very similar IQ scores.	**Not valid:** The test <u>did not measure</u> intelligence as it was designed to do. **Reliable:** Repeated testing <u>did result</u> in very similar IQ scores.	**Not valid:** The test <u>did not measure</u> intelligence as it was designed to do. **Not reliable:** Repeated testing <u>did not result</u> in very similar IQ scores.

The task is to identify the missing shape in this sequence.

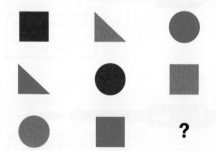

Choose from the eight shapes below to complete the sequence above:

The answer is the first triangle in the bottom row:

groups. That is, doing well on intelligence tests often requires knowing the language and culture of the mainstream.

For instance, consider this analogy:

STRING is to GUITAR as REED is to

a. TRUMPET

b. OBOE

c. VIOLIN

d. TROMBONE

Are you familiar with all these instruments? Do you know what a reed is? To solve this analogy, you need to know that an oboe uses a reed to make music, just as a guitar uses strings to make music. If you were not exposed to this information, you could not answer the question.

What it means to be intelligent also varies across cultures. Most measures of IQ reflect values of what is considered important in

FIGURE 8.32

Removing Bias from Tests

According to the creators of this test, the task should not yield differences in intelligence based on a person's culture.

modern Western culture, such as being quick-witted or speaking well. But what is adaptive in one society is not necessarily adaptive in others. One approach to dealing with cultural bias is to use items that do not depend on language. The nonverbal performance measures on the WAIS, for example, may be a more neutral way to test intelligence. Other culture-neutral tests show a series of patterns and ask the test taker to identify the missing pattern (**Figure 8.32**). The use of these nonverbal tests helps assessors ensure that cultural bias does not affect test scores.

8.12 Intelligence Is Associated with Cognitive Performance

8.12 LEARNING GOAL ACTIVITIES

To maximize your learning, complete the following learning goal activities.

a. Understand all bold and italic terms by writing explanations of them in your own words.

b. Understand the relationship between cognitive performance and intelligence by describing in your own words three ways that cognitive performance reveals intelligence.

Psychometric tests provide a good way to measure IQ based on the premise that intelligence is a single factor. But as you learned in study unit 8.9, other models propose that intelligence has multiple aspects. In the late 1800s, the scientist Sir Francis Galton believed that intelligence was related to the speed of neural responses and the sensitivity of sensory-perceptual systems. The smartest people, Galton believed, had the quickest responses, keenest perceptions, and most efficient brains. Other psychologists believe that intelligence is supported by cognitive performance. Cognitive performance can be observed through processes such as mental processing, working memory, and attention. How can such aspects of intelligence be measured?

SPEED OF MENTAL PROCESSING   People who do not seem very intelligent are sometimes described as "a bit slow." Though that description may sometimes be hurtful, it actually might be accurate. People who score lower on intelligence tests consistently respond more slowly on tests of reaction time than those who score higher on intelligence tests (Deary, 2000). Psychologists test reaction time in two ways.

A test of *simple reaction time* might require you to press a computer key as quickly as possible whenever a stimulus appears on the screen. For example, "Press the X key every time you see an X." A more difficult test might require you to choose, again as quickly as possible, the correct response for the stimulus presented. For example, "Press the X key every time you see an X, or press the A key every time you see an A." Scores on intelligence tests are related even more strongly to this *choice reaction time* (Jensen, 1998).

WORKING MEMORY AND ATTENTION   General intelligence scores are also closely related to working memory (Conway, Kane, & Engle, 2003). As you learned in

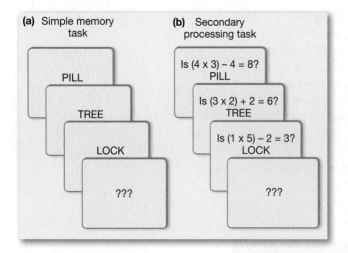

(a) Simple memory task

PILL

TREE

LOCK

???

(b) Secondary processing task

Is (4 x 3) − 4 = 8?
PILL

Is (3 x 2) + 2 = 6?
TREE

Is (1 x 5) − 2 = 3?
LOCK

???

FIGURE 8.33

Memory Tasks

(a) In a simple test of memory, you listen to a short list of words and then repeat the words in order. **(b)** Memory tests that have two components show a stronger association between working memory and general intelligence. In this case, you have to solve math operations as words are presented. Once again, you have to repeat the words in the order they are presented (adapted from Conway et al., 2003).

FIGURE 8.34

Stephen Wiltshire

Despite his autism, Stephen Wiltshire had published a book of his remarkably accurate, expressive, memory-based drawings by the time he was a young teenager. Here, in October 2010, he holds his drawing of an architectural site in London, England. Wiltshire observed the site briefly, then completed the picture largely from memory.

study unit 7.5, working memory is the ability to keep information in mind as you work with it. Many studies of the relationship between working memory and intelligence differentiate between simple tests of memory and memory tests that require some form of secondary processing. On a simple test of memory, you would be asked to listen to a list of words and then repeat the list in the same order (**Figure 8.33a**). Performance on these tests is related only weakly to general intelligence (Engle, Tuholski, Laughlin, & Conway, 1999). In contrast, memory tests that have two components show a strong relation between working memory and general intelligence (**Figure 8.33b**; Gray & Thompson, 2004; Kane, Hambrick, & Conway, 2005; Oberauer, Schulze, Wilhelm, & Süfs, 2005).

The link between working memory and general intelligence may be attention. Paying attention (focusing mental resources on information to be processed; see study unit 3.3) enables you to stick to a task until you complete it successfully (Engle & Kane, 2004). The connection between paying attention and completing a task is especially strong when you are being bombarded with competing information or other distractions. The importance of staying focused makes sense in light of the relationship between general intelligence and the accomplishment of novel, complex tasks. The question, then, is whether brain regions that support working memory are involved in general intelligence.

SAVANTS   How would you like to be able to read a page of this textbook in 8 to 10 seconds? Perhaps less useful but even more impressive would be the ability to recite all the zip codes and area codes in the United States by their assigned regions, or to name hundreds of classical music pieces by hearing only a few notes of each work. These amazing abilities are just a few of the extraordinary memory feats demonstrated by Kim Peek (Treffert & Christensen, 2006).

Peek, who died in 2008, was the inspiration for the character played by Dustin Hoffman in the 1988 movie *Rain Man*. He memorized the contents of over 9,000 books, but he could not button his own clothes or manage any of the usual chores of daily living, such as making change. Peek was born, in 1951, with an enlarged head and many brain anomalies, including a missing corpus callosum, the thick band of nerves that connects the brain's two halves. He also had abnormalities in several other parts of his brain, especially the left hemisphere. He scored 87 on an intelligence test, but clearly this number did not adequately describe his intelligence.

Peek and people like him are known as *savants*. They have minimal intellectual capacities in most domains, but at a very early age each savant shows an exceptional ability in some "intelligent" process. For example, a savant's exceptional ability may be related to math, music, or art. The neurologist and author Oliver Sacks (1995) recounts the story of Stephen Wiltshire, an artistic savant. Wiltshire has autism spectrum disorder. In childhood, it took him the utmost effort to acquire enough language to accomplish simple verbal communication. Even so, years after taking a single glance at a place, Wiltshire can draw a highly accurate picture of it (**Figure 8.34**). We know very little about savants. The combination of prodigious memory and the inability to learn seemingly basic tasks is a great mystery.

8.13 Many Factors Determine Group Differences in Intelligence

8.13 LEARNING GOAL ACTIVITIES

To maximize your learning, complete the following learning goal activities.

a. Understand all bold and italic terms by writing explanations of them in your own words.

b. Apply the concept of stereotype threat to the real world by providing an example of how you have experienced stereotype threat in your life, have seen it in others, or can imagine it happening.

When you hear that Nobel Prize winners, Supreme Court justices, or members of Mensa have high IQs, you probably are not surprised or bothered. The idea that some people may be smarter than the average person is not very controversial. A more controversial claim is that there are differences in intelligence between people of different races.

The most controversial aspect of intelligence testing over the last century has been the idea that genetics can explain overall differences in intelligence scores between racial groups. In a 1969 paper, Arthur Jensen created a huge controversy by stating that African Americans are, on average, less intelligent than white Americans. Given the importance of intelligence to educational and career attainment, claims that some groups are superior to others require close scrutiny, and it is important to discuss controversial and sensitive topics with an eye to being as fair to all sides as possible.

The debate continues about differences in African Americans' and white Americans' scores on measures of intelligence. Multiple studies over the past 30 years have found that—although many African Americans have higher intelligence scores than most white Americans—on average whites score about 10–15 points higher than African Americans on most measures of intelligence. What might be the cause of this group difference?

ENVIRONMENTAL DIFFERENCES   Even if there are differences in IQ score between races, we cannot conclude that race causes the differences if there are any environmental differences between the groups. On average, African Americans have very different life circumstances than white Americans. On average, African Americans make less money, are more likely to live in poverty, generally go to under-funded schools, have fewer years of education and lower-quality health care, and are more likely to face prejudice and discrimination.

Around the world, minority groups that are the targets of discrimination—such as the Maori in New Zealand, the burakumin in Japan, and the Dalits in India—have lower intelligence scores on average. John Ogbu (1994) argues that poor treatment of minority-group members can make them pessimistic about their chances of success within their cultures. This may make them less likely to believe that hard work will pay off for them, in turn lowering their motivational level and therefore their performance. This explanation is plausible, but it is not a clear-cut basis for understanding the differences in test scores between African Americans and white Americans (Neisser et al., 1996). Consider one other explanation: stereotype threat.

STEREOTYPE THREAT   Research from social psychology provides one possible explanation that might contribute to why some racial groups may score lower

FIGURE 8.35

Stereotype Threat

Stereotype threat may lead black students to perform poorly on some standardized tests.

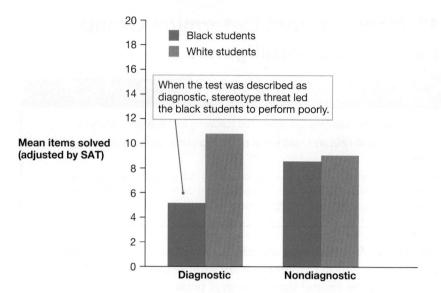

When the test was described as diagnostic, stereotype threat led the black students to perform poorly.

stereotype threat

Apprehension about confirming negative stereotypes related to a person's own group.

on standardized tests of intelligence. **Stereotype threat** is the worry or fear that some people might experience if they believe that their performances on tests might confirm negative beliefs about their racial group (Steele & Aronson, 1995; **Figure 8.35**). As noted by the psychologist Toni Schmader (2010), stereotype threat causes distraction and anxiety, interfering with performance by reducing the capacity of short-term memory and undermining confidence and motivation. As described in Has It Happened to You?, knowing you are experiencing stereotype threat can help you overcome it.

Steven Spencer and his colleague Gregory Walton researched many stereotype threat studies involving a number of different groups from several countries and reached two general conclusions. First, they found that stereotyped groups perform worse than non-stereotyped groups when they are being evaluated. This effect is reversed when the threat is reduced, such as when an exam is presented as non-evaluative (Walton & Spencer, 2009). Second, they found that interventions to reduce the effects of stereotype threat are often successful. For instance, even simply informing people about the negative consequences of stereotype threat can prevent them from showing the effects (Johns, Schmader, & Martens, 2005).

In another study, encouraging African American students to write about important personal values appeared to protect them from stereotype threat, perhaps because it led them to focus on positive aspects of their lives rather than on stereotypes about their group (Cohen, Garcia, Apfel, & Master, 2006). Other studies have found that strengthening peer relations and social connections can help prevent stereotype threat. Indeed, Canadian aboriginal children performed better academically in school environments that provided opportunities to develop social skills and create friendships (Baydala et al., 2009).

Stereotype threat applies to any group that is subject to a negative stereotype (Spencer, Logel, & Davies, 2016). For instance, women tend to do more poorly than men when taking an exam on which they believe men typically outscore women, but they often perform as well as men on the same test if they do not hold such a belief (Schmader, Johns, & Forbes, 2008; Spencer, Steele, & Quinn, 1999). One study used fMRI to examine the neural mechanisms underlying stereotype threat (Krendl, Richeson, Kelley, & Heatherton, 2008). The researchers found that women who had been reminded about the negative stereotypes concerning women's math ability solved fewer math problems correctly and responded more slowly. Most important, they had more activation in the brain regions involved in social and emotional processing, suggesting that they were anxious about their performance. By contrast, the women in the control group who had not been told the negative stereotypes showed greater activation in neural networks associated with mathematical learning. These results support the idea that anxiety about confirming stereotypes interferes with performance.

 How Is Intelligence Measured?

To make sure you learned what you just read, write answers to the following questions and check your answers.

8.11 Suppose a 2-year-old child is able to perform at the level of a 4-year-old on the Stanford-Binet. What are the 2-year-old's mental age and IQ score?

8.12 What is the relationship between intelligence and speed of processing?

8.13 How does stereotype threat sometimes interfere with minority students' performance on intelligence tests?

See Appendix B for answers to the red Q questions.

BIG PICTURE

Want to earn a better grade on your test? Go to **INQUIZITIVE** to practice actively with this chapter's content and get personalized feedback along the way.

What Is Thinking?

8.1 Thinking Is the Mental Manipulation of Representations

Review the learning goal activities on p. 294. Thinking is the mental manipulation of representations of information that people encounter in their environments. Thinking involves both analogical representations (which usually correspond to images) and symbolic representations (which usually correspond to words or ideas). Thinking also involves using mental maps, which include both analogical and symbolic representations. Together, these representations form the basis of human thought, intelligence, and the ability to solve complex problems or special challenges.

8.2 Schemas Are the Basis of Thinking

Review the learning goal activities on p. 296. Schemas are mental structures—collections of ideas, prior knowledge, and experience—that help organize information and guide thought and behavior. Schemas are made up of categories, which are groupings of information based on properties that are shared. In turn, categories are made up of concepts, which are single mental representations of items. According to the prototype model, a concept that is the most typical member of a category is called a prototype. According to the exemplar model, there is no one best concept in a category. Instead, representations of all the examples (exemplars) of a category ever encountered by a person become the basis for the category.

8.3 Schemas Are the Basis of Stereotypes

Review the learning goal activities on p. 299. Schemas are helpful because they allow for efficient thinking about groups of people, events, or objects. However, schemas can have unintended consequences, such as creating stereotypes. Stereotypes are generalizations—about people, events, or objects—that can lead to biases in how people think or act.

KEY TERMS

thinking (p. 295)	schemas (p. 296)
analogical representations (p. 295)	prototype model (p. 298)
	exemplar model (p. 299)
symbolic representations (p. 295)	stereotypes (p. 299)

How Do You Use Thinking?

8.4 You Use Thinking in Three Ways

Review the learning goal activities on p. 302. Three common forms of thinking are: (1) reasoning, (2) decision making, and (3) problem solving. Reasoning is using information to determine if a conclusion is valid. Reasoning can be informal (that is, based on opinion, hearsay, or personal experience) or formal (as in the scientific method).

8.5 How You Think Biases Decision Making

Review the learning goal activities on p. 303. Decision making is a process of choosing among different alternatives. Decision making is often based on using heuristics, which are mental shortcuts that allow quick and easy ways of thinking about information. Three common heuristics that can lead to errors are the: (1) availability heuristic (making decisions based on how easily information comes to mind), (2) representativeness heuristic (making decisions based on how information seems to represent a group), and (3) affective heuristic (making decisions based on one's emotions). Unfortunately, these mental shortcuts can also lead to faulty thinking. Decision making is also affected by framing, that is, how information is presented. The paradox of choice—that is, having too many options—contributes to the difficulty of decision making.

8.6 You Solve Problems to Achieve Goals

Review the learning goal activities on p. 308. In problem solving, obstacles are overcome to reach a desired goal. Four common problem solving strategies are: (1) subgoals (working to reach smaller goals on the path to a larger goal), (2) working backward (starting at the goal state and proceeding to the start state, (3) analogy (using a problem that is similar to the current one), and (4) insight (suddenly realizing a solution to the problem when you stop thinking about the problem).

8.7 You Overcome Obstacles to Solve Problems

Review the learning goal activities on p. 310. Difficult problems can be solved by changing mental representations to overcome an obstacle to thinking. People can successfully change these representations to solve problems in three ways, by: (1) restructuring the representation (changing the way one thinks about a problem), (2) overcoming mental sets (avoiding old, unsuccessful ways of thinking about the problem), and (3) overcoming functional fixedness (thinking of new uses for objects to solve a problem).

What Is Intelligence?

8.8 One General Factor May Underlie Intelligence

Review the learning goal activities on p. 312. General intelligence is the idea that a single common factor underlies intelligence. General intelligence is thought to be revealed by intelligence tests with many different types of questions that provide one intelligence quotient (IQ) score. High general intelligence tends to be seen in higher IQ scores.

8.9 There May Be Multiple Aspects of Intelligence

Review the learning goal activities on p. 314. Several theories suggest that people can have many different intelligences, including: (1) fluid intelligence (thinking quickly and flexibly in processing information) and crystallized intelligence (about facts, knowledge, and past experience), (2) multiple intelligences (seven unique types according to Gardner's theory), (3) the three intelligences included in triarchic theory (analytical, creative, and practical), and (4) emotional intelligence (about recognizing emotions and how to appropriately regulate emotions).

8.10 Intelligence Is a Result of Genes and Environment

Review the learning goal activities on p. 317. Both nature (genes and biology) and nurture (environment and upbringing) affect intelligence. Behavioral genetics has demonstrated that genes influence intelligence, but no single gene underlies intelligence. Instead, it is likely that thousands of genes contribute to intelligence. However, environmental factors also influence intelligence, beginning in the womb and extending through one's upbringing. Although some factors (such as poverty) can have negative effects on intelligence, others (such as breast feeding and being in enriched environments) can positively affect intelligence.

How Is Intelligence Measured?

8.11 Intelligence Is Assessed with Psychometric Tests

Review the learning goal activities on p. 319. Psychometric tests are designed to test various aspects of intelligence and share three common aspects. All are standardized, so they are given in a consistent way and scored objectively. They must also be reliable, which means that they must give similar results over time. Finally, they must be valid, which means that they must actually measure what they are meant to, which is intelligence. Three different types of psychometric tests allow a measure of intelligence: (1) achievement (tests what a person knows), (2) aptitude (tests a person's capacity to develop skills), and (3) intelligence tests (IQ tests). For adults, modern IQ tests have an average score of 100 within each age group. A child's IQ is computed by dividing the child's estimated mental age by the child's chronological age, then multiplying this number by 100.

8.12 Intelligence Is Associated with Cognitive Performance

Review the learning goal activities on p. 325. Intelligence is related to how a person processes information, which is called cognitive performance. Three aspects of cognitive performance are related to intelligence: (1) the speed of mental processing (how quickly one thinks), (2) working memory (the ability to keep information in mind as one manipulates it), and (3) attention (focusing mental resources on information to be processed).

8.13 Many Factors Determine Group Differences in Intelligence

Review the learning goal activities on p. 327. Differences in intelligence across races and ethnicities are hard to assess because of environmental differences. Stereotype threat influences test scores when people believe that their performances might confirm negative stereotypes about their sex or race.

CHAPTER 8 SELF-QUIZ

To make sure you learned the information in this chapter, write answers to the following questions and check your answers. **See Appendix B for answers to the self-quiz.**

1. Camden is learning to play pool. He thinks about how his knowledge of math formulas in physics can help him make different types of shots. Camden is using a(n) _____ to think about how to play pool.
   a. prototype
   b. analogical representation
   c. symbolic representation
   d. heuristic

2. Ayanna doesn't know what a "clunker" is, so her friend Hilary says, "You know that old car Bruce has? That's the best example of a 'clunker.' It has all the characteristics: It's an older car, it looks terrible, and it's always breaking down, yet it's still driveable." Hilary's thinking about Bruce's clunker is based on the _____ model of thought.
   a. prototype
   b. exemplar
   c. schema
   d. stereotype

3. Dawson thinks about going to Las Vegas on his vacation. But he remembers the recent mass shooting and decides that Las Vegas is too dangerous. So he books a flight to Sarasota instead. Dawson's overestimation of the danger in Las Vegas is a result of _____.
   a. formal reasoning
   b. the availability heuristic
   c. framing
   d. the representativeness heuristic

4. When he works on a sudoku puzzle, Armando begins by filling in all the number 1's. Then he moves on to all the 2's, then 3's, and so on until he finishes with the number 9's. Armando's problem solving strategy of filling in one number at a time until the entire puzzle is complete is based on _____.
   a. using an analogy
   b. creating subgoals
   c. working backward
   d. experiencing insight

5. Florin wants to go out on Halloween, but he doesn't have a costume. His wife, Ashley, replies, "No problem. Just use this sheet." But Florin doesn't see how the sheet could be a costume. His wife says, "Put this sheet over your head, poke out two holes for your eyes, and now you're a ghost!" The fact that Florin didn't see how he could use the sheet as a ghost costume is most likely explained by his experiencing _____.
   a. restructuring
   b. framing
   c. insight
   d. functional fixedness

6. Mrs. Tomaselli knows that her student Eli has an average IQ. She also has observed him having difficulty spelling long words and multiplying double-digit numbers. Because of these facts, Mrs. Tomaselli assumes that Eli will have trouble with other specific abilities, such as solving science problems. Mrs. Tomaselli's assessment of Eli's abilities is best explained by a belief in _____.
   a. general intelligence
   b. multiple intelligences
   c. crystallized intelligence
   d. the triarchic theory of intelligence

7. Fritz is an "A" student who easily learns and remembers facts from school and recalls them for tests. Jason is skilled at diagnosing car troubles and solving them creatively so he can get around. Fritz is most likely considered to be intelligent based on _____, while Jason is most likely considered to be intelligent based on _____.
   a. fluid intelligence; multiple intelligences
   b. fluid intelligence; triarchic theory
   c. crystallized intelligence; triarchic theory
   d. crystallized intelligence; multiple intelligences

8. Carla conducts a study and finds evidence supporting a correlation between nurture and intelligence. Which of the following is Carla most likely to have found?
   a. Identical twins receive similar scores on a traditional IQ test.
   b. Adopted siblings vary greatly in their ability to learn new tasks.
   c. Children who are able to teach themselves to read are more likely to go to college.
   d. Children whose parents provide them with many books perform better academically.

9. Dr. Cantor puts several questions about his political views on an American history exam. Students complain that those questions have nothing to do with how well they know American history and should not be used to determine their grades. The students are arguing that the test _____.
   a. lacks reliability
   b. does not have a normal distribution
   c. lacks validity
   d. measures aptitude, not achievement

10. Felicia has a high IQ and is excellent at trivia. Felicia always answers the questions several seconds before anyone else. Felicia's cognitive performance suggests she is intelligent, because she _____.
    a. has fast reaction times
    b. has high general intelligence
    c. has good working memory
    d. is a savant

How Can Understanding Thinking Help You Succeed in Your Career?

Have you ever been frustrated by a mechanical problem with your car? As automotive systems have grown increasingly complex and reliant on computers, the job of automotive technician has become more demanding. Pinpointing and repairing malfunctions can require multiple tests, attempts, and approaches. Technicians now need to understand various forms of technology. They also need to understand how to reason, make decisions, and solve problems. All jobs require thinking, but understanding how thinking works from a psychological perspective can be especially helpful to automotive industry professionals.

Using a process or algorithm is an effective strategy for figuring out what is wrong with a car. A technician may ask a series of questions that identify or rule out explanations for the problem, such as whether it happens only in cold weather, or whenever the car turns to the right, or when it has been too long since the spark plugs were replaced. On the PBS radio show Car *Talk*, the hosts used this strategy with great success to figure out car complaints from their listeners.

Most jobs in health care also require problem solving and decision making. Nurse practitioners and paramedics, for example, often have to make quick decisions about a person's illness with incomplete information. These are exactly the kinds of situations in which heuristics, shortcuts or informal guidelines, are most used. Health care providers are cautioned to be aware of how frequently something occurs (the base rate) in making decisions, such as first looking for the most likely cause of the person's health complaints. In addition, understanding how framing and avoiding risk may influence a patient's choice of medical treatment is crucial in any discussion between patient and health care provider.

Generally, understanding how people think is valuable when you need to hire or supervise people. People in human resources positions need to understand how aptitude is

related to job performance. Knowing about the several complicated issues involved in assessing intelligence means they understand that there is more to being a good employee than knowing some relatively obscure piece of information on an IQ test. Human resources officers understand that people possess different types of intellectual skills that might benefit the job. Knowing also that people who face discrimination may be at a disadvantage on traditional assessments enables those who hire to look for other qualities that diverse candidates bring to the workplace. Having this knowledge about thinking helps create productive companies with employees who feel valued and respected.

TAKEAWAY POINT: Knowing how thinking works can help you in any job, especially one in which you must deal creatively with technology. Whether you work with sick cars or sick people, the material in this chapter can help you because reasoning, decision making, and problem solving are crucial to diagnosing system failures and fixing them.

Ψ You can look up job descriptions, education requirements, salaries, and more at the Bureau of Labor Statistics: www.bls.gov. Visit the site and start putting psychology to work!

9 Motivation and Emotion

MALALA YOUSAFZAI WAS JUST A GIRL GOING TO SCHOOL, but that is why armed gunmen tried to assassinate her. It was 2012, and girls in Pakistan were forbidden from getting an education by the Taliban, a religious group with extremist views. Malala was 15 years old when she survived the attempt on her life and became an activist for the right of all girls to safely get a free, quality education (**Figure 9.1**).

In the two years following the attack, Malala spoke at the United Nations in support of educating girls, published the book *I Am Malala* (Yousafzai, 2013), and won a Nobel Peace Prize. How did she achieve so much, during years when she was constantly threatened with death? According to Malala, "When I survived the attack and when I woke up in the hospital, my mind was very, very clear, that this life is for a cause. This is a second life, and it is given to me for something greater than what I was before" (Gidda, 2017).

BIG QUESTIONS

What Motivates Your Behavior?

What Are Your Most Important Motivated Behaviors?

How Do You Experience Emotions?

How Do Emotions Affect You?

FIGURE 9.1

Malala Yousafzai

Even in the face of death threats, Malala **(left)** has fought for the education of girls worldwide. To learn more about Malala and her campaign, visit www.malala.org.

Indeed, Malala considers herself very lucky to "be the voice" of all of the millions of girls who are denied the opportunity to get an education ("Malala Yousafzai," 2016).

Malala's work has produced real-world results. For example, Nigerian girls who escaped from Boko Haram, a militant religious group, were given counseling and full high school scholarships. In Lebanon, a school was opened for children who were refugees from Syria. Malala donated $50,000 of the Nobel Prize money to help rebuild a school in Gaza. Malala now plans to study philosophy, politics, and economics at England's Oxford University. "As our politicians are doing nothing for us, nothing for peace, nothing for education," she explains, "I want to become prime minister of my country" (Gidda, 2017).

One key to success in achieving goals is strong motivation, as shown by Malala. This chapter begins by examining what motivates people to act in certain ways. For example, where does the motivation to achieve come from? What makes people persevere toward their goals?

In addition, this chapter examines how motivation and emotion are tied together. On the one hand, people are motivated to act because of the emotions they experience. You know this if you have ever felt angry at an injustice and decided to act to improve the situation. On the other hand, being motivated to act and successfully reaching goals can produce emotions. Indeed, if you have worked hard to do well in a course and experienced a positive outcome, you may have felt satisfaction, even joy. As Malala's story shows, motivation can keep people moving toward their goals and lead to deep feelings of satisfaction.

What Motivates Your Behavior?

What inspires you to get up in the morning? Why do you choose to eat certain foods? How important is it to you to achieve your goals at school or at work? Specific questions such as these lead to general questions about the reasons for behaviors. As the example of Malala Yousafzai shows, your behavior is strongly influenced by your motivation to do—or not do—certain things. The following study unit considers factors that influence motivation.

9.1 Many Factors Influence Motivation

9.1 LEARNING GOAL ACTIVITIES

To maximize your learning, complete the following learning goal activities.

a. Understand all bold and italic terms by writing explanations of them in your own words.

b. Apply the four internal factors that affect motivation by describing one example each of how your motivation is affected by needs, drives, arousal, and pleasure.

c. Understand the one external factor that affects motivation by explaining how incentives motivate you to achieve positive outcomes and avoid negative outcomes.

Most of the general theories of motivation emphasize four basic qualities. First, motivation is *activating*—it stimulates you to do something. For instance, the desire to be fit might motivate you to get up and go for a run on a cold morning. Second, motivation is *directive*—it guides your behaviors toward meeting specific goals or needs. Hunger motivates you to eat, thirst motivates you to drink, and pride (or fear, or many other feelings) motivates you to study for exams. Third, motivation helps you *sustain* your behavior until you achieve your goals or satisfy your needs. For example, hunger gnaws at you until you find something to eat, whereas a desire to win drives you to practice foul shots until you succeed. Fourth, motives *differ in strength*, depending on the person and on the situation. You might feel a strong motivation to exercise to get in better shape, but another person might not feel such a strong motivation to exercise. Thus **motivation** refers to factors of differing strength that energize, direct, or sustain behavior (**Figure 9.2**). A wide range of factors have an impact on the motivation to perform particular behaviors, as described in **Table 9.1**.

SATISFACTION OF NEEDS What do you really need to do to stay alive? Of course, you need air, food, and water to survive. But satisfying your basic biological needs is not enough to live a fully satisfying life. People also have social needs, including the need for achievement and the need to be with others. A **need**, then, is a state of deficiency that can be either biological (for example, water) or social (for example, being with other people). Either way, needs make people behave in goal-directed ways. Failure to satisfy a need leads to psychological or physical problems.

In the 1940s, the psychologist Abraham Maslow proposed a "need theory" of motivation that became very influential, although it has not since been supported by research. Maslow believed that people are driven by many needs, which can be

(a)   (b)

(c)   (d)

FIGURE 9.2

What Motivates People?

When you look at people, in life or in photos, you see their behaviors. For example, they may be **(a)** dressing warmly, **(b)** studying, **(c)** eating with friends and family, or **(d)** embracing and kissing. And while you may think you know why people act as they do, you actually can't see their internal motivations. Throughout this chapter, you will refer back to the examples in this figure as you consider people's motivations and behaviors.

TABLE 9.1
Factors That Motivate Behavior

Factor	Description	Example
Satisfaction of needs	A need is a state of being deficient in biological or social factors. The deficiency motivates the person to engage in behaviors that make up for it (that is, help satisfy the need).	Your job doesn't pay enough money to guarantee that you can pay for housing and food for your family. You take a second job to help pay the bills.
Drive reduction	A drive is an internal psychological state that motivates behaviors that will satisfy a certain need. When the need is satisfied, the drive is reduced.	You feel very cold in your apartment. This feeling creates a drive that motivates you to put on a sweater to satisfy your need for warmth. Once you feel warmed, the drive is reduced.
Optimal level of arousal	Each person has an optimal level of arousal, somewhere from low to high. People are motivated to engage in behaviors that fit with their preferred level of arousal.	You and your partner are an odd couple. Preferring calmness, you stay in and watch movies in the evening. Preferring excitement, your partner goes out to clubs at night.
Pleasure principle	The pleasure principle says that people are motivated to engage in behaviors that make them feel good and to avoid behaviors that cause them pain.	You are completely full after dinner. You order the flourless chocolate cake anyway because you know how good it will taste.
Incentives	Incentives are external factors that motivate behaviors.	Knowing you can win the tennis championship is a good incentive that motivates you to practice hard.

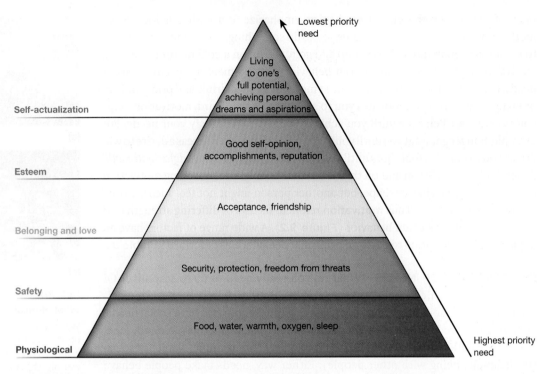

FIGURE 9.3

Need Hierarchy

According to Maslow's hierarchy of needs, people must satisfy basic needs (such as for food and water) before they can address higher needs for personal growth (such as for self-actualization).

described in a **need hierarchy** (**Figure 9.3**). Survival needs (such as food and water) can be placed at the bottom of the hierarchy, based on the idea that they must be satisfied first. Needs such as personal growth can be placed at the top of the hierarchy. To experience personal growth, Maslow believed, people must not only meet their biological needs. They must also meet the needs to feel safe and secure, to feel loved, and to have a good opinion of themselves.

Maslow's theory is an example of *humanistic psychology*. As you learned in study unit 1.6, the humanistic school views people as striving toward personal fulfillment. From this perspective, human beings are unique among animals because people continually try to improve themselves. In considering motivation, humanists focus on the person. For example, they suggest that it is the person who desires food, not the person's stomach. A state of *self-actualization* occurs when people achieve their personal dreams and aspirations. A self-actualized person is living up to that person's unique potential and therefore is truly happy. Maslow writes, "A musician must make music, an artist must paint, a poet must write, if he is ultimately to be at peace with himself. What a man *can* be, he *must* be" (Maslow, 1968, p. 46).

Maslow's need hierarchy has long been embraced in education and business. Even so, this order lacks scientific support. Self-actualization might or might not be a requirement for happiness. And the ranking of needs is not as simple as Maslow suggests. For instance, think of political activists who starve themselves in hunger strikes to demonstrate the importance of their personal beliefs. Some people who have satisfied their physiological and security needs prefer to be left alone rather than to be part of a community. Maslow's hierarchy, therefore, is more useful as a description of how important various needs might be.

DRIVE REDUCTION Many bars set out free snacks, such as nuts or potato chips, for their customers. Doing so is good for business, because the saltiness of the

motivation
Factors of differing strength that energize, direct, and sustain behavior.

need
A state of biological or social deficiency.

need hierarchy
An arrangement of needs, in which basic survival needs must be met before people can satisfy higher needs.

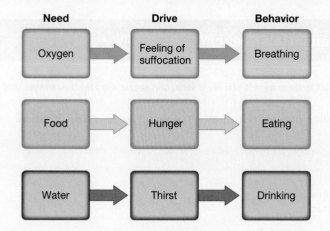

Need	Drive	Behavior
Oxygen	Feeling of suffocation	Breathing
Food	Hunger	Eating
Water	Thirst	Drinking

snacks makes people thirsty and so they drink more. By providing salty treats, bars are creating a need for fluids. What motivates people to satisfy their needs? A **drive** is a psychological state that motivates a person to satisfy a need. A particular drive encourages behaviors that will satisfy a particular need (**Figure 9.4**). In this example, because people have a need for water, the salty snacks create the drive of thirst. The drive of thirst then encourages the purchase of a beverage to drink.

Basic biological drives, such as thirst or hunger, help people maintain a stable condition. A stable condition is also called equilibrium. In the 1920s, the physiologist Walter Cannon coined the term *homeostasis* to describe the tendency for bodily functions to remain in equilibrium. A good analogy for homeostasis is a home heating and cooling system controlled by a thermostat. You set the thermostat to some desired temperature. The temperature is a *set point*. This set point indicates homeostasis for the system. If the actual temperature is different from the set point, the furnace or air conditioner gets feedback that makes it adjust the temperature. Similarly, the human body regulates temperature to a set point (**Figure 9.5**).

When you are too warm or too cold, brain mechanisms initiate responses such as sweating (to cool the body) or shivering (to warm the body). At the same time, you may become motivated to take off or put on clothes (as suggested in the case of the woman dressing warmly in Figure 9.2a). Models such as this are useful for describing various basic biological drives, such as hunger and thirst.

drive
A psychological state that, by creating arousal, motivates an organism to engage in a behavior to satisfy a need.

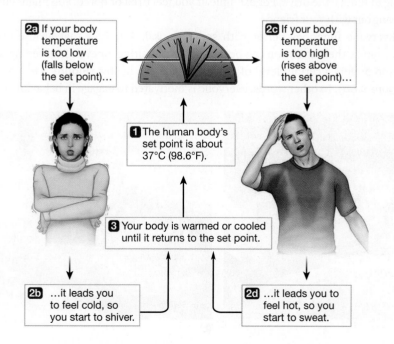

2a If your body temperature is too low (falls below the set point)…

2c If your body temperature is too high (rises above the set point)…

1 The human body's set point is about 37°C (98.6°F).

3 Your body is warmed or cooled until it returns to the set point.

2b …it leads you to feel cold, so you start to shiver.

2d …it leads you to feel hot, so you start to sweat.

Do you prefer more rather than less arousal? Use this chart to determine if you are a sensation seeker. Choose the number that reflects how you feel about each statement.

Strongly disagree	Somewhat disagree	Neither disagree nor agree	Somewhat agree	Strongly agree
1	2	3	4	5

(a) I would like to explore strange places. _____
(b) I like to do frightening things. _____
(c) I like new and exciting experiences, even if I have to break the rules. _____
(d) I prefer friends who are exciting and unpredictable. _____

Scoring:
Add your four answers and divide by four. Your score reveals whether you tend to avoid or seek out new sensations.

1.0 to 1.99: You may strongly avoid sensation seeking; you may prefer a very low level of internal arousal.
2.0 to 2.99: You may mildly avoid sensation seeking; you may prefer a somewhat low level of internal arousal.
3.0 to 3.99: You may mildly tend toward sensation seeking; you may prefer a somewhat high level of internal arousal.
4.0 and above: You may strongly tend toward sensation seeking; you may prefer a very high level of internal arousal.

Your score is a rough indication of whether you are motivated toward activities that raise or lower your level of arousal. It also suggests your optimal level of arousal. This level is the point at which you will perform the best in most circumstances.

Source: Stephenson, Hoyle, Palmgreen, & Slater (2003).

arousal
Physiological activation (such as increased brain activity) or increased autonomic responses (such as increased heart rate, sweating, or muscle tension).

If a behavior consistently reduces a drive over time, it becomes a *habit*. The likelihood that a behavior will occur is due to both drive and habit. For instance, suppose you sometimes feel hungry at night. To satisfy that need for food, you eat a late-night snack. The snack reduces your hunger, and that outcome reinforces further late-night snacking. Over time, you might develop the habit of eating late at night.

OPTIMAL AROUSAL AND PERFORMANCE   When you are deprived of some need (such as water or sleep), a drive increases in proportion to the degree of deprivation. The hungrier you are, the more driven you are to find food. The drive creates **arousal**. Arousal is a sense of physiological tension that encourages you to do something to reduce the drive. For example, if you feel tired or bored, you might choose to hang out with your friends.

Everyone functions better with some arousal. Activities that arouse people and capture their attention can be stimulating, exciting, or even frightening. Each person prefers a certain level of arousal, which can be low (**Figure 9.6a**) or high (**Figure 9.6b**). In other words, everyone is motivated to engage in behaviors based

FIGURE 9.6

People Differ in Their Optimal Level of Arousal

Each of us has a different level of optimal arousal that motivates us to behave in certain ways. **(a)** Some people have a lower level of optimal arousal. These people tend to prefer calmer activities, such as reading, which keep arousal at an optimal lower level. **(b)** Other people have a higher level of optimal arousal. They tend to prefer exciting activities, such as skydiving, which raise arousal to an optimal higher level.

(a)

(b)

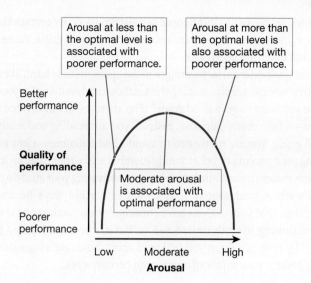

FIGURE 9.7

Graph of the Yerkes-Dodson Law
According to this law, performance increases with arousal until an optimal point. Here, the optimal point is the top of the curve. Below that point of moderate arousal and above it, arousal levels impair performance.

Arousal at less than the optimal level is associated with poorer performance.

Arousal at more than the optimal level is also associated with poorer performance.

Better performance

Quality of performance

Moderate arousal is associated with optimal performance

Poorer performance

Low   Moderate   High

Arousal

on their own *optimal level of arousal*. Too much arousal may overwhelm a person. Too little arousal may leave a person bored. Answer the questions in Try It Yourself on p. 340 to determine what your optimal level of arousal is.

You might think that more arousal will lead to more motivation and thus to better performance. But that's not necessarily the case. The *Yerkes-Dodson law* describes the relationship between arousal, motivation, and performance. This law was named after the two researchers who formulated it, in 1908. This law states that performance improves with arousal up to an optimal point. After that point, more arousal will result in declining performance. A graph of this relationship is shaped like an upside-down U (**Figure 9.7**).

As the Yerkes-Dodson law predicts, students perform best on exams when they feel moderate anxiety. Too little anxiety can make them inattentive or unmotivated, and too much anxiety can interfere with their thinking ability. Likewise, athletes have to pump themselves up for their events, but they can fall apart under too much stress.

PLEASURE   Sigmund Freud proposed that needs are satisfied based on the *pleasure principle*. According to Freud, the pleasure principle motivates people to seek pleasure and avoid pain. This idea is central to many theories of motivation. People do things that feel good. If something feels good, they do it again. The fact that certain foods make them feel good is an excellent example. When asked what foods bring them a lot of pleasure, people often name comfort foods, such as macaroni and cheese, steak, specific desserts, or dishes that their relatives often made.

The idea that pleasure motivates behavior helps explain why people behave in ways that do not necessarily satisfy biological needs. For example, they eat dessert even when they are not hungry. But the pleasure principle also makes sense from an evolutionary perspective. Both positive and negative motivations are adaptive. For instance, big, fierce animals are associated with pain, so people are motivated to avoid them (Watson, Wiese, Vaidya, & Tellegen, 1999). Food is typically associated with pleasure, so people are motivated to seek out foods they like to eat. A good example of this principle is the finding that animals prefer to eat sweet foods (Steiner, 1977). Sweetness usually indicates that food is safe to eat. By contrast, most poisons and toxins taste bitter, so it is not surprising that animals avoid bitter tastes. However, as you will see later in this chapter, the inborn preference for sweet tastes over bitter ones can lead to eating too many sugary foods.

INCENTIVES   So far, you have seen how internal factors "push" people to act in certain ways—for example, to satisfy needs, reduce drives, reach optimal levels

incentives
External objects or external goals, rather than internal drives, that motivate behaviors.

of arousal, and feel pleasure. But people are also "pulled" by certain things in their environments. **Incentives** are external objects or external goals, rather than internal factors, that motivate behaviors.

Think about what external factors might make a person study hard, like the person in Figure 9.2b. In your case, are you reading this textbook and studying for your psychology class because you want to get a good grade? If so, then you are motivated to get a positive outcome—a high grade. Suppose, instead, you are reading and studying to avoid getting a bad grade. You are motivated to avoid a bad outcome—a low grade, or even disappointing your parents or other family members. In either case, an incentive—an external factor, rather than an internal drive—is motivating your studying behavior.

Incentives affect your motivations to act in certain ways because you have learned over time that your actions have consequences. You learned about this idea, operant conditioning, in study units 6.8–6.12. But it is not necessarily a good thing to be motivated by rewards. Soon you will read about how receiving external rewards may actually reduce your motivation to act in certain ways.

9.2 Some Behaviors Are Motivated for Their Own Sake

9.2 LEARNING GOAL ACTIVITIES

To maximize your learning, complete the following learning goal activities.

a. Understand all bold and italic terms by writing explanations of them in your own words.

b. Apply intrinsic and extrinsic motivation by explaining how you use intrinsic motivation to meet one goal and extrinsic motivation to meet a different goal.

Imagine that you have a big exam coming up in one of your classes. You are motivated to make a study plan and start studying. But why are you motivated to act in that way? On the one hand, you may be motivated to study because you like the subject and want to master the material. This is an internal factor, something inside you, that prompts you to study. On the other hand, you might want to earn an A on the exam. This is an external factor that is the basis for your studying. Both kinds of factors—ones inside you and ones outside you—motivate you to act.

INTRINSIC MOTIVATION Consider the activities people find most satisfying, such as reading a good novel, taking a walk, or listening to music. Many of these activities seem to fulfill no obvious purpose other than enjoyment. Such activities are directed toward **intrinsic motivation**. Intrinsic motivation is the desire to get the value or pleasure from the activity with no apparent external goal (**Figure 9.8a**). The desire to master a topic in a course you are taking is an example of intrinsic motivation. In the chapter opening story, you read about how Malala Yousafzai found herself in the position "to be the voice" for girls who are deprived of an education. Because Malala was serving this role for its own sake, without concrete goals, she may have been experiencing intrinsic motivation.

Some intrinsically motivated activities may satisfy natural curiosity and creativity. After playing with a new toy for a long time, children start to lose interest and will seek out something new. Playful exploration is characteristic of all mammals and especially primates. For example, monkeys will work hard, without an external reward, to solve relatively complex puzzles (Harlow, Harlow, & Meyer, 1950). One

(a)

(b)

FIGURE 9.8

Intrinsic Motivation and Extrinsic Motivation

(a) Intrinsic motivation causes you to behave in a certain way simply because the activity, or the result of the activity, is valuable or enjoyable. **(b)** Extrinsic motivation is an external factor that causes you to behave in a certain way. One factor is a reward, such as money.

function of play is that it helps you learn about the objects in an environment. This activity clearly has survival value. That is, knowing how things work lets you use those objects for more serious tasks.

Similarly, you may be driven toward creative pursuits. Maybe you produce artwork. Maybe you modify recipes with new ingredients. You may do these things simply because you enjoy activities that allow you to express your creativity. Creativity is the tendency to generate ideas or alternatives that may be useful in solving problems, communicating, and entertaining yourself and others (Franken, 2007).

EXTRINSIC REWARDS CAN REDUCE INTRISIC MOTIVATION However, sometimes people are not motivated by internal factors. **Extrinsic motivation** is the desire to perform an activity to achieve an external goal. For example, when you work to earn a good grade or a paycheck, you are extrinsically motivated (**Figure 9.8b**).

Unfortunately, extrinsic rewards may actually reduce intrinsic motivation. In a classic study, children were invited to draw with colored marking pens (Lepper, Greene, & Nisbett, 1973). Most children find this activity intrinsically motivating because they liked it. One group of children was extrinsically motivated to draw by being led to expect a "good player award." Another group of children was rewarded unexpectedly after the task. A third group was neither rewarded nor led to expect a reward. Later, there was a free-play period.

Children who were expecting an extrinsic reward spent much less time playing with the pens than did the children who were never rewarded or the children who received an unexpected reward. The first group of children responded as though it was their job to draw with the colored pens. In other words, why would they play with the pens for free when they were used to being paid? This seems to contradict a basic principle of learning discussed in study unit 6.10: When a behavior is reinforced, you will increase that behavior. However, there are two explanations for why intrinsic motivation may be reduced by extrinsic rewards.

According to *self-determination theory*, people are motivated by a desire to feel good about themselves, which inspires them to do their most creative work (Deci & Ryan, 1987). For example, self-determination theory states that people are motivated to engage in certain behaviors because they need to feel successful at something, have personal control, or develop personal relationships with others. However, extrinsic rewards may reduce the feeling that you are choosing to do something for yourself. So as in the research by Lepper et al. (1973), the presence of a reward, such as a "good player award," can reduce the intrinsic value of a certain behavior, such as coloring.

Self-perception theory can also explain why the presence of extrinsic rewards can reduce internal motivation. According to this theory, people are seldom aware of their specific motives. Instead, people make inferences about their motives according to what seems to make the most sense (Bem, 1967). Suppose someone gives you a big glass of water and you drink it all. Then you exclaim, "Wow, I must have been thirsty!" You believe you were thirsty because you drank the whole glass. You make this assumption even though you were not aware of being thirsty. When you cannot come up with an obvious explanation for your behavior—that you expected a reward, for instance—you may conclude that you simply like the behavior. Being rewarded for engaging in an activity, such as coloring in the Lepper et al. (1973) study, gives you an alternative explanation for engaging in it. The alternative explanation is that you performed the behavior, coloring, to get the reward, the "good player award," instead of just doing it for fun. So without the reward, you have no reason to engage in the behavior. The reward has replaced the goal of pure pleasure.

intrinsic motivation
A desire to perform an activity because of the value or pleasure associated with that activity, rather than for an apparent external goal or purpose.

extrinsic motivation
A desire to perform an activity to achieve an external goal that activity is directed toward.

So is it better to be intrinsically motivated than extrinsically motivated? The research suggests that, depending on the person and the situation, both intrinsic and extrinsic motivation can influence your behavior (Cerasoli, Nicklin, & Ford, 2014). Think of it this way: You work hard to get an external reward, such as a good salary or a good grade. But your internal desire to master new skills at work, or to learn the material in your classes, affects the quality of your work and your ability to achieve your goals. Together, these two forms of motivation influence the outcome of your behavior in many situations, including in your personal life, in your academic work, and in your career. This chapter's Putting Psychology to Work feature, on p. 375, explains how understanding motivation (and emotion) can help you succeed professionally.

You'll learn more about the topic of motivation in the next section, which considers the motivations behind a few important behaviors: eating, bonding with others, and successfully achieving long-term goals.

 What Motivates Your Behavior?

To make sure you learned what you just read, write answers to the following questions and check your answers.

9.1 What is the difference between a need and a drive?

9.2 If a child enjoys studying for school, will paying that child for getting good grades increase the child's motivation to study? Why or why not?

See Appendix B for answers to the red Q questions.

What Are Your Most Important Motivated Behaviors?

Do you love to eat good food? What about spending time with friends and family? Is it important for you to work hard and achieve your goals at school and work? Many of us are highly motivated to engage in these behaviors and others, such as having sex. Our motivations about sexual relations are described in detail in study units 10.9–10.11. This section explores our motivations to eat, create social ties, and work hard to be successful in academics and the workplace.

9.3 Motivation to Eat Is Affected by Biology

 9.3 LEARNING GOAL ACTIVITIES

To maximize your learning, complete the following learning goal activities.

a. Understand all bold and italic terms by writing explanations of them in your own words.

b. Analyze how four biological systems influence motivation to eat by describing how your stomach, glucose, hormones, and brain increase or decrease your desire to eat.

Three main biological factors combine to influence your motivation to eat: (1) levels of glucose in your bloodstream, (2) hormones such as insulin, ghrelin, and leptin, and (3) signals from your brain, especially from your hypothalamus. In contrast with what you might think, signals from your stomach do not strongly motivate eating.

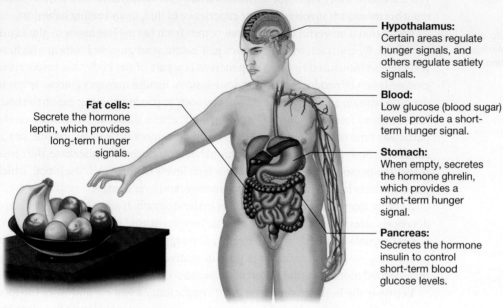

Hypothalamus: Certain areas regulate hunger signals, and others regulate satiety signals.

Blood: Low glucose (blood sugar) levels provide a short-term hunger signal.

Stomach: When empty, secretes the hormone ghrelin, which provides a short-term hunger signal.

Pancreas: Secretes the hormone insulin to control short-term blood glucose levels.

Fat cells: Secrete the hormone leptin, which provides long-term hunger signals.

Everyone needs to eat to survive. But eating is also one of life's greatest pleasures, and we do a lot of it. Most people in industrialized countries consume between 80,000 and 90,000 meals during their lives—that's more than 40 tons of food! For a long time, scientists believed that eating was a classic homeostatic system. That is, people would normally eat when they felt hungry and stop eating when they were full. Some sort of "detector" would notice deviations from the set point and would signal that a person should start or stop eating. But where did the hunger signals come from? The search for the hunger detector has led scientists from the stomach and the chemistry of the bloodstream to hormones and the brain. So it is not surprising that many different biological mechanisms encourage eating (Rogers & Brunstrom, 2016). This study unit looks at the three main biological mechanisms that motivate eating, which are shown in the Learning Tip above.

STOMACH AND BLOOD CHEMISTRY Your stomach rumbles in the middle of class or while you are at work. You immediately know what that means: You are hungry. But is this really true? Internal contractions and expansions of the stomach can indeed make your stomach growl. However, over the past century, research has established that while these movements are associated with hunger, they are not the sole cause of hunger. Indeed, people who have had their stomachs surgically removed due to illness continue to report feeling hungry even though they no longer have a stomach that growls (Bergh, Sjöstedt, Hellers, Zandian, & Sodersten, 2003). So signals from the stomach have a weak influence on the motivation to eat.

Other research has pointed to the existence of receptors in the bloodstream that monitor levels of vital nutrients. One theory proposes that the bloodstream is monitored for its glucose levels. *Glucose*, also known as blood sugar, is the primary fuel for metabolism and is especially crucial for neuronal activity. It therefore makes sense

insulin
A hormone, secreted by the pancreas, that controls glucose levels in the blood.

ghrelin
A hormone, secreted by an empty stomach, that is associated with increasing eating behavior based on short-term signals in the bloodstream.

leptin
A hormone, secreted by fat cells, that is associated with decreasing eating behavior based on long-term body fat regulation.

for animals to become hungry when they are deficient in glucose. So what happens when your glucose levels drop? You probably get crabby. In addition, your body sends chemical signals about hunger. These signals are ultimately what prompt you to eat a snack to alleviate your hunger.

HORMONES   Other chemicals that help regulate hunger signals are hormones. As you learned in study unit 2.10, hormones affect your thoughts and behaviors. Three main hormones are involved in your experience of hunger and eating behaviors.

Recall that a powerful hunger signal comes from having low levels of glucose in the blood. By contrast, when you have just eaten, your glucose levels are high, so you are less motivated to eat. The pancreas is a part of the body that responds to glucose levels by producing the hormone **insulin**. Insulin manages glucose levels in the bloodstream and allows the cells of the body to process the glucose so the body has energy to function. Do you know anybody who is diabetic? Depending on the particular type of diabetes, the person's body produces little or no insulin, or the cells of the body do not process the insulin that is produced. In either case, the result is that the person's body cannot process high levels of glucose in the blood, which can ultimately lead to blindness, nerve damage, and liver damage.

Another hormone, **ghrelin**, originates in the stomach. It surges before meals and decreases after you eat, so it may play an important role in triggering short-term hunger signals (Abizaid, 2009; Higgins, Gueorguiev, & Korbonits, 2007). When people lose weight, an increase in ghrelin motivates additional eating, in part by making food more rewarding (Zorrilla et al., 2006).

Leptin is the hormone involved in fat regulation. As you eat and store the food energy as fat, leptin is released from your fat cells. The released leptin travels to the hypothalamus, the brain region that controls many homeostatic systems. There it acts to stop eating behavior, perhaps by making food less appetizing (Farooqi et al., 2007). Because leptin acts slowly, however, it takes considerable time after eating before leptin levels change in the body. Therefore, leptin may be more important for long-term body fat regulation than for short-term eating control. With obesity on the rise around the world, considerable research is under way to find out whether leptin is associated with the condition.

THE BRAIN   While hormones contribute greatly to your motivation to eat, so does the brain. The hypothalamus is the brain structure that most influences eating. Early research revealed that damage to the hypothalamus could dramatically change eating behavior and body weight. One of the first observations occurred in 1939, when researchers discovered that patients with tumors of the hypothalamus became obese. To examine whether obesity could be caused in animals of normal weight, researchers selectively damaged a specific area of the hypothalamus in rats (Graff & Stellar, 1962). When the middle, or *ventromedial*, region of the hypothalamus (VMH) is damaged, rats eat great quantities of food. This condition, *hyperphagia*, causes the rats with VMH damage to grow extremely obese. Sometimes damage to the VMH can cause obesity in humans (**Figure 9.9**).

Brain structures other than the hypothalamus are also involved in eating behavior. A region of the frontal cortex called the gustatory cortex processes taste cues such as sweetness and saltiness (Rolls, 2007; see Figure 5.24). Seeing tasty food makes you crave it (**Figure 9.10**). This response is associated with activity in the limbic system, the main brain region involved in emotion and rewards (Rapuano et al., 2017; Volkow, 2007).

Of course, sometimes you may eat when you are not hungry. At other times, you may avoid eating even though you are not full. How much any one biological mechanism contributes to eating behavior, including the eating disorders described in

FIGURE 9.9

Hyperphagia in Humans

(a) In 2012, Alexis Shapiro underwent brain surgery that accidentally damaged her hypothalamus. **(b)** This damage caused her to feel extremely hungry all the time and resulted in a large weight gain.

study unit 11.2—anorexia nervosa and bulimia nervosa—is unclear. Many factors influence eating. They include learning and culture, which you will read about in the next study unit.

9.4 Motivation to Eat Is Also Influenced by Learning

9.4 LEARNING GOAL ACTIVITIES

To maximize your learning, complete the following learning goal activities.

a. Understand all bold and italic terms by writing explanations of them in your own words.

b. Apply the idea that learning affects motivation to eat by providing examples of how conditioning, familiarity, flavor, and culture influence your motivation to eat.

As you learned in the previous study unit, your body gives you a lot of information about when to eat and when not to eat. But do you sometimes eat when you are not hungry, such as by eating too much at a special holiday meal? And do you sometimes not eat when you are hungry, such as during religious observances when fasting is required? Around the globe, much of the social world revolves around when people should and should not eat. This aspect of eating is greatly affected by learning. The eating behaviors shown in Figure 9.2c, on p. 337, are most likely motivated by learning what foods to eat, what time to eat, and how to eat from common plates of food.

CONDITIONED TO EAT   What time did you eat lunch yesterday? Most people, all around the world, eat lunch at about the same time of day—somewhere between noon and 2 PM. On a physiological level, this practice makes little sense. After all, people differ greatly in metabolic rate, the amount they eat for breakfast, and the amount of fat they have stored for long-term energy needs. But people don't eat lunch at noon because they have deficient energy stores. They do it because they have been classically conditioned to associate eating with regular mealtimes.

To understand how your watch telling you it is noon leads to hunger and eating, recall Pavlov's metronome, which you read about in study unit 6.4. Like the metronome, the time of day is a stimulus associated with food. This association makes the time of day—indicated by hearing a lunch bell or noticing your watch says it is noon—a conditioned stimulus that produces a learned response, a conditioned response. In this case, regular mealtimes lead to various anticipatory responses that motivate eating behavior and prepare the body for digestion. The sight and smell of tasty foods activates physiological systems that increase hunger. Just thinking about treats—freshly baked bread, pizza, a decadent dessert—may initiate similar reactions that make you hungry.

FAMILIARITY   As a child, were you raised in a household that ate whole grain bread or white bread (**Figure 9.11**)? Or maybe rice or tortillas? Now as an adult, which do you prefer? If you are like most people, you probably eat the same type of food that you ate as a child. Familiarity generally shapes food preferences. The more experience you have with a food, the more you will continue to eat it.

(a)   (b)

FIGURE 9.11
Familiarity Influences Food Preferences
People tend to prefer eating the foods they are familiar with. **(a)** If as a child you ate wheat or multigrain bread, you are likely to do so as an adult. **(b)** By contrast, if you ate white bread as a child, then as an adult you are more likely to still eat white bread.

FIGURE 9.12

The Impact of Variety on Eating Behavior

When people are presented with a variety of foods, they tend to eat more than when they are presented with only a few foods.

People's avoidance of unfamiliar foods makes evolutionary sense because unfamiliar foods may be dangerous or poisonous, so avoiding them is adaptive (Galef & Whiskin, 2000). Getting children to like new foods often involves exposing them to small amounts at a time until they grow accustomed to the taste. Infants and toddlers also learn to try foods by observing their parents and siblings. Children are much more likely to eat a new food offered by their mother than the same food offered by a friendly stranger. This behavior, too, makes sense from an evolutionary standpoint. After all, if a child sees a parent eat something, then it must be safe to eat.

FLAVOR An important factor that motivates eating is flavor. Humans have an inborn preference for sweetness, which likely is adaptive. Over the course of human evolution, sweetness was most often obtained through fruits, which provided healthy nutrients. However, a modern diet that includes added sugar leads children to find natural foods, such as fruits, not sweet enough (Mennella, Bobowski, & Reed, 2016). This change encourages people to select diets high in added sugars (Foterek et al., 2016).

Having a variety of flavors also promotes eating. Animals, including humans, will stop eating relatively quickly if they have just one type of food to eat, but they will continue eating if presented with a different type of food. Thus, they tend to eat much more when various foods are available than when only one or two types of food are available (**Figure 9.12**).

FIGURE 9.13

Our Culture Influences What We View as Tasty

Crickets are a popular snack among Cambodians. This vendor in Phnom Penh is offering what is considered to be a tasty treat in that culture: fried crickets.

CULTURAL INFLUENCES Would you eat a bat? In the Seychelles islands, bat is a delicacy. (It tastes something like chicken.) What we will eat has little to do with logic and everything to do with what we learn is "food" (see Has It Happened to You? on p. 349). Some of the most nutritious foods are not eaten in North America, because they are viewed as disgusting. For instance, fried termites, a favorite in Zaire, have more protein than beef. Insects are nutritious, and in many countries they are eaten as tasty treats (**Figure 9.13**). At the same time, people from other cultures might be nauseated by some North American favorites, such as Jell-O or peanut butter.

Of course, what we prefer to eat is also determined by the ethnic, cultural, and religious values of our own upbringing and experiences. For example, Kosher Jews eat beef but not pork. Hindus eat pork but not beef. Ethnic differences in food preference often continue when a family moves to a new country, so culturally transmitted food preferences powerfully affect our eating habits.

9.5 People Have a Need to Belong

9.5 LEARNING GOAL ACTIVITIES

To maximize your learning, complete the following learning goal activities.

a. Understand all bold and italic terms by writing explanations of them in your own words.

b. Apply the need to belong by describing one way you show a need to belong, one positive effect of belonging, and one negative effect of failing to belong.

When you eat, do you prefer to eat alone or with friends or family? We often hear that "humans are social animals." This statement is not just a way of saying that people like to dine together or go to parties. Over the course of human evolution, our ancestors who lived with others were more likely to survive, reproduce, and pass along their genes. Children who stayed with adults were more likely to survive until their reproductive years, because the adults would protect and take care of them. Similarly, adults who developed long-term, committed relationships were more likely to reproduce and to have children who survived to reproduce. Successful groups shared food, provided mates, and helped care for children, including orphans. Some survival tasks (such as hunting large mammals or looking out for predatory enemies) were best accomplished by group cooperation. It therefore makes great sense that, over the millennia, humans have lived in groups.

PEOPLE ARE MOTIVATED TO FORM GROUPS The **need to belong theory** states that the need for social relations is a fundamental motive that has evolved for adaptive reasons (Baumeister & Leary, 1995). This theory explains why most people make friends easily (**Figure 9.14**). All societies have some form of group membership, though the types of groups may differ (Brewer & Caporael, 1990). Not belonging to a group increases risk for various negative consequences, such as illness and premature death (Elovainio et al., 2017; Rico-Uribe et al., 2018). Such ill effects suggest that the need to belong is a basic motive that drives behavior. The need to belong motivates people the same way that hunger drives people to seek food and avoid dying from starvation.

If humans have a fundamental need to belong, then it is reasonable to expect that we have ways of detecting whether we are included in particular groups. In other words, given the importance of being a group member, people need to be sensitive to signs that the group might reject them. Indeed, evidence indicates that people feel anxious when facing exclusion from their social groups (MacDonald & Leary, 2005). Further, people who are shy and lonely tend to worry most about social evaluation and pay much more attention to social information (Gardner, Pickett, Jefferis, & Knowles, 2005). The take-home message is that just as a lack of food causes hunger, a lack of social contact causes emptiness and despair.

In the movie *Cast Away*, Tom Hanks's character becomes stranded on a desert island. The man has such a strong need for companionship that he begins carrying on a friendship with a volleyball he calls Wilson (named for the manufacturer, whose name is on the ball). As the film reviewer Susan Stark (2000) notes, this film convinces us that "human company, as much as shelter, water, food and fire, is essential to life as most of us understand it." To see how you can satisfy a need to belong, read Using Psychology in Your Life on p. 350.

HAS IT HAPPENED TO YOU?
Food and Traditions

Do you eat turkey and cranberries in July? Many Americans eat these foods at Thanksgiving but not at other times of the year. Every family has its own traditions for what and how they eat. The particular choices may be due to ethnicity, religion, or other reasons. Family food traditions are especially strong around particular holidays. Does the culture of your family sometimes set up a motivation for you to eat (or not eat) certain things? If so, you have learned the motivation to eat based on cultural experiences.

need to belong theory
The need for interpersonal attachments is a fundamental motive that has evolved for adaptive purposes.

FIGURE 9.14
Making Friends
We generally have a need to belong. This need motivates us to form friendships and join social groups.

9.6 People Have a Need to Achieve Long-Term Goals

9.6 LEARNING GOAL ACTIVITIES

To maximize your learning, complete the following learning goal activities.

a. Understand all bold and italic terms by writing explanations of them in your own words.

b. Apply achievement motivation by describing three changes you can make to demonstrate high achievement motivation in your schoolwork or job.

So far, this chapter has focused on motivation to fulfill short-term goals, such as satisfying hunger or bonding with loved ones. But motivation applies to long-term

How Can You Satisfy a Need to Belong?

People have a strong need to form stable and satisfying relationships with friends, family, romantic partners, colleagues, and the community. But we are also often told to "look out for number one," suggesting that our self-interest should be a primary motivator. Jennifer Crocker is a research psychologist interested in the ways that motivations influence our sense of well-being. Crocker has examined two motivational perspectives. These perspectives are based on *egosystem goals* and *ecosystem goals*. Both perspectives have important implications for our ability to satisfy the need to belong.

*Ego*system goals motivate us to build and maintain other people's impressions of us. People motivated by egosystem goals focus on proving themselves, showing their good qualities, and validating their worth. Such people prioritize their own perceived needs over those of others (Crocker, Olivier, & Nuer, 2009). When we are so focused on building and maintaining others' perceptions of us, we see relationships with others in terms of winning and losing: If I win, you lose. If you win, I lose. Crocker's research shows that students who hold these goals became more depressed and anxious during their first semester in college. These goals are also associated with problematic alcohol use (Moeller & Crocker, 2009).

In contrast, people with *eco*system goals perceive themselves as part of a system where their own circumstances are linked to those of others. They prioritize the needs of others because they understand these social connections and care about the well-being of others (Crocker et al., 2009). These individuals are likely to think that both people can benefit from a situation, and that they are responsible for working together to make that happen. Students who hold ecosystem goals tend to be less depressed and anxious during their first semester in college. They are more engaged in their courses and more eager to learn from failure. In a nutshell, people with ecosystem goals seem to enjoy a host of positive benefits.

How might you cultivate your ecosystem goals and satisfy your need to belong? Three strategies will help you see yourself as more interconnected in relationships with others.

1. **Think and write about your personal values and priorities.** The ability to think beyond the self is at the heart of ecosystem goals. Interestingly, you can do this by clarifying your own values. Write down the values (that is, personal principles or standards of behavior) that are important to you, and explain why they are important. A study by Crocker and her colleagues found that people who did that felt more loving, joyful, giving, empathic, connected, sympathetic, grateful, and so on (Crocker, Niiya, & Mischkowski, 2008).

2. **Think about goals you have that would help other people.** Ask yourself how the tasks in your everyday life support your other-oriented goals. For example, if you are interested in studying medicine, you might say, "I want to help relieve other people's physical pain." You might then see your organic chemistry class as an opportunity to learn something that will help in future work with patients rather than as a difficult barrier that could show the world you are not cut out to be a doctor.

3. **Be grateful.** Other people touch our lives in many ways that we can be thankful for. One way to identify and appreciate moments of humanity and moments of connection is to keep a gratitude journal. Each evening before you go to bed, think of an instance or two where you were affected in a good way by another person. The event might be something small, such as when a kind driver made room for you to merge into traffic. It might be something larger, such as when a friend sat with you for hours as you grieved the loss of a loved one.

aspirations as well. Consider: What would you like to be doing 10 years from now? What things about yourself would you change? Your aspirations might not be as newsworthy as Malala Yousafzai's dreams of ensuring that all girls have access to educational opportunities, but they matter greatly. What might motivate you to fulfill those long-term goals?

achievement motivation
The need, or desire, to attain a certain standard of excellence.

ACHIEVEMENT MOTIVATION   In the 1930s, the personality psychologist Henry Murray (1938) proposed four *psychosocial needs*: the needs for power, autonomy, achievement, and play. The study of psychosocial needs has yielded important insights into what motivates human behavior. A key insight is that people are especially motivated to achieve long-term personal goals. But people differ in how much they pursue challenging goals.

Achievement motivation is the need, or desire, to do well relative to standards of excellence. Indeed, achievement may be the motivation for the student studying hard in Figure 9.2b. Compared with those low in achievement motivation, students high in achievement motivation sit closer to the front of classrooms, score higher on exams, and obtain better grades in courses relevant to their career goals (McClelland, 1987). Students with high achievement motivation also are more realistic in their career aspirations. Those high in achievement motivation set challenging but attainable personal goals. Those low in achievement motivation set extremely easy or impossibly high goals.

Four other factors affect your ability to achieve long-term goals: the goals themselves, your sense of self-efficacy, your ability to delay gratification, and grit.

GOALS AFFECT ACHIEVEMENT   Good goals should motivate you to work hard, but what is a good goal? Challenging—but not overly difficult—and specific goals are best (Locke & Latham, 1990). Challenging goals encourage effort, persistence, and concentration. In contrast, goals that are too easy or too hard can undermine motivation and lead to failure. Dividing specific goals into concrete steps also leads to success, just as setting subgoals is helpful in solving problems (see study unit 8.6). If you are interested in running the Boston Marathon, for instance, your first goal might be gaining the stamina to run 1 mile. When you can run a mile, you can set another goal and eventually build up to running the 26-mile marathon. Focusing on concrete, short-term goals helps in achieving long-term goals.

SELF-EFFICACY AFFECTS ACHIEVEMENT   Personal expectations for success also play an important role in motivation to achieve long-term goals. For instance, if you believe studying hard will lead to a good grade on an exam, you will be motivated to study. *Self-efficacy* is the expectation that your efforts will lead to success (Bandura, 1977a). This expectation helps get you going. If you have low self-efficacy—if you do not believe your efforts will pay off—you may be too discouraged even to study for the exam. People with high self-efficacy often set challenging goals that lead to success. However, those with inflated self-views may set goals they cannot possibly achieve. Again, goals that are challenging but not overwhelming usually are most likely to lead to success.

ABILITY TO DELAY GRATIFICATION   Suppose that you are applying to graduate school and the entrance exam is coming up soon. You know you should stay in and study, but all your friends are going out to the basketball game and are begging you to come with them. Which would you do?

One common challenge in meeting our long-term goals is postponing immediate gratification. In a series of now-classic studies, children were given the choice of

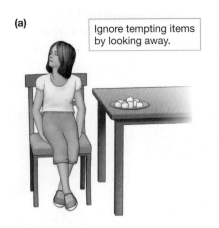

(a)

Ignore tempting items by looking away.

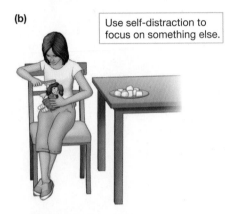

(b)

Use self-distraction to focus on something else.

FIGURE 9.15

Delaying Gratification

It is often hard to meet long-term goals because there is no immediate reward, or gratification, for our hard work. Luckily, several techniques can help you cope with delaying gratification, including: **(a)** ignoring a tempting item and **(b)** distracting yourself from thinking about it.

FIGURE 9.16

Grit

(a) The nature of grit is symbolized by this sign. **(b)** Grit is perfectly characterized by the musician, actor, and producer Will Smith, when he explains how he achieved so many goals even though he came from a humble background in Philadelphia: "The only thing that I see that is distinctly different about me is I'm not afraid to die on a treadmill. I will not be outworked, period. You might have more talent than me, you might be smarter than me, you might be sexier than me, you might be all of those things—you got it on me in nine categories. But if we get on the treadmill together, there's two things: You're getting off first, or I'm going to die. It's really that simple."

waiting to receive a preferred toy or food item or having a less preferred toy or food item right away (Mischel, Shoda, & Rodriguez, 1989). Some children were better at delaying gratification than other children were.

How did some of the children in these studies manage to delay gratification? Given the choice between eating one marshmallow right away or eating two after several minutes, some 4-year-olds used strategies to help them not eat the marshmallow while they waited. One strategy was simply ignoring the tempting item rather than looking at it (**Figure 9.15a**). For example, some of them covered their eyes or looked away. Alternatively, some children were able to use the related strategy of self-distraction to focus on something else (**Figure 9.15b**). For example, they sang, played games, or pretended to sleep. On average, older children were better at delaying gratification. Very young children tended to look directly at the item they were trying to resist, making the delay especially difficult.

The ability to delay gratification is an indicator of success in life (Mischel, 2014). Children able to delay gratification at age 4 were rated 10 years later as being more socially competent and better able to handle frustration. The ability to delay gratification in childhood has also been found to predict higher SAT scores and better school grades (Mischel et al., 1989).

GRIT   One final, very important factor that is related to your ability to achieve long-term goals is *grit*. People with grit have a deep passion for their goals and a willingness to keep working toward them, even in spite of hardships and pitfalls (Duckworth, Peterson, Matthews, & Kelly, 2007; **Figure 9.16a**). Malala Yousafzai, the activist who survived an attack by the Taliban to continue promoting education for girls, clearly has grit. By contrast, people who have less grit get discouraged more easily, lose steam in the middle of pursuing their goals, or get sidetracked from their goals by new interests.

Is it true that grit is even more important than having natural talent? Recent research suggests that the answer may be yes. For example, grit has been shown to be a better predictor than intelligence for achieving long-term goals in several areas, such as educational attainment, retention in the United States Military Academy at West Point, and ranking in a national spelling bee (Duckworth et al., 2007). In addition, grit has been shown to be a significant predictor for the grades of college students (Duckworth et al., 2007; Duckworth & Quinn, 2009), especially those of African American men (Strayhom, 2014). Why is grit so important to achieving

(a)

(b)

long-term goals? Because one component of grit is perseverance, which is the determination to keep working toward your goals. Research suggests that perseverance is the most important aspect of grit for predicting student outcomes (Muenks, Wigfied, Yang, & O'Neal, 2017; Wolters & Hussain, 2015). This great news means that as long as you work hard and keep trying, you can achieve your long-term goals (**Figure 9.16b**). And in turn, achieving your goals can bring you joy.

 What Are Your Most Important Motivated Behaviors?

To make sure you learned what you just read, write answers to the following questions and check your answers.

9.3 What brain structure most influences eating?

9.4 What are the four learned factors that affect eating?

9.5 What is the need that motivates people to develop social relationships?

9.6 What are two ways that people can delay gratification to help them achieve long-term goals?

See Appendix B for answers to the red Q questions.

How Do You Experience Emotions?

In the previous sections, you learned about various factors that motivate your behavior. An additional factor that motivates your behavior is how you feel. In fact, the words "motivation" and "emotion" come from the same Latin word: *movere*, "to move." You seek out people, activities, and objects that make you feel good. You avoid events, activities, and objects that make you feel bad. When you work toward goals, you feel emotions, such as happiness or sadness. Consider the emotions, from fear to triumph, that Malala Yousafzai must have experienced in her journey from near assassination to powerful advocacy.

But what does it mean to feel an emotion? What are emotions? And how can you understand your experience of emotions? The second half of this chapter will answer these questions, and more, about your emotions.

9.7 Emotions Are Personal but Labeled and Described Consistently

 9.7 LEARNING GOAL ACTIVITIES

To maximize your learning, complete the following learning goal activities.

a. Understand all bold and italic terms by writing explanations of them in your own words.

b. Apply emotions to your life by naming one of your emotions, describing it as primary or secondary, and explaining the valence and the level of arousal of the emotion.

You have an intuitive sense of what an emotion is. It's how you feel, for example, about a romantic partner, about exercising, and even about buying the latest iPhone.

emotion
An immediate, specific, negative or positive response to environmental events or internal thoughts.

primary emotions
Evolutionarily adaptive emotions that are shared across cultures and associated with specific physical states; they include anger, fear, sadness, disgust, happiness, and possibly surprise and contempt.

secondary emotions
Blends of primary emotions; they include remorse, guilt, submission, shame, and anticipation.

But from the perspective of psychology, an **emotion** is an immediate, specific, negative or positive response to environmental events or internal thoughts. An emotion may seem like it is just one unified experience. However, an emotion has three components.

First, emotions are based on physical, bodily responses. For example, how does your body react when you ride a roller coaster? Your heart probably beats faster. Second, emotions affect thoughts and actions. For example, on that roller coaster, you may have thought, "How can I get off this thing?" Or you may have vowed to never ride one again. And third, emotions are subjective, so each person experiences positive emotions and negative emotions differently (**Figure 9.17**). You may have felt the excitement of going on a roller coaster as a positive emotion. Another person might have felt that excitement negatively. So a person's feeling is a unique experience of the emotion. In other words, the person may feel scared, but that person's feeling is just one version of the emotion, not the only possible experience of it.

Even though people experience emotions in their own unique ways, psychological research reveals that emotions can be labeled in general ways and the experience of them can be described consistently.

EMOTIONS ARE LABELED AS PRIMARY OR SECONDARY Psychologists commonly use two labels that distinguish between emotions. Basic emotions, or **primary emotions**, are evolutionarily adaptive, shared across cultures, and associated with specific physical states. They include anger, fear, sadness, happiness, disgust, and possibly surprise and contempt. **Secondary emotions** are blends of primary emotions. They include remorse, guilt, submission, shame, and anticipation. To see the difference between these two types of emotion, imagine that your boyfriend or girlfriend reports feeling ignored by you. Your first emotional response might be a primary one: anger at being accused, because you did not mean to neglect your companion. Your second emotional response might also be primary: sadness, because you accidentally hurt your companion. Your anger and sadness might then combine into a secondary emotion: guilt, because through neglect you brought pain to someone you care about.

By contrast with emotions, *moods* are spread-out, long-lasting emotional states that do not have an identifiable object or trigger. Rather than interrupting what is happening, moods influence thought and behavior. Often people who are in good or bad moods have no idea why they feel the way they do. Thus, moods refer to people's vague senses that they feel certain ways. Think of the difference this way: Getting cut off in traffic can make a person angry (emotion), but for no apparent reason a person can be irritable (mood).

FIGURE 9.17

Negative Emotions and Positive Emotions Can Both Make You Cry

Emotions can be positive or negative. Your experience of them is very personal. So you can show the same response, such as crying, to either negative or positive emotions. **(a)** The tears shed by the family and friends of a fallen police officer reflect their sadness. **(b)** This bride is crying because of the happiness she feels during her wedding.

(a)

(b)

EMOTIONS ARE DESCRIBED BY VALENCE AND AROUSAL Psychological research has also revealed that people's experience of emotions can be described consistently. One way to describe emotions is based on the *circumplex model*. In this model, emotions are plotted along two dimensions that lie along a continuum: valence and arousal (Kuppens, Tuerlinckx, Russell, & Barrett, 2013; Russell, 2003; **Figure 9.18a, b**). "Valence" refers to how negative or positive the emotion is. "Arousal" describes how the emotion causes physiological activation (such as increased brain activity) or increased autonomic nervous system responses (such as quickened heart rate, increased sweating, or muscle tension; see study unit 2.9).

To understand the difference between valence and arousal, imagine you discover that you have lost the $1 bill that was in your pants pocket. This experience will most likely make you unhappy, so you will judge it to have a negative valence. It also might make you slightly aroused (increase your autonomic responses a little bit). Now imagine that you find a lottery ticket that turns out to be worth a million dollars. This experience will most likely make you very, very happy, so you will judge it as on the extremely positive side of the valence scale. Your arousal will probably be very high—topping the chart. Psychologists have debated the names for these emotion dimensions and even the whole idea of dimensions. However, circumplex models have proved useful as a basic way to classify emotions (Barrett, Mesquita, Ochsner, & Gross, 2007).

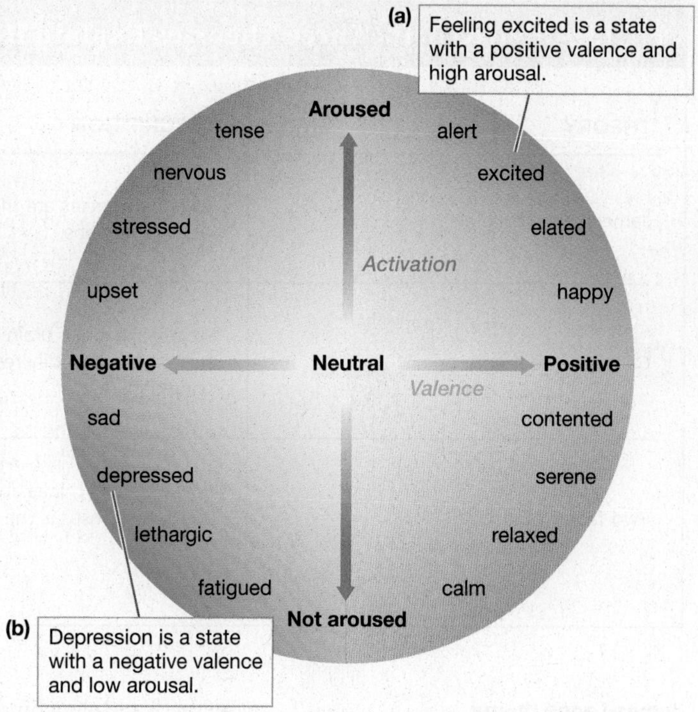

(a) Feeling excited is a state with a positive valence and high arousal.

Aroused

Activation

tense · alert
nervous · excited
stressed · elated
upset · happy

Negative — Neutral — Positive

Valence

sad · contented
depressed · serene
lethargic · relaxed
fatigued · calm

(b) Depression is a state with a negative valence and low arousal.

Not aroused

FIGURE 9.18

Circumplex Map of Emotion

Your experience of emotions can be categorized by a certain degree of valence (negative to positive) and by a certain level of arousal (low to high). For example, **(a)** excitement has a positive valence and high arousal, whereas **(b)** depression has a negative valence and low arousal.

9.8 Three Major Theories Explain Your Emotions

9.8 LEARNING GOAL ACTIVITIES

To maximize your learning, complete the following learning goal activities.

a. Understand all bold and italic terms by writing explanations of them in your own words.

b. Analyze the three theories of emotion by differentiating how each theory explains how you would feel excited happiness on seeing a good friend you haven't seen in a long time.

At different times, you feel happy, sad, angry, and impatient—but what causes you to feel these and other emotions? Three theories explain how you experience emotion. The James-Lange theory explains emotions based on your bodily (physiological) responses. The Cannon-Bard theory focuses on how the brain processes information. The two-factor theory focuses on our thought processes. The Learning Tip on p. 356 summarizes each theory.

JAMES-LANGE THEORY Common sense suggests that emotions lead to physical changes. Maybe your stomach is in knots because you're so worried about how you will do on an exam. Or someone makes you very angry, and you respond by gritting

THEORY	DESCRIPTION	EXAMPLE
James-Lange theory	Bodily responses are the basis for feeling emotions.	You have to give a presentation to 50 people. Your palms are sweating, and you are breathing heavily. You feel very scared. (See Figure 9.19.)
Cannon-Bard theory	Processing in the brain is the cause of emotions and bodily responses at the same time.	When your son graduates from college, your brain processes the information. You feel overwhelming joy at the same time as your heart beats rapidly. (See Figure 9.21.)
Two-factor theory	How a person thinks about and labels bodily responses is the basis for emotions.	When you are in a car crash, your heart races incredibly fast. You attribute your heart beating so quickly to fear caused by the scary event. (See Figure 9.22.)

James-Lange theory
Emotions result from the experience of physiological reactions in the body.

your teeth and clenching your fists. When you feel angry or sad or embarrassed, your body responds. But in 1884, William James argued that it was just the opposite.

James stated that the physical changes you experience because of a situation actually lead you to feel an emotion. As he put it, "We feel sorry *because* we cry, angry *because* we strike, afraid *because* we tremble, [it is] not that we cry, strike, or tremble because we are sorry, angry, or fearful" (1884, p. 190). James believed that physical changes in the body occur in distinct patterns that translate directly into specific emotions.

Around the same time, the physician and psychologist Carl Lange independently proposed a similar theory. Psychologists now refer to these ideas as the **James-Lange theory** of emotion. According to this theory, you experience specific patterns of bodily responses. When you perceive those physical responses, you feel emotions. In the example shown in **Figure 9.19**, the man sees the bear. As a result, his heart rate increases. This response is the basis for the man's emotional response of fear.

One implication of the James-Lange theory is that if you mold your facial muscles to mimic an emotional state, it is thought that you will activate the associated emotion. In other words, moving your muscles to create facial expressions triggers your experience for emotions, not the other way around. In 1963, Silvan Tomkins proposed this idea as the *facial feedback hypothesis*. Researchers tested the idea by having people hold a pencil between their teeth or with their mouths

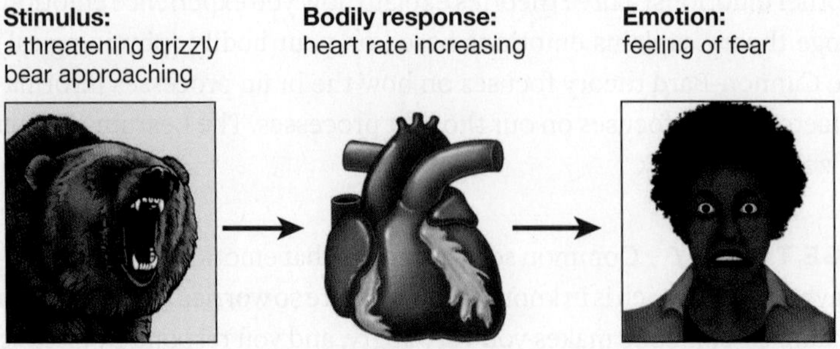

Stimulus:
a threatening grizzly bear approaching

Bodily response:
heart rate increasing

Emotion:
feeling of fear

FIGURE 9.19
James-Lange Theory of Emotion
According to this theory, when you experience a stimulus, you have a bodily response. Then you feel the emotion.

(a) 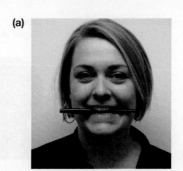 (b)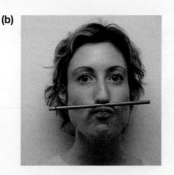

FIGURE 9.20
Facial Feedback Hypothesis
According to this hypothesis, the muscles used to create a facial expression trigger your experience of emotion. **(a)** When you hold a pencil this way, your cheek muscles draw up into a smile. **(b)** But when you hold a pencil this way, the cheek muscles draw down into a frown. In each case, the resulting expression affects your emotions.

in a way that produced a smile (**Figure 9.20a**) or a frown (**Figure 9.20b**). When participants rated cartoons, those in a posed smile found the cartoons the funniest (Strack, Martin, & Stepper, 1988). Using slightly different methods, another team of researchers recently failed to replicate this effect (Wagenmakers et al., 2016). However, the general idea that changing facial expression alters emotions has been shown many times (Strack, 2016).

CANNON-BARD THEORY   In 1927, the physiologist Walter B. Cannon noted that the human mind and the human body do not experience emotions at the same speed. The mind—in other words, the brain—is quick to experience emotions. The body is much slower, taking at least a second or two to respond. Cannon also noted that many emotions produce similar bodily responses. For instance, anger, excitement, and sexual interest all produce similar changes in heart rate and blood pressure. The similarities make it too difficult for people to determine quickly which emotion they are experiencing. Therefore, Cannon, along with Philip Bard, proposed that the mind and body experience emotions independently.

According to the **Cannon-Bard theory** of emotion, the information from an emotion-producing stimulus is processed in the brain. As a result of this processing, you experience two separate things at roughly the same time: an emotion and a physical reaction. In the example in **Figure 9.21,** the man sees the bear. The man's brain processes the information about the bear. The processing in the brain produces, at the same time, both the emotion of fear and bodily changes, such as an increase in heart rate.

Cannon-Bard theory
Emotions and bodily responses both occur simultaneously due to how parts of the brain process information.

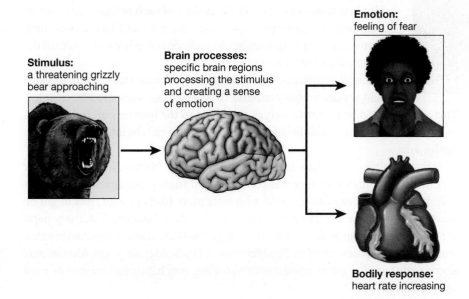

Stimulus:
a threatening grizzly bear approaching

Brain processes:
specific brain regions processing the stimulus and creating a sense of emotion

Emotion:
feeling of fear

Bodily response:
heart rate increasing

FIGURE 9.21
Cannon-Bard Theory of Emotion
According to this theory, when you experience a stimulus, the information is processed in your brain. Then, simultaneously, you feel the emotion and the bodily reaction.

FIGURE 9.22

Two-Factor Theory of Emotion

According to this theory, when you experience a stimulus, you have a bodily response. Then you apply an emotion label to explain the changes. Finally, you feel the emotion brought on by the situation.

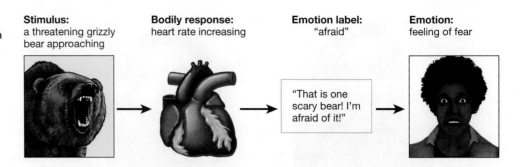

Stimulus: a threatening grizzly bear approaching

Bodily response: heart rate increasing

Emotion label: "afraid"

"That is one scary bear! I'm afraid of it!"

Emotion: feeling of fear

two-factor theory

How we experience an emotion is influenced by the cognitive label we apply to explain the physiological changes we have experienced.

TWO-FACTOR THEORY The social psychologists Stanley Schachter and Jerome Singer (1962) proposed a **two-factor theory** of emotion. According to this theory, a situation evokes both a physiological response, such as arousal, and a cognitive interpretation. The cognitive interpretation is called an emotion label. In other words, when you experience arousal, you search for its source so you can explain it cognitively. **Figure 9.22** shows a man seeing a bear. The man feels a bodily response, such as an increase in heart rate. The man then interprets that his heart rate increased because the bear is scary and threatening. Thus the interpretation of the bodily response leads to the feeling of fear. Most researchers now agree that thought processes, including interpretation of bodily responses, are a part of emotions (Barrett, 2006).

Often the search for a cognitive explanation is quick and straightforward. That is, you generally recognize the event that led to your emotional state. But what happens when the situation is not so clear? The two-factor theory proposes that whatever you believe caused the emotion will determine how you label the emotion.

One interesting implication of the two-factor theory is that physical states caused by a situation can be attributed to the wrong emotion. Such mistaken identification of the source of your arousal is called *misattribution of arousal*.

In one exploration of this phenomenon, researchers tried to see whether people could feel romantic attraction through misattribution (Dutton & Aron, 1974). Each participant, a heterosexual male, chose to cross either of two bridges over the Capilano River, in British Columbia. One was a narrow suspension bridge with a low rail that swayed 230 feet above raging, rocky rapids (**Figure 9.23**). The other was a sturdy modern bridge just above the river. At the middle of each bridge, an attractive female research assistant approached the man and interviewed him. She gave him her phone number and offered to explain the results of the study at a later date if he was interested.

FIGURE 9.23

Misattribution of Arousal

Some men walked across this scary bridge. These men displayed more attraction to the female experimenter on the bridge than did the men who crossed on a safer bridge. This result suggests that the men on this bridge misattributed their physiological responses. They assumed their fast heartbeats and increased sweating were related to being attracted to the female, not to being scared by crossing the high bridge.

According to the two-factor theory of emotion, the less stable bridge would produce bodily arousal (sweaty palms, increased heart rate). This arousal could be misattributed as attraction to the interviewer. Indeed, men interviewed on the less stable bridge were more likely to call the interviewer and ask her for a date.

Many possible confounds could affect this study (as you learned in study unit 1.11, confounds are factors that provide an alternative explanation for what is found in a study). For instance, men who were more likely to take risks might be more likely to choose a scary bridge *and* to call for a date. Nevertheless, the general idea—that people can mistake arousal for attraction—has been supported in other studies. In fact, as described in The Methods of Psychology on p. 359, arousal may also be attributed to other causes, such as feeling very happy and excited or even feeling angry.

Hypothesis: Whatever a person believes caused an emotion will determine how the person experiences and labels the emotion.

1 Participants were injected with a stimulant (adrenaline) or a placebo.

2 Informed participants in the adrenaline condition were told the drug they were given might make them feel shaky, cause their hearts to beat faster, and make their faces feel flushed. All of these bodily activities are physical effects of taking adrenaline. Uninformed participants were not told anything about the drug's effects.

3 In the happy condition, each participant was exposed to a person who was working with the researchers. This person was in a great mood, played with a hula hoop, and made paper airplanes.

In the angry condition, each participant was seated with a person working with the researchers. Both the participant and the person working with the researchers were asked to fill out a questionnaire that included very insulting questions, such as a question that implied their mothers had cheated on their fathers. The person working with the researchers became angry, tore up the questionnaire, and stormed out of the room.

4 The researchers noted behavioral indicators of happiness, such as joining in the fun. They also noted behavioral indicators of anger, such as agreeing with the angry person. In addition, participants were asked about their emotional states, such as whether they felt happy or angry.

Happy condition   **Angry condition**

Result: When participants received the adrenaline and were told how their bodies would respond to the drug, they had an easy explanation for their arousal. They attributed it to the adrenaline, not to the situation. In contrast, when participants received adrenaline but were not given information about its effects, they looked to the environment to explain or label their bodies' responses.

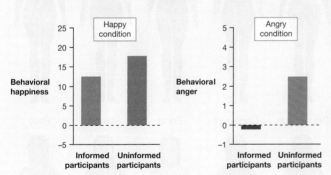

When uninformed participants waited with the happy people, they displayed behavioral indicators of happiness (see left-side graph). They also reported feeling happy. When uninformed participants waited with the angry people, they displayed behavioral indicators of anger (see right-side graph). They also reported feeling angry. These results happened because the uninformed participants attributed their feelings to what was happening in the environment. Informed participants did not react in the same ways or make the same attributions. For example, in the angry condition, their behavioral indicators of anger decreased.

Conclusion: Feelings of arousal can be attributed to events in the environment, thereby shaping people's emotions.

QUESTION: Why did the actions of the person working with the researchers not affect the participants in the informed condition?

ANSWER: Those participants had an explanation for their arousal, so they did not attribute how they felt to the person working with the researchers.

Source: Schachter, S., & Singer, J. (1962). Cognitive, social, and physiological determinants of emotional state. *Psychological Review, 69,* 379–399.

9.9 Your Body and Brain Influence Your Emotions

9.9 LEARNING GOAL ACTIVITIES

To maximize your learning, complete the following learning goal activities.

a. Understand all bold and italic terms by writing explanations of them in your own words.

b. Understand how the body and the brain influence emotions by summarizing these influences in a table.

As you just learned, different theories of emotion focus on the idea that you feel something based primarily on how your body or your brain responds to a situation. You feel fear because you see a bear and your heart starts beating quickly, or because your brain processes information about the bear. Let's look more closely now at exactly what parts of your body and your brain influence your experience of emotions.

EMOTIONS FROM BODILY RESPONSES How does your body feel when you are happy or angry? On the one hand, some research suggests that your body responds the same way across different emotions. This type of response may occur if all emotions share core physical properties related to valence and arousal, as suggested by the circumplex model of emotions (Wilson-Mendenhall, Feldman Barrett, & Barselou, 2013). But if this is the case, then many emotions

FIGURE 9.24

Body Maps of Emotion

These maps represent areas of the body that are more active (warm colors) or less active (cool colors) when people consider how various emotions make their bodies feel. The color bar reflects the extent of increasing activity (yellow) or decreasing activity (blue).

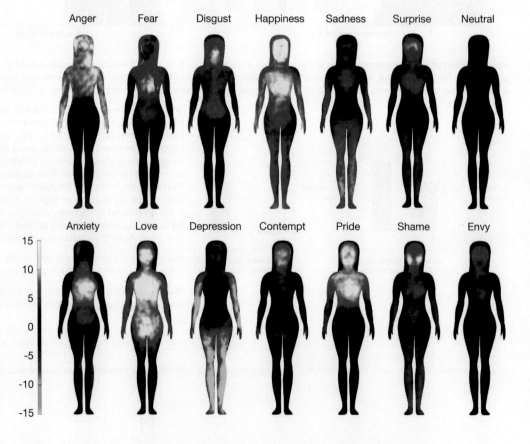

would be difficult to distinguish based on bodily responses alone. This difficulty would occur because many of the bodily responses to emotion produced by the autonomic nervous system may overlap. For example, if your heart beats quickly when you are scared and when you are excited, how can you tell what you are feeling?

On the other hand, some research suggests that your body responds differently when you experience specific emotions. This type of response may happen if each emotion has a specific pattern of bodily responses from the autonomic nervous system (Lench, Flores, & Bench, 2011). Indeed, research shows that certain emotional states do influence the body in predictable ways (Comtesse & Stemmler, 2016; Eisenbarth, Chang, & Wager, 2016; Levenson, 2014). When you are frightened, your heart beats faster, but your muscles also become tense. When you are nervous, you perspire. Other autonomic bodily responses—such as changes in blood pressure, blood temperature, breathing rate, and pupil size—are also associated with certain emotional states.

To study the relationship between different bodily responses and specific emotions, Finnish researchers asked people from various cultures to use a computer program to color what areas of the body were involved in feeling various emotions (Nummenmaa, Glerean, Hari, & Hietanen, 2014). Across five studies, emotions were experienced by having participants imagine the emotions, read short stories, or watch movies. The participants reported activation of certain body parts based on the emotions they felt and what body parts felt activated that overlapped somewhat across emotions. However, overall, specific emotions were characterized by different patterns of activity in the body (**Figure 9.24**). The researchers concluded that people's perception of their bodily responses may play a role in how different emotions are experienced.

EMOTIONS FROM BRAIN PROCESSES   When you feel happy or angry, this feeling is not just the result of bodily processes. Instead, many parts of the brain regions are involved in producing emotions, including cortical areas such as the prefrontal cortex. However, the region most important for understanding emotion is the subcortical region of the amygdala (**Figure 9.25a**).

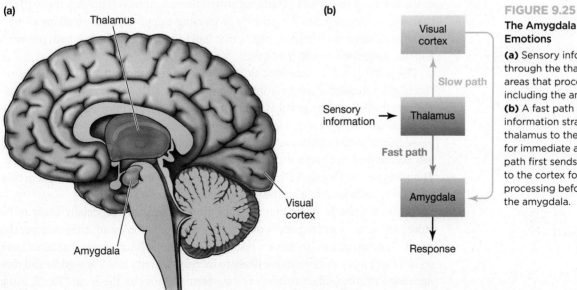

(a)

Thalamus

Visual cortex

Amygdala

(b)

Visual cortex

Slow path

Sensory information → Thalamus

Fast path

Amygdala

Response

FIGURE 9.25

The Amygdala Processes Emotions

(a) Sensory information passes through the thalamus to brain areas that process emotion, including the amygdala.
(b) A fast path sends information straight from the thalamus to the amygdala for immediate action. A slow path first sends information to the cortex for additional processing before it reaches the amygdala.

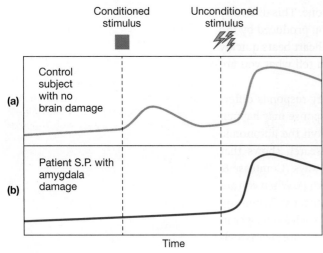

Conditioned stimulus

Unconditioned stimulus

(a) Control subject with no brain damage

(b) Patient S.P. with amygdala damage

Time

Lines show changes in perspiration.

FIGURE 9.26

Lack of Fear Conditioning After Damage to the Amygdala

(a) In a classical conditioning task, people have a physiological response, such as increased sweating, to a shock (unconditioned stimulus). Most people also learn to fear a blue square (conditioned stimulus) that consistently precedes the shock, as also shown by increased sweating. **(b)** However, patient S.P., with damage to the amygdala, never learned the conditioned fear response to the blue square and doesn't show increased sweating to that stimulus, only to the unconditioned stimulus of the shock.

The amygdala processes the emotional significance of stimuli, and it generates immediate emotional and behavioral reactions (Phelps, 2006). According to Joseph LeDoux (2007, 2015), the processing of emotion in the amygdala is a circuit that has developed over the course of evolution to protect animals from danger. LeDoux and his colleagues (LeDoux & Pine, 2016) have established the amygdala as the brain structure most important for emotional learning. For an example of emotional learning, remember how fear responses can be classically conditioned (see study unit 6.6).

People with damage to the amygdala might know certain objects are dangerous, but they do not seem afraid of those objects. These same people do not develop conditioned fear responses to objects associated with negative events, such as being shocked each time the object is presented. Consider the case of S.P. This patient had a portion of her amygdala removed to reduce the frequency of epileptic seizures (Anderson & Phelps, 2000). The surgery was reasonably successful, and S.P. retained most of her intellectual abilities, but she does not show fear conditioning. A person with an intact amygdala will show increased sweating in response to a blue square (conditioned stimulus) that the person has learned to associate with an electrical shock (unconditioned stimulus; **Figure 9.26a**). By contrast, when S.P. sees a picture of a blue square that has previously been accompanied by an electric shock, S.P. can tell you that the blue square is associated with shock. However, her body shows no physiological evidence of having learned a fear response to the blue square, because she does not show increased sweating (Phelps, 2006; **Figure 9.26b**).

When the amygdala is intact, it contributes to the processing of emotions in two ways: through a fast path and a slow path (**Figure 9.25b**). The fast pathway is a "quick and dirty" system that processes sensory information nearly instantaneously. Recall from Chapter 5 that except for smell, all sensory information travels to the thalamus before going on to other brain structures and the related portions of the cortex. Along the fast path, sensory information travels quickly through the thalamus to the amygdala for priority processing. Suppose you are walking along a hiking trail and come across an object that looks like a snake. The fast path prepares you to take action to avoid the snake.

The second path is somewhat slower, but it leads to more-deliberate and more-thorough evaluation of information. Along this slow path, sensory information travels from the thalamus to cortical areas that process sensory information, such as the visual cortex. In the cortex, the information is analyzed in greater depth before it is passed along to the amygdala. This slower processing may determine that what you saw on the trail was just a stick shaped like a snake, and you can step right over it. Theorists believe that the fast system prepares animals to respond to a threat in case the slower pathway confirms the threat (LeDoux, 2000).

As you learned in study unit 7.15, emotional events are especially likely to be stored in memory and to persist over time, even if you don't want to remember the event. The amygdala also plays a role in this process. Brain imaging studies have shown that emotional events are likely to increase activity in the amygdala and that increased activity is likely to improve long-term memory for the event (Talmi, 2013;

(a)  **(b)**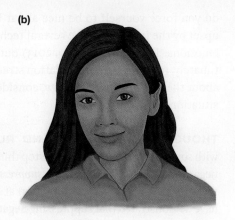

FIGURE 9.27
Evaluating Trustworthiness from Facial Expressions
People with damage to the amygdala cannot determine whether the facial expression in **(a)** or **(b)** shows trustworthiness. People with damage to the amygdala tend to be unusually friendly and not cautious with strangers.

Manns & Bass, 2016). In short, thanks to the amygdala, emotions such as fear strengthen memories. This adaptive mechanism lets us remember harmful situations so we can potentially avoid them.

The amygdala also plays one final role in the processing of emotions: It is involved in the perception of social stimuli. For instance, when we "read" someone's facial expressions, the amygdala helps us interpret them (Öhman, 2002). Brain imaging studies demonstrate that this perception is particularly useful in the case of fearful faces (Whalen et al., 1998; Méndez-Bértolo et al., 2016). People with damage to the amygdala often have difficulty evaluating the intensity of fearful faces. The amygdala also enables people to quickly and easily assess the trustworthiness of a face (Willis & Todorov, 2006). Furthermore, the amygdala seems to process trustworthiness of a face even if the facial image is presented too quickly to see (Freeman, Stolier, Ingbretsen, & Hehman, 2014). By contrast, people with damage to the amygdala have difficulty using photographs to assess people's trustworthiness (Adolphs, Sears, & Piven, 2001; **Figure 9.27**). This difficulty leads them to be unusually friendly with people they do not know. Their extra friendliness might result from lacking the normal mechanisms for being cautious around strangers and for feeling that some people should be avoided.

9.10 Most People Try to Regulate Their Emotional States

 9.10 LEARNING GOAL ACTIVITIES

To maximize your learning, complete the following learning goal activities.

a. Understand all bold and italic terms by writing explanations of them in your own words.

b. Apply the regulation of emotional states by giving examples of how you can use positive reappraisal, humor, and distraction to regulate your negative emotions more successfully than by thought suppression and rumination.

You need emotions to function normally, but your emotions can be disruptive and troublesome. In your daily life, circumstances often require you to control your emotional responses. Doing so is not easy, of course. How do you mask your expression of disgust when, to be polite, you must eat something you dislike? How do you force yourself to be nice about losing a competition when you are very upset by the loss? There are several techniques that you can use to regulate your emotions. James Gross (1999, 2013) outlined several of these strategies. Unfortunately, not all emotion regulation strategies are equally successful. As you read about the five techniques below, consider how you might apply them in specific situations.

THOUGHT SUPPRESSION AND RUMINATION   Have you ever broken up with someone and been unable to stop thinking about the person? Trying to suppress negative thoughts is called *thought suppression*. Suppressing thoughts is a way of trying not to feel or respond to the emotion at all. Daniel Wegner and colleagues (1990) have demonstrated that suppressing negative thoughts is extremely difficult. In fact, doing so often leads to a rebound effect. As a result of the rebound, you actually think more about something after suppression than before. Sometimes people who are dieting try not to think about the foods they can't eat. These people often end up thinking about those foods more than if they had engaged in a distracting activity.

Rumination involves thinking about, elaborating, and focusing on undesired thoughts or emotions. Instead of helping a person to regulate their emotions, this strategy actually prolongs the emotions. It also makes it harder to use more successful regulation strategies, such as reappraisal, humor, and distraction (Lyubomirsky & Nolen-Hoeksema, 1995).

POSITIVE REAPPRAISAL   One way to regulate emotions is based on your thoughts about the event, which is called appraisal. In Chapter 11, you will learn more about how you engage in appraisal to judge an event or reappraisal to change your judgment. In *positive reappraisal,* you directly alter your emotional reactions to an event by thinking about the events in more neutral or even positive terms. So if you get scared while watching a movie, you can remind yourself that the movie is fictional and no one is actually being hurt. You can use positive reappraisal to successfully reduce any fear you experience about exams (**Figure 9.28**). Studies have found that engaging in positive reappraisal actually changes the activity of brain regions involved in the experience of emotion (Ochsner, Bunge, Gross, & Gabrieli, 2002). The following two subsections look at some other strategies for regulating emotional states. However, not all of these strategies are equally successful.

HUMOR   "Laughter is the best medicine" is a common saying. Indeed, *humor* is a simple, effective method of regulating negative emotions. In fact, humor has many mental and physical health benefits. Most obviously, humor increases positive emotion. When you find something humorous, you smile, laugh, and enter a state of pleasurable, relaxed excitation. Research shows that laughter improves the immune system and stimulates the release of hormones, dopamine, serotonin, and endorphins. When you laugh, you experience rises in circulation, blood pressure, skin temperature, and heart rate, along with a decrease in pain perception. All of these responses are similar to those resulting from physical exercise. They are considered beneficial to short-term and long-term health.

Sometimes we laugh in situations that do not seem very humorous. For example, telling funny stories about someone at her funeral may seem odd. According to one theory, laughing in such situations helps people distance themselves from their negative emotions and strengthens their connections to others. In one study on the topic, Dacher Keltner and George Bonanno (1997)

FIGURE 9.28
Using Positive Reappraisal Can Reduce Negative Emotions About Exams

Positive reappraisal, changing one's thoughts about an event in a positive way, can be used to successfully regulate emotions. Thinking of an exam as a threat can lead to fear and anxiety. But thinking of it as a positive challenge, or a chance to show what you know, can help create more positive emotions toward the exam.

interviewed 40 people who had recently lost a spouse. The researchers found that genuine laughter during the interview was associated with positive mental health and fewer negative feelings, such as grief. Laughing was a way of coping with a difficult situation.

DISTRACTION You're going to the dentist tomorrow morning. Just thinking about the root canal work you're going to have is making your evening unpleasant. So you distract yourself by going out with friends. *Distraction* involves doing or thinking about something other than the troubling activity or thought. By focusing attention elsewhere, distraction temporarily helps you stop focusing on your difficulties.

Some distractions backfire, however. You may end up thinking about other problems. Or you may engage in maladaptive behaviors, such as overeating or binge drinking. A healthier strategy might involve watching a movie that captures your attention. Choose a movie that will not remind you of your troubled situation. Otherwise, you might simply find yourself wallowing in mental anguish.

Q How Do You Experience Emotions?

To make sure you learned what you just read, write answers to the following questions and check your answers.

9.7 Is jealousy a primary emotion or a secondary emotion?

9.8 According to the James-Lange theory, which comes first, the emotion or the bodily response?

9.9 You are swimming in the ocean and see a jellyfish, so you freeze in fear. When you see it is a plastic bag, you relax and continue swimming. How are your visual experiences related to the fast and slow paths for processing emotions?

9.10 Is thought suppression a good way to control negative emotions? Why or why not?

See Appendix B for answers to the red Q questions.

How Do Emotions Affect You?

You know that you experience emotions, such as joy at a great achievement or sorrow at the passing of a loved one. And you just learned how you feel emotions. But how do emotions influence your behavior?

One answer is that over the course of human evolution, emotions have helped people respond appropriately in any given situation. For example, when faced with attack, people experience fear. That emotion prompts an appropriate response, such as running away. In other words, emotions are adaptive because they influence thoughts and behaviors that increase the likelihood that people will survive and reproduce. Of course, not everyone is motivated to act in the same way in the face of danger. Recall that Malala Yousafzai responded to the threats against her, even the assassination attempt, by becoming an even more vocal activist for girls' education.

Another answer is that emotions help promote social relationships. This happens in two ways. First, emotions help teach social rules, which are necessary for living together in groups. For example, you most likely learned at a young age that in many cultures it is not appropriate to laugh during a funeral. Second, people detect emotions in others and try to help regulate other people's emotional experiences

(Reeck, Ames, & Ochsner, 2016). For example, you might try to cheer up a friend who is sad over a breakup.

In short, emotions help you achieve certain goals, including surviving and creating social connections by preparing you for actions aimed at achieving those goals (Frijda, 1994). Let's explore now the several ways that emotions influence you.

9.11 You Use Facial Expressions to Interpret Emotions

 9.11 LEARNING GOAL ACTIVITIES

To maximize your learning, complete the following learning goal activities.

a. Understand all bold and italic terms by writing explanations of them in your own words.

b. Apply the interpretation of facial expressions by describing how you can tell the emotions of another person based on the eyes and also based on the mouth.

Suppose someone scowls at you intensely. You are likely to feel afraid or at least wary of that person. You interpret facial expressions of emotion to predict other people's behavior. Facial expressions also provide clues about whether your behavior is pleasing to others or whether your behavior is likely to make other people reject, attack, or cheat you. In his 1872 book, *The Expression of the Emotions in Man and Animals*, Charles Darwin argued that the expression of emotion is adaptive because it communicates how people are feeling. Thus facial expressions, like emotions themselves, provide information that helps you understand a situation and respond appropriately.

EYES AND MOUTH One way that people show emotions is through the eyes and mouth. Much of the research on facial expression is conducted by having participants view isolated faces. In the real world, however, you see faces in contexts that give you cues about what emotions people are experiencing. In one study, researchers showed identical facial expressions in different contexts and found that the context profoundly affected how participants interpreted the emotion (Aviezer et al., 2008; **Figure 9.29**). Look at the photos in Try It Yourself on p. 367 to see if you can tell when a smile is sincere.

FACIAL EXPRESSIONS ARE SIMILAR ACROSS CULTURES Does a smile mean the same thing in Bolivia or Vietnam that it means in the United States? According to Darwin, the face innately communicates emotions to others. He argued that these communications are understandable by all people, regardless of culture. Paul Ekman and colleagues (Ekman, Sorenson, & Friesen, 1969) tested this hypothesis in Argentina, Brazil, Chile, Japan, and the United States. In each country, participants viewed photographs of posed emotional expressions and then were asked to identify the emotional responses. In all five countries, the participants recognized the expressions as anger, fear, disgust, happiness, sadness, and surprise.

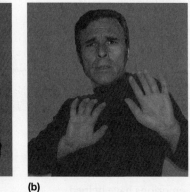

(a)   (b)

FIGURE 9.29

Contextual Effects on Categorizing Emotional Expression

Research participants were shown images such as these and asked to categorize them as showing anger, fear, pride, sadness, disgust, surprise, or happiness. **(a)** This photo pairs a sad face with a sad posture. When the face appeared in this context, most participants categorized the expression as sad. **(b)** This photo pairs the same sad face with a fearful posture. When the face appeared in this context, most participants categorized the expression incorrectly, as fearful.

TRY IT YOURSELF: Genuine Versus Fake Smiles

When people smile, they don't always mean it. Try to determine whether the man below is showing a genuine smile (really feeling happy) or a "fake" smile (being sociable but not actually feeling happy). The answer is below.

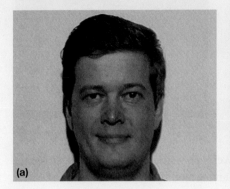

There are real differences between a genuine smile and a fake one. These differences are processed by different regions of the brain. Focusing on the mouth does not provide information about whether the smile is genuine. Instead, the eyes tell it all: When a person is genuinely happy, you will see a small crinkle at the corners of the eyes.

Answers: (a) fake, (b) genuine.

Because people in these countries had a lot of exposure to each other's cultures, however, learning and not biology could have been responsible for the cross-cultural agreement. To control for that potential confounding factor, Ekman and Friesen (1971) traveled to a remote area in New Guinea. The native inhabitants there had little exposure to outside cultures and received little formal education. Nonetheless, they were able to identify the emotions shown in the photos fairly well, but agreement was not quite as high as in other cultures. The researchers also asked participants in New Guinea to display certain facial expressions. They found that evaluators from other countries identified the expressions at a level better than chance.

Subsequent research has found general support for cross-cultural identification of some facial expressions (**Figure 9.30**). Support is strongest for happiness and weakest for fear and disgust (Elfenbein & Ambady, 2002). The evidence showing that many facial expressions are universal suggests they probably have a biological basis (Sievers, Polansky, Casey, & Wheatley, 2013).

FACIAL EXPRESSIONS OF PRIDE ARE INNATE Would you expect the physical expression of pride to be biologically based or culturally specific? The psychologist Jessica Tracy has found that young children can recognize when a person feels pride. Moreover, she found that isolated populations with minimal Western contact also accurately identify the physical signs. These signs include a smiling face, raised arms, an expanded chest, and a pushed-out torso (Tracy & Robins, 2008).

Tracy and David Matsumoto (2008) examined pride responses among people competing in judo matches in the 2004 Olympic and Paralympic Games. Sighted and blind athletes from 37 nations competed. After victory, the behaviors

FIGURE 9.30

A Smile Indicates Happiness Across Cultures

Research suggests that across cultures people identify certain facial expressions in similar ways, especially happiness.

FIGURE 9.31

Expressions of Pride May Be Biologically Determined

In response to victory in separate judo matches, **(a)** a sighted athlete and **(b)** an athlete who was born blind both expressed their pride through similar behaviors. Because such similarities occur across cultures, the physical expression of pride appears to be biologically based.

(a)

(b)

displayed by sighted and blind athletes were very similar. This finding suggests that pride responses are innate rather than learned by observing them in others (**Figure 9.31**).

9.12 Your Display of Emotion Varies

9.12 LEARNING GOAL ACTIVITIES

To maximize your learning, complete the following learning goal activities.

a. Understand all bold and italic terms by writing explanations of them in your own words.

b. Understand display rules by comparing when the display rules of your culture do or do not permit showing two of the emotions that are usually recognized across cultures.

Do you think of Americans as loud and obnoxious? Are the British cold and bland? Are Italians warm and emotional? Most people are familiar with such cultural stereotypes, which appear in everything from movies to advertising. While basic emotions seem to be expressed similarly across cultures, people learn what emotions they should show based on their experiences in their cultures.

DISPLAY RULES INDICATE WHAT EMOTIONS TO SHOW Display rules are the learned rules about what emotions should be shown in certain situations. Because display rules are learned, they vary across cultures. For example, research suggests that Japanese people are less likely than people in North America to display anger or disgust when observed by others (Sadfar et al., 2009). Display rules also may explain why the identification of facial expressions is much better within a culture than between cultures (Elfenbein & Ambady, 2002).

From culture to culture, display rules tend to be different for women and men. In particular, the rules for smiling and crying differ between the sexes (**Figure 9.32**). At least in North America, it is generally believed that women display emotions more readily, frequently, easily, and intensely (Plant, Hyde, Keltner, & Devine, 2000; Chaplin, 2015). There is evidence that this belief is true—except perhaps for emotions related to dominance, such as anger (LaFrance & Banaji, 1992). For example, women may be less likely to show anger in the workplace, although this behavior may be influenced as much by differences in status as by gender (Domagalski & Steelman, 2007).

display rules
Rules that are learned through socialization and that indicate what emotions are suitable in certain situations.

Women may be more likely to display many emotions. They do not necessarily experience those emotions more intensely. Even when women report more-intense emotions, their reports might reflect societal norms about how women are supposed to feel (Grossman & Wood, 1993). Perhaps because of differences in upbringing in modern Western society, women tend to be better than men at describing their emotions (Feldman Barrett, Lane, Sechrest, & Schwartz, 2000).

Men and women may vary in their emotional expressiveness for evolutionary reasons: The emotions most closely associated with women are related to caregiving, nurturance, and interpersonal relationships. The emotions associated with men are related to dominance, defensiveness, and competitiveness.

Ultimately, do sex differences in emotional expression reflect learned patterns of behaviors? Or do they reflect biologically based differences? Nature and nurture work together here. It is difficult—often impossible—to distinguish the effects of nature versus nurture.

FIGURE 9.32

Display Rules for Emotions Vary Across Genders

Males and females tend to show different emotions even in majority American culture. For example, in a single situation a woman might show emotion while a man remains expressionless.

9.13 Emotions Influence Your Thoughts

9.13 LEARNING GOAL ACTIVITIES

To maximize your learning, complete the following learning goal activities.

a. Understand all bold and italic terms by writing explanations of them in your own words.

b. Understand how emotions affect people by summarizing in your own words how emotions affect people's decision making and judgments.

affect-as-information theory
People use their current emotions to make decisions, judgments, and appraisals, even if they do not know what caused their emotions.

For a long time, psychologists considered thinking and feeling as separate. Researchers studied decision making, memory, and other mental processes as if people were evaluating the information from a purely rational perspective. Yet our immediate emotional responses arise quickly and automatically, coloring our perceptions at the very instant we notice an object. As Robert Zajonc put it, "We do not just see 'a house': We see a *handsome* house, an *ugly* house, or a *pretentious* house" (1980, p. 154). These instantaneous evaluations subsequently guide our decision making, memory, and behavior. Therefore, psychologists now generally acknowledge that it is unrealistic to try to separate emotion from cognition (Phelps, 2006).

EMOTIONS AFFECT DECISION MAKING AND JUDGMENTS As study unit 8.5 emphasizes, everyday cognition is far from rational. Our decisions and judgments are affected by our feelings. For example, when we are experiencing positive emotions, we tend to be persistent and to find creative, elaborate responses to challenging problems (Isen, 1993). When we are pursuing goals, positive feelings signal that we are making satisfactory progress and thereby encourage us to keep trying. According to the **affect-as-information theory** (Schwarz & Clore, 1983), we use our current emotions to make decisions, judgments, and appraisals (**Figure 9.33**). We draw on our emotions even if we do not know their sources. For example, when you are upset but don't know why, this feeling may affect what you buy at the grocery store, what you watch on TV, or whether you do your homework.

FIGURE 9.33

Emotions Affect Your Decisions

Your feelings affect how you judge information and make decisions about it. For example, if you're happy when talking about or holding a product, you may be more likely to seal the deal.

Would you rather go rock climbing in the Alps or attend a performance by a small dance troupe in Paris? In considering this question, did you think rationally about all the implications of either choice? Or did you flash on how you would feel in either situation? Emotions influence our decision making in different ways. For example, anticipating how different choices might make us feel can serve as a guide in decision making. In this way, we are able to make decisions more quickly and more efficiently. And in the face of complex, multifaceted situations, emotions serve as heuristic guides (see study unit 8.5). That is, emotions provide feedback for making quick decisions (Slovic, Finucane, Peters, & MacGregor, 2002).

As noted above, we use our emotions to make judgments. For example, Schwarz and Clore (1983) asked people to rate their overall life satisfaction. To answer this question, people potentially must consider many factors, including living situations, expectations, personal goals, and accomplishments. In arriving at their answers, however, the research participants did not carefully consider all these factors. Instead, the participants seemed to rely on their current feelings. People experiencing positive emotions rated their lives as satisfactory, whereas people experiencing negative emotions gave lower overall ratings.

9.14 Emotions Strengthen Your Interpersonal Relations

9.14 LEARNING GOAL ACTIVITIES

To maximize your learning, complete the following learning goal activities.

a. Understand all bold and italic terms by writing explanations of them in your own words.

b. Apply the social effects of guilt and embarrassment by providing one example each of how guilt and embarrassment have strengthened your interpersonal relationships.

Because humans are social animals, many of our emotions involve interpersonal factors. We feel hurt when teased, angry when insulted, happy when loved, and proud when complimented. In interacting with others, we use emotional expressions as powerful tools for social communication (**Figure 9.34**).

Nevertheless, for most of the twentieth century, psychologists paid little attention to interpersonal emotions. Guilt, embarrassment, and similar phenomena were associated with Freudian thinking and therefore not studied in mainstream psychological science. Theorists have since reconsidered interpersonal emotions in view of humans' evolutionary need to belong to social groups. Thus social emotions may be important for maintaining social bonds.

GUILT STRENGTHENS SOCIAL BONDS When we believe we did something that directly or indirectly harmed another person, we experience feelings of anxiety, tension, and remorse. We label such feelings as **guilt**. The typical guilt experience occurs when we feel responsible for another person's negative emotional state. Occasionally, however, guilt can arise even when we know we are not responsible. A familiar example is survivor guilt. That is, people feel guilty for having survived accidents or catastrophes in which others have died.

Excessive feelings of guilt may have negative consequences. Guilt itself is not entirely negative. According to one theory, guilt protects and strengthens interpersonal relationships in three ways (Baumeister, Heatherton, & Tice, 1994). First,

FIGURE 9.34

Emotions Influence Social Bonds

Emotions can help strengthen social relationships between people. Here, the clear expressions of joy will help cement the decision of this couple to get married.

guilt
A negative emotional state associated with anxiety, tension, and agitation.

feelings of guilt discourage us from doing things that would harm our relationships and encourage behaviors that strengthen relationships. For example, guilt keeps us from cheating on our partners and leads us to phone our parents regularly. Second, displays of guilt demonstrate that people care about their relationship partners, thereby affirming social bonds. Third, guilt can be used to manipulate others. This aspect of guilt is especially effective when people hold power over us and it is difficult to get them to do what we want. For instance, you might try to make your boss feel guilty so you do not have to work overtime. Children may use guilt to get adults to buy them presents or grant them privileges.

There is evidence that socialization is more important than biology in determining specifically how children experience guilt. One study involving identical and fraternal twins (Zahn-Waxler & Robinson, 1995) found that all the negative emotions showed considerable genetic influence, but guilt was unique in being highly influenced by social environment. Perhaps surprisingly, parental warmth is associated with greater guilt in children. This finding suggests that feelings of guilt arise in healthy and happy relationships. As children become citizens in a social world, they develop the capacity to empathize. As a result, they experience feelings of guilt when they transgress against others.

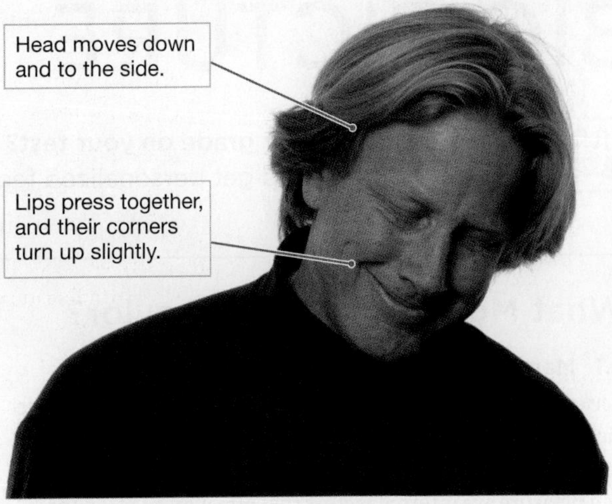

EMBARRASSMENT AND BLUSHING   We have all experienced embarrassment, probably many times. We tend to feel embarrassed after violating a cultural norm, doing something clumsy, being teased, or experiencing a threat to our self-image (Miller, 1996). Some theories suggest that embarrassment remedies interpersonal awkwardness and restores social bonds. Embarrassment represents recognition of the unintentional social error. Like guilt, embarrassment may reaffirm close relationships after wrongdoing (**Figure 9.35**).

Embarrassment is often accompanied by blushing. The writer Mark Twain once said, "Man is the only animal that blushes. Or needs to." Darwin, in his 1872 book, called blushing the "most peculiar and the most human of all expressions," thereby separating it from emotional responses he deemed necessary for survival.

According to recent theory and research, blushing occurs most often when people believe others might view them negatively, and blushing communicates an understanding that some type of social awkwardness occurred. This nonverbal apology is an appeasement that brings out forgiveness in others, thereby repairing and maintaining relationships (Keltner & Anderson, 2000).

Head moves down and to the side.

Lips press together, and their corners turn up slightly.

FIGURE 9.35

Embarrassment

Embarrassment is another emotion that can increase social bonds. In this photo, the psychologist Dacher Keltner is demonstrating the classic facial signals of embarrassment.

Q How Do Emotions Affect You?

To make sure you learned what you just read, write answers to the following questions and check your answers.

9.11 What six emotions are recognized in facial expressions across cultures?

9.12 According to cultural stereotypes, Italians are very emotional, whereas the English are unemotional. How might display rules influence the development of these stereotypes?

9.13 Imagine that you are in a bad mood and everything your romantic partner does is annoying you. Name the theory that explains why you should not make a big decision about ending the relationship while you are in a bad mood.

9.14 What two emotions strengthen the social bonds between people?

See Appendix B for answers to the red Q questions.

BIG PICTURE

Want to earn a better grade on your test? Go to **INQUIZITIVE** to practice actively with this chapter's content and get personalized feedback along the way.

What Motivates Your Behavior?

9.1 Many Factors Influence Motivation

Review the learning goal activities on p. 336. Motivations include factors of differing strengths that activate, direct, and sustain behaviors that satisfy a need. Needs, drives, arousal, and pleasure are internal factors that affect motivation for particular behaviors. Incentives are external factors that affect our motivation to act in particular ways.

9.2 Some Behaviors Are Motivated for Their Own Sake

Review the learning goal activities on p. 342. Intrinsic motivation influences people to act in certain ways because those activities have value, are pleasurable, or both. Extrinsic motivation influences people to act in certain ways to obtain external goals. Receiving an extrinsic reward may reduce intrinsic motivation.

KEY TERMS
motivation (p. 337)
need (p. 337)
need hierarchy (p. 338)
drive (p. 339)
arousal (p. 340)
incentives (p. 342)
intrinsic motivation (p. 342)
extrinsic motivation (p. 343)

What Are Your Most Important Motivated Behaviors?

9.3 Motivation to Eat Is Affected by Biology

Review the learning goal activities on p. 344. The motivation to eat is not strongly influenced by signals from the stomach. Instead, this motivation is influenced primarily by three factors: (1) signals from the bloodstream (glucose), (2) hormones (insulin, ghrelin, and leptin), and (3) specific regions of the brain (hypothalamus, gustatory cortex, and limbic system).

9.4 Motivation to Eat Is Also Influenced by Learning

Review the learning goal activities on p. 347. Learning influences the motivation to eat through four factors: (1) classical conditioning, (2) familiarity, (3) flavor, and (4) culture.

9.5 People Have a Need to Belong

Review the learning goal activities on p. 348. People have a fundamental need for social relationships and to be in groups. This need to belong motivates people to make friends and avoid social exclusion. But this need creates feelings of emptiness and despair in the absence of other people.

9.6 People Have a Need to Achieve Long-Term Goals

Review the learning goal activities on p. 349. People are motivated to achieve their long-term goals. People with high achievement motivation are more likely to achieve long-term goals, especially when they: (1) have good goals, (2) have a high sense of self-efficacy, (3) can delay gratification, and (4) have grit, which lets them persevere toward their goals.

KEY TERMS
insulin (p. 346)
ghrelin (p. 346)
leptin (p. 346)
need to belong theory (p. 349)
achievement motivation (p. 351)

How Do You Experience Emotions?

9.7 Emotions Are Personal but Labeled and Described Consistently

Review the learning goal activities on p. 353. Emotions are immediate, specific, negative or positive responses to environmental events or internal thoughts. Even though emotions are experienced personally, they are labeled and are described consistently. Primary emotions are universal across cultures. Secondary emotions are blends of the primary emotions. Emotions have both valence, positive or negative, and a level of arousal that ranges from low to high.

9.8 Three Major Theories Explain Your Emotions

Review the learning goal activities on p. 355. Three theories explain how we experience emotions, based primarily on physiological or cognitive components: (1) James-Lange theory, (2) Cannon-Bard theory, and (3) two-factor theory. The James-Lange theory states that specific bodily responses create the perception of emotions. The Cannon-Bard theory proposes that processing in the brain simultaneously activates both bodily responses and the perception of emotions. The two-factor theory states that people interpret bodily changes, which leads them to label their emotions. People often experience misattribution of arousal, where they wrongly think that their emotions are caused by their situations.

9.9 Your Body and Brain Influence Your Emotions

Review the learning goal activities on p. 360. The emotions that people experience are influenced by physiological responses in the body, such as increased or decreased blood pressure and breathing rate. People's perceptions of those responses in certain areas of their bodies influence what emotions they experience. People's experience of emotion is also influenced by processing in certain areas of the brain, such as the prefrontal cortex and especially the amygdala. The amygdala processes emotional significance of stimuli and is associated with emotional learning, memory of emotional events, and the interpretation of facial expressions of emotion. The amygdala processes emotions in two ways: (1) a fast route, where sensory input moves through the thalamus and directly to the amygdala for immediate response, and (2) a slow route, where sensory input moves through the thalamus and then cortical sensory processing areas, such as the primary visual cortex, for more careful processing, before being processed in the amygdala.

9.10 Most People Try to Regulate Their Emotional States

Review the learning goal activities on p. 363. People may try to regulate their negative emotional states with thought suppression (not thinking about an event) or rumination (thinking continually about an event), but research suggests these techniques are not effective. Instead, people can successfully regulate their negative emotional states by using three strategies: (1) positive reappraisal (changing one's thoughts about an event), (2) humor, and (3) distraction (focusing one's attention elsewhere).

KEY TERMS

emotion (p. 354)	James-Lange theory (p. 356)
primary emotions (p. 354)	Cannon-Bard theory (p. 357)
secondary emotions (p. 354)	two-factor theory (p. 358)

How Do Emotions Affect You?

9.11 You Use Facial Expressions to Interpret Emotions

Review the learning goal activities on p. 366. We communicate emotion through facial expressions, especially with the eyes and mouth. Certain expressions of emotion are universally recognized, such as anger, fear, disgust, happiness, sadness, and surprise. In addition, expressions of pride also seem to be innate, because they are seen even in blind people who have never observed pride.

9.12 Your Display of Emotion Varies

Review the learning goal activities on p. 368. Display rules are the learned ways that people express certain emotions in certain situations. Display rules vary across cultures and between the sexes.

9.13 Emotions Influence Your Thoughts

Review the learning goal activities on p. 369. Emotions serve cognitive functions. According to the affect-as-information theory, people use their emotions to make decisions and evaluate information.

9.14 Emotions Strengthen Your Interpersonal Relations

Review the learning goal activities on p. 370. Guilt and embarrassment strengthen interpersonal relations by helping to maintain and repair social bonds.

KEY TERMS

display rules (p. 368)
affect-as-information theory (p. 369)
guilt (p. 370)

CHAPTER 9 SELF-QUIZ

To make sure you learned the information in this chapter, write answers to the following questions and check your answers. **See Appendix B for answers to the self-quiz.**

1. Dwayne enjoys spending calm, quiet evenings at home watching old movies. Debbie likes to do exciting activities, such as skydiving, on her days off. The fact that Dwayne and Debbie choose to spend their free time in these ways is best explained by _____.
   a. satisfaction of needs
   b. incentives
   c. optimal level of arousal
   d. drive reduction

2. Vince and Edith are training for a marathon. When asked why they are running the race, Vince says he wants the medal they give out to everyone who crosses the finish line. Edith responds that she enjoys trying new things. Vince's behavior is most likely explained by _____, whereas Edith's behavior is most likely explained by _____.
   a. extrinsic motivation; intrinsic motivation
   b. intrinsic motivation; extrinsic motivation
   c. self-perception theory; self-determination theory
   d. self-determination theory; self-perception theory

3. When Terry's stomach starts growling, he decides it's time for lunch. After eating a burrito and tortilla chips, he feels full and does not want to eat more. Which of the following does NOT play a role in his short-term feeling of fullness?
   a. increased glucose in his bloodstream
   b. decreased ghrelin in his stomach
   c. activation of his hypothalamus
   d. release of leptin in his saliva

4. Thomas sends his daughter Sophia to spend the summer with her grandparents, who eat dinner at 5:00 PM. Upon her return home, Sophia wants to eat dinner at 5:00 PM every night, because she now associates that time of day with eating. Sophia's change in desired mealtime has most likely been influenced by _____.
   a. drive reduction
   b. classical conditioning
   c. optimal arousal
   d. low levels of the hormone ghrelin

5. Mr. Ray is a middle school math teacher who wants to help his students learn achievement motivation so they can reach the long-term goal of doing well on the state math tests. Mr. Ray helps the students develop achievement motivation through all of the following ways EXCEPT _____.
   a. helping them develop grit
   b. showing them their hard work leads to success
   c. training them to wait for delayed gratification
   d. making sure they have a need to belong

6. Hannah enjoys playing video games because every time she scores a point, processing in her brain simultaneously causes an excited emotion and an increase in her heart rate. The theory that has been proposed to explain emotion in the way Hannah experienced it is the _____ theory.
   a. Cannon-Bard
   b. Grison-Gazzaniga
   c. James-Lange
   d. two-factor

7. After Bernadette is in a car accident, she is extra friendly to people she meets. In fact, she does not seem to realize when she might be revealing personal information to untrustworthy strangers. This information suggests that Bernadette may have brain damage in her _____.
   a. right prefrontal cortex
   b. left prefrontal cortex
   c. amygdala
   d. thalamus

8. Bianca is sad and anxious because her sister is moving across the country for a new job. To make herself feel better, Bianca thinks of her sister's new city as a vacation destination—a place Bianca can visit and explore. Bianca is successfully regulating her emotional state by using _____.
   a. rumination
   b. distraction
   c. thought suppression
   d. positive reappraisal

9. Tori sometimes refrains from arguing with her colleagues in staff meetings because she believes it is not appropriate for women to show anger. Tori's belief about emotional expressiveness in women is best explained by _____.
   a. self-determination theory
   b. thought suppression
   c. display rules
   d. affect-as-information theory

10. Madison frequently checks the cell phone of her husband, Max, to see if he is texting other women. Max catches her and is very hurt by her behavior. Madison loves Max very much and feels bad that she hurt him. In this situation, Madison is most likely to feel the emotion of _____.
    a. guilt
    b. pride
    c. embarrassment
    d. fear

How Can Understanding Motivation and Emotion Help You Work with Customers?

Have you ever walked into a store to buy something, but were put off by the salesperson being overly aggressive? Most likely you left without buying anything. Working in sales—helping people purchase items and feel satisfied with their purchases—involves understanding what makes people think and act in certain ways. In short, a good salesperson has a knowledge of motivation. Emotion, too, is involved in sales. For example, as discussed in study unit 9.13, a customer who feels good about a product is more likely to buy that item. So the knowledge this chapter gives you about motivation and emotion can be very helpful in dealing with customers.

If you complete an associate's degree, you can be qualified to work as a customer service representative. In the quickly growing field of customer service, a person helps customers by processing their orders or handling complaints, in person, on the phone, or through e-mail or Internet chat tools. Because people who call to complain are often angry, understanding how emotions affect their thoughts and actions may assist you in responding effectively to their complaints. You can also use your knowledge of emotion regulation to calm yourself in dealing with customers who have lost their cool.

Perhaps you would like to work in the financial services industry, such as being a bank teller, loan officer, bookkeeper, or financial planner. In one of these positions, you will help customers handle their money. Because incentives such as money are an important source of motivation, knowing how incentives work will help you understand your customers. People often struggle between their short-term desires and their long-term interests. As noted in this chapter, delaying gratification is hard. As a bank teller or loan officer, you can describe products in terms of how they satisfy customers' real needs and goals.

Understanding how emotions affect thinking is also valuable for working in financial services. Many people worry a lot about money, and many have serious financial problems that cause them distress. Helping customers control their emotions is part of guiding them toward good financial decisions.

TAKEAWAY POINT: Dealing with customers requires you to know how their motivations and emotions affect their thoughts and actions. You can use this knowledge to excel as a salesperson or customer service representative, or in any occupation that involves helping people manage their finances. But being able to improve your own motivation, and those of people you work with, can help you succeed in almost any job.

 You can look up job descriptions, education requirements, salaries, and more at the Bureau of Labor Statistics: www.bls.gov. Visit the site and start putting psychology to work!

10 Sex, Gender, and Sexuality

WHEN A BABY IS BORN, the first thing people usually say is "Congratulations!" Then they ask, "Is it a boy or a girl?" When Coy Mathis was born, in Colorado in 2007, the family answered, "We have a boy!" Coy's parents dressed him as a boy, gave him firefighter and knight costumes, and encouraged him to play with Matchbox cars and Iron Man figures (Erdely, 2013). But by the time Coy was 18 months old, as soon as he started communicating, he began expressing that he was, in fact, a girl. His parents initially took these feelings to mean that Coy was a boy who liked to wear girls' things, preferred pink to blue, and wanted to play with girls' toys. However, within a few years, Coy showed signs of distress. He would not leave the house wearing boys' clothes. At school, when teachers placed him in the boys' line, he cried. And he began feeling depressed and anxious.

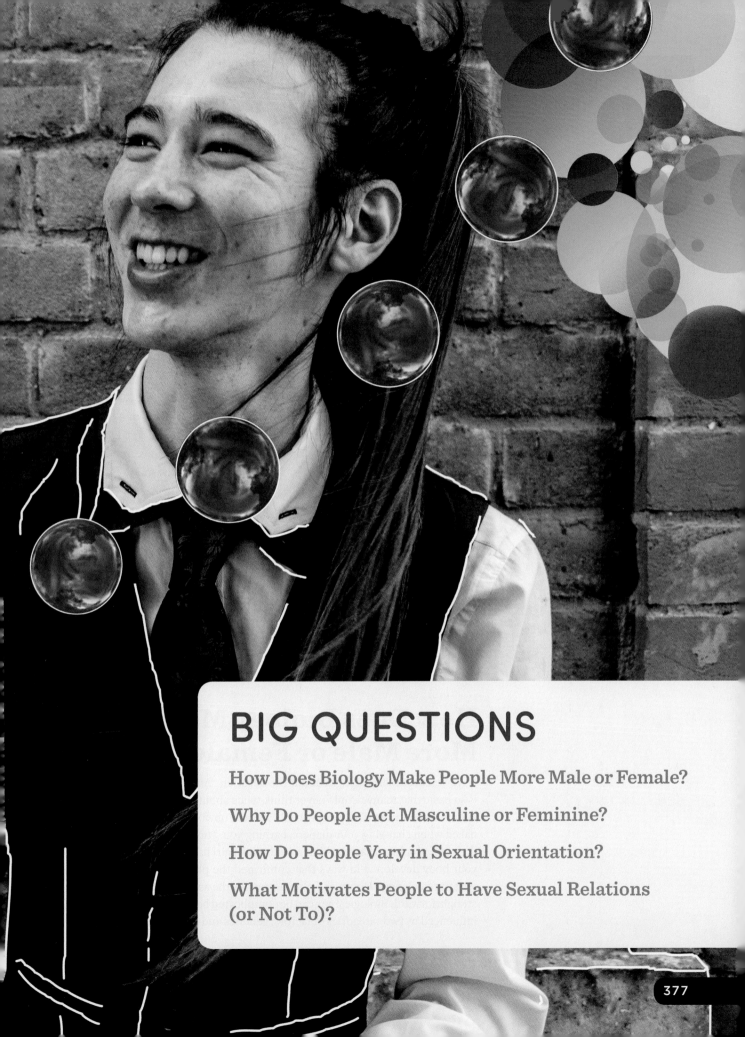

BIG QUESTIONS

How Does Biology Make People More Male or Female?

Why Do People Act Masculine or Feminine?

How Do People Vary in Sexual Orientation?

What Motivates People to Have Sexual Relations (or Not To)?

FIGURE 10.1

Coy Mathis Is Transgender

Coy Mathis was born male, but by the time she was a year and a half old she consistently stated she was a girl. Coy's case reveals that a person's gender is not always the same as the sex assigned at birth. When this mismatch happens, the person is experiencing a transgender identity.

Experts helped Coy's parents understand that their child is transgender. That is, although Coy was assigned the sex of male at birth, she says that she is a girl (**Figure 10.1**). The experts suggested that Coy's parents help her transition to living as a girl. So by the time she was 5 years old, Coy's state identification from Colorado identified her as female, as did her passport. Coy wore frilly dresses and princess costumes with a flowered headpiece, played with a Barbie doll and other girls' toys, and ate off a pink plate. She also started attending kindergarten as a girl. After her parents won a land-mark civil rights case, 6-year-old Coy was allowed to use the girls' restroom at school. Her depression and anxiety started to fade. She was a happy little girl in a body that most people would think of as male.

The experiences of Coy and her parents, which are presented in the 2017 documentary *Growing Up Coy,* reveal a fact that surprises many people: *Biological sex,* the physical aspects of being male or female, is different from *gender,* the psychological experience of being a boy or a girl. Most people feel that their gender matches their biological sex. But approximately 1–3 percent of the population reports being transgender, where their gender is different from the sex they were assigned at birth (Conron, Scott, Stowell, & Landers, 2012; Gates, 2011; Olyslager & Conway, 2007). In addition, gender can extend beyond the two traditional choices of a boy or a girl. Some people don't consider their gender to be a boy or a girl. Other people say they feel more like a boy (or a man) in some situations and more like a girl (or a woman) in others. We simply do not know how many people experience *gender nonconformity.*

In this chapter, you will explore what factors determine biological sex and how this label differs from people's understanding of what gender is. You will also learn about the many variations in whom people are attracted to, which is their sexual orientation. And you will discover the many ways in which biological sex, gender, and sexual orientation influence thoughts and actions. By the end of the chapter, you should understand that biological sex, gender, and sexual orientation reflect complex and important aspects of each person's sense of self, rather than a set of boxes that a person can check off.

How Does Biology Make People More Male or Female?

Have you ever really thought about the question "Am I male or female?" The idea is so basic that many people never think twice about it. When you were born, you were assigned a sex. That sex probably seemed obvious to the people who saw you naked when changing your diapers, bathing you, and so on. Even very young children will proclaim that a boy has a penis and a girl has a vagina. As you grew older, your body developed in ways that confirmed the physical aspects of your maleness or femaleness. However, for some people, the answer to the question is not so straightforward. Biological sex can be complicated because being male or female is influenced by two categories of factors: genetics and hormones.

10.1 Genetics and Hormones Influence Biological Sex

biological sex
The physical aspects of a person's sex.

10.1 LEARNING GOAL ACTIVITIES

To maximize your learning, complete the following learning goal activities.

a. Understand all bold and italic terms by writing explanations of them in your own words.

b. Understand biological sex by summarizing in your own words the two ways that genetics and the two ways that hormones make people biologically male or female.

Biological sex refers to the physical aspects of a person's sex. As described in the Learning Tip, the two categories of factors that influence biological sex can be broken down into four aspects. When all these aspects of a person are consistent with each other, we usually say the person is either male or female. When at least one aspect of biological sex is inconsistent with the others, it becomes harder to describe a person's sex as clearly "male" or "female."

LEARNING TIP: Four Aspects of Biological Sex

This tip will help you understand the four aspects of biological sex that reveal differences between males and females.

FOUR ASPECTS OF BIOLOGICAL SEX	TYPICALLY FEMALE	TYPICALLY MALE
GENETIC INFLUENCES ON BIOLOGICAL SEX		
Sex chromosomes: genetic material determined at conception by the 23rd pair of chromosomes in the new zygote	XX sex chromosomes	XY sex chromosomes
Sex glands: organs that release sex hormones and contain the cells used for sexual reproduction	Ovaries release more estrogens and develop mature egg cells.	Testes release more androgens and develop mature sperm cells.
HORMONAL INFLUENCES ON BIOLOGICAL SEX		
Secondary sex characteristics: changes during puberty that are indirectly related to sexual reproduction	Increased release of estradiol Defining of waist Increase in fat Breast development Body hair (armpits) Pubic hair	Increased release of testosterone Greater muscle mass Facial hair Deepening voice Angular jaw Body hair (armpits and chest) Pubic hair
Primary sex characteristics: changes during puberty that are directly related to sexual reproduction	Mature internal organs (uterus and ovaries with egg cells) Mature genitals (vagina) Menarche	Mature internal organs (testes with sperm cells) Mature genitals (penis) Spermarche

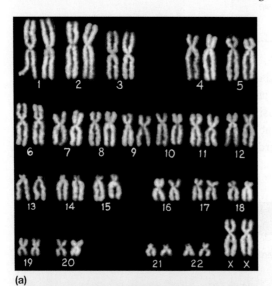

(a)

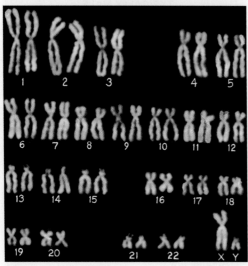

(b)

FIGURE 10.2

Sex Chromosomes Influence Biological Sex

These images show the chromosomes of two zygotes. Each image reveals the 23 pairs of chromosomes. The 23rd pair is the sex chromosomes. **(a)** The sex chromosomes are XX, so this zygote is biologically female. **(b)** The sex chromosomes are XY, so this zygote is biologically male.

SEX CHROMOSOMES ARE DETERMINED BY GENETICS Biological sex is determined at conception. As you learned in study unit 2.11, genes are a person's hereditary makeup, which is determined the moment that the father's sperm fertilizes the mother's egg. The result is the zygote, the first cell of a new life, which is created in the germinal period of prenatal development (see Figures 4.4a and 4.5a). When developing normally, the zygote contains all the genetic information from both parents in 23 paired chromosomes (46 chromosomes in total). Out of each pair, one chromosome is from the father and one is from the mother. Together with the individual's environment, these chromosomes help determine physical traits (such as height), psychological characteristics (such as personality), and predispositions for diseases, such as alcoholism (Epps & Holt, 2011). However, it is the 23rd chromosome from each parent that determines the zygote's biological sex.

The mother's egg cell always contributes an X chromosome as the 23rd chromosome of the zygote. In about half of conceptions, the father's sperm cell also contributes an X chromosome so that the zygote has **XX sex chromosomes.** This means that the zygote is female (**Figure 10.2a**). In about the other half of conceptions, the father's sperm cell contributes a Y chromosome instead so the zygote has **XY sex chromosomes.** In this case, the zygote is male (**Figure 10.2b**). Put simply, the sex of a zygote is determined by whether an egg is fertilized by a sperm carrying an X chromosome or a sperm carrying a Y chromosome. As a result, about half of babies are born with female sex chromosomes and about half are born with male sex chromosomes.

SEX GLANDS ARE ALSO INFLUENCED BY GENETICS Once the sex chromosomes of a zygote are determined, they further influence biological sex. They do so by affecting what sex glands, or *gonads,* the zygote will eventually develop. The Y chromosome contains a special gene that affects how the gonads develop. This gene is called *SRY,* which stands for "sex determining region on the Y chromosome." As the name suggests, the SRY gene is absent on the X chromosome. So at about six to seven weeks of development, in the embryonic period (see Figures 4.4b and 4.5b), embryos with XY sex chromosomes start to develop the male sex glands, called **testes** (see Figure 2.24). By contrast, embryos with XX chromosomes do not develop male sex glands because they do not have the Y chromosome with the SRY gene (Ngun, Gjahramani, Sánchez, Bocklandt, & Vilain, 2011). Instead, the female sex glands will develop. These sex glands are called **ovaries** (see Figure 2.24). The male and female sex glands are critical in making people's bodies develop into their adult male and adult female forms and also in helping those bodies reach sexual maturity and reproduce.

These sex glands are part of the endocrine system. As you learned in study unit 2.10, the endocrine system is a communication network that releases chemicals called hormones into the bloodstream. The hormones released by the sex glands affect physical development, thoughts, and behavior. Specifically, as children reach adolescence and enter *puberty,* the hormones released by the ovaries and testes cause their bodies to become more adult-like.

During puberty, females' ovaries begin to release more of one class of sex hormones, called **estrogens.** Within the class of estrogens, one specific hormone, *estradiol,* increases to about 8 times the level it was before puberty (Malina, Bouchard, & Bar-Or, 2004). In males, the testes release greater amounts of another class of hormones, called **androgens**. Of the androgens, one particular hormone, *testosterone*, increases to 20 times the level it was before puberty (Roche & Sun, 2003). All people have both estrogens and androgens. It is the increases in estradiol for females and testosterone for males that cause the first physical changes experienced during puberty, which are called *secondary sex characteristics*.

SECONDARY SEX CHARACTERISTICS DEVELOP DUE TO HORMONES

The secondary sex characteristics are not directly related to sexual reproduction. That is why they are called "secondary." But as described in study unit 4.8, these characteristics make particular aspects of adolescents' bodies look more male or more female (**Figure 10.3a–b**). These changes signal that the adolescents are becoming capable of reproduction.

These changes start to appear in girls at about 8 years of age and in boys at about 9 or 10 (Ge, Natsuaki, Neiderhiser, & Reiss, 2007; Herman-Giddens, Wang, & Koch, 2001; Sun et al., 2005). For both sexes, the secondary sex characteristics include the development of darker and thicker body hair on the legs, in the armpits, and in the pubic area (Tanner, 1972). The skin secretes more oil, and body odor increases as a result (Katchadourian, 1977). Both sexes experience a growth spurt. However, in girls this rapid increase in height begins at about age 10 and peaks at 12, whereas in boys it begins at about age 12 and peaks at 14 (Malina, Bouchard, & Beunen, 1988; Tanner & Davies, 1985). Girls gain more fat, their waists become more defined, and their breasts develop. Boys gain more muscle mass and develop facial hair, their voices deepen, and their jaws become more angular (Lee, 1980). After about four years of puberty, both boys and girls stop looking like children. They physically look like young men and young women.

PRIMARY SEX CHARACTERISTICS ARE ALSO A RESULT OF HORMONES

Recall that the most obvious way that we determine whether a person is biologically male or female is by looking at the *genitals*. Sound waves can be used to create a visual image of the developing fetus, through a technique called sonography, or ultrasound. By 14 weeks after conception, ultrasound can detect early signs of the developing genitals with considerable accuracy (Odeh, Grinin, Kais, Ophir, & Bornstein, 2009). However, the genitals don't reach full maturity until about two years after the adolescent growth spurt, which is when the hormones released by the sex glands prepare our bodies for sexual reproduction. The changes that result from the increased hormones, called *primary sex characteristics*, are described in study unit 4.8. These changes are "primary" because they are directly related to sexual reproduction.

In females, increases in estrogens cause primary sex characteristics such as the maturation of the uterus, the vagina, and the two ovaries, including the egg cells

ovaries
The female gonads (sex glands); they release the sex hormones and produce the cells that females use for sexual reproduction, called eggs.

estrogens
A class of hormones, including estradiol, that are more prevalent in females; they are associated with the development of the secondary and primary sex characteristics and with sexual behavior.

androgens
A class of hormones, including testosterone, that are more prevalent in males; they are associated with the development of the secondary and primary sex characteristics and with sexual behavior.

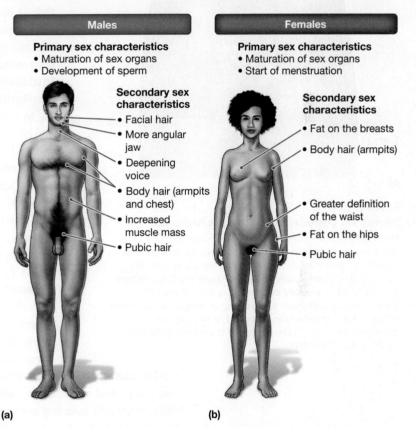

(a)

(b)

FIGURE 10.3

Secondary Sex Characteristics Cause People's Bodies to Look More Female or More Male

Compare these graphics with Figure 4.23a–b. The previous images show how, as a result of hormones, people's bodies change from childhood through puberty, developing a physical appearance that is more male or more female. Here, the secondary sex characteristics are shown for **(a)** the mature male and **(b)** the mature female.

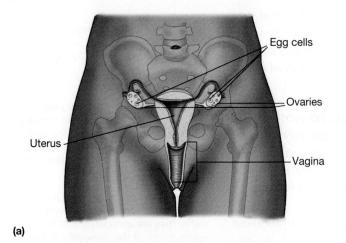

(a)

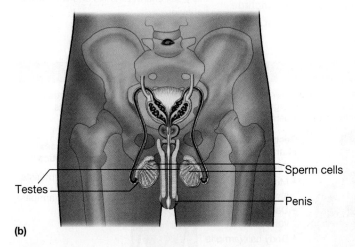

(b)

FIGURE 10.4

Primary Sex Characteristics Let People Reproduce

These graphics show how hormones change people's bodies during puberty so that females and males become able to reproduce. Other aspects of male and female sexual and reproductive anatomy are shown in Figure 10.26. **(a)** Female development of primary sex characteristics affects the uterus, vagina, and ovaries, including the egg cells contained in the ovaries. **(b)** Male development of primary sex characteristics affects the penis and the testes, including the sperm cells in the testes.

menarche
A primary sex characteristic in females; a female's first menstrual period, which signals the ability to reproduce sexually.

spermarche
A primary sex characteristic in males; a male's first production of mature sperm, which signals the ability to reproduce sexually.

contained in the ovaries (**Figure 10.4a**). In males, increases in androgens cause primary sex characteristics that include the maturation of the penis and the two testes and beginning of sperm cell production in the testes (**Figure 10.4b**).

If you are female, think back to when you were in puberty. What is the biggest change that happened to your body? The clearest sign of primary sex characteristics in a female occurs when she experiences **menarche** (pronounced "MEN-ar-key"), which is her first menstrual period. Menarche occurs when one of the female's ovaries releases an egg cell. When the egg cell is not fertilized by a sperm cell, the egg leaves the uterus, along with the tissue lining the uterus. This "flow" is what a female experiences as her first menstrual period. Once puberty is complete, a female will experience menstruation each month unless an egg is fertilized by a sperm.

Menarche usually occurs at about 12 years of age (Rosenfield, Lipton, & Drum, 2009). However, it is beginning earlier than it did 50 years ago (Herman-Giddens et al., 2001). What explains the declining age of menarche? Consider that a female typically must weigh at least 100 pounds to experience menarche (Berkey, Gardner, Frazier, & Colditz, 2000). In addition, a female's level of body fat is a trigger for puberty (Kaplowitz, 2008). Now consider that obesity is increasing in many cultures, so females on average weigh more and have greater body fat than they did in previous generations. This may be one reason why females who are higher than average on the body mass index experience menarche earlier (Lin-Su, Vogiatzi, & New, 2002). By contrast, females who have lower body fat than average—for example, those who practice ballet or perform gymnastics—experience menarche later (Robert-McComb, 2008).

In the majority North American culture, most females report feeling more "grown up" after menarche begins (Brooks-Gunn & Ruble, 1982). In addition to increased maturity, they enjoy higher social ranking with peers and greater self-esteem (Archibald, Graber, & Brooks-Gunn, 2003). By contrast, when females in North America learn negative information about menarche from their mothers or other sources, they tend to report greater discomfort during menarche (Teitelman, 2004). And according to a study of various cultures in Turkey, Malaysia, and Wales, when girls have not been given information to prepare them for menarche, they tend to experience the event fearfully (Howie & Shail, 2005). In short, the research suggests that girls tend to experience this important life event positively when they have accurate information and a positive outlook.

If you are male, how do you remember the physical changes of puberty? You may remember your muscles developing or your voice changing, but in terms of reproduction, the most important aspect of your physical development was not outwardly visible. The beginning of sperm cell production in the testes, **spermarche** (pronounced "sperm-AR-kee"), usually occurs at about age 12 (Bancroft, 2006). A male won't know that his sperm production has begun until he experiences an outward sign of it: the release of sperm from the penis in *semenarche* ("see-men-AR-kee"). Usually, semenarche first happens when a sleeping male experiences an emission of semen, commonly known as a "wet dream." Indeed, the "wetness" may lead him to think he has urinated rather than ejaculated. However, semenarche may also occur during masturbation.

Most adolescent males experience semenarche with a mix of pleasure and confusion, but their reactions depend on how prepared they are for the event (Stein & Reiser, 1994). Unfortunately, parents rarely bring up semenarche with their sons, who also tend to remain silent about the experience (Frankel, 2002).

10.2 Biological Sex Is Not Always Clear

10.2 LEARNING GOAL ACTIVITIES

To maximize your learning, complete the following learning goal activities.

a. Understand all bold and italic terms by writing explanations of them in your own words.

b. Analyze the two main biological causes of being intersex by describing these causes in your own words.

Let's return to the question that began this discussion of biological sex: Are you male or female? You probably answered right away. But then you learned that being male or female involves more aspects than most people ever consider. Are you sure that *all* of the aspects of your biological sex are male or that they *all* are female?

SOME PEOPLE EXPERIENCE INCONSISTENCIES IN BIOLOGICAL SEX

For example, do you know whether your sex chromosomes are XX (female) or XY (male)? Believe it or not, most of us don't know. We simply assume that our sex chromosomes match the sex reflected in our genitals. So our biological answer to the question of being male or female seems clear. However, for approximately 2 percent of people, the issue of being "male or female" is much more complicated (Blackless et al., 2000). For these people, some aspects of biological sex are either ambiguous or inconsistent with each other.

Consider the South African middle-distance runner Caster Semenya. When Semenya competed in the 2009 African Junior Championships, she blew past the competition twice, winning gold in the 800-meter and 1,500-meter events. She went on to win gold in the 800-meter race at the World Championships. Because her amazing athletic achievements included dramatically improving her personal best time, however, she was forced to undergo testing to determine her biological sex. Her competitors argued that although Semenya had been assigned the sex of female at birth, she was such a fast runner because she was male. Regardless of the controversy, Semenya went on to win gold in the 800 meters event in both the 2012 and 2016 Olympics.

For privacy reasons, the results of the tests were not officially released. According to newspaper reports, Semenya may lack ovaries and a uterus and have internal testes that produce high levels of testosterone. The publicly available information suggests that Semenya may experience inconsistencies in biological sex (**Figure 10.5a**), but Semenya has not confirmed this information. In 2018, the International Association of Athletics Federations introduced new and highly controversial rules that limit the amount of testosterone for females who compete in long-distance events. Those with levels higher than the limits, such as Semenya, will be required to take medications to reduce their testosterone levels. The point here is that athletics may have separate events for males and females, but biological sex in humans is not that simple.

When people, such as Semenya, do not clearly fall into either category of biologically male or biologically female they are commonly described as **intersex.** However,

(a)

(b)

FIGURE 10.5

Biological Sex Is Not Always Consistent

(a) According to her birth certificate, Caster Semenya **(right)** is a female. Her female competitors have argued that Semenya is so fast because she is male. If Semenya has inconsistencies in her biological sex, then she is intersex. **(b)** Sara Kelly Keenan **(right),** here posing with her husband, is the first person in the United States to have her biological sex listed as "intersex" on her birth certificate. Although her sex chromosomes suggest she is male, her genitals appear female, and her internal reproductive system is neither clearly male nor clearly female.

intersex
When a person experiences conflicting or ambiguous aspects of biological sex.

some advocacy groups, such as the Accord Alliance, prefer to say that these people have differences of sex development. In December 2016, New York City issued the first birth certificate in the United States listing "intersex" in the sex field instead of "male" or "female." It was issued to 55-year-old Sara Kelly Keenan (**Figure 10.5b**), who was born with male genes, female genitals, and internal reproductive organs inconsistent with being biologically male or female.

The main causes of intersex are conflicting or ambiguous biological sex indicators, including abnormalities in the sex chromosomes or in hormones, which can affect how the genitals look (American Psychiatric Association, 2013). When an inclusive definition of intersex is used, research suggests that about 1 or 2 of every 100 people experience some ambiguity in their biological sex (Blackless et al., 2000; Arboleda, Sandberg, & Vilain, 2014).

AMBIGUITY IN SEX CHROMOSOMES One cause of intersex is present from conception, when the merging sperm cell and egg cell do not provide the usual combination of XX or XY sex chromosomes to the new zygote (Juul, Main, & Skakkebaek, 2011). It is estimated that about 1 in 426 people does not have the typical sex chromosomes (Nielsen & Wohlert, 1990). Such babies generally have normal genitals, so they may never be aware that they are intersex until puberty or when they try to reproduce.

For example, zygotes may inherit three sex chromosomes. Two female sex chromosomes and one male sex chromosome together create a zygote with XXY sex chromosomes. This very common abnormality results in *Klinefelter syndrome,* which affects between 1 in 500 and 1 in 1,000 births (National Institutes of Health, 2018a). Children with Klinefelter syndrome seem to develop normally as males until puberty. At that point, lower than normal production of testosterone for a male results in secondary sex characteristics that are more typical of females. That is, adolescents with Klinefelter syndrome develop breasts, have higher voices than would be expected, and have less facial and body hair than most men. In addition, although the penis of a male with XXY chromosomes is anatomically normal, the adult size is much smaller than for a male born with XY chromosomes. Testosterone replacement therapy can stimulate the development of more typically male physical characteristics. However, this therapy has serious risks, such as the possibility of liver damage.

By contrast, some zygotes have inherited only one sex chromosome, an X. In such cases, where there is just one (female) sex chromosome, the zygote is described as having XO sex chromosomes. The O refers to the missing chromosome. This very rare chromosomal abnormality results in *Turner syndrome,* which occurs in about 1 in 2,500 births (National Institutes of Health, 2018b). These children are born with vaginas that appear typical. However, their ovaries do not develop in a typical way, so they have reduced amounts of estrogen. As a result, during puberty, they do not show many of the typically female secondary sex characteristics, such as breast growth. Estrogen replacement therapy during adolescence may improve breast development and even start menarche.

CONFLICTS IN HORMONES Another group of people are intersex due to a conflict between their sex chromosomes and the presence of certain hormones. Because of this conflict, they exhibit some characteristics of another sex. For example, a zygote with XX sex chromosomes—genetically female—may be exposed to greater amounts of androgens in utero. People with this condition, called *congenital adrenal hyperplasia* (CAH), may be born with genitals that are not clearly male or female, or their genitals may look more like a penis. Mild forms of CAH occur in as many as 1 in 1,000 births worldwide (Merke & Kabbani, 2001), while severe forms occur in about 1 in every 15,000–18,000 births (Merke & Kabbani, 2001; Khalid et al., 2012).

By contrast, a zygote with XY sex chromosomes—genetically male—may be born with what looks like a vagina. People who are intersex in this way are experiencing *androgen insensitivity syndrome (AIS)*. The rates of AIS vary, depending on the severity of the form, but it is expected to occur in at least 1 in every 99,000 people (Boehmer et al., 2001) but possibly as many as 5 in 100,000 people (Farhud, Zarif Veganeh, Sadighi, & Zandvakili, 2016). The XY chromosomes should cause development of the testes, but in AIS the cells of the body do not respond to the testosterone released by the testes. Because of this lack of response, the testes remain in the body, and the penis does not fully develop.

Overall, hormonal abnormalities such as these, and other forms, are the most common reason that newborns (about 1 in every 1,500) have genitals that are not clearly a penis or a vagina (American Psychological Association, 2006). In these cases, should the child be assigned the sex that most closely aligns with the genitals or with the sex chromosomes?

One study investigated this question with 16 genetically male infants (with XY sex chromosomes) who were born with unclear genitals (Reiner & Gearhart, 2004). The parents of 14 of the children had their children's genitals surgically altered to be female and raised the children as girls. By early childhood, 8 of these 14 children had declared themselves to be boys, as did the 2 children who did not undergo surgical intervention. The results of this study suggest that biological sex is determined more by the sex chromosomes and their associated levels of prenatal testosterone than by the appearance of the genitals and the assigned sex. For this reason, intersex advocacy groups strongly urge people to avoid genital surgeries for children until they are old enough to understand and communicate whether they are boys or girls.

Given what you just learned about people who are intersex, it should be clear that biological sex is more complicated than just being male or female. Instead, biological sex can be viewed as a continuum that includes greater or lesser physical aspects of each sex (**Figure 10.6**). However, the story of Coy Mathis, the transgender child discussed at the start of this chapter, is a reminder to look past biological aspects of sex, and the sex a person is assigned at birth, in understanding each person. In the next section, you will learn how your social experiences, and your thoughts and feelings about yourself, heavily influence who you are. If you want to understand people in terms of variations in biological sex, gender, and sexual orientation, then a career in the social services could be a good fit for you. You can learn about this field in Putting Psychology to Work on p. 419.

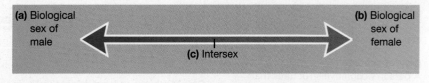

(a) Biological sex of male

(c) Intersex

(b) Biological sex of female

FIGURE 10.6

Biological Sex Can Be Viewed as a Continuum

Some people have biological traits of both sexes, so it may be appropriate to view biological sex as a continuum of being more or less physically female or male. **(a)** Males have biological traits that are consistently male. **(b)** Females have biological traits that are consistently female. **(c)** People who are intersex have aspects of biological sex that are both male and female.

Q How Does Biology Make People More Male or Female?

To make sure you learned what you just read, write answers to the following questions and check your answers.

10.1 What is the relationship between primary sex characteristics and biological sex?

10.2 Biologically, why can a person with XXY sex chromosomes be considered neither male nor female?

See Appendix B for answers to the red Q questions.

gender
The social, cultural, and psychological aspects of masculinity and femininity.

gender schemas
A person's cognitive structures that organize information about gender into categories, which include gender roles and gender identity.

Why Do People Act Masculine or Feminine?

Coy Mathis was born biologically male. However, from the age of 18 months Coy rejected "boy clothes," "boy activities," and language that referred to Coy as "he" or "him." Instead, Coy would wear only "girl clothes," such as dresses. She preferred "girl activities," such as playing with dolls. And she insisted on being called "she," "her," and so on. How did Coy come to understand the differences between what is masculine and what is feminine?

10.3 People Have Mental Categories of What Is Masculine and What Is Feminine

10.3 LEARNING GOAL ACTIVITIES

To maximize your learning, complete the following learning goal activities.

a. Understand all bold and italic terms by writing explanations of them in your own words.

b. Analyze your gender schemas by organizing a chart that shows what you consider to be more masculine and more feminine with respect to clothes, hair, jobs, traits, and habits.

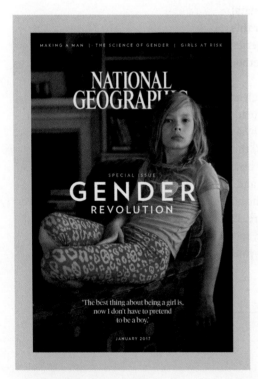

FIGURE 10.7

***National Geographic* Explores the Growing Understanding of Gender**

The January 2017 issue of *National Geographic* magazine looked at advances in the scientific and social understanding of gender. The cover portrayed Avery Jackson, a nine-year-old transgender girl.

Coy followed a path we all take, where her experiences over time (in Coy's case, a very short time) helped her develop knowledge about **gender.** That is, she organized information she experienced into mental categories about masculinity and femininity. She also learned about the social expectations for boys and girls. Ultimately, she viewed herself as being a girl, which affected how she acted, thought, and felt about herself. So, unlike biological sex, gender refers to the social, cultural, and psychological aspects of masculinity and femininity. Right now, the scientific understanding of gender is changing so rapidly that some suggest we are experiencing a gender revolution (**Figure 10.7**). This section looks at what research has revealed about both gender and how people learn about it.

GENDER SCHEMAS ENCOURAGE CATEGORIZATION OF GENDER INFORMATION As you learned in Chapters 4 and 8, your experiences provide information. You organize that information into mental structures called schemas. Individual schemas can include many types of information, such as what distinguishes birds from butterflies (see Learning Tip: Assimilation and Accommodation, on p. 146) or the similarities and differences between country music instruments and orchestral instruments (see Figure 8.5, on p. 297).

Your schemas about gender specifically organize the information you experience about being a woman or a man. Even as a very young child, you were probably so curious about gender that you were naturally compelled to categorize information about it all the time. As described by the psychologist Sandra Bem (1981), **gender schemas** are knowledge structures that contain information about aspects of gender, including social expectations, traits, interests, thoughts, and feelings. In ways that can be helpful or harmful, gender schemas often divide the world into two categories: what is masculine and what is feminine. The Try It Yourself feature on p. 387 may give you some insight into your gender schemas. But recall from study unit 8.3 that using stereotypes to categorize people as masculine or feminine may promote sexist attitudes or behavior. Being aware of how easily you categorize people according to your existing gender schemas may help you avoid sexist stereotyping.

The process of creating gender schemas starts by 6 months of age, when infants have categorized men's voices as low-pitched and women's voices as high-pitched. By 9 months, they have categorized visual differences between men's faces and women's faces. By the time they are toddlers, children categorize physical aspects of men and women (Martin, Ruble, & Szkrybalo, 2002). However, when young children create gender schemas, the categories are usually simplistic and incorrect. For example, children raised in North America may categorize "boys" as people who have short hair and wear masculine clothes and "girls" as people who have long hair and wear feminine clothes.

Sometimes gender schemas serve as mental shortcuts for processing information and responding to it. As you learned in study unit 8.3, such shortcuts are generally called stereotypes. **Gender stereotypes** reflect people's most commonly held beliefs about men and women. For example, by about age 5, children's gender schemas include information about boys' toys and girls' toys. Such groupings can result in very rigid gender stereotypes, such as that boys play with boats and building blocks and girls do not (Martin & Ruble, 2004; **Figure 10.8a**). Fortunately, over time and experience, children can update their gender schemas with additional information about what it means to be a woman or a man, such as their personal traits, actions, thoughts, feelings, and jobs. For example, if the North American children referred to above met girls with short hair, who wore masculine clothes, or who played with building blocks (**Figure 10.8b**), the children would update their gender schemas to incorporate this information. If the children were interested in activities or professions usually associated with genders different from their own, they might make their gender schemas even more flexible when it comes to associating jobs with people of one gender or another (Liben & Bigler, 2002).

YOUR GENDER SCHEMAS ARE UNIQUE Everyone has gender schemas, but individuals develop their own personal gender schemas based on the culture they live in. For example, some cultures do not view gender as a simple difference between men and women. In South Asia, particularly in India, the *hijra* are people who think of themselves as a gender that is between these two categories. In fact, by

gender stereotypes
Common beliefs about people of particular genders, based on similarities across many people's gender schemas.

(a)

(b)

FIGURE 10.8

Gender Stereotypes Can Be Overcome
(a) Historically, manufacturers of children's toys have promoted gender stereotyping by categorizing toys as either for boys or for girls. **(b)** Currently, some toy companies are helping to overcome gender stereotyping by creating toys that appeal to both boys and girls.

 TRY IT YOURSELF: **How Do You Categorize What Is Masculine or Feminine?**

Identify whether each trait is more likely to be seen in college students who are men or in college students who are women.

	Masculine	Feminine		Masculine	Feminine
1. Independent			5. Emotional		
2. Competitive			6. Helpful		
3. Self-confident			7. Kind		
4. Decisive			8. Understanding		

Scoring
People generally categorize traits 1–4 as more typical of men who are college students and traits 5–8 as more typical of women who are college students. This split suggests that people usually organize information about what is masculine and feminine into distinct, conventional categories. Which traits did you categorize as masculine? Which did you categorize as feminine? Your answers reveal whether your gender schemas are organized in a way that is similar to, or different from, other people's.

Source: Adapted from Spence, Helmreich, & Stapp (1975).

gender roles
The positions, characteristics, and interests that are considered normal and are expected for boys/men or for girls/women in a particular culture; this social information is stored in each person's gender schemas.

gender role socialization
The idea that people learn culture-specific expectations about gender roles passively, through exposure to social information in the environment.

2014, India and Bangladesh had officially recognized the hijra as a third gender. So when people in South Asian countries develop gender schemas, those schemas may include information about three genders: men, women, and hijra. Unless you are from this region, you probably don't have hijra as part of your gender schemas.

Although we can't say what specific information is included in any one person's gender schemas because of these types of cultural differences, we can say what *kind* of information is included in everyone's gender schemas. Two main types of information get organized.

On the one hand, people incorporate into their gender schemas the social information about the traits and positions of men and women. These traits and positions are called gender roles. In the next study unit, you will learn about gender roles and how these affect the way that people behave.

On the other hand, people also incorporate into their gender schemas cognitive information—their thoughts and feelings—about being a boy or a girl. This cognitive information leads people to develop a sense of gender identity, which affects how they think, feel, and act. In study units 10.5 and 10.6, you will learn more about gender identity and the various types of gender identities a person can have.

10.4 Gender Roles Affect How People Act

10.4 LEARNING GOAL ACTIVITIES

To maximize your learning, complete the following learning goal activities.

a. Understand all bold and italic terms by writing explanations of them in your own words.

b. Apply gender role socialization by describing the three ways that social interactions helped you learn the gender roles for men and women in your culture.

In your culture, what are the social expectations for men and for women? What jobs and characteristics do men usually have and women usually have? What behaviors are typically exhibited by men and typically exhibited by women? You most likely can answer these questions because over time your interactions with people have led you to store the necessary information. This information concerns **gender roles,** which are all the positions, characteristics, and interests considered normal and expected for boys/men or for girls/women in a particular culture. How you learn gender roles and how they influence your behavior depend on your gender role socialization.

GENDER ROLE SOCIALIZATION **Gender role socialization** is the idea that you develop culture-specific expectations about gender roles passively, by being exposed to social information in the environment around you (Ruble, Martin, & Berenbaum, 2006; **Figure 10.9**). In short, the social environment molds you into acting in ways that are masculine or feminine (Mischel, 1966).

Specifically, you learn about gender roles in three ways, all of which are described in detail in Chapter 6. First, you watch what other people do, in a process called observational learning (see study unit 6.13). Second, you imitate people's actions, in a process called modeling (also see study unit 6.13). Third, your behavior has either positive or negative consequences, which make you either repeat or avoid the same behavior in the future. This process is called operant conditioning (see study unit 6.10). Together,

FIGURE 10.9

Learning Gender Roles from the Environment

Gender role socialization is the idea that you learn gender roles through social experiences. For example, the child in this photo is learning that Mom stays at home to raise the children while Dad works to provide for the family.

these three forces of gender role socialization cause you to behave in specific ways. For example, they can explain why young children choose certain toys, play with them in specific ways (Martin et al., 2002), and prefer objects of a particular color.

Here's an example. Suppose a young man watches his father and other men compete to hold leadership roles. He is learning that in his culture it is socially expected that men be leaders. In other words, he is learning what gender roles are expected of him. If the young man chooses to follow the example of other men, he might model their behavior by running for student body president at school. If his candidacy yields positive consequences, such as praise and respect, this positive reinforcement would make him likely to conform even more with gender roles in the future. Of course, cultures vary widely, so the specific gender roles that you learn during gender role socialization depend on the experiences in your environment.

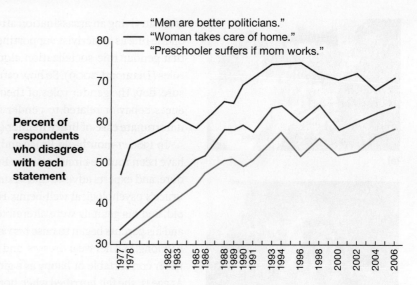

Percent of respondents who disagree with each statement

— "Men are better politicians."
— "Woman takes care of home."
— "Preschooler suffers if mom works."

FIGURE 10.10

People Increasingly Disagree with Statements about Traditional Gender Roles

This figure shows data from the United States General Social Survey between 1977 and 2006 (adapted from Cotter et al., 2011). Over time, more people have disagreed with statements that present traditional gender roles. These changes suggest that attitudes about gender roles are shifting for men and women.

GENDER ROLE SOCIALIZATION ACROSS CULTURES What are the gender roles in modern North America? Research shows that they are changing rapidly. The General Social Survey (GSS) shows that since 1977, American adults are less likely to hold traditional gender role expectations about men's jobs, women working outside the home, and who is responsible for the housework (Cotter, Hermsen, & Vanneman, 2011; **Figure 10.10**). This changing view about gender roles is also affecting how children behave in North America and in other nontraditional cultures.

In many nontraditional cultures like North America—especially the Netherlands, Germany, Italy, and England (Best & Williams, 2001)—boys and girls are encouraged to develop their individual uniqueness and personal expression, including with respect to gender roles. As a result, it is now much more acceptable for girls and women to act in ways that are more consistent with gender roles for boys and men, such as by being tomboys and by playing sports.

For example, girls in North America often receive a lot of admiration and praise for their athletic achievements, which encourages them to continue to pursue athletics. Consider Mo'ne Davis, who in 2014 became the first girl to pitch a shutout in the Little League World Series as a member of a boys' baseball team. Mo'ne's accomplishments led to her being the first Little League player to appear on the cover of *Sports Illustrated*—indeed, of any major U.S. sports magazine. She was subsequently named the *Sports Illustrated* SportsKid of the Year (**Figure 10.11**).

By contrast, in many traditional cultures—especially Nigeria, Pakistan, and Japan—boys and girls are taught to obey authority and conform to expectations, including the traditional gender roles of their cultures (Best & Williams, 2001). In 2012, as a young girl in Pakistan, Malala was brutally attacked and nearly killed for attending school and speaking out against Islamic militants opposed to education for females.

BIOLOGY CAN OVERRIDE GENDER ROLE SOCIALIZATION If the idea of gender role socialization is correct, then children who are punished for not conforming with their society's gender roles should change their behavior. But even

FIGURE 10.11

Girls' Gender Roles in a Nontraditional Culture

When Mo'ne Davis defied gender roles in the nontraditional culture of North America by becoming the first girl to pitch a shutout on a boy's baseball team in the Little League World Series, she was celebrated.

(a)

(b)

FIGURE 10.12

Brian and Brenda (Bruce, David) Reimer

(a) This photo shows identical twins Brian **(left)** and Bruce Reimer **(right)** as children. The photograph was taken after Bruce's damaged penis was removed and he was being raised as a girl, named Brenda. Bruce's unfortunate situation became a case study of whether a child born with a clear biological sex could be influenced by social forces into becoming another sex. **(b)** The answer to that question seems to be no, since Brenda never accepted herself as a girl and, in adolescence, identified as male and changed his name to David. This photo shows David as an adult.

after surviving an assassination attempt, Malala Yousafzai continues to put her life on the line as an activist supporting girls' right to an education. Most experts agree that gender role socialization alone does not explain behavior related to gender roles (Diamond, 2009). So how can we explain that some children, even under pressure, defy the gender roles of their culture? One answer is that biology also influences behavior related to gender roles. This biological influence is shown by the unfortunate case of Bruce Reimer (Colapinto, 2000).

In 1966, 7-month-old Bruce and his twin brother, Brian, underwent what should have been routine circumcisions. But Bruce's penis was destroyed during the procedure, and experts advised that sexual reassignment was the best course of action for Bruce's psychological well-being. His testes were removed when he was 22 months old, and his genitals were altered to look like a vagina. Bruce was renamed Brenda, and his parents began to raise him as a girl (**Figure 10.12a**). Brenda's parents kept her hair long, had her wear dresses, and encouraged her to play with dolls. But Brenda was never comfortable or happy as a girl. She was teased for being rough and aggressive. At age 11, she felt horrified when hormone therapy led her to start developing breasts.

Ultimately, Brenda's parents were forced to acknowledge that she would never act like a girl. When Brenda was told that she was born a boy, her feelings suddenly made sense to her. She knew that she wasn't "crazy." Brenda immediately decided to live as a boy (**Figure 10.12b**). He changed his name to David and later had surgery to replace the apparent vagina he had been given as a toddler with a functional penis. Even though he seemed to have a satisfying adult life, even marrying a woman, ultimately David's story ended tragically in 2004, when he committed suicide at the age of 38.

What are we to learn from this sad story? David Reimer was biologically male with respect to his sex chromosomes (XY) and his hormones (higher in testosterone), regardless of the loss of his male genitals. David felt like a man and thought of himself as a man, so he rejected his parents' attempts to make him dress and act like a girl. Now recall the findings of Reiner and Gearhart (2004), discussed in study unit 10.2. This research looked at 14 infants who were genetically male but who had unclear genitals. These infants were surgically altered to be female and were raised as girls. Eight of these children ultimately decided they were boys and began acting in ways consistent with their genetic sex of male.

Together, the David Reimer story and this research suggest that people do not conform to gender roles just because of what they learn through socialization. Instead, biology also influences behavior. Consider that prenatal exposure to chemicals that affect the impact of androgens, such as testosterone, is associated with preschool-aged boys' showing less masculine play (Swan et al., 2010). In addition, biology may also influence a person's sense of being a man or a woman. The following study unit looks at how that sense develops.

10.5 Gender Identity Also Affects How People Act

 10.5 LEARNING GOAL ACTIVITIES

To maximize your learning, complete the following learning goal activities.

a. Understand all bold and italic terms by writing explanations of them in your own words.

b. Apply gender to yourself by describing your own gender identity and gender expression.

Do you think of yourself as a man or a woman? Do you feel more like a man or a woman? If you can answer these questions, then you have developed a **gender identity.** This term refers to your overall sense of being a woman or a man. How have you come to understand your gender identity? On the one hand, some research suggests that gender identity is related to biology, even from the time of prenatal development. For example, the presence of testosterone prenatally makes a person more likely to identify as being a man (Swaab, 2004). On the other hand, coming to have a sense of gender identity is a normal part of cognitive development.

COGNITIVE DEVELOPMENT OF GENDER IDENTITY According to **cognitive development theory,** as children develop mentally and experience information about gender, they begin to think of other people and themselves as associated with one gender more than another. The cognitive development of gender is usually thought to occur in three main stages (Martin et al., 2002). First, children between ages 2 and 3 start to think about what a boy is and what a girl is, but they apply these terms interchangeably to themselves and to others. For example, a 2-year-old boy may call himself a boy or a girl any time you ask him which he is. If he were looking at **Figure 10.13,** he might say that any of the people shown is a boy. He might say that any one is a girl. Furthermore, he might use different labels each time you ask him.

By about age 4, children think of themselves and others in a stable way as boys or girls. The boy just discussed would now be much more likely to consistently call himself a boy. He would also be more likely to correctly label other people as boys or girls. This 4-year-old boy would be much more likely to consistently state that the person in Figure 10.13a is a boy and the person in Figure 10.13d is a girl.

Between ages 5 and 7, children recognize that their gender identity does not change even if they dress or act in ways associated with the other gender. So the 7-year-old boy will most likely still consider himself male even if he grows his hair long. At this point, he may state that any of the photographs in Figure 10.13 could be boys or girls, because he understands that external appearances do not necessarily indicate a person's gender identity.

SITUATIONS CAN AFFECT GENDER EXPRESSION According to cognitive development theory, gender identity stabilizes in childhood. But even with a stable gender identity, people may not present themselves in a way you might expect based on their gender identity. In other words, people's *gender expression*—the way they communicate their gender through clothes, interests, and language—is completely unrelated to their gender identity. According to a theory proposed by the social psychologists Kay Deaux and Brenda Major (1987), people are influenced by situations to act in ways that are masculine or feminine.

Consider a study of young women talking on the telephone. When the women talked to their boyfriends, their voices changed to a higher pitch and became softer and more relaxed than when they talked to their male friends. The way they spoke to their boyfriends was also more baby-like, feminine, and absentminded (as rated by objective judges). When asked, the women said they knew they took on a different manner of speaking to their boyfriends and did it in order to communicate affection (Montepare & Vega, 1988). Even when a person has a clear gender identity, a particular situation can alter the person's gender expression in a variety of ways. For a review of the relationship between gender schemas, gender roles, and gender identity, see the Learning Tip on p. 392.

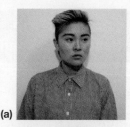

(a)

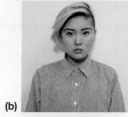

(b)

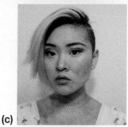

(c)

(d)

FIGURE 10.13

Cognitive Development of Gender Identity

Cognitive development explains how, over time and experiences, people develop thoughts and feelings about what is masculine and what is feminine. These thoughts and feelings allow categorization of people by gender. Ultimately, people develop an understanding that another person's gender is not necessarily related to that person's appearance. Despite the different details, all of these photographs are of the same woman, the artist Coco Layne.

gender identity
The thoughts and feelings that make up a person's sense of being a boy/man or a girl/woman. This cognitive information is stored in each person's gender schemas.

cognitive development theory
The idea that each individual develops a gender identity by actively processing thoughts and feelings about gender.

GENDER SCHEMAS	SOCIAL INFORMATION ABOUT GENDER	COGNITIVE INFORMATION ABOUT GENDER
<u>What</u> information is learned	Gender roles: Information about the social positions, traits, interests, and behaviors of boys/men and of girls/women are stored in gender schemas.	Gender identity: Personal thoughts and feelings about being a boy/man or a girl/woman are stored in gender schemas.
<u>How</u> the information becomes incorporated into gender schemas	Gender role socialization: People learn gender roles passively from the social environment through observational learning, modeling, and operant conditioning.	Cognitive development theory: People actively process their thoughts and feelings to place themselves in the category of being a boy/man or a girl/woman.

10.6 People Vary in Gender Identity

10.6 LEARNING GOAL ACTIVITIES

To maximize your learning, complete the following learning goal activities.

a. Understand all bold and italic terms by writing explanations of them in your own words.

b. Understand gender identity by using your own words to name and explain the four main variations in gender identity.

Most people develop a stable gender identity that is consistent with their biological sex (Diamond & Butterworth, 2008). Typically, such a person may be described as having a gender identity of *cisgender* (Stryker, 2008). The prefix "cis" comes from Latin and means "on this side of." So someone who is cisgender has a gender identity that is "on the same side of" the sex assigned at birth. A person who is biologically male and who identifies as a man may be considered "cis male" (**Figure 10.14a**). A person who is biologically female and who identifies as a woman may be considered "cis female" (**Figure 10.14b**).

The term "cisgender" is somewhat controversial. Some people see it as suggesting that "on the same side of" is the "norm" for gender identity (Enke, 2013). Other people see it as focusing on just two genders—of being a woman or a man. Instead, just like

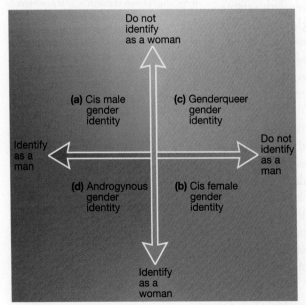

FIGURE 10.14

Gender Identity Can Be Viewed as a Continuum

It may be more accurate to view gender identity as a continuum.
(a) People with a cis male gender identity identify as men, not women.
(b) By contrast, people with a cis female gender identity identify as women, not men. **(c)** Some people do not identify as either men or women, or their gender identity may vary. These people sometimes have a gender identity called genderqueer. **(d)** People who identify as being both a man and a woman have a gender identity called androgynous.

biological sex, gender identity is not an either/or decision. It can be considered a continuum, to reflect how different kinds of people think and feel about themselves. To understand these issues, let's consider people who may not view themselves as cisgender.

VARIATIONS IN GENDER IDENTITY ARE NORMAL

When talking with *Out* magazine in 2014, the singer Miley Cyrus stated, "I don't relate to what people would say defines a girl or a boy, and I think that's what I had to understand: Being a girl isn't what I hate, it's the box that I get put into" (Krochmal, 2015). Cyrus's statement suggests that she is neutral in terms of her sense of gender. Like Cyrus, other people also don't have a sense of being particularly men or women. The term *genderqueer* is sometimes used to describe this gender identity (**Figure 10.14c**).

By contrast, some people have the sense they are both a man and a woman. This gender identity is called *androgynous* (**Figure 10.14d**). The late musician Prince presented his gender in a way that can be described as androgynous. For example, in the 1984 song "I Would Die 4 U," the lyrics declare, "I'm not a woman / I'm not a man / I am something that you'll never understand." On the cover of his 1988 album, *Lovesexy,* Prince displays a hairy chest and facial hair, in what seems to be a presentation of masculine traits. However, Prince also appears to have shaved his legs, and he is covering a nipple in a way that might be seen as feminine (**Figure 10.15**).

The actor Laverne Cox, of the show *Orange Is the New Black,* also experiences a normal variation in gender identity. While interviewing Cox on *CBS This Morning,* the anchorperson Gayle King said, "Let's let people know about you, Laverne, because you were born a boy" (Nichols, 2014). Cox interrupted her and stated, "I was assigned male at birth is the way I like to put it, because I think we're born who we are and the gender thing is something someone imposes on you. And so I was assigned male at birth but I always felt like I was a girl." Cox is **transgender,** because her gender identity differs from the sex she was assigned at birth (American Psychological Association, 2014; **Figure 10.16**). Like "cis," the prefix "trans" comes from Latin. It means "on the other side of," indicating that the person has a gender identity "on the other side of" the sex assigned at birth. According to the American Psychiatric Association (2013), being transgender is not a psychological disorder. Instead, psychologists are increasingly viewing people who are transgender as experiencing normal variations in gender identity.

As discussed in the chapter opener, Coy Mathis is transgender. She was assigned a male sex at birth, but before the age of 2 years, Coy consistently said she was a girl. Could a young child such as Coy simply be confused or playacting when it comes to her gender identity? Research suggests that the answer is no. One study looked at 32 transgender children who were 5–12 years old (Olson, Key, & Eaton, 2015). The research methods included self-reports and implicit measures of gender identity. The results indicated that the children thought of themselves in terms of gender identity, not assigned sex. In addition, the pattern of responses of the transgender children was similar to the pattern of responses from children who accepted their assigned sex as their gender identity.

There may be a biological basis to a transgender identity. For example, brain imaging studies have shown that the brains of transgender people are more similar to those who share their gender identity than to those who share their biological sex (Nawata et al., 2010). In addition, the brain networks of those who are transgender

FIGURE 10.15
Prince's Androgynous Gender Identity

On the cover of *Lovesexy,* Prince seems to identify as female and male simultaneously. Imagery of this kind embraces an androgynous gender identity.

transgender
When a person's gender identity and/or gender expression differs from the sex assigned at birth.

FIGURE 10.16
Some People Are Transgender

Laverne Cox is transgender because her gender identity (as a woman) differs from the sex she was assigned at birth (male).

may be wired differently than the brain networks of those who are cisgender (Hahn et al., 2015).

Some transgender people choose to live as what they feel is their true gender instead of their sex assigned at birth. To varying degrees, they change their behaviors and appearances to match their personal experience of their gender. They may use hormones, surgery, or both to transform their bodies. We should not assume to know a person's gender identity based on that person's appearance or actions.

At this point, you may be wondering what the future holds for Coy Mathis. Will she someday change her body, transitioning to having physical traits of a female? No one can predict her choices, but even as a very young child, Coy asked her parents when they would take her to a doctor to get her "girl parts" (Erdely, 2013). It may be surprising that a preschool-aged child could have such feelings. However, in Europe (de Vries & Cohen-Kettenis, 2012) and in North America (Wood et al., 2013), many more people are being referred to clinics that specialize in gender identity, and there is a sharp decline in the ages of people who are making requests for medical interventions for gender reassignment. These changes are especially true for cases where people, even very young children, experience extreme distress about their gender identities.

GENDER DYSPHORIA IS A PSYCHOLOGICAL DISORDER   Although being transgender is not a psychological disorder, feeling discontent with the sex one was assigned at birth can become a problem if the feelings are present for six months or more and also cause significant personal distress (American Psychiatric Association, 2013; Lawrence, 2014). The feeling of living in a body that doesn't match a person's feeling of his or her true gender identity is often the cause of that distress, which can result in extreme anxiety and depression. In these circumstances, a person may be experiencing **gender dysphoria.**

Distress, anxiety, and depression are bad enough to face. But when people who are transgender experience discrimination, victimization, or rejection by family and friends, they have a higher risk of attempting suicide than people in the general population (Herman, Hass, & Rogers, 2014). In 2014, the plight of transgender people who experience harassment came to light with the suicide of 17-year-old Leelah Alcorn. Born biologically male, Leelah declared herself a girl at age 14. She was cut off socially, her family did not accept her gender identity, and she was forced to endure conversion therapy. Leelah hoped that her death would spur legislative action to help people who are transgender gain legal protection. She wrote on social media, "The only way I will rest in peace is if one day transgender people aren't treated the way I was, they're treated like humans, with valid feelings and human rights" (Coolidge, 2014).

LEGAL PROTECTION FOR PEOPLE WHO ARE TRANSGENDER   When Coy Mathis entered first grade, the public school notified Coy's parents that she would no longer be allowed to use the girls' bathroom. A letter from the school explained that "as Coy grows older and his male genitals develop along with the rest of his body, at least some parents and students are likely to become uncomfortable with his continued use of the girls' restroom" (Erdely, 2013). Was it legal for the school to deny Coy access to the girls' restroom on this basis? In 2013, the Colorado Civil Rights Division determined that the school had violated Coy's right to use the bathroom that she preferred. At the age of 6, Coy was allowed to use the school bathroom that she felt best matched her gender identity: the girls' room.

gender dysphoria
A psychological disorder characterized by significant distress about the difference between a person's gender assigned at birth and that person's experience of his or her true gender identity.

Similarly, in 2012, the U.S. Equal Employment Opportunity Commission (EEOC) addressed this question by declaring that it is illegal to discriminate against people who are transgender and gender nonconforming (*Macy v. Bureau of Alcohol, Tobacco, Firearms and Explosives*, 2012). In addition, as of 2018, 20 states and Washington, D.C., have adopted employment laws that prohibit discrimination on the basis of gender identity (Movement Advancement Project, 2018). These legislative advances are important in recognizing the existence of variations in gender identity and gender expression. Furthermore, these legal changes clarify that it is illegal to prevent a person from using a gender-specific facility because the person's biological sex does not match the person's gender identity (American Psychological Association, 2014). Indeed, as of 2017, over 200 municipalities have passed legislation allowing people to use the bathroom that matches their gender identity. Furthermore, communities in California, Philadelphia, Texas, Oregon, and Washington, D.C., have passed legislation requiring gender-neutral bathrooms.

These communities are aiming to provide facilities that are welcoming and safe for all people, including those whose gender expression or gender identity differs from their biological sex. However, not everyone supports such changes. In 2017, the U.S. federal government withdrew its support for schools that allow transgender students to use their bathrooms of choice (de Vogue, Mallonee, and Grinberg, 2017). If you would like to help spare people of all gender identities from social isolation, prejudice, and discrimination, see Has It Happened to You?

sexual orientation
The nature of a person's enduring sexual, emotional, and/or romantic attraction to other people.

heterosexual (straight)
A sexual orientation where a person is sexually, emotionally, and/or romantically attracted to people of another sex; the more commonly used term is "straight."

homosexual (gay or lesbian)
A sexual orientation where a person is sexually, emotionally, and/or romantically attracted to people of the same sex. Males who are attracted to males are commonly described as gay, while females who are attracted to females are commonly described as lesbian.

bisexual
A sexual orientation where a person is sexually, emotionally, and/or romantically attracted to people of the same sex and people of another sex.

asexual
A sexual orientation where a person does not experience sexual attraction but may experience emotional and/or romantic attraction.

 Why Do People Act Masculine or Feminine?

To make sure you learned what you just read, write answers to the following questions and check your answers.

10.3 What is the difference between gender schemas and gender stereotypes?

10.4 How do people come to understand their culture's gender roles?

10.5 According to cognitive development theory, at about what age do children develop a stable gender identity?

10.6 What is the difference between transgender and gender dysphoria?

See Appendix B for answers to the red Q questions.

How Do People Vary in Sexual Orientation?

In learning about biological sex and gender identity, you considered the question of whether you think of yourself as a man or a woman or both or neither. Now consider another question: Do you feel sexual attraction to other people? If so, whom do you feel attracted to?

10.7 Variations in Sexual Orientation Are Normal

✎ **10.7 LEARNING GOAL ACTIVITIES**

To maximize your learning, complete the following learning goal activities.

a. Understand all bold and italic terms by writing explanations of them in your own words.

b. Understand variations in sexual orientation by summarizing in your own words the four main types of sexual orientation.

Sexual orientation is a person's enduring sexual, emotional, and/or romantic attraction to other people (Bailey et al., 2016). To be clear: Sexual orientation is not about whom a person actually has sexual relations with. Rather, sexual orientation describes whom a person is sexually attracted to or emotionally close with, and/or establishes a romantic or committed relationship with. Much like biological sex and gender identity, sexual orientation is complex and multifaceted. The different types of sexual orientation are completely normal variations in attraction. As you read about the four main sexual orientations, consider which one or which ones might apply to you.

VARIATIONS IN SEXUAL ORIENTATION ARE NORMAL Most people experience sexual attraction to other people. How can that attraction be described? Most people—throughout history and across cultures—experience attraction to people of another sex (Bullough, 1990). This

FIGURE 10.17

Most People Have a Straight Sexual Orientation
Bud Holt, 96, hugs his wife, Jo, 93, on their 75th anniversary.

sexual orientation is traditionally called **heterosexual** (from the Greek word *hetero,* meaning "other"; **Figure 10.17**). A male who is heterosexual, or **straight,** is attracted to females. A female who is straight is attracted to males. However, not everyone is straight or even consistently attracted to the same types of people. Indeed, it is normal for people to experience variations in sexual orientation.

For example, some people report being attracted to people of the same sex. This sexual orientation has traditionally been described as **homosexual** (from the Greek word *homo,* meaning "same"). However, many people see the term "homosexual" as a negative way to describe those who are attracted to people of the same sex. Because of this, a male who is attracted to other males may call himself **gay,** whereas a female who is attracted to other females may call herself **lesbian** (American Psychological Association, 2008; **Figure 10.18**). Although it is hard to accurately determine, studies suggest that 2–5 percent of the population in the United States reports being exclusively gay or lesbian (Bailey et al., 2016; Norris, Marcus, & Green, 2015).

About 1.8 percent of the population reports being attracted to both males and females (Gates, 2011). This sexual orientation is called **bisexual** (**Figure 10.19**). Even among people who consider themselves bisexual, however, there is great variation in sexual attraction. According to one survey, 27 percent of respondents who claimed a bisexual orientation reported they were mainly attracted to people of the same sex (Herek, Norton, Allen, & Sims, 2010). By contrast, 39 percent stated they were primarily attracted to people of another sex, and 34 percent were attracted equally to both sexes.

While both males and females may consider themselves bisexual, females are much more likely to report having that sexual orientation (Mosher, Chandra, & Jones, 2005). This difference may be in part because females experience greater *sexual fluidity* (Diamond, 2016). That is, the sexual interests, motivations, and behaviors of females tend to vary more than those of males. For example, straight females show genital arousal when viewing photographs of male and female genitals, but straight males show genital arousal only when viewing photographs of female genitals (Spape et al., 2014). Similarly, neuroimaging studies have shown that lesbian and straight females have patterns of brain activity that are similar when they view erotic photographs of either males or females (Sylva et al., 2013). By contrast, gay and straight males have greater differences in their neural responses when they view erotic photographs showing people of the sex they are more attracted to. Research using pupil dilation as an indicator of sexual arousal has also found that bisexual arousal is more common in females than in males (Rieger et al., 2015). In addition, over time and across situations, the sexual behaviors of females seem to vary more than those of males, and their sexual behaviors are less consistent with their attitudes (Baumeister, 2000). Taken together, these findings suggest that females experience greater sexual fluidity than males. So for females—as for a smaller number of males—the difference between being bisexual and having another sexual orientation tends to reflect where they view themselves on a continuum of sexual attraction at that point in their lives.

Finally, some people who do not experience sexual attraction are described as having a sexual orientation called **asexual** (Bogaert, 2004). Estimates vary on the proportion of people whose sexual orientation is asexual. When nearly 700 college students in the United States were surveyed, about 5 percent of males and 10 percent of females described their sexual attraction as low enough to be categorized as asexual (Nurius, 1983). By contrast, about 1 percent of nearly

FIGURE 10.18

Some People Have a Gay or Lesbian Sexual Orientation

In January 2015, after a judge lifted Florida's same-sex marriage ban, Todd Delmay **(far right)**, and his partner, Jeff Delmay, got married, as did Catherina Pareto **(far left)**, and her partner, Karla Arguello.

FIGURE 10.19

Some People Experience a Bisexual Sexual Orientation

The model, actor, and women's rights activist Amber Rose is bisexual. She has stated, "I'm extremely open with my sexuality. I can be in love with a woman, I can be in love with a man. I definitely find beauty in everybody, whether they're heavy-set, super-skinny, if they're white, black, Indian, Asian, Spanish."

FIGURE 10.20

Some People Experience an Asexual Sexual Orientation

David Jay is asexual. To increase awareness of this sexual orientation, he founded the Asexual Visibility and Education Network. He also appeared in the documentary *(A)Sexual* (2011).

19,000 people surveyed in the United Kingdom stated that they had never felt any sexual attraction (Bogaert, 2004). To date, the 1 percent statistic is the best one available.

Very little research has been done on asexuality. However, in 2001, the asexuality activist David Jay started the Asexual Visibility and Education Network (AVEN) to educate people about this sexual orientation (**Figure 10.20**). According to AVEN, people with an asexual sexual orientation are not simply choosing to not have sex. Instead, they feel the absence of sexual attraction as a core part of their identity. By contrast, they do have emotional needs and may form close romantic relationships with other people.

So far, this discussion makes it seem as though sexual orientation is a very straightforward concept. In fact, understanding and describing sexual orientation is quite complex. Let's see why that is.

CHALLENGES IN DESCRIBING SEXUAL ORIENTATION   One difficulty in describing sexual orientation is that some people think of themselves in complicated ways (Savin-Williams & Vrangalova, 2013; Kinsey, Pomeroy, & Martin, 1948). For example, when people are asked to report their sexual orientation, some label themselves as completely straight (**Figure 10.21a**), others label themselves as completely gay or lesbian (**Figure 10.21e**), and yet others state they are bisexual (**Figure 10.21c**). However, some people consider themselves to be either mostly straight (**Figure 10.21b**) or mostly gay or lesbian (**Figure 10.21d**). This research suggests that people consider their own sexual orientation as existing on a continuum (Savin-Williams, 2016; **Figure 10.22**). As you learned in study unit 10.6, gender identity can also be viewed on a continuum (see Figure 10.14).

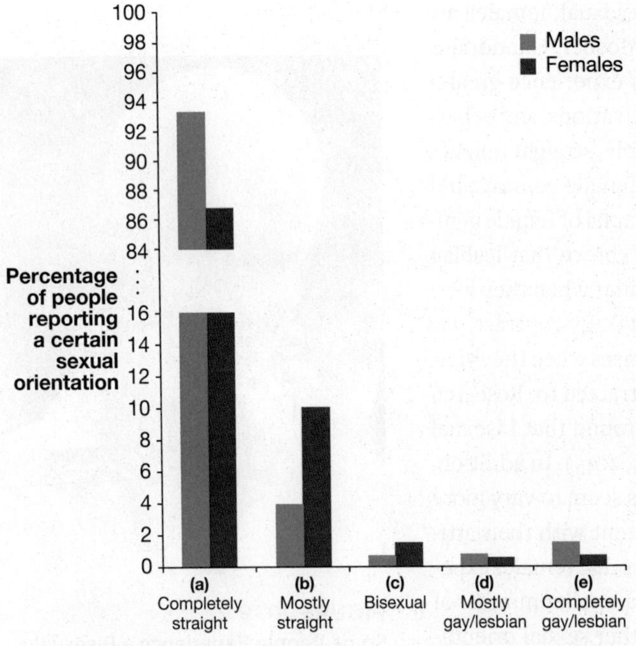

Another difficulty in describing sexual orientation is that sexual attraction, and the labeling of sexual orientation, is not necessarily consistent with sexual behavior (Savin-Williams & Vrangalova, 2012). For example, people who label themselves as primarily gay or lesbian report sometimes engaging in sexual behaviors with people of another sex. The same is true of people who identify as straight. In the United States, less than 5 percent of people who label themselves only straight report engaging in any same-sex sexual behaviors, though females report more same-sex behaviors than males do (4.6 versus 2.8 percent; Chandra, Mosher, Copen, & Sionean, 2011). However, for people who label themselves as mostly straight, the rates are much higher, with 47.4 percent of females and 20.6 percent of males reporting engaging in same-sex sexual behavior (Chandra et al., 2011). Once again, these data suggest that sexual orientation is best described on a continuum (see Figure 10.22).

A final difficulty in describing sexual orientation is based on the terminology itself. Consider that the terms "homosexual" and "heterosexual" mean that a person has a specific assigned sex or a self-identified gender and is attracted to people of either the same sex or gender or another sex or gender. But as you have learned, some people experience variations in biological sex or identified gender. First, people may be intersex. Second, people may not clearly identify as being either a man or a woman. Finally, people may not necessarily be attracted to people with a specific gender identity. So how should we describe their sexual orientation? One woman, Danielle Flink, perfectly describes the difficulty in searching for the right term:

FIGURE 10.21

People Vary in How They Label Their Sexual Orientation

When given multiple categories to classify their sexual orientation, people vary from describing themselves as **(a)** completely straight, **(b)** to mostly straight, **(c)** to bisexual, **(d)** to mostly gay or lesbian, **(e)** to completely gay or lesbian.

When I first came out, I identified as bisexual. Over time, I realized that I really was way more attracted to women so I identified as a lesbian. Then the [female] person I fell in love with came out to me as transgender [having a male gender identity]. I wasn't sure where I fit anymore. I was confused. I asked myself a million questions before I came to a self-understanding that my sexual orientation wasn't fixed. It never had been. Even before I placed a label on myself upon coming out, I didn't feel like I belonged in any "group" or "box" or "label" that society currently had to offer me. So then I came across queer. At the time, I was pretty gender nonconforming as well so it really seemed to fit everything I wanted into a word that I could tell people when they asked. (Parents, Families and Friends of Lesbians and Gays [PFLAG], 2015)

As Flink's experience illustrates, some people who experience fluidity in sexual orientation may prefer the term *queer*. Other people simply avoid the most common terms used for sexual orientation (see Figure 10.22) and simply describe whether they are attracted to males, females, people who are genderqueer, or some combination of people.

Ultimately, people tend to identify themselves with the people they have the most in common with. Groups tend to adopt the label of sexual orientation that they feel is appropriate for themselves. In this way, choices of words to describe sexual orientation are very much based on cultural, social, and emotional influences.

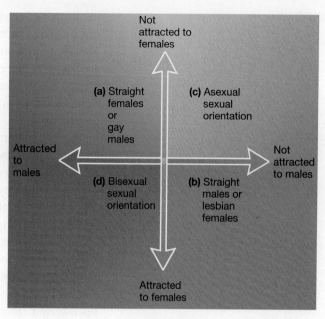

FIGURE 10.22

Sexual Orientation Can Be Viewed as a Continuum

It may be more accurate to view sexual orientation as a continuum. **(a)** Some people are attracted to males, not females. If they are female, their sexual orientation is straight. If they are male, their sexual orientation is gay. **(b)** Some people are attracted to females, not males. If they are male, their sexual orientation is straight. If they are female, their sexual orientation is lesbian. **(c)** Some people are not attracted to either males or females, in which case their sexual orientation is asexual. **(d)** People who are attracted to both males and females have a bisexual sexual orientation.

10.8 Biology Influences the Development of Sexual Orientation

10.8 LEARNING GOAL ACTIVITIES

To maximize your learning, complete the following learning goal activities.

a. Understand all bold and italic terms by writing explanations of them in your own words.

b. Analyze how biology relates to sexual orientation by describing in your own words the four biological factors that are associated with sexual orientation.

If you experience sexual attraction, when did such feelings start? Most people know whether they are sexually attracted to females, males, or both by their late teens or shortly thereafter (Elliott & Brantley, 1997). Regardless of whom a person may actually have sex with, this initial sexual orientation tends to remain stable over time. The question is: What causes a person to have a certain sexual orientation? On the one hand, environment, including parenting, could influence sexual orientation. On the other hand, biology—including factors such as genetics, hormones, maternal antibodies, and the brain—could influence sexual orientation. Let's investigate both of these possibilities.

ENVIRONMENT AND SEXUAL ORIENTATION Early psychoanalytic theories suggested that parenting influences sexual orientation. For example, families with a domineering mother and a submissive father were thought to cause children to identify with the parent of another sex (in this case, a boy might identify with his mother). Such identifications were thought to translate into a sexual attraction toward a sex that is different from that of the parent whom the child identified with. That is, a boy would develop a same-sex attraction. However, most children who are raised by gay or lesbian parents are in fact straight. The majority of studies have found little or no evidence that parents affect the sexual orientation of their children, regardless of their own sexual orientation (Bailey et al., 2016; Fedewa, Black, & Soveon, 2015).

The most common finding that relates environment to sexual orientation is that attraction to the same sex, for males and females, is associated with gender nonconformity in childhood (Bailey et al., 2016). Gender nonconformity may be seen, for example, when boys dress like girls and play with dolls and when girls prefer rough play and competitive sports. However, this relationship reflects a correlation only (see study unit 1.10), so following or not following gender roles cannot be said to cause sexual orientation. Instead another factor, a third variable, could provide a link between following or not following gender roles and sexual orientation. Recall from study unit 10.4 that preschool-aged boys showed less masculine play when they were exposed prenatally to chemicals that reduce the prenatal impact of testosterone (Swan et al., 2010). This finding suggests that biology may influence sex roles. The following subsections of this study unit consider the possibility that biology might also affect sexual orientation.

Another way to explore whether the environment influences sexual orientation is based on the idea that if sexual orientation can be learned, then it can be unlearned. "Homosexual conversion" therapy is proposed to do just this: change a person's sexual orientation from gay, lesbian, or bisexual to straight. "Treatments" that try to convert people's sexual orientations also tend to emphasize that homosexual behavior is immoral, so treatment failures can lead to feelings of shame. Because of this, so-called conversion therapy may inflict significant harm on mental health (Flentje, Heck, & Cochran, 2014). Indeed, the American Psychological Association issued a report in 2009 stating that conversion therapy efforts involve some risk of harm (Anton, 2010). In addition, despite reports of successful conversion therapy in the popular media, there is little empirical evidence that these programs do any more than suppress a person's sexual behavior with another person of the same sex.

LEARNING TIP: Four Biological Contributions to Sexual Orientation

BIOLOGICAL FACTORS	RELATIONSHIP TO SEXUAL ORIENTATION
Genetics	Identical twins (who share more genetic material) are more likely to have the same sexual orientation than non-identical twins.
	The X sex chromosome inherited from the mother seems to be related to males being gay. However, there is no single "gay gene."
Influences of hormones	Greater prenatal exposure to androgens is related to females being lesbian.
	Lesser exposure to androgens produced by the testes during childhood is related to males being gay.
Prenatal influences of maternal immune system	With repeated pregnancies of male fetuses, it is hypothesized that mothers may develop an antibody that affects the prenatal development of later-born male siblings in ways that increase the probability of these males being gay.
Brain structure and mental processes	The size and processing of the hypothalamus in gay males is closer to that of straight females than to that of straight males, so this structure may differ naturally in gay males or may come to differ due to their experiences.

Based on these reports, one prominent group that had been trying for nearly 40 years to "convert" people who are gay and lesbian to a straight sexual orientation was disbanded in 2013, when the group's leader concluded that sexual orientation cannot be changed (Lovett, 2013). Furthermore, as of this time, several U.S. states and Canadian provinces have passed legislation banning the use of conversion therapy on minors (Drescher et al., 2016).

Today, few psychologists or physicians believe that sexual orientation—as opposed to specific sexual behaviors—is a choice or that it can be changed (Haldeman, 1994, 2002; Myers & Scanzoni, 2005). So if environment does influence sexual orientation, research has not revealed what these environmental factors are. However, as you will soon see, biological differences exist between people who are primarily straight and people who are primarily gay or lesbian. In other words, according to the best available evidence, sexual orientation is related to biological factors. The four biological factors that seem to be most related to sexual orientation are described in the Learning Tip on p. 400.

GENETIC EXPLANATIONS OF SEXUAL ORIENTATION If biology contributes to sexual orientation through genetics, sexual orientation might be an inherited trait. Identical and fraternal (non-identical) twins provide an excellent opportunity to investigate this idea. For example, research has explored in twins the incidence of gender-atypical behavior in childhood or having a gay sexual orientation in adulthood. This research reveals that there is a greater similarity in gender-atypical childhood behavior and in adult sexual orientation in identical twins, who have the same genetic makeup, than in fraternal twins, who are no more similar genetically than any other siblings born to the same parents (Alanko et al., 2010).

In one study of almost 4,000 pairs of twins in Finland, statistical modeling indicated that shared genetics accounted for nearly 40 percent of male twins' homosexual behavior but only about 20 percent of female twins' homosexual behavior (Långström, Rahman, Carlström, & Lichtenstein, 2010). This finding suggests that shared genetics accounts for some part of homosexual behavior. Another study found similar results. This research with 143 sisters found that in the identical female twins, 48 percent were both lesbian (Bailey, Pillard, Neale, & Agyei, 1993). In the fraternal female twins, only 16 percent were both lesbian. In adopted female siblings, only 6 percent were both lesbian. This research is consistent with the idea that genetics influences sexual orientation.

Other evidence also points to this genetic influence. For example, the fact that gay males tend to have more gay relatives than other people do suggests that attraction to other males tends to run in families (Camperio-Ciani, Corna, & Capiluppi, 2004; Camperio-Ciani, Iemmola, & Blecher, 2009; Mustanski & Bailey, 2003). This association is especially true for the males on the mother's side of the family. Consistent with this finding, a link was found between a marker on the X chromosome—the sex chromosome passed by the mother—and sexual orientation in males (Hamer, Hu, Magnuson, Hu, & Pattatucci, 1993). The popular media quickly dubbed the marker "the gay gene." However, since then other researchers have failed to find any specific gene for sexual orientation (O'Riordan, 2012). In short, it seems unlikely that a single gene carries this trait. However, several genes may interact to influence sexual orientation. While it remains unclear how sexual orientation might be encoded in the genes (Bailey et al., 2016), other biological factors may influence sexual orientation.

HORMONAL INFLUENCES ON SEXUAL ORIENTATION According to the best available evidence, exposure to androgens in utero might play some role in sexual orientation (Bailey et al., 2016; Hines, 2011; Mustanski, Chivers, & Bailey, 2002). For

Fraternal Birth Order Effect May Explain Why Later-Born Males Are More Likely to Be Gay

Hypothesis: Being repeatedly pregnant with male fetuses is associated with later-born males being gay as adults.

Research Method: Analyses of data from several studies investigated the probability that a man would be gay based on the number of older male siblings he had. The researchers also explored whether this effect would depend on the man's being right-handed.

Results: Only later-born males who were right-handed were about 24 percent more likely to be gay for each additional older male sibling they had. Later-born males who were non-right-handed showed no increase in their likelihood of being gay.

Conclusion: Sexual orientation of later-born males seems to be related to prenatal factors that arise from being repeatedly pregnant with male fetuses.

QUESTION: Is this research using an experimental method or correlational method? Based on your answer, can you say that being a male with older male siblings and right-handed causes a man to be gay? Explain how the research method relates to this statement.

ANSWER: This study uses a correlational method, so you cannot say that being a male with older male siblings causes a male to be gay. Only experimental research can demonstrate a cause-and-effect relationship, because it allows control of the variables being manipulated and tested.

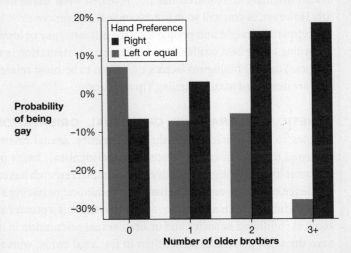

Source: Blanchard, R., Cantor, J. M., Bogaert, A. F., Breedlove, S. M., & Ellis, L. (2006). Interaction of fraternal birth order and handedness in the development of male homosexuality. *Hormones and Behavior*, 49, 405–414.

females, there is good evidence that higher levels of androgens prenatally are associated with greater same-sex attraction. For example, this effect is seen in girls with congenital adrenal hyperplasia (CAH), who experience greater levels of androgens prenatally. As these girls grow, they have typically masculine characteristics and a greater tendency toward being lesbian or bisexual (Hines, Brook, & Conway, 2004). For males, the evidence is less consistent, but it is still suggestive (Balthazart, 2011). For example, in males, higher levels of androgens during childhood are associated with bone development in the hands, feet, and arms. Research suggests that males who are sexually attracted to males have less long bone growth in those areas than do males who are sexually attracted to females (Martin & Nguygen, 2004). This finding suggests an association between low levels of childhood androgens and being gay as a man.

MATERNAL IMMUNE SYSTEM   In addition, according to some research, males who have older brothers are more likely to be gay as adults than are first-born males (Williams et al., 2000). This finding is called the *fraternal birth order effect* (Blanchard, 1997, 2008; Bogaert, 2003; but see McConaghy et al., 2006). As you can see in The Methods of Psychology above, this effect is limited to males who are right-handed (Blanchard, Cantor, Bogaert, Breedlove, & Ellis, 2006; Bogaert, Blanchard, & Crosthwait, 2007). The fraternal birth order effect has not been seen with adopted boys, so simply being raised with older brothers does not seem to be associated with being gay (Bogaert, 2006). Instead, the effect seems to be biological.

One hypothesis is that with repeated pregnancies of male fetuses, mothers may develop an immune response against substances produced by male fetuses but not by female fetuses (Blanchard, 2008). Accordingly, these *male-specific antigens* may cause mothers to develop antibodies against these substances produced by male fetuses (Bogaert et al., 2018). The maternal antibodies may then influence the development of male fetuses in a way that influences the males' later sexual orientation. Why might this effect occur for only right-handed males? It is possible that mothers of non-right-handed fetuses do not produce the antibodies. Alternatively, male fetuses that will not be right-handed may have distinctive brain features that leave them unaffected by maternal antibodies. Future research is likely to investigate both of these possibilities.

SEXUAL ORIENTATION AND THE BRAIN Finally, some research suggests that the hypothalamus (the brain's master regulatory structure; see study unit 2.6) is related to sexual orientation. In examinations of males that occurred after death, the neuroscientist Simon LeVay (1991) found that an area of the hypothalamus that typically differs between males and females was only half as large in males who were gay versus straight. In fact, the size of this area in gay males was comparable to its size in straight females. Likewise, in a recent brain imaging study, straight males showed greater activation of the hypothalamus when they smelled a female pheromone, a hormone that travels through the air, than when they sniffed a male pheromone. By contrast, straight females showed greater activation when they sniffed a male pheromone rather than a female pheromone (Savic, Berglund, & Lindström, 2005). However, gay males showed a pattern of activation in the hypothalamus in response to the male pheromone that was more similar to that of females than that of straight males.

Of course, both of these studies can be criticized on the grounds that an association between factors (a correlation) does not mean that one causes another (causation). That is, a size difference or activation difference in any one part of the brain doesn't indicate if this area determines sexual orientation, whether being straight or gay results in changes to brain structure or function, or whether a third variable is responsible for all these effects. For instance, some researchers have proposed that the size of the hypothalamus is determined by prenatal exposure to androgens.

Remember, too, that the brain changes with use. The size of the hypothalamus might reflect the impact of the experiences of gay males and straight males over the years. Thus, although these studies' findings are suggestive, the current evidence can't establish a causal connection between brain regions and sexual orientation. However, when considered together, the evidence is consistent that biological processes play some role in sexual orientation. Researchers continue to investigate how, when, and to what degree biology might contribute to the sexual orientations of people who are gay, lesbian, bisexual, or straight. Unfortunately, regardless of the association between biology and sexual orientation, people who are not straight often suffer mistreatment in response to their sexual orientation.

ACCEPTANCE OF VARIATIONS IN SEXUAL ORIENTATION In 2012, John Mace, a resident of New York City, got married. At the time of his wedding, Mr. Mace was 91 years old. What is even more remarkable is that he waited 62 years to marry his soul mate, 84-year-old Richard Dorr (**Figure 10.23**). The two men met in 1948, at the Juilliard School of Music, and became a couple in 1950. At the time that Mr. Mace and Mr. Dorr met, homosexual behavior was illegal in every state in the United States. In most Western cultures, having sex with someone of the same sex was regarded as deviant. In fact, experiencing same-sex sexual attraction was considered a mental illness until the diagnosis of "homosexuality" was removed from the *Diagnostic and Statistical Manual of Mental Disorders, Second Edition*

FIGURE 10.23

Changing Perspectives on Sexual Orientation

When Richard Dorr **(left)** and John Mace became a couple in 1950, homosexual behavior was illegal in every state in the United States. Sixty-two years after the start of their relationship, Mr. Dorr, 84, and Mr. Mace, 91, were finally married. Mr. Dorr died in 2016, and Mr. Mace in 2017.

(American Psychiatric Association, 1973). But homosexual behavior has been noted in various forms throughout recorded history, and attitudes toward it have varied over time and place. Right now, as with issues of gender identity, public opinion about people who are gay and lesbian is shifting in the United States. In 2011, Dorr and Mace, who lived in New York City, helped encourage the New York State Senate to pass the Marriage Equality Act. New York became the fifth state to recognize marriage equality. The next year, Dorr and Mace married, viewing the relationship change as "a completion" after so many years of feeling like second-class citizens.

Indeed, attitudes toward gays and lesbians are becoming more positive (Loftus, 2001; Tucker & Potocky-Tripodi, 2006). Canada, Spain, Norway, Sweden, South Africa, and Portugal have legalized marriage equality, and other places around the world recognize same-sex relationships in varying ways. In 2015, the Supreme Court of the United States ruled that the Constitution guarantees marriage equality. This ruling legalizes marriage equality in all states of the country. In some ways, the contemporary world is starting to catch up with human history. Homosexual behavior has always existed, whether or not gay, lesbian, and bisexual people were free to be themselves (see Has It Happened to You?).

Q How Do People Vary in Sexual Orientation?

To make sure you learned what you just read, write answers to the following questions and check your answers.

10.7 What are the four main normal variations in sexual orientation?

10.8 According to the research, is sexual orientation more influenced by environment or biology?

See Appendix B for answers to the red Q questions.

What Motivates People to Have Sexual Relations (or Not To)?

The Internet, movies, television, video games, advertising—sex is all around, and people seem endlessly fascinated by it. As you have learned, most people report feeling sexual attraction. If you are part of that majority, you know that attraction is only the first step toward having sex. You also need to be motivated to engage in sexual behavior. The next several subsections consider what factors might motivate you to engage in sexual behaviors, or not.

10.9 Biology Influences the Motivation for Sexual Activity

 10.9 LEARNING GOAL ACTIVITIES

To maximize your learning, complete the following learning goal activities.

a. Understand all bold and italic terms by writing explanations of them in your own words.

b. Understand the two ways that biology influences the motivation to have sex by summarizing in your own words how the sexual response cycle and hormones influence sexual motivation.

For much of the history of psychology, the study of sex was taboo. The idea that people were motivated to have sex was not discussed. In fact, many early theorists argued that females were incapable of enjoying sex. Whether the motives for sexual behavior are discussed or not, they are incredibly powerful, vital to the survival of our species, and potentially important to individuals' well-being. The motivation to engage in sexual activity is called **desire**. While many people have a significant desire for sex, what motivates them to have sex varies considerably among individuals and across circumstances. Sexual motivation is generally influenced by three factors: biology, environment and culture, and individual differences. As you learn about these factors, consider how each one influences your motivation to have sex (or not to).

In the 1950s, the pioneering work of Alfred Kinsey and his colleagues provided what was then shocking evidence that females' sexual attitudes and behaviors were in many ways similar to males' (Kinsey, Pomeroy, Martin, & Gebhard, 1953). In his surveys of thousands of Americans, Kinsey found that more than half of both males and females reported premarital sexual behavior, that masturbation was common in both sexes, that women enjoyed orgasms, and that homosexual behaviors were much more common than most people realized (Kinsey, Pomeroy, & Martin, 1948; Kinsey et al., 1953).

Kinsey's surveys have been criticized over the years for their sampling methods, such as their inclusion of large numbers of prisoners (Gebhard, 1972). These problems produced inflated estimates for some sexual behaviors, such as homosexuality and extramarital affairs (Diamond, 1993; Laumann, Gagnon, Michaels, & Michaels, 1994; Pruitt, 2002). However, overall the Kinsey studies were valuable for shedding light on a topic that had previously received little research attention. Kinsey showed a deep respect for collecting data as a way of answering a research question. More than 50 years after his work, we know a great deal more about sexual behavior based on the responses of his participants. However, his surveys did not reveal how the physical aspects of sex might affect the motivation for sex. This section examines our current understandings of biological motivation for sex.

THE SEXUAL RESPONSE CYCLE AFFECTS MOTIVATION TO HAVE SEX

Although Kinsey's research revealed what people were willing to describe in terms of their sexual behavior, these self-reports could not reveal many aspects of their sex lives. In 1957, the researcher William Masters and his assistant (later his wife), Virginia Johnson, began conducting laboratory studies to actually observe and record people's sexual behavior (**Figure 10.24**). Masters and Johnson gained considerable insight into the biology of human sexual behavior and sexual responses and how these influence people's desire for sexual activities.

The most enduring contribution of Masters and Johnson's research was the identification of the **sexual response cycle** (Masters & Johnson, 1966). This predictable pattern of physical and psychological responses consists of four phases. However, males and females experience the phases differently (**Figure 10.25**).

FIGURE 10.24

Masters of Sex

The Showtime series *Masters of Sex* portrayed the lives and work of William Masters and Virginia Johnson. Masters and Johnson pioneered research investigating the physiological aspects of sex by observing sex acts and recording physical responses to sexual stimulation.

desire

A person's psychological experience of wanting to engage in sexual activity.

sexual response cycle

A four-stage pattern of physiological and psychological responses during sex; the four stages are experienced differently by males than by females.

FIGURE 10.25

The Sexual Response Cycle as Experienced by Males and by Females

The four phases of the sexual response cycle are: **(1)** excitement, **(2)** plateau, **(3)** orgasm, and **(4)** resolution. However, **(a)** males and **(b)** females experience these phases differently.

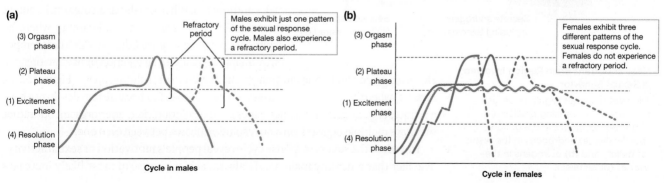

The *excitement phase* (see Figure 10.25a and b, Phase 1) occurs when people think about sexual activity or begin kissing and touching in a sensual manner (Graham, Sanders, Milhausen, & McBride, 2004). During this stage, blood flows to the male and female genitals, and often people experience feelings of sexual arousal. For males, the penis, which is a structure that actually extends into the pelvis, begins to become erect. For females, the tip of the clitoris becomes visibly swollen, although research shows that the clitoris is a large structure that also extends into the pelvis (O'Connell, Sanjeevan, & Hutson, 2005). In addition, for females the vagina expands and secretes fluids, and the nipples become erect. However, this excitement phase is not always associated with feelings of arousal. As you will soon learn, other aspects of the context affect arousal, and this is especially true for women, for whom emotional closeness and intimacy are often related to arousal (Basson, 2001).

As excitement continues into the *plateau phase* (Figure 10.25a and 10.25b, Phase 2), pulse rate, breathing, and blood pressure increase, as do the various other signs of arousal. For many people, this stage is the frenzied phase of sexual activity. Inhibitions are lifted, and passion takes control.

The plateau phase culminates in the *orgasm phase* (Figure 10.25a and 10.25b, Phase 3). This stage consists of involuntary muscle contractions throughout the body, dramatic increases in breathing and heart rate, rhythmic contractions of the vagina for females, and ejaculation of semen for males. For healthy males, orgasm nearly always occurs. For females, orgasm is more variable because they may not always experience orgasm or they may have multiple orgasms (Basson, 2000). Indeed, females have three separate patterns of sexual response, ranging from one orgasm (Figure 10.25b, blue line) to multiple orgasms (pink line) to repeated plateaus without orgasm (green line). In addition, females may experience orgasm from stimulation of the external area of the clitoris, parts of the clitoris located inside the pelvis (O'Connell, et al., 2005), or from a dime-sized area, the G-spot, that is proposed to be in the front wall of the vagina, above the pubic bone (Jannini et al., 2012; Ostrzenski, 2012). Regardless of the type of orgasm experienced, females and males report nearly identical pleasurable sensations during orgasm, which they describe as being like waves of electricity, the release of tension like an explosion, like a roller coaster where all your muscles tense and then release, and so on.

After an orgasm, sexual tension is dramatically decreased, and the person may slowly return to a normal state of arousal. However, this pattern varies between males and females. When a male has an orgasm, he enters the *resolution phase* (Figure 10.25a, Phase 4), where he experiences a *refractory period*, during which he is temporarily unable to maintain an erection or have an orgasm. However, when a female has an orgasm, she may enter a resolution phase (Figure 10.25b, Phase 4) where her arousal decreases to a normal level. But because females do not have a refractory period, they may not experience resolution right after orgasm, but rather may have multiple orgasms with no resolution phases between each one.

How does the sexual response cycle reveal people's motivation or sexual activity? The fact that a healthy male nearly always achieves orgasm most likely increases

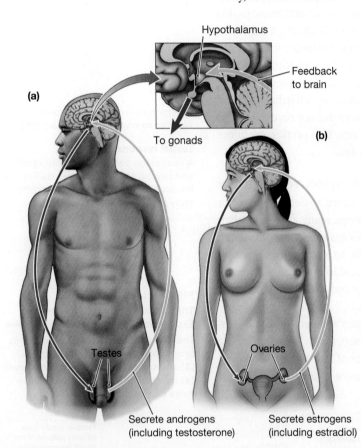

(a)

Hypothalamus

Feedback to brain

To gonads

(b)

Testes

Ovaries

Secrete androgens
(including testosterone)

Secrete estrogens
(including estradiol)

FIGURE 10.26

Most Important Brain Region Involved in Sexual Behavior

The hypothalamus regulates sexual behavior by influencing production of the sex hormones in the gonads, specifically: **(a)** androgens in the testes (of males) and **(b)** estrogens in the ovaries (of females).

his motivation for sex. However, each female's individual pattern of orgasm may increase or decrease her motivation for sex. In all, Masters and Johnson's research made clear that the pleasure associated with orgasm creates a strong desire for sexual activity. This desire in turn creates an internal motivation for people to engage in sexual relations (Peplau, 2003).

HORMONES AFFECT SEXUAL DESIRE AND BEHAVIOR   In study unit 10.1, you learned that hormones affect human biological sex by influencing the physical development of the brain and body during puberty. But hormones also help motivate sexual behavior (Schulz & Sisk, 2016). That is, hormones are involved in producing and terminating sexual behaviors. Given the important role of the hypothalamus (**Figure 10.26**) in controlling the release of these hormones into the bloodstream, it is no surprise that the hypothalamus is the most important brain region for stimulating sexual behavior.

Females and males both have some amount of all the sex hormones. However, after puberty, males have a greater amount of androgens, and females have a greater amount of estrogens. Androgens are the most important hormone for sexual desire, at least for humans. Testosterone—as you know, a type of androgen—is involved in both male and female sexual desire (Sherwin, 2008). The fact that males usually have higher levels of testosterone may partially account for the noticeable and consistent finding that males, on average, have a higher level of sexual motivation than females do. In general, males masturbate more frequently than females, think and fantasize about sex more often, spend more time and money (and other resources) in the effort to obtain sex, desire a greater variety of sexual activities, initiate sex more and refuse sex less, rate their own sex drives as stronger than females', and want sex earlier in the relationship (Baumeister, Catanese, & Vohs, 2001).

For example, males are much more willing than females to have sex with someone they do not know. In one study of 96 university students, a moderately attractive stranger approached a person of another sex and said, "I have been noticing you around campus. I find you attractive. Would you go to bed with me tonight?" Not one woman said yes to the stranger's request, but three-quarters of the men agreed to the request. In fact, the men were more likely to agree to have sex with the stranger than they were to agree to go on a date with her (Clark & Hatfield, 1989; **Figure 10.27**). Other researchers have found similar results using paper-and-pencil methods (Tappé, Bensman, Hayashi, & Hatfield, 2013). However, women may be more accepting of propositions in situations they deem to be safer, such as on a university campus versus in a nightclub (Baranowski & Hecht, 2015).

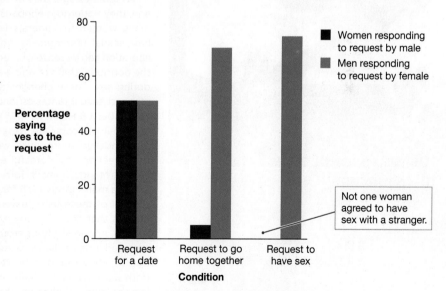

FIGURE 10.27

Sexual Behaviors and Responses

Men and women were propositioned by a stranger of another sex. Both sexes were equally likely to accept a date. Men were much more willing than women to agree to go home with or have sex with the stranger.

Even though males usually have more testosterone and therefore have greater sexual desire, they still need a certain amount of testosterone to be interested in sex. For example, when men have testosterone replacement therapy, their sexual desire increases (Yates, 2000). However, the evidence is inconsistent about whether testosterone replacement improves sexual function (Wang et al., 2000) or not (Brill et al., 2002).

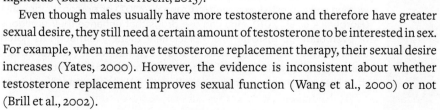

While testosterone can trigger sexual desire in males, sexual desire can also increase the testosterone of males. In one study, male skateboarders who viewed an attractive female experienced increases in testosterone (Ronay & von Hippel, 2010). Unfortunately, this hormone increase led to the males' making riskier skateboarding moves and crashing more often. In another study, males showed greater increases in testosterone when they smelled the T-shirts of females who were ovulating—and therefore fertile—than when they smelled the T-shirts of females who were not ovulating (Miller & Maner, 2010, 2011). In short, in males at least, increased testosterone can be both a cause and an effect of sexual desire.

So far, you have read about how testosterone influences the sexual desire of males. What about the sexual desire of females? As you know, females typically have lower levels of testosterone than males. But the more of a certain type of testosterone females have, the more likely they are to have sexual thoughts and desires. For example, adolescent females with higher than average levels of this type of testosterone for their age are more likely to engage in sexual intercourse (Halpern, Udry, & Suchindran, 1997). *Oxytocin* is another important hormone that affects sexual desire in females, and also in males. Oxytocin is released during sexual arousal and orgasm, is associated with feelings of romantic love, and promotes a sense of sexual gratification (Bartels & Zeki, 2004). In addition, oxytocin also seems to be involved in

USING PSYCHOLOGY IN YOUR LIFE

Changes in Sexual Desire and Sexual Activity over the Life Span

When you were a teenager, did you experience the first stirrings of sexual attraction? When you saw or spoke to a certain person, did you feel a rush of attraction? If so, you have experienced the physical intensity of sexual desires influenced by hormones. But your hormone levels, like everyone else's, will change throughout life. In middle age and beyond, hormone levels decrease, and those decreases can affect sexual desire and sexual activity.

As females age, they experience a decline in estrogen. In late middle age, they undergo menopause. The end of reproductive capacity makes many women feel liberated—free from menstrual periods and free to have sexual intercourse without concerns about pregnancy. This sense of liberation can increase women's interest in sex (Dillaway, 2005). However, the hormonal shifts of aging also lead to vaginal dryness and discomfort during sex. These changes are associated with reduced sexual desire, reduced sexual fantasies, and reduced frequency of sexual intercourse (Leitenberg & Henning, 1995). Similarly, as males age, they experience a decline in testosterone. Researchers have begun to investigate whether men undergo andropause, which has physical symptoms such as a less firm erection, less forceful ejaculation, and a longer refractory period (Buvat, Maggi, Guay, & Torres, 2013). Clearly these symptoms will also affect a man's motivation for sex.

If all of these facts leave you picturing a sexless old age, the good news is that not everyone experiences age-related reduced motivation for sex. In one study of around 3,000 people aged 57–85, participants reported little decline in sexual interest (Herbenick et al., 2010). Through age 74, they reported no reduction in sexual intercourse. In addition, both women and men can improve their sexual experiences by addressing the physical changes they experience. To combat vaginal dryness, women can use estrogen creams (Crandall, 2002) or personal lubricants (Herbenick et al., 2011). Men can use drugs that enhance their erections or even undergo testosterone replacement therapy, although as noted earlier, serious risks are associated with such treatment (Kolata, 2002). Generally, healthy older adults report that sexuality is an important part of their lives and that they enjoy sex with their intimate partners.

promoting social behavior in general (Carter, 2014). Finally, for females, estrogen has an impact on sexual desire, although the impact is less direct. As females age, their hormone levels decline, so they often experience reductions in sexual fantasies and in sexual activity (Leitenberg & Henning, 1995). However, when women undergoing *menopause*—the termination of a female's menstrual cycle and her ability to reproduce—receive estrogen hormone replacement therapy, they often experience increased sexual desire, arousal, and sexual activity (Braunstein et al., 2005; Buster et al., 2005; Petersen & Hyde, 2011). As the Using Psychology in Your Life feature on p. 408 explains, sexual desire and sexual activity do not always decline as people age.

10.10 Environmental Context Influences the Motivation for Sexual Activity

10.10 LEARNING GOAL ACTIVITIES

To maximize your learning, complete the following learning goal activities.

a. Understand all bold and italic terms by writing explanations of them in your own words.

b. Apply the three ways that environment influences the motivation for sex by explaining how culture, mate preferences, and stimuli in your environment have affected your motivation (or the motivation of someone you know) for sex.

If you are like most people, you have experienced times when the situation affected your desire to have sex or your ability to engage in sexual activity. Perhaps there have been times when your sexual partner was of a culture that differed from yours in their beliefs about sex. Maybe at some point you have had a partner who was particularly attractive to you. Or you watched a movie that set just the right mood—or the totally wrong mood. In many ways, the environmental context influences the motivation to engage in sexual behavior.

CULTURAL DIFFERENCES IN SEXUAL BEHAVIOR   The Pfizer Global Study of Sexual Attitudes and Behaviors reveals how sexual behavior varies by culture (Laumann et al., 2006). For example, the frequency with which people have sex varies by cultures. People in Greece and Croatia report having the most sex, between 134 and 138 times per year, whereas people in Japan have the least amount of sex, at 45 times per year. Americans reported that they have sex about twice per week, or 113 times per year.

Before the 1960s, sexual intercourse outside of marriage was strongly discouraged because of the risk of unwanted pregnancies and the lack of reliable birth control. With the advent of oral contraceptives in the 1960s, sexual attitudes became more permissive and casual sex before marriage became more commonplace (Smith, 1990; Thornton & Young-DeMarco, 2001; Tyrer, 1999). Yet before the 1990s, men in the United States viewed casual sex before marriage as being more acceptable than did women (Laumann et al., 1994). Nowadays, young men and young women tend to have more-similar views about the acceptability of casual sex before marriage. Young adults who see premarital sex as acceptable may engage in hookup behavior, a modern trend involving very brief sexual encounters in people who are not romantically involved (Garcia, Reiber, Massey, & Merriwether, 2012). Anything from kissing to touching body parts above or below the waist to oral sex and even intercourse can be considered a hookup.

Which of these two people do you think is more physically attractive?

(a)   **(b)**

What about these two?

(c)   **(d)**

People from Western cultures who are attracted to Caucasians often find specific features to be more attractive. The woman labeled **(b)** is typically seen as sexy due to being tanner, having higher and more prominent cheekbones, and being thinner. The man labeled **(d)** is seen as sexy because of his square jaw and prominent cheekbones. However, because what is physically attractive varies greatly across cultures and experience, it is entirely possible that you don't find any of these people attractive.

MATE PREFERENCES AFFECT OUR MOTIVATION FOR SEX What do people want in their mates? To judge from all the self-help books on the subject, the question isn't easily answered. It may be easier to say what they do not want. In seeking mates, both sexes avoid certain characteristics, such as insensitivity, bad manners, loudness or shrillness, and the tendency to brag about sexual conquests (Cunningham, Barbee, & Druen, 1996).

We can assume that people seek physically attractive partners, because conventional aspects of attractiveness (youth and beauty) imply potential fertility. You can explore the nature of attraction in Try It Yourself. But according to the *sexual strategies theory*, females should be choosier than males in selecting mates. Because females can produce a limited number of offspring, they should seek males who can provide resources that will help them successfully nurture their children. In other words, males should judge potential mates mainly on looks because looks imply fertility, whereas females should also look for indications that their mates will be good providers. Is there any scientific support for these ideas?

According to a study of 92 married couples in 37 cultures, females generally prefer males who are considerate, honest, dependable, kind, understanding, fond of children, well-liked by others, good earners, ambitious, career oriented, from a good family, and fairly tall. By contrast, males tend to value good looks, cooking skills, and sexual faithfulness. Females value a good financial prospect more than males do. In all 37 cultures, women tend to marry older men, who often are more settled and financially stable (Buss, 1989). In short, males and females differ in the relative emphases they place on social status and physical appearance, at least for long-term relationships.

The evolutionary account of human mating is controversial. Some researchers have argued that behaviors shaped by evolution have little impact on contemporary relationships. After all, instinctive behaviors are affected by cultural context, which is very different now than it was in early human societies. Modern human sexual behavior is influenced by contemporary norms. For example, from a biological view, it might seem advantageous for humans to reproduce as soon as they are able. But many contemporary cultures discourage sexual behavior until people are older and better able to care for their offspring. The critical point is that human behavior emerges to solve adaptive problems. To some degree, the modern world presents new adaptive challenges based on societal standards of conduct. These standards shape the context in which males and females view sexual behavior as desirable and appropriate.

INNER THOUGHTS AND EXTERNAL STIMULI AFFECT MOTIVATION FOR SEX If you fantasize about sex, you are not alone. Most people think about sex, although males tend to have different kinds of fantasies than females do. For example, more males than females fantasize about sexual activities with people other than their romantic partner (Hicks & Leitenberg, 2001). In addition, males' fantasies tend to be more physical, faster paced, and less personal and romantic (Leitenberg & Henning, 1995).

If you have ever become sexually aroused while watching an explicit scene, you are also not alone. Many people experience arousal from external stimuli, such as watching pornographic movies or reading erotic material (Murnen & Stockton, 1997) and even from sexting (see Has It Happened to You?). However, males tend to find different material arousing than females do. For example, when males watch pornographic movies that show full-frontal nudity, oral sex, and penile-vaginal intercourse, they become more aroused than females do (Mosher & MacIan, 1994). When females watch versions of the same movies modified to appeal more to females—focusing less on genitals and male pleasure—females become more aroused than they did toward the original versions. Similarly, males tend to be aroused by explicit written descriptions of sex acts, whereas females tend to be aroused by suggestive written descriptions (Scott & Cortez, 2011).

Although experiencing arousal from what we see is generally considered normal, exposure to erotic material can have negative effects. After viewing sexually attractive females on TV or in magazines, straight male college students rate average females and their own female sex partners as less attractive (Kenrick & Gutierres, 1980; Kenrick, Gutierres, & Goldberg, 1989; Weaver, Masland, & Zillmann, 1984). In addition, watching pornographic movies can reduce people's satisfaction with their own sex partners (Zillmann, 1989). Most importantly, when pornographic movies depict nonconsensual sex acts, males become more willing to hurt females (Malamuth & Check, 1981; Zillmann, 1989). Finally, when a person is repeatedly sexually aroused by specific objects or situations, the person may become dependent on those objects or situations to experience arousal. In such cases, people's motivations for sex can be considered disordered (American Psychiatric Association, 2013).

10.11 Individual Differences Influence the Motivation for Sexual Activity

10.11 LEARNING GOAL ACTIVITIES

To maximize your learning, complete the following learning goal activities.

a. Understand all bold and italic terms by writing explanations of them in your own words.

b. Understand individual differences in sexual motivation by naming and explaining the two categories of individual differences that can increase or decrease a person's motivation for sex.

As you have learned, biological and environmental factors motivate people to have sex or not. Inner thoughts also play a role, as people experience sexual fantasies and particular desires. Some people experience unusual sexual desires that increase their motivation to have those specific sexual experiences. Alternatively, some people experience sexual dysfunctions that decrease their motivation for sex. This section looks at such individual differences in motivation.

PARAPHILIAS CAN INCREASE MOTIVATION FOR SPECIFIC SEXUAL EXPERIENCES A *paraphilia* is unchanging sexual interest, arousal, and/or behavior in association with an object, type of person, or situation that is not usually associated with sex (American Psychiatric Association, 2013). Regardless of whether the focus of a paraphilia is on an object, a person, or a behavior, the sexual interest is

Have you ever sexted anyone? Or received a sext? Sending sexually explicit text messages and/or photos is a new way that some people increase sexual desire and interest through the use of external stimuli. But be careful! Sexting may be sexy, but it can also get you into trouble. For example, anything you send can be saved, forwarded, shared, and posted online. It can live on to affect your future. People have even been lured into sharing explicit sexual content electronically and then blackmailed for money or actual sexual contact. Don't let immediate temptations lead you into dangerous territory.

paraphilic disorder
A psychological disorder where sexual activity is associated with a paraphilia (atypical sexual interest, arousal, and/or behavior), causing distress in the person or others and impairing the person's life; may cause the person to pursue sexual activity without consent.

sexual dysfunction
A psychological disorder that reduces sexual activity due to a significant and enduring problem in sexual functioning or pleasure, causing distress and impairing the person's life.

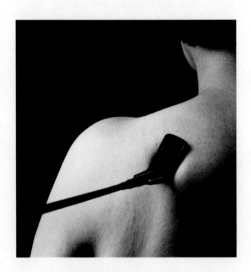

FIGURE 10.28

Some Paraphilias Can Be Paraphilic Disorders

The *Fifty Shades* books and movies show bondage, domination, sadism, and masochism (BDSM). Because Ana does not seem to fully consent to or feel comfortable with these sexual activities with Christian, it may be that sexual sadism disorder and sexual masochism disorder are being depicted.

very specific and unchanging. Indeed, the person may become dependent on engaging with the object, type of person, or situation to experience sexual satisfaction. However, even though paraphilias are atypical and intense sexual desires, they are not considered psychological disorders if all the people involved are consenting adults and if the paraphilias do not cause distress.

One group of paraphilias may revolve around a particular object. For example, some people have sexual interest in nonsexual objects, such as shoes. Other people are aroused by nonsexual body parts, such as feet. When a person focuses on nonsexual objects for sexual arousal, this paraphilia is called *fetishism*.

Alternatively, people may be sexually interested in certain acts. *Exhibitionism* is sexual arousal from exposing one's naked body to others. *Voyeurism* is sexual arousal from watching people disrobe and/or engage in sex. *Frotteurism* involves being sexually aroused by touching or rubbing against another person. *Transvestism*, not to be confused with being transgender (see study unit 10.6), is when one experiences sexual arousal from dressing and acting as a person of a different sex. Two other paraphilias of this type include *sexual sadism*, which is being sexually aroused by the physical or psychological humiliation or suffering of another person, and *sexual masochism*, which is when a person is aroused by being humiliated, beaten, bound, or made to suffer in some way.

Sexual sadism and sexual masochism, and some of the other paraphilias, can be practiced in psychologically healthy ways by consenting adults. However, healthy participation requires each person's consent as well as a great deal of communication, emotional maturity, and honesty between the adults engaging in these unusual sexual practices. Unfortunately, this kind of interaction does not always happen.

When does a paraphilia become a psychological disorder? According to the *Diagnostic and Statistical Manual of Mental Disorders* (DSM-5; American Psychiatric Association, 2013; First, 2014), a **paraphilic disorder** exists when a paraphilia causes distress to the person or others and impairs the person's life. In addition, someone may be experiencing a paraphilic disorder if the person is being harmed by the paraphilia or harming another person through it. Such harm includes failing to obtain consent for the sexual activities. One such psychological disorder is *pedophilia*. This paraphilia is related to sexual fantasies, urges, and/or behaviors focused on prepubescent children, usually under the age of 13. Pedophilia is a crime because by law minors cannot give consent. In addition, pedophilia traumatizes the children who are victimized.

E. L. James's *Fifty Shades* book trilogy (2011, 2012a, 2012b) and the movie adaptations (2015, 2017, 2018) have received lots of attention for portraying two people, Christian and Ana, engaging in bondage, domination, sadism, and masochism (BDSM; **Figure 10.28**). Some critics have suggested that *Fifty Shades* does not depict psychologically healthy sexual activities, in part because Ana does not seem truly comfortable with their sexual activities. If Ana is not fully consenting, then *Fifty Shades* may unfortunately be depicting *sexual sadism disorder* and *sexual masochism disorder*.

SEXUAL DYSFUNCTION CAN REDUCE MOTIVATION FOR SEX Whereas a paraphilia increases a person's motivation to pursue a particular unusual sexual activity, sexual problems decrease a person's motivation for sex. That is, the person loses motivation due to a problem with sexual desire, functioning during the sexual response cycle, or receiving pleasure from sex. When a person experiences an enduring pattern of sexual problems, distress about the situation, and impairment in daily functioning, the person is considered to have a **sexual dysfunction** (American Psychiatric Association, 2013).

Sexual dysfunctions are generally categorized in terms of females' and males' difficulties with sexual desire and arousal, orgasm, or pain, or problems caused by taking substances or medications (**Table 10.1**). For males, poor physical health is a risk factor for all sexual dysfunctions, but for females poor health is associated only with pain during sex (Laumann, Paik, & Rosen, 1999).

According to a large survey of sexual behavior in the United States, approximately 43 percent of females and 31 percent of males report experiencing some kind of sexual problem at some point in their lives (Laumann et al., 1999). Sexual problems tend to increase with age for males but to decrease with age for females. In addition, married people report fewer sexual problems than do unmarried people.

TABLE 10.1
Sexual Dysfunctions

Females	Males
Sexual Desire/Arousal Disorders	
Sexual interest/arousal disorder: reduced or absent interest/arousal about sexual desire, thoughts, and activities	**Male hypoactive sexual desire disorder:** reduced or absent interest/arousal about sexual desire, thoughts, and activities **Erectile disorder:** difficulty achieving or maintaining an erection during sexual activities with a partner
Orgasmic Disorders	
Female orgasmic disorder: delayed, infrequent, or absent orgasm or reduced intensity of the feeling of orgasm	**Delayed ejaculation:** difficulty or inability to achieve ejaculation during sexual activities with a partner **Premature (early) ejaculation:** ejaculation during sexual activity with a partner within 1 minute following penetration or before individual wishes it
Sexual Pain Disorders	
Genitopelvic pain/penetration disorder: difficulties with vaginal penetration during intercourse, pain during intercourse, or fear or anxiety about pain or penetration	Not applicable
Substance/Medication-Induced Disorders	
Substance/medication-induced sexual dysfunction: sexual dysfunction experienced when taking an illegal drug or prescription drug, but ending after the substance or drug is not taken	**Substance/medication-induced sexual dysfunction:** sexual dysfunction experienced when taking an illegal drug or prescription drug, but ending after the substance or drug is not taken

Finally, people of lower educational status report having less pleasurable sex and increased anxiety about sex.

While these data are illuminating, the very high statistics have been criticized by some researchers as potentially misrepresenting sexual problems (Moynihan, 2003). For example, some argue that reduced sexual desire can be a completely healthy and functional response for people who are tired, face high levels of stress, or experience psychological or physical threats from their partners (Bancroft, 2002). In other words, while the symptoms of sexual dysfunction are physical in terms of how they affect the human sexual response cycle, the underlying causes can be either physical or psychological.

Many psychological factors are associated with sexual dysfunction. For example, changes in finances are associated with increased risk for certain dysfunctions, perhaps due to the stress associated with such changes. In addition, feeling less physical and emotional satisfaction and happiness is associated with all types of sexual dysfunction except premature ejaculation. And a traumatic sexual experience can decrease sexual functioning, even years after the event (Browning & Laumann, 1997). Research that focuses solely on the genital-function aspects of sexual dysfunction may fail to identify how problematic thoughts, feelings, and actions may contribute to the issue (Tiefer, 2000). In Chapter 11, you will learn about how the physical and psychological aspects of sexually transmitted infections are related to the motivation for sex.

Clearly, people's experiences, including their thoughts and feelings, affect their motivation for sex. The desire to have sex or not is intensely personal. It is influenced by the major aspects of sexuality that you have learned about in this chapter: biological sex, gender identity, and sexual orientation. Because these factors interact differently in each individual, it is not safe to make assumptions about the sexuality or gender of any one person or group of people. Whether you are interacting with a young person who is transgender, a middle-aged person who is gender nonconforming, an elderly person who is straight, and so on, remember to keep an open mind about the person's private life.

 ## What Motivates People to Have Sexual Relations (or Not To)?

To make sure you learned what you just read, write answers to the following questions and check your answers.

10.9 Are androgens or estrogens more important for sexual behavior in humans?

10.10 According to the sexual strategies theory, why are females more cautious than males about having sex?

10.11 According to the American Psychiatric Association (APA), what are the two common characteristics of people who are experiencing a paraphilic disorder or a sexual dysfunction?

See Appendix B for answers to the red Q questions.

BIG PICTURE

Want to earn a better grade on your test? Go to **INQUIZITIVE** to practice actively with this chapter's content and get personalized feedback along the way.

How Does Biology Make People More Male or Female?

10.1 Genetics and Hormones Influence Biological Sex

Review the learning goal activities on p. 379. Each person has a biological sex, which is determined by four aspects of the person's physical attributes: two genetic aspects and two hormonal aspects. The two genetic aspects of biological sex are the sex chromosomes and how the sex chromosomes shape the development of the sex glands. The two hormonal aspects of biological sex emerge in puberty. Estradiol increases in girls, and testosterone increases in boys. Both hormones yield sex differences in secondary sex characteristics and primary sex characteristics.

10.2 Biological Sex Is Not Always Clear

Review the learning goal activities on p. 383. When people experience inconsistencies in biological sex, they are intersex.

Such inconsistencies may be related to genetics, as is the case with Klinefelter syndrome and Turner syndrome, or hormones, as occurs in congenital adrenal hyperplasia (CAH) and androgen insensitivity syndrome (AIS). The fact that some people are intersex indicates that biological sex is experienced on a continuum, where people may be biologically more male or more female.

KEY TERMS
biological sex (p. 379)
XX sex chromosomes (p. 380)
XY sex chromosomes (p. 380)
testes (p. 380)
ovaries (p. 380)
estrogens (p. 380)
androgens (p. 381)
menarche (p. 382)
spermarche (p. 382)
intersex (p. 383)

Why Do People Act Masculine or Feminine?

10.3 People Have Mental Categories of What Is Masculine and What Is Feminine

Review the learning goal activities on p. 386. Gender is not the same as biological sex. Gender refers to social, cultural, and psychological aspects of masculinity and femininity. People learn about gender by organizing information about what is masculine and what is feminine into cognitive structures called gender schemas, which affect how people then process information about gender. Gender schemas that lead to commonly held beliefs about males and females are called gender stereotypes.

10.4 Gender Roles Affect How People Act

Review the learning goal activities on p. 388. Gender roles are the positions, characteristics, and interests considered normal and expected for males and females. People learn gender roles through gender role socialization within their culture. However, biology may also influence the development of gender roles.

10.5 Gender Identity Also Affects How People Act

Review the learning goal activities on p. 390. Gender identity is a person's sense of being more male or more female. A person's gender identity emerges during three stages of cognitive development, but is complete by about the age of 7 or 8.

10.6 People Vary in Gender Identity

Review the learning goal activities on p. 392. People experience several normal variations in gender identity, including being cisgender, genderqueer, androgynous, or transgender. Variations in gender identity are associated with the psychological disorder of gender dysphoria only when they lead to distress and impairment in life.

KEY TERMS
gender (p. 386)
gender schemas (p. 386)
gender stereotypes (p. 387)
gender roles (p. 388)
gender role socialization (p. 388)
gender identity (p. 391)
cognitive development theory (p. 391)
transgender (p. 393)
gender dysphoria (p. 394)

How Do People Vary in Sexual Orientation?

10.7 Variations in Sexual Orientation Are Normal

Review the learning goal activities on p. 396. Sexual orientation is the nature of a person's enduring sexual, emotional, and/or romantic attraction to other people. It does not refer to whom people may actually have sex with. There are several normal variations in sexual orientation. Most people are straight (heterosexual), some are gay or lesbian (homosexual), others are bisexual, and some are asexual.

10.8 Biology Influences the Development of Sexual Orientation

Review the learning goal activities on p. 399. There is little or no evidence that environmental factors, such as a person's parents, cause sexual orientation. Instead, research suggests that sexual orientation is associated with four biological factors: (1) genetics, (2) fetal hormones, (3) prenatal impacts on the maternal immune system, and (4) brain structures and processes.

KEY TERMS
sexual orientation (p. 396)
heterosexual (straight) (p. 397)
homosexual (gay or lesbian) (p. 397)
bisexual (p. 397)
asexual (p. 397)

What Motivates People to Have Sexual Relations (or Not To)?

10.9 Biology Influences the Motivation for Sexual Activity

Review the learning goal activities on p. 404. Biology influences the motivation for sex through the four phases of the sexual response cycle: (1) excitement, (2) plateau, (3) orgasm, and (4) resolution. Biology also influences the motivation for sexual activity through hormones, especially testosterone, which is related to sexual desire in males and females. However, oxytocin is also related to sexual motivation in both sexes, and estrogen affects sexual desire in females.

10.10 Environmental Context Influences the Motivation for Sexual Activity

Review the learning goal activities on p. 409. Environmental context influences the motivation for sex based on the culture, the attractiveness of a person's mate, and the person's inner thoughts and external stimuli in the situation.

10.11 Individual Differences Influence the Motivation for Sexual Activity

Review the learning goal activities on p. 411. People with paraphilias are sexually aroused by atypical objects, types of people, and/or situations. Paraphilic disorders are psychological disorders where a person's atypical sexual interest, arousal, or behavior causes distress to the person or others and impairs the person's life. A paraphilic disorder may also lead the person to not get consent for sexual activity. By contrast, sexual dysfunction is a psychological disorder where reduced desire or arousal, orgasm, increased sexual pain, and/or problems caused by taking substances or medications cause distress or impair daily functioning.

KEY TERMS
desire (p. 405)
sexual response cycle (p. 405)
paraphilic disorder (p. 412)
sexual dysfunction (p. 412)

CHAPTER 10 SELF-QUIZ

To make sure you learned the information in this chapter, write answers to the following questions and check your answers. **See Appendix B for answers to the self-quiz.**

1. Michelle is a doctor who has just delivered a newborn. She sees that the baby has a vagina, not a penis, and announces, "It's a girl!" Michelle's statement is about the new baby's _____.
   a. gender identity
   b. sex chromosomes
   c. gender schemas
   d. biological sex

2. Daniel is an adult with XXY chromosomes. Since puberty, his penis has been unusually small. His voice never deepened, and he does not have chest or facial hair. He has breasts. Given this information regarding Daniel's genetics and his _____ sex characteristics, Daniel may be intersex due to a condition called _____.
   a. primary; Klinefelter syndrome
   b. primary; congenital adrenal hyperplasia
   c. secondary; Klinefelter syndrome
   d. secondary; congenital adrenal hyperplasia

3. Tara and her mother prefer to take baths, whereas her father and brother prefer to take showers. As a result, Tara has mentally categorized baths as "girl things" and showers as "boy things." This organization of knowledge about what is feminine and what is masculine is part of Tara's gender _____.
   a. roles
   b. identity
   c. dysphoria
   d. schemas

4. One day, Aidan, a 4-year-old boy, plays dress-up by wearing his sister's princess gown. When Aidan's mother sees him, she reprimands him and says, "Boys don't wear dresses. Girls do." Aidan quickly takes off the dress. In this example, Aidan is learning about gender roles in his culture through _____.
   a. gender role socialization
   b. cognitive developmental theory
   c. gender stereotypes
   d. gender expression

5. Gloria identifies as male when she puts on rocker clothes, puts her hair in a bun, plugs in her bass guitar, and plays AC/DC songs with the guys in her band. However, she identifies as female when she lets her hair down and wears a dress to her job at a day care center. Based on this information, Gloria's gender identity is best described as _____.
   a. transgender
   b. genderqueer
   c. androgynous
   d. gender dysphoria

6. Derek is sexually attracted to women, and all of his romantic relationships have been with women. He finds some men very attractive, though, and often fantasizes about having sex with these men. Based on this information, Derek's sexual orientation is best described as _____.
   a. gay
   b. straight
   c. lesbian
   d. bisexual

7. You and a friend are debating how sexual orientation develops in people. You correctly tell your friend, "According to the best scientific evidence, sexual orientation is _____."
   a. determined by one specific gene
   b. influenced by how parents treat their children
   c. related to genetics, prenatal hormones, the maternal immune system, and brain structure and processes
   d. a direct result of community values

8. Belinda, a woman, and Joe, a man, are in excellent health and are highly motivated to have sexual relations with each other. According to the research of Masters and Johnson, the sexual response cycles of Belinda and Joe are likely to differ in all of the following ways EXCEPT _____.
   a. only Joe will experience increased blood flow to his genitals in the excitement phase
   b. Belinda is more likely to remain in the plateau phase for a long period of time
   c. Joe will almost always reach the orgasm phase
   d. Belinda will have no refractory period between her orgasms

9. Rachel, an 18-year-old woman, has a lot of sexual thoughts and desires. In response, she engages in frequent sexual behavior. Rachel's motivation for sexual activity is most likely influenced by her having _____ levels of a certain class of hormones called _____ .
   a. lower; androgens
   b. higher; androgens
   c. lower; estrogens
   d. higher; estrogens

10. Which of the following people could be described as experiencing a sexual dysfunction?
    a. Elle's friends often use Tinder and other apps to find hookups for brief sexual encounters, but Elle has no desire to engage in casual sexual activities.
    b. Dylan never feels any sexual attraction to his girlfriends, but he enjoys being in romantic relationships that do not include sex.
    c. Logan experiences such strong sexual arousal from women's feet that he tries not to go out in public anywhere there are likely to be women wearing high heels.
    d. Claudia is upset and worried because she never has an orgasm when she has sexual intercourse with her husband.

How Can Psychology Lead to a Career Supporting People with Variations in Sex, Gender, and Sexuality?

Most people, at some point in their lives, need extra support to confront issues they are facing. Some people may be especially likely to need extra support. For example, as you have learned in this chapter, there are people who feel anxious, depressed, socially isolated, or discriminated against due to their biological sex, gender identity, or sexual orientation. Luckily, there are professionals who can help people get the support they need to lead happy, fulfilling lives. If you like to help others, then a career in social services might be for you.

A social services assistant works with clients to find services, benefits, and support for individuals and for families. Social services assistants work in various settings, including nonprofit organizations, for-profit social services organizations, and local, state, and federal government. For example, the Accord Alliance, mentioned in study unit 10.2, is a nonprofit organization that supports the needs of intersex people. The information in this chapter about how some people experience inconsistencies in biological sex due to conflicts in genes or hormones will help you understand what it means to be intersex. To become a social services assistant, you need to earn an associate's degree.

With a bachelor's degree in psychology, sociology, social work, or a related field, you can become a social worker. The information in this chapter about how society has responded to those with nontraditional identities or sexual orientations will provide insights into people's social environments and their feelings of acceptance. As noted in the chapter, experiences of discrimination, harassment, or rejection contribute to gender dysphoria. Social workers help clients address issues in their daily lives and cope with problems. Some of these clients may be people who are intersex or who are seeking support around their gender identity and/or sexual orientation. Social workers also help a broad array of clients with varying issues and needs. The need for social workers is on the rise, and the field is experiencing more growth

than the average career, with 16 percent growth expected between 2016 and 2026. So if you are interested in using psychology to help others, now is a great time to become a social worker.

Many social workers go on to earn a master's degree in social work (MSW), which requires about two to three more years in school and a practicum or internship providing services to clients in the community. You may need to pass certain exams and have field experience to become a licensed clinical social worker. As a clinical social worker, you would help assess the mental health of clients and their needs, develop a care plan, and provide case management for all of the services that the person might need.

TAKEAWAY POINT: Understanding psychology can help you understand people's thoughts, feelings, and actions. With this knowledge, you can support people's needs and help them lead happy, fulfilling lives. This application of psychology is especially true in careers associated with social work.

Ψ You can look up job descriptions, education requirements, salaries, and more at the Bureau of Labor Statistics: www.bls.gov. Visit the site and start putting psychology to work!

11 Health and Well-Being

FAT SHAMING, making fun of people for their body shape or weight, is widespread in North American culture. It occurs frequently in social media, particularly for women. And some industries are especially prone to it, such as show business. Consider the actor Gabourey Sidibe. In a review of the 2009 movie *Precious,* a *New York* magazine critic described Sidibe's head as "a balloon on the body of a zeppelin, her cheeks so inflated they squash her eyes into slits" (Breslaw, 2014; **Figure 11.1a**). The late actor Carrie Fisher was asked to lose weight for the 2015 movie *Star Wars: The Force Awakens* (**Figure 11.1b**). In an interview, Fisher noted, "I'm in a business where the only thing that matters is weight and appearance. That is so messed up" (Good Housekeeping Features Team, 2016). Jennifer Lawrence has confirmed that most women in Hollywood experience fat shaming,

BIG QUESTIONS

What Affects Your Health?

How Does Stress Affect Your Health?

How Do Mediating Factors Affect Your Stress?

Can a Positive Attitude Keep You Healthy?

(a)

(b)

FIGURE 11.1

Fat Shaming

Many people, most likely including people you know, have felt the negative effects of being shamed for their body shape or weight. Actors such as **(a)** Gabourey Sidibe and **(b)** Carrie Fisher have spoken out about the pressure to be thin.

but she refuses to be bothered by it. "What are you gonna do," Lawrence has asked, "be hungry every single day to make other people happy?" (Saad, 2013). But for most people it is not so easy to ignore insults and jokes about weight.

Fat shaming can do more than hurt people's feelings. It can have serious health consequences. For example, a recent study found that the more women believed they had negative traits associated with obesity, the more likely they were to have poor health (Pearl et al., 2017). This effect was true even taking into account the person's body weight. Being stigmatized about body weight is associated with mental health problems, anxiety, perceived stress, substance abuse, and poor coping strategies (Papadopoulos & Brennan, 2015). Indeed, feeling that one is being discriminated against because of body weight decreases life expectancy (Sutin, Stephan, & Terracciano, 2015). This effect may occur for two reasons. Overweight people might avoid physicians who lecture them about their body weight, and physicians might actually hold negative attitudes about overweight patients, attitudes that interfere with treatment (Chrisler & Barney, 2017).

This chapter explores how health and well-being are closely connected to psychological states. The first section discusses common behaviors that place health at risk and examines the social, psychological, and biological factors that affect these outcomes. The second section looks at the many ways that stress can harm health. The third section then looks at how people cope with stress and suggests methods for doing so successfully. The final section considers the benefits of a positive attitude on health and well-being.

What Affects Your Health?

If you ask yourself, "What affects my health?" you may think first about germs, viruses, and disease. Indeed, most people think about their health in only biological and medical terms. So you may be surprised to learn that your attitudes and behavior affect your health.

11.1 Biology, Psychology, and Social Factors Influence Your Health

 11.1 LEARNING GOAL ACTIVITIES

To maximize your learning, complete the following learning goal activities.

a. Understand all bold and italic terms by writing explanations of them in your own words.

b. Apply the biopsychosocial model of health to your life by providing a description of how your health could be explained by this model.

The traditional Western medical model sees health essentially as the absence of disease. According to this model, people are patients—passive recipients of disease. The focus is on medical treatments, including drugs, designed to return patients to health. The assumption is that health professionals know best and thus should maintain control over what happens to the patients.

Psychologists and most health-care professionals take a more integrated approach to health and well-being. They believe that attitudes and behaviors are critical in staying healthy, regaining health following illness, and achieving well-being throughout life. In this approach, the individual plays a more active role.

Health psychology integrates research on health and on psychology. This field was launched nearly four decades ago. At that time, psychologists, physicians, and other health professionals came to appreciate the importance of lifestyle factors to physical health (**Figure 11.2**). Health psychologists do not think of health as merely the absence of disease. Instead, they apply their knowledge of psychological principles to promote health and well-being.

Before the twentieth century, most people died from infections and from diseases transmitted person to person. Infectious diseases remain the leading causes of death in some developing nations, especially for children, but in most countries the causes have shifted dramatically. For example, in the United States people are now more likely to die from heart disease, cancer, strokes, lung disease, and accidents than from infectious diseases (Heron, 2016). All of these causes of death are at least partially outcomes of lifestyle. Daily habits such as poor nutrition, overeating, smoking, alcohol use, and lack of exercise contribute to nearly every major cause of death in developed nations (Smith, Orleans, & Jenkins, 2004).

What does it mean to be healthy, then? If being healthy is defined as being physically active, not smoking, eating a healthy diet, and not having too much body fat, then fewer than 3 percent of Americans meet all those criteria (Loprinzi, Branscum, Hanks, & Smit, 2017). Congratulations if you are one of them, but most people struggle with one or more of these issues. Partially for this reason, in 2015 and 2016 life expectancy dropped in the United States, the first time this has happened in several decades (Kochanek, Murphy, Xu, & Arias, 2017; Xu, Murphy, Kochanek, & Arias, 2016). Lifestyle factors, such as substance abuse and obesity, are responsible for much of this decline (Woolf et al., 2018). Research in health psychology helps explain why people engage in healthy or unhealthy lifestyles that shorten their lives and often make them miserable.

Well-being is a positive state in which you feel your best. To achieve this state, you need to strive for optimal health and life satisfaction. To achieve optimal health, you need to actively participate in health-enhancing behaviors.

Health and well-being is a growing area of psychology. Psychologists who study in this area want to understand the complex relationships between thoughts (health-related cognitions), actions, and physical and mental health. To understand those relationships, psychologists rely on the research methods of psychology. They study how behavior and social systems affect health. They study how ethnic and sex differences influence health outcomes. And they study how health-related behaviors and health outcomes affect actions, thoughts, and emotions.

BIOPSYCHOSOCIAL MODEL How can your personality, thoughts, or behavior affect your health? To answer this question, you need to understand the **biopsychosocial model** (**Figure 11.3**). This model is central to understanding the difference between the traditional medical model and the approach taken by health psychologists. Here, health and illness result from a combination of factors, including biological

FIGURE 11.2

The Longest-Living People

The Japanese tend to live very long lives. Their longevity is no doubt due to a combination of genetics and behavior. Pictured here are 99-year-old Matsu and 91-year-old Taido, both of Ogimi Village.

health psychology
A field that integrates research on health and on psychology; it involves the application of psychological principles to promoting health and well-being.

well-being
A positive state that includes striving for optimal health and life satisfaction.

biopsychosocial model
A model of health that integrates the effects of biological, behavioral, and social factors on health and illness.

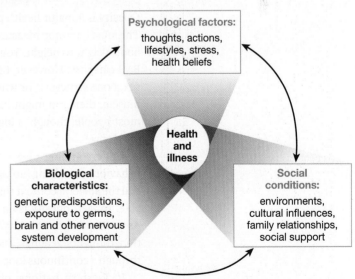

FIGURE 11.3

The Biopsychosocial Model

This model illustrates how health and illness result from a combination of biological, psychological, and social factors.

characteristics (for example, genetic predisposition), psychological factors (for example, behaviors, lifestyle, stress, health beliefs), and social conditions (for example, cultural influences, family relationships, social support).

As Figure 11.3 illustrates, your thoughts and actions affect the environments you find yourself in. Those environments affect the biological underpinnings of your thoughts and actions. The result is a kind of continuous loop.

Suppose you are an anxious person. You have particular ways of dealing with high-anxiety situations, such as before an exam, or when you are having relationship difficulties, or if you have financial worries. For example, in such situations, eating comfort foods such as mashed potatoes, macaroni and cheese, and ice cream calms you down. If you consume these foods in excess, you will probably gain weight and eventually become overweight. Extra weight can make even moderate exercise difficult, so you may decrease your physical activity. That decrease will slow down your metabolism. A slowed metabolism will cause you to gain more weight. Being overweight may make you even more anxious. And so the circle would continue.

This chapter explores how obesity, eating disorders, sexually transmitted infections, smoking, and stress affect health. Such effects always involve the interplay between biological, social, and psychological factors.

11.2 Obesity and Disordered Eating Have Many Health Consequences

11.2 LEARNING GOAL ACTIVITIES

To maximize your learning, complete the following learning goal activities.

a. Understand all bold and italic terms by writing explanations of them in your own words.

b. Analyze how overeating, anorexia, bulimia, and binge-eating disorder affect health by differentiating between these four types of disordered eating and the causes and health effects of each.

Obesity is a major health problem with physical and psychological consequences. The most common measure of obesity is **body mass index (BMI)**. BMI is the ratio of body weight to height. You can use the chart in Try It Yourself on p. 425 to see your BMI category. However, BMI is far from perfect. It does not take into account age, sex, bone structure, or where body fat is stored. If you are athletic or have a lot of muscle, then you might have a high BMI even though you are in great shape. For most people, though, a high BMI indicates excess weight that might cause health problems.

Understanding obesity requires a complex approach. You have to examine behavior, underlying biology, cognition (how people think about food and obesity), and the societal context that makes cheap, tasty, and high-calorie food readily available. In fact, obesity is an ideal example of the biopsychosocial model of health. As you read about obesity, keep in mind the linkages between genetic predisposition, thoughts, feelings, and behaviors. Also keep in mind that these variables cycle through a continuous loop.

In Western nations, obesity has increased dramatically in recent years. For example, obesity rates have increased significantly in the United States. Fewer than 15 percent of the U.S. population met the criteria for obesity in 1980, but more than 38 percent met the criteria in 2014 (Flegal, Kruszon-Moran, Carroll, Fryar, & Ogden, 2016). The numbers are even higher for racial and ethnic minorities. Nearly half of

body mass index (BMI)
A ratio of body weight to height, used to measure obesity.

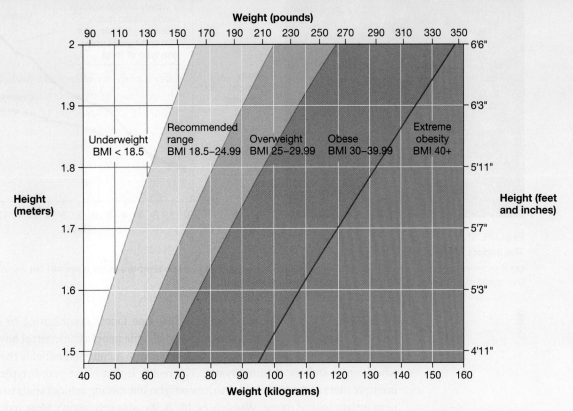

To see your body mass index (BMI) category, find the point at which your weight and height meet on the graph. If your BMI is above or below the optimal range (shown in yellow), then you are at greater risk for health problems.

African American women and Mexican American women are classified as obese. Likewise, the percentage of obese children has quadrupled since the 1960s (Ogden et al., 2016). Being overweight or obese in childhood strongly predicts weight and health problems throughout adulthood (Ward et al., 2017).

Extreme obesity is having a BMI over 40. This condition was almost unheard of in 1960, but it now characterizes nearly 1 in 12 Americans (Fryar, Carroll, & Ogden, 2016; **Figure 11.4**). The increase in extreme obesity is a concern because the health consequences of being overweight are most apparent when people have BMIs over 35 (Flegal, Kit, Orpana, & Graubard, 2013).

Obesity is not a problem just in the United States. According to the World Health Organization (WHO), obesity has doubled around the globe since 1980 (World Health Organization, 2016). Given the many health consequences associated with obesity, there has been great interest in understanding why people are gaining weight and what might be done to reverse this trend.

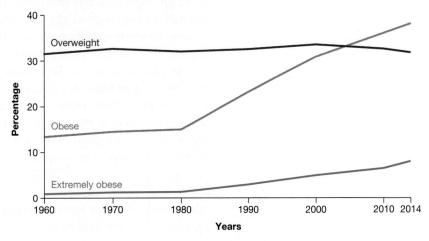

FIGURE 11.4

Changing Trends in Body Mass

This graph shows the trends in people characterized as overweight, obese, and extremely obese among adults over age 20 in the United States, 1960–2014.

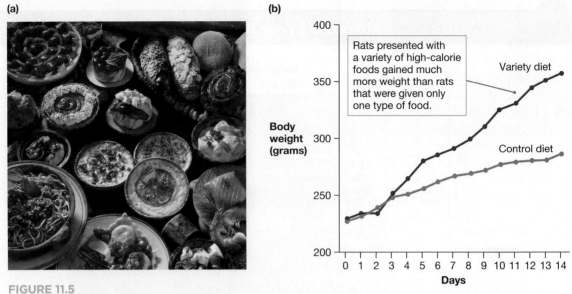

FIGURE 11.5
The Impact of Variety on Eating Behavior
(a) If you were presented with this table full of delicious foods, would you be tempted to try them all? **(b)** As shown in this graph, rats gain more weight when given variety in their diet.

OVEREATING It may seem obvious that one factor contributing to obesity is overeating. But scientists do not know why some people can control how much they eat and others struggle with eating behaviors. A common belief is that those who overeat are lazy or unmotivated. The reality is that obese people typically try multiple diets and other "cures" to lose weight, but dieting seldom leads to permanent weight loss (Aronne, Wadden, Isoldi, & Woodworth, 2009). Most individuals who lose weight through dieting eventually regain the weight. Often, these individuals gain back more than they lost.

Think of a buffet table at a party, or perhaps at a hotel you've visited. You see platter after platter of different foods. You don't eat many of these foods at home, and you want to try them all (**Figure 11.5a**). But trying them all might mean eating more than your usual meal size. The availability of different types of food is one factor in gaining weight. Scientists have seen this behavior in studies with rats. Rats that normally maintain a steady body weight when eating one type of food eat huge amounts and become obese when they are presented with a variety of high-calorie foods, such as chocolate bars, crackers, and potato chips (Sclafani & Springer, 1976; **Figure 11.5b**). The same is true of humans. We eat much more when a variety of good-tasting foods are available than when only one or two types of food are available (Epstein, Robinson, Roemmich, Marusewski, & Roba, 2010). We also eat more when portions are larger (Rolls, Roe, & Meengs, 2007). In addition, overweight people show more activity in reward regions of the brain when they look at good-tasting foods than do individuals who are at an optimal weight (Rapuano et al., 2017). Together, these findings suggest that, in industrialized nations, the increase in obesity over the past few decades is partly explained by three factors: the availability of a variety of high-calorie foods, the large portions served in many restaurants, and individual differences in response to food cues.

SOCIAL AND GENETIC INFLUENCES Body weight may be socially contagious. One study found that close friends of the same sex tend to be similar in body weight (Christakis & Fowler, 2007). This study also found that even when close friends live far apart from each other, if one friend is obese, the other one is likely to be obese as well. Studies of the social transmission of obesity suggest that the critical factor is not eating the same meals or cooking together. Instead, what matters is the unstated agreement on acceptable body weight (**Figure 11.6**). If many of your close friends are obese, you learn that obesity is normal. Subtle communications of this kind might affect how you think and act when you eat.

A trip to the local mall, a tourist attraction, or any place that families gather reveals one obvious fact about body weight: Obesity tends to run in families. Various family and adoption studies indicate that approximately half the variability in body weight can be considered to be the result of genetics (Klump & Culbert, 2007). One of the best and largest studies, carried out in Denmark during the 1980s, found that the BMI of adopted children was strongly related to the BMI of their biological parents and not at all to the BMI of their adoptive parents (Sorensen, Holst, Stunkard, & Skovgaard, 1992). Studies of twins provide even stronger evidence of the genetic control of body weight. Identical twins tend to have similar body weights whether they are raised together or raised apart (Bouchard & Pérusse, 1993; Wardle, Carnell, Haworth, & Plomin, 2008).

If genes primarily determine body weight, why has the percentage of Americans who are obese doubled over the past few decades? Genetics determines whether a person *can* become obese, but environment determines whether that person *will* become obese (Stunkard, 1996). In an important study, identical adult twins were overfed by approximately 1,000 calories a day for 100 days (Bouchard, Tremblay, et al., 1990). Most of the twins gained some weight, but there was great variability among pairs in how much they gained (ranging from 4.3 kilograms to 13.3 kilograms, or 9.5 pounds to 29.3 pounds). Further, within each pair, there was striking similarity in how much weight the two twins gained and in which parts of the body they stored the fat. Thus genes predispose some people to obesity in environments that promote overfeeding, such as contemporary industrialized societies.

THE STIGMA OF OBESITY   Think back to the fat shaming experienced by Gabourey Sidibe and Carrie Fisher, which you read about at the beginning of this chapter. Such criticism illustrates the stigma, or social negativity, associated with being overweight. In most Western cultures, obese individuals are viewed as less attractive, less socially adept, less intelligent, and less productive than their normal-weight peers (Dejong & Kleck, 1986).

Not surprisingly, obesity can give rise to various psychological problems. Perceiving yourself as overweight is linked to depression, anxiety, and low self-esteem (Stice, 2002). Bear in mind, however, that human obesity research is correlational. We cannot say that one factor causes the other. Maybe people with low self-esteem are more likely to put on weight.

Not all cultures stigmatize obesity. In some developing countries, being obese is a sign of being a member of the upper class. Obesity may be desirable in developing countries because it helps prevent some infectious diseases and reduces the likelihood of starvation. It may also serve as a status symbol, indicating that a person can afford to eat luxuriously. In Pacific Island countries such as Tonga and Fiji, being obese is a source of personal pride, and dieting is uncommon. In 2013, more than

FIGURE 11.6
Body Weight Is Socially Contagious
Friends tend to influence one another's sense of what body weight is appropriate. Thus friends often have similar body types.

half of men and nearly two-thirds of women living in Tonga were obese (Ng et al., 2014; **Figure 11.7a**).

In most industrialized cultures, food is generally abundant. Because citizens of those countries are thus able to take food for granted, being overweight is not associated with upper-class status. Instead, it is associated with lower socioeconomic status. Indeed, in the United States fresh and nutritious food is often more expensive than high-calorie fast food. The relative affordability of fast food may contribute to people becoming overweight if they have limited finances.

The upper classes in Western cultures have a clear preference for very thin body types. For example, think about the fashion industry (**Figure 11.7b**). The typical female fashion model is 5 feet 11 inches tall and weighs approximately 110 pounds. In other words, the standard represented by models is 7 inches taller and 55 pounds lighter than the average woman in the United States. As you can see in Try It Yourself on p. 425, this standard places the average model in the underweight range in BMI. Such extreme thinness represents a body weight that is nearly impossible for most people to achieve. Nevertheless, women report holding body weight ideals that are not only lower than average weight but also lower than what men find attractive (Fallon & Rozin, 1985).

RESTRICTIVE DIETING   In contemporary Western societies, we are constantly bombarded with advertising for the latest weight-loss systems, miracle diets, and food plans that "guarantee" the shedding of pounds. Indeed, about half of American adults report dieting to try to lose weight within the previous 12 months (Martin, Herrick, Sarafrazi, & Ogden, 2018). But as noted earlier, dieting is not a very effective way to lose weight permanently.

Most diets fail primarily because of the body's natural defense against weight loss (Kaplan, 2007). Body weight is regulated around a set point determined mainly by genetic influence. Consider two examples. In 1966, several inmates at a Vermont prison for men were challenged to increase their body weight by 25 percent (Sims et al., 1968). For six months, these inmates consumed more than 7,000 calories a day, nearly double their usual intake. If each inmate was eating about 3,500 extra calories a day (the equivalent of seven large cheeseburgers), simple math suggests that he should have gained approximately 170 pounds over the six months. In reality, few inmates gained more than 40 pounds. Most lost the weight when they went back to normal eating. Those who did not lose the weight had family histories of obesity.

At the other end of the spectrum, researchers investigated the short-term and long-term effects of semistarvation (Keys, Brozek, Henschel, Mickelsen, & Taylor, 1950). During World War II, more than 100 men volunteered to take part in this study as an alternative to military service. Over six months of being forced to reduce their food intake, the participants lost an average of 25 percent of their body weight. Most found this weight reduction very hard to accomplish. Some had great difficulty losing more than 10 pounds. The men underwent dramatic changes in emotions, motivation, and attitudes toward food. They became anxious, depressed, and listless. They lost interest in sex and other activities. They became obsessed with eating. Many of these outcomes are similar to those experienced by people with eating disorders.

Maybe you or someone you know has tried to diet to reduce weight, only to regain the weight and perhaps gain more. Unfortunately, dieting can be a vicious cycle (**Figure 11.8**). Although it is possible to alter body weight, the body responds to weight loss by slowing down metabolism and using less energy.

(a)

(b)

FIGURE 11.7

Variations in Body Image

(a) In some places, people find larger body shapes more desirable. Consider these welcoming women on the island of Fatu Hiva, in French Polynesia. **(b)** By contrast, consider the thinness shown by these models in the United States.

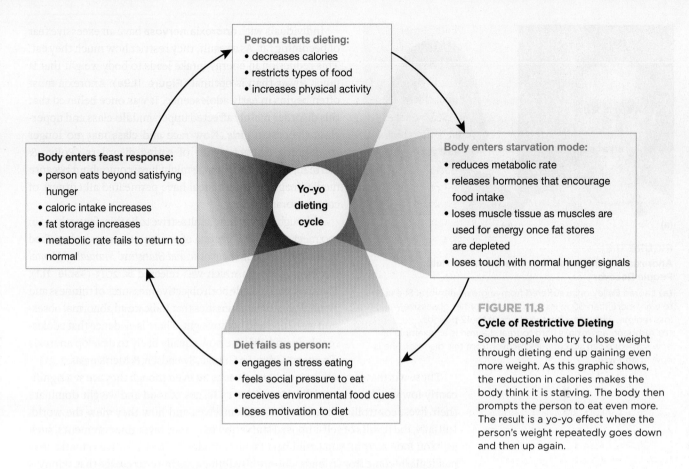

Person starts dieting:
- decreases calories
- restricts types of food
- increases physical activity

Body enters feast response:
- person eats beyond satisfying hunger
- caloric intake increases
- fat storage increases
- metabolic rate fails to return to normal

Yo-yo dieting cycle

Body enters starvation mode:
- reduces metabolic rate
- releases hormones that encourage food intake
- loses muscle tissue as muscles are used for energy once fat stores are depleted
- loses touch with normal hunger signals

Diet fails as person:
- engages in stress eating
- feels social pressure to eat
- receives environmental food cues
- loses motivation to diet

FIGURE 11.8
Cycle of Restrictive Dieting
Some people who try to lose weight through dieting end up gaining even more weight. As this graphic shows, the reduction in calories makes the body think it is starving. The body then prompts the person to eat even more. The result is a yo-yo effect where the person's weight repeatedly goes down and then up again.

Therefore, after the body has been deprived of food, it needs less food to maintain a given body weight. Likewise, weight gain occurs much faster after weight loss (Brownell, Greenwood, Stellar, & Shrager, 1986). This pattern might explain why "yo-yo dieters" tend to become heavier over time. To avoid this pattern, try to reduce calories slowly over time and keep your eating at a level that is maintainable over a long period of time to prevent bingeing on food.

For weight-loss programs to be successful, people need to make permanent lifestyle changes. These changes include altering eating habits, increasing exercise, dealing with temptations to eat, and enlisting family members to help. People who are not obese but want to shed extra pounds can join support groups to help them exercise more and eat better. Physical exercise helps control appetite, increase metabolism, and burn calories. For these reasons, exercise is an essential element of any weight control program.

DISORDERED EATING When dieters fail to lose weight, they often blame their lack of willpower. They may vow to redouble their efforts on the next diet. Repeatedly failing may have harmful and permanent physiological and psychological consequences. In physiological terms, weight-loss and weight-gain cycles alter the dieter's metabolism and may make future weight loss more difficult. Psychologically, repeated failures diminish satisfaction with body image and damage self-esteem. Over time, chronic dieters tend to feel helpless and depressed. Some eventually engage in more extreme behaviors to lose weight, such as taking drugs, fasting, exercising excessively, or purging (Heatherton & Polivy, 1992).

For a vulnerable individual, chronic dieting may promote the development of a clinical eating disorder. The three most common eating disorders are anorexia nervosa, bulimia nervosa, and binge-eating disorder (Wiseman, Harris, & Halmi, 1998).

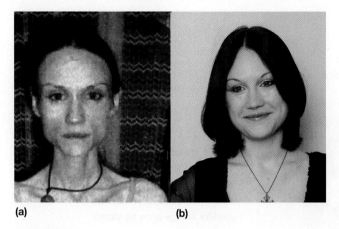

(a)   **(b)**

FIGURE 11.9

Anorexia Can Be Deadly, but Treatment Can Help People Recover

(a) Lauren Bailey once suffered from anorexia nervosa. She used to walk more than 30 miles a day as part of her obsessive weight loss regime, which saw her weight drop to 42 pounds.
(b) Although anorexia is hard to treat, Lauren is an example of how someone can successfully recover from this disorder. She is now fit and well.

Individuals with **anorexia nervosa** have an excessive fear of becoming fat. As a result, they restrict how much they eat. This reduction in energy intake leads to body weight that is much lower than is optimal (**Figure 11.9a**). Anorexia most often begins in early adolescence. It was once believed that this disorder mainly affected upper-middle-class and upper-class Caucasian girls. Now race and class may no longer be defining characteristics of eating disorders (Polivy & Herman, 2002). This change might have come about because media images of a thin ideal have permeated all corners of contemporary society.

Although many young adults strive to be thin, fewer than 1 in 100 meet the clinical criteria of anorexia nervosa as described by the most recent *Diagnostic and Statistical Manual of Mental Disorders (DSM-5)*, which was released in 2013 (**Table 11.1**). These criteria include both objective measures of thinness and psychological characteristics that indicate an abnormal obsession with food and body weight. There is evidence that adolescent boys and girls are now equally likely to develop anorexia (Swanson, Crow, Le Grange, Swendsen, & Merikangas, 2011).

Those who have anorexia view themselves as fat even though they are at a significantly low weight, often with BMIs under 17. Issues of food and weight dominate their lives, controlling how they view themselves and how they view the world. Initially, the results of self-imposed starvation may draw favorable comments, such as "You look so thin, you could be a fashion model!" These positive remarks may particularly come from friends who are also influenced by the message that skinny is beautiful. But as people with anorexia lose more and more weight, family and friends usually become concerned. People with anorexia not only starve themselves, but often engage in activities such as vomiting, abuse of laxatives, or excessive exercise

TABLE 11.1

Diagnosing Eating Disorders

DSM-5 Disorder	Criteria
Anorexia nervosa	Food restriction that leads to a body weight significantly below what is expected for age, sex, and health; exaggerated fear of weight gain or of becoming overweight; dissatisfaction with body shape or weight; believing oneself to be much heavier than in reality; denial of seriousness of the disorder.
Bulimia nervosa	Regularly and repeatedly eating within a short period of time (for example, two hours) an amount of food much greater than people would normally eat (that is, binge eating); a feeling that eating is out of control; offset the calories from binge eating by vomiting, extreme exercise, misusing laxatives or other medications; feelings about oneself overly influenced by body weight and shape.
Binge-eating disorder	Regularly and repeatedly eating within a short period of time (for example, two hours) an amount of food much greater than people would normally eat (that is, binge eating); a feeling that eating is out of control; binge eating episode typically involves eating alone because of embarrassment, consuming food very rapidly, continuing to eat beyond when one feels full, and feeling guilty, depressed, or disgusted about overeating; overall dissatisfaction with eating behavior.

Adapted from American Psychiatric Association (2013).

to further reduce the impact of food energy that is consumed. In many cases, medical attention is required.

Anorexia is difficult to treat (**Figure 11.9b**). Those with this dangerous disorder cling to the belief that they are overweight or not as thin as they would like to be, even when they are severely emaciated. Anorexia causes a number of serious health problems, in particular a loss of bone density and heart disease. About 15 percent to 20 percent of those with anorexia eventually die from the disorder—they literally starve themselves to death (American Psychiatric Association, 2000).

Individuals with **bulimia nervosa** alternate between dieting and binge eating. Bulimia often develops during late adolescence. Approximately 1 to 2 percent of women in high school and college meet the criteria for bulimia nervosa (see Table 11.1). These women tend to be of average weight or slightly overweight. Bulimia is much more common in females than in males (Klump, Culbert, & Sisk, 2017).

Those with bulimia regularly binge eat, feel their eating is out of control, worry excessively about body weight issues, and engage in one or more compensatory behaviors, such as self-induced vomiting, excessive exercise, or the abuse of laxatives. For both women and men, bulimia is more common than anorexia nervosa. However, most people with bulimia are women.

Whereas those with anorexia nervosa cannot easily hide their self-starvation, binge eating tends to occur secretly. When ordering large quantities of food, those with bulimia nervosa pretend they are ordering for a group. They often hide the massive quantities of food they buy for binges. They try to vomit quietly or seek out little-used bathrooms to avoid being heard while they vomit. Although bulimia is associated with serious health problems, such as dental and cardiac disorders, it is seldom fatal (Keel & Mitchell, 1997).

A disorder similar to bulimia is **binge-eating disorder**. The American Psychiatric Association officially recognized binge eating as a disorder in 2013. People with this disorder engage in binge eating at least once a week, but they do not purge (see Table 11.1). These individuals often eat very quickly, even when they are not hungry. Those with binge-eating disorder often experience feelings of guilt and embarrassment, and they may binge eat alone to hide the behavior. Many people with binge-eating disorder are obese. Compared with bulimia, binge-eating disorder is more common among males and ethnic minorities (Wilfley, Bishop, Wilson, & Agras, 2007).

anorexia nervosa
An eating disorder characterized by excessive fear of becoming fat and therefore restricting energy intake to obtain a significantly low body weight.

bulimia nervosa
An eating disorder characterized by dieting, binge eating, and purging.

binge-eating disorder
An eating disorder characterized by binge eating that causes significant distress.

11.3 Exercise Benefits You Physically, Cognitively, and Emotionally

11.3 LEARNING GOAL ACTIVITIES

To maximize your learning, complete the following learning goal activities.

a. Understand all bold and italic terms by writing explanations of them in your own words.

b. Apply the positive effects of exercise to your life by describing one physical, one cognitive, and one emotional effect of getting more exercise.

Are you more of a couch potato or a gym rat? Perhaps your idea of exercise is running after your children, spending an afternoon gardening, or playing a game of pickup basketball. By contrast to most societies in human history, modern Western society encourages people to use little physical energy. They drive to work; take elevators; spend hours watching remote-controlled television; spend even more hours online; use various labor-saving devices, such as dishwashers; and then complain about not having time to exercise. Once people are out of shape, it is difficult for them to start exercising regularly. But in general, the more people exercise, the better their health. In fact, exercise can improve physical, cognitive, and emotional health.

EXERCISE IMPROVES YOUR PHYSICAL HEALTH   The physical benefits of exercise are well-known. People who exercise are at much lower risk for most types of cancer (Moore et al., 2016), and they are less likely to have heart problems (Arem et al., 2015). One type of exercise, aerobics, is especially good for temporarily increasing heart rate and breathing. Because of this effect, aerobic exercise helps improve cardiovascular health. That is, it lowers blood pressure and strengthens the heart and lungs (Lavie et al., 2015). Even weekend warriors who exercise only once or twice a week show reductions in heart disease and cancer (O'Donovan, Lee, Hamer, & Stamatakis, 2017). And people with better fitness in middle age are likely to live much longer (Ladenvall et al., 2016).

EXERCISE AIDS YOUR THINKING ABILITIES   In addition, exercise can help improve cognition, including memory (Harburger, Nzerem, & Frick, 2007; **Figure 11.10**). These benefits may occur because exercise enhances brain functioning. One study explored the benefits of exercise on cognition in sedentary adults between the ages of 60 and 79 (Colcombe et al., 2006). These participants were randomly assigned to either six months of aerobic training (such as running or fast dancing) or six months of a control group. Those who received aerobic training increased their brain volume, including both white (myelinated) matter and gray matter. The control group experienced no comparable changes. Another study focused on the impact of exercise in older adults with moderate memory problems (Lautenschlager et al., 2008). These participants were randomly assigned to an exercise group (three hours a week for two weeks) or to a control group. The exercise group improved in their overall cognition, including memory. The control group showed no changes. The researchers concluded that exercise reduces cognitive decline in older adults with moderate memory problems.

EXERCISE BENEFITS YOUR EMOTIONS AND MOOD   In addition to improving physical health and thinking, exercise also benefits emotion and mood. It can make you feel good because you know it is good for you. It can help you build self-confidence and cope with stress. It affects neurotransmitter systems involved in reward, motivation, and emotion. In fact, as little as 10 minutes of exercise can promote feelings of vigor and enhance mood, although at least 30 minutes of daily exercise is associated with the most positive mental state (Hansen, Stevens, & Coast, 2001). Exercise may contribute to positive outcomes for the treatment of depression (Schuch et al., 2016). It may also help in the treatment of addiction and alcoholism (Read & Brown, 2003). (The use and abuse of alcohol is discussed in study unit 3.12, and addiction is discussed in study unit 3.13. The treatment of psychological disorders, including depression, is the subject of Chapter 15.)

Fortunately, it is never too late to start exercising and receiving its positive benefits. If you are interested in using your understanding of psychology to help others become healthier through exercise, there are many career paths that you can explore, as described in Putting Psychology to Work on p. 461.

FIGURE 11.10
Exercise Improves Your Health
The scientific evidence shows that exercise improves your health physically, cognitively, and emotionally.

11.4 Sexually Transmitted Infections Can Be Prevented by Practicing Safer Sex

11.4 LEARNING GOAL ACTIVITIES

To maximize your learning, complete the following learning goal activities.

a. Understand all bold and italic terms by writing explanations of them in your own words.

b. Understand safer sex by describing three ways that a person can reduce the risk of getting sexually transmitted infections (STIs).

sexually transmitted infections (STIs) Infections that can be, but are not always, transmitted from one person to the next through sexual contact.

Eating is a huge part of life, so it makes sense that physical and psychological health depends on eating right. Similarly, for most people, having sexual relations is an important part of life. In study units 10.9–10.11, you learned about motivation to engage in sexual activity (or not to). This study unit discusses how risky sexual behavior can affect health by increasing the risk of contracting **sexually transmitted infections (STIs)**.

STIs AFFECT THE HEALTH OF MANY PEOPLE Each year in the United States, there are nearly 20 million new cases of STIs. That means that about 54,000 people each day in the United States are being diagnosed with an STI. About half of these new infections are in people ranging from 15 to 24 years old, even though this group represents just 25 percent of the sexually experienced population (Centers for Disease Control and Prevention, 2013b). These young males and young females contract STIs at about equal rates. What do these statistics mean for you? If you are between 15 and 24, approximately one in four people your age has an STI. That's a lot of people, potentially creating a lot of risk for further infection. So you need to know: How do people get exposed to STIs?

STIs are generally transmitted through sexual contact with a partner who carries the bacteria, virus, or parasite that causes the infection (see **Table 11.2**, on p. 434). This contact often includes vaginal intercourse, anal intercourse, and oral-genital contact. However, some STIs can be spread through other means. For example, certain STIs—including chlamydia, gonorrhea, genital herpes, syphilis, human papillomavirus (HPV), and human immunodeficiency virus (HIV)—can be passed from a pregnant mother to her baby either before birth or during birth. These mother-to-child infections can have devastating effects on the infant, ranging from blindness to death. In addition, HIV can be transmitted through sharing needles that were used by an infected person. Syphilis can be transmitted by touching the open sore of an infected person.

Herpes is a very misunderstood STI that can be transmitted through kissing or other skin-to-skin contact, such as sexual activity. As described in Has It Happened to You?, cold sores, also called fever blisters, are caused by the herpes virus. In the past, it was believed that only one form of the herpes virus led to genital herpes, while another form of herpes led to the cold sores seen in oral herpes. However, it is now known that both forms of the virus (HSV-1 and HSV-2) can produce the same symptoms. And both forms can be transmitted to another person on the lips, genitals, or another area on the skin. Because herpes is easily caught, and because many people do not understand its symptoms, children often contract oral herpes through contact with an infected parent (Xu et al., 2006). Adults can easily pass oral herpes to a partner through sexual activity, in

HAS IT HAPPENED TO YOU?

Cold Sores Are Symptoms of Herpes

Anyone who gets a cold sore has herpes. This is true even if the sore is invisible, because the virus lives in the skin. Since the virus can be passed from person to person, someone with herpes needs to be extremely considerate and careful when coming into contact with other people. Suppose you know you have herpes. What can you do to avoid transmitting the virus to someone else? Do not be embarrassed. Be honest with your doctor and, if you are sexually active, with your sex partner(s). Talk with your doctor about medicines that help reduce the likelihood of passing the virus to someone else. Once you feel the tingling sensation that comes before a cold sore or fever blister, avoid touching other people. Don't have sex during an outbreak. Above all, always use a barrier method of protection (discussed on pp. 435–36) when engaging in sexual activity. By following these simple rules, you can avoid passing this virus to others and still have a satisfying romantic life.

TABLE 11.2
Common Sexually Transmitted Infections

Disease (and Number of New Cases in U.S. Each Year)	Type of Infection	Symptoms	Treatment
Chlamydia (2,860,000)	Bacterial	90% of people show no symptoms. Symptoms include thin, clear discharge from vagina or penis; irritation during urination.	Easily cured with antibiotics
Gonorrhea (820,000)	Bacterial	Sometimes no symptoms. Painful urination; abnormal discharge from vagina or thick discharge (puslike) from the penis; swollen testicles	Two different antibiotics at the same time
Syphilis (55,400)	Bacterial	Painless, round sores around the genitals; skin rash and fever; large sores on other body parts	Long-acting antibiotic
Trichomoniasis (1,090,000)	Parasite	Most people do not have symptoms; itching, burning, or unusual discharge in the genitals; pain during sexual activity.	Easily cured with drug therapy; all sexual partners must be treated.
Human Papillomavirus (HPV) (14,100,000)	Viral	Usually no symptoms; itchy genital warts; throat warts; various cancers	Treat symptoms; vaccinations may provide protection.
Herpes (776,000)	Viral	Burning or itching at site of infection; painful blisters that break and then crust over; fever and flulike symptoms; body aches and swollen glands	No cure for the virus; infections can spread when blisters occur; antiviral drugs may relieve symptoms.
Human Immunodeficiency Virus (HIV) (41,400)	Viral (Retrovirus)	Often no initial symptoms; flulike symptoms; fatigue; weight loss; persistent headaches. Without treatment, HIV can progress to AIDS, where the person has a severely compromised immune system and is susceptible to numerous infections.	No cure for the virus; long-term treatment with multiple antiretroviral drugs controls HIV; without treatment, progression to AIDS is often fatal.

SOURCES: Satterwhite et al., 2013; Centers for Disease Control and Prevention, 2018a.

which case the partner then might contract genital herpes. Approximately 48 percent of people in the United States between the ages of 14 and 49 have HSV-1, and approximately 12 percent have HSV-2 (McQuillan, Kruszon-Moran, Flagg, & Paulose-Ram, 2018). While this STI can be managed with drugs, there is no cure for it.

While some STIs—such as chlamydia, gonorrhea, syphilis, and trichomoniasis—are treated fairly easily and may have no long-term negative impact, these same STIs also may have no symptoms, so they go undetected. The lack of treatment can have long-term impacts on health. For example, women with untreated chlamydia or gonorrhea can experience chronic pain from pelvic inflammatory disease (PID) and increased risk of infertility. In addition, in the twentieth century, an estimated 100 million deaths worldwide have been due to untreated syphilis infections (Chiappa & Fornish, 1976). Other STIs, including certain strains of HPV (the most common STI), are related to the development of cancer, including cancers of the cervix and vulva (the area outside the vagina) in women and oral/throat cancers. Finally, some STIs, such as HIV and herpes, can never be cured. Instead, the infected person must manage the symptoms of the infection throughout life. To reduce the likelihood of being infected, all of us must know the facts about STIs and practice safer sex.

PEOPLE CAN PRACTICE SAFER SEX IN THREE WAYS Even though you are aware of how STIs can damage your health, you may be thinking, "It won't happen to me" (Kusseling, Shapiro, Greenberg, & Wenger, 1996). However, over the course of their lives, 1 in every 2 people will get an STI (Satterwhite et al., 2013). In other words, there is a 50/50 chance that it will happen to you! The good news is that you can reduce the likelihood of contracting an STI by engaging in **safer sex.**

One aspect of safer sex practices pertains to your intimate relationships with others. For example, there is an association between the number of sexual partners a person has had and having an STI (Joffe et al., 1992). So when you abstain from sex or limit your sexual partners, you limit the risk of your exposure to STIs. Despite this fact, many people have multiple sexual partners (Eaton et al., 2012). Similarly, waiting to engage in sexual activities until you enter a mutually faithful, long-term, monogamous relationship also limits the likelihood of contracting an infection.

Because not all relationships are monogamous (Haupert et al., 2017), a second important aspect of safer sex includes getting information about your sexual health and the sexual health of your partner(s). For example, sexually active people should get STI testing regularly, and females should get annual pelvic exams and PAP tests. In addition, when beginning a sexual relationship, it is vital to have honest discussions with a partner about sexual experiences, injection drug use, history of STIs, and treatments. All of this information will help each partner avoid spreading or catching infection.

A third aspect of safer sex practices can be summarized with this well-known phrase: An ounce of prevention is worth a pound of cure. One aspect of prevention can occur before girls and boys are sexually active, when they receive vaccinations against HPV. Research is currently being done on the effectiveness of these vaccinations. One study in Australia showed that after a national HPV vaccination program began in 2007, cases of genital warts in teenage girls had nearly disappeared (Read et al., 2011). Another method of prevention is when sexually active people use barrier methods of protection. These are simple devices that may reduce the risk of many, but not all, STIs.

BARRIER METHODS OF PROTECTION AGAINST STIs Three barrier methods of protection can help protect against STIs: male condoms, female condoms, and dental dams. Male condoms (**Figure 11.11a**) are a very effective method of preventing infection with an STI. For example, more-consistent use of male condoms among commercial sex workers in Thailand was associated with a decrease in bacterial STIs over a four-year period, from over 400,000 reported cases to about 28,000 reported cases (World Health Organization, 2000). Similarly, male condoms have been shown to be about 80 percent effective in preventing the transmission of HIV (Weller & Davis-Beaty, 2002). Female condoms (**Figure 11.11b**) are just beginning to be developed and produced, so there is less research on their effectiveness against STIs.

Lastly, although many people consider oral sex to be safer sex, this is simply not the case! HPV that is transmitted through oral sex has been linked to a large increase in mouth cancer and throat cancer (Scudellari, 2013). In addition, one's risk of contracting oral HPV rises with the number of partners a person has (Gillison et al., 2012). Proper use of a condom when performing oral sex on a male and proper use of a dental dam (**Figure 11.11c**) while performing oral sex on a female are important to limit the possibility of these infections. However, a common reason for not using these important preventative measures is that people do not have them on hand when they start to engage in sexual activity. To avoid this situation, buy condoms, dental dams, or both, ahead of time and carry them with you. In addition, use of drugs and alcohol reduces the correct use of condoms and dental dams

safer sex
Sexual behaviors that decrease the likelihood of contracting a sexually transmitted infection.

(a)

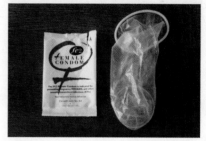
(b)

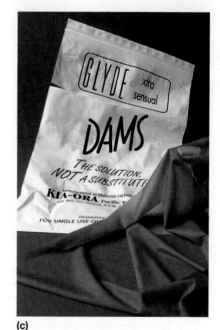
(c)

FIGURE 11.11
Barrier Methods Can Help Prevent STIs

During sexual activity, three barrier methods may be used to reduce the risk of contracting an STI: **(a)** male condoms, **(b)** female condoms, and **(c)** dental dams.

(George et al., 2009), so to best protect yourself, avoid drugs and alcohol if you might be sexually active. These safer sex practices will help safeguard your physical health and emotional well-being.

11.5 Smoking Is Dangerous to Your Health

11.5 LEARNING GOAL ACTIVITIES

To maximize your learning, complete the following learning goal activities.

a. Understand all bold and italic terms by writing explanations of them in your own words.

b. Understand the three main reasons why people may start to smoke and continue smoking by explaining each one.

Like obesity, eating disorders, and sexually transmitted infections, smoking has a large impact on health. Despite overwhelming evidence that smoking cigarettes leads to premature death, millions of people around the globe continue to light up (Fiore, Schroeder, & Baker, 2014). Increasing numbers of people in low-income countries are smoking (**Figure 11.12**). Thirty percent of all smokers worldwide are in China, 10 percent are in India, and an additional 25 percent come from Indonesia, Russia, the United States, Japan, Brazil, Bangladesh, Germany, and Turkey combined. The U.S. Surgeon General reports that in 2014, about 1 in 5 American adults was a current smoker (United States Department of Health and Human Services [USDHHS], 2014). Smoking is blamed for more than 480,000 deaths per year in the United States and decreases the typical smoker's life by more than 12 years (Jha et al., 2013). According to the World Health Organization (2008), tobacco causes 5.4 million deaths worldwide every year.

Smoking causes numerous health problems, including heart disease, respiratory ailments, and various cancers. Cigarette smoke also causes health problems for nonsmoking bystanders. As a result, smoking has been banned in many public and private places. Smokers also endure scoldings from physicians and loved ones concerned for their health and welfare. Besides spending money on cigarettes, smokers pay significantly more for life insurance and health insurance. Why do they continue to smoke? Why does anyone start?

STARTING SMOKING Most smokers begin in childhood or early adolescence. This early start concerns health care workers because of how nicotine may affect the developing brain. Every day, about 3,200 Americans ages 11 to 17 smoke their first cigarette (USDHHS, 2014). About half of young smokers will likely continue smoking into adulthood, and one-third of those will die from smoking (USDHHS, 2014). Fortunately, after an increase in the 1990s, adolescent smoking decreased significantly in the early 2000s (Johnston, O'Malley, Bachman, & Schulenberg, 2011; **Figure 11.13**). Regular

(a)

(b)

FIGURE 11.12

Smoking Is a Global Phenomenon

(a) These men are smoking in Tiananmen Square, in Beijing, China. **(b)** These smokers belong to the Mentawi people, a seminomadic hunter-gatherer tribe in the coastal and rain forest regions of Indonesia.

At the end of the 1990s, the percentage of adolescents who smoked leveled off and then began to decline.

FIGURE 11.13

Adolescents and Smoking

This graph shows the percentages of adolescents who smoked in the given years.

smoking dropped from approximately 13 percent to 7 percent of adolescents, and the number of adolescents who even try smoking dropped by 33 percent (Centers for Disease Control and Prevention, 2010; USDHHS, 2014).

It is hard to imagine any good reason to start smoking. First attempts at smoking often involve a great deal of coughing, watering eyes, a terrible taste in the mouth, and feelings of nausea. Yet, by the 12th grade, 50 percent to 70 percent of adolescents in the United States have had some experience with tobacco products (Centers for Disease Control and Prevention, 2010; Mowery, Brick, & Farrelly, 2000). Of course, it is hard to look tough while gasping and retching. So even though most adolescents try one or two cigarettes, most of them do not become regular smokers. Still, many of the adolescents who experiment with smoking do go on to smoke on a regular basis (Baker, Brandon, & Chassin, 2004).

So why do kids continue to smoke? Most researchers point to powerful social influences as the leading cause of adolescent smoking (Chassin, Presson, & Sherman, 1990). Adolescents are more likely to smoke if their parents or friends smoke (Hansen et al., 1987; **Figure 11.14**). They often smoke their first cigarettes in the company of other smokers, or at least with the encouragement of their peers. Though many adolescent smokers overestimate the number of adolescent and adult smokers (Sherman, Presson, Chassin, Corty, & Olshavsky, 1983), they may take it up to fit in with the crowd.

Other studies have pointed out that kids continue to smoke because "being a smoker" can have a powerful influence on young people. Adolescents might also be affected by media images of smokers. Television shows and movies often portray smokers in glamorous ways that appeal to adolescents (see Figure 6.25). Researchers in Germany found that among German children aged 10 to 16, the more they watched popular North American movies that depicted smoking, the more likely they were to try smoking (Hanewinkel & Sargent, 2008). Children take up smoking partially to look "tough, cool, and independent of authority" (Leventhal & Cleary, 1980, p. 384). Thus smoking may be one way for adolescents to enhance their self-image as well as their image with peers (Chassin et al., 1990).

However, the most important reason why kids and other people continue to smoke is that over time, casual smokers become addicted (review study unit 3.13 for the physical and psychological aspects of addiction). Nicotine is the active drug in tobacco, and this drug is widely acknowledged as the primary factor in motivating and maintaining smoking behavior (Fagerström & Schneider, 1989; USDHHS, 2004). Once the smoker becomes hooked on nicotine, going without cigarettes will lead to unpleasant withdrawal symptoms, including distress and heightened anxiety (Russell, 1990). Some people appear especially susceptible to nicotine addiction, perhaps because of genetics (Sabol et al., 1999). Nicotine leads to increased activation of dopamine neurons. This activation has a reinforcing effect and encourages further use.

ELECTRONIC CIGARETTES   People continue to smoke in order to obtain nicotine. Within the past few years, a new way to get nicotine has become increasingly popular: electronic cigarettes, or e-cigarettes. According to the 2014 U.S. Surgeon General's report (USDHHS, 2014), approximately 6 percent of U.S. adults have used e-cigarettes. Most e-cigarette use is by current smokers or those trying to quit.

A positive aspect of e-cigarettes is that they do not contain tobacco or the thousands of chemicals, many of them cancer causing, that are in regular

FIGURE 11.14
Social Influence on Smoking
Adolescents are strongly affected by social situations. They are more likely to smoke if their friends or parents smoke.

(a)

(b)

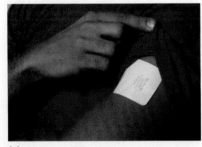

(c)

FIGURE 11.15

Nicotine Replacement Therapy

Three ways to quit smoking can include replacing the nicotine delivery system: **(a)** smoking e-cigarettes with lower doses of nicotine, **(b)** chewing nicotine gum, or **(c)** wearing the patch.

cigarettes. It is currently unclear if the vapor from e-cigarettes can be harmful to nonsmokers. Health officials do not know whether e-cigarettes are better or worse for individuals and society than traditional tobacco products (Fagerström, Etter, & Unger, 2015; Glynn, 2014). Scientific data are lacking regarding the levels of nicotine in and safety of e-cigarettes. Researchers also have not determined if, for smokers, e-cigarettes substitute for the look and feel of real cigarettes. Although some research suggests that e-cigarettes modestly help smokers quit (Bullen et al., 2013), other evidence indicates that e-cigarettes may hinder attempts to quit smoking (Al-Delaimy, Myers, Leas, Strong, & Hofstetter, 2015).

Between 2011 and 2014, there was a dramatic increase of e-cigarette use by U.S. high school students. More high school students now use e-cigarettes (13.4 percent) than any other tobacco product (Arrazola et al., 2015). Recent studies have found that adolescents and young adults who used e-cigarettes were much more likely to become regular smokers—nicotine addicts—than those who did not use e-cigarettes (Primack, Soneji, Stoolmiller, Fine, & Sargent, 2015; Wills et al., 2017).

QUITTING SMOKING   Many people who smoke worry about the health risks and want to quit. But how can people quit smoking cigarettes? Their best chances involve several actions at once. Prescription medications may play a part in efforts to quit. As you learned in study unit 2.3, agonists can mimic the effects of drugs by stimulating the receptors on neurons' dendrites. One method of quitting smoking is based on a drug, called Chantix, that acts as a partial agonist for nicotine receptors. Because the drug binds with nicotine receptors, it reduces cravings and provides some of the desirable effects of smoking without the need to smoke cigarettes. To assist with the withdrawal symptoms, smokers can also try using nicotine replacement, such as e-cigarettes with lower doses of nicotine, patches, or gum (**Figure 11.15**). As mentioned above, though, the data suggest that e-cigarettes are not very effective at helping people reduce smoking. By contrast, those people who are trying to quit can avoid places where other people smoke. In addition, they can substitute behaviors that are healthier than smoking, such as chewing sugar-free gum.

Around 90 percent of people who successfully quit do so on their own, going "cold turkey" (Smith & Chapman, 2014). Many smokers may need to "hit rock bottom" before realizing they have to change their behavior. The psychologist David Premack discusses a case study of a man who quit smoking because of something that happened as he was picking up his children at the city library:

> A thunderstorm greeted him as he arrived there; and at the same time a search of his pockets disclosed a familiar problem: he was out of cigarettes. Glancing back at the library, he caught a glimpse of his children stepping out in the rain, but he continued around the corner, certain that he could find a parking space, rush in, buy the cigarettes and be back before the children got seriously wet. (Premack, 1970)

For the smoker, it was a shocking vision of himself "as a father who would actually leave the kids in the rain while he ran after cigarettes." According to Premack, the man quit smoking on the spot. Not everyone can quit smoking by going "cold turkey." Because it is so difficult to quit, much of the current research on smoking examines ways to prevent people from smoking in the first place (USDHHS, 2014).

Q What Affects Your Health?

To make sure you learned what you just read, write answers to the following questions and check your answers.

11.1 What percentage of Americans are considered healthy based on having all four of the criteria of: being physically active, not smoking, eating a healthy diet, and maintaining the recommended body fat level?

11.2 How does anorexia nervosa differ from bulimia nervosa?

11.3 How often does a person have to exercise to see health benefits?

11.4 Are cold sores a symptom of an STI or not?

11.5 What is the main reason that smokers continue to smoke despite the health consequences?

See Appendix B for answers to the red Q questions.

How Does Stress Affect Your Health?

What is causing you stress right now? You might be experiencing stress because of schoolwork, family, your job, or a romantic relationship. Maybe several factors are involved.

You may think of stress as something objective, outside yourself. But the biological effects of stress result directly from the ways you think about events in your life and the way social factors influence you. For example, some students find final exams so stressful that they get sick at exam time. Other students may see exams simply as inconveniences or even challenges to be overcome. For these students, exams do not have negative health consequences. In short, stress is another perfect example of how the biopsychosocial model explains health. So when psychologists talk about stress, what do they mean?

11.6 Stress Has a Negative Impact on Your Health

11.6 LEARNING GOAL ACTIVITIES

To maximize your learning, complete the following learning goal activities.

a. Understand all bold and italic terms by writing explanations of them in your own words.

b. Apply the idea of stressors by naming the two types of stressors and giving an example of each type in your life.

Stress is the set of behavioral, mental, and physical processes that occur as an organism attempts to deal with an environmental event or stimulus that it perceives as threatening. As the Learning Tip on p. 440 summarizes, stress has three components. The event perceived as threatening is called a **stressor**. The stressor elicits one or more behavioral, mental, and/or physical **stress responses**. However, *mediating factors* can increase or decrease the likelihood that a stressor will elicit a stress response. Mediating factors may include personality and coping strategies.

stress
The set of behavioral, mental, and physical processes that occur as an organism attempts to deal with an environmental event or a stimulus that it perceives as threatening.

stressor
An environmental event or a stimulus that an organism perceives as threatening.

stress responses
Behavioral, mental, and/or physical responses to stressors.

LEARNING TIP: Stressors, Responses, and Mediating Factors

You can't see "stress." It is not a physical object. Instead, it is a set of processes within your body. You can understand these processes in terms of the three components of stress.

You can see stressors—events in your life that force you to make adjustments and lead to the process of stress. You also experience responses to stressors. Finally, the effects of stressors in eliciting responses can be increased or decreased by mediating factors, such as your personality and your coping strategies.

You have experienced the connections between these three factors many times. Maybe you were in a situation where a loved one became ill. You started to feel anxious about this person's health, but the support of your family helped get everyone through the tough time. Or the situation could have been as simple as losing your keys. Looking for your keys made you late for work, and you became angry.

Stressors	Mediating factors	Stress responses
Major life stressors Daily hassles	⟷ Personality Coping strategies ⟷	Physical Psychological Behavioral

major life stressors
Large disruptions, especially unpredictable and uncontrollable catastrophic events, that affect central areas of people's lives.

daily hassles
Everyday irritations that cause small disruptions, the effects of which can add up to a large impact on health.

FIGURE 11.16

Two Main Types of Stressors

(a) Hurricane Maria, in 2017, was the worst storm to hit Puerto Rico in over 80 years. The effects of the hurricane have been a major life stressor for millions of people on the island. Here, in the aftermath of the storm, a woman copes with the lack of electricity by cooking outside over a wood fire. **(b)** By contrast, waiting on a long line at the supermarket is an example of a daily hassle. If the impacts of daily hassles add up, these stressors can have as much effect on health as major life stressors.

TYPES OF STRESSORS Psychologists typically think of stressors as falling into two categories: **major life stressors** and **daily hassles**. Major life stressors are changes or disruptions that strain central areas of people's lives. Unpredictable and uncontrollable catastrophic events are especially stressful. In the fall of 2017, Hurricane Maria, a massive storm, became a major stressor that affected Puerto Rico's 3.4 million residents (**Figure 11.16a**). Months after the hurricane, people in Puerto Rico lacked reliable access to power, water, and basic services.

Major life stressors can be choices you make as well as things out of your control. For instance, you might decide to move somewhere new. Experiencing this major event is stressful even though you made the choice. We tend to think of major life stressors as negative events, but positive experiences may also be stressors. Consider the birth of a baby. Many parents call this event one of the most exhausting—but rewarding—experiences of their lives. Other positive stressors can include starting a new job, starting school, or getting married.

By contrast, daily hassles are stressors that are small, day-to-day irritations and annoyances. Examples include driving in heavy traffic, dealing with difficult people, or waiting in a long line (**Figure 11.16b**). The combined effects of constant daily

(a)

(b)

To determine the amount of stress in your life, select the events that have happened to you in the past 12 months.

Event	Life Change Units	Event	Life Change Units	Event	Life Change Units
Death of close family member	100	Change in financial status	39	Change in sleeping habits	29
Death of close friend	73	Change in major	39	Change in social activities	29
Divorce between parents	65	Trouble with parents	39	Change in eating habits	28
Jail term	63	New girlfriend or boyfriend	38	Chronic car trouble	26
Major personal injury or illness	63	Increased workload at school	37	Change in number of family get-togethers	26
Marriage	58	Outstanding personal achievement	36	Too many missed classes	25
Being fired from job	50	First term in college	35	Change of college	24
Failing important course	47	Change in living conditions	31	Dropping more than one class	23
Change in health of family member	45	Serious argument with instructor	30	Minor traffic violations	20
Pregnancy	45	Lower grades than expected	29		
Sex problems	44				
Serious argument with close friend	40				

Scoring

Next to each event is a score that indicates how much a person has to adjust as a result of the change. Both positive events (outstanding personal achievement) and negative events (major personal injury or illness) can be stressful because they require us to make adjustments. Add together the life change unit scores to determine how likely you are to experience illness or mental health problems as a result of the stress of these events.

300 life change units or more: A person has a high risk for a serious health change.
150–299 life change units: About 1 of every 2 people is likely to have a serious health change.
149 life change units or less: About 1 of every 3 people is likely to have a serious health change.

SOURCE: Adapted from Holmes & Rahe (1967).

hassles can be comparable to the effects of major life changes. By slowly wearing down personal resources, these hassles pose a threat to our coping abilities. People may get used to some hassles but not to others. For example, conflicts with other people or living in a crowded, noisy, or polluted place appear to add up to have negative effects on health and well-being. For some research studies, participants keep diaries of their daily activities. The researchers find consistently that the more intense and frequent the hassles, the poorer the physical and mental health of the participant.

To understand what stressors may be affecting you, add up your stress events using the scale in Try It Yourself above. In doing the activity, you will notice that some stressors cause more stress than others. These results are indicated by higher life-change unit scores for the more-stressful events. These events are more likely to elicit stress responses and require some sort of coping mechanisms. Notice also that some of the stressors are positive life events, such as getting married.

The next two study units will build on your new understanding of stressors. You will learn how you are responding to stressors. You will also learn what coping tools you are, or should be, using.

11.7 You Can Have Several Responses to Stress

11.7 LEARNING GOAL ACTIVITIES

To maximize your learning, complete the following learning goal activities.

a. Understand all bold and italic terms by writing explanations of them in your own words.

b. Understand the general adaptation syndrome (GAS) by naming and describing each of the three phases of the GAS stress response in your own words.

c. Apply stress responses by providing an example of how you responded to a stressor in one of the five ways described in this study unit.

When you experience stressors, how do you react to them? Does your heart beat faster? Do you get upset? Perhaps you turn to friends for help? Or maybe you eat too much ice cream or drink too much alcohol? Let's explore five main stress responses now. As you read about them, consider which stress responses you tend to experience.

GENERAL ADAPTATION SYNDROME IS A PHYSICAL STRESS RESPONSE
In the early 1930s, the endocrinologist Hans Selye (1936) found that different stressors produced roughly the same pattern of physiological responses. These changes include enlarged adrenal glands. They also include damage to part of the **immune system,** resulting in decreased levels of white blood cells in the blood. Selye concluded that the enlarged adrenal glands and immune system damage reduce the organism's potential ability to resist additional stressors. These effects represent a nonspecific physical stress response, which Selye called the **general adaptation syndrome (GAS).** The general adaptation syndrome consists of three stages: alarm, resistance, and exhaustion (**Figure 11.17**).

immune system
The body's mechanism for dealing with invading microorganisms, such as allergens, bacteria, and viruses.

general adaptation syndrome (GAS)
A consistent pattern of physical responses to stress that consists of three stages: alarm, resistance, and exhaustion.

FIGURE 11.17
The General Adaptation Syndrome
Selye described three stages of physical response to stress. As shown here, the body may progress from alarm to resistance to exhaustion. At each stage, the ability of the body to resist more stressors is influenced. Ultimately, in the exhaustion stage, the person will be more likely to experience adverse health effects.

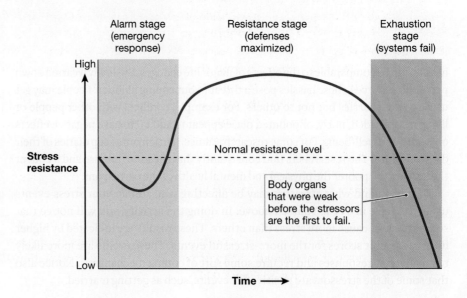

Alarm stage (emergency response) · Resistance stage (defenses maximized) · Exhaustion stage (systems fail)

High

Stress resistance — Normal resistance level

Body organs that were weak before the stressors are the first to fail.

Low

Time →

Think about a time when you were frightened. Suppose you heard a strange noise while walking alone late at night. Your heart probably started to beat faster. Maybe your palms became sweaty. This physical response is what happens in the *alarm stage* of the general adaptation syndrome. As an emergency reaction, these effects prepare your body to respond physically. That is, immediate bodily responses are aimed at boosting your physical abilities to fight or run away. At this point, your resistance decreases, making you less able to cope with additional stressors. At the same time, action starts in the immune system, which will protect you if you are injured while fighting or running away.

By contrast, some stressors last much longer than a temporary frightening experience. For example, students and people with difficult jobs both experience a lot of stress in an effort to do well. These people might be described as experiencing the *resistance stage* of the general adaptation syndrome. Here, the body physically prepares for a longer, more sustained attack against a stressor. The immunity to infection and disease increases somewhat as the body maximizes its defenses. Unfortunately, the body's physical fight against stress is not sustainable.

After being exposed to a stressor for a long time, the body reaches the *exhaustion stage*. The body's ability to respond to stress begins to decline. Various physiological systems, such as the immune system, begin to fail. Most of us have experienced this stage in a small way: We get sick immediately after a longer period of stress, such as when studying for exams or preparing important work at our jobs. But the effects of the exhaustion stage can also have a much more severe impact. Bodily systems that were already weak before the stress become more likely to fail. This effect is one reason that people with high levels of chronic stress in their lives are more susceptible to some serious diseases.

IMMUNE RESPONSE One of Selye's central points was that stress alters the functions of the immune system. Normally, when foreign substances such as viruses, bacteria, or allergens enter the body, the immune system launches into action to destroy the invaders. Stress interferes with this natural process. More than 300 studies have demonstrated that short-term stress boosts the immune system— such as occurs during the end of the fight-or-flight response—whereas chronic stress weakens it, leaving the body less able to deal with infection (Segerstrom & Miller, 2004).

The effects of long-term stress make the body less capable of warding off foreign substances. In a clear demonstration that stress affects the immune system, shown in The Methods of Psychology on p. 444, Sheldon Cohen and colleagues (1991) paid healthy volunteers to have cold viruses swabbed into their noses. Those who reported the highest levels of stress before being exposed to the viruses developed worse cold symptoms and higher viral counts than those who reported being less stressed.

Apparently, when we experience high stress levels for a long time, the function of the immune system is impaired, and the probability and severity of poor health increase (Herbert & Cohen, 1993; McEwen, 2008). People who have very stressful jobs—such as air traffic controllers, combat soldiers, and firefighters—tend to have many health problems that presumably are due partly to the effects of high levels of chronic stress. Indeed, as you will see in the next study unit, stress is associated with health problems that include increased blood pressure, cardiac disease, diabetes, and declining sexual interest.

FIGHT-OR-FLIGHT RESPONSE The behavioral and bodily responses to stress help prepare a person or animal for dealing with potential danger. This preparation is called a **fight-or-flight response (Figure 11.18)**.

fight-or-flight response
The physiological preparedness of animals to deal with danger.

FIGURE 11.18

Fight-or-Flight Response

Fight-or-flight is a physical response to stressors, which occurs during the alarm stage of the general adaptation syndrome. It prepares a person's body to fight or run away. Here, the man on the left appears to be experiencing a tendency to fight, not flee. If he strikes, the man on the right will need to respond, either by fighting or fleeing.

THE METHODS OF PSYCHOLOGY: Stress and the Immune System

Hypothesis: Stress affects the immune system.

Research Method: Researchers swabbed the noses of healthy volunteers with cold viruses.

Results: Participants who reported a higher level of stress before being exposed to the cold virus developed worse cold symptoms.

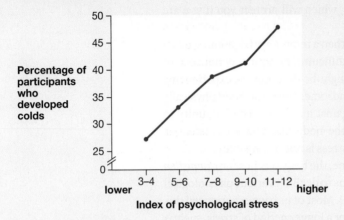

Conclusion: The functioning of the immune system can be impaired by high levels of stress.

QUESTION: According to the results of this research, would students tend to be more susceptible to colds during spring break or final exams?

ANSWER: Students are more likely to colds during final exams, because final exams tend to be more stressful than spring break.

Source: Cohen, S., Tyrrell, D. A. J., & Smith, A. P. (1991). Psychological stress and susceptibility to the common cold. *New England Journal of Medicine, 325*, 606–612.

Within seconds or minutes, the fight-or-flight response lets the organism direct its energy to dealing with the threat. In other words, immediate physiological responses are aimed at boosting physical abilities while reducing activities that make the organism vulnerable. Recall from study unit 2.9 that the physical reaction by the sympathetic nervous system includes increased heart rate, redistribution of the blood supply from skin and digestive organs to muscles and brain, deepening of respiration, and dilation of the pupils. At the same time, the body postpones less critical processes—such as food digestion—that can occur after the stressor is removed. In the fight-or-flight response, the body is also most likely to be exposed to infection and disease. For example, the body might be injured in an attack. So the immune system kicks in, and the body begins fighting back.

The ability to respond immediately and effectively to stressors is important to survival and reproduction. Thus this stress response was adaptive for our ancestors because it gave them the energy they needed to either outrun a predator or stand their ground and fight it.

TEND-AND-BEFRIEND RESPONSE The generalizability of the fight-or-flight response has been questioned by Shelley Taylor and colleagues (Taylor, 2006; Taylor et al., 2002). They note that in the past, stress research has been conducted primarily with male participants—fewer than 1 in 5 of the participants were female. The result is a sex inequality in laboratory stress studies that can blind us to the

tend-and-befriend response
Females' tendency to respond to stressors by protecting and caring for their offspring and forming social alliances.

fact that men and women often respond differently to stressors. Indeed, Taylor's research has revealed that females generally respond by protecting and caring for their offspring as well as by forming alliances with social groups to reduce risks to individuals, including themselves (Taylor, 2006; Taylor et al., 2002). Taylor and colleagues coined the phrase **tend-and-befriend response** to describe this pattern (**Figure 11.19**). Laboratory research supports the idea that stressed women are more attentive to the distress of an infant than stressed men are (Probst et al., 2017).

Tend-and-befriend responses make sense from an evolutionary perspective. After all, females typically bear a greater responsibility for the care of offspring. Responses that protect their offspring as well as themselves would be most adaptive. When a threat appears, hiding or quieting the offspring may be a more effective means of avoiding harm than trying to flee while pregnant or with a clinging infant. Furthermore, affiliating with others might provide additional protection and support.

NEGATIVE STRESS RESPONSES   Some people who feel stress head to the gym for a workout. Unfortunately, many of us have less positive responses to stress. Indeed, many problem drinkers explain that they abuse alcohol as a response to stress in their lives. When people are stressed, they also eat junk food, smoke cigarettes, use drugs, and so on (Baumeister, Heatherton, & Tice, 1994). In addition, some people are especially likely to respond to stress by overeating (Heatherton & Baumeister, 1991; see Has It Happened to You?). One study of more than 12,000 people from Minnesota found that high stress was associated with greater intake of fat, less frequent exercise, and heavier smoking (Ng & Jeffrey, 2003). As mentioned in study unit 11.1, such habits contribute to nearly every major cause of death in modern society.

 ## How Does Stress Affect Your Health?

To make sure you learned what you just read, write answers to the following questions and check your answers.

11.6 What is the difference between stress and stressors?

11.7 Explain how three specific stress responses can be associated with poor health.

See Appendix B for answers to the red Q questions.

How Do Mediating Factors Affect Your Stress?

Is the stress of modern life making people sick? Jobs, school, family, relationships, money, time, pressure to succeed, pressure to conform, and pressure to be different are mediating factors in how individuals deal with stress. Mediating factors can increase or decrease the chances that someone will become ill because of stress.

Consider heart disease. In this illness, blood vessels around the heart become narrow or are blocked by fatty plaque. When pieces of plaque break off from the wall of a blood vessel, blood clots form around the plaque and interrupt blood flow. If a clot blocks a blood vessel that feeds the heart, the blockage causes a heart attack. If a clot blocks a vessel that feeds the brain, the blockage causes a stroke. This stress-related condition is the leading cause of death for adults in the industrialized world. According to a World Health Organization (WHO) report in 2011, each year more

FIGURE 11.19
Tend-and-Befriend Stress Response
Tend-and-befriend occurs when, in response to stressors, females form social groups and care for offspring. Here, a group of women work together to guide schoolchildren at a museum.

HAS IT HAPPENED TO YOU?

Stress Eating

Have you ever found yourself eating a box of cookies, a bag of potato chips, or a pint of ice cream after something bad happened to you? If that's the case, then you have experienced *stress eating*. Stress eating is just what it sounds like: a response to stressors by eating, usually overeating junk foods.

Most people have experienced stress eating at one time or another. But eating as a consistent response to stress can lead to obesity and have other adverse effects on health. Instead of stress eating, try to find other ways to distract you from your stress. Consider taking a walk, reading a good book, or watching an engaging movie (Heatherton & Baumeister, 1991).

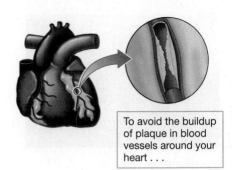

To avoid the buildup of plaque in blood vessels around your heart . . .

. . . don't smoke

. . . eat healthfully

. . . exercise.

FIGURE 11.20

Heart Disease

To decrease your risk of heart disease, follow these simple steps to reduce the impact of stressors.

type A behavior pattern
Personality traits characterized by competitiveness, achievement orientation, aggressiveness, hostility, restlessness, impatience with others, and an inability to relax.

type B behavior pattern
Personality traits characterized by being noncompetitive, relaxed, easygoing, and accommodating.

than 7 million people die from heart attacks (**Figure 11.20**). The rate of heart disease is lower in women than in men, but heart disease is the number one killer of both men and women.

Genetics is one of the many factors that influence heart disease. However, other critical factors are how you respond to stressors and how you cope with them. Do you respond with negative behaviors such as overeating and smoking, which are major risk factors for heart disease? Or do you respond by directing your energy into healthy behaviors? Your responses depend partly on your personality.

11.8 Personality Influences the Impact of Stress on Heart Disease

11.8 LEARNING GOAL ACTIVITIES

To maximize your learning, complete the following learning goal activities.

a. Understand all bold and italic terms by writing explanations of them in your own words.

b. Understand how personality affects stress by summarizing in your own words how different personality styles can increase or decrease the effects of stressors.

Stress and negative emotions increase the risk of heart disease in two ways (Albus, 2010; Sirois & Burg, 2003). First, as discussed in previous study units, people often cope with these states through behaviors that are bad for health, such as overeating, drinking excessively, or smoking. Second, over time, stress causes wear and tear on the heart, making the heart more likely to fail. Chronic stress leads to overstimulation of the sympathetic nervous system. That overstimulation causes higher blood pressure, constriction of blood vessels, changes in blood chemistry, and greater buildup of plaque on arteries. In turn, each of these conditions contributes to heart disease. For these reasons, people who tend to be stressed out are more likely to have heart disease than are people who tend to be laid back.

TYPE A AND B BEHAVIOR PATTERNS   The Western Collaborative Group conducted one of the earliest tests of the hypothesis that personality affects heart disease (Rosenman et al., 1964). In 1960, this group of physicians began an $8^1/_2$-year study. The participants were 3,500 men from northern California who were free of heart disease at the start of the study. The men were screened annually for established risk factors such as high blood pressure, accelerated heart rate, and high cholesterol. Their overall health practices were assessed. Personal details—such as education level, medical and family history, income, and personality traits—also were assessed.

The results indicated that a particular set of personality traits predicted heart disease. This set of traits is now known as the **type A behavior pattern**. Type A describes people who are competitive, achievement oriented, aggressive, impatient, and time-pressed (feeling hurried, restless, unable to relax; **Figure 11.21a**). Men who exhibited these traits were much more likely to develop heart disease than were those who exhibited the **type B behavior pattern**. Type B describes noncompetitive, relaxed, easygoing, accommodating people (**Figure 11.21b**). In fact, this study found that having a type A behavior pattern was as strong a predictor of heart disease as having high blood pressure, high cholesterol, or smoking (Rosenman et al., 1975). Although the initial work on heart disease was done only with men, recent research shows that personality matters for women as well (Knox, Weidner, Adelman, Stoney, & Ellison, 2004; Krantz & McCeney, 2002).

HOSTILE PERSONALITIES AND DEPRESSION   Research done over the 50 years since the original study has found that the original list of traits was too broad. Today we know that only certain components of the type A behavior pattern are related to heart disease for women and men. For example, researchers have found that the most toxic factor on the list is *hostility* (Williams, 1987). Hot-tempered people who are frequently angry, cynical, and combative are much more likely to die at an early age from heart disease (Eaker, Sullivan, Kelly-Hayes, D'Agostino, & Benjamin, 2004). Indeed, having a high level of hostility while in college predicts greater risk for heart disease later in life (Siegler et al., 2003). At the same time, there is considerable evidence that negative emotional states not viewed as part of a type A or B behavior pattern—especially depression—also predict heart disease (Carney & Freedland, 2017).

Of course, having a heart condition might *make* someone angry and depressed. Still, having a hostile personality and being depressed also predict the worsening of heart disease. Causes and effects might be connected in a vicious cycle. In contrast, optimistic people tend to be at lower risk for heart disease (Maruta, Colligan, Malinchoc, & Offord, 2002). How might a negative personality increase the risk of heart disease?

Think about a time when you were very angry. How did it feel? Your body likely responded by increasing your heart rate, shutting down digestion, moving more blood to your muscles—in short, preparing for fight or flight. Some people even turn red with anger or start to shake. People with hostile personalities frequently experience such physiological responses (**Figure 11.21c**). These responses take a toll on the heart. Chronic hostility can lead to the same physical symptoms as chronic stress, causing wear and tear on the heart and making it more likely to fail.

11.9 Coping Mediates the Impact of Stress

11.9 LEARNING GOAL ACTIVITIES

To maximize your learning, complete the following learning goal activities.

a. Understand all bold and italic terms by writing explanations of them in your own words.

b. Apply strategies for coping with stress by giving an example of how you use emotion-focused coping in one stressful situation and problem-focused coping in another.

Maybe it's an exam in a course you have to pass. Maybe you're starting a new job. Maybe the hurricane left you in the cold and dark for a week. As you deal with the stressors in your life, two ways of thinking let you manage stressors more objectively. Richard Lazarus (1993) described a two-part appraisal process: You use **primary appraisals** to decide whether stimuli are stressful, benign, or irrelevant. When you decide that stimuli are stressful, you use **secondary appraisals** to consider how to cope with the stressor. Such thoughts also affect your perceptions of potential stressors and your reactions to stressors in the future. In other words, making cognitive appraisals can help you cope with stressful events. They can also help you prepare for stressful events.

(a)

(b)

(c)

FIGURE 11.21

Personality Traits Predict Heart Disease

(a) People with type A behavior pattern are ambitious, aggressive, and impatient. They tend to respond more to stressors and are more likely to develop heart disease. **(b)** People with type B behavior pattern are noncompetitive, easygoing, and relaxed. They are less adversely affected by stressors and so are less likely to develop heart disease. **(c)** People with hostile personalities are hot-tempered, angry, and combative. They have strong physical responses to stressors and are especially likely to develop heart disease.

primary appraisals
Part of coping that involves making decisions about whether a stimulus is stressful or not.

secondary appraisals
Part of coping where people decide how to manage and respond to a stressful stimulus.

(a)

(b)

FIGURE 11.22
Emotion-Focused Coping and Problem-Focused Coping

(a) In emotion-focused coping, you avoid the stressor, minimize it, distance yourself, or try to escape by eating or drinking. **(b)** In problem-focused coping, you try to address the stressor by solving problems.

emotion-focused coping
A type of coping in which people try to prevent having an emotional response to a stressor.

problem-focused coping
A type of coping in which people take direct steps to confront or minimize a stressor.

TYPES OF COPING Susan Folkman and Richard Lazarus (1988) have grouped coping strategies into two general categories. In **emotion-focused coping**, you try to prevent an emotional response to the stressor. That is, you adopt strategies to numb the pain. Such strategies include avoidance, minimizing the problem, trying to distance yourself from the outcomes of the problem, or engaging in behaviors such as eating or drinking (**Figure 11.22a**). For example, if you are having difficulty at school, you might avoid the problem by skipping class, minimize the problem by telling yourself school is not all that important, distance yourself from the outcome by saying you can always get a job if college does not work out, or overeat and drink alcohol to dull the pain of the problem. These strategies do not solve the problem or prevent it from happening again in the future.

Problem-focused coping involves taking direct steps to solve the problem: generating alternative solutions, weighing their costs and benefits, and choosing between them (**Figure 11.22b**). For example, if you are having academic trouble, you might arrange for a tutor, minimize the distractions in your life, or ask for an extension on a paper you're struggling with. Given these alternatives, you could consider how likely a tutor is to be helpful, discuss the problem with your professors, and so on. People adopt problem-focused behaviors when they perceive stressors as controllable and are experiencing only moderate levels of stress. Conversely, emotion-focused behaviors may let people continue functioning in the face of uncontrollable stressors or high levels of stress.

The best way to cope with stress depends on personal resources and on the situation. Most people report using both emotion-focused coping and problem-focused coping. Emotion-based strategies are usually effective only in the short run. For example, if your partner is in a bad mood and is giving you a hard time, just ignoring the person until the mood passes can be the best option. In contrast, ignoring your partner's drinking problem will not make it go away, and eventually you will need a better coping strategy. Problem-focused coping strategies tend to work better in the long run. However, that is true only if the person can do something about the situation.

Besides problem-focused coping, two other strategies can help you use positive thoughts to deal with stress (Folkman & Moskowitz, 2000). When using this cognitive process, you focus on possible good things—the proverbial silver lining—in the current situation. One strategy is to compare yourself to those who are worse off. This *downward comparison* has been shown to help people cope with serious illnesses. For example, if you were diagnosed with diabetes, you could recognize that diabetes is not as serious as cancer. That is, your situation is not as bad as for those who have cancer (downward comparison). Another strategy is to give positive meaning to ordinary events. For example, you could take time to enjoy the positive moments in your life, such as eating a delicious meal or enjoying a sunset. Finding the positive in events can help distract us from feeling stressed. Using Psychology in Your Life, on p. 449, describes how the various coping mechanisms can help you reduce the effects of stress in an area that almost all students experience: exam anxiety.

INDIVIDUAL DIFFERENCES IN COPING Does spending time with your family during a major holiday make you feel anxious? Perhaps you're dreading all the food preparation or having to see your cranky uncle. Meanwhile, your friend may be looking forward to the holiday as a chance to spend relaxing time with his relatives. People differ widely in their perceptions of how stressful life events are.

Reducing Exam Anxiety

Almost everyone has felt nervous about an upcoming exam. But sometimes exam jitters can seem to get out of hand. You walk into the exam room and suddenly your heart is beating rapidly, your breathing rate increases, and your palms get sweaty. When you begin the exam, all the information you knew seems to fly from your brain and be totally inaccessible. Later on, after the exam, you may have wondered, "How could I have gotten so many questions wrong? I knew those answers!" This extremely common experience of stress is called exam anxiety.

Recalling the three components of stress can help you understand and cope with this experience. The stressor is the actual exam. The stress response is in part physical: Your sympathetic nervous system prepares you to "fight or flee" from the test, which causes the increase in heart rate, respiration, and perspiration. There are also emotional responses, including fear and anxiety, and cognitive responses, which prevent you from accessing information that you had stored in your brain. Fortunately, you can use four coping strategies to reduce the impact of the stressor and these responses.

1. **Change how you think about the exam.** You might find yourself thinking about the worst-case scenario: "I'll flunk the course, I'll never get a job, and everyone will think I'm stupid." But thinking repeatedly about this scenario will increase the impact of the stressor. Instead, use a technique called positive reappraisal. Rather than viewing the exam as scary, view it as a challenge that you can meet successfully.

2. **Get plenty of sleep the night before the exam.** Avoid unhealthy behaviors, such as drinking alcohol. Many of the behaviors that stressed-out college students may engage in—skipping sleep, drinking alcohol, smoking cigarettes—further exacerbate the problem of stress (Glaser & Kiecolt-Glaser, 2005).

3. **Arrive at the exam several minutes early.** Relax and take some deep breaths. Your body can keep up the sympathetic nervous system response for only a short time. So if you can get there early and give your body time to overcome the response, your heart rate and breathing will return to normal. Taking a few minutes to write down what is making you anxious about the exam may also help you reduce stress and get a higher exam grade (Ramirez & Beilock, 2011).

4. **Finally, use good test-taking skills as you work through the exam.** Underline important parts of questions. Cross off answers you know are wrong. Take time to check every answer and come back to ones you are unsure of. Reconsider them after you have worked through all the questions, because you continue to learn as you take the exam.

If you follow these steps, you are likely to experience less exam anxiety and also get better exam grades. This result creates a positive cycle. As you get better grades on your exams, you will find it easier to eliminate exam anxiety.

(a)

(b)

FIGURE 11.23

Hardiness and Resilience

Some people are better at coping with stressors than others are. **(a)** People with hardiness seem less affected by stressors because they view them as an opportunity to do something constructive. Former congresswoman Gabrielle Giffords has displayed hardiness in campaigning for gun control and background checks in the wake of being shot. **(b)** People who show resilience in the face of stressors tend to respond flexibly and bounce back quickly. This woman shows resilience after the 2011 floods in Taiwan by using a bike to transport supplies.

Some people seem stress resistant because they are so capable of adapting to life changes by viewing events constructively (**Figure 11.23a**). This trait is called *hardiness* (Kobasa, 1979). Hardiness has three components: commitment, challenge, and control. People high in hardiness are committed to their daily activities, view threats as challenges or as opportunities for growth, and see themselves as being in control of their lives. People low in hardiness typically feel alienated, fear or resist change, and view events as beyond their control (for example, being under someone else's control).

A related idea is *resilience*. Generally, some people are more resilient than others, better able to cope in the face of adversity (Block & Kremen, 1996). When faced with hardships or difficult circumstances, resilient individuals "bend without breaking." As a result, they are able to bounce back quickly when bad things happen (**Figure 11.23b**). Those who are highest in resilience are able to use their emotional resources flexibly to meet the demands of stressful situations (Bonanno, 2004).

Can resilience be taught? Some researchers believe that people can become more resilient by following particular steps (Algoe & Fredrickson, 2011). The steps in this process include coming to understand when particular emotions are adaptive, learning specific techniques for regulating both positive and negative emotions, and working to build healthy social and emotional relations with others.

INVOLVING THE FAMILY One of the most stressful events in life is dealing with illness or pain. At some point in life, many of us will experience a serious medical condition, or our loved ones may suffer from illness or chronic pain. Can family members help each other cope with such situations?

Including family members in a treatment plan for a chronically ill person might seem important. According to the research, however, such inclusion often is not effective (Martire & Schulz, 2007). A major problem is that the ill person may feel that family members are being controlling, not helpful. And as noted, being in control of essential decisions in your life is a central component of hardiness.

Family involvement can be beneficial when family members promote the person's feeling of being in control. Some behaviors that seem to help when a family member has a chronic illness include motivating the patient to make health and life choices, letting the person carry out the activities of everyday living, modeling healthy behaviors, providing rewards for displaying those behaviors, and pointing out the positive consequences of caring for the person (Martire & Schulz, 2007). By providing motivation, encouragement, and emotional support, families can also assist the patient in adjusting to life with the illness.

 How Do Mediating Factors Affect Your Stress?

To make sure you learned what you just read, write answers to the following questions and check your answers.

11.8 What personality characteristics place people most at risk for developing heart disease?

11.9 Which is better for dealing with stress over the long term, emotion-focused coping or problem-focused coping?

See Appendix B for answers to the red Q questions.

Can a Positive Attitude Keep You Healthy?

As you have seen throughout this chapter, stress and negative emotions, especially hostility, can affect your health in negative ways. What about the opposite? Can positive experiences and a positive attitude keep you healthy? Can they even make you healthier?

11.10 Positive Psychology Emphasizes Well-Being

11.10 LEARNING GOAL ACTIVITIES

To maximize your learning, complete the following learning goal activities.

a. Understand all bold and italic terms by writing explanations of them in your own words.

b. Understand happiness by summarizing the three characteristics of happiness.

In the 1990s, some psychologists began studying what is positive in the human experience. The **positive psychology** movement encouraged the scientific study of qualities such as faith, values, creativity, courage, and hope (Seligman & Csikszent-mihalyi, 2000). The earliest emphasis in positive psychology was on understanding what makes people truly happy. According to positive psychologists, happiness has three components: (1) positive emotion and pleasure, (2) engagement in life, and (3) living a meaningful life (Seligman, Steen, Park, & Peterson, 2005).

For example, college students high in authentic happiness might experience pleasure when interacting with other students (component 1), might be actively engaged in class discussions and course readings (component 2), and might find meaning in how the material influences their lives (component 3). More recently, the positive psychology movement has placed a greater emphasis on overall well-being. In his book *Flourish* (2011), Seligman argues that a truly successful life is not just about happiness (that is, pleasure, engagement, and meaning). It is also about good relationships and a history of accomplishment.

A SENSE OF WELL-BEING The new positive psychology emphasizes the strengths and virtues that help people thrive. Its primary aim is an understanding of psychological well-being (Diener, 2000). Recall from study unit 11.1 that to achieve well-being, a positive state where you feel your best, you need to strive for optimal health and life satisfaction by actively participating in health-enhancing behaviors. But might an action as simple as petting a dog increase happiness and well-being? You can investigate this possibility in Evaluating Psychology in the Real World on p. 452.

Enhancing well-being has become an important issue for governments. In 2010, the prime minister of the United Kingdom, David Cameron, announced a new well-being scale that would be used to understand the state of the nation. In the United States, a new biannual survey called the Well-Being Index investigates people's sense of well-being across six areas. These areas include life evaluation, emotional

positive psychology
The study of the strengths and virtues that allow people and communities to thrive.

If you are like most college students, you experience a lot of stress. That stress can have a negative impact on your health and also on your feelings of happiness and well-being. Perhaps at some point you found time to relax and unwind by playing with a pet. Many people feel good when they are with their pets, but can just stroking a dog help a person feel happier and less stressed? Explore the research in the article excerpted below (from https://www.sciencedaily.com/releases/2018/03/180312085045.htm) and decide whether you should accept the claim made in the article.

To answer this question, use the three steps in critical thinking:

ACTIVITY: To determine if you should accept the claim in this article, review the Learning Tip on p. 7 and follow these steps:

Step 1 What is the claim I am being asked to accept?

Step 2 What evidence, if any, is provided to support the claim?

Step 3 Given the evidence, what are the most reasonable conclusions about the claim?

If you have rejected the claim or found the evidence lacking, why did you do so? If you have found that the evidence supports the claim, how might this information change how you think and act?

Sit, Stay, Heal: Study Finds Therapy Dogs Help Stressed University Students

Therapy dog sessions for stressed-out students are an increasingly popular offering at North American universities. Now, new research from the University of British Columbia confirms that some doggy one-on-one time really can do the trick of boosting student wellness.

"Therapy dog sessions are becoming more popular on university campuses, but there has been surprisingly little research on how much attending a single drop-in therapy dog session actually helps students," said Emma Ward-Griffin, the study's lead author and research assistant in the UBC department of psychology. "Our findings suggest that therapy dog sessions have a measurable, positive effect on the wellbeing of university students, particularly on stress reduction and feelings of negativity."

In research published today in *Stress and Health*, researchers surveyed 246 students before and after they spent time in a drop-in therapy dog session. Students were free to pet, cuddle and chat with seven to 12 canine companions during the sessions. They also filled out questionnaires immediately before and after the session, and again about 10 hours later.

The researchers found that participants reported significant reductions in stress as well as increased happiness and energy immediately following the session, compared to a control group of students who did not spend time at a therapy dog session. While feelings of happiness and life satisfaction did not appear to last, some effects did.

"The results were remarkable," said Stanley Coren, study co-author and professor emeritus of psychology at UBC. "We found that, even 10 hours later, students still reported slightly less negative emotion, feeling more supported, and feeling less stressed, compared to students who did not take part in the therapy dog session."

While previous research suggested that female students benefit from therapy dog sessions more than male students, the researchers found the benefits were equally distributed across both genders in this study.

Since the strong positive effects of the therapy dog session were short-lived, the researchers concluded that universities should be encouraged to offer them at periods of increased stress.

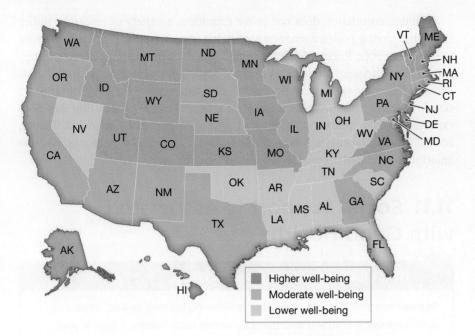

FIGURE 11.24

Well-Being in the United States

These 2009 data are from Gallup's Well-Being Index. Each day, 500 people in the United States were surveyed about their lives, emotional health, work environment, physical health, healthy behaviors, and access to food and shelter. The data reveal a general pattern of people's satisfaction with their lives.

health, work environment, physical health, healthy behavior, and basic access (to housing, food, water, etc.; **Figure 11.24**). These new tools should help governments understand individual and collective issues about well-being. The new understanding, in turn, should help leaders develop strategies and policies to enhance people's well-being.

Well-being tends to vary across cultures. The wealthiest countries often have the highest levels of satisfaction. These findings fit well with the proposal, described in study unit 9.1, that people need to satisfy basic needs such as food, shelter, and safety before they can address self-esteem needs. People who are resilient—that is, who can bounce back from negative events—experience positive emotions even when under stress (Tugade & Fredrickson, 2004). According to the broaden-and-build theory, positive emotions prompt people to consider novel solutions to their problems. Thus resilient people tend to draw on their positive emotions in dealing with setbacks or negative life experiences (Fredrickson, 2001).

HEALTH BENEFITS OF POSITIVITY AND WELL-BEING   Can positive emotions and well-being be linked with good health (**Figure 11.25**)? To address this question, one team of researchers asked more than 1,000 patients in a large medical practice to fill out questionnaires about their emotional traits (Richman et al., 2005). The questionnaires measured positive emotions (hope and curiosity) and negative emotions (anxiety and anger). Two years after receiving the questionnaires, the researchers used the patients' medical files to see if there was a relationship between these emotions and three broad types of diseases: hypertension, diabetes, and respiratory tract infections. Higher levels of hope were associated with reduced risk of these diseases. Higher levels of curiosity were associated with reduced risk of hypertension and diabetes.

Of course, it is possible that poor health can cause both unhappiness and increased health problems. One large study from the United Kingdom found that once researchers controlled for people's initial self-rated health, positivity did not predict lower mortality (Liu et al., 2016). As mentioned in study unit 11.7, it is possible that unhappy people, such as those who are stressed, engage in a variety of unhealthy behaviors, such as alcohol or drug use or overeating.

FIGURE 11.25

Health Effects of Laughter

Laughing clubs, such as this one in India, believe in laughter as therapy and as a way to keep in shape.

Although correlation does not prove causation, a variety of research studies show that having positive emotions, or being generally positive, predicts living longer (Lawrence, Rogers, & Wadsworth, 2015). This may happen because happy people have stronger immune systems. People with a positive attitude show enhanced immune system functioning and live longer than their less positive peers (Dockray & Steptoe, 2010; Xu & Roberts, 2010). They have fewer illnesses after exposure to cold germs and flu viruses (Cohen, Alper, Doyle, Treanor, & Turner, 2006). In other words, across multiple studies and types of measures, positive emotions are related to considerable health benefits.

11.11 Social Support Is Associated with Good Health

11.11 LEARNING GOAL ACTIVITIES

To maximize your learning, complete the following learning goal activities.
a. Understand all bold and italic terms by writing explanations of them in your own words.
b. Understand how social support benefits health by explaining the two ways that social support reduces the effects of stress.

Isolation and loneliness are associated with depression and other psychological problems. But social interaction appears to be beneficial for physical as well as mental health. For example, one study has shown that people with larger social networks—more people they interact with regularly—are less likely to catch colds (Cohen, Doyle, Skoner, Rabin, & Gwaltney, 1997). People who have more friends also appear to live longer than those who have fewer friends. A study that used a random sample of almost 7,000 adults found that people with smaller social networks were more likely to die during the 9-year study period than people with more friends (Berkman & Syme, 1979). Indeed, there is accumulating evidence that loneliness predicts both physical illness and mortality (Hawkley & Cacioppo, 2010). One meta-analysis concluded that the increased likelihood of death was 26 percent for subjective loneliness, 29 percent for lack of social contacts, and 32 percent for living alone (Holt-Lunstad, Smith, Baker, Harris, & Stephenson, 2015). Either being or feeling alone is associated with poor health outcomes.

Social support helps people cope and maintain good health in two basic ways. First, people with social support experience less stress overall. Consider single parents who have to juggle the demands of both job and family. The lack of a partner means more tasks to handle. It also means having no one who shares the emotional challenges. Social support can take tangible forms, such as providing material help or assisting with daily chores. Second, social support lets people better cope with stressors. To be most effective, social support needs to imply that other people care. When family, friends, or organized support groups offer expressions of caring and willingness to listen to problems, it can lessen the negative effects of stress.

Marriage is generally people's most intimate and long-lasting supportive relationship, and it has many health advantages (see study unit 4.12). The benefit of social support is particularly seen in research showing that married people tend to be in better health than others in a similar age range (Centers for Disease

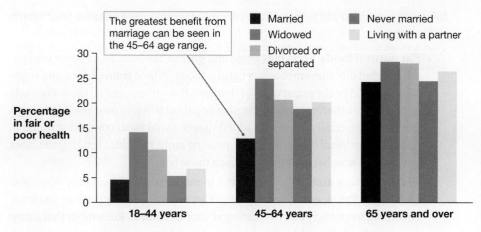

The greatest benefit from marriage can be seen in the 45–64 age range.

Legend:
- Married
- Widowed
- Divorced or separated
- Never married
- Living with a partner

Percentage in fair or poor health

18–44 years   45–64 years   65 years and over

FIGURE 11.26

Relationship Between Marriage and Health

Positive social relationships, including marriage, are good for health.

Control and Prevention, 2004; **Figure 11.26**). However, marriage is not a guaranteed path to good health. Troubled marriages are associated with increased stress, and unmarried people can be happier than people in bad marriages. For instance, research shows that people with troubled marriages and people going through a divorce or bereavement all had compromised immune systems (Kiecolt-Glaser & Glaser, 1988).

SPIRITUALITY CONTRIBUTES TO WELL-BEING For many people, religion or spirituality provides a sense of meaning or purpose in life. In many studies, people who are religious report greater feelings of well-being than do people who are not religious. This feeling can be derived from a number of things. Religious people are better at coping with crises in their lives, because their religious beliefs serve as a buffer against hard knocks (Myers, 2000). On a daily basis, religious beliefs can help people achieve and maintain well-being through the social support provided by faith communities. The support can also be physical. Many religions promote healthy behaviors, such as avoiding alcohol and tobacco or eating a vegetarian diet.

The positive effects are not associated with any single religion, however. Instead, the benefits come from a sense of spirituality that occurs across religions (**Figure 11.27**). As Rabbi Harold Kushner notes, people need to feel they are "something more than just a momentary blip in the universe" (quoted in Myers 2000, p. 64).

FIGURE 11.27

Spirituality and Well-Being

A sense of spirituality can have positive effects on well-being. That sense does not have to be connected with a particular religion.

11.12 Several Strategies Can Help You Stay Healthy

11.12 LEARNING GOAL ACTIVITIES

To maximize your learning, complete the following learning goal activities.

a. Understand all bold and italic terms by writing explanations of them in your own words.

b. Apply strategies for healthy living by describing three strategies you can use to increase your health.

Over the last three decades, psychologists have learned much about the complex relations between stress and health. We now know that to be healthy, we need to cope with stress, regulate our emotions, and control our daily habits. Adopting the following strategies will help you take control of your life and enhance your health and well-being.

- **Eat natural foods.** Food fads come and go, but the basic rules never change: Eat a varied diet that emphasizes natural foods. Whole grains, fruits, and vegetables should be the major parts of that diet. But various animal products, such as poultry or other lean meats, can also be part of it. Avoid processed foods and fast foods, especially those with added sugars. Avoid foods containing trans fat and other artificial types of fat that prolong store shelf life. Reading the label will tell you whether a product contains these fats.

- **Watch portion size.** Eat a varied diet in moderation, and eat only when you are hungry. Eating small, healthy snacks between meals may prevent you from becoming too hungry and overeating at your next meal. Remember that many prepared foods are sold in large portions, and large portions encourage overeating. Over time, the extra calories from large portions may contribute to obesity.

- **Drink alcohol in moderation, if at all.** According to some research, one glass of wine per day, or a similar quantity of other alcohol-containing drinks, may have cardiovascular benefits (Klatsky, 2009). But excessive alcohol consumption can cause serious health problems, including alcoholism, liver problems, some cancers, heart disease, and immune system deficiencies.

- **Keep active.** Exercise is an excellent daily strategy for keeping stress in check. Four times a week or more, engage in at least a half hour of moderate physical activity. Ignore the saying "No pain, no gain," because discomfort may actually keep you from exercising over the long run. Start with moderate exercise that will not leave you breathless, and gradually increase the intensity. Look for other ways to be active, such as taking the stairs or walking to work or school.

- **Do not smoke.** Many college students and other adults begin smoking each year. Smoking eventually produces undesirable physical effects for all smokers. These problems include a hacking cough, unpleasant odor, bad breath, some cancers and other lung disease, and death at a younger age.

- **Practice safe sex.** Sexually transmitted infections (STIs) affect millions of people worldwide—including college students. Many new HIV cases are occurring among those under age 25, who are infected through heterosexual or homosexual activity. Despite the devastating consequences of some STIs, many young adults engage in risky sexual practices, such as not using barrier protection methods. They are especially likely to engage in risky practices when using alcohol or other drugs. Ways to avoid STIs include abstinence and use of barrier protection methods.

- **Learn to relax.** Stress can cause many health problems. For example, conditions such as insomnia can interfere with your ability to function. By contrast, relaxation exercises can help soothe the body and mind. You might also try a relaxing activity, such as yoga (**Figure 11.28**). You can also seek help from trained counselors. One method that counselors teach is using biofeedback to measure your physiological activity so you can learn to control your bodily responses to stress.

- **Learn to cope.** Negative events are a part of life. Learn to assess them realistically. See what might be positive about the events even as you accept the difficulties they pose. You can learn strategies for dealing with stressors: seeking advice or assistance, attempting new solutions, distracting yourself with more-pleasant thoughts or activities, reinterpreting situations humorously,

FIGURE 11.28

Relaxing

You can improve your health and work toward a positive sense of well-being in many ways. One good method is to relax, such as by practicing yoga.

and so on. Find out which strategies work best for you. The important thing is to prevent stress from consuming your life.

- **Build a strong support network.** Friends and family can help you deal with much of life's stress, from daily frustrations to serious catastrophes. Avoid people who encourage you to act in unhealthy ways or who are threatened by your efforts to be healthy. Instead, find people who share your values, who understand what you want from life, and who can listen and provide advice, assistance, or simply encouragement. Trusting others is a necessary part of social support, and it is associated with positive health outcomes.

- **Consider your spiritual life.** If you have spiritual beliefs, try incorporating them into your daily living. Benefits can come from living a meaningful life and from experiencing the support provided by faith communities.

- **Try some happiness exercises.** Many low-risk activities can quickly increase your happiness (Lyubomirsky, King, & Diener, 2005). For example, you can write and deliver a letter of gratitude to someone you want to thank. Once a week, write down three things that went well and describe why they went well. Act like a happy person. Sometimes just going through the motions of being happy will create happiness. By focusing on positive events and more-positive explanations of troubling ones, you may become a happier—and healthier—person.

Q Can a Positive Attitude Keep You Healthy?

To make sure you learned what you just read, write answers to the following questions and check your answers.

11.10 What is the association between hope and good health?

11.11 Is social support from being married always associated with better health?

11.12 What is the relationship between drinking alcohol and health?

See Appendix B for answers to the red Q questions.

BIG PICTURE

 Want to earn a better grade on your test? Go to INQUIZITIVE to practice actively with this chapter's content and get personalized feedback along the way.

What Affects Your Health?

11.1 Biology, Psychology, and Social Factors Influence Your Health

Review the learning goal activities on p. 422. Health psychology is a field that applies psychological principles to issues related to health. Researchers in this field believe that good health is not just the absence of disease, but it is a positive state of well-being. The biopsychosocial model explains health and illness based on biological characteristics, psychological factors, and social conditions.

11.2 Obesity and Disordered Eating Have Many Health Consequences

Review the learning goal activities on p. 424. Obesity is excessive weight, which may be revealed by a high body mass index (BMI). Obesity is a major health problem with physical and psychological effects. Obesity is influenced by genetics, overeating, and how people think about food and their environments. There are also three types of eating disorders: (1) anorexia nervosa, where people starve themselves, (2) bulimia nervosa, where people binge on food and then purge it to lose weight, and (3) binge-eating disorder, which is characterized by feeling distress about eating a lot of food in a short time.

11.3 Exercise Benefits You Physically, Cognitively, and Emotionally

Review the learning goal activities on p. 431. Exercising just a couple of days each week can have positive effects on your physical, cognitive, and emotional health. Exercise strengthens the heart and lungs, improves cognitive abilities, such as memory, and leads to a more positive mood.

11.4 Sexually Transmitted Infections Can Be Prevented by Practicing Safer Sex

Review the learning goal activities on p. 433. Sexually transmitted infections (STIs) can be caused by bacteria, viruses, or parasites. They can be transmitted through birth, sexual contact, kissing, or even casual touching of the skin. STIs are very common, and if they are untreated they can have severe health consequences. However, practicing safer sex can reduce the risk of contracting an STI. The three ways to practice safer sex are by (1) limiting sexual partners and being faithful to one partner, (2) getting regular testing and openly communicating with a partner, and (3) preventing human papillomavirus (HPV) through vaccination and by using barrier methods of protection during sexual activities.

11.5 Smoking Is Dangerous to Your Health

Review the learning goal activities on p. 436. Smoking contributes to heart disease, cancer, and many other deadly diseases. Young people may start smoking because of learning from their environments. Successful methods for quitting smoking include prescription medications for use during therapy, nicotine replacement therapy (such as nicotine gum or the patch), and avoiding places where people smoke.

KEY TERMS
health psychology (p. 423)
well-being (p. 423)
biopsychosocial model (p. 423)
body mass index (BMI) (p. 424)
anorexia nervosa (p. 430)
bulimia nervosa (p. 431)
binge-eating disorder (p. 431)
sexually transmitted infections (STIs) (p. 433)
safer sex (p. 435)

How Does Stress Affect Your Health?

11.6 Stress Has a Negative Impact on Your Health

Review the learning goal activities on p. 439. Stress is the combination of behavioral, mental, and physical processes that occur when an organism perceives that it is facing a threat. The three components of stress are: (1) stressors (the events that cause stress), (2) stress responses (the physical and psychological effects of stress), and (3) mediating factors (the fact that personality and coping strategies increase or decrease the impact of stress). Stress can negatively affect health when stressors, either major life stressors or daily hassles, require life adjustments over long periods of time.

11.7 You Can Have Several Responses to Stress

Review the learning goal activities on p. 442. People experience five main stress responses. (1) The general adaptation syndrome is a physical response to stress. This response consists of an initial alarm stage, resistance, and, if the stressor continues, exhaustion. (2) Over time, stress can negatively affect the immune system, increasing the risk of illness. (3) Males tend to respond to stress with the fight-or-flight response. (4) Females often respond to stress with the tend-and-befriend response. (5) Some people have negative stress responses, such as over-eating and smoking.

How Do Mediating Factors Affect Your Stress?

11.8 Personality Influences the Impact of Stress on Heart Disease

Review the learning goal activities on p. 446. Chronic stress is associated with adverse health effects, both directly (due to bad habits associated with stress, such as overeating, drinking alcohol, and smoking) and indirectly (by increasing the risk of heart disease). Personality differences—including type A and B behavior patterns, hostility, and depression—can explain both the varied effects of stress on people and disparities in health across individuals.

11.9 Coping Mediates the Impact of Stress

Review the learning goal activities on p. 447. How people think about stressors, in deciding if they are harmful (primary appraisals) and how to cope with them (secondary appraisals), affects the influence of stress. Emotion-focused coping and problem-focused coping can mediate stress and the effects on health. In the long run, problem-focused coping may be more helpful in dealing with stress, especially if the stressor can be controlled.

Can a Positive Attitude Keep You Healthy?

11.10 Positive Psychology Emphasizes Well-Being

Review the learning goal activities on p. 451. Positive psychology investigates happiness and emphasizes the strengths and virtues associated with psychological well-being. There appear to be three components of happiness: (1) positive emotion and pleasure, (2) engagement in life, and (3) living a meaningful life. In short, a positive, optimistic outlook provides many health benefits.

11.11 Social Support Is Associated with Good Health

Review the learning goal activities on p. 454. Social support can benefit good health by reducing the stress people feel because tasks can be shared and by helping people cope with stressors. Good marriages can be an important form of social support, and married people tend to be in better health than those who are not married. Spirituality and social and physical support from faith communities can also contribute to a person's sense of well-being.

11.12 Several Strategies Can Help You Stay Healthy

Review the learning goal activities on p. 455. To be healthy, people need to cope with stress, regulate their emotions, and control their daily habits. People can use several effective strategies to take control of their lives and enhance their health, happiness, and well-being.

CHAPTER 11 SELF-QUIZ

To make sure you learned the information in this chapter, write answers to the following questions and check your answers. **See Appendix B for answers to the self-quiz.**

1. Chuck is often stressed because he suffers from severe arthritis. If Chuck is also very dissatisfied with his life and has very few close friends, then he is likely to become ill according to the _____.
   a. theory of well-being
   b. biopsychosocial model
   c. fight-or-flight response
   d. general adaptation syndrome

2. Emilia is of average weight. However, she often hides food in her bedroom and eats late at night when she feels anxious. She compensates for this behavior by chroni-cally abusing laxatives to help her get rid of calories. This information suggests that Emilia is most likely to be diagnosed with _____.
   a. bulimia nervosa
   b. binge-eating disorder
   c. anorexia nervosa
   d. obesity

3. Dante is working with a personal trainer to create an exercise program to improve his health. Dante is surprised to learn that exercising has so many benefits, including all of the following EXCEPT _____.
   a. creating a more positive emotional state
   b. reducing the risk of anorexia nervosa
   c. improving memory and cognitive abilities
   d. reducing the chance of heart problems

4. Chang wants to quit smoking. Which of the following methods is most likely to help him be successful?
   a. trying to convince other smokers to quit
   b. using e-cigarettes with high doses of nicotine instead of smoking cigarettes with tobacco
   c. avoiding the places where he used to smoke, and using an agonist drug that blocks nicotine receptors
   d. smoking several packs of cigarettes at once so he feels nauseated and vomits

5. Logan works at an investment company and has been embezzling money from his clients. Last year, he was arrested and sentenced to 10 years in prison. As Logan adjusts to life in prison, he is most likely experiencing stress due to _____.
   a. the alarm stage of the general adaptation syndrome
   b. this daily hassle
   c. the exhaustion stage of the general adaptation syndrome
   d. this major life stressor

6. Kenny has to give an oral presentation in 15 minutes. He is very anxious and experiencing shortness of breath, dilated pupils, and a huge lump in his throat. Kenny is most likely experiencing the _____ stage of Selye's general adaptation syndrome.
   a. immune
   b. resistance
   c. alarm
   d. exhaustion

7. When faced with stress, Ross reacts with aggressiveness and impatience, whereas Tia is more relaxed and easy-going. In these situations, Ross exhibits a _____ behavior pattern and is _____ likely than Tia to develop heart disease.
   a. type A; less
   b. type B; less
   c. type A; more
   d. type B; more

8. Preston told his supervisor that he is unable to work when he has soccer practice, but she keeps scheduling him for shifts during those times. Preston uses problem-focused coping when he decides to _____.
   a. talk to his friends to reduce his stress
   b. think about whether the situation is stressful enough for him to deal with
   c. take up smoking to relieve some of his stress
   d. remind his supervisor about his schedule conflicts

9. When Lauren is feeling down, she makes an extra effort to feel optimistic about the future and maintain a happy attitude. Lauren is most likely to benefit from her posi-tive attitude by _____.
   a. experiencing less hypertension and not developing diabetes
   b. having a better-functioning immune system
   c. living longer than her peers
   d. all of the above

10. Brian and Zariah have been dating for years and have a good relationship. If they get married, they are likely to experience _____.
    a. better health than other people their ages who are not married
    b. a lower risk of heart problems related to stress
    c. less need for social support from friends
    d. all of the above

Can Psychology Help You Be Successful in a Career in Fitness?

Do you like to exercise? Would you enjoy using what you know about how people think, feel, and act to help them improve their health and their lives? If you answered yes to these questions, then a career in fitness, combined with a knowledge of psychology, may be a perfect fit for you.

For example, a personal trainer works with clients to help them develop exercise routines, exercise in a healthy way, stay motivated to keep exercising, and generally develop a healthier lifestyle. Many clients seek a personal trainer not only because they are out of shape, but also because they are overweight. Understanding the factors that contribute to obesity will be useful in developing healthy eating plans for clients. This chapter notes that restrictive dieting is not the best way to lose weight. A better strategy includes healthy eating and regular exercise. Related careers that encourage healthy lifestyles include nutritionists and dieticians. Both advise people about what to eat to maximize health.

Knowledge of psychology can also help a personal trainer understand how people think about health, what stressors affect them, and how to motivate them as individuals. As discussed in this chapter, exercise is not only good for the body. It also improves mood and enhances thinking abilities. A personal trainer must have education in a field related to exercise, such as an associate's degree in exercise science or kinesiology, or specialized certification in personal training. With a bachelor's degree, you could become an exercise physiologist and help clients recover from disease by developing exercise programs to improve specific aspects of their health.

Some people choose to fully combine exercise and psychology together in a career as a sports psychologist. Sports psychologists can work with individual athletes or with an entire team, to help them develop their mental skills and

physical abilities. They may, for example, use visualization techniques and simulation techniques to mimic a real-world athletic event during practice and have athletes practice thinking about the best ways to respond in that athletic event. You would need an advanced degree, such as a master's or doctorate, to become a sports psychologist. In this quickly growing career, you can work with athletes in colleges and universities (Voelker, 2012). You might also work with professional sports teams.

TAKEAWAY POINT: If you enjoy exercising, healthy living, and working with people, then a career in exercise might be a perfect fit for you. Along with your degree, getting expertise in psychology can help you understand psychological factors that affect health, including why people get stressed and what places them at risk for obesity. This knowledge can help you do your best to help others become healthy.

Ψ You can look up job descriptions, education requirements, salaries, and more at the Bureau of Labor Statistics: www.bls.gov. Visit the site and start putting psychology to work!

12 Social Psychology

UNITED STATES SENATOR CORY BOOKER gives new meaning to the phrase "public servant." In 2012, when he was mayor of Newark, New Jersey, Booker noticed that his neighbor's house was in flames. He then heard someone screaming that a woman was trapped inside. Booker's security guards initially tried to hold him back. Later, one of the guards explained what happened. "He basically told me, 'This woman is going to die if we don't help her,' and what can I say to that? I let him go and without thinking twice, he just ran into the flames and rescued this young lady."

Booker rushed to the second floor of the home. He felt flames behind him and saw nothing but smoky blackness in front of him. He found the woman and carried her back through the house,

BIG QUESTIONS

How Do You Think About Other People?

How Do Your Attitudes Affect You?

How Do Other People Influence You?

How Can You Develop Strong Relationships?

FIGURE 12.1

Cory Booker's Helping Behavior

During his tenure as mayor of Newark, New Jersey, Cory Booker demonstrated many ways that people can help each other and develop strong relationships with others. Here, Booker helps dig out the snowbound car of a Newark resident. "It was very nice," said the car's owner. "I didn't expect it, so it was shocking."

which by then was engulfed in flames. Although they managed to escape, Booker sustained second-degree burns and was treated for smoke inhalation.

This story shows how people sometimes risk their lives for other people. Every day we read about how people can be cruel to each other. We hear about bullying that leads to teen suicide, wars that victimize the innocent, gang shootouts—the list of horrors seems endless. Yet people such as Cory Booker perform acts of compassion on both large and small scales every day (**Figure 12.1**). Their stories not only impress us. They also can inspire us to help others.

This chapter considers how and why we help or hurt each other, how situations and people influence the ways we think and act, and how we develop strong relationships with the people in our lives. These concerns are the realm of *social psychology*. Because almost every human activity has a social dimension, research in social psychology covers a lot of territory. Let's begin by looking at how people think about other people.

How Do You Think About Other People?

We are social animals who live in a highly complex social world. At any moment, hundreds of millions of people are talking with friends, forming impressions of strangers, arguing with family members, falling in love, and helping other people, as Cory Booker has done. Our regular interactions with others—even imagined others, including online "avatars"—shape who we are and how we understand the world.

12.1 You Tend to Make Snap Judgments About Other People

 12.1 LEARNING GOAL ACTIVITIES

To maximize your learning, complete the following learning goal activities:

a. Understand all bold and italic terms by writing explanations of them in your own words.

b. Apply the principles of snap judgments by providing an example of how you have experienced snap judgments based on thin slices of behavior and/or facial expressions.

Think about what goes through your mind when you first meet someone, or even when you see someone in passing. Most likely, you very quickly make several snap judgments. You might think: This is someone attractive, or someone to be wary of, or someone about as intelligent as you are, or someone you'd like to know better. Many factors affect your initial impressions of someone and the way you react to that person. These factors include how others describe the person and how you feel about the person's nonverbal behavior, or body language—movements, gestures, and facial expressions (**Figure 12.2**).

NONVERBAL BEHAVIOR How much can you learn from body language? The psychologists Nalini Ambady and Robert Rosenthal have found that people can

FIGURE 12.2

Reading Body Language

People's body language affects your impressions of them and their situations. How do the facial expressions and gestures of the men in this photo influence your judgment of the situation?

make accurate judgments based on only a few seconds of observation (Ambady & Rosenthal, 1993). Ambady and Rosenthal refer to such quick views as *thin slices of behavior.* Thin slices of behavior are powerful cues for forming impressions of others.

In one research study, participants viewed soundless 30-second film clips of college teachers lecturing (Ambady & Rosenthal, 1993). The participants were asked to rate the lecturers' teaching ability. Based solely on thin slices of behavior, the participants' ratings agreed strongly with the ratings given by the instructors' actual students. Here's another example: Videotapes of judges giving instructions to juries reveal that a judge's nonverbal actions can predict whether a jury will find the defendant guilty or not guilty (Rosenthal, 2003). Perhaps unconsciously, judges may indicate their beliefs about guilt or innocence through facial expressions, tone of voice, and gestures (**Figure 12.3**).

Another good example of thin slices is "gaydar." Indeed, substantial evidence shows that people are quite accurate in judging sexual orientation based on nonverbal behavior (Rule & Alaei, 2016).

FACIAL EXPRESSIONS   One of the first things you usually notice about another person is the face. In fact, when human babies are less than an hour old, they prefer to look at a picture of a human face rather than a blank outline of a head (Morton & Johnson, 1991). The face communicates information such as emotional state, interest, and trustworthiness. Young children's rating of faces as nice or mean match adult ratings of whether a face is trustworthy or not (Cogsdill, Todorov, Spelke, & Banaji, 2014).

This ability to communicate is particularly true for the eyes. We use our eyes to indicate anger, to flirt, or to catch the attention of a passing waiter. Eye contact is important in social situations, though how you perceive it depends on your culture. People from Western cultures tend to seek eye contact when they speak to someone. If the other person does not meet their eyes, they might assume—perhaps incorrectly—that the person is embarrassed, ashamed, or lying. Westerners tend to view a person who looks them in the eyes as truthful and friendly. For this reason, people wearing sunglasses are often described as cold and aloof, and police officers sometimes wear sunglasses partly to seem intimidating. In other groups, such as certain Native American tribes, making direct eye contact, especially with the elderly, is considered disrespectful.

FIGURE 12.3

Thin Slices of Behavior

Even having a few seconds to read body language can provide enough cues for you to form general impressions about people. Here, the judge's expression and upraised finger indicate her disapproval of the defendant.

12.2 You Make Attributions About Other People

12.2 LEARNING GOAL ACTIVITIES

To maximize your learning, complete the following learning goal activities:

a. Understand all bold and italic terms by writing explanations of them in your own words.

b. Analyze how we make attributions based on the actor/observer bias by distinguishing between the attributions you would make if you were fired from a job versus if a coworker were fired.

When other people act kindly and heroically, you probably assume they are kind and heroic people. You may neglect to consider the situation in which they have acted. For instance, Cory Booker said that he just did what most neighbors would do if they realized someone was trapped in a burning building. He noted also that firefighters and police officers perform those kinds of actions every day. One key finding from social psychology is that people are usually more affected by situations than anyone realizes. It is important to keep this lesson in mind when explaining why certain events happened or why people behaved as they did. Explanations for events or actions, including other people's behavior, are called *attributions*.

TYPES OF ATTRIBUTIONS   In any situation, there are dozens of likely explanations for how things turn out. For example, you might have done well on a test because you studied hard, the test was easy, or a combination of these factors.

The explanations people give for outcomes are called attributions. **Personal attributions** are explanations based on people's internal characteristics, such as abilities, traits, moods, or efforts. **Situational attributions** are explanations based on external events, such as the weather, luck, accidents, or other people's actions. Bernard Weiner (1974) noted that attributions can also vary on other dimensions. For example, attributions can be stable over time (permanent) or unstable (temporary). They can be controllable or uncontrollable. The weather, for instance, is situational, unstable, and uncontrollable. How would you classify good study habits?

Humans generally like order and predictability. We prefer to think that things happen for reasons, because explanations enable us to anticipate future events. But the world can be dangerous—many unexpected things happen. Suppose that a violent act, such as a rape or murder, appears to be senseless. We may make attributions about the victim, such as "She deserved it because she was wearing sexy clothes," or "He provoked it by starting the fight." Attributions of this kind are part of the *just world hypothesis*. From this perspective, victims must have done something to justify what happened to them. Such attributions make the violent act seem more understandable and more justified. Though simplistic, these types of attributions are appealing because they make the world seem safer and saner.

BIAS IN ATTRIBUTIONS   When explaining other people's behavior, you probably tend to overemphasize personality traits and underestimate situations. This tendency is so pervasive that it has been called the **fundamental attribution error**. By contrast, when you make attributions about yourself, you probably tend to focus on situations rather than on your personality traits. This tendency is called the **actor/observer bias.**

The actor/observer bias refers to two tendencies. When you are the *actor* in a particular situation, your interpretation of a behavior or outcome is based on the situation. For example, you might say, "I failed the exam because it was unfair." When you are the *observer*, you interpret the same behavior, or the same outcome, based on others' personality traits. For example, you might say, "They failed the exam because they did not study." One reason for this difference in attributions between yourself and others is simply that you know more about the situations that you are involved in. Because you know less about the situations of other people, you tend to think that what happened was based on their personality traits. Some researchers have found that people in Eastern cultures, such as those in Asia, are more likely than Westerners to believe that human behavior is the outcome of both personal and situational factors (Choi, Dalal, Kim-Prieto, & Park, 2003; Miyamoto & Kitayama, 2002). The Learning Tip on p. 467 will help you remember the actor/observer bias.

personal attributions
People's explanations for why events or actions occur that refer to people's internal characteristics, such as abilities, traits, moods, or efforts.

situational attributions
People's explanations for why events or actions occur that refer to external events, such as the weather, luck, accidents, or other people's actions.

fundamental attribution error
In explaining other people's behavior, the tendency to overemphasize personality traits and underestimate situations.

actor/observer bias
When interpreting our own behavior, the tendency to focus on situations rather than personality traits.

LEARNING TIP: Attributions and the Actor/Observer Bias

Here's an easy way to remember the actor/observer bias based on a common situation: a fender bender.

WHEN YOU SEE	PLEASE THINK	FENDER BENDER EXAMPLE
Actor	When you are the <u>actor</u>, you attribute the outcome to the <u>situation</u>.	I had a fender bender because: • The road was slippery. • The other driver went through the red light.
Observer	When you are the <u>observer</u>, you attribute the outcome to another person's <u>personality traits.</u>	That person had a fender bender because: • She's a careless driver. • His eyesight is really bad.

12.3 You Tend to Stereotype Other People

12.3 LEARNING GOAL ACTIVITIES

To maximize your learning, complete the following learning goal activities:

a. Understand all bold and italic terms by writing explanations of them in your own words.

b. Apply self-fulfilling prophecy by describing how a positive stereotype can lead to one outcome and a negative stereotype can lead to a different outcome.

Do all Italians have fiery tempers? Do all Canadians like hockey? Can Asian American women rap? As you learned in study unit 8.3, stereotypes are mental shortcuts that allow for easy, fast processing of social information (**Figure 12.4**). Stereotyping occurs automatically and, in most cases, outside of awareness. In and of themselves, stereotypes are neutral. They simply reflect efficient cognitive processes. Indeed, some stereotypes are based in truth: Men tend to be more violent than women, and women tend to be more nurturing than men. However, these statements are true on average. Not all men are violent, nor are all women nurturing.

MAINTAINING STEREOTYPES Once you form a stereotype, you tend to maintain it. For instance, you might perceive a behavior in a way that is consistent with a stereotype you hold. Suppose you hear that a person acted aggressively. If that person is a lawyer, you may form one mental image of the aggressiveness. If the person is a construction worker, you may form a very different image.

When you encounter someone who does not fit a stereotype, you may put that person in a special category rather than change the stereotype. This practice is called *subtyping*. Thus a racist who believes African Americans are lazy may categorize the superstar Beyoncé or the politicians Cory Booker and Barack Obama as exceptions to the rule rather than as evidence that the stereotype is wrong. Forming a subtype of successful African Americans allows the racist to maintain the stereotype that most African Americans are unsuccessful.

(a)

(b)

FIGURE 12.4

Stereotypes

Mental stereotypes are a fast, easy way to think about social information. Unfortunately, they are not always correct. **(a)** Does this photo, of fans at a 2010 Olympic gold medal hockey game between Canada and the United States, lead you to think that all Canadians like hockey? **(b)** When you think of a rapper, do you picture an Asian American woman? Probably not. But Awkwafina is a well-regarded performer in a field traditionally dominated by men of color.

(a)

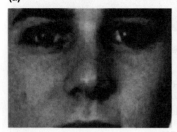

(b)

FIGURE 12.5

Stereotypes and Perception

(a) In one study, participants were shown a picture of a white face or a picture of a black face. **(b)** Then participants were immediately shown a picture of an object and asked to classify it as a gun or a tool. Participants primed by seeing black faces identified guns more quickly and mistook tools for guns. The study revealed that stereotypes can influence basic perceptual processes.

STEREOTYPES AND PERCEPTION   Social psychological research has shown that stereotypes can influence basic perceptual processes. Because you may not be conscious of your stereotypes, you may be unaware of how those stereotypes influence your perceptions.

In an experiment that demonstrated this influence, white participants were briefly shown a picture of a white face or a black face (Payne, 2001; **Figure 12.5a**). The picture appeared so briefly that participants were not aware of seeing it. After each face, a picture of either a tool or a gun appeared (**Figure 12.5b**). Participants were asked to classify the object as a "tool" or a "gun" as quickly as possible. Participants who were shown a black face identified the gun more quickly and also more often mistook the tool for a gun.

SELF-FULFILLING PROPHECY   If you are treated as a member of a stereotyped group, how might that treatment affect you? Stereotypes that start out being untrue can later become true. The **self-fulfilling prophecy** is the tendency to behave in ways that confirm expectations, whether those expectations are your own or others'.

In the 1960s, the psychologist Robert Rosenthal and a school principal, Lenore Jacobsen, conducted impressive research on this process. In one of their studies, elementary school students took a test that supposedly identified those who were especially likely to show large increases in their intelligence quotient (IQ, discussed in study unit 8.8) during the school year. These students were labeled bloomers. Teachers were given a list of the bloomers in their classes. The purpose of this label was to create a positive stereotype in the minds of the teachers. At the end of the year, standardized testing revealed that the bloomers showed large increases in IQ. However, as you might have guessed, students on the bloomer lists had actually been chosen at random. These students had not necessarily scored higher on the earlier test. Therefore, their increases in IQ likely resulted from the extra attention and encouragement provided by the teachers. The teachers' expectations turned into reality—a self-fulfilling prophecy.

Of course, negative stereotypes can become self-fulfilling as well. When teachers expect certain students to fail, they might subtly, however unconsciously, undermine those students' self-confidence or motivation (McKown & Weinstein, 2008). For instance, offering unwanted help, even with the best intentions, can send the message that the teacher does not believe the student has what it takes to succeed. Have you ever experienced a self-fulfilling prophecy, either positive or negative? To explore this outcome, see Has It Happened to You?

12.4 Stereotypes Can Have Negative Effects

 12.4 LEARNING GOAL ACTIVITIES

To maximize your learning, complete the following learning goal activities:

a. Understand all bold and italic terms by writing explanations of them in your own words.

b. Understand prejudice and discrimination by summarizing the similarities and differences between them and explaining how they are increased by competition and reduced by cooperation.

When stereotypes are negative, they can lead to prejudice and discrimination. **Prejudice** involves negative feelings, opinions, and beliefs associated with a stereotype. **Discrimination** is the inappropriate and unjustified treatment of people based on the groups they belong to. Prejudice and discrimination are responsible for much of the conflict and warfare around the world. Within nearly all cultures, some groups of people are discriminated against because of prejudice. Over the last half century, social psychologists have studied the causes and consequences of prejudice. They have looked for ways to reduce the destructive effects of prejudice.

Why do stereotypes so often lead to prejudice and discrimination? Psychologists have developed various theories. According to one theory, only certain types of people are prejudiced. According to a second theory, people treat others as scapegoats to relieve the tensions of daily living. According to a third theory, people discriminate against others to protect their own self-esteem. Yet another explanation, consistent with evolutionary theory, is that it is adaptive to favor our own groups over other groups. As a result, we tend to discriminate against people who pose threats to our groups.

INGROUP/OUTGROUP BIAS   It's the big game. You are wearing the team colors, cheering yourself hoarse, and maybe even doing silly dances—all in the name of team spirit. You tend to be powerfully connected to the groups you belong to. You not only cheer them on, you may fight for them, and you might even be willing to die for them. Those groups that you belong to are *ingroups*. Those that you do not belong to are *outgroups* (**Figure 12.6**).

According to *social identity theory* (Tajfel & Turner, 1979), your group memberships are an important part of how you view yourself. Membership contributes to each group member's overall sense of self-esteem. Believing that the groups you belong to are good groups makes you feel better about yourself. The separation of people into ingroup and outgroup members appears to occur early in development. Beginning in infancy, humans readily differentiate between ingroups and outgroups (Guassi Moreira, Van Bavel, & Telzer, 2017).

Once you categorize others as ingroup or outgroup members, you treat them differently. For instance, you may view outgroup members as less varied than ingroup members. St. Cloud State students may think Minnesota Duluth students are all alike. But when they think about St. Cloud State students, they cannot help noticing the wide diversity in students. Of course, Minnesota Duluth students have the same view in reverse: They see that their student body is diverse, but they think that one St. Cloud State student is not much different from any other.

One consequence of categorizing people as ingroup or outgroup members is *ingroup favoritism*. For example, you may be more willing to do favors for ingroup members or to forgive their mistakes or errors. The power of group membership is so strong that people show ingroup favoritism even if the groups are formed by chance. In one study, researchers randomly assigned volunteers to two groups by flipping a coin (Billig & Tajfel, 1973). This procedure is known as the *minimal group paradigm*. Participants were then given a task in which they divided up money. Not surprisingly, they gave more money to their ingroup members. But they also tried to prevent the outgroup members from receiving any money. This behavior happened even when the participants were reminded that the groups were formed randomly.

Why might you value members of your own groups more highly than you value other people? One possible explanation is that over the course of human evolution, personal survival has depended on group survival. Those who work together to keep resources within their group and deny resources to outgroup members have a

self-fulfilling prophecy
People's tendency to behave in ways that confirm their own expectations or other people's expectations.

prejudice
Negative feelings, opinions, and beliefs associated with a stereotype.

discrimination
The inappropriate and unjustified treatment of people based on the groups they belong to.

FIGURE 12.6
Ingroup/Outgroup Bias
People tend to identify strongly with the groups they are a part of. Here, St. Cloud State hockey players compete against Minnesota Duluth players.

selective advantage over those who are willing to share with the outgroup. This advantage becomes especially important when groups are competing for scarce resources.

MODERN PREJUDICE   Even people who believe they are not prejudiced may hold negative attitudes about certain groups of people. In 2014, when the Dallas Mavericks owner Mark Cuban said he would cross the street to avoid a black man in a hoodie or a white person looking like a skinhead, he was acknowledging his prejudices even as he condemned himself for having them. Nowadays few people openly admit they are racist, and many explicitly reject racist attitudes. However, there are still subtle forms of prejudice. Social psychologists have introduced the idea of **modern racism,** which refers to subtle forms of prejudice that coexist with the rejection of racist beliefs. Modern racists tend to believe that discrimination is no longer a serious problem. They think that minority groups are demanding too many changes to traditional values (Henry & Sears, 2002). Modern racism often appears more like indifference to the concerns of minority group members than outright hostility. For instance, people may condemn racist attitudes toward Latinos but be unwilling to help a Latino in need (Abad-Merino, Newheiser, Dovidio, Tabernero, & González, 2013).

Because people are reluctant to admit racist attitudes, researchers use questionnaires that get at subtle prejudices (McConahay, 1986). For example, a version of this scale was used to assess subtle racism against Asians in Canada (Son Hing, Chung-Yan, Hamilton, & Zanna, 2008). Participants were asked to agree or disagree with statements such as "There are too many foreign students of Asian descent being allowed to attend university in Canada," "Discrimination against Asians is no longer a problem in Canada," and "It is too easy for Asians to illegally arrive in Canada and receive refugee status."

Modern racism happens because the equal treatment of minorities seems to challenge traditions associated with the majority. Other prejudices also have modern subtle forms. For example, some people say that gays should not face discrimination, but these same people do not support marriage equality. They argue that same-sex marriage threatens the traditional definition of marriage as being between a man and a woman (**Figure 12.7**).

COMPETITION AND COOPERATION   Can the findings of social psychology be used to reduce prejudice? Can they be used to encourage peace? Since the 1950s, social psychologists have worked with politicians, activists, and others in many attempts to lessen the hostility and violence between factions.

Social psychology may be able to offer strategies for promoting intergroup harmony and producing greater tolerance for outgroups. The first study to suggest this possibility was conducted in the 1950s by Muzafer Sherif and colleagues (1961). Sherif arranged for 22 well-adjusted and intelligent white fifth-grade boys from Oklahoma City to attend a summer camp at a lake. The boys did not know each other. Before arriving at camp, they were randomly divided into two groups, the Eagles and the Rattlers. The next week, over a four-day period, the groups were pitted against each other in competition.

Group pride was extremely strong, and animosity between the groups quickly escalated. The Eagles burned the Rattlers' flag. The Rattlers retaliated by trashing the Eagles' cabin. Eventually, confrontations and physical fights had to be broken up by the experimenters. Sherif had shown how easy it was to make people hate each other: Simply divide them into groups, have the groups compete against each other, and prejudice and mistreatment will result. If you've ever watched *Survivor*, you've seen this happen.

FIGURE 12.7

Controversy and Modern Prejudice

Many opponents of marriage equality, such as this protester in Utah, do not advocate prejudice or discrimination against people who are gay. They argue that same-sex marriage threatens traditional marriage.

The next part of the study then explored whether the hostility could be undone. Sherif reasoned that if competition led to hostility, then cooperation should reduce hostility. The experimenters created situations in which members of both groups had to cooperate to achieve necessary goals. For instance, the experimenters rigged a truck to break down. Getting the truck moving required all the boys to pull together. In an ironic twist, the boys had to use the same rope they had used earlier in a tug-of-war. After a series of tasks that required cooperation, the walls between the two sides broke down. The boys became friends across the groups. Among strangers, competition and isolation tend to create enemies (**Figure 12.8a**). Among enemies, cooperation tends to create friends (**Figure 12.8b**).

COOPERATION IN THE CLASSROOM The programs that most successfully bring groups together involve person-to-person interaction. A good example is the jigsaw classroom. The social psychologist Eliot Aronson developed this program with his students in the 1970s.

In the jigsaw classroom, students work together in mixed-race or mixed-sex groups. Each group member is an expert on one aspect of the assignment. For instance, when studying Mexico, one group member might focus on the country's geography, another on its history, and so on. The various geography experts from each group get together and master the material. They then return to their own groups and teach the material to their team members. In other words, each group member cooperates both within and outside of the group.

More than 800 studies of the jigsaw classroom have demonstrated that this program leads to more-positive treatment of other ethnicities. According to Aronson (2002), children in jigsaw classrooms grow to like each other more and develop higher self-esteem than do children in traditional classrooms. The lesson is clear: Communal work toward goals can reduce prejudice and benefit all the workers.

(a)

(b)

FIGURE 12.8
Competition and Cooperation
(a) Competition can increase rivalry. For example, when the tennis greats Serena Williams (top, about to return the ball) and Venus Williams play against each other in singles matches, each sister seeks to defeat the other. **(b)** By contrast, cooperation can increase tolerance and friendship. As a team in doubles matches, the Williams sisters unite to defeat their opponents.

Q How Do You Think About Other People?

To make sure you learned what you just read, write answers to the following questions and check your answers.

12.1 When you walk into your psychology class on the first day, your professor is at the door and says hello to you, welcomes you to class, and shakes your hand. If you decide based on this behavior that your professor is a nice person, then what was the basis of your snap judgment?

12.2 What does the actor/observer bias predict about how you would attribute your being late for work compared with another employee's being late for work?

12.3 Giuseppe comes from an Italian family that believes that Italians are great cooks. If Giuseppe cooks a lot to show what he sees as his inherited talent in the kitchen, then what two aspects of social psychology have influenced Giuseppe?

12.4 What is the difference between prejudice and discrimination?

See Appendix B for answers to the red Q questions.

How Do Your Attitudes Affect You?

Do you have a religion? Do you belong to a political party? Do you have strong feelings about a movie you saw recently or a brand of shampoo? We all have feelings and beliefs about serious things, such as religion and politics. We also have feelings and beliefs about more trivial things, such as movies and hair products.

attitudes
People's evaluations of objects, of events, or of ideas.

attitude accessibility
Ease or difficulty of retrieving an attitude from memory.

mere exposure effect
The increase in liking due to repeated exposure.

All of your feelings and beliefs are shaped by your social context. As a result, they play important roles in how you evaluate and interact with other people. For example, how you were raised influences your religious and political beliefs. Your beliefs in turn affect whether you attend a religious institution as well as which religious institution you might attend, and whether you engage in political campaigning and for which candidate. Moreover, your engagement in these behaviors further influences and refines your attitudes. For all these reasons, understanding your feelings and beliefs and how they affect daily life is an important issue in social psychology.

12.5 You Form Attitudes Through Experience and Socialization

12.5 LEARNING GOAL ACTIVITIES

To maximize your learning, complete the following learning goal activities:

a. Understand all bold and italic terms by writing explanations of them in your own words.

b. Understand the three main ways attitudes develop by summarizing each way and giving an example of an attitude that could be formed in that way.

The feelings and beliefs that you hold are called **attitudes**. Attitudes affect behavior, and behavior affects attitudes (**Figure 12.9**). Sometimes your behavior matches your attitude. For example, if you believe smoking is bad for you and you do not smoke, then your behavior is consistent with your attitude. That is, you have a *simple attitude* toward smoking. Other times, your behavior doesn't match your attitude.

For example, if you believe smoking is bad for you and you do smoke, then your behavior is not consistent with your attitude. In this case, you have a *complex attitude*. You probably have some attitude toward exercising, either simple or complex, as described in Try It Yourself on p. 473.

ATTITUDES CAN PREDICT BEHAVIOR   In general, the stronger and more personally relevant an attitude is, the more likely it is to predict behavior. A strong and personally relevant attitude also leads to consistent actions in different situations related to that attitude. Consider someone who grew up in a strongly Democratic household. Suppose the person frequently heard negative comments about Republicans. That person is more likely to register as a Democrat and vote Democratic than someone who grew up in a more politically neutral environment.

The more specific the attitude, the more predictive it is. For instance, your attitude toward recycling is more predictive of whether you take your soda cans to a recycling bin than are your general environmental beliefs. Attitudes formed through direct experience also tend to be better predictors of behavior. For example, think about parenthood. If you aren't a parent but plan to have children, what kind of parent do you think you will be? Your expectations aren't yet informed by direct experience of parenting. But if you have seen one child through toddlerhood, you will have formed very strong attitudes about child-rearing techniques. These attitudes will predict how you approach the early months and years of parenting your second child.

Actions

Attitudes

FIGURE 12.9

Attitudes and Behavior

Here, in 2005, the Vietnam veteran Don Sioss, a member of the Disabled Vietnam Veterans, talks with Major Ladda Tammy Duckworth (now a United States senator from Illinois) about her treatment for injuries she suffered while serving as a helicopter pilot in Iraq. Here, Don Sioss's attitude about helping injured soldiers is likely to become stronger from his positive visits, and this positive attitude will encourage him to help again in the future.

Is your attitude toward exercising simple or complex? To figure out your attitude, answer the questions in the table below. If you answer both questions the same way— both yes or both no—then you have a simple attitude toward exercising. That is, your behavior is consistent with your attitude. If you answer one question differently, then you have a complex attitude toward exercising. That is, like many people, your behavior is inconsistent with your attitude.

	Simple attitude (consistent)		Complex attitude (inconsistent)	
Attitude: Do you believe exercising makes you healthier?	Yes	No	Yes	No
Behavior: Do you exercise?	Yes	No	No	Yes

The ease or difficulty of retrieving an attitude from memory is called **attitude accessibility.** The accessibility of an attitude predicts how consistent with the attitude a behavior is likely to be. Russell Fazio (1995) has shown that easily activated attitudes are more stable, predictive of behavior, and resistant to change. Thus the more quickly you recall that recycling is important to you, the more likely you are to discard a soda can into a recycling bin rather than a trash can.

ATTITUDES DEVELOP IN THREE WAYS Think about a food you like that you could not stand when you first tried it—for instance, coffee or sushi. How did you come to like it? Attitudes develop in three ways. In the first way, the more you are exposed to something, the more you tend to like it. You acquire a taste for it— sometimes literally. In a classic set of studies, Robert Zajonc (1968, 2001) exposed people to unfamiliar items either a few times or many times. Greater exposure to the item, and therefore greater familiarity with it, caused people to have more-positive attitudes about the item. This process is called the **mere exposure effect**.

The mere exposure effect is also seen in relation to faces. That is, you tend to prefer seeing a face the way you normally see it. If you looked at normal photographs of yourself and compare them with photos with the same images reversed, you would probably prefer the reversed versions. Why would this be the case? The reversed images correspond to what you usually see when you look in the mirror, or how you are used to seeing yourself (**Figure 12.10**). Your friends and family members would prefer the true photographs, which correspond to how they are used to seeing you. You can try this yourself by taking a "selfie" and then flipping it. Which image do you prefer?

The second way attitudes develop is through learning. Because your associations between things and their meanings can change, your attitudes can be conditioned. (To refresh your memory about conditioning, see Chapter 6, especially study units 6.4 and 6.10.) Advertisers often use classical conditioning to create positive attitudes about a product. When you see a celebrity whom you are attracted to (say, Brad Pitt) paired with a product that you have neutral feelings about (for example, a certain perfume), you tend to develop more-positive attitudes about the product (**Figure 12.11**). After this conditioning, the formerly neutral stimulus (the perfume) alone triggers the same positive attitude response as the positively viewed object (Brad Pitt). Operant conditioning also shapes attitudes: If you are rewarded with praise each time you recycle, you will develop a more positive attitude toward

FIGURE 12.10

The Mere Exposure Effect

If she is like most people, Meghan Markle, now formally known as Meghan, Duchess of Sussex, will prefer **(left)** her mirror image to **(right)** her photographic image. Meghan is more familiar with her mirror image, which—like most of us—she no doubt sees many times every day.

FIGURE 12.11

Classical Conditioning in Advertising to Change Attitudes

Advertisers depend on the idea that positive feelings about a celebrity can often condition a person to have a positive response to a product that is paired with that celebrity. This effect usually translates into greater sales for the product.

recycling. If you enjoy the challenges of shaping people's attitudes about products, then you might be interested in a career in advertising or marketing. The Putting Psychology to Work feature on p. 501 can help you get started.

The third way attitudes develop is through socialization. Here, you observe other people's attitudes and then model them in your own behavior. Caregivers, peers, teachers, religious leaders, politicians, and media figures guide attitudes about many things. As mentioned in study unit 6.13, teenagers' attitudes about clothing styles and music, about behaviors such as smoking and drinking alcohol, and about the latest celebrities are heavily influenced by their peers' beliefs. Society instills many basic attitudes.

EXPLICIT AND IMPLICIT ATTITUDES Most white Americans say that they view African Americans positively and that they are not racist. Yet earlier in life, they may have learned societal stereotypes of African Americans that are at odds with their expressed beliefs. How do you know what your real attitude is about something?

As you learned in study units 3.3–3.4, your access to your mental processes is limited, and unconscious processes can influence your behavior. Your conscious awareness of your attitudes can be limited by what you want to believe, but your actions may reveal your less positive attitudes (Nosek, Hawkins, & Frazier, 2011). These unconscious attitudes can reveal themselves through subtle responses. Suppose, for example, that a nonracist white person feels more uneasy when seeing a black person than when seeing a white person.

Attitudes can be explicit or implicit. These different attitudes have different effects on behavior. An **explicit attitude** is one you know about and can report to other people. If you say you like bowling, you are stating your explicit attitude toward it. But maybe you always say no when friends invite you to go bowling. This behavior suggests an unconscious outlook that is different. An unconscious attitude is also known as an **implicit attitude**. Your many implicit attitudes influence your feelings and behaviors at an unconscious level (Greenwald & Banaji, 1995).

You access implicit attitudes from memory quickly, with little conscious effort or control. In this way, implicit attitudes function like implicit memories. As you learned in study unit 7.10, implicit memories make it possible for you to perform actions, such as riding a bicycle, without thinking through all the required steps. Similarly, you might purchase a product endorsed by a celebrity even though you have no conscious memory of having seen the celebrity use the product. The product might simply look familiar to you. Some evidence suggests that implicit attitudes involve brain regions associated with implicit rather than explicit memory (Lieberman, 2000).

To assess implicit attitudes, researchers use indirect means. One method researchers have used to assess implicit attitudes is a reaction time test called the Implicit Association Test (IAT; Greenwald, McGhee, & Schwartz, 1998). The IAT measures how quickly a person associates concepts or objects with positive or negative words.

Another way to assess implicit attitudes is to observe behavior. Consider the 2008 presidential election, when many observers wondered how attitudes about African Americans would affect people's willingness to vote for Barack Obama. People higher in self-reported (explicit) prejudice were indeed less likely to vote for Obama. In addition, though, people who reported low levels of prejudice but whose scores on the IAT indicated negative attitudes about blacks also were less likely to vote for Obama (Payne et al., 2010). For this second group of people, their implicit attitudes were better predictors of behavior than their explicit attitudes.

explicit attitude
An attitude that a person is consciously aware of and can report.

implicit attitude
An attitude that influences a person's feelings and behavior at an unconscious level.

Use of the IAT has become controversial. An early meta-analysis of more than 100 studies found that in socially sensitive situations in which people might not want to admit their real attitudes, the IAT is a better predictor of behavior than explicit self-reports are (Greenwald, Poehlman, Uhlmann, & Banaji, 2009). However, some recent evidence suggests that the IAT may not effectively predict racial and ethnic discrimination (Oswald, Mitchell, Blanton, Jaccard, & Tetlock, 2015). Indeed, there is strong concern that the public perception of the IAT exaggerates its ability to accurately identify racial bias or predict biased behavior. At this time, there is no reliable way to measure whether someone has unconscious bias.

12.6 Discrepancies Between Attitudes and Behavior Lead to Dissonance

12.6 LEARNING GOAL ACTIVITIES

To maximize your learning, complete the following learning goal activities:

a. Understand all bold and italic terms by writing explanations of them in your own words.

b. Apply the idea of cognitive dissonance by providing an example of cognitive dissonance in your life and explaining how you resolved the conflict.

Generally, we expect attitudes to guide behavior. We expect people to vote for candidates they like and avoid eating foods they do not like. What happens when people hold conflicting attitudes? In 1957, the social psychologist Leon Festinger answered that question by proposing the theory of **cognitive dissonance**.

COGNITIVE DISSONANCE THEORY Dissonance is a lack of agreement. According to Festinger's theory, cognitive dissonance occurs when there is a contradiction between two attitudes or between an attitude and a behavior. For example, people experience cognitive dissonance when they smoke even though they know that smoking might kill them.

A basic assumption of cognitive dissonance theory is that dissonance causes anxiety and tension. Anxiety and tension cause displeasure. Displeasure motivates people to reduce dissonance. People may reduce dissonance by changing their attitudes or behaviors. Smokers may reduce dissonance by quitting smoking or by deciding that smoking isn't so bad. They sometimes rationalize or trivialize the discrepancies, as the Learning Tip on this page illustrates.

Cognitive dissonance also arises when you have positive attitudes about different options, but you have to choose one option. For example, you might have trouble deciding which apartment to rent. You narrow the choice to two or three alternatives, and then you have to choose one. Once you've made your choice, *postdecisional dissonance* motivates you to focus on the chosen apartment's positive aspects and the other apartments' negative aspects. This effect occurs automatically, with little cognitive processing, and apparently without awareness, since people with amnesia who are unable to remember their choices

LEARNING TIP: Cognitive Dissonance

What happens when you have a complex attitude? Suppose your attitude is that it is healthy to exercise (Cognition A). However, you do not exercise (Behavior B). This inconsistency creates some internal conflict, or cognitive dissonance, which feels uncomfortable.

You can reduce the discomfort of cognitive dissonance in two ways. You can bring your attitude in line with your behavior—for example, by saying, "Exercising won't affect my health that much" (change Cognition A). Or you might bring your behavior in line with your attitude by beginning to exercise (change Behavior B). Either way, the dissonance is reduced and the consistency between your attitude and your behavior will make you feel better.

cognitive dissonance
An uncomfortable mental state due to a contradiction between two attitudes or between an attitude and a behavior.

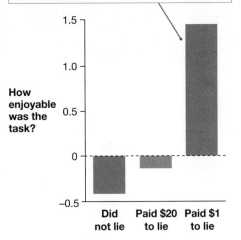

Participants who were paid only $1 to mislead a fellow participant experienced the effect of insufficient justification, a form of cognitive dissonance. This dissonance led them to increase their attitudes about how pleasurable the task had been.

FIGURE 12.12

Insufficient Justification Effect

Participants in one study performed an extremely boring task and then reported to other participants how enjoyable it was. Some participants were paid $20 to lie, and some were paid $1.

FIGURE 12.13

The Aftermath of Hazing

Hazing can have dangerous effects and tragic consequences. Here, the family members of California State University, Northridge student Armando Villa mourn Villa's death, which happened during a fraternity-hazing hike in 2014. Why do fraternity candidates submit to dangerous hazing activities?

show the effects of postdecisional dissonance (Lieberman, Ochsner, Gilbert, & Schacter, 2001).

JUSTIFICATION OF EFFORT   In one of the original dissonance studies, each participant was asked to perform an extremely boring task for an hour (Festinger & Carlsmith, 1959). People did not like the task, but the experimenter offered the participants either $1 or $20 to lie and tell the next participant that the task was really interesting, educational, and worthwhile. Almost all the participants went along with this setup and lied to the next participant.

Later, in an apparently unrelated study, the same participants were asked how worthwhile and enjoyable the task in the earlier study actually had been. You might think that those paid $20 remembered the task as more enjoyable, but just the opposite happened. Participants who were paid $1 rated the task much more favorably than those who were paid $20 (**Figure 12.12**).

According to the researchers, this *insufficient justification effect* occurred because those paid $1 did not have a strong enough reason to lie. Therefore, to justify why they went along with the lie, they changed their attitudes about performing the dull task. Those paid $20 had plenty of justification for lying, because $20 was a large amount of money in 1959 (roughly equivalent to $150 today). Therefore, these participants did not experience dissonance and did not have to change their attitudes about the task.

As research has shown (Aronson & Mills, 1959), when people put themselves through pain, embarrassment, or discomfort to join a group, they experience a great deal of dissonance. After all, these people typically would not choose to be in pain, embarrassed, or uncomfortable. Yet they made such a choice. They resolve the dissonance by exaggerating the importance of the group and their commitment to it. Tragically, justification of effort may help explain why people who give up connections to family and friends to join cults or to follow charismatic leaders are willing to die rather than leave the groups. If they have sacrificed so much to join a group, they believe, the group must be extraordinarily important.

The justification of effort helps explain why people are willing to subject themselves to humiliating experiences such as hazing. The groups require new recruits to undergo embarrassing or difficult rites of passage because these endurance tests make membership in the group seem much more valuable. The tests also make the group more cohesive. In 2011, band members at Florida A&M University were hazing the drum major Robert Champion on a school bus. They ended up beating Champion to death. Hazing and initiation rites are major problems on college campuses (**Figure 12.13**). Administrators impose rules and penalties to discourage hazing, yet some groups, such as fraternities and sororities, continue to do it.

12.7 Your Attitudes Can Be Changed Through Persuasion

 12.7 LEARNING GOAL ACTIVITIES

To maximize your learning, complete the following learning goal activities:

a. Understand all bold and italic terms by writing explanations of them in your own words.

b. Apply the elaboration likelihood model by finding one advertisement that uses the central route and one that uses the peripheral route and explaining why each ad is an example of that type of persuasion.

You may feel bombarded by advertisements; lectures from parents, teachers, and physicians; pressure from peers; public service announcements; politicians appealing for your vote; and on and on. These messages attempt to persuade you to think or do something. **Persuasion** is the active and conscious effort to change an attitude by sending a message. In the earliest scientific work on persuasion, Carl Hovland and colleagues (1953) emphasized that persuasion is most likely to occur when you pay attention to a message, understand it, and find it convincing. You also have to remember it.

THREE FACTORS AFFECT PERSUASIVENESS Three factors affect the persuasiveness of a message (Petty & Wegener, 1998). These factors include the source (who delivers the message), the content (what the message says), and the receiver (who processes the message). Sources that are both attractive and credible tend to be very persuasive. Thus television ads for medicines and medical services often feature attractive people playing the roles of physicians. Even better, of course, is when a drug company ad uses a spokesperson who is both attractive and an actual doctor. A message also may be more credible and persuasive when you perceive the source as similar to yourself.

Of course, the content of the message, including the arguments that are made, are important for persuasion (Greenwald, 1968). Strong arguments that appeal to emotions are the most persuasive. Advertisers also use the mere exposure effect: They repeat the message over and over in the hope that multiple exposures will make it more persuasive. For this reason, politicians often make the same statements seemingly endlessly during campaigns.

Those who want to persuade (including, of course, politicians) also have to decide whether to deliver one-sided arguments or to consider both sides of a particular issue. One-sided arguments work best when the audience is more likely to be on the speaker's side or is gullible. With a more skeptical crowd, speakers who acknowledge both sides but argue that one is superior tend to be more persuasive than those who completely ignore the opposing view.

TWO ROUTES OF PERSUASION What happens when you encounter a persuasive message? According to Richard Petty and John Cacioppo's *elaboration likelihood model* (1986), you sometimes think carefully and sometimes do not think too deeply. When you are motivated to process information and are able to process that information, persuasion takes the **central route** (**Figure 12.14a**). That is, you elaborate the information. You pay attention to the arguments, consider all the information, and use rational cognitive processes. This route leads to strong attitudes that last over time and that you actively defend.

When we are either not motivated or unable to process information, persuasion takes the **peripheral route** (**Figure 12.14b**). In this route, you don't think too deeply. That is, you minimally elaborate the message. When you don't think carefully, cues

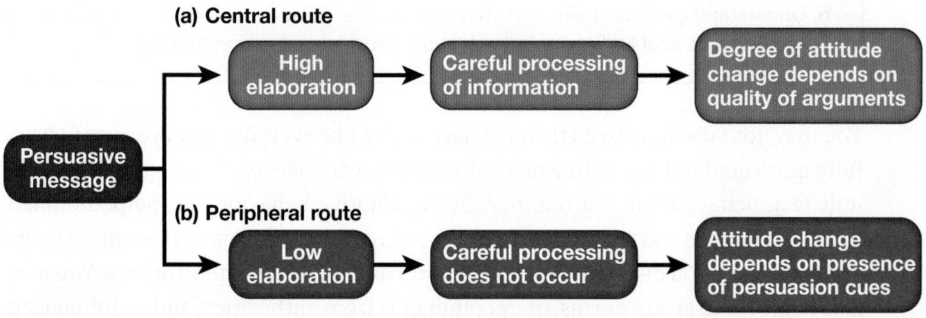

persuasion
The active and conscious effort to change an attitude through the transmission of a message.

central route
A method of persuasion that uses high elaboration—where people pay attention to the arguments and consider all the information in the message. This method usually results in development of stronger attitudes.

peripheral route
A method of persuasion that uses low elaboration—where people minimally process the message. This method usually results in development of weaker attitudes.

(a) Central route

Persuasive message → High elaboration → Careful processing of information → Degree of attitude change depends on quality of arguments

(b) Peripheral route

Persuasive message → Low elaboration → Careful processing does not occur → Attitude change depends on presence of persuasion cues

FIGURE 12.14

The Elaboration Likelihood Model

(a) When you are motivated and able to consider information, you process the information via the central route. As a result, your attitude changes reflect high elaboration. **(b)** When you are either not motivated or not able to consider information, you process the information via the peripheral route. As a result, your attitude changes reflect low elaboration.

such as the attractiveness or status of the person making the argument influence what attitude is adopted. This route leads to more-impulsive action, as when you purchase a product because a celebrity has endorsed it or because of how an advertisement makes you feel (for example, consider the situation in Has It Happened to You?). Attitudes developed through the peripheral route are weaker and more likely to change over time.

Q How Do Your Attitudes Affect You?

To make sure you learned what you just read, write answers to the following questions and check your answers.

12.5 As a child, Saskia did not want to eat mushrooms. Over time, her parents had her try one bite of a mushroom any time it was in a meal. After tasting mushrooms repeatedly, Saskia began to like them. What explains Saskia's change in attitude?

12.6 Before buying a car, your aunt spent months choosing between two options. After she decided what car to buy, she claimed that the right choice was always obvious because the one car is so much better. What explains your aunt's attitude?

12.7 At the grocery store, Steward buys a particular cereal because the nutrition label says it has very little sugar and is high in protein, so he knows it's a healthy choice. According to the elaboration likelihood model, what route of persuasion influenced Steward's decision, and how did it do so?

See Appendix B for answers to the red Q questions.

How Do Other People Influence You?

"As soon as I'm around my parents, I act as if I'm seven years old again!" It's a common lament, and you may have said it yourself. Do you behave the same way when you are with your parents, a teacher or employer, or a romantic interest? And do you act the same way when you are alone as when you're in a group? Of course not. So how are you affected by other people?

12.8 Groups Affect Your Behavior

12.8 LEARNING GOAL ACTIVITIES

To maximize your learning, complete the following learning goal activities:

a. Understand all bold and italic terms by writing explanations of them in your own words.

b. Understand the four main ways that groups affect you by summarizing social facilitation, social loafing, deindividuation, and group decision making.

You may not be willing to go through hazing. But like everyone else, you are powerfully motivated to fit in with whatever group you are part of. As discussed in study unit 12.4, being part of a group may be an adaptive behavior that helped human ancestors survive and reproduce. One way you may try to fit in is by presenting yourself positively. You display your best behavior and try not to offend others. You may also conform to group norms, obey commands from authorities, and be influenced

(a)

(b)

FIGURE 12.15

Influence of Groups on Behavior

(a) In social facilitation, the presence of others often improves performance. For example, you may run faster in a group than alone. (b) In social loafing, the presence of others impairs performance. For example, when other people are around to do the work, you may tend to slack off.

by others in your social group. In fact, the desire to fit in with the group and avoid being ostracized is so great that under some circumstances, you might willingly engage in behaviors that you otherwise would condemn. Perhaps the single most important lesson from social psychology is that the power of the social situation is much greater than most people believe.

social facilitation
When the mere presence of others improves performance.

social loafing
The tendency for people to work less hard in a group than when working alone.

SOCIAL FACILITATION AND SOCIAL LOAFING   In the first social psychology experiment, conducted in 1897, Norman Triplett showed that bicyclists pedal faster when they ride with other people than when they ride alone. They do so because of **social facilitation** (**Figure 12.15a**). That is, the presence of others often improves performance, particularly for tasks that are easy or well learned. For difficult tasks, though, sometimes the presence of other people can negatively affect performance.

Some people slack off when working in groups. That is, people tend to work less hard in a group than when working alone. This effect is called **social loafing** (**Figure 12.15b**). Social loafing occurs when efforts are pooled, so individuals do not feel personally responsible for the group's output.

In a classic study, six blindfolded people wearing headphones were told to shout as loudly as they could. Some were told they were shouting alone. Others were told they were shouting with other people. Participants did not shout as loudly when they believed that others were also shouting (Latané, Williams, & Harkins, 1979). When people know that their individual efforts can be monitored, however, they do not engage in social loafing. Thus if a group is working on a project, each person must feel personally responsible for some component of the project for everyone to exert maximum effort (Williams, Harkins, & Latané, 1981).

(a)

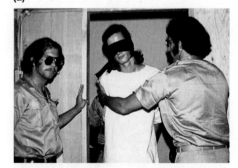

(b)

FIGURE 12.16

Effect of Groups in the Stanford Prison Study and at Abu Ghraib

(a) In the Stanford prison study, student-guards took on their roles with such vigor that the study was ended early because of concerns for the well-being of the "guards" and the "prisoners." (b) Were soldier-guards at Abu Ghraib who harassed, threatened, and tortured prisoners just a few "bad apples," or were they normal people reacting to an extreme situation?

DEINDIVIDUATION   In a classic study, the psychologists Philip Zimbardo and Chris Haney had male undergraduates at Stanford University play the roles of prisoners and guards in a mock prison (Haney, Banks, & Zimbardo, 1973). The students had all been screened and found to be psychologically stable. They were randomly assigned to their roles. What the authors reported happening was unexpected and shocking. Within days, some of the "guards" became brutal and sadistic. They constantly harassed the "prisoners," forcing them to engage in meaningless and tedious tasks and exercises. The prisoners became helpless to resist. Although the study was scheduled to last two weeks, the researchers stopped it after only six days. The study lacked many of the features of a true experiment, and recent critiques have noted that there was considerable variability in the behavior of the guards (Bartels, 2015; Bartels, Milovich, & Moussier, 2016). Indeed, some evidence suggests that the guards were even coached how to act in the study (Blum, 2018). Nonetheless, the results demonstrate what some people are willing to do when put in a situation with defined social roles (**Figure 12.16a**). Even if they were acting the part, some of the guards were willing to mistreat the prisoners.

deindividuation
A state of reduced individuality, reduced self-awareness, and reduced attention to personal standards; this phenomenon may occur when people are part of a group.

In a real-life situation that has been likened to the Stanford experiment, the Abu Ghraib prison in Iraq, now named the Baghdad Central Prison, will always be remembered as the site of horrible abuses of power. During 2003, the first year of the Iraq War, American soldiers brutalized Iraqi detainees at Abu Ghraib. The soldiers raped prisoners, threatened them with dogs, beat them, placed them in humiliating positions, and forced them to perform or simulate oral sex and masturbation (**Figure 12.16b**).

When the news media began to reveal the abuse at Abu Ghraib, U.S. military and government officials were quick to claim that these were isolated incidents carried out by a small group of wayward soldiers. They emphasized that even amid the horrors of war, soldiers are expected to behave in a civilized and professional manner. The idea that only a few troubled individuals were responsible for the abuses is strangely comforting, but is it true?

The soldiers at Abu Ghraib, like the students in the Stanford study, were probably normal people who were caught up in overwhelming situations where being part of the group influenced their actions in extreme ways. Essentially, they lost their individuality, and their self-awareness, when they became part of the group. **Deindividuation** occurs when people are not self-aware and therefore are not paying attention to their personal standards.

Being self-aware typically causes people to act in ways that are consistent with their values and beliefs. When self-awareness disappears, so do inhibitions. Deindividuated people often do things they would not do if they were alone or self-aware. For example, most of us like to think we would try to help a person who was threatening suicide. But people in crowds often fail to intercede in such situations. Disturbingly, they may even egg the person on, yelling "Jump! Jump!" to someone teetering on a ledge.

People are especially likely to become deindividuated when they are aroused and anonymous and when responsibility is not clear. Rioting by fans, looting following disasters, and other mob behaviors are the products of deindividuation. Not all deindividuated behavior is so serious, of course. Fans dressing alike at a sports event and people dancing the funky chicken while under the influence of alcohol at a wedding are most likely in deindividuated states and acting in ways they would avoid if they were self-aware (**Figure 12.17**).

GROUP DECISION MAKING Think back to when you were younger and all your friends were going to do something risky. Maybe they were going to dive off a high cliff or steal something from a convenience store. Did you join in?

In the 1960s, James Stoner found that groups often make riskier decisions than individuals do. Stoner called this phenomenon the *risky-shift effect*. The risky-shift effect accounts for why people in a group may try something dangerous that none of them would have tried alone. People in groups tend to make decisions that are more extreme than those made by people on their own.

Sometimes, however, groups become more cautious. Whether the group accepts more risk or becomes more cautious depends on the initial attitudes of the group members. If most of the group members are somewhat cautious, then the group becomes even more cautious. This process is known as *group polarization* (Myers & Lamm, 1976). For example, a jury that is initially skeptical is likely to become even more so after its members discuss the case. Through mutual persuasion, the decision making individuals come to agreement.

Sometimes group members are particularly concerned with maintaining a good atmosphere within the group. Therefore, for the sake of cordiality, the group may end up making a bad decision. In 1972, the social psychologist Irving Janis coined the term *groupthink* to describe this extreme form of group polarization.

(a)

(b)

FIGURE 12.17

Deindividuation

(a) When people are excited and anonymous, like the fans at this basketball game, they tend to become less self-aware and to pay less attention to their personal standards. **(b)** When this process of deindividuation happens, people tend to act in ways that they would not normally behave.

To avoid groupthink the next time you are working in a group, try these tips.

1. Try to keep the group small: In a smaller group, members are more likely to speak their minds.
2. Be open to alternative ideas: Sometimes the best idea is the one you have not considered yet.
3. Express your ideas: Even one dissenting opinion can decrease group conformity.
4. Treat dissenters respectfully: Making fun of others may make them afraid to speak up.
5. List the pros and cons of all options: Sorting through the positive and negative aspects will help you choose the best option.

Being open to new ideas and carefully weighing options can help you avoid groupthink and come to the best group decision.

Many examples of groupthink have occurred throughout history. In 2003, the United States went to war with Iraq over weapons of mass destruction that did not exist (as later investigations showed). Even though some members of the administration had doubts, they kept those doubts to themselves to avoid rocking the boat. Groupthink typically occurs when a group is under intense pressure, is facing external threats, or is biased in a particular direction. The group does not carefully process all the information available to it. Dissension is discouraged. Group members assure each other that they are doing the right thing.

To prevent groupthink, leaders must refrain from expressing their opinions too strongly at the beginning of discussions. The group should be encouraged to consider alternative ideas. Either a group member can play devil's advocate or the group can carefully examine outside opinions. Of course, a group can make a bad decision even without falling victim to groupthink. Other factors, such as political values, can bias a group's decision making. But carefully going through the alternatives and weighing their pros and cons can help people avoid groupthink. The next time you work in a group, you can test some of the suggestions in Try It Yourself above.

12.9 You Conform to and Comply with Others

12.9 LEARNING GOAL ACTIVITIES

To maximize your learning, complete the following learning goal activities:

a. Understand all bold and italic terms by writing explanations of them in your own words.

b. Apply conformity and compliance by providing one example each of how two different people influenced you, one to conform and the other to comply.

When you enter an elevator, do you face the doors or the other people? Most likely you face the doors. If you can't, you look at the floor. Looking directly at strangers in an elevator will make you and them uncomfortable. As a result, you conform to the expected behavior. **Conformity** is altering your behaviors or opinions to match those of others or to match what is expected of you. And conformity is a powerful form of social influence. What causes conformity?

conformity
The altering of your own behaviors and opinions to match those of other people or to match other people's expectations.

FIGURE 12.18

Normative and Informational Influence

People behave in the ways that others do for two main reasons. **(a)** They do this to be liked or to avoid looking foolish due to normative influence. An example of this behavior is the way that people generally stand facing the door in an elevator. **(b)** They also behave like others do when they think the group provides information about what should be done. This effect of informational influence is seen in crowds, when people start running in a particular direction—presumably away from a particular danger.

(a)

(b)

NORMATIVE AND INFORMATIONAL INFLUENCE Social psychologists have identified two primary reasons that you might conform. *Normative influence* occurs when—to be liked, to be accepted, or to avoid looking foolish—you go along with what the group does. This effect leads you to face the door in the elevator (**Figure 12.18a**). *Informational influence* occurs when you assume that the behavior of a group provides information about the right way to act. Suppose you are in a public place and see a mass of people running for the exit. In such a situation, you might assume that their behavior is giving you information about a potential emergency. If you suspect they are exiting for a good reason, informational influence would lead you to conform by running in the same direction (**Figure 12.18b**).

We have all seen examples of conformity to a group. Solomon Asch (1955) provided remarkable evidence of this behavior. Asch assembled male participants for a study of visual acuity. The participants looked at a reference line and three comparison lines. They decided which of the three comparison lines matched the reference line and said their answers aloud (**Figure 12.19**).

Normally, people are able to perform this easy task with a high level of accuracy. In these studies, Asch included just one naive (real) participant with a group of five confederates. The confederates pretended to be participants, but they actually were working for the experimenter. The real participant always gave his answer last, after the five confederates gave theirs.

On 12 of the 18 trials, the confederates deliberately gave the same wrong answer. After hearing five wrong answers, the participant then had to state his answer. About one third of the time, the participant went along with the confederates: He knowingly gave an answer that was obviously false. When the trials were repeated, three out of four real participants conformed to the incorrect response at least once. Why would they do this? It was not because they knew others were providing the right answer. In other words, it was not due to informational influence. Instead, people conformed because they did not want to look foolish by going against the group. That is, they conformed due to normative influence.

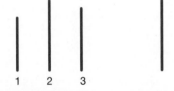

1	2	3	

Comparison lines   Reference line

FIGURE 12.19

Asch's Research on Conformity

In Asch's study, participants in a group had to decide which of the three comparison lines matched the reference line and to say their answers aloud. He found that people tended to conform to social norms by giving the wrong answer, even when those norms were obviously wrong.

SOCIAL NORMS You may complain about all the rules you have to follow, but society needs rules in order to function. Imagine what would happen if you woke up one morning and decided that you would start driving on the wrong side of the road. Normative influence relies on the societal need for rules. Expected standards of conduct are called **social norms**. Social norms influence behavior in many ways. For example, they indicate which behavior is appropriate in a given situation and also how people will respond to those who violate norms. Standing in line is a social

social norms

Expected standards of conduct, which influence behavior.

norm, and people who violate that norm by cutting in line are often sternly told to move to the back of the line. Normative influence works because people tend to feel embarrassed when they break social norms. The next time you enter an elevator, try standing with your back to the elevator door and facing people. You may find it quite difficult to defy even this simple social norm.

People conform due to normative influence in daily life: Adolescents conform to peer pressure to smoke, jury members go along with the group rather than state their own opinions, and people stand in line to buy tickets. Sometimes, of course, people reject social norms. In a series of follow-up studies, Asch (1956) found that small group size and lack of unanimity among the group both diminish our tendency to conform.

Groups tend to enforce social norms. Research (for example, Schachter, 1951) has shown that dissenters are typically not treated well by groups. Groups enforce conformity, and those who fail to go along are rejected. The need to belong, and worry about the possibility of being excluded from a social group, gives a group powerful influence over its members.

COMPLIANCE You may follow social norms because you are afraid not to. You also behave in certain ways simply because others ask you to. Say your friends ask you to do a favor for them. If you do what they request, you are exhibiting **compliance.**

A number of factors increase compliance. Joseph Forgas (1998) has demonstrated if you are in a good mood, you are especially likely to comply. This tendency may be the basis for "buttering up" others when you want things from them.

As shown in **Table 12.1,** some powerful strategies can be used to influence others to comply. Consider the *foot-in-the-door* strategy: Once you agree to a small request, you are more likely to comply with a large and undesirable request. Jonathan Freedman and Scott Fraser (1966) asked homeowners to place a large, unattractive "DRIVE CAREFULLY" sign on their front lawns. Few people agreed to do so. However, when homeowners were first asked to sign a petition supporting legislation to reduce traffic accidents, many later agreed to put up the lawn signs. Once you commit to a course of action, you behave in ways consistent with that course.

The opposite strategy is the *door-in-the-face*: You are more likely to agree to a small request after you have refused a large request. The second request seems modest in comparison, and you want to seem reasonable. Salespeople often use this technique when they try to sell you a moderately priced item after you've rejected an expensive one.

compliance
The tendency to agree to do things requested by others.

TABLE 12.1
The Three Ways of Inducing Compliance

Strategy	Technique	Example
Foot-in-the-door	If you agree to a small request, you are more likely to comply with a large request.	You agree to help a friend move a couch. Now you are more likely to comply when she asks you to help her move all of her belongings to her new apartment.
Door-in-the-face	If you refuse a large request, you are more likely to comply with a smaller request.	A marketer calls, and you refuse to answer a product questionnaire that takes 20 minutes. Now you are likely to agree to answer 5 questions about a product.
Lowballing	When you agree to buy a product for a certain price, you are likely to comply with a request to pay more for the product.	You agree to buy a used car for $4,750. When the salesman says he forgot to add some charges, you agree to buy the car for $5,275.

Another favorite sales tactic is the *lowballing* strategy. Here, a salesperson offers a product—for example, a car—for a very low price. Once the customer agrees, the salesperson may claim that the manager did not approve the price or that there will be additional charges. Whatever the reason, someone who has already agreed to buy a product will often agree to pay the increased cost.

12.10 You Probably Obey People Who Have Authority

12.10 LEARNING GOAL ACTIVITIES

To maximize your learning, complete the following learning goal activities:

a. Understand all bold and italic terms by writing explanations of them in your own words.

b. Understand obedience by explaining what it is and describing the two factors that affect people's willingness to obey others.

In the early 1960s, Stanley Milgram conducted what turned out to be one of the most famous and most disturbing psychology experiments ever done. Milgram wanted to understand why apparently normal German citizens willingly obeyed orders to injure or kill innocent people during World War II. Milgram was interested in the determinants of **obedience**. That is, he wanted to find out what factors influence people to follow orders given by an authority.

MILGRAM'S CLASSIC EXPERIMENT ON OBEDIENCE Milgram's experiment is summarized in The Methods of Psychology on p. 485. One participant was assigned to serve as a "teacher." The experimenter sat next to the teacher. Another participant, located in the next room, was the "learner." The learner was asked questions. Each time he gave a wrong answer, the teacher gave him what the teacher was told was an electric shock. As the test proceeded, the teacher was supposed to gradually increase the strength of the shocks.

In fact, the learner was a confederate of the experimenter, and the "shocks" were not real. A recording made it sound as though the learner was getting extremely painful shocks. The learner also complained of a heart condition and begged for the shocks to stop. Almost all the teachers tried to quit, especially when the learner screamed in pain. Each time, however, the experimenter ordered the teacher to continue. The experimenter stated: "The experiment requires that you continue," "It is essential that you go on," "There is no other choice; you must go on!"

Milgram was quite surprised by the results of his study. When he had asked people to predict the results, very few expected the research participants would follow orders to hurt others (**Figure 12.20**). Although some teachers resisted authority by saying no to the experimenter's orders, nearly two-thirds obeyed all the experimenter's directives. Indeed, most of the teachers were willing to administer an apparently dangerous amount of electricity to the learner with a heart condition. These findings have been replicated by Milgram and others around the world. The conclusion of all the studies is that ordinary people can be coerced into obedience by insistent authorities. This effect occurs even when the coerced behavior goes against the way people usually would behave.

Milgram's results do not mean that people are always obedient. Instead, two factors affect obedience. First, some types of people, such as those who are concerned about how others view them, are more likely to be obedient (Blass, 1991).

obedience
When a person follows the orders of a person of authority.

Hypothesis: People will obey authority figures.

Research Method:

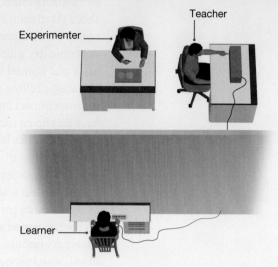

1. The participant ("teacher") was told that he must administer a shock to the "learner," located in another room, whenever he answered a question incorrectly. The learner was secretly working with the experimenter as a confederate.

2. The teacher helped the experimenter strap the learner into the machine that supposedly delivered the shocks. During the experiment, when the teacher believed he was shocking the learner, he heard a recording of the learner screaming in pain and begging the teacher to stop.

3. The teacher initially wanted to stop the study, but the experimenter insisted that he give the learner increasingly severe shocks. The real purpose of the experiment was to determine whether the teacher would obey the authority of the experimenter.

4. According to Milgram, each participant teacher was introduced to the confederate learner after the experiment so the teacher could see that the learner had not been harmed.

Results: Almost all of the participants tried to quit. However, nearly two-thirds of them obeyed the experimenter's directives to continue delivering shocks.

Conclusion: Most people will obey orders given by insistent authority figures. This willingness may be reduced depending on personality and making people more personally responsible for what is occurring.

QUESTION: Why might people follow an order even if they disagree with the order?

ANSWER: People obey orders from those whom they perceive to be authority figures.

Source: Milgram, S. (1974). Obedience to authority: An experimental view. New York: Harper & Row.

In addition, Milgram also found that some situations produced less obedience. For instance, if the teacher could see or had to touch the learner, obedience decreased. When the experimenter gave the orders over the telephone and thus was more removed from the situation, obedience dropped dramatically. So both personality and situational factors affected obedience.

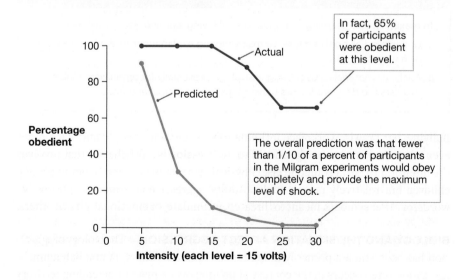

In fact, 65% of participants were obedient at this level.

The overall prediction was that fewer than 1/10 of a percent of participants in the Milgram experiments would obey completely and provide the maximum level of shock.

FIGURE 12.20

Predicted and Actual Results

Psychiatrists, college sophomores, middle-class adults, and both graduate students and professors in the behavioral sciences offered predictions about the results of Milgram's experiments. Their predictions were incorrect. Most people continued shocking participants.

RETHINKING MILGRAM'S RESEARCH   Over the fifty years since the Milgram studies were conducted, a number of criticisms have emerged (Brannigan, Nicholson, & Cherry, 2015; Griggs, 2017). For instance, some participants seem to have received stronger orders than others did (Gibson, 2013). It also appears that many participants did not really believe that the victim was receiving a life-threatening shock (Hoffman, Myerberg, & Morawski, 2015). Some researchers have even questioned whether participants were truly obedient, or whether they were following the experimenter's directives because they believed in the value of the scientific enterprise and wanted to help the experimenter (Haslam, Reicher, Millard, & McDonald, 2015). Telling people they have to continue for the sake of the experiment has a greater impact on participants than telling them that they must obey because they have no choice (Burger, Girgis, & Manning, 2011). From this view, participants are willing to inflict harm because they identify with the goals of science and believe they are being virtuous (Haslam, Reicher, & Birney, 2016). Still, people were willing to inflict significant pain on an innocent victim for the cause.

The earliest and most persistent critiques revolve around the ethical treatment of the research participants (Baumrind, 1964). Even though Milgram claimed to be highly concerned with his participants' mental states, not all participants received timely debriefings, in which they learned the true nature of the experiments (Nicholson, 2011; Perry, 2013). In an attempt to understand the long-term impact of taking part in the research, Milgram (1974) followed his participants over time and reported that most people were glad they had participated. They felt they had learned something about themselves and about human nature. Nowadays, researchers follow clear guidelines to protect the physical and mental health of research participants (as discussed in study unit 1.12).

Even given these faults, the Milgram studies document just how powerful situational influences can be. Most of us assume that only evil people would willingly inflict injury on others when ordered to do so. Milgram's research, and studies that followed up on it, demonstrated that ordinary people may do horrible things when ordered to do so by an authority. Although some people have speculated that these results would not be true today, a recent replication found that 70 percent of the participants were obedient up to the maximum voltage in the experiment (Burger, 2009).

12.11 You May Hurt or Help Other People

 12.11 LEARNING GOAL ACTIVITIES

To maximize your learning, complete the following learning goal activities:

a. Understand all bold and italic terms by writing explanations of them in your own words.

b. Analyze what makes us act aggressively or prosocially by organizing a table that lists the different factors behind these two types of actions.

Bullying, bar brawls, workplace intimidation—sometimes people hurt each other even when they are not being ordered to. **Aggression** is any behavior that involves the intention to harm someone else. Physical aggression is common among young children but relatively rare in adults. Adults' aggressive acts more often involve words, or other symbols, meant to threaten, intimidate, or emotionally harm others.

BIOLOGY AND THE SITUATION AFFECT AGGRESSION   The biology of aggression has been studied primarily in nonhuman animals. Among nonhuman animals, aggression often occurs in the context of fighting over a mate or defending territory

aggression
Any behavior that involves the intention to harm someone else.

from intruders. Research with nonhuman animals has shown that stimulating certain brain regions or altering brain chemistry can lead to substantial changes in the level of aggression displayed. Several lines of evidence suggest that serotonin is especially important in the control of aggressive behavior (Caramaschi, de Boer, & Koolhaus, 2007). In humans, low levels of serotonin have been associated with aggression in adults and with hostility and disruptive behavior in children (Kruesi et al., 1992; Moffitt et al., 1998). A second factor that affects aggression is the situation. Imagine the following: You are driving to an important meeting. Traffic is barely moving. As the minutes go by, you start imagining the consequences of being late. Then another driver cuts in front of you. It's a perfect setup for road rage, a common form of aggression.

In the 1930s, John Dollard and colleagues proposed the **frustration-aggression hypothesis**. This hypothesis suggests that the more frustrated you feel, the more likely you are to be aggressive. The more your goals are blocked, the greater your frustration, and therefore the greater your aggression (**Figure 12.21**).

Frustration may lead to aggression by eliciting negative emotions. Similarly, any situation that induces negative emotions—such as being insulted, afraid, or in pain—can trigger physical aggression even if it does not induce frustration. Being overly hot can also make you more aggressive (Van Lange, Rinderu, & Bushman, 2017). Negative emotions may lead to aggression because negative events activate thoughts related to fighting or escaping, and those thoughts prepare you to act aggressively. Whether you actually behave aggressively depends on the situation. If you have recently been exposed to cues of violence—for example, if you have recently watched a violent movie or been in the presence of weapons—you are more likely to act aggressively (Bushman & Anderson, 2015).

SOCIAL AND CULTURAL FACTORS AFFECT AGGRESSION If you consider aggression in terms of human evolution, you might expect all societies to show similar patterns of aggressive behavior. After all, if aggression provided a selective advantage for human ancestors, it should have done so for all humans. But the data show that violence varies dramatically across cultures and even within cultures at different times. For example, over the course of 300 years, Sweden went from being one of the most violent nations on Earth to being one of the most peaceable. Moreover, murder rates are far higher in some countries than in others (**Figure 12.22**). And analysis of crime statistics in the United States reveals that

FIGURE 12.21
Frustration Predicts Aggression
Frustration generally leads to aggression. For example, when traffic is heavy and drivers feel frustrated, they are more likely to behave aggressively. That aggressive behavior may include yelling and displaying road rage.

frustration-aggression hypothesis
The idea that the more frustrated a person feels, the more likely the person is to act aggressively.

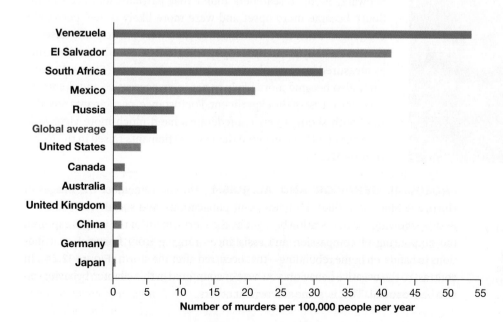

FIGURE 12.22
Aggression Varies Across Cultures
The numbers in this chart are the most recent available, from 2012. They come from the United Nations Office on Drugs and Crime (2013a).

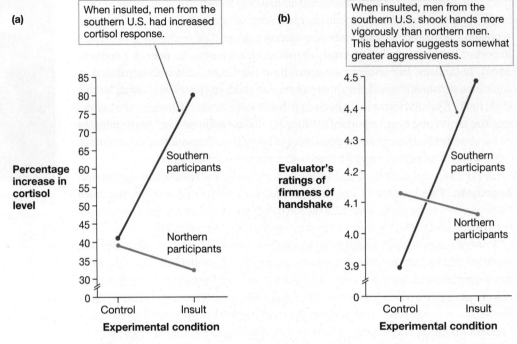

(a)

When insulted, men from the southern U.S. had increased cortisol response.

Percentage increase in cortisol level

Southern participants

Northern participants

Control   Insult
Experimental condition

(b)

When insulted, men from the southern U.S. shook hands more vigorously than northern men. This behavior suggests somewhat greater aggressiveness.

Evaluator's ratings of firmness of handshake

Southern participants

Northern participants

Control   Insult
Experimental condition

FIGURE 12.23

Aggressive Responses to Insults

According to results from studies at the University of Michigan, men in the southern United States tend to respond more aggressively to personal insults than do men in the North. This effect may partly be due to the Southerners having been raised in a culture of honor.

prosocial
Acting in ways that tend to benefit others.

FIGURE 12.24

Prosocial Behavior and Hurricane Maria

During and after Hurricane Maria, many people acted in prosocial ways by helping others. Here, volunteers use excavators and small boats to rescue neighbors from flooded areas of Loiza, Puerto Rico.

physical violence is much more prevalent in the South than in the North. Aggression may be part of human nature, but society and culture influence people's tendencies to commit acts of physical violence.

Some cultures may be violent because they subscribe to a culture of honor. In this belief system, men are primed to protect their reputations through physical aggression. For example, men in the southern United States traditionally were—and perhaps still are—raised to be ready to fight for their honor and to respond aggressively to personal threats. In a 1996 study (Cohen, Nisbett, Bowdle, & Schwarz, 1996), researchers found that participants raised in the South became more upset and were more likely to feel personally challenged when they were insulted than were participants raised in the North. They became more physiologically aroused after the insult, as measured by cortisol and testosterone increases (**Figure 12.23a**). They also became more likely to act in an aggressive and dominant way for the rest of the experiment. For instance, participants raised in the South shook a new confederate's hand much more vigorously after they had been insulted than did participants raised in the North (**Figure 12.23b**).

PROSOCIAL BEHAVIOR AND ALTRUISM Do you remember the images of Hurricane Maria that filled TV news, print publications, and social media in 2017? Besides showing the devastation brought by the storm, many of the images captured the outpouring of compassion and assistance—ranging from financial contributions to hands-on home rebuilding—that occurred after the storm (**Figure 12.24**). In contrast to the negative behaviors you have encountered in this chapter, behavior can also be **prosocial**. That is, some acts benefit others.

Prosocial behaviors include offering assistance, doing favors, paying compliments, resisting the temptation to insult or throttle another person, or simply being pleasant and cooperative. By benefiting others, prosocial behaviors lead to positive interpersonal relationships. Group living, which requires you to engage in prosocial behaviors such as sharing and cooperating, may be a central human survival strategy. After all, a group that works well together is a strong group, and belonging to a strong group benefits the individual members.

Altruism is one type of prosocial behavior where you provide help when it is needed, with no apparent reward for doing so. But doesn't helping others, and even risking personal safety to do so, seem contrary to evolutionary principles? After all, those who protect themselves first would appear to have an advantage over those who risk their lives to help others. Perhaps this is why Cory Booker was viewed as so heroic after saving his neighbor from the burning house, as described in the chapter opener.

You will probably be most altruistic toward those whose genes you share. This behavior makes evolutionary sense, because you are helping to ensure that your common genes survive into future generations. Of course, you will also sometimes help nonrelatives, just as Cory Booker risked his life to save his neighbor. Nonhuman animals exhibit this type of behavior as well. For example, dolphins and lions look after orphans within their own species.

Another explanation for altruism toward nonrelatives is the idea of *reciprocal helping*. According to Robert Trivers (1971), one animal helps another because the other may return the favor in the future. In a literal example of "You scratch my back, and I'll scratch yours," primates take turns cleaning each other's fur. For reciprocal helping to be adaptive, the benefits must outweigh the costs. Indeed, you are less likely to help others when the costs of doing so are high. Reciprocal helping is also much more likely to occur among animals, such as humans, that live in social groups because their species survival depends on cooperation.

BYSTANDER INTERVENTION EFFECT In 1964, a young woman named Kitty Genovese was walking home from work in a relatively safe area of New York City. An assailant savagely attacked her for half an hour, eventually killing her. At the time, a newspaper reported that 38 people had witnessed the crime, and none of them tried to help or called the police (**Figure 12.25**). That story appears to have been wrong, however. Few of the witnesses were in a position to see what was happening to Genovese (Manning, Levine, & Collins, 2007), and at least two people did call the police.

As you might imagine, the idea that 38 people could stand by and watch a brutal murder provoked outrage at the time. The public response prompted social psychologists to undertake research on how people react in emergencies. Shortly after the Genovese murder, Bibb Latané and John Darley examined situations that produce what they called **bystander intervention effect**. This term refers to the failure to offer help by those who observe someone in need. Common sense might suggest that when more people are available to help, a victim is more likely to be helped. Latané and Darley claimed, however, that each person is less likely to offer help if other bystanders are around.

To test their theory, Latané and Darley placed people in situations that indicated they should seek help. In one of the first situations, male college students were in a room, filling out questionnaires (Latané & Darley, 1968). Pungent smoke started puffing in through the heating vents. Some participants were alone. Some

altruism
The act of providing help when it is needed, with no apparent reward for doing so.

bystander intervention effect
The failure to offer help to people in need.

38 Who Saw Murder Didn't Call the Police

A young woman name Kitty Genovese was walking home from work in a relatively safe area of New York City. The assailant savagely attacked her for half an hour, eventually killing her. At the time, a newspaper reported that 38 people had witnessed the crime, and none of them tried to help or called the police

FIGURE 12.25

Kitty Genovese: A True Case of the Bystander Intervention Effect?

The idea that 38 people watched Kitty Genovese's murder provoked research on the bystander intervention effect. Although the reporting of the case was incorrect, the bystander intervention effect does occur.

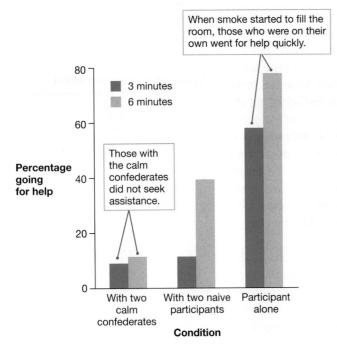

When smoke started to fill the room, those who were on their own went for help quickly.

Those with the calm confederates did not seek assistance.

Percentage going for help

- 3 minutes
- 6 minutes

FIGURE 12.26

The Bystander Intervention Effect

In Latané and Darley's experiments, participants were asked to wait with two calm confederates, with two other naive participants, or alone. This chart records the participants' reactions to smoke filling the room.

were with two other naive participants. Some were with two confederates, who noticed the smoke, shrugged, and continued filling out their questionnaires. When participants were on their own, most went for help. When three naive participants were together, however, few initially went for help. With the two calm confederates, only 10 percent of participants went for help in the first 6 minutes (**Figure 12.26**). The other 90 percent "coughed, rubbed their eyes, and opened the window—but they did not report the smoke" (p. 218).

In later studies, the researchers confronted the participants with mock crimes, apparent heart attack victims in subway cars, and people passed out in public places. The experimenters got similar results each time. The bystander intervention effect has been shown to occur in a wide variety of contexts. In one recent study, children as young as 5 years of age were less likely to help in the presence of others (Plötner, Over, Carpenter, & Tomasello, 2015).

Years of research have indicated four major reasons for bystander intervention effect. First, bystanders expect other bystanders to help. Thus the greater the number of people who witness someone in need of help, the less likely any of them are to step forward. Second, people fear making social blunders in ambiguous situations. In the Genovese murder, the few witnesses found the situation unclear and therefore might have been reluctant to call the police. There is evidence that people feel freer to seek help as the need for help becomes clearer. Third, people are less likely to help when they are anonymous and can remain so. Therefore, if you need help, it is often wise to point to a specific person and say something like, "You, in the red shirt, call an ambulance!"

A fourth factor in deciding whether to help involves weighing two factors: How much personal harm do you risk by helping someone? And what benefits might you have to forgo if you help? Imagine you are walking to a potentially dull class on a beautiful day. Right in front of you, someone falls down, twists an ankle, and needs transportation to the nearest clinic. You probably would be willing to help. Now imagine you are running to a final exam that counts for 90 percent of your grade. In this case, you probably would be much less likely to offer assistance.

Q How Do Other People Influence You?

To make sure you learned what you just read, write answers to the following questions and check your answers.

12.8 How does social facilitation differ from social loafing?

12.9 A woman dining at an Ethiopian restaurant picks up the food with her fingers because everyone else around her is doing so and she does not want to look foolish. Does this behavior represent normative or informational influence?

12.10 According to the research on obedience by Milgram, when is a person less likely to obey an authority's order to hurt someone?

12.11 According to the frustration-aggression hypothesis, why is aggression more likely in hot climates than in cold ones?

See Appendix B for answers to the red Q questions.

How Can You Develop Strong Relationships?

When you think about the social relationships that have been the most important to you, most likely you think about a romantic partner or your closest friends. These people have powerful effects on you. Whom do you choose to be your friends or lovers, how do these core social bonds develop, and why do some succeed and others fail?

Some people think that love and friendship are mysterious states to be considered only by poets. But relationships can be explored scientifically. Recently, researchers have begun to make considerable progress in identifying the factors that lead us to form relationships (Berscheid & Regan, 2005). Many of these findings support the idea that developing strong, lasting relationships with others is important to our survival as a species.

12.12 Situations and Personalities Affect Your Relationships

12.12 LEARNING GOAL ACTIVITIES

To maximize your learning, complete the following learning goal activities:

a. Understand all bold and italic terms by writing explanations of them in your own words.

b. Apply information about how situations and personalities affect relationships by describing how proximity, similarity, a person's admirable characteristics, and the person's physical attractiveness influenced the development of one of your friendships.

How did you become close with your best friend? If you are like most people, your best friend is someone that you grew up with or have lived near for a long time. The person is probably also similar to you in numerous ways, including core values and beliefs. In addition, your best friend probably has a lot of characteristics that you find positive. Psychologists have discovered that all these factors promote the development of friendships.

PROXIMITY   In 1950, Leon Festinger, Stanley Schachter, and Kurt Back examined the effects of proximity on friends in a college dorm. *Proximity* here simply means how often people come into contact. The researchers found that the more often students come into contact, the more likely they are to become friends. Indeed, friendships often form among people who belong to the same groups, clubs, and so on. Proximity might have its effects because of familiarity: People like familiar things more than unfamiliar ones. And, as we saw earlier, when we are repeatedly exposed to something, we tend to like the thing more over time. The mere exposure effect may apply to people as well as objects.

SIMILARITY   Birds of a feather really do flock together, and so do people who are like each other (**Figure 12.27**). People with similar attitudes, values, interests, backgrounds, personalities, and levels of attractiveness tend to like each other more than people who are dissimilar (Youyou, Schwartz, Stillwell, & Kosinski, 2017). In high school, people tend to be friends with those of the same sex, race or ethnicity, age, and year in school. College roommates who are most similar at the beginning of the school

FIGURE 12.27

Similarity in Attitudes and in Attractiveness

Friends and romantic partners tend to be similar in personal characteristics, attitudes, beliefs, and attractiveness. A good example of this matching is Beyoncé and Jay-Z, both of whom are very attractive and successful musicians and entrepreneurs.

year are most likely to become good friends (Neimeyer & Mitchell, 1988). In addition, the most successful romantic couples also tend to be the most physically similar (Bentler & Newcomb, 1978; Caspi & Herbener, 1990). Of course, people can and do become friends or romantic partners with people of other races, people who are much older or younger, and so on. Such friendships and relationships tend to be based on other important similarities, such as values, education, and socioeconomic status.

ADMIRABLE PERSONAL CHARACTERISTICS   You probably tend to like people who have admirable personality characteristics. This tendency holds true whether you are choosing friends or lovers. In a now-classic study, Norman Anderson (1968) asked college students to rate how much they would like others who possessed 555 different traits. As you might suspect, people most like those who have personal characteristics valuable to the group, such as kindness, dependability, and trustworthiness (**Table 12.2**). They dislike others with characteristics such as dishonesty, insincerity, and lack of personal warmth, which tend to drain group resources. People who seem overly competent or too perfect, however, make others feel uncomfortable or inadequate, and small mistakes can make a person seem more human and therefore more likable (Helmreich, Aronson, & LeFan, 1970).

PHYSICAL ATTRACTIVENESS   People also value physical attractiveness in forming relationships. But what determines physical attractiveness? Some standards of beauty, such as preferences for particular body types, appear to change over time and across cultures. Nevertheless, how people rate attractiveness is generally similar across all cultures (Cunningham, Roberts, Barbee, Druen, & Wu, 1995). For example, across all cultures, people who look after themselves, such as by having good hygiene, are viewed as more attractive.

TABLE 12.2
The Ten Most Positive and Most Negative Personal Characteristics

Most Positive	Most Negative
1. Sincere	1. Unkind
2. Honest	2. Untrustworthy
3. Understanding	3. Malicious
4. Loyal	4. Obnoxious
5. Truthful	5. Untruthful
6. Trustworthy	6. Dishonest
7. Intelligent	7. Cruel
8. Dependable	8. Mean
9. Open-minded	9. Phony
10. Thoughtful	10. Liar

Source: Anderson (1968).

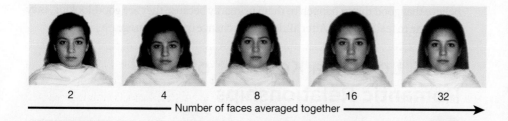

2   4   8   16   32

⟵ Number of faces averaged together ⟶

Most people find symmetrical faces more attractive than asymmetrical ones. This preference may be adaptive, because a lack of symmetry could indicate poor health or a genetic defect. A cleverly designed study of what people find attractive (Langlois & Roggman, 1990) used a computer program to combine (or average) various faces without regard to individual attractiveness. The more faces that were combined, the more the "averaged" faces were rated as attractive (**Figure 12.28**). What explains this result? People may view averaged faces as attractive because of the mere exposure effect. In other words, averaged faces may be more familiar than unusual faces. Other researchers have found that the ratings depend on what types of faces are averaged together. When composites are made from individual faces that have been judged to be more attractive, those composites are rated more favorably than composites made from faces initially rated as less attractive (Perrett, May, & Yoshikawa, 1994). Look at the photos in Try It Yourself below to see if you agree.

Attractiveness can bring many important social benefits. Most people are drawn to those they find physically attractive (Langlois et al., 2000). Attractive people are less likely to be perceived as criminals, and they are given lighter sentences when convicted of crimes. They are typically rated as happier, more intelligent, more sociable, more capable, more gifted, more successful, and less socially deviant (Feingold, 1992). They are paid more for doing the same work, and they have greater career opportunities. These findings point to what Karen Dion and colleagues (1972) dubbed the *"what is beautiful is good" stereotype*.

The preference for attractiveness begins early. Children as young as 6 months prefer to look at attractive faces, and young children prefer attractive playmates over unattractive ones (Rubenstein, Kalakanis, & Langlois, 1999). Even mothers treat their attractive children more positively than their less attractive children (Langlois, Ritter, Casey, & Sawin, 1995).

Although attractive people typically receive preferential treatment, do they actually have characteristics consistent with the stereotype that what is beautiful is good? The evidence on this issue is mixed. Attractive people tend to be more popular, more socially skilled, and healthier, but they are not necessarily smarter or happier (Feingold, 1992). Among studies of college students, for instance, the correlation between objective ratings of attractiveness and other characteristics, such as grades or number of personal relationships, appears small.

So why does having all the benefits of attractiveness not lead to greater happiness? Possibly, attractive people learn to distrust attention from others, especially romantic attention (Reis et al., 1982). If they

TRY IT YOURSELF
Which Face Is More Attractive?

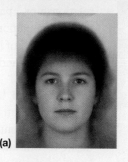 

(a)   (b)

Which face do you find more attractive? Image **(a)** represents the averaging of the faces of 60 women. Image **(b)** is the composite of the 15 faces that were initially rated as the most attractive out of that 60. Given the choice between (a) and (b), most people prefer (b). Female faces tend to be rated as most attractive when they are very symmetrical between the left and right sides and when they have stereotypically feminine features, such as larger eyes, a smaller nose, plumper lips, and a smaller chin.

passionate love
A type of romantic relationship that includes intense longing and sexual desire.

companionate love
A type of romantic relationship that includes strong commitment to supporting and caring for a partner.

believe that good things happen to them primarily because they are good-looking, they may come to feel insecure. After all, looks can change or fade with age.

12.13 Love Is a Key Part of Romantic Relationships

12.13 LEARNING GOAL ACTIVITIES

To maximize your learning, complete the following learning goal activities:

a. Understand all bold and italic terms by writing explanations of them in your own words.

b. Understand the two types of love by comparing them and describing the main aspects of each.

c. Apply to your life two methods of working to stay in love by providing two examples of how you can manage conflict and change your attributional style to make your romantic relationships stronger.

"Who Wrote the Book of Love?" was a hit song in 1958. But long before then, people were questioning what love is. We still do today. Thanks to the pioneering work of Ellen Berscheid and Elaine (Walster) Hatfield (1969), researchers now can use scientific methods to examine this important interpersonal bond (Bradbury & Karney, 2013).

(a)

(b)

FIGURE 12.29
Passionate Versus Companionate Love
(a) Some romantic relationships focus on passionate love. **(b)** Other romances show the development of companionate love.

PASSIONATE AND COMPANIONATE LOVE Hatfield and Berscheid have drawn an important distinction between **passionate love** and **companionate love**. Passionate love is a state of intense longing and sexual desire, the stereotype of love shown in movies and on television. In passionate love, people fall head over heels for each other. They feel an overwhelming urge to be together. When they are together, they are continually aroused sexually (**Figure 12.29a**). Brain imaging studies show that passionate love is associated with activity in dopamine reward systems, the same systems involved in drug addiction (Fisher, Aron, & Brown, 2006; Ortigue, Bianchi-Demicheli, Hamilton, & Grafton, 2007).

People experience passionate love early in relationships. In most enduring relationships, passionate love evolves into companionate love (Sternberg, 1986). Companionate love is a strong commitment to care for and support a partner. This kind of love develops slowly over time because it is based on friendship, trust, respect, and intimacy (**Figure 12.29b**).

CHANGES IN LOVE OVER TIME Romantic relationships change over time, as the long-term pattern of sexual activity rises and then declines. Typically, for a period of months or even years, the two people experience frequent, intense desire for one another. They have sex as often as they can arrange it. Past that peak, however, their interest in having sex with each other decreases. For example, from the first year of marriage to the second, frequency of sex declines by about half. After that, the frequency continues to decline, though more gradually. In addition, people typically experience less passion for their partners over time. Unless people develop other forms of satisfaction in their romantic relationships—such as friendship, social support, and intimacy—the loss of passion leads to dissatisfaction and often to the eventual dissolution of the relationship (Berscheid & Regan, 2005).

Perhaps unsurprisingly, then, relatively few marriages meet the blissful ideals that newlyweds expect. Many contemporary Western marriages fail. In North America,

Overlooking Flaws to Have a Great Romantic Life

Some couples seem loving and supportive. You may look at them and think, "That's the kind of relationship I'd like to have!" With other couples you may think, "That relationship seems so toxic! Why are they even together?" What different factors help create healthy and unhealthy relationships? How can their successes and failures help you create a healthy relationship that will thrive?

Sandra Murray, John Holmes, and Dale Griffin reasoned that people who fall in love and maintain that love tend to be biased toward positive views of their partners. This bias enables the lovers to reconcile two conflicting thoughts: "I love my partner" and "My partner sometimes does things that drive me crazy!" After all, people in love relationships often have to make accommodations for one another's failings.

To investigate this hypothesis, Murray and colleagues (1996) investigated partners' perceptions of each other. Their study included couples who were dating as well as married couples. The results were consistent with their predictions. Those people who loved their partners the most also idealized their partners the most. That is, they viewed their partners in unrealistically positive terms compared with how they viewed other people *and* compared with how their partners viewed themselves. Those people with the most positively biased views of their partners were more likely to be in a relationship with the same partner several months later than were those people with more realistic views of their partners.

How can you benefit from this research? Suppose your romantic partner has annoying habits, such as frequently coming home late from work or always leaving dirty dishes around the house. According to Murray and colleagues, paying attention to your partner's flaws or placing too much importance on occasional failures may make it very difficult to remain in love. If, however, you can put a positive spin on your partner's behavior, you should encounter fewer conflicting thoughts. For example, you might think of your partner's lateness as reflecting that "he's trying his best to provide for the family by working hard." In other words, if you try to idealize your partner a bit, this view may protect your relationship. This technique is one way that you can use psychology to improve your romantic life.

approximately half of all marriages end in divorce or separation, often within the first few years. Moreover, many couples that do not get divorced live together unhappily. Some "partners" exist in a constant state of tension or as strangers sharing a home. The social psychologist Rowland Miller notes that "married people are meaner to each other than they are to total strangers" (1997, p. 12). Given that relationships inevitably change, you have to make staying in love something you are willing to work at.

WORKING TO STAY IN LOVE Even in the best relationships, some conflict is inevitable. Couples continually need to resolve such problems. Managing conflict is clearly an important aspect of any relationship, because it often determines whether the relationship will last.

John Gottman (1994) describes four interpersonal styles that typically lead couples to discord and dissolution. These maladaptive strategies are being overly critical, holding the partner in contempt (that is, having disdain and lacking respect), being defensive, and mentally withdrawing from the relationship. For example, when one partner voices a complaint, the other partner responds with his or her own complaint. The responder may raise the stakes by recalling all of the other person's failings. People use sarcasm and sometimes insult or demean their

FIGURE 12.30

Having Positive Experiences to Stay in Love

Positive interactions, such as doing things you enjoy together, are ways to keep love lasting.

partners. Inevitably, any disagreement, no matter how small, escalates into a major fight over the core problems. Often, the core problems center on a lack of money, a lack of sex, or both.

When a couple is more satisfied with their relationship, the partners tend to express concern for each other even while they are disagreeing. They manage to stay relatively calm and try to see each other's point of view. They may also deliver criticism lightheartedly and playfully (Keltner, Young, Heerey, Oemig, & Monarch, 1998).

Happy couples also differ from unhappy couples in attributional style. This term refers to how one partner explains the other's behavior (Bradbury & Fincham, 1990). Happy couples overlook bad behavior or respond constructively, a process called *accommodation* (Rusbult & Van Lange, 1996). Unhappy couples tend to view each other in the most negative ways possible. Essentially, happy couples attribute good outcomes to each other, and they attribute bad outcomes to situations. Unhappy couples attribute good outcomes to situations, and they attribute bad outcomes to each other. For example, if a couple is happy and one partner brings home flowers as a gift, the other partner reflects on the gift giver's generosity and sweetness. If a couple is unhappy and one of the partners brings home flowers as a gift, the other partner wonders what bad deed the first partner is making up for. Above all, then, viewing your partner in a positive light—even to the point of idealization—may be the key to maintaining a loving relationship (**Figure 12.30**). To read more about how to maintain a positive long-term relationship, see Using Psychology in Your Life on p. 495.

How Can You Develop Strong Relationships?

To make sure you learned what you just read, write answers to the following questions and check your answers.

12.12 In terms of relationships, why don't opposites attract?

12.13 How does passionate love differ from companionate love?

See Appendix B for answers to the red Q questions.

BIG PICTURE

 Want to earn a better grade on your test? Go to **INQUIZITIVE** to practice actively with this chapter's content and get personalized feedback along the way.

How Do You Think About Other People?

12.1 You Tend to Make Snap Judgments About Other People

Review the learning goal activities on p. 464. Snap judgments are first impressions of people. All people tend to form first impressions quickly, based on thin slices of behavior and facial expressions.

12.2 You Make Attributions About Other People

Review the learning goal activities on p. 465. People make two types of attributions about other people's behavior: (1) personal attributions and (2) situational attributions. This tendency to make attributions leads to two common biases. The fundamental attribution error is the tendency to overemphasize personality traits and underestimate situations. The actor/observer bias is the tendency to make situational attributions to explain our own behavior and personal attributions to explain other people's behavior.

12.3 You Tend to Stereotype Other People

Review the learning goal activities on p. 467. Stereotypes allow for fast, easy processing of social information. Once a stereotype is created, it is difficult to change. Stereotypes can even affect basic perceptual processes. Self-fulfilling prophecy is people's tendency to behave in ways that confirm their own or others' expectations.

12.4 Stereotypes Can Have Negative Effects

Review the learning goal activities on p. 468. Stereotypes can lead to prejudice, which includes negative feelings, opinions, and beliefs about people in a particular group. Stereotypes can also lead to discrimination, which is the inappropriate and unjustified treatment of people based on the groups they belong to. Stereotypes also lead to ingroup/outgroup bias, where people treat members of ingroups and outgroups differently. Finally, stereotypes can lead to modern racism, which is a subtle form of prejudice that is found even in people who reject racist beliefs. Engaging in activities that reduce competition and increase cooperation reduces stereotypes and prejudice.

KEY TERMS

personal attributions (p. 466)
situational attributions (p. 466)
fundamental attribution error (p. 466)
actor/observer bias (p. 466)
self-fulfilling prophecy (p. 468)
prejudice (p. 469)
discrimination (p. 469)
modern racism (p. 470)

How Do Your Attitudes Affect You?

12.5 You Form Attitudes Through Experience and Socialization

Review the learning goal activities on p. 472. Attitudes are evaluations of objects, of events, or of ideas. Attitudes affect behavior. Attitudes can be simple, where behavior is consistent with beliefs, or complex, where behavior is inconsistent with beliefs. Attitudes are created in three ways: through (1) the mere exposure effect, (2) conditioning, and (3) socialization. Explicit attitudes reflect conscious awareness of both the attitudes and how they affect behavior. Implicit attitudes operate at an unconscious level and affect behavior without awareness.

12.6 Discrepancies Between Attitudes and Behavior Lead to Dissonance

Review the learning goal activities on p. 475. Cognitive dissonance is an uncomfortable mental state produced by conflict between attitudes or between an attitude and a behavior. This state is characterized by anxiety, tension, and displeasure. People reduce dissonance by changing their attitudes or behaviors, trivializing the discrepancies (such as through postdecisional dissonance), or rationalizing the discrepancies (such as through the insufficient justification effect).

12.7 Your Attitudes Can Be Changed Through Persuasion

Review the learning goal activities on p. 476. Persuasion is an active and conscious effort to use a message to change an attitude. Three factors affect the persuasiveness of a message: (1) who delivers the message, (2) what the message says, and (3) the receiver who processes the message. According to the elaboration likelihood model, attitudes are changed by persuasion through two routes: (1) the central route, which requires deeper thought about the message, and (2) the peripheral route, which requires less thought about a message.

How Do Other People Influence You?

12.8 Groups Affect Your Behavior

Review the learning goal activities on p. 478. Being with other people in social situations can influence how people behave. Groups influence behavior in four ways, through: (1) social facilitation, (2) social loafing, (3) deindividuation, and (4) group decision making.

12.9 You Conform to and Comply with Others

Review the learning goal activities on p. 481. Social situations provide information about appropriate behavior. Normative influence occurs when you go along with what the group does, whereas informational influence occurs when you assume that the behavior of a group reveals the correct way to act. So people conform to match the behaviors, opinions, or expectations of others even if they are not asked to. But people also comply with the requests of others. The three main strategies that tend to make a person comply with a request are (1) foot-in-the-door, (2) door-in-the-face, and (3) lowballing.

12.10 You Probably Obey People Who Have Authority

Review the learning goal activities on p. 484. The presence of an authority figure influences how people act because they are more likely to obey someone who is an authority. However, personal traits can reduce obedience, such as concern about the effects of an action on other people. In addition, the situation also affects obedience, because people are less likely to obey an authority who is removed from them.

12.11 You May Hurt or Help Other People

Review the learning goal activities on p. 486. People sometimes intend to hurt others through aggression. Aggression is influenced by biological and situational factors. The frustration-aggression hypothesis says that increasing frustration in a situation causes aggressive responses. Aggression is also influenced by social and cultural factors. People help others through prosocial behaviors and altruism that maintain social relations. But people sometimes fail to help others when other people are around, which is called the bystander intervention effect.

How Can You Develop Strong Relationships?

12.12 Situations and Personalities Affect Your Relationships

Review the learning goal activities on p. 491. The development of both strong friendships and romantic relationships is influenced by situations and personal traits. Specifically, you are more likely to become close with people for four reasons: (1) you have proximity to them, (2) you are similar in some way, (3) you admire their personal characteristics, and (4) they are physically attractive.

12.13 Love Is a Key Part of Romantic Relationships

Review the learning goal activities on p. 494. Passionate love and companionate love are important aspects of romantic relationships. Passionate love is a state of intense longing and sexual desire, which happens early in a relationship. Companionate love is a strong commitment to support and care for a partner, which develops over time. You can work to stay in love, and increase satisfaction with your romantic relationships, by learning how to manage conflict and by seeing your partner in a positive way.

CHAPTER 12 SELF-QUIZ

To make sure you learned the information in this chapter, write answers to the following questions and check your answers. **See Appendix B for answers to the self-quiz.**

1. Within a few seconds of meeting her new coworker, Greg, Lucy noticed his nice smile. Because of his smile, Lucy assumed she would enjoy working with Greg. Lucy most likely made a judgment based on _____.
   a. thin slices of behavior
   b. the actor/observer bias
   c. a situational attribution
   d. a self-fulfilling prophecy

2. When Elizabeth's fellow students show up late to class, she thinks they are irresponsible and lazy. But when Elizabeth is late to class, she tells her professor that it is not her fault because her bus was late. Elizabeth's explanations best illustrate the _____.
   a. fundamental attribution error
   b. just world hypothesis
   c. self-fulfilling prophecy
   d. actor/observer bias

3. Troy believes that exercise contributes to positive self-esteem. If Troy formed this attitude through operant conditioning, which of the following situations is most likely?
   a. He drives by a local gym every morning and sees good-looking, happy people.
   b. He exercises on a daily basis, consistently doing the same workout on his treadmill.
   c. He begins exercising and is pleased that he can now buy jeans in a smaller size.
   d. His parents routinely exercise and encourage him to do the same.

4. Before a big charity event, Bridget decides to get a hair-cut at an expensive salon. Afterward, she doesn't think it looks any different from her normal cut and is worried that she wasted money. A few hours later, she tells her friends that it was the best haircut she has ever gotten. Bridget's change in attitude is best explained by _____.
   a. cognitive dissonance
   b. postdecisional dissonance
   c. the mere exposure effect
   d. attitude accessibility

5. In an advertisement for Activist Group A, a beautiful actor says she is against using animals for testing cosmetics. In an advertisement for Activist Group B, an average-looking research scientist explains how animals are physically harmed in cosmetic testing. According to the elaboration likelihood model, Activist Group A is using the _____ route to influence attitudes, whereas Activist Group B is using the _____ route to influence attitudes.
   a. personal; situational
   b. peripheral; central
   c. situational; personal
   d. central; peripheral

6. Marco will be singing with three other people in his glee club's upcoming performance and has put in many hours of practice. Which of the following statements is the best example of how social facilitation is likely to influence his performance?
   a. Marco will not sing as loudly during the chorus because everyone else is singing very well.
   b. Marco will sing very well because of the presence of other singers.
   c. Marco will forget the words to the song because everyone is watching him.
   d. Marco will pay less attention to his personal standards of singing because all the singers are wearing the same costume.

7. Most of the students in David's introductory psychology class sit in the same seat every day, so David also sits in the same seat every day. On Monday, he has to switch seats because his instructor tells him to move to the front row to help with an in-class demonstration. David's usual choice of seat is influenced by _____, but on Monday he displayed _____.
   a. deindividuation; compliance
   b. conformity; compliance
   c. deindividuation; obedience
   d. conformity; obedience

8. Darren is walking through a busy grocery store when he knocks over a display full of paper towel rolls. Many people see the paper towels fall, but no one helps him pick them up. People's failure to help can most likely be attributed to _____.
   a. altruism
   b. reciprocal helping
   c. the frustration-aggression hypothesis
   d. the bystander intervention effect

9. Glenda is 30 and single. Because of the impact of proximity, she is most likely to date which of the following bachelors?
   a. Leon, a friend-of-a-friend she has met twice, who shares her passion for volleyball and vacations in Europe
   b. Dion, a thoughtful and sincere man she met through a dating service
   c. Martin, whom she sees at the dog park several times a week
   d. Jay, who lives across town and whom she sometimes sees at the grocery store

10. Victoria and Ryne have been married for five years. They still have as much sexual desire for each other as when they first started dating. This information suggests that Victoria and Ryne experience _____.
   a. passionate love
   b. prosocial behavior
   c. companionate love
   d. accommodation

How Can Psychology Help You Succeed in a Career in Advertising and Marketing?

Has an advertisement ever made you want to buy a product? Maybe you were hooked by a catchy song, you were persuaded by a celebrity endorsement, or the ad spoke to you because it showed up on a favorite YouTube channel. If an ad has persuaded you, then you have experienced the power of marketing. In general terms, marketing is the promotion of a product to potential customers. Key to such promotion is understanding the thoughts, feelings, and actions of potential customers to convince them to buy the product. Having a background in social psychology can help you create advertisements that successfully market products.

Social psychology research in persuasion and attitude formation has long been used in advertising and marketing. As discussed in this chapter, attitudes form through processes such as the mere exposure effect, in which people come to like items the more often they are exposed to them. This is why the same advertisements appear so often. The more you are exposed to an ad, the more you like it. And the more you like the ad, the more likely you are to have a favorable attitude toward the advertised product and buy it. And, of course, the use of celebrities in advertisements encourages consumers to associate the products with these stars. Such strategies increase sales.

People employed in advertising and marketing benefit from knowledge about social psychology. A marketer might study the purchasing trends of customers, help companies develop good public relations, design sales strategies and advertisements to go with them, and sell advertisements to media sources (print, radio, television, online). A market research analyst studies the products people want and how much they will pay for them. Due to the growth of marketing and advertising on the Internet, the need for workers in this area is expected to grow anywhere from 9 percent to 23 percent by 2026. Another job that involves

attitudes is public relations, which involves creating a positive image of a company or a product through means such as media releases and social media programs. Politicians employ workers with expertise in public relations to design successful campaigns that can change attitudes. If helping people or companies present their best possible selves appeals to you, then applying your knowledge of social psychology in public relations might work for you.

TAKEAWAY POINT: Careers in advertising and marketing depend on understanding the thoughts, feelings, and actions of potential buyers. Knowing how attitudes are formed and how consumers can be persuaded to change their attitudes or behavior is crucial to success in these fields. Knowledge of social psychology will increase your skills in this area.

Ψ You can look up job descriptions, education requirements, salaries, and more at the Bureau of Labor Statistics: www.bls.gov. Visit the site and start putting psychology to work!

13 Self and Personality

WHAT DO DRAKE, Mark Zuckerberg, and Selena Gomez have in common? As you might have answered, they are all part of the millennial generation, those people born roughly from the early 1980s to the mid-1990s (Dimock, 2018; **Figure 13.1**). People in this generation may be described as too focused on themselves (Stein, 2013). However, compared with prior generations, millennials are more politically aware, more interested in social justice, and less interested in money than prior generations (Winograd & Hais, 2014).

The generation of people born roughly after 1995—called Generation Z, GenZ, iGen, or plurals— is notable for being the first truly digital natives. In other words, they have been connected to the Internet all their lives. What do we know about people in this generation? Some research

BIG QUESTIONS

How Do You Know Yourself?

How Can You Understand Personality?

How Does Biology Affect Personality?

How Can Personality Be Assessed?

(a)

(b)

(c)

FIGURE 13.1

Characteristics of Millennials

Well-known millennials include **(a)** the musician Drake, **(b)** the Facebook founder Mark Zuckerberg, and **(c)** the singer and actor Selena Gomez. As members of the millennial generation, these people share characteristics. That is, they are likely to differ from members of other generations. But apart from belonging to the same generation, these people are also likely to differ from each other in terms of their individual traits.

suggests that their constant exposure to social media has surprisingly made them more lonely, anxious, and depressed than previous generations (Twenge, 2017). Although their group identity is still forming, they appear to differ from millennials and other generations before them. For example, they prefer to work independently, they spend more time multitasking, and they see themselves as global citizens (Seemiller & Grace, 2017). The differences in the traits of millennials versus GenZ-ers suggest that social forces can shape people's characteristics. But what else determines who people are?

We constantly try to figure out other people—to understand them and predict their thoughts, feelings, and actions. This chapter explains how people view each other and themselves, what personality is and where it comes from, how psychologists study personality, and what knowing someone's personality can tell you about predicting that person's thoughts and behaviors. As you read the information here, you will learn about what makes other people tick. You might even gain insight into how you tick.

How Do You Know Yourself?

If you know anything about Drake, Mark Zuckerberg, and Selena Gomez, you might have ideas about who they are as individuals. But your sense of them—of other people—is not the same as your sense of yourself. To understand the difference between these ideas, let's start with how you perceive yourself. This section focuses on how you know yourself—how you see yourself and how this view shapes who you are. In other words, in this section you will look at one of the most enduring questions in psychology: "Who am I?"

13.1 Your Sense of Self Is Who You Believe You Are

 13.1 LEARNING GOAL ACTIVITIES

To maximize your learning, complete the following learning goal activities:

a. Understand all bold and italic terms by writing explanations of them in your own words.

b. Apply your sense of self by describing who you believe you are, providing one example each of your self-schema and working self-concept.

Personality consists of a person's typical thoughts, emotional responses, and behaviors that are relatively stable over time and across circumstances. Like everyone else, you have a sense of your own personality. It's part of what you mean when you say "myself." But what makes up your sense of "self"?

Your sense of self involves your mental representations of your personal experiences, such as memories and perceptions of what is going on at any particular moment. Your sense of self also includes your physical body and your conscious awareness of being separate from others and unique. In short, your sense of self is who you believe you are. This sense is sometimes called the self-concept. As you learned in study unit 8.2, a concept is a mental representation about an object. So your self-concept is your mental representation of you.

For college students, the sense of self typically includes gender, age, student status, family status (son, daughter), interpersonal style (shy, friendly), personal characteristics (moody, optimistic), and physical traits (tall, short). Stop and think for a moment about 10 ways that you can answer the question "Who am I?" Your answers reveal your sense of self (**Figure 13.2**).

Your sense of self influences you in several ways. It affects how you think, by guiding your attention to information relevant to you. It also influences the way you behave. As you will see in study unit 13.2, your sense of self also has an impact on how you feel. Because of all these connections, your self affects you every day. For example, think back to your 10 ideas about who you are. Now think about concrete ways that those ideas have influenced your thoughts, behaviors, and feelings. If you think of yourself as shy, you may avoid parties. However, even if you think of yourself as shy, you may need to be outgoing on job interviews. These examples highlight the two cognitive aspects of your sense of self, who you believe you are. The cognitive aspects of your sense of self are your self-schema and your working self-concept.

YOUR SENSE OF SELF INCLUDES YOUR SELF-SCHEMA Picture yourself at a loud, crowded party. You can barely hear yourself speak. But when someone across the room mentions your name, your ears perk up. As you learned in study unit 7.2, psychologists explain that this effect occurs because you pay attention to and process information about yourself deeply, thoroughly, and automatically. So all of the information you have about yourself becomes part of your **self-schema**.

Your self-schema consists of an integrated set of memories, beliefs, and generalizations about yourself (Markus, 1977). The information is organized as a network of interconnected knowledge about yourself (**Figure 13.3**). Your self-schema helps you perceive, organize, interpret, and use information about yourself. It also helps you filter information so that you are likely to notice things that are relevant to you, such as your name. Examples of your behavior and aspects of your personality that are important to you become prominent in your self-schema. For instance, being a successful student may be a major component of your self-schema, but having few cavities probably is not. Thus, if you are asked whether you are ambitious, you can answer without sorting through occasions when you did or did not act ambitiously. Your self-schema summarizes the relevant past information.

Your self-schema may increase your memory for information that is relevant to you. Tim Rogers and colleagues (1977) showed that you are likely to remember adjectives better when they are used to describe your own traits than when they are used only generally. For instance, suppose you are asked, "What does the word 'honest' mean?" If you are later asked to recall the word you were asked about, you might or might not recall "honest." Suppose, however, the initial question is, "Does the word 'honest' describe you?" When asked later to recall the word, you will be more likely to remember it.

What brain activity is involved in this effect? Researchers typically find that when people process information about themselves, there is activity in the middle of the frontal lobes of the brain (Gillihan & Farah, 2005; Kelley et al., 2002). Damage to the frontal lobes tends to reduce or eliminate self-awareness. Activation of the frontal lobes seems to be important for processing information about the self (Heatherton, 2011; Meyer & Lieberman, 2018).

WORKING SELF-CONCEPT SHOWS THAT YOUR SENSE OF SELF CAN VARY Psychologists refer to the immediate experience of the self in the

FIGURE 13.2
Your Sense of Self
Like any person, you have a sense of who you are. Your sense of self includes your memories, experiences, personal characteristics, and physical appearance.

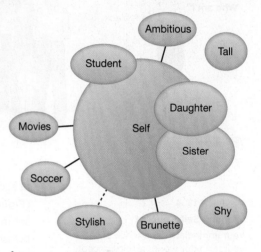

FIGURE 13.3
Self-Schema
Your self-schema consists of interrelated knowledge about yourself. Here, the concepts that are most strongly related to one specific person's sense of self (student, daughter, and sister) are shown overlapping with the self. Concepts that are not quite as strongly related to this person's sense of self (ambitious, movies, soccer, and brunette) are connected to the self with a solid line. Weakly related concepts (stylish) are connected to the self with a dotted line. Concepts that do not relate to the person's sense of self (tall, shy) have no connecting lines.

personality
A person's typical thoughts, emotional responses, and behaviors that are relatively stable over time and across circumstances.

self-schema
An integrated set of memories, beliefs, and generalizations about the self.

(a)

Who am I?

I am male.

(b)

Who am I?

I am black.

FIGURE 13.4

Working Self-Concept

Your immediate experience of yourself, your working self-concept, varies depending on which aspect of yourself is most relevant at that moment. **(a)** Suppose a black man is working with a group of women. In that situation, his working self-concept might focus on awareness that he is a man. **(b)** Now suppose the same man is working with a group of white people. In that situation, his working self-concept might focus on awareness that he is black.

working self-concept
The immediate experience of the self in the here and now.

here and now as the **working self-concept**. This experience is limited to the amount of personal information that is being processed at one moment in time. Because the working self-concept includes only part of the vast array of self-knowledge, the sense of self varies from moment to moment. Your self-descriptions depend on which memories you retrieve, which situation you are in, which people you are with, and your role in that situation. And they affect how you act in different situations. For instance, suppose your sense of self includes the traits "fun-loving" and "intelligent." At a party, you might think of yourself more as fun-loving than intelligent. This working self-concept will influence your behavior at the party. In other words, you become more likely to act in ways that show you are fun. By contrast, when you are in class, you might think of yourself as intelligent. In that situation, your working self-concept will lead you to participate actively in the discussion.

When you consider who you are or think about different features of your personality, you probably emphasize characteristics that make you distinct from others. Think back to your 10 responses to the question "Who am I?" Which answers stressed your similarity to other people or membership in a group? Which stressed your differences from other people, or at least from the people immediately around you? In studies using this question, respondents are especially likely to mention features such as ethnicity, gender, or age if they differ in these respects from other people around them at the moment (**Figure 13.4**). For example, Canadians are more likely to note their nationality if they are in Missouri than if they are in Alberta. Because the working self-concept guides behavior, this tendency implies that Canadians are also more likely to feel and act like "Canadians" when in Missouri than when in Alberta. Most people do not want to be too distinctive, however, because generally they want to avoid standing out too much from the crowd.

13.2 Self-Esteem Is How You Feel About Your Sense of Self

 13.2 LEARNING GOAL ACTIVITIES

To maximize your learning, complete the following learning goal activities:

a. Understand all bold and italic terms by writing explanations of them in your own words.

b. Apply how you feel about your sense of self by describing two ways that your self-esteem has been positively influenced by reflected appraisal and sociometer theory.

If you think of yourself as shy and so you avoid parties, does that make you feel positively or negatively about yourself? If you believe you are optimistic in some situations but not others, do you feel good about that or not? These questions show that you have a sense of self and that you also evaluate your personal characteristics.

Self-esteem is how you feel about your sense of self. Although self-esteem is related to your sense of self, you can objectively believe positive things about yourself and still have low self-esteem—that is, not like yourself very much. Conversely, you can like yourself very much, and therefore have high self-esteem, even when objective indicators do not support such positive self-views.

Many theories propose that self-esteem is based on how you believe others perceive you. This view is known as *reflected appraisal*. When you internalize the values and beliefs expressed by people who are important in your life, you adopt those attitudes (and related behaviors) as your own. Consequently, you come to respond to yourself in ways that are consistent with how others respond to you. From this perspective, if you believe that important people in your life do not value you, you may find it hard to value yourself.

One recent perspective suggests that if you want to feel better about yourself, you should treat yourself as you would treat a good friend. If a good friend were having a hard time because of doing something foolish, you would probably try to comfort the person by pointing out that no one is perfect and we all make mistakes at times. In other words, you would be compassionate to your friend. *Self-compassion* refers to treating yourself with care, acceptance, and kindness during difficult times, just as you would treat a good friend (Neff, 2011). There appear to be many benefits to being self-compassionate, including greater life satisfaction and fewer feelings of depression (Phillips, Hine, & Marks, 2018). Why not try being self-compassionate and seeing if you feel these positive effects? See Evaluating Psychology in the Real World on p. 508.

YOUR SELF-ESTEEM DEPENDS ON SOCIAL ACCEPTANCE OR REJECTION   One theory argues that self-esteem is a mechanism for monitoring the likelihood of social acceptance or rejection (Leary et al., 1995). As described in study unit 9.5, humans have a fundamental, adaptive need to belong. When you behave in ways that make you more likely to be rejected from a social group, your self-esteem most likely decreases. Thus self-esteem is a *sociometer*, an internal monitor of social acceptance or rejection.

When your sociometer indicates a high possibility of rejection, you may experience low self-esteem (**Figure 13.5a**). In this case, you are highly motivated to improve your public image. When your sociometer indicates a low probability of rejection, you tend to experience high self-esteem (**Figure 13.5b**). In this case, you will probably not worry about how others perceive you. One line of evidence that supports sociometer theory is the finding that low self-esteem is highly correlated with social anxiety (Leary, 2004; Leary & MacDonald, 2003).

SELF-ESTEEM AND LIFE OUTCOMES   With so much emphasis placed on self-esteem in Western culture, you might expect that having high self-esteem is the key to life success. But the evidence from psychology indicates that self-esteem may be less important than is commonly believed. A review of several hundred studies found that although people with high self-esteem report being much happier, self-esteem is weakly related to objective life outcomes (Baumeister, Campbell, Krueger, & Vohs, 2003, 2005). For instance, people with high self-esteem who consider themselves smarter, more attractive, and better liked do not necessarily have higher IQs and are not necessarily thought of more highly by others. In other words, your self-esteem has little to do with whether other people actually like you. Instead, your self-esteem influences your perception of how other people feel about you.

Many people with high self-esteem are successful in their careers, but so are many people with low self-esteem. Although self-esteem has a slight relationship to

self-esteem
How you feel about your sense of self.

(a)
Probability of rejection

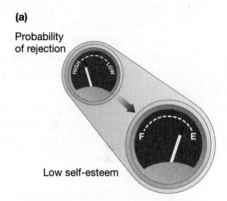

Low self-esteem

(b)
Probability of rejection

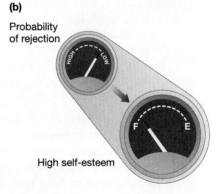

High self-esteem

FIGURE 13.5
Sociometers
(a) If the probability of rejection seems high, your self-esteem will tend to be low. **(b)** If the probability of rejection seems low, your self-esteem will tend to be high.

People sometimes feel badly about themselves. A common way to make people feel better when they are down is to praise them. If they hear about how amazing they are, people may feel better about their mistakes, get over their regrets, and experience increased self-esteem. But can practicing self-compassion have the same or similar effects? To consider this question, read the article below (from https://www.livescience.com/55254-overcome-regrets -self-compassion.html) and explore the claim about self-compassion by using the three steps in critical thinking:

ACTIVITY: To determine if you should accept the claims in this article, review the Learning Tip on p. 7 and follow these steps:

Step 1 What is the claim I am being asked to accept?

Step 2 What evidence, if any, is provided to support the claim?

Step 3 Given the evidence, what are the most reasonable conclusions about the claim?

If you have rejected the claim or found the evidence lacking, why did you do so? If you have found that the evidence supports the claim, how might this information change how you think and act?

Science Finds a Way to Overcome Life's Regrets

If you can't seem to let go of a regret, a little self-compassion may help you move on, a recent study finds.

The people in the study who practiced self-compassion, or being kind to oneself, were more likely to overcome regrets than the people who did not do so, according to the study, published in February in the journal *Personality and Social Psychology Bulletin*. . . .

In the study, the researchers zeroed in on self-compassion as a potential factor in why some people have an easier time leaving their regrets behind them.

In an experiment, 400 students ages 18 to 49 sat down at computers for a writing exercise. First, the students were asked to write about their biggest regret. Half were randomly assigned to write about a regret of action, or something that they did but wish they had not done; the other half were asked to write about a regret of inaction, or something they did not do but wish they had, according to the study.

Then, the participants were randomly assigned to one of three groups: self-compassion, self-esteem, and a control group. The self-compassion group was asked to respond to the prompt, "Imagine that you are talking to yourself about this regret from a compassionate and understanding perspective. What would you say?" The self-esteem group was asked to respond to the prompt, "Imagine that you are talking to yourself about this regret from a perspective of validating your positive

(rather than negative) qualities," according to the study.

The control group was not asked to write about the regret; rather, these participants were asked to write about a hobby they enjoyed.

Then, the researchers asked the participants a series of questions about their feelings of forgiveness, acceptance, and personal improvement following the exercise.

They found that the people in the self-compassion group reported greater feelings of acceptance, forgiveness, and personal improvement, compared with not only the control group but also the self-esteem group. In other words, focusing on your best qualities is not what helps you feel better about a regret. Rather, being compassionate toward yourself is what may make a difference, the researchers found.

It's possible that people who practice self-compassion are able to confront their regrets and see what went wrong, so they can make a better choice in the future. . . .

some outcomes, such as academic success, the success might be what leads to high self-esteem. That is, people might have higher self-esteem because they have done well in school.

In fact, having a high opinion of yourself could even have some downsides. Violent criminals commonly have very high self-esteem. Some people become violent when they think others are not treating them with an appropriate level of respect (Baumeister, Smart, & Boden, 1996). School bullies also often have high self-esteem (Baumeister, Campbell, Krueger, & Vohs, 2003). Ultimately, having high self-esteem seems to make people happier, but it does not necessarily lead to successful social relationships or life success.

NARCISSISTS HAVE INFLATED SELF-ESTEEM One characteristic associated with inflated self-esteem is *narcissism*. The term comes from a Greek myth, in which a young man named Narcissus rejected the love of others and fell in love with his own reflection in a pond. In the psychological sense, people who are narcissistic are self-centered, view themselves in grandiose terms, feel entitled to special treatment, and are manipulative. Because narcissists' greatest love is for the self, they tend to have poor relations with others (Campbell, Bush, Brunell, & Shelton, 2005), they become angry when challenged (Rhodewalt & Morf, 1998), and they tend to be unfaithful (Campbell, Foster, & Finkel, 2002).

An analysis of many studies found increasing narcissism among American college students between 1979 and 2006 (Twenge, Konrath, Foster, Campbell, & Bushman, 2008). This was the basis for the information mentioned at the beginning of this chapter, that millennials may be overly focused on themselves. The researchers point to a few possible contributing factors to increases in narcissism: programs aimed at increasing self-esteem among young schoolchildren (such as having them sing songs about how they are special), grade inflation that makes students feel more capable than they really might be, and a rise in the use of self-promotion Web sites such as Facebook and LinkedIn. However, other research has not found the same increase in narcissism, so debate continues about whether it is appropriate to say that people in the millennial generation are members of "Generation Me" (Trzesniewski, Donnellan, & Roberts, 2008).

Even though we might encourage children to have high self-esteem, there is a tendency for self-esteem to fall during adolescence and be at its lowest for people, especially young women, aged 18 to 22 years (Robins, Trzesniewski, Tracy, Gosling, & Potter, 2002; **Figure 13.6**). Self-esteem then typically increases across adulthood, peaking when people are in their sixties and falling off toward the end of life.

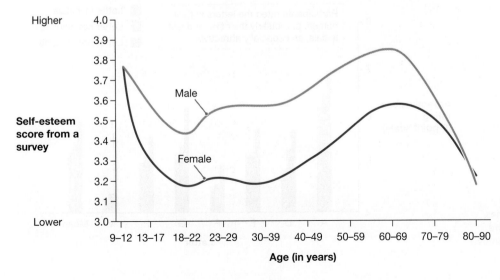

FIGURE 13.6

Self-Esteem Across the Life Span

People's self-esteem varies over their lives. Low points in self-esteem are seen in the late teens and early twenties, especially for females. Low self-esteem is also experienced toward the end of life. Self-esteem typically peaks when people are in their sixties.

HAS IT HAPPENED
TO YOU?

Social Comparisons

You have probably engaged in social comparisons at some point. To find out, ask yourself these questions.

1. Have you ever compared yourself with someone who seemed to be worse off than you in some way? This downward comparison probably made you feel good and increased your self-esteem.

2. Have you compared yourself with someone whom you saw as better off than you in some way? This upward comparison probably made you feel bad and decreased your self-esteem.

3. Have you ever compared some version of yourself with a version from some point in the past? Usually we view our present selves as better than our past selves. This temporal comparison also likely increased your self-esteem.

This pattern appears to be true in cultures around the world (Bleidorn et al., 2016). Studies typically find that females have lower self-esteem than males, particularly during adolescence. However, the gap between females and males appears to be decreasing (Zuckerman, Li, & Hall, 2016).

13.3 You Try to Create a Positive Sense of Self

13.3 LEARNING GOAL ACTIVITIES

To maximize your learning, complete the following learning goal activities:

a. Understand all bold and italic terms by writing explanations of them in your own words.

b. Evaluate your sense of self by examining how positive illusions, social comparisons, and the self-serving bias create your positive sense of self.

A consistent theme that emerges from research is that people show favoritism to anything associated with themselves. For example, people consistently prefer things they own to things they do not own (Beggan, 1992). They even prefer the letters of their own names, especially their initials, to other letters (Koole, Dijksterhuis, & van Knippenberg, 2001; **Figure 13.7**).

Sometimes these positive views of self can seem inflated. Statistically, it is impossible for *everyone* to be above average, but things are different when it comes to self-esteem. For instance, 90 percent of adults claim they are better-than-average drivers, even if they once were the driver in a car accident that landed them in the hospital (Guerin, 1994; Svenson, 1981). Similarly, when the College Entrance Examination Board surveyed more than 800,000 college-bound seniors, no seniors rated themselves as below average, and a whopping 25 percent rated themselves in the top 1 percent (Gilovich, 1991). Most people describe themselves as above average in nearly every way. Psychologists refer to this phenomenon as the *better-than-average effect* (Alicke, Klotz, Breitenbecher, Yurak, & Vredenburg, 1995). People with high self-esteem are especially likely to exhibit this effect.

Though life is filled with failure, rejection, and disappointment, most of us feel pretty good about ourselves. How do we maintain such positive views? Psychologists

FIGURE 13.7

Favoritism

People rate letters in their own names, especially their initials, as being more beautiful than letters not in their names.

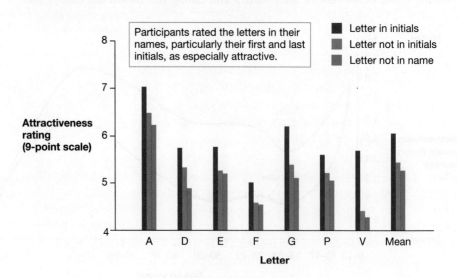

have cataloged several unconscious strategies that help us maintain a positive sense of self. Some of the most common are having positive illusions, making social comparisons, and having self-serving biases. As you read the following descriptions, bear in mind that psychologists do not necessarily recommend these strategies.

MOST PEOPLE HAVE POSITIVE ILLUSIONS ABOUT THE SENSE OF SELF According to research, most people have *positive illusions*—overly favorable and unrealistic beliefs about themselves—in at least three areas (Taylor & Brown, 1988). First, most people continually experience the better-than-average effect. Second, they have unrealistic beliefs about how much they can control what happens. For example, some fans believe they help their favorite sports teams win if they attend games or wear their lucky jerseys. Third, most people are unrealistically optimistic about their personal futures. They believe they probably will be successful, marry happily, and live long lives. Positive illusions can be adaptive when they promote optimism in meeting life's challenges, but they can lead to trouble when people overestimate their skills and underestimate their vulnerabilities.

SOCIAL COMPARISONS AFFECT THE SENSE OF SELF Social comparison occurs when you evaluate your own actions, abilities, and beliefs by contrasting them with those of other people (Festinger, 1954). That is, you compare yourself with others to see where you stand. You are especially likely to make such comparisons when there is no objective standard. For instance, you might think you are doing better financially than someone else, even though a number of factors, from income to savings to lifestyle, affect financial success. Social comparisons are an important means of understanding actions and emotions.

In general, people with high self-esteem make **downward comparisons**. That is, they contrast themselves with people whom they view as inferior to themselves in the characteristic they are evaluating. People with low self-esteem tend to make **upward comparisons**. They contrast themselves with people they see as superior to them. *Temporal comparison* is another form of downward comparison where people view their current selves as better than their former selves (Wilson & Ross, 2001; **Figure 13.8**). Thinking of yourself as better than others, or as better than you used to be, tends to make you feel good about yourself. But constantly comparing yourself with others who do better may only confirm your negative feelings about yourself. To consider whether you have engaged in social comparisons, read Has It Happened to You? on p. 510.

THE SELF-SERVING BIAS SUPPORTS A POSITIVE SENSE OF SELF People with high self-esteem tend to take credit for success but blame failure on outside factors. Psychologists refer to this tendency as the **self-serving bias**. For instance, students who do extremely well on exams often explain their performance by referring to their skills or hard work. Those who do poorly might describe the test as an arbitrary examination of trivial details. People with high self-esteem also assume that criticism is motivated by envy or prejudice. According to one theory, members of groups prone to discrimination (for example, a person with disabilities; ethnic minorities) maintain positive self-esteem by taking credit for success and blaming negative feedback on prejudice (Crocker & Major, 1989). Thus if they succeed, the success is due to personal strengths and occurs despite the odds. If they fail, the failure is due to external factors and unfair obstacles.

downward comparisons
Comparing oneself with another person who is seen as less competent or in a worse situation, which tends to protect a person's high self-esteem.

upward comparisons
Comparing oneself with another person who is seen as more competent or in a better situation, which tends to confirm a person's low self-esteem.

self-serving bias
The tendency for people to take personal credit for success but blame failure on external factors.

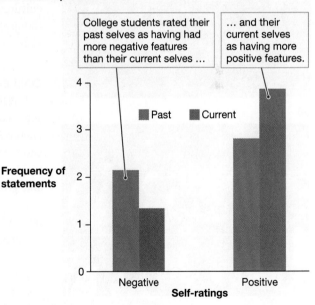

FIGURE 13.8

Temporal Comparisons of the Self

People tend to make temporal comparisons that indicate more positive perceptions of themselves now than in the past. This form of downward comparison has the effect of protecting a person's positive sense of self.

Over the last 40 years, psychologists have documented many ways that we show self-serving bias (Campbell & Sedikides, 1999). In thinking about our failures, for example, we compare ourselves with others who did worse, we diminish the importance of the challenge, we think about the things we are really good at, and we bask in the reflected glory of both family and friends. The overall picture suggests we are extremely well equipped to protect our positive beliefs about ourselves. Some researchers have argued that self-serving biases reflect healthy psychological functioning (Mezulis, Abramson, Hyde, & Hankin, 2004; Taylor & Brown, 1988). Still, the earlier discussion of narcissism should make us wary of that perspective.

13.4 Your Sense of Self Is Influenced by Cultural Factors

13.4 LEARNING GOAL ACTIVITIES

To maximize your learning, complete the following learning goal activities:

a. Understand all bold and italic terms by writing explanations of them in your own words.

b. Understand how the sense of self can vary by summarizing how people from collectivist and individualist cultures differ in their senses of self.

(a)

(b)

FIGURE 13.9

Collectivist and Individualist Cultures

(a) People in collectivist cultures tend to value following group norms and obedience to authority figures. **(b)** People in individualist cultures tend to emphasize individuality and freedom of self-expression.

Do you like to stand out in a crowd? If so, then maybe you have body art, color your hair brightly, wear unusual clothes, or do something that makes you seem unique. In Western cultures, particularly the United States, people often take pride in expressing themselves in ways that make them stand out from the crowd. But this is not the case for all people. In some cultures, people prefer to blend into the group. Whether people view themselves as fundamentally separate from or connected to other people also affects the sense of self.

COLLECTIVIST AND INDIVIDUALIST CULTURES EMPHASIZE DIFFERENT SENSES OF SELF Harry Triandis (1989) has noted that some cultures emphasize the collective self more than the personal self. Such *collectivist cultures* include those in Japan, Greece, Pakistan, China, and some regions of Africa. Collectivist cultures emphasize connections to family, social groups, and ethnic groups; conformity to societal norms; and group cohesiveness. In Japan, people tend to dress similarly and respect situational norms (**Figure 13.9a**). When a family goes to a restaurant in China, all the people at the table share multiple dishes. In collectivist cultures, one's sense of self is influenced largely by people's social roles and personal relationships (Markus & Kitayama, 1991; **Figure 13.10a**). Children in collectivist cultures are raised to follow group norms and to obey parents, teachers, and other people in authority. They are expected to find their proper place in society and not to challenge or complain about their status.

In contrast, *individualist cultures* emphasize individual rights and freedoms, self-expression, and diversity. Individualist cultures include those in northern and western Europe, Australia, Canada, New Zealand, and the United States. In the United States, people dress differently from one another, cultivate personal interests, and often enjoy standing out from the crowd (**Figure 13.9b**). When an American family goes to a restaurant, each person usually orders what he or she prefers.

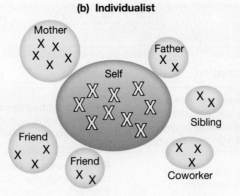

FIGURE 13.10
Cultural Differences in Self
The sense of self differs across cultures, and some aspects are more important to the self (as shown by the larger Xs). **(a)** In collectivist cultures, the most important elements of a person's sense of self tend to reside in areas where the person's sense of self is connected with others. **(b)** In individualist cultures, the most important elements of a person's sense of self tend to reside within the person.

In individualist cultures, parents and teachers encourage children to be self-reliant and to pursue personal success, even at the expense of interpersonal relationships. Thus children's senses of self are based on their feelings of being distinct from others (**Figure 13.10b**).

Note, however, that within these broad patterns there is variability. Some people in individualist cultures have interdependent senses of self. Some people in collectivist cultures have independent senses of self.

Q How Do You Know Yourself?

To make sure you learned what you just read, write answers to the following questions and check your answers.

13.1 A teenager sees herself as carefree when she is with her friends but responsible when she is watching her little brother. What concept best explains this difference in her sense of self?

13.2 Mr. Englund sees himself as the best biology teacher ever and feels that he is entitled to special privileges in how he teaches his classes and treats his students. Based on this description, what is the most accurate way to describe Mr. Englund's high sense of self-esteem?

13.3 What is the main way you may engage in social comparisons with other people to create a positive sense of self?

13.4 Would a person from a collectivist culture or from an individualist culture be more likely to have a sense of self that emphasizes strong relationships with family?

See Appendix B for answers to the red Q questions.

How Can You Understand Personality?

What do you know about the personalities of the millennials mentioned at the beginning of the chapter? Is Drake outgoing? Is Mark Zuckerberg funny? Is Selena Gomez a responsible person? Now that you understand more about the sense of self, let's turn to the second topic in this chapter: personality.

Because humans are so complex, the discussion of personality brings together a host of topics from across psychology: How is personality influenced by nature and nurture? How much does behavior reveal about personality? How much does personality vary across situations? In an attempt to answer these questions and more, in the past century, psychologists have studied personality based on four

TABLE 13.1
Approaches to Personality

Approach	Description	Example
Psychodynamic theory	Personality is based on unconscious wishes that create conflict between the id, ego, and superego.	**Freud's psychodynamic theory:** You will do anything to get what you want. According to Freud, your personality may be dominated by your id.
Humanistic approaches	Personality is based on the tendency to fulfill potential through personal growth.	**Rogers's person-centered approach:** You always tell your children that you love them even if you disapprove of some of their actions. According to Rogers, by expressing unconditional positive regard, you are helping your children reach their full potential for growth.
Social cognitive approaches	Personality is based on how a person thinks.	**Rotter's expectancy theory:** You know that if you work hard in college, you will get high grades and this will help you get a good job. According to Rotter, you have an internal locus of control. **Bandura's reciprocal determinism:** According to Bandura, your competence at work is due to three interacting factors: environment (for example, supportive), person factors (such as your self-confidence), and behavior (perhaps working late to finish projects).
Trait approaches	Personality can be described by the individual's characteristics.	**Five-factor theory:** You are described by friends as very dependable but not very outgoing. According to the five-factor theory, you are highly conscientious and very introverted. **Eysenck's biological trait theory:** You are highly introverted and somewhat emotionally unstable. According to Eysenck, you could be described as moody. However, you also show moderate constraint, so you are able to control your moodiness.

different general approaches (**Table 13.1**). In the next several study units, you will learn more about each approach to personality.

13.5 Psychodynamic Theory Emphasizes Unconscious Conflicts

13.5 LEARNING GOAL ACTIVITIES

To maximize your learning, complete the following learning goal activities:

a. Understand all bold and italic terms by writing explanations of them in your own words.

b. Apply psychodynamic theory by explaining how, according to Freud, the id, ego, and superego could be in conflict when a person is tempted by a very large piece of cake.

As you learned in study unit 1.5, Sigmund Freud was a physician who developed many ideas about personality by observing his patients. Freud came to believe that many of their problems were caused by psychological rather than physical factors. From his clinical work, Freud developed his **psychodynamic theory** of personality. The central idea of this theory is that unconscious forces—such as wishes, desires, and hidden memories—determine behavior and influence personality. Many of Freud's ideas are controversial and not well supported by scientific research, but his theories had an enormous influence over psychological thinking for much of its early history.

psychodynamic theory
Freudian theory that unconscious forces determine behavior.

FREUD BELIEVED HIDDEN MOTIVES INFLU-ENCED PERSONALITY   For Freud, the powerful forces that drive behavior often conflict with each other. He also emphasized that people are typically unaware of those forces or their conflicts. For instance, you might unknowingly want to steal an object you desire. That impulse would conflict with your implicit knowledge that you could get in trouble for the theft or that society considers theft a crime. Freud believed that conscious awareness is only a small fraction of mental activity. That is, according to psychodynamic theory, conscious awareness represents the proverbial tip of the iceberg, and most mental processes happen under the surface (**Figure 13.11**).

According to this model, the *conscious* level of your mental activity consists of the thoughts that you are aware of. The *preconscious* level consists of content that is not currently in your awareness but that could be brought to awareness. This level is roughly analogous to long-term memory. The *unconscious* level contains material that the mind cannot easily retrieve. These hidden memories, wishes, desires, and motives are often in conflict. The conflicts between them produce anxiety or other psychological discomfort. To protect you from this distress, these forces and their conflicts are kept hidden from awareness. Sometimes, however, this information leaks into consciousness in "Freudian slips." For example, you may accidentally reveal a hidden motive by saying, when you meet an attractive person, "I don't think we've been seduced" instead of "introduced." Freud said these slips were not accidents. Instead, they offered a glimpse into unconscious conflicts that determine behavior.

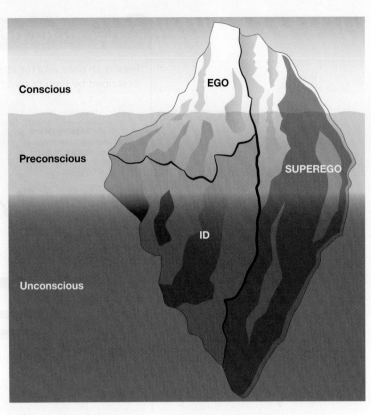

FIGURE 13.11

Freud's Psychodynamic Theory of Personality

Sigmund Freud theorized that unconscious mental activity can result in conflict between the three personality structures: the id, the superego, and the ego.

THREE STRUCTURES OF PERSONALITY   Freud also proposed a model of how personality is organized. In this model, personality consists of three interacting structures, and these structures vary in their access to consciousness (see Figure 13.11). The first structure, the **id,** exists at the most basic level: completely submerged in the unconscious. The id operates according to the *pleasure principle*, which pushes you to seek pleasure and avoid pain. Freud called the force that drives the pleasure principle the *libido*. Although today the term "libido" has a specifically sexual connotation, Freud used it to refer more generally to the energy that promotes pleasure seeking. In other words, the libido acts on impulses and desires. The id is like an infant, crying to be fed whenever hungry, held whenever anxious.

The second structure, the **superego,** acts as a brake on the id. Largely existing in the unconscious, the superego develops in childhood and is the internalization of parental and societal standards of behavior. It is a rigid structure of morality, or conscience.

The third structure, the **ego,** mediates between the id and the superego. That is, the ego tries to satisfy the wishes of the id while being responsive to the rules of the superego. The ego operates according to the *reality principle*, which involves rational thought and problem solving. According to psychodynamic theory, unique interactions of the id, superego, and ego produce individual differences in personality. For help remembering these three aspects of Freud's theory of personality, review the Learning Tip on p. 516.

id

In psychodynamic theory, the component of personality that is completely submerged in the unconscious and operates according to the pleasure principle.

superego

In psychodynamic theory, the component of personality that reflects the internalization of societal and parental standards of conduct.

ego

In psychodynamic theory, the component of personality that tries to satisfy the wishes of the id while being responsive to the superego.

LEARNING TIP: Id, Superego, and Ego

Here is an easy way for you to remember the three aspects of personality described by Freud's psychodynamic theory.

The **id** is the desire for pleasure and avoidance of pain.

The **ego** resolves the conflict between the id and the superego.

The **superego** is the conscience for what is socially acceptable and moral.

Conflicts between the id and the superego lead to anxiety. The ego then copes with anxiety through various **defense mechanisms**. Defense mechanisms are unconscious mental strategies that the mind uses to protect itself from distress (**Table 13.2**). For instance, according to psychodynamic theory, you may rationalize your behavior by blaming the situation. Maybe you tell your parents that you didn't call them because you were too busy studying for an exam. Finding good excuses keeps you from feeling bad and can also prevent others from feeling annoyed at you.

Much of the theoretical work on defense mechanisms can be credited to Freud's daughter, Anna Freud (1936; see Figure 1.10c). Over the past 40 years, psychological research has provided a great deal of support for the existence of many of the defense mechanisms (Baumeister, Dale, & Sommers, 1998). According to contemporary researchers, however, these mechanisms do not relieve unconscious conflict over libidinal desires. Rather, defense mechanisms protect self-esteem.

PSYCHOSEXUAL DEVELOPMENT An important component of Freudian thinking is the idea that early childhood experiences have a major impact on the development of personality. Freud believed that children unconsciously aim to satisfy libidinal urges to experience pleasure. In their pursuit of these satisfactions, children go through developmental stages that correspond to the different urges. These developmental stages are called *psychosexual stages*.

In each psychosexual stage, libido is focused on one of the body's erogenous zones. *Erogenous* means "sexually arousing," and these zones are the mouth, the anus, and the genitals.

defense mechanisms
In psychodynamic theory, unconscious mental strategies that the mind uses to protect itself from distress.

TABLE 13.2
Common Defense Mechanisms According to Psychodynamic Theory

Mechanism	Definition	Example
Denial	Refusing to acknowledge source of anxiety	Tanya has been diagnosed with cancer but refuses to get treatment, saying her symptoms are caused by something other than cancer.
Repression	Excluding source of anxiety from awareness	Louis cannot remember the night that he was mugged at gunpoint.
Projection	Attributing unacceptable qualities of the self to someone else	Emily is very competitive but accuses others of being super-competitive.
Reaction formation	Warding off an uncomfortable thought by overemphasizing its opposite	Simon is attracted to a person of the same sex, but bullies that person for being gay.
Rationalization	Creating a seemingly logical reason or excuse for behavior that might otherwise be shameful	Pamela drives after drinking alcohol because "everyone does it."
Displacement	Shifting the attention of emotion from one object to another, easier target	Franklin has a terrible day at work with his boss and then goes home and yells at his children.
Sublimation	Channeling socially unacceptable impulses into constructive, even admirable, behavior	Lakisha has an eating disorder and becomes a nutritionist who works with people trying to lose weight.

The *oral stage* lasts from birth to approximately 18 months. During this time, infants seek pleasure through the mouth. Because hungry infants experience relief when they breast-feed, they come to associate pleasure with sucking. When children are 2 to 3 years old, they enter the *anal stage*. During this time, toilet training—learning to control the bowels—leads them to focus on the anus. From age 3 to 5, children are in the *phallic stage*. That is, they direct their libidinal energies toward the genitals. Children often discover the pleasure of rubbing their genitals during this time, although they have no real sexual intent. The phallic stage is followed by a brief *latency stage*. During this time, children suppress libidinal urges or channel them into doing schoolwork or building friendships. Finally, in the *genital stage*, adolescents and adults attain mature attitudes about sexuality and adulthood. They center their libidinal urges on the capacities to reproduce and to contribute to society.

One of the most controversial Freudian theories applies to children in the phallic stage. According to Freud, children desire an exclusive relationship with the opposite-sex parent. For this reason, children consider the same-sex parent a rival. As a result, they develop hostility toward that parent. In boys, this phenomenon is known as the *Oedipus complex* (**Figure 13.12**). The complex is named after the ancient Greek character Oedipus, who unknowingly killed his father and married his mother. Freud believed that children develop unconscious wishes to kill their same-sex parent so they can claim the other parent. He suggested that children resolve this conflict by repressing their desires for the opposite-sex parent and identifying with the same-sex parent. That is, they take on many of that parent's values and beliefs. This theory applied mostly to boys. Freud's theory for girls was more complex and even less convincing. There is little research support for either theory.

According to Freud, progression through these psychosexual stages profoundly affects personality. For example, some people become *fixated*, or stuck, at a stage during which they receive excessive parental restriction or indulgence. Those fixated at the oral stage develop *oral personalities*. They seek pleasure through the mouth, such

FIGURE 13.12

Freud's Theory of the Oedipus Complex During Psychosexual Development

Freud proposed that during one of the stages of psychosexual development, young boys form an attachment to their mothers and compete with their fathers for the mothers' affection. Because this unconscious desire causes conflict, Freud suggested that it is repressed, resulting in young boys' identifying more strongly with their fathers.

as by smoking. They also are excessively needy. Those fixated at the anal phase may have *anal-retentive personalities*. They are stubborn and highly regulating. Anal fixation may arise from overly strict toilet training or excessively rule-based child rearing.

PSYCHODYNAMIC THEORY TODAY Sigmund Freud is the thinker most closely identified with psychodynamic theory. A number of influential scholars have modified Freud's ideas. While rejecting aspects of Freudian thinking, these scholars have embraced the notion of unconscious conflict and the importance of early childhood on personality. Contemporary *neo-Freudians* focus on social interactions, especially children's emotional attachments to their parents or primary caregivers. This focus is embodied in *object relations theory*. According to this theory, your mind and sense of self develop in relation to others ("objects") in your environment, and how you relate to these others shapes your personality. The concept of object relations is important to many professionals who conduct counseling to help people improve their relations with others.

Today, Freud's work has to be understood in the context of his time and the methods available to him. Freud was a keen observer of behavior and a creative theorist. Indeed, Freud's theory is still used extensively in the humanities and arts, where scholars are more interested in interpretation than in an empirical approach. Yet Freud had no way to use objective methods to explore mental processes, such as using brain imaging to examine emotional reactions to things that might produce the conflicts predicted by psychodynamic theory. Because Freud's central premises cannot be examined through accepted scientific methods, psychologists have largely abandoned psychodynamic theories. Still, Freud's observations and ideas continue to affect personality psychology and have framed much of the research in personality over the last century (Hines, 2003; Westen, 1998).

13.6 Humanistic Approaches Emphasize Goodness in People

13.6 LEARNING GOAL ACTIVITIES

To maximize your learning, complete the following learning goal activities:

a. Understand all bold and italic terms by writing explanations of them in your own words.

b. Apply humanistic approaches to personality by providing an example of how conditions of worth or unconditional positive regard may have influenced your personality (or the personality of someone you know).

Until the early 1950s, most theories of personality painted a rather bleak view of people. For example, Freud's theories emphasized a dark side filled with anxiety and conflict. Against this backdrop, a new and more positive view of personality began to emerge. **Humanistic approaches** emphasize how your unique goodness, growth, and self-understanding influence your personality. These approaches propose that you seek to fulfill your potential for personal growth through greater self-understanding. This process is called self-actualization. Abraham Maslow's theory of motivation is an example. As discussed in study unit 9.1, Maslow believed that the desire to become self-actualized is the ultimate human motive (see Figure 9.3).

The most prominent humanistic psychologist, Carl Rogers, introduced a *person-centered approach* to understanding personality and human relationships. In the therapeutic technique Rogers developed, the therapist would create a supportive

humanistic approaches
Ways of studying personality that emphasize self-actualization, where people seek to fulfill their potential through greater self-understanding.

and accepting environment. The therapist and the client would deal with the client's problems and concerns as the client understood them.

Rogers emphasized two issues as crucial in the development of personality. The first issue is your personal understanding of your life—that is, your sense of self (see study unit 13.1). The second issue is how others see you and evaluate you, which affects your self-esteem (see study unit 13.2).

PERSONALITY IS SHAPED BY THE EVALUATIONS OF OTHERS Rogers's theory highlights the importance of the way parents show affection for their children and how parents can affect personality development. Rogers believed that most parents provide love and support that is conditional. That is, the parents love their children on the condition that the children do what the parents want them to do and live up to the parents' standards. This condition creates a discrepancy between the children's sense of self and how their parents evaluate them. In turn, this discrepancy leads to development of a personality based on *conditions of worth* (**Figure 13.13a**). Parents who do not approve of their children's behavior may withhold their love. As a result, children quickly abandon their true feelings, dreams, and desires. They accept only those parts of themselves that elicit parental love and support. Thus, as children grow older they may lose touch with their true selves as they attempt to develop a personality that depends on getting approval from others.

To prevent conditions of worth, Rogers encouraged parents to accept and prize their children no matter how the children behave or how close they come to meeting parents' expectations. This approach, called *unconditional positive regard,* helps children develop a sense of self that is consistent with how their parents evaluate them. This consistency helps children develop personalities based on their true selves (**Figure 13.13b**).

In other words, the best way parents can help children develop their true personalities is to express disapproval of the children's bad behavior while at the same time expressing their love for the children. According to Rogers, children raised with unconditional positive regard would develop a healthy sense of self-esteem and have a better chance to fulfill their personal growth.

a If parents' affection for a child is conditional on the child acting in an acceptable way, the child's personality develops based solely on the aspects that get approval from others. That is, the child's personality is based on *conditions of worth.*

or

b When parents' affection for a child is unconditional, and expressed regardless of how the child acts, the child's personality can develop freely. That is, the child's personality will be based on *unconditional positive regard.*

FIGURE 13.13

Rogers's Person-Centered Approach to Personality

According to a humanistic approach to personality, Rogers's person-centered approach, personality is influenced by how you understand yourself and how others evaluate you, which can lead to **(a)** conditions of worth or **(b)** unconditional positive regard.

social cognitive approaches
Ways of studying personality that recognize the influence of how people think.

13.7 Social Cognitive Approaches Focus on How Thoughts Shape Personality

13.7 LEARNING GOAL ACTIVITIES

To maximize your learning, complete the following learning goal activities:

a. Understand all bold and italic terms by writing explanations of them in your own words.

b. Understand social cognitive approaches to personality by describing how expectancy theory and reciprocal determinism can influence personality.

As you learned in study units 6.8–6.12, learning theory dominated most areas of psychology for the first half of the twentieth century. From this perspective, personality resulted from learned responses to patterns of reinforcement. By the 1950s, however, there was growing agreement that cognition—thinking—is important in understanding many aspects of human behavior, including personality. This change in focus was the basis for development of **social cognitive approaches** to personality.

EXPECTANCY THEORY EXPLAINS HOW PERSONALITY IS LEARNED

Julian Rotter (1954) developed one of the first theories of personality that included cognition. According to Rotter's *expectancy theory,* your behaviors are part of your personality. They result from how you think about two things: your *expectancies* for reinforcement and the *values* you place on particular reinforcers. For instance, suppose you are deciding whether to study for an exam or go to a party. You will probably consider whether studying will lead to a good grade and how much that grade matters to you. Then you will weigh those two considerations against two others: the likelihood that the party will be fun, and how much you value having fun.

Expectancy theory led Rotter to propose that people's personalities are based on their *locus of control.* Locus of control means whether people control the rewards and punishments that they experience. People with an *internal locus of control* believe that they themselves influence outcomes (**Figure 13.14a**). For example, if you have an internal locus of control, you might believe that you got a promotion because you worked hard. Those with an *external locus of control* believe that outcomes—and therefore their personal fates—result from forces beyond their control (**Figure 13.14b**). If you have an external locus of control, you might view the same promotion as being due to luck, not because of your hard work. These generalized beliefs reflect personality. What is your locus of control? To find out, see Try It Yourself on p. 521.

RECIPROCAL DETERMINISM EXPLAINS PERSONALITY BASED ON THREE FACTORS

In another influential social cognitive theory of personality, Albert Bandura (1977a) argued that three factors influence how you act. The first factor is your environment. The second factor is multiple *person factors,* which

a People who expect that their own actions influence events and outcomes have a personality based on an *internal locus of control.*

or

b People who expect that forces outside of their control influence events and outcomes have developed a personality based on an *external locus of control.*

FIGURE 13.14

Rotter's Expectancy Theory of Personality

According to one of the social cognitive approaches to personality, Rotter's expectancy theory, personality is influenced by expectations, which can lead to having **(a)** an internal locus of control or **(b)** an external locus of control.

Do you believe that your efforts will lead to positive outcomes? To determine your locus of control, decide which statement (A or B) best represents your position in each of these five situations.

1. A. People's misfortunes result from the mistakes they make.

   B. Many of the unhappy things in people's lives are partly due to bad luck.

2. A. There is a direct connection between how hard I study and the grades I get.

   B. Sometimes I can't understand how teachers arrive at the grades they give.

3. A. Getting a good job is a matter of hard work, not luck.

   B. Getting a good job depends mainly on being in the right place at the right time.

4. A. People who can't get others to like them don't understand how to get along with others.

   B. No matter how hard you try, some people just don't like you.

5. A. What happens to me is my own doing.

   B. Sometimes I feel that I don't have enough control over the direction my life is taking.

Scoring:

- If you chose A more often, you may tend to have an internal locus of control. That is, you expect that you can control the outcome of events.

- If you chose B more often, you may tend to have an external locus of control. In other words, you expect that the outcome of events is outside your control.

SOURCE: Adapted from Rotter (1966).

include your characteristics, self-confidence, and expectations. The third factor is behavior itself. This approach to personality explains how each of these three factors affects the others to determine how personality is expressed through behavior. Because personality is explained by the interaction of all three factors, the model is called *reciprocal determinism*.

Let's look at how these factors affect how someone's personality is expressed in a situation. Imagine that you go to a party. According to Bandura's model, the party is the environment. The specific features of the environment affect your behavior. To judge the effects, we need to know the specifics. Therefore, let's specify that you don't know most of the people at the party (**Figure 13.15a**). In addition, you have particular person factors. Let's say you are outgoing and sociable. These characteristics have probably been rewarded by your environment in the past. For example, people may have responded positively to your friendliness (**Figure 13.15b**). Lastly,

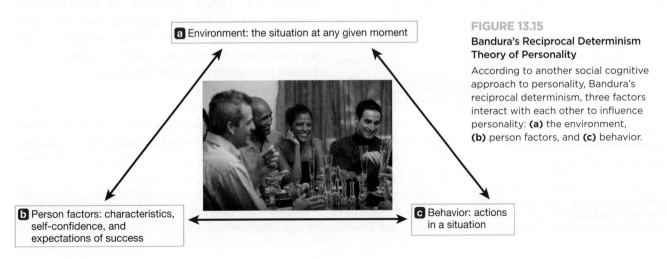

a Environment: the situation at any given moment

b Person factors: characteristics, self-confidence, and expectations of success

c Behavior: actions in a situation

FIGURE 13.15

Bandura's Reciprocal Determinism Theory of Personality

According to another social cognitive approach to personality, Bandura's reciprocal determinism, three factors interact with each other to influence personality: **(a)** the environment, **(b)** person factors, and **(c)** behavior.

your behavior in this situation will reflect both the environment and your person factors. Specifically, at this party, you most likely will be talkative with new people (**Figure 13.15c**). In turn, your behavior will affect the environment (see Figure 13.15c→a). Furthermore, because you are friendly, the party may become more fun for everyone (see Figure 13.15b→a).

But if any of the three factors change, then your behavior will also change. For example, if the environment changes and several people leave the party, your behavior is likely to change.

13.8 Trait Approaches Describe Characteristics

13.8 LEARNING GOAL ACTIVITIES

To maximize your learning, complete the following learning goal activities:

a. Understand all bold and italic terms by writing explanations of them in your own words.

b. Apply the trait approaches to personality by using Eysenck's theory and the five-factor theory to each explain the personality of a person you know.

According to the personality theories you have just learned about, the same underlying processes occur in everyone. Individuals differ because they experience different conflicts, think differently, and so on. Other approaches to personality focus more on description than explanation. Most contemporary personality psychologists focus on **trait approaches** to personality. These approaches describe the behavioral tendencies that are generally consistent over time and across most situations.

According to this approach, your traits exist on a continuum (**Figure 13.16**). Most people fall somewhere in the middle, and relatively few are at the extremes. For instance, some of the people you know may be very shy and some just the opposite. But most are probably in the middle—they are shy in some situations but not in others. Let's look at how two trait approaches to personality focus on the ways individuals differ in basic personality characteristics.

EYSENCK'S TRAIT THEORY In the 1960s, the psychologist Hans Eysenck proposed that personality traits had three major dimensions: how outgoing people were, whether their emotions tended to be stable or unstable, and their ability to control selfish impulses (Eysenck, 1967) (**Figure 13.17a-c**).

First, according to Eysenck, people vary in how outgoing they are (see Figure 13.17a). *Introversion* refers to how shy, reserved, and quiet people are. *Extraversion* refers to how sociable, outgoing, and bold people are. As you will see in the next study unit, 13.9, Eysenck believed that this dimension reflects differences in biological processes.

Eysenck's second dimension refers to variability in people's moods and emotions (see Figure 13.17b). People who are *stable* in emotionality tend to show consistency in moods and emotions. People who have *unstable* emotions experience frequent

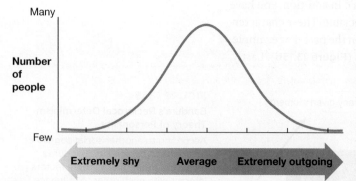

FIGURE 13.16

Personality Trait on a Continuum

Personality traits can be viewed on a continuum. For example, in shyness, people range from extremely shy to extremely outgoing. Most people are in the middle. Relatively few people are at the extremes of any personality trait.

Do Personalities Matter in Roommate Relationships?

If you are like most college students, you share your living space with at least one roommate. Positive roommate relationships can be a highlight of your college experience and can provide a foundation for lifelong friendships. Negative roommate relationships can make your life miserable and add significant stress to your college experience. How can you use a psychological understanding of personality to help ensure a positive roommate relationship? There are no guarantees in the realm of interpersonal relationships, but the research on this topic points to some useful advice.

Carli and colleagues (1991) examined the association between personality similarity and relationship satisfaction among 30 college roommate pairs. The roommates had been randomly assigned to live together during the fall of their freshman year. After living together for six months, they completed questionnaires asking about their personality traits. The researchers found that personality similarity between roommates was positively correlated with both relationship satisfaction and intent to live together the following year. Simply put, students liked their roommates when they were similar to them.

What do the results of this study mean for you? When it comes time to select a roommate, look for someone who is similar to you, especially in the personality traits that are most important to you. But how do you do this? You have at least three options for figuring out how a potential roommate compares with you. You can ask the potential roommate, you can ask her previous roommates, or you can rely on your own observations.

Preference for—and comfort with—a tidy versus a messy living space is a personality characteristic related to conscientiousness and is therefore a trait worth paying attention to. Ogletree and colleagues (2005) found that a third of the college-age people they studied reported experiencing roommate conflict related to the cleanliness of their living space. So it would be a good idea to ask potential roommates questions such as those in **Table 13.3.**

Many colleges and universities ask students to complete personality questionnaires before matching roommates in dorms. You might already have responded to questions like those in Table 13.3 as part of your application for residence. If you and your roommate are a good fit, the system has worked.

TABLE 13.3
Level of Cleanliness Scale

Answer each item on a scale of 1 to 5, where 1 represents "very strongly disagree" and 5 represents "very strongly agree." If your answers are quite similar to those of your potential roommate, you've got at least one good indication of a satisfying arrangement.

1. I don't mind having a messy apartment.

2. It is important to me that my house or apartment is nice and neat.

3. If my house is cluttered when guests drop by, I apologize for the mess.

4. Leaving a stack of dirty dishes in the sink overnight is disgusting.

5. An overflowing trash can does not bother me.

6. It is important that anyone I live with share my cleanliness standards.

7. Leaving clothes that have been worn on a chair is an acceptable way of dealing with dirty clothes until doing laundry.

SOURCE: Ogletree et al. (2005).

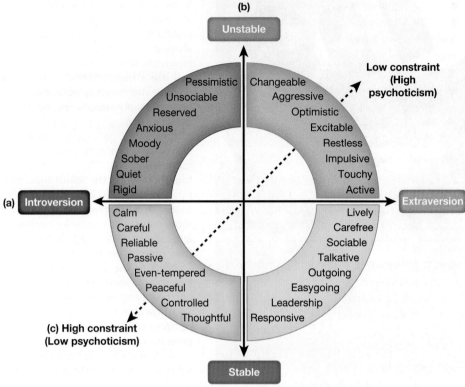

FIGURE 13.17

Eysenck's Trait Theory of Personality

According to Eysenck, personality is composed of traits that occur in three dimensions: **(a)** introversion/extraversion, **(b)** unstable/stable, and **(c)** high constraint/low constraint.

and dramatic mood swings, especially toward negative emotions, compared with people who are more stable. Eysenck referred to these people as being *neurotic*. Neurotic people often feel anxious, moody, and depressed and generally hold very low opinions of themselves.

Eysenck also proposed a third dimension of personality traits (see Figure 13.17c). Psychoticism reflects a mix of aggression, poor impulse control, self-centeredness, or a lack of empathy. The term *psychoticism* implies a level of psychological disorder that Eysenck did not intend. As a result, more-recent conceptions of this trait call it *constraint*. According to this view of the trait, people range from generally controlling their impulses to generally not controlling them (Watson & Clark, 1997).

THE FIVE-FACTOR TRAIT THEORY   Since Eysenck's initial proposal, many personality psychologists have embraced the *five-factor theory*. This theory identifies

---

LEARNING TIP: Remembering the Big Five

According to the five-factor theory, there are five personality traits, called the Big Five: openness, conscientiousness, extraversion, agreeableness, and neuroticism. Each person ranges from low to high on each personality trait. To remember the personality dimensions of the five-factor theory, just look at this graphic. Notice that, when taken together, the first letters of the five dimensions can be used to create a mnemonic by spelling the word "OCEAN." So when you need to remember the personality traits of the five-factor theory, just think of the OCEAN.

Openness to experience	**C**onscientiousness	**E**xtraversion	**A**greeableness	**N**euroticism
Imaginative vs. down-to-earth Likes variety vs. likes routine Independent vs. conforming	Organized vs. disorganized Careful vs. careless Self-disciplined vs. weak-willed	Social vs. retiring Fun-loving vs. sober Affectionate vs. reserved	Softhearted vs. ruthless Trusting vs. suspicious Helpful vs. uncooperative	Worried vs. calm Insecure vs. secure Self-pitying vs. self-satisfied

five basic personality traits, which are often called the Big Five: *extraversion, neuroticism, conscientiousness, agreeableness,* and *openness to experience* (McCrae & Costa, 1999). The Learning Tip on p. 524 will help you remember the Big Five personality traits.

Two of the Big Five traits are highly consistent with Eysenck's theory, where extraversion reflects Eysenck's introversion/extraversion dimension and neuroticism reflects Eysenck's unstable/stable dimension. The conscientiousness trait in the Big Five is also believed to reflect Eysenck's constraint dimension, which refers to how careful and organized you are. The Big Five trait of agreeableness reflects the extent to which you are trusting and helpful. Finally, if you are high in openness to experience, you are imaginative and independent. If you are low in this basic trait, you are down-to-earth and conformist. For each of the five factors, your personality may be anywhere on a continuum from low to high. Which of the five traits do you think you are highest on? Which do you think you are lowest on?

Considerable evidence supports the five-factor theory (John, 1990). The Big Five emerge across cultures, among adults and children, even when vastly different questionnaires assess the factors. The same five factors appear whether people rate themselves or are rated by others. Furthermore, people's "scores" on the five-factor theory traits have been shown to predict a wide variety of behaviors (Paunonen & Ashton, 2001). Their scores also have been shown to predict satisfaction with job, marriage, and life generally (Heller, Watson, & Ilies, 2004). As shown in Using Psychology in Your Life on p. 523, your personality according to the five-factory theory may also predict whether you will get along with a roommate or not. Today, the five-factor theory dominates much of the way that psychologists study personality in humans.

 How Can You Understand Personality?

To make sure you learned what you just read, write answers to the following questions and check your answers.

13.5 According to Freud's psychodynamic approach to personality, which personality structure operates according to the reality principle?

13.6 A parent says to a child, "I love you, but I am disappointed that you were careless and broke the vase." According to Rogers's person-centered approach to personality, what does this statement reveal?

13.7 In explaining why his date was unsuccessful, Joe blamed bad weather for forcing cancellation of the concert his date was excited to attend. Based on this explanation, analyze whether Rotter's theory of personality would suggest that Joe most likely has an internal or external locus of control.

13.8 Which of the following is NOT one of the Big Five personality traits: agreeableness, conscientiousness, openness to experience, dominance, neuroticism, or extraversion?

See Appendix B for answers to the red Q questions.

How Does Biology Affect Personality?

As you have seen in many chapters throughout this textbook, nature and nurture work together to make you think, feel, and act as you do. This theme is particularly true for personality. Over the past few decades, evidence has emerged that biological factors—such as genes, brain structures, and neurochemistry—play an important role in determining personality.

13.9 Personality Has a Biological Basis

13.9 LEARNING GOAL ACTIVITIES

To maximize your learning, complete the following learning goal activities:

a. Understand all bold and italic terms by writing explanations of them in your own words.

b. Understand how extraversion/introversion is related to biological factors by summarizing how introverts and extraverts differ in their optimal levels of arousal.

Do you like to read by a fire, chat with one or two friends, or take a gentle walk? Or perhaps you prefer to drive fast, go to big parties, or engage in strenuous exercise? Either way, these tendencies reflect your personality. And there is evidence that certain aspects of your personality—including your thoughts, emotions, and behaviors—are based on biological processes (Canli, 2006). For example, most research on the neurobiological underpinnings of personality has explored the dimension of introversion/extraversion.

Recall from the previous study unit, 13.8, that Hans Eysenck developed a trait theory with one dimension that describes introversion/extraversion (see Figure 13.17a). Eysenck believed that differences in arousal produce the behavioral differences between introverts and extraverts. A person's degree of arousal is based on processing in a part of the brain called the *reticular activating system (RAS)*. The RAS affects alertness. It is also involved in inducing and terminating the different stages of sleep. Eysenck proposed that the RAS differs between introverts and extraverts.

As you learned in study unit 9.1, each person prefers some level of arousal that is optimal for that person. And each person also functions best at that level of arousal (see Figure 9.7). Eysenck proposed that extraverts typically are below their optimal level of arousal. In other words, extraverts are chronically underaroused relative to their optimal level of arousal. So they often engage in activities that will increase their arousal. They seek out new situations and new emotional experiences, such as going to parties or meeting new people. And extraverts tend to perform better in stimulating situations such as these (**Figure 13.18a**). By contrast, introverts typically are above their optimal levels of arousal. These people are often overaroused in relation to their optimal level of arousal. Because they do not want any additional arousal, they seek out quiet solitude with few stimuli, and they perform better in these situations (**Figure 13.18b**). In short, if you are an introvert, a noisy environment will distract you. If you are an extravert, quiet places will bore you. Either way, you won't be able to complete tasks to the best of your ability.

As with many areas of psychology, the recent advances in brain imaging are also starting to provide new insights into the biological basis of personality traits (Abram & DeYoung, 2017). Based on this research it is likely that multiple brain areas influence how personality develops and is expressed. For example, extraversion is associated with many brain areas involved in reward, whereas neuroticism involves brain regions involved in threat and negative affect (DeYoung et al., 2010; Eisenberger, Lieberman, & Satpute, 2005). Patterns such as these show that the Big Five traits can be distinguished from each other based on patterns of brain activity.

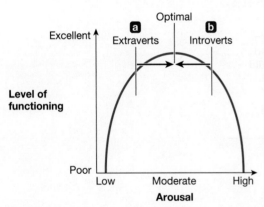

FIGURE 13.18

Optimal Arousal Influences Personality

(a) People who are extraverted have lower levels of arousal. To function optimally, they tend to seek out exciting activities. **(b)** By contrast, people who are introverted have higher levels of arousal. To function optimally, they tend to seek out calming activities.

13.10 Personality Is Influenced by Genes

Did you do the Try It Yourself exercise on p. 340, in Chapter 9? If so, then you might have learned whether you are a sensation seeker, who enjoys new experiences and seeks adventure. For these and other aspects of your personality, you can thank your genes (see study unit 2.11), because they are likely to be at least somewhat responsible.

TWIN STUDIES SHOW THAT GENES INFLUENCE PERSONALITY There is overwhelming evidence that nearly all personality traits are influenced by genes (Plomin, DeFries, Knopik, & Neiderhiser, 2016). For example, research with twins provides insight into how genes influence personality. As you learned in study unit 2.12, monozygotic twins are identical, and they share nearly the same genes, whereas dizygotic twins, or fraternal twins, do not necessarily share genes (**Figure 13.19a**). Numerous studies have shown that identical twins are more similar than fraternal twins in personality traits described by the five-factor theory (for example, Jang, Livesley, & Vernon, 1996; **Figure 13.19b**). The majority of twin studies have found that genetic influence explains about half of the variability (40–60 percent) between individuals for all personality traits (Vukasović, & Bratko, 2015).

This statistic does not mean that half of personality comes from genes. Instead, it means that when researchers look at how people differ in their personality traits, differences in genes explain about half of why people differ on a given trait. At the same time, however, it is also not the case that there are specific genes for any

FIGURE 13.19

Identical Twins Have Similar Personalities

(a) Identical twins **(top)** have the same genes, are the same sex, and look the same. Fraternal twins **(bottom)** have no more genes in common than do any two siblings. **(b)** Researchers examined the similarity between personality traits for 123 pairs of identical twins and 128 pairs of fraternal twins. Their findings showed that identical twins are more similar in personality traits than are fraternal twins.

(a)

(b)

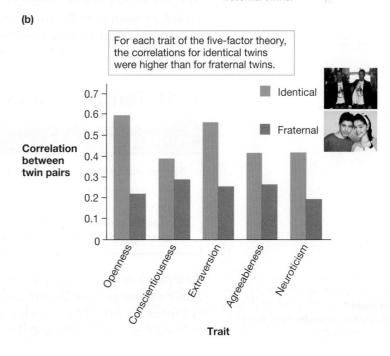

For each trait of the five-factor theory, the correlations for identical twins were higher than for fraternal twins.

particular personality trait. Instead, the combined actions of hundreds of genes influence personality overall (Chabris, Lee, Cesarini, Benjamin, & Laibson, 2015).

As you learned in study unit 8.10, studies that explored intelligence in twins raised apart have found that they are often as similar as, or even more similar than, twins raised together (Bouchard et al., 1990). One possible explanation for this finding is that when identical twins are raised together, parenting style may foster differences rather than similarities. If this explanation is correct, we might expect stronger correlations between personality traits for older twins than for younger twins, since the effects of parenting would diminish over time and the effects of genes would become stronger. And indeed, identical twins become more alike as they grow older. However, siblings and fraternal twins do not become more alike.

ADOPTION STUDIES SHOW THAT GENES INFLUENCE PERSONALITY

Further evidence for the genetic basis of personality comes from adoption studies. Two children who are not biologically related but raised as siblings in the same household tend to be no more alike in personality than any two strangers randomly plucked off the street (Plomin & Caspi, 1999). Why might this be the case?

One explanation is that these siblings do not share genes. Another explanation is that, even though the siblings are raised in the same home, their environments differ. After all, their ages may be different, they may have younger or older sisters or brothers, and their parents no doubt respond to each child differently. Further, the lives of siblings become less similar as they establish friendships outside the home. Their personalities slowly become increasingly individualized as their initial differences become magnified through their interactions with the world. Moreover, the personalities of adopted children bear no significant relationship to those of their adoptive parents.

These findings and other current evidence suggest that parenting style has much less impact than has long been assumed. In other words, the similarities in personality between biological siblings and between children and their biological parents seem to have some genetic component.

The small correlations in personality among siblings might imply that parenting style has little effect. Still, parents are important. David Lykken is a leading researcher in behavioral genetics. Lykken (2000) has argued that children raised with inadequate parenting are not socialized properly. Improperly socialized children, according to Lykken, are much more likely to become delinquent or to display antisocial behavior. Thus children need adequate parenting, which most parents provide. However, the particular style of parenting may not have a major impact on children's personalities.

13.11 Temperament Is Innate

13.11 LEARNING GOAL ACTIVITIES

To maximize your learning, complete the following learning goal activities:

a. Understand all bold and italic terms by writing explanations of them in your own words.

b. Apply temperament to children by providing one example of each of the three aspects of temperament to children you know or can imagine.

Have you heard stories about yourself as a baby? Or have you spent time with babies? Either way, you probably know that it's easy to make judgments about babies' characteristics. We do it all the time when we say things such as "She's a fussy baby," "He smiles at everyone," or "She really loves to run around!"

temperament
Biologically based tendency to feel or act in certain ways.

Each of these statements describes the child's **temperament**. Temperament is the biologically based tendency to feel or act in certain ways. This sense of a person is broader than personality traits. Life experiences may alter personality traits, but temperament is the innate biological structure of your personality.

THREE ASPECTS OF TEMPERAMENT Arnold Buss and Robert Plomin (1984) have argued that personality characteristics make up a child's temperament. *Activity level* is the overall amount of energy and behavior the child exhibits (**Figure 13.20a**). For example, some children race around the house. Other children are less vigorous. Still others are slow paced. *Emotionality* describes the intensity of the child's emotional reactions (**Figure 13.20b**). For example, some children cry often or become frightened easily. Some children anger quickly. Finally, *sociability* refers to the child's tendency to affiliate with others (**Figure 13.20c**). Children high in sociability prefer to be with others rather than to be alone. According to Buss and Plomin, these three aspects of temperament are the main personality factors influenced by genes. There is evidence from twin studies, adoption studies, and family studies that genes have a powerful effect on these core temperaments. And these core temperaments, which are evident when we are children, endure throughout our lives.

LONG-TERM EFFECTS OF TEMPERAMENT You are clearly different as an adult than you were as a child. Yet early childhood temperament appears to influence behavior and personality significantly throughout a person's development (Caspi, 2000).

One study focused on the health, development, and personalities of more than 1,000 people born during a one-year period (Caspi et al., 2016; Rivenbark et al., 2018). These individuals were examined approximately every two years, and 95 percent remained in the study through their 38th birthdays (Poulton, Moffitt, & Silva, 2015). When they were 3 years old, they were classified into temperament types. The classification at age 3 turned out to be a good predictor of personality and behaviors that appeared in early adulthood. Children whose temperaments were classified as well adjusted were less likely at the age of 21 to abuse alcohol or show antisocial disorders than were children whose temperaments had been classified as undercontrolled at age 3 (**Figure 13.21**). In addition, inhibited children were much more likely, as adults, to be anxious, to become depressed, to be unemployed, to have less social support, and to attempt suicide.

Research also has shown that children as young as 6 weeks show behaviors and reactions, such as being easily startled, that identify them as likely to be shy (Kagan & Snidman, 1991). This finding suggests that shyness has a strong biological influence. However, shyness has a social component as well. To reduce shyness in their children, parents can create supportive and calm environments in which children

(a)

(b)

(c)

FIGURE 13.20

Three Aspects of Temperament

Temperament is the biological structure of personality. The three aspects of temperament are **(a)** activity level, **(b)** emotionality, and **(c)** sociability.

FIGURE 13.21

Predicting Adolescent Behavior Based on Temperament at Age 3

Researchers investigated the personality development of more than 1,000 people. As shown in these graphs, the individuals who were judged as undercontrolled at age 3 were later more likely to be antisocial or to have alcohol problems. In the graphs, the dotted line indicates the average for the entire sample.

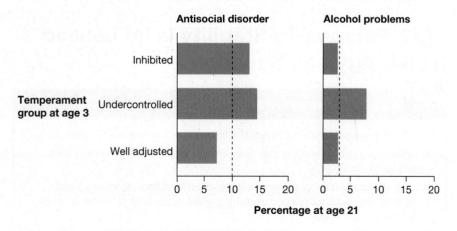

Hypothesis: People who had an inhibited temperamental style as children are more likely to show signs of social anxiety later in life.

Research method:

1 Adults received brain scans while viewing pictures of familiar faces and of novel faces. One group of these adults had been categorized as inhibited before age 2. The other group had been categorized as uninhibited before age 2.

2 Two regions of the brain were more activated by novel faces. These areas were the amygdala (marked "Amy" in the brain scan below) and the occipitotemporal cortex (marked "OTC"). The amygdala is normally active when people are threatened. The occipitotemporal cortex is normally active when people see faces, whether the faces are novel or familiar.

Results: Compared with the uninhibited group, the inhibited group showed significantly greater activation of the amygdala while viewing novel faces. That activation indicated that, when seeing novel faces, the inhibited group showed greater brain activity associated with threat.

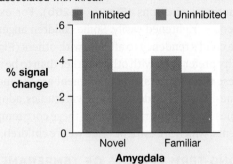

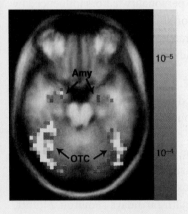

Conclusion: The results suggest that some aspects of childhood temperament are preserved in the adult brain. In particular, biological factors seem to play an important role in social anxiety.

QUESTION: Did adults who were inhibited as children show increased amygdala activity to all faces?

ANSWER: No. They showed increased activity mainly to novel faces.

Source: Schwartz, C. E., Wright, C. I., Shin, L. M., Kagan, J., & Rauch, S. L. (2003). Inhibited and uninhibited infants "grown up": Adult amygdalar response to novelty. *Science, 300,* 1952–1953.

can deal with stress and novelty at their own pace. Approximately one quarter of young children identified as potentially shy are not shy later in childhood (Kagan, 2011). Once again, nature and nurture work together to influence who we are.

Furthermore, as shown in The Methods of Psychology above, adults who were rated as more inhibited as children were more likely to show brain activity, in the amygdala, that is associated with social anxiety (Schwartz, Wright, Shin, Kagan, & Rauch, 2003). In other words, according to the research, early childhood temperament may be a good predictor of later behavior and personality.

13.12 Personality Stability Is Influenced by Biology and Situation

13.12 LEARNING GOAL ACTIVITIES

To maximize your learning, complete the following learning goal activities:

a. Understand all bold and italic terms by writing explanations of them in your own words.

b. Understand the stability of personality by describing basic tendencies and characteristic adaptations and explaining which of these tend to change more as a person gets older.

basic tendencies
Personality traits that are largely determined by biology and are stable over time.

characteristic adaptations
Changes in behavioral expression of basic tendencies based on the demands of specific situations.

Your genes may predispose you to have certain personality traits or characteristics. Whether these genes are expressed depends on the unique circumstances that you face during your development. This idea is expressed in the maxim "Give me a child until he is seven, and I will show you the man." The movie directors Paul Almond and Michael Apted have explored this maxim in the *Up* series of documentary films. Through the series, which started in 1964, Almond and Apted have followed the development of 14 British people. Most of the participants have been interviewed every seven years from age 7 until age 56. A striking aspect of the films is the apparent stability of personality over time. For example, the boy who was interested in the stars and science becomes a physics professor. The reserved, well-mannered, upper-class 7-year-old girl grows into the reserved, well-mannered woman living in the country at age 35.

PERSONALITY TRAITS ARE GENERALLY STABLE OVER TIME Are all people's personalities really so stable? Childhood temperament may predict behavioral outcomes in early adulthood, but what about change during adulthood? Clinical psychology is based on the belief that people can and do change important aspects of their lives. In fact, they use a lot of energy trying to change, attending self-help groups, reading self-help books, paying for therapy sessions, and struggling to make their lives different. But how much can people really change their personalities?

Whether personality is fixed or changeable depends largely on how we define the essential features of personality. Continuity over time and across situations is inherent in the definition of "trait." Most research finds personality traits to be quite stable over the adult life span (McCrae & Costa, 1990). An analysis of 150 studies—in which nearly 50,000 participants were followed for at least one year—found strong evidence for stability in personality (Roberts & Friend-DelVecchio, 2000). People's rankings, low or high, on any personality trait were quite stable over long periods across all age ranges. Stability was lowest for young children and highest for those over age 50 (**Figure 13.22**). This finding suggests that personality traits change somewhat in childhood but become more stable by middle age.

CERTAIN ASPECTS OF PERSONALITY CAN CHANGE OVER THE LIFE COURSE In describing changes in personality over time, Robert McCrae and Paul Costa (1999) emphasize an important distinction. They separate basic tendencies of personality from characteristic adaptations. **Basic tendencies** are traits determined largely by biological processes. As such, they are very stable (**Figure 13.23a**). **Characteristic adaptations** are adjustments to situational demands (**Figure 13.23b**). Such adaptations tend to be somewhat consistent because they are based on skills, habits, roles, and so on. But changes in behavior produced by characteristic adaptations do not indicate changes in basic tendencies. Consider a highly extraverted man. In his youth, he may go to parties frequently, be a thrill seeker, and have multiple sexual partners. When he is older, he will be

> Consistency is lowest in childhood and highest after age 50.

(bar chart: Rank-order trait consistency vs. Age periods)

Age periods: 0–2, 3–5, 6–11, 12–17, 18–21, 22–29, 30–39, 40–49, 50–59, 60–73

FIGURE 13.22
The Stability of Personality
After childhood, people's personality traits tend to be quite stable over time.

ⓐ Basic tendencies: traits determined largely by biological processes that are very stable over time. For example, being a highly extraverted person.

ⓑ Characteristic adaptation: behavior changes caused by adjustments to the situation, which tend to be consistent. For example, a highly extraverted young man will still be very extraverted as an older man, but will show that extraversion in different ways, based on what he can do at that age.

FIGURE 13.23
McCrae and Costa's Model of Personality
According to this model, personality is made up of two tendencies: **(a)** basic tendencies and **(b)** characteristic adaptations.

less likely to do these things, but he may have many friends and enjoy traveling. Although the exact behaviors differ, they reflect the basic tendency of extraversion. As discussed in Has It Happened to You?, people often have to adjust their behavior to new circumstances.

Even though basic tendencies remain stable, so that people who are very shy remain so over time, there are consistent patterns of personality change as people age. For instance, people generally develop increased self-control and emotional stability as they get older (Caspi, Roberts, & Shiner, 2005). They become less neurotic, less extraverted, and less open to new experiences as they get older (Milojev & Sibley, 2017). They also tend to become more agreeable and more conscientious (Srivastava, John, Gosling, & Potter, 2003). Moreover, this pattern holds in different cultures (McCrae et al., 2000; **Figure 13.24**). These cross-cultural findings suggest that age-related changes in personality occur independently of environmental influences and therefore that personality change itself may be based in human biology.

Overall, personality appears to be quite stable, especially among older adults. However, when behaviors, thoughts, or emotions change, and do so repeatedly over time, people can come to see themselves in a new light. Personality may change in adulthood because people's lives change as they form long-term relationships, have children, and build careers (Roberts, 2009). For instance, a first job requires that a person show up on time, work hard, and get along with others. Doing so over time may make the person more conscientious. Likewise, having a good job makes people happier. It is no surprise, then, that greater job satisfaction can decrease neuroticism over time (Le, Donnellan, & Conger, 2014).

Life events can also change personality. One study examined personality change among people who were caregivers for a spouse dying from cancer. The researchers measured personality before and approximately seven months after the spouse's death. Compared with a control group, the bereaved caregivers became more agreeable, sociable (a component of extraversion), and conscientious (Hoerger et al., 2014; **Figure 13.25**). The take-home message is that personality is usually stable because environments tend to be relatively stable. However, major life events can lead to changes in personality.

FIGURE 13.24

Conscientiousness at Different Ages in Three Cultures

The tendency for people to show an increase in conscientiousness as they age occurs across cultures, suggesting that such personality changes have a biological component.

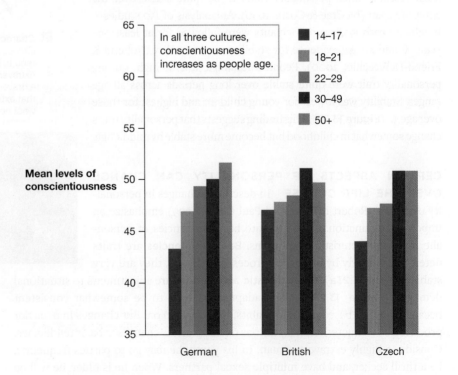

In all three cultures, conscientiousness increases as people age.

- 14–17
- 18–21
- 22–29
- 30–49
- 50+

Mean levels of conscientiousness

German   British   Czech

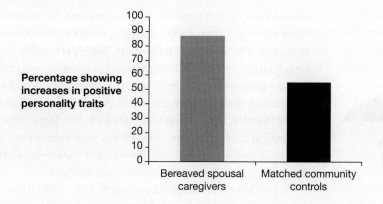

FIGURE 13.25

Caregiving and Personality Change

As this graph illustrates, a greater percentage of caregivers for spouses dying from cancer experienced increases in personality traits considered to be positive (agreeableness, sociableness, and conscientiousness) than did people in a control group.

Q How Does Biology Affect Personality?

To make sure you learned what you just read, write answers to the following questions and check your answers.

13.9 Given the biological underpinnings of introversion, explain whether an introvert would prefer to study in a noisy café or a quiet library.

13.10 On average, how similar are the personalities of adopted children to the personalities of the parents who adopt them and raise them?

13.11 What are the three aspects of temperament seen in children?

13.12 If Sheri is highly extraverted in her 20s, how extraverted is she likely to be in her 50s?

See Appendix B for answers to the red Q questions.

How Can Personality Be Assessed?

At the start of this chapter you saw photos of Drake, Mark Zuckerberg, and Selena Gomez. You most likely had immediate thoughts about these people, including what their personalities are like. But if personality is all about understanding ourselves and other people, how can we be sure that our intuition about personalities is accurate? Psychology is a science. To understand personality from an objective psychological perspective, psychologists must be able to assess what we're talking about. Let's consider several different methods.

13.13 Several Methods Are Used to Assess Personality

13.13 LEARNING GOAL ACTIVITIES

To maximize your learning, complete the following learning goal activities:

a. Understand all bold and italic terms by writing explanations of them in your own words.

b. Understand the four ways that personality is assessed by summarizing how projective measures, self-report measures, electronically activated records, and observational methods are used to assess personality.

(a)

(b)

FIGURE 13.26

Projective Measures of Personality
Projective measures provide insight into personality by allowing you to project unconscious thoughts onto ambiguous images, as shown here in **(a)** a Rorschach inkblot test and **(b)** the Thematic Apperception Test (TAT).

projective measures
Personality tests that examine unconscious processes by having people interpret ambiguous stimuli.

self-report measures
Personality tests that use questionnaires to let people respond to items that reveal traits and behaviors.

Researchers do not agree on the best method for assessing the three aspects of personality: thoughts, emotional responses, and behaviors. The way they choose to measure personality depends largely on their theoretical orientation. For instance, trait researchers use personality descriptions. Humanistic psychologists use approaches that consider the whole person at once. Psychodynamic theorists try to assess unconscious forces. Regardless of the theoretical approach taken, personality can be assessed using four methods: projective measures, self-report measures, electronically activated records, and observational methods.

If you have ever applied for a job, you might have taken a personality test as part of the application. Companies use self-report measures and observational methods to assess the personalities of prospective employees. To further explore the connections between psychology and human resources, read Putting Psychology to Work on p. 543.

PROJECTIVE MEASURES As you learned in study unit 13.5, psychodynamic theory considers unconscious conflicts to be an influence on personality. **Projective measures** explore the unconscious by having people describe or tell stories about stimulus items that are ambiguous. The general idea is that people will project their mental contents onto the ambiguous items. This process is used by followers of psychodynamic theory to reveal hidden aspects of personality, such as motives, wishes, and unconscious conflicts. Many of these procedures have been criticized for being too subjective and insufficiently validated.

One of the best-known projective measures is the *Rorschach inkblot test* (**Figure 13.26a**). In this procedure, you look at an apparently abstract inkblot and describe what it appears to be. How you describe the inkblot is supposed to reveal unconscious conflicts and other problems. The Rorschach has been criticized for many reasons, chief among them that the test appears to reveal psychological disorders in many normal adults and children (Wood, Garb, Lilienfeld, & Nezworski, 2002).

Another classic projective measure is the *Thematic Apperception Test* (TAT). Christiana Morgan and Henry Murray (1935) developed the TAT to study motives related to personality, such as achievement. In this test, you look at an ambiguous picture and tell a story about it (**Figure 13.26b**). The story is scored based on the motivational schemes that emerge. The schemes are assumed to reflect your personal motives. Indeed, the TAT has been useful for measuring motivational traits—especially those related to achievement, power, and affiliation—and it continues to be used in contemporary research (McClelland, Koestner, & Weinberger, 1989; Serfass & Sherman, 2013). The TAT also reliably predicts how interpersonally dependent you are (Bornstein, 1999). For example, this test predicts how likely you are to seek approval and support from others.

SELF-REPORT MEASURES Many assessments of personality involve **self-report measures**, where you respond to items on questionnaires (**Figure 13.27**). These assessments measure only what you report. They do not attempt to uncover hidden wishes or conflicts. Personality researchers use self-reports to assess how much the answers predict behavior. A questionnaire might target a specific trait, such as how much excitement you seek out of life. More often, a questionnaire will include a large inventory of traits. For example, the *NEO Personality Inventory* consists of 240 items that are designed to assess the five-factor theory personality traits (Costa & McCrae, 2010).

A problem with self-reports is that they can be affected by the desire to avoid looking bad and even by the desire to view yourself in a good light. In addition, it can be difficult for researchers to compare different people's self-reported measures, because people do not have objective standards to rate themselves against. Suppose you are asked to rate yourself for shyness on a scale from 1 to 7. What does a 5 mean to you? Two individuals reporting a 5 on a 7-point shyness scale may not be equally shy, because the term can mean different things to different people.

FIGURE 13.27

Self-Reports of Personality

Self-reports provide insight into personality based on your responses on questionnaires.

ELECTRONICALLY RECORDING INFORMATION ABOUT PERSONALITY
Researchers have developed a number of measures to assess how personality emerges in daily life. One example is the *electronically activated record*, or EAR (Mehl, Pennebaker, Crow, Dabbs, & Price, 2001). Here, you wear a device that unobtrusively tracks your real-world moment-to-moment interactions, picking up snippets of conversation and other auditory information. Through studies using the device, researchers have discovered various aspects of personality. One study found that the stereotype that women talk more than men is false (Mehl, Vazire, Ramirez-Esparza, Slatcher, & Pennebaker, 2007). The EAR also has been used to show that self-reports on the five-factor theory traits predict real-world behavior (Mehl, Gosling, & Pennebaker, 2006). For instance, extraverts talk more and spend less time alone. Agreeable people swear less often. Conscientious people attend class more often. And people open to experience spend more time in restaurants, bars, and coffee shops. Several ongoing studies are using smartphone sensors to provide information about how personality predicts behavior during daily life (Harari et al., 2016).

Do you keep your bedroom tidy or messy, warm or cold? Such aspects of your environment may predict your personality. In his 2008 book *Snoop*, Sam Gosling notes that each person's personality leaks out in many situations, such as through a Facebook profile, a personal Web page, or the condition of the person's bedroom or office. In a number of unrelated studies, participants who viewed public information about other people were able to form reasonably accurate impressions of how those people rated themselves on the five-factor theory personality traits.

OBSERVATIONAL METHODS   Someone might be able to judge your personality by looking at your bedroom and your Facebook profile. Still, how well does that person really know you? Suppose you feel shy in new situations, as many people do. Would others know that shyness is part of your personality? Some shy people force themselves to be outgoing to mask their feelings, so their friends might have no idea that they feel shy. Other people react to their fear of social situations by remaining quiet, so observers might believe them to be cold, arrogant, and unfriendly. Ultimately, how well do observers' personality judgments predict others' behavior?

One study found a surprising degree of accuracy for trait judgments (Funder, 1995). For instance, your close acquaintances may predict your behavior more

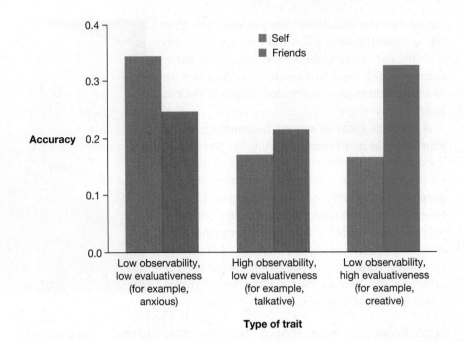

FIGURE 13.28

Self-Ratings Versus Friends' Ratings for Different Traits

This chart shows the average accuracy scores for ratings of three types of traits. As shown in the pair of bars on the left, self-ratings tend to be more accurate than friends' ratings for traits that are low in both observability and evaluativeness. As shown in the middle, friends' ratings tend to be more accurate than self-ratings for traits that are high in observability and low in evaluativeness. As shown on the right, friends' ratings tend to be especially accurate for traits that are low in observability and high in evaluativeness.

accurately than you do. This effect may occur because your friends actually observe how you behave in situations. By contrast, you may be preoccupied with evaluating other people and fail to notice your own behavior. Not surprisingly, there is evidence that you come to know others better over time, as you witness their behavior across different circumstances. Thus you will be probably be more accurate in predicting a close friend's behavior than in predicting the behavior of a mere acquaintance (Biesanz, West, & Millevoi, 2007).

How accurate are people's self-judgments in comparison to the way their friends describe them? Research suggests that you have blind spots about aspects of your personality, because you want to feel good about yourself (Vazire & Carlson, 2011). This tendency is particularly true for highly evaluative traits—those that you care strongly about. Thus you might be accurate in knowing whether you are anxious or optimistic, because those traits are associated with feelings that can be ambiguous to observers. By contrast, your friends might be more accurate in knowing whether you are talkative or charming, because the behaviors associated with those traits are easy to observe. A key insight of this research is that a trait that is easy to observe but also highly meaningful to people, such as creativity, is more likely to be judged accurately by friends than by the person with the trait (**Figure 13.28**).

13.14 Behavior Is Influenced by Personality and Situation

 13.14 LEARNING GOAL ACTIVITIES

To maximize your learning, complete the following learning goal activities:

a. Understand all bold and italic terms by writing explanations of them in your own words.

b. Apply the person/situation debate by providing one example each of how your behavior is influenced more by personality traits in weak situations and more by the situation in strong situations.

Suppose you are looking for a parking space on a busy street. You see one, but you'd have to make an illegal U-turn to get it. You probably wouldn't do it if a police officer was nearby. But would you do it if there was no officer to see you? There is considerable evidence that personality traits predict behavior over time and across situations. Nevertheless, people are also highly sensitive to social context. Even though personality can be assessed reliably across situations, social norms influence behavior regardless of personality.

PERSON/SITUATION DEBATE In 1968, Walter Mischel dropped a bombshell on the field of personality. Mischel proposed that behaviors are determined more by situations than by personality traits. This idea has come to be called **situationism**. For evidence, Mischel referred to studies in which people who were dishonest in one situation were completely honest in another. Suppose you attended a party instead of finishing your paper. You aren't totally honest with your instructor in explaining why your paper is late. According to Mischel, you may be no more likely to steal or to cheat on your taxes than another student who admits to attending the party instead of finishing the paper.

Mischel's critique of personality traits caused considerable rifts between social psychologists and personality psychologists. After all, social psychologists emphasize situational forces. Personality psychologists focus on individual traits. And the most basic definition of personality holds that personality is relatively stable across situations and circumstances. If Mischel was correct and there is relatively little stability, the whole concept of personality seems empty. As you might expect, there was a vigorous response to Mischel's critique. The discussion has come to be called the *person/situation debate*. Personality psychologists now agree that both the person and the situation are important.

INTERACTION OF PERSONALITY AND SITUATION How much your behavior expresses your personality varies from situation to situation (Kenrick & Funder, 1991). Suppose you are highly extraverted, aggressive, and boisterous. Your friend is shy, thoughtful, and restrained. At a party, the two of you would probably act quite differently. At a funeral, you might display similar or even nearly identical behavior. Personality psychologists differentiate between *strong situations* and *weak situations*. Strong situations (for example, elevators, religious services, job interviews) tend to mask differences in personality, thanks to the power of the social environment (**Figure 13.29a**). Weak situations (for example, parks, bars, one's house) tend to reveal differences in personality (**Figure 13.29b**). Most trait theorists believe that behavior is determined jointly by situations and underlying disposition. This idea is called **interactionism**.

However, you also affect your social environments. First, you choose many of the situations you find yourself in. Introverts tend to avoid parties or other situations where they might feel anxious. Extraverts seek out social opportunities. Once you are in situations, your behavior affects those around you. Some extraverts may draw people out and encourage them to have fun. Other extraverts might act aggressively and turn people off. As Bandura noted in his social cognitive approach to personality, reciprocal determinism means that interactions occur between the person and the social environment so that they simultaneously influence each other.

(a)

(b)

FIGURE 13.29

Strong and Weak Situations

(a) A strong situation, such as a funeral, tends to discourage displays of personality. **(b)** A weak situation, such as hanging out with friends, tends to let people behave more freely.

situationism
The theory that behavior is determined more by situations than by personality traits.

interactionism
The idea that behavior is determined jointly by situations and underlying traits.

13.15 Assessment Can Reveal Cultural and Gender Differences in Personality

13.15 LEARNING GOAL ACTIVITIES

To maximize your learning, complete the following learning goal activities:

a. Understand all bold and italic terms by writing explanations of them in your own words.

b. Apply cultural and gender differences in personality assessment by describing how you would rate yourself in agreeableness if you were a different gender or grew up in a different culture.

How similar are people around the world in terms of their personalities? As we have seen, there are stereotypes about people from different countries as well as about men and women. Is there any truth to these stereotypes? Does scientific evidence document differences in personality between cultures or between women and men?

One research team conducted a careful investigation of personality differences across 56 nations (Schmitt, Allik, McCrae, & Benet-Martinez, 2007). They found the five-factor theory personality traits in all 56 countries, but there were modest differences across the countries. For example, people from East Asia (Japan, China, Korea) rated themselves comparatively lower than other respondents on extraversion, agreeableness, and conscientiousness, and comparatively higher on neuroticism (**Figure 13.30**). By contrast, respondents from countries in Africa rated themselves as more agreeable, more conscientious, and less neurotic than people from most other countries rated themselves. Keep in mind, however, that the ratings might have reflected differences in cultural norms for saying good and bad things about oneself. People from East Asian countries might simply be the most modest. Thus, assessing personality across cultures presents many challenges.

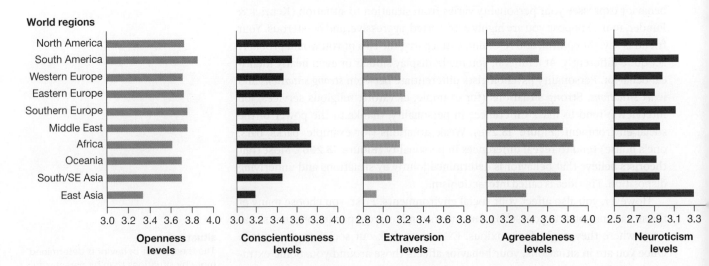

FIGURE 13.30

Cross-Cultural Research on Personality Traits

A team of more than 120 scientists investigated the five-factor theory personality traits around the world, from Argentina to Zimbabwe. This chart presents some of their findings.

What about the personalities of men and women? Are the stereotypes about their personalities accurate? As you read in study unit 13.13, one study found that the stereotype that women talk more than men is false. In addition, women and men are much more similar than different in terms of personality. But the differences between women and men largely support the stereotypes. That is, across various studies, women typically report and are rated as being more empathetic and agreeable than men, but also as being somewhat more neurotic and concerned about feelings. By contrast, men tend to report, and are rated as, being more assertive (Costa, Terracciano, & McCrae, 2001; Feingold, 1994; Maccoby & Jacklin, 1974). One study found that gender differences in personality, although fairly small, were similar across 23 diverse cultures (De Bolle et al., 2015).

 ## How Can Personality Be Assessed?

To make sure you learned what you just read, write answers to the following questions and check your answers.

13.13 What are the four main scientific methods of assessing personality?

13.14 Why might it be difficult to tell an introvert from an extravert at a funeral?

13.15 When personality is assessed across the genders, what are the main personality differences that are found?

See Appendix B for answers to the red Q questions.

BIG PICTURE

 Want to earn a better grade on your test? Go to **INQUIZITIVE** to practice actively with this chapter's content and get personalized feedback along the way.

How Do You Know Yourself?

13.1 Your Sense of Self Is Who You Believe You Are

Review the learning goal activities on p. 504. Personality is your typical thoughts, emotional responses, and behaviors, which tend to be relatively stable over time and across circumstances. Your sense of self is based on two cognitive aspects: (1) self-schema (your integrated memories, beliefs, and generalizations about yourself) and (2) working self-concept (your immediate experience of yourself in the here and now).

13.2 Self-Esteem Is How You Feel About Your Sense of Self

Review the learning goal activities on p. 506. Self-esteem is how you feel about your sense of self. Self-esteem is thought to depend on: (1) reflected appraisal (how you believe other people perceive you), and (2) an internal sociometer (reflecting the likelihood that you will be socially accepted or rejected). People with overly positive self-esteem may experience narcissism.

13.3 You Try to Create a Positive Sense of Self

Review the learning goal activities on p. 510. You tend to create a positive view of yourself through three main unconscious strategies: (1) positive illusions (overly favorable and unrealistic beliefs about yourself), (2) social comparisons (such as downward comparisons, that is, contrasting yourself with people you see as inferior to yourself; upward comparisons, that is, contrasting yourself with people you see as superior to yourself; and temporal comparisons, that is, having more positive perceptions of yourself now than in the past), and (3) the self-serving bias (by taking credit for your successes but blaming failure on external factors).

13.4 Your Sense of Self Is Influenced by Cultural Factors

Review the learning goal activities on p. 512. People from collectivist cultures tend to have interdependent senses of self, which emphasize connections to family, social groups, and other ethnic groups; conformity to societal norms; and group cohesiveness. People from individualist cultures tend to have more individual senses of self, which focus on individual rights and freedoms, self-expression, and diversity.

KEY TERMS

personality (p. 504)
self-schema (p. 505)
working self-concept (p. 506)
self-esteem (p. 507)

downward comparisons (p. 511)
upward comparisons (p. 511)
self-serving bias (p. 511)

How Can You Understand Personality?

13.5 Psychodynamic Theory Emphasizes Unconscious Conflicts

Review the learning goal activities on p. 514. Freud's psychodynamic theory proposes that unconscious forces—such as wishes, desires, and hidden memories—determine behavior. Unique interactions between the id, superego, and ego are the basis of personality. Any of seven defense mechanisms may be used to protect a person from distressing unconscious conflicts—although contemporary researchers have found that defense mechanisms instead protect self-esteem. According to Freud, personality is profoundly affected by progression through three psychosexual stages: (1) oral stage, (2) phallic stage, and (3) genital stage. Contemporary *neo-Freudians* focus on social interactions, especially children's emotional attachments to caregivers. According to object relations theory, the mind and sense of self develop in relation to others, and that relation shapes personality.

13.6 Humanistic Approaches Emphasize Goodness in People

Review the learning goal activities on p. 518. Humanistic approaches to personality emphasize that personality is influenced by inherent goodness. People seek to fulfill their potential for personal growth through greater self-understanding, a process called self-actualization. According to Rogers's person-centered humanistic approach, personality is shaped by the evaluation of others in two ways: through (1) conditions of worth and (2) unconditional positive regard.

13.7 Social Cognitive Approaches Focus on How Thoughts Shape Personality

Review the learning goal activities on p. 520. Social cognitive approaches to personality propose that thinking influences personality. Two main social cognitive approaches to personality are: (1) Rotter's expectancy theory (where people have either an internal locus of control or an external locus of control) and (2) Bandura's reciprocal determinism theory (where personality is shaped by the environment; person factors, which include your characteristics, self-confidence, and expectations; and your behavior).

13.8 Trait Approaches Describe Characteristics

Review the learning goal activities on p. 522. Trait approaches to personality describe personality based on people's tendencies to act in a certain way over time and across most situations. Two main trait approaches to personality are: (1) Eysenck's trait theory and (2) the five-factor theory. Eysenck's theory describes three main personality dimensions: (1) introversion/ extraversion, (2) unstable/stable, and (3) high constraint/low constraint. By contrast, the five-factor theory describes five personality dimensions: (1) openness, (2) conscientiousness, (3) extraversion, (4) agreeableness, and (5) neuroticism.

KEY TERMS

psychodynamic theory (p. 514)

id (p. 515)

superego (p. 515)

ego (p. 515)

defense mechanisms (p. 516)

humanistic approaches (p. 518)

social cognitive approaches (p. 520)

trait approaches (p. 522)

How Does Biology Affect Personality?

13.9 Personality Has a Biological Basis

Review the learning goal activities on p. 526. Personality traits such as introversion/extraversion are linked to biological processes. Eysenck suggested that the introversion/extraversion dimension of his biological trait theory was linked to activity in the reticular activating system (RAS), which influences level of arousal.

13.10 Personality Is Influenced by Genes

Review the learning goal activities on p. 527. The results of twin studies suggest that genes influence personality, because identical twins (who share more genes) are more similar in personality than fraternal twins (who share fewer genes). Adoption studies show similar results, because siblings who are not biologically related, yet raised in the same household, are no more similar in personality than any two people chosen at random.

13.11 Temperament Is Innate

Review the learning goal activities on p. 528. Temperament is the biologically based personality tendency to feel or act in a certain way. There are three aspects of temperament: (1) activity level, (2) emotionality, and (3) sociability. Early childhood temperament also seems to be a good long-term predictor of later behavior and personality.

13.12 Personality Stability Is Influenced by Biology and Situation

Review the learning goal activities on p. 530. Basic tendencies are personality traits that are largely determined by biology and are stable over time. However, characteristic adaptations are traits that are expressed differently, depending on the situation. Accordingly, characteristic adaptations reveal how major life events can affect personality.

KEY TERMS

temperament (p. 529)

basic tendencies (p. 531)

characteristic adaptations (p. 531)

How Can Personality Be Assessed?

13.13 Several Methods Are Used to Assess Personality

Review the learning goal activities on p. 533. Researchers use four main scientific methods to assess personality: (1) projective measures, (2) self-report measures, (3) electronically activated records, and (4) observational methods. Projective measures provide an ambiguous stimulus, where a person's interpretation of the stimulus is thought to reveal personality. Self-report measures provide insight into personality based on how a person responds to items on a questionnaire. An electronically activated record is provided when a wearable device records a person's conversations and behavior, which are then analyzed to gain insight into personality. Observational methods provide insight into personality based on how a person behaves in a situation.

13.14 Behavior Is Influenced by Personality and Situation

Review the learning goal activities on p. 536. In the past, behavior was thought to be primarily influenced by the situation (situationism). However, it is now known that behavior is influenced by the interaction of personality traits and situations (interactionism). Behavior in strong situations depends more on the situation, whereas behavior in weak situations depends more on personality traits.

13.15 Assessment Can Reveal Cultural and Gender Differences in Personality

Review the learning goal activities on p. 538. The five-factor theory personality traits are universal across cultures, but personality assessment reveals modest differences between cultures for each of the factors. Gender differences in personality tend to be consistent with common gender stereotypes.

KEY TERMS

projective measures (p. 534)

self-report measures (p. 534)

situationism (p. 537)

interactionism (p. 537)

CHAPTER 13 SELF-QUIZ

To make sure you learned the information in this chapter, write answers to the following questions and check your answers. **See Appendix B for answers to the self-quiz.**

1. Lee is riding an elevator to the top floor of a tall building. During a brief conversation with a stranger in the elevator, Lee mentions that he is afraid of heights, which is not how he normally thinks of himself. After arriving at the top floor, Lee realizes that his fear of heights came to mind because of the elevator ride. This example best illustrates how Lee's thoughts were influenced by
   _____.
   a. his working self-concept
   b. a sociometer
   c. a self-serving bias
   d. his self-esteem

2. Kelly decides that she is an excellent graduate student because she has several more publications than the other students in her research group. Kelly's positive sense of self in this situation is based on _____.
   a. an upward comparison
   b. reflected appraisal
   c. a downward comparison
   d. self-serving bias

3. Holly was raised in a collectivist culture. At school, Holly is most likely to experience a sense of self that is valued in collectivist cultures when _____.
   a. she works well with a group of students to promote a social event
   b. she expresses her own unique viewpoint during science class
   c. her artwork is displayed in the school's hallway
   d. her teacher praises her work in front of other students

4. When Delaney asks Harvey to give him the cookies from his lunch, Harvey says no. Delaney tells him he is mean. Delaney's negative evaluations have created conditions of worth in Harvey. These conditions of worth may influence the development of Harvey's personality, according to _____.
   a. psychodynamic theory
   b. expectancy theory
   c. the five-factor theory
   d. the person-centered approach

5. Justin believes that bad things just happen to him and that he has bad luck. Justin's belief is most consistent with the cognitive approach to personality called
   _____.
   a. expectancy theory
   b. object relations theory
   c. reciprocal determinism
   d. biological trait theory

6. Whenever Ella gets an assignment in one of her classes, she immediately writes it down in her planner. At home, Ella keeps a notepad and calendar on her desk so she can stay organized with all her coursework. This information suggests that Ella is likely to score high on the five-factor personality trait of _____.
   a. extraversion
   b. conscientiousness
   c. agreeableness
   d. neuroticism

7. Julian, a researcher, conducts an adoption study and concludes that "nature" affects shyness. Which of these findings is most consistent with the conclusion of Julian's study?
   a. Children who are biologically related are dissimilar in their degree of shyness.
   b. Children who are biologically related but who are raised in different households are similar in shyness.
   c. A child raised by nonbiological parents is more likely to be shy.
   d. Identical twins are likely to be dissimilar in their levels of shyness.

8. Three-year-old Morris loves being with other children at the park. When his mom tells him it is time to go home, he typically cries and yells at her. This information suggests that Morris is exhibiting two aspects of temperament: _____ and _____.
   a. low sociability; low emotionality
   b. low activity level; low emotionality
   c. high sociability; high emotionality
   d. high activity level; high emotionality

9. Tameka takes a personality test in which she is asked to write lyrics for a piece of music. The personality test that Tameka is most likely taking is a(n) _____.
   a. objective measure
   b. Thematic Apperception Test
   c. projective measure
   d. Rorschach test

10. Jerome, an office worker with a background in psychology, attends a picnic for work. He is surprised to see his usually reserved coworker Ralph singing karaoke and playing games. Jerome believes that the environmental cues at the picnic directly influenced Ralph's personality. This type of environmental influence is called _____. Jerome sees the picnic as a _____.
    a. interactionism; weak situation
    b. situationism; strong situation
    c. interactionism; strong situation
    d. situationism; weak situation

How Can Understanding People's Personalities Become a Career?

Are you a Gryffindor or a Slytherin? If you're familiar with *Harry Potter* lore, perhaps you have occasionally wished that a real-life Sorting Hat could assess your skills and preferences and assign you to the perfect major or career. As you have learned in this chapter, you may not be the best judge of your own personality traits, skills, and preferences. You might be able to get a more-accurate assessment from other people or, if possible, from an evidence-based measure of personality. And knowing how to best use your traits, skills, and preferences can have important implications for your satisfaction at work and in life generally. In addition, knowledge of personality can help you at the workplace.

Almost every entry-level job, from restaurant worker to retail salesperson, involves training of some kind. New employees must learn their jobs, and veteran employees must develop their skills. Even as you pursue an associate's degree, you can put your knowledge of personality to good use in training people at a company. For example, knowing the traits of the employees can help you think of the best ways to explain their duties to them, use the most successful strategies to teach them skills, and help them be productive in their jobs.

But what if you really want to use all that you know about psychology, including personality, to improve the workplace? In that case, you might want to become an industrial/organizational (I/O) psychologist. The path to this field starts with an undergraduate degree in psychology, perhaps combined with a business minor. You would then have to earn a master's degree or even a doctorate in psychology. I/O psychologists apply psychological research to selecting, recruiting, and training employees. They may also use personality tests, such as the Big Five, to get the best fit between an employee's traits and particular job requirements. They may observe how employees work in a team and make suggestions to improve productivity

or to minimize interpersonal conflicts. I/O psychologists can work in various settings. Some conduct research as university faculty in psychology or business departments. Others are hired by companies as human resource specialists or as training and development managers, working directly with employees. Finally, I/O psychologists can work as independent consultants who are contracted by companies to help with particular problems. This career can be very rewarding, because you can have a lot of influence on employees' work lives.

TAKEAWAY POINT: Assessing and applying personality traits can be valuable in any workplace, because they can help you train employees, improve worker productivity, and help increase job satisfaction. An undergraduate degree in psychology, along with courses in business, can lead to entry-level training positions. Advanced degrees open up more employment opportunities to influence employees in the workplace, especially as an I/O psychologist, and also lead to higher starting salaries.

Ψ You can look up job descriptions, education requirements, salaries, and more at the Bureau of Labor Statistics: www.bls.gov. Visit the site and start putting psychology to work!

14 Psychological Disorders

IN 2012, 15-YEAR-OLD AMANDA TODD posted a soundless YouTube video displaying a series of handwritten messages that described her years of being bullied (**Figure 14.1**). The bullying had begun in the seventh grade, when Amanda used video chat to meet people over the Internet. One man convinced her to pose topless and then threatened to blackmail Amanda unless she posted even more explicit sexual images of herself. Police informed Amanda's parents that her pictures had been widely circulated over the Internet. Students at her school started to tease her and call her names. Amanda went into a tailspin, experiencing feelings of anxiety and depression.

BIG QUESTIONS

What Is a Psychological Disorder?

How Do People Experience Disorders of Emotion?

How Do People Experience Disorders of Thought?

How Do People Experience Disorders of Self?

What Disorders Affect Children?

FIGURE 14.1

The Case of Amanda Todd

Amanda Todd is shown here in a school portrait (courtesy of her mother, Carol Todd). Amanda experienced repeated cyberbullying so extreme that she suffered from anxiety and depression. Despite attempts to treat Amanda's problems, she ended her life. This case highlights how debilitating psychological disorders can be and how important it is to address the factors that cause disorders. To learn about how to prevent bullying and what to do when it happens, visit www.stopbullying.gov. For more information about Amanda Todd, see the family's tribute site at amandatoddlegacy.org.

Amanda moved to a new school, but she didn't get the fresh start she had hoped for. Her tormenter followed her online, sending the damaging pictures to students and teachers at her new school. As students from both her old and new schools continued to bully Amanda, her psychological state worsened and she began to harm herself by cutting. Then Amanda attempted suicide. Frantic to help Amanda, her parents arranged for counseling. Amanda attended another new school. She was diagnosed with anxiety and depression and given drugs to treat her symptoms. Despite these efforts, Amanda committed suicide a month after posting her YouTube video.

Unfortunately, Amanda's case is not isolated. As you learned in Chapter 4 (see Using Psychology in Your Life, p. 157) many adolescents and young adults are bullied, in person and over the Internet. It's natural for someone who is the victim of bullying to feel anxious or sad. Such feelings may pass with time, but if the feelings become so overwhelming that they begin to interfere with daily living, the person may be experiencing a psychological disorder. There is a strong relationship between bullying and psychological disorders. A recent study of over 1,400 participants found that being bullied during childhood is associated with psychological disorders such as anxiety and depression (Copeland, Wolke, Angold, & Costello, 2013).

The tragic case of Amanda Todd has some important messages. First, bullying can cause deep psychological harm, so we each need to do our part to prevent it, avoid taking part in it, and support people involved. Second, we need to be aware of the signs of psychological disorders so that we can seek help for ourselves, our families, and our friends. For instance, the desire to commit suicide is a symptom of the psychological disorder called major depressive disorder. This chapter will help you understand the most common psychological disorders, including their symptoms and causes. In the next chapter, you will learn about some ways professionals can treat these disorders to help people recover so that they can improve their lives.

What Is a Psychological Disorder?

Psychological disorders, sometimes called mental disorders, are common around the globe, in all countries and all societies (Patel et al., 2016). Psychological disorders account for the greatest amount of disability in developed countries, surpassing even cancer and heart disease (Centers for Disease Control and Prevention, 2011). Indeed, in any given year about 1 in 4 Americans over age 18 has a psychological disorder (Kessler, Chiu, Demler, & Walters, 2005). Nearly 1 in 2 Americans will develop some form of psychological disorder at some point in life, most commonly depression, attention-deficit/hyperactivity disorder (ADHD), an anxiety disorder, or a substance abuse disorder (Kessler & Wang, 2008). There are enormous differences in psychopathology across the sexes: Some disorders, such as depression, are much more common in women. Others, such as antisocial personality disorder and childhood ADHD, are more common in men (**Figure 14.2**).

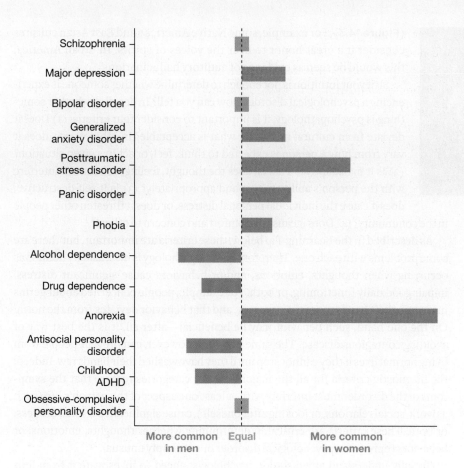

Schizophrenia

Major depression

Bipolar disorder

Generalized
anxiety disorder

Posttraumatic
stress disorder

Panic disorder

Phobia

Alcohol dependence

Drug dependence

Anorexia

Antisocial personality
disorder

Childhood
ADHD

Obsessive-compulsive
personality disorder

More common   Equal   More common
in men   in women

FIGURE 14.2
Sex Differences in Psychological Disorders

The bars in this graph represent how common particular psychological disorders are for men and for women. Note that these are relative rates, and they do not reflect the frequency of disorders for the entire population. For example, anorexia is much more likely in women than in men, but it is relatively uncommon in the population.

14.1 Disorders Interfere with Our Lives

14.1 LEARNING GOAL ACTIVITIES

To maximize your learning, complete the following learning goal activities:

a. Understand all bold and italic terms by writing explanations of them in your own words.

b. Apply psychopathology by considering whether the criterion "interferes with life" applies to the thoughts, emotions, or behaviors of either a person you know or a person depicted in a movie or TV show.

Most of us have felt really sad on occasion or anxious when facing some difficult challenge. How can we tell if those feelings are a reasonable response to the situation or an indication of something more serious? Drawing the line between "normal" emotions, thoughts, and behaviors and a psychological disorder can be difficult. After all, different people respond to events differently, and the level of personal suffering is hard to measure objectively. However, as a rule of thumb, when the emotions, thoughts, and/or behaviors disrupt a person's life, cause significant distress over a long period, or both, the problem is considered a disorder rather than merely a low point of everyday life. At this point, the symptoms reflect **psychopathology**, a sickness or disorder of the mind.

How do you know if someone is experiencing psychopathology? Behavior, especially unusual behavior, must always be considered in context. A woman running through the streets screaming, sobbing, and grabbing and hugging people might have some form of psychological disorder—or she might be celebrating because she just won the lottery. Many thoughts, emotions, and behaviors that are considered acceptable in one setting may be considered deviant in other settings

psychopathology
A sickness or disorder of the mind.

FIGURE 14.3

Psychological Disorder or Not?

According to the sociocultural model, psychopathology results from the interaction between individuals and their cultures. This woman's eccentric behavior might signal that she has a psychological disorder. However, eccentric behavior by the wealthy is often tolerated.

etiology
Factors that contribute to the development of disordered thoughts, emotions, and/or behaviors.

(**Figure 14.3**). For example, some Native American and East Asian cultures consider it a great honor to hear the voices of spirits. In urban America, this would be seen as evidence of auditory hallucinations.

So if your intuition is not enough to determine whether someone is experiencing a psychological disorder, how can you tell? In deciding whether something is psychopathology, it is important to consider four criteria: (1) Does it deviate from cultural norms for what is acceptable? In other words, does it vary from how a person is expected to think, feel, or act in a given situation? (2) Is it maladaptive? That is, does the thought, feeling, or behavior interfere with the person's ability to respond appropriately? (3) Is it self-destructive, does it cause the individual personal distress, or does it threaten other people in the community? (4) Does it cause discomfort and concern to others?

As described in the Learning Tip below, these criteria are important, but there are some problems with each one. Therefore, psychopathology is increasingly defined as occurring when thoughts, emotions, and/or behaviors cause significant distress, impair good daily functioning, or both. For example, people concerned about germs may wash their hands more than average, and that behavior deviates from the norm. On the one hand, such behavior may be beneficial—after all, it is the best way of avoiding contagious disease. The same behavior, however, can prevent people from living normal lives if they cannot stop until they have washed their hands raw. Indeed, the diagnostic criteria for all the major disorder categories require that the symptoms of the disorder must interfere with at least one aspect of the person's life (such as work, social relations, or looking after oneself), cause significant personal distress, or both. These criteria are critical in determining whether thoughts, emotions, or behaviors represent a psychological disorder or are simply unusual.

To fully understand any disorder, psychologists need to investigate it from four perspectives. First, they have to determine **etiology**—the factors that contribute to

 LEARNING TIP: Limitations of the Criteria for Disordered Emotions, Thoughts, and/or Behaviors

This table will help you understand the limitations of the four specific criteria for determining when emotions, thoughts, and/or behaviors are disordered.

CRITERIA	LIMITATION	EXAMPLE
1. Does it deviate from cultural norms for what is acceptable?	People differ in their beliefs of whether something deviates from the cultural norm.	The behavior of the eccentric woman in Figure 14.3 may be more tolerated in the wealthy.
2. Is it maladaptive?	Just because it is maladaptive doesn't make it a disorder.	Talking on your cell phone while driving puts you at risk for a crash, but it is not necessarily a psychological disorder.
3. Does it cause the individual personal distress or threaten other people?	It is possible to experience distress without having a psychological disorder.	A person might be distressed about how others respond to the person's sexual orientation, even though that orientation is not a psychological disorder.
	It is also possible to experience a psychological disorder without distress.	A person who is a psychopath will take advantage of and hurt others without any concern or remorse.
4. Does it cause discomfort and concern to others?	Something that is not a disorder can cause discomfort to others.	Several people cyberbullied Amanda Todd. This behavior caused Amanda great pain, but it does not mean the bullies had psychological disorders.

the development of the disordered thoughts, emotions, and/or behaviors. Second, they need to identify and assess the *symptoms* of the disorder to understand what is occurring. Third, they must group symptoms into meaningful *categories* to make a diagnosis. This process of categorization and diagnosis is critical to the fourth perspective, which is identifying possible *treatments*.

For example, the causes of depression may be quite different from the causes of schizophrenia. Likewise, people with depression may show different symptoms than people with schizophrenia. By grouping people into disorder categories, you can look for what is shared by the people within those categories. You can then explore what treatments might help people with similar symptoms. The following study unit looks at how psychologists generally view the causes of psychological disorders. Before you begin that study unit, however, read Try It Yourself to understand why it is important to avoid the temptation to "diagnose" someone with a psychological disorder.

14.2 There Are Two General Ways to View the Causes of Disorders

14.2 LEARNING GOAL ACTIVITIES

To maximize your learning, complete the following learning goal activities:

a. Understand all bold and italic terms by writing explanations of them in your own words.

b. Apply the diathesis-stress model to psychopathology by describing how Amanda Todd's anxiety and depression might be explained by the diathesis-stress model.

Psychologists do not completely agree about the causes of most psychological disorders. And as you have learned throughout this book, both nature and nurture make people who they are, so it doesn't make sense to say that either biology or environment is solely responsible for a given disorder. At the same time, psychologists have general ways to view the causes of disorders.

THE DIATHESIS-STRESS MODEL The **diathesis-stress model** (Riboni & Belzung, 2017; **Figure 14.4**) offers an explanation for the mechanism that leads to a psychological disorder. This explanation is based on two factors. First, an individual may have an underlying vulnerability, a predisposition (known as a *diathesis*), to a psychological disorder. This vulnerability can be biological, such as a genetic predisposition to a specific disorder. Alternatively, the vulnerability can be environmental, such as childhood trauma. By itself, the vulnerability may not be enough to trigger a psychological disorder. Instead, the disorder can be brought on by the addition of a second factor, which is stress. If the stress level is more than the person can cope with, the symptoms of a psychological disorder may emerge. For example, the stress that Amanda Todd experienced due to bullying may have been a factor in the decline in her mental health. To investigate whether bullying can be a factor in someone's long-term mental health, see Evaluating Psychology in the Real World on p. 550.

In short, according to the diathesis-stress model, a family history of at least one psychological disorder raises the possibility that someone may be vulnerable to mental

diathesis-stress model
The idea that a disorder may develop when an underlying vulnerability is coupled with stress.

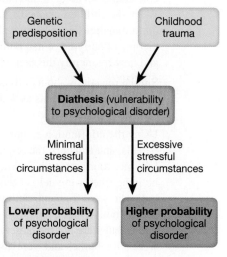

FIGURE 14.4

Diathesis-Stress Model of the Onset of Psychological Disorders

This model illustrates how nature and nurture work together in the onset of psychological disorders.

Many people, including parents and teachers, dismiss bullying by saying things like "Boys will be boys" or "Girls can be cruel at this age." However, others say that bullying can have long-term negative effects. What is the truth?

Consider the article below, which is excerpted from https://www.livescience.com/53034-childhood-bullying-lasting-mental-health-effects.html. Should you accept or reject the claim being made here about the long-term effects of bullying? To answer this question, use the three steps in critical thinking:

ACTIVITY: To determine if you should accept the claim in this article, review the Learning Tip on p. 7 and follow these steps:

Step 1 What is the claim I am being asked to accept?

Step 2 What evidence, if any, is provided to support the claim?

Step 3 Given the evidence, what are the most reasonable conclusions about the claim?

If you have rejected the claim or found the evidence lacking, why did you do so? If you have found that the evidence supports the claim, how might this information change how you think and act?

Childhood Bullying Can Have Lasting Effects on Mental Health

Bullying can have a lasting effect on a person's mental health: A new study finds that children who were bullied frequently when they were 8 years old were more likely to develop a psychiatric disorder that needed treatment as an adult, compared with kids who were not bullied.

The scientists also found strong evidence that being bullied as a child puts kids at high risk for depression as a young adult, according to the study, published online [December 9, 2015] in the journal *JAMA Psychiatry*. . . .

In the study, the researchers analyzed data collected from about 5,000 children in Finland. When the children reached age 8, they filled out questionnaires that asked whether they were victims of bullying or had bullied other children, and how frequently this behavior occurred.

Similar questions about bullying were also asked of the children's parents as well as the children's second-grade teachers.

Using the information gathered from children, parents, and teachers, the researchers divided the kids into four groups: kids who were uninvolved in bullying (they were neither bullies nor bullied); kids who were frequent victims of bullying but did not bully others; kids who were frequent bullies but were not the targets of it; and kids who were often bullies and were also often victims of bullying. . . .

Then, the researchers looked at the mental health outcomes of the children from ages 16 to 29 by examining data from a nationwide hospital register that includes all inpatient and outpatient mental health visits in Finland.

They found that the vast majority of the children, or 90 percent of them, were not involved in bullying, and among this group, about 12 percent had been diagnosed with a psychiatric disorder before age 30.

But about 20 percent of those who were bullies as children had a mental health problem that needed medical treatment as a teen or young adult, and 23 percent of the kids who were victims of frequent bullying had sought help for a psychiatric problem before age 30.

The group that fared the worst in terms of adult mental health were the 8-year-olds who were frequently bullies and were also bullied themselves. About 31 percent of these children had psychiatric problems that required treatment, and these kids also had the highest rates of depression, anxiety disorders, schizophrenia, and substance abuse of all four groups analyzed in the study. . . .

Bullying behavior should be taken seriously by teachers, parents, and [children's] peers because early intervention in childhood bullying can help prevent its long-term mental health consequences. . . .

health problems. A family history does not mean that a person will develop psychopathology. Instead, the person's environment matters. Is the environment creating the kind and amount of stress that might push the vulnerability into a disorder? As you can imagine, maintaining good mental health in yourself and others involves managing the effects of stressors. (For a refresher on the effects of stressors, see study units 11.8–11.9.)

BIOPSYCHOSOCIAL APPROACH The diathesis-stress model focuses on how stress can trigger psychological disorders in people with vulnerabilities to them. Today most psychologists recognize that in addition to vulnerability and stress, several factors contribute to psychological disorders. As the name suggests, the *biopsychosocial approach* states that most psychological disorders are influenced by biological, psychological, and sociocultural factors (**Figure 14.5**).

The biological aspect of this approach focuses on how physiological factors—such as brain function, neurotransmitter imbalances, and genetics—contribute to psychological disorders (Gatt, Burton, Williams, & Schofield, 2015; Kandel, 1998). Studies comparing the rates of psychological disorders between identical and fraternal twins and individuals who have been adopted have revealed the importance of genetic factors (Kendler, Prescott, Myers, & Neale, 2003; Krueger, 1999; also see study unit 2.12).

The psychological aspect of this approach considers that thoughts, emotions, personality, and learned experiences influence the development of psychological disorders. For example, recall the story in study unit 6.6 of how Little Albert learned to fear white rats after experiencing a loud clanging noise that was paired with a rat.

Lastly, sociocultural factors—such as family relationships, socioeconomic status, and the cultural context in which a person is born and raised—are related to the development of psychological disorders. Certain disorders, such as schizophrenia, appear to be more common among the lower socioeconomic classes. This increased occurrence may be due to differences in lifestyles, in expectations, and in opportunities between the classes. In addition, people may be biased in how they view disorders in different social classes. For example, odd behavior by a wealthy person might be tolerated or viewed as amusing. The same behavior by a person living in poverty might be taken as evidence of a psychological disorder.

The biopsychosocial approach recognizes that each of these factors alone can influence psychological disorders. More important, however, is the idea that the three factors interact with each other in disordered thoughts, emotions, and/or behaviors (Halldorsdottir & Binder, 2017).

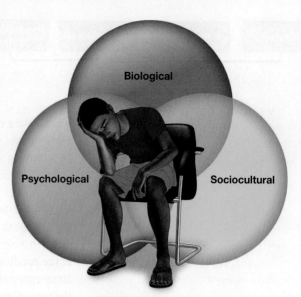

FIGURE 14.5

Biopsychosocial Approach to Psychological Disorders

According to this approach, most psychological disorders are influenced by three factors: biological processes, such as brain function and genetics; psychological processes, including how people think and feel; and sociocultural factors, such as socioeconomic status.

14.3 Disordered Thoughts, Emotions, and/or Behaviors Can Be Assessed and Categorized

 14.3 LEARNING GOAL ACTIVITIES

To maximize your learning, complete the following learning goal activities:

a. Understand all bold and italic terms by writing explanations of them in your own words.

b. Understand the classification systems for psychological disorders by summarizing how the *DSM-5* classification system is similar to and different from the dimensional approach to psychological disorders.

Interviews → Self-reports → Observations → Psychological testing

↓

Assessment

↓

Diagnosis

↓

Treatment

↓

Ongoing assessment

FIGURE 14.6

Assessing the Symptoms of a Patient

Clinical psychologists examine a person's mental functions and psychological health to diagnose a psychological disorder and determine an appropriate treatment. This flowchart shows the factors that lead to treatment.

If you have a discolored patch on your skin, a medical test called a biopsy can evaluate the cause. If you have an infection, a blood test will reveal the bacteria involved. Determining whether someone has a psychological disorder is not as straightforward. Clinical psychologists often work like detectives, tracking down information from sources through interviews, self-reports, observations, and psychological testing (**Figure 14.6**). This *assessment* of a person's mental functions and actions allows psychologists to categorize the individual's thoughts, emotions, and behaviors in order to make a *diagnosis* so that appropriate treatment can be provided. The course of the condition and its probable outcome, or *prognosis*, will depend on the particular category of psychological disorder that is diagnosed. A correct diagnosis will help the person, and perhaps the person's family, understand what the future might bring.

ASSESSING SYMPTOMS Most psychological problems develop over a fairly long time. Frequently, family members or a physician will notice symptoms and encourage the person to seek help. During assessment, four methods can be used to determine what symptoms the person is experiencing. Once assessment begins, the person is referred to as a client (not a patient).

A psychologist's first step in an assessment is often to conduct an *interview*. That is, the psychologist asks the client about current symptoms and about recent experiences that might be causing distress. For example, if someone is feeling depressed, the psychologist is likely to ask whether the person recently experienced some sort of loss. A *self-report* can reveal a lot of important information.

A psychologist can also gain information through *observation* of the client's behavior. For instance, a person who avoids eye contact during an examination might be experiencing social anxiety disorder (social phobia) or have attention-deficit/hyperactivity disorder. A person whose eyes dart around nervously may feel paranoid. Behavioral assessments often are useful with children. Observing their interactions with other children or seeing whether they can sit still in a classroom, for instance, may tell a psychologist more than the children could.

Another way to conduct assessment is through *psychological testing*. Personality tests, such as those described in study unit 13.13, are one example. Other psychological tests ask the client to perform actions—such as copying a picture or placing blocks into slots on a board while blindfolded—that require abilities such as planning, coordinating, or remembering (**Figure 14.7**). By discovering actions that the person performs poorly, the assessment might indicate problems with a particular brain region. For instance, people who have difficulty categorizing objects may have impairments in the frontal lobes. Subsequent assessment with brain imaging might show brain damage caused by a tumor or by an injury.

Once assessment reveals that someone is experiencing disordered thoughts, emotions, and/or behaviors, the next step is to make a diagnosis in one or more categories of psychological disorder.

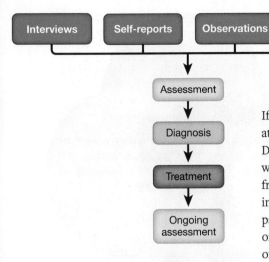

FIGURE 14.7

Psychological Testing

The assessment depicted here uses a neuropsychological test to examine mental function.

FIGURE 14.8

Historical View of Psychological Disorders

Throughout history, people believed that the gods, witches, or evil spirits caused psychological disorders.

CATEGORIZING DISORDERED EMOTIONS, THOUGHTS, AND/OR BEHAVIORS Throughout most of human history, people showing signs of what we now consider psychological disorders were viewed as suffering from madness. Their problems were believed to be caused by the gods, witches, or evil spirits (**Figure 14.8**). But with advances in the medical understanding and treatment of diseases, recognition grew that psychological disorders were not caused by these entities. Eventually, doctors such as Sigmund Freud began to study psychological disorders to find out what caused them. In the late 1800s, the psychiatrist Emil Kraepelin noticed that not all patients experienced the same disorder. Kraepelin identified psychological disorders based on the groups of symptoms that occurred together. For instance, he separated disorders of mood (such as depression) from disorders that focus on thought disturbances (such as schizophrenia).

The idea of categorizing psychological disorders systematically was not officially adopted until 1952, when the American Psychiatric Association published the first edition of the *Diagnostic and Statistical Manual of Mental Disorders (DSM)*. Since then, the *DSM* has undergone several revisions and remains the standard tool used by professionals to sort patients' symptoms into categories of psychological disorders. In the current edition, the *DSM-5* (released in 2013), disorders are described in terms of observable symptoms. A patient must meet specific criteria to receive a particular diagnosis. The *DSM-5* consists of three sections: (1) an introduction with instructions for using the manual; (2) diagnostic criteria for all of the disorders, which are grouped so that similar disorders are located near each other; and (3) a guide for future psychopathology research that describes conditions not yet officially recognized as disorders, such as excessive Internet gaming.

However, people seldom fit neatly into the precise categories of psychological disorders. An alternative to categorization by type is the *dimensional approach*, where people's symptoms are placed on a continuum based on their severity (Clark, Cuthbert, Lewis-Fernández, Narrow, & Reed, 2017). With categorization, the approach can be compared to a simple switch that turns a light either on or off. By contrast, the dimensional approach is like a dimmer switch, which can provide light in varying amounts. A dimensional approach recognizes that many symptoms of psychological disorders are extreme versions of what people often experience. For example, you might feel worried sometimes. When you feel worried, you may be slightly anxious (**Figure 14.9,** line A), somewhat anxious (**Figure 14.9,** line B), or very anxious (**Figure 14.9,** line C). There is no minimum level you have to reach to be diagnosed with an anxiety disorder. In the third section of the *DSM-5*, researchers are encouraged to examine whether a dimensional approach might be helpful for understanding many psychological disorders, such as personality disorders.

Further, scientific research indicates that many psychological disorders occur together even though the *DSM-5* treats them as separate disorders. For example, depression and anxiety often are experienced together, as are depression and substance abuse. This state is known as *comorbidity* (**Figure 14.10**). Accordingly, people who are found to be depressed should also be assessed for comorbid conditions. Though they may be diagnosed with two or more disorders, a dual diagnosis offers no advantages in terms of treatment because both conditions usually will respond to the same treatment.

Despite the limitations of *DSM-5* categorization, the rest of this chapter considers some of the most common psychological disorders described in the manual. The *DSM-5* describes 19 major categories of disorders, each of which has several variations or types (**Table 14.1,** on p. 554). Nearly all psychological disorders involve disturbances in how people feel, think, and behave, but emotions are more central to some disorders, thoughts are more central to others, and behaviors are more central to yet others. The next study unit considers the most common disorders involving emotions.

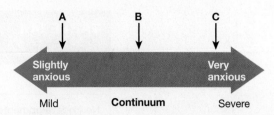

FIGURE 14.9

Dimensional Approach to Psychological Disorders

An alternative to categorizing a psychological disorder as present or absent is to describe the severity of the symptoms along a continuum from mild to severe.

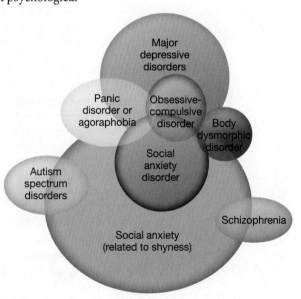

FIGURE 14.10

Comorbidity of Psychological Disorders

As this diagram illustrates, psychological disorders commonly overlap. For instance, social anxiety disorder is often seen with many other psychological disorders, such as panic disorder, agoraphobia, obsessive-compulsive disorder, and/or body dysmorphic disorder.

TABLE 14.1
DSM-5 Disorders

Category	Examples
Neurodevelopmental disorders	Autism spectrum disorder
Schizophrenia spectrum and other psychotic disorders	Schizophrenia
Bipolar and related disorders	Bipolar I disorder
Depressive disorders	Major depressive disorder
Anxiety disorders	Panic disorder
Obsessive-compulsive and related disorders	Body dysmorphic disorder
Trauma- and stressor-related disorders	Posttraumatic stress disorder
Dissociative disorders	Dissociative amnesia
Somatic symptom and related disorders	Conversion disorder
Feeding and eating disorders	Anorexia nervosa
Elimination disorders	Enuresis (bed wetting)
Sleep-wake disorders	Narcolepsy
Sexual dysfunctions	Erectile disorder
Gender dysphoria	Gender dysphoria in adolescents and adults
Disruptive, impulse-control, and conduct disorders	Pyromania
Substance-related and addictive disorders	Alcohol use disorder
Neurocognitive disorders	Delirium
Personality disorders	Borderline personality disorder
Paraphilic disorders	Exhibitionist disorder

Source: Adapted from American Psychiatric Association (2013).

What Is a Psychological Disorder?

To make sure you learned what you just read, write answers to the following questions and check your answers.

14.1 At what point are a person's emotions, thoughts, and/or behaviors said to reflect psychopathology?

14.2 According to the biopsychosocial model, what are the three categories of factors that affect the development of psychopathology?

14.3 What are the four assessment methods that can be used to investigate a person's symptoms?

See Appendix B for answers to the red Q questions.

How Do People Experience Disorders of Emotion?

Almost certainly, you can think of times in your life when you've felt rather emotional, perhaps a bit anxious or down. These feelings are a common experience for most people, and feeling some anxiety is useful. It can prepare you for upcoming events and motivate you to learn new ways of coping with life's challenges. Being anxious about tests may remind you to keep up with your homework and study. Being slightly anxious when meeting new people may help you avoid doing bizarre things and making bad impressions. For some people, however, anxiety can become debilitating and interfere with every aspect of life.

Like emotions, moods color every aspect of our lives (for a refresher on the difference between emotions and moods, see study unit 9.7). When we are happy, the world seems like a wonderful place, and we are filled with boundless energy. When we are sad, we view the world in a decidedly less rosy light, feeling hopeless and isolated. Few of us, however, experience these symptoms day after day. When a person's emotions—such as feeling sad or anxious—go from being a normal part of daily living to being extreme enough to disrupt the ability to work, learn, and play, the person's emotions are considered to be disordered.

14.4 Anxiety Disorders Make People Fearful and Tense

14.4 LEARNING GOAL ACTIVITIES

To maximize your learning, complete the following learning goal activities:

a. Understand all bold and italic terms by writing explanations of them in your own words.

b. Apply anxiety disorders by describing five imaginary people who show the symptoms of the five anxiety disorders.

We all feel anxious in stressful or threatening situations, but it is abnormal to feel strong chronic anxiety without cause. *Anxiety disorders* are characterized by excessive fear in the absence of danger. Anxious individuals tend to perceive ambiguous situations as threatening, whereas nonanxious individuals assume they are nonthreatening (Eysenck, Mogg, May, Richards, & Matthews, 1991; **Figure 14.11**). Anxious individuals also focus excessive attention on perceived threats (Rinck, Reinecke, Ellwart, Heuer, & Becker, 2005), and they recall threatening events more easily than nonthreatening events. These biases in thinking help to exaggerate the threat and contribute to greater anxiety. More than 1 in 4 Americans will develop some type of anxiety disorder during their lifetime (**Figure 14.12**; Kessler & Wang, 2008). In one survey of over 94,000 college students, more than half reported overwhelming anxiety within the last 12 months (American College Health Association, 2014).

People who experience anxiety disorders feel fearful, tense, and worried about the future. Anxiety disorders are also responsible for many physical ailments, some of which are potentially serious. Constant worry can make falling asleep and staying asleep difficult, and attention span and concentration can be impaired.

By continually arousing the autonomic nervous system, chronic anxiety also causes bodily symptoms such as sweating, dry mouth, rapid pulse, shallow breathing,

The statement *The doctor examined little Emma's growth...*

tends to be perceived by anxious individuals as...

tends to be perceived by nonanxious individuals as...

"The doctor looked at little Emma's cancer."

"The doctor measured little Emma's height."

FIGURE 14.11

Anxiety Disorders Are Characterized by Excessive Fear

As this example illustrates, people who are anxious tend to perceive ambiguous situations as more threatening than do people who are not anxious.

FIGURE 14.12

Anxiety Disorders Are Very Common

Like 15 million other Americans, the football player Ricky Williams has been diagnosed with social anxiety disorder. Some people thought that Williams was shy or aloof. Instead, he was afraid of interacting with people. Williams could not look people in the eye, dreaded meeting fans on the street, talked to reporters with his helmet on, and could not interact with his daughter. After Williams sought treatment, he began to realize that he wasn't crazy. Soon he was able, he said, "to start acting like the real Ricky Williams."

specific phobia
An anxiety disorder marked by fear of a specific object or situation that is out of proportion with any actual threat.

social anxiety disorder
An anxiety disorder characterized by fear of social situations or performance where a person is anxious about being negatively evaluated by others.

and increased muscular tension. Chronic arousal can also result in hypertension, headaches, and intestinal problems. It can even cause brain damage (McEwen, 2017). Due to their high levels of autonomic arousal, people who experience anxiety disorders also exhibit restless and useless motor behaviors, such as toe tapping and excessive fidgeting. Problem solving and judgment may be impaired as well. Because chronic stress can damage the body, including the brain, it is important to identify and effectively treat disorders that involve chronic anxiety. Let's consider five main types of anxiety disorders, which are summarized in **Table 14.2**.

SYMPTOMS OF SPECIFIC PHOBIA As you learned in study unit 6.6, a phobia is an unreasonable fear of something that is not likely to hurt you. According to the *DSM-5*, if that fear impairs your life, causes significant distress, or both, you may have a **specific phobia**. Specific phobia, a fear of a specific object or situation that is exaggerated and out of proportion to the actual danger, affects about 1 in 8 people around the globe (Wardenaar et al., 2017). A specific phobia is classified based on the object of the fear. Common specific phobias include fear of snakes (ophidiophobia), fear of enclosed spaces (claustrophobia), and fear of heights (acrophobia). Another common specific phobia is fear of flying (aviophobia). Some people find flying terrifying, even though the odds of dying in a plane crash, compared with a car crash, are extraordinarily small. For those who need to travel frequently for their jobs, a fear of flying can cause significant impairment in daily living. **Table 14.3** lists some unusual specific phobias.

SYMPTOMS OF SOCIAL ANXIETY DISORDER Social anxiety disorder is a fear of being negatively evaluated by others. It includes fears of being in social situations, public speaking, speaking up in class, meeting new people, and eating

TABLE 14.2
Five Types of Anxiety Disorders

Category	Description	Example
Specific phobia	Fear of a specific object or situation that is disproportionate to the threat	You are so afraid of snakes that if you see even a picture of a snake, your heart begins to pound and you feel the need to run away.
Social anxiety disorder	Fear of being negatively evaluated by others in a social setting or performance situation	You worry intensely that you will say or do the wrong thing around other people and they will think badly of you. So you prefer to be by yourself and avoid being around lots of people.
Generalized anxiety disorder	Nearly constant anxiety not associated with a specific thing	You feel very worried and have been for months, but you can't figure out why. It seems as though you are anxious about everything.
Panic disorder	Sudden attacks of overwhelming terror	You have had several panic attacks and worry you will have another one. This worry brings on more panic attacks, where you feel extreme fear and your heart pounds in your chest.
Agoraphobia	Fear of being in a situation from which one cannot escape	You work for a company located in a skyscraper, but you are so terrified of not being able to get out of the building that you have panic attacks at work.

Source: Adapted from American Psychiatric Association (2013).

TABLE 14.3
Some Unusual Specific Phobias

Arachibutyrophobia: fear of peanut butter sticking to the roof of one's mouth
Automatonophobia: fear of ventriloquists' dummies
Barophobia: fear of gravity
Dextrophobia: fear of objects at the right side of the body
Geliophobia: fear of laughter
Gnomophobia: fear of garden gnomes
Hippopotomonstrosesquippedaliophobia: fear of long words
Ochophobia: fear of being in a moving automobile
Panophobia: fear of everything
Pentheraphobia: fear of mothers-in-law
Triskaidekaphobia: fear of the number 13

in front of others. About 1 in 8 people will develop social anxiety disorder at some point in their lifetimes, and around 1 in 14 are experiencing social anxiety disorder at any given time (Ruscio et al., 2008). It is one of the earliest forms of anxiety disorder to develop, often beginning around age 13. The more social anxiety people have, the more likely they are to develop other disorders, particularly depression and substance abuse problems. Indeed, assessment must consider the overlap between social anxiety disorder and related disorders to make an informed diagnosis (Stein & Stein, 2008).

SYMPTOMS OF GENERALIZED ANXIETY DISORDER   Whereas the fear in specific phobias has a specific focus, the anxiety in **generalized anxiety disorder** is not focused on one object or situation and is always present. People with this disorder are constantly anxious and worry incessantly about even minor matters (Newman, Llera, Erickson, Przeworski, & Castonguay, 2013). They even worry about being worried! Because the anxiety is not focused, it can occur in response to almost anything, so the person is constantly on the alert for problems. This high level of alertness results in distractibility, fatigue, irritability, and sleep problems as well as headaches, restlessness, lightheadedness, and muscle pain (Stein & Sareen, 2015). Just under 6 percent of the U.S. population is affected by this disorder at some point in their lives, though women are diagnosed more often than men (Kessler et al., 1994; Kessler & Wang, 2008).

SYMPTOMS OF PANIC DISORDER   **Panic disorder** consists of sudden, overwhelming attacks of terror and worry about having additional panic attacks. The attacks seemingly come out of nowhere, though they may be brought on by external stimuli or internal thought processes. Panic attacks typically last for several minutes. Symptoms include sweating and trembling, racing heart, shortness of breath, chest pain, dizziness, lightheadedness, and numbness and tingling in the hands and feet.

generalized anxiety disorder
An anxiety disorder with a state of constant anxiety not associated with any specific object or event.

panic disorder
An anxiety disorder that consists of sudden, overwhelming attacks of terror.

agoraphobia
An anxiety disorder marked by fear of being in situations from which escape is difficult or impossible.

People experiencing panic attacks often feel that they are going crazy, that they are dying, or as if they are about to be hit by a train and cannot escape. Panic disorder affects an estimated 3 percent of the population in a given year, and women are twice as likely to be diagnosed as men (Kessler & Wang, 2008). Those who experience panic attacks attempt suicide much more frequently than those in the general population (Fawcett, 1992; Korn et al., 1992; Noyes, 1991).

SYMPTOMS OF AGORAPHOBIA Loosely translated, *agoraphobia* means "fear of a gathering place." People who have **agoraphobia** fear being in situations from which escape is difficult or impossible. A wide range of situations may bring on their fears—for example, being in a crowded shopping mall or using public transportation. Their fear is so strong that being in such situations causes panic attacks. Indeed, agoraphobia without panic attacks is quite rare (Kessler & Wang, 2008). As a result, people who experience agoraphobia avoid going into open spaces or to places that might have crowds. In extreme cases, these people may feel unable to leave their homes. In addition to fearing the particular situations, many people with agoraphobia fear having a panic attack in public.

DEVELOPMENT OF ANXIETY DISORDERS Although people are anxious about different things, the etiology of various types of anxiety is best explained by the biopsychosocial approach. For example, as you learned in study unit 13.11, temperaments are biologically determined aspects of personality. Children who have an inhibited temperamental style are usually shy and tend to avoid unfamiliar people and novel objects. These inhibited children are more likely to develop anxiety disorders later in life (Buss & McDoniel, 2016; Fox, Henderson, Marshall, Nichols, & Ghera, 2005). They are especially at risk for developing social anxiety disorder (Biederman et al., 2001). Recall from Chapter 13 that people who had been categorized as inhibited before age 2 showed a threat response to novel faces even as adults many years later (Schwartz, Wright, Shin, Kagan, & Rauch, 2003). This finding suggests that some aspects of childhood temperament are preserved in the adult brain (see "The Methods of Psychology: Inhibition and Social Anxiety," on p. 530).

In addition, many fears are learned. As you learned in study unit 6.6, a person might come to associate something with fear through classical conditioning, such as developing a phobia of dentists by learning to associate going to the dentist with pain. Observational learning might also contribute to anxiety disorders. For example, someone could develop a fear of flying by observing another person's fearful reaction to the closing of cabin doors. Such a fear might then generalize to other enclosed spaces, resulting in claustrophobia.

14.5 Some Disorders Have Unwanted and Intrusive Thoughts that Increase Anxiety

14.5 LEARNING GOAL ACTIVITIES

To maximize your learning, complete the following learning goal activities:

a. Understand all bold and italic terms by writing explanations of them in your own words.

b. Analyze the symptoms of obsessive-compulsive disorder (OCD) by differentiating between obsessions and compulsions.

c. Understand posttraumatic stress disorder (PTSD) by explaining how a traumatic event can lead to persistent and unwanted thoughts about the trauma.

The comedian and game show host Howie Mandel is famous for giving his guests a fist bump rather than shaking hands with them. What viewers didn't know was that Mandel had a serious psychological reason for using his signature greeting: He was obsessed with germs. In 2009, Mandel publicly announced that he had been diagnosed with obsessive-compulsive disorder (OCD), a condition that had been ruling his life for many years (**Figure 14.13**).

So far you have read that many psychological disorders involve both emotional and cognitive impairments. In some cases, the occurrence of unwanted thoughts leads to emotional distress. The *DSM-5* categorizes a number of disorders that involve experiencing unwanted thoughts or the desire to engage in maladaptive behaviors.

SYMPTOMS OF OBSESSIVE-COMPULSIVE DISORDER   Obsessive-compulsive disorder (OCD) involves frequent intrusive thoughts and compulsive actions. Affecting 1 percent to 2 percent of the population, OCD is more common in women than men, and it generally begins in early adulthood (Ruscio, Stein, Chiu, & Kessler, 2010; Weissman et al., 1994). OCD includes two aspects of disordered thoughts and behaviors. *Obsessions* are recurrent, intrusive, and unwanted thoughts or urges or mental images that increase anxiety. They often include intense worry and fears of contamination, of accidents, or of one's own aggression. *Compulsions* are particular acts that the person feels driven to perform over and over again that reduce anxiety. The most common compulsive behaviors are cleaning, checking, and counting. The key in this disorder is that when the person engages in the compulsive behavior, she experiences a temporary reduction in the anxiety caused by the obsession. For instance, a person who has an obsessive fear of germs might engage in the compulsion of repeatedly washing his hands. People diagnosed with OCD are aware that their obsessions and compulsions are irrational, yet they are unable to stop them.

DEVELOPMENT OF OBSESSIVE-COMPULSIVE DISORDER   OCD is another example of how the biopsychosocial approach explains the causes of some psychological disorders. One explanation is that the disorder results from psychological factors, such as learning by conditioning. Anxiety is somehow paired to a specific event, probably through classical conditioning. The person then engages in behavior that reduces anxiety. The reduction of anxiety is negatively reinforced through operant conditioning, and the chances of engaging in that behavior again are increased (negative reinforcement is discussed in study unit 6.10). This type of learning can happen to anyone. For instance, if you are forced to shake hands with a man who has a bad cold, you will likely feel anxious or uncomfortable because you do not want to get sick (**Figure 14.14**, part 1). As soon as the pleasantries are over, you run to the bathroom and wash your hands (**Figure 14.14**, part 2). Afterward, you feel relieved (**Figure 14.14**, part 3). Because you have paired hand-washing with a reduction in anxiety, you are more likely to wash your hands in a similar situation in the future. For people who develop OCD, however, the compulsive behavior will reduce the anxiety only temporarily, so they will continue to experience repeated, disruptive obsessive thoughts— for example, about germs (**Figure 14.14**, part 4). In turn, they will perform the behavior again and again in attempts to reduce the anxiety.

However, there is also good evidence that the etiology of OCD is in part biological (Pauls, Abramovitch, Rauch, & Geller, 2014). Specifically, OCD seems to have a genetic origin. Various research methods, such as twin studies, have shown that OCD runs in families. The specific mechanism has not been identified, but the OCD-related genes appear to control the neurotransmitter glutamate (Pauls, 2008). As discussed in study unit 2.3, glutamate is the major excitatory transmitter in the brain. It increases neural firing.

FIGURE 14.13

Howie Mandel's Obsessions and Compulsions

Howie Mandel has been diagnosed with obsessive-compulsive disorder. Like many people with OCD, Mandel experiences a strong fear of germs. His trademark shaved head helps him with this problem by making him feel cleaner. Mandel even built a second, sterile house, where he can retreat if he feels he might be contaminated by anyone around him. Here, Mandel promotes his autobiography, *Here's the Deal: Don't Touch Me* (2009), in which he "comes clean" about his experiences with OCD and other disorders.

obsessive-compulsive disorder (OCD)

A psychological disorder characterized by frequent intrusive thoughts that create anxiety and compulsive actions that temporarily reduce the anxiety.

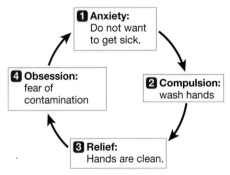

FIGURE 14.14

The Cycle of Obsession and Compulsion

As shown here, the obsession and compulsion aspects of obsessive-compulsive disorder feed into each other in a continuous cycle.

Brain imaging has also provided some evidence regarding a brain system involved in OCD. In people with OCD, the caudate, a brain structure involved in suppressing impulses, is smaller and has structural abnormalities (Baxter, 2000; Fineberg et al., 2018). It is possible that in people with OCD, the caudate does not function properly to prevent impulses from reaching conscious awareness.

SYMPTOMS OF POSTTRAUMATIC STRESS DISORDER OCD is not the only type of psychopathology that can produce unwanted and intrusive thoughts. Such cognitive problems can also be caused by disorders that result from experiencing or witnessing life-threatening events or sexual violations. The *DSM-5* categorizes a number of disorders together that result from trauma or excessive stress. This category describes *trauma and stressor-related disorders*. For example, a person who cries continually, has difficulty studying, and avoids social settings for 6 months after a romantic breakup may have an *adjustment disorder*. This person is having difficulty adjusting to the stressor.

When people experience severe stress or emotional trauma, they often have negative reactions long after the danger has passed. In severe cases, they develop **posttraumatic stress disorder (PTSD)**. This disorder involves frequent and recurring unwanted thoughts related to the trauma, including nightmares, intrusive thoughts, and flashbacks. Various types of traumatic experiences can lead to PTSD, such as having a serious accident, experiencing sexual assault or rape, fighting in active combat, or surviving a natural disaster. Around 4 percent of people having experienced a trauma are likely to develop PTSD, although the risk of PTSD varies greatly by the type of trauma that is experienced (Liu et al., 2017; **Table 14.4**). In addition, there are gender differences in PTSD, where women are more likely to develop the disorder (Kessler et al., 2005).

An opportunity to study susceptibility to PTSD came about because of a tragedy at Northern Illinois University in 2008. On the campus, in front of many observers, a lone gunman killed five people and wounded 21. Among a sample of female students,

TABLE 14.4
Risk of Developing PTSD Based on Type of Trauma Experienced

Type of Trauma	Risk of PTSD (percent)
War-related trauma	3.5
Physical violence	2.8
Intimate partner or sexual violence	11.4
Accident	2.0
Unexpected death of loved one	5.4
Other traumas of loved ones or witnessed	2.4
Other traumas	9.2

Source: Adapted from "Trauma and PTSD in the WHO World Mental Health Surveys," by R. C. Kessler et al., 2017, *European Journal of Psychotraumatology*, 8(Suppl. 5), 1353383, doi:10.1080/20008198.2017.1353383.

those with certain genetic markers related to serotonin functioning were much more likely to show PTSD symptoms in the weeks after the shooting (Mercer et al., 2012). In support of the diathesis-stress model, this finding suggests that some individuals may be more at risk than others for developing PTSD after exposure to a stressful event.

Those with PTSD often have chronic tension, anxiety, and health problems, and they may experience memory and attention problems in their daily lives. PTSD involves an unusual problem in memory—the inability to forget. People with PTSD also pay a lot of attention to stimuli associated with their traumatic events. For instance, soldiers with combat-induced PTSD show increased physiological responsiveness to pictures of troops, sounds of gunfire, and even words associated with combat. It is as if the severe emotional event is "overconsolidated" and incredibly memorable, so the person is always on the alert to experience a similar situation. In effect, PTSD interferes with the various brain processes that normally lead to extinction in fear learning, so it is difficult to "unlearn" the fear associated with the event (Marin et al., 2016). (For a review of consolidation and reconsolidation of memory, see study unit 7.12; for extinction, see study unit 6.5; for counterconditioning of fear responses, see study unit 6.6.)

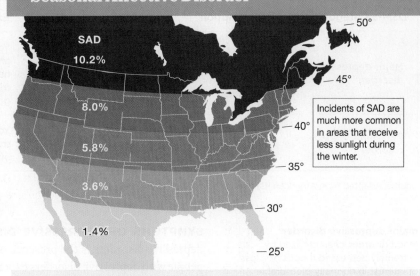

Seasonal Affective Disorder

SAD
10.2%
8.0%
5.8%
3.6%
1.4%

— 50°
— 45°
— 40°
— 35°
— 30°
— 25°

Incidents of SAD are much more common in areas that receive less sunlight during the winter.

Do you tend to feel depressed during the winter? If this happens every winter and the sadness is severe enough to cause significant distress, impair daily functioning, or both, then it may be a depressive disorder with seasonal pattern, more informally called *seasonal affective disorder (SAD)*. People are more likely to experience this cyclical pattern of depression due to the particularly short days and reduced sunlight in winter. The good news is that people with SAD don't just need to wait for summer to come. Effective treatments are available, as described in Chapter 15.

14.6 Depressive Disorders Consist of Sad, Empty, or Irritable Mood

14.6 LEARNING GOAL ACTIVITIES

To maximize your learning, complete the following learning goal activities:

a. Understand all bold and italic terms by writing explanations of them in your own words.

b. Understand depressive disorders by distinguishing between the symptoms of major depressive disorder and persistent depressive disorder.

When people feel down, or sad about something, they often say they are "depressed." These emotions are relatively common—perhaps for some people, during the winter. In fact, if you have ever experienced "the blues" during winter, then you may have had a mild form of depression (see Has It Happened to You? above). However, only lasting episodes of depressed mood that impair a person's life, cause significant distress, or both, are diagnosed as depressive disorders. *Depressive disorders* are a type of mood disorder that features persistent and pervasive feelings of sadness, and they are very common (**Figure 14.15**). Two types of depressive disorders are summarized in **Table 14.5,** on p. 562.

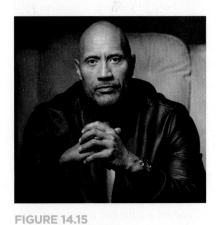

FIGURE 14.15

Many People Experience Depressive Disorders

In 2018, the actor Dwayne "The Rock" Johnson publicly acknowledged that he has suffered from depression. "Took me a long time to realize it," he tweeted, "but the key is not to be afraid to open up. Especially us dudes have a tendency to keep it in. You're not alone."

TABLE 14.5
Two Types of Depressive Disorders

DSM-5 Category	Description	Example
Major depressive disorder	Extremely depressed mood or loss of interest in pleasurable activities, lasting for two weeks or more, plus other symptoms, such as changes in weight or sleep	You had been deeply depressed for months and had no hope that you would ever feel happy again. You didn't enjoy seeing your friends, you were tired all the time, and you gained a lot of weight.
Persistent depressive disorder	Mild or moderate depressed mood most days for at least 2 years	You used to be a very happy person, but for the past few years you have felt "down" most of the time.

Source: Adapted from American Psychiatric Association (2013).

major depressive disorder
Mood disorder, characterized by extremely depressed moods or a loss of interest in normally pleasurable activities, that persists for two weeks or more.

persistent depressive disorder
Mood disorder, characterized by mildly or moderately depressed moods, that persists for at least two years.

SYMPTOMS OF DEPRESSIVE DISORDERS The common feature of all depressive disorders is the presence of sad, empty, or irritable mood. In addition, people with depressive disorders experience bodily symptoms, and cognitive problems, that interfere with daily life.

The classic disorder in this category is **major depressive disorder.** According to *DSM-5* criteria, to be diagnosed with major depressive disorder a person must have one of two symptoms: very depressed (often irritable) mood, or loss of interest in pleasurable activities for two weeks or more (**Figure 14.16**). In addition, the person must have other symptoms, such as appetite and weight changes, sleep disturbances, loss of energy, difficulty concentrating, feelings of self-reproach or guilt, and frequent thoughts of death, perhaps by suicide. Amanda Todd, whose tragic story opened this chapter, had many of these symptoms.

Major depressive disorder affects about 7–8 percent of Americans in any given year (Pratt & Brody, 2014), and approximately 16 percent of Americans will develop major depressive disorder at some point in their lives (Kessler & Wang, 2008). Although major depressive disorder varies in severity, those who receive a diagnosis are highly impaired by the condition (Otte et al., 2016). It tends to persist over several months, sometimes lasting for years (Kessler, Merikangas, & Wang, 2007; see Figure 14.16). Some people experience repeated episodes of major depressive disorder over their lives. Women are nearly twice as likely as men to be diagnosed with major depressive disorder (Kessler et al., 2003).

Unlike major depressive disorder, **persistent depressive disorder** is of mild to moderate severity. People with persistent depressive disorder—approximately

FIGURE 14.16

Depressed Mood in Two Depressive Disorders

This graphic provides a general way to understand the two main types of depressive disorders in relation to "normal mood." People with major depressive disorder tend to experience extremely depressed moods for at least two weeks but often months or longer. By contrast, people with persistent depressive disorder experience mildly or moderately depressed moods but for many years.

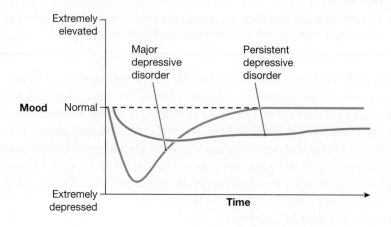

2–3 percent of the population—may have many of the same symptoms as those with major depressive disorder, but the symptoms are less intense (see Figure 14.16). To be diagnosed with persistent depressive disorder, someone must have a depressed mood most of the day, more days than not, for at least two years. Periods of persistent depressive disorder last from 2 to 20 or more years, although the typical duration is about 5 to 10 years.

Depression is so prevalent that it is sometimes called the common cold of psychological disorders. In its most severe form, depression is the leading cause of disability in the United States and worldwide (Worley, 2006). Depression is the leading risk factor for suicide, which claims approximately 800,000 lives annually around the world (World Health Organization, 2018a) and is among the top three causes of death for people between 15 and 35 years of age (Insel & Charney, 2003). Unfortunately, some people do not seek treatment because of the stigma associated with having a psychological disorder. One way to combat this stigma is to focus attention on how common they are and to educate more people about effective treatments (**Figure 14.17**).

"I lost interest in doing things with the kids...going to the movies, things that families do."

—Rene Ruballo, Police Officer

Real Men. Real Depression. "They would ask their mother. 'Why is Daddy not getting up?' They didn't do anything to me. I just didn't want to do anything. I'm thinking there's got to be something wrong because I'm waking up and going, but I feel like nothing matters." Depression is a real disease that can be successfully treated. For information, call 1-866-227-6464, visit www.nimh.nih.gov, or contact your health care provider.

It takes courage to ask for help. Rene did.

NIMH
National Institute of Mental Health
National Institutes of Health

14.7 Many Factors Influence the Development of Depressive Disorders

14.7 LEARNING GOAL ACTIVITIES

To maximize your learning, complete the following learning goal activities:

a. Understand all bold and italic terms by writing explanations of them in your own words.

b. Understand what causes depressive disorders by describing the three aspects of the cognitive triad that contribute to their development.

FIGURE 14.17

Informing the Public

Advertisements such as this one, from the National Institute of Mental Health, are meant to increase understanding about psychological disorders. The more we hear about how common psychological disorders are, the more inclined we may be to visit doctors when problems arise.

Depressive disorders are so common that people often wonder what causes them. The answer is not simple. As with other psychological disorders, biopsychosocial factors play a role in the etiology of depression. Let's look at each of these influences.

BIOLOGICAL FACTORS IN DEPRESSIVE DISORDERS Studies of twins, of families, and of adoptive children support the notion that depression has a genetic component. Although there is some variability among studies, it is more likely that both identical twins will have depression than that both fraternal twins will (Levinson, 2006). The existence of a genetic component implies that biological factors are involved in depression. In fact, there is evidence that major depression involves various neurotransmitters that regulate emotion. As you will learn about in Chapter 15, medications that increase or decrease the availability of specific neurotransmitters are used in the treatment of depression.

In addition, studies of brain function have suggested that certain neural structures may be involved in mood disorders. Damage to the left prefrontal cortex can lead to depression, but damage to the right prefrontal cortex does not. Biological rhythms also have been implicated in depression. People who experience depression enter REM sleep more quickly and have more of it. In fact, one symptom of depression is excessive sleeping and tiredness.

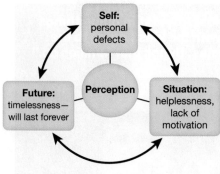

FIGURE 14.18

Cognitive Triad

People who experience depression perceive themselves, their situations, and the future negatively. These perceptions influence each other and contribute to the disorder.

PSYCHOLOGICAL FACTORS IN DEPRESSIVE DISORDERS Psychological factors also play a role in the cause of depression. A number of studies have implicated life stressors, such as the death of a loved one, a divorce, or multiple negative events, in many cases of depression (Hammen, 2005).

How people react to stress, however, can be influenced by their interpersonal relationships, and relationships play an extremely important role in depression. A person who has a close friend or group of friends is less likely to become depressed when faced with stress. This protective factor is related not to the number of friends, but to the quality of the friendships: One good friend is more protective than a large number of casual acquaintances.

The psychologist Aaron Beck has hypothesized that a psychological factor associated with depression is how people think of themselves. Specifically, people with depression think negatively about themselves ("I am worthless"; "I am a failure"; "I am ugly"), about their situations ("Everybody hates me"; "The world is unfair"), and about the future ("Things are hopeless"; "I can't change"). Beck refers to these negative thoughts about self, situation, and the future as the *cognitive triad* (Beck, 1967, 1976; **Figure 14.18**).

From Beck's perspective, people likely to develop depression blame misfortunes on personal defects and see positive occurrences as the result of luck. People who are not prone to depression do the opposite. Beck also notes that people likely to become depressed make errors in logic. For example, they overgeneralize based on single events, exaggerate the seriousness of bad events, think in extremes (such as believing they should either be perfect or not try), and take responsibility for bad events that actually have little to do with them.

A second cognitive theory of depression is based on *learned helplessness* (Seligman, 1974, 1975). In this case, people come to see themselves as unable to have any effect on events in their lives. The psychologist Martin Seligman based this model on years of research with nonhuman animals. When animals are placed in unpleasant situations they cannot escape (such as receiving an inescapable shock), the animals eventually become passive and unresponsive. They end up lacking the motivation to try new methods of escape even when given the opportunity. Similarly, people who are experiencing learned helplessness come to expect that bad things will happen to them and believe they are powerless to avoid negative events. Their explanations for negative events refer to personal factors that are unchanging rather than to situational factors that are temporary. This pattern leads them to feel hopeless about making positive changes in their lives (Abramson, Metalsky, & Alloy, 1989). Unfortunately, this hopelessness is a key symptom of depression that can lead to thoughts of suicide. At some point in your life, you may know someone who is considering suicide. To learn what signs to look for, read Using Psychology in Your Life on p. 565. The information you gain might just save a life.

SOCIAL FACTORS IN DEPRESSIVE DISORDERS In its most severe form, depression is the leading cause of disability worldwide and affects more than 300 million people (World Health Organization, 2018b). For example, major depressive disorder affects about 41 million people in India and 49 million people in China (Baxter et al., 2016). Unfortunately, in both countries there are large gaps between the numbers of people who have psychological disorders and the resources to treat those people (Patel et al., 2017). The stigma associated with depressive disorder has especially bad consequences in developing countries, where people do not take advantage of the treatment options because they do not want to admit to being depressed (Andrade et al., 2014).

What to Do if a Person Might Be Thinking of Suicide

Many people consider suicide at some point in their lives. Tragically, as of 2015, suicide is the second leading cause of death among Americans 10–24 years old (Centers for Disease Control and Prevention, 2018). Indeed, in 2010–15, suicide rates increased for adolescents, and the increased use of social media may be responsible (Twenge, Joiner, Rogers, & Martin, 2018). As a result, many college students will be or have been touched by suicide. Perhaps you know a family member who died by suicide. Perhaps a friend of yours talks about wanting to die. Or maybe you have thought about taking your own life. Understanding the risk factors associated with suicide is an important step toward preventing suicide. Knowing where and how to find support can save lives.

In helping explain suicide, Thomas Joiner, in his book *Why People Die by Suicide* (2005), argues that "people desire death when two fundamental needs are frustrated" (p. 47). The first of these fundamental needs is the need to belong, to feel connected with others. We all want to have positive interactions with others who care about us. Without such interactions, our need to belong is not met. The second fundamental need is the need for competence. If we do not perceive ourselves as able to do the things we think we should be able to do, our need for competence is not met. According to Joiner, when the need to belong and the need for competence are frustrated, we might desire death.

What can you do if you think someone you care about might be suicidal?

1. **Take all threats of suicide seriously.** You have to assume the person is actually capable of committing suicide.

2. **Get help.** Someone who is considering suicide should talk with a trained professional as soon as possible. Contact a counselor at your school, call a local suicide prevention hotline, or speak to someone at the National Suicide Prevention Lifeline: 1-800-273-TALK (8255). These individuals can help get the necessary support for someone at risk.

3. **Let the person know you care.** Remember, suicide risk is particularly high when people do not feel a sense of connection with others. You can remind the suicidal person that you value your relationship, that you care about the person's well-being, and that you would be devastated if this person were no longer in your life. These forms of support can challenge your loved one's sense of not belonging. You can also challenge a perceived sense of incompetence by expressing your genuine admiration for the person, or you can ask the person for help on a project or issue you are genuinely struggling with.

Suicide is forever, but the problems that prompt someone to feel suicidal are often temporary. If you ever find yourself or someone you care about feeling that suicide offers the best way out of an overwhelming or hopeless situation, know that other options exist. You or your loved one might not be able to see those options right away. Reach out to someone who can help you or your loved one see the ways out of current problems and into the future.

FIGURE 14.19

People with Bipolar Disorder Experience Elevated Mood

The singer Demi Lovato was diagnosed with bipolar disorder at age 22. In 2018, she continued to struggle with alcohol and drug problems. Lovato has made her diagnosis public in the hope of reducing the stigma associated with psychological disorders.

Across multiple countries and contexts, twice as many women as men are diagnosed with depression (Ustün, Ayuso-Mateos, Chatterji, Mathers, & Murray, 2004; Pratt & Brody, 2014). Furthermore, gender roles may lead to discrepancies in the experience of depression. One theory is that women respond to stressful events by internalizing their feelings, which leads to depression and anxiety, whereas men externalize with alcohol, drugs, and violence (Holden, 2005).

14.8 Bipolar Disorders Involve Mania

14.8 LEARNING GOAL ACTIVITIES

To maximize your learning, complete the following learning goal activities:

a. Understand all bold and italic terms by writing explanations of them in your own words.

b. Understand bipolar disorders by describing the similarities and differences between bipolar I disorder and bipolar II disorder.

How have you been feeling for the past week? Perhaps on some days you were happy, and on others you were sad. We all experience variations in mood. Our typical fluctuations from happiness to sadness seem small, however, compared with the extremes experienced by people with *bipolar disorders,* who experience episodes of greatly elevated mood. These periods of greatly elevated mood can vary in degree and are accompanied by major shifts in energy level, physical activity, and creativity. For example, the singer Demi Lovato, who has been diagnosed with bipolar disorder, has described episodes in which she stayed up all night writing one song after another (**Figure 14.19**). The two main types of bipolar disorders, each of which are characterized by different degrees of elevated mood, are summarized in **Table 14.6**.

SYMPTOMS OF BIPOLAR DISORDERS   True *manic episodes* last one week or longer and are characterized by abnormally and persistently elevated mood, increased activity, diminished need for sleep, grandiose ideas, racing thoughts, and extreme distractibility. For some people, mania involves a sense of agitation

TABLE 14.6

Two Types of Bipolar Disorders

DSM-5 Category	Description	Example
Bipolar I Disorder	Extremely elevated moods (mania) lasting at least one week	For two weeks, you feel extremely happy and excited, need very little sleep, and impulsively spend your life savings.
Bipolar II Disorder	Alternating between mildly elevated mood (hypomania) for at least four days and extremely depressed mood for two weeks	You experience weeks of deep sadness when you feel unable to accomplish much. Then your mood improves, you feel happy, and you have the energy to get things done.

Source: Adapted from American Psychiatric Association (2013).

and restlessness rather than positivity (Garriga et al., 2016). During episodes of mania, heightened levels of activity and extreme happiness often result in excessive involvement in pleasurable but foolish activities. People may engage in sexual indiscretions, buying sprees, risky business ventures, and similar "out of character" behaviors that they regret once the mania has subsided. This condition is known as **bipolar I disorder**. Bipolar I disorder is based on the presence of extreme mania. Although those with bipolar I disorder often have depressive episodes, such episodes are not necessary for a *DSM-5* diagnosis (**Figure 14.20**). Furthermore, the mania experienced in bipolar I disorder can be so severe as to make it hard for a person to know what is real, such as if the person experiences severe thought disturbances or hallucinations. This extreme form of mania can cause significant impairment in daily living and often can result in hospitalization.

Compared with bipolar I disorder, in which people experience true manic episodes, those with **bipolar II disorder** may experience less extreme mood elevations, called *hypomania* (see Figure 14.20). These episodes are often characterized by heightened creativity and productivity, and they can be extremely pleasurable and rewarding. Although these less extreme mood elevations may be somewhat disruptive to a person's life, they do not cause significant impairment in daily living or require hospitalization. However, the bipolar II diagnosis does require at least one episode of major depression. Therefore the depression might cause significant impairments, distress, or both. Thus the impairments to daily living for bipolar I disorder are the manic episodes, whereas the impairments for bipolar II disorder are the major depressive episodes.

A CASE STUDY OF BIPOLAR DISORDER The psychology professor Kay Redfield Jamison acknowledged her own struggles with bipolar disorder in her award-winning memoir *An Unquiet Mind* (1995; **Figure 14.21**). Her work has helped shape the study of the disorder. Her 1990 textbook, coauthored with Frederick Goodwin, is considered the standard for the field (Goodwin & Jamison, 1990).

In *An Unquiet Mind,* Jamison details how as a child she was intensely emotional and occasionally obsessive. When she was 17, she had her first serious bout of what she describes as profoundly suicidal depression. Jamison experienced deepening swings from wild exuberance to paralyzing depression throughout her undergraduate years. In 1975, after obtaining her Ph.D. in clinical psychology, she joined the UCLA Department of Psychiatry, where she directed the Affective Disorders Clinic.

Within months after she began this job, her condition deteriorated dramatically. She began hallucinating and feared that she was losing her mind. This state so terrified her that she sought out a psychiatrist, who quickly diagnosed her as having bipolar disorder and prescribed a drug called lithium. Although lithium has helped Jamison, she also credits the psychological support of her psychiatrist as well as her family and friends.

An unfortunate side effect of lithium is that it blunts positive feelings. People with bipolar disorder experience profoundly enjoyable highs during their manic phases, so they often resent the drug and refuse to take it. Jamison has made the point that lithium can rob people of creative energy. In her 1993 book *Touched with Fire,* Jamison

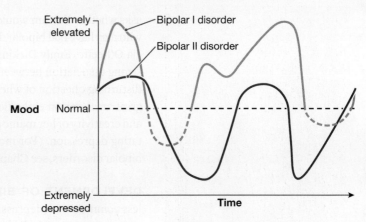

FIGURE 14.20

Elevated and Depressed Moods in Two Bipolar Disorders

This graphic provides a general way to understand two types of bipolar disorders based on what is considered "normal mood." People with bipolar I tend to experience extremely elevated moods, called mania. They may also experience major depressive disorder, but this symptom is not required for a diagnosis of bipolar I (as indicated by the dashed green line). People with bipolar II disorder tend to experience mildly elevated moods, called hypomania, along with major depressive disorder.

bipolar I disorder
Mood disorder characterized by extremely elevated moods during manic episodes.

bipolar II disorder
Mood disorder characterized by alternating periods of extremely depressed and mildly elevated moods.

FIGURE 14.21

Kay Redfield Jamison

Jamison was able to overcome bipolar disorder to succeed as a teacher, researcher, and author.

asks whether lithium would have dampened the genius of major artists and writers who may have had bipolar disorders, such as Michelangelo, Vincent van Gogh, Georgia O'Keeffe, Emily Dickinson, and Ernest Hemingway. Jamison demonstrates the strong association between bipolar disorder and artistic genius, and she raises the disturbing question of whether eradicating the disorder would rob society of much great art. Jamison embodies this irony: Her early career benefited from the energy and creativity of her manic phases even as her personal life was threatened by devastating depression. (For more information about lithium and other treatments for bipolar disorders, see Chapter 15.)

DEVELOPMENT OF BIPOLAR DISORDERS Bipolar disorders are much less common than depressive disorders. Around 3–4 percent of the population will experience a bipolar disorder in their lifetimes (Kessler & Wang, 2008). Whereas depression is more common in women, bipolar disorders are equally prevalent in women and men. Bipolar disorders emerge most commonly during late adolescence or early adulthood. Bipolar I disorder is typically diagnosed at an earlier age than bipolar II disorder.

There is a very strong genetic component to bipolar disorders (Ament et al., 2015). Twin studies reveal that if one twin has the disorder, an identical twin is three times more likely to have the disorder than a fraternal twin is (Nurnberger, Goldin, & Gershon, 1994). In the 1980s, the Amish community—a self-contained religious community centered largely in Pennsylvania—was involved in a genetic research study. The Amish were an ideal population for this sort of research because they keep good family history records and few outsiders marry into the community. In addition, substance abuse is virtually nonexistent among Amish adults, so psychological disorders are less likely to be confused with it. The research results revealed that bipolar disorders ran in a limited number of families and that all of those afflicted had a similar genetic defect (Egeland et al., 1987). Subsequent studies of this Amish group have identified several other potential genes involved in bipolar disorder (Georgi et al., 2014).

Indeed, recent genetic research has found that the hereditary nature of bipolar disorders is complex and not linked to just one gene. Current research focuses on identifying several genes that may be involved (Wray, Byrne, Stringer, & Mowry, 2014). In addition, it appears that in families with bipolar disorders, the disorders are more severe and appear at younger ages in successive generations (Petronis & Kennedy, 1995; Post et al., 2013). Research on this pattern may help reveal the genetics of the disorders, but the specific nature of the heritability of bipolar disorders remains to be discovered.

How Do People Experience Disorders of Emotion?

To make sure you learned what you just read, write answers to the following questions and check your answers.

14.4 How does specific phobia differ from generalized anxiety disorder?

14.5 What is the difference between an obsession and a compulsion?

14.6 How do major depressive disorder and persistent depressive disorder differ with respect to (a) depth of the depressed mood and (b) duration of the depressed mood?

14.7 Which psychological cause of depressive disorders involves people seeing themselves as unable to change their lives?

14.8 What is the difference between the type of mania experienced in bipolar I disorder and the type experienced in bipolar II disorder?

See Appendix B for answers to the red Q questions.

How Do People Experience Disorders of Thought?

As you have learned in this chapter so far, many psychological disorders are characterized primarily by impairments in emotion. Those impairments can influence thinking. For example, people with depression can have distorted thoughts about themselves or their futures. By contrast, some disorders are characterized primarily by extreme thought disturbances. The *DSM-5* category of schizophrenia spectrum and other related disorders includes a number of such conditions. In all of them, a break from reality causes a person to have difficulty distinguishing real thoughts from imagined ones, and the person has extreme difficulty functioning in everyday life.

14.9 Schizophrenia Involves a Disconnection from Reality

14.9 LEARNING GOAL ACTIVITIES

To maximize your learning, complete the following learning goal activities:

a. Understand all bold and italic terms by writing explanations of them in your own words.

b. Understand schizophrenia by naming and explaining each of the five symptoms.

c. Understand the six types of delusions by naming each one and describing the symptoms of each type of delusion.

The term *schizophrenia* literally means "splitting of the mind." The psychological disorder **schizophrenia** is characterized by extreme alterations in thought, in perceptions, and/or in consciousness. These disturbances result in a break from reality, so the person experiences *psychosis*, the inability to tell what is real from what is imagined. According to current estimates, around 1 in 200 persons around the globe have schizophrenia (Simeone, Ward, Rotella, Collins, & Winisch, 2015). The rates for men and women are similar (Saha, Chant, Welham, & McGrath, 2006).

For the person and for the family, schizophrenia may be the most devastating psychological disorder. It is characterized by a combination of motor, cognitive, behavioral, and perceptual abnormalities. These abnormalities result in impaired social, personal, or occupational functioning or in some combination of these impairments. According to the *DSM-5*, to be diagnosed with schizophrenia a person has to have shown continuous signs of disturbances for at least 6 months. There are five major *DSM-5* symptoms for schizophrenia: (1) delusions, (2) hallucinations, (3) disorganized speech, (4) disorganized behavior, and (5) negative symptoms. A diagnosis of schizophrenia requires a person to show two or more of these symptoms. At least one of these has to be from among the first three symptoms listed above (delusions, hallucinations, and disorganized speech). By tradition, researchers tend to group these five sets of symptoms into two categories: **Positive symptoms** are excesses. They are positive not in the sense of being good or desirable, but in the sense of adding abnormal behaviors. As you will see, **negative symptoms** are deficits in functioning, such as apathy, lack of emotion, slowed speech, and slowed movement.

schizophrenia
A psychological disorder characterized by extreme alterations in thought, in perceptions, and/or in consciousness that result in a break from reality.

positive symptoms
Symptoms of schizophrenia that are marked by excesses in functioning, such as delusions, hallucinations, and disorganized speech or behavior.

negative symptoms
Symptoms of schizophrenia that are marked by deficits in functioning, such as apathy, lack of emotion, slowed speech, and slowed movement.

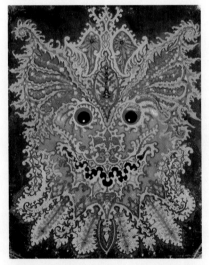

FIGURE 14.22

Louis Wain's Paintings May Reveal Symptoms of Schizophrenia

According to some commentators, Wain painted his realistic but fanciful paintings when he was experiencing fewer symptoms of schizophrenia. In this view, the increasingly abstract, frenetic, and hostile feel of his work may reflect his worsening symptoms, including delusions of persecution and visual disturbances.

delusions
False beliefs that reflect breaks from reality.

TABLE 14.7	
Common Delusions and False Beliefs Associated with Schizophrenia	
Persecution	Belief that others are persecuting, spying on, or trying to harm you
Referential	Belief that objects, events, or other people have particular significance to you, such as a belief that a stop sign has a particular personal message for you
Grandiose	Belief that you have great power, knowledge, or talent
Identity	Belief that you are someone else, such as Jesus Christ or the president of the United States
Guilt	Belief that you have committed a terrible sin
Control	Belief that your thoughts and behaviors are being controlled by external forces

DELUSIONS Delusions are positive symptoms (an excess in function) most commonly associated with schizophrenia. Delusions are a psychotic symptom because they are false beliefs that reflect breaks from reality. People with bipolar disorder who have severe episodes of mania may also experience delusions. There are six common types of delusions experienced by people with schizophrenia (**Table 14.7**). Delusional people persist in their beliefs despite clear evidence to the contrary, because their cognitive processes misinform them about what is real and what is not. For example, in his 50s, the early 20th-century artist Louis Wain began to experience delusions of persecution and to have difficulty separating reality from fantasy. Wain was subsequently diagnosed with schizophrenia. Many people believe that changes in his art over time reflect periods where he was experiencing milder or more-severe symptoms (**Figure 14.22**).

Delusions are characteristic of schizophrenia in all cultures, but the type of delusion can be influenced by cultural factors. For instance, Tateyama and colleagues (1993) found that German and Japanese patients with schizophrenia had similar rates of *grandiose delusions,* believing themselves much more powerful and important than they really were. The two groups differed significantly, however, for other types of delusions. The German patients had delusions that involved guilt and sin, particularly as these concepts related to religion. By contrast, the Japanese patients showed beliefs that they were being slandered by others.

HALLUCINATIONS Hallucinations are another positive symptom commonly associated with schizophrenia. **Hallucinations** are perceptual disturbances that are experienced without an external source, so they are another psychotic symptom. While they are frequently auditory, they can also be visual, olfactory, or bodily. Auditory hallucinations are often accusatory voices. They may accuse a person of being evil or stupid, or they may command the person to do dangerous things. Sometimes the person hears a racket of sounds with voices intermingled. As with delusions, people with bipolar disorder may experience this form of psychosis during manic episodes.

The cause of hallucinations is unclear. According to neuroimaging studies, auditory hallucinations may be associated with increased activity in brain areas that are usually engaged when people hear external sounds or engage in inner speech (Kühn & Gallinat, 2012). This finding has led to speculation that auditory hallucinations might be caused by a difficulty in distinguishing the inner speech of talking to oneself (inside the person's mind) from external sounds. To function in society, people with schizophrenia have to learn to ignore the voices in their heads, but doing so is extremely difficult and sometimes impossible.

FIGURE 14.23

Disorganized Behavior in Schizophrenia

Individuals with schizophrenia may act strangely, such as talking to themselves and inappropriately wearing multiple layers of clothing.

DISORGANIZED SPEECH   Another key positive symptom of schizophrenia is **disorganized speech**. The speech is disorganized in the sense that it is incoherent, failing to follow a normal conversational structure. It is very difficult or impossible to follow what people with schizophrenia are talking about because they frequently change topics, which is known as a *loosening of associations*. More-extreme cases involve *clang associations*: the stringing together of words that rhyme but have no other apparent link. People with schizophrenia may also display strange and inappropriate emotions while talking. Such strange speaking patterns make it very difficult for people with schizophrenia to communicate (Docherty, 2005).

hallucinations
Perceptual disturbances that are experienced without an external source.

disorganized speech
Speaking in an incoherent way and displaying strange or inappropriate emotions while talking.

DISORGANIZED BEHAVIOR   A final common positive symptom of schizophrenia is **disorganized behavior**. In other words, people with schizophrenia often act strangely (**Figure 14.23**). They might wear multiple layers of clothing even on hot summer days, walk along muttering to themselves, alternate between anger and laughter, or pace and wring their hands as if extremely worried. They have problems performing many activities, which interferes with daily living.

disorganized behavior
Acting in strange or unusual ways, including strange movement of limbs and inappropriate self-care, such as failing to dress properly or bathe.

NEGATIVE SYMPTOMS   About 1 out of 4 people with schizophrenia show reductions in typical behavior, which are called negative symptoms (Üçok & Ergül, 2014). For example, they avoid eye contact and seem apathetic. They do not express emotion even when discussing emotional subjects. Their speech is slowed, they say less than most people, and they use a monotonous tone of voice. Their speech may be characterized by long pauses before answering, failure to respond to a question, or inability to complete saying something after they start it. There is often a similar reduction in their behavior: Patients' movements may be slowed and their overall amount of movement reduced (Fusar-Poli et al., 2015). They may engage in little initiation of behavior and have no interest in social participation. These negative symptoms, though less dramatic than delusions and hallucinations and other positive symptoms, can be equally serious and result in patients' becoming withdrawn and isolated. Negative symptoms are more common in men than in women (Mendrek & Mancini-Marie, 2016). To consider how disorganized behavior is depicted in popular media, see Try It Yourself.

TRY IT YOURSELF
Recognizing Disordered Behavior

Psychological disorders are often represented in the popular media, on television shows, and in the movies. For example, the 2001 movie *A Beautiful Mind* stars Russell Crowe as the late Princeton mathematics professor and Nobel laureate John Forbes Nash, who was diagnosed with schizophrenia. Watch the movie, and try to identify the positive and the negative symptoms of the disorder.

14.10 Schizophrenia Is Caused by Biological and Environmental Factors

FIGURE 14.24

Genetics and Schizophrenia

As this graph illustrates, the more closely related a person is to someone with schizophrenia, the more likely the person is to develop schizophrenia. This finding is evidence of at least a partially genetic basis for schizophrenia.

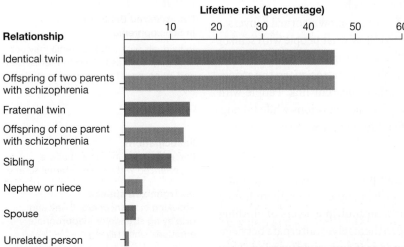

The etiology of schizophrenia is not well understood. Early theories attributed the development of this disorder to the patient's mother, who may have simultaneously accepted and rejected the individual during childhood. Research has revealed, however, that the causes of the disorder are much more complex.

BIOLOGICAL FACTORS INFLUENCE THE DEVELOPMENT OF SCHIZO-PHRENIA Schizophrenia runs in families, and genetics clearly plays a role in the development of the disorder (**Figure 14.24**). For instance, if one twin develops schizophrenia, the likelihood of the other twin's developing it is almost 50 percent if the twins are identical but only 14 percent if the twins are fraternal. If one parent has schizophrenia, the risk of a child's developing the disorder is 13 percent. If both parents have schizophrenia, the risk jumps to almost 50 percent (Gottesman, 1991; Wray & Gottesman, 2012). However, a person inherits a genetic predisposition for schizophrenia, not the disorder itself. Other factors must activate that predisposition for the person to develop schizophrenia. If genetics alone caused schizophrenia, the likelihood of both identical twins having the disorder would approach 100 percent.

Schizophrenia is primarily a brain disorder (Walker, Kestler, Bollini, & Hochman, 2004). As seen in brain imaging, the ventricles are enlarged in people with schizophrenia (**Figure 14.25**). In other words, there is actually less brain tissue, especially in the frontal lobes and medial temporal lobes. Some researchers have speculated, however, that schizophrenia is more likely a problem of connection between brain regions than the result of diminished or changed functions of any particular brain region (Walker et al., 2004).

One possibility is that schizophrenia results from abnormality in neurotransmitters. Since the 1950s, scientists have believed that dopamine may play an important role. Drugs that block dopamine activity decrease symptoms of schizophrenia, whereas drugs that increase dopamine activity increase symptoms. Other neurotransmitters may also be involved.

If schizophrenia is a brain disorder, when do these brain abnormalities emerge? Schizophrenia is most often diagnosed when people are in their 20s or 30s, but it is hard to assess whether brain impairments occur earlier. There is evidence that some

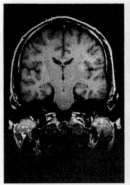
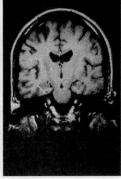

FIGURE 14.25

The Brains of Twins, One of Whom Has Schizophrenia

These brain MRIs are from twins, one without schizophrenia **(left)** and one with schizophrenia **(right)**. The MRI of the twin with schizophrenia shows larger ventricles. These fluid-filled cavities, which appear dark in the image, suggest that the brain may be deteriorating over time for this person (and others with schizophrenia).

neurological signs of schizophrenia can be observed long before the disorder is diagnosed. Elaine Walker and colleagues (2004) have analyzed home movies taken by parents whose children later developed schizophrenia. Compared with their siblings, those who developed the disorder displayed unusual social behaviors, more-severe negative emotions, and motor disturbances. All of these differences often went unnoticed during the children's early years. Such studies suggest that schizophrenia develops over the life course but that obvious symptoms often emerge by late adolescence. Hints of future problems, however, may be evident even in young children.

ENVIRONMENTAL FACTORS AFFECT THE DEVELOPMENT OF SCHIZOPHRENIA
Because genetics do not account fully for the onset and severity of schizophrenia, other factors must also be at work. In those genetically at risk for schizophrenia, environmental stress seems to contribute to its development (Walker et al., 2004). This finding is consistent with the diathesis-stress model, discussed in study unit 14.2. One study looked at adopted children whose biological mothers were diagnosed with schizophrenia (Tienari et al., 1990, 1994). If the adoptive families were severely disturbed, 11 percent of the children developed schizophrenia and 41 percent had severe psychological disorders. If the adoptive families were psychologically healthy, none of the children developed psychosis. More generally, growing up in a dysfunctional family may increase the risk of developing schizophrenia for those who are genetically at risk (Tienari et al., 2004; Walder, Faraone, Glatt, Tsuang, Seidman, 2014; **Figure 14.26a**). By contrast, without a genetic risk, a child has a low risk for developing schizophrenia, regardless of whether the family environment is dysfunctional or healthy (**Figure 14.26b**).

Some researchers have also theorized that the increased stress of urban environments can trigger the onset of the disorder. In fact, being born or raised in an urban area approximately doubles the risk of developing schizophrenia later in life (Torrey, 1999). Others have speculated that some kind of virus causes schizophrenia. If so, the close quarters of a big city increases the likelihood of the virus spreading. In support of the virus hypothesis, there is now strong evidence

FIGURE 14.26

Effects of Biology and Environment on Schizophrenia

(a) If a child has a genetic risk for schizophrenia and is raised in a dysfunctional family environment, that child will have a high risk of developing schizophrenia. But if that child is raised in a healthy family environment, that child will have a low risk of developing the disorder. **(b)** By contrast, if a child has no genetic risk of developing schizophrenia, the child will have a low risk of developing the disorder whether the child is raised in a dysfunctional or a healthy family environment.

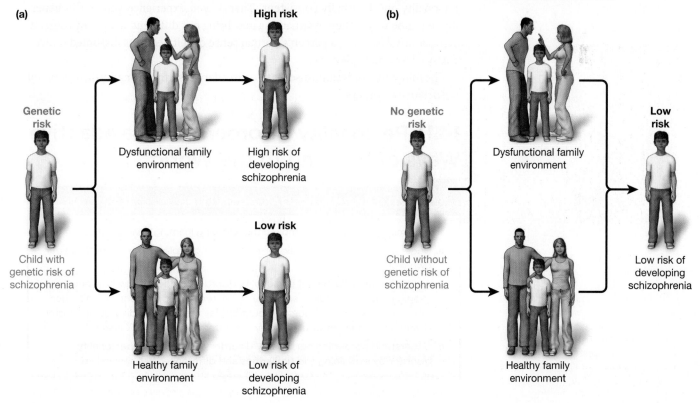

(a)

Genetic risk

Child with genetic risk of schizophrenia

Dysfunctional family environment

High risk

High risk of developing schizophrenia

Healthy family environment

Low risk

Low risk of developing schizophrenia

(b)

No genetic risk

Child without genetic risk of schizophrenia

Dysfunctional family environment

Low risk

Low risk of developing schizophrenia

Healthy family environment

that maternal inflammation, such as occurs from a virus, plays a significant role in schizophrenia (Brown & Derkits, 2009; Canetta et al., 2014). Ultimately, according to the evidence, multiple factors may serve as triggers for the development of schizophrenia for those who are genetically susceptible.

Q How Do People Experience Disorders of Thought?

To make sure you learned what you just read, write answers to the following questions and check your answers.

14.9 Explain whether disorganized behavior is a positive or negative symptom of schizophrenia.

14.10 How does the diathesis-stress model explain the development of schizophrenia?

See Appendix B for answers to the red Q questions.

How Do People Experience Disorders of Self?

As you learned in study units 13.5–13.8, your personality reflects your unique response to your environment. It is part of your identity and your sense of self. Although you change over time, the ways that you interact with the world and cope with events are pretty much set by the end of adolescence. Some people's identities cause them to interact with the world in maladaptive and inflexible ways. When this style of interaction is long-lasting and causes problems in work and in social situations, it becomes a *personality disorder*. Although people with personality disorders do not hallucinate or experience radical mood swings, their ways of interacting with the world can have serious consequences for the individual, family and friends, and society.

And as you learned in study unit 13.1, your sense of self is how you view your own personality and is usually consistent. That is, you experience yourself in generally the same way, although situations may bring out different aspects of yourself. In *dissociative disorders,* a person's normal sense of self becomes disrupted or even fractured into multiple selves.

The following study units discuss two disorders of self: personality disorders and dissociative disorders.

14.11 Personality Disorders Are Maladaptive Ways of Relating to the World

14.11 LEARNING GOAL ACTIVITIES

To maximize your learning, complete the following learning goal activities:

a. Understand all bold and italic terms by writing explanations of them in your own words.

b. Apply the three clusters of personality disorders by describing how one imaginary person would display the characteristics of a personality disorder from Cluster A, another person would display them from a disorder in Cluster B, and a third person would display them from a disorder in Cluster C.

c. Understand borderline personality disorder and antisocial personality disorder by explaining the similarities and differences between them.

The *DSM-5* divides personality disorders into three groups, as listed in **Table 14.8**. Disorders in the first group (Cluster A) are characterized by odd or eccentric behavior. People with *paranoid, schizoid,* and *schizotypal* personality disorders are often reclusive and suspicious. They have difficulty forming personal relationships because of their strange behavior and aloofness. As you might expect, people with personality disorders in this category show some similarities to people with schizophrenia, but their symptoms are far less severe.

Disorders in the second group (Cluster B) are characterized by dramatic, emotional, or erratic behaviors. *Antisocial, borderline, histrionic,* and *narcissistic* personality disorders make up this group. Borderline and antisocial personality disorders have been the focus of much research, so they are discussed in more detail in the next subsections.

Disorders in the third group (Cluster C)—*avoidant, dependent,* and *obsessive-compulsive* personality disorders—are characterized by anxious or fearful behavior. These disorders share some characteristics of anxiety disorders such as social phobia or generalized anxiety disorder. However, personality disorders in this third group refer more to maladaptive ways of interacting with others and of responding to events. People with obsessive-compulsive disorder (OCD) have true obsessions and compulsions, but people with obsessive-compulsive personality disorder do not. For instance, whereas people with OCD may be obsessed with germs and have the compulsion to wash their hands, people with an obsessive-compulsive personality

TABLE 14.8
Personality Disorders and Associated Characteristics

Cluster A: Odd or Eccentric Behavior	
Paranoid	Distrust; suspiciousness
Schizoid	Detachment from social relationships; restricted emotional expression
Schizotypal	Peculiarities of thought, appearance, and behavior that are disconcerting to others; acute discomfort in social relationships
Cluster B: Dramatic, Emotional, or Erratic Behavior	
Antisocial	Disregard for and violation of the rights of others
Borderline	Unstable moods, personal relationships, and self-image; impulsivity
Histrionic	Excessive emotionality; attention seeking
Narcissistic	Pattern of grandiosity; need for admiration; lack of empathy
Cluster C: Anxious or Fearful Behavior	
Avoidant	Social inhibition; feelings of inadequacy; easily hurt and embarrassed
Dependent	Submissive and clinging behavior; excessive need to be taken care of
Obsessive-compulsive	Perfectionistic; preoccupied with orderliness and control

Source: Adapted from American Psychiatric Association (2013).

borderline personality disorder
A personality disorder characterized by disturbances in identity, in moods, and in impulse control.

disorder may be excessively neat and orderly. They might always eat the same food at precisely the same time or perhaps read a newspaper in a particular order each time. People with OCD are often distressed by their rituals. By contrast, people with personality disorders view their behavior as problematic only when it interferes with their lives. For example, people with personality disorders may find it impossible to travel or to maintain relationships.

SYMPTOMS AND DEVELOPMENT OF BORDERLINE PERSONALITY DISORDER Borderline personality disorder is characterized by disturbances in identity, in emotional states, and in impulse control. This complex disorder was officially recognized as a diagnosis in 1980. The term *borderline* was initially used because people with these disorders were considered on the border between normal and psychotic (Knight, 1953). Approximately 1–2 percent of adults meet the criteria for borderline personality disorder, and the disorder is more than twice as common in women as in men (Lenzenweger, Lane, Loranger, & Kessler, 2007).

People with borderline personality disorder seem to lack a strong sense of self. They cannot tolerate being alone and have an intense fear of abandonment. Because they desperately need an exclusive and dependent relationship with another person, they can be very manipulative in their attempts to control relationships. In addition to problems with identity, borderline individuals have affective disturbances. Emotional instability is a key feature (Hazlett, 2016). Episodes of depression, anxiety, anger, irritability, or some combination of these states can last from a few hours to a few days. Shifts from one mood to another usually occur for no obvious reason.

The third key feature of borderline personality disorder is impulsivity, which may explain the much higher rate of the disorder in prisons than in the general population (Conn et al., 2010). Impulsivity can include sexual promiscuity, physical fighting, and binge eating and purging. Self-mutilation, such as cutting and burning of the skin, is commonly associated with this disorder, as is a high risk for suicide. Those with borderline personality disorder show abnormal functioning of the frontal lobes, which are important for controlling behavior (Salvador et al., 2016).

Borderline personality disorder may have an environmental component because of the strong relationship that exists between the disorder and trauma or abuse (Lieb, Zanarini, Schmahl, Linehan, & Bohus, 2004). Some studies have reported that 70–80 percent of patients with borderline personality disorder have experienced physical or sexual abuse or observed some kind of extreme violence. Other theories propose that borderline patients may have had caretakers who did not accept them or were unreliable or unavailable. The constant rejection and criticism made it difficult for the patients to learn to regulate their emotions and understand emotional reactions to events (Linehan, 1987). An alternative theory is that caregivers encouraged dependence, preventing the individuals in their charge from adequately developing a sense of self. As a result, the individuals became overly sensitive to others' reactions: If rejected by others, they reject themselves.

FIGURE 14.27
Ted Bundy
The convicted serial killer Ted Bundy would have been given a diagnosis of antisocial personality disorder. He also showed psychopathic traits.

SYMPTOMS AND DEVELOPMENT OF ANTISOCIAL PERSONALITY DISORDER During the 1970s, a handsome and charismatic law student named Ted Bundy kidnapped, raped, and murdered 30 or more young women and girls and violated their bodies in appalling ways (**Figure 14.27**). Most people can't understand Bundy's behavior. Even one of Bundy's defense attorneys described him as heartless and evil. Bundy was eventually executed for his crimes.

According to the *DSM-5,* **antisocial personality disorder (APD)** is the diagnosis for individuals who behave in socially undesirable ways, such as breaking the law and being deceitful and irresponsible. People with APD are willing to take advantage of others and hurt them without showing any concern or remorse for their behavior. Instead, people with this disorder tend to be focused on pleasure, seeking immediate gratification of wants and needs with no thought about others. For example, such individuals could be superficially charming and rational, but they also could be insincere, unsocial, and incapable of love; lack insight; and be shameless. However, not all criminals can be described as having APD.

The term *psychopath* is used to refer to a disorder that is related, but not identical, to APD. People with psychopathic tendencies display more-extreme behaviors than those with APD. They also tend to have other personality characteristics not found in those with APD, such as being smooth-talking, having extremely high sense of self-worth, being unemotional, and being manipulative. They have no remorse, lie and cheat, and lack empathy. Their behavior is particularly dangerous because they can be extremely hard-hearted (Coid & Ullrich, 2010). For instance, one study of murderers found that those with psychopathic tendencies nearly always kill intentionally. They want to gain something, such as money, sex, or drugs. Those without psychopathic tendencies are much more likely to commit murder impulsively, such as when provoked or angry (Woodworth & Porter, 2002). Because of this difference, psychopaths fit the stereotype of cold-blooded killers such as Ted Bundy. A career that involves identifying psychopaths is forensic psychology. To learn about this field, see Putting Psychology to Work on p. 591.

Ironically, people with psychopathic traits are often seen as charming and intelligent. For this reason, some psychopaths manage to be successful professionals and conceal their uncaring and devious tendencies. Their psychopathic traits may even provide advantages in some occupations, such as business and politics (**Figure 14.28**).

In the United States, about 1–4 percent of the population has APD (Compton, Conway, Stinson, Colliver, & Grant, 2005). Less common are people with this condition who also show more-extreme psychopathic traits (Lenzenweger et al., 2007). APD is much more common in men than in women (Goldstein et al., 2017). The disorder is most apparent in late adolescence and early adulthood, and people who have this disorder generally improve on their own around age 40 (Hare, McPherson, & Forth, 1988), at least for those without psychopathic traits.

Various physiological abnormalities may play a role in APD. In 1957, David Lykken reported that those with APD do not become anxious when they experience unpleasant stimuli. Lykken and other investigators have continued this line of research, showing that such individuals do not seem to feel fear or anxiety (Lykken, 1995). They do not learn from punishment, because they do not experience punishment as particularly unpleasant. This pattern of reduced psychophysiological response in the face of punishment also occurs in adolescents at risk for developing APD (Fung et al., 2005). Abnormalities in multiple brain regions involved in responding to fear and controlling impulses have been found in those with APD or whose behavior in adolescence places them at risk for developing APD (Marsh et al., 2013). You can read more about this research in The Methods of Psychology on p. 578.

antisocial personality disorder (APD)
A personality disorder marked by disregard for and violation of the rights of others and by lack of remorse.

FIGURE 14.28
American Psychopath
In the 2000 movie *American Psycho,* Christian Bale plays Patrick Bateman, who appears to be a suave man-about-town and a successful professional but may also be a serial killer.

Amygdala Activity in Children at Risk for Antisocial Personality Disorder

Hypothesis: Youths who show callous-unemotional traits that place them at risk for developing antisocial personality disorder will show abnormal amygdala activity when viewing faces displaying fear expressions.

Research Method:

1 Children and adolescents ages 10–17 were shown pictures of faces displaying emotional expressions while in the brain scanner. One group of children had been identified as possessing callous-unemotional traits (including limited empathy, a lack of guilt, and superficial emotions), another group had ADHD, and the final group was comparison children who did not have a psychological disorder.

2 Brain activity was contrasted between when the participant was viewing emotional expressions (anger, fear) versus when the participant was viewing the neutral expression.

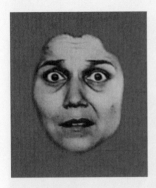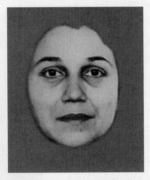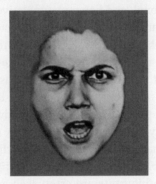

Result: Youths with callous-unemotional traits showed less activity in the amygdala in response to the fearful expressions (compared to the neutral expression) than did either those with ADHD or the healthy comparison youths. There were no differences in brain activity in response to the angry expressions (compared to the neutral expression).

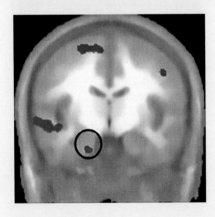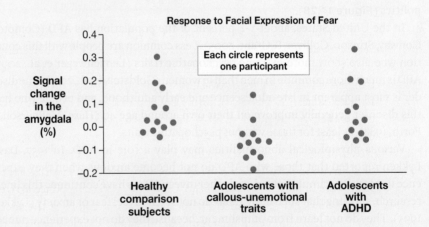

Conclusion: The results suggest that children at risk for developing antisocial personality disorder have reduced responses to distress-based social cues such as fear. In such children, the lack of amygdala response may produce impaired processing of social cues that indicate social distress. Therefore these at-risk youths may not avoid behaviors that distress others.

Question: Did those who exhibited callous-unemotional traits show reduced amygdala activity to all emotional expressions?

ANSWER: No. They showed reduced amygdala activity only in response to fearful expressions.

Source: Marsh, A. A., Finger, E. C., Mitchell, D. G., Reid, M. E., Sims, C., et al. (2008). Reduced amygdala response to fearful expressions in children and adolescents with callous-unemotional traits and disruptive behavior disorders. *American Journal of Psychiatry, 165,* 712–720.

14.12 Dissociative Disorders Involve Disruptions in the Sense of Self

Sometimes you may get lost in your thoughts or daydreams, even to the point of losing track of what is going on around you. Maybe you have had the experience of forgetting what you are doing while in the middle of an action ("Why was I headed to the kitchen?"). When you wake up in an unfamiliar location, you may be disoriented for a short time and not know where you are. In other words, your thoughts and experiences can become dissociated, or split, from the external world.

Dissociative disorders are extreme versions of this phenomenon. These disorders involve disruptions of identity, memory, or conscious awareness (Spiegel et al., 2013). In all of them, some parts of memory are split off from a person's conscious awareness. Dissociative disorders are believed to result from extreme stress. That is, the person with a dissociative disorder has split off a traumatic event in order to protect the person's sense of self. Some researchers believe that people prone to dissociative disorders are also prone to PTSD (Cardeña & Carlson, 2011).

SYMPTOMS AND DEVELOPMENT OF DISSOCIATIVE AMNESIA   In **dissociative amnesia**, a person forgets that an event happened or loses awareness of a large block of time. For example, someone with this disorder may suddenly lose memory for personal facts, including the person's own name and address. These memory failures cannot be accounted for by ordinary forgetting (such as briefly forgetting where you parked your car) or by the effects of drugs or alcohol.

Consider the case of Dorothy Joudrie, from Calgary, Canada. In 1995, after suffering years of physical abuse from her husband, Joudrie shot him six times. Her husband survived, and he described her behavior during the shooting as very calm, as if she were detached from what she was doing. When the police arrived, however, Joudrie was extremely distraught. She had no memory of the shooting and told the police that she simply found her husband shot and lying on the garage floor, at which time she called for help. Joudrie was found not criminally responsible for her actions because of her dissociative state (Butcher, Mineka, & Hooley, 2007).

The rarest and most extreme form of dissociative amnesia is *dissociative fugue*. The disorder involves a loss of identity. In addition, it involves traveling to another location (the Latin word *fuga* means "flight") and sometimes assuming a new identity. The fugue state often ends suddenly, leaving people unsure of how they ended up in unfamiliar surroundings. Typically, they do not remember events that took place during the fugue state.

dissociative amnesia
Psychological disorder that involves disruptions of memory for personal facts or loss of conscious awareness for a period of time.

dissociative identity disorder (DID) The occurrence of two or more distinct identities in the same individual.

SYMPTOMS AND DEVELOPMENT OF DISSOCIATIVE IDENTITY DISORDER An individual with **dissociative identity disorder (DID)** has developed two or more distinct identities. (The condition was formerly called *multiple personality disorder*.) Most people diagnosed with DID are women who report being severely abused as children. According to the most common theory, children who are likely to develop DID cope with abuse by pretending it is happening to someone else. They enter a trancelike state in which they separate their mental states from their physical bodies. Over time, this dissociated state takes on its own identity. Different identities develop to deal with different traumas.

Often the identities have periods of amnesia, and sometimes only one identity is aware of the others. Indeed, diagnosis often occurs only when a person has difficulty accounting for large chunks of time. The separate identities usually differ substantially in gender, sexual orientation, age, language spoken, interests, physiological profiles, and patterns of brain activation (Reinders et al., 2003). Even their handwriting can differ (**Figure 14.29**).

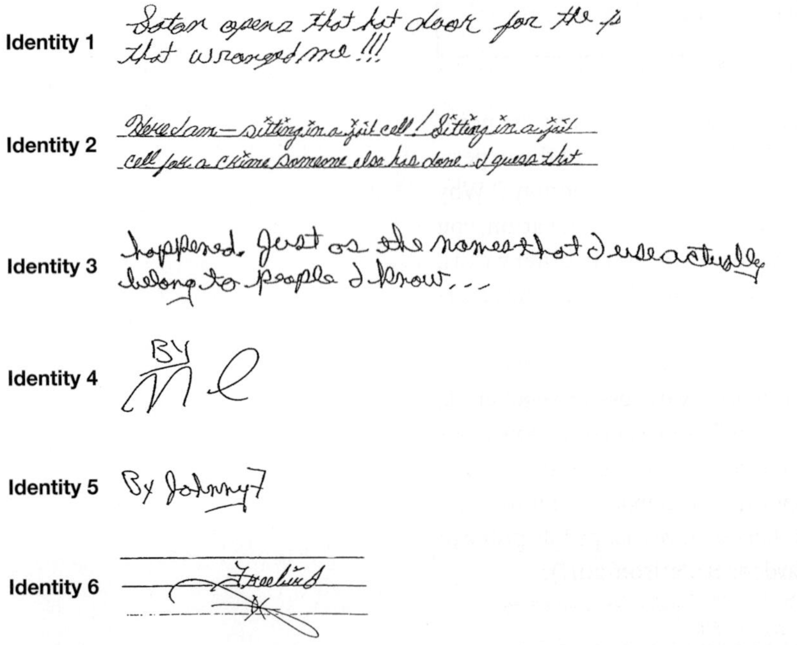

Despite this evidence, many researchers remain skeptical about whether DID is a genuine psychological disorder or even whether it exists at all (Kihlstrom, 2005). In part, they have doubts because DID first received popular attention when it was portrayed in the 1976 movie *Sybil*. After the movie, there was a sharp rise in reported cases. Therapists in the 1980s and 1990s who used hypnosis were the most likely to diagnose their clients as having DID. Skeptics claim that it was the therapists' beliefs that led to the increased diagnoses. Moreover, some people may have hidden motives for claiming DID. A diagnosis of DID often occurs after someone has been accused of committing a crime, raising the possibility that the suspect is pretending to have multiple identities to avoid conviction. Ultimately, how can we know whether a diagnosis of DID is valid? As noted in study unit 14.3, most often there is no objective, definitive test for diagnosing a psychological disorder. It can be difficult to tell if a person is faking, has come to believe what a therapist said, or has a genuine psychological disorder.

Identity 1

Identity 2

Identity 3

Identity 4

Identity 5

Identity 6

FIGURE 14.29

Handwriting Samples from a Person with Dissociative Identity Disorder

When researchers studied 12 murderers diagnosed with DID, writing samples from 10 of the participants revealed markedly different handwriting in each of their identities. Here, handwriting samples from one of the participants demonstrate the expression of several different identities.

Q How Do People Experience Disorders of Self?

To make sure you learned what you just read, answer the following questions and check your answers.

14.11 How do people with antisocial personality disorder, as that condition is defined by the *DSM-5*, differ from psychopaths?

14.12 What is the difference between dissociative amnesia and dissociative fugue?

See Appendix B for answers to the red Q questions.

What Disorders Affect Children?

In his classic text on the classification of psychological disorders, published in 1883, Emil Kraepelin did not mention childhood disorders. The first edition of the *DSM*, published 70 years later, essentially considered children as small versions of adults and did not consider childhood disorders separately from adulthood disorders. We now know that many children and adolescents experience anxiety and depressive disorders, along with emerging symptoms of schizophrenia.

An important lesson here is that psychological disorders found in adults often started when those individuals were children or teenagers. All children and adolescents need support to develop and maintain positive mental health.

14.13 Children May Experience Neurodevelopmental Disorders

14.13 LEARNING GOAL ACTIVITIES

To maximize your learning, complete the following learning goal activities:

a. Understand all bold and italic terms by writing explanations of them in your own words.

b. Apply the characteristics of one of the neurodevelopmental disorders by naming one of the six neurodevelopmental disorders and describing a real or imaginary child who shows the symptoms of that disorder.

The *DSM-5* groups disorders that most commonly emerge in children as **neurodevelopmental disorders**. This category includes a wide range of disorders. Some—such as specific learning disorders and communication disorders, such as stuttering—affect only very specific areas of a child's world. Other conditions—such as autism spectrum disorder, attention-deficit/hyperactivity disorder, and others listed in **Table 14.9,** on p. 582—affect every aspect of a child's life.

All of the neurodevelopmental disorders should be considered within the context of normal childhood development. Some symptoms of childhood psychological disorders are extreme examples of normal behavior or are actually normal behaviors for much younger children. For example, bed-wetting is normal for 2-year-olds but not for 10-year-olds. Other behaviors, however, deviate significantly from normal development. The following study units consider autism spectrum disorder and attention-deficit/hyperactivity disorder as examples of neurodevelopmental disorders.

neurodevelopmental disorders
Psychological disorders that most commonly develop in childhood.

TABLE 14.9
Neurodevelopmental Disorders That Affect Children

Disorder	Description	Example
Intellectual disabilities	Deficits in intellectual functioning and in adaptive functioning that begin during childhood or adolescence	At age 5, you have difficulty learning in a variety of areas. Your problems adapting to the demands of daily living suggest that you will need support at school and in daily functioning.
Communication disorders	Deficits in language, speech, or communications; for example, difficulty learning a language, stuttering, or failure to follow social rules for communication; symptoms begin in childhood	Although you are very intelligent, you had a hard time learning to speak as a child. As a teenager, you still often make inappropriate responses in conversation, which greatly affects your social life.
Autism spectrum disorder	Persistent impairment in social interaction; unresponsiveness; impaired language, social, cognitive development; restricted, repetitive behavior; symptoms begin in early childhood	At age 2, you suddenly stopped speaking, stopped looking people in the eyes and responding to your name, and began to flap your arms repeatedly when upset.
Attention-deficit/ hyperactivity disorder	Hyperactive, inattentive, and impulsive behavior that causes social or academic impairment; begins before age 12	You fidget all the time at school, can't pay attention to the teacher or follow instructions to complete tasks, and often disrupt other students.
Specific learning disorder	Difficulty learning and using academic skills; for example, much lower performance in reading, mathematics, or writing than expected for age, education, and intelligence; begins during school-age years	You are in third grade and show normal intelligence, but your reading skills are closer to those of a first grader.
Motor disorders	Recurrent motor and/or vocal tics that cause marked distress or impairment or deficits in developing or being able to show coordinated motor skills; symptoms begin in childhood	You are an adolescent who for several years has experienced uncontrollable muscle spasms, called tics, in your face and head.

Source: Adapted from American Psychiatric Association (2013).

14.14 Autism Spectrum Disorder Involves Social Deficits and Restricted Interests

14.14 LEARNING GOAL ACTIVITIES

To maximize your learning, complete the following learning goal activities:

a. Understand all bold and italic terms by writing explanations of them in your own words.

b. Analyze the severity of autism spectrum disorder by differentiating the symptoms of the severe form from those of the mild form.

autism spectrum disorder
A developmental disorder characterized by deficits in social interaction, by impaired communication, and by restricted, repetitive behavior and interests.

Autism spectrum disorder is characterized by deficits in social interaction, by impaired communication, and by restricted, repetitive behavior and interests (Volkmar, Chawarska, & Klin, 2005). The disorder was first described in 1943, by the psychiatrist Leo Kanner. Struck by the profound isolation of some children, Kanner coined the term *early infantile autism*.

Approximately 1–2 percent of children show signs of autism spectrum disorder, and males with the disorder outnumber females 5 to 1 (Christensen et al., 2015). From 1991 to 1997, there was a dramatic increase—of 556 percent—in the number of children diagnosed with autism (Stokstad, 2001). This increase was likely due to a greater awareness of symptoms by parents and physicians and a willingness to apply the diagnosis to a wider array of behaviors (Rutter, 2005).

This probable explanation is important to recognize because some parents are worried that childhood vaccinations, or chemicals in the solutions used to administer the vaccines, might have caused an epidemic of autism. However, there is overwhelming evidence that vaccines do not cause autism spectrum disorder (DeStefano, Price, & Weintraub, 2013; Jain et al., 2015).

Why might people falsely believe that vaccines cause autism? The disorder tends to first appear in early childhood, when many children are receiving vaccinations. As a critical thinker, you might recognize that other characteristics emerge at the same time in development, such as talking. Are these characteristics also associated with vaccinations? Few people would suggest that being vaccinated causes children to talk. So what is the apparent connection between vaccines and developing autism? It may simply be that both happen when children are young.

The classification of autism is an excellent example of a dimensional approach to assessment. Autism spectrum disorder varies in severity, from mild social impairments to severe social and intellectual impairments. Although not an official *DSM-5* disorder, high-functioning autism has sometimes been called *Asperger syndrome*, named after the pediatrician who first described it. A child with Asperger's has normal intelligence but deficits in social interaction. These deficits reflect an underdeveloped theory of mind. As you learned in study unit 4.6, theory of mind is both the understanding that other people have mental states and the ability to predict their behavior accordingly.

SYMPTOMS OF AUTISM SPECTRUM DISORDER Children with a severe form of autism spectrum disorder are seemingly unaware of others. As babies, they do not smile at their caregivers, do not respond to vocalizations, and may actively reject physical contact with others. These children do not establish eye contact and do not use their gaze to gain or direct the attention of those around them (Moriuchi, Klin, & Jones, 2016). One group of researchers had participants view video footage of the first birthdays of children with autism to see if characteristics of autism spectrum disorder could be detected before the children were diagnosed (Osterling & Dawson, 1994). By considering only the number of times a child looked at another person's face, the participants were able to classify the children with impressive accuracy, as either having autism (**Figure 14.30a**) or not having autism (**Figure 14.30b**).

Deficits in communication are a second characteristic of autism spectrum disorder. Children with autism show severe impairments in verbal and nonverbal communication. Even if they vocalize, it is often not because they are trying to communicate. Such deficits are evident by 14 months of age (Landa, Holman, & Garrett-Mayer, 2007).

A third set of deficits includes restricted, repetitive behaviors and interests. Though children with autism spectrum disorder seem not to notice people around them, they are acutely aware of their surroundings. Most children automatically pay attention to the social aspects of a situation, but those with autism may focus on seemingly trivial details, such as objects in the environment (Klin, Jones, Schultz, & Volkmar, 2003; **Figure 14.31**).

Any changes in daily routine or in the placement of furniture or toys are very upsetting for children with autism spectrum disorder. Once they are upset, the

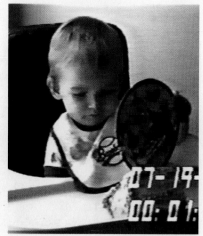

(a)

(b)

FIGURE 14.30

Scenes from Videotapes of Children's Birthday Parties

(a) This child focused more on objects than on people. The child was later diagnosed with autism. **(b)** This child focused appropriately on objects and on people. The child developed normally.

Viewer (2-year-old with autism)

Area focused on by a 2-year-old with autism.

D:088 H:443 V:327   23:13:37:51

FIGURE 14.31

Toddler with Autism Watching Television

This image from a 1994 study shows the television program being viewed by a 2-year-old with autism and the image of the child's eye as he watches the program **(top left)**. The circled area **(bottom right)** is where the child was looking when watching the television show. This pattern suggested that children with autism will focus on the unimportant details in the scene rather than on the social interaction.

children can become extremely agitated or throw tantrums. The play of children with severe autism spectrum disorder tends to be repetitive and obsessive, and they focus on the sensory aspects of objects. The children may smell and taste objects, or they may spin and flick them for visual stimulation. Other aspects of their behavior also tend to be repetitive and can include strange hand movements, body rocking, and hand flapping. Self-injury is common, and some children must be forcibly restrained to keep them from hurting themselves.

DEVELOPMENT OF AUTISM SPECTRUM DISORDER   It is now well established that autism is the result of biological factors. For example, there is evidence for a genetic component to this disorder (Holmboe et al., 2013; Hyman, 2008). Although autism spectrum disorder is heritable, environmental or other factors are also important.

Research into the causes of autism also points to prenatal and/or early childhood events that may result in brain dysfunction. The brains of children with autism spectrum disorder grow unusually large during the first two years of life, and then growth slows until age 5 (Courchesne et al., 2007). The brains of children with autism spectrum disorder also do not develop normally during adolescence (Amaral, Schumann, & Nordahl, 2008; Hazlett et al., 2017). Researchers are investigating genetic factors, such as gene mutations, and nongenetic factors that might explain this overgrowth/undergrowth pattern.

In addition, there is evidence that the brains of people with autism have faulty wiring in a large number of areas (Minshew & Williams, 2007). Some of those brain areas are associated with social thinking, and others might support attention to social aspects of the environment.

14.15 Attention-Deficit/Hyperactivity Disorder Is a Disruptive Impulse Control Disorder

 14.15 LEARNING GOAL ACTIVITIES

To maximize your learning, complete the following learning goal activities:

a. Understand all bold and italic terms by writing explanations of them in your own words.

b. Apply the symptoms of attention-deficit/hyperactivity disorder (ADHD) by providing a description of a real or imaginary child who shows the symptoms of ADHD.

What kind of childhood behavior counts as hyperactivity? At home, children exhibiting hyperactivity might have difficulty remembering not to trail their dirty hands along clean walls as they run from room to room. While playing games with their peers, they might spontaneously change the rules. At school, they might make warbling noises or other strange sounds that inadvertently disturb anyone nearby. They might seem to have more than their share of accidents. For example, they might knock over the tower their classmates are building or trip over the television cord while chasing the family cat (Whalen, 1989).

SYMPTOMS OF ATTENTION-DEFICIT/HYPERACTIVITY DISORDER Symptoms such as these can seem funny when you read about them, but the reality is a different story. Children with **attention-deficit/hyperactivity disorder (ADHD)** are overly active, inattentive, and impulsive. They need to have directions repeated and rules explained over and over. Although they are often friendly and talkative, these children can have trouble making and keeping friends because they miss subtle social cues and make unintentional social mistakes. Many of these symptoms are exaggerations of typical toddler behavior, and thus the line between normal and abnormal behavior is hard to draw. According to the *DSM-5*, children must show symptoms before age 12 to be diagnosed with ADHD.

Estimates of the prevalence of ADHD vary widely. The best available evidence for children in the United States is that 7 percent of children have the disorder, with it being more common in boys than girls (Thomas, Sanders, Doust, Beller, & Glasziou, 2015). Around the globe, an estimated 5 percent of children have ADHD (Sayal, Prasad, Daley, Ford, & Coghill, 2018). Although ADHD traditionally has been most common among white boys, recently girls and minorities have increasingly been diagnosed with the disorder (Collins & Cleary, 2016; Siegel, Laska, Wanderling, Hernandez, & Levenson, 2015). In addition, ADHD was once associated with being thin or normal weight, but children with ADHD are now more likely to be obese (Cortese et al., 2016). One possible explanation for these differences is that practitioners may be more willing to look beyond stereotypes of who has the disorder (**Figure 14.32**).

DEVELOPMENT OF ADHD The causes of ADHD are unknown. One of the difficulties in pinpointing its etiology is that the behavioral profiles of children with ADHD vary, so the causes of the disorder most likely vary as well. Environmental factors may contribute to the onset of symptoms, as is true for all psychological disorders. Still, ADHD clearly has a genetic component (Larsson, Chang, D'Onofrio, & Lichtenstein, 2014; Sherman, McGue, & Iacono, 1997).

In an early imaging study, Alan Zametkin and colleagues (1990) found that adults who had been diagnosed with ADHD in childhood had reduced metabolism in brain regions involved in the self-regulation of motor functions and of attentional systems. A general finding is that there is reduced tissue in many brain regions for those with ADHD, particularly in areas involving attention, cognitive and motor control, emotional regulation, and motivation (Gallo & Posner, 2016; Hoogman et al., 2017). This pattern suggests that the brains of those with ADHD develop more slowly than average (Friedman & Rapoport, 2015; Shaw et al., 2012).

ADHD ACROSS THE LIFE SPAN Children generally are not diagnosed with ADHD until they enter structured settings where they must conform to rules, get along with peers, and sit in their seats for long periods. In the past, these things happened when children entered school, between ages 5 and 7. Now, with more structured day care settings, the demands on children to conform are occurring much earlier.

According to longitudinal studies, children do not outgrow ADHD by the time they enter adulthood (Agnew-Blais et al., 2016; McGough & Barkley, 2004). The

attention-deficit/hyperactivity disorder (ADHD)
A disorder characterized by excessive activity or fidgeting, inattentiveness, and impulsivity.

FIGURE 14.32
ADHD in Girls
The stereotype of ADHD is a thin and overactive white male. However, ADHD is increasingly diagnosed in girls and minorities, possibly because practitioners are looking beyond stereotypical characteristics in their assessment of disordered behaviors.

Do you know any children who seem to always be on the move? Maybe they do silly things on impulse and can't seem to control themselves. And they seem to not hear directions and reprimands to change their behavior. Many of us can see the characteristics of attention-deficit/hyperactivity disorder (ADHD) in children, or possibly adults, we know. This makes sense because ADHD is one of the most commonly diagnosed disorders of childhood, and the symptoms continue into adulthood. With support, children can learn ways to reduce distractions, follow directions, and stay on task, which can reduce the effects of ADHD in adulthood. On the plus side, both children and adults with ADHD are often friendly and talkative, so they can be fun to be with—as long as they learn social rules and pay attention to subtle social cues.

FIGURE 14.33

Living with ADHD

Paula Luper, of North Carolina, was diagnosed with ADHD in elementary school. Here, as a senior in high school, she is taking a quiz in the teachers' lounge to avoid being distracted.

DSM-5 recognizes that many of the symptoms of ADHD continue well into adulthood. Adults with ADHD symptoms, about 4 percent of the population (Kessler et al., 2006), may struggle academically and vocationally. They generally reach a lower-than-expected socioeconomic level and change jobs more frequently than other adults (Klein et al., 2012). At the same time, many adults with ADHD learn how to adapt to their condition, such as by reducing distractions while they work (**Figure 14.33**). To consider examples of ADHD in your life, see Has It Happened to You?

Q What Disorders Affect Children?

To make sure you learned what you just read, answer the following questions and check your answers.

14.13 If a third-grader has normal intelligence but reads and writes at a first-grade level, then which of the six neurodevelopmental disorders might that child be diagnosed with?

14.14 How does brain development in autism spectrum disorder differ from typical brain development?

14.15 What are the three main symptoms of ADHD?

See Appendix B for answers to the red Q questions.

BIG PICTURE

Want to earn a better grade on your test? Go to **INQUIZITIVE** to practice actively with this chapter's content and get personalized feedback along the way.

What Is a Psychological Disorder?

14.1 Disorders Interfere with Our Lives

Review the learning goal activities on p. 547. People experiencing psychopathology have emotions, thoughts, and/or behaviors that impair their lives.

14.2 There Are Two General Ways to View the Causes of Disorders

Review the learning goal activities on p. 549. The diathesis-stress model suggests that psychopathology arises from vulnerability (diathesis) paired with stress. Psychopathology may also arise from biopsychosocial factors, which includes biological, psychological, and sociocultural factors.

14.3 Disordered Thoughts, Emotions, and/or Behaviors Can Be Assessed and Categorized

Review the learning goal activities on p. 551. Assessment is the process of examining mental functions and actions to classify symptoms into categories. Four main methods of assessment are used: (1) interviews, (2) self-reports, (3) observations, and (4) psychological testing. Based on the assessment, the *DSM-5* allows categorization of the symptoms into one or more of 19 major psychological disorders, which allows for diagnosis and treatment.

KEY TERMS
psychopathology (p. 547)
etiology (p. 548)
diathesis-stress model (p. 549)

How Do People Experience Disorders of Emotion?

14.4 Anxiety Disorders Make People Fearful and Tense

Review the learning goal activities on p. 555. Anxiety disorders are characterized by excessive fear in the absence of danger. The *DSM-5* describes five main types of anxiety disorders: (1) specific phobia, (2) social anxiety disorder, (3) generalized anxiety disorder, (4) panic disorder, and (5) agoraphobia. The development of anxiety disorders is influenced by biopsychosocial factors, such as innate temperament and learning to fear certain situations or objects.

14.5 Some Disorders Have Unwanted and Intrusive Thoughts that Increase Anxiety

Review the learning goal activities on p. 558. Two disorders described in the *DSM-5* are characterized by the presence of anxiety-provoking thoughts. Obsessive-compulsive disorder (OCD) involves repeated intrusive thoughts that cause great anxiety and compulsive behaviors that temporarily relieve the anxiety. OCD is caused by biopsychosocial factors, such as genetics and processing in certain brain areas as well as classically conditioned fear responses. Posttraumatic stress disorder (PTSD) is characterized by unwanted, recurring thoughts about a trauma that caused great anxiety, which include nightmares and flashbacks.

14.6 Depressive Disorders Consist of Sad, Empty, or Irritable Mood

Review the learning goal activities on p. 561. Depressive disorders include a depressed mood that features persistent and pervasive feelings of sadness. The *DSM-5* includes two main depressive disorders: (1) major depressive disorder, which is severe episodes of depression that last for two weeks or longer, and (2) persistent depressive disorder, which is mild to moderate depression that lasts for two years or more.

14.7 Many Factors Influence the Development of Depressive Disorders

Review the learning goal activities on p. 563. The development of depressive disorders is influenced by biopsychosocial factors. Biological factors include genetics, damage to certain brain structures (left prefrontal cortex), and alterations in biological rhythms. Psychological factors include the presence of stressors; negative thoughts about oneself, the situation, and the future (the cognitive triad); and learned helplessness. Social factors include aspects of culture (such as gender and stigmas about psychological disorders).

14.8 Bipolar Disorders Involve Mania

Review the learning goal activities on p. 566. Bipolar disorders include an elevated mood that varies in intensity. According to the *DSM-5*, two main types of bipolar disorders are: (1) bipolar I disorder, with episodes of extreme mania and possibly major depression, and (2) bipolar II disorder, with episodes of mild hypomania as well as major depression. The development of bipolar disorders seems to be primarily influenced by genetics.

KEY TERMS
specific phobia (p. 556)
social anxiety disorder (p. 556)
generalized anxiety disorder (p. 557)
panic disorder (p. 557)
agoraphobia (p. 558)
obsessive-compulsive disorder (OCD) (p. 559)
posttraumatic stress disorder (PTSD) (p. 560)
major depressive disorder (p. 562)
persistent depressive disorder (p. 562)
bipolar I disorder (p. 567)
bipolar II disorder (p. 567)

How Do People Experience Disorders of Thought?

14.9 Schizophrenia Involves a Disconnection from Reality

Review the learning goal activities on p. 569. Schizophrenia is a psychotic disorder that is characterized by extreme alterations in thought, in perceptions, and in consciousness that are associated with a break from reality. According to the *DSM-5*, it is diagnosed according to five criteria: (1) delusions (false beliefs), (2) hallucinations (perceptions in the absences of environmental input), (3) disorganized speech (language that is incoherent), (4) disorganized behavior (strange behavior), and (5) negative symptoms (the reduction of typical behavior—for example, apathy, lack of emotion, slowed speech, and slowed movements).

14.10 Schizophrenia Is Caused by Biological and Environmental Factors

Review the learning goal activities on p. 572. Schizophrenia is a genetically related disorder characterized by abnormal brain structures and processes. Environmental factors, such as the stress of dysfunctional family dynamics or urban environments, may trigger the onset of schizophrenia.

KEY TERMS
schizophrenia (p. 569)
positive symptoms (p. 569)
negative symptoms (p. 569)
delusions (p. 570)
hallucinations (p. 570)
disorganized speech (p. 571)
disorganized behavior (p. 571)

How Do People Experience Disorders of Self?

14.11 Personality Disorders Are Maladaptive Ways of Relating to the World

Review the learning goal activities on p. 574. Personality disorders result from a person's identity causing problems with how the person interacts with others. The *DSM-5* categorizes personality disorders into three groups: (1) Cluster A: odd or eccentric behavior; (2) Cluster B: dramatic, emotional, or erratic behavior; (3) Cluster C: anxious or fearful behavior. People with borderline personality disorder lack a strong sense of self and are very emotionally unstable and impulsive. Antisocial personality disorder (APD) includes behaving in socially undesirable ways, a willingness to take advantage of and hurt others, and a lack of remorse.

14.12 Dissociative Disorders Involve Disruptions in the Sense of Self

Review the learning goal activities on p. 579. Dissociative disorders are disruptions in one's identity, memory, or conscious awareness. Dissociative amnesia involves forgetting that events happened or losing awareness of a large block of time. A certain form of dissociative amnesia, called dissociative fugue, also includes a person traveling to another location and perhaps even assuming a new identity. A person with dissociative identity disorder (DID) has two or more identities, which may have developed to help the person cope with severe trauma. This diagnosis is controversial.

KEY TERMS
borderline personality disorder (p. 576)
antisocial personality disorder (APD) (p. 577)
dissociative amnesia (p. 579)
dissociative identity disorder (DID) (p. 580)

What Disorders Affect Children?

14.13 Children May Experience Neurodevelopmental Disorders

Review the learning goal activities on p. 581. The DSM-5 describes six neurodevelopmental disorders that can affect children: (1) intellectual disabilities, (2) communication disorders, (3) autism spectrum disorder, (4) attention-deficit/hyperactivity disorder, (5) specific learning disorder, and (6) motor disorders.

14.14 Autism Spectrum Disorder Involves Social Deficits and Restricted Interests

Review the learning goal activities on p. 582. Autism spectrum disorder is characterized by deficits in social interactions; impaired communication; and restricted, repetitive behavior and interests. A mild form of autism, which has been called Asperger syndrome, is characterized by similar impairments but normal intellectual capacities. Autism has genetic and environmental causes.

14.15 Attention-Deficit/Hyperactivity Disorder Is a Disruptive Impulse Control Disorder

Review the learning goal activities on p. 584. Children with attention-deficit/hyperactivity disorder (ADHD) are overly active, inattentive, and impulsive. The causes of ADHD are still being investigated. Environmental factors, genetics, and brain function all contribute to the development of ADHD.

KEY TERMS
neurodevelopmental disorders (p. 581)
autism spectrum disorder (p. 582)
attention-deficit/hyperactivity disorder (ADHD) (p. 585)

CHAPTER 14 SELF-QUIZ

To make sure you learned the information in this chapter, write answers to the following questions and check your answers. **See Appendix B for answers to the self-quiz.**

1. Which of the following college students is most likely at risk of developing psychopathology?
   a. Elijah, who has frequent disagreements with classmates that make them uncomfortable
   b. Jan, who likes to sing and dance at her desk even though her teachers sometimes yell at her for doing it
   c. Jeremy, who has uncontrollable urges to eat nonedible objects, such as chalk, so often that these urges interfere with his life
   d. Emily, who likes to ride the elevator facing backward, even though most people face forward

2. Crystal points out that abuse in childhood can create a predisposition in women for depression, which can be triggered by stress later in life. Based on this statement, Crystal seems to adhere to the _____ to the cause of disorders.
   a. assessment approach
   b. biopsychosocial approach
   c. psychopathology model
   d. diathesis-stress model

3. Kat constantly worries, even over small things. She is always on high alert and is so easily distracted that she had to quit her job. This information suggests that Kat would most likely be diagnosed with _____.
   a. social anxiety disorder
   b. generalized anxiety disorder
   c. panic disorder
   d. agoraphobia

4. Mary experiences feelings of deep sadness that last for several months at a time and make it hard for her to get out of bed to care for her children. However, she sometimes experiences short periods where she is a bit more creative and energized than normal and is able to succeed at her job as a book illustrator. Mary is most likely experiencing _____ disorder.
   a. bipolar I
   b. major depressive
   c. bipolar II
   d. persistent depressive

5. William hears a voice inside his head that urges him to steal money and lab equipment from a medical research center. William is most likely experiencing _____, which are a _____ symptom of schizophrenia.
   a. hallucinations; positive
   b. delusions; positive
   c. hallucinations; negative
   d. delusions; negative

6. Warren has schizophrenia. He believes that a chip has been implanted in his brain and that it lets his boss spy on his thoughts about the company. Warren's belief is best characterized as a _____ delusion.
   a. grandiose
   b. control
   c. referential
   d. persecution

7. During conversations with his therapist, Paul often makes comments that reveal his vast mood swings, unstable relationships, and impulsivity. As a result, Paul's therapist would probably characterize him as having _____ personality disorder.
   a. avoidant
   b. borderline
   c. paranoid
   d. dependent

8. Twin sisters Molly and Holly both have peculiar psychological conditions. Once, Molly woke up on her kitchen floor, not knowing her name or how she came to be in her house. Holly disappeared and turned up a month later in a different state, living as "Nicole" and with no memory of her former life. Molly most likely has dissociative _____, whereas Holly most likely has dissociative _____.
   a. fugue; amnesia
   b. identity disorder; amnesia
   c. amnesia; fugue
   d. identity disorder; fugue

9. Rhiannon is a 3-year-old who does not talk yet. When her parents talk to her, Rhiannon does not look at them or smile. Rhiannon's attention is mainly captured by anything related to dinosaurs. For hours, she will play with dinosaur figures or watch TV shows about dinosaurs. Based on this information, Rhiannon is most likely to be diagnosed with _____.
   a. a specific learning disorder
   b. an intellectual disability
   c. a motor disorder
   d. autism spectrum disorder

10. Louis, a 7-year-old, has a hard time keeping friends. Although he can be very friendly and outgoing, he is inattentive to classmates. During recess, he acts impulsively, often running from group to group and interrupting their games. Louis's behavior is most consistent with having _____.
    a. autism spectrum disorder
    b. attention-deficit/hyperactivity disorder
    c. Asperger's syndrome
    d. a motor disorder

How Can Understanding Psychological Disorders Become a Career?

On television crime dramas such as *Criminal Minds* and *CSI*, FBI investigators in the Behavioral Analysis Unit rush to identify murderers. A case is often solved when the show's forensic psychologist creates a psychological profile that leads to the suspect. Forensic psychology involves applying what is known from the science of psychology to the legal system. With the popularity of crime shows, there has been increased interest in forensic psychology as a career. Although FBI agents, rather than forensic psychologists, are responsible for "criminal profiling," what you learn in this chapter is relevant to many careers that involve legal questions and settings.

Mental health issues arise for both criminals and the victims of their crimes. As discussed in this chapter, people with antisocial personality disorder take advantage of or hurt others, and they frequently break the law. Once criminals have been caught, law-enforcement officials who work with them benefit from understanding how to identify psychopathology and how to deal with those who have it. Understanding psychological disorders helps corrections officers keep prison inmates safe and secure. Understanding how certain disorders, such as those that include impulsivity, may increase the likelihood of reoffending helps probation officers predict whether individuals will commit new crimes once those individuals are released from prison. Probation officers can also encourage individuals to seek mental health support for psychological disorders those individuals are experiencing.

The victims of crime can develop psychological disorders related to anxiety or depression. In addition, being the victim of a violent crime can lead to PTSD. Victim advocates help crime victims navigate the legal system, such as explaining their rights, attending court with them, and helping them fill out difficult paperwork. The job of victim advocate requires understanding how life circumstances contribute to the development of psychological disorders. Many jobs related to forensic psychology involve assessing people who are involved with the legal system. For instance, as a forensic interviewer, you may be called on to assess children who are victims of physical or sexual abuse.

The job duties of forensic psychologists may include evaluating child custody disputes, treating crime victims, designing treatment programs for criminal offenders, and assessing the risk of a criminal's reoffending. Forensic psychologists can also be very influential in court cases. They may testify about the reliability of eyewitness testimony, or they may be called on to assess a defendant's state of mind, particularly in regard to an "insanity defense." Insanity is a legal rather than psychological concept. But a forensic psychologist might conclude that the accused is suffering from a psychological disorder, such as schizophrenia, that prevents the person from distinguishing between right and wrong.

TAKEAWAY POINT: Understanding the development and effects of psychological disorders can help those working with criminals or with crime victims perform their jobs supportively. Knowledge of clinical assessments has important applications in legal settings and can lead to careers in forensic psychology.

 You can look up job descriptions, education requirements, salaries, and more at the Bureau of Labor Statistics: www.bls.gov. Visit the site and start putting psychology to work!

15 Psychological Treatments

WHAT IS IT LIKE to be the parent of a child with autism spectrum disorder? In 2004, John O'Neil, who was then an editor at the *New York Times,* described the diagnosis and treatment of his son James. As a toddler, James had begun to show signs of being "different." He had difficulty looking his parents in the eye and did not display a strong sense of emotional connection with them. James showed little interest in objects, even toys that were given or shown to him. Instead, he repeated behaviors to the point of harming himself. For example, he pulled his cowboy boots on and off until his feet were raw. He responded to loud noises by crying.

BIG QUESTIONS

How Are Psychological Disorders Treated?

What Are the Most Effective Treatments?

Can Personality Disorders Be Treated?

How Can Disorders Be Treated in Children and Adolescents?

FIGURE 15.1

James O'Neil

At the time of this photo, James **(center)** was 8 years old. At left is his friend Larry, also 8. At right is James's brother, Miles, who was 6.

James's behavior really started to change for the worse when he was 2½, following the birth of a baby brother and a move to a new house. His parents assumed he was overwhelmed, but the director of James's new preschool noticed the telltale signs of autism spectrum disorder. On her recommendation, a professional assessed James and diagnosed him with the disorder. During the first visit to a speech therapist, James's condition had reached the point that he forgot his own name.

As you will learn in this chapter, the best type of therapy for autism requires that parents and teachers spend hours working closely with the child. James's day might begin with physical activities to strengthen coordination and build body awareness. During a snack break, his appropriate social behaviors (such as saying "please") would be reinforced. Each part of the day was devoted to work on James's problem areas. He spent up to eight hours every day performing tasks that most children would find extremely boring. For example, he had to repeatedly imitate the therapist's placing two blocks next to each other or touching her nose. Along the way, his progress was charted to guide upcoming sessions. If James was going to be able to attend mainstream school, his language skills had to improve. Encouraged by being given any treat he asked for, James learned to talk.

He started school with the assistance of one of his full-time instructors, who attended class with him. Despite some rocky moments, James made tremendous progress. He still had problems in some areas, such as reading comprehension, math, attention, and social skills. He did not understand why he had a disorder and other kids did not. But James triumphed. Perhaps his biggest accomplishment was making friends with a classmate named Larry (**Figure 15.1**).

James's father wondered what brought James and Larry together as friends. Perhaps it was their shared love of potty humor. Perhaps they were similarly warm and enthusiastic. One day, O'Neil overheard the two friends engaged in silly conversation. They were telling stupid jokes and gossiping about their "girlfriends." In that moment, O'Neil realized how many of his dreams for James had been realized.

Psychological research continues to aid in the development of effective treatments for disorders such as autism. The goal of this research is to help people like James live happy and healthy lives. The resulting treatments improve the lives of people who have the disorders and their families, and thus the treatments have a positive influence on society. This chapter discusses the latest treatments for many psychological disorders.

How Are Psychological Disorders Treated?

Throughout history, the treatment of psychological disorders has been based on what people believed was the cause of the disorders. For example, the earliest views of psychopathology explained "madness" as resulting from possession by spirits or demons. "Treatments" to cast out these evil influences included magic potions, exorcism, bloodletting, and drilling holes into the skull to release the spirits or demons.

Of course, none of these treatments worked, and people with psychological problems were often seen as a nuisance to society. During the second half of the

Middle Ages, people with psychopathology were often removed from society so that they would not bother others. They were placed in overcrowded institutions called asylums (**Figure 15.2**). People in asylums were often chained up and lived in incredibly filthy conditions. The "treatments" they received included starvation, beatings, and isolation.

In 1793, Philippe Pinel, a French physician, argued that treatments should be based on what actually works to reduce psychopathology. Pinel removed patients from their chains and ended physical punishment. He began what came to be known as *moral treatment,* which involved close contact with patients and careful observation of them. Pinel's kinder approach gained a foothold in Europe. Later, the Massachusetts schoolteacher Dorothea Dix promoted moral treatment in America. However, this method often did little to reduce the symptoms of psychopathology.

There are no instant cures for psychological disorders. Some treatments are more successful than others. Disorders need to be managed over time through treatment that helps reduce symptoms so people can function well in their daily lives. This approach includes a continuous cycle of assessment, diagnosis, and treatment, followed by ongoing assessment and continued treatment. The choice of treatment depends on the type and severity of symptoms as well as on the specific diagnosis. In the following study units, you will learn about how particular treatments may be more likely to reduce the symptoms of particular disorders.

(a)

(b)

15.1 Some Types of Psychotherapy Focus on Providing Insight

15.1 LEARNING GOAL ACTIVITIES

To maximize your learning, complete the following learning goal activities:

a. Understand all bold and italic terms by writing explanations of them in your own words.

b. Understand psychodynamic therapy by explaining its main goal and naming and describing the two main techniques that were used in psychoanalysis.

c. Understand humanistic therapy by describing its main goal and naming and explaining the two main techniques used in client-centered therapy.

FIGURE 15.2

A Scandalous Example of Psychological "Treatment"

(a) Bethlem Hospital was opened in 1247, in London, England. Its nickname, Bedlam, has come to mean uproar and confusion. This definition initially described the terrible conditions at the hospital. **(b)** James Norris, an American, was a patient at Bethlem in 1814. His mistreatment prompted laws to treat patients in asylums more humanely.

The name for any formal psychological treatment aimed at changing thoughts and behavior is **psychotherapy**. The particular techniques used may depend on the practitioner's training, but all forms of psychotherapy involve interactions between practitioner and client. These interactions are vital in helping clients understand their symptoms and problems as well as providing solutions for those symptoms and problems.

Therapists generally use psychotherapy to change their clients' thought patterns, feelings, and/or behavior. The methods used to bring about such changes can differ dramatically, however. One researcher estimated that more than 400 approaches to treatment are available (Kazdin, 1994). Many therapists follow an *eclectic* approach. That is, they use various techniques that seem appropriate for the particular client. Study units 15.1–15.3 highlight the most common psychotherapy treatments that have been used over the past century, which are summarized in **Table 15.1,** on p. 596. Unfortunately, psychological disorders are very common, but many people who need help do not seek treatment. You may know someone who has resisted getting treatment for a psychological disorder, as described in Has It Happened to You? on p. 596.

psychotherapy
Treatment for psychological disorders where a therapist works with clients to help them overcome their psychological problems and disorders.

TABLE 15.1
Seven Approaches to Psychotherapy

Approach	Therapy Goals	Therapy Methods
Psychodynamic therapy	Help clients become aware of unconscious conflicts and defense mechanisms	Psychoanalysis with free association and dream analysis
Humanistic therapy	Help clients fulfill their potential for personal growth	Client-centered therapy with active listening and unconditional positive regard
Behavior therapy	Help clients replace harmful behaviors with beneficial ones	Behavior modification, including rewards and punishments, token economies, social skills training, and modeling
Cognitive therapy	Help clients eliminate distorted thoughts and replace them with more-realistic ones	Cognitive therapy that includes cognitive restructuring and/or rational-emotive therapy
Cognitive-behavioral therapy	Help clients change both distorted thoughts and maladaptive behavior	May use a mix of any behavior therapy and cognitive therapy
Group therapy	Provide support while also improving social skills cost-effectively	Often uses an eclectic mix of psychotherapy approaches
Family therapy	Heal family relationships	Systems approach; often uses an eclectic mix of psychotherapy approaches

PSYCHODYNAMIC THERAPY   One of the first people to develop treatments for psychological disorders was Sigmund Freud. Along with Josef Breuer, Freud pioneered the method of *psychoanalysis*. This method was based on the idea that psychological disorders were caused by prior experiences, especially early traumatic experiences, that created unconscious conflicts in the people with the disorders.

Freud's psychoanalytic treatment involved identifying these unconscious conflicts. They existed, he believed, in feelings and drives that created maladaptive thoughts and behaviors. Techniques for finding inner conflicts included *free association* and *dream analysis*. In free association, the client would say whatever came to mind and the therapist would look for signs of unconscious conflicts, especially where the client appeared resistant to discussing certain topics. In dream analysis, the therapist would interpret the hidden meaning of the client's dreams. In early forms of psychoanalysis, the client would lie on a couch while the therapist sat out of view (**Figure 15.3**). This method was meant to reduce the client's inhibitions and allow freer access to unconscious thought processes.

The general goal of psychoanalysis is to increase clients' awareness of their own unconscious psychological processes and how these processes affect daily functioning. This awareness is called *insight*. By gaining this insight, clients were thought to be freed from these unconscious influences. According to psychoanalysis, clients' symptoms should reduce as a result of addressing unconscious conflicts.

Psychotherapists later revised some of Freud's ideas and developed a number of adaptations. These later developments are known collectively as **psychodynamic therapy.** In using the psychodynamic approach, a therapist aims to help clients examine their unconscious needs, motives, and defenses. The insight that results from this process is important because it is meant to help clients understand why they are distressed. Most supporters of the psychodynamic perspective today continue to embrace Freud's "talking therapy." They have replaced the couch with a chair, and the talking tends to be more conversational. During the past few decades, the use of psychodynamic therapy has become increasingly controversial. Traditional psychodynamic therapy is expensive and time-consuming, sometimes continuing for many years. Moreover, there is little scientific evidence for the effectiveness of psychodynamic therapy in treating psychological disorders.

Recently, a briefer form of psychodynamic therapy, such as focusing on emotional conflicts that result from defense mechanisms, has been found to be more effective than no treatment at all (Lilliengren et al., 2016). However, it is not clear whether the psychodynamic parts of the treatment are better than other brief forms of therapy, such as simply talking about personal problems to a caring therapist. The chance to talk about your problems with someone who listens is important for any type of therapy.

HUMANISTIC THERAPY As you learned in study unit 13.6, the humanistic approach to personality emphasizes personal experience and the individual's belief systems. So **humanistic therapy** likewise works to help people learn to understand themselves and their goals and supports them in fulfilling their potential for personal growth.

One of the best-known humanistic therapies is *client-centered therapy.* This approach was developed by the psychologist Carl Rogers. Client-centered therapy encourages people to fulfill their potential for personal growth through greater self-understanding. In other words, when clients gain insight into their problems, they have the chance to become the best people they can be.

One key aspect of client-centered therapy is the creation of a safe and comforting setting for clients to access their true feelings. An important factor in achieving this goal is the relationship between therapist and client. A good relationship can provide hope that help will be received (Miller, 2000; Talley, Strupp, & Morey, 1990).

Another key aspect of humanistic therapy is the technique *active listening.* Here, the therapist listens attentively to clients, repeats the clients' concerns to help them clarify their feelings, and asks for further clarification when necessary (**Figure 15.4**). Therapists strive to be genuine and empathic, to take the clients' perspectives, and to accept the clients through *unconditional positive regard.* The therapist does not direct the clients' behavior or pass judgment on their actions or thoughts. Instead, the therapist helps the clients focus on their subjective experiences. Relatively few practitioners follow the principles of humanistic theory strictly. But in establishing a good therapeutic relationship between therapist and client, many practitioners use techniques advocated by Rogers.

FIGURE 15.3

Psychodynamic Therapy Aims to Resolve Unconscious Conflicts

As part of the treatment process of psychoanalysis, Freud sat behind his desk (partly visible in the lower left corner). His clients would lie on the couch, facing away from him. Through free association, dream analysis, and other techniques, Freud worked to help the client become aware of unconscious conflicts that were causing distress.

psychodynamic therapy
Treatment for psychological disorders where a therapist works with clients to help them gain insight about how their unconscious processes may be causing inner conflict and impairing daily functioning.

humanistic therapy
Treatment for psychological disorders where a therapist works with clients to help them develop their full potential for personal growth through greater insight.

FIGURE 15.4

Humanistic Therapy Aims to Help People Fulfill Their Potential

Carl Rogers founded the form of humanistic therapy called client-centered therapy. Here, Rogers (far right, wearing glasses) leads a group therapy session, demonstrating the importance of a safe and comforting environment in the pursuit of greater self-understanding.

FIGURE 15.5

Behavior Therapy Helps People Learn Desired Behaviors

A person can use operant conditioning as a form of behavior therapy. For example, someone who bites his nails can snap a rubber band on his finger or wrist when he performs this behavior. Even this small punishment will decrease the behavior.

15.2 Behavioral and Cognitive Treatments Aim to Change Behavior, Emotion, and/or Thought Directly

15.2 LEARNING GOAL ACTIVITIES

To maximize your learning, complete the following learning goal activities:

a. Understand all bold and italic terms by writing explanations of them in your own words.

b. Understand the three therapies that aim to change behavior, emotion, and/or thought by naming and explaining each therapy.

Many of the most successful therapies involve trying to change a client's behavior, emotion, or thought directly. These therapies are behavioral, cognitive, or a combination of the two. Recall that psychodynamic therapies consider maladaptive behavior the result of an underlying problem. By contrast, behavior and cognitive therapies treat the thoughts, emotions, and behaviors as the problems. For example, the therapist is not particularly interested in *why* someone has developed a fear of elevators. Instead, the therapist targets the client's thoughts and behaviors as a way of helping the client overcome the fear.

BEHAVIOR THERAPY The main idea behind **behavior therapy** is that maladaptive behaviors can be replaced with adaptive ones through the use of classical and operant conditioning (**Figure 15.5**). As discussed in study units 6.8–6.12, behavior modification is based on operant conditioning. It is a method of helping people to learn desired behaviors and unlearn unwanted behaviors. Desired behaviors are reinforced (reinforcers might include small treats or praise). Unwanted behaviors are ignored or punished (punishments might include groundings, time-outs, or the administration of unpleasant tastes). Many treatment centers use *token economies*. Through these systems, people earn tokens for good behavior and can trade the tokens for rewards or privileges. This technique also increases a person's likelihood of engaging in a desired behavior.

For a desired behavior to be rewarded, however, the client first must exhibit the behavior. A therapist can use *social skills training* to elicit desired behavior. A client who has particular interpersonal difficulties, such as with initiating a conversation, can learn appropriate ways to act in specific social situations. The first step is often *modeling*. Here, the therapist acts out an appropriate behavior. Recall from study unit 6.13 that people learn many behaviors by watching others perform them. In modeling, the client is encouraged to imitate the displayed behavior, rehearse it in therapy, and later use the learned behavior in real-world situations. The successful use of newly acquired social skills is itself rewarding and encourages the continued use of those skills.

COGNITIVE THERAPY **Cognitive therapy** is based on the theory that distorted thoughts can produce maladaptive behaviors and emotions. Thus treatment strategies that modify the distorted thought patterns should eliminate the maladaptive behaviors and emotions. Various approaches to cognitive therapy have been proposed. For example, Aaron Beck has advocated *cognitive restructuring*. Through this approach, a clinician seeks to help clients recognize distorted thought patterns and replace them with ways of viewing the world that are more in tune with reality

behavior therapy
Treatment for psychological disorders where a therapist works with clients to replace maladaptive behaviors with adaptive ones.

cognitive therapy
Treatment for psychological disorders where a therapist works with clients to help them change distorted thought patterns.

(**Figure 15.6**). Albert Ellis, another major thinker in this area, introduced *rational-emotive therapy*. In this approach, the therapist acts as a teacher, explaining clients' errors in thinking and demonstrating more-adaptive ways to think and feel. Although both of these therapies are considered to be cognitive because they primarily target clients' distorted thoughts and feelings, they also include a behavioral component to help clients change their actions.

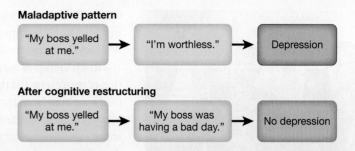

Maladaptive pattern

"My boss yelled at me." → "I'm worthless." → Depression

After cognitive restructuring

"My boss yelled at me." → "My boss was having a bad day." → No depression

FIGURE 15.6

Cognitive Therapy Helps Change Distorted Thought Patterns

A therapist can use cognitive restructuring to help a client learn to replace distorted thought patterns with more-realistic, positive ones.

COGNITIVE-BEHAVIORAL THERAPY Cognitive-behavioral therapy (CBT) incorporates techniques from both behavior therapy and cognitive therapy. CBT tries to correct clients' faulty cognitions and train them to engage in new behaviors. Suppose clients have social anxiety disorder—a fear of being viewed negatively by others. The therapist will encourage the clients to examine other people's reactions to them and understand how they might be wrong about how other people view them. At the same time, the therapist will teach the clients how to change their behavior. CBT is perhaps the most widely used version of psychotherapy. It is one of the most effective therapies for many types of psychological disorders, especially anxiety disorders and depressive disorders (Deacon & Abramowitz, 2004; Hollon, Thase, & Markowitz, 2002). Because anxiety disorders and depressive disorders are often comorbid, CBT that addresses symptoms of both disorders at the same time is especially effective (Newby, McKinnon, Kuyken, Gilbody, & Dalgleish, 2015; for a refresher on comorbidity, see study unit 14.3).

15.3 The Context of Therapy Matters

15.3 LEARNING GOAL ACTIVITIES

To maximize your learning, complete the following learning goal activities:

a. Understand all bold and italic terms by writing explanations of them in your own words.

b. Understand how the context of therapy matters by explaining group therapy, family therapy, and how culture affects therapy.

Some people seek treatment because symptoms, possibly of a psychological disorder, are interfering with their lives. For example, some people would like to overcome feelings of social anxiety that keep them trapped in lonely isolation. By contrast, some people are sent to treatment because their behavior may upset others, such as addicts whose behavior causes conflicts with their families. People's unique circumstances affect their symptoms, psychological disorders, and treatments. As a result, treatments differ depending on family involvement, client resources, and the cultures in which the people needing treatment live. Therapists need to be sensitive both to the cultural meanings of disorders and to how psychological treatments are viewed within those cultures.

GROUP THERAPY In the mid-twentieth century, because of the many stresses related to World War II, many people needed therapy. But there were not enough therapists available to treat them. As a result, the idea of treating people in groups became popular. This form of treatment is called *group therapy*. Therapists came to realize that in some instances, group therapy offers advantages over individual therapy. The most obvious benefit is cost. Group therapy is often much less expensive

cognitive-behavioral therapy (CBT)
Treatment for psychological disorders where a therapist incorporates techniques from cognitive therapy and behavior therapy to correct faulty thinking and maladaptive behaviors.

Family Therapy Heals Relationships
A person with a psychological disorder is part of a larger context. To see the person within at least part of that context, many practitioners take a systems approach to treatment and include family members in therapy.

than individual treatment. Because it is less expensive, it is available to more people. In addition, the group setting gives people an opportunity to improve their social skills and learn from each other's experiences.

Group therapies vary widely in the types of clients enrolled in the group, the duration of treatment, the theoretical perspective of the therapist running the group, and the group size (some practitioners believe the ideal number is around eight clients). Many groups are organized around a particular type of problem (for example, sexual abuse) or a particular type of client (such as for people who are transgender, as described in study unit 10.6). Many groups continue over long periods, during which some members leave the group and others join it at various intervals.

Depending on the therapist's preferred treatment approach, the group may be highly structured. Or it may be more loosely organized to encourage open discussion. For example, behavior therapy groups and cognitive-behavioral therapy groups usually are highly structured. They have specific goals and techniques designed to modify the behavior and thought patterns of group members. This type of group has been effective for disorders such as bulimia and obsessive-compulsive disorder. The social support that group members can provide each other is one of the most helpful aspects of this type of therapy. Those who are experiencing similar issues in their lives might more easily empathize with the experiences of other group members (Heck, 2016).

FAMILY THERAPY   During treatment for a psychological disorder, the therapy the client receives is of course an important element. But the client's family often plays an almost equally important role, and therefore family therapy attempts to include all family members in the process of therapy (**Figure 15.7**).

According to a *systems approach,* an individual is part of a larger context. Any change in individual behavior will affect the whole system. This effect is often easiest to see within families. Each person in a family plays a particular role and interacts with the other members in specific ways. Over the course of therapy, the way the individual thinks, behaves, and interacts with others may change. Such changes can greatly affect the family dynamics. For instance, an alcoholic who gives up drinking may start to criticize other family members when they drink. In turn, the family members might provide less support for the client's continuing to avoid alcohol. After all, if the family members do not have drinking problems, they might resent being criticized. If they do have drinking problems, they might be irritated by the comments because they do not want to give up drinking. The goal of family therapy is to heal these problems for the entire family.

CULTURAL BELIEFS AFFECT TREATMENT   Different cultures have different views of what psychological disorders are and how or whether they should be treated. For example, the primary symptoms for a particular psychological disorder may vary from one culture to another. How these symptoms are used in diagnosis and treatment will also vary across cultures. As a result, culture has multiple influences on the way psychological disorders are expressed, on which people with psychological disorders are likely to recover, and on people's willingness to seek help.

Psychotherapy is accepted to different extents in different countries. Some countries, such as China and India, have relatively few psychotherapists. Many of these countries are seeing a growing need, as the last two decades or so of economic expansion have brought increasingly stressful lifestyles and an awareness of the mental health problems that come with them. However, the people in some of these countries are resistant to even discussing psychological problems, much less treating them. Because of traditional cultural beliefs, many Chinese distrust emotional expression and avoid seeking help for depression, anger, or grief (Magnier, 2008). Likewise, in India, because of the stigma of psychological disorders, terms such as mental illness, depression, and anxiety are avoided; instead, terms such as tension and strain are used to communicate psychological health problems (Kohn, 2008). Thus, providers need to be sensitive both to the cultural meanings of disorders and to how psychological treatments are regarded within those cultures (**Figure 15.8**).

15.4 Biological Therapies Are Effective for Certain Disorders

15.4 LEARNING GOAL ACTIVITIES

To maximize your learning, complete the following learning goal activities:

a. Understand all bold and italic terms by writing explanations of them in your own words.

b. Understand the types of psychotropic medications by comparing the differences between the five main classes of psychotropic medications.

The psychotherapies you have read about so far are based on the idea that psychological disorders arise from cognition, emotion, and behavior. **Biological therapy,** in contrast, is based on the notion that psychological disorders result from abnormalities in bodily processes, so treatment must address these physical problems. Accordingly, biological therapies reflect medical approaches to illness and to disease.

PSYCHOTROPIC MEDICATIONS For some psychological disorders, drugs have provided effective treatment. Their use is based on the assumption that psychological disorders result from imbalances in specific neurotransmitters or from improperly functioning receptors for those neurotransmitters. Drugs that affect mental processes are called **psychotropic medications.** They act by changing brain neurochemistry, such as by altering how neurotransmitters work in the brain (see Table 2.1, on p. 55) to affect thoughts, emotions, and behavior.

Most psychotropic medications fall into five categories: *anti-anxiety drugs, antidepressants, mood stabilizers, antipsychotics,* and *stimulants.* The use of psychotropic medications is very common in the United States. In 2013, about 1 in 6 U.S. adults reported filling one or more prescriptions for drugs to treat psychological disorders, mostly antidepressants, less commonly anti-anxiety drugs or sleeping pills, and a small percentage of antipsychotics (Moore & Mattison, 2017).

Psychotropics are generally used to treat specific disorders (see **Table 15.2,** on p. 602). Note, however, that drugs from one category are sometimes used to treat a disorder from another category, such as when antidepressant drugs are used to treat anxiety. One reason for this approach is comorbidity. For example, as noted in study unit 14.3, many people experiencing a depressive disorder also meet the diagnostic criteria for an anxiety disorder. Another reason is that in most cases, there is not enough evidence about why a particular drug is effective in reducing symptoms of a psychological disorder. Many questions remain about how brain chemistry is related to psychological disorders, and many drug treatments have been based on trial-and-error clinical trials in which different drugs have been tried to see if they reduce symptoms. Later study units in this chapter go into greater detail about how some of these drugs are effective in treating specific disorders.

biological therapy
Treatment for psychological disorders that is based on medical approaches to illness and to disease.

psychotropic medications
Drugs that affect mental processes and that can be used to treat psychological disorders.

TABLE 15.2
Five Classes of Psychotropic Medications

Drug Classification	Treatment Provided	Drug Type	Side Effects	Drug Brand Names
Anti-anxiety drugs	Temporarily increase sense of calm	Minor tranquilizers	Drowsiness, addiction	• Valium • Xanax • Ativan
Antidepressant drugs	Increase positive mood; reduce emotionality, impulsiveness, and arousal	Selective serotonin reuptake inhibitors (SSRIs)	Sexual dysfunction, nausea, nervousness, weight gain	• Prozac • Paxil • Zoloft
		Tricyclics	Weight gain, dizziness, sexual and digestive problems	• Anafranil • Tofranil • Elavil
Mood stabilizer drugs	Help even out moods, especially manic episodes	Mineral	Blunting of positive affect	• Lithium
Antipsychotic drugs	Reduce positive symptoms of schizophrenia (delusions, hallucinations, disorganized speech and behavior)	Conventional antipsychotics (early antipsychotics)	Tardive dyskinesia, seizures, lethargy	• Thorazine • Haldol
	Reduce positive and some negative symptoms of schizophrenia (lethargy, lack of emotion) and disturbed thoughts in mania in bipolar disorders	Atypical antipsychotics (recent antipsychotics)	Potentially fatal loss of white blood cells, seizures, heart rate problems, weight gain, Type 2 diabetes	• Clozaril • Risperdal • Zyprexa • Seroquel
Stimulants	Decrease hyperactivity, distractibility; increase attention, concentration	Methylphenidate	Insomnia, reduced appetite, body twitches, temporary suppression of growth	• Ritalin
		Amphetamine	Insomnia, nausea, weight loss, vomiting, nervousness	• Adderall

FIGURE 15.9

Electroconvulsive Therapy Can Relieve Depression

A woman being prepared for ECT has a soft object placed between her teeth to prevent her from hurting her tongue. ECT is most commonly used to treat severe depression that has not been responsive to medication or psychotherapy.

ALTERNATIVE TREATMENTS FOR EXTREME CASES Unfortunately, not all people experiencing psychological disorders are treated successfully with psychotherapy, medication, or a combination of both. In extreme treatment-resistant cases, practitioners may suggest alternative biological treatments, such as electrical or magnetic stimulation of the brain, or brain surgery in the most extreme cases.

Electroconvulsive therapy (ECT) involves placing electrodes on a client's head and administering an electrical current strong enough to produce a seizure (Figure 15.9). This procedure was developed in Europe in the 1930s. It was first tried on a human in 1938. In the 1950s and 1960s, it was commonly and successfully used to treat some psychological disorders, including schizophrenia and depression. However, researchers still do not know precisely how ECT achieves these positive treatment effects.

The general public has a very negative view of ECT. This view comes partly from Ken Kesey's 1962 novel *One Flew over the Cuckoo's Nest,* as well as the award-winning 1975

FIGURE 15.10

Transcranial Magnetic Stimulation Treats Depression

In TMS, a wire coil is placed over the scalp where a brain area is to be stimulated. When electrical current passes through the coil, a magnetic field is created. When the coil is turned on and off, this action interrupts brain function in the stimulated region (for example, see the area in yellow). TMS is used mainly to treat severe depression.

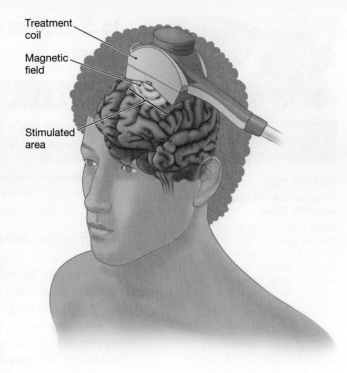

film version. Kesey graphically depicted ECT and its extreme side effects, as well as the tragic effects of brain surgeries such as lobotomy and abuses in mental health care generally. Although care for those with psychological disorders is still far from perfect, many reforms have been made. ECT now generally occurs under anesthesia, using powerful muscle relaxants to eliminate muscular convulsions. As discussed in study unit 15.8, ECT is particularly effective for some cases of severe depression, but this treatment still involves some risks.

During **transcranial magnetic stimulation (TMS),** which you first read about in study unit 2.4, an electrical current produces a powerful magnetic field. When rapidly switched on and off, this magnetic field creates an electrical current in the brain region directly below the coil, thereby interrupting the activity of neurons in that region (**Figure 15.10**). TMS has been used with some success in cases of depression, as discussed in study unit 15.8.

One of the most dramatic new techniques for treating severe psychological disorders is **deep brain stimulation (DBS).** This brain surgery technique involves surgically implanting electrodes deep within the brain, at differing sites depending on the disorder. Mild electricity is then used to stimulate the particular region of the brain at an optimal frequency and intensity, much the way a pacemaker stimulates the heart (**Figure 15.11**). DBS is being tested for treating various psychological disorders. As discussed in study unit 15.8, DBS might be especially valuable for treating severe obsessive-compulsive disorder (OCD) and depression.

electroconvulsive therapy (ECT)
Treatment for psychological disorders that involves administering a strong electrical current to the client's brain to produce a seizure; ECT is effective in some cases of severe depression.

transcranial magnetic stimulation (TMS)
Treatment for psychological disorders that uses a magnetic field to interrupt function in specific regions of the brain.

deep brain stimulation (DBS)
Treatment for psychological disorders that involves passing electricity through electrodes planted in the client's brain to stimulate the brain at a certain frequency and intensity.

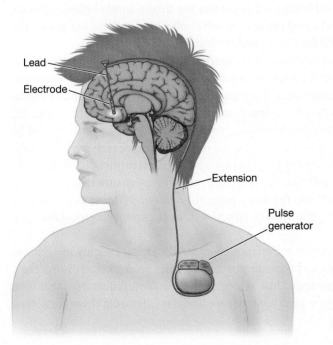

FIGURE 15.11

Deep Brain Stimulation Is Used to Treat Depression and Obsessive-Compulsive Disorder

In DBS, an electrical generator placed just under the skin below the collarbone sends out continuous stimulation to electrodes implanted in the brain (see the area in yellow). DBS is used to treat OCD and major depressive disorder.

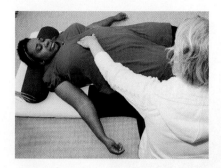

FIGURE 15.12

Rebirthing: A "Therapy" with No Scientific Basis

Some practitioners claim that rebirthing therapy can promote attachment and reduce traumas remaining from birth. However, there is no scientific evidence that rebirthing therapy has any benefit.

15.5 Scientific Evidence Indicates Which Treatments Are Safe and Effective

15.5 LEARNING GOAL ACTIVITIES

To maximize your learning, complete the following learning goal activities:

a. Understand all bold and italic terms by writing explanations of them in your own words.

b. Understand the importance of evidence-based psychotherapies by explaining how you can know a treatment is safe and effective.

Reenacting your own birth, screaming, and having body parts manipulated are a few activities that have been offered as "psychotherapy" (**Figure 15.12**). Do they work? Many available "therapies," such as those just mentioned, have no scientific basis. Just as you need to use critical thinking to recognize flawed science, you also need to recognize therapies that do not have scientific evidence of effectiveness.

Some treatments widely believed to be effective not only lack scientific support, but can be counterproductive or even dangerous (Hines, 2003; Lilienfeld, 2007). For instance, exposing adolescents to prisoners or tough treatments supposedly scares them away from committing crimes, but teens in "scared straight" programs show an increase in conduct problems. Children in drug education programs such as DARE are more likely to drink alcohol and smoke cigarettes than children who do not attend such programs. In addition, many self-help books make questionable claims. Given what you know about critical thinking (and emotion and personality), would you trust the information in a book called *Make Anyone Fall in Love with You in 5 Minutes*, or another called *Three Easy Steps for Having High Self-Esteem*?

It is important to recognize the difference between evidence-based psychotherapies and "fringe" therapies because the latter can prevent people from getting effective treatment and may even be dangerous. In one tragic case, a 10-year-old girl died from suffocation after being wrapped in a blanket for 70 minutes during a supposed rebirthing therapy session to simulate her own birth. This was an untested and unscientific method being used to correct the child's unruly behavior (Lowe, 2001). The people conducting the session were unlicensed and had not passed the tests that certify knowledge about psychotherapy.

As with the various psychological theories discussed throughout this book, the only way to know whether a treatment is valid is to conduct empirical research. The researchers should compare the treatment with a control condition, such as receiving helpful information or having supportive listeners (Kazdin, 2008). In keeping with good scientific principles, client-participants should be randomly assigned to conditions. The use of *randomized clinical trials* is a hallmark of good research to establish whether a particular treatment is effective. As you learned in study unit 1.11, random assignment helps ensure that groups are comparable, and it controls for many potential confounds. Most psychologists recommend treatments shown to be effective through careful empirical research (Kazdin, 2008).

Three features characterize evidence-based psychological treatments (Barlow, 2004). First, treatments vary according to the particular psychological disorder and the client's specific symptoms. Just as treatment for asthma differs from that for a broken leg, treatments for panic disorder are likely to differ from those for autism spectrum disorder. Second, the techniques used in these treatments have been developed in the laboratory by psychologists, especially behavioral, cognitive, and social psychologists. Third, treatment is not guided by one single theory about what causes the disorder. Instead, treatment is based on evidence of its effectiveness. If you are interested in a career that uses the best and most effective treatments to help clients overcome psychological disorders, see Putting Psychology to Work on p. 635.

15.6 Various Providers Assist in Treatment for Psychological Disorders

As noted at the start of Chapter 14, nearly half of all Americans meet the criteria for a psychological disorder at some point in their lives. Given the societal impact of such widespread disorders, it's especially important for people with symptoms of disorders to get treatment from qualified professionals. Who provides this treatment? As summarized in **Table 15.3,** on p. 606, the providers of psychological treatment range from those with advanced degrees in clinical psychology (**Figure 15.13a**) to psychiatrists, who have medical degrees (**Figure 15.13b**), to paraprofessionals, who have limited training and provide peer counseling (**Figure 15.13c**). Each type of professional works in different settings and provides different services to people who have psychological disorders or who are experiencing life problems. In addition to mental health specialists, regular health care providers (such as internists and pediatricians), human-services workers (such as school counselors), and volunteers (for example, with self-help groups) provide services related to treatment. No matter who administers the treatment, however, most of the techniques used today have emerged from psychological laboratories.

Choosing the right treatment provider is extremely important for ensuring successful treatment (see Using Psychology in Your Life on p. 607). That professional must have the appropriate training and experience for the specific psychological disorder or life problem, and the person seeking help must believe the therapist is trustworthy and caring. The initial consultation should make the client feel at ease and hopeful that the psychological problem can be resolved. If not, the client should seek another provider.

In most places, psychotropic medication is normally prescribed only by psychiatrists, because they have a medical degree. However, the ability to prescribe medication should play a minor role in the choice of therapist. Efforts are under way to give more practitioners, such as clinical psychologists, the ability to prescribe medications. In New Mexico and Louisiana, clinical

(a)

(b)

(c)

FIGURE 15.13

Providers of Psychological Treatment

Many types of professionals provide treatment for psychological disorders. **(a)** Clinical psychologists either work with clients by providing therapy or conduct research on the effectiveness of various treatments. **(b)** Psychiatrists work in hospitals and treatment centers. They can prescribe psychotropic medications. **(c)** Paraprofessionals often work in the community and provide outreach services to people with psychological disorders.

TABLE 15.3
Providers of Psychological Treatment

Specialty	Training	Degree	Employment
Clinical psychologists	5–7 years of graduate school conducting research on psychological disorders and treatment, including 1 year of clinical internship	PhD	Academics, private practice, hospitals, schools, mental health centers, substance abuse programs
	4–6 years of graduate school developing clinical skills to treat people with psychological disorders, followed by 1 year of internship	PsyD	Private practice, medical settings, mental health centers, substance abuse programs
Psychiatrists	4 years of medical school with 3–5 years of additional specialization in residency programs to treat people with psychological disorders and prescribe psychotropic medications	MD	Hospitals, private practice, mental health centers, academics, substance abuse programs
Counseling psychologists	3–6 years of graduate school developing clinical skills to treat clients' adjustment and life stress problems (academic, relationship, work) but not psychological disorders	Master's degree or PhD	University student health clinics, mental health centers, private practice, schools, wellness programs, rehabilitation facilities, business and organization settings
Psychiatric social workers	2–3 years of graduate training on directing clients to appropriate social and community agency resources, plus specialized training in mental health care	MSW	Mental health centers, private practice, hospitals, community and social service agencies, substance abuse programs
Psychiatric nurses	2 years for an associate's degree (ASN, RN), 4 years for a bachelor's degree (BSN), or 2–3 additional years of graduate training (MSN), but all focus on nursing plus special training in the care of clients with psychological disorders	ASN; RN; BSN; MSN	Hospitals, mental health centers, residential treatment programs
Paraprofessionals	Work under supervision to assist those with mental health problems in the challenges of daily living	Limited advanced training, no advanced degree	Community outreach programs, crisis centers, substance abuse centers, pastoral counseling, mental health hotlines

Note: PhD = Doctor of Philosophy in Psychology; PsyD = Doctor of Psychology; MD = Doctor of Medicine; MSW = Master of Social Work; ASN = Associate of Science in Nursing; RN = Registered Nurse; BSN = Bachelor of Science in Nursing; MSN = Master of Science in Nursing.

psychologists with specialized training in psychoactive drugs can prescribe medications; similar legislation is being proposed elsewhere in the United States (McGrath, 2010). In addition, almost all practitioners have arrangements with physicians who can prescribe medications if necessary. In searching for a provider who is right for you, the most important thing is to find someone who is both empathic and experienced in the methods known to be effective in treating specific psychological disorders.

It is most important that individuals not feel hopeless in their struggles with psychological disorders. They should seek help just as they would for any illness or injury. College students usually have access to low-cost or free therapies at their schools. Most communities have sliding-fee, low-cost, or free facilities to help people who do not have insurance coverage.

How Do You Find a Provider Who Can Help You?

Have you ever felt that the stresses or problems of your life were more than you could cope with alone? Perhaps you thought about seeking therapeutic support but were hesitant. That hesitation is understandable. It's not easy to admit—to yourself or others—that you need extra support. And stepping into a stranger's office and disclosing your personal thoughts and feelings is not easy either. Here are some questions and answers that can help you decide if the time has come, and how to find the right therapist.

How can I know if I need therapy? Many times family members, friends, professors, or physicians encourage college students to seek help for psychological problems. For example, if you go to the health center because you feel tired all the time, the doctor might ask if you have been under stress or feeling sad. These conditions might indicate that you are experiencing depression and could be helped by a therapist. Of course, you might already be aware that you have a psychological problem. For example, if you struggle night after night to fall asleep because of constant worry about your academic performance, you might seek help for dealing with anxiety.

You don't have to be 100 percent certain that you need therapy before seeking it out. You can think of the first couple of sessions as a trial period to help you figure out if therapy would be a valuable tool in your situation.

What kinds of issues can therapists help with? According to the psychologist Katherine Nordal, "Psychologists [and other therapists] work with clients who are looking for help in making lifestyle and behavior changes that lead to better physical and mental health. [They] can help people learn to cope with anxiety or depression, deal with stressful situations, overcome addictions, manage chronic illnesses, both physical and psychological, and break past barriers that might prevent them from reaching their goals" (American Psychological Association, 2010). In other words, therapists can help you deal with various issues, ranging from acute stressors (for example, preparing to move across the country) to chronic concerns (such as managing anxiety).

How do I find a therapist who is a good fit for me and my needs? Most college campuses have counselors who can direct students to appropriate treatment providers. In addition, you can ask your friends, teachers, or clergy if they can recommend someone in your area. And organizations such as the American Psychological Association host referral services, many of which are free and Web based.

But just having a name and phone number does not mean that therapist will be a good fit for you. To figure that out, you will want to do some information gathering up front. First, what are your preferences? Do you think you would be more comfortable working with someone who is the same gender as you? Is it important for the therapist to have a cultural background similar to yours? Second, it is a good idea to make sure the therapist is qualified to treat people with your particular psychological disorder (for example, anxiety or depression) or stressor (such as procrastination or coming out to your parents). Third, pay attention to your comfort level as you interact with the therapist during the first session or two. It is critical for you to find a therapist who is trustworthy and caring. The initial consultation should make you feel at ease and hopeful that your issue can be resolved.

If you do not feel a connection with one therapist, seek another. It might take more than one try to find someone you want to work with, but the effort will be well spent. Remember, therapy involves a kind of relationship. Just as you would not expect every first date to be a love connection, do not expect every therapist to be a good fit for you. Finding someone you connect with can be difficult, but it is extremely important for ensuring successful treatment.

Q How Are Psychological Disorders Treated?

To make sure you learned what you just read, write answers to the following questions and check your answers.

15.1 Why is insight important in psychodynamic and humanistic therapy?

15.2 Why is cognitive-behavioral therapy effective for many disorders, especially anxiety and depressive disorders?

15.3 Why is a systems approach important in family therapy?

15.4 What is the main difference between ECT and TMS?

15.5 How can a person know whether a psychological treatment for a disorder is effective?

15.6 Can all treatment providers prescribe psychotropic medications?

See Appendix B for answers to the red Q questions.

What Are the Most Effective Treatments?

Think back to the story of James that opened this chapter. Although James's parents found an effective treatment for his autism spectrum disorder, the treatment was time-consuming and difficult. Indeed, some psychological disorders are especially hard to treat. In addition, the outcomes of treatment are influenced by how the particular clients and therapists interact, so it is difficult to make comparisons across disorders and therapists. Nevertheless, research over the past three decades has shown that certain types of treatments are particularly effective for specific types of disorders (Barlow, Bullis, Comer, & Ametaj, 2013). The best-practice treatments for anxiety, obsessive-compulsive disorder, mood disorders, and schizophrenia are described in this section and are summarized in **Table 15.4**, on p. 609.

15.7 Anxiety and Obsessive-Compulsive Disorders Are Best Treated with Cognitive-Behavioral Therapy

FIGURE 15.14

Anxiety Disorders Can Be Successfully Treated

The actor Kim Basinger is one of the thousands of people who receive treatment each year for anxiety disorders. After extreme social anxiety led to panic attacks, Basinger did not leave her house for six months. While she still feels "shy," psychotherapy has helped Basinger manage her panic disorder and agoraphobia.

 15.7 LEARNING GOAL ACTIVITIES

To maximize your learning, complete the following learning goal activities:

a. Understand all bold and italic terms by writing explanations of them in your own words.

b. Apply cognitive-behavioral therapy (CBT) to panic disorder by describing how cognitive restructuring and exposure therapy could be used to treat people who feel like they are dying when they have a panic attack.

c. Analyze the impact of different treatments on obsessive-compulsive disorder (OCD) by differentiating the effects of cognitive-behavioral, drug, and alternative treatments for the disorder.

TABLE 15.4

Types of Treatment for Common Psychological Disorders

Category	Examples of Specific Disorders	Types of Treatment	Sample of Possible Techniques
Anxiety disorders	*Specific phobia:* fear of something out of proportion to the threat	CBT	• changing thoughts about feared stimulus • exposure • systematic desensitization
	Panic disorder: sudden attacks of overwhelming terror	CBT	• cognitive restructuring about panic attacks • exposure
Obsessive-compulsive and related disorders	*Obsessive-compulsive disorder:* frequent anxiety-provoking intrusive thoughts (obsessions) and actions that are performed repeatedly to reduce anxiety (compulsions)	CBT	• cognitive restructuring to recognize that all people have intrusive thoughts • exposure and response prevention
		psychotropic medications	• antidepressants
		alternative treatment	• DBS
Depressive disorders	*Major depressive disorder:* depression that is severe, plus other symptoms	psychotropic medications	• antidepressants
		CBT	• alter thinking to address cognitive triad of negative thoughts
		alternative treatments	• phototherapy • exercise • ECT, TMS, DBS
Bipolar and related disorders	*Bipolar disorders:* elevated mood that can range from mild (hypomania) to severe (mania), possibly with symptoms of depression	psychotropic medications	• lithium • atypical antipsychotics • antidepressants may be used cautiously for symptoms of depression
Schizophrenia spectrum and other psychotic disorders	*Schizophrenia:* psychotic disorder with motor, cognitive, behavioral, and perceptual abnormalities	psychotropic medications	• atypical antipsychotics
		behavior therapy	• social skills training • behavioral training for life skills

Note: CBT = cognitive-behavioral therapy; DBS = deep brain stimulation; ECT = electroconvulsive therapy; TMS = transcranial magnetic stimulation.

Most evidence suggests that cognitive-behavioral therapy (CBT) works best to treat nearly all disorders that include anxious thoughts (Hofmann & Smits, 2008; **Figure 15.14**). A key part of behavior therapies for anxiety disorders is an **exposure** component (Abramowitz, 2013; Foa & McLean, 2016). In this technique, which is based on classical conditioning, the client is exposed repeatedly to the

exposure
Therapy technique that involves repeatedly exposing a client to an anxiety-producing stimulus or situation and has the goal of reducing the client's fear.

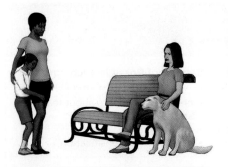

1 The little girl in the white shirt (on the left) has a phobia about dogs.

2 She is encouraged to approach a dog that scares her.

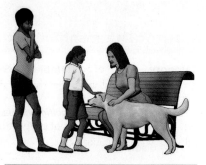

3 From this mild form of exposure she learns that the dog is not dangerous, and she overcomes her fear.

FIGURE 15.15

Using Exposure to Reduce Phobias

Exposure is a common feature of many cognitive-behavioral therapies. In this sequence, exposure is used to help a little girl overcome her fear of dogs. She is not allowed to avoid a dog, and her level of exposure to the dog is gradually increased.

systematic desensitization
Therapy technique that involves exposing a client to increasingly anxiety-producing stimuli or situations while having the client relax at the same time.

FIGURE 15.16

Using Computer Simulations to Conquer Phobias

Computer-generated images can simulate feared environments or social interactions as part of treatment for phobias. For example, in this "virtual world," the client can stand on the edge of a tall building or fly in an aircraft and practice relaxing to get rid of fear. By using a process of systematic desensitization, the client can conquer the virtual situation before taking on the feared situation in real life.

anxiety-producing stimulus or situation (**Figure 15.15**). By confronting feared stimuli in the absence of negative consequences, the person learns new, nonthreatening associations. That is, exposure to the feared object in a safe environment eventually produces extinction.

Anti-anxiety drugs (see Table 15.2, on p. 602) are also beneficial in some cases because they have a sedative effect that makes people feel calmer. With drugs, however, there are risks of side effects and, after drug treatment is terminated, the risk of relapse. For instance, anti-anxiety drugs work in the short term for generalized anxiety disorder, but they do little to lessen the source of anxiety and are addictive. Therefore, they are not a treatment of choice. By contrast, the effects of CBT persist long after treatment, so this remains the best treatment in general for anxiety disorders (Hollon, Stewart, & Strunk, 2006).

Studies have suggested that antidepressants (see Table 15.2) might be useful for social anxiety disorder. In one comprehensive study, researchers found that undergoing CBT was just as effective as taking an antidepressant in treating social anxiety disorder (Davidson et al., 2004). Those taking the antidepressant, however, had more physical complaints, such as lack of sexual interest. This again indicates that CBT rather than drugs is the best choice for social anxiety disorder.

SPECIFIC PHOBIAS Learning theory suggests that specific phobias are acquired either by experiencing a trauma or by observing similar fear in others. However, phobias often develop without being brought about by any particular event. Although learning theory cannot completely explain the development of phobias, behavior techniques are the treatment of choice.

A gradual form of exposure therapy is **systematic desensitization**. In this method, the client imagines increasingly anxiety-producing situations while learning to relax. First, the client makes a *fear hierarchy*, a list of situations in which fear develops, from least fear to greatest. An example of a fear hierarchy is shown in Try It Yourself on p. 611. The next step is relaxation training, in which the client learns to alternate muscular tension with muscular relaxation and to use other relaxation techniques. Exposure therapy is often the next step. While relaxed, the client is asked to enact or imagine scenarios from the fear hierarchy that become more and more upsetting.

A recent alternative is to expose clients to fearful situations without putting them in danger by using computers to simulate the environments and the feared objects (**Figure 15.16**). There is substantial evidence that exposure to these virtual environments can reduce fear responses (Freeman et al., 2017).

PANIC DISORDER Panic disorder has multiple components, and each symptom may require a different treatment. When people feel anxious, they tend to

Everyone is afraid of something. But even if your fears are not as extreme as specific phobias, you can use systematic desensitization to help you conquer fears. First, create a fear hierarchy about something you are afraid of. This sample fear hierarchy was created by a person who wanted to conquer a fear of heights so he could go mountain climbing.

Once you have created your own hierarchy, take yourself through it. Begin by putting yourself in the least fearful situation, either in real life or in your imagination. Then practice relaxation and breathing until you are calm in that situation. Then proceed to the next fearful situation and repeat the process until you are quite relaxed even in the most fearful situation. This technique may take a while. But by going step by step, you may overcome your fear.

Degree of fear	Situation
10	I'm standing on the balcony of the top floor of an apartment tower.
20	I'm sitting on the slope of a mountain, looking out over the horizon.
30	I'm riding a ski lift 8 feet above the ground.
40	I'm climbing a ladder outside the house to reach a second-story window.
50	I'm scrambling up a rock that is 8 feet high.
60	I'm walking on a wide plateau, 2 feet from the edge of a cliff.
70	I'm walking over a railway trestle.
80	I'm riding a chairlift 15 feet above the ground.
90	I'm walking up (or down) a 15-degree slope on a 3-foot-wide trail. On one side of the trail, the terrain drops down sharply; on the other side is a steep upward slope.
100	I'm walking on a 2-foot-wide ridge. The trail slopes on either side are more than 25 degrees.

overestimate the probability of danger, potentially contributing to their rising feelings of panic. To break the learned association between the physical symptoms of anxiety, such as hyperventilation or heart palpitations, and the feeling of impending doom, CBT can be effective.

Cognitive restructuring (see study unit 15.2) is a technique used in cognitive therapy to address ways of reacting to the symptoms of a panic attack. For example, first the clients identify their specific fears, such as having a heart attack or fainting. Then the clients estimate how many panic attacks they have experienced. Therapists help the clients assign percentages to specific fears and then compare these numbers with the actual number of times the fears have been realized. For example, clients might estimate that they fear having a heart attack during 90 percent of their panic attacks and fainting during 85 percent of their attacks. Therapists can then point out that the actual rate of occurrence was zero. In fact, people do not faint during panic attacks. The physical symptoms of a panic attack, such as having a racing heart, are the opposite of fainting.

Even if clients recognize the irrationality of their fears, they may still experience panic attacks. From a cognitive-behavioral perspective, the attacks continue because of a conditioned response to the trigger (such as shortness of breath). The goal of therapy is to break the connection between the trigger symptom and the resulting panic. This break can be made by exposure treatment.

In the treatment of panic attacks, CBT appears to be as effective as or more effective than medication (Schmidt & Keough, 2011). For example, David Barlow and colleagues (2000) found that in the short term, the results were the same for CBT alone as for an antidepressant alone. Six months after treatment ended, however, those who had received CBT were less likely to relapse than those who had taken medication. These results support the conclusion that CBT is the treatment of choice for panic disorder, as it is for other anxiety disorders.

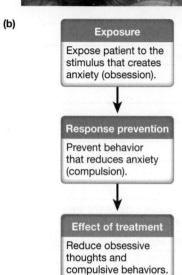

(a)

(b)

Exposure
Expose patient to the stimulus that creates anxiety (obsession).

↓

Response prevention
Prevent behavior that reduces anxiety (compulsion).

↓

Effect of treatment
Reduce obsessive thoughts and compulsive behaviors.

FIGURE 15.17

Using Exposure and Response Prevention to Treat Obsessive-Compulsive Disorder

(a) Someone who obsesses about germs might engage in a compulsive behavior, such as excessive hand washing. **(b)** In exposure and response prevention therapy, the person would be asked to touch something dirty, and then would be prevented from immediately hand washing. The effect should be to break the link between the obsession and the compulsion, reducing both.

FIGURE 15.18

Effectiveness of Treatments for Obsessive-Compulsive Disorder

This graph shows how the numbers of symptoms of OCD changed over a period of 12 weeks based on each type of treatment. The results indicated that treatment with an antidepressant alone did not reduce symptoms as much as did treatment with exposure and response prevention alone.

OBSESSIVE-COMPULSIVE DISORDER As you learned in study unit 14.5, obsessive-compulsive disorder (OCD) is a combination of recurrent intrusive thoughts that cause anxiety (obsessions) and behaviors that a person feels compelled to perform over and over to reduce the anxiety temporarily (compulsions). Once again, cognitive-behavioral therapy (CBT) is the best choice for OCD, although in this case adding an antidepressant might bring additional benefit (Franklin & Foa, 2011).

A common therapy for OCD is **exposure and response prevention**. This treatment is based on the theory that a particular stimulus triggers anxiety and that performing the compulsive behavior is what reduces the anxiety. For example, clients might obsess about germs and then compulsively wash their hands to reduce anxiety after touching a doorknob, using a public telephone, or shaking hands with someone (**Figure 15.17a**). In this variation of exposure therapy, clients are directly exposed to the anxiety-producing stimuli but are prevented from engaging in the compulsive behavior that reduces the anxiety. So clients who obsess about germs would be required to touch a dirty doorknob and then be instructed not to immediately engage in the compulsive behavior of washing their hands afterward (**Figure 15.17b**). As with exposure therapy for panic disorder, the goal is to break the conditioned link between a particular stimulus and a compulsive behavior. When this happens, the avoidance response to stimuli that cause obsessive thoughts is eventually extinguished. Anxiety is reduced, which then reduces the need for the compulsive behavior. This form of therapy is highly effective for treating people with OCD.

Some cognitive therapies are also useful for OCD. For example, cognitive restructuring (see study unit 15.2) may help clients recognize that most people occasionally experience unwanted thoughts and compulsions. Indeed, unwanted thoughts and compulsions are a normal part of human experience.

How does drug treatment with an antidepressant compare with CBT for OCD? In one study, the use of exposure and response prevention proved superior to the use of a specific tricyclic antidepressant, although both were better than *placebos*, which are "sugar pills" that contain no active drugs (Foa et al., 2005; **Figure 15.18**). CBT may thus be a more effective way of treating OCD than medication, especially over the long term. There is evidence that, at a minimum, adding CBT to drug treatment with certain antidepressant drugs may improve outcomes (Simpson et al., 2008).

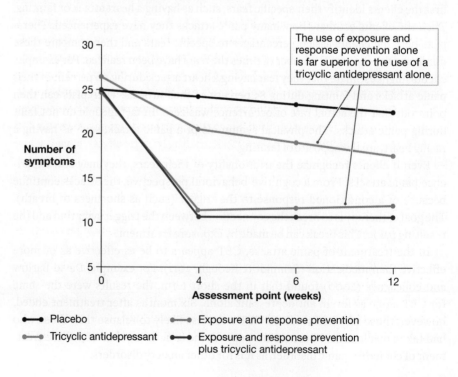

The use of exposure and response prevention alone is far superior to the use of a tricyclic antidepressant alone.

Number of symptoms

Assessment point (weeks)

● Placebo   ● Exposure and response prevention
● Tricyclic antidepressant   ● Exposure and response prevention plus tricyclic antidepressant

One exciting possibility is that deep brain stimulation (DBS) may be an effective treatment for those with OCD who have not found relief from CBT or medications (Ooms et al., 2014). Early studies used psychosurgery, such as lobotomy, to remove brain regions thought to contribute to OCD. There were promising outcomes at times, but these techniques could involve destroying large areas of brain tissue, especially in the frontal lobes. And brain surgery is inherently a risky therapy because it is irreversible. DBS offers new hope.

15.8 Many Effective Treatments Are Available for Depressive Disorders

15.8 LEARNING GOAL ACTIVITIES

To maximize your learning, complete the following learning goal activities:

a. Understand all bold and italic terms by writing explanations of them in your own words.

b. Understand how cognitive-behavioral therapy (CBT) is used to treat people with depressive disorders by explaining in your own words how people with depression can benefit from treatment of the cognitive triad.

As you learned in study unit 14.6, depressive disorders involve depressed moods that range from mild to extreme, lasting anywhere from two weeks to years. Depression is one of the most widespread psychological disorders among adolescents and adults, and it has become more common over the past few decades (Weinberger et al., 2018). Fortunately, scientific research has validated a number of effective treatments. There is no one "best" way to treat depression. Many approaches are available (**Figure 15.19**). Ongoing research is determining which type of therapy works best for which types of individuals.

PSYCHOTROPIC MEDICATIONS FOR DEPRESSIVE DISORDERS In the 1950s, tuberculosis was a major health problem in the United States, particularly in urban areas. A common drug treatment reduced tuberculosis-related bacteria in patients' saliva. It also stimulated patients' appetites, increased their energy levels, and gave them an overall sense of well-being. In 1957, researchers who had noted the drug's effect on mood reported preliminary success in using it to treat depression. In the following year, nearly half a million people experiencing depression were given the drug, although it is no longer used. Since then, various drugs have been used to treat depression (see Table 15.2, on p. 602). Each drug has side effects, however, and different antidepressants can affect people in different ways.

Researchers have attempted to determine how particular types of people will respond to antidepressants. Still, physicians often must resort to a trial-and-error approach in treating clients who are experiencing depression to determine what will work for them. Because of this, no single drug stands out as being most effective. Often the decision of which drug to use depends on the client's overall medical health and the possible side effects of each medication. In general, though, because selective serotonin reuptake inhibitors (SSRIs) have fewer serious side effects than other drugs used (see Table 15.2), they tend to be the first-line medication (Olfson et al., 2002). If a client does not respond to SSRIs, then other antidepressants are used, such as tricyclics, which target different neurotransmitters (see Table 15.2).

exposure and response prevention
Exposing a client to a stimulus that causes anxiety because it triggers obsessive thoughts and then preventing the client from engaging in compulsive behavior to reduce that anxiety.

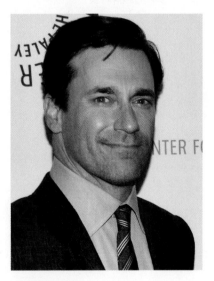

FIGURE 15.19

Depressive Disorders Can Be Successfully Treated

The actor Jon Hamm, from *Mad Men,* has talked publicly about his experiences with chronic depression after the death of his father when Hamm was 20 years old. He credits both psychotherapy and psychotropic medications with helping him overcome the disorder. By using antidepressants, he says, "You can change your brain chemistry enough to think: 'I want to get up in the morning; I don't want to sleep until four in the afternoon. I want to get up and . . . go to work and . . . kick-start the engine!'"

The use of antidepressants is based on the belief that depression (like other psychological disorders) is caused by an imbalance in neurotransmitters or problems with neural receptors. For instance, recall from study unit 2.3 that low levels of serotonin are associated with sad and anxious moods. As a result, SSRIs are designed to leave more serotonin in the synapse to bind with the postsynaptic neurons. Recently, some critics have challenged this view. These critics argue that there is no evidence that people with depression had abnormal brain functioning before drug treatment (Angell, 2011).

Indeed, the treatment of depression with drugs may be based on faulty reasoning. The fact that drugs seem to help symptoms of depression has been viewed as evidence that depression is caused by an abnormality in neurotransmitter function. As a critical thinker, you probably recognize that this connection is not necessarily proof of causation. After all, when you have a cold, you might take a medication that treats your runny nose. Doing so does not prove that your cold was caused by your runny nose. Thus antidepressants may help treat the symptoms of depression without having any influence on the underlying cause.

Other critics have questioned whether antidepressants are more effective than placebos in treating depression. Research generally shows that antidepressants provide somewhat more relief from depressive symptoms than placebos. A recent meta-analysis of studies assessing more than 116,000 clients taking different antidepressants confirmed that most of the 21 drugs studied were better than a placebo at relieving depression, but that some of the drugs were more effective than others or produced fewer side effects (Cipriani et al., 2018). Placebos that produce some side effects (such as a dry mouth) are called active placebos, and they are more likely to produce therapeutic gains than placebos that have no side effects (Kirsch, 2011). This result occurs because the placebos' side effects lead clients to think they are receiving real drugs. So when antidepressants are compared with active placebos, the benefits of antidepressants are more modest. Only drug trials that involve individuals with severe depression show clear benefits of drugs over placebos, in part because people with severe depression show less response to placebo treatments (Kirsch et al., 2008).

COGNITIVE-BEHAVIORAL THERAPY Not all clients benefit from antidepressant medications. In addition, some clients cannot or will not tolerate the side effects. Fortunately, research has shown that cognitive-behavioral therapy (CBT) is just as effective as antidepressants in treating depressive disorders (Hollon et al., 2002).

From a cognitive perspective, people become depressed because of automatic, distorted thoughts. According to the cognitive distortion model developed by Aaron Beck, depression is the result of a cognitive triad of negative thoughts about oneself, the situation, and the future (see Figure 14.18). People with depression think about how they have failed in the past, how poorly they are dealing with the present situation, and how terrible the future will be. The goal of CBT for depression is to identify, reevaluate, and change negative thoughts associated with depression. Ultimately, this approach helps the client think more appropriately and eliminate the cognitive triad of negative thoughts. This change is intended to improve mood and behavior. The specific treatment is adapted to the individual client, but some general principles apply. Clients may be asked to recognize and record negative thoughts. Thinking about situations in a negative way can become automatic, and recognizing these thought patterns can be difficult. Once the patterns are identified and monitored, the clinician can help the client recognize other ways of viewing the same situation that are not so dysfunctional (see Try It Yourself on p. 615).

phototherapy
Treatment for depressive disorder with seasonal pattern, informally called seasonal affective disorder (SAD), through which the client is exposed to high-intensity light each day.

TRY IT YOURSELF: Using a Journal to Reduce Negative Thoughts

We all have negative thoughts at times. These thoughts may be rational or irrational, but they may lead us to feel anxious or sad. In fact, sometimes negative thoughts and the feelings that go with them can appear in patterns. These patterns can be severe enough to be diagnosed as depression.

How can you avoid negative thoughts and negative emotions? Keep a journal to write down your thoughts and emotions. As shown in this sample from a person experiencing depression, you should note the day, the event, your thoughts, and your feelings. Look for patterns in how you think and feel. Use the far column to write down ways to make positive changes in your thoughts and feelings.

Date	Event	Thought	Feeling	Change(s)
April 4	Boss seemed annoyed	*Oh, what have I done now? If I keep making him angry, I am going to get fired.*	Sad, anxious, worried	Explore alternative interpretations. • *Is he annoyed at something other than me?* Don't think of a situation as a catastrophe. • *I am overestimating and probably won't get fired.*
April 5	Husband did not want to make love	*I'm so fat and ugly.*	Sad	Check to see if thinking is influenced by negative views. • *There are positive aspects of my body.*
April 7	Boss yelled at another employee	*I'm next.*	Anxious	Make the best of a bad situation. • *See if I can do anything to help so my boss is less annoyed.*
April 9	Husband said he's taking a long business trip next month	*He's probably got a mistress somewhere. My marriage is falling apart.*	Sad, defeated	Question whether there is evidence to support this idea. • *Is there evidence of an affair?*
April 10	Neighbor brought over some cookies	*She probably thinks that I can't cook. I look like such a mess all the time. And my house was a disaster when she came in.*	A little happy, mostly sad	Stop a cascade of negative thoughts and replace them with positive ones. • *The neighbor just wants to help me.*

CBT can be effective on its own, but combining it with antidepressant medication can be more effective than either one of these approaches alone (Craighead & Dunlop, 2014). The issue is not drugs versus psychotherapy. The issue is what provides relief for each client. For instance, drug treatment may be the most effective option for clients who are suicidal, in acute distress, or unable to regularly attend treatment sessions with a therapist, for example, due to scheduling conflicts. For most clients, especially those who have physical problems such as liver impairment or cardiac problems, CBT may be the treatment of choice because it is long-lasting and does not have the side effects associated with medications (Hollon et al., 2006).

ALTERNATIVE TREATMENTS In clients with a depressive disorder with seasonal pattern, informally called seasonal affective disorder (SAD), episodes of depression are most likely to occur during winter. Many of these clients respond favorably to **phototherapy**. This treatment involves exposure to a high-intensity light source for part of each day (**Figure 15.20**). Research conducted with clients diagnosed with SAD find that phototherapy is effective (Meesters & Gordijn, 2016; Winkler et al., 2017).

FIGURE 15.20

Phototherapy

Phototherapy is one treatment for a depressive disorder with seasonal pattern called SAD. In this method, the client sits in front of strong lighting for several hours each day to reduce symptoms of depression.

THE METHODS OF PSYCHOLOGY
Mayberg's Study of Deep Brain Stimulation for Depression

Hypothesis: Deep brain stimulation of an area of the prefrontal cortex may alleviate depression.

Research Method:

1 A pair of small holes were drilled into the skulls of six participants.

2 A pulse generator was attached under the collarbone, connecting to electrodes that passed through the holes in the skull to a specific area of the prefrontal cortex (see Figure 15.11).

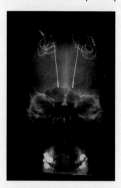

Results: Some participants reported relief as soon as the electrodes were switched on, and two thirds of the participants felt significantly better within months.

Conclusion: DBS may be an especially effective method for clients with depression that is resistant to other treatments.

QUESTION: Is DBS used as an initial treatment for depression?

ANSWER: No. It is used only for those with treatment-resistant depression for whom other treatments do not produce relief.

Source: Mayberg, H. S., Lozano, A. M., Voon, V., McNeely, H. E., Seminowicz, D., Hamani, C., et al. (2005). Deep brain stimulation for treatment-resistant depression. *Neuron, 45,* 651–660.

For some clients with depression, regular aerobic exercise can reduce the symptoms and prevent recurrence (Pollock, 2004). Aerobic exercise may reduce depression because it releases endorphins. As discussed in study unit 2.3, the release of endorphins can cause an overall feeling of well-being (a feeling runners sometimes experience as "runner's high"). Aerobic exercise may also regularize bodily rhythms, improve self-esteem, and provide social support if people exercise with others. However, clients with depression may have difficulty finding the energy and motivation to begin an exercise regimen.

An alternative treatment that alters the brain's electrical function, such as electroconvulsive therapy (ECT), is very effective for those who are severely depressed and do not respond to conventional treatments (Hollon et al., 2002). ECT might be a preferred treatment for a number of reasons. Antidepressants can take weeks to be effective, whereas ECT works quickly. For a suicidal client, waiting several weeks for relief can literally be deadly. In addition, ECT may be the treatment of choice for pregnant women, because there is no evidence that the seizures harm the developing fetus. Many psychotropic medications, in contrast, can cause birth defects. Most important, ECT has proved effective in clients for whom other treatments have failed.

ECT does, however, have some serious limitations, including memory impairments and a high rate of relapse (often making repeated treatments necessary; Fink, 2001). In most cases, memory loss is limited to the day of ECT treatment, but some clients experience substantial permanent memory loss (Donahue, 2000). Some treatment centers perform ECT only over the brain hemisphere not dominant for language, and this approach seems to reduce memory disruption (Papadimitriou, Zervas, & Papakostas, 2001).

A series of studies have demonstrated that changing brain function by using transcranial magnetic stimulation (TMS) over the left frontal regions of the brain also reduces depression significantly (Brunoni et al., 2017; Padberg & George, 2009; Pascual-Leone, Catala, & Pascual-Leone, 1996). Because TMS does not involve anesthesia or have any major side effects other than headache, it can be administered outside hospital settings. Moreover, it is effective even for those who have not responded to treatment with antidepressants (Fitzgerald et al., 2003). In October 2008, the Food and Drug Administration (FDA) approved TMS for the treatment of severe major depressive disorder in clients who are not helped by traditional therapies.

As with obsessive-compulsive disorder, deep brain stimulation (DBS) might be valuable for treating severe depression when all other treatments have failed. As described in The Methods of Psychology above, neurosurgeons inserted electrodes into the prefrontal cortex in six clients who had been diagnosed with major depressive disorder (Mayberg et al., 2005; McNeely, Mayberg, Lozano, & Kennedy, 2008). Four of the clients had stunning results. In fact, some of them felt relief as soon as the switch was turned on. For all four, it was as if a horrible noise had stopped and a weight had been lifted. The clients described the result as feeling like they had emerged into a more beautiful world (Dobbs, 2006; Ressler & Mayberg, 2007).

Several studies have been done of using DBS for treatment-resistant depression, and each time at least half the clients benefited from the treatment (Bewernick et al., 2010; Malone et al., 2009). One study followed 20 clients for three to six years and found that about two thirds showed long-lasting benefits from DBS (Kennedy et al., 2011). Before DBS, only 10 percent of the client-participants had been able to work or engage in meaningful activities outside the house, whereas two-thirds were able to do so after DBS. Such studies demonstrate that DBS is useful for helping some clients lead more productive lives. Research using DBS to treat severe depressive disorders is now under way at a number of facilities around the globe (Ryder & Holtzheimer, 2016).

15.9 Psychotropic Medications Are Most Effective for Bipolar Disorders

15.9 LEARNING GOAL ACTIVITIES

To maximize your learning, complete the following learning goal activities:

a. Understand all bold and italic terms by writing explanations of them in your own words.

b. Understand the treatment of bipolar disorders by describing the two recommended drug treatments for bipolar disorders.

Bipolar disorders are one of the few psychological disorders for which there is a clear optimal treatment (**Figure 15.21**). The best practice is to use psychotropic medications that stabilize mood or reduce psychotic thoughts (see Table 15.2, on p. 602; Geddes, Burgess, Hawton, Jamison, & Goodwin, 2004; Geddes & Miklowitz, 2013). The first substance found to stabilize mood was lithium, a naturally occurring mineral. Just how lithium stabilizes mood is not well understood, but the drug seems to modulate neurotransmitter levels, balancing excitatory and inhibitory activities (Jope, 1999).

The mania in bipolar disorders can include unusual thoughts that seem out of touch with reality. These disturbed thoughts are similar to the delusions found in people with schizophrenia. It is not surprising, then, that medications used to treat schizophrenia have been found to be effective in stabilizing moods and reducing episodes of extreme mania. The drug quetiapine (better known as Seroquel) is an atypical antipsychotic and is now the most commonly prescribed drug for bipolar disorders (Hooshmand et al., 2014). Quetiapine and lithium work through different mechanisms, but both are effective in treating bipolar disorder (Ketter, Miller, Dell'Osso, & Wang, 2016). Combining lithium with quetiapine improves treatment outcomes (Buoli, Serati, & Altamura, 2014).

Because lithium and quetiapine work better on elevated moods than on depressed moods, clients may also be given an antidepressant to manage symptoms of depression. This has to be done very carefully, however, as there is a risk of triggering mania (Fornaro et al., 2018; Pacchiarotti et al., 2013). When viewed as necessary, SSRIs are preferable to other antidepressants because they are less likely to trigger episodes of mania (Gijsman, Geddes, Rendell, Nolen, & Goodwin, 2004). At this time, however, little evidence supports the usefulness of antidepressants in the treatment of bipolar disorder (Nivoli et al., 2011).

As with all psychological disorders, compliance with drug therapy can be a problem for various reasons. Lithium has unpleasant side effects, including thirst, hand tremors, excessive urination, and memory problems. These side effects often diminish after several weeks on the drug. To reduce these effects, some clients may skip doses or stop taking the medication completely. In such situations, cognitive-behavioral

FIGURE 15.21

Bipolar Disorders Can Be Successfully Treated

The actor Catherine Zeta-Jones has been diagnosed with bipolar II disorder. Zeta-Jones manages her symptoms through psychotropic medications and periodic residential treatment.

therapy (CBT) can help clients stay on their medication regimens (Miller, Norman, & Keitner, 1989). Clients with bipolar disorder also may stop taking their medications because they miss the "highs" of their manic episodes. Again, psychological therapy can help clients accept their need for medication and understand how much their disorder affects those around them as well as themselves (Oud et al., 2016).

15.10 Atypical Antipsychotic Medications Are the Best Treatment for Schizophrenia

15.10 LEARNING GOAL ACTIVITIES

To maximize your learning, complete the following learning goal activities:

a. Understand all bold and italic terms by writing explanations of them in your own words.

b. Analyze drug treatments for schizophrenia by distinguishing the pros and cons in using conventional versus atypical antipsychotics to treat schizophrenia and explain why atypical antipsychotics are now the treatment of choice.

In the early 1900s, Freud's psychoanalytic theory and treatments based on it were widely touted as the answer to many psychological disorders. However, even Freud admitted that his techniques were unlikely to benefit people with more-severe psychotic disorders, such as schizophrenia. Psychotic people were difficult to handle and even more difficult to treat, so they generally were institutionalized as patients in large mental hospitals with extremely poor conditions. In such institutions in New York State, for instance, the physician-to-patient ratio in 1934 was less than 1 to 200.

In this undesirable situation, the staff and administration of mental hospitals were willing to try any inexpensive treatment that might help decrease the patient population or that at least might make patients more manageable. Brain surgery, such as lobotomy, was often used for patients with severe psychological disorders. But those with schizophrenia did not seem to improve following the operation, although it did make them easier to handle. Fortunately, the introduction of medications in the 1950s eliminated the use of lobotomy.

PSYCHOTROPIC MEDICATIONS FOR SCHIZOPHRENIA   Early antipsychotic drugs, called *conventional antipsychotics* (see Table 15.2, on p. 602), reduced the positive symptoms of schizophrenia, such as delusions, hallucinations, and disorganized speech and behavior. These drugs became the most frequently used treatment for this disorder, and they revolutionized the treatment of schizophrenia. Patients who had been hospitalized for years were able to walk out of mental institutions and live independently—although as you will learn, many of these patients had problems over the long term. Moreover, although these drugs were effective in reducing positive symptoms, they had little to no effect on the negative symptoms of schizophrenia, such as apathy and lack of emotion. What's more, they have significant side effects. For instance, conventional antipsychotics have significant motor effects that resemble symptoms of Parkinson's disease: lack of movement of facial muscles, trembling of extremities, muscle spasms, uncontrollable salivation, and a shuffling walk. *Tardive dyskinesia*—involuntary movement of body parts—is another devastating side effect of these medications and is irreversible once it appears (**Figure 15.22**).

In the late 1980s, practitioners began prescribing a new group of drugs, called the *atypical antipsychotics* (see Table 15.2). These are significantly different from conventional antipsychotic medications in three main ways. First, they act on different

FIGURE 15.22

A Side Effect of Conventional Antipsychotics Was Tardive Dyskinesia

Conventional antipsychotics were the earliest drugs used to treat schizophrenia. They unfortunately left some clients with a permanent motor disorder called tardive dyskinesia. This disorder caused involuntary movements of the face and neck as well as abnormal posture.

neurotransmitters. Second, they are beneficial in treating both the positive symptoms of schizophrenia (**Figure 15.23a**) and some of the negative symptoms (**Figure 15.23b**). Indeed, many clients who had not responded to the previously available conventional antipsychotics improved after taking a specific atypical antipsychotic. Third, fewer signs of tardive dyskinesia appeared in the clients taking this drug.

While atypical antipsychotics have fewer side effects than earlier antipsychotic medications, early versions had serious side effects. These effects included seizures, heart rate problems, and large weight gain. An even greater concern was that some of the drugs could cause a fatal reduction in white blood cells. Newer atypical antipsychotics are safer and as effective for treating positive symptoms, but they may not be as successful for treating negative symptoms (Leucht et al., 2009). Atypical antipsychotics are now the drug of choice for treating schizophrenia.

BEHAVIOR THERAPY   Medication is essential in the treatment of schizophrenia. Without medication, clients may deteriorate, experiencing more-frequent and more-severe psychotic episodes. When antipsychotic drugs became available, practitioners mostly stopped using other types of therapies for schizophrenia. Over time, however, it became clear that although medication can effectively reduce symptoms, clients might still have long-standing social problems. Thus antipsychotic drugs should be combined with other treatments to help people lead productive lives.

Specifically, behavior therapy can include social skills training to help produce desired behavior. For example, clients can learn appropriate ways to act in specific social situations. These clients can also benefit from intensive training in regulating their expressions of emotion, recognizing social cues, and predicting the effects of their behavior in social situations. With intensive long-term training, clients with schizophrenia can take the skills they learn in therapy and generalize them to other social environments. In fact, the successful use of newly acquired social skills is itself rewarding and encourages the clients to continue using those skills. Similarly, when clients' self-care skills are poor, behavioral interventions can focus on areas such as grooming and bathing, managing medications, and financial planning. By contrast, training in specific cognitive skills, such as modifying thinking patterns and coping with auditory hallucinations, has been less effective.

PROGNOSIS IN SCHIZOPHRENIA   Some people with schizophrenia have positive outcomes that could be considered progress toward recovery. Eventually, they may overcome disruptive symptoms and be able to function in daily life. However, knowing how often people actually recover depends on how you define recovery. For instance, how long does a person have to go without symptoms before being considered recovered? An analysis of outcomes across 50 long-term studies tried to identify the number of people who had reduced symptoms and good social function for at least two years (Jääskeläinen et al., 2013). By these standards, only about 1 in 7 individuals achieved recovery.

This result is troubling because it suggests that in spite of major advances in diagnoses and treatment, the **prognosis**, or prospect of recovery, for those with schizophrenia has not improved in recent years (Jääskeläinen et al., 2013; Millan et al., 2016). Several questions remain unclear, such as whether some treatments are better than others. What seems clear is that the longer a person with psychotic symptoms does not receive treatment, the worse the person's prognosis (Penttilä, Jääskeläinen, Hirvonen, Isohanni, & Miettunen, 2014).

The evidence confirms that atypical antipsychotics are extremely valuable in the short-term for people experiencing psychotic symptoms (Goff et al., 2017; Harrow & Jobe, 2013). But how long should the people remain on the medication?

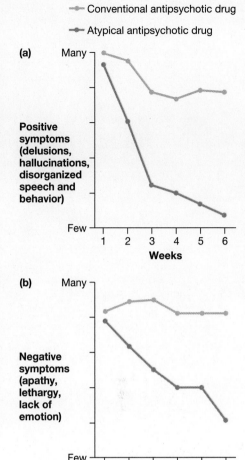

— Conventional antipsychotic drug
— Atypical antipsychotic drug

(a)

Positive symptoms (delusions, hallucinations, disorganized speech and behavior)

(b)

Negative symptoms (apathy, lethargy, lack of emotion)

FIGURE 15.23

Effectiveness of Conventional Versus Atypical Antipsychotics

(a) While conventional antipsychotics reduced positive symptoms somewhat, atypical antipsychotics reduced positive symptoms much more. **(b)** By contrast, only atypical antipsychotics reduced negative symptoms.

prognosis
A prediction of the likely course of a psychological (or physical) disorder.

It is possible that long-term use of these drugs may be associated with worse outcomes, possibly because long-term use changes the brain so that the antipsychotics become less effective (Harrow, Jobe, & Faull, 2014).

The prognosis for people with schizophrenia also depends on the age when the disorder first appears. People diagnosed later in life tend to have a more favorable prognosis than people who experience their first symptoms during childhood or adolescence (McGlashan, 1988). This difference could be because of delays in treatment or because schizophrenia affects brain development, much of which occurs during childhood and adolescence (Millan et al., 2016).

Q What Are the Most Effective Treatments?

To make sure you learned what you just read, write answers to the following questions and check your answers.

15.7 Why is exposure therapy a part of treatment for anxiety disorders?

15.8 For depressive disorders, what psychotherapy treatment can be just as effective as antidepressants?

15.9 What two classes of psychotropic drugs are best for treatment of the elevated moods seen in bipolar disorders?

15.10 What are the three differences between the atypical antipsychotics and the conventional antipsychotics used to treat schizophrenia?

See Appendix B for answers to the red Q questions.

Can Personality Disorders Be Treated?

Most therapists agree that personality disorders are very difficult to treat. Clients with these disorders see the environment, not their own behavior, as the cause of their problems. As a result, individuals with personality disorders rarely seek therapy, or such individuals are very difficult to engage in therapy. Nevertheless, some therapies have proven to be helpful for two of the most disruptive personality disorders, as shown in **Table 15.5**.

TABLE 15.5
Types of Treatment for Specific Personality Disorders

Category	Examples of Specific Disorders	Types of Treatment	Sample of Possible Techniques
Cluster B: dramatic, emotional, or erratic behavior	*Borderline personality disorder:* intense, unstable moods, relationships, and self-image; impulsivity	cognitive-behavioral therapy (CBT) psychotropic medications	• dialectical behavior therapy (DBT) • antidepressants
	Antisocial personality disorder (APD): disregard for and violation of the rights of others; manipulativeness; lack of guilt	behavior therapy	• operant procedures

15.11 Dialectical Behavior Therapy Is the Best Treatment for Borderline Personality Disorder

15.11 LEARNING GOAL ACTIVITIES

To maximize your learning, complete the following learning goal activities:

a. Understand all bold and italic terms by writing explanations of them in your own words.

b. Apply dialectical behavior therapy (DBT) to the treatment of borderline personality disorder by describing how a therapist would go through three steps in DBT to treat someone with borderline personality disorder.

FIGURE 15.24

Marsha Linehan

The psychologist Marsha Linehan pioneered the therapeutic technique of DBT. Linehan has publicly described her experience of the kind of psychological disorder this technique is used to treat.

The impulsivity, emotional disturbances, and identity disturbances characteristic of borderline personality disorder make it challenging to provide therapy for the people affected. Traditional psychotherapy approaches have been largely unsuccessful, so therapists have attempted to develop approaches specific to borderline personality disorder.

The most successful treatment approach so far was developed by the psychologist Marsha Linehan in the 1980s (**Figure 15.24**). Two decades earlier, as a young woman, Linehan had suffered from extreme social withdrawal, physical self-destructiveness, and recurrent thoughts of suicide (Carey, 2011). Diagnosed as having schizophrenia, she was institutionalized, locked in a seclusion room, treated with various medications, given Freudian psychoanalysis (see study unit 15.1), and treated with electroconvulsive therapy (ECT). Eventually, after being released from the hospital with little hope of surviving, Linehan learned to manage her disorder by changing the way she thought. She began to accept herself rather than striving for some impossible ideal.

This idea of "radical acceptance," as she puts it, enabled Linehan to function. She earned her PhD in psychology with the goal of helping people who are chronically self-destructive or even suicidal. She developed a method in which people use a dialectical approach, which means discussing ideas that are in conflict using logic and reasoning. Linehan's **dialectical behavior therapy (DBT)** combines elements of behavior, cognitive, and psychodynamic therapies with a mindfulness approach based on Eastern meditative practices (Lieb, Zanarini, Schmahl, Linehan, & Bohus, 2004). All clients are seen in both group and individual sessions, and the responsibilities of the client and the therapist are made explicit.

DBT proceeds in three phases (**Figure 15.25**). In Phase 1, therapists target the clients' most extreme and dysfunctional behaviors. Often these behaviors involve self-cutting and threats of suicide or suicide attempts. The focus is on replacing these behaviors with less destructive ones. The clients learn problem-solving techniques and effective ways of coping with their emotions. The clients are taught to control their attention to focus on the present. Strategies for controlling attention

dialectical behavior therapy (DBT)
Form of therapy, used to treat borderline personality disorder, that combines behavior therapy, cognitive therapy, psychodynamic therapy, and a mindfulness approach.

(a)

(b)

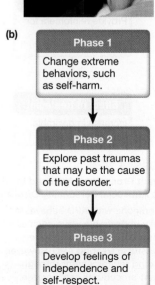

FIGURE 15.25

Dialectical Behavior Therapy Is Used to Treat Borderline Personality Disorder

(a) Suppose that clients with borderline personality disorder want to hurt themselves. **(b)** In Phase 1 of DBT, the clients learn to change extreme behaviors by using mindfulness to focus on the present to improve problem solving and coping. In Phase 2, the clients explore past traumas underlying their emotional problems. In Phase 3, the clients work to increase their self-esteem and stop depending on others for validation.

operant procedures
Form of therapy used to treat antisocial personality disorder (APD) where a therapist helps the client learn to associate certain behaviors with specific desirable outcomes.

are based on mindfulness meditation. In Phase 2, therapists help the clients explore past traumatic experiences that may be at the root of their emotional problems. In Phase 3, therapists help the clients develop self-respect and independent problem solving. This phase is crucial because clients with borderline personality disorder depend heavily on others for support and validation. These clients must be able to develop the appropriate attitudes and necessary skills themselves. Otherwise, they are likely to return to their previous behavior patterns.

Therapeutic approaches targeted at borderline personality disorder—for example, DBT—may improve the prognosis for these clients. Studies have demonstrated that when clients with borderline personality disorder undergo DBT, they are more likely to remain in treatment and less likely to be suicidal than are clients with borderline personality disorder who undergo other types of therapy (Linehan, Armstrong, Suarez, Allmon, & Heard, 1991; Linehan, Heard, & Armstrong, 1993). SSRI antidepressants are often prescribed along with DBT to treat feelings of depression.

15.12 Antisocial Personality Disorder Is Extremely Difficult to Treat

15.12 LEARNING GOAL ACTIVITIES

To maximize your learning, complete the following learning goal activities:

a. Understand all bold and italic terms by writing explanations of them in your own words.

b. Understand the barriers to treatment of antisocial personality disorder (APD) by explaining in your own words why it is so difficult to treat APD.

Treating clients with borderline personality disorder can be difficult. Treating those with antisocial personality disorder (APD) often seems impossible. These clients lie without thinking twice about it, care little for other people's feelings, and live for the present without considering the future. All these factors decrease the possibility of developing a therapeutic relationship and motivating the client to change. Individuals with this disorder are often more interested in manipulating their therapists than in changing their own behavior. Therapists working with these clients must constantly be on guard.

Numerous treatment approaches have been tried for APD and for the related but more extreme disorder, where a person may be a psychopath (see study unit 14.11). Individuals with APD apparently have less arousal in the cortex. For this reason, stimulants have been prescribed to normalize arousal levels. There is evidence that these drugs are beneficial in the short term but not the long term. Anti-anxiety drugs may lower hostility levels somewhat, and lithium has shown promise in treating the aggressive, impulsive behavior of violent criminals who are psychopathic. Overall, however, psychotropic medications have not been effective in treating this disorder.

Similarly, most psychotherapies seem of little use in treating APD. Individual therapy sessions, for instance, rarely produce any change in antisocial behavior. Behavior therapy approaches have had some success when they use **operant procedures**. As you learned in study unit 6.8, operant conditioning is a form of learning where people learn to associate certain behaviors with specific outcomes. It can be applied to treatment when a therapist uses reinforcers to increase desirable behaviors (**Figure 15.26**). In this way, treatment using operant procedures can replace maladaptive behavior patterns with behavior patterns that are more socially appropriate. These approaches seem to work best when the therapist

(a)

(b)

Reinforcement

Provide reinforcers for desirable behaviors, such as telling the truth.

Effect of treatment

Increase in desirable behaviors.

FIGURE 15.26

Operant Procedures Are Used to Treat Antisocial Personality Disorder

(a) Someone with APD behaves in socially undesirable ways, such as stealing. **(b)** No treatment is very successful in treating APD. However, providing reinforcement through operant procedures can increase desired behaviors.

controls reinforcement, the client cannot leave treatment, and the client is part of a group. This behavior therapy cannot be implemented on an outpatient basis, because the client could then leave treatment at any time and, once outside of therapy, might receive reinforcement for antisocial behavior. For these reasons, therapy for APD is most effective in a residential treatment center or a correctional facility.

However, the prognosis is poor that clients with APD will change their behaviors as a result of any therapy. This conclusion is especially true for clients with psychopathic traits. Some of the more recently developed cognitive techniques show promise, but there is no good evidence that they produce long-lasting or even real changes. Fortunately for society, individuals with APD, but without the more severe disease of psychopathy, typically improve after age 40 with or without treatment.

The reasons for this improvement are unknown, but it may be due to a reduction in biological drives. One alternative theory is that these individuals may gain insight into their self-defeating behaviors. Another possibility is that they may just get worn out and be unable to continue their manipulative ways. The improvement, however, is mainly in the realm of antisocial behavior. The underlying egocentricity, callousness, and manipulativeness can remain unchanged (Harpur & Hare, 1994), especially for those who are psychopathic. Criminal acts and imprisonment decrease among those with APD after age 40 (**Figure 15.27**). Even so, more than half of the individuals with the more severe disorder, psychopathy, continue to be arrested after age 40 (Hare, McPherson, & Forth, 1988). Thus, although some aspects of the behavior of people with APD mellow with age, people with psychopathy remain indifferent to traditional societal norms.

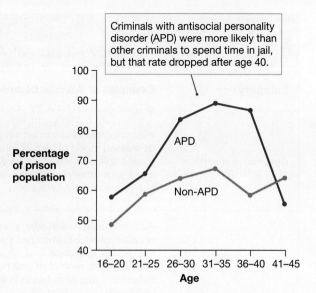

FIGURE 15.27
Rates of Imprisonment for People of Different Ages with Antisocial Personality Disorder

For this longitudinal study, the percentage of participants in prison during each five-year period is shown. After age 40, the percentage declined for those with APD.

Q Can Personality Disorders be Treated?

To make sure you learned what you just read, write answers to the following questions and check your answers.

15.11 What role does mindfulness play in dialectical behavior therapy (DBT)?

15.12 What is the general prognosis for those with antisocial personality disorder (APD)?

See Appendix B for answers to the red Q questions.

How Can Disorders Be Treated in Children and Adolescents?

In the United States, an estimated 12–20 percent of children and adolescents experience psychological disorders (Merikangas et al., 2010). As you have seen throughout this book, experiences and development during early life are critical to psychological health in adulthood. Problems not addressed during childhood or adolescence may persist into adulthood. Accordingly, there is a benefit to getting treatment early (**Figure 15.28**). In this section, you will learn about the psychotropic medications, cognitive therapy, and behavior therapy approaches that are most effective for

FIGURE 15.28
Children and Adolescents Benefit from Treatment for Psychological Disorders

By receiving appropriate treatment early in life, young people can overcome psychological disorders. **(a)** Children may benefit from play therapy. **(b)** Adolescents can benefit from group therapy.

TABLE 15.6

Types of Treatment for Children and Adolescents Experiencing Psychological Disorders

Category	Examples of Specific Disorders	Types of Treatment	Sample of Possible Techniques
Depressive disorders	*Major depressive disorder*: severely depressed mood or loss of interest in pleasurable activities for two weeks or more, plus other symptoms, such as changes in weight or in sleep	psychotropic medications	antidepressants
		cognitive-behavioral therapy (CBT)	changing negative thoughts associated with depression
Neurodevelopmental disorders	*Autism spectrum disorder*: persistent unresponsiveness; impaired social interaction, language, and cognitive development; restricted and repetitive behavior; symptoms begin in early childhood	behavior therapy	applied behavioral analysis
	Attention-deficit/hyperactivity disorder (ADHD): hyperactivity, inattentiveness, and impulsive behavior with social or academic impairment; begins before age 12	psychotropic medications	stimulants
		behavior therapy	operant procedures

adolescent depressive disorders, autism spectrum disorder, and attention-deficit/hyperactivity disorder (ADHD) (see **Table 15.6**).

15.13 Using Medication to Treat Depressive Disorders in Adolescents Is Controversial

15.13 LEARNING GOAL ACTIVITIES

To maximize your learning, complete the following learning goal activities:

a. Understand all bold and italic terms by writing explanations of them in your own words.

b. Evaluate the two treatment options for adolescents with depressive disorders by assessing the pros and cons of treating adolescents with antidepressants versus psychotherapy.

Adolescent depression is a serious problem. Approximately 8 percent of 12- to 17-year-olds in the United States have reported experiencing a major depressive episode that met *Diagnostic and Statistical Manual (DSM)* criteria (Substance Abuse and Mental Health Services Administration, 2011; **Figure 15.29**). Approximately 5,000 U.S. teenagers kill themselves each year, making suicide now the second leading cause of death for that age group (Centers for Disease Control and Prevention, 2018). For many years, depression in children and adolescents was ignored or seen as a typical part of growing up. Even today, only about one third of adolescents with psychological disorders receive any form of treatment (Merikangas et al., 2011). The percentage is even lower for adolescents from racial and ethnic minorities

(Cummings & Druss, 2010). Untreated adolescent depression is associated with drug abuse, dropping out of school, and suicide. Understandably, then, many mental health professionals reacted favorably to the initial use of antidepressants to treat adolescent depression.

RISKS OF ANTIDEPRESSANTS FOR ADOLESCENTS

Shortly after SSRIs (see Table 15.2, on p. 602) were introduced as treatments for adolescent depression, some mental health researchers raised concerns that the drugs might cause some adolescents to become suicidal (Jureidini et al., 2004). These concerns arose partly from studies with adults that found SSRIs caused some people to feel restless, impulsive, and suicidal. Following a report by one drug company of an increase in suicidal thoughts among adolescents taking its product, the FDA asked all drug companies to analyze their records for similar reports. An analysis of reports on more than 4,400 children and adolescents found that for those taking SSRIs, the number who reported having suicidal thoughts (4 percent) was about twice as high as for those taking a placebo (2 percent).

None of the children or adolescents in the reports actually committed suicide. But evidence of increased thoughts of suicide led the FDA, in 2004, to require warning labels on antidepressant packaging. Physicians also were advised to watch their young clients closely, especially in the first few weeks of treatment. Suddenly, many parents were wondering whether SSRIs were safe for their children.

Many questions about SSRIs and young people need to be answered. First, are SSRIs effective for young people? If so, are they more effective than other treatments? Second, do these drugs cause suicidal feelings, or are young people with depression likely to feel suicidal whether or not they take medication? Finally, how many children and adolescents would be suicidal if their depression were left untreated?

Some of these questions were addressed in the Treatment for Adolescents with Depression Study (Treatment for Adolescents with Depression Study [TADS] Team, 2004). This ambitious research program was supported by the U.S. National Institutes of Health. TADS provided clear evidence that SSRIs are effective in treating adolescent depression. The study examined 439 adolescents who had experienced depression for an average of 40 weeks before the study began. Participants were assigned randomly to a type of treatment and followed for 12 weeks (**Figure 15.30**). Sixty-one percent of participants taking an SSRI showed improvement in symptoms, compared with 43 percent receiving cognitive-behavioral therapy (CBT) and 35 percent taking a placebo. The group that received both an SSRI antidepressant and therapy did best (71 percent improved). This latter finding is consistent with studies of adults.

A follow-up study three years after the initial TADS research (March et al., 2007) found that the combined group still had the best outcomes (86 percent improvement). Improvement with CBT alone was similar to that with SSRIs alone (81 percent for both groups). In short, combining drugs and psychotherapy often produces the strongest results for treating depression in adolescents. The original

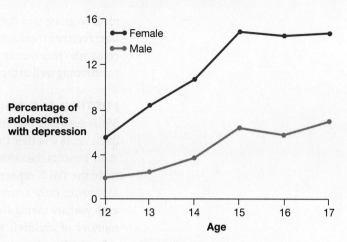

FIGURE 15.29

Rates of Depression in Adolescents

This graph shows results from the National Survey on Drug Use and Health. The survey was undertaken by the Substance Abuse and Mental Health Services Administration (SAMHSA), a branch of the U.S. Department of Health and Human Services. The graph shows the percentage of adolescents reporting depression at each age in 2009.

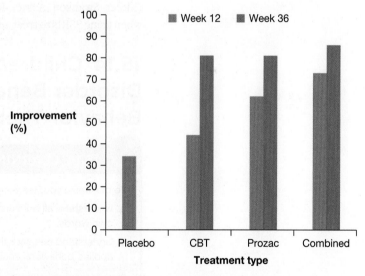

FIGURE 15.30

Treatment Outcomes in the TADS Study

At 12 weeks, treatment for adolescent depression with Prozac or Prozac combined with CBT was more effective than use of a placebo treatment with CBT alone. However, by 36 weeks, CBT and Prozac were equally effective. Combining CBT with Prozac was slightly more effective at both times.

placebo group was not included in the follow-up study because all the participants later received treatment. A follow-up study nearly four years later found that adolescents who received any of the treatments maintained positive outcomes and were functioning well in their daily lives (Peters et al., 2016).

FURTHER THOUGHTS ON TREATMENT APPROACHES   So can we say that SSRIs are a safe and effective treatment for adolescent depression? Ultimately, the question is whether the millions of children who take antidepressants experience more benefits than risks.

In the TADS report, suicide attempts were quite uncommon (7 of 439 clients). Moreover, only a small number of the 5,000 adolescents who kill themselves each year are taking antidepressants of any kind. The question is whether the large number of children who take antidepressants experience more benefits than risks (Walkup, 2017).

According to some researchers, the relative success of psychotherapy for teenage depression makes it a better treatment choice (Mufson et al., 2004). But getting adolescents to comply with psychotherapy can be challenging. Young adolescents may lack the cognitive, emotional, or social skills necessary to benefit from treatment, thereby requiring changing therapy to match the adolescent's current abilities (Garber, Frankel, & Herrington, 2016). Psychotherapy is also time consuming and expensive, and many health insurance companies provide only minimal support (Rifkin & Rifkin, 2004). In addition, it is unrealistic to expect that sufficient resources will be available to provide psychotherapy to all adolescents who need it now or in the near future.

By contrast, it is relatively easy for pediatricians and family physicians to prescribe drugs. But care needs to be taken. According to recent research, higher doses of SSRIs are especially likely to trigger suicidal attempts among adolescents (Miller, Swanson, Azrael, Pate, & Stürmer, 2014). The best advice to practitioners when using SSRIs to treat adolescents is "start low, go slow" (Brent & Gibbons, 2014).

15.14 Children with Autism Spectrum Disorder Benefit from Structured Behavior Therapy

15.14 LEARNING GOAL ACTIVITIES

To maximize your learning, complete the following learning goal activities:

a. Understand all bold and italic terms by writing explanations of them in your own words.

b. Understand behavior therapy for autism spectrum disorder by describing applied behavioral analysis in the treatment of a child with autism.

The treatment of children with autism spectrum disorder presents unique challenges to mental health professionals. The core symptoms of autism spectrum disorder are impaired communication, restricted interests, and deficits in social interaction. These symptoms make the children particularly difficult to work with. Their sometimes extreme behaviors—such as hand waving, rocking, humming, and jumping up and down—must be reduced or eliminated before the children can make progress in other areas. Changing these extreme behaviors is difficult to do because effective reinforcers are hard to find. Children without autism respond positively to social praise and small prizes, but children with autism often show no response to these rewards. In some cases, food is the only effective reinforcer in the initial stages of treatment.

Children with autism also tend to be quite selective in what they pay attention to. This tendency to focus on specific details while ignoring others interferes with generalizing learned behavior to other stimuli and situations. For example, children who learn to set the table with plates may not know what to do when they are asked to use bowls instead. Generalization of skills must be explicitly taught. Thus, for children with autism, structured therapies are more effective than unstructured interventions such as play therapy (in which the therapist tries to engage the child in conversation while the child plays with toys).

BEHAVIOR THERAPY FOR AUTISM SPECTRUM DISORDER

One of the best-known and perhaps most effective treatments was developed in the 1980s by Ivar Lovaas and his colleagues (Lovaas, 1987). This program, **applied behavioral analysis,** is based on principles of operant conditioning. As you learned in study unit 6.8, behaviors that are reinforced should increase in frequency, and behaviors that are not reinforced should diminish (**Figure 15.31**). There is evidence that this method can be used successfully to treat autism spectrum disorder (Warren et al., 2011), particularly if treatment is started early in life (Vismara & Rogers, 2010). James, the boy with autism spectrum disorder you read about in the chapter opener, received a form of applied behavioral analysis.

This intensive approach requires a minimum of 40 hours of treatment per week. In Lovaas's study (1987), preschool-age children with autism were treated by teachers and by their parents, who received specific training. After more than two years of treatment, the children had gained about 20 IQ points on average. Most of them were able to enter a normal kindergarten program. In contrast, IQ did not change in a control group that received no treatment. Children who received only 10 hours of treatment per week fared no better than those in the control group. Initiating treatment at a younger age yielded better results. Children with better language skills before entering treatment also had better outcomes than those with language impairments.

Lovaas's applied behavioral analysis program has some drawbacks. The most obvious is the time commitment. Parents of children with autism essentially become full-time teachers for years, as James's parents did. The financial and emotional drains on the family can be substantial. And other children in the family may feel neglected or jealous due to the amount of time and energy devoted to the child with autism.

BIOLOGICAL TREATMENT FOR AUTISM SPECTRUM DISORDER

There is good evidence that autism spectrum disorder is caused by brain dysfunction, although the nature of that dysfunction is unknown. Many attempts have been made to use this knowledge to treat the disorder. It is easy to find compelling case studies of children who appear to have benefited from alternative treatment approaches. When the treatments are assessed in controlled studies, however, there is little or no evidence that any of them are effective. Attempts to use psychopharmacology to treat the disorder have led to some improvements in behavior, but much remains to be learned.

PROGNOSIS IN AUTISM SPECTRUM DISORDER

Despite a few reports of remarkable recovery from autism spectrum disorder, such as with James, the long-term prognosis is generally discouraging. One follow-up study revealed that men in

applied behavioral analysis
An intensive behavior therapy used to treat autism; this treatment is based on operant conditioning.

FIGURE 15.31

Applied Behavioral Analysis Is Used to Treat Autism Spectrum Disorder

Applied behavioral analysis involves intensive interaction between children with autism and their teachers and parents. Over time, the children increase socially desired and appropriate behaviors due to the rewards they receive for performing these actions.

their early 20s continued to show the ritualistic, self-stimulating behavior typical of autism spectrum disorder. In addition, nearly three-quarters had severe social difficulties and were unable to live and work independently (Howlin, Mawhood, & Rutter, 2000).

Several factors affect the chances of recovery. Therapists once believed the prognosis was particularly poor for children whose symptoms were apparent before age 2 (Hoshino et al., 1980). However, it is possible that, before public recognition of the disorder increased, only the most severe cases of autism were diagnosed that early. Early diagnosis clearly allows for more-effective treatments (National Research Council, Committee on Educational Interventions for Children with Autism, 2001). Still, severe cases are less likely to improve with treatment. Cases involving notable cognitive deficiencies are particularly resistant to treatment. Early language ability is associated with better outcomes (Howlin et al., 2000). Higher IQ is also associated with better outcomes. Children with autism have difficulty generalizing from the therapeutic setting to the real world, and this limitation severely restricts their social functioning (Handleman, Gill, & Alessandri, 1988). A higher IQ may mean a better ability to generalize learning and therefore a better overall prospect of improvement.

15.15 Children with ADHD Can Benefit from Various Approaches

15.15 LEARNING GOAL ACTIVITIES

To maximize your learning, complete the following learning goal activities:

a. Understand all bold and italic terms by writing explanations of them in your own words.

b. Apply the treatments for attention-deficit/hyperactivity disorder (ADHD) by providing an example of how a therapist might use psychotropic medications and behavior therapy treatments for an 11-year-old with ADHD.

Is attention-deficit/hyperactivity disorder (ADHD) a psychological disorder that should be treated, or is it simply a troublesome behavior pattern that children eventually outgrow? You may remember from study unit 14.15 that people have different opinions about this question.

Some individuals diagnosed with ADHD as children do grow out of it. Many more continue to experience the disorder throughout adolescence and adulthood. These people are more likely to drop out of school and to reach a lower socioeconomic level than expected. They show continued patterns of inattention, impulsivity, and hyperactivity, and they are at increased risk for other psychiatric disorders (Wilens, Faraone, & Biederman, 2004). Because of this somewhat bleak long-term prognosis, effective treatment early in life may be crucial.

PSYCHOTROPIC MEDICATIONS FOR ADHD The most common treatment for ADHD is a central nervous system stimulant (see Table 15.2, on p. 602), such as methylphenidate. This drug is most commonly known by the brand name Ritalin. The drug's actions are not fully understood, but it may affect multiple neurotransmitters, particularly dopamine. Another drug used to treat ADHD is Adderall, which combines stimulants. These drugs appear to stimulate activity in frontal lobe regions that support both cognition and behavioral control (Spencer, Devilbiss, & Berridge, 2015).

At appropriate doses, these drugs decrease overactivity and distractibility. They increase attention and the ability to concentrate. Children on these drugs experience a small increase in positive behaviors (**Figure 15.32a**) and a large decrease in negative behaviors (**Figure 15.32b**). They are able to work more effectively on a task without interruption and are less impulsive. Studies have shown that children taking Ritalin also are happier, more adept socially, and modestly more successful academically (Chronis, Jones, & Raggi, 2006; Van der Oord, Prins, Oosterlaan, & Emmelkamp, 2008).

Such improvements quite likely have contributed to increases in the number of children who take this medication. Parents often feel pressured by school systems to medicate children who have ongoing behavior problems, and parents often pressure physicians to prescribe Ritalin because its effects can make home life much more manageable.

Drugs such as Ritalin have drawbacks, however. Side effects include sleep problems, reduced appetite, body twitches, and temporary slowing of growth (Rapport & Moffitt, 2002; Schachter, Pham, King, Langford, & Moher, 2001). There is evidence that the short-term benefits of stimulants may not be maintained over the long term.

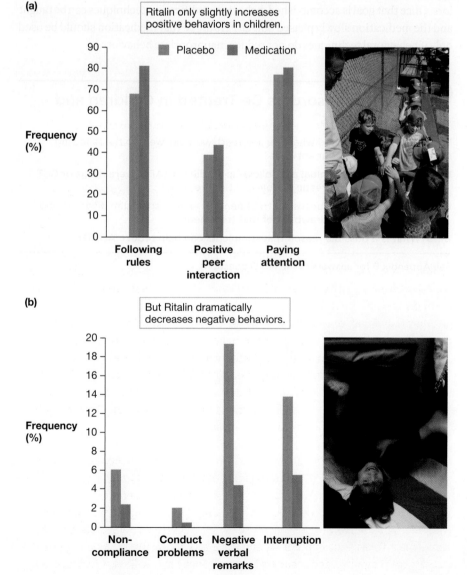

(a) Ritalin only slightly increases positive behaviors in children.

(b) But Ritalin dramatically decreases negative behaviors.

FIGURE 15.32

The Effects of Ritalin on the Symptoms of ADHD

These graphs compare the effects of Ritalin on the symptoms of ADHD. **(a)** Ritalin only slightly increases positive behaviors in children with ADHD. **(b)** But Ritalin has a large effect on decreasing their negative behaviors.

In addition, because stimulants affect everyone who takes them, not just those with a diagnosed condition, drug abuse is a very real risk. There are many cases of children and adolescents buying and selling drugs such as Ritalin and Adderall. One study found that nearly 8 percent of college students had taken a nonprescribed stimulant in the past 30 days, and 60 percent reported knowing students who misused stimulants (Weyandt et al., 2009).

Perhaps most important, some children on medication may see their problems as beyond their control. They may not feel responsible for their behaviors and may not learn coping strategies they will need if they stop taking their medication or if it becomes ineffective. Most therapists believe medication should be supplemented by psychological therapies, such as behavior modification. Some therapists even urge that medication be replaced by other treatment approaches when possible.

BEHAVIOR THERAPY FOR ADHD   Behavior therapy for ADHD aims to use operant procedures (see study unit 15.12) to reinforce positive behaviors and ignore or punish problem behaviors. An analysis of 174 studies consisting of over 2,000 research participants found clear support for the effectiveness of behavior therapy for ADHD (Fabiano et al., 2009). Many therapists advocate combining behavioral approaches with medication. The medication is used to gain control over the behaviors. Once that goal is accomplished, behavior modification techniques can be taught and the medication slowly phased out. Others argue that medication should be used only if behavioral techniques do not reduce inappropriate behaviors.

 How Can Disorders Be Treated in Children and Adolescents?

To make sure you learned what you just read, write answers to the following questions and check your answers.

15.13 According to the initial and follow-up studies in TADS, were drugs or CBT most effective in treating adolescent depression?

15.14 What is the most successful treatment for autism spectrum disorder, and what is the major drawback of that treatment?

15.15 What is a possible reason that stimulants can help reduce ADHD?

See Appendix B for answers to the red Q questions.

BIG PICTURE

Want to earn a better grade on your test? Go to **INQUIZITIVE** to practice actively with this chapter's content and get personalized feedback along the way.

How Are Psychological Disorders Treated?

15.1 Some Types of Psychotherapy Focus on Providing Insight

Review the learning goal activities on p. 595. Psychotherapy is formal treatment for psychological disorders where trained practitioners work to change clients' thoughts, feelings, and/ or behaviors. Psychodynamic therapy was an early method that adapted psychoanalysis (including free association and dream analysis) to help clients examine their unconscious needs, motives, and defenses to gain insight into their distress. However, this treatment is controversial because it is time-consuming and expensive and its effectiveness is unclear. Humanistic therapy uses client-centered therapy (with active listening and unconditional positive regard) to help people gain insight so they can work to become their best.

15.2 Behavioral and Cognitive Treatments Aim to Change Behavior, Emotion, and/or Thought Directly

Review the learning goal activities on p. 598. Many of the successful psychotherapies involve trying to change clients' behaviors, emotions, or thoughts directly. Three of these successful treatments include: (1) behavior therapy, (2) cognitive therapy, and (3) cognitive-behavioral therapy (CBT). Behavior therapy changes a client's behavior with techniques such as rewards, punishments, token economies, social skills training, and modeling. Cognitive therapy changes clients' distorted thoughts based on cognitive restructuring and rational-emotive therapy. CBT uses a combination of both behavior therapy and cognitive therapy to alter clients' actions and thoughts.

15.3 The Context of Therapy Matters

Review the learning goal activities on p. 599. Because people experience psychological disorders differently, the treatment for them must be appropriate. Some people may benefit from group therapy with others experiencing similar issues. Other people may benefit from family therapy with a systems approach that helps all members of the family function well together. Culture also affects both how psychological disorders are viewed and how the disorders are treated.

15.4 Biological Therapies Are Effective for Certain Disorders

Review the learning goal activities on p. 601. Biological treatments include psychotropic medications that change neurochemistry.

The five main categories of psychotropic medications are: (1) anti-anxiety drugs, (2) antidepressants, (3) mood stabilizers, (4) antipsychotics, and (5) stimulants. When traditional treatments are not successful, alternative biological treatments may be used, such as electroconvulsive therapy (ECT), transcranial magnetic stimulation (TMS), and deep brain stimulation (DBS).

15.5 Scientific Evidence Indicates Which Treatments Are Safe and Effective

Review the learning goal activities on p. 604. Therapies not supported by scientific evidence can be dangerous. Evidence-based treatments are safe and effective. There are three features of evidence-based psychological treatments: (1) They vary according to the particular disorder and the client's symptoms, (2) the techniques have been developed in the laboratory by psychologists, and (3) no single theory guides treatment—instead, treatments are chosen based on evidence of their effectiveness.

15.6 Various Providers Assist in Treatment for Psychological Disorders

Review the learning goal activities on p. 605. The various specialized mental health practitioners have different training that allows them to provide treatment in diverse settings. However, in most places only psychiatrists with medical degrees can prescribe psychotropic medications.

KEY TERMS
psychotherapy (p. 595)
psychodynamic therapy (p. 597)
humanistic therapy (p. 597)
behavior therapy (p. 598)
cognitive therapy (p. 598)
cognitive-behavioral therapy (CBT) (p. 599)
biological therapy (p. 601)
psychotropic medications (p. 601)
electroconvulsive therapy (ECT) (p. 602)
transcranial magnetic stimulation (TMS) (p. 603)
deep brain stimulation (DBS) (p. 603)

What Are the Most Effective Treatments?

15.7 Anxiety and Obsessive-Compulsive Disorders Are Best Treated with Cognitive-Behavioral Therapy

Review the learning goal activities on p. 608. Cognitive-behavioral therapy (CBT) works best to treat nearly all disorders that include anxious thoughts. Specific phobias are best treated with therapies that include exposure and systematic desensitization. Panic disorder can be treated with exposure therapy and cognitive restructuring. Obsessive-compulsive disorder (OCD) is best treated with exposure and response prevention, cognitive restructuring, and antidepressant medications. Deep brain stimulation (DBS) also holds promise for the treatment of OCD.

15.8 Many Effective Treatments Are Available for Depressive Disorders

Review the learning goal activities on p. 613. Many treatments are effective for depressive disorders. The options include antidepressants, cognitive-behavioral therapy (CBT), and alternative therapies such as phototherapy (for seasonal affective disorder), electroconvulsive therapy (ECT), transcranial magnetic stimulation (TMS), and deep brain stimulation (DBS).

15.9 Psychotropic Medications Are Most Effective for Bipolar Disorders

Review the learning goal activities on p. 617. Bipolar disorders are best treated with a combination of psychotropic medications.

Mood stabilizers such as lithium and quetiapine are the most effective treatments for bipolar disorders. They are especially effective for episodes of mania. When patients with bipolar disorders have symptoms of depression, then an antidepressant may also be used cautiously for treatment. Psychotherapy can help support compliance with drug treatment.

15.10 Atypical Antipsychotic Medications Are the Best Treatment for Schizophrenia

Review the learning goal activities on p. 618. Atypical antipsychotics reduce positive and negative symptoms of schizophrenia and do not elicit the side effect of tardive dyskinesia. Therefore, atypical antipsychotics are the current treatment of choice for schizophrenia. Psychotropic medications are most effective when combined with behavior therapy, especially social skills training and behavioral training for life skills.

KEY TERMS
exposure (p. 609)
systematic desensitization (p. 610)
exposure and response prevention (p. 612)
phototherapy (p. 615)
prognosis (p. 619)

Can Personality Disorders Be Treated?

15.11 Dialectical Behavior Therapy Is the Best Treatment for Borderline Personality Disorder

Review the learning goal activities on p. 621. Dialectical behavior therapy (DBT) is the most successful treatment for borderline personality disorder. DBT combines elements of behavior therapy, cognitive therapy, psychodynamic therapy, and mindfulness meditation. DBT therapy has three phases: (1) Mindfulness is used to focus on the present and replace extreme behaviors with more-appropriate ones, (2) past traumatic experiences are explored with psychoanalysis, and (3) self-respect and independent problem solving are developed.

15.12 Antisocial Personality Disorder Is Extremely Difficult to Treat

Review the learning goal activities on p. 622. Antisocial personality disorder (APD) is extremely difficult to treat. Treatment

with operant procedures has had some success to help clients learn to associate certain behaviors with specific outcomes and increase desirable behaviors. This treatment has the best chance of having a benefit when it occurs in a controlled residential treatment center or a correctional facility.

KEY TERMS
dialectical behavior therapy (DBT) (p. 621)
operant procedures (p. 622)

How Can Disorders Be Treated in Children and Adolescents?

15.13 Using Medication to Treat Depressive Disorders in Adolescents Is Controversial

Review the learning goal activities on p. 624. The use of SSRIs to treat adolescent depression is increasingly common, but it is controversial due to the possible risk of suicide. Cognitive-behavioral treatment (CBT) is also effective, particularly when combined with drug treatment.

15.14 Children with Autism Spectrum Disorder Benefit from Structured Behavior Therapy

Review the learning goal activities on p. 626. Children with autism spectrum disorder benefit from applied behavioral analysis, an intensive treatment based on operant conditioning. This treatment diminishes unwanted extreme behaviors and increases socially desirable behaviors.

15.15 Children with ADHD Can Benefit from Various Approaches

Review the learning goal activities on p. 628. Stimulants such as Ritalin are effective at treating children with attention-deficit/hyperactivity disorder (ADHD). Many therapists advocate combining behavioral approaches with medication. Others argue medication should be used only if behavioral techniques do not reduce inappropriate behaviors.

KEY TERMS
applied behavioral analysis (p. 627)

CHAPTER 15 SELF-QUIZ

To make sure you learned the information in this chapter, write answers to the following questions and check your answers. **See Appendix B for answers to the self-quiz.**

1. Eileen, a psychotherapist, interacts with her clients as equals as she helps them fulfill their potential for personal growth. She does not give clients advice, but provides the acceptance and support that will allow them to change their own behavior. Eileen most likely uses a _____ therapy approach with clients.
   a. cognitive
   b. psychodynamic
   c. humanistic
   d. behavior

2. The last time Ryan experienced a manic phase, he proposed marriage to four women in one day, maxed out all his credit cards, and quit his job. Ryan's psychiatrist will most likely prescribe a(n) _____ to control his symptoms.
   a. antidepressant drug
   b. antipsychotic drug
   c. stimulant drug
   d. anti-anxiety drug

3. Craig has been successfully treated for severe depression. He has an associate's degree and now volunteers at a suicide crisis center, conducting intake interviews with new patients as a way to help others. Craig is most likely a _____.
   a. clinical psychologist
   b. psychiatric social worker
   c. paraprofessional
   d. counseling psychologist

4. Jonah has panic attacks when he has to give presentations in class. Jonah's therapist helps him change the way he thinks about the symptoms of a panic attack. He also has Jonah practice reading aloud in front of a few people so Jonah will get used to it. Jonah's therapist is using _____ to treat his panic attacks.
   a. exposure and response prevention
   b. psychodynamic therapy
   c. systematic desensitization
   d. group therapy

5. Aidan's therapist believes that cognitive-behavioral therapy will help to relieve the symptoms of his major depressive disorder. As part of this therapy, his therapist will most likely suggest that Aidan _____.
   a. take an antidepressant for 8 weeks before coming back for another visit
   b. sit under a high-intensity light source for a short period each day
   c. expose himself to situations that make him feel depressed until his mood improves
   d. keep a journal to track his negative thoughts and then work to change his thoughts

6. Peter, a man with schizophrenia, experiences auditory hallucinations, slow speech, and apathy. His doctor is likely to prescribe a(n) _____ to treat all of these symptoms.
   a. conventional antipsychotic
   b. mood stabilizer drug
   c. atypical antipsychotic
   d. stimulant

7. Cindy has come to Dr. Lindstrom for assistance with borderline personality disorder. Which of the following treatment approaches is least likely to be part of a successful treatment using dialectical behavior therapy?
   a. discussing childhood abuse
   b. prescribing mood stabilizer drugs
   c. using mindfulness meditation
   d. working to develop self-respect

8. Hugh, a 35-year-old man, has been diagnosed with anti-social personality disorder. His doctor is concerned that Hugh's prognosis is poor because people with antisocial personality disorder _____.
   a. have a lack of empathy that makes it difficult to develop a therapeutic relationship
   b. have symptoms that get worse after age 40
   c. respond only to extreme measures, such as a type of psychosurgery called lobotomy
   d. are not able to learn positive behaviors through operant procedures

9. Samantha, a 14-year-old, seeks help for depression. Her doctor reviews the literature on treating adolescent depression and concludes that taking Prozac, an SSRI antidepressant medication, will likely be _____ in treating Samantha's symptoms. He also concludes that cognitive-behavioral therapy may _____ the impact of her drug treatment.
   a. effective; increase
   b. effective; decrease
   c. ineffective; increase
   d. ineffective; decrease

10. Every time her name is spoken, Simone is rewarded with her favorite candy if she makes eye contact with her teacher. Simone most likely has been diagnosed with _____ and is being treated with _____.
    a. ADHD; play therapy
    b. ADHD; applied behavioral analysis
    c. autism spectrum disorder; play therapy
    d. autism spectrum disorder; applied behavioral analysis

Do You Want to Become a Counselor or Clinical Psychologist?

Early in her career, the singer/songwriter Ellie Goulding experienced panic attacks that prevented her from leaving her house or going to the recording studio (McNamara, 2016). Cognitive behavioral therapy (CBT) helped Goulding manage her anxiety and function successfully in her private and public life. Goulding's experience with a psychological disorder and treatment for it is consistent with the material in this chapter.

As discussed in previous Putting Psychology to Work features, if you work as a substance abuse counselor, social services assistant, or social worker, you can support people struggling with psychological issues. As summarized in Table 15.3, on p. 606, a wide variety of mental health providers can administer treatments. They range from paraprofessionals, who may have little advanced training, to clinical psychologists, who have doctoral degrees.

This chapter also explains why particular treatments are used for different disorders. For example, Ellie Goulding received CBT because it is the most effective treatment for anxiety and panic disorders. Although all types of providers can help people who are experiencing mental health issues, it is typically counselors or clinical psychologists who use CBT to treat clients with serious psychological problems, such as anxiety disorders.

Perhaps after reading this chapter, or because of a personal or family experience with therapy, you are interested in a career that involves treating people with psychological disorders. Counseling and clinical psychology are the most popular advanced degrees in psychology, accounting for more than half of all graduate degrees awarded each year (Norcross & Sayette, 2016). Admission to these graduate programs is very competitive, but you can take steps now to make you a stronger candidate for admission in the years to come.

In addition to working hard at your studies, other factors that increase your chances at getting admission to graduate school include letters of recommendation from your professors, research or practical experience, and a good personal statement. To receive strong letters of recommendation, get to

know your professors. Attend class regularly, ask informed questions, and take advantage of office hours. If a professor is conducting research that interests you, see whether you can become involved in that work. Some schools offer academic credit for research, such as completing an independent project or an honors thesis.

Along with engaging in research, you can explore possible areas of interest, and gain experience, by working in a clinical setting. For example, you might volunteer at a crisis hotline, community mental health center, women's resource center, or drug and alcohol treatment program.

TAKEAWAY POINT: If a career in counseling or clinical psychology is your goal, keep admission criteria in mind to increase your chances of acceptance in a graduate program. Doing well in your courses, gaining experience in research or clinical work, and getting to know your professors will all help. In applying to a graduate program, you will need to craft a personal statement explaining your interest in and commitment to psychology, and it's never too early to start putting those aspects of your life into words.

Ψ You can look up job descriptions, education requirements, salaries, and more at the Bureau of Labor Statistics: www.bls.gov. Visit the site and start putting psychology to work!

APPENDIX A: How Do Psychologists Analyze Research Data?

A.1 Descriptive Statistics Summarize the Data

A.1 LEARNING GOAL ACTIVITIES

To maximize your learning, complete the following learning goal activities:

a. Understand all bold and italic terms by writing explanations of them in your own words.

b. Apply descriptive statistics by calculating the mean, median, and mode of the number of hours that a group of college students reported actively reading their introductory psychology textbook: 4, 0, 1, 6, 7, 4, 2, 3, 5, 8, 4.

c. Apply correlations by describing one positive correlation from your life and one negative correlation from your life.

After conducting research, you need to analyze the data to see whether your hypothesis is supported (see Figure 1.19, Step 4). Recall that in your experiment the hypothesis was: "Using either a hands-free cell phone or a handheld cell phone impairs driving." One way you measured this relationship was based on the number of crashes participants had while driving in the simulator. These measurements are raw data, which are as close as possible to the form in which they were collected. So the first step in analyzing research results is to inspect the raw data. In examining raw data, researchers look for errors in data recording. For instance, they remove any responses from the data set that seem especially unlikely (for example, 50,000 accidents in one hour of driving on the simulator).

CENTRAL TENDENCY DESCRIBES THE MIDDLE OF THE DATA SET Once the researchers are satisfied that the raw data make sense, they summarize the basic patterns. *Descriptive statistics* provide an overall summary of the study's results. For example, descriptive statistics might show how many accidents participants had during one hour in the driving simulator across each of the three groups (when not talking on a cell phone in the control group, talking on a hands-free phone or talking on a handheld phone in the two experimental groups). The simplest descriptive statistics are measures of **central tendency** (**Figure A.1a**). This single value describes a numerical response in the middle of the data set as a whole.

A common measure of central tendency is the *mean*. The mean is the arithmetic average of a set of numbers. As shown in Figure A.1a, to find the mean, you add up all of the scores and divide by the total number of scores you had. The class average on an exam is an example of a mean score. To find the mean of a test you would add up all 31 students' scores and then divide by 31. In your experiment on how using a cell phone affects driving performance, you might calculate three means, one for each group. Each of these means would show the average number of car crashes during one hour of simulated driving. You would calculate one mean for those participants who did not use a cell phone while driving (control group), another mean for participants who talked on a hands-free cell phone while driving (experimental group 1),

central tendency
A group of descriptive statistics, including mean, median, and mode, where one number represents the middle numerical response in a data set.

and another mean for the participants who talked on a handheld cell phone while driving (experimental group 2). If using a cell phone in these different ways affects driving, you would see a difference in the mean number of car accidents in one hour of simulated driving across these conditions.

A second measure of central tendency is the *median*. The median is the value in a set of numbers that falls exactly halfway between the lowest and highest values. To find the median (Figure A.1a), you order all of the scores, from lowest to highest, and the score in the middle is the median. For instance, for a class of 31 students, if you received the median score on a test, then half of the people who took the test scored lower than you (15 students) and half the people scored higher (15 students).

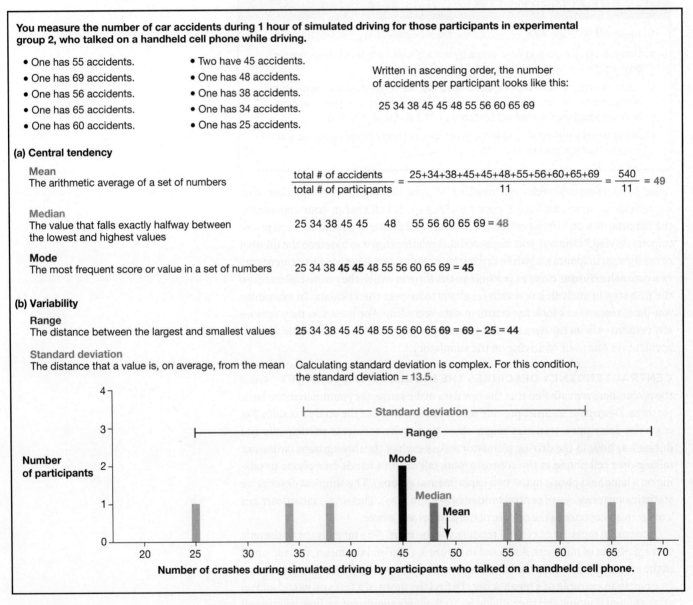

You measure the number of car accidents during 1 hour of simulated driving for those participants in experimental group 2, who talked on a handheld cell phone while driving.

- One has 55 accidents.
- One has 69 accidents.
- One has 56 accidents.
- One has 65 accidents.
- One has 60 accidents.
- Two have 45 accidents.
- One has 48 accidents.
- One has 38 accidents.
- One has 34 accidents.
- One has 25 accidents.

Written in ascending order, the number of accidents per participant looks like this:

25 34 38 45 45 48 55 56 60 65 69

(a) Central tendency

Mean
The arithmetic average of a set of numbers

$$\frac{\text{total \# of accidents}}{\text{total \# of participants}} = \frac{25+34+38+45+45+48+55+56+60+65+69}{11} = \frac{540}{11} = 49$$

Median
The value that falls exactly halfway between the lowest and highest values

25 34 38 45 45   48   55 56 60 65 69 = 48

Mode
The most frequent score or value in a set of numbers

25 34 38 **45 45** 48 55 56 60 65 69 = **45**

(b) Variability

Range
The distance between the largest and smallest values

25 34 38 45 45 48 55 56 60 65 **69** = 69 − 25 = **44**

Standard deviation
The distance that a value is, on average, from the mean

Calculating standard deviation is complex. For this condition, the standard deviation = **13.5**.

Number of crashes during simulated driving by participants who talked on a handheld cell phone.

FIGURE A.1

Descriptive Statistics for an Experiment on Cell Phone Use and Driving Performance

Here, descriptive statistics summarize the numerical results of a data set for a sample experiment investigating the relationship between cell phone use and driving performance. Here, the data are shown for one of three groups, experimental group 2, where participants used a handheld cell phone while driving in a simulator. **(a)** Three different measures of central tendency are shown for the sample experiment: mean, median, and mode. **(b)** Two measures of variability are shown for the sample experiment: range and the standard deviation.

At some point in your life you are likely to negotiate a salary for a job. The best way to do this is to get information about what people usually get paid to do that job. "Usually" suggests that you need to use a measure of central tendency to calculate the average salary so you know what your salary should be. But what measure should you use? You want to use the measure that will end up getting you the highest salary possible. So if many people have a high salary in that position, you should calculate the mean salary. This measure gives you a higher salary to negotiate around. But if many people make a low salary at the job, then the mean will be quite low, so you would not want to use that figure as the basis for your salary negotiation. In that case, you would use the median, which will be higher than the mean. Once you have calculated the mean or median salary information, you would make your pitch that your salary should at least match that level.

In other words, your score is ranked 16th out of the 31 students. To find the median when there is an even number of scores, you must calculate the mean of the two numbers ranked in the middle of the data set. In your study, you could also calculate the median number of accidents for each of the three groups to describe how using a cell phone affects driving.

Sometimes researchers will summarize data using a median instead of a mean. The median will be more useful than the mean if some of the numbers in the set are dramatically larger or smaller than all the others, because the mean will then give either an inflated or a deflated summary of the average. This effect occurs in studies of average income. Perhaps about 50 percent of Americans make more than $56,000 per year, but a small percentage of people make so much more (multiple millions or billions for the richest people) that the mean income is much higher than the median and is not an accurate measure of what the typical person earns. The median provides a better estimate of how much money the average person makes. Understanding the difference between these measures is information that you can use to your advantage. Think about it by reading Try It Yourself above.

A third measure of central tendency is the *mode*. The mode is the most frequent score or value in a set of numbers (Figure A.1a). It is useful for seeing what value is typical or common. For instance, the mode in the number of children in an American family is two, which means that more American families have two children than have any other number of children. In the case of the test scores for the 31 students, the mode is the most frequently earned test score. In our sample experiment, you would also calculate the mode of the number of accidents for each of the three groups who used cell phones in different ways.

VARIABILITY IS THE SPREAD OF DATA POINTS Consider two neighborhoods. One neighborhood is suburban, and most of its residents earn similar salaries. The other neighborhood is urban, and its residents have incomes ranging from low to high. In both neighborhoods, the mean income is $45,000 per year. Despite the differences between these populations, their mean incomes are the same. What does this example show? Measures of central tendency are not the only important way to describe data. Another important descriptive statistic for a set of numbers is the **variability,** the spread in numerical responses (**Figure A.1b**).

variability
A group of descriptive statistics, including range and standard deviation, where one number represents the spread between numerical responses in a data set.

A simple measure of variability is the *range*, the distance between the largest and smallest values. As seen in Figure A.1b, this value is easily calculated by ordering the data points, from lowest to highest, and subtracting the lowest number from the highest number. Say that out of 31 exam scores, the top score for an exam is 95 out of a possible 100. The bottom score is 52. The range is 43. This result could be considered large, in that it shows great variability in student performance on the exam. It suggests that the person who scored 52 might need extra help—as do people who earned similar scores. In the research on cell phone use, you could also calculate the range in numbers of accidents during 1 hour of simulated driving for each of the three groups.

One common measure of variability is the *standard deviation*. While the calculation of the standard deviation is complex, it is easy to understand what the measure describes and to see it reflected in data (see Figure A.1b). In short, this measure reflects how far away each value is, on average, from the mean. As an example, if the mean score for an exam is 75 percent and the standard deviation is 5, most people scored between 70 percent and 80 percent. If the mean remains the same but the standard deviation becomes 15, most people scored between 60 and 90—a much larger spread. This would be the last statistic that you would need in your sample experiment on how using a cell phone affects driving. You would calculate the standard deviation in number of crashes for each of the groups in the experiment to determine how much spread there is in the data around the mean for each group. This result tells you how consistent each group is in terms of driving performance, as affected by the particular group's use, or not, of a cell phone during the simulated driving task.

CORRELATIONS MEASURE RELATIONSHIPS The descriptive statistics you have learned about so far are used for summarizing the central tendency and variability in a set of numbers. Descriptive statistics can also be used to summarize how two variables relate to each other.

Remember that finding the relationship between two variables is the goal of correlational methods. In study unit 1.10, you learned about using correlational methods to test the hypothesis "More frequent use of a cell phone while driving is related to having more crashes." In this case, your first step in examining the relationship between these two variables would be to create a *scatterplot*. This type of graph provides a convenient picture of the data (**Figure A.2**).

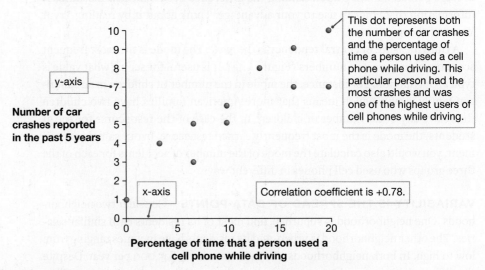

FIGURE A.2

Scatterplot of Correlation Between Cell Phone Use and Car Crashes

Scatterplots are graphs that illustrate the correlation between two variables. This scatterplot shows the data from sample correlational research revealing that across a five-year period, more frequent use of a cell phone while driving is related to greater numbers of crashes.

In addition to visually showing the relationship in a scatterplot, you would compute a **correlation coefficient**. The correlation coefficient is a descriptive statistic to summarize what is shown visually in the scatterplot. This descriptive statistic provides a numerical value between +1.0 and –1.0. In your sample correlational research, the correlation coefficient for using a cell phone while driving and the number of crashes a person had in the past five years is +0.78 (see Figure A.2). This correlation coefficient provides two pieces of information that help you understand the relationship between the two variables: It describes the *direction of the relationship* and the *strength of the relationship*.

Both the direction and the strength of relationships are shown in the scatterplots in **Figure A.3**. If two variables have a *positive correlation,* they change in the same direction. That is, they both increase together or decrease together, as shown by a "+" sign before the number in a correlation coefficient (see Figure A.3, graphs 1 and 2). For example, in your sample research the correlation coefficient is +0.78, and the "+" indicates a positive correlation between the two variables. So in your study, using a cell phone *more* while driving is related to having *more* car crashes (see Figure A.2).

If two variables have a *negative correlation,* they change in opposite directions: As one variable increases in value, the other decreases in value (see Figure A.3, graphs 4 and 5). This relationship would be shown by a "–" sign before the number in a correlation coefficient. Consider that instead of accidents, you measured how quickly drivers travel through an obstacle course. Maybe you have noticed that people who drive while talking on a cell phone often drive slowly. So an example of a negative correlation could be that when a person uses a cell phone *more* while driving, this increase is related to a *decrease* in the speed at which the person drives in the simulator. This negative correlation might be revealed by a correlation coefficient of –0.62.

Besides indicating the direction of the relationship between variables, a correlation coefficient also tells you about the strength of that relationship. Knowing how people measure on one variable lets you predict how they will measure on the other variable. What signifies a strong relationship? The closer the correlation coefficient

correlation coefficient
A descriptive statistic that indicates the direction (positive or negative) and strength (from 0 to 1) of the relationship between variables; taken together these result in numbers ranging from +1 to 0 to –1.

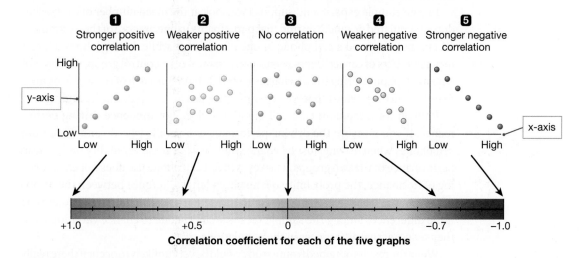

FIGURE A.3

Direction and Strength of Correlations

Correlations can have different values between +1.0 and –1.0. These values reveal the strength and direction of relationships between two variables. The greater the scatter of values, the lower the correlation. A perfect correlation occurs when all the values fall on a straight line.

is to 1, either +1 or –1, the stronger the relationship. A perfect positive correlation is indicated by a value of +1.0 (see Figure A.3, graph 1). A perfect negative correlation is indicated by a value of –1.0 (see Figure A.3, graph 5). By contrast, the closer a correlation coefficient is to 0, the weaker the relationship. If two variables show no apparent relationship, the value of the correlation will be zero (see Figure A.3, graph 3).

In your sample correlational research, the correlation coefficient of +0.78 includes the number 0.78, which is very close to 1. This is a very strong relationship between the two variables, indicating that people who use their cell phones more while driving are more likely to have car crashes (see Figure A.2). Statistical information of this kind is important for people to know because it may help them drive safely.

A.2 Inferential Statistics Rule Out Chance Findings

 A.2 LEARNING GOAL ACTIVITIES

To maximize your learning, complete the following learning goal activities:

a. Understand all bold and italic terms by writing explanations of them in your own words.

b. Evaluate inferential statistics in a sample experiment. In a control group, student participants read a text passage and highlighted it. In an experimental group, student participants read the same passage and answered questions about it. Inferential statistics showed that the mean number of facts remembered was greater for the experimental group than for the control group. If there was no actual difference between the groups, this outcome was likely to happen by chance less than 3 percent of the time. How would you describe the results of this research?

Researchers use descriptive statistics to summarize data sets. They also need to estimate whether their results are due to chance or whether differences actually exist in the populations they have drawn their study samples from. In order to do this, researchers use *inferential statistics*.

In your sample experiment, suppose you look at the mean number of car crashes during simulated driving. You find that participants in one or more of the experimental groups, who used a cell phone in one of two ways while driving, showed larger mean numbers of car accidents versus participants in the control group, who did not have a cell phone during the driving task. How different do each of these means need to be for you to conclude that your finding is not just an isolated, chance finding?

Pretend for a moment that cell phone use does not influence driving performance. If you measure the driving performance of people who do and do not use cell phones when driving, just by chance there will be some variability in the mean performance of the two groups. The key is that if cell phone use does not affect driving performance, the probability of showing a large difference between the means of the groups is relatively small. Researchers use statistical techniques to determine if the differences among the sample means are likely due to chance variations or if they reflect actual differences in the populations.

When the results obtained from a study would be very unlikely to occur if there really were no real differences between the groups of subjects, the researchers conclude that the results have **statistical significance**. According to generally accepted standards, researchers typically conclude that research findings have statistical significance only if the results would occur by chance less than 5 percent of the time.

statistical significance
A measure of the likelihood that research results are large enough to be a result of factors other than chance.

Now apply this idea to your sample research. In study unit 1.11, the hypothesis for the experiment was: "Using either hands-free or handheld cell phones impairs driving." In a study to test that hypothesis, the control group did not use a cell phone while driving. The first experimental group talked on a hands-free cell phone, and the second talked on a handheld cell phone. In evaluating the data from this experiment, you would need to compare the means across all three conditions.

Figure A.4 shows the mean number of crashes during simulated driving in each condition. Compared with the control group, the mean number of crashes is visibly higher for experimental group 2, where participants talked on a handheld cell phone (Figure A.4a), and for experimental group 1, where participants talked on a hands-free cell phone (Figure A.4b). But are these differences larger than would be expected by chance? The error bars show a measure of variability for the groups in the study. The difference between the means is much larger than the observed variability within each group. Thus, these differences between the groups do not appear to have happened by chance. Inferential statistics suggest that these differences appear to be real, and they suggest that talking on a cell phone impairs driving performance.

By contrast, Figure A.4c also shows that the means and error bars are overlapping for the two experimental conditions where participants talked on a cell phone, regardless of whether the participants held the phone. That is, there seems to be no significant difference in the mean number of crashes when drivers talked on a hands-free cell phone and when they talked on a handheld cell phone. This outcome might occur because both conditions require the driver's focus on the distracting conversation.

This pattern of inferential statistics for the sample experiment suggests that the manual task of holding a cell phone while using it is not what impairs driving.

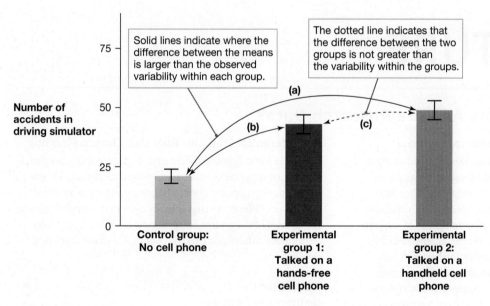

FIGURE A.4

Evaluating Differences in Research Results

This hypothetical experiment shows the mean number of crashes in a driving simulator by participants in three conditions. Error bars have been added to show the variability of data within each condition. The differences in the means of the various groups show that compared to the control group, participants had significantly more crashes when **(a)** talking on a handheld cell phone or **(b)** talking on a hands-free cell phone. However, participants crashed about as much when **(c)** talking on either a hands-free or a handheld phone. The data suggest that talking on a cell phone, whether hands-free or handheld, interferes with driving.

Instead, driving is impaired by the phone conversation, regardless of whether the phone is in the driver's hand. This result is generally consistent with other research in the field. A review of 206 studies found that the skills necessary to drive a car can become impaired when people perform a second task at the same time (Ferdinand & Menachemi, 2014). The takehome message is that hands-free cell phone use is far from safe. It is more dangerous than holding a regular conversation with a passenger because passengers notice the driving conditions and understand when not to distract the driver (Strayer & Drews, 2007).

In reading this appendix, you now have a good understanding of why it is so dangerous to use a cell phone while driving, even if you are using a hands-free phone. Cell phone use interferes with your focus on driving, and you need to avoid distractions to drive as well as possible to avoid crashes. This knowledge can empower you to change your behavior—to never use a cell phone while driving—and to inspire that change in others.

 How Do Psychologists Analyze Research Data?

To make sure you learned what you just read, write answers to the following questions and check your answers.

A.1 If two variables are completely unrelated to each other, what would the correlation coefficient be?

A.2 What does it mean if an observed difference between groups in a research study is described as statistically significant?

See Appendix B for answers to the red Q questions.

BIG PICTURE

How Do Psychologists Analyze Research Data?

A.1 Descriptive Statistics Summarize the Data

Review the learning goal activities on p. A1. Descriptive statistics provide an overall summary of a study's results. Measures of central tendency (mean, median, and mode) describe a numerical response in the middle of a data set. Measures of variability (range and standard deviation) describe the spread of numerical responses in a data set. A correlation coefficient describes the direction and strength of the relationship between variables. The sign of a correlation shows whether the variables change in the same way (positive) or in opposite ways (negative). Correlation coefficients may range from +1.0 to 0 to –1.0. The strength of a correlation indicates how related the variables are, where 0 indicates no relationship between the variables and +1 or –1 indicates a very strong relationship.

A.2 Inferential Statistics Rule Out Chance Findings

Review the learning goal activities on p. A6. Inferential statistics indicate whether differences seen in the data obtained from two or more groups are due to chance variations or whether they reflect differences that actually exist in the mental activity or behavior of the groups being compared. When the results are unlikely to have occurred by chance, they have statistical significance.

KEY TERMS
central tendency (p. A1)
variability (p. A3)
correlation coefficient (p. A5)
statistical significance (p. A6)

Appendix B: Answers to Red Q Questions and Self-Quiz Questions

Chapter 1: Answers to Red Q Questions

1.1 Psychology is (1) a science that studies (2) mental activity, (3) behavior, and (4) how mental activity and behavior are processed in the brain.

1.2 The three steps in critical thinking are (1) understanding the claim that is being made; (2) determining what evidence, if any, is presented to support the claim; and (3) deciding if the evidence supports the claim.

1.3 Answering learning goal activities forces you to actively process the information, whereas highlighting material, rereading it, or both are more passive processes that do not require much thought and lead to poorer memory.

1.4 The nature/nurture debate and the mind/body problem are appropriate for psychology because they explore mental activity, behavior, and underlying brain processes.

1.5 The theory of natural selection is related to functionalism, a historical school of thought that said the mind serves the function of supporting adaptive behavior.

1.6 Humanism is a historical school of thought in psychology that focuses on people's goodness and how we should accept ourselves, work toward achieving our personal goals, and fulfill our potential to be the best we can be.

1.7 The subfield of psychology that is most likely to investigate attention processes in any situation, including using a cell phone while driving, is cognitive psychology.

1.8 A hypothesis is a specific, testable prediction about the results one might expect to find in empirical research.

1.9 One limitation of case studies is that they are subjective. Another is that the findings might not generalize, or apply, to people beyond the particular case being investigated.

1.10 No, you should not grow your hair in order to lose weight, because a limitation of the correlational research method is that you cannot determine what causes the relationship between variables.

1.11 In an experiment, the independent variable is manipulated and the dependent variable is measured.

1.12 Informed consent is the ethical issue that requires a researcher to tell potential participants about the study so they can choose whether to participate.

Chapter 1: Answers to Self-Quiz Questions

1. **D:** Psychology is the study of human mental activity and behavior. Refer to Learning Goal Activity 1.1b.

2. **C:** The nature/nurture debate considers how mental processes and behaviors are influenced by biological and/or environmental factors. Refer to Learning Goal Activity 1.4b.

3. **A:** Structuralism is the school of psychology that explores conscious experiences by breaking them down into their component parts. Refer to Learning Goal Activity 1.5b.

4. **C:** Cognitive psychology investigates mental activity associated with functions such as intelligence, learning, thinking, attention, and memory. Refer to Learning Goal Activity 1.6b.

5. **A:** Personality psychology is the study of enduring characteristics that people display over time (for example, shyness). Cultural psychology examines how people's behavior is influenced by the societal rules, values, and beliefs from their environment. Refer to Learning Goal Activity 1.7b.

6. **B:** Simon has come up with a specific, testable prediction—a hypothesis. He is using the number of words remembered during a visual task as the dependent variable that will let him measure his participants' visual memories. Refer to Learning Goal Activities 1.8c and 1.11b.

7. **D:** By strictly watching the children and not manipulating any variables, Jool is using one of the three descriptive methods, an observational study. Refer to Learning Goal Activity 1.9b.

8. **B:** Because the research shows a relationship between two variables (reading actively and higher quiz grades), a correlational method was used. Refer to Learning Goal Activity 1.10b.

9. **A:** Remember that the control group receives the baseline condition while the experimental group gets the treatment of interest. Refer to Learning Goal Activity 1.11b.

10. **C:** According to the ethical guidelines regarding privacy, the couples in a study of this kind must be observed in public settings only, not in private settings. Refer to Learning Goal Activity 1.12b.

Chapter 2: Answers to Red Q Questions

2.1 The four main parts of a neuron are dendrites, cell body, axon, and terminal buttons.

2.2 When the axon becomes sufficiently positively charged on the inside relative to the outside, an action potential moves down the axon, toward the terminal buttons.

2.3 Agonists increase the effects of a neurotransmitter, whereas antagonists decrease the effects of a neurotransmitter.

2.4 EEG provides information on the electrical activity in the brain, fMRI provides information about where in the brain activity occurs, and TMS disrupts brain activity in specific locations to examine which regions are necessary for specific psychological functions.

2.5 Your spinal cord is the part of your CNS that sends information to and receives information from another part of your CNS, your brain.

2.6 The thalamus is called the gateway to the cortex, because almost all sensory information (except smell) goes first to the thalamus before being sent to the appropriate regions of the cortex for more processing.

2.7 The prefrontal cortex is organized differently in humans, and it supports processing of the complex demands of human social life, such as understanding other people and having a sense of self.

2.8 Your somatic nervous system, in your PNS, detects the sensory input on your skin and sends that information about water temperature to your CNS.

2.9 Your parasympathetic nervous system, in your autonomic nervous system, calms your body.

2.10 The gonads of males, called testes, and the gonads of females, called ovaries, release hormones such as androgens and estrogens, which influence sexual development.

2.11 Genotype is your genes. Phenotype is your observable physical and psychological traits, which result from your genes and your environment.

2.12 Behavioral genetics is the exploration of how genes and environment interact to influence psychology (mental activity and behavior).

2.13 Influenced by environment, plasticity can change your brain by growing new neurons, strengthening or weakening neural connections, and building new connections (reorganization).

Chapter 2: Answers to Self-Quiz Questions

1. **C:** If a presynaptic neuron has an action potential, then neurotransmitters are released from the terminal buttons at the end of the axon, cross the synapse, and bind with the receptors on the dendrites of the postsynaptic neuron. But action potentials are never stronger or weaker—they fire or do not fire, but they always fire at a constant rate. Refer to Learning Goal Activity 2.2b.

2. **A:** Glutamate is the primary excitatory neurotransmitter that assists in learning and memory by reinforcing neural pathways. Refer to Learning Goal Activity 2.3b.

3. **A:** The hindbrain is the portion of the brain that contains the cerebellum, which is crucial for motor learning, coordination, and balance. Refer to Learning Goal Activity 2.5b.

4. **C:** The hippocampus plays a crucial role in the formation of new memories. Refer to Learning Goal Activity 2.6b.

5. **D:** The occipital lobes house the primary visual cortex and process visual information. Refer to Learning Goal Activity 2.7b.

6. **D:** The somatic nervous system, part of the peripheral nervous system (PNS), transmits sensory information to the central nervous system (CNS), using receptors in the skin, muscles, and joints. It also processes information from the CNS to move muscles and joints. Refer to Learning Goal Activity 2.8b.

7. **A:** The sympathetic nervous system, in the autonomic portion of the peripheral nervous system (PNS), prepares the body for action and is in charge of the fight-or-flight response. It would most likely be responsible for the increased heart rate that lets Ricardo run from the bear. Refer to Learning Goal Activity 2.9b.

8. **A:** Androgens are hormones, found in greater levels in males, that influence the development of secondary sex characteristics, such as the growth of facial hair. Refer to Learning Goal Activity 2.10b.

9. **B:** A behavioral geneticist examines how genes and environment interact to influence psychology. To focus on how "nature" influences siblings, behavioral geneticists study monozygotic (identical) and dizygotic (fraternal) twins in the same home, because similarities between the twins are thought to be due to genetics. To focus on how "nurture" influences siblings, behavioral geneticists use adoption studies, because similarities between biological and adopted siblings are thought to be due to environment. Refer to Learning Goal Activity 2.12b.

10. **B:** Plasticity is a property of the brain that lets it change through experience. Refer to Learning Goal Activity 2.13b.

Chapter 3: Answers to Red Q Questions

3.1 A person's level of consciousness refers to how aware the person is of both the external world and mental activity, whereas a person's state of consciousness refers to the person's clarity of awareness.

3.2 Dualism is the idea that the brain and the mind are separate, whereas materialism is the idea that they are inseparable. The global workspace model supports materialism by describing how consciousness is associated with activity in certain areas of the brain.

3.3 Automatic processing is fast and does not require a lot of attention resources, whereas controlled processing is slower and requires more attention resources.

3.4 This unconscious influence on thinking is an example of subliminal perception, which can affect simple responses to information.

3.5 A person is fully asleep and less conscious in stage 2 sleep. During this stage, EEGs reveal sleep spindles and K-complexes.

3.6 You most likely had a non-REM dream, as the content is dull and not bizarre as dreams tend to be during REM sleep.

3.7 Sleeping for a long time after great exertion, such as running a marathon, is consistent with the restorative theory, which says that sleep helps repair the body.

3.8 According to research, good sleeping habits depend on going to bed at the same time every night, regardless of what that hour is.

3.9 No, not everyone can be hypnotized. Hypnosis works only for certain people who are willing to go along with the experience.

3.10 By focusing on a specific image, the person is practicing concentrative meditation.

3.11 Flow is an altered state of consciousness that results from being deeply immersed in a completely enjoyable and satisfying experience that may have no consequences beyond itself.

3.12 These substances are stimulants. They increase behavior and mental activity.

3.13 The two physical aspects of addiction are tolerance, which is the need to ingest more of a drug to get the desired effect, and withdrawal, which is the experience of anxiety, tension, and craving for the drug after use of it has been decreased.

Chapter 3: Answers to Self-Quiz Questions

1. **A:** The global workspace model states that brain activity gives rise to consciousness. Specifically, our conscious experiences are a result of which brain circuits are active at a given time. Refer to Learning Goal Activity 3.2b.

2. **C:** Automatic processing occurs when we execute well-learned, routine tasks without devoting much of our attention to the tasks, so we are not fully aware of doing them. Refer to Learning Goal Activity 3.3b.

3. **B:** The left hemisphere of the brain is responsible for producing language, so Clark will be able to say "dog." But the left hand is controlled by the right hemisphere. Because his right hemisphere did not receive the image of the dog due to his corpus callosum having been cut, Clark will be unable to pick up the toy with his left hand. Refer to Learning Goal Activity 3.4b.

4. **D:** Slow-wave sleep is characterized by the presence of delta waves. Consciousness is very different in this stage of sleep. People can respond to important information in an environment, such as a baby's cries. But if they wake up from slow-wave sleep, they are often disoriented. Refer to Learning Goal Activity 3.5b.

5. **A:** According to consolidation theory, the main benefit of sleeping is to help us strengthen and consolidate the neural connections that let us learn and remember. Refer to Learning Goal Activity 3.7b.

6. **D:** REM behavior disorder occurs when the body's muscles are not paralyzed during REM sleep and people act out their dreams. Refer to Learning Goal Activity 3.8b.

7. **C:** According to the dissociation theory of hypnosis, hypnosis is a truly altered state of consciousness in which people's awareness of their conscious experiences are suspended or inaccessible. Refer to Learning Goal Activity 3.9b.

8. **C:** During many pleasurable daily activities, such as watching television or looking at a fire, a person may experience flow, an altered state of consciousness where thoughts and external events seem either more or less clear. Refer to Learning Goal Activity 3.11b.

9. **B:** Hallucinogenic drugs create an altered state of consciousness by changing a person's perceptions, thoughts, and emotions. Refer to Learning Goal Activity 3.12b.

10. **A:** The evidence suggests that Jerry has developed a tolerance for caffeine. This form of physical dependence occurs when the body becomes accustomed to certain levels of a substance and needs more of the substance to feel the same effect as when the person first started using it. Refer to Learning Goal Activity 3.13b.

Chapter 4: Answers to Red Q Questions

4.1 An intentional smile reflects development of the brain (physical domain), development of thought processes about what is interesting or entertaining (cognitive domain), and development of feelings, such as happiness (socio-emotional domain).

4.2 At 16 weeks, the unborn baby is in the fetal period of development.

4.3 Alcohol is a teratogen that—through exposure from the father, mother, or both—can impair an unborn baby's prenatal development.

4.4 Young infants have poor color vision and low visual acuity, so they most easily perceive objects with stark contrasts, such as black against a white background.

4.5 An infant showing these responses most likely has a secure attachment.

4.6 According to Piaget, the 8-month-old stops crying because a child of that age does not have object permanence. That is, the child cannot understand that the toy, while hidden, still exists.

4.7 Before about 24 months of age, a toddler typically uses telegraphic speech, combining two words to convey the meaning of an entire sentence.

4.8 Because the limbic system matures before the frontal lobes, adolescents may experience motivations and emotions that are stronger than their ability to exert control and make good decisions.

4.9 Adolescents must resolve the crisis of identity versus role confusion, by figuring out who they are with respect to factors such as gender, sexual orientation, ethnicity, parents, and peers.

4.10 Bullies might not feel the moral emotions of guilt and shame. In addition, bullies with high self-esteem tend to exhibit moral disengagement, such as indifference or pride, and to rationalize or justify their behavior.

4.11 Good nutrition and physical exercise—the earlier in life the better—are the two main ways to sustain health in adulthood.

4.12 In heterosexual marriages, husbands receive the most benefit from marriage partly because their wives encourage healthy lifestyles and provide social support.

4.13 Dementia is a brain condition that over time causes declines in thinking, memory, and behavior.

Chapter 4: Answers to Self-Quiz Questions

1. **A:** From 2 months until the birth of the baby, a developing human is a fetus and the woman is in the fetal period of prenatal development. Although most pregnancies end with a birth at about 40 weeks of gestation, a fetus can often survive outside the womb after about 28 weeks of gestation. Refer to Learning Goal Activity 4.2b.

2. **D:** Alcohol is an example of a teratogen (that happens to be a legal drug) with severe effects on a developing human. Alcohol may lead to birth defects such as facial and limb malformations, heart defects, and intellectual disabilities. Refer to Learning Goal Activity 4.3b.

3. **B:** The process of maturation occurs when children develop a predictable set of motor skills in the same sequential order within a similar range of time. Maturation was thought to be a purely biological process that reflected the influence of nature on development. But we now know that the influence of nurture—experiences and environment—helps shape an infant's physical development. Refer to Learning Goal Activity 4.4b.

4. **A:** An ambivalent attachment is an insecure attachment. Children with ambivalent attachments cry when their caregiver leaves and are inconsolable upon being reunited with the caregiver. Refer to Learning Goal Activity 4.5b.

5. **D:** If Shay is out of the preoperational stage of cognitive development, he is now in the concrete operational stage. In this stage, he is able to think logically and perform and understand operations on concrete objects. For example, he can do simple math if he uses his fingers or blocks or some other object to help him. Refer to Learning Goal Activity 4.6b.

6. **C:** Eric is able to put words together using correct grammar for English. But as a normal part of his language development, he is overapplying certain rules, which is called overregularization. In this case, Eric incorrectly added "-ed" to "forget" to make "forgetted." Instead of using the regular past tense, he should have used the irregular past tense, "forgot." Refer to Learning Goal Activity 4.7b.

7. **D:** Secondary sex characteristics are changes in the adolescent body that make it look more adult. Primary sex characteristics are the bodily changes that directly relate to the ability to reproduce. Both of these changes happen during puberty. Refer to Learning Goal Activity 4.8b.

8. **D:** People in the conventional level of moral reasoning are likely to make moral decisions based on laws or social rules. Their moral reasoning about breaking laws and going against social norms is based on when doing so would bring about disapproval. Refer to Learning Goal Activity 4.10b.

9. **B:** According to Erickson, when most people reach middle age—between about age 40 and 50—they face the challenge of generativity versus stagnation. This challenge reflects the tension between a desire to work hard in one's career and raise children to leave something for future generations versus focusing only on oneself. Refer to Learning Goal Activity 4.12b.

10. **C:** As people age, they experience cognitive impairments such as reacting quickly to information, doing two things at one time, and learning new information. But they tend to retain knowledge for facts they learned in the past. Refer to Learning Goal Activity 4.13b.

Chapter 5: Answers to Red Q Questions

5.1 Transduction is the translation of physical stimuli received by sensory receptors into signals the brain can interpret.

5.2 The just-noticeable difference is related to the difference threshold, because the just-noticeable difference explains that the amount of stimulus needed to detect a change in input between two stimuli (the difference threshold) is based on a proportional change between the two stimuli.

5.3 The fovea has only cones, no rods.

5.4 Afterimages are best explained by opponent-process theory, because some ganglion cells make it seem that green and red are opposites and others make it seem that yellow and blue are opposites.

5.5 We perceive people together as a crowd because we group close objects due to the principle of proximity and we group objects that share aspects due to the principle of similarity.

5.6 The main difference is the number of eyes involved. Binocular depth cues require the use of two eyes, whereas monocular depth cues are available with just one eye.

5.7 Stroboscopic motion explains why individual blinking lights appear to run in a continuous line.

5.8 The four types of object constancy are size constancy, shape constancy, color constancy, and brightness constancy.

5.9 Loud sounds have higher-amplitude sound waves that ultimately damage hair cells in the cochlea by forcing them to repeatedly bend in response to the input.

5.10 Temporal coding lets you hear low pitches. That is, lower-pitched sounds are perceived due to the firing rate of the auditory nerve, which matches the lower frequency of the sound wave.

5.11 The five basic taste qualities that are confirmed by research are sweet, sour, salty, bitter, and umami (savory).

5.12 Olfactory information is not processed through the thalamus. Instead, it goes directly to the olfactory bulb.

5.13 When you shake hands, pressure receptors in the skin detect the touch. Perception of the touch is processed in the somatosensory cortex.

5.14 Rubbing activates sensory receptors that can close the pain gate, reducing the experience of pain.

Chapter 5: Answers to Self-Quiz Questions

1. **B:** The technician is attempting to determine when Mia can detect an auditory stimulus half the time. The absolute threshold represents the smallest amount of input needed to detect a stimulus. By contrast, a difference threshold is the ability to distinguish a difference between two or more stimuli. Refer to Learning Goal Activity 5.2b.

2. **D:** The process of detecting physical stimuli is called sensation. For vision, sensation of light waves occurs in the retina. The rods are the sensory receptors that detect dim light to let us see in the dark. By contrast, cones are the sensory receptors in the retina that allow us to see colors and details. Ultimately, perception is our unique experience of a stimulus, and this occurs in the brain. Refer to Learning Goal Activity 5.3b.

3. **A:** The fact that we see some colors as opposites can be explained by opponent-process theory. Activity in some types of ganglion cells makes red and green seem like opposites. Activity in other types of ganglion cells makes yellow and blue seem like opposites. Refer to Learning Goal Activity 5.4b.

4. **C:** Binocular disparity is a binocular depth cue, which means that it requires two eyes. It allows you to see depth because the brain calculates how far away objects are based on the slightly different image received by the retina of each eye. This cue works only for objects that are close to you. Refer to Learning Goal Activity 5.6b.

5. **B:** The hair cells are responsible for transduction in the auditory system. That is, the hair cells change sound waves into signals that the brain ultimately processes as sounds. The auditory nerve then relays this neural signal to the auditory cortex, in the brain. Refer to Learning Goal Activity 5.9b.

6. **C:** Because Kai is having problems hearing high-pitched sounds, she is having difficulty processing high-frequency sound waves. According to place theory, these waves are encoded by hair cells at different locations on the basilar membrane in the cochlea. Refer to Learning Goal Activity 5.10b.

7. **A:** Papillae are structures on the tongue that contain many taste buds. The taste buds contain the sensory receptors for the gustatory system, called taste receptors. People who have many papillae also have more taste receptors and are more sensitive to certain tastes. Refer to Learning Goal Activity 5.11b.

8. **D:** Sensory information is processed through the thalamus for all the senses except smell. If Cosette's sense of smell is declining, then any of the other three structures—olfactory cortex, olfactory bulb, or olfactory nerve—might be damaged. Refer to Learning Goal Activity 5.12b.

9. **C:** Pressure receptors, including those that are sensitive to vibration and different types of pressure, are located in the skin and detect tactile stimuli. Refer to Learning Goal Activity 5.13b.

10. **B:** Fast fibers carry information that we perceive as sharp pain. These messages are transmitted immediately because the axons of fast fibers are insulated by myelin. Refer to Learning Goal Activity 5.14b.

Chapter 6: Answers to Red Q Questions

6.1 Learning is a change in behavior, resulting from a person's experiences.

6.2 Habituation decreases a behavioral response, whereas sensitization increases a behavioral response.

6.3 Long-term potentiation is the strengthening of synaptic connections when one neuron repeatedly activates another.

6.4 Food was the unconditioned stimulus in Pavlov's research, because it naturally elicited a response with no prior learning.

6.5 Stimulus discrimination will help you learn how to identify the different species of flowers.

6.6 If a child fears dogs (where CS [dog] → CR1 [fear]), then by association dogs with calmly petting them, the child will learn to relax around dogs (where CS [dog] → CR2 [relaxation]).

6.7 When a person eats a particular food and then feels nausea, the person is more likely to learn a conditioned taste aversion to the food, because the food (CS) predicts the nausea (US).

6.8 The operant was the action (studying), and the reinforcer was the consequence (the grade of A on the exam).

6.9 A cash bonus is a secondary reinforcer because it does not serve a biological need. A primary reinforcer serves a biological need.

6.10 All reinforcements increase behavior. In positive reinforcement, something is added that increases behavior. In negative reinforcement, something is removed that increases behavior.

6.11 This learning system is called a token economy.

6.12 Latent learning challenges traditional operant conditioning theory because it takes place without reinforcement, which is central to operant conditioning.

6.13 You are less likely to cheat when you see someone suspended for this behavior because your behavior has been affected by vicarious conditioning.

6.14 Mirror neurons are thought to be the basis of observational learning and even empathy, because they are activated by watching someone perform an action.

Chapter 6: Answers to Self-Quiz Questions

1. **A:** Habituation is a form of non-associative learning. In this case, Sanjay became habituated to the noise of his roomate chewing gum, so he didn't notice it anymore. Refer to Learning Goal Activity 6.2b.

2. **C:** In this scenario, seeing Erin's boyfriend is the unconditioned stimulus. It causes an unconditioned physiological response of a fast heartbeat. For Erin, five knocks have become associated with seeing her boyfriend at her dorm room. So five knocks are now a conditioned stimulus that elicits a conditioned response, a fast heartbeat. Refer to Learning Goal Activity 6.4b.

3. **A:** Acquisition is the process of learning an association between two stimuli over a period of time. Refer to Learning Goal Activity 6.5b.

4. **B:** Stimulus generalization occurs when stimuli that are similar to a conditioned stimulus cause the same conditioned response. Refer to Learning Goal Activity 6.5b.

5. **D:** Rosie is attempting to teach the cat a relationship between two things: the doorbell ringing and the consequences of the cat meowing when the doorbell rings. This relationship represents operant conditioning. Refer to Learning Goal Activity 6.8b.

6. **B:** Negative reinforcement *increases* the likelihood of a certain behavior by *removing* a negative stimulus. In this case, Ajeet lets his sister play the game more because doing so reduces the amount of time she bugs him. Refer to Learning Goal Activity 6.10b.

7. **B:** With a fixed ratio schedule, a behavior is reinforced after a person does the desired behavior a specific number of times (if Glen is paid $3 per bag and rakes three bags of leaves, he will earn $9). With a fixed interval schedule, a behavior is reinforced after a person does the desired behavior for a specific length of time (if Lynda rakes for an hour, she will earn $7, regardless of how many bags of leaves she rakes). Refer to Learning Goal Activity 6.10a.

8. **C:** Latent learning is an example of how learning is influenced by cognition, where learning can occur even without reinforcement. Refer to Learning Goal Activity 6.12b.

9. **D:** Modeling occurs when someone learns a behavior by watching the actions of another person and then imitates that behavior. Refer to Learning Goal Activity 6.13b.

10. **D:** Through vicarious conditioning, we can learn to not perform a behavior because we see another person being punished for that behavior, as in the case with Jung. Or, through vicarious conditioning, we can learn to perform a behavior if we see another person being reinforced for it. Refer to Learning Goal Activity 6.13b.

Chapter 7: Answers to Red Q Questions

7.1 There are three stages of information processing in memory: (1) encoding information, (2) storage of the information for a period of time, and (3) retrieval of the information when it is needed.

7.2 Darren's ability to use selective attention to focus on the lesson means he will be more likely to create new memories about the material than Luisa will.

7.3 Information first passes into sensory storage before it can be processed into short-term storage and then long-term storage.

7.4 Sensory memory lets you have a continuous experience of the world around you—for example, so what you see or hear doesn't have "holes" in it.

7.5 Working memory processes, such as chunking, can be used to keep information available in short-term storage.

7.6 To retain information in long-term storage, you should use elaborative rehearsal, where you link new information with what you already know.

7.7 The main idea behind the speading activation models of memory is that activating one node increases the likelihood that closely associated nodes will also be activated, making that information easier to retrieve.

7.8 You are experiencing retrograde amnesia, which is a loss of memory for events that occurred before a brain injury.

7.9 Recalling a vacation is an explicit memory, because you can retrieve it consciously and talk about it.

7.10 Practicing a dance routine requires procedural memory, because it involves motor skills.

7.11 Prospective memory lets you remember to do something at a future time.

7.12 Consolidation is the original storage of a memory. By contrast, reconsolidation is subsequent storage after retrieval, which involves changes to the original memory to include new information.

7.13 The context that you create a memory in helps provide a retrieval cue when you try to remember information later on. So students are more likely to remember material when they take a test in the same room where they learned it.

7.14 You have a hard time remembering to call your friend her new name, Kathleen, because the old name, Katie, proactively interferes with your ability to remember the new name.

7.15 You are likely to remember more information from an exciting speech because emotional states, such as being excited, are associated with stronger consolidation, which makes memories easier to retrieve.

7.16 People often do not pay attention to the relevant details when an event happens. Because they are not paying attention, they do not encode and store the information so that it can be remembered accurately later.

Chapter 7: Answers to Self-Quiz Questions

1. **A:** When Johanna recalled hearing an s, her answer implied that she had stored and retrieved a memory. However, since she recalled the wrong letter, her brain most likely processed the incorrect information during encoding. Refer to Learning Goal Activity 7.1b.

2. **D:** In this case, storing information for use the next day is an example of long-term storage. To store memories and retrieve them later on, we must devote attentional resources to the information. Refer to Learning Goal Activity 7.3b.

3. **C:** Chunking is the process of using working memory to organize information into meaningful units to maintain it in short-term storage. This process can ultimately allow for better transfer into long-term storage. Refer to Learning Goal Activity 7.5b.

4. **C:** The ability to keep track of a few variables in the mind while solving math problems indicates a functioning working memory. The inability to remember the math formulas during a test suggests the information was not retained in long-term storage. Refer to Learning Goal Activity 7.6b.

5. **B:** According to spreading activation models of memory, activating one idea in semantic long-term storage activates closely linked ideas. Refer to Learning Goal Activity 7.7b.

6. **C:** In a case of anterograde amnesia caused by brain injury, someone loses the ability to form new memories. However, the person can remember information learned before the brain injury. Refer to Learning Goal Activity 7.8b.

7. **A:** Recalling information about personally experienced events—such as the time, place, and circumstances—is episodic memory. Episodic memory is a type of explicit memory. Explicit memory means memories we are consciously aware of and can describe. Refer to Learning Goal Activity 7.9b.

8. **D:** The cerebellum plays a vital role in implicit memory, including procedural memory used to perform many motor behaviors, such as playing the piano. By contrast, the temporal lobe is important for explicit memories, the hippocampus is important for the consolidation of new memories and for spatial memory, and the amygdala is crucial in processing implicit memories about fear learning. Refer to Learning Goal Activity 7.12b.

9. **B:** State-dependent memory allows us to retrieve memories that occurred when we were in a physical state that is similar to what we are in now. Because Cadence is currently frustrated with her coworker, it is easier for her to recall events when she was also frustrated with her student, Jamie. Refer to Learning Goal Activity 7.13b.

10. **C:** Russell's opinion of his grandmother used to be negative because he thought hoarding was unhealthy. Now that he is displaying the same type of behavior, he has changed his memory of his grandmother so that it is consistent with his attitude toward his own behavior. This shift is an example of memory bias, which is one of the ways our memories become distorted. Refer to Learning Goal Activity 7.16b.

Chapter 8: Answers to Red Q Questions

8.1 A blueprint is an analogical representation because aspects of this two-dimensional rendering correspond to a physical layout.

8.2 A prototype is the best example of a category, whereas exemplars are average examples of a category.

8.3 Schemas are mental structures—collections of ideas, knowledge, and experiences—that you use to think in generalized ways about people, events, or objects. Those generalized thoughts are stereotypes.

8.4 By deciding that the statement was valid, you have engaged in reasoning—specifically, you have engaged in informal reasoning, because it was based on opinion.

8.5 Your decision making was influenced by the availability heuristic, which is relying on information that comes easily to mind.

8.6 Whereas the other three strategies require active processing, insight is a passive process where you do not actively think about the problem but rather put it aside for a while.

8.7 A mental set is a problem solving strategy that seems reliable because it has always worked in the past, even though it might not be the best solution.

8.8 IQ is a mathematical measure of intelligence, whereas general intelligence is the theory that one general factor underlies intelligence.

8.9 Knowing the answers to trivia questions is related to crystallized intelligence, which is knowledge gained through experience.

8.10 Intelligence has a genetic aspect, and environment affects the expression of that aspect.

8.11 The mental age is 4, and the IQ is 200, because the formula for IQ is mental age (4) divided by chronological age (2) and multiplied by 100.

8.12 Those with high IQs tend to have quicker reaction times, especially on choice reaction time tests.

8.13 When minority students focus on stereotypes about their groups, they may become anxious about confirming such stereotypes through their test results. This distraction makes them less likely to do well on the tests.

Chapter 8: Answers to Self-Quiz Questions

1. **C:** Camden is using a symbolic representation because his thoughts are abstract mental connections consisting of words or ideas about how principles of physics can help him play pool. Refer to Learning Goal Activity 8.1b.

2. **A:** Hilary is describing Bruce's car as a prototype of the category "clunker." A prototype is the concept that is the "most typical" member of a given category. According to the exemplar model, there is no one concept that is the "best" member of a category. Instead, all concepts are examples of the category. Refer to Learning Goal Activity 8.2b.

3. **B:** The availability heuristic is a rule of thumb where our decisions tend to be made based on information that is easily retrieved from memory. Refer to Learning Goal Activity 8.5b.

4. **B:** Armando is using subgoals to solve the puzzle. In this case, he is completing one number at a time—all the 1's, then the 2's, and so on. Each number he gets correct places him one step closer to reaching his ultimate goal of finishing the sudoku. Refer to Learning Goal Activity 8.6b.

5. **D:** Functional fixedness is an obstacle to problem solving that arises when we rely too heavily on our mental representation of the typical functions for ordinary objects. Refer to Learning Goal Activity 8.7b.

6. **A:** General intelligence is the idea that one general factor underlies intelligence. It is responsible for IQ scores and for a person's performance across a range of tasks that show specific abilities, such as math, writing, drawing, and problem solving. Refer to Learning Goal Activity 8.8b.

7. **C:** Fritz's skills reveal crystallized intelligence, which is long-term memory about facts and knowledge. Jason's skills reflect the triarchic theory of intelligence, which posits that intelligence consists of practical intelligence, analytical intelligence, and creative intelligence. Refer to Learning Goal Activity 8.9b.

8. **D:** Nurture can play a large role in the development of intelligence through a person's environment, social characteristics, upbringing, and experiences. Thus, out of these options, Carla most likely found that children with lots of books (having access to lots of books is an environmental factor) do best academically. Refer to Learning Goal Activity 8.10b.

9. **C:** Validity is an assessment of whether a test measures what it is intended to measure. In this case, the test may be invalid if the questions don't assess knowledge of American history. Refer to Learning Goal Activity 8.11a.

10. **A:** Because Felicia answers the questions quickly, her reaction times are faster. The faster reaction times indicate that her mental processing is more efficient. Indeed, many people argue that fast reaction times indicate increased intelligence. Refer to Learning Goal Activity 8.12bc.

Chapter 9: Answers to Red Q Questions

9.1 A need is a lack of something (such as food), which creates a drive (such as hunger), which is a motivation to fulfill the need through a certain behavior (such as by eating).

9.2 No. Paying the child for studying if that is an intrinsic motivation might actually decrease motivation and therefore reduce studying.

9.3 The hypothalamus is the brain structure that most influences eating.

9.4 People learn what and when to eat through conditioning, familiarity, flavor, and cultural influence.

9.5 The need to belong motivates people to form relationships with others.

9.6 People can delay gratification by ignoring temptation and distracting themselves from temptation.

9.7 Jealousy is a secondary emotion, as being jealous involves multiple primary emotions (such as anger, fear, and sadness).

9.8 According to the James-Lange theory, the bodily response comes first, which is then experienced by the person as an emotion.

9.9 Your emotional processing and response to danger happen because visual information is sent via the fast path (from the thalamus to the amygdala), and then your further evaluation and relief happen because visual information also takes the slow path (from the thalamus to the visual cortex and on to the amygdala).

9.10 Thought suppression, trying not to think about a problem, is not effective because that effort can lead to a rebound effect, where you think about the problem even more.

9.11 The six emotions that are recognized in facial expressions across cultures are anger, fear, disgust, happiness, sadness, and surprise.

9.12 Because the display rules for emotions differ from culture to culture, people in Italy might feel freer to express their emotions than people in England do.

9.13 The affect-as-information theory states that because your mood will affect your decisions and judgments, you should not make a big decision about your relationship if you are in a bad mood.

9.14 Guilt and embarrassment strengthen the social bonds between people.

Chapter 9: Answers to Self-Quiz Questions

1. **C:** Each person has an optimal level of arousal, which motivates the person to behave in certain ways. Too much arousal overwhelms us, and we need a break; too little arousal leaves us bored. Refer to Learning Goal Activity 9.1b.

2. **A:** Extrinsic motivation is the desire to perform an action to achieve certain external goals. Intrinsic motivation is

the desire to perform an action because of the enjoyment it brings. Refer to Learning Goal Activity 9.2b.

3. **D:** Leptin is involved in the biological process of eating. However, this hormone is released by fat cells (not in our saliva) and acts on the hypothalamus. In addition, it affects long-term fat regulation, not short-term motivation for eating. Refer to Learning Goal Activity 9.3b.

4. **B:** Eating meals at a specific time of day is an example of classical conditioning. After spending time with her grandparents, Sophia learned to associate eating dinner with a very specific time of day, so she now prefers to eat at that time. Refer to Learning Goal Activity 9.4b.

5. **D:** The need to belong is an important motivation for us to develop strong interpersonal attachments, but it doesn't affect our motivation to achieve our goals. Instead, achievement motivation is affected by four other factors: setting good goals, feeling a sense of self-efficacy, being able to delay gratification, and having grit. Refer to Learning Goal Activity 9.5b.

6. **A:** The Cannon-Bard theory of emotion proposes that processing in the brain creates the experience of emotion and physical response in the body at the same time. Refer to Learning Goal Activity 9.8b.

7. **C:** The amygdala is associated with various emotional functions. It plays a major role in the perception of social stimuli, such as evaluating the trustworthiness of a stranger or feeling cautious around strangers. Refer to Learning Goal Activity 9.9b.

8. **D:** Positive reappraisal is a method of emotion regulation in which we alter our emotional reactions by thinking of events in more neutral (as opposed to negative) terms. Refer to Learning Goal Activity 9.10b.

9. **C:** Tori's belief that women should not show anger suggests she is following display rules, which are rules learned through socialization that dictate how and when people express emotions. These rules are often heavily influenced by factors such as whether a person is male or female and what culture the person is from. Refer to Learning Goal Activity 9.12b.

10. **A:** Guilt can arise from anxiety and remorse in situations when we have harmed another person. Displays of guilt also demonstrate that we care about our relationship partners. By showing that we care, the displays can help strengthen our social bonds. Refer to Learning Goal Activity 9.14b.

Chapter 10: Answers to Red Q Questions

10.1 Hormone differences between females and males produce different primary sex characteristics, which allow sexual reproduction. These include, for females, mature internal organs (ovaries), genitals (vagina), and menarche. For males, these include mature internal organs (testes), genitals (penis), and spermarche.

10.2 Whereas XX sex chromosomes make a person biologically female and XY sex chromosomes make a person biologically male, XXY sex chromosomes make a person intersex.

10.3 Gender schemas are thought structures about maleness and femaleness, which can lead to gender stereotypes, which are common beliefs about gender.

10.4 People come to understand gender roles through gender role socialization, although biological factors may also be involved.

10.5 According to cognitive development theory, children develop a stable gender identity (sense of maleness or femaleness) by about the age of 4.

10.6 People who are transgender are experiencing a normal variation in gender identity, whereas people experiencing the psychological disorder of gender dysphoria have extreme distress over their gender identity for at least 6 months.

10.7 The four main normal variations in sexual orientation include being straight, gay or lesbian, bisexual, and asexual.

10.8 Research has not found any environmental factors that influence sexual orientation, but it has found that sexual orientation is related to several biological factors: genetics, hormones, prenatal influences of the maternal immune system, and brain structures and processes.

10.9 Androgens are more important for the sexual behavior of both males and females.

10.10 According to the sexual strategies theory, females are more cautious about having sex because they risk becoming pregnant and pregnancy leads to a much more intensive commitment for females than for males.

10.11 According to the APA, people experiencing a paraphilic disorder or a sexual dysfunction are distressed and their lives are impaired.

Chapter 10: Answers to Self-Quiz Questions

1. **D:** There is a difference between biological sex and gender identity. Biological sex consists of the physical aspects of being male or female: sex chromosomes, sex glands, secondary sex characteristics, and primary sex characteristics. Refer to Learning Goal Activity 10.1b.

2. **C:** Secondary sex characteristics are traits that develop in puberty that make a person look like a mature male (deeper voice, chest and facial hair, etc.) or female (breasts, wider hips, etc.). These traits are not directly related to reproduction. By contrast, primary sex characteristics are traits that develop in puberty that enable a person to reproduce as a sexually mature male (who produces sperm) or female (who produces eggs). Daniel's secondary sex characteristics, together with his XXY sex chromosomes, suggest that he is experiencing Klinefelter syndrome. Refer to Learning Goal Activity 10.2b.

3. **D:** Gender schemas are the ways that we mentally organize information about gender into categories of what is masculine and what is feminine. Gender schemas include information about gender roles, which are the social aspects of being male or female (such as positions and characteristics). Gender

schemas also include information about gender identity, which is one's sense of being more male (cis male) or more female (cis female) or having a variation in gender identity (such as genderqueer, androgynous, or transgender). Refer to Learning Goal Activity 10.3b.

4. **A:** Gender role socialization is the idea that people learn culture-specific expectations about gender roles through exposure to social information in the environment. In this example, gender role socialization is occurring through operant conditioning. That is, the consequences of Aidan's actions (in this case, negative consequences) are teaching him to modify his behavior (not wear girls' clothes in the future). The question doesn't discuss Aidan's gender identity; how people become aware of their sense of gender is best explained by cognitive development theory. Refer to Learning Goal Activity 10.4b.

5. **C:** People with an androgynous gender identity have the sense of being male and being female. By contrast, people who are genderqueer do not always strongly identify as male or female, or their identity shifts over time. People who are transgender identify as a gender that is different from the sex they were assigned at birth. Gender dysphoria is a psychological condition characterized by enduring significant distress about one's assigned sex as different from what they experience as their true gender identity. Refer to Learning Goal Activity 10.6b.

6. **D:** Sexual orientation refers to a person's enduring sexual, emotional, and/or romantic attraction to other people. Derek is attracted to people of a different sex (females) and people of the same sex (males). Even though he is only fantasizing about having sex with males, not actually having sex with them, his sexual orientation is best described as bisexual. Refer to Learning Goal Activity 10.7b.

7. **C:** According to the best scientific evidence, the development of sexual orientation is not associated with environmental factors (nurture). By contrast, there is evidence that the development of sexual orientation is associated with the four biological factors (nature) listed in this answer. Refer to Learning Goal Activity 10.8b.

8. **A:** Masters and Johnson identified the four phases of the sexual response cycle: (1) excitement, where blood engorges the genitals; (2) plateau, where the physical aspects of arousal continue to increase; (3) orgasm, with involuntary muscle contractions throughout the body; and (4) resolution, where arousal decreases. Males and females experience the excitement phase in a similar way, with increased blood flow to the genitals. However, males and females experience some of these phases differently. For example, females are more likely to stay in a plateau phase without reaching orgasm, and females are more likely to have multiple orgasms. Only males have a refractory period after reaching orgasm, where they cannot maintain an erection or have another orgasm in a short period of time. Refer to Learning Goal Activity 10.9b.

9. **B:** Androgens—for example, testosterone—are hormones that are more important in influencing sexual behavior than estrogens are. In particular, the more testosterone a female has, the more likely she is to have sexual thoughts and desires, and the more likely she is to engage in sexual behavior. Refer to Learning Goal Activity 10.9b.

10. **D:** Elle's choice to abstain from casual sex may be unique in her social environment, but it is not a sexual dysfunction. Dylan is not distressed by what appears to be his asexual sexual orientation, so he is not experiencing a sexual dysfunction. Logan is experiencing fetishism, which is not a sexual dysfunction, but which may be a paraphilic disorder because it impairs his life. Only Claudia is experiencing a sexual dysfunction. Sexual dysfunction occurs when a person experiences distress and impairment in life from an ongoing problem with sexual desire, with function during the sexual response cycle, or with receiving pleasure from sex. Refer to Learning Goal Activity 10.11b.

Chapter 11: Answers to Red Q Questions

11.1 Fewer than 3 percent of Americans are healthy based on all four of these criteria.

11.2 People with anorexia tend to starve themselves to achieve extreme thinness, whereas people with bulimia alternate between dieting, binge eating, and purging (self-induced vomiting).

11.3 A person who exercises even once or twice a week will experience the benefits of exercise.

11.4 Cold sores are a symptom of herpes and may be caused by two forms of the herpes virus: HSV-1 and HSV-2.

11.5 The main reason that people continue to smoke is that they have become addicted to nicotine.

11.6 Stressors are environmental events that you experience as threatening, whereas stress is the combination of behavioral, mental, and physical effects that you experience as you cope with stressors you experience.

11.7 Stress reduces the effectiveness of the immune system, causing illness. Over long periods of time, stress can lead to the exhaustion phase of the GAS, where people may become chronically ill. Stress also causes negative stress responses, such as poor eating, not exercising, and drinking alcohol, all of which are associated with poor health.

11.8 The personality traits that place people at greatest risk for heart disease are hostility and the negative emotional state of depression.

11.9 Emotion-focused coping can help you deal with stress in the short term. Problem-focused coping is better for lasting results, but only if you can do something about the stressor.

11.10 Hope is associated with lower rates of hypertension, diabetes, and respiratory tract infections.

11.11 People in troubled marriages, who are getting divorced, or who are coping with the death of a spouse do not usually show the health benefits typically seen with social support.

11.12 One glass of wine or another alcoholic drink per day is associated with health benefits, but drinking to excess is associated with poor health.

Chapter 11: Answers to Self-Quiz Questions

1. **B:** The biopsychosocial model suggests that health (or illness) results from the combined influence of biological, social, and psychological characteristics. In Chuck's case, arthritis (a biological factor), life dissatisfaction (a psychological factor), and having few friends (a social factor) have the potential to make him ill. Refer to Learning Goal Activity 11.1b

2. **A:** Bulimia nervosa is an eating disorder characterized by alternating between dieting, binge eating, and purging by vomiting or using laxatives. Refer to Learning Goal Activity 11.2b.

3. **B:** Exercise has many physical, cognitive, and emotional benefits. However, exercise does not reduce the risk of anorexia nervosa, which is an eating disorder. Refer to Learning Goal Activity 11.3b.

4. **C:** A person is most likely to be successful in quitting smoking if they do several things simultaneously, including taking a drug like Chantix, chewing nicotine gum, and avoiding the places they used to go to smoke and the people they used to smoke with. However, using e-cigarettes has not been shown to help people quit smoking. Refer to Learning Goal Activity 11.5b.

5. **D:** A major life stressor—such as adapting to life in prison—is a large disruption that is unpredictable or uncontrollable and that affects the central areas of a person's life. Refer to Learning Goal Activity 11.6b.

6. **C:** The alarm stage of the general adaptation syndrome occurs when the body has an emergency response to a stressor. This response physically prepares us to fight or run away. Refer to Learning Goal Activity 11.7b.

7. **C:** People with a type A behavior pattern display competitiveness, aggression, impatience, and hostility, whereas people with a type B behavior pattern are more laid-back, easygoing, and accommodating. Research has shown that people with type A behavior patterns are more likely to develop heart disease, among other health problems. Refer to Learning Goal Activity 11.8b.

8. **D:** A problem-focused coping method involves taking direct steps to reduce the stressor. In this case, Preston would most likely discuss his scheduling conflicts with his supervisor. Refer to Learning Goal Activity 11.9b.

9. **D:** Positivity—positive emotions, attitudes, and outlooks—helps people to maintain good mental and physical health in all of these ways. Refer to Learning Goal Activity 11.10b.

10. **A:** Research shows that people who are in marriages that are not troubled have better health than other people of similar ages. Refer to Learning Goal Activity 11.11b.

Chapter 12: Answers to Red Q Questions

12.1 You made a snap judgment of your professor based on observing just a few seconds of behavior, so this judgment was based on thin slices of behavior.

12.2 You would attribute your lateness to the situation, such as bad traffic, whereas you would attribute your coworker's lateness to personality traits, such as unreliability.

12.3 Giuseppe has been exposed to a stereotype that his family holds about Italians being great cooks, which has resulted in a self-fulfilling prophecy because Giuseppe now behaves in a way that is consistent with this stereotype.

12.4 Prejudice involves negative attitudes that are associated with stereotypes, whereas discrimination is the inappropriate and unjustified treatment of people because of prejudice.

12.5 Saskia's attitude changed due to the mere exposure effect, because greater exposure to an item leads to a more positive attitude about it.

12.6 Postdecisional dissonance explains her attitude, because it makes her focus on the positive features of the car she chose and the negative features of the car she rejected.

12.7 Steward was persuaded to buy the cereal through the central route, which requires a person to think more deeply about the information being presented in the persuasive message.

12.8 In social facilitation, the presence of others improves performance, whereas in social loafing, the presence of others leads to worse performance.

12.9 When the diner picks up the food with her fingers, she is exhibiting normative influence because she is going along with what other people are doing.

12.10 A person is less likely to obey the authority when able to see or touch the person who is supposed to be hurt or if the authority is somewhat removed from the situation.

12.11 Being overly hot can produce more of a negative emotion than being overly cold, and a negative emotion tends to bring out aggression.

12.12 Birds of a feather flock together, which means that people in relationships tend to be similar in important qualities, such as attitudes, values, interests, and personalities.

12.13 Passionate love, which happens at the start of a relationship, is based on intense longing and sexual desire, whereas companionate love, which builds over a long period, includes friendship, trust, and intimacy that are the basis of a commitment to care for another person.

Chapter 12: Answers to Self-Quiz Questions

1. **A:** When Lucy determines her feeling about Greg after viewing his facial expression for just a few seconds, she is making a snap judgment based on thin slices of behavior. Refer to Learning Goal Activity 12.1b.

2. **D:** Elizabeth is displaying the actor/observer bias because she is making a personal attribution about her classmates' behavior (observer bias: they are late because they are lazy) and a situational attribution about her own behavior (actor bias: she is late because of her bus). Refer to Learning Goal Activity 12.2b.

3. **C:** If Troy has formed an attitude about exercising through operant conditioning, he was most likely reinforced for working out by being able to buy smaller jeans. Refer to Learning Goal Activity 12.5b.

4. **A:** Cognitive dissonance occurs when there is a contradiction between two attitudes or between an attitude and a behavior. Bridget held two conflicting attitudes: An expensive haircut should be better than a cheap haircut, and her expensive haircut did not look any different from her normal one. Taken together, these conflicting ideas led her to be anxious and change her attitude about how her hair looked. Refer to Learning Goal Activity 12.6b.

5. **B:** The peripheral route to persuasion does not elaborate information in a meaningful way or encourage someone to process the information carefully. As a result, persuasion to change attitudes is achieved based on the attractiveness of the messenger. By contrast, the central route for persuasion uses high elaboration and provides the opportunity for someone to carefully process the information presented. In this case, persuasion to change attitudes depends on the quality of the arguments. Refer to Learning Goal Activity 12.7b.

6. **B:** Social facilitation occurs when the mere presence of other people improves a person's performance. Refer to Learning Goal Activity 12.8b.

7. **D:** When you alter your behavior to match the behavior or expectations of others, you are conforming. Another way you alter your behavior, obedience, occurs when an authority figure such as a parent, teacher, or police officer tells you to behave in a specific way. Refer to Learning Goal Activity 12.9b.

8. **D:** The bystander intervention effect is when people fail to offer help to someone in need. This effect is particularly strong when many bystanders are present. In that situation, people will generally expect someone else to offer assistance, relieving them of this responsibility. Refer to Learning Goal Activity 12.11b.

9. **C:** Proximity influences our relationships based on how frequently we come into contact with each other. In particular, the more frequently you come into contact with someone, the greater the chance you will like that person. Increased liking may also result from increased familiarity caused when you repeatedly are exposed to someone. Refer to Learning Goal Activity 12.12b.

10. **A:** Passionate love describes romantic relationships that include intense physical and/or sexual desire. Refer to Learning Goal Activity 12.13b.

Chapter 13: Answers to the Red Q Questions

13.1 The teenager has a working self-concept that allows her to see certain traits as relevant in some situations but not in others.

13.2 Mr. Englund seems to be experiencing narcissism, an overly inflated sense of self-esteem.

13.3 You can create a positive sense of self by making downward comparisons.

13.4 A person from a collectivist culture would be more likely to have a sense of self that emphasizes strong relationships with family.

13.5 In Freud's view, the ego is the part of the personality that operates according to the reality principle, because it uses rational thought and problem solving to mediate between the desires of the id and morals of the superego.

13.6 The statement reveals unconditional positive regard, which should help the child develop a personality based on the child's true self, resulting in higher self-esteem.

13.7 Joe's explanation for his unsuccessful date suggests that, according to Rotter, Joe has an external locus of control, because he blames the weather, which is beyond his control.

13.8 As represented by the mnemonic OCEAN, the Big Five traits are openness, conscientiousness, extraversion, agreeableness, and neuroticism. Dominance is not one of the Big Five traits.

13.9 Because introverts tend to have internal levels of arousal, possibly in the reticular activating system, that are above their optimal levels, an introvert would probably prefer a setting that provides less stimulation, such as a quiet library.

13.10 There is little relation between the personalities of adopted children and the personalities of those who raise them.

13.11 The three aspects of temperament seen in children are activity level, emotionality, and sociability.

13.12 As Sheri grows older, she is likely to still be extraverted, but she is likely to become somewhat less extraverted as she ages.

13.13 Personality can be assessed using projective measures, self-report measures, the electronically activated record (EAR), and observational methods.

13.14 A funeral is a strong situation, and the social norms for how one behaves at a funeral tend to mask individual differences in personality.

13.15 In general, assessments find that the personalities of females are more empathetic, agreeable, and neurotic, whereas the personalities of males are more assertive.

Chapter 13: Answers to the Self-Quiz Questions

1. **A:** Working self-concept reflects how a person thinks about himself and processes personal information at a given moment. Refer to Learning Goal Activity 13.1b.

2. **C:** When a person makes a downward comparison, she is contrasting herself with people worse off than herself in the characteristic she is evaluating. This type of social comparison helps maintain a positive sense of self. Refer to Learning Goal Activity 13.3b.

3. **A:** A collectivist culture emphasizes the value of an interdependent sense of self more than an individual sense of self and teaches its members to value connections to family, social groups, and group cohesiveness. Thus Holly most likely feels good about herself when she is working well with others to promote an event that will bring other people together. Refer to Learning Goal Activity 13.4b.

4. **D:** According to one humanistic approach to personality, Carl Rogers's person-centered approach to personality, an individual's personality is influenced by the person's sense of self and how others evaluate him. Inconsistencies between a person's self-concept and the way others evaluate him may lead to conditions of self-worth. Conditions of worth lead to the development of a personality based only on the aspects of the person that are accepted by others. Refer to Learning Goal Activity 13.6b.

5. **A:** Justin's explanation that he "has bad luck" is consistent with having an external locus of control, one of two types of personality described by Rotter's expectancy theory, a social cognitive approach to personality. Rotter's work in personality is a cognitive approach because it states that (1) our behaviors are part of our personality and (2) our actions are shaped by our expectations for reinforcement and the values that we ascribe to different reinforcers. Refer to Learning Goal Activity 13.7b.

6. **B:** According to the information presented, Ella appears to be high in conscientiousness. The characteristics of this five-factor personality trait include being organized, careful, and self-disciplined. Refer to Learning Goal Activity 13.8b.

7. **B:** Adoption studies can examine siblings who are biologically related but are raised in different households; similarities between siblings can be attributed to the effect of nature. In this study, the children display similar shyness. This finding suggests that biology (nature) influenced the degree of shyness but that parenting differences (nurture) across the two households did not influence the degrees of shyness. Refer to Learning Goal Activity 13.10b.

8. **C:** The description indicates that Morris tends to affiliate with others and to display intense emotional reactions. Morris's temperament is based on high sociability and high emotionality. Refer to Learning Goal Activity 13.11b.

9. **C:** A projective personality test presents an ambiguous stimulus or prompt and allows the person to respond freely. The hope is that the person will project her hidden mental processes onto the prompt. This projection may reveal hidden aspects of her personality, such as her unconscious wishes, desires, and so on. Refer to Learning Goal Activity 13.13b.

10. **D:** The person/situation debate is about whether personality or situational cues directly influence behavior. Situationism argues that personality is determined more by situational cues, but it recognizes that there are strong situations (those that mask individual differences in personality due to environment) and weak situations (those that reveal individual differences in personality due to environment). Refer to Learning Goal Activity 13.14b.

Chapter 14: Answers to Red Q Questions

14.1 When the emotions, thoughts, and/or behaviors disrupt a person's life, the person is said to be experiencing psychopathology (a psychological disorder).

14.2 According to the biopsychosocial model, the three categories of factors that affect the development of psychopathology are: (1) biological factors, (2) psychological factors, and (3) social factors.

14.3 Assessment can involve interviews, self-reports, observation, and psychological testing to investigate a person's symptoms.

14.4 With specific phobia, a particular object is associated with fear, whereas generalized anxiety disorder involves no specific threat but a general sense of anxiety.

14.5 An obsession is a repeated, intrusive thought that increases anxiety, whereas a compulsion is a behavior that is performed to temporarily reduce the anxiety of the obsession.

14.6 Major depressive disorder is characterized by a deeper depression than persistent depressive disorder, but it lasts for less time than persistent depressive disorder.

14.7 Learned helplessness is a cause of depressive disorders in which people see themselves as unable to change their lives.

14.8 Bipolar I disorder includes an extremely elevated mood, called mania, whereas bipolar II disorder includes a somewhat elevated mood, called hypomania.

14.9 Disorganized behavior is a positive symptom of schizophrenia because it is the presence, not the absence, of strange behaviors.

14.10 According to the diathesis-stress model, a person has a greater or lesser predisposition for schizophrenia (diathesis), and stress in the person's environment may cause the person to show symptoms of schizophrenia.

14.11 Psychopaths are people with the *DSM-5* disorder APD who are also extremely uncaring and willing to injure others for their personal gain.

14.12 Dissociative amnesia is the loss of memory for a specific event or for a period of time, whereas dissociative fugue is a form of dissociative amnesia that involves a complete loss of identity and travel to a new location.

14.13 When a school-age child has normal intelligence but great difficulty learning and using academic skills—such as reading, writing, and/or math—the child may be experiencing a neurodevelopmental disorder called specific learning disorder.

14.14 The brains of those who develop autism spectrum disorder show unusually large growth beginning as early as 6 months of age, do not grow normally in adolescence, and may have faulty wiring in several areas.

14.15 The three main symptoms of ADHD are: (1) being overly active, (2) being inattentive, and (3) being impulsive.

Chapter 14: Answers to Self-Quiz Questions

1. **C:** Psychopathology arises from disordered thoughts, emotions, and/or behaviors that deviate from cultural norms, are maladaptive, cause personal distress, and cause discomfort for others. However, the most important criteria for something to be a psychopathology is that it must interfere with the life of the person being diagnosed. Refer to Learning Goal Activity 14.1b.

2. **D:** Crystal seems to adhere to the diathesis-stress model: When an individual has a predisposition for a psychopathology, this predisposition may trigger the disorder under stressful circumstances. Refer to Learning Goal Activity 14.2b.

3. **B:** Generalized anxiety disorder is a state of constant anxiety not associated with a specific stimulus or event, resulting in distractibility, fatigue, irritability, and sleep problems. Refer to Learning Goal Activity 14.4b.

4. **C:** Mary is most likely to be diagnosed with bipolar II disorder—alternating periods of extreme depression and mildly elevated mood (hypomania)—because her daily functioning is more impaired by her depressive episodes than by her heightened mood. Refer to Learning Goal Activity 14.8b.

5. **A:** William is experiencing hallucinations, which are perceptual disturbances (in this case, auditory) that arise without any actual sensory input. Hallucinations are a positive symptom of schizophrenia, because they represent the addition of an abnormal behavior. Refer to Learning Goal Activity 14.9b.

6. **D:** A person with schizophrenia has a delusion of persecution if he believes that others are persecuting, spying on, or trying to harm him. Refer to Learning Goal Activity 14.9c.

7. **B:** Cluster B personality disorders are characterized by dramatic, emotional, or erratic behaviors. They include antisocial, borderline (as described in the question), histrionic, and narcissistic personality disorders. Refer to Learning Goal Activity 14.11b.

8. **C:** Dissociative amnesia is a disorder that involves disruptions of memory for personal facts, plus loss of conscious awareness for a period of time. Dissociative fugue is a disorder that involves a loss of identity in conjunction with travel to a new location and sometimes assuming a new identity. Refer to Learning Goal Activity 14.12b.

9. **D:** Rhiannon most likely has autism spectrum disorder. Autism is one of the six neurodevelopmental disorders. The symptoms include deficits in social interaction, impaired communication, and restricted, repetitive behavior and interests. Refer to Learning Goal Activity 14.14b.

10. **B:** Attention-deficit/hyperactivity disorder is characterized by excessive activity, inattentiveness, and impulsivity in a child under the age of 12. This disorder often leads to social difficulties. Refer to Learning Goal Activity 14.15b.

Chapter 15: Answers to the Red Q Questions

15.1 In psychodynamic therapy, insight makes people aware of their unconscious conflicts so that they can resolve them. In humanistic therapy, insight helps people see how they can fulfill their potential for growth and become the best person they can be.

15.2 Cognitive-behavioral therapy is so effective because it treats both the distorted thoughts and maladaptive behaviors that are seen in both anxiety and depressive disorders.

15.3 A systems approach is important in family therapy because all of the members of the family are interconnected with each other; if one person experiences a psychological disorder and gets treatment, then everyone is affected.

15.4 Although both forms of these biological treatments disrupt brain activity, ECT uses electrical currents, whereas TMS uses a strong magnetic field.

15.5 If a treatment for a psychological disorder is effective, then there should be research on the treatment showing that it works.

15.6 In most places, only psychiatrists can prescribe psychotropic medications.

15.7 Exposure to a feared object in a safe environment helps the person extinguish a learned fear that is associated with that object.

15.8 For depressive disorders, the psychotherapy treatment of cognitive-behavioral therapy (CBT) can be just as effective as antidepressants.

15.9 The two classes of psychotropic drugs that are best for treatment of the elevated moods seen in bipolar disorders are mood stabilizer drugs (such as lithium) and antipsychotics (such as Seroquel).

15.10 The three differences between atypical antipsychotics and conventional antipsychotics are that the atypical antipsychotics: (1) act on different neurotransmitters; (2) reduce negative, not just positive, symptoms of schizophrenia; and (3) do not produce the side effect of tardive dyskinesia.

15.11 Mindfulness meditation is used in the first stage of dialectical behavior therapy (DBT) to help the person control attention to focus on the present to replace extreme behaviors.

15.12 Few therapies work for people with antisocial personality disorder (APD), but most people with APD show a reduction in antisocial behavior after about age 40.

15.13 Both were equally effective over the long term.

15.14 Applied behavior analysis is the most successful treatment, especially when combined with symbolic play or joint attention, but it requires great commitment from the client and the client's family because it is very intensive and takes years.

15.15 These drugs stimulate brain regions involved in behavioral control and paying attention.

Chapter 15: Answers to the Self-Quiz Questions

1. **C:** The humanistic therapy approach encourages clients to fulfill their potential for personal growth through active listening and unconditional positive regard. Refer to Learning Goal Activity 15.1c.

2. **B:** The most commonly prescribed psychotropic medication to treat bipolar disorder is Seroquel, an antipsychotic, to control disturbed thoughts that break from reality. Refer to Learning Goal Activity 15.4b.

3. **C:** A paraprofessional has little or no advanced training or education in psychology, but works under supervision in the community to assist people with psychological disorders. Refer to Learning Goal Activity 15.6b.

4. **B:** Effective therapies for panic attacks, such as cognitive-behavioral therapy, aim to change how people think about their responses to their physical symptoms and may also address the triggers of the attack through exposure techniques. Refer to Learning Goal Activity 15.7b.

5. **D:** Cognitive-behavioral therapy can be used to treat the symptoms of depression by identifying, evaluating, and replacing negative thoughts. This treatment will in turn help the patient improve his mood. Refer to Learning Goal Activity 15.8b.

6. **C:** Atypical antipsychotics are used for treating both positive and negative symptoms of schizophrenia. Early antipsychotics reduced only positive symptoms and were associated with the negative side effect of tardive dyskinesia. Refer to Learning Goal Activity 15.10b.

7. **B:** The most effective treatment for borderline personality disorder is dialectical behavior therapy (DBT). DBT involves three steps: (1) replacing destructive behaviors with less destructive actions and teaching problem-solving skills, (2) exploration of past traumatic experiences, and (3) development of self-respect, independent problem solving, and self-acceptance. Refer to Learning Goal Activity 15.11b.

8. **A:** The prognosis for treatment of antisocial personality disorder is poor. In particular, psychotherapy does not work because the manipulative, egotistical characteristics of the patient prevent a positive therapeutic relationship from forming. Moderate gains have been made only in treating antisocial personality disorder with stimulants (in the short term) and operant procedures in residential treatment centers. Refer to Learning Goal Activity 15.12b.

9. **A:** Several studies have found that SSRIs are effective at treating depression in adolescents. Cognitive-behavioral therapy is also effective at treating depression on its own, and it enhances the effect of drug treatment with SSRIs. Refer to Learning Goal Activity 15.13b.

10. **D:** Autism spectrum disorder, which is marked by difficulties with social and communication skills, can be effectively treated with applied behavioral analysis. In this intensive behavior therapy, desirable behaviors are rewarded in the hope that their frequency will increase. Refer to Learning Goal Activity 15.14b.

Appendix A: Answers to Red Q Questions

A.1 If two variables have no relationship to each other, the correlation coefficient is zero. Refer to Learning Goal Activity A.1c.

A.2 When an observed difference between research groups is statistically significant, the difference is unlikely to have occurred by chance. Refer to Learning Goal Activity A.2b.

GLOSSARY

absolute threshold (p. 175) The smallest amount of physical stimulation required to detect a sensory input half of the time it is present.

accommodation (p. 144) The process we use to create new schemas (mental representations) or drastically alter existing ones to incorporate new information that otherwise would not fit.

achievement motivation (p. 351) The need, or desire, to attain a certain standard of excellence.

achievement test (p. 320) A psychometric test that is designed to test a person's knowledge and skills.

acquisition (p. 222) The gradual formation of an association between conditioned and unconditioned stimuli.

action potential (p. 52) The neural impulse that travels along the axon and then causes the release of neurotransmitters into the synapse.

activation-synthesis theory (p. 104) The idea that dreams are the result of the brain's attempts to make sense of random brain activity by combining the activity with stored memories.

actor/observer bias (p. 466) When interpreting our own behavior, the tendency to focus on situations rather than personality traits.

addiction (p. 122) Compulsive drug craving and use, despite the negative consequences of using the drug.

affect-as-information theory (p. 369) People use their current emotions to make decisions, judgments, and appraisals, even if they do not know what caused their emotions.

aggression (p. 486) Any behavior that involves the intention to harm someone else.

agoraphobia (p. 558) An anxiety disorder marked by fear of being in situations from which escape is difficult or impossible.

altered state of consciousness (p. 90) A state that deviates from a normal waking state of consciousness. It may reflect either a more vivid awareness of the external world and inner mental activity or a less clear awareness of them.

altruism (p. 489) The act of providing help when it is needed, with no apparent reward for doing so.

ambivalent attachment (p. 142) The attachment style for infants who are unwilling to explore an unfamiliar environment but seem to have mixed feelings about the caregiver—they cry when the caregiver leaves the room, but they cannot be consoled by the caregiver upon the caregiver's return.

amygdala (p. 65) A subcortical forebrain structure; it serves a vital role in our learning to associate things with emotional responses and in processing emotional information.

analogical representations (p. 295) Mental representations that have some of the physical characteristics of objects.

androgens (p. 381) A class of hormones, including testosterone, that are more prevalent in males; they are associated with the development of the secondary and primary sex characteristics and with sexual behavior.

anorexia nervosa (p. 430) An eating disorder characterized by excessive fear of becoming fat and therefore restricting energy intake to obtain a significantly low body weight.

anterograde amnesia (p. 269) A condition in which people lose the ability to form new memories after experiencing a brain injury.

antisocial personality disorder (APD) (p. 577) A personality disorder marked by disregard for and violation of the rights of others and by lack of remorse.

applied behavioral analysis (p. 627) An intensive behavior therapy used to treat autism; this treatment is based on operant conditioning.

aptitude test (p. 320) A psychometric test that is designed to test a person's ability to learn—that is, the person's future performance.

arousal (p. 340) Physiological activation (such as increased brain activity) or increased autonomic responses (such as increased heart rate, sweating, or muscle tension).

asexual (p. 397) A sexual orientation where a person does not experience sexual attraction but may experience emotional and/or romantic attraction.

assimilation (p. 144) The process we use to incorporate new information into existing schemas (mental representations).

attention (p. 93) The focusing of mental resources on specific information to become consciously aware of that information.

attention-deficit/hyperactivity disorder (ADHD) (p. 585) A disorder characterized by excessive activity or fidgeting, inattentiveness, and impulsivity.

attitude accessibility (p. 473) Ease or difficulty of retrieving an attitude from memory.

attitudes (p. 472) People's evaluations of objects, of events, or of ideas.

autism spectrum disorder (p. 582) A developmental disorder characterized by deficits in social interaction, by impaired communication, and by restricted, repetitive behavior and interests.

autonomic nervous system (p. 72) A subdivision of the peripheral nervous system (PNS); it transmits sensory signals and motor signals back and forth between the central nervous system (CNS) and the body's glands and internal organs.

avoidant attachment (p. 142) The attachment style for infants who are somewhat willing to explore an unfamiliar environment but do not look at the caregiver when the caregiver leaves or returns, as though they have little interest in the caregiver.

axon (p. 49) A long, narrow outgrowth of a neuron's cell body that lets the neuron transmit information to other neurons.

babbling (p. 150) Intentional vocalization, often by an infant, that does not have a specific meaning.

basic tendencies (p. 531) Personality traits that are largely determined by biology and are stable over time.

behaviorism (p. 18) A school of thought that emphasizes the role of environmental forces in producing behavior.

behavior therapy (p. 598) Treatment for psychological disorders where a therapist works with clients to replace maladaptive behaviors with adaptive ones.

binge-eating disorder (p. 431) An eating disorder characterized by binge eating that causes significant distress.

binocular depth cues (p. 186) Cues of depth perception that arise because people have two eyes.

biological sex (p. 379) The physical aspects of a person's sex.

biological therapy (p. 601) Treatment for psychological disorders that is based on medical approaches to illness and to disease.

biopsychosocial model (p. 423) A model of health that integrates the effects of biological, behavioral, and social factors on health and illness.

bipolar I disorder (p. 567) Mood disorder characterized by extremely elevated moods during manic episodes.

bipolar II disorder (p. 567) Mood disorder characterized by alternating periods of extremely depressed and mildly elevated moods.

bisexual (p. 397) A sexual orientation where a person is sexually, emotionally, and/or romantically attracted to people of the same sex and people of another sex.

body mass index (BMI) (p. 424) A ratio of body weight to height, used to measure obesity.

borderline personality disorder (p. 576) A personality disorder characterized by disturbances in identity, in moods, and in impulse control.

bottom-up processing (p. 185) Perception based on the physical features of the stimulus.

Broca's area (p. 59) A small portion of the left frontal region of the brain; this area is crucial for producing speech.

bulimia nervosa (p. 431) An eating disorder characterized by dieting, binge eating, and purging.

bystander intervention effect (p. 489) The failure to offer help to people in need.

Cannon-Bard theory (p. 357) Emotions and bodily responses both occur simultaneously due to how parts of the brain process information.

cell body (p. 49) Part of the neuron where information from thousands of other neurons is collected and integrated.

central nervous system (CNS) (p. 47) The part of the nervous system that consists of the brain and the spinal cord.

central route (p. 477) A method of persuasion that uses high elaboration—where people pay attention to the arguments and consider all the information in the message. This method usually results in development of stronger attitudes.

central tendency (p. A1) A group of descriptive statistics, including mean, median, and mode, where one number represents the middle numerical response in a data set.

cerebellum (p. 62) A hindbrain structure behind the medulla and pons; this structure is essential for coordinated movement and balance.

change blindness (p. 94) A failure to be aware of visual information when one's attention is directed elsewhere.

characteristic adaptations (p. 531) Changes in behavioral expression of basic tendencies based on the demands of specific situations.

chunking (p. 262) Using working memory to organize information into meaningful units to make it easier to remember.

circadian rhythms (p. 100) The regulation of biological cycles into regular, daily patterns.

classical conditioning (p. 218) A type of learned response in which a neutral object comes to elicit a response when it is associated with a stimulus that already produces a response.

cochlea (p. 192) A coiled, bony, fluid-filled tube in the inner ear that houses the sensory receptors.

cognitive-behavioral therapy (CBT) (p. 599) Treatment for psychological disorders where a therapist incorporates techniques from cognitive therapy and behavior therapy to correct faulty thinking and maladaptive behaviors.

cognitive development theory (p. 391) The idea that each individual develops a gender identity by actively processing thoughts and feelings about gender.

cognitive dissonance (p. 475) An uncomfortable mental state due to a contradiction between two attitudes or between an attitude and a behavior.

cognitive map (p. 239) A visuospatial mental representation of an environment.

cognitive psychology (p. 19) A school of thought that studies how people think, learn, and remember.

cognitive therapy (p. 598) Treatment for psychological disorders where a therapist works with clients to help them change distorted thought patterns.

cold receptors (p. 203) Sensory receptors in the skin that detect the temperature of stimuli and transduce it into information processed in the brain as cold.

companionate love (p. 494) A type of romantic relationship that includes strong commitment to supporting and caring for a partner.

compliance (p. 483) The tendency to agree to do things requested by others.

concrete operational stage (p. 147) The third stage in Piaget's theory of cognitive development; during this stage, children begin to think about and understand logical operations, and they are no longer fooled by appearances.

conditioned response (CR) (p. 221) A response to a conditioned stimulus; a response that has been learned.

conditioned stimulus (CS) (p. 221) A stimulus that elicits a response only after learning has taken place.

cones (p. 178) Sensory receptors in the retina that detect light waves and transduce them into signals that are processed in the brain as vision. Cones respond best to higher levels of illumination, and therefore they are responsible for seeing color and fine detail.

conformity (p. 481) The altering of your own behaviors and opinions to match those of other people or to match other people's expectations.

conscious (p. 89) A level of consciousness that reflects awareness of the external world and inner mental activity.

consciousness (p. 89) The combination of a person's subjective experience of the external world and the person's internal mental activity; this combination results from brain activity.

consolidation (p. 275) A process where immediate memories become lasting memories when new neural connections are created and prior neural connections get stronger.

control group (p. 35) In an experiment, a comparison group of participants that does not receive the experimental treatment.

conventional level (p. 156) Middle level of moral reasoning; at this level, strict adherence to societal laws and the approval of others determine what is moral.

correlational methods (p. 31) Research methods that examine how variables are naturally related in the real world. The researcher makes no attempt to alter the variables or assign causation between them.

correlation coefficient (p. A5) A descriptive statistic that indicates the direction (positive or negative) and strength (from 0 to 1) of the relationship between variables; taken together these result in numbers ranging from +1 to 0 to −1.

critical thinking (p. 7) Systematically evaluating information to reach conclusions best supported by evidence.

crystallized intelligence (p. 315) Intelligence that reflects both knowledge gained through experience and the ability to use that knowledge.

culture (p. 19) The beliefs, values, rules, and customs that exist within a group of people who share a common language and environment and that are transmitted through learning from one generation to the next.

daily hassles (p. 440) Everyday irritations that cause small disruptions, the effects of which can add up to a large impact on health.

decision making (p. 303) Attempting to select the best alternative among several options.

deep brain stimulation (DBS) (p. 603) Treatment for psychological disorders that involves passing electricity through electrodes planted in the client's brain to stimulate the brain at a certain frequency and intensity.

defense mechanisms (p. 516) In psychodynamic theory, unconscious mental strategies that the mind uses to protect itself from distress.

deindividuation (p. 480) A state of reduced individuality, reduced self-awareness, and reduced attention to personal standards; this phenomenon may occur when people are part of a group.

delusions (p. 570) False beliefs that reflect breaks from reality.

dementia (p. 164) Severe impairment in intellectual capacity and personality, often due to damage to the brain.

dendrites (p. 49) Branchlike extensions of the neuron's cell body with receptors that receive information from other neurons.

dependent variable (p. 34) In an experiment, the variable that is measured to determine how it was affected by the manipulation of the independent variable.

depressants (p. 117) Psychoactive drugs that cause an altered state of consciousness by decreasing behavior and mental activity.

descriptive methods (p. 27) Research methods that provide a systematic and objective description of what is occurring.

desire (p. 405) A person's psychological experience of wanting to engage in sexual activity.

developmental psychology (p. 131) The scientific study of how humans change over the life span, from conception until death.

dialectical behavior therapy (DBT) (p. 621) Form of therapy, used to treat borderline personality disorder, that combines behavior therapy, cognitive therapy, psychodynamic therapy, and a mindfulness approach.

diathesis-stress model (p. 549) The idea that a disorder may develop when an underlying vulnerability is coupled with stress.

difference threshold (p. 176) The minimum difference in physical stimulation required to detect a difference between sensory inputs.

discrimination (p. 469) The inappropriate and unjustified treatment of people based on the groups they belong to.

disorganized behavior (p. 571) Acting in strange or unusual ways, including strange movement of limbs and inappropriate self-care, such as failing to dress properly or bathe.

disorganized speech (p. 571) Speaking in an incoherent way and displaying strange or inappropriate emotions while talking.

display rules (p. 368) Rules that are learned through socialization and that indicate what emotions are suitable in certain situations.

dissociation theory of hypnosis (p. 111) The idea that hypnotized people are in an altered state of consciousness where their awareness is separated from other aspects of consciousness.

dissociative amnesia (p. 579) Psychological disorder that involves disruptions of memory for personal facts or loss of conscious awareness for a period of time.

dissociative identity disorder (DID) (p. 580) The occurrence of two or more distinct identities in the same individual.

distortion (p. 284) Human memory is not a perfectly accurate representation of the past, but is flawed.

dizygotic twins (p. 77) Fraternal twins; these siblings result from two separately fertilized eggs, so they are no more similar genetically than nontwin siblings are.

downward comparisons (p. 511) Comparing oneself with another person who is seen as less competent or in a worse situation, which tends to protect a person's high self-esteem.

dreams (p. 103) Products of consciousness during sleep in which a person confuses images and fantasies with reality.

drive (p. 339) A psychological state that, by creating arousal, motivates an organism to engage in a behavior to satisfy a need.

eardrum (p. 191) A thin membrane that marks the beginning of the middle ear; sound waves cause the eardrum to vibrate.

ego (p. 515) In psychodynamic theory, the component of personality that tries to satisfy the wishes of the id while being responsive to the superego.

elaborative rehearsal (p. 263) Using working memory processes to think about how new information relates to yourself or your prior knowledge (semantic information); provides deeper encoding of information for more successful long-term storage.

electroconvulsive therapy (ECT) (p. 602) Treatment for psychological disorders that involves administering a strong electrical current to the client's brain to produce a seizure; ECT is effective in some cases of severe depression.

embryonic period (p. 132) The period in prenatal development from three through eight weeks after conception, when the brain, spine, major organs, and bodily structures begin to form in the embryo.

emotion (p. 354) An immediate, specific, negative or positive response to environmental events or internal thoughts.

emotion-focused coping (p. 448) A type of coping in which people try to prevent having an emotional response to a stressor.

encoding (p. 253) The processing of information so it can be stored in the brain.

endocrine system (p. 74) A communication system that uses hormones to influence mental activity and behavior.

episodic memory (p. 270) A type of explicit memory that includes a person's personal experiences.

estrogens (p. 380) A class of hormones, including estradiol, that are more prevalent in females; they are associated with the development of the secondary and primary sex characteristics and with sexual behavior.

etiology (p. 548) Factors that contribute to the development of disordered thoughts, emotions, and/or behaviors.

exemplar model (p. 299) A way of thinking about concepts: All concepts in a category are examples (exemplars); together, they form the category.

experimental group (p. 35) In an experiment, one or more treatment groups of participants that receive the manipulation of the independent variable being investigated.

experimental methods (p. 33) Research methods that test causal hypotheses by manipulating independent variables and measuring the effects on dependent variables.

explicit attitude (p. 474) An attitude that a person is consciously aware of and can report.

explicit memory (p. 270) The system for long-term storage of conscious memories that can be verbally described.

exposure (p. 609) Therapy technique that involves repeatedly exposing a client to an anxiety-producing stimulus or situation and has the goal of reducing the client's fear.

exposure and response prevention (p. 612) Exposing a client to a stimulus that causes anxiety because it triggers obsessive thoughts and then preventing the client from engaging in compulsive behavior to reduce that anxiety.

extinction (p. 223) A process in which the conditioned response is weakened when the conditioned stimulus is repeated without the unconditioned stimulus.

extrinsic motivation (p. 343) A desire to perform an activity to achieve an external goal that activity is directed toward.

fast fibers (p. 206) Sensory receptors in skin, muscles, organs, and membranes around both bones and joints; these myelinated fibers quickly convey intense sensory input to the brain, where it is perceived as sharp, immediate pain.

fetal period (p. 133) The period in prenatal development from nine weeks after conception until birth, when the brain continues developing, bodily structures are refined, and the fetus grows in length and weight and accumulates fat in preparation for birth.

fight-or-flight response (p. 443) The physiological preparedness of animals to deal with danger.

fixed interval schedule (FI) (p. 234) Reinforcing the occurrence of a particular behavior after a predetermined amount of time since the last reinforcement.

fixed ratio schedule (FR) (p. 234) Reinforcing a particular behavior after that behavior has occurred a predetermined number of times.

flow (p. 114) A highly focused, altered state of consciousness, when awareness of self and time diminishes due to being completely engrossed in an enjoyable activity.

fluid intelligence (p. 315) Intelligence that reflects the ability to process information, particularly in novel or complex circumstances.

forgetting (p. 280) The inability to access a memory from long-term storage.

formal operational stage (p. 147) The final stage in Piaget's theory of cognitive development; during this stage, people can think abstractly, and they can formulate and test hypotheses through logic.

framing (p. 305) How information is presented affects how that information is perceived and influences decisions.

frontal lobes (p. 69) Regions of the cerebral cortex at the front of the brain; these regions are important for movement and complex processes (rational thought, attention, social processes, etc.).

frustration-aggression hypothesis (p. 487) The idea that the more frustrated a person feels, the more likely the person is to act aggressively.

functional fixedness (p. 311) A tendency to think of things based on their usual functions, which may make it harder to solve a problem.

functionalism (p. 16) An early school of thought concerned with the adaptive purpose, or function, of mind and behavior.

fundamental attribution error (p. 466) In explaining other people's behavior, the tendency to overemphasize personality traits and underestimate situations.

gender (p. 386) The social, cultural, and psychological aspects of masculinity and femininity.

gender dysphoria (p. 394) A psychological disorder characterized by significant distress about the difference between a person's gender assigned at birth and that person's experience of his or her true gender identity.

gender identity (p. 391) The thoughts and feelings that make up a person's sense of being a boy/man or a girl/woman. This cognitive information is stored in each person's gender schemas.

gender roles (p. 388) The positions, characteristics, and interests that are considered normal and are expected for boys/men or for girls/women in a particular culture; this social information is stored in each person's gender schemas.

gender role socialization (p. 388) The idea that people learn culture-specific expectations about gender roles passively, through exposure to social information in the environment.

gender schemas (p. 386) A person's cognitive structures that organize information about gender into categories, which include gender roles and gender identity.

gender stereotypes (p. 387) Common beliefs about people of particular genders, based on similarities across many people's gender schemas.

general adaptation syndrome (GAS) (p. 442) A consistent pattern of physical responses to stress that consists of three stages: alarm, resistance, and exhaustion.

general intelligence (p. 314) The theory that one common factor underlies intelligence.

generalized anxiety disorder (p. 557) An anxiety disorder with a state of constant anxiety not associated with any specific object or event.

generativity versus stagnation (p. 160) Seventh stage of Erikson's theory of psychosocial development, where middle-aged adults face the challenge of leaving behind a positive legacy and caring for future generations.

genes (p. 76) The units of heredity, which partially determine an organism's characteristics.

germinal period (p. 132) The period in prenatal development from conception to two weeks after conception, when the zygote divides rapidly and implants in the uterine wall.

Gestalt theory (p. 18) The idea that the whole of personal experience is different from simply the sum of its parts.

ghrelin (p. 346) A hormone, secreted by an empty stomach, that is associated with increasing eating behavior based on short-term signals in the bloodstream.

global workspace model (p. 91) Consciousness is a product of activity in specific brain regions.

grouping (p. 184) The visual system's organization of features and regions to create the perception of a whole, unified object.

guilt (p. 370) A negative emotional state associated with anxiety, tension, and agitation.

habituation (p. 216) A decrease in behavioral response after lengthy or repeated exposure to a stimulus.

hair cells (p. 192) Sensory receptors located in the cochlea that detect sound waves and transduce them into signals that ultimately are processed in the brain as sound.

hallucinations (p. 570) Perceptual disturbances that are experienced without an external source.

hallucinogens (p. 117) Psychoactive drugs that create an altered state of consciousness by affecting perceptual experiences and evoking sensory images even without sensory input.

health psychology (p. 423) A field that integrates research on health and on psychology; it involves the application of psychological principles to promoting health and well-being.

heterosexual (straight) (p. 397) A sexual orientation where a person is sexually, emotionally, and/or romantically attracted to people of another sex; the more commonly used term is "straight."

heuristic (p. 304) A shortcut (rule of thumb or informal guideline) used to reduce the amount of thinking that is needed to make decisions.

hippocampus (p. 64) A subcortical forebrain structure; it is associated with the formation of new memories.

homosexual (gay or lesbian) (p. 397) A sexual orientation where a person is sexually, emotionally, and/or romantically attracted to people of the same sex. Males who are attracted to males are commonly described as gay, while females who are attracted to females are commonly described as lesbian.

hormones (p. 74) Chemical substances, released from endocrine glands, that travel through the bloodstream to targeted tissues; the tissues are later influenced by the hormones.

humanistic approaches (p. 518) Ways of studying personality that emphasize self-actualization, where people seek to fulfill their potential through greater self-understanding.

humanistic psychology (p. 18) A school of thought that investigates how people grow to become happier and more fulfilled; it focuses on the basic goodness of people.

humanistic therapy (p. 597) Treatment for psychological disorders where a therapist works with clients to help them develop their full potential for personal growth through greater insight.

hypnosis (p. 111) A social interaction during which a person, responding to suggestions, experiences changes in memory, perception, and/or voluntary action.

hypothalamus (p. 64) A subcortical forebrain structure involved in regulating bodily functions. The hypothalamus also influences our basic motivated behaviors.

hypothesis (p. 25) A specific prediction of what should be observed in a study if a theory is correct.

id (p. 515) In psychodynamic theory, the component of personality that is completely submerged in the unconscious and operates according to the pleasure principle.

identity versus role confusion (p. 154) Fifth stage of Erikson's theory of psychosocial development, where adolescents face the challenge of figuring out who they are.

immune system (p. 442) The body's mechanism for dealing with invading microorganisms, such as allergens, bacteria, and viruses.

implicit attitude (p. 474) An attitude that influences a person's feelings and behavior at an unconscious level.

implicit memory (p. 271) The system for long-term storage of unconscious memories that cannot be verbally described.

incentives (p. 342) External objects or external goals, rather than internal drives, that motivate behaviors.

independent variable (p. 34) In an experiment, the variable that the experimenter manipulates to examine its impact on the dependent variable.

insight learning (p. 240) A sudden understanding of how to solve a problem after a period of either inaction or thinking about the problem.

insomnia (p. 107) A disorder characterized by a repeated inability to sleep.

institutional review boards (IRBs) (p. 38) Groups of people responsible for reviewing proposed research to ensure that it meets the accepted standards of science and provides for the physical and emotional well-being of research participants.

insulin (p. 346) A hormone, secreted by the pancreas, that controls glucose levels in the blood.

integrity versus despair (p. 160) Eighth stage of Erikson's theory of psychosocial development, where older adults face the challenge of feeling satisfied that they have lived a good life and developed wisdom.

intelligence (p. 312) The ability to use knowledge to reason, make decisions, make sense of events, solve problems, understand complex ideas, learn quickly, and adapt to environmental challenges.

intelligence quotient (IQ) (p. 313) A mathematical measure of intelligence (originally computed by dividing a child's estimated mental age by the child's chronological age, then multiplying this number by 100).

interactionism (p. 537) The idea that behavior is determined jointly by situations and underlying traits.

intersex (p. 383) When a person experiences conflicting or ambiguous aspects of biological sex.

intimacy versus isolation (p. 160) Sixth stage of Erikson's theory of psychosocial development, where young adults face the challenge of forming committed long-term friendships and romances.

intrinsic motivation (p. 342) A desire to perform an activity because of the value or pleasure associated with that activity, rather than for an apparent external goal or purpose.

James-Lange theory (p. 356) Emotions result from the experience of physiological reactions in the body.

latent learning (p. 240) Learning that takes place in the absence of reinforcement.

learning (p. 215) A change in behavior, resulting from experience.

lens (p. 178) The adjustable, transparent structure behind the pupil; this structure focuses light on the retina, resulting in a crisp visual image.

leptin (p. 346) A hormone, secreted by fat cells, that is associated with decreasing eating behavior based on long-term body fat regulation.

long-term storage (p. 263) A memory storage system that allows relatively permanent storage, probably of an unlimited amount of information.

maintenance rehearsal (p. 263) Using working memory processes to repeat information based on how it sounds (auditory information); provides only shallow encoding of information and less successful long-term storage.

major depressive disorder (p. 562) Mood disorder, characterized by extremely depressed moods or a loss of interest in normally pleasurable activities, that persists for two weeks or more.

major life stressors (p. 440) Large disruptions, especially unpredictable and uncontrollable catastrophic events, that affect central areas of people's lives.

maturation (p. 138) Physical development of the brain and body that prepares an infant for voluntary movement, such as rolling over, sitting, and walking.

meditation (p. 113) A practice in which intense contemplation leads to a deep sense of calmness that has been described as an altered state of consciousness.

medulla (p. 62) A hindbrain structure at the top of the spinal cord; it controls survival functions such as heart rate and breathing.

melatonin (p. 100) A hormone that aids regulation of circadian rhythms; bright light reduces production and darkness increases production.

memory (p. 253) The nervous system's ability to obtain and retain information and skills for later retrieval.

menarche (p. 382) A primary sex characteristic in females; a female's first menstrual period, which signals the ability to reproduce sexually.

mental age (p. 320) An assessment of a child's intellectual standing compared with that of same-age peers; determined by comparing the child's test score with the average score for children of each chronological age.

mental sets (p. 311) A tendency to approach a problem in the same way that has worked in the past, which may make it harder to solve a problem.

mere exposure effect (p. 473) The increase in liking due to repeated exposure.

modeling (p. 242) Demonstrating a behavior to imitate a behavior that was previously observed.

modern racism (p. 470) Subtle forms of prejudice that coexist with the rejection of racist beliefs.

monocular depth cues (p. 186) Cues of depth perception that are available to each eye alone.

monozygotic twins (p. 77) Identical twins; these siblings result from one zygote splitting in two, so they share the same genes.

motivation (p. 337) Factors of differing strength that energize, direct, and sustain behavior.

multiple intelligences (p. 316) The idea that people have many different types of intelligence that are independent of one another.

myelin sheath (p. 52) A fatty material that covers and insulates some axons to allow for faster movement of electrical impulses along the axon.

narcolepsy (p. 108) A disorder in which a person experiences excessive sleepiness during normal waking hours, sometimes going limp and collapsing.

natural selection (p. 16) The basis of evolution; the idea that those who inherit characteristics that help them adapt to their particular environments have a selective advantage over those who do not.

need (p. 337) A state of biological or social deficiency.

need hierarchy (p. 338) An arrangement of needs, in which basic survival needs must be met before people can satisfy higher needs.

need to belong theory (p. 349) The need for interpersonal attachments is a fundamental motive that has evolved for adaptive purposes.

negative punishment (p. 233) The removal of a stimulus to decrease the probability that a behavior will recur.

negative reinforcement (p. 232) The removal of a stimulus to increase the probability that a behavior will be repeated.

negative symptoms (p. 569) Symptoms of schizophrenia that are marked by deficits in functioning, such as apathy, lack of emotion, slowed speech, and slowed movement.

nervous system (p. 47) A network of billions of cells in the brain and the body, responsible for all aspects of what we think, feel, and do.

neurodevelopmental disorders (p. 581) Psychological disorders that most commonly develop in childhood.

neurons (p. 48) The basic units of the nervous system; cells that receive, integrate, and transmit information in the nervous system. Neurons operate through electrical impulses, communicate with other neurons through chemical signals, and form neural networks.

neurotransmitters (p. 49) Chemical substances that carry signals from one neuron to another.

normal waking state of consciousness (p. 90) A state of consciousness that reflects a clear awareness of the external world and inner mental activity.

obedience (p. 484) When a person follows the orders of a person in authority.

object constancy (p. 189) Correctly perceiving objects as staying the same in their size, shape, color, and lightness, across viewing conditions that yield different physical input to the eyes.

observational learning (p. 241) The acquisition or modification of a behavior after exposure to at least one performance of that behavior.

obsessive-compulsive disorder (OCD) (p. 559) A psychological disorder characterized by frequent intrusive thoughts that create anxiety and compulsive actions that temporarily reduce the anxiety.

occipital lobes (p. 67) Regions of the cerebral cortex at the back of the brain; these regions are important for vision.

olfactory bulb (p. 201) A brain structure above the olfactory epithelium in the nasal cavity; from this structure, the olfactory nerve carries information about smell to the brain.

olfactory epithelium (p. 201) A thin layer of tissue, deep within the nasal cavity, containing the olfactory receptors; these sensory receptors produce information that is processed in the brain as smell.

operant (p. 229) An action that is performed on an environment and has consequences.

operant conditioning (p. 228) A learning process in which an action's consequences determine how likely an action is to be performed in the future.

operant procedures (p. 622) Form of therapy used to treat antisocial personality disorder (APD) where a therapist helps the client learn to associate certain behaviors with specific desirable outcomes.

opioids (p. 117) Psychoactive drugs that create an altered state of consciousness by reducing pain and producing pleasure.

opponent-process theory (p. 183) The idea that ganglion cells in the retina receive excitatory input from one type of cone and inhibitory input from another type of cone, creating the perception that some colors are opposites.

ovaries (p. 380) The female gonads (sex glands); they release the sex hormones and produce the cells that females use for sexual reproduction, called eggs.

overregularization (p. 150) The tendency for young children to incorrectly use a regular grammar rule where they should use an exception to the rule.

panic disorder (p. 557) An anxiety disorder that consists of sudden, overwhelming attacks of terror.

papillae (p. 197) Structures on the tongue that contain groupings of taste buds.

paraphilic disorder (p. 412) A psychological disorder where sexual activity is associated with a paraphilia (atypical sexual interest, arousal, and/or behavior), causing distress in the person or others and impairing the person's life; may cause the person to pursue sexual activity without consent.

parietal lobes (p. 67) Regions of the cerebral cortex in front of the occipital lobes and behind the frontal lobes; these regions are important for the sense of touch and for picturing the layout of spaces in an environment.

partial-reinforcement extinction effect (p. 234) The greater persistence of behavior under partial reinforcement than under continuous reinforcement.

passionate love (p. 494) A type of romantic relationship that includes intense longing and sexual desire.

perception (p. 173) The processing, organization, and interpretation of sensory signals in the brain; these processes result in an internal neural representation of the physical stimulus.

peripheral nervous system (PNS) (p. 47) The part of the nervous system that consists of all the nerves cells throughout the body except those in the brain and spinal cord.

peripheral route (p. 477) A method of persuasion that uses low elaboration—where people minimally process the message. This method usually results in development of weaker attitudes.

persistence (p. 283) The continual recurrence of unwanted memories from long-term storage.

persistent depressive disorder (p. 562) Mood disorder, characterized by mildly or moderately depressed moods, that persists for at least two years.

personal attributions (p. 466) People's explanations for why events or actions occur that refer to people's internal characteristics, such as abilities, traits, moods, or efforts.

personality (p. 504) A person's typical thoughts, emotional responses, and behaviors that are relatively stable over time and across circumstances.

persuasion (p. 477) The active and conscious effort to change an attitude through the transmission of a message.

phototherapy (p. 615) Treatment for depressive disorder with seasonal pattern, informally called seasonal affective disorder (SAD), through which the client is exposed to high-intensity light each day.

place coding (p. 195) The perception of higher-pitched sounds that is a result of the location on the basilar membrane where hair cells are stimulated by sound waves of varying higher frequencies.

plasticity (p. 80) A property of the brain that causes it to change through experience, drugs, or injury.

pons (p. 62) A hindbrain structure above the medulla; it regulates sleep and arousal and coordinates movements of the left and right sides of the body.

positive psychology (p. 451) The study of the strengths and virtues that allow people and communities to thrive.

positive punishment (p. 233) The addition of a stimulus to decrease the probability that a behavior will recur.

positive reinforcement (p. 232) The addition of a stimulus to increase the probability that a behavior will be repeated.

positive symptoms (p. 569) Symptoms of schizophrenia that are marked by excesses in functioning, such as delusions, hallucinations, and disorganized speech or behavior.

postconventional level (p. 156) Highest level of moral reasoning; at this level, decisions about morality depend on abstract principles and the value of all life.

posttraumatic stress disorder (PTSD) (p. 560) A psychological disorder that involves frequent nightmares, intrusive thoughts, and flashbacks related to an earlier trauma.

preconventional level (p. 156) Lowest level of moral reasoning; at this level, self-interest and event outcomes determine what is moral.

prejudice (p. 469) Negative feelings, opinions, and beliefs associated with a stereotype.

preoperational stage (p. 146) The second stage in Piaget's theory of cognitive development; during this stage, children think symbolically about objects, but they reason based on intuition and superficial appearances rather than logic.

pressure receptors (p. 203) Sensory receptors in the skin that detect tactile stimulation and transduce it into information processed in the brain as different types of pressure on the skin.

primary appraisals (p. 447) Part of coping that involves making decisions about whether a stimulus is stressful or not.

primary emotions (p. 354) Evolutionarily adaptive emotions that are shared across cultures and associated with specific physical states; they include anger, fear, sadness, disgust, happiness, and possibly surprise and contempt.

primary sex characteristics (p. 152) Physical development during puberty that results in sexually mature reproductive organs and genitals.

proactive interference (p. 281) When access to newer memories is impaired by older memories.

problem-focused coping (p. 448) A type of coping in which people take direct steps to confront or minimize a stressor.

problem solving (p. 303) Finding a way around an obstacle to reach a goal.

procedural memory (p. 272) A type of implicit memory that involves motor skills and behavioral habits.

prognosis (p. 619) A prediction of the likely course of a psychological (or physical) disorder.

projective measures (p. 534) Personality tests that examine unconscious processes by having people interpret ambiguous stimuli.

prosocial (p. 488) Acting in ways that tend to benefit others.

prospective memory (p. 273) Remembering to do something at some future time.

prototype model (p. 298) A way of thinking about concepts: Within each category, there is a best example—a prototype—for that category.

psychoanalytic theory (p. 17) The idea that our thoughts and actions are influenced by specific unconscious forces.

psychodynamic theory (p. 514) Freudian theory that unconscious forces determine behavior.

psychodynamic therapy (p. 597) Treatment for psychological disorders where a therapist works with clients to help them gain insight about how their unconscious processes may be causing inner conflict and impairing daily functioning.

psychology (p. 5) The scientific study of mental activity and behavior, which are based on brain processes.

psychopathology (p. 547) A sickness or disorder of the mind.

psychotherapy (p. 595) Treatment for psychological disorders where a therapist works with clients to help them overcome their psychological problems and disorders.

psychotropic medications (p. 601) Drugs that affect mental processes and that can be used to treat psychological disorders.

puberty (p. 151) The physical changes in the body that are a part of sexual development.

random assignment (p. 37) Placing research participants into the conditions of an experiment in such a way that each participant has an equal chance of being assigned to any level of the independent variable.

random sample (p. 36) A sample of participants that fairly represents the population because each member of the population had an equal chance of being included.

reasoning (p. 302) Using information to determine if a conclusion is valid.

reinforcer (p. 229) A consequence of an action that affects the likelihood of the action being repeated, or not, in the future.

reliability (p. 319) How consistently a psychometric test produces similar results each time it is used.

REM sleep (p. 102) The stage of sleep where a person experiences rapid eye movements, dreaming, and paralysis of motor systems; EEGs show beta wave activity, which is also associated with an awake, conscious mind.

replication (p. 23) Repetition of a research study to confirm or contradict the results.

restructuring (p. 311) Thinking about a problem in a new way in order to solve it.

retina (p. 178) The thin inner surface of the back of the eyeball; this surface contains the sensory receptors.

retrieval (p. 254) The act of accessing stored information when it is needed.

retrieval cue (p. 278) Anything that helps a person access information in long-term storage.

retroactive interference (p. 281) When access to older memories is impaired by newer memories.

retrograde amnesia (p. 269) A condition in which people lose the ability to access memories they had before a brain injury.

rods (p. 178) Sensory receptors in the retina that detect light waves and transduce them into signals that are processed in the brain as vision. Rods respond best to low levels of illumination, and therefore they do not support color vision or seeing fine detail.

safer sex (p. 435) Sexual behaviors that decrease the likelihood of contracting a sexually transmitted infection.

schemas (p. 296) Mental structures—collections of ideas, prior knowledge, and experiences—that help organize information and guide thought and behavior.

schizophrenia (p. 569) A psychological disorder characterized by extreme alterations in thought, in perceptions, and/or in consciousness that result in a break from reality.

scientific method (p. 23) A systematic procedure of observing and measuring phenomena (observable things) to answer questions about *what* happens, *when* it happens, *what* causes it, and *why*. This process involves a dynamic interaction between theories, hypotheses, and research methods.

secondary appraisals (p. 447) Part of coping where people decide how to manage and respond to a stressful stimulus.

secondary emotions (p. 354) Blends of primary emotions; they include remorse, guilt, submission, shame, and anticipation.

secondary sex characteristics (p. 152) Physical changes during puberty that are not directly related to reproduction but that indicate the differences between the sexes.

secure attachment (p. 142) The attachment style for most infants, who are confident enough to play in an unfamiliar environment as long as the caregiver is present and are readily comforted by the caregiver during times of distress.

selective attention (p. 255) The ability to direct mental resources to relevant information in order to process that information further, while also ignoring irrelevant information.

self-esteem (p. 507) How you feel about your sense of self.

self-fulfilling prophecy (p. 468) People's tendency to behave in ways that confirm their own expectations or other people's expectations.

self-report measures (p. 534) Personality tests that use questionnaires to let people respond to items that reveal traits and behaviors.

self-schema (p. 505) An integrated set of memories, beliefs, and generalizations about the self.

self-serving bias (p. 511) The tendency for people to take personal credit for success but blame failure on external factors.

semantic memory (p. 270) A type of explicit memory that includes a person's knowledge about the world.

sensation (p. 173) The sense organs' detection of external physical stimulus and the transmission of information about this stimulus to the brain.

sensitization (p. 216) An increase in behavioral response after lengthy or repeated exposure to a stimulus.

sensorimotor stage (p. 145) The first stage in Piaget's theory of cognitive development; during this stage, infants acquire information about the world through their senses and motor skills.

sensory adaptation (p. 176) A decrease in sensitivity to a constant level of stimulation.

sensory receptors (p. 174) Sensory organs that detect physical stimulation from the external world and change that stimulation into information that can be processed by the brain.

sensory storage (p. 260) A memory storage system that very briefly holds a vast amount of information from the five senses in close to their original sensory formats.

sexual dysfunction (p. 412) A psychological disorder that reduces sexual activity due to a significant and enduring problem in sexual functioning or pleasure, causing distress and impairing the person's life.

sexually transmitted infections (STIs) (p. 433) Infections that can be, but are not always, transmitted from one person to the next through sexual contact.

sexual orientation (p. 396) The nature of a person's enduring sexual, emotional, and/or romantic attraction to other people.

sexual response cycle (p. 405) A four-stage pattern of physiological and psychological responses during sex; the four stages are experienced differently by males than by females.

short-term storage (p. 261) A memory storage system that briefly holds a limited amount of information in awareness.

situational attributions (p. 466) People's explanations for why events or actions occur that refer to external events, such as the weather, luck, accidents, or other people's actions.

situationism (p. 537) The theory that behavior is determined more by situations than by personality traits.

sleep apnea (p. 108) A disorder in which a person, while asleep, stops breathing because the throat closes; the condition results in frequent awakenings during the night.

slow fibers (p. 206) Sensory receptors in skin, muscles, organs, and membranes around both bones and joints; these unmyelinated fibers slowly convey intense sensory input to the brain, where it is perceived as chronic, dull, steady pain.

slow-wave sleep (p. 101) Stages 3 and 4 of deep sleep, where a person is substantially less conscious and is hard to awaken; EEGs reveal large, regular delta waves.

social anxiety disorder (p. 556) An anxiety disorder characterized by fear of social situations or performance where a person is anxious about being negatively evaluated by others.

social cognitive approaches (p. 520) Ways of studying personality that recognize the influence of how people think.

social facilitation (p. 479) When the mere presence of others improves performance.

social loafing (p. 479) The tendency for people to work less hard in a group than when working alone.

social norms (p. 482) Expected standards of conduct, which influence behavior.

sociocognitive theory of hypnosis (p. 111) Theory that hypnotized people are not in an altered state of consciousness, but they behave in a way that is expected in that situation.

somatic nervous system (p. 71) A subdivision of the peripheral nervous system (PNS); it transmits sensory signals and motor signals back and forth between the central nervous system (CNS) and the skin, muscles, and joints.

specific phobia (p. 556) An anxiety disorder marked by fear of a specific object or situation that is out of proportion with any actual threat.

spermarche (p. 382) A primary sex characteristic in males; a male's first production of mature sperm, which signals the ability to reproduce sexually.

split brain (p. 97) A condition in which the corpus callosum is surgically cut and the two hemispheres of the brain do not receive information directly from each other.

spontaneous recovery (p. 223) A process in which a previously extinguished response reemerges after the conditioned stimulus is presented again.

stage 1 sleep (p. 101) First stage of sleep, where a person is drifting off; EEGs show slower theta waves, and conscious awareness of both the external world and inner mental activity starts to decline.

stage 2 sleep (p. 101) Second stage of sleep, where a person is truly asleep; EEGs show K-complexes and sleep spindles, and there is much less conscious awareness of both the external world and inner mental activity.

statistical significance (p. A6) A measure of the likelihood that research results are large enough to be a result of factors other than chance.

stereotypes (p. 299) Schemas that allow for easy, fast processing of information about people, events, or objects, based on their membership in particular groups.

stereotype threat (p. 328) Apprehension about confirming negative stereotypes related to a person's own group.

stimulants (p. 117) Psychoactive drugs that result in an altered state of consciousness by increasing behavior and mental activity.

stimulus generalization (p. 223) Learning that occurs when stimuli that are similar but not identical to the conditioned stimulus produce the conditioned response.

stimulus discrimination (p. 223) Learning to differentiate between two similar stimuli when only one of them is consistently associated with the unconditioned stimulus.

storage (p. 254) The retention of information in the brain over time.

stress (p. 439) The set of behavioral, mental, and physical processes that occur as an organism attempts to deal with an environmental event or a stimulus that it perceives as threatening.

stressor (p. 439) An environmental event or a stimulus that an organism perceives as threatening.

stress responses (p. 439) Behavioral, mental, and/or physical responses to stressors.

structuralism (p. 14) An approach to psychology based on the idea that conscious experience can be broken down into its basic underlying components.

subliminal perception (p. 95) The processing of information by sensory systems without a person's conscious awareness.

superego (p. 515) In psychodynamic theory, the component of personality that reflects the internalization of societal and parental standards of conduct.

symbolic representations (p. 295) Abstract mental representations that consist of words or ideas.

synapse (p. 49) The space between neurons where communication takes place through neurotransmitters.

systematic desensitization (p. 610) Therapy technique that involves exposing a client to increasingly anxiety-producing stimuli or situations while having the client relax at the same time.

taste buds (p. 197) Structures, located in papillae on the tongue, that contain the sensory receptors called taste receptors.

telegraphic speech (p. 150) The tendency for toddlers to speak by combining basic words in a logical syntax, but not a complete sentence, to convey a wealth of meaning.

temperament (p. 529) Biologically based tendency to feel or act in certain ways.

temporal coding (p. 194) The perception of lower-pitched sounds that results from the timing of firing of the auditory nerve when the basilar membrane vibrates from sound waves of lower frequencies.

temporal lobes (p. 68) Regions of the cerebral cortex below the parietal lobes and in front of the occipital lobes; these regions are important for hearing and for recognizing objects, such as faces.

tend-and-befriend response (p. 445) Females' tendency to respond to stressors by protecting and caring for their offspring and forming social alliances.

teratogens (p. 134) Environmental substances that can harm prenatal development.

terminal buttons (p. 49) Parts of the neuron, at the end of axons, that release chemical signals from the neuron into the synapse.

testes (p. 380) The male gonads (sex glands); they release the sex hormones and produce the cells that males use for sexual reproduction, called sperm.

thalamus (p. 64) A subcortical forebrain structure; the gateway to the brain for almost all incoming sensory information before that information reaches the cortex.

theory (p. 25) A model of interconnected ideas or concepts that explains what is observed and makes predictions about future events.

thinking (p. 295) The mental manipulation of representations of information we encounter in our environments.

tolerance (p. 122) A physical aspect of addiction that occurs when a person needs to take larger doses of a drug to experience its effect.

top-down processing (p. 185) Perception based on knowledge, expectations, or past experiences, which affect the interpretation of sensory information.

trait approaches (p. 522) Ways of studying personality that are based on people's characteristics, their tendencies to act in a certain way over time and across most situations.

transcranial magnetic stimulation (TMS) (p. 603) Treatment for psychological disorders that uses a magnetic field to interrupt function in specific regions of the brain.

transduction (p. 174) A process by which sensory receptors change physical stimuli into signals that are eventually sent to the brain.

transgender (p. 393) When a person's gender identity and/or gender expression differs from the sex assigned at birth.

triarchic theory (p. 316) The idea that people have three types of intelligence: analytical, creative, and practical.

trichromatic theory (p. 182) The idea that three types of cone receptor cells in the retina are responsible for color perception. Each type responds optimally to different, but overlapping, ranges of wavelengths.

two-factor theory (p. 358) How we experience an emotion is influenced by the cognitive label we apply to explain the physiological changes we have experienced.

type A behavior pattern (p. 446) Personality traits characterized by competitiveness, achievement orientation, aggressiveness, hostility, restlessness, impatience with others, and an inability to relax.

type B behavior pattern (p. 446) Personality traits characterized by being noncompetitive, relaxed, easygoing, and accommodating.

unconditioned stimulus (US) (p. 219) A stimulus that elicits a response that is innate and does not require any prior learning.

unconditioned response (UR) (p. 219) A response that does not have to be learned, such as a reflex.

unconscious (p. 89) A level of consciousness that reflects a lack of awareness of the external world and inner mental activity.

upward comparisons (p. 511) Comparing oneself with another person who is seen as more competent or in a better situation, which tends to confirm a person's low self-esteem.

validity (p. 320) How well a psychometric test measures what it is intended to measure.

variable (p. 29) Something in the world that can vary and that a researcher can manipulate (change), measure (evaluate), or both.

variability (p. A3) A group of descriptive statistics, including range and standard deviation, where one number represents the spread between numerical responses in a data set.

variable interval schedule (VI) (p. 234) Reinforcing the occurrence of a particular behavior after an unpredictable and varying amount of time since the last reinforcement.

variable ratio schedule (VR) (p. 234) Reinforcing a particular behavior after the behavior has occurred an unpredictable and varying number of times.

vicarious conditioning (p. 244) Learning the consequences of an action by watching others being reinforced or punished for performing the action.

warm receptors (p. 203) Sensory receptors in the skin that detect the temperature of stimuli and transduce it into information processed in the brain as warmth.

well-being (p. 423) A positive state that includes striving for optimal health and life satisfaction.

withdrawal (p. 122) A physical and psychological aspect of addiction that occurs when a person experiences anxiety, tension, and cravings after stopping use of an addictive drug.

working memory (p. 261) An active processing system that allows manipulation of different types of information to keep it available for current use.

working self-concept (p. 506) The immediate experience of the self in the here and now.

XX sex chromosomes (p. 380) The genetic material that is one aspect of the biological sex of a human female.

XY sex chromosomes (p. 380) The genetic material that is one aspect of the biological sex of a human male.

REFERENCES

Abad-Merino, S., Newheiser, A. K., Dovidio, J. F., Tabernero, C., & González, I. (2013). The dynamics of intergroup helping: The case of subtle bias against Latinos. *Cultural Diversity and Ethnic Minority Psychology, 19*, 445–452.

Abizaid, A. (2009). Ghrelin and dopamine: New insights on the peripheral regulation of appetite. *Journal of Neuroendocrinology, 21*, 787–793.

Abram, S. V., & DeYoung, C. G. (2017). Using personality neuroscience to study personality disorder. *Personality Disorders: Theory, Research, and Treatment, 8*, 2–13.

Abramowitz, J. S. (2013). The practice of exposure therapy: Relevance of cognitive-behavioral theory and extinction theory. *Behavior Therapy, 44*, 548–558.

Abramson, L. Y., Metalsky, G., & Alloy, L. (1989). Hopelessness depression: A theory-based subtype of depression. *Psychological Review, 96*, 358–372.

Adolphs, R., Sears, L., & Piven, J. (2001). Abnormal processing of social information from faces in autism. *Journal of Cognitive Neuroscience, 13*, 232–240.

Agnew-Blais, J. C., Polanczyk, G. V., Danese, A., Wertz, J., Moffitt, T. E., & Arseneault, L. (2016). Evaluation of the persistence, remission, and emergence of attention-deficit/hyperactivity disorder in young adulthood. *JAMA Psychiatry, 73*, 713–720.

Ainsworth, M. D. S., Blehar, M. C., Waters, E., & Wall, S. (1978). *Patterns of attachment: A psychological study of the strange situation*. Hillsdale, NJ: Erlbaum.

Aizpurua, A., & Koutstaal, W. (2015). A matter of focus: Detailed memory in the intentional autobiographical recall of older and younger adults. *Consciousness and Cognition, 33*, 145–155.

Alanko, K., Santtila, P., Harlaar, N., Witting, K., Varjonen, M., Jern, P., Johansson, A., von der Pahlen, B., & Sandnabba, N. K. (2010). Common genetic effects of gender atypical behavior in childhood and sexual orientation in adulthood: A study of Finnish twins. *Archives of Sexual Behavior, 39*, 81–92.

Alberini, C. M., & LeDoux, J. E. (2013). Memory reconsolidation. *Current Biology, 23*, B746–B750.

Albus, C. (2010). Psychological and social factors in coronary heart disease. *Annals of Medicine, 42*, 487–494.

Al-Delaimy, W. K., Myers, M. G., Leas, E. C., Strong, D. R., & Hofstetter, C. R. (2015). E-cigarette use in the past and quitting behavior in the future: A population-based study. *American Journal of Public Health, 105*, 1213–1219.

Algoe, S. B., & Fredrickson, B. L. (2011). Emotional fitness and the movement of affective science from lab to field. *American Psychologist, 66*, 35–42.

Ali, K., Ahmed, N., & Greenough, A. (2012). Sudden infant death syndrome (SIDS), substance misuse, and smoking in pregnancy. *Research and Reports in Neonatology, 2*, 95–101.

Alicke, M. D., Klotz, M. L., Breitenbecher, D. L., Yurak, T. J., & Vredenburg, D. S. (1995). Personal contact, individuation, and the better-than-average effect. *Journal of Personality and Social Psychology, 68*, 804–825.

Amaral, D. G., Schumann, C. M., & Nordahl, C. W. (2008). Neuroanatomy of autism. *Trends in Neurosciences, 3*, 137–145.

Amato, P. R., Johnson, D. R., Booth, A., & Rogers, S. J. (2003). Continuity and change in marital quality between 1980 and 2000. *Journal of Marriage and Family, 65*, 1–22.

Ambady, N., & Rosenthal, R. (1993). Half a minute: Predicting teacher evaluations from thin slices of nonverbal behavior and physical attractiveness. *Journal of Personality and Social Psychology, 64*, 431–441.

Ament, S. A., Szelinger, S., Glusman, G., Ashworth, J., Hou, L., Akula, N., . . . Roach, J. C. (2015). Rare variants in neuronal excitability genes influence risk for bipolar disorder. *Proceedings of the National Academy of Sciences, 112*, 3576–3581.

American College Health Association (2014). *Spring 2014 reference group executive summary*. Hanover, MD: American College Health Association.

American Psychiatric Association. (1973). *Diagnostic and statistical manual of mental disorders* (2nd ed., text rev.). Washington, DC: Author.

American Psychiatric Association. (2000). Practice guidelines for the treatment of patients with eating disorders (revised). *American Journal of Psychiatry, 157*(Suppl.), 1–39.

American Psychiatric Association. (2013). *Diagnostic and statistical manual of mental disorders* (5th ed.). Washington, DC: Author.

American Psychological Association. (2006). Answers to your questions about individuals with intersex conditions. Retrieved from http://www.apa.org/topics/lgbt/intersex.aspx

American Psychological Association. (2008). Answers to your questions: For a better understanding of sexual orientation and homosexuality. Retrieved from http://www.apa.org/topics/lgbt/orientation.pdf

American Psychological Association (2010, May 13). Dr. Katherine C. Nordal on how to find a therapist. Retrieved from http://apa.org/news/press/releases/2010/05/locate-a-therapist.aspx

American Psychological Association. (2014). Answers to your questions about transgender people, gender identity, and gender expression. Retrieved from http://www.apa.org/topics/lgbt/transgender.pdf

Anderson, A. K., Christoff, K., Stappen, I., Panitz, D., Ghahremani, D. G., Glover, G., . . . Sobel, N. (2003). Dissociated neural representations of intensity and valence in human olfaction. *Nature Neuroscience, 6*, 196–202.

Anderson, A. K., & Phelps, E. A. (2000). Expression without recognition: Contributions of the human amygdala to emotional communication. *Psychological Science, 11*, 106–111.

Anderson, N. H. (1968). Likableness ratings of 555 personality-trait words. *Journal of Personality and Social Psychology, 9,* 272–279.

Andrade, L. H., Alonso, J., Mneimneh, Z., Wells, J. E., Al-Hamzawi, A., Borges, G., . . . Kessler, R. C. (2014). Barriers to mental health treatment: Results from the WHO World Mental Health surveys. *Psychological Medicine, 44,* 1303–1317.

Angell, M. (2011, June 23). The epidemic of mental illness: Why? *The New York Review of Books,* p. 14. Retrieved from http://www.nybooks.com/articles/archives/2011/jun/23/epidemic-mental-illness-why/

Anton, B. S. (2010). Proceedings of the American Psychological Association for the legislative year 2009: Minutes of the annual meeting of the Council of Representatives and minutes of the meetings of the Board of Directors. *American Psychologist, 65,* 385–475.

Arboleda, V. A., Sandberg, D. E., & Vilain, E. (2014). DSDs: Genetics, underlying pathologies and psychosexual differentiation. *Nature Reviews Endocrinology, 10,* 603–615.

Archibald, A. B., Graber, J. A., & Brooks-Gunn, J. (2003). Pubertal processes and physiological growth in adolescence. In G. Adams & M. Berzonsky (Eds.), *Blackwell handbook of adolescence* (pp. 24–47). Malden, MA: Blackwell.

Arem, H., Moore, S. C., Patel, A., Hartge, P., de Gonzalez, A. B., Visvanathan, K., . . . Matthews, C. E. (2015). Leisure time physical activity and mortality: A detailed pooled analysis of the dose-response relationship. *JAMA Internal Medicine, 175,* 959–967.

Aronne, L. J., Wadden, T., Isoldi, K. K., & Woodworth, K. A. (2009). When prevention fails: Obesity treatment strategies. *American Journal of Medicine, 122*(4 Suppl. 1), S24–S32.

Aronson, E. (2002). Building empathy, compassion, and achievement in the jigsaw classroom. In J. Aronson (Ed.), *Improving academic achievement: Impact of psychological factors on education* (pp. 209–225). San Diego, CA: Academic Press.

Aronson, E., & Mills, J. (1959). The effects of severity of initiation on liking for a group. *Journal of Abnormal and Social Psychology, 59,* 177–181.

Arrazola, R. A., Singh, T., Corey, C. G., Husten, C. G., Neff, L. J., Apelberg, B. J., . . . Caraballo, R.S. (2015). Tobacco use among middle and high school students—United States, 2011–2014. *Morbidity and Mortality Weekly Report (MMWR), 64,* 381–385.

Asch, S. E. (1955). Opinions and social pressure. *Scientific American, 193,* 31–35.

Asch, S. E. (1956). Studies of independence and conformity: A minority of one against a unanimous majority. *Psychological Monographs, 70,* Whole No. 416.

Atkinson, R. C., & Shiffrin, R. M. (1968). Human memory: A proposed system and its control processes. *The Psychology of Learning and Motivation, 2,* 89–195.

Austin, E. J., Saklofske, D. H., & Mastoras, S. M. (2010). Emotional intelligence, coping and exam-related stress in Canadian undergraduate students. *Australian Journal of Psychology, 62,* 42–50.

Aviezer, H., Hassin, R. R., Ryan, J., Grady, C., Susskind, J., Anderson, A., . . . Bentin, S. (2008). Angry, disgusted, or afraid? Studies on the malleability of emotion perception. *Psychological Science, 19,* 724–732.

Axelsson, J., Sundelin, T., Ingre, M., Van Someren, E. J. W., Olsson, A., & Lekander, M. (2010). Beauty sleep: Experimental study on the perceived health and attractiveness of sleep deprived people. *British Medical Journal, 341,* c6614.

Baars, B. (1988). *A cognitive theory of consciousness.* Cambridge, UK: Cambridge University Press.

Baddeley, A. D. (2002). Is working memory still working? *European Psychologist, 7,* 85–97.

Baddeley, A. D., & Hitch, G. (1974). Working memory. In G. H. Bower (Ed.), *The psychology of learning and motivation: Advances in research and theory* (Vol. 8, pp. 47–89). New York, NY: Academic Press.

Bailes, J. E., Petraglia, A. L., Omalu, B. I., Nauman, E., & Talavage, T. (2013). Role of subconcussion in repetitive mild traumatic brain injury: A review. *Journal of Neurosurgery, 119,* 1235–1245.

Bailey, J. M., Pillard, R. C., Neale, M. C., & Agyei, Y. (1993). Heritable factors influence sexual orientation in women. *Archives of General Psychiatry, 50,* 217–223.

Bailey, J. M., Vasey, P. L., Diamond, L. M., Breedlove, S. M., Vilain, E., & Epprecht, M. (2016). Sexual orientation, controversy, and science. *Psychological Science in the Public Interest, 17,* 45–101.

Baillargeon, R. (1987). Object permanence in 3½ and 4½ month old infants. *Developmental Psychology, 23,* 655–664.

Baillargeon, R., Li, J., Ng, W., & Yuan, S. (2009). A new account of infants' physical reasoning. In A. Woodward & A. Needham (Eds.), *Learning and the infant mind* (pp. 66–116). New York, NY: Oxford University Press.

Baillargeon, R., Scott, R. M., & Bian, L. (2016). Psychological reasoning in infancy. *Annual Review of Psychology, 67,* 159–186.

Baker, T. B., Brandon, T. H., & Chassin, L. (2004). Motivational influences on cigarette smoking. *Annual Review of Psychology, 55,* 463–491.

Baldwin, D. A., & Baird, J. A. (2001). Discerning intentions in dynamic human action. *Trends in Cognitive Sciences, 5,* 171–178.

Baldwin, G. T., Breiding, M. J., & Sleet, D. (2016). Commentary—Using the public health model to address unintentional injuries and TBI: A perspective from the Centers for Disease Control and Prevention (CDC). *NeuroRehabilitation: An Interdisciplinary Journal, 39,* 1–4.

Baler, R. D., & Volkow, N. D. (2006). Drug addiction: The neurobiology of disrupted self-control. *Trends in Molecular Medicine, 12,* 559–566.

Ballantyne, J. C., & LaForge, K. S. (2007). Opioid dependence and addiction during opioid treatment of chronic pain. *Pain, 129,* 235–255.

Balthazard, C. G., & Woody, E. Z. (1992). The spectral analysis of hypnotic performance with respect to "absorption." *International Journal of Clinical and Experimental Hypnosis, 40,* 21–43.

Balthazart, J. (2011). Minireview: Hormones and human sexual orientation. *Endocrinology, 152,* 2937–2947.

Bancroft, J. (2002). The medicalization of female sexual dysfunction: The need for caution. *Archives of Sexual Behavior, 31,* 451–455.

Bancroft, J. (2006). Normal sexual development. In H. E. Barbaree & W. L. Marshall (Eds.), *The juvenile sex offender* (2nd ed., pp. 19–57). New York, NY: Guilford Press.

Bandura, A. (1977a). Self-efficacy: Toward a unifying theory of behavioral change. *Psychological Review, 84,* 191–215.

Bandura, A. (1977b). *Social learning theory.* Englewood Cliffs, NJ: Prentice-Hall.

Bandura, A. (1978). The self system in reciprocal determinism. *American Psychologist, 33,* 344–358.

Bandura, A., Ross, D., & Ross, S. (1961). Transmission of aggression through imitation of aggressive models. *Journal of Abnormal and Social Psychology, 66,* 3–11.

Bandura, A., Ross, D., & Ross, S. A. (1963). Vicarious reinforcement and imitative learning. *The Journal of Abnormal and Social Psychology, 67,* 601–607.

Baranowski, A., & Hecht, H. (2015). Gender differences and similarities in receptivity to sexual invitations: Effects of location and risk perception. *Archives of Sexual Behavior, 44,* 2257–2265.

Bargh, J. (2017). *Before you know it: The unconscious reasons we do what we do.* New York, NY: Touchstone.

Barlow, D. H. (2004). Psychological treatments. *American Psychologist, 59,* 869–878.

Barlow, D. H., Bullis, J. R., Comer, J. S., & Ametaj, A. A. (2013). Evidence-based psychological treatments: An update and a way forward. *Annual Review of Clinical Psychology, 9*, 1–27.

Barlow, D. H., Gorman, J. M., Shear, M. K., & Woods, S. W. (2000). Cognitive-behavioral therapy, imipramine, or their combination for panic disorder: A randomized controlled trial. *Journal of the American Medical Association, 283*, 2529–2536.

Barr, A. M., Panenka, W. J., MacEwan, G. W., Thornton, A. E., Lang, D. J., Honer, W. G., & Lecomte, T. (2006). The need for speed: An update on methamphetamine addiction. *Journal of Psychiatry & Neuroscience, 31*, 301–313.

Barrett, L.F. (2006). Are emotions natural kinds? *Perspectives on Psychological Science, 1*, 28–58.

Barrett, L. F., Mesquita, B., Ochsner, K. N., & Gross, J. J. (2007). The experience of emotion. *Annual Review of Psychology, 58*, 373–403.

Barretto, R. P., Gillis-Smith, S., Chandrashekar, J., Yarmolinsky, D. A., Schnitzer, M. J., Ryba, N. J., & Zuker, C. S. (2015). The neural representation of taste quality at the periphery. *Nature, 517*, 373–376.

Bartels, A., & Zeki, S. (2004). The neural correlates of maternal and romantic love. *Neuroimage, 21*, 1155–1166.

Bartels, J. M. (2015). The Stanford prison experiment in introductory psychology textbooks: A content analysis. *Psychology Learning & Teaching, 14*, 36–50.

Bartels, J. M., Milovich, M. M., & Moussier, S. (2016). Coverage of the Stanford Prison Experiment in introductory psychology courses: A survey of introductory psychology instructors. *Teaching of Psychology, 42*, 136–141.

Bartlett, F. C. (1932). *Remembering: A study in experimental and social psychology.* Cambridge, UK: Cambridge University Press.

Bartoshuk, L. M. (2000). Comparing sensory experiences across individuals: Recent psychophysical advances illuminate genetic variation in taste perception. *Chemical Senses, 25*, 447–460.

Basson, M. D., Bartoshuk, L. M., Dichello, S. Z., Panzini, L., Weiffenbach, J. M., & Duffy, V. B. (2005). Association between 6-n-propylthiouracil (PROP) bitterness and colonic neoplasms. *Digestive Diseases and Sciences, 50*, 483–489.

Basson, R. (2000). The female sexual response: A different model. *Journal of Sex and Marital Therapy, 26*, 51–65.

Basson, R. (2001). Human sex-response cycles. *Journal of Sex and Marital Therapy, 27*, 33–43.

Baugh, C. M., Stamm, J. M., Riley, D. O., Gavett, B. E., Shenton, M. E., Lin, A., ... Stern, R. A. (2012). Chronic traumatic encephalopathy: Neurodegeneration following repetitive concussive and subconcussive brain trauma. *Brain Imaging and Behavior, 6*, 244–254.

Baumeister, R. F. (1991). *Escaping the self: Alcoholism, spirituality, masochism, and other flights from the burden of selfhood.* New York, NY: Basic Books.

Baumeister, R. F. (2000). Gender differences in erotic plasticity: The female sex drive as socially flexible and responsive. *Psychological Bulletin, 126*, 347–374.

Baumeister, R. F., Campbell, J. D., Krueger, J. I., & Vohs, K. D. (2003). Does high self-esteem cause better performance, interpersonal success, happiness, or healthier lifestyles? *Psychological Science in the Public Interest, 4*, 1–44.

Baumeister, R. F., Campbell, J. D., Krueger, J. I., & Vohs, K. D. (2005). Exploding the self-esteem myth. *Scientific American, 292*, 84–91.

Baumeister, R. F., Catanese, K. R., & Vohs, K. D. (2001). Is there a gender difference in strength of sex drive? Theoretical views, conceptual distinctions, and a review of the relevant literature. *Social Psychology Review, 5*, 242–273.

Baumeister, R. F., Dale, K., & Sommers, K. L. (1998). Freudian defense mechanisms and empirical findings in modern social psychology: Reaction formation, projection, displacement, undoing, isolation, sublimation, and denial. *Journal of Personality, 66*, 1081–1124.

Baumeister, R. F., Heatherton, T. F., & Tice, D. (1994). *Losing control: How and why people fail at self-regulation.* San Diego, CA: Academic Press.

Baumeister, R. F., & Leary, M. R. (1995). The need to belong: Desire for interpersonal attachments as a fundamental human motivation. *Psychological Bulletin, 117*, 497–529.

Baumeister, R. F., Smart, L., & Boden, J. M. (1996). Relation of threatened egotism to violence and aggression: The dark side of high self-esteem. *Psychological Review, 103*, 5–33.

Baumrind, D. (1964). Some thoughts on ethics of research: After reading Milgram's "Behavioral Study of Obedience." *American Psychologist, 19*, 421.

Baumrind, D., Larzelere, R. E., & Cowan, P. A. (2002). Ordinary physical punishment: Is it harmful? Comment on Gershoff (2002). *Psychological Bulletin, 128*, 580–589.

Baxter, A. J., Charlson, F. J., Cheng, H. G., Shidhaye, R., Ferrari, A. J., & Whiteford, H. A. (2016). Prevalence of mental, neurological, and substance use disorders in China and India: A systematic analysis. *The Lancet Psychiatry, 3*, 832–841.

Baxter, L. R. (2000). Functional imaging of brain systems mediating obsessive-compulsive disorder. In D. S. Charney, E. J. Nestler, & B. S. Bunney (Eds.), *Neurobiology of mental illness* (pp. 534–547). New York, NY: Oxford University Press.

Baydala, L., Rasmussen, C., Birch, J., Sherman, J., Wikman, E., Charchun, J., ... Bisanz, J. (2009). Self-beliefs and behavioural development as related to academic achievement in Canadian Aboriginal children. *Canadian Journal of School Psychology, 24*, 19–33.

Beck, A. T. (1967). *Depression: Clinical, experimental and theoretical aspects.* New York, NY: Harper & Row.

Beck, A. T. (1976). *Cognitive therapy and the emotional disorders.* New York, NY: International Universities Press.

Beckerman, J., & Gray, T. (2014). *The sonic boom: How sound transforms the way we think, feel, and buy.* Boston, MA: Houghton Mifflin Harcourt.

Beggan, J. K. (1992). On the social nature of nonsocial perception: The mere ownership effect. *Journal of Personality and Social Psychology, 62*, 229–237.

Behne, T., Carpenter, M., Call, J., & Tomasello, M. (2005). Unwilling versus unable: Infants' understanding of intentional action. *Developmental Psychology, 41*, 328–337.

Behnke, M., & Smith, V. C. (2013). Prenatal substance abuse: Short- and long-term effects on the exposed fetus. *Pediatrics, 131*, e1009–e1024.

Belsky, J. (1990). Children and marriage. In F. D. Fincham & T. N. Bradbury (Eds.), *The psychology of marriage: Basic issues and applications* (pp. 172–200). New York, NY: Guilford Press.

Belsky, J., Houts, R. M., & Fearon, R. M. P. (2010). Infant attachment security and the timing of puberty: Testing an evolutionary hypothesis. *Psychological Science, 21*, 1195–1201.

Bem, D. J. (1967). Self-perception: An alternative explanation of cognitive dissonance phenomena. *Psychological Review, 74*, 183–200.

Bem, S. L. (1981). Gender schema theory: A cognitive account of sex typing. *Psychological Review, 88*, 354–364.

Bennett, Tara. (2014, July 11). "Boyhood" star Ellar Coltrane talks about 12-year movie adventure. *Today.* Retrieved from https://www.today.com/popculture/boyhood-star-ellar-coltrane-talks-about-12-year-film-1D79899208?

Bentler, P. M., & Newcomb, M. D. (1978). Longitudinal study of marital success and failure. *Journal of Consulting and Clinical Psychology, 46*, 1053–1070.

Berger, S. L., Kouzarides, T., Shiekhattar, R., & Shilatifard, A. (2009). An operational definition of epigenetics. *Genes & Development, 23*, 781–783.

Bergh, C., Sjöstedt, S., Hellers, G., Zandian, M., & Sodersten, P. (2003). Meal size, satiety and cholecystokinin in gastrectomized humans. *Physiology & Behavior, 78*, 143–147.

Berkey, C. S., Gardner, J. D., Frazier, A. L., & Colditz, G. A. (2000). Relation of childhood diet and body size to menarche and adolescent growth in girls. *American Journal of Epidemiology, 152,* 446–452.

Berkman, L. F., & Syme, S. L. (1979). Social networks, host resistance, and mortality: A nine-year follow-up study of Alameda County residents. *American Journal of Epidemiology, 109,* 186–204.

Berridge, K. C., & Kringelbach, M. L. (2013). Neuroscience of affect: Brain mechanisms of pleasure and displeasure. *Current Opinion in Neurobiology, 23,* 294–303.

Berridge, K. C., & Kringelbach, M. L. (2015). Pleasure systems in the brain. *Neuron, 86,* 646–664.

Berscheid, E., & Regan, P. (2005). *The psychology of interpersonal relationships.* New York, NY: Prentice-Hall.

Berscheid, E., & Walster, E. H. (1969). *Interpersonal attraction.* Reading, MA: Addison-Wesley.

Best, D. L., & Williams, J. E. (2001). Gender and culture. In D. Matsumoto (Ed.), *The handbook of culture and psychology* (pp. 195–219). New York, NY: Oxford University Press.

Bewernick, B. H., Hurlemann, R., Matusch, A., Kayser, S., Grubert, C., Hadrysiewicz, B., ... Schlaepfer, T. E. (2010). Nucleus accumbens deep brain stimulation decreases ratings of depression and anxiety in treatment-resistant depression. *Biological Psychiatry, 67,* 110–116.

Bidell, T. R., & Fischer, K. W. (1995). Between nature and nurture: The role of agency in the epigenesis of intelligence. In R. Sternberg & E. Grigorenko (Eds.), *Intelligence: Heredity and environment* (pp. 193–242). New York, NY: Cambridge University Press.

Biederman, J., Hirshfeld-Becker, D. R., Rosenbaum, J. F., Herot, C., Friedman, D., Snidman, N., ... Faraone, S. V. (2001). Further evidence of association between behavioral inhibition and social anxiety in children. *American Journal of Psychiatry, 158,* 1673–1679.

Biesanz, J., West, S. G., & Millevoi, A. (2007). What do you learn about someone over time? The relationship between length of acquaintance and consensus and self-other agreement in judgments of personality. *Journal of Personality and Social Psychology, 92,* 119–135.

Billig, M., & Tajfel, H. (1973). Social categorization and similarity in intergroup behaviour. *European Journal of Social Psychology, 3,* 27–52.

Bjorklund, D. F. (2007). *Why youth is not wasted on the young: Immaturity in human development.* Malden, MA: Blackwell.

Blackless, M., Charuvastra, A., Derryck, A., Fausto-Sterling, A., Lauzanne, K., & Lee, E. (2000). How sexually dimorphic are we? Review and synthesis. *American Journal of Human Biology, 12,* 151–166.

Blakemore, S. J., & Choudhury, S. (2006). Development of the adolescent brain: Implications for executive function and social cognition. *Journal of Child Psychology and Psychiatry, 47,* 296–312.

Blanchard, R. (1997). Birth order and sibling sex ratio in homosexual versus heterosexual males and females. *Annual Review of Sex Research, 8,* 27–67.

Blanchard, R. (2008). Review and theory of handedness, birth order, and homosexuality in men. *Laterality, 13,* 51–70.

Blanchard, R., Cantor, J. M., Bogaert, A. F., Breedlove, S. M., & Ellis, L. (2006). Interaction of fraternal birth order and handedness in the development of male homosexuality. *Hormones and Behavior, 49,* 405–414.

Blasiman, R. N., Dunlosky, J., & Rawson, K. A. (2017). The what, how much, and when of study strategies: Comparing intended versus actual study behaviour. *Memory, 25,* 784–792.

Blass, T. (1991). Understanding behavior in the Milgram obedience experiment: The role of personality, situations, and their interactions. *Journal of Personality and Social Psychology, 60,* 398–413.

Bleidorn, W., Arslan, R. C., Denissen, J. J., Rentfrow, P. J., Gebauer, J. E., Potter, J., & Gosling, S. D. (2016). Age and gender differences in self-esteem—A cross-cultural window. *Journal of Personality and Social Psychology, 111,* 396–410.

Block, J., & Kremen, A. M. (1996). IQ and ego-resiliency: Conceptual and empirical connections and separateness. *Journal of Personality and Social Psychology, 70,* 349–361.

Blum, B. (2018). The lifespan of a lie. *Medium.* June 7, 2018. https://medium.com/s/trustissues/the-lifespan-of-a-lie-d869212b1f62

Boehmer, A. L. M., Brinkmann, A. O., Bruggenwirth, H., Van Assendelft, C., Otten, B. J., Verleun-Mooijman, M. C. T., ... Drop, S. L. S. (2001). Genotype versus phenotype in families with androgen insensitivity syndrome. *Journal of Clinical Endocrinology and Metabolism, 86,* 4151–4160.

Bogaert, A. F. (2003). Number of older brothers and sexual orientation: New texts and the attraction/behavior distinction in two national probability samples. *Journal of Personality and Social Psychology, 84,* 644–652.

Bogaert, A. F. (2004). Asexuality: Prevalence and associated factors in a national probability sample. *Journal of Sex Research, 41,* 279–287.

Bogaert, A. F. (2006). Biological versus nonbiological older brothers and men's sexual orientation. *Proceedings of the National Academy of Sciences, 103,* 10771–10774.

Bogaert, A. F., Blanchard, R., & Crosthwait, L. E. (2007). Interaction of birth order, handedness, and sexual orientation in the Kinsey interview data. *Behavioral Neuroscience, 121,* 845–853.

Bogaert, A. F., Skorska, M. N., Wang, C., Gabrie, J., MacNeil, A. J., Hoffarth, M. R., ... Blanchard, R. (2018). Male homosexuality and maternal immune responsivity to the Y-linked protein NLGN4Y. *Proceedings of the National Academy of Sciences, 115,* 302–306.

Bohlin, G., Hagekull, B., & Rydell, A. M. (2000). Attachment and social functioning: A longitudinal study from infancy to middle childhood. *Social Development, 9,* 24–39.

Boldrini, M., Fulmore, C.A., Tartt, A. N., Simeon, L. R., Pavlova, I., Poposka, V., ... Mann, J. J. (2018). Human hippocampal neurogenesis persists throughout aging. *Cell Stem Cell, 22,* 589–599.

Bolles, R. C. (1970). Species-specific defense reactions and avoidance learning. *Psychological Review, 77,* 32–48.

Bonanno, G. A. (2004). Loss, trauma, and human resilience: Have we underestimated the human capacity to thrive after extremely aversive events? *American Psychologist, 59,* 20–28.

Bootzin, R. R., & Epstein, D. R. (2011). Understanding and treating insomnia. *Annual Review of Clinical Psychology, 7,* 435–458.

Bornstein, R. F. (1999). Criterion validity of objective and projective dependency tests: A meta-analytic assessment of behavioral prediction. *Psychological Assessment, 11,* 48–57.

Bouchard, C., & Pérusse, L. (1993). Genetics of obesity. *Annual Review of Nutrition, 13,* 337–354.

Bouchard, C., Tremblay, A., Despres, J. P., Nadeau, A., Lupien, J. P., Theriault, G., ... Fournier, G. (1990). The response to long-term overfeeding in identical twins. *New England Journal of Medicine, 322,* 1477–1482.

Bouchard, T. J., Jr., Lykken, D. T., McGue, M., Segal, N. L., & Tellegen, A. (1990). Sources of human psychological differences: The Minnesota study of twins reared apart. *Science, 250,* 223–228.

Bouton, M. E. (1994). Context, ambiguity, and classical conditioning. *Current Directions in Psychological Science, 3,* 49–53.

Bouton, M. E., Trask, S., & Carranza-Jasso, R. (2016). Learning to inhibit the response during instrumental (operant) extinction. *Journal of Experimental Psychology: Animal Learning and Cognition, 42,* 246–258.

Bowlby, J. (1982). Attachment and loss: Retrospect and prospect. *American Journal of Orthopsychiatry, 52,* 664–678.

Bradbury, T. N. & Karney, B. R. (2013). *Intimate relationships.* New York, NY: Norton.

Bradbury, T. N., & Fincham, F. D. (1990). Attributions in marriage: Review and critique. *Psychological Bulletin, 107,* 3–33.

Brannigan, A., Nicholson, I., & Cherry, F. (2015). Introduction to the special issue: Unplugging the Milgram machine. *Theory & Psychology, 25,* 551–563.

Bransford, J. D., & Johnson, M. K. (1972). Contextual prerequisites for understanding: Some investigations of comprehension and recall. *Journal of Verbal Learning and Verbal Behavior, 11,* 717–726. (Reprinted and modified in *Human memory,* p. 305, by E. B. Zechmeister & S. E. Nyberg, Eds., Pacific Grove, CA: Brooks Cole, 1982.)

Braunstein, G. D., Sundwall, D. A., Katz, M., Shifren, J. L., Buster, J. E., Simon, J. A., . . . Watts, N. B. (2005). Safety and efficacy of a testosterone patch for the treatment of hypoactive sexual desire disorder in surgically menopausal women: A randomized, placebo-controlled trial. *Archives of Internal Medicine, 165,* 1582-1589.

Breland, K., & Breland, M. (1961). The misbehavior of organisms. *American Psychologist, 16,* 681–684.

Brent, D. A., & Gibbons, R. (2014). Initial dose of antidepressant and suicidal behavior in youth: Start low, go slow. *JAMA Internal Medicine, 174,* 909–911.

Breslaw, A. (2014, January 16). Is Gabourey Sidibe the most fat-shamed actress in Hollywood? *Cosmopolitan.* Retrieved from https://www.cosmopolitan.com/sex-love/advice/a5365/gabourey-sidibe-fat-shaming/

Brewer, M. B., & Caporael, L. R. (1990). Selfish genes vs. selfish people: Sociobiology as origin myth. *Motivation and Emotion, 14,* 237–243.

Brill, K. T., Weltman, A. L., Gentili, A., Patrie, J. T., Fryburg, D. A., Hanks, J. B., . . . Veldhuis, J. D. (2002). Single and combined effects of growth hormone and testosterone administration on measures of body composition, physical performance, mood, sexual function, bone turnover, and muscle gene expression in healthy older men. *The Journal of Clinical Endocrinology and Metabolism, 87,* 5649–5657.

Britt, R. R. (2006, June 29). Cell phones make drivers as bad as drunks. *LiveScience.* Retrieved from https://www.livescience .com/872-cell-phones-drivers-bad-drunks.html

Broadbent, D. E. (1958). *Perception and communication.* New York, NY: Oxford University Press.

Brody, G. H., Gray, J. C., Yu, T., Barton, A. W., Beach, S. R., Galván, A., . . . Sweet, L. H. (2017). Protective prevention effects on the association of poverty with brain development. *JAMA Pediatrics, 171,* 46–52.

Bromley, S. M., & Doty, R. L. (1995). Odor recognition memory is better under bilateral than unilateral test conditions. *Cortex, 31,* 25–40.

Brooks-Gunn, J., & Ruble, D. N. (1982). The development of menstrual-related beliefs and behaviors during early adolescence. *Child Development, 53,* 1567–1577.

Brown, A. S., & Derkits, E. J. (2009). Prenatal infection and schizophrenia: A review of epidemiologic and translational studies. *American Journal of Psychiatry, 167,* 261–280.

Brown, B. B., Mounts, N., Lamborn, S. D., & Steinberg, L. (1993). Parenting practices and peer group affiliations in adolescence. *Child Development, 64,* 467–482.

Brown, R. (1973). Development of the first language in the human species. *American Psychologist, 28,* 97–106.

Brown, R., & Kulik, J. (1977). Flashbulb memories. *Cognition, 5,* 73–99.

Brown, R., & McNeill, D. (1966). The "tip-of-the-tongue" phenomenon. *Journal of Verbal Learning and Verbal Behavior, 5,* 325–337.

Brownell, K. D., Greenwood, M. R. C., Stellar, E., & Shrager, E. E. (1986). The effects of repeated cycles of weight loss and regain in rats. *Physiology & Behavior, 38,* 459–464.

Browning, C. R., & Laumann, E. O. (1997). Sexual contact between children and adults: A life course perspective. *American Sociological Review, 62,* 540-560.

Brunetti, D., De Luca, M., and James, E. L. (Producers), & Taylor-Johnson, S. (Director). (2015). *Fifty shades of grey* [Motion picture]. United States: Universal Pictures.

Bruni, F. (2000, September 13). The 2000 campaign: The Texas governor; Bush says rats reference in ad was unintentional. *The New York Times,* p. A19.

Brunoni, A. R., Chaimani, A., Moffa, A. H., Razza, L. B., Gattaz, W. F., Daskalakis Z. J., & Carvalho, A. F. (2017). Repetitive transcranial magnetic stimulation for the acute treatment of major depressive episodes: A systematic review with network meta-analysis. *JAMA Psychiatry, 74,* 143–152.

Bullen, C., Howe, C., Laugesen, M., McRobbie, H., Parag, V., Williman, J., & Walker, N. (2013). Electronic cigarettes for smoking cessation: A randomised controlled trial. *The Lancet, 352,* 1629–1637.

Bullough, V. (1990). The Kinsey scale in historical perspective. In D. P. Whirter, S. A. Sanders, & J. M. Reinisch (Eds.), *Homosexuality/heterosexuality: Concepts of sexual orientation* (pp. 3–15). New York, NY: Oxford University Press.

Buoli, M., Serati, M., & Altamura, A. (2014). Is the combination of a mood stabilizer plus an antipsychotic more effective than mono-therapies in long-term treatment of bipolar disorder? A systematic review. *Journal of Affective Disorders, 152,* 12–18.

Burger, J. M. (2009). Replicating Milgram: Would people still obey today? *American Psychologist, 64,* 1–11.

Burger, J. M., Girgis, Z. M., & Manning, C. C. (2011). In their own words: Explaining obedience to authority through an examination of participants' comments. *Social Psychological and Personality Science, 2,* 460–466.

Burger, N. E., Kaffine, D. T., & Yu, B. (2014). Did California's hand-held cell phone ban reduce accidents? *Transportation Research Part A: Policy and Practice, 66,* 162–172.

Bush, E. C., & Allman, J. M. (2004). The scaling of frontal cortex in primates and carnivores. *Proceedings of the National Academy of Sciences, USA, 101,* 3962–3966.

Bushdid, C., Magnasco, M. O., Vosshall, L. B., & Keller, A. (2014). Humans can discriminate more than 1 trillion olfactory stimuli. *Science, 343,* 1370–1372.

Bushman, B. J., & Anderson, C. A. (2015). Understanding causality in the effects of media violence. *American Behavioral Scientist, 59,* 1807–1821.

Buss, A. H., & Plomin, R. (1984). *Temperament: Early developing personality traits.* Hillsdale, NJ: Erlbaum.

Buss, D. M. (1989). Sex differences in human mate preferences: Evolutionary hypotheses tested in 37 cultures. *Behavioral and Brain Sciences, 12,* 1–49.

Buss, K. A., & McDoniel, M. E. (2016). Improving the prediction of risk for anxiety development in temperamentally fearful children. *Current Directions in Psychological Science, 25,* 14–20.

Buster, J. E., Kingsberg, S. A., Aguirre, O., Brown, C., Breaux, J. G., Buch, A., . . . Casson, P. (2005). Testosterone patch for low sexual desire in surgically menopausal women: A randomized trial. *Obstetrics and Gynecology, 105,* 944–952.

Butcher, J. N., Mineka, S., & Hooley, J. M. (2007). *Abnormal psychology* (13th ed.). Boston, MA: Allyn & Bacon.

Buvat, J., Maggi, M., Guay, A., & Torres, L. O. (2013). Testosterone deficiency in men: Systematic review and standard operating procedures for diagnosis and treatment. *Journal of Sexual Medicine, 10,* 245–284.

Byers-Heinlein, K., Burns, T. C., & Werker, J. F. (2010). The roots of bilingualism in newborns. *Psychological Science, 21,* 343–348.

Cahn, B. R., & Polich, J. (2006). Meditation states and traits: EEG, ERP, and neuroimaging studies. *Psychological Bulletin, 132,* 180–211.

Cairns, R. B., & Cairns, B. D. (1994). *Lifelines and risks: Pathways of youth in our times.* Cambridge, UK: Cambridge University Press.

Califf, R. M., Woodcock, J., & Ostroff, S. (2016). A proactive response to prescription opioid abuse. *New England Journal of Medicine, 374,* 1480–1485.

Campbell, W. K., Bush, C. P., Brunell, A. B., & Shelton, J. (2005). Understanding the social costs of narcissism: The case of tragedy of the commons. *Personality and Social Psychology, 31,* 1358–1368.

Campbell, W. K., Foster, C. A., & Finkel, E. J. (2002). Does self-love lead to love for others? A story of narcissistic game playing. *Journal of Personality and Social Psychology, 83,* 340–354.

Campbell, W. K., & Sedikides, C. (1999). Self-threat magnifies the self-serving bias: A meta-analytic integration. *Review of General Psychology, 3,* 23–43.

Camperio-Ciani, A., Corna, F., & Capiluppi, C. (2004). Evidence for maternally inherited factors favouring male homosexuality and promoting female fecundity. *Proceedings of the Royal Society of London B, 271,* 2217–2221.

Camperio-Ciani, A., Iemmola, F., & Blecher, S. R. (2009). Genetic factors increase fecundity in female maternal relatives of bisexual men as in homosexuals. *The Journal of Sexual Medicine, 6,* 449–455.

Canetta, S., Sourander, A., Surcel, H. M., Hinkka-Yli-Salomäki, S., Leiviskä, J., Kellendonk, C., . . . Brown, A. S. (2014). Elevated maternal C-reactive protein and increased risk of schizophrenia in a national birth cohort. *American Journal of Psychiatry, 171,* 960–968.

Canli, T. (2006). *Biology of personality and individual differences.* New York, NY: Guilford Press.

Cannon, W. B. (1927). The James-Lange theory of emotion: A critical examination and an alternative theory. *American Journal of Psychology, 39,* 106–124.

Cantu, D., Walker, K., Andresen, L., Taylor-Weiner, A., Hampton, D., Tesco, G., & Dulla, C. G. (2015). Traumatic brain injury increases cortical glutamate network activity by compromising GABAergic control. *Cerebral Cortex, 25,* 2306–2320.

Caramaschi, D., de Boer, S. F., & Koolhaus, J. M. (2007). Differential role of the 5-HT receptor in aggressive and non-aggressive mice: An across-strain comparison. *Physiology & Behavior, 90,* 590–601.

Cardeña, E., & Carlson, E. (2011). Acute stress disorder revisited. *Annual Review of Clinical Psychology, 7,* 245–267.

Carey, B. (2011, June 23). Expert on mental illness reveals her own fight. *The New York Times.* Retrieved from http://www.nytimes.com/2011/06/23/health/23lives.html

Carli, L. L., Ganley, R., & Pierce-Otay, A. (1991). Similarity and satisfaction in roommate relationships. *Personality and Social Psychology Bulletin, 17,* 419–426.

Carney, C. E., Edinger, J. D., Kuchibhatla, M., Lachowski, A. M., Bogouslavsky, O., Krystal, A. D., & Shapiro, C. M. (2017). Cognitive behavioral insomnia therapy for those with insomnia and depression: A randomized controlled clinical trial. *Sleep, 40,* zsx019.

Carney, R. M., & Freedland, K. E. (2017). Depression and coronary heart disease. *Nature Reviews Cardiology, 14,* 145–155.

Carrère, S., Buehlman, K. T., Gottman, J. M., Coan, J. A., & Ruckstuhl, L. (2000). Predicting marital stability and divorce in newlywed couples. *Journal of Family Psychology, 14,* 42–58.

Carstensen, L. L. (1995). Evidence for a life-span theory of socioemotional selectivity. *Current Directions in Psychological Science, 4,* 151–156.

Carter, C. S. (2014). Oxytocin pathways and the evolution of human behavior. *Annual Review of Psychology, 65,* 17–39.

Case, R. (1992). The role of the frontal lobes in development. *Brain and Cognition, 20,* 51–73.

Casey, B. J., Jones, R. M., & Somerville, L. H. (2011). Braking and accelerating of the adolescent brain. *Journal of Research in Adolescence, 21,* 21–33.

Caspi, A. (2000). The child is father of the man: Personality continuities from childhood to adulthood. *Journal of Personality and Social Psychology, 78,* 158–172.

Caspi, A., & Herbener, E. S. (1990). Continuity and change: Assortative marriage and the consistency of personality in adulthood. *Journal of Personality and Social Psychology, 58,* 250–258.

Caspi, A., Houts, R. M., Belsky, D. W., Harrington, H., Hogan, S., Ramrakha, S., . . . Moffitt, T. E. (2016). Childhood forecasting of a small segment of the population with large economic burden. *Nature Human Behaviour, 1,* 0005.

Caspi, A., Roberts, B. W., & Shiner, R. L. (2005). Personality development: Stability and change. *Annual Review of Psychology, 56,* 453–485.

Cattell, R. B. (1971). *Abilities: Their structure, growth, and action.* Boston, MA: Houghton Mifflin.

CBC News. (2012, June 15). 2nd hypnotist rescues students stuck in trance. Retrieved from http://www.cbc.ca/news/canada/montreal/2nd-hypnotist-rescues-students-stuck-in-trance-1.1240499

Ceci, S. J. (1999). Schooling and intelligence. In S. J. Ceci & W. M. Williams (Eds.), *The nature-nurture debate: The essential readings* (pp. 168–175). Oxford, UK: Blackwell.

Centers for Disease Control and Prevention. (2004, July). Summary health statistics for U.S. adults: National health interview survey, 2002. *Vital and Health Statistics* series 10, no. 222. Retrieved from https://www.cdc.gov/nchs/data/series/sr_10/sr10_222.pdf

Centers for Disease Control and Prevention. (2010). Tobacco use and United States students. Retrieved from http://www.cdc.gov/HealthyYouth/yrbs/pdf/us_tobacco_combo.pdf

Centers for Disease Control and Prevention. (2011). Mental illness surveillance among adults in the United States. *Morbidity and Mortality Weekly Report, 60,* 1–32.

Centers for Disease Control and Prevention. (2013). Noise-induced hearing loss. Retrieved from https://www.cdc.gov/ncbddd/hearingloss/noise.html

Centers for Disease Control and Prevention. (2018a). Sexually transmitted diseases (STDs). Retrieved from https://www.cdc.gov/std/default.htm

Centers for Disease Control and Prevention. (2018b). 10 leading causes of death by age group, United States—2014. Retrieved from https://www.cdc.gov/injury/images/lc-charts/leading_causes_of_death_age_group_2014_1050w760h.gif

Cepeda, N. J., Pashler, H., Vul, E., Wixted, J. T., & Rohrer, D. (2006). Distributed practice in verbal recall tasks: A review and quantitative synthesis. *Psychological Bulletin, 132,* 354–380.

Cerasoli, C. P., Nicklin, J. M., & Ford, M. T. (2014). Intrinsic motivation and extrinsic incentives jointly predict performance: A 40-year meta-analysis. *Psychological Bulletin, 140,* 980–1008.

Chabas, D., Taheri, S., Renier, C., & Mignot, E. (2003). The genetics of narcolepsy. *Annual Review of Genomics & Human Genetics, 4,* 459–483.

Chabris, C. F., Lee, J. J., Cesarini, D., Benjamin, D. J., & Laibson, D. I. (2015). The fourth law of behavior genetics. *Current Directions in Psychological Science, 24,* 304–312.

Chadwick, M. J., Anjum, R. S., Kumaran, D., Schacter, D. L., Spiers, H. J., & Hassabis, D. (2016). Semantic representations in the temporal pole predict false memories. *Proceedings of the National Academy of Sciences, 113,* 10180–10185.

Chandra, A., Mosher, W. D., Copen, C., & Sionean, C. (2011). Sexual behavior, sexual attraction, and sexual identity in the United States: Data from the 2006–2008 National Survey of Family Growth. *National Health Statistics Reports, 36,* 1–36.

Chaplin, T. M. (2015). Gender and emotion expression: A developmental contextual perspective. *Emotion Review, 7,* 14–21.

Charles, S. T., Mogle, J., Urban, E. J., & Almeida, D. M. (2016). Daily events are important for age differences in mean and duration for negative affect but not positive affect. *Psychology and Aging, 31,* 661–671.

Chase, W. G., & Simon, H. A. (1973). Perception in chess. *Cognitive Psychology, 4,* 55–81.

Chassin, L., Presson, C. C., & Sherman, S. J. (1990). Social psychological contributions to the understanding and prevention of adolescent cigarette smoking. *Personality and Social Psychology Bulletin, 16,* 133–151.

Chavez, R. S., Heatherton, T. F., & Wagner, D. D. (2017). Neural population decoding reveals the intrinsic positivity of the self. *Cerebral Cortex, 27*, 5222–5229.

Chen, Q., Yan, W., & Duan, E. (2016). Epigenetic inheritance of acquired traits through sperm RNAs and sperm RNA modifications. *Nature Reviews Genetics, 17*, 733–743.

Cherry, E. C. (1953). Some experiments on the recognition of speech, with one and two ears. *Journal of the Acoustical Society of America, 25*, 975–979.

Chiappa, J. A., & Fornish, J. J. (1976). *The VD book*. New York, NY: Holt, Rinehart, & Winston.

Choi, I., Dalal, R., Kim-Prieto, C., & Park, H. (2003). Culture and judgment of causal relevance. *Journal of Personality and Social Psychology, 84*, 46–59.

Chrisler, J. C., & Barne, A. (2017). Sizeism is a health hazard. *Fat Studies, 6*, 38–53.

Christakis, N. A., & Fowler, J. H. (2007). The spread of obesity in a large social network over 32 years. *New England Journal of Medicine, 357*, 370–379.

Christensen, D. L., Baio, J., Braun, K. V., Bilder, D., Charles, J., Constantino, J. N., . . . Yeargin-Allsopp, M. (2015). Prevalence and characteristics of autism spectrum disorder among children aged 8 years—Autism and developmental disabilities monitoring network, 11 sites, United States, 2012. *Morbidity and Mortality Weekly Report. Surveillance Summaries, 65*, 1–23.

Christian, K. M., Song, H., & Ming, G. L. (2014). Functions and dysfunctions of adult hippocampal neurogenesis. *Annual Review of Neuroscience, 37*, 243–262.

Christianson, S. (1992). Emotional stress and eyewitness memory: A critical review. *Psychological Bulletin, 112*, 284–309.

Christopher, F. S., & Sprecher, S. (2000). Sexuality in marriage, dating, and other relationships: A decade review. *Journal of Marriage and Family, 62*, 999–1017.

Chronis, A. M., Jones, H. A., & Raggi, V. L. (2006). Evidence-based psychosocial treatments for children and adolescents with attention-deficit/hyperactivity disorder. *Clinical Psychology Review, 26*, 486–502.

Chun, M. M., Golomb, J. D., & Turk-Browne, N. B. (2011). A taxonomy of external and internal attention. *Annual Review of Psychology, 62*, 73–101.

Cipriani, A., Furukawa, T. A., Salanti, G., Chaimani, A., Atkinson, L. Z., Ogawa, Y., . . . Geddes, J. R. (2018). Comparative efficacy and acceptability of 21 antidepressant drugs for the acute treatment of adults with major depressive disorder: A systematic review and network meta-analysis. *The Lancet, 391*, 1357–1366.

Clark, L. A., Cuthbert, B., Lewis-Fernández, R., Narrow, W. E., & Reed, G. M. (2017). Three approaches to understanding and classifying mental disorder: ICD-11, DSM-5, and the National Institute of Mental Health's Research Domain Criteria (RDoC). *Psychological Science in the Public Interest, 18*, 72–145.

Clark, R. D., & Hatfield, E. (1989). Gender differences in receptivity to sexual offers. *Journal of Psychology and Human Sexuality, 2*, 39–55.

Cogsdill, E. J., Todorov, A. T., Spelke, E. S., & Banaji, M. R. (2014). Inferring character from faces: A developmental study. *Psychological Science, 25*, 1132–1139.

Cohen, D., Nisbett, R. E., Bowdle, B. F., & Schwarz, N. (1996). Insult, aggression, and the southern culture of honor: An "experimental ethnography." *Journal of Personality and Social Psychology, 70*, 945–960.

Cohen, G. L., Garcia, J., Apfel, N., & Master, A. (2006). Reducing the racial achievement gap: A social-psychological intervention. *Science, 313*, 1307–1310.

Cohen, S., Alper, C. M., Doyle, W. J., Treanor, J. J., & Turner, R. B. (2006). Positive emotional style predicts resistance to illness after experimental exposure to rhinovirus or influenza A virus. *Psychomatic Medicine, 68*, 809–815.

Cohen, S., Doyle, W. J., Skoner, D. P., Rabin, B. S., & Gwaltney, J. M. J. (1997). Social ties and susceptibility to the common cold. *Journal of the American Medical Association, 277*, 1940–1944.

Cohen, S., Tyrrell, D. A. J., & Smith, A. P. (1991). Psychological stress and susceptibility to the common cold. *New England Journal of Medicine, 325*, 606–612.

Coid, J., & Ullrich, S. (2010). Antisocial personality disorder is on a continuum with psychopathy. *Comprehensive Psychiatry, 51*, 426–433.

Colapinto, J. (2000). *As nature made him: The boy who was raised as a girl*. New York, NY: HarperCollins.

Colcombe, S. J., Erickson, K. I., Scalf, P., Kim, J., Prakash, R., McAuley, E., . . . Kramer, A. F. (2006). Aerobic exercise training increases brain volume in aging humans. *Journal of Gerontology: Medical Sciences, 61A*, 1166–1170.

Collins, A. M., & Loftus, E. F. (1975). A spreading activation theory of semantic processing. *Psychologial Review, 82*, 407–428.

Collins, K. P., & Cleary, S. D. (2016). Racial and ethnic disparities in parent-reported diagnosis of ADHD: National Survey of Children's Health (2003, 2007, and 2011). *The Journal of Clinical Psychiatry, 77*, 52–59.

Compton, W. M., Conway, K. P., Stinson, F. S., Colliver, J. D., & Grant, B. F. (2005). Prevalence, correlates, and comorbidity of *DSM-IV* antisocial personality syndromes and alcohol and specific drug use disorders in the United States: Results from the national epidemiologic survey on alcohol and related conditions. *Journal of Clinical Psychiatry, 66*, 677–685.

Compton, W. M., Jones, C. M., & Baldwin, G. T. (2016). Relationship between nonmedical prescription-opioid use and heroin use. *New England Journal of Medicine, 374*, 154–163.

Comstock, R. D., Currie, D. W., Pierpoint, L. A., Grubenhoff, J. A., & Fields, S. K. (2015). Original investigation: An evidence-based discussion of heading the ball and concussions in high school soccer. *JAMA Pediatrics, 169*, 830–837.

Comtesse, H., & Stemmler, G. (2016). Fear and disgust in women: Differentiation of cardiovascular regulation patterns. *Biological Psychology, 123*, 166–176.

Conn, C., Warden, R., Stuewig, R., Kim, E., Harty, L., Hastings, M., & Tangney, J. P. (2010). Borderline personality disorder among jail inmates: How common and how distinct? *Corrections Compendium, 35*, 6–13.

Conron, K. J., Scott, G., Stowell, G. S., & Landers, S. L. (2012). Transgender health in Massachusetts: Results from a household probability sample of adults. *American Journal of Public Health, 102*, 118–122.

Conway, A. R. A., Kane, M. J., & Engle, R. W. (2003). Working memory capacity and its relation to general intelligence. *Trends in Cognitive Sciences, 7*, 547–552.

Cook, G. I., Marsh, R. L., Clark-Foos, A., & Meeks, J. T. (2007). Learning is impaired by activated intentions. *Psychonomic Bulletin and Review, 14*, 101–106.

Cook, M., & Mineka, S. (1989). Observational conditioning of fear to fear-relevant versus fear-irrelevant stimuli in rhesus monkeys. *Journal of Abnormal Psychology, 98*, 448–459.

Cooke, S. F., & Bliss, T. V. P. (2006). Plasticity in the human central nervous system. *Brain: A Journal of Neurology, 129*, 1659–1673.

Coolidge, S. (2014, December 31). Transgender teen: "My death needs to mean something." *USA Today*. Retrieved from http://www.usatoday.com/story/news/nation-now/2014/12/30/transgender-teen-death-means-something/21059923

Cooper, C. R., Denner, J., & Lopez, E. M. (1999). Cultural brokers: Helping Latino children on pathways toward success. *The Future of Children, 9*, 51–57.

Copeland, W. E., Wolke, D., Angold, A., & Costello, E. J. (2013). Adult psychiatric outcomes of bullying and being bullied by peers in childhood and adolescence. *Journal of the American Medical Association Psychiatry, 70*, 419–426.

Coren, S. (1996). Daylight savings time and traffic accidents. *New England Journal of Medicine, 334,* 924.

Cortese, S., Moreira-Maia, C. R., St. Fleur, D., Morcillo-Peñalver, C., Rohde, L. A., & Faraone, S. V. (2016). Association between ADHD and obesity: A systematic review and meta-analysis. *American Journal of Psychiatry, 173,* 34–43.

Cortiella, C., & Horowitz, S. H. (2014). *The state of learning disabilities: Facts, trends and emerging issues* (3rd ed.). New York, NY: National Center for Learning Disabilities.

Costa, P. T., & McCrae, R. R. (2010). *The NEO Personality Inventory: 3.* Odessa, FL: Psychological Assessment Resources.

Costa, P. T., Terracciano, A., & McCrae, R. R. (2001). Gender differences in personality traits across cultures: Robust and surprising findings. *Journal of Personality and Social Psychology, 81,* 322–331.

Cotter, D., Hermsen, J. M., & Vanneman, R. (2011). The end of the gender revolution? Gender role attitudes from 1977 to 2008. *American Journal of Sociology, 117,* 259–289.

Courchesne, E., Pierce, K., Schumann, C. M., Redcay, E., Buckwalter, J. A., Kennedy, D. P., & Morgan, J. (2007). Mapping early brain development in autism. *Neuron, 56,* 399–413.

Cowan, C. P., & Cowan, P. A. (1988). Who does what when partners become parents? Implications for men, women, and marriage. In R. Palkovitz & M. B. Sussman (Eds.), *Transitions to parenthood* (pp. 105–132). New York, NY: The Haworth Press.

Cowan, N. (2010). The magical mystery four: How is working memory capacity limited, and why? *Current Directions in Psychological Science, 19,* 51–57.

Cowell, P. E., Turetsky, B. E., Gur, R. C., Grossman, R. I., Shtasel, D. L., & Gur, R. E. (1994). Sex differences in aging of the human frontal and temporal lobes. *Journal of Neuroscience, 14,* 4748–4755.

Craighead, W. E., & Dunlop, B. W. (2014). Combination psychotherapy and antidepressant medication treatment for depression: For whom, when, and how. *Annual Review of Psychology, 65,* 267–300.

Craik, F. I. M., & Lockhart, R. S. (1972). Levels of processing: A framework for memory research. *Journal of Verbal Learning and Verbal Behavior, 11,* 671–684.

Craik, F. I. M., & Tulving, E. (1975). Depth of processing and the retention of words in episodic memory. *Journal of Experimental Psychology: General, 104,* 268–294.

Crandall, C. (2002). Vaginal estrogen preparations: A review of safety and efficacy for vaginal atrophy. *Journal of Women's Health, 11,* 857–877.

Crawford, H. J., Corby, J. C., & Kopell, B. (1996). Auditory event-related potentials while ignoring tone stimuli: Attentional differences reflected in stimulus intensity and latency responses in low and highly hypnotizable persons. *International Journal of Neuroscience, 85,* 57–69.

Crocker, J., & Major, B. (1989). Social stigma and self-esteem: The self-protective properties of stigma. *Psychological Review, 96,* 608–630.

Crocker, J., Niiya, Y., & Mischkowski, D. (2008). Why does writing about important values reduce defensiveness? Self-affirmation and the role of positive other-directed feelings. *Psychological Science, 19,* 740–747.

Crocker, J., Olivier, M., & Nuer, N. (2009). Self-image goals and compassionate goals: Costs and benefits. *Self and Identity, 8,* 251–269.

Crosnoe, R., & Elder, G. H., Jr. (2002). Successful adaptation in the later years: A life-course approach to aging. *Social Psychology Quarterly, 65,* 309–328.

Crothers, T. (2012). *The queen of Katwe: A story of life, chess, and one extraordinary girl's dreams of becoming a grandmaster.* New York, NY: Scribner.

Csikszentmihalyi, M. (1990). *Flow: The psychology of optimal experience.* New York, NY: Harper & Row.

Csikszentmihalyi, M. (1999). If we are so rich, why aren't we happy? *American Psychologist, 54,* 821–827.

Csikszentmihalyi M. (2014). Toward a psychology of optimal experience. In *Flow and the foundations of positive psychology.* Dordrecht: Springer. Retrieved from https://link.springer.com/chapter/10.1007%2F978-94-017-9088-8_14

Cummings, J. L., Morstorf, T., & Zhong, K. (2014). Alzheimer's disease drug-development pipeline: Few candidates, frequent failures. *Alzheimer's Research & Therapy, 6,* 37.

Cummings, J. R., & Druss, B. G. (2010). Racial/ethnic differences in mental health service use among adolescents with major depression. *Journal of the American Academy of Child & Adolescent Psychiatry, 50,* 160–170.

Cunningham, M. R., Barbee, A. P., & Druen, P. B. (1996). Social allergens and the reactions they produce: Escalation of annoyance and disgust in love and work. In R. M. Kowalski (Ed.), *Aversive interpersonal behaviors* (pp. 189–214). New York, NY: Plenum Press.

Cunningham, M. R., Roberts, A. R., Barbee, A. P., Druen, P. B., & Wu, C. (1995). Their ideas of beauty are, on the whole, the same as ours: Consistency and variability in the cross-cultural perception of female physical attractiveness. *Journal of Personality and Social Psychology, 68,* 261–279.

Curatolo, P., D'Agati, E., & Moavero, R. (2010). The neurobiological basis of ADHD. *Italian Journal of Pediatrics, 36,* 79.

Dalton, M. A., Bernhardt, A. M., Gibson, J. J., Sargent, J. D., Beach, M. L., Adachi-Mejia, A., . . . Heatherton, T. F. (2005). "Honey, have some smokes." Preschoolers use cigarettes and alcohol while role playing as adults. *Archives of Pediatrics & Adolescent Medicine, 159,* 854–859.

Damasio, H., Grabowski, T., Frank, R., Galaburda, A. M., & Damasio, A. R. (1994). The return of Phineas Gage: Clues about the brain from the skull of a famous patient. *Science, 264,* 1102–1105.

Darwin, C. R. (1872). *The expression of the emotions in man and animals.* London, UK: John Murray.

Davidson, J. R., Foa, E. B., Huppert, J. D., Keefe, F. J., Franklin, M. E., Compton, J. S., et al. (2004). Fluoxetine, comprehensive cognitive behavioral therapy, and placebo in generalized social phobia. *Archives of General Psychiatry, 61,* 1005–1013.

Daxinger, L., & Whitelaw, E. (2012). Understanding transgenerational epigenetic inheritance via the gametes in mammals. *Nature Reviews Genetics, 13,* 153–162.

Deacon, B. J., & Abramowitz, J. S. (2004). Cognitive and behavioral treatments for anxiety disorders: A review of meta-analytic findings. *Journal of Clinical Psychology, 60,* 429–441.

Deary, I. J. (2000). *Looking down on human intelligence.* New York, NY: Oxford University Press.

Deaton, A., & Stone, A. A. (2014). Evaluative and hedonic well-being among those with and without children at home. *Proceedings of the National Academy of Science, 111,* 1328–1333.

Deaux, K., & Major, B. (1987). Putting gender into context: An interactive model of gender-related behavior. *Psychological Review, 94,* 369–389.

De Bolle, M., De Fruyt, F., McCrae, R. R., Löckenhoff, C. E., Costa Jr., P. T., & Avdeyeva, T. V. (2015). The emergence of sex differences in personality traits in early adolescence: A cross-sectional, cross-cultural study. *Journal of Personality and Social Psychology, 108,* 171–185.

DeCasper, A. J., & Fifer, W. P. (1980). Of human bonding: Newborns prefer their mothers' voices. *Science, 208,* 1174–1176.

DeCasper, A. J., & Spence, M. J. (1986). Prenatal maternal speech influences newborns' perception of speech sounds. *Infant Behavior and Development, 9,* 133–150.

Deci, E. L., & Ryan, R. M. (1987). The support of autonomy and the control of behavior. *Journal of Personality and Social Psychology, 53,* 1024–1037.

Decyk, B. N. (1994).Using examples to teach concepts. In *Changing college classrooms: New teaching and learning strategies for an increasingly complex world* (pp. 39–63). San Francisco: Jossey-Bass.

Deeb, S. S. (2005). The molecular basis for variation in human color vision. *Clinical Genetics, 67,* 369–377.

Dehaene, S., Changeux, J. P., Naccache, L., Sackur, J., & Sergent, C. (2006). Conscious, preconscious, and subliminal processing: A testable taxonomy. *Trends in Cognitive Sciences, 10,* 204–211.

Dejong, W., & Kleck, R. E. (1986). The social psychological effects of overweight. In C. P. Herman, M. P. Zanna, & E. T. Higgins (Eds.), *Physical appearance, stigma and social behavior: The Ontario Symposium* (pp. 65–87). Hillsdale, NJ: Erlbaum.

Demerouti, E. (2006). Job characteristics, flow, and performance: The moderating role of conscientiousness. *Journal of Occupational Health Psychology, 11,* 266–280.

DeStefano, F., Price, C. S., & Weintraub, E. S. (2013). Increasing exposure to antibody-stimulating proteins and polysaccharides in vaccines is not associated with risk of autism. *The Journal of Pediatrics, 163,* 561–567.

de Vries, A. L., & Cohen-Kettenis, P. T. (2012). Clinical management of gender dysphoria in children and adolescents: The Dutch approach. *Journal of Homosexuality, 59,* 301–320.

de Vogue, A., Mallonee, M. K., & Grinberg, E. (2017, February 23). Trump administration withdraws federal protections for transgender students. *CNN Politics.* Retrieved from https://www.cnn.com/2017/02/22/politics/doj-withdraws-federal-protections-on-transgender-bathrooms-in-schools/index.html

de Wijk, R. A., Schab, F. R., & Cain, W. S. (1995). Odor identification. In F. R. Schab (Ed.), *Memory for odors* (pp. 21–37). Mahwah, NJ: Erlbaum.

DeYoung, C. G., Hirsh, J. B., Shane, M. S., Papademetris, X., Rajeevan, N., & Gray, J. R. (2010). Testing predictions from personality neuroscience: Brain structure and the big five. *Psychological Science, 21,* 820–828.

Diamond, L. M. (2016). Sexual fluidity in male and females. *Current Sexual Health Reports, 8,* 249–256.

Diamond, L. M., & Butterworth, M. (2008). Questioning gender and sexual identity: Dynamic links over time. *Sex Roles, 59,* 365–376.

Diamond, M. (1993). Homosexuality and bisexuality in different populations. *Archives of Sexual Behavior, 22,* 291–310.

Diamond, M. (2009). Clinical implications of the organizational and activational effects of hormones. *Hormones and Behavior, 55,* 621–632.

Diener, E. (2000). Subjective well-being: The science of happiness and a proposal for a national index. *American Psychologist, 55,* 34–43.

Dillaway, H. E. (2005). Menopause is the "good old": Women's thoughts about reproductive aging. *Gender & Society, 19,* 398–417.

Dimock, M. (2018). Defining generations: Where millennials end and post-millennials begin. Pew Research Center. Retrieved from http://www.pewresearch.org/fact-tank/2018/03/01/defining-generations-where-millennials-end-and-post-millennials-begin/

Dion, K., Berscheid, E., & Walster, E. (1972). What is beautiful is good. *Journal of Personality and Social Psychology, 24,* 285–290.

Diotallevi, M. (2008). Testimonials versus evidence. *Canadian Medical Association Journal, 179,* 449.

Dobbs, D. (2006). Turning off depression. *Scientific American Mind, 17,* 26–31.

Doblin, R., Greer, G., Holland, J., Jerome, L., Mithoefer, M. C., & Sessa, B. (2014). A reconsideration and response to Parrott, A. C. (2013). Human psychobiology of MDMA or 'Ecstasy': An overview of 25 years of empirical research. *Human Psychopharmacology: Clinical and Experimental, 29,* 105–108.

Docherty, N. M. (2005). Cognitive impairments and disordered speech in schizophrenia: Thought disorder, disorganization, and communication failure perspectives. *Journal of Abnormal Psychology, 114,* 269–278.

Dockray, A., & Steptoe, A. (2010). Positive affect and psychobiological process. *Neuroscience and Biobehavioral Reviews, 35,* 69–75.

Dolan, P., & Metcalfe, R. (2010). "Oops . . . I did it again": Repeated focusing effects in reports of happiness. *Journal of Economic Psychology, 31,* 732–737.

Doleac, J. L., & Mukherjee, A. (2018). The moral hazard of lifesaving innovations: Naloxone access opioid abuse, and crime. Retrieved from https://ssrn.com/abstract=3135264

Dollard, J., Miller, N. E., Doob, L. W., Mowrer, O. H., & Sears, R. R. (1939). *Frustration and aggression.* New Haven, CT: Yale University Press.

Domagalski, T. A., & Steelman, L. A. (2007). The impact of gender and organizational status on workplace anger expression. *Management Communication Quarterly, 20,* 297–315.

Domhoff, G. W. (2003). *The scientific study of dreams: Neural networks, cognitive development, and content analysis.* Washington, DC: American Psychological Association.

Donahue, A. B. (2000). Electroconvulsive therapy and memory loss: A personal journey. *Journal of ECT, 16,* 133–143.

Dowd, K. E. (2017, April 28). Michael Phelps opens up about ADHD struggles. *Sports Illustrated.* Retrieved from https://www.si.com/olympics/2017/04/28/michael-phelps-opens-about-adhd-struggles-teacher-told-me-id-never-amount-anything

Drescher, J., Schwartz, A., Casoy, F., McIntosh, C. A., Hurley, B., Ashley, K., . . . Tompkins, D. A. (2016). The growing regulation of conversion therapy. *Journal of Medical Regulation, 102,* 7–12.

Drosopoulos, S., Schulze, C., Fischer, S., & Born, J. (2007). Sleep's function in the spontaneous recovery and consolidation of memories. *Journal of Experimental Psychology: General, 136,* 169–183.

Duckworth, A. L., Peterson, C., Matthews, M. D., & Kelly, D. R. (2007). Grit: Perseverance and passion for long-term goals. *Journal of Personality and Social Psychology, 92,* 1087–1101.

Duckworth, A.L., & Quinn, P.D. (2009). Development and validation of the short grit scale (Grit-S). *Journal of Personality Assessment, 91,* 166–174.

Duckworth, A. L., & Seligman, M. E. P. (2005). Self-discipline outdoes IQ in predicting academic performance of adolescents. *Psychological Science, 16,* 939–944.

Duncker, K. (1945). On problem solving. *Psychological Monographs, 58,* i–113.

Dunlosky, J., Rawson, K. A., Marsh, E. J., Nathan, M. J., & Willingham, D. T. (2013). Improving students' learning with effective learning techniques: Promising directions from cognitive and educational psychology. *Psychological Science in the Public Interest, 14,* 4–58.

Dutton, D. G., & Aron, A. P. (1974). Some evidence for heightened sexual attraction under conditions of high anxiety. *Journal of Personality and Social Psychology, 30,* 510–517.

Dutton, J. (2007, April). They will make you proud. *Attitude Magazine.* Retrieved from https://www.additudemag.com/michael-phelps-adhd-advice-from-the-olympians-mom/

Eaker, E. D., Sullivan, L. M., Kelly-Hayes, M., D'Agostino, R. B., Sr., & Benjamin, E. J. (2004). Anger and hostility predict the development of atrial fibrillation in men in the Framingham Offspring Study. *Circulation, 109,* 1267–1271.

Eaton, D. K, Kann, L., Kinchen, S., Shanklin, S., Flint, K. H., Hawkins, J., . . . Wechsler, H. (2012). Youth risk behavior surveillance—United States. *Morbidity and Mortality Weekly Report, 61,* 1–162.

Ebbinghaus, H. (1964). *Memory* (H. A. Ruger & C. E. Bussenius, Trans.) New York, NY: Teachers College. (Original work published as *Das Gedächtnis,* 1885.)

Egeland, J. A., Gerhard, D. S., Pauls, D. L., Sussex, J. N., Kidd, K. K., Allen, C. R., . . . Housman, D. E. (1987). Bipolar affective disorders linked to DNA markers on chromosome 11. *Nature, 325,* 783–787.

Eichenbaum, H. (2004). Hippocampus: Cognitive processes and neural representations that underlie declarative memory. *Neuron, 44,* 109–120.

Einstein, G. O., & McDaniel, M. A. (2005). Prospective memory. Multiple retrieval processes. *Current Directions in Psychological Science, 14,* 286–290.

Eisenbarth, H., Chang, L. J., & Wager, T. D. (2016). Multivariate brain prediction of heart rate and skin conductance responses to social threat. *Journal of Neuroscience, 36,* 11987–11998.

Eisenberger, N. I., Lieberman, M. D., & Satpute, A. B. (2005). Personality from a controlled processing perspective: An fMRI study of neuroticism, extraversion, and self-consciousness. *Cognitive, Affective, & Behavioral Neuroscience, 5,* 169–181.

Ekman, P., & Friesen, W. V. (1971). Constants across cultures in the face and emotion. *Journal of Personality and Social Psychology, 17,* 124–129.

Ekman, P., Sorenson, E. R., & Friesen, W. V. (1969). Pancultural elements in facial displays of emotions. *Science, 164,* 86–88.

Elfenbein, H. A., & Ambady, N. (2002). On the universality of cultural specificity of emotion recognition: A meta-analysis. *Psychological Bulletin, 128,* 203–235.

Elliott, L., & Brantley, C. (1997). *Sex on campus: The naked truth about the real sex lives of college students.* New York, NY: Random House.

Elovainio, M., Hakulinen, C., Pulkki-Råback, L., Virtanen, M., Josefsson, K., Jokela, M., . . . Kivimäki, M. (2017). Contribution of risk factors to excess mortality in isolated and lonely individuals: An analysis of data from the UK Biobank cohort study. *The Lancet Public Health, 2,* e260–e266.

Engle, R. W., & Kane, M. J. (2004). Executive attention, working memory capacity, and a two-factor theory of cognitive control. In B. Ross (Ed.), *The psychology of learning and motivation* (pp. 145–199). New York, NY: Elsevier.

Engle, R. W., Tuholski, S. W., Laughlin, J. E., & Conway, A. R. A. (1999). Working memory, short-term memory, and general fluid intelligence: A latent variable approach. *Journal of Experimental Psychology: General, 128,* 309–331.

Engwall, M., & Duppils, G. S. (2009). Music as a nursing intervention for postoperative pain: A systematic review. *Journal of Perianesthesia Nursing, 24,* 370–383.

Enke, A. F. (2013). The education of Little Cis: Cisgender and the discipline of opposing bodies. In S. Stryker & A. Z. Aizura (Eds.), *The transgender studies reader* (Vol. 2, pp. 234–247). New York, NY: Routledge.

Enns, J. (2005). *The thinking eye, the seeing brain.* New York, NY: Norton.

Epps, C., & Holt, L. (2011). The genetic basis of addiction and relevant cellular mechanisms. *International Anesthesiology Clinics, 49,* 3–14.

Epstein, L. H., Robinson, J. L., Roemmich, J. N., Marusewski, A. L., & Roba, L. G. (2010). What constitutes food variety? Stimulus specificity of food. *Appetite, 54,* 23–29.

Era, P., Jokela, J., & Heikkinen, E. (1986). Reaction and movement times in men of different ages: A population study. *Perceptual and Motor Skills, 63,* 111–130.

Erdely, S. R. (2013, November 7). About a girl: Coy Mathis' fight to change gender. *Rolling Stone.* Retrieved from http://www.rollingstone.com/culture/news/about-a-girl-coy-mathis-fight-to-change-change-gender-20131028

Erickson, K. I., Voss, M. W., Prakash, R. S., Basak, C., Szabo, A., Chaddock, L., . . . Kramer, A. F. (2011). Exercise training increases size of hippocampus and improves memory. *Proceedings of the National Academy of Sciences of the United States of America, 108,* 3017–3022.

Erikson, E. H. (1959). *Identity and the life cycle.* New York, NY: International Universities Press.

Erikson, E. H. (1968). *Identity: Youth and crisis.* New York, NY: Norton.

Erikson, E. H. (1980). *Identity and the life cycle.* New York, NY: Norton.

Eriksson, P. S., Perfilieva, E., Bjork-Eriksson, T., Alborn, A. M., Nordborg, C., Peterson, D. A., & Gage, F. H. (1998). Neurogenesis in the adult human hippocampus. *Nature Medicine, 4,* 1313–1317.

Espelage, D. L., & Holt, M. K. (2012). Understanding and preventing bullying and sexual harassment in school. In K. R. Harris & M. Zeidner (Eds.), *APA educational psychology handbook, Vol. 2: Individual differences and cultural contextual factors* (pp. 391–416). Washington, DC: American Psychologial Association.

Espie, C. A. (2002). Insomnia: Conceptual issues in the development, persistence, and treatment of sleep disorders in adults. *Annual Review of Psychology, 53,* 215–243.

Eysenck, H. J. (1967). *The biological basis of personality.* Springfield, IL: Thomas.

Eysenck, M. W., Mogg, K., May, J., Richards, A., & Matthews, A. (1991). Bias in interpretation of ambiguous sentences related to threat in anxiety. *Journal of Abnormal Psychology, 100,* 144–150.

Fabiano, G. A., Pelham, W. E., Coles, E. K., Gnagy, E. M., Chronis-Tuscano, A., & O'Connor, B. C. (2009). A meta-analysis of behavioral treatments for attention-deficit/hyperactivity disorder. *Clinical Psychology Review, 29,* 129–140.

Fagerström, K., Etter, J. F., & Unger, J. B. (2015). E-cigarettes: A disruptive technology that revolutionizes our field? *Nicotine & Tobacco Research, 17,* 125–126.

Fagerström, K. O., & Schneider, N. G. (1989). Measuring nicotine dependence: A review of the Fagerström tolerance questionnaire. *Journal of Behavioral Medicine, 12,* 159–181.

Fallon, A. E., & Rozin, P. (1985). Sex differences in perceptions of desirable body shape. *Journal of Abnormal Psychology, 94,* 102–105.

Fantz, R. L. (1966). Pattern discrimination and selective attention as determinants of perceptual development from birth. In A. H. Kidd & L. J. Rivoire (Eds.), *Perceptual development in children* (pp. 143–173). New York, NY: International Universities Press.

Farb, N. A., Anderson, A. K., Mayberg, H., Bean, J., McKeon, D., & Segal, Z. V. (2010). Minding one's emotions: Mindfulness training alters the neural expression of sadness. *Emotion, 10,* 25–33.

Farhud, D. D., Zarif Yeganeh, M., Sadighi, H., & Zandvakili, S. (2016). Testicular feminization or androgen insensitivity syndrome (AIS) in Iran: A retrospective analysis of 30-year data. *Iranian Journal of Public Health, 45,* 1–5.

Farooqi, I. S., Bullmore, E., Keogh, J., Gillard, J., O'Rahilly, S., & Fletcher, P. C. (2007). Leptin regulates striatal regions and human eating behavior. *Science, 317,* 1355.

Faul, M., Xu, L., Wald, M. M., & Coronado, V. G. (2010). *Traumatic brain injury in the United States: Emergency department visits, hospitalizations, and deaths.* Atlanta, GA: Centers for Disease Control and Prevention, National Center for Injury Prevention and Control.

Fawcett, J. (1992). Suicide risk factors in depressive disorders and in panic disorders. *Journal of Clinical Psychiatry, 53,* 9–13.

Fazio, R. H. (1995). Attitudes as object-evaluation associations: Determinants, consequences, and correlates of attitude accessibility. In R. E. Petty & J. A. Krosnick (Eds.), *Attitude strength: Antecedents and consequences* (pp. 247–282). Hillsdale, NJ: Erlbaum.

Fedewa, A. L., Black, W. W., & Soyeon, A. (2015). Children and adolescents with same-gender parents: A meta-analytic approach in assessing outcomes. *Journal of GLBT Family Studies, 11,* 1–34.

Feingold, A. (1992). Good-looking people are not what we think. *Psychological Bulletin, 111,* 304–341.

Feingold, A. (1994). Gender differences in personality: A meta-analysis. *Psychological Bulletin, 116,* 429–456.

Feldman, S. S., & Rosenthal, D. A. (1991). Age expectations of behavioural autonomy in Hong Kong, Australian and American youth: The influence of family variables and adolescents' values. *International Journal of Psychology, 26,* 1–23.

Feldman Barrett, L., Lane, R. D., Sechrest, L., & Schwartz, G. E. (2000). Sex differences in emotional awareness. *Personality and Social Psychology Bulletin, 26,* 1027–1035.

Ferdinand, A. O., & Menachemi, N. (2014). Associations between driving performance and engaging in secondary tasks: A systematic review. *American Journal of Public Health, 104,* e39–e48.

Fernald, A. (1989). Intonation and communicative intent in mothers' speech to infants: Is the melody the message? *Child Development, 60,* 1497–1510.

Ferrari, P. F., Visalberghi, E., Paukner, A., Fogassi, L., Ruggiero, A., & Suomi, S. (2006). Neonatal imitation in rhesus macaques. *PLOS Biology, 4,* 1501–1508.

Ferry, G. (Writer/Broadcaster). (2002, 12 & 19 November). Hearing colours, eating sounds. *BBC Radio 4, Science.* Retrieved from http://www.bbc.co.uk/radio4/science/hearingcolours.shtml

Festinger, L. (1954). A theory of social comparison processes. *Human Relations, 7,* 117–140.

Festinger, L. (1957). *A theory of cognitive dissonance.* Evanston, IL: Row, Peterson.

Festinger, L. (1987). A personal memory. In N. E. Grunberg, R. E. Nisbett, J. Rodin, & J. E. Singer (Eds.), *A distinctive approach to psychological research: The influence of Stanley Schachter* (pp. 1–9). New York, NY: Erlbaum.

Festinger, L., & Carlsmith, J. M. (1959). Cognitive consequences of forced compliance. *Journal of Abnormal and Social Psychology, 58,* 203–210.

Festinger, L., Schachter, S., & Back, K. W. (1950). *Social pressures in informal groups.* New York, NY: Harper.

Fibiger, H. C. (1993). Mesolimbic dopamine: An analysis of its role in motivated behavior. *Seminars in Neuroscience, 5,* 321–327.

Fineberg, N. A., Apergis-Schoute, A. M., Vaghi, M. M., Banca, P., Gillan, C. M., Voon, V., ... Bullmore, E. T. (2017). Mapping compulsivity in the DSM-5 obsessive compulsive and related disorders: Cognitive domains, neural circuitry, and treatment. *International Journal of Neuropsychopharmacology, 21,* 42–58.

Finger, S. (1994). *Origins of neuroscience.* Oxford, UK: Oxford University Press.

Fink, M. (2001). Convulsive therapy: A review of the first 55 years. *Journal of Affective Disorders, 63,* 1–15.

Fiore, M. C., Schroeder, S. A., & Baker, T. B. (2014). Smoke, the chief killer—Strategies for targeting combustible tobacco use. *New England Journal of Medicine, 37,* 297–299.

First, M. B. (2014). DSM-5 and paraphilic disorders. *Journal of the American Academy of Psychiatry and the Law Online, 42,* 191–201.

Fischer, K. (1980). A theory of cognitive development: The control and construction of hierarchies of skills. *Psychological Review, 87,* 477–531.

Fisher, H. E., Aron, A., & Brown, L. L. (2006). Romantic love: A mammalian brain system for mate choice. *Philosophical Transactions of the Royal Society of London, 361B,* 2173–2186.

Fitzgerald, P. B., Brown, T. L., Marston, N. A., Daskalakis, Z. J., De Castella, A., & Kulkarni, J. (2003). Transcranial magnetic stimulation in the treatment of depression: A double-blind, placebo-controlled trial. *Archives of General Psychiatry, 60,* 1002–1008.

Fixx, J. F. (1978). *Solve it.* New York, NY: Doubleday.

Flegal, K. M., Kit, B. K., Orpana, H., & Graubard, B. I. (2013). Association of all-case mortality with overweight and obesity using standard body mass index categories. *Journal of the American Medical Asssociation, 309,* 71–82.

Flegal, K. M., Kruszon-Moran, D., Carroll, M. D., Fryar, C. D., & Ogden, C. L. (2016). Trends in obesity among adults in the United States, 2005 to 2014. *Journal of the American Medical Association, 315,* 2284–2291.

Flentje, A., Heck, N. C., & Cochran, B. N. (2014). Experiences of ex-ex-gay individuals in sexual reorientation therapy: Reasons for seeking treatment, perceived helpfulness and harmfulness of treatment, and post-treatment identification. *Journal of Homosexuality, 61,* 1242–1268.

Flynn, J. R. (2007). Solving the IQ puzzle. *Scientific American Mind, 18,* 24–31.

Foa, E. B., Liebowitz, M. R., Kozak, M. J., Davies, S., Campeas, R., Franklin, M. E., ... Tu, X. (2005). Randomized, placebo-controlled trial of exposure and ritual prevention, clomipramine, and their combination in the treatment of obsessive-compulsive disorder. *American Journal of Psychiatry, 162,* 151–161.

Foa, E. B., & McLean, C. P. (2016). The efficacy of exposure therapy for anxiety-related disorders and its underlying mechanisms: The case of OCD and PTSD. *Annual Review of Clinical Psychology, 12,* 1–28.

Foer, Joshua. (2005). Forget me not: How to win the U.S. memory championship. *Slate.* Retrieved from http://www.slate.com/articles/news_and_politics/dispatches/2005/03/forget_me_not.html

Fogel, S. M., & Smith, C. T. (2011). The function of the sleep spindle: A physiological index of intelligence and a mechanism for sleep-dependent memory consolidation. *Neuroscience & Biobehavioral Reviews, 35,* 1154–1165.

Folkman, S., & Lazarus, R. S. (1988). Coping as a mediator of emotion. *Journal of Personality and Social Psychology, 54,* 466–475.

Folkman, S., & Moskowitz, J. T. (2000). Positive affect and the other side of coping. *American Psychologist, 55,* 647–654.

Forgas, J. P. (1998). Asking nicely: Mood effects on responding to more or less polite requests. *Personality and Social Psychology Bulletin, 24,* 173–185.

Fornaro, M., Anastasia, A., Novello, S., Fusco, A., Solmi, M., Monaco, F., ... de Bartolomeis, A. (2018). Incidence, prevalence and clinical correlates of antidepressant-emergent mania in bipolar depression: A systematic review and meta-analysis. *Bipolar Disorders, 20,* 195–227.

Foterek, K., Buyken, A. E., Bolzenius, K., Hilbig, A., Nöthlings, U., & Alexy, U. (2016). Commercial complementary food consumption is prospectively associated with added sugar intake in childhood. *The British Journal of Nutrition, 115,* 2067–2074.

Fox, N. A., Henderson, H. A., Marshall, P. J., Nichols, K. E., & Ghera, M. M. (2005). Behavioral inhibition: Linking biology and behavior within a developmental framework. *Annual Review of Psychology, 56,* 235–262.

Franke, B., Faraone, S. V., Asherson, P., Buitelaar, J., Bau, C. H., Ramos-Quiroga, J. A., ... Reif, A. (2012). The genetics of attention deficit/hyperactivity disorder in adults, a review. *Molecular Psychiatry, 17,* 960–987.

Frankel, L. (2002). "I've never thought about it": Contradictions and taboos surrounding American males' experiences of their first ejaculation (semenarche). *Journal of Men's Studies, 11,* 37–54.

Franken, R. E. (2007). *Human motivation* (6th ed.). Boston, MA: Cengage.

Franklin, M. E., & Foa, E. B. (2011). Treatment of obsessive compulsive disorder. *Annual Review of Clinical Psychology, 7,* 229–243.

Fratiglioni, L., Paillard-Borg, S., & Winblad, B. (2004). An active and socially integrated lifestyle in late life might protect against dementia. *Lancet Neurology, 3,* 343–353.

Fredrickson, B. L. (2001). The role of positive emotions in positive psychology: The broaden-and-build theory of positive emotions. *American Psychologist, 56,* 218–226.

Freedman, J. L., & Fraser, S. C. (1966). Compliance without pressure: The foot-in-the-door technique. *Journal of Personality and Social Psychology, 4,* 196–202.

Freeman, D., Reeve, S., Robinson, A., Ehlers, A., Clark, D., Spanlang, B., & Slater, M. (2017). Virtual reality in the assessment, understanding, and treatment of mental health disorders. *Psychological Medicine, 47,* 2393–2400.

Freeman, J. B., Stolier, R. M., Ingbretsen, Z. A., & Hehman, E. A. (2014). Amygdala responsivity to high-level social information from unseen faces. *The Journal of Neuroscience, 34,* 10573–10581.

Freud, A. (1936). *The ego and the mechanisms of defense.* New York, NY: International Universities Press.

Freud, S. (1900). *The interpretation of dreams: The standard edition of the complete psychological works of Sigmund Freud* (vols. 4 and 5). London, UK: Hogarth Press.

Friedman, L. A., & Rapoport, J. L. (2015). Brain development in ADHD. *Current Opinion in Neurobiology, 30,* 106–111.

Frijda, N. H. (1994). Emotions are functional, most of the time. In P. Ekman & R. J. Davidson (Eds.), *The nature of emotion: Fundamental questions, Vol. 4: Series in affective science* (pp. 112–122). New York, NY: Oxford University Press.

Frisen, J. (2016). Neurogenesis and gliogenesis in nervous system plasticity and repair. *Annual Review of Cell and Developmental Biology, 32,* 127–141.

Fryar, C. D., Carroll, M. D., & Ogden, C. L. (2016). Prevalence of overweight, obesity, and extreme obesity among adults aged 20 and over: United States, 1960–1962 through 2013–2014. *Division of Health and Nutrition Examination Surveys.* Hyattsville, MD: National Center for Health Statistics.

Funder, D. C. (1995). On the accuracy of personality judgment: A realistic approach. *Psychological Review, 102,* 652–670.

Fung, H. H., & Carstensen, L. L. (2004). Motivational changes in response to blocked goals and foreshortened time: Testing alternatives to socioemotional selectivity theory. *Psychology and Aging, 19,* 68–78.

Fung, M. T., Raine, A., Loeber, R., Lynam, D. R., Steinhauer, S. R., Venables, P. D., & Stouthamer-Loeber, M. (2005). Reduced electrodermal activity in psychopathy-prone adolescents. *Journal of Abnormal Psychology, 114,* 187–196.

Fusar-Poli, P., Papanastasiou, E., Stahl, D., Rocchetti, M., Carpenter, W., Shergill, S., & McGuire, P. (2015). Treatments of negative symptoms in schizophrenia: Meta-analysis of 168 randomized placebo-controlled trials. *Schizophrenia Bulletin, 41,* 892–899.

Galanter, E. (1962). Contemporary psychophysics. In R. Brown (Ed.), *New directions in psychology* (pp. 87–156). New York, NY: Holt, Rinehart & Winston.

Galef, B. G., Jr., & Whiskin, E. E. (2000). Social influences on the amount eaten by Norway rats. *Appetite, 34,* 327–332.

Gallagher, D. T., Hadjiefthyvoulou, F., Fisk, J. E., Montgomery, C., Robinson, S. J., & Judge, J. (2014). Prospective memory deficits in illicit polydrug users are associated with the average long-term typical dose of ecstasy typically consumed in a single session. *Neuropsychology, 28,* 43–54.

Gallo, E. F., & Posner, J. (2016). Moving towards causality in attention-deficit hyperactivity disorder: Overview of neural and genetic mechanisms. *The Lancet Psychiatry, 3,* 555–567.

Gallup. (1995). *Disciplining children in America: A Gallup poll report.* Princeton, NJ: Author.

Gana, K., Bailly, N., Saada, Y., Joulain, M., & Alaphilippe, D. (2013). Does life satisfaction change in old age: Results from an 8-year longitudinal study. *Journals of Gerontology, Series B.*

Garber, J., Frankel, S. A., & Herrington, C. G. (2016). Developmental demands of cognitive behavioral therapy for depression in children and adolescents: Cognitive, social, and emotional processes. *Annual Review of Clinical Psychology, 12,* 181–216.

Garcia, J., & Koelling, R. A. (1966). Relation of cue to consequence in avoidance learning. *Psychonomic Science, 4,* 123–124.

Garcia, J. R., Reiber, C., Massey, S. G., & Merriwether, A. M. (2012). Sexual hookup culture: A review. *Review of General Psychology, 16,* 161–176.

Gardner, H. (1983). *Frames of mind: The theory of multiple intelligences.* New York, NY: Basic Books.

Gardner, W. L., Pickett, C. L., Jefferis, V., & Knowles, M. (2005). On the outside looking in: Loneliness and social monitoring. *Personality and Social Psychology Bulletin, 31,* 1549–1560.

Garon, N., Bryson, S. E., & Smith, I. M. (2008). Executive function in preschoolers: A review using an integrative framework. *Psychological Bulletin, 134,* 31–60.

Garriga, M., Pacchiarotti, I., Kasper, S., Zeller, S. L., Allen, M. H., Vázquez, G., . . . Vieta, E. (2016). Assessment and management of agitation in psychiatry: Expert consensus. *The World Journal of Biological Psychiatry, 17,* 86–128.

Gartrell, N., & Bos, H. (2010). US National Longitudinal Lesbian Family Study: Psychological adjustment of 17-year-old adolescents. *Pediatrics, 126,* 28–36.

Gates, G. J. (2011). How many people are lesbian, gay, bisexual and transgender? Los Angeles, CA: The Williams Institute, UCLA School of Law. Retrieved from http://williamsinstitute.law.ucla.edu/wp-content/uploads/Gates-How-Many-People-LGBT-Apr-2011.pdf

Gatt, J. M., Burton, K. L., Williams, L. M., & Schofield, P. R. (2015). Specific and common genes implicated across major mental disorders: A review of meta-analysis studies. *Journal of Psychiatric Research, 60,* 1–13.

Gazzaniga, M. S. (2000). Cerebral specialization and interhemispheric communication: Does the corpus callosum enable the human condition? *Brain, 123,* 1293–1326.

Gazzaniga, M. S. (2015). *Tales from both sides of the brain: A life in neuroscience.* New York, NY: HarperCollins.

Gazzaniga, M. S., Doron, K. W., & Funk, C. M. (2009). Looking toward the future: Perspective on examining the architecture and function of the human brain as a complex system. In M. S. Gazzaniga, *The cognitive neurosciences* (4th ed., pp. 1245–1252). Cambridge, MA: MIT Press.

Gazzaniga, M. S., & LeDoux, J. E. (1978). *The integrated mind.* New York, NY: Plenum Press.

Gazzaniga, M. S., & Sperry, R. W. (1967). Language after section of the cerebral commissures. *Brain, 90,* 131–148.

Ge, X., Natsuaki, M. N., Neiderhiser, J. M., & Reiss, D. (2007). Genetic and environmental influences on pubertal timing: Results from two national sibling studies. *Journal of Research on Adolescence, 17,* 767–788.

Gebhard, P. H. (1972). Incidence of overt homosexuality in the United States and Western Europe. *NIMH task force on homosexuality: Final report and background papers* (pp. 22–29). Rockville, MD: National Institute of Mental Health.

Geddes, J. R., Burgess, S., Hawton, K., Jamison, K., & Goodwin, G. M. (2004). Long-term lithium therapy for bipolar disorder: Systematic review and meta-analysis of randomized controlled trials. *American Journal of Psychiatry, 161,* 217–222.

Geddes, J. R., & Miklowitz, D. J. (2013). Treatment of bipolar disorder. *The Lancet, 381,* 1672–1682.

George, W. H., Davis, K. C., Norris, J., Heiman, J. R., Stoner, S. A., Schacht, R. L., . . . Kajumulo, K. F. (2009). Indirect effects of acute alcohol intoxication on sexual risk-taking: The roles of subjective and physiological sexual arousal. *Archives of Sexual Behavior, 38,* 498–513.

Georgi, B., Craig, D., Kember, R. L., Liu, W., Lindquist, I., Nasser, S., . . . Bućan, M. (2014). Genomic view of bipolar disorder revealed by whole genome sequencing in a genetic isolate. *PLOS Genetics, 10,* e1004229.

Gergely, G., & Csibra, G. (2003). Teleological reasoning in infancy: The naïve theory of rational action. *Trends in Cognitive Sciences, 7,* 287–292.

Gershman, S. J., & Daw, N. D. (2017). Reinforcement learning and episodic memory in humans and animals: An integrative framework. *Annual Review of Psychology, 68,* 101–128.

Gershoff, E. T. (2002). Parental corporal punishment and associated child behaviors and experiences: A meta-analytic and theoretical review. *Psychological Bulletin, 128,* 539–579.

Gershoff, E. T., & Grogan-Kaylor, A. (2016). Spanking and child outcomes: Old controversies and new meta-analyses. *Journal of Family Psychology, 30,* 453–469.

Gibson, S. (2013). Milgram's obedience experiments: A rhetorical analysis. *British Journal of Social Psychology, 52,* 290–309.

Gidda, M. (2017, January). Malala Yousafzai's new mission: Can she still inspire as an adult? *Newsweek.*

Gijsman, H. J., Geddes, J. R., Rendell, J. M., Nolen, W. A., & Goodwin, G. M. (2004). Antidepressants for bipolar depression: A systematic review of randomized, controlled trials. *American Journal of Psychiatry, 161,* 1537–1547.

Gilbert, D. T., Pinel, E. C., Wilson, T. D., Blumberg, S. J., & Wheatley, T. (1998). Immune neglect: A source of durability bias in affective forecasting. *Journal of Personality and Social Psychology, 75,* 617–638.

Gilbert, D. T., & Wilson, T. D. (2007). Prospection: Experiencing the future. *Science, 317,* 1351–1354.

Gilligan, C. (1977). In a different voice: Women's conceptions of self and of morality. *Harvard Educational Review, 47,* 481–517.

Gillihan, S. J., & Farah, M. J. (2005). Is self special? A critical review of evidence from experimental psychology and cognitive neuroscience. *Psychological Bulletin, 131,* 76–97.

Gillison, M. L., Broutian, T., Pickard, R. K. L., Tong, Z.-Y., Xiao, W., Kahle, L., . . . Chaturvedi, A. K. (2012). Prevalence of oral HPV infection in the United States, 2009–2010. *Journal of the American Medical Association, 307,* 693–703.

Gillogley, K. M., Evans, A. T., Hansen, R. L., Samuels, S. J., & Batra, K. K. (1990). The perinatal impact of cocaine, amphetamine, and opiate use detected by universal intrapartum screening. *American Journal of Obstetrics and Gynecology, 163,* 1535–1542.

Gilovich, T. (1991). *How we know what isn't so: The fallibility of human reason in everyday life.* New York, NY: The Free Press.

Gingerich, A. C., & Lineweaver, T. T. (2014). OMG! Texting in class = U fail: Empirical evidence that text messaging during class disrupts comprehension. *Teaching of Psychology, 41,* 44–51.

Glaser, R., & Kiecolt-Glaser, J. K. (2005). Stress-induced immune dysfunction: Implications for health. *Nature Reviews, 5,* 243–251.

Glynn, T. J. (2014). E-cigarettes and the future of tobacco control. *Cancer Journal for Clinicians, 64,* 164–168.

Godden, D. B., & Baddeley, A. D. (1975). Context-dependent memory in two natural environments: On land and underwater. *British Journal of Psychology, 66,* 325–331.

Goff, D. C., Falkai, P., Fleischhacker, W. W., Girgis, R. R., Kahn, R. M., Uchida, H., . . . Lieberman, J. A. (2017). The long-term effects of antipsychotic medication on clinical course in schizophrenia. *American Journal of Psychiatry, 174,* 840–849.

Goldin, C., & Rouse, C. (2000). Orchestrating impartiality: The impact of "blind" auditions on female musicians. *The American Economic Review, 90,* 715–741.

Goldstein, R. B., Chou, S. P., Saha, T. D., Smith, S. M., Jung, J., Zhang, H., . . . Grant, B. F. (2017). The epidemiology of antisocial behavioral syndromes in adulthood: Results from the National Epidemiologic Survey on Alcohol and Related Conditions–III. *The Journal of Clinical Psychiatry, 78,* 90–98.

Gonzales, R., Mooney, L., & Rawson, R. A. (2010). The methamphetamine problem in the United States. *Annual Review of Public Health, 31,* 385–398.

Good Housekeeping Features Team (2016, January). "I'm in a business where the only things that matter are weight and appearance." *Good Housekeeping.* Retrieved from http://www.goodhousekeeping.co.uk/lifestyle/gh-women-celebrity-interviews/carrie-fisher

Goodall, G. (1984). Learning due to the response-shock contingency in signaled punishment. *Quarterly Journal of Experimental Psychology, 36,* 259–279.

Goodman, S. N., Fanelli, D., & Ioannidis, J. P. (2016). What does research reproducibility mean? *Science Translational Medicine, 8,* 341ps12.

Goodwin, F. K., & Jamison, K. R. (1990). *Manic-depressive illness.* New York, NY: Oxford University Press.

Gosling, S. D. (2008). *Snoop: What your stuff says about you.* New York, NY: Basic Books.

Gottesman, I. I. (1991). *Schizophrenia genesis: The origins of madness.* New York, NY: Freeman.

Gottfredson, L. S. (2004a). Intelligence: Is it the epidemiologists' elusive "fundamental cause" of social class inequalities in health? *Journal of Personality and Social Psychology, 86,* 174–199.

Gottfredson, L. S. (2004b, Summer). Schools and the g factor. *Wilson Quarterly, 28,* 35–45.

Gottman, J. (1994). *Why marriages succeed or fail . . . and how you can make yours last.* New York, NY: Simon & Schuster.

Graf, P., & Uttl, B. (2001). Prospective memory: A new focus for research. *Consciousness and Cognition, 10,* 437–450.

Graff, H., & Stellar, E. (1962). Hyperphagia, obesity, and finickiness. *Journal of Comparative and Physiological Psychology, 55,* 418–424.

Graham, C. A., Sanders, S. A., Milhausen, R. R., & McBride, K. R. (2004). Turning on and turning off: A focus group study of the factors that affect women's sexual arousal. *Archives of Sexual Behavior, 33,* 527–538.

Granot, D., & Mayseless, O. (2001). Attachment security and adjustment to school in middle childhood. *International Journal of Behavioral Development, 25,* 530–541.

Gray, J. R., & Thompson, P. M. (2004). Neurobiology of intelligence: Science and ethics. *Nature Reviews Neuroscience, 5,* 471–482.

Greenwald, A. G. (1968). Cognitive learning, cognitive response to persuasion, and attitude change. In A. G. Greenwald, T. C. Brock, & T. M. Ostrom (Eds.), *Psychological foundations of attitudes* (pp. 147–170). New York, NY: Academic Press.

Greenwald, A. G. (1992). New look 3: Reclaiming unconscious cognition. *American Psychologist, 47,* 766–779.

Greenwald, A. G., & Banaji, M. R. (1995). Implicit social cognition: Attitudes, self-esteem, and stereotypes. *Psychological Review, 102,* 4–27.

Greenwald, A. G., McGhee, D., & Schwartz, J. (1998). Measuring individual differences in implicit cognition: The implicit association test. *Journal of Personality and Social Psychology, 74,* 1464–1480.

Greenwald, A. G., Poehlman, T. A., Uhlmann, E. L., & Banaji, M. R. (2009). Understanding and using the Implicit Association Test: III. Meta-analysis of predictive validity. *Journal of Personality and Social Psychology, 97,* 17–41.

Griggs, R. A. (2015). Psychology's lost boy: Will the real Little Albert please stand up? *Teaching of Psychology, 42,* 14–18.

Griggs, R. A. (2017). Milgram's obedience study: A contentious classic reinterpreted. *Teaching of Psychology, 44,* 32–37.

Gross, J. J. (1999). Emotion and emotion regulation. In L. A. Pervin & O. P. John (Eds.), *Handbook of personality: Theory and research* (2nd ed., pp. 525–552). New York, NY: Guilford Press.

Gross, J. J. (2013). Emotion regulation: Taking stock and moving forward. *Emotion, 13,* 359–365.

Grossman, L. (2005, January 24). Grow up? Not so fast. *Time, 165,* 42–53.

Grossman, M., & Wood, W. (1993). Sex differences in intensity of emotional experience: A social role interpretation. *Journal of Personality and Social Psychology, 65,* 1010–1022.

Gruber, S. A., Silveri, M. M., & Yurgelun-Todd, D. A. (2007). Neuropsychological consequences of opiate use. *Neuropsychological Review, 17,* 299–315.

Gruzelier, J. H. (2000). Redefining hypnosis: Theory, methods, and integration. *Contemporary Hypnosis, 17,* 51–70.

Guassi Moreira, J. F., Van Bavel, J. J., & Telzer, E. H. (2017). The neural development of "Us and Them." *Social Cognitive and Affective Neuroscience, 12,* 184–196.

Guerin, B. (1994). What do people think about the risks of driving? Implications for traffic safety interventions. *Journal of Applied Social Psychology, 24,* 994–1021.

Guerri, C. (2002). Mechanisms involved in central nervous system dysfunctions induced by prenatal ethanol exposure. *Neurotoxicity Research, 4,* 327–335.

Hahn, A., Kranz, G. S., Küblböck, M., Kaufmann, U., Ganger, S., Hummer, A., . . . Lanzenberger, R. (2015). Structural connectivity networks of transgender people. *Cerebral Cortex, 25,* 3527–3534.

Halász, P. (2016). The K-complex as a special reactive sleep slow wave—A theoretical update. *Sleep Medicine Reviews, 29,* 34–40.

Haldeman, D. C. (1994). The practice and ethics of sexual orientation conversion therapy. *Journal of Consulting and Clinical Psychology, 62,* 221–227.

Haldeman, D. C. (2002). Gay rights, patient rights: The implications of sexual orientation conversion therapy. *Professional Psychology: Research and Practice, 33,* 260–264.

Halldorsdottir, T., & Binder, E. B. (2017). Gene × environment interactions: From molecular mechanisms to behavior. *Annual Review of Psychology, 68,* 215–241.

Halpern, C. T., Udry, J. R., & Suchindran, C. (1997). Testosterone predicts initiation of coitus in adolescent females. *Psychosomatic Medicine, 59,* 161–171.

Halpin, L. E., Collins, S. A., & Yamamoto, B. K. (2014). Neurotoxicity of methamphetamine and 3,4-methylenedioxymethamphetamine. *Life Sciences, 97,* 37–44.

Hamer, D. H., Hu, S., Magnuson, V. L., Hu, N., & Pattatucci, A. M. (1993). A linkage between DNA markers on the X chromosome and male sexual orientation. *Science, 261,* 321–327.

Hamilton, N. A., Gallagher, M. W., Preacher, K. J., Stevens, N., Nelson, C. A., Karlson, C., & McCurdy, C. (2007). Insomnia and well-being. *Journal of Consulting and Clinical Psychology, 75,* 939–946.

Hammen, C. (2005). Stress and depression. *Annual Review of Clinical Psychology, 1,* 293–319.

Handleman, J. S., Gill, M. J., & Alessandri, M. (1988). Generalization by severely developmentally disabled children: Issues, advances, and future directions. *Behavior Therapist, 11,* 221–223.

Hanewinkel, R., & Sargent, J. D. (2008). Exposure to smoking in internationally distributed American movies and youth smoking in Germany: A cross-cultural cohort study. *Pediatrics, 121,* 108–117.

Haney, C., Banks, C., & Zimbardo, P. (1973). Interpersonal dynamics in a simulated prison. *International Journal of Criminology and Penology, 1,* 69–97.

Hansen, C. J., Stevens, L. C., & Coast, J. R. (2001). Exercise duration and mood state: How much is enough to feel better? *Health Psychology, 20,* 267–275.

Hansen, T. (2012). Parenthood and happiness: A review of folk theories versus empirical evidence. *Social Indicators Research, 108,* 29–64.

Hansen, W. B., Graham, J. W., Sobel, J. L., Shelton, D. R., Flay, B. R., & Johnson, C. A. (1987). The consistency of peer and parental influences on tobacco, alcohol, and marijuana use among young adolescents. *Journal of Behavioral Medicine, 10,* 559–579.

Harari, G. M., Lane, N. D., Wang, R., Crosier, B. S., Campbell, A. T., & Gosling, S. D. (2016). Using smartphones to collect behavioral data in psychological science: Opportunities, practical considerations, and challenges. *Perspectives on Psychological Science, 11,* 838–854.

Harburger, L. L., Nzerem, C. K., & Frick, K. M. (2007). Single enrichment variables differentially reduce age-related memory decline in female mice. *Behavioral Neuroscience, 121,* 679–688.

Hare, R. D., McPherson, L. M., & Forth, A. E. (1988). Male psychopaths and their criminal careers. *Journal of Consulting and Clinical Psychology, 56,* 710–714.

Harlow, H. F., & Harlow, M. K (1966). Learning to love. *American Scientist, 54,* 244–272.

Harlow, H. F., Harlow, M. K., & Meyer, D. R. (1950). Learning motivated by a manipulation drive. *Journal of Experimental Psychology, 40,* 228–234.

Harmon, K. G., Drezner, J. A., Gammons, M., Guskiewicz, K. M., Halstead, M., Herring, S. A., . . . Roberts, W. O. (2013). American Medical Society for Sports Medicine position statement: Concussion in sport. *British Journal of Sports Medicine, 47,* 15–26.

Harpur, T. J., & Hare, R. D. (1994). Assessment of psychopathy as a function of age. *Journal of Abnormal Psychology, 103,* 604–609.

Harrow, M., & Jobe, T. H. (2013). Does long-term treatment of schizophrenia with antipsychotic medications facilitate recovery? *Schizophrenia Bulletin, 39,* 962–965.

Harrow, M., Jobe, T. H., & Faull, R. N. (2014). Does treatment of schizophrenia with antipsychotic medications eliminate or reduce psychosis? A 20-year multi-follow-up study. *Psychological Medicine, 44,* 3007–3016.

Hartmann, P., Reuter, M., & Nyborg, H. (2006). The relationship between date of birth and individual differences in personality and general intelligence: A large-scale study. *Personality and Individual Differences, 40,* 1349–1362.

Haslam, S. A., Reicher, S. D., & Birney, M. E. (2016). Questioning authority: New perspectives on Milgram's "obedience" research and its implications for intergroup relations. *Current Opinion in Psychology, 11,* 6–9.

Haslam, S. A., Reicher, S. D., Millard, K., & McDonald, R. (2015). "Happy to have been of service": The Yale archive as a window into the engaged followership of participants in Milgram's "obedience"experiments. *British Journal of Social Psychology, 54,* 55–83.

Haupert, M. L., Gesselman, A. N., Moors, A. C., Fisher, H. E., & Garcia, J. R. (2017). Prevalence of experiences with consensual nonmonogamous relationships: Findings from two national samples of single Americans. *Journal of Sex & Marital Therapy, 43,* 424–440.

Hawkley, L., & Cacioppo, J. T. (2010). Loneliness matters: A theoretical and empirical review of consequences and mechanisms. *Annals of Behavioral Medicine, 40,* 218–227.

Hayakawa, S., Kawai, N., & Masataka, N. (2011). The influence of color on snake detection in visual search in human children. *Scientific Reports, 1,* 1–4.

Hazlett, E. A. (2016). Neural substrates of emotion-processing abnormalities in borderline personality disorder. *Biological Psychiatry, 7,* 74–75.

Hazlett, H. C., Gu, H., Munsell, B. C., Kim, S. H., Styner, M., Wolff, J. J., . . . Statistical Analysis (2017). Early brain development in infants at high risk for autism spectrum disorder. *Nature, 542,* 348–351.

Heatherton, T. F. (2011). Neuroscience of self and self-regulation. *Annual Review of Psychology, 62,* 363–390.

Heatherton, T. F., & Baumeister, R. F. (1991). Binge eating as escape from self-awareness. *Psychological Bulletin, 110,* 86–108.

Heatherton, T. F. & Polivy, J. (1992). Chronic dieting and eating disorders: A spiral model. In J. H. Crowther, S. E. Hobfall, M. A. P. Stephens, & D. L. Tennenbaum (Eds.), *The etiology of bulimia nervosa: The individual and familial context* (pp. 133–155). Washington, DC: Hemisphere Publishers.

Hebb, D. O. (1949). *The organization of behavior: A neuropsychological approach.* New York, NY: Wiley.

Heck, N. C. (2016). Group psychotherapy with transgender and gender nonconforming adults: Evidence-based practice applications. *Psychiatric Clinics of North America, 40,* 157–175.

Heller, D., Watson, D., & Ilies, R. (2004). The role of person versus situation in life satisfaction: A critical examination. *Psychological Bulletin, 130,* 574–600.

Helmreich, R., Aronson, E., & LeFan, J. (1970). To err is humanizing sometimes: Effects of self-esteem, competence, and a pratfall on interpersonal attraction. *Journal of Personality and Social Psychology, 16,* 259–264.

Henrich, J., Heine, S. J., & Norenzayan, A. (2010). The weirdest people in the world? *Behavioral and Brain Sciences, 33,* 61–83, 111–135.

Henry, P. J., & Sears, D. O. (2002). The Symbolic Racism (2000) Scale. *Political Psychology, 23,* 253–283.

Herbenick, D., Reece, M., Hensel, D., Sanders, S., Jozkowski, K., & Fortenberry, J. D. (2011). Association of lubricant use with women's sexual pleasure, sexual satisfaction, and genital symptoms: A prospective daily diary study. *Journal of Sexual Medicine, 8,* 202–212.

Herbenick, D., Reece, M., Schick, V., Sanders, S. A., Dodge, B., & Fortenberry, J. D. (2010). Sexual behavior in the United States: Results from a national probability sample of men and women ages 14–94. *The Journal of Sexual Medicine, 7,* 255–265.

Herbert, T. B., & Cohen, S. (1993). Stress and immunity in humans: A meta-analytic review. *Psychosomatic Medicine, 55,* 364–379.

Herek, G. M. (2006). Legal recognition of same-sex relationships in the United States: A social science perspective. *American Psychologist, 61,* 607–621.

Herek, G. M., Norton, A. T., Allen, T. J., & Sims, C. L. (2010). Demographic, psychological, and social characteristics of self-identified lesbian, gay, and bisexual adults in a US probability sample. *Sexuality Research and Social Policy, 7,* 176–200.

Herman, A. L., Hass, A. P., & Rogers, P. L. (2014). Suicide attempts among transgender and gender non-conforming adults. Los Angeles, CA: The Williams Institute, UCLA School of Law. Retrieved from http://williamsinstitute.law.ucla.edu/wp-content/uploads/AFSP-Williams-Suicide-Report-Final.pdf

Herman-Giddens, M., Wang, L., & Koch, G. (2001). Secondary sexual characteristics in boys. *Archives of Pediatrics and Adolescent Medicine, 155,* 1022–1028.

Heron, M. (2016). Deaths: Leading causes for 2014. *National Vital Statistics Reports,* Vol. 65, No. 5. Hyattsville, MD: National Center for Health Statistics.

Herring, B. E., & Nicoll, R. A. (2016). Long-term potentiation: From CaMKII to AMPA receptor trafficking. *Annual Review of Physiology, 78,* 351–365.

Hicks, T. V., & Leitenberg, H. (2001). Sexual fantasies about one's partner versus someone else: Gender differences in incidence and frequency. *The Journal of Sex Research, 38,* 43–50.

Higgins, S. C., Gueorguiev, M., & Korbonits, M. (2007). Ghrelin, the peripheral hunger hormone. *Annals of Medicine, 39,* 116–136.

Hilgard, E. R., & Hilgard, J. R. (1975). *Hypnosis in the relief of pain.* Los Altos, CA: Kaufmann.

Hines, M. (2011). Gender development and the human brain. *Annual Review of Neuroscience, 34,* 69–88.

Hines, M., Brook, C., & Conway, G. S. (2004). Androgen and psychosexual development: Core gender identity, sexual orientation and recalled childhood gender role behavior in women and men with congenital adrenal hyperplasia (CAH). *Journal of Sex Research, 41,* 75–81.

Hines, T. (2003). *Pseudoscience and the paranormal.* Amherst, NY: Prometheus.

Hirst, W., & Phelps, E. A. (2016). Flashbulb memories. *Current Directions in Psychological Science, 25,* 36–41.

Hirst, W., Phelps, E. A., Meksin, R., Vaidya, C. J., Johnson, M. K., Mitchell, K., . . . Olsson A. (2015). A ten-year follow-up of a study of memory for the attack of September 11, 2001: Flashbulb memories and memories for flashbulb events. *Journal of Experimental Psychology: General, 144,* 604–623.

Hobson, J. A. (1999). Sleep and dreaming. In M. J. Zigmond, F. E. Bloom, S. C. Landis, J. L. Roberts, & L. R. Squire (Eds.), *Fundamental neuroscience* (pp. 1207–1227). San Diego: Academic Press.

Hobson, J. A. (2009). REM sleep and dreaming: Towards a theory of protoconsciousness. *Nature Reviews Neuroscience, 10,* 803–814.

Hobson, J. A., & McCarley, R. (1977.) The brain as a dream state generator: An activation-synthesis hypothesis of the dream process. *American Journal of Psychiatry, 134,* 1335–1348.

Hobson, J. A., Pace-Schott, E. F., & Stickgold, R. (2000). Dreaming and the brain: Toward a cognitive neuroscience of conscious states. *Behavioral and Brain Sciences, 23,* 793–842.

Hockley, W. E. (2008). The effect of environmental context on recognition memory and claims of remembering. *Journal of Experimental Psychology: Learning, Memory, and Cognition, 34,* 1412–1429.

Hoerger, M., Chapman, B. P., Prigerson, H. G., Fagerlin, A., Mohile, S. G., Epstein, R. M., . . . Duberstein, P. R. (2014). Personality change pre- to post-loss in spousal caregivers of patients with terminal lung cancer. *Social Psychological and Personality Science, 5,* 722–729.

Hoffman, E., Myerberg, N. R., & Morawski, J. G. (2015). Acting otherwise: Resistance, agency, and subjectivities in Milgram's studies of obedience. *Theory & Psychology, 25,* 670–689.

Hofmann, S. G., & Smits, J. A. J. (2008). Cognitive-behavioral therapy for adult anxiety disorders: A meta-analysis of randomized placebo-controlled trials. *Journal of Clinical Psychiatry, 69,* 621–632.

Hogan, M. J., Parker, J. D., Wiener, J., Watters, C., Wood, L. M., & Oke, A. (2010). Academic success in adolescence: Relationships among verbal IQ, social support and emotional intelligence. *Australian Journal of Psychology, 62,* 30–41.

Holden, C. (2005). Sex and the suffering brain. *Science, 308,* 1574.

Holliday, R. (1987). The inheritance of epigenetic defects. *Science, 238,* 163–170.

Hollon, S. D., Stewart, M. O., & Strunk, D. (2006). Enduring effects for cognitive behavior therapy in the treatment of depression and anxiety. *Annual Review of Psychology, 57,* 285–315.

Hollon, S. D., Thase, M. E., & Markowitz, J. C. (2002). Treatment and prevention of depression. *Psychological Science in the Public Interest, 3,* 39–77.

Holmbeck, G. N. (1996). A model of family relational transformations during the transition to adolescence: Parent-adolescent conflict and adaptation. In J. A. Graber, J. Brooks-Gunn, & A. C. Petersen (Eds.), *Transitions through adolescence* (pp. 67–200). Mahwah, NJ: Erlbaum.

Holmboe, K., Rijsdijk, F. V., Hallett, V., Happé, F., Plomin, R., & Ronald, A. (2013). Strong genetic influences on the stability of autistic traits in childhood. *Journal of the American Academy of Child & Adolescent Psychiatry, 53,* 221–230.

Holmes, T. H., & Rahe, R. H. (1967). The social readjustment rating scale. *Journal of Psychosomatic Research, 11,* 213–218.

Holstein, S. B., & Premack, D. (1965). On the different effects of random reinforcement and presolution reversal on human concept-identification. *Journal of Experimental Psychology, 70,* 335–337.

Holt-Lunstad, J., Smith, T. B., Baker, M., Harris, T., & Stephenson, D. (2015). Loneliness and social isolation as risk factors for mortality: A meta-analytic review. *Perspectives on Psychological Science, 10,* 227–237.

Honein, M. A., Dawson, A. L., Petersen, E. E., Jones, A. M., Lee, E. H., Yazdy, M. M., . . . Jamieson, D. J. (2017). Birth defects among fetuses and infants of US women with evidence of possible Zika virus infection during pregnancy. *Journal of the American Medical Association, 317,* 59–68.

Hoogman, M., Bralten, J., Hibar, D. P., Mennes, M., Zwiers, M. P., Schweren, L. S., . . . de Zeeuw, P. (2017). Subcortical brain volume differences in participants with attention deficit hyperactivity disorder in children and adults: A cross-sectional mega-analysis. *The Lancet Psychiatry, 4,* 310–319.

Hooshmand, F., Miller, S., Dore, J., Wang, P. W., Hill, S. J., Portillo, N., & Ketter, T. A. (2014). Trends in pharmacotherapy in patients referred to a bipolar specialty clinic, 2000–2011. *Journal of Affective Disorders, 155,* 283–287.

Horn, J. L. (1968). Organization of abilities and the development of intelligence. *Psychological Review, 75,* 242–259.

Hoshino, Y., Kumashiro, H., Yashima, Y., Tachibana, R., Watanabe, M., & Furukawa, H. (1980). Early symptoms of autism in children and their diagnostic significance. *Japanese Journal of Child and Adolescent Psychiatry, 21,* 284–299.

House, J. S., Landis, K. R., & Umberson, D. (1988). Social relationships and health. *Science, 241,* 540–545.

Hovland, C. I., Janis, I. L., & Kelley, H. H. (1953). *Communication and persuasion: Psychological studies of opinion change.* New Haven, CT: Yale University Press.

Howard, D. J., Gengler, C., & Jain, A. (1995). What's in a name? A complimentary means of persuasion. *Journal of Consumer Research, 22,* 200–211.

Howard, D. J., Gengler, C., & Jain, A. (1997). The name remembrance effect: A test of alternative explanations. *Journal of Social Behaviour and Personality, 12,* 801–810.

Howes, O. D., McCutcheon, R., Owen, M. J., & Murray, R. M. (2017). The role of genes, stress, and dopamine in the development of schizophrenia. *Biological Psychiatry, 81,* 9–20.

Howie, G., & Shail, A. (Eds.). (2005). *Menstruation: A cultural history.* New York, NY: Palgrave Macmillan.

Howlin, P., Mawhood, L., & Rutter, M. (2000). Autism and developmental receptive language disorder—A follow-up comparison in early adult life. II: Social, behavioural, and psychiatric outcomes. *Journal of Child Psychology and Psychiatry and Allied Disciplines, 41,* 561–578.

Hoyme, H. E., Kalberg, W. O., Elliott, A. J., Blankenship, J., Buckley, D., Marais, M. S., . . . May, P. A. (2016). Updated clinical guidelines for diagnosing fetal alcohol spectrum disorders. *Pediatrics, 138,* e20154256.

Hughes, M. E., & Waite, L. J. (2009). Marital biography and health at mid-life. *Journal of Health and Social Behavior, 50,* 344–358.

Hulse, G. K., Milne, E., English, D. R., & Holman, C. D. J. (1998). Assessing the relationship between maternal opiate use and ante-partum haemorrhage. *Addiction, 93,* 1553–1558.

Hyman, S. E. (2008). A glimmer of light for neuropsychiatric disorders. *Nature, 455,* 890–893.

Hymel, S., Rocke-Henderson, N., & Bonanno, R. A. (2005). Moral disengagement: A framework for understanding bullying among adolescents. *Journal of Social Sciences, 8,* 1–11.

Iacoboni, M. (2009). Imitation, empathy, and mirror neurons. *Annual Review of Psychology, 60,* 653–670.

Imbach, L. L., Büchele, F., Valko, P. O., Li, T., Maric, A., Stover, J. F., . . . Baumann, C. R. (2016). Sleep-wake disorders persist 18 months after traumatic brain injury but remain underrecognized. *Neurology, 86,* 1945–1949.

Insel, T. R., & Charney, D. S. (2003). Research on major depression. *Journal of the American Medical Association, 289,* 3167–3168.

Institute of Medicine (IOM) and National Research Council (NRC). (2015). *Transforming the workplace for children birth through age 8: A unifying foundation.* Washington, DC: National Academies Press.

Isen, A. M. (1993). Positive affect and decision making. In M. Lewis & J. M. Haviland (Eds.), *Handbook of emotions* (pp. 261–277). New York, NY: Guilford Press.

Iyengar, S. S., & Lepper, M. R. (2000). When choice is demotivating: Can one desire too much of a good thing? *Journal of Personality and Social Psychology, 79,* 995–1006.

Iyengar, S. S., Wells, R. E., & Schwartz, B. (2006). Doing better but feeling worse: Looking for the best job undermines satisfaction. *Psychological Science, 17,* 143–150.

Jääskeläinen, E., Juola, P., Hirvonen, N., McGrath, J. J., Saha, S., Isohanni, M., . . . Miettunen, J. (2013). A systematic review and meta-analysis of recovery in schizophrenia. *Schizophrenia Bulletin, 39,* 1296–1306.

Jain, A., Marshall, J., Buikema, A., Bancroft, T., Kelly, J., & Newschaffer, C. (2015). Autism occurrence by MMR vaccine status among US children with older siblings with and without autism. *Journal of the American Medical Association, 313,* 1534–1540.

Jakubovski, E., Varigonda, A. L., Freemantle, N., Taylor, M. J., & Bloch, M. H. (2016). Systematic review and meta-analysis: Dose-response relationship of selective serotonin reuptake inhibitors in major depressive disorder. *American Journal of Psychiatry, 173,* 174–183.

James, E. L. (2011). *Fifty shades of grey.* New York, NY: Vintage.

James, E. L. (2012a). *Fifty shades darker.* New York, NY: Vintage.

James, E. L. (2012b). *Fifty shades freed.* New York, NY: Vintage.

James, W. (1884). What is an emotion? *Mind, 9,* 188–205.

Jamieson, G. A. (2007). *Hypnosis and conscious states: The cognitive neuroscience perspective.* New York, NY: Oxford University Press.

Jamison, K. R. (1993). *Touched with fire: Manic-depressive illness and the artistic temperament.* New York, NY: Free Press.

Jamison, K. R. (1996). *An unquiet mind.* New York, NY: Vintage Books.

Jang, K. L., Livesley, W. J., & Vernon, P. A. (1996). Heritability of the big five personality dimensions and their facets: A twin study. *Journal of Personality, 64,* 577–592.

Janis, I. L. (1972). *Victims of groupthink: A psychological study of foreign policy decisions and fiascoes.* Boston, MA: Houghton Mifflin.

Jannini, E. A., Rubio-Casillas, A., Whipple, B., Buisson, O., Komisaruk, B. R., & Brody, S. (2012). Female orgasm(s): One, two, several. *Journal of Sexual Medicine, 9,* 956–965.

Jensen, A. R. (1998). *The g factor: The science of mental ability.* Westport, CT: Praeger.

Jha, P., Ramasundarahettige, C., Landsman, V., Rostron, B., Thun, M., Anderson, R. N., . . . Peto, R. (2013). 21st-century hazards of smoking and benefits of cessation in the United States. *New England Journal of Medicine, 368,* 341–350.

Joffe, G. P., Foxman, B., Schmidt, A. J., Farris, K. B., Carter, R., Neumann, S., . . . Walters, A. M. (1992). Multiple partners and partner choice as risk factors for sexually transmitted disease among female college students. *Sexually Transmitted Diseases, 19,* 272–278.

John, O. P. (1990). The "Big Five" factor taxonomy: Dimensions of personality in the natural language and in questionnaires. In L. A. Pervin & O. P. John (Eds.), *Handbook of personality: Theory and research* (pp. 66–100). New York, NY: Guilford Press.

Johns, F., Schmader, T., & Martens, A. (2005). Knowing is half the battle— Teaching stereotype threat as a means of improving women's math performance. *Psychological Science, 16,* 175–179.

Johnston, L. D., O'Malley, P. M., Bachman, J. G., & Schulenberg, J. E. (2011). *Monitoring the future national results on adolescent drug use: Overview of key findings, 2010.* Ann Arbor: Institute for Social Research, University of Michigan.

Joiner, T. E. (2005). *Why people die by suicide.* Cambridge, MA: Harvard University Press.

Jones, M. C. (1924). A laboratory study of fear: The case of Peter. *Pedagogical Seminary, 31,* 308–315.

Jope, R. S. (1999). Anti-bipolar therapy: Mechanism of action of lithium. *Molecular Psychiatry, 4,* 117–128.

Jorm, A. F. (2000). Does old age reduce the risk of anxiety and depression? A review of epidemiological studies across the adult life span. *Psychological Medicine, 30,* 3011–3022.

Junco, R., & Cotten, S. R. (2012). No A 4 U: The relationship between multitasking and academic performance. *Computers & Education, 59*, 505–514.

Jureidini, J. N., Doecke, C. J., Mansfield, P. R., Haby, M., Menkes, D. B., & Tonkin, A. L. (2004). Efficacy and safety of antidepressants for children and adolescents. *British Medical Journal, 328*, 879–883.

Juul, A., Main, K. M., & Skakkebaek, N. E. (2011). Development: Disorders of sex development—the tip of the iceberg? *Nature Reviews Endocrinology, 7*, 504–505.

KABC-TV. (2014). Three-year-old Arizona girl accepted into Mensa for high IQ. Retrieved from http://abclocal.go.com/kabc/story?id=9435453

Kagan, J. (2011). Three lessons learned. *Perspectives in Psychological Science, 6*, 107–113.

Kagan, J., & Snidman, N. (1991). Infant predictors of inhibited and uninhibited profiles. *Psychological Science, 2*, 40–44.

Kahneman, D. (2011). *Thinking, fast and slow*. London, UK: Macmillan.

Kallio, S., & Revonsuo, A. (2003). Hypnotic phenomena and altered states of consciousness: A multi-level framework of description and explanation. *Contemporary Hypnosis, 20*, 111–164.

Kandall, S. R., & Gaines, J. (1991). Maternal substance use and subsequent sudden infant death syndrome (SIDS) in offspring. *Neurotoxicology and Teratology, 13*, 235–240.

Kandel, E. R. (1998). A new intellectual framework for psychiatry. *American Journal of Psychiatry, 155*, 457–469.

Kane, M. J., Hambrick, D. Z., & Conway, A. R. A. (2005). Working memory capacity and fluid intelligence are strongly related constructs: Comment on Ackerman, Beier, and Boyle (2005). *Psychological Bulletin, 131*, 66–71.

Kanner, L. (1943). Autistic disturbances of affective contact. *Nervous Child: Journal of Psychopathology, Psychotherapy, Mental Hygiene, and Guidance of the Child, 2*, 217–250.

Kaplan, R. M. (2007). Should Medicare reimburse providers for weight loss interventions? *American Psychologist, 62*, 217–219.

Kaplowitz, P. B. (2008). Link between body fat and the timing of puberty. *Pediatrics, 121*, S208–S217.

Kapoula, Z., Ruiz, S., Spector, L., Mocorovi, M., Gaertner, C., Quilici, C., & Vernet, M. (2016). Education influences creativity in dyslexic and non-dyslexic children and teenagers. *PLOS ONE, 11*, e0150421.

Kapur, S. E., Craik, F. I. M., Tulving, E., Wilson, A. A., Houle, S., & Brown, G. R. (1994). Neuroanatomical correlates of encoding in episodic memory: Levels of processing effects. *Proceedings of the National Academy of Sciences, USA, 91*, 2008–2011.

Katchadourian, H. (1977). *The biology of adolescence*. San Francisco: Freeman.

Kawas, C., Gray, S., Brookmeyer, R., Fozard, J., & Zonderman, A. (2000). Age-specific incidence rates of Alzheimer's disease: The Baltimore longitudinal study of aging. *Neurology, 54*, 2072–2077.

Kazdin, A. E. (1994). Methodology, design, and evaluation in psychotherapy research. In A. E. Bergin & S. L. Garfield (Eds.), *International handbook of behavior modification and behavior change* (4th ed., pp. 19–71). New York, NY: Wiley.

Kazdin, A. E. (2008). Evidence-based treatment and practice: New opportunities to bridge clinical research and practice, enhance the knowledge base, and improve patient care. *American Psychologist, 63*, 146–159.

Kazdin, A. E., & Benjet, C. (2003). Spanking children: Evidence and issues. *Current Directions in Psychological Science, 12*, 99–103.

Keane, M. (1987). On retrieving analogues when solving problems. *Quarterly Journal of Experimental Psychology, 39A*, 29–41.

Keel, P. K., & Mitchell, J. E. (1997). Outcome in bulimia nervosa. *American Journal of Psychiatry, 154*, 313–321.

Keller, J., & Bless, H. (2008). Flow and regulatory compatibility: An experimental approach to the flow model of intrinsic motivation. *Personality and Social Psychology Bulletin, 34*, 196–209.

Kelley, W. T., Macrae, C. N., Wyland, C., Caglar, S., Inati, S., & Heatherton, T. F. (2002). Finding the self? An event-related fMRI study. *Journal of Cognitive Neuroscience, 14*, 785–794.

Keltner, D., & Anderson, C. (2000). Saving face for Darwin: The functions and uses of embarrassment. *Current Directions in Psychological Science, 9*, 187–192.

Keltner, D., & Bonanno, G. A. (1997). A study of laughter and dissociation: Distinct correlates of laughter and smiling during bereavement. *Journal of Personality and Social Psychology, 73*, 687–702.

Keltner, D., Young, R. C., Heerey, E. A., Oemig, C., & Monarch, N. D. (1998). Teasing in hierarchical and intimate relations. *Journal of Personality and Social Psychology, 75*, 1231–1247.

Kendler, K. S., Prescott, C. A., Myers, J., & Neale, M. C. (2003). The structure of genetic and environmental risk factors for common psychiatric and substance use disorders in men and women. *Archives of General Psychiatry, 60*, 929–937.

Kennedy, D. P., & Adolphs, R. (2010). Impaired fixation to eyes following amygdala damage arises from abnormal bottom-up attention. *Neuropsychologia, 48*, 3392–3398.

Kennedy, S. H., Giacobbe, P., Rizvi, S., Placenza, F. M., Nishikawa, Y., Mayberg, H. S., & Lozano, A. M. (2011). Deep brain stimulation for treatment-resistant depression: Follow-up after 3 to 6 years. *American Journal of Psychiatry, 168*, 502–510.

Kenrick, D. T., & Funder, D. C. (1991). The person-situation debate: Do personality traits really exist? In V. J. Derlega, B. A. Winstead, & W. H. Jones (Eds.), *Personality: Contemporary theory and research* (pp. 149–174). Chicago, IL: Nelson Hall.

Kenrick, D. T., & Gutierres, S. E. (1980). Contrast effects and judgments of physical attractiveness: When beauty becomes a social problem. *Journal of Personality and Social Psychology, 38*, 131–140.

Kenrick, D. T., Gutierres, S. E., & Goldberg, L. L. (1989). Influence of popular erotica on judgments of strangers and mates. *Journal of Experimental Social Psychology, 25*, 159–167.

Kesey, K. (1962). *One flew over the cuckoo's nest: A novel*. New York, NY: Viking.

Kessler, R. C., Adler, L., Barkley, R., Biederman, J., Conners, C. K., Demler, O., . . . Zaslavsky, A. M. (2006). The prevalence and correlates of adult ADHD in the United States: Results from the national comorbidity survey replication. *American Journal of Psychiatry, 163*, 716–723.

Kessler, R. C., Aguilar-Gaxiola, S., Alonso, J., Benjet, C., Bromet, E. J., Cardoso, G., . . . Koenen, K. C. (2017). Trauma and PTSD in the WHO World Mental Health Surveys. *European Journal of Psychotraumatology, 8*, 1353383.

Kessler, R. C., Berglund, P., Demler, O., Jin, R., Koretz, D., Merikangas, K. R., . . . Wang, P. S. (2003). The epidemiology of major depressive disorder: Results from the national comorbidity survey replication (NCS-R). *Journal of the American Medical Association, 289*, 3095–3105.

Kessler, R. C., Chiu, W. T., Demler, O., & Walters, E. E. (2005). Prevalence, severity, and comorbidity of twelve-month *DSM-IV* disorders in the national comorbidity survey replication (NCS-R). *Archives of General Psychiatry, 62*, 617–627.

Kessler, R. C., Demler, O., Frank, R. G., Olfson, M., Pincus, M. A., Walters, E. E., . . . Zaslavsky, A. M. (2005). Prevalence and treatment of mental disorders, 1990 to 2003. *New England Journal of Medicine, 352*, 2515–2523.

Kessler, R. C., McGonagle, K. A., Zhao, S., Nelson, C. B., Hughes, M., Eshleman, S., . . . Kendler, K. S. (1994). Lifetime and 12-month prevalence of *DSM-III-R* psychiatric disorders in the United States: Results from the national comorbidity study. *Archives of General Psychiatry, 51*, 8–19.

Kessler, R. C., Merikangas, K. R., & Wang, P. S. (2007). Prevalence, comorbidity, and service utilization for mood disorders in the United States at the beginning of the twenty-first century. In

S. NolenHoeksema, T. Cannon, & T. Widiger (Eds.), *Annual Review of Clinical Psychology* (Vol. 3, pp. 137–158). Palo Alto, CA: Annual Reviews.

Kessler, R. C., & Wang, P. S. (2008). The descriptive epidemiology of commonly occurring mental disorders in the United States. *Annual Review of Public Health, 29,* 115–129.

Ketter, T. A., Miller, S., Dell'Osso, B., & Wang, P. W. (2016). Treatment of bipolar disorder: Review of evidence regarding quetiapine and lithium. *Journal of Affective Disorders, 191,* 256–273.

Keys, A., Brozek, J., Henschel, A. L., Mickelsen, O., & Taylor, H. L. (1950). *The biology of human starvation.* Minneapolis: University of Minnesota Press.

Khalid, J. M., Oerton, J. M., Dezateux, C., Hindmarsh, P. C., Kelnar, C. J., & Knowles, R. L. (2012). Incidence and clinical features of congenital adrenal hyperplasia in Great Britain. *Archives of Disease in Childhood, 97,* 101–106.

Kiecolt-Glaser, J. K., & Glaser, R. I. (1988). Immunological competence. In E. A. Blechman & K. D. Brownell (Eds.), *Handbook of behavioral medicine for women* (pp. 195–205). Elmsford, NY: Pergamon Press.

Kihlstrom, J. F. (2005). Dissociative disorder. *Annual Review of Clinical Psychology, 1,* 227–253.

Kihlstrom, J. F. (2016a). Unconscious mental life. In H. S. Friedman (Ed.), *Encyclopedia of mental health* (2nd ed., pp. 345–349). Waltham, MA: Academic Press.

Kihlstrom, J. F. (2016b). Hypnosis. In H. S. Friedman (Ed.), *Encyclopedia of mental health* (2nd ed., Vol. 2, pp. 361–365).Waltham, MA: Academic Press.

Kihlstrom, J. F., & Eich, E. (1994). Altering states of consciousness. In D. Druckman & R. A. Bjork (Eds.), *Learning, remembering, and believing: Enhancing performance* (pp. 207–248). Washington, DC: National Academy Press.

Kim, K. S., & Kim, J. (2012). Disorders of sex development. *Korean Journal of Urology, 53,* 1–8.

Kim, M. J., Solomon, K. M., Neta, M., Davis, F. C., Oler, J. A., Mazzulla, E. C., & Whalen, P. J. (2016). A face versus non-face context influences amygdala responses to masked fearful eye whites. *Social Cognitive and Affective Neuroscience, 11,* 1933–1941.

Kim, S. J., Lyoo, I. K., Hwang, J., Chung, A., Hoon Sung, Y., Kim, J., ... Renshaw, P. F. (2006). Prefrontal grey-matter changes in short-term and long-term abstinent methamphetamine abusers. *International Journal of Neuropsychopharmacology, 9,* 221–228.

Kinsey, A. C., Pomeroy, W. B., & Martin, C. E. (1948). *Sexual behavior in the human male.* Philadelphia: Saunders.

Kinsey, A. C., Pomeroy, W. B., Martin, C. E., & Gebhard, P. H. (1953). *Sexual behavior in the human female.* Philadelphia: Saunders.

Kirk, M., Wiser, M., Fainaru, S., & Fainaru-Wada, M. (Writers), & Kirk, M. (Director). (2013, October 8). League of denial: The NFL's concussion crisis [Television series episode]. In M. Kirk, J. Gilmore, & M. Wiser (Producers), *Frontline.* Boston, MA: WGBH. Retrieved from https://www.pbs.org/wgbh/frontline/film/league-of-denial/

Kirsch, I. (2011). The placebo effect has come of age. *Journal of Mind-Body Regulation, 1,* 106–109.

Kirsch, I., Deacon, B. J., Huedo-Medina, T. B., Scoboria, A., Moore, T. J., & Johnson, B. T. (2008). Initial severity and antidepressant benefits: A meta-analysis of data submitted to the Food and Drug Administration. *PLOS Medicine, 5,* e45.

Kirsch, I., & Lynn, S. J. (1995). The altered state of hypnosis: Changes in the theoretical landscape. *American Psychologist, 10,* 846–858.

Klatsky, A. (2009). Alcohol and cardiovascular health. *Physiology and Behavior, 100,* 76–81.

Klein, R. G., Mannuzza, S., Olazagasti, M. A. R., Roizen, E., Hutchison, J. A., Lashua, E. C., & Castellanos, F. X. (2012). Clinical and functional outcome of childhood attention-deficit/hyperactivity disorder 33 years later. *Archives of General Psychiatry, 69,* 1295–1303.

Klin, A., Jones, W., Schultz, R., & Volkmar, F. (2003). The enactive mind, or from actions to cognition: Lessons from autism. *Philosophical Transactions of the Royal Society of London, 358B,* 345–360.

Klump, K. L., & Culbert, K. M. (2007). Molecular genetic studies of eating disorders: Current status and future directions. *Current Directions in Psychological Science, 16,* 37–41.

Klump, K. L., Culbert, K. M., & Sisk, C. L. (2017). Sex differences in binge eating: Gonadal hormone effects across development. *Annual Review of Clinical Psychology, 13,* 183–207.

Knight, R. (1953). Borderline states. *Bulletin of the Menninger Clinic, 17,* 1–12.

Knox, S. S., Weidner, G., Adelman, A., Stoney, C. M., & Ellison, R. C. (2004). Hostility and physiological risk in the National Heart, Lung, and Blood Institute Family Heart Study. *Archives of Internal Medicine, 164,* 2442–2447.

Kobasa, S. C. (1979). Personality and resistance to illness. *American Journal of Community Psychology, 7,* 413–423.

Kochanek, K. D., Murphy, S. L., Xu, J., & Arias, E. (2017). *Mortality in the United States, 2016.* (NCHS Data Brief No. 293). Hyattsville, MD: National Center for Health Statistics.

Koen, J. D., & Yonelinas, A. P. (2014). The effects of healthy aging, amnestic mild cognitive impairment, and Alzheimer's disease on recollection and familiarity: A meta-analytic review. *Neuropsychology Review, 24,* 332–354.

Kohlberg, L. (1984). *Essays on moral development: Vol. 2. The psychology of moral development.* San Francisco: Harper & Row.

Köhler, W. (1925). *The mentality of apes.* New York, NY: Harcourt Brace.

Kohn, D. (2008, March 11). Cases without borders: Psychotherapy for all. *New York Times.* Retrieved from http://www.nytimes.com/2008/03/11/health/11psych.html

Kolata, G. (2002, July 9). Citing risks, US will halt study of drugs for hormones. *The New York Times.* Retrieved from http://www.nytimes.com/2002/07/09/national/09HORM.html

Koole, S. L., Dijksterhuis, A., & van Knippenberg, A. (2001). What's in a name: Implicit self-esteem and the automatic self. *Journal of Personality and Social Psychology, 80,* 669–685.

Korn, M. L., Kotler, M., Molcho, A., Botsis, A. J., Grosz, D., Chen, C., ... Herman, M. (1992). Suicide and violence associated with panic attacks. *Biological Psychiatry, 31,* 607–612.

Kosslyn, S. M., Thompson, W. L., Constantine-Ferrando, M. F., Alpert, N. M., & Spiegel, D. (2000). Hypnotic visual illusion alters color processing in the brain. *American Journal of Psychiatry, 157,* 1279–1284.

Kowalski, P., & Taylor, A. K. (2004). Ability and critical thinking as predictors of change in students' psychological misconceptions. *Journal of Instructional Psychology, 31,* 297–303.

Kraepelin, E. (1883). *Compendium der Psychiatrie.* Leipzig, Germany: Abel.

Kragel, P. A., & LaBar, K. S. (2016). Decoding the nature of emotion in the brain. *Trends in Cognitive Sciences, 20,* 444–455.

Krantz, D. S., & McCeney, M. K. (2002). Effects of psychological and social factors on organic disease: A critical assessment of research on coronary heart disease. *Annual Review of Psychology, 53,* 341–369.

Krendl, A. C., Richeson, J. A., Kelley, W. M., & Heatherton, T. F. (2008). The negative consequences of threat: An fMRI investigation of the neural mechanisms underlying women's underperformance in math. *Psychological Science, 19,* 168–175.

Kringelbach, M. L., & Berridge, K. C. (2009). Toward a functional neuroanatomy of pleasure and happiness. *Trends in Cognitive Sciences, 13,* 479–487.

Krochmal, S. N. (2015, May 5). Exclusive: Miley Cyrus launches anti-homelessness, pro-LGBT "Happy Hippie Foundation." *Out.* Retrieved from https://www.out.com/music/2015/5/05/exclusive-miley-cyrus-launches-anti-homelessness-pro-lgbt-happy-hippie-foundation

Kroes, M. C., Schiller, D., LeDoux, J. E., & Phelps, E. A. (2016). Translational approaches targeting reconsolidation. *Current Topics in Behavioral Neurosciences, 28,* 197–230.

Krueger, R. F. (1999). The structure of common mental disorders. *Archives of General Psychiatry, 56,* 921–926.

Kruesi, M. J., Hibbs, E. D., Zahn, T. P., Keysor, C. S., Hamburger, S. D., Bartko, J. J., & Rapoport, J. L. (1992). A 2-year prospective follow-up study of children and adolescents with disruptive behavior disorders: Prediction by cerebrospinal fluid 5-hydroxyindoleacetic acid, homovanillic acid, and autonomic measures. *Archives of General Psychiatry, 49,* 429–435.

Kuhl, P. K. (2006). Is speech learning "gated" by the social brain? *Developmental Science, 10,* 110–120.

Kuhl, P. K., Stevens, E., Hayashi, A., Deguchi, T., Kiritani, S., & Iverson, P. (2006). Infants show a facilitation effect for native language phonetic perception between 6 and 12 months. *Developmental Science, 9,* F13–F21.

Kuhl, P. K., Tsao, F. M., & Liu, H. M. (2003). Foreign-language experience in infancy: Effects of short-term exposure and social interaction on phonetic learning. *Proceedings of the National Academy of Sciences, USA, 100,* 9096–9101.

Kuhn, C., Swartzwelder, S., & Wilson, W. (2003). *Buzzed: The straight facts about the most used and abused drugs from alcohol to ecstasy* (2nd ed.). New York, NY: Norton.

Kühn, S., & Gallinat, J. (2012). Quantitative meta-analysis on state and trait aspects of auditory verbal hallucinations in schizophrenia. *Schizophrenia Bulletin, 38,* 779–786.

Kuncel, N. R., Hezlett, S. A., & Ones, D. S. (2004). Academic performance, career potential, creativity, and job performance: Can one construct predict them all? *Journal of Personality and Social Psychology, 86,* 148–161.

Kuppens, P., Tuerlinckx, F., Russell, J. A., & Barrett, L. F. (2013). The relation between valence and arousal in subjective experience. *Psychological Bulletin, 139,* 917.

Kusseling, F. S., Shapiro, M. F., Greenberg, J. M., & Wenger, N. S. (1996). Understanding why heterosexual adults do not practice safer sex: A comparison of two samples. *AIDS Education and Prevention, 8,* 247–257.

Ladenvall, P., Persson, C. U., Mandalenakis, Z., Wilhelmsen, L., Grimby, G., Svärdsudd, K., & Hansson, P. O. (2016). Low aerobic capacity in middle-aged men associated with increased mortality rates during 45 years of follow-up. *European Journal of Preventive Cardiology, 23,* 1557–1564.

LaFrance, M. L., & Banaji, M. (1992). Toward a reconsideration of the gender-emotion relationship. In M. Clarke (Ed.), *Review of personality and social psychology* (pp. 178–201). Beverly Hills, CA: Sage.

Landa, R., Holman, K., & Garrett-Mayer, E. (2007). Social and communication development in toddlers with early and later diagnosis of autism spectrum disorders. *Archives of General Psychiatry, 64,* 853–864.

Langlois, J. H., Kalakanis, L., Rubenstein, A. J., Larson, A., Hallam, M., & Smoot, M. (2000). Maxims or myths of beauty? A meta-analytic and theoretical review. *Psychological Bulletin, 126,* 390–423.

Langlois, J. H., Ritter, J. M., Casey, R. J., & Sawin, D. B. (1995). Infant attractiveness predicts maternal behaviors and attitudes. *Developmental Psychology, 31,* 464–472.

Langlois, J. H., & Roggman, L. A. (1990). Attractive faces are only average. *Psychological Science, 1,* 115–121.

Långström, N., Rahman, Q., Carlström, E., & Lichtenstein, P. (2010). Genetic and environmental effects on same-sex sexual behavior: A population study of twins in Sweden. *Archives of Sexual Behavior, 39,* 75–80.

Lansford, J. E., Alampay, L. P., Al-Hassan, S., Bacchini, D., Bombi, A. S., Bornstein, M. H., . . . Zelli, A. (2010). Corporal punishment of children in nine countries as a function of child gender and parent gender. *International Journal of Pediatrics, 2010,* 1–12.

Larson, E. B., Wang, L., Bowen, J. D., McCormick, W. C., Teri, L., Crane, P., & Kukull, W. (2006). Exercise is associated with reduced risk for incident dementia among persons 65 years of age and older. *Annals of Internal Medicine, 144,* 73–81.

Larsson, H., Chang, Z., D'Onofrio, B. M., & Lichtenstein, P. (2014). The heritability of clinically diagnosed attention deficit hyperactivity disorder across the lifespan. *Psychological Medicine, 44,* 2223–2229.

Latané, B., & Darley, J. M. (1968). Group inhibition of bystander intervention in emergencies. *Journal of Personality and Social Psychology, 10,* 215–221.

Latané, B., Williams, K., & Harkins, S. G. (1979). Many hands make light the work: The causes and consequences of social loafing. *Journal of Personality and Social Psychology, 37,* 822–832.

Laumann, E. O., Gagnon, J. H., Michael, R. T., & Michaels, S. (1994). *The social organization of sexuality: Sexual practices in the United States.* Chicago, IL: University of Chicago Press.

Laumann, E. O., Paik, A., Glasser, D. B., Kang, J. H., Wang, T., Levinson, B., . . . Gingell, C. (2006). A cross-national study of subjective sexual well-being among older women and men: Findings from the Global Study of Sexual Attitudes and Behaviors. *Archives of Sexual Behavior, 35,* 143–159.

Laumann, E. O., Paik, A., & Rosen, R. C. (1999). Sexual dysfunction in the United States: Prevalence and predictors. *Journal of the American Medical Association, 281,* 537–544.

Laureys, S., Celesia, G. G., Cohadon, F., Lavrijsen, J., León-Carrión, J., Sannita, W. G., . . . Dolce, G. (2010). Unresponsive wakefulness syndrome: A new name for the vegetative state or apallic syndrome. *BMC Medicine, 8,* 68.

Lautenschlager, N. T., Cox, K. L., Flicker, L., Foster, J. K., van Bockxmeer, F. M., Xiao, J., et al. (2008). Effect of physical exercise on cognitive function in older adults at risk for Alzheimer disease. *Journal of the American Medical Association, 300,* 1027–1037.

Lavie, C. J., Arena, R., Swift, D. L., Johannsen, N. M., Sui, X., Lee, D., . . . Blair, P. E. D. (2015). Exercise and the cardiovascular system: Clinical science and cardiovascular outcomes. *Circulation Research, 117,* 207–219.

Lawrence, A. A. (2014). Gender assignment dysphoria in the DSM-5. *Archives of Sexual Behavior, 43,* 1263–1266.

Lawrence, E. M., Rogers, R. G., & Wadsworth, T. (2015). Happiness and longevity in the United States. *Social Science & Medicine, 145,* 115–119.

Lazarus, R. S. (1993). From psychological stress to the emotions: A history of changing outlooks. *Annual Review of Psychology, 44,* 1–21.

Lazer, D. M. J., Baum, M. A., Benkler, Y., Berinsky, A. J., Greenhill, K. M., Menczer, F., . . . Zittrain, J. L. (2018). The science of fake news. *Science, 359,* 1094–1096.

Le, K., Donnellan, M. B., & Conger, R. (2014). Personality development at work: Workplace conditions, personality changes, and the correspansive principle. *Journal of Personality, 82,* 44–56.

Leach, J., & Patall, E. A. (2013). Maximizing and counterfactual thinking in academic major decision making. *Journal of Career Assessment, 21,* 414–429.

Leary, M. R. (2004). The function of self-esteem in terror management theory and sociometer theory: Comment on Pyszczynski et al. *Psychological Bulletin, 130,* 478–482.

Leary, M. R., & MacDonald, G. (2003). Individual differences in self-esteem: A review and theoretical integration. In M. R. Leary & J. P. Tangney (Eds.), *Handbook of self and identity* (pp. 401–418). New York, NY: Guilford Press.

Leary, M. R., Tambor, E. S., Terdal, S. K., & Downs, D. L. (1995). Self-esteem as an interpersonal monitor: The sociometer hypothesis. *Journal of Personality and Social Psychology, 68,* 518–530.

LeDoux, J. E. (2000). Emotion circuits in the brain. *Annual Review of Neuroscience, 23,* 155–184.

LeDoux, J. E. (2015). *Anxious: Using the brain to understand and treat fear and anxiety.* New York, NY: Penguin.

LeDoux, J. E., & Pine, D. S. (2016). Using neuroscience to help understand fear and anxiety: A two-system framework. *American Journal of Psychiatry, 173,* 1083–1093.

Lee, D., Pate, R. R., Lavie, C. J., Sui, X., Church, T. S., & Blair, S. N. (2014). Leisure-time running reduces all-cause and cardiovascular mortality risk. *Journal of the American College of Cardiology, 64,* 472–481.

Lee, P. A. (1980). Normal ages of pubertal events among American males and females. *Journal of Adolescent Health Care, 1,* 26–29.

Leigh, B. C., & Schafer, J. C. (1993). Heavy drinking occasions and the occurrence of sexual activity. *Psychology of Addictive Behaviors, 7,* 197–200.

Leigh, B. C., & Stacy, A. W. (2004). Alcohol expectancies and drinking in different age groups. *Addiction, 99,* 215–217.

Leitenberg, H., & Henning, K. (1995). Sexual fantasy. *Psychological Bulletin, 117,* 469.

Lench, H. C., Flores, S. A., & Bench, S. W. (2011). Discrete emotions predict changes in cognition, judgment, experience, behavior, and physiology: A meta-analysis of experimental emotion elicitations. *Psychological Bulletin, 137,* 834–855.

Lenzenweger, M. F., Lane, M. C., Loranger, A. W., & Kessler, R. C. (2007). *DSM-IV* personality disorders in the national comorbidity survey replication. *Biological Psychiatry, 62,* 553–564.

Lepper, M. R., Greene, D., & Nisbett, R. E. (1973). Undermining children's intrinsic interest with extrinsic reward: A test of the "overjustification" hypothesis. *Journal of Personality and Social Psychology, 28,* 129–137.

Lerner, J. S., Li, Y., Valdesolo, P., & Kassam, K. S. (2015). Emotion and decision making. *Annual Review of Psychology, 66,* 799–823.

Leucht, S., Corves, C., Arbter, D., Engel, R. R., Li, C., & Davis, J. M. (2009). Second-generation versus first-generation antipsychotic drugs for schizophrenia: A meta-analysis. *The Lancet, 373,* 31–41.

Leuthardt, E. C., Roland, J. L., & Ray, W. Z. (2014, November). Neuroprosthetics: Linking the human nervous system to computers is providing unprecedented control of artificial limbs and restoring lost sensory function. *The Scientist.* Retrieved from https://www.the-scientist.com/?articles.view/articleNo/41324/title/Neuroprosthetics/

LeVay, S. (1991). A difference in hypothalamic structure between heterosexual and homosexual men. *Science, 253,* 1034–1037.

Levenson, R. W. (2014). The autonomic nervous system and emotion. *Emotion Review, 6,* 100–112.

Leventhal, H., & Cleary, P. D. (1980). The smoking problem: A review of research and theory in behavioral risk modification. *Psychological Bulletin, 88,* 370–405.

Levinson, D. F. (2006). The genetics of depression: A review. *Biological Psychiatry, 60,* 84–92.

Li, N., & DiCarlo, J. J. (2008). Unsupervised natural experience rapidly alerts invariant object representation in the visual cortex. *Science, 321,* 1502–1506.

Liben, L. S., & Bigler, R. S. (2002). The developmental course of gender differentiation: Conceptualizing, measuring, and evaluating constructs and pathways. *Monographs of the Society for Research in Child Development, 67,* 76–95.

Lick, D. J., Cortland, C. I., & Johnson, K. L. (2016). The pupils are the windows to sexuality: Pupil dilation as a visual cue to others' sexual interest. *Evolution and Human Behavior, 37,* 117–124.

Lieb, K., Zanarini, M. C., Schmahl, C., Linehan, M. M., & Bohus, M. (2004). Borderline personality disorder. *Lancet, 364,* 453–461.

Lieberman, M. D. (2000). Intuition: A social cognitive neuroscience approach. *Psychological Bulletin, 126,* 109–137.

Lieberman, M. D., Ochsner, K. N., Gilbert, D. T., & Schacter, D. L. (2001). Do amnesiacs exhibit cognitive dissonance reduction? The role of explicit memory and attention in attitude change. *Psychological Science, 121,* 135–140.

Lilienfeld, S. O. (2007). Psychological treatments that cause harm. *Perspectives on Psychological Science, 2,* 53–67.

Lilliengren, P., Johansson, R., Lindqvist, K., Mechler, J., & Andersson, G. (2016). Efficacy of experiential dynamic therapy for psychiatric conditions: A meta-analysis of randomized controlled trials. *Psychotherapy, 53,* 90–104.

Lin, J. Y., Arthurs, J., & Reilly, S. (2017). Conditioned taste aversions: From poisons to pain to drugs of abuse. *Psychonomic Bulletin & Review, 24,* 335–351.

Linehan, M. M. (1987). Dialectical behavior therapy for borderline personality disorder: Theory and method. *Bulletin of the Menninger Clinic, 51,* 261–276.

Linehan, M. M., Armstrong, H. E., Suarez, A., Allmon, D., & Heard, H. (1991). Cognitive behavioral treatment of chronically parasuicidal borderline patients. *Archives of General Psychiatry, 48,* 1060–1064.

Linehan, M. M., Heard, H., & Armstrong, H. E. (1993). Naturalistic follow-up of a behavioral treatment for chronically parasuicidal borderline patients. *Archives of General Psychiatry, 50,* 971–974.

Lin-Su, K., Vogiatzi, M. G., & New, M. I. (2002). Body mass index and age at menarche in an adolescent clinic population. *Clinical Pediatrics, 41,* 501–507.

Liu, B., Floud, S., Pirie, K., Green, J., Peto, R., Beral, V., & Million Women Study Collaborators (2016). Does happiness itself directly affect mortality? The prospective UK Million Women Study. *The Lancet, 387,* 874–881.

Liu, H., Petukhova, M. V., Sampson, N. A., Aguilar-Gaxiola, S., Alonso, J., Andrade, L. H., . . . Kessler, R. C. (2017). Association of DSM-IV posttraumatic stress disorder with traumatic experience type and history in the World Health Organization World Mental Health Surveys. *JAMA Psychiatry, 74,* 270–281.

Lledo, P. M., Gheusi, G., & Vincent, J. D. (2005). Information processing in the mammalian olfactory system. *Physiological Review, 85,* 281–317.

Locke, E. A., & Latham, G. P. (1990). *A theory of goal setting and task performance.* Englewood Cliffs, NJ: Prentice-Hall.

Loftus, E. F. (1993). The reality of repressed memories. *American Psychologist, 48,* 518–537.

Loftus, E. F., Miller, D. G., & Burns, H. J. (1978). Semantic integration of verbal information into a visual memory. *Journal of Experimental Psychology: Human Learning and Memory, 4,* 19–31.

Loftus, E. F., & Palmer, J. C. (1974). Reconstruction of automobile destruction: An example of the interaction between language and memory. *Journal of Learning and Verbal Behavior, 13,* 585–589.

Loftus, J. (2001). America's liberalization in attitudes toward homosexuality, 1973 to 1998. *American Sociological Review, 66,* 762–782.

Loprinzi, P. D., Branscum, A., Hanks, J., & Smit, E. (2016). Healthy lifestyle characteristics and their joint association with cardiovascular disease biomarkers in US adults. *Mayo Clinic Proceedings, 91,* 432–442.

Lovaas, O. I. (1987). Behavioral treatment and normal educational and intellectual functioning in young autistic children. *Journal of Consulting and Clinical Psychology, 55,* 3–9.

Lovett, I. (2013). Law banning "gay cure" is upheld in California. *The New York Times.* Retrieved from http://www.nytimes.com/2013/08/30/us/law-banning-gay-cure-is-upheld-in-california.html?_r=0

Lowe, P. (2001, October 12). No prison for Candace's adoptive mom. *Denver Rocky Mountain News,* p. 26A.

Lubinski, D. (2004). Introduction to the special section on cognitive abilities: 100 years after Spearman's (1904) "'General intelligence,' objectively determined and measured." *Journal of Personality and Social Psychology, 86,* 96–111.

Luria, A. R. (1968). *The mind of a mnemonist.* New York, NY: Avon.

Lykken, D. T. (1957). A study of anxiety in the sociopathic personality. *Journal of Abnormal Social Psychology, 55,* 6–10.

Lykken, D. T. (1995). *The antisocial personalities*. Hillsdale, NJ: Erlbaum.

Lykken, D. T. (2000). The causes and costs of crime and a controversial cure. *Journal of Personality, 68,* 560–605.

Lyubomirsky, S., King, L., & Diener, E. (2005). The benefits of frequent positive affect: Does happiness lead to success? *Psychological Bulletin, 131,* 803–855.

Lyubomirsky, S., & Nolen-Hoeksema, S. (1995). Effects of self-focused rumination on negative thinking and interpersonal problem solving. *Journal of Personality and Social Psychology, 69,* 176–190.

Maccoby, E. E., & Jacklin, C. N. (1974). *The psychology of sex differences.* Stanford, CA: Stanford University Press.

MacDonald, G., & Leary, M. R. (2005). Why does social exclusion hurt? The relationship between social and physical pain. *Psychological Bulletin, 131,* 202–223.

Macrae, C. N., Bodenhausen, G. V., & Calvini, G. (1999). Contexts of cryptomnesia: May the source be with you. *Social Cognition, 17,* 273–297.

Macy v. Bureau of Alcohol, Tobacco, Firearms and Explosives (April 20, 2012). EEOC Appeal No. 0120120821.

Magnier, M. (2008, May 26). China quake survivors show signs of post-traumatic stress. *Los Angeles Times,* p. 1.

Maguire, E. A., Spiers, H. J., Good, C. D., Hartley, T., Frackowiak, R. S. J., & Burgess, N. (2003). Navigation expertise and the human hippocampus: A structural brain imaging analysis. *Hippocampus, 13,* 250–259.

Malala Yousafzai: Why I fight for education. (2016, March). *National Geographic Magazine.* Retrieved from https://www.national-geographic.com/magazine/2016/03/3-questions-malala-yousafzai/

Malamuth, N. M., & Check, J. V. (1981). The effects of mass media exposure on acceptance of violence against women: A field experiment. *Journal of Research in Personality, 15,* 436–446.

Malina, R. M., Bouchard, C., & Bar-Or, O. (2004). *Growth, maturation, and physical activity* (2nd ed.). Champaign, IL: Human Kinetics.

Malina, R. M., Bouchard, C., & Beunen, G. (1988). Human growth: Selected aspects of current research on well-nourished children. *Annual Review of Anthropology, 17,* 187–219.

Malone, D. A., Jr., Dougherty, D. D., Rezai, A. R., Carpenter, L. L., Friehs, G. M., Eskandar, E. N., ... Greenberg, B. D. (2009). Deep brain stimulation of the ventral capsule/ventral striatum for treatment-resistant depression. *Biological Psychiatry, 65,* 267–275.

Mandel, H. (2009). *Here's the deal: Don't touch me.* New York, NY: Bantam.

Manning, R., Levine, M., & Collins, A. (2007). The Kitty Genovese murder and the social psychology of helping: The parable of the 38 witnesses. *American Psychologist, 62,* 555–562.

Manns, J. R., & Bass, D. I. (2016). The amygdala and prioritization of declarative memories. *Current Directions in Psychological Science, 25,* 261–265.

March, J. S., Silva, S., Petrycki, S., Curry, J., Wells, K., Fairbank, J., ... Severe, J. (2007). The Treatment for Adolescents with Depression Study (TADS): Long-term effectiveness and safety outcomes. *Archives of General Psychiatry, 64,* 1132–1143.

Marcus, G. F. (1996). Why do children say "breaked"? *Current Directions in Psychological Science, 5,* 81–85.

Marcus, G. F., Pinker, S., Ullman, M., Hollander, M., Rosen, T. S., & Xu, F. (1992). Overregularization in language acquisition. *Monographs of the Society for Research in Child Development, 57,* 1–178.

Marin, M. F., Song, H., VanElzakker, M. B., Staples-Bradley, L. K., Linnman, C., Pace-Schott, E. F., ... Milad, M. R. (2016). Association of resting metabolism in the fear neural network with extinction recall activations and clinical measures in trauma-exposed individuals. *American Journal of Psychiatry, 173,* 930–938.

Marin, M. M., Rapisardi, G., & Tani, F. (2015). Two-day-old newborn infants recognise their mother by her axillary odour. *Acta Paediatrica, 104,* 237–240.

Markon, J. (2001, October 8). Elderly judges handle 20 percent of U.S. caseload. *The Wall Street Journal,* p. A15.

Markus, H. R. (1977). Self-schemata and processing information about the self. *Journal of Personality and Social Psychology, 35,* 63–78.

Markus, H. R., & Kitayama, S. (1991). Culture and the self: Implications for cognition, emotion, and motivation. *Psychological Review, 98,* 224–253.

Marlatt, G. A. (1999). Alcohol, the magic elixir? In S. Peele & M. Grant (Eds.), *Alcohol and pleasure: A health perspective* (pp. 233–248). Philadelphia: Brunner/Mazel.

Marsh, A. A., Finger, E. C., Fowler, K. A., Adalio, C. J., Jurkowitz, I. T., Schechter, J. C., ... Blair, R. J. (2013). Empathic responsiveness in amygdala and anterior cingulate cortex in youths with psychopathic traits. *Journal of Child Psychology and Psychiatry, 54,* 900–910.

Marshall, W. A., & Tanner, J. M. (1970). Variations in the pattern of pubertal changes in boys. *Archives of Disease in Childhood, 45,* 13–23.

Martin, C. B., Herrick, K. A., Sarafrazi, N., & Ogden, C. L. (2018). *Attempts to lose weight among adults in the United States, 2013–2016.* (NCHS Data Brief No. 313). Hyattsville, MD: National Center for Health Statistics.

Martin, C. L., & Ruble, D. (2004). Children's search for gender cues: Cognitive perspectives on gender development. *Current Directions in Psychological Science, 13,* 67–70.

Martin, C. L., Ruble, D. N., & Szkrybalo, J. (2002). Cognitive theories of early gender development. *Psychological Bulletin, 128,* 903–933.

Martin, J. T., & Nguyen, D. H. (2004). Anthropometric analysis of homosexuals and heterosexuals: Implications for early hormone exposure. *Hormones and Behavior, 45,* 31–39.

Martire, L. M., & Schulz, R. (2007). Involving family in psychosocial interventions for chronic illness. *Current Directions in Psychological Science, 16,* 90–94.

Maruta, T., Colligan, R. C., Malinchoc, M., & Offord, K. P. (2002). Optimism-pessimism assessed in the 1960s and self-reported health status 30 years later. *Mayo Clinic Proceedings, 77,* 748–753.

Maslow, A. (1968). *Toward a psychology of being.* New York, NY: Van Nostrand.

Masters, W. H., & Johnson, V. E. (1966). *Human sexual response.* Boston, MA: Little, Brown.

Matsui, M., Tanaka, C., Niu, L., Noguchi, K., Bilker, W. B., Wierzbicki, M., & Gur, Ruben C. (2016). Age-related volumetric changes of prefrontal gray and white matter from healthy infancy to adulthood. *International Journal of Clinical and Experimental Neurology, 4,* 1–8.

Mayberg, H. S., Lozano, A. M., Voon, V., McNeely, H. E., Seminowicz, D., Hamani, C., ... Kennedy, S. H. (2005). Deep brain stimulation for treatment-resistant depression. *Neuron, 45,* 651–660.

Mayhew, D. R., Brown, S. W., & Simpson, H. M. (2002). *The alcohol-crash problem in Canada: 1999.* Ottawa, Canada: Transport Canada.

Mazza, S., Gerbier, E., Gustin, M. P., Kasikci, Z., Koenig, O., Toppino, T. C., & Magnin, M. (2016). Relearn faster and retain longer along with practice, sleep makes perfect. *Psychological Science, 27,* 1321–1330.

McAdams, D. P., & Olson, B. D. (2010). Personality development: Continuity and change over the life course. *Annual Review of Psychology, 61,* 517–542.

McCabe, D. P., Roediger, H. L., McDaniel, M. A., Balota, D. A., & Hambrick, D. Z. (2010). The relationship between working memory capacity and executive functioning: Evidence for a common executive attention construct. *Neuropsychology, 24,* 222–243.

McClelland, D. C. (1987). *Human motivation.* New York, NY: Cambridge University Press.

McClelland, D. C., Koestner, R., & Weinberger, J. (1989). How do self-attributed and implicit motives differ? *Psychological Review, 96,* 690–702.

McConaghy, N., Hadzi-Pavlovic, D., Stevens, C., Manicavasagar, V., Buhrich, N., & Volimer-Conna, U. (2006). Fraternal birth order and ratio of heterosexual/homosexual feelings in women and men. *Journal of homosexuality, 51,* 161–174.

McConahay, J. B. (1986). Modern racism, ambivalence, and the Modern Racism Scale. In J. F. Dovidio & S. L. Gaertner (Eds.), *Prejudice, discrimination, and racism* (pp. 91–125). San Diego, CA: Academic Press.

McCrae, R. R., & Costa, P. T., Jr. (1990). *Personality in adulthood.* New York, NY: Guilford Press.

McCrae, R. R., & Costa, P. T., Jr. (1999). A five-factor theory of personality. In L. A. Pervin & O. P. John (Eds.), *Handbook of personality: Theory and research* (2nd ed., pp. 139–153). New York, NY: Guilford Press.

McCrae, R. R., Costa, P. T., Ostendorf, F., Angleitner, A., Hrebickova, M., Avia, M. D., . . . Smith, P. B. (2000). Nature over nurture: Temperament, personality, and life span development. *Journal of Personality and Social Psychology, 78,* 173–186.

McEwen, B. S. (2008). Central effects of stress hormones in health and disease: Understanding the protective and damaging effects of stress and stress mediators. *European Journal of Pharmacology, 583,* 174–185.

McEwen, B. S. (2017). Neurobiological and systemic effects of chronic stress. *Chronic Stress, 1,* 1–11.

McGaugh, J. L. (2015). Consolidating memories. *Annual Review of Psychology, 66,* 1–24.

McGlashan, T. H. (1988). A selective review of recent North American long-term follow-up studies of schizophrenia. *Schizophrenia Bulletin, 14,* 515–542.

McGough, J. J., & Barkley, R. A. (2004). Diagnostic controversies in adult attention deficit hyperactivity disorder. *American Journal of Psychiatry, 161,* 1948–1956.

McGrath, R.W. (2010). Prescriptive authority for psychologists. *Annual Review of Clinical Psychology, 6,* 21–47.

McGregor, H. R., Cashaback, J. G., & Gribble, P. L. (2016). Functional plasticity in somatosensory cortex supports motor learning by observing. *Current Biology, 26,* 921–927.

McKinnon, M. C., Palombo, D. J., Nazarov, A., Kumar, N., Khuu, W., & Levine, B. (2015). Threat of death and autobiographical memory: A study of passengers from flight AT236. *Clinical Psychological Science, 3,* 487–502.

McKown, C., & Weinstein, R. S. (2008). Teacher expectations, classroom context, and the achievement gap. *Journal of School Psychology, 46,* 235–261.

McNamara, B. (2016, May 24). How Ellie Goulding learned to cope with her debilitating panic attacks. *Teen Vogue.* Retrieved from http://www.teenvogue.com/story/ellie-goulding-panic-attacks-anxiety

McNeely, H. E., Mayberg, H. S., Lozano, A. M., & Kennedy, S. H. (2008). Neuropsychological impact of Cg25 deep brain stimulation for treatment-resistant depression: Preliminary results over 12 months. *Journal of Nervous and Mental Disease, 196,* 405–410.

McNeil, D. G., Jr. (2006, November 23). For rare few, taste is in the ear of the beholder. *The New York Times.* Retrieved from http://www.nytimes.com/2006/11/23/science/23taste.html

McQuillan, G., Kruszon-Moran, D., Flagg, E. W., & Paulose-Ram, R. (2018). *Prevalence of herpes simplex virus type 1 and type 2 in persons aged 14–49: United States, 2015–2016.* (NCHS Data Brief No. 304). Hyattsville, MD: National Center for Health Statistics.

Meddis, R. (1977). *The sleep instinct.* London, UK: Routledge & Kegan Paul.

Meesters, Y., & Gordijn, M. C. (2016). Seasonal affective disorder, winter type: Current insights and treatment options. *Psychology Research and Behavior Management, 9,* 317.

Mehl, M. R., Gosling, S. D., & Pennebaker, J. W. (2006). Personality in its natural habitat: Manifestations and implicit folk theories of personality in daily life. *Journal of Personality and Social Psychology, 90,* 862–877.

Mehl, M. R., Pennebaker, J. W., Crow, M. D., Dabbs, J., & Price, J. H. (2001). The electronically activated recorder (EAR): A device for sampling naturalistic daily activities and conversations. *Behavior Research Methods, Instruments, and Computers, 33,* 517–523.

Mehl, M. R., Vazire, S., Ramírez-Esparza, N., Slatcher, R. B., & Pennebaker, J. W. (2007). Are women really more talkative than men? *Science, 317,* 82.

Melzack, R., & Wall, P. D. (1982). *The challenge of pain.* New York, NY: Basic Books.

Méndez-Bértolo, C., Moratti, S., Toledano, R., Lopez-Sosa, F., Martínez-Alvarez, R., Mah, Y. H., . . . Strange, B. A. (2016). A fast pathway for fear in human amygdala. *Nature Neuroscience, 19,* 1041–1049.

Mendrek, A., & Mancini-Marïe, A. (2016). Sex/gender differences in the brain and cognition in schizophrenia. *Neuroscience & Biobehavioral Reviews, 67,* 57–78.

Mennella, J. A., Bobowski, N. K., & Reed, D. R. (2016). The development of sweet taste: From biology to hedonics. *Reviews in Endocrine and Metabolic Disorders, 17,* 171–178.

Mennella, J. A., Jagnow, C. P., & Beauchamp, G. K. (2001). Prenatal and postnatal flavor learning by human infants. *Pediatrics, 107,* e88.

Mercer, K. B., Orcutt, H. K., Quinn, J. F., Fitzgerald, C. A., Conneely, K. N., Barfield, R. T., & Ressler, K. J. (2012). Acute and posttraumatic stress symptoms in a prospective gene x environment study of a university campus shooting. *Archives of General Psychiatry, 69,* 89–97.

Merikangas, K. R., Burstein, M., Swanson, S. A., Avenevoli, S., Cui, L., Benjet, C., . . . Swendsen, J. (2010). Lifetime prevalence of mental disorders in U.S. adolescents: Results from the National Comorbidity Survey Replication–Adolescent Supplement (NCS–A). *Journal of the American Academy of Child and Adolescent Psychiatry, 49,* 980–989.

Merikangas, K., He, J., Burstein, M., Swendsen, J., Avenevoli, S., Case, B., . . . Olfson, M. (2011). Service utilization for lifetime mental disorders in U.S. adolescents: Results of the National Comorbidity Survey–Adolescent Supplement (NCS–A). *Journal of the American Academy of Child and Adolescent Psychiatry, 50,* 32–45.

Merke, D., & Kabbani, M. (2001). Congenital adrenal hyperplasia: Epidemiology, management and practical drug treatment. *Paediatric Drugs, 3,* 599–611.

Meyer, M. L., & Lieberman, M. D. (2018). Why people are always thinking about themselves: Medial prefrontal cortex activity during rest primes self-referential processing. *Journal of Cognitive Neuroscience, 30,* 714–721.

Mez, J., Daneshvar, D. H., Kiernan, P. T., Abdolmohammadi, B., Alvarez, V. E., Huber, B. R., . . . McKee, A. C. (2017). Clinicopathological evaluation of chronic traumatic encephalopathy in players of American football. *Journal of the American Medical Association, 318,* 360–370.

Mezulis, A. H., Abramson, L. Y., Hyde, J. S., & Hankin, B. L. (2004). Is there a universal positivity bias in attributions? A meta-analytic review of individual, developmental, and culture differences in the self-serving attributional bias. *Psychological Bulletin, 130,* 711–747.

Michalski, D., Kohout, J., Wicherski, M., & Hart, B. (2011, May). *2009 Doctorate employment survey.* Retrieved from http://www.apa.org/workforce/publications/09-doc-empl/table-3.pdf

Michel, C., Velasco, C., Gatti, E., & Spence, C. (2014). A taste of Kandinsky: Assessing the influence of the artistic visual presentation of food on the dining experience. *Flavour, 3,* 7.

Milgram, S. (1974). *Obedience to authority: An experimental view.* New York, NY: Harper & Row.

Millan, M. J., Andrieux, A., Bartzokis, G., Cadenhead, K., Dazzan, P., Fusar-Poli, P., . . . Weinberger, D. (2016). Altering the course of schizophrenia: Progress and perspectives. *Nature Reviews Drug Discovery, 15,* 485–515.

Miller, G. (1956). The magical number seven, plus or minus two: Some limits on our capacity for processing information. *Psychological Review, 63,* 81–97.

Miller, G. (2004). Axel, Buck share award for deciphering how the nose knows. *Science, 306,* 207.

Miller, I. W., Norman, W. H., & Keitner, G. I. (1989). Cognitive-behavioral treatment of depressed inpatients: Six- and twelve-month follow-up. *American Journal of Psychiatry, 146,* 1274–1279.

Miller, M., Swanson, S. A., Azrael, D., Pate, V., & Stürmer, T. (2014). Antidepressant dose, age, and the risk of deliberate self-harm. *JAMA Internal Medicine, 174,* 899–909.

Miller, R. S. (1996). *Embarrassment: Poise and peril in everyday life.* New York, NY: Guilford Press.

Miller, R. S. (1997). We always hurt the ones we love: Aversive interactions in close relationships. In R. M. Kowalski (Ed.), *Aversive interpersonal behaviors* (pp. 11–29). New York, NY: Plenum Press.

Miller, S. L., & Maner, J. K. (2010). Evolution and relationship maintenance: Fertility cues lead committed men to devalue relationship alternatives. *Journal of Experimental Social Psychology, 46,* 1081–1084.

Miller, S. L., & Maner, J. K. (2011). Ovulation as a male mating prime: Subtle signs of women's fertility influence men's mating cognition and behavior. *Journal of Personality and Social Psychology, 100,* 295–308.

Miller, W. T. (2000). Rediscovering fire: Small interventions, large effects. *Psychology of Addictive Behaviors, 14,* 6–18.

Milojev, P., & Sibley, C. G. (2017). Normative personality trait development in adulthood: A 6-year cohort-sequential growth model. *Journal of Personality and Social Psychology, 112,* 510–526.

Minshew, N. J., & Williams, D. L. (2007). The new neurobiology of autism: Cortex, connectivity, and neuronal organization. *Archives of Neurology, 64,* 945–950.

Mischel, W. (1966). A social-learning view of sex differences in behavior. In E. E. Maccoby (Ed.), *The development of sex differences* (pp. 56–81). Stanford: Stanford University Press.

Mischel, W. (1968). *Personality and assessment.* New York, NY: Wiley.

Mischel, W. (2014). *The marshmallow test: Understanding self-control and how to master it.* New York, NY: Little, Brown.

Mischel, W., Shoda, Y., & Rodriguez, M. L. (1989). Delay of gratification in children. *Science, 244,* 933–938.

Mithoefer, M. C., Wagner, M. T., Mithoefer, A. T., Jerome, L., Martin, S. F., Yazar-Klosinski, B., & Doblin, R. (2013). Durability of improvement in post-traumatic stress disorder symptoms and absence of harmful effects or drug dependency after 3,4-methylenedioxymethamphetamine-assisted psychotherapy: A prospective long-term follow-up study. *Journal of Psychopharmacology, 27,* 28–39.

Miyamoto, Y., & Kitayama, S. (2002). Cultural variation in correspondence bias: The critical role of attitude diagnosticity of socially constrained behavior. *Journal of Personality and Social Psychology, 83,* 1239–1248.

Moeller, S. J., & Crocker, J. (2009). Drinking and desired self-images: Path models of self-image goals, coping motives, heavy-episodic drinking, and alcohol problems. *Psychology of Addictive Behaviors, 23,* 334–340.

Moffitt, T. E., Brammer, G. L., Caspi, A., Fawcett, J. P., Raleigh, M., Yuwiler, A., & Silva, P. (1998). Whole blood serotonin relates to violence in an epidemiological study. *Biological Psychiatry, 43,* 446–457.

Moll, J., & de Oliveira-Souza, R. (2007). Moral judgments, emotions and the utilitarian brain. *Trends in Cognitive Sciences, 11,* 319–321.

Montepare, J. M., & Vega, C. (1988). Women's vocal reactions to intimate and casual male friends. *Personality and Social Psychology Bulletin, 14,* 103–113.

Montgomery, G. H., DuHamel, K. N., & Redd, W. H. (2000). A meta-analysis of hypnotically induced analgesia: How effective is hypnosis? *International Journal of Clinical and Experimental Hypnosis, 48,* 138–153.

Montgomery, S., Hiyoshi, A., Burkill, S., Alfredsson, L., Bahmanyar, S., & Olsson, T. (2017). Concussion in adolescence and risk of multiple sclerosis. *Annals of Neurology, 82,* 554–561.

Monti, M. M., Vanhaudenhuyse, A., Coleman, M. R., Boly, M., Pickard, J. D., Tshibanda, L., . . . Laureys, S. (2010). Willful modulation of brain activity in disorders of consciousness. *New England Journal of Medicine, 362,* 579–589.

Moore, D. W. (2005, June 16). Three in four Americans believe in paranormal. *Gallup News.* Retrieved from http://www.gallup.com/poll/16915/Three-Four-Americans-Believe-Paranormal.aspx

Moore, S. C., Lee, I. M., Weiderpass, E., Campbell, P. T., Sampson, J. N., . . . Patel, A. V. (2016). Association of leisure-time physical activity with risk of 26 types of cancer in 1.44 million adults. *JAMA Internal Medicine, 176,* 816–825.

Moore, T. J., & Mattison, D. R. (2017). Adult utilization of psychiatric drugs and differences by sex, age, and race. *JAMA Internal Medicine, 177,* 274–275.

Morefield, K. M., Keane, M., Felgate, P., White, J. M., & Irvine, R. J. (2011). Pill content, dose and resulting plasma concentrations of 3,4-methylenedioxymethamphetamine (MDMA) in recreational "ecstasy" users. *Addiction, 106,* 1293–1300.

Morgan, C. D., & Murray, H. A. (1935). A method for investigating fantasies: The Thematic Apperception Test. *Archives of Neurology & Psychiatry, 34,* 289–306.

Morin, C. M., Vallières, A., Guay, B., Ivers, H., Savard, J., Mérette, C., . . . Baillargeon, L. (2009). Cognitive behavioral therapy, singly and combined with medication, for persistent insomnia: A randomized controlled trial. *Journal of the American Medical Association, 301,* 2005–2015.

Moriuchi, J. M., Klin, A., & Jones, W. (2016). Mechanisms of diminished attention to eyes in autism. *American Journal of Psychiatry, 174,* 26–35.

Mortensen, E. L., Michaelsen, K. F., Sanders, S. A., & Reinisch, J. M. (2002). The association between duration of breastfeeding and adult intelligence. *Journal of the American Medical Association, 287,* 2365–2371.

Morton, J., & Johnson, M. H. (1991). CONSPEC and CONLERN: A two-process theory of infant face recognition. *Psychological Review, 98,* 164–181.

Mosher, D. L., & MacIan, P. (1994). College men and women respond to X-rated videos intended for male or female audiences: Gender and sexual scripts. *Journal of Sex Research, 31,* 99–113.

Mosher, W. D., Chandra, A., & Jones, J. (2005). *Sexual behavior and selected health measures: Men and women 15–44 years of age, United States, 2002* (Advance Data From Vital and Health Statistics, No. 362). Washington, DC: Centers for Disease Control and Prevention, National Health Center for Statistics. Retrieved from http://www.cdc.gov/nchs/data/ad/ad362.pdf

Moss, M. (2014). *Salt, sugar, fat: How the food giants hooked us.* New York, NY: Random House.

Movement Advancement Project (2018, May 15). "Non-Discrimination Laws." Retrieved from http://www.lgbtmap.org/equality-maps/non_discrimination_laws

Mowery, P. D., Brick, P. D., & Farrelly, M. (2000). *Pathways to established smoking: Results from the 1999 national youth tobacco survey (Legacy First Look Report No. 3).* Washington, DC: American Legacy Foundation.

Moynihan, R. (2003). The making of a disease: Female sexual dysfunction. *BMJ: British Medical Journal, 326,* 45.

Mroczek, D. K., & Kolarz, C. M. (1998). The effect of age on positive and negative affect: A developmental perspective on happiness. *Journal of Personality and Social Psychology, 75,* 1333–1349.

Mueller, P. A., & Oppenheimer, D. M. (2014). The pen is mightier than the keyboard: Advantages of longhand over laptop note taking. *Psychological Science, 25,* 1159–1168.

Muenks, K., Wigfield, A., Yang, J. S., & O'Neal, C. R. (2017). How true is grit? Assessing its relations to high school and college students' personality characteristics, self-regulation, engagement, and achievement. *Journal of Educational Psychology, 109,* 599.

Mufson, L., Dorta, K. P., Wickramaratne, P., Nomura, Y., Olfson, M., & Weissman, M. M. (2004). A randomized effectiveness trial of interpersonal psychotherapy for depressed adolescents. *Archives of General Psychiatry, 61,* 577–584.

Mukherjee, R. A. S., Hollins, S., Abou-Saleh, M. T., & Turk, J. (2005). Low levels of alcohol consumption and the fetus. *British Medical Journal, 330,* 375–385.

Munson, J. A., McMahon, R. J., & Spieker, S. J. (2001). Structure and variability in the developmental trajectory of children's externalizing problems: Impact of infant attachment, maternal depressive symptomatology, and child sex. *Development and Psychopathology, 13,* 277–296.

Murnen, S. K., & Stockton, M. (1997). Gender and self-reported sexual arousal in response to sexual stimuli: A meta-analytic review. *Sex Roles, 37,* 135–153.

Murray, H. A. (1938). *Explorations in personality.* New York, NY: Oxford University Press.

Murray, S. L., Holmes, J. G., & Griffin, D. W. (1996). The benefits of positive illusions: Idealization and the construction of satisfaction in close relationships. *Journal of Personality and Social Psychology, 70,* 79–98.

Mustanski, B. S., & Bailey, J. M. (2003). A therapist's guide to the genetics of human sexual orientation. *Sexual and Relationship Therapy, 18,* 429–436.

Mustanski, B. S., Chivers, M. L., & Bailey, J. M. (2002). A critical review of recent biological research on human sexual orientation. *Annual Review of Sex Research, 13,* 89–140.

Myers, D. G. (2000). The funds, friends, and faith of happy people. *American Psychologist, 55,* 56–67.

Myers, D. G., & Lamm, H. (1976). The group polarization phenomenon. *Psychological Bulletin, 83,* 602–627.

Myers, D. G., & Scanzoni, L. D. (2005). *What God has joined together: The Christian case for gay marriage.* San Francisco: HarperSanFrancisco.

Nadel, L., Hoscheidt, S., & Ryan, L. R. (2013). Spatial cognition and the hippocampus: The anterior–posterior axis. *Journal of Cognitive Neuroscience, 25,* 22–28.

Nader, K., & Einarsson, E. O. (2010). Memory reconsolidation: An update. *Annals of the New York Academy of Sciences, 1191,* 27–41.

Nader, K., Schafe, G. E., & Le Doux, J. E. (2000). Fear memories require protein synthesis in the amygdala for reconsolidation after retrieval. *Nature, 406,* 722–726.

Nash, M., & Barnier, A. (2008). *The Oxford handbook of hypnosis.* New York, NY: Oxford University Press.

National Association of Colleges and Employers. (2016, April 6). Economics projected as top-paid class of 2016 social sciences major. Retrieved from http://www.naceweb.org/s04062016/top-paid-social-sciences-major-economics.aspx

National Center for Education Statistics (2017, April). *The condition of education: Postsecondary education.* Chap. 3. Retrieved from https://nces.ed.gov/programs/digest/d15/ch_3.asp

National Highway Traffic Safety Administration. n.d. Distracted driving. Retrieved from https://www.nhtsa.gov/risky-driving/distracted-driving

National Institute of Drug Abuse. (2014). National Survey of Drug Use and Health. Retrieved from http://www.drugabuse.gov/national-survey-drug-use-health

National Institutes of Health. (2018a). Klinefelter syndrome. *Genetics Home Reference: Your Guide to Understanding Genetic Conditions.* Retrieved from https://ghr.nlm.nih.gov/condition/klinefelter-syndrome#statistics

National Institutes of Health. (2018b). Turner syndrome. *Genetics Home Reference: Your Guide to Understanding Genetic Conditions.* Retrieved from https://ghr.nlm.nih.gov/condition/turner-syndrome#statistics

National Research Council. (2006). *When I'm 64.* Washington, DC: National Academy Press.

National Research Council, Committee on Educational Interventions for Children with Autism. (2001). *Educating young children with autism.* Washington, DC: National Academy Press.

Nawata, H., Ogomori, K., Tanaka, M., Nishimura, R., Urashima, H., Yano, R., . . . Kuwabara, Y. (2010). Regional cerebral blood flow changes in female to male gender identity disorder. *Psychiatry and Clinical Neurosciences, 64,* 157–161.

Neff, K. D. (2011). Self-compassion, self-esteem, and well-being. *Social and Personality Psychology Compass, 5,* 1–12.

Neimeyer, R. A., & Mitchell, K. A. (1988). Similarity and attraction: A longitudinal study. *Journal of Social and Personal Relationships, 5,* 131–148.

Neisser, U., Boodoo, G., Bouchard, T. J., Jr., Boykin, A. W., Brody, N., Ceci, S. J., . . . Urbina, S. (1996). Intelligence: Knowns and unknowns. *American Psychologist, 51,* 77–101.

Nelson, S. K., Kushlev, K., English, T., Dunn, E. W., & Lyubomirsky, S. (2013). In defense of parenthood: Children are associated with more joy than misery. *Psychological Science, 24,* 3–10.

Newby, J. M., McKinnon, A., Kuyken, W., Gilbody, S., & Dalgleish, T. (2015). Systematic review and meta-analysis of transdiagnostic psychological treatments for anxiety and depressive disorders in adulthood. *Clinical Psychology Review, 40,* 91–110.

Newman, M. G., Llera, S. J., Erickson, T. M., Przeworski, A., & Castonguay, L. G. (2013). Worry and generalized anxiety disorder: A review and theoretical synthesis of evidence on nature, etiology, mechanisms, and treatment. *Annual Review of Clinical Psychology, 9,* 275–297.

Ng, D. M., & Jeffrey, E. W. (2003). Relationships between perceived stress and health behaviors in a sample of working adults. *Health Psychology, 22,* 638–642.

Ng, M., Fleming, T., Robinson, M., Thomson, B., Graetz, N., Margono, C., . . . Gakidou, E. (2014). Global, regional, and national prevalence of overweight and obesity in children and adults during 1980–2013: A systematic analysis for the Global Burden of Disease Study 2013. *The Lancet, 384,* 766–781.

Ngun, T. C., Gjahramani, N., Sánchez, F. J., Bocklandt, S., & Vilain, E. (2011). The genetics of sex differences in brain and behavior. *Frontiers in Neuroendocrinology, 32,* 227–246.

Nichols, J. (2014, August 4). Laverne Cox corrects Gayle King after "Born a Boy" comment. *The Huffington Post.* Retrieved from https://www.huffingtonpost.com/2014/08/04/laverne-cox-gayle-king_n_5647816.html

Nicholson, I. (2011). "Torture at Yale": Experimental subjects, laboratory torment and the "rehabilitation" of Milgram's "Obedience to Authority." *Theory & Psychology, 21,* 737–761.

Nielsen, J., & Wohlert, M. (1991). Chromosome abnormalities found among 34,910 newborn children: Results from a 13-year incidence study in Århus, Denmark. *Human Genetics, 87,* 81–83.

Nigg, J. T. (2005). Neuropsychologic theory and findings in attention-deficit/hyperactivity disorder: The state of the field and salient challenges for the coming decade. *Biological Psychiatry: A Journal of Psychiatric Neuroscience and Therapeutics, 57,* 1424–1435.

Nisbett, R. E., & Wilson, T. D. (1977). Telling more than we can know: Verbal reports on mental processes. *Psychological Review, 84,* 231–259.

Nishino, S. (2007). Narcolepsy: Pathophysiology and pharmacology. *Journal of Clinical Psychiatry, 68*(Suppl. 13), 9–15.

Nivoli, A., Colom, F., Murru, A., Pacchiarotti, I., Castro-Loli, P., González-Pinto, A., . . . Vieta, E. (2011). New treatment guidelines for acute bipolar depression: A systematic review. *Journal of Affective Disorders, 129,* 14–26.

Noble, K. G., Korgaonkar, M. S., Grieve, S. M., & Brickman, A. M. (2013). Higher education is an age-independent predictor of white matter integrity and cognitive control in late adolescence. *Developmental Science, 16,* 653–664.

Nomura, Y., Halperin, J. M., Newcorn, J. H., Davey, C., Fifer, W. P., Savitz, D. A., & Brokks-Gunn, J. (2009). The risk for impaired learning-related abilities in childhood and educational achievement among adults born near-term. *Journal of Pediatric Psychology, 34,* 406–418.

Norcross, J. C., & Sayette, M. A. (2016). *Insider's guide to graduate programs in clinical and counseling psychology* (2016–2017 ed.). New York, NY: Guilford Press.

Norman, K. A., Polyn, S. M., Detre, G. J., & Haxby, J. V. (2006). Beyond mind-reading: Multi-voxel pattern analysis of fMRI data. *Trends in Cognitive Sciences, 10,* 424–423.

Norris, A. L., Marcus, D. K., & Green, B. A. (2015). Homosexuality as a discrete class. *Psychological Science, 26,* 1843–1853.

Nosek, B. A., Hawkins, C. B., & Frazier, R. S. (2011). Implicit social cognition: From measures to mechanisms. *Trends in Cognitive Sciences, 15,* 152–159.

Noyes, R. (1991). Suicide and panic disorder: A review. *Journal of Affective Disorders, 22,* 1–11.

Null, J. (2016). Heatstroke deaths of children in vehicles. Retrieved from http://noheatstroke.org

Nummenmaa, L., Glerean, E., Hari, R., & Hietanen, J. K. (2014). Bodily maps of emotions. *Proceedings of the National Academy of Sciences, 111,* 646–651.

Nurius, P. S. (1983). Mental health implications of sexual orientation. *Journal of Sex Research, 19,* 119–136.

Nurnberger, J. J., Goldin, L. R., & Gershon, E. S. (1994). Genetics of psychiatric disorders. In G. Winokur & P. M. Clayton (Eds.), *The medical basis of psychiatry* (pp. 459–492). Philadelphia: Saunders.

Oberauer, K., Schulze, R., Wilhelm, O., & Süß, H. M. (2005). Working memory and intelligence—Their correlation and their relation: Comment on Ackerman, Beier, and Boyle (2005). *Psychological Bulletin, 131,* 61–65.

Ochsner, K. N., Bunge, S. A., Gross, J. J., & Gabrieli, J. D. E. (2002). Rethinking feelings: An fMRI study of the cognitive regulation of emotion. *Journal of Cognitive Neuroscience, 14,* 1215–1299.

O'Connell, H. E., Sanjeevan, K. V., & Hutson, J. M. (2005). Anatomy of the clitoris. *The Journal of Urology, 174*(Pt. 1), 1189–1195.

Odeh, M., Grinin, V., Kais, M., Ophir, E., & Bornstein, J. (2009). Sonographic fetal sex determination. *Obstetrical & Gynecological Survey, 64,* 50–57.

O'Donovan, G., Lee, I. M., Hamer, M., & Stamatakis, E. (2017). The "weekend warrior" and other leisure-time physical activity patterns and the risks of all-cause, cardiovascular disease and cancer mortality. *JAMA Internal Medicine, 177,* 335–342.

Ogbu, J. U. (1994). From cultural differences to differences in cultural frames of reference. In P. M. Greenfield & R. R. Cocking (Eds.), *Cross cultural roots of minority child development* (pp. 365–392). Hillsdale, NJ: Erlbaum.

Ogden, C. L., Carroll, M. D., Lawman, H. G., Fryar, C. D., Kruszon-Moran, D., Kit, B. K. & Flegal, K. M. (2016). Trends in obesity prevalence among children and adolescents in the United States, 1988–1994 through 2013–2014. *Journal of the American Medical Association, 315,* 2292–2299.

Ogletree, S. M., Turner, G., Vieira, A., & Brunotte, J. (2005). College living: Issues related to housecleaning attitudes. *College Student Journal, 39,* 729–733.

Ohla, K., & Lundström, J. N. (2013). Sex differences in chemosensation: Sensory or emotional? *Frontiers in Human Neuroscience, 7,* 607.

Öhman, A. (2002). Automaticity and the amygdala: Nonconscious responses to emotional faces. *Current Directions in Psychological Science, 11,* 62–66.

O'Leary, S. G. (1995). Parental discipline mistakes. *Current Directions in Psychological Science, 4,* 11–13.

Olfson, M., Marcus, S. C., Druss, B., Elinson, L., Tanielian, T., & Pincus, H. A. (2002). National trends in the outpatient treatment of depression. *Journal of the American Medical Association, 287,* 203–209.

Oliveira-Pinto, A. V., Santos, R. M., Coutinho, R. A., Oliveira, L. M., Santos, G. B., Alho, A. T., . . . Lent, R. (2014). Sexual dimorphism in the human olfactory bulb: Females have more neurons and glial cells than males. *PLOS ONE, 9,* e111733.

Olson, H. C., Ohlemiller, M. M., O'Connor, M. J., Brown, C. W., Morris, C. A., & Damus, K. (March, 2009). A call to action: Advancing essential services and research on fetal alcohol spectrum disorders—A report of the national task force on fetal alcohol syndrome and fetal alcohol effect. U.S. Department of Health and Human Services.

Olson, K. R., Key, A. C., & Eaton, N. R. (2015). Gender cognition in transgender children. *Psychological Science, 26,* 467–474.

Olyslager, F., & Conway, L. (2007, September). On the calculation of the prevalence of transsexualism. Paper presented at the World Professional Association for Transgender Health 20th International Symposium, Chicago, IL.

O'Neil, J. (2004, December 29). Slow-motion miracle: One boy's journey out of autism's grasp. *The New York Times,* p. B8.

O'Neil, S. (1999). Flow theory and the development of musical performance skills. *Bulletin of the Council for Research in Music Education, 141,* 129–134.

Onishi, K. H., & Baillargeon, R. (2005). Do 15-month-old infants understand false beliefs? *Science, 308,* 255–258.

Ooms, P., Mantione, M., Figee, M., Schuurman, P. R., van den Munckhof, P., & Denys, D. (2014). Deep brain stimulation for obsessive-compulsive disorders: Long-term analysis of quality of life. *Journal of Neurology, Neurosurgery & Psychiatry, 85,* 153–158.

Organization for Economic Cooperation and Development (2013). Health care at a glance—2013. *OECD Indicators,* OECD Publishing, Paris, France.

Ortigue, S., Bianchi-Demicheli, F., Hamilton, C., & Grafton, S. T. (2007). The neural basis of love as a subliminal prime: An event-related functional magnetic resonance imaging study. *Journal of Cognitive Neuroscience, 19,* 1218–1230.

O'Riordan, K. (2012). The life of the gay gene: From hypothetical genetic marker to social reality. *Journal of Sex Research, 49,* 362–368.

Osterling, J., & Dawson, G. (1994). Early recognition of children with autism: A study of first birthday home videotapes. *Journal of Autism and Developmental Disorders, 24,* 247–257.

Ostrzenski, A. (2012). G-spot anatomy: A new discovery. *The Journal of Sexual Medicine, 9,* 1355–1359.

Oswald, F. L., Mitchell, G., Blanton, H., Jaccard, J., & Tetlock, P. E. (2015). Using the IAT to predict ethnic and racial discrimination: Small effect sizes of unknown societal significance. *Journal of Personality and Social Psychology, 108,* 562–571.

O'Toole, A. J., Natu, V., An, X., Rice, A., Ryland, J., & Phillips, P. J. (2014). The neural representation of faces and bodies in motion and at rest. *NeuroImage, 84,* 698–711.

Otte, C., Gold, S. M., Penninx, B. W., Pariante, C. M., Etkin, A., Fava, M., . . . Schatzberg, A. F. (2016). Major depressive disorder. *Nature Reviews. Disease Primers, 2,* 16065.

Ottieger, A. E., Tressell, P. A., Inciardi, J. A., & Rosales, T. A. (1992). Cocaine use patterns and overdose. *Journal of Psychoactive Drugs, 24,* 399–410.

Oud, M., Mayo-Wilson, E., Braidwood, R., Schulte, P., Jones, S. H., Morriss, R., . . . & Kendall, T. (2016). Psychological interventions for adults with bipolar disorder: Systematic review and meta-analysis. *The British Journal of Psychiatry, 208,* 213–222.

Owen, A. M., Coleman, M. R., Boly, M., Davis, M. H., Laureys, S., & Pickard, J. D. (2006). Detecting awareness in the vegetative state. *Science, 313,* 1402.

Pacchiarotti, I., Bond, D. J., Baldessarini, R. J., Nolen, W. A., Grunze, H., Licht, R. W., . . . Vieta, E. (2013). The International Society for Bipolar Disorders (ISBD) Task Force Report on antidepressant use in bipolar disorders. *American Journal of Psychiatry, 170,* 1249–1262.

Pack, A. I., & Pien, G. W. (2011). Update on sleep and its disorders. *Annual Review of Medicine, 62,* 447–460.

Padberg, F., & George, M. S. (2009). Repetitive transcranial magnetic stimulation of the prefrontal cortex in depression. *Experimental Neurology, 219,* 2–13.

Pagnoni, G., & Cekic, M. (2007). Age effects on gray matter volume and attentional performance in Zen meditation. *Neurobiology of Aging, 28,* 1623–1627.

Palombo, D. J., McKinnon, M. C., McIntosh, A. R., Anderson, A. K., Todd, R. M., & Levine, B. (2016). The neural correlates of memory for a life-threatening event: An fMRI study of passengers from flight AT236. *Clinical Psychological Science, 4,* 312–319.

Papadimitriou, G. N., Zervas, I. M., & Papakostas, Y. G. (2001). Unilateral ECT for prophylaxis in affective illness. *Journal of ECT, 17,* 229–231.

Papadopoulos, S., & Brennan, L. (2015). Correlates of weight stigma in adults with overweight and obesity: A systematic literature review. *Obesity, 23,* 1743–1760.

Paredes, M. F., James, D., Gil-Perotin, S., Kim, H., Cotter, J. A., Ng, C., . . . Alvarez-Buylla, A. (2016). Extensive migration of young neurons into the infant human frontal lobe. *Science, 354,* aaf7073.

Parents, Families and Friends of Lesbians and Gays (PFLAG). (2015). A definition of "queer." Retrieved from http://community.pflag.org/abouttheq

Parrott, A. C. (2013). MDMA, serotonergic neurotoxicity, and the diverse functional deficits of recreational "ecstasy" users. *Neuroscience & Biobehavioral Reviews, 37,* 1466–1484.

Pascual-Leone, A., Catala, M. D., & Pascual-Leone, P. A. (1996). Lateralized effect of rapid-rate transcranial magnetic stimulation of the prefrontal cortex on mood. *Neurology, 46,* 499–502.

Patel, V., Chisholm, D., Parikh, R., Charlson, F. J., Degenhardt, L., Dua, T., . . . DCP MNS Author Group (2016). Addressing the burden of mental, neurological, and substance use disorders: Key messages from Disease Control Priorities. *The Lancet, 387,* 1672–1685.

Patel, V., Xiao, S., Chen, H., Hanna, F., Jotheeswaran, A. T., Luo, D., . . . Saxena, S. (2017). The magnitude of and health system responses to the mental health treatment gap in adults in India and China. *The Lancet, 388,* 3074–3084.

Patrick, M. E., Schulenberg, J. E., Martz, M. E., Maggs, J. L., O'Malley, P. M., & Johnston, L.D. (2013). Extreme binge drinking among 12th-grade students in the United States: Prevalence and predictors. *JAMA Pediatrics, 167,* 1019–1025.

Patterson, D., & Jensen, M. (2003). Hypnosis and clinical pain. *Psychological Bulletin, 129,* 495–521.

Paul-Labrador, M., Polk, D., Dwyer, J. H., Velasquez, I., Nidich, S., Rainforth, M., . . . Merz, C.N.B. (2006). Effects of a randomized controlled trial of transcendental meditation on components of the metabolic syndrome in subjects with coronary heart disease. *Archives of Internal Medicine, 166,* 1218–1224.

Pauls, D. L. (2008). The genetics of obsessive compulsive disorder: A review of the evidence. *American Journal of Medical Genetics, 148C,* 133–139.

Pauls, D. L., Abramovitch, A., Rauch, S. L., & Geller, D. A. (2014). Obsessive-compulsive disorder: An integrative genetic and neurobiological perspective. *Nature Reviews Neuroscience, 15,* 410–424.

Paunonen, S. V., & Ashton, M. C. (2001). Big five factors and facets and the prediction of behavior. *Journal of Personality and Social Psychology, 81,* 524–539.

Pavlov, I. P. (1927). *Conditioned reflexes: An investigation of the physiological activity of the cerebral cortex.* (Translated and edited by G. V. Anrep.) London, UK: Oxford University Press; Humphrey Milford.

Payne, B. K. (2001). Prejudice and perception: The role of automatic and controlled processes in misperceiving a weapon. *Journal of Personality and Social Psychology, 81,* 181–192.

Payne, B. K., Krosnick, J. A., Pasek, J., Lelkes, Y., Akhtar, O., & Tompson, T. (2010). Implicit and explicit prejudice in the 2008 American presidential election. *Journal of Experimental Social Psychology, 46,* 367–374.

Pearl, R. L., Wadden, T. A., Hopkins, C. M., Shaw, J. A., Hayes, M. R., Bakizada, Z. M., . . . Alamuddin, N. (2017). Association between weight bias internalization and metabolic syndrome among treatment-seeking individuals with obesity. *Obesity, 25,* 317–322.

Penfield, W., & Jasper, H. (1954). *Epilepsy and the functional anatomy of the human brain.* Boston, MA: Little, Brown.

Penttilä, M., Jääskeläinen, E., Hirvonen, N., Isohanni, M., & Miettunen, J. (2014). Duration of untreated psychosis as predictor of long-term outcome in schizophrenia: Systematic review and meta-analysis. *The British Journal of Psychiatry, 205,* 88–94.

Peplau, L. A. (2003). Human sexuality: How do men and women differ? *Current Directions in Psychological Science, 12,* 37–40.

Perrett, D. I., May, K. A., & Yoshikawa, S. (1994). Facial shape and judgments of female attractiveness. *Nature, 368,* 239–242.

Perry, B. D. (2002). Childhood experience and the expression of genetic potential: What childhood neglect tells us about nature and nurture. *Brain and Mind, 3,* 79–100.

Perry, G. (2013). *Behind the shock machine: The untold story of the notorious Milgram psychology experiments.* New York, NY: The New Press.

Pert, C. B., & Snyder, S. H. (1973). Opiate receptor: Demonstration in nervous tissue. *Science, 179,* 1011–1014.

Peters, A. T., Jacobs, R. H., Feldhaus, C., Henry, D. B., Albano, A. M., Langenecker, S. A., . . . Curry, J. F. (2016). Trajectories of functioning into emerging adulthood following treatment for adolescent depression. *Journal of Adolescent Health, 58,* 253–259.

Petersen, J. L., & Hyde, J. S. (2011). Gender differences in sexual attitudes and behaviors: A review of meta-analytic results and large datasets. *Journal of Sex Research, 48,* 149–165.

Peterson, L. R., & Peterson, M. J. (1959). Short-term retention of individual verbal items. *Journal of Experimental Psychology, 58,* 193–198.

Petronis, A., & Kennedy, J. L. (1995). Unstable genes—Unstable mind? *American Journal of Psychiatry, 152,* 164–172.

Petty, R. E., & Cacioppo, J. T. (1986). *Communication and persuasion: Central and peripheral routes to attitude change.* New York, NY: Springer-Verlag.

Petty, R. E., & Wegener, D. T. (1998). Attitude change: Multiple roles for persuasion variables. In D. T. Gilbert, S. T. Fiske, & G. Lindzey (Eds.), *The handbook of social psychology* (4th ed., pp. 323–390). Boston, MA: McGraw- Hill.

Pew Research (2018). *Millennials.* Retrieved from http://www.pewresearch.org/topics/millennials/

Phelps, E. A. (2006). Emotion and cognition: Insights from studies of the human amygdala. *Annual Review of Psychology, 57,* 27–53.

Phelps, E. A., Ling, S., & Carrasco, M. (2006). Emotion facilitates perception and potentiates the perceptual benefits of attention. *Psychological Science, 17,* 292–299.

Phillips, W. J., Hine, D. W., & Marks, A. D. (2018). Self-compassion moderates the predictive effects of implicit cognitions on subjective well-being. *Stress and Health, 34,* 143–151.

Phinney, J. S. (1990). Ethnic identity in adolescents and adults: Review of research. *Psychological Bulletin, 108,* 499–514.

Pickrell, T. M., & Li, H. (2017, June). Driver electronic device use in 2016 (Traffic Safety Facts Research Note. Report No. DOT HS 812 426). Washington, DC: National Highway Traffic Safety Administration.

Pinker, S. (1984). *Language learnability and language development.* Cambridge, MA: Harvard University Press.

Plant, E. A., Hyde, J. S., Keltner, D., & Devine, P. G. (2000). The gender stereotyping of emotions. *Psychology of Women Quarterly, 24,* 81–92.

Plomin, R., & Caspi, A. (1999). Behavioral genetics and personality. In L. A. Pervin & O. P. John (Eds.), *Handbook of personality: Theory and research* (2nd ed., pp. 251–276). New York, NY: Guilford Press.

Plomin, R., DeFries, J. C., Knopik, V. S., & Neiderhiser, J. M. (2016). Top 10 replicated findings from behavioral genetics. *Perspectives on Psychological Science, 11,* 3–23.

Plomin, R., & Spinath, F. M. (2004). Intelligence: Genetics, genes, and genomics. *Journal of Personality and Social Psychology, 86,* 112–129.

Plötner, M., Over, H., Carpenter, M., & Tomasello, M. (2015). Young children show the bystander effect in helping situations. *Psychological Science, 26,* 499–506.

Polivy, J., & Herman, C. P. (2002). Causes of eating disorders. *Annual Review of Psychology, 53,* 187–213.

Pollock, K. M. (2004). Exercise in treating depression: Broadening the psychotherapist's role. *Journal of Clinical Psychology, 57,* 1289–1300.

Post, R. M., Leverich, G. S., Kupka, R., Keck, P., McElroy, S., Altshuler, L., . . . Nolen, W. A. (2013). Increased parental history of bipolar disorder in the United States: Association with early age of onset. *Acta Psychiatrica Scandinavica, 129,* 375–382.

Poulton, R., Moffitt, T. E., & Silva, P. A. (2015). The Dunedin Multidisciplinary Health and Development Study: Overview of the first 40 years, with an eye to the future. *Social Psychiatry and Psychiatric Epidemiology, 50,* 679–693.

Powell, R. A., Digdon, N., Harris, B., & Smithson, C. (2014). Correcting the record on Watson, Rayner, and Little Albert: Albert Barger as "psychology's lost boy." *American Psychologist, 69,* 600–611.

Prakash, R. S., Voss, M. W., Erickson, K. I., & Kramer, A. F. (2015). Physical activity and cognitive vitality. *Annual Review of Psychology, 66,* 769–797.

Pratt, L. A., & Brody, D. J. (2014). *Depression in the US Household Population, 2009–2012.* (NCHS Data Brief No. 172). Hyattsville, MD: National Center for Health Statistics.

Premack, D. (1959). Toward empirical behavior laws: 1. Positive reinforcement. *Psychological Review, 66,* 219–233.

Premack, D. (1970). Mechanisms of self-control. In W. A. Hunt (Ed.), *Learning mechanisms in smoking* (pp. 107–123). Chicago, IL: Aldine.

Prentiss, D., Power, R., Balmas, G., Tzuang, G., & Israelski, D. (2004). Patterns of marijuana use among patients with HIV/AIDS followed in a public health care setting. *Journal of Acquired Immune Deficiency Syndromes, 35,* 38–45.

Price, D. D., Harkins, S. W., & Baker, C. (1987). Sensory-affective relationships among different types of clinical and experimental pain. *Pain, 28,* 297–307.

Primack, B. A., Soneji, S., Stoolmiller, M., Fine, M. J., & Sargent, J. D. (2015). Progression to traditional cigarette smoking after electronic cigarette use among U.S. adolescents and young adults. *JAMA Pediatrics, 169,* 1018–1023.

Probst, F., Meng-Hentschel, J., Golle, J., Stucki, S., Akyildiz-Kunz, C., & Lobmaier, J. S. (2017). Do women tend while men fight or flee? Differential emotive reactions of stressed men and women while viewing newborn infants. *Psychoneuroendocrinology, 75,* 213–221.

Pruitt, M. V. (2002). Size matters: A comparison of anti- and pro-gay organizations' estimates of the size of the gay population. *Journal of Homosexuality, 42,* 21–29.

Putnam, A. L., Sungkhasettee, V. W., & Roediger, H. L. (2016). Optimizing learning in college: Tips from cognitive psychology. *Perspectives on Psychological Science, 11,* 652–660.

Rainville, P., Duncan, G. H., Price, D. D., Carrier, B., & Bushnell, M. C. (1997). Pain affect encoded in human anterior cingulate but not somatosensory cortex. *Science, 277,* 968–971.

Rainville, P., Hofbauer, R. K., Bushnell, M. C., Duncan, G. H., & Price, D. D. (2002). Hypnosis modulates activity in brain structures involved in the regulation of consciousness. *Journal of Cognitive Neuroscience, 14,* 887–901.

Ram, S., Seirawan, H., Kumar, S. K., & Clark, G. T. (2010). Prevalence and impact of sleep disorders and sleep habits in the United States. *Sleep Breath, 14,* 63–70.

Ramachandran, V. S., & Hubbard, E. M. (2003). Hearing colors, tasting shapes: Color-coded world. *Scientific American, 288,* 42–49.

Ramirez, G., & Beilock, S. L. (2011). Writing about testing worries boosts exam performance in the classroom. *Science, 331,* 211–213.

Rapport, M. D., & Moffitt, C. (2002). Attention-deficit/hyperactivity disorder and methylphenidate: A review of the height/weight, cardiovascular, and somatic complaint side effects. *Clinical Psychology Review, 22,* 1107–1131.

Rapuano, K. M., Zieselman, A. L., Kelley, W. M., Sargent, J. D., Heatherton, T. F., & Gilbert-Diamond, D. (2017). Genetic risk for obesity predicts nucleus accumbens size and responsivity to real-world food cues. *Proceedings of the National Academy of Sciences, 114,* 160–165.

Rasmussen, S. A., Jamieson, D. J., Honein, M. A., & Petersen, L. R. (2016). Zika virus and birth defects—reviewing the evidence for causality. *New England Journal of Medicine, 374,* 1981–1987.

Rauscher, F. H., Shaw, G. L., & Ky, K. N. (1993). Music and spatial task performance. *Nature, 365,* 611.

Rayner, K., Schotter, E. R., Masson, M. E., Potter, M. C., & Treiman, R. (2016). So much to read, so little time: How do we read, and can speed reading help? *Psychological Science in the Public Interest, 17,* 4–34.

Read, J. P., & Brown, R. A. (2003). The role of exercise in alcoholism treatment and recovery. *Professional Psychology: Research and Practice, 34,* 49–56.

Read, T. R. H., Hocking, J. S., Chen, M. Y., Donovan, B., Bradshaw, C. S., & Fairley, C. K. (2011). The near disappearance of genital warts in young women four years after commencing a national human papillomavirus (HPV) vaccination program. *Sexually Transmitted Diseases, 87,* 544–547.

Reeck, C., Ames, D. R., & Ochsner, K. N. (2016). The social regulation of emotion: An integrative, cross-disciplinary model. *Trends in Cognitive Sciences, 20,* 47–63.

Reeves, L. M., & Weisberg, R. W. (1994). The role of content and abstract information in analogical transfer. *Psychological Bulletin, 115,* 381–400.

Reinders, A. A., Nijenhuis, E. R., Paans, A. M., Korf, J., Willemsen, A. T., & den Boer, J. A. (2003). One brain, two selves. *Neuroimage, 20,* 2119–2125.

Reiner, W. G., & Gearhart, J. P. (2004). Discordant sexual identity in some genetic males with cloacal exstrophy assigned to female sex at birth. *New England Journal of Medicine, 350,* 333–341.

Reis, D. L., Brackett, M. A., Shamosh, N. A., Kiehl, K. A., Salovey, P., & Gray, J. R. (2007). Emotional intelligence predicts individual differences in social exchange reasoning. *Neuroimage, 35,* 1385–1391.

Reis, H. X, Wheeler, L., Spiegel, N., Kernis, M. H., Nezlek, J., & Perri, M. (1982). Physical attractiveness in social interaction: II. Why does appearance affect social experience? *Journal of Personality and Social Psychology, 43,* 979–996.

Rescorla, R. (1966). Predictability and number of pairings in Pavlovian fear conditioning. *Psychonomic Science, 4,* 383–384.

Ressler, K. J., & Mayberg, H. S. (2007). Targeting abnormal neural circuits in mood and anxiety disorders: From the laboratory to the clinic. *Nature Neuroscience, 10,* 1116–1124.

Rhodewalt, F., & Morf, C. C. (1998). On self-aggrandizement and anger: A temporal analysis of narcissism and affective reactions to success and failure. *Journal of Personality and Social Psychology, 74,* 672–685.

Riboni, F. V., & Belzung, C. (2017). Stress and psychiatric disorders: From categorical to dimensional approaches. *Current Opinion in Behavioral Sciences, 14,* 72–77.

Richman, L. S., Kubzansky, L., Maselko, J., Kawachi, I., Choo, P., & Bauer, M. (2005). Positive emotion and health: Going beyond the negative. *Health Psychology, 24,* 422–429.

Rico-Uribe, L. A., Caballero, F. F., Martín-María, N., Cabello, M., Ayuso-Mateos, J. L., & Miret, M. (2018). Association of loneliness with all-cause mortality: A meta-analysis. *PLOS ONE, 13,* e0190033.

Rieger, G., Cash, B. M., Merrill, S. M., Jones-Rounds, J., Muralidharan Dharmavaram, S., & Savin-Williams, R. C. (2015). *Sexual arousal: The correspondence of eyes and genitals, 104,* 56–64.

Rifkin, A., & Rifkin, W. (2004). Adolescents with depression. *Journal of the American Medical Association, 292,* 2577–2578.

Rinck, M., Reinecke, A., Ellwart, T., Heuer, K., & Becker, E. S. (2005). Speeded detection and increased distraction in fear of spiders: Evidence from eye movements. *Journal of Abnormal Psychology, 114,* 235–248.

Rivenbark, J. G., Odgers, C. L., Caspi, A., Harrington, H., Hogan, S., Houts, R. M. Poulton, R., & Moffitt, T. E. (2018). The high societal costs of childhood conduct problems: Evidence from administrative records up to age 38 in a longitudinal birth cohort. *Journal of Child Psychology and Psychiatry, 59,* 703–710.

Robert-McComb, J. J. (2008). Nutritional guidelines and energy needs for the female athlete: Determining energy and nutritional needs to alleviate the consequences of functional amenorrhea caused by energy imbalance. In J. J. Robert-McComb, R. L. Norman, & M. Zumwalt (Eds.), *The active female: Health issues throughout the lifespan* (pp. 299–310). Totowa, NJ: Humana Press.

Roberts, B. W. (2009). Back to the future: Personality and assessment and personality development. *Journal of Research in Personality, 43,* 137–145.

Roberts, B. W., & Friend-DelVecchio, W. (2000). The rank-order consistency of personality traits from childhood to old age: A quantitative review of longitudinal studies. *Psychological Bulletin, 126,* 3–25.

Robins, R. W., Trzesniewski, K., Tracy, J. L., Gosling, S. D., & Potter, J. (2002). Global self-esteem across the life span. *Psychology and Aging, 17,* 423–434.

Robles, T. F., & Kiecolt-Glaser, J. K. (2003). The physiology of marriage: Pathways to health. *Physiology & Behavior, 79,* 409–416.

Roche, A. F., & Sun, S. S. (2003). *Human growth: Assessment and interpretation.* Cambridge, UK: Cambridge University Press.

Roediger, H. L., III, & Karpicke, J. D. (2006). The power of testing memory: Basic research and implications for educational practice. *Psychological Science, 1,* 181–210.

Roediger, H. L., III, & McDermott, K. B. (1995). Creating false memories: Remembering words not presented in lists. *Journal of Experimental Psychology: Learning, Memory, and Cognition, 21,* 803–814.

Rogers, P. J., & Brunstrom, J. M. (2016). Appetite and energy balancing. *Physiology & Behavior, 164,* 465–471.

Rogers, T. B., Kuiper, N. A., & Kirker, W. S. (1977). Self-reference and the encoding of personal information. *Journal of Personality and Social Psychology, 35,* 677–688.

Rolls, B. J., Roe, L. S., & Meengs, J. S. (2007). The effect of large portion sizes on energy intake is sustained for 11 days. *Obesity Research, 15,* 1535–1543.

Rolls, E. T. (2007). Sensory processing in the brain related to the control of food intake. *Proceedings of the Nutritional Society, 66,* 96–112.

Rolls, E. T., Burton, M. J., & Mora, F. (1980). Neurophysiological analysis of brain-stimulation reward in the monkey. *Brain Research, 194,* 339–357.

Ronay, R., & von Hippel, W. (2010). The presence of an attractive woman elevates testosterone and physical risk taking in young men. *Social Psychological and Personality Science, 1,* 57–64.

Rosenfield, R. L., Lipton, R. B., & Drum, M. L. (2009). Thelarche, pubarche, and menarche attainment in children with normal and elevated body mass index. *Pediatrics, 123,* 84–88.

Rosenman, R. H., Brand, R. J., Jenkins, C. D., Friedman, M., Straus, R., & Wurm, M. (1975). Coronary heart disease in the Western Collaborative Group Study: Final follow-up experience of 8½ years. *Journal of the American Medical Association, 233,* 872–877.

Rosenman, R. H., Friedman, M., Straus, R., Wurm, M., Kositchek, R., Hahn, W., . . . Werthessen, N. T. (1964). A predictive study of heart disease. *Journal of the American Medical Association, 189,* 15–22.

Rosenthal, R. (2003). Covert communication in laboratories, classrooms, and the truly real world. *Current Directions in Psychological Science, 12,* 151–154.

Rosenthal, R., & Jacobson, L. (1968). *Pygmalion in the classroom: Teacher expectation and pupils' intellectual development.* New York, NY: Holt, Rinehart and Winston.

Ross, C. E., Mirowsky, J., & Goldsteen, K. (1990). The impact of the family on health: The decade in review. *Journal of Marriage and the Family, 52,* 1059–1078.

Rotter, J. B. (1954). *Social learning and clinical psychology.* New York, NY: Prentice-Hall.

Rotter, J. B. (1966). Generalized expectancies for internal versus external control of reinforcements. *Psychological Monographs, 80,* Whole No. 609.

Rubenstein, A. J., Kalakanis, L., & Langlois, J. H. (1999). Infant preferences for attractive faces: A cognitive explanation. *Developmental Psychology, 35,* 848–855.

Ruble, D. N., Martin, C. L., & Berenbaum, S. A. (2006). Gender development: Social, emotional, and personality development. In W. Damon, R. M. Lerner, & N. Eisenberg (Eds.), *Handbook of child psychology* (6th ed., pp. 858–932). Hoboken, NJ: Wiley.

Rudd, R. A., Aleshire, N., Zibbell, J. E., & Gladden, R. M. (2016). Increases in drug and opioid overdose deaths—United States, 2000–2014. *Morbidity and Mortality Weekly Report, 64,* 1378–1382.

Rule, N. O., & Alaei, R. (2016). "Gaydar": The perception of sexual orientation from subtle cues. *Current Directions in Psychological Science, 25,* 444–448.

Rusbult, C. E., & Van Lange, P. A. M. (1996). Interdependence processes. In E. T. Higgins & A. Kruglanski (Eds.), *Social psychology: Handbook of basic principles* (pp. 564–596). New York, NY: Guilford Press.

Ruscio, A. M., Brown, T. A., Chiu, W. T., Sareen, J., Stein, M. B., & Kessler, R. C. (2008). Social fears and social phobia in the USA: Results from the national comorbidity survey replication. *Psychological Medicine, 35,* 15–28.

Ruscio, A. M., Stein, D. J., Chiu, W. T., & Kessler, R. C. (2010). The epidemiology of obsessive-compulsive disorder in the National Comorbidity Survey Replication. *Molecular Psychiatry, 15,* 53–63.

Russell, J. A. (2003). Core affect and the psychological construction of emotion. *Psychological Review, 110,* 145–172.

Russell, M. A. H. (1990). The nicotine trap: A 40-year sentence for four cigarettes. *British Journal of Addiction, 85,* 293–300.

Rutter, M. (2005). Incidence of autism disorders: Changes over time and their meaning. *Acta Paediatrica, 94,* 2–15.

Ryder, J. G., & Holtzheimer, P. E. (2016). Deep brain stimulation for depression: An update. *Current Behavioral Neuroscience Reports, 3,* 102–108.

Saad, N. (2013, November 8). Jennifer Lawrence explains pixie cut, slams "Fashion Police." *Los Angeles Times.* Retrieved from http://articles.latimes.com/2013/nov/08/entertainment/la-et-mg-jennifer-lawrence-pixie-cut-reaction-dye-hunger-games-20131108

Sabol, S. Z., Nelson, M. L., Fisher, C., Gunzerath, L., Brody, C. L., Hu, S., . . . Hamer, D. H. (1999). A genetic association for cigarette smoking behavior. *Health Psychology, 18,* 7–13.

Sacks, O. (1995). *An anthropologist on Mars: Seven paradoxical tales.* New York, NY: Knopf.

Safdar, S., Friedlmeier, W., Matsumoto, D., Yoo, S. H., Kwantes, C. T., Kakai, H., & Shigemasu, E. (2009). Variations of emotional display rules within and across cultures: A comparison between Canada, USA, and Japan. *Canadian Journal of Behavioural Science / Revue canadienne des sciences du comportement, 41,* 1–10.

Saha, S., Chant, D. C., Welham, J. L., & McGrath, J. J. (2006). The incidence and prevalence of schizophrenia varies with latitude. *Acta Psychiatrica Scandinavica, 114,* 36–39.

Sala Frigerio, C., & De Strooper, B. (2016). Alzheimer's disease mechanisms and emerging roads to novel therapeutics. *Annual Review of Neuroscience, 39,* 57–79.

Salovey, P., & Grewel, D. (2005). The science of emotional intelligence. *Current Directions in Psychological Science, 14,* 281–286.

Salovey, P., & Mayer, J. D. (1990). Emotional intelligence. *Imagination, Cognition, and Personality, 9,* 185–211.

Salvador, R., Vega, D., Pascual, J. C., Marco, J., Canales-Rodríguez, E. J., Aguilar, S., . . . Pomarol-Clotet, E. (2016). Converging medial frontal resting state and diffusion-based abnormalities in borderline personality disorder. *Biological Psychiatry, 79,* 107–116.

Sana, F., Weston, T., & Cepeda, N. J. (2012). Laptop multitasking hinders classroom learning for both users and nearby peers. *Computers & Education, 62,* 24–31.

Sanbonmatsu, D. M., Strayer, D. L., Behrends, A. A., Ward, N., & Watson, J. M. (2016). Why drivers use cell phones and support legislation to restrict this practice. *Accident Analysis & Prevention, 92,* 22–33.

Sanford, A. J., Fay, N., Stewart, A., & Moxey, L. (2002). Perspective in statements of quantity, with implications for consumer psychology. *Psychological Science, 13,* 130–134.

Sargent, J. D., Beach, M. L., Adachi-Mejia, A. M., Gibson, J. J., Titus-Ernstoff, L. T., Carusi, C. P., . . . Dalton, M. A. (2005). Exposure to movie smoking: Its relation to smoking initiation among U.S. adolescents. *Pediatrics, 116,* 1183–1191.

Satterwhite, C. L., Torrone, E., Meites, E., Dunne, E. F., Mahajan, R., Ocfemia, M. C. B., Su, J., Xu, F., & Weinstock, H. (2013). Sexually transmitted infections among U.S. women and men: Prevalence and incidence estimates, 2008. *Sexually Transmitted Diseases, 40,* 187-193.

Savic, I., Berglund, H., & Lindström, P. (2005). Brain response to putative pheromones in homosexual men. *Proceedings of the National Academy of Sciences of the United States of America, 102,* 7356-7361.

Savin-Williams, R. C. (2016). Sexual orientation: Categories or continuum? Commentary on Bailey et al. (2016). *Psychological Science in the Public Interest, 17,* 37–44.

Savin-Williams, R. C., & Vrangalova, Z. (2012). Mostly heterosexual and mostly gay/lesbian: Evidence for new sexual orientation identities. *Archives of Sexual Behavior, 41,* 85–101.

Savin-Williams, R. C., & Vrangalova, Z. (2013). Mostly heterosexual as a distinct sexual orientation group: A systematic review of the empirical evidence. *Developmental Review, 33,* 58–88.

Savitz, D. A., Schwingle, P. J., & Keels, M. A. (1991). Influences of paternal age, smoking, and alcohol consumption on congenital anomalies. *Teratology, 44,* 429–440.

Sayal, K., Prasad, V., Daley, D., Ford, T., & Coghill, D. (2018). ADHD in children and young people: Prevalence, care pathways, and service provision. *The Lancet Psychiatry, 5,* 175–186.

Sayette, M. A. (1993). An appraisal-disruption model of alcohol's effects on stress responses in social drinkers. *Psychological Bulletin, 114,* 459–476.

Schacter, D. L., & Tulving, E. (1994). What are the memory systems of 1994? In D. L. Schacter & E. Tulving (Eds.), *Memory systems 1994* (pp. 1–38). Cambridge, MA: MIT Press.

Schachter, H. M., Pham, B., King, J., Langford, S., & Moher, D. (2001). How efficacious and safe is short-acting methylphenidate for the treatment of attention-deficit hyperactivity disorder in children and adolescents? A meta-analysis. *Canadian Medical Association Journal, 165,* 1475-1488.

Schachter, S. (1951). Deviation, rejection, and communication. *Journal of Abnormal Psychology, 46,* 190–207.

Schachter, S., & Singer, J. (1962). Cognitive, social, and physiological determinants of emotional state. *Psychological Review, 69,* 379–399.

Schagdarsurengin, U., & Steger, K. (2016). Epigenetics in male reproduction: Effect of paternal diet on sperm quality and offspring health. *Nature Reviews Urology, 13,* 584–595.

Schaie, K. W. (1990). Intellectual development in adulthood. In J. E. Birren & K. W. Schaie (Eds.), *Handbook of the psychology of aging* (3rd ed., pp. 291–319). New York, NY: Van Nostrand Reinhold.

Scheerer, M. (1963). Problem-solving. *Scientific American, 208,* 118–128.

Schmader, T. (2010). Stereotype threat deconstructed. *Current Directions in Psychological Science, 19,* 14–18.

Schmader, T., Johns, M., & Forbes, C. (2008). An integrated process model of stereotype threat effects on performance. *Psychological Review, 115,* 336–356.

Schmidt, N. B., & Keough, M. E. (2011). Treatment of panic. *Annual Review of Clinical Psychology, 6,* 241–256.

Schmitt, D. P., Allik, J., McCrae, R. R., & Benet-Martinez, V. (2007). The geographic distribution of big five personality traits: Patterns and profiles of human self-description across 56 nations. *Journal of Cross-Cultural Psychology, 38,* 173–212.

Schoenemann, P. T., Sheehan, M. J., & Glotzer, L. D. (2005). Prefrontal white matter volume is disproportionately larger in humans than in other primates. *Nature Neuroscience, 8,* 242–252.

Schooler, J. W., Mrazek, M. D., Baird, B., & Winkielman, P. (2015). Minding the mind: The value of distinguishing among unconscious, conscious, and metaconscious processes. In M. Mikulincer, P. R. Shaver, E. Borgida, & Bargh, J. A. (Eds.), *APA handbook of personality and social psychology, Volume 1: Attitudes and social cognition* (pp. 179–202). Washington, DC: American Psychological Association.

Schuch, F. B., Vancampfort, D., Richards, J., Rosenbaum, S., Ward, P., & Stubbs, B. (2016). Exercise as a treatment for depression: A meta-analysis adjusting for publication bias. *Journal of Psychiatric Research, 77,* 42–51.

Schultz, W. (2016). Dopamine reward prediction-error signalling: A two-component response. *Nature Reviews Neuroscience, 17,* 183–185.

Schulz, K. M., & Sisk, C. L. (2016). The organizing actions of adolescent gonadal steroid hormones on brain and behavioral development. *Neuroscience & Biobehavioral Reviews, 70,* 148–158.

Schumacher, J., Hoffmann, P., Schmäl, C., Schulte-Körne, G., & Nöthen, M. M. (2007). Genetics of dyslexia: The evolving landscape. *Journal of Medical Genetics, 44,* 289–297.

Schwartz, B. (2004). *The paradox of choice: Why more is less.* New York, NY: Ecco.

Schwartz, B., Ward, A., Monterosso, J., Lyubomirsky, S., White, K., & Lehman, D. R. (2002). Maximizing versus satisficing: Happiness is a matter of choice. *Journal of Personality and Social Psychology, 83,* 1178–1197.

Schwartz, C. E., Wright, C. I., Shin, L. M., Kagan, J., & Rauch, S. L. (2003). Inhibited and uninhibited infants "grown up": Adult amygdalar response to novelty. *Science, 300,* 1952–1953.

Schwartz, D. (2014). Arizona toddler with 160 IQ admitted to Mensa. Retrieved from http://www.reuters.com/article/2014/02/19/us-usa-arizona-genius-idUSBREA1I21020140219

Schwartz, S., & Maquet, P. (2002). Sleep imaging and the neuropsychological assessment of dreams. *Trends in Cognitive Sciences, 6,* 23–30.

Schwarz, N., & Clore, G. L. (1983). Mood, misattribution, and judgments of well-being: Informative and directive functions of affective states. *Journal of Personality and Social Psychology, 45,* 513–523.

Sclafani, A., & Springer, D. (1976). Dietary obesity in adult rats: Similarities to hypothalamic and human obesity syndromes. *Physiology and Behavior, 17,* 461–471.

Scott, C. L., & Cortez, A. (2011). No longer his and hers, but ours: Examining sexual arousal in response to erotic stories designed for both sexes. *Journal of Sex and Marital Therapy, 37,* 165–175.

Scudellari, M. (2013). Sex, cancer and a virus. *Nature, 503,* 330–332.

Seemiller, C., & Grace, M. (2017). Generation Z: Educating and engaging the next generation of students. *About Campus, 22,* 21–26.

Seery, M. D., Weisbuch, M., Hetenyi, M. A., & Blascovich, J. (2010). Cardiovascular measures independently predict performance in a university course. *Psychophysiology, 47,* 535–539.

Segerstrom, S. C., & Miller, G. E. (2004). Psychological stress and the human immune system: A meta-analytic study of 30 years of inquiry. *Psychological Bulletin, 130,* 601–630.

Seligman, M. E. P. (1970). On the generality of the laws of learning. *Psychological Review, 77,* 406–418.

Seligman, M. E. P. (1974). Depression and learned helplessness. In R. J. Friedman & M. M. Katz (Eds.), *The psychology of depression: Contemporary theory and research* (pp. 83–113). Washington, DC: V. H. Winston.

Seligman, M. E. P. (1975). *Helplessness: On depression, development, and death.* San Francisco: Freeman.

Seligman, M. E. P. (2011). *Flourish.* New York, NY: Simon & Schuster.

Seligman, M. E. P., & Csikszentmihalyi, M. (2000). Positive psychology: An introduction. *American Psychologist, 55,* 5–14.

Seligman, M. E. P., Steen, T. A., Park, N., & Peterson, C. (2005). Positive psychology progress: Empirical validation of interventions. *American Psychologist, 60,* 410–421.

Selkie, E. M., Fales, J. L., & Moreno, M. A. (2016). Cyberbullying prevalence among US middle and high school–aged adolescents: A systematic review and quality assessment. *Journal of Adolescent Health, 58,* 125–133.

Selye, H. (1936). A syndrome produced by diverse nocuous agents. *Nature, 138,* 32.

Serfass, D. G., & Sherman, R. A. (2013). Personality and perceptions of situations from the Thematic Apperception Test. *Journal of Research in Personality, 47,* 708–718.

Shapiro, A. F., Gottman, J. M., & Carrère, S. (2000). The baby and the marriage: Identifying factors that buffer against decline in marital satisfaction after the first baby arrives. *Journal of Family Psychology, 14,* 59–70.

Shaw, P., Malek, M., Watson, B., Sharp, W., Evans, A., & Greenstein, D. (2012). Development of cortical surface area and gyrification in attention-deficit/hyperactivity disorder. *Biological Psychiatry, 72,* 191–197.

Shedler, J., & Block, J. (1990). Adolescent drug use and psychological health: A longitudinal inquiry. *American Psychologist, 45,* 612–630.

Shenkin, S. D., Starr, J. M., & Deary, I. J. (2004). Birth weight and cognitive ability in childhood: A systematic review. *Psychological Bulletin, 130,* 989–1013.

Shephard, R. J. (1997). *Aging, physical activity, and health.* Champaign, IL: Human Kinetics Publishers.

Sher, K. J., Grekin, E. R., & Williams, N. A. (2005). The development of alcohol use disorders. *Annual Review of Clinical Psychology, 1,* 493–523.

Sherif, M., Harvey, O. J., White, B. J., Hood, W. R., & Sherif, C. W. (1961). *Intergroup cooperation and competition: The Robbers Cave experiment.* Norman, OK: University Book Exchange.

Sherman, D. K., McGue, M. K., & Iacono, W. G. (1997). Twin concordance for attention deficit hyperactivity disorder: A comparison of teacher's and mother's reports. *American Journal of Psychiatry, 154,* 532–535.

Sherman, S. J., Presson, C., Chassin, L., Corty, E., & Olshavsky, R. (1983). The false consensus effect in estimates of smoking prevalence: Underlying mechanisms. *Personality and Social Psychology Bulletin, 9,* 197–207.

Sherwin, B. B. (2008). Hormones, the brain, and me. *Canadian Psychology/ Psychologie Canadienne, 49,* 42–48.

Sherwood, R. A., Keating, J., Kavvadia, V., Greenough, A., & Peters, T. J. (1999). Substance misuse in early pregnancy and relationship to fetal outcome. *European Journal of Pediatrics, 158,* 488–492.

Shetty, A. K., & Upadhya, D. (2016). GABA-ergic cell therapy for epilepsy: Advances, limitations and challenges. *Neuroscience & Biobehavioral Reviews, 62,* 35–47.

Siegel, C. E., Laska, E. M., Wanderling, J. A., Hernandez, J. C., & Levenson, R. B. (2015). Prevalence and diagnosis rates of childhood ADHD among racial-ethnic groups in a public mental health system. *Psychiatric Services, 67,* 199–205.

Siegler, I. C., Costa, P. T., Brummett, B. H., Helms, M. J., Barefoot, J. C., Williams, R., . . . Rimer, B. K. (2003). Patterns of change in hostility from college to midlife in the UNC alumni heart study predict high-risk status. *Psychosomatic Medicine, 65,* 738–745.

Sievers, B., Polansky, L., Casey, M., & Wheatley, T. (2013). Music and movement share a dynamic structure that supports universal expressions of emotion. *Proceedings of the National Academy of Sciences, 110,* 70–75.

Siklenka, K., Erkek, S., Godmann, M., Lambrot, R., McGraw, S., Lafleur, C., . . . Kimmins, S. (2015). Disruption of histone methylation in developing sperm impairs offspring health transgenerationally. *Science, 350,* 651.

Silber, M., Ancoli-Israel, S., Bonnet, M., Chokroverty, S., Grigg-Damberger, M., Hirshkowitz, M., . . . Iber, C. (2007). The visual scoring of sleep in adults. *Journal of Clinical Sleep Medicine, 3,* 121–131.

Silva, C. E., & Kirsch, I. (1992). Interpretive sets, expectancy, fantasy proneness, and dissociation as predictors of hypnotic response. *Journal of Personality and Social Psychology, 63,* 847–856.

Simeone, J. C., Ward, A. J., Rotella, P., Collins, J., & Windisch, R. (2015). An evaluation of variation in published estimates of schizophrenia prevalence from 1990–2013: A systematic literature review. *BMC Psychiatry, 15,* 193.

Simner, J., Mulvenna, C., Sagiv, N., Tsakanikos, E., Witherby, S. A., Fraser, C., . . . Ward, J. (2006). Synaesthesia: The prevalence of atypical cross-modal experiences. *Perception, 35,* 1024–1033.

Simons, D. J., & Levin, D. T. (1998). Failure to detect changes to people during a real-world interaction. *Psychonomic Bulletin and Review, 5,* 644–649.

Simpson, H. B., Foa, E. B., Liebowitz, M. R., Ledley, D. R., Huppert, J. D., Cahill, S., . . . Petkova, E. (2008). A randomized, controlled trial of cognitive-behavioral therapy for augmenting pharmacotherapy in obsessive-compulsive disorder. *American Journal of Psychiatry, 165,* 621–630.

Sims, H. E. A., Goldman, R. F., Gluck, C. M., Horton, E., Kelleher, P., & Rowe, D. (1968). Experimental obesity in man. *Transactions of the Association of American Physicians, 81,* 153–170.

Sirois, B. C., & Burg, M. M. (2003). Negative emotion and coronary heart disease: A review. *Behavior Modification, 27,* 83–102.

Slovic, P., Finucane, M., Peters, E., & MacGregor, D. (2002). The affect heuristic. In T. Gilovich, D. Griffin, & D. Kahneman (Eds.), *Heuristics and biases: The psychology of intuitive judgment* (pp. 397–420). New York, NY: Cambridge University Press.

Smith, A. L., & Chapman, S. (2014). Quitting smoking unassisted: The 50-year research neglect of a major public health phenomenon. *Journal of the American Medical Association, 311,* 137–138.

Smith, A., Floerke, V., & Thomas, A. (2016). Retrieval practice protects memory against acute stress. *Science, 354,* 1046–1048.

Smith, C., & Lapp, L. (1991). Increases in number of REMs and REM density in humans following an intensive learning period. *Sleep, 14,* 325–330.

Smith, T. W. (1990). A report: The sexual revolution? *Public Opinion Quarterly, 54,* 415–435.

Smith, T. W., Orleans, C. T., & Jenkins, C. D. (2004). Prevention and health promotion: Decades of progress, new challenges, and an emerging agenda. *Health Psychology, 23,* 126–131.

Snarey, J. R. (1985). Cross-cultural universality of social-moral development: A critical review of Kohlbergian research. *Psychological Bulletin, 97,* 202–232.

Snowling, M. J., & Melby-Lervåg, M. (2016). Oral language deficits in familial dyslexia: A meta-analysis and review. *Psychological Bulletin, 142,* 498–545.

Solms, M. (2000). Dreaming and REM sleep are controlled by different brain mechanisms. *Behavioral and Brain Sciences, 23,* 793.

Sommerville, J. A., & Woodward, A. L. (2005). Pulling out the intentional structure of action: The relation between action processing and action production in infancy. *Cognition, 95,* 1–30.

Son Hing, L. S., Chung-Yan, G. A., Hamilton, L. K., & Zanna, M. P. (2008). A two-dimensional model that employs explicit and implicit attitudes to characterize prejudice. *Journal of Personality and Social Psychology, 94,* 971–987.

Sorensen, T., Holst, C., Stunkard, A. J., & Skovgaard, L. T. (1992). Correlations of body mass index of adult adoptees and their biological and adoptive relatives. *International Journal of Obesity and Related Metabolic Disorders, 16,* 227–236.

Sorrells, S. F., Paredes, M. F., Cebrian-Silla, A., Sandoval, K., Qi, D., Kelley, K. W., ... Alvarez-Buylla, A. (2018). Human hippocampal neurogenesis drops sharply in children to undetectable levels in adults. *Nature, 555,* 377–381.

Spanos, N. P., & Coe, W. C. (1992). A social-psychological approach to hypnosis. In E. Fromm & M. Nash (Eds.), *Contemporary hypnosis research* (pp. 102–130). New York, NY: Guilford Press.

Spape, J., Timmers, A. D., Yoon, S., Ponseti, J., & Chivers, M. L. (2014). Gender-specific genital and subjective sexual arousal to prepotentsexual features in heterosexual women and men. *Biological Psychology, 102,* 1–9.

Spearman, C. (1904). "General intelligence," objectively determined and measured. *American Journal of Psychology, 15,* 201–293.

Spelke, E. S. (2016). Cognitive abilities of infants. In R. J. Sternberg, S. T. Fiske, & D. J. Foss (Eds.), *Scientists making a difference: One hundred eminent behavioral and brain scientists talk about their most important contributions* (pp. 22–234). Cambridge, UK: Cambridge University Press.

Spence, C. (2012). Auditory contributions to flavour perception and feeding behaviour. *Physiology & Behavior, 107,* 505–515.

Spence, J. T., Helmreich, R., & Stapp, J. (1975). Ratings of self and peers on sex role attributes and their relation to self-esteem and conceptions of masculinity and femininity. *Journal of Personality and Social Psychology, 32,* 29–39.

Spencer, R. C., Devilbiss, D. M., & Berridge, C. W. (2015). The cognition-enhancing effects of psychostimulants involve direct action in the prefrontal cortex. *Biological Psychiatry, 77,* 940–950.

Spencer, S. J., Logel, C., & Davies, P. G. (2016). Stereotype threat. *Annual Review of Psychology, 67,* 415–437.

Spencer, S. J., Steele, C. M., & Quinn, D. M. (1999). Stereotype threat and women's math performance. *Journal of Experimental Social Psychology, 35,* 4–28.

Sperling, G. (1960). The information available in brief visual presentations. *Psychological Monographs, 74,* 1–29.

Spiegel, D., Lewis-Fernández, R., Lanius, R., Vermetten, E., Simeon, D., & Friedman, M. (2013). Dissociative disorders in DSM-5. *Annual Review of Clinical Psychology, 9,* 299–326.

Spurr, K. F., Graven, M. A., & Gilbert, R. W. (2008). Prevalence of unspecified sleep apnea and the use of continuous positive airway pressure in hospitalized patients, 2004 national hospital discharge survey. *Sleep and Breathing, 12,* 229–234.

Squire, L. R., & Moore, R. Y. (1979). Dorsal thalamic lesion in a noted case of human memory dysfunction. *Annals of Neurology, 6,* 503–506.

Squire, L. R., Stark, C. E. L., & Clark, R. E. (2004). The medial temporal lobe. *Annual Review of Neuroscience, 27,* 279–306.

Srivastava, S., John, O. P., Gosling, S. D., & Potter, J. (2003). Development of personality in early and middle adulthood: Set like plaster or persistent change? *Journal of Personality and Social Psychology, 84,* 1041–1053.

Stark, S. (2000, December 22). "Cast Away" lets Hanks fend for himself. *The Detroit News.* Retrieved from http://www.detnews.com

Steele, C. M., & Aronson, J. (1995). Stereotype threat and the intellectual test performance of African-Americans. *Journal of Personality and Social Psychology, 69,* 797–811.

Stein, J. (2013). *Millennials: The me me me generation. Time,* May 20, 2013. Retrieved from http://time.com/247/millennials-the-me-me-me-generation/

Stein, J. H., & Reiser, L. W. (1994). A study of white middle-class adolescent boys' responses to "semenarche" (the first ejaculation). *Journal of Youth and Adolescence, 23,* 373–384.

Stein, M. B., & Sareen, J. (2015). Generalized anxiety disorder. *New England Journal of Medicine, 373,* 2059–2068.

Stein, M. B., & Stein, D. J. (2008). Social anxiety disorder. *Lancet, 371,* 1115–1125.

Steinberg, L., & Sheffield, A. M. (2001). Adolescent development. *Journal of Cognitive Education and Psychology, 2,* 55–87.

Steiner, J. E. (1977). Facial expressions of the neonate infant indicating the hedonics of food-related chemical stimuli. In J. M. Weiffenbach (Ed.), *Taste and development* (pp. 173–189). Bethesda, MD: National Institutes of Health.

Stephenson, M. T., Hoyle, R. H., Palmgreen, P., & Slater, M. D. (2003). Brief measures of sensation seeking for screening and large-scale surveys. *Drug and Alcohol Dependence, 72,* 279–286.

Sternberg, R. J. (1986). A triangular theory of love. *Psychological Review, 93,* 119–135.

Sternberg, R. J. (1999). The theory of successful intelligence. *Review of General Psychology, 3,* 292–316.

Stewart, P. A. (2008). Subliminals in the 2000 presidential election: Policy implications of applied neuroscience. *Public Integrity, 10,* 215–232.

Stice, E. (2002). Risk and maintenance factors for eating pathology: A meta-analytic review. *Psychological Bulletin, 128,* 825–848.

Stokstad, E. (2001). New hints into the biological basis of autism. *Science, 294,* 34–37.

Stoner, J. A. (1968). Risky and cautious shifts in group decisions: The influence of widely held values. *Journal of Experimental Social Psychology, 4,* 442–459.

Strack, F. (2016). Reflection on the smiling registered replication report. *Perspectives on Psychological Science, 11,* 929–930.

Strack, F., Martin, L. L., & Stepper, S. (1988). Inhibiting and facilitating conditions of the human simile: A nonobtrusive test of the facial feedback hypothesis. *Journal of Personality and Social Psychology, 54,* 768–777.

Strayer, D. L. & Drews, F. A. (2007). Cell-phone-induced driver distraction. *Current Directions in Psychological Science, 16,* 128–131.

Strayhorn, T.L. (2014). What role does grit play in the academic success of black male collegians at predominantly white institutions? *Journal of African American Studies, 18,* 1–10.

Stryker, S. (2008). *Transgender history.* Berkeley, CA: Seal.

Stunkard, A. J. (1996). Current views on obesity. *American Journal of Medicine, 100,* 230–236.

Substance Abuse and Mental Health Services Administration (SAMHSA). (2011). Major depressive episode and treatment among adolescents: 2009. *National Survey on Drug Use and Health.* Retrieved from http://www.oas.samhsa.gov/2k11/ 009/AdolescentDepression .htm

Substance Abuse and Mental Health Services Administration (SAMHSA). (2014). *Results from the 2013 National Survey on Drug Use and Health: Summary of national findings.* NSDUH Series H-48, HHS Publication No. (SMA) 14-4863. Rockville, MD: Substance Abuse and Mental Health Services Administration.

Suchecki, D., Tiba, P., & Machado, R. (2012). REM sleep rebound as an adaptive response to stressful situations. *Frontiers in Neurology, 3,* 41.

Sun, S. S., Schubert, C. M., Liang, R., Roche, A. F., Kulin, H. E, Lee, P. A, . . . Chumlea, W. C. (2005). Is sexual maturity occurring earlier among U.S. children? *Journal of Adolescent Health, 37,* 345–355.

Sutin, A. R., Stephan, Y., & Terracciano, A. (2015). Weight discrimination and risk of mortality. *Psychological Science, 26,* 1803–1811.

Svenson, O. (1981). Are we all less risky and more skillful than our fellow drivers? *Acta Psychologica, 47,* 143–148.

Swaab, D. F. (2004). Sexual differentiation of the human brain: Relevance for gender identity, transsexualism and sexual orientation. *Gynecological Endocrinology, 19,* 301–312.

Swan, S. H., Liu, F., Hines, M., Kruse, R. L., Wang, C., Redmon, J. B., . . . Weiss, B. (2010). Prenatal phthalate exposure and reduced masculine play in boys. *International Journal of Andrology, 33,* 259–269.

Swanson, S. A., Crow, S. J., Le Grange, D., Swendsen, J., & Merikangas, K. R. (2011). Prevalence and correlates of eating disorders in adolescents: Results from the national comorbidity survey replication adolescent supplement. *Archives of General Psychiatry, 68,* 714–723.

Swendsen, J., Burstein, M., Case, B., Conway, K. P., Dierker, L., He, J., & Merikangas, K. R. (2012). Use and abuse of alcohol and illicit drugs in U.S. adolescents: Results of the National Comorbidity Survey— Adolescent supplement. *Archives of General Psychiatry, 69,* 390–398.

Sylva, D., Safron, A., Rosenthal, A. M., Reber, P. J., Parrish, T. B., Bailey, J. M. (2013). Neural correlates of sexual arousal in heterosexual and homosexual women and men. *Hormones and Behavior, 64,* 673–684.

Tajfel, H., & Turner, J. C. (1979). An integrative theory of intergroup conflict. In W. G. Austin & S. Worchel (Eds.), *The social psychology of intergroup relations* (pp. 33–47). Monterey, CA: Brooks/Cole.

Talarico, J. M., & Rubin, D. C. (2003). Confidence, not consistency, characterizes flashbulb memories. *Psychological Science, 14,* 455–461.

Talley, P. R., Strupp, H. H., & Morey, L. C. (1990). Matchmaking in psychotherapy: Patient-therapist dimensions and their impact on outcome. *Journal of Consulting and Clinical Psychology, 58,* 182–188.

Talmi, D. (2013). Enhanced emotional memory: Cognitive and neural mechanisms. *Current Directions in Psychological Science, 22,* 430–436.

Tang, Y. Y., Ma, Y. H., Wang, J., Fan, Y., Feng, S., Lu, Q. L., . . . Posner, M.I. (2007). Short-term meditation training improves attention and self-regulation. *Proceedings of the National Academy of Sciences, USA, 104,* 17152–17156.

Tangney, J. P., Stuewig, J., & Mashek, D. J. (2007). Moral emotions and moral behavior. *Annual Review of Psychology, 58,* 345–372.

Tanner, J. M. (1972). Human growth hormone. *Nature, 237,* 433–439.

Tanner, J. M., & Davies, P. S. W. (1985). Clinical longitudinal standards for height and height velocity for North American children. *Journal of Pediatrics, 107,* 317–329.

Tappé, M., Bensman, L., Hayashi, K., & Hatfield, E. (2013). Gender differences in receptivity to sexual offers: A new research prototype. *Interpersona, 7,* 323–344.

Tate, M. C., Herbet, G., Moritz-Gasser, S., Tate, J. E., & Duffau, H. (2014). Probabilistic map of critical functional regions of the human cerebral cortex: Broca's area revisited. *Brain, 137,* 2773–2782.

Tateyama, M., Asai, M., Kamisada, M., Hashimoto, M., Bartels, M., & Heimann, H. (1993). Comparison of schizophrenic delusions between Japan and Germany. *Psychopathology, 26,* 151–158.

Taylor, S. E. (2006). Tend and befriend: Biobehavioral bases of affiliation under stress. *Current Directions in Psychological Science, 15,* 273–277.

Taylor, S. E., & Brown, J. D. (1988). Illusion and well-being: A social psycho-logical perspective on mental health. *Psychological Bulletin, 103,* 193–210.

Taylor, S. E., Lewis, B. P., Gruenewald, T. L., Gurung, R. A. R., Updegraff, J. A., & Klein, L. C. (2002). Sex differences in biobehavioral responses to threat: Reply to Geary and Flinn. *Psychological Review, 109,* 751–753.

Teitelman, A. M. (2004). Adolescent girls' perspectives of family interactions related to menarche and sexual health. *Qualitative Health Research, 14,* 1292–1308.

Teller, D. Y., Morse, R., Borton, R., & Regal, C. (1974). Visual acuity for vertical and diagonal gratings in human infants. *Vision Research, 14,* 1433–1439.

Tessler, L. G. (1997). How college students with learning disabilities can advocate for themselves. Retrieved from http://www.ldanatl.org/ aboutld/adults/post_secondary/print_college.asp

Thomas, R., Sanders, S., Doust, J., Beller, E., & Glasziou, P. (2015). Prevalence of attention-deficit/hyperactivity disorder: A systematic review and meta-analysis. *Pediatrics, 135,* e994.

Thompson, P. M., Hayashi, K. M., Simon, S. L., Geaga, J. A., Hong, M. S., Sui, Y., . . . London, E. D. (2004). Structural abnormalities in the brains of human subjects who use methamphetamine. *Journal of Neuroscience, 24,* 6028–6036.

Thornton, A., & Young-DeMarco, L. (2001). Four decades of trends in attitudes toward family issues in the United States: The 1960s through the 1990s. *Journal of Marriage and Family, 63,* 1009–1037.

Tickle, J. J., Sargent, J. D., Dalton, M. A., Beach, M. L., & Heatherton, T. F. (2001). Favorite movie stars, their tobacco use in contemporary movies and its association with adolescent smoking. *Tobacco Control, 10,* 16–22.

Tiefer, L. (2000). Sexology and the pharmaceutical industry: The threat of co-optation. *Journal of Sex Research, 37,* 273–283.

Tienari, P., Lahti, I., Sorri, A., Naarala, M., Moring, J., Kaleva, M., . . . Wynne, L. C. (1990). Adopted-away offspring of schizophrenics and controls: The Finnish adoptive family study of schizophrenia. In L. Robins & M. Rutter (Eds.), *Straight and devious pathways from childhood to adulthood* (pp. 365–379). New York, NY: Cambridge University Press.

Tienari, P., Wynne, L. C., Moring, J., Lahti, I., Naarala, M., Sorri, A., . . . Laksy, K. (1994). The Finnish adoptive family study of schizophrenia: Implications for family research. *British Journal of Psychiatry, 23*(Suppl.), 20–26.

Tienari, P., Wynne, L. C., Sorri, A., Lahti, I., Laksy, K., Moring, J., . . . Wahlberg, K. E. (2004). Genotype-environment interaction in schizophrenia spectrum disorder. *British Journal of Psychiatry, 184,* 216–222.

Tolman, E. C., & Honzik, C. H. (1930). Introduction and removal of reward, and maze performance in rats. *University of California Publications in Psychology, 4,* 257–275.

Tomkins, S. S. (1963). *Affect imagery consciousness: Vol. 2. The negative affects.* New York, NY: Tavistock/Routledge.

Tong, F., Nakayama, K., Vaughan, J. T., & Kanwisher, N. (1998). Binocular rivalry and visual awareness in human extrastriate cortex. *Neuron, 21,* 753–759.

Torrey, E. F. (1999). Epidemiological comparison of schizophrenia and bipolar disorder. *Schizophrenia Research, 39,* 101–106.

Tracy, J. L., & Matsumoto, D. (2008). The spontaneous display of pride and shame: Evidence for biologically innate nonverbal displays. *Proceedings of the National Academy of Sciences, USA, 105,* 11655–11660.

Tracy, J. L., & Robins, R. W. (2008). The nonverbal expression of pride: Evidence for cross-cultural recognition. *Journal of Personality and Social Psychology, 94,* 516–530.

Treanor, M., Brown, L. A., Rissman, J., & Craske, M. G. (2017). Can memories of traumatic experiences or addiction be erased or modified? A critical review of research on the disruption of memory reconsolidation and its applications. *Perspectives on Psychological Science, 12,* 290–305.

Treatment for Adolescents with Depression Study (TADS) Team. (2004). Fluoxetine, cognitive-behavioral therapy, and their combination for adolescents with depression: Treatment for Adolescents with Depression Study (TADS) randomized controlled trial. *Journal of the American Medical Association, 292,* 807–820.

Treffert, D. A., & Christensen, D. D. (2006). Inside the mind of a savant. *Scientific American Mind, 17,* 50–55.

Treisman, A., & Gelade, G. (1980). A feature-integration theory of attention. *Cognitive Psychology, 12,* 97–136.

Triandis, H. C. (1989). The self and social behavior in differing cultural contexts. *Psychological Review, 96,* 506–520.

Trivers, R. L. (1971). The evolution of reciprocal altruism. *Quarterly Review of Biology, 46,* 35–57.

Trzesniewski, K. H., Donnellan, M. B., & Roberts, R. W. (2008). Is "generation me" really more narcissistic than previous generations? *Journal of Personality, 76,* 903–918.

Tucker, E. W., & Potocky-Tripodi, M. (2006). Changing heterosexuals' attitudes toward homosexuals: A systematic review of the empirical literature. *Research on Social Work Practice, 16,* 176–190.

Tugade, M. M., & Fredrickson, B. L. (2004). Resilient individuals use positive emotions to bounce back from negative emotional experiences. *Journal of Personality and Social Psychology, 86,* 320–333.

Tulving, E. (1972). Episodic and semantic memory. In E. Tulving & W. Donaldson (Eds.), *Organization of memory* (pp. 381–403). New York, NY: Academic Press.

Twenge, J. M. (2017). *iGen: Why today's super-connected kids are growing up less rebellious, more tolerant, less happy—and completely unprepared for adulthood (and what this means for the rest of us).* New York, NY: Atria Books.

Twenge, J. M., Joiner, T. E., Rogers, M. L., & Martin, G. N. (2018). Increases in depressive symptoms, suicide-related outcomes, and suicide rates among US adolescents after 2010 and links to increased new media screen time. *Clinical Psychological Science, 6,* 3–17.

Twenge, J. M., Konrath, S., Foster, J. D., Campbell, K. W., & Bushman, B. J. (2008). Egos inflating over time: A cross-temporal meta-analysis of the narcissistic personality inventory. *Journal of Personality, 76,* 875–902.

Tyrer, L. (1999). Introduction of the pill and its impact. *Contraception, 59,* 11S–16S.

Üçok, A., & Ergül, C. (2014). Persistent negative symptoms after first episode schizophrenia: A 2-year follow-up study. *Schizophrenia Research, 158,* 241–246.

Umberson, D. (1992). Gender, marital status and the social control of health behavior. *Social Science & Medicine, 34,* 907–917.

United Nations Office on Drugs and Crime. (2013a). *Global study on homicide 2013: Trends, contexts, data.* Vienna, Austria: Author.

United Nations Office on Drugs and Crime. (2013b). *World drug report 2013.* United Nations publication, Sales No. E.13.XI.6.

U.S. Bureau of Labor Statistics, U.S. Department of Labor. (2017a). Psychologists. *Occupational outlook handbook, 2016–2017 edition.* Retrieved from https://www.bls.gov/ooh/life-physical-and-social-science/psychologists.htm

U.S. Bureau of Labor Statistics, U.S. Department of Labor. (2017b). Substance abuse, behavioral disorder, and mental health counselors. *Occupational outlook handbook, 2016–2017 edition.* Retrieved from https://www.bls.gov/ooh/community-and-social-service/substance-abuse-and-behavioral-disorder-counselors.htm

United States Department of Health and Human Services (USDHHS). (2008). Physical activity guidelines for Americans. Retrieved from http://www.health.gov/paguidelines

United States Department of Health and Human Services (USDHHS). (2014). *The health consequences of smoking— 50 years of progress: A report of the Surgeon General.* Atlanta, GA: U.S. Government Printing Office.

United States Department of Health and Human Services (USDHHS), Office of the Surgeon General. (2004, May 27). *The health consequences of smoking: A report of the Surgeon General.* Retrieved from http://www.surgeongeneral.gov/library/reports/smokingconsequences

Urberg, K. A., Değirmencioğlu, S. M., Tolson, J. M., & Halliday-Scher, K. (1995). The structure of adolescent peer networks. *Developmental Psychology, 31,* 540–547.

Ustün, T. B., Ayuso-Mateos, J. L., Chatterji, S., Mathers, C., & Murray, C. J. (2004). Global burden of depressive disorders in the year 2000. *British Journal of Psychiatry, 184,* 386–392.

Vallabha, G. K., McClelland, J. L., Pons, F., Werker, J. F., & Amano, S. (2007). Unsupervised learning of vowel categories from infant-directed speech. *Proceedings of the National Academy of Sciences, USA, 104,* 13273–13278.

Van der Oord, S., Prins, P. J. M., Oosterlaan, J., & Emmelkamp, P. M. G. (2008). Efficacy of methylphenidate, psychosocial treatments and their combination in school-aged children with ADHD: A meta-analysis. *Clinical Psychology Review, 28,* 783–800.

van IJzendoorn, M. H. (1995). Adult attachment representations, parental responsiveness, and infant attachment: A meta-analysis on the predictive validity of the Adult Attachment Interview. *Psychologial Bulletin, 117,* 387–403.

Van Ijzendoorn, M. H., & Kroonenberg, P. M. (1988). Cross-cultural patterns of attachment: A meta-analysis of the strange situation. *Child Development, 59,* 147–156.

Van Lange, P. A. M., Rinderu, M. I., & Bushman, B. J. (2017). Aggression and violence around the world: A model of CLimate, Aggression, and Self-control in Humans (CLASH). *Behavioral and Brain Sciences, 40,* e75.

Van Luling, T. (2017, updated October 11). Austin Rogers explains the real secrets to his "Jeopardy!" success: Spending a night in Brooklyn watching "Jeopardy!" with the current champion. *The Huffington Post.* Retrieved from https://www.huffingtonpost.com/entry/austin-rogers-jeopardy_us_59dcd961e4b0b34afa5c74c2

Vargas-Reighley, R. V. (2005). *Bicultural competence and academic resilience among immigrants.* El Paso, TX: LFB Scholarly Publishing.

Vargha-Khadem, F., Gadian, D. G., Watkins, K. E., Connelly, A., Van Paesschen, W., & Mishkin, M. (1997). Differential effects of early hippocampal pathology on episodic and semantic memory. *Science, 277,* 376–380.

Varley, T. (2015, July 16). "Iron Mike" anchored the Steelers line. *Steelers.com.* Retrieved from http://www.steelers.com/news/article-1/Iron-Mike-anchored-the-Steelers-line/b636ea92-0fb6-4b53-be6d-040c953b6142

Vazire, S., & Carlson, E. N. (2011). Others sometimes know us better than we know ourselves. *Current Directions in Psychological Science, 20,* 104–108.

Venkatraman, V., Dimoka, A., Pavlou, P. A., Vo, K., Hampton, W., Bollinger, B., . . . Winer, R. S. (2015). Predicting advertising success beyond traditional measures: New insights from neurophysiological measures and market response modeling. *Journal of Marketing Research, 52,* 436–452.

Villemagne, V. L., Burnham, S., Bourgeat, P., Brown, B., Ellis, K. A., Salvado, O., . . . Masters, C. L. (2013). Amyloid β deposition, neurodegeneration, and cognitive decline in sporadic Alzheimer's disease: A prospective cohort study. *The Lancet Neurology, 12*, 357–367.

Vismara, L., & Rogers, S. (2010). Behavioral treatments in autism spectrum disorders: What do we know? *Annual Review of Clinical Psychology, 6*, 447–468.

Voelker, R. (2012, November). Hot careers: Sport psychology. *gradPSYCH Magazine*. Retrieved from http://www.apa.org/gradpsych/2012/11/sport-psychology.aspx

Volkmar, F., Chawarska, K., & Klin, A. (2005). Autism in infancy and early childhood. *Annual Review of Psychology, 56*, 1–21.

Volkow, N. D. (2007). This is your brain on food. Interview by Kristin Leutwyler-Ozelli. *Scientific American, 297*, 84–85.

Volkow, N. D. (2016). Opioids in pregnancy. *British Medical Journal, 352*, i19.

Volkow, N. D., Wang, G. J., & Baler, R. D. (2011). Reward, dopamine, and the control of food intake: Implications for obesity. *Trends in Cognitive Science, 15*, 37–46.

von Stumm, S., & Plomin, R. (2015). Socioeconomic status and the growth of intelligence from infancy through adolescence. *Intelligence, 48*, 30–36.

Vrangalova, Z., & Savin-Williams, R. C. (2012). Mostly heterosexual and mostly gay/lesbian: Evidence for new sexual orientation identities. *Archives of Sexual Behavior, 41*, 85–101.

Vukasović, T., & Bratko, D. (2015). Heritability of personality: A meta-analysis of behavior genetic studies. *Psychological Bulletin, 141*, 769.

Vygotsky, L. S. (1978). *Mind in society*. Cambridge, MA: Harvard University Press.

Wagenmakers, E. J., Beek, T., Dijkhoff, L., Gronau, Q. F., Acosta, A., Adams Jr., R. B., . . . Zwaan, R. (2016). Registered replication report: Strack, Martin, & Stepper (1988). *Perspectives on Psychological Science, 11*, 917–928.

Waite, L. J. (1995). Does marriage matter? *Demography, 32*, 483–507.

Walder, D. J., Faraone, S. V., Glatt, S. J., Tsuang, M. T., & Seidman, L. J. (2014). Genetic liability, prenatal health, stress and family environment: Risk factors in the Harvard Adolescent Family High Risk for Schizophrenia Study. *Schizophrenia Research, 157*, 142–148.

Walker, E., Kestler, L., Bollini, A., & Hochman, K. M. (2004). Schizophrenia: Etiology and course. *Annual Review of Psychology, 55*, 401–430.

Walker, M. P., & Stickgold, R. (2006). Sleep, memory, and plasticity. *Annual Review of Psychology, 57*, 139–166.

Walkup, J. T. (2017). Antidepressant efficacy for depression in children and adolescents: Industry- and NIMH-funded studies. *American Journal of Psychiatry, 174*, 430–437.

Walton, G. M., & Spencer, S. J. (2009). Latent ability: Grades and test scores systematically underestimate the intellectual ability of negatively stereotyped students. *Psychological Science, 20*, 1132–1139.

Wamsley, E. J., Tucker, M., Payne, J. D., Benavides, J. A., & Stickgold, R. (2010). Dreaming of a learning task is associated with enhanced sleep-dependent memory consolidation. *Current Biology, 20*, 850–855.

Wang, C., Swerdloff, R. S., Iranmanesh, A., Dobs, A., Snyder, P. J., Cunningham, G., . . . Berman, N.: Testosterone Gel Study Group. (2000). Transdermal testosterone gel improves sexual function, mood, muscle strength, and body composition parameters in hypogonadal men. *The Journal of Clinical Endocrinology & Metabolism, 85*, 2839–2853.

Ward, Z. J., Long, M. W., Resch, S. C., Giles, C. M., Cradock, A. L., & Gortmaker, S. L. (2017). Simulation of growth trajectories of childhood obesity into adulthood. *New England Journal of Medicine, 377*, 2145–2153.

Wardenaar, K. J., Lim, C. C. W., Al-Hamzawi, A. O., Alonso, J., Andrade, L. H., Benjet, C., . . . de Jonge, P. (2017). The cross-national epidemiology of specific phobia in the World Mental Health Surveys. *Psychological Medicine, 47*, 1744–1760.

Wardle, J., Carnell, S., Haworth, C. M., & Plomin, R. (2008). Evidence for a strong genetic influence on childhood adiposity despite the force of the obesogenic environment. *American Journal of Clinical Nutrition, 87*, 398–404.

Warren, Z., McPheeters, M., Sathe, N., Foss-Feig, J. H., Glasser, A., & Veenstra-Vanderweele, J. (2011). A systematic review of early intensive intervention for autism spectrum disorders. *Pediatrics, 127*, e1303–e1311.

Washburn, M. F. (1908). *The animal mind: A textbook of comparative psychology*. New York, NY: Macmillan.

Waters, E., Matas, L., & Sroufe, L. A. (1975). Infants' reactions to an approaching stranger: Description, validation, and functional significance of wariness. *Child Development, 46*, 348–356.

Watson, D., & Clark, L. A. (1997). Extraversion and its positive emotional core. In R. Hogan, J. Johnson, & S. Briggs (Eds.), *Handbook of personality psychology* (pp. 767–793). San Diego, CA: Academic Press.

Watson, D., Wiese, D., Vaidya, J., & Tellegen, A. (1999). The two general activation systems of affect: Structural findings, evolutionary considerations, and psychobiological evidence. *Journal of Personality and Social Psychology, 76*, 820–838.

Watson, J. B. (1924). *Behaviorism*. New York, NY: Norton.

Weaver, J. B., Masland, J. L., & Zillmann, D. (1984). Effect of erotica on young men's aesthetic perception of their female sexual partners. *Perceptual and Motor Skills, 58*, 929–930.

Wedge, M. (2012, September 4). From ADHD kid to Olympic gold medalist. *Psychology Today*. Retrieved from https://www.psychologytoday.com/blog/suffer-the-children/201209/adhd-kid-olympic-gold-medalist

Wegner, D., Shortt, J., Blake, A., & Page, M. (1990). The suppression of exciting thoughts. *Journal of Personality and Social Psychology, 58*, 409–418.

Weinberger, A. H., Gbedemah, M., Martinez, A. M., Nash, D., Galea, S., & Goodwin, R. D. (2018). Trends in depression prevalence in the USA from 2005 to 2015: Widening disparities in vulnerable groups. *Psychological Medicine, 48*, 1308–1315.

Weiner, B. (1974). *Achievement motivation and attribution theory*. Morristown, NJ: General Learning Press.

Weissman, M. M., Bland, R. C., Canino, G. J., Greenwald, S., Hwu, H. G., Lee, C. K., . . . Yeh, E. K. (1994). The cross national epidemiology of obsessive compulsive disorder. The cross national collaborative group. *Journal of Clinical Psychiatry, 55*, 5–10.

Weller, S., & Davis-Beaty, K. (2002). The effectiveness of male condoms in prevention of sexually transmitted diseases (protocol). *Cochrane Database of Systematic Reviews*, Issue 4, Art. No. CD004090.

Wells, G. L., Small, M., Penrod, S., Malpass, R. S., Fulero, S. M., & Brimacombe, C. A. E. (1998). Eyewitness identification procedures: Recommendations for lineups and photospreads. *Law and Human Behavior, 22*, 603–647.

Wen, C. P., Wai, J. P. M., Tsai, M. K., Yang, Y. C., Cheng, T. Y. D., Lee, M.-C., . . . Wu, X. (2011). Minimal amount of physical activity for reduced mortality and extended life expectancy: A prospective cohort study. *Lancet, 378*, 1244–1253.

Wermeling, D. P. (2013). A response to the opioid overdose epidemic: Naloxone nasal spray. *Drug Delivery and Translational Research, 3*: 63–74.

West, G., Anderson, A., & Pratt, J. (2009). Motivationally significant stimuli show visual prior entry: Direct evidence for attentional capture. *Journal of Experimental Psychology: Human Perception and Performance, 35*, 1032–1042.

Westen, D. (1998). The scientific legacy of Sigmund Freud: Toward a psychodynamically informed psychological science. *Psychological Bulletin, 124*, 333–371.

Weyandt, L. L., Janusis, G., Wilson, K., Verdi, G., Paquin, G., Lopes, J., . . . Dussault, C. (2009). Nonmedical prescription stimulant use among a sample of college students: Relationships with psychological variables. *Journal of Attention Disorders, 13*, 284–296.

Weyandt, L. L., Marraccini, M. E., Gudmundsdottir, B. G., Zavras, B. M., Turcotte, K. D., Munro, B. A., & Amoroso, A. J. (2013). Misuse of prescription stimulants among college students: A review of the literature and implications for morphological and cognitive effects on brain functioning. *Experimental and Clinical Psychopharmacology, 21,* 385–407.

Whalen, C. K. (1989). Attention deficit and hyperactivity disorders. In T. H. Ollendick & M. Herson (Eds.), *Handbook of child psychopathology* (2nd ed., pp. 131–169). New York, NY: Plenum Press.

Whalen, P. J., Raila, H., Bennett, R., Mattek, A., Brown, A., Taylor, J., . . . Palmer, A. (2013). Neuroscience and facial expressions of emotion: The role of amygdala–prefrontal interactions. *Emotion Review, 5,* 78–83.

Whalen, P. J., Rauch, S. L., Etcoff, N. L., McInerney, N. L., Lee, M. B., & Jenike, M. A. (1998). Masked presentations of emotional facial expressions modulate amygdala activity without explicit knowledge. *Journal of Neuroscience, 18,* 411–418.

Wheatley, T., & Haidt, J. (2005). Hypnotic disgust makes moral judgments more severe. *Psychological Science, 16,* 780–784.

White, C. M. (2014). 3, 4-Methylenedioxymethamphetamine's (MDMA's) impact on posttraumatic stress disorder. *Annals of Pharmacotherapy, 48,* 908–915.

Wierson, M., Long, P. J., & Forehand, R. L. (1993). Toward a new understanding of early menarche: The role of environmental stress in pubertal timing. *Adolescence, 28,* 913–924.

Wight, R. G., LeBlanc, A. J., & Lee Badgett, M. V. (2013). Same-sex legal marriage and psychological well-being: Findings from the California Health Interview Survey. *American Journal of Public Health, 103,* 339–346.

Wilens, T. E., Faraone, S. V., & Biederman, J. (2004). Attention-deficit/hyperactivity disorder in adults. *Journal of the American Medical Association, 292,* 619–623.

Wilfley, D. E., Bishop, M., Wilson, G. T., & Agras, W. S. (2007). Classification of eating disorders: Toward *DSM-V*. *International Journal of Eating Disorders, 40*(Suppl.), S123–S129.

Williams, K., Harkins, S. G., & Latané, B. (1981). Identifiability as a deterrent to social loafing: Two cheering experiments. *Journal of Personality and Social Psychology, 40,* 303–311.

Williams, M. E., & Fredriksen-Goldsen, K. I. (2014). Same-sex partnerships and the health of older adults. *Journal of Community Psychology, 42,* 558–570.

Williams, R. B., Jr. (1987). Refining the type A hypothesis: Emergence of the hostility complex. *American Journal of Cardiology, 60,* 27J–32J.

Williams, T. J., Pepitone, M. E., Christensen, S. E., Cooke, B. M., Huberman, A. D., Breedlove, N. J., . . . Breedlove, S. M. (2000). Finger-length ratios and sexual orientation. *Nature, 404,* 455–456.

Willis, J., & Todorov, A. (2006). First impressions: Making up your mind after a 100-ms exposure to a face. *Psychological Science, 17,* 592–598.

Wills, T. A., DuHamel, K., & Vaccaro, D. (1995). Activity and mood temperament as predictors of adolescent substance use: Test of a self-regulation mediational model. *Journal of Personality and Social Psychology, 68,* 901–916.

Wills, T. A., Knight, R., Sargent, J. D., Gibbons, F. X., Pagano, I., & Williams, R. J. (2017). Longitudinal study of e-cigarette use and onset of cigarette smoking among high school students in Hawaii. *Tobacco Control, 26,* 34–39.

Wilson, A. E., & Ross, M. (2001). From chump to champ: People's appraisals of their earlier and present selves. *Journal of Personality and Social Psychology, 80,* 572–584.

Wilson, M. A., & McNaughton, B. L. (1994). Reactivation of hippocampal ensemble memories during sleep. *Science, 265,* 676–679.

Wilson, T. D., & Gilbert, D. T. (2003). Affective forecasting. In M. Zanna (Ed.), *Advances in experimental social psychology* (Vol. 35, pp. 345–411). New York, NY: Elsevier.

Wilson-Mendenhall, C. D., Barrett, L. F., & Barsalou, L. W. (2013). Neural evidence that human emotions share core affective properties. *Psychological Science, 24,* 947–956.

Winberg, J., & Porter, R. H. (1998). Olfaction and human neonatal behaviour: Clinical implications. *Acta Paediatrica, 87,* 6–10.

Winkler, D., Pjrek, E., Spies, M., Willeit, M., Dorffner, G., Lanzenberger R., & Kasper S. (2017). Has the existence of seasonal affective disorder been disproven? *Journal of Affective Disorders, 208,* 54–55.

Winograd, M. & Hais, M. (2014). How millennials could upend Wall Street and corporate America. Brookings Institute. Retrieved from https://www.brookings.edu/wp-content/uploads/2016/06/Brookings_Winogradfinal.pdf

Wiseman, C. V., Harris, W. A., & Halmi, K. A. (1998). Eating disorders. *Medical Clinics of North America, 82,* 145–159.

Wolpe, J. (1997). Thirty years of behavior therapy. *Behavior Therapy, 28,* 633–635.

Wolters, C. A., & Hussain, M. (2015). Investigating grit and its relations with college students' self-regulated learning and academic achievement. *Metacognition and Learning, 10,* 293–311.

Wong, B. (2011). Point of view: Color blindness. *Nature Methods, 8,* 441.

Wood, D. M., Stribley, V., Dargan, P. I., Davies, S., Holt, D. W., & Ramsey, J. (2011). Variability in the 3, 4-methylenedioxymethamphetamine content of "ecstasy" tablets in the UK. *Emergency Medicine Journal, 28,* 764–765.

Wood, H., Sasaki, S., Bradley, S. J., Singh, D., Fantus, S., Owen-Anderson, A., . . . Zucker, K. J. (2013). Patterns of referral to a gender identity service for children and adolescents (1976–2011): Age, sex ratio, and sexual orientation. *Journal of Sex & Marital Therapy, 39,* 1–6.

Wood, J. M., Garb, H. N., Lilienfeld, S. O., & Nezworski, M. T. (2002). Clinical assessment. *Annual Review of Psychology, 53,* 519–543.

Woodworth, M., & Porter, S. (2002). In cold blood: Characteristics of criminal homicides as a function of psychopathy. *Journal of Abnormal Psychology, 111,* 436–445.

Woolf, S. H., Chapman, D. A., Buchanich, J. M., Bobby, K. J., Zimmerman, E. B., & Blackburn, S. M. (2018). Changes in midlife death rates across racial and ethnic groups in the United States: Systematic analysis of vital statistics. *BMJ, 362,* k3096.

Woolfe, Z. (2017, November 7). At the Met Opera, a note so high, it's never been sung before. *The New York Times,* C1.

World Health Organization. (2000). Effectiveness of male latex condoms in protecting against pregnancy and sexually transmitted infections. Retrieved from http://www.who.int/mediacentre/factsheets/fs243/en

World Health Organization. (2008). WHO Report on the global tobacco epidemic. Retrieved from http://www.who.int/tobacco/mpower/en/

World Health Organization. (2011). Fact sheet: The top ten causes of death. Retrieved from http://www.who.int/mediacentre/factsheets/fs310/en/index.html

World Health Organization. (2016). Fact sheet: Obesity and overweight. Retrieved from http://www.who.int/mediacentre/factsheets/fs311/en/

World Health Organization. (2018a). Fact sheet: Suicide. Retrieved from http://www.who.int/mediacentre/factsheets/fs398/en/

World Health Organization. (2018b). Fact sheet: Depression. Retrieved from http://www.who.int/mediacentre/factsheets/fs369/en/

Worley, H. (2006, June). Depression: A leading contributor to global burden of disease; Myriad obstacles—particularly stigma—block better treatment in developing countries. Retrieved from http://www.prb.org/Articles/2006/DepressionaLeadingContributortoGlobalBurdenofDisease.aspx

Wray, N. R., Byrne, E. M., Stringer, S., & Mowry, B. J. (2014). Future directions in genetics of psychiatric disorders. In S. H. Rhee & A. Ronald (Eds.), *Behavior genetics of psychopathology* (pp. 311–337). New York, NY: Springer.

Wray, N. R., & Gottesman, I. I. (2012). Using summary data from the Danish National Registers to estimate heritabilities for schizophrenia, bipolar disorder, and major depressive disorder. *Frontiers in Genetics, 3,* 118.

Xu, F., Sternberg, M. R., Kottiri, B. J., McQuillan, G. M., Lee, F. K., Nahmias, A. J., ... Markowitz. L. E. (2006). Trends in herpes simplex virus type 1 and type 2 seroprevalence in the United States. *Journal of the American Medical Association, 296,* 964–973.

Xu, J., Murphy, S. L., Kochanek, K. D., & Arias, E. (2016). *Mortality in the United States, 2015.* (NCHS Data Brief No. 267). Hyattsville, MD: National Center for Health Statistics.

Xu, J., & Roberts, R. E. (2010). The power of positive emotions: It's a matter of life or death—subjective well-being and longevity in a general population. *Health Psychology, 29,* 9–19.

Yates, W. R. (2000). Testosterone in psychiatry: Risks and benefits. *Archives of General Psychiatry, 57,* 155–156.

Yazdy, M. M., Desai, R. J., & Brogly, S. B. (2015). Prescription opioids in pregnancy and birth outcomes: A review of the literature. *Journal of Pediatric Genetics, 4,* 56–70.

Yeager, D. S., & Dweck, C. S. (2012). Mindsets that promote resilience: When students believe that personal characteristics can be developed. *Educational Psychologist, 47,* 302–314.

Yerkes, R. M., & Dodson, J. D. (1908). The relation of strength of stimulus to rapidity of habit formation. *Journal of Comparative Neurology & Psychology, 18,* 459–482.

Yeshurun, Y., & Sobel, N. (2010). An odor is not worth a thousand words: From multidimensional odors to unidimensional odor objects. *Annual Review of Psychology, 61,* 219–241.

Yoo, S. S., Hu, P. T., Gujar, N., Jolesz, F. A., & Walker, M. P. (2007). A deficit in the ability to form new human memories without sleep. *Nature Neuroscience, 10,* 385–392.

Youngstedt, S. D., & Kline, C. E. (2006). Epidemiology of exercise and sleep. *Sleep and Biological Rhythms, 4,* 215–221.

Yousafzai, M. (2013). *I am Malala: The girl who stood up for education and was shot by the Taliban.* New York, NY: Little, Brown.

Youyou, W., Stillwell, D., Schwartz, H. A., & Kosinski, M. (2017). Birds of a feather do flock together: Behavior-based personality-assessment method reveals personality similarity among couples and friends. *Psychological Science, 28,* 276–284.

Zahn-Waxler, C., & Robinson, J. (1995). Empathy and guilt: Early origins of feelings of responsibility. In J. P. Tangney & K. W. Fischer (Eds.), *Self-conscious emotions: The psychology of shame, guilt, embarrassment, and pride* (pp. 143–173). New York, NY: Guilford Press.

Zajonc, R. B. (1968). Attitudinal effects of mere exposure. *Journal of Personality and Social Psychology Monographs, 9,* 1–27.

Zajonc, R. B. (1980). Feeling and thinking: Preferences need no inferences. *American Psychologist, 35,* 151–175.

Zajonc, R. B. (2001). Mere exposure: A gateway to the subliminal. *Current Directions in Psychological Science, 10,* 224–228.

Zametkin, A. J., Nordahl, T. E., Gross, M., King, A. C., Stemple, W. E., Rumsey, J., ... Cohen, R. M. (1990). Cerebral glucose metabolism in adults with hyperactivity of childhood onset. *New England Journal of Medicine, 323,* 1361–1366.

Zellner, D. A., Siemers, E., Teran, V., Conroy, R., Lankford, M., Agrafiotis, A., ... Locher, P. (2011). Neatness counts: How plating affects liking for the taste of food. *Appetite, 57,* 642–648.

Zetterberg, H., Smith, D. H., & Blennow, K. (2013). Biomarkers of mild traumatic brain injury in cerebrospinal fluid and blood. *Nature Reviews Neurology, 9,* 201–210.

Zillmann, D. (1989). Aggression and sex: Independent and joint operations. In H. Wagner & A. Manstead (Eds.), *Handbook of social psychophysiology* (pp. 229–259). New York, NY: Wiley.

Zorrilla, E. P., Iwasaki, S., Moss, J. A., Chang, J., Otsuji, J., Inoue, K., ... Janda, K. D. (2006). Vaccination against weight gain. *Proceedings of the National Academy of Sciences, USA, 103,* 13226–13231.

Zou, Z., Li, F., & Buck, L. B. (2005). From the cover: Odor maps in the olfactory cortex. *Proceedings of the National Academy of Sciences, 102,* 7724–7729.

Zucchi, F. C., Yao, Y., Ward, I. D., Ilnytskyy, Y., Olson, D. M., Benzies, K., ... Metz, G. A. (2013). Maternal stress induces epigenetic signatures of psychiatric and neurological diseases in the offspring. *PLOS ONE, 8,* e56967.

Zuckerman, M., Li, C., & Hall, J. A. (2016). When men and women differ in self-esteem and when they don't: A meta-analysis. *Journal of Research in Personality, 64,* 34–51.

PERMISSIONS ACKNOWLEDGMENTS

FRONT MATTER

Meet the Authors Sarah Grison: Photo Courtesy of Daniel Kolen (dkmedia.productions); Michael Gazzaniga: Baron Stafford
Mission of *Psychology in Your Life* Laura Scaletta: Courtesy of Deb Vukelich; Gabrielle (Gabby) Wessels: Courtesy of Kathy Northcott; Jon Skalski: Courtesy of Rockford University (Brian Thomas Photography); James Sturges: Courtesy of Trés Palmer; Salman Khan: Courtesy of Salman Khan; Thipachan (Mia) Radanavong: Courtesy of Nina Lüttel; Krishna Stilianos: Courtesy of Crist Stilianos; Robin Musselman: Courtesy of Kate Stauter/Frank Mitman Studio **Table of Contents** (in chronological order): Getty Images/Cultura RF; Joe McBride/Getty Images; Sverre Haugland/Image Source/Corbis; Rhea Anna/Gallery Stock; Ollyy/Shutterstock; Bela Szandelszky/AP; Adam Hester/Getty Images; Muro/F1 Online/Media Bakery; Getty Images/Blend Images; Jemma Jones/Alamy; Maridav/Shutterstock; Nisian Hughes/Iconica/Getty Images; Alys Tomlinson/Getty Images; Vetta/Getty Images; Tom Merton/Getty Images

CHAPTER 1

pp. 2–3 Getty Images/Cultura RF **4** Photo provided by the Raffaele family **5** Kevin Mazur/Getty Images **6 left** Paper Boat Creative/Getty Images **6 second from left** Prisma/SuperStock **6 center** Will Steacy/Getty Images **6 second from right** Blue Jean Images/SuperStock **6 right** iStockphoto **8 bottom** Editorial Image, LLC/Alamy Stock Photo **9** Blue Jean Images/Alamy **11 top** Design Pics/Ron Nickel/Getty Images **11 middle** Steve Debenport/iStock/Getty Images **11 bottom** Weekend Images Inc./Getty Images **12** Geomphotography/Alamy **14** Center for the History of Psychology/The University of Akron **15** YAY Media AS/Alamy **16 top left** Wikimedia Commons **16 top center** Archives of the History of American Psychology **16 top right** Imagno/Getty Images **21** Pie Chart: "Where Psychologists Work," from American Psychological Association, *Careers in Psychology*. Copyright © 2011 by the American Psychological Association. Adapted with permission. **21 top right** Exactostock/SuperStock **21 second from top right** Turba/Corbis **21 second from bottom right** Aflo Co. Ltd./Alamy Stock Photo **21 bottom right** monkeybusinessimages/Getty Images **22** Steve Debenport/iStock/Getty Images **24 text** "Cell Phones Make Drivers as Bad as Drunks," by Robert Roy Britt from LiveScience.com, June 29, 2006. Reprinted by permission of EnVeritas Group, Inc. **24 photo** Jim Moulin, University of Utah **25 top** Christina Kennedy/Getty Images **25 second from top** Leren Lu/Getty Images **25 third from top** © 2014 Department of Psychology, Clemson University. All Rights Reserved. **25 bottom** Christy Varonfakis Johnson/Alamy **27** Courtesy of Kristen Frosio **28 left** Lawrence S. Sugiyama, University of Oregon **28 right** Karl Ammann/Getty Images **29 left** Janine Wiedel Photolibrary/Alamy **29 right** John Birdsall/The Image Works **30 left** AP Photo/Jason DeCrow **30 right** Kateleen Foy/Getty Images **31** Blend Images/Alamy Stock Photo **35** Marmaduke St. John/Alamy **38** University of Pittsburgh, Department of Psychology **42** From "Datapoint: What do people do with their psychology degrees?" *Monitor on Psychology*, June 2012, p. 12. Copyright © 2012 by the American Psychological Association. Adapted with permission.

CHAPTER 2

pp. 44–45 Joe McBride/Getty Images **46** Andrew Mills/The Star-Ledger/The Image Works **48** Derek Storm/Splash News/Newscom **49 left** Alamy **49 right** James Cavallini/Science Source **50** David Aguilera/BuzzFoto/FilmMagic/Getty Images **56** Thinkstock/Getty Images **57** AP Photo/Ross D. Franklin **58** Hybrid Images/Getty Images **59 top** Alamy **59 bottom** Bettmann/Getty Images **60 top left** *Nature Reviews Neuroscience 5*, 812–819, © October 2004. **60 second from top left** AJPhoto/Science Source **60 second from top right** James Cavallini/Science Source **60 third from top left** Mark Harmel/Alamy **60 third from top right** Courtesy of Psych Central **60 bottom left** Marcello Massimini/University of Wisconsin-Madison **60 bottom right** Dr K Singh, Liverpool University/Dr S Hamdy & Dr Q Aziz, Manchester University **68 top left and right** From Penfield, Wilder (1958), The excitable cortex in conscious man. Liverpool University Press **68 bottom** Ramachandran, V.S., and Blakeslee, S. Fig. 6.1, Drawing made by a hemineglect patient, from *Phantoms in the brain*. Copyright © 1998 by V. S. Ramachandran and Sandra Blakeslee **70 top left** Science Source **70 top center** Warren Anatomical Museum in the Francis A. Countway Library of Medicine, Gift of Jack and Beverly Wilgus **70 top right** Damasio et al. (1994) The Return of Phineas Gage. *Science*. Copyright © 1994, AAAS. **70 bottom** Bettmann/Getty Images **72** Simone Vandenberg/Getty Images **75 bottom** George Burns/Handout/Corbis via Getty Images **78 top** George Shelley/Getty Images **78 center** Brand New Images/Getty Images **78 bottom** AP Photo **79 top** Provided by the Mack Family **79 bottom** Provided by the Mack Family **85** Dean Hanson/Albuquerque Journal/Albuquerque Journal via ZUMA Wire/Alamy

CHAPTER 3

pp. 86–87 Sverre Haugland/Image Source/Corbis **88 top** George Gojkovich/Getty Images **88 bottom** American Academy of Physical Medicine and Rehabilitation. Stern, et al. Vol. 3, S460–S467, October 2011 **89** iStockphoto **92** Detecting Awareness in the Vegetative State. Adrian M. Owen, Martin R. Coleman, Melanie Boly, Matthew H. Davis, Steven Laureys, and John D. Pickard. *Science*, 8 September 2006: 1402 **93** travelif/iStock **94 top** Monkey Business/AgeFotostock **94 bottom** travelif/iStock/Getty Images **95 all** Simons, D. J., & Levin, D. T. (1998). Failure to detect changes to people during a real-world interaction. *Psychonomic Bulletin and Review, 5*, 644–649. © 1998 Psychonomic Society, Inc. Figure courtesy Daniel J. Simons. **96** Republican National Committee, 2000 **104 top** Rob Byron/Shutterstock **104 bottom** Cavan Images/Shutterstock **106 top** Rafael Ben-Ari/Chameleons Eye/Newscom **106 bottom** Chris Rout/Alamy **108** Phototake Inc./Alamy **109 top** Greg Ceo/Getty Images **109 bottom** Heidi Coppock-Beard/Getty Images **111** Carlos Osorio/Getty Images **112** Monika Wisniewska/Alamy Stock Photo **113 top** Jupiterimages/Getty Images **113 bottom** Minding one's emotions: Mindfulness training alters the neural expression of sadness, Farb, Norman A. S.; Anderson, Adam K.; Mayberg, Helen; Bean, Jim; McKeon, Deborah; Segal, Zindel V. *Emotion*. Vol 10(2), Apr 2010, p. 215 **114 top** Ed Kashi/National Geographic Creative **114 bottom** Fernando Nuñez/EyeEm/Getty Images **115 text** © 2014 National Public Radio, Inc. NPR news report titled "Mindfulness Meditation Can Help Relieve Anxiety and Depression" by Allison Aubrey was originally published on npr.org on January 7, 2014, and is used with the permission of NPR. Any unauthorized duplication is strictly prohibited. **115 photo** mediaphotos/iStockphoto/Getty Images **116** Eckehard Schultz/AP **118 top** Wikimedia Commons **118 bottom** Prefrontal grey-matter changes in short-term and long-term abstinent methamphetamine abusers. Seog Ju Kim, et al. *International Journal of Neuropsychopharmacology*, Volume 9, Issue 2, pp. 221–228 **119** Multnomah County Sheriff's Office **120** Wikimedia Commons **121** Gary Tramontina/The New York Times/Redux **123 top** Janine Wiedel Photolibrary/Alamy **123 bottom** Blend Images/SuperStock **127** Spencer Platt/Getty Images

CHAPTER 4

pp. 128–29 Rhea Anna/Gallery Stock **130 top** Sebastien Micke/Paris Match via Getty Images **130 bottom left** Atlaspix/Alamy Stock Photo **130 bottom right** AF Archive/Alamy Stock Photo **131 top left** Tony Garcia/Getty Images **131 top right** © Ellen Senisi **131 bottom** Gale Zucker/Getty Images **132 left** Dr. Yorgos Nikas/Phototake **132 center** Petit Format/Science Source **132 right** Biophoto Associates/Science Source **133** Gallo Images/Alamy **134** Miami Herald/Getty Images **136 top** Courtesy of Sterling K. Clarren, MD Clinical Professor of Pediatrics, University of British Columbia Faculty of Medicine **136 bottom** Diego Herculano/Brazil Photo Press/LatinContent/Getty Images **137 left** © Ellen Senisi **138 center** Petit Format/Science Source **138 right** Petit Format/Science Source **139 bottom** Jacky Chapman/Photofusion Picture Library/Alamy **140** jacoblund/Getty Images **141 both** Nina Leen/Time Life Pictures/Getty Images **142 left** Mcimage/Shutterstock **144** Angela Georges/Getty Images **145 top** Sally and Richard Greenhill/Alamy **145 second from top** Tom Mareschal/Alamy **145 third from top** Ian Shaw/Alamy **145 bottom** Jon Feingersh/Getty Images **146 bottom** Sarah Grison **147 all** Marmaduke St. John/Alamy **149 bottom** © Ellen Senisi **153 top** Bob Daemmrich/The Image Works **154 top** Gale Zucker/Getty Images **154 bottom** Peter Turnley/Corbis/VCG via Getty Images **157** John S. Powell/fotolibra **158** Monkey Business Images/Shutterstock **159 top** WDC Photos/Alamy Stock Photo **159 center** Araya Diaz/WireImage/Getty Images **159 bottom** Patrick Kovarik/AFP/Getty Images **161 top** Arcticphoto/Alamy **161 center** © John Sanders **161 bottom** dbimages/Alamy **162 left** Ted Foxx/Alamy **162 right** maxriesgo/Shutterstock **164 top** Figure 1A from "Exercise training increases size of hippocampus and improves memory," *PNAS 108*(7), pp. 3017–3022, February 2011. Reprinted by permission of PNAS. **164 bottom** Stephanie Maze/Getty Images **165** Tony Garcia/Getty Images **169** Michelle Del Guercio/Getty Images

CHAPTER 5

pp. 170–71 Ollyy/Shutterstock **173** Robert Ashton/Massive Pixels/Alamy Stock Photo **175 left** Blend Images/Super Stock **176 bottom** PhotoAlto/Alamy **177** Wayhome studio/Shutterstock **179 right** GlowImages/Alamy **185 top** Rick Price/Getty Images **185 bottom** A Hawthorne/Arctic Photo **187** Kumar Sriskandan/Alamy **189 bottom** Figure: "Turning Tables" from the book *Mind Sights: Original Visual Illusions, Ambiguities and Other Anomalies, With a Commentary on the Play of Mind in Perception and Art* by Roger N. Shepard. Copyright © 1990 by Roger N. Shepard. Reprinted by permission of Henry Holt and Company. All rights reserved. **191 right** andresr/Getty Images **192** Marcos Welsh/AgeFotostock **195 top** Stephen Dalton/NHPA/Science Source **196 top** Andre Bernardo/Getty Images **197 right** Marcy Maloy/Getty Images **198** Linus Gelber/Alert the Medium/Getty Images **199 left** Steven Errico/Digital Vision/Getty Images **199 right** Jose Luis Pelaez Inc/Blend Images/Getty Images **201 right** Anna Zielinska/Getty Images **202 top** Blend Images/SuperStock **202 bottom** Mark Edward Atkinson/Tracey Lee/Getty Images **204 bottom** Jose Luis Pelaez Inc/Getty Images **205 right** John Bazemore/AP **206** Westend61 GmbH/Alamy **207** Art Directors & TRIP/Alamy **211** jacoblund/Getty Images

CHAPTER 6

pp. 212–13 Bela Szandelszky/AP **214** Angelo Gandolfi/Nature Picture Library **217 top** Mark Peterson/Corbis via Getty Images

217 bottom Marjorie Kamy Cotera/Daemmrich Photos/The Image Works **218** fourohfour/iStockphoto **219 left** Bettman/Getty Images **221** Courtesy Everett Collection **223 top** Scott Camazine/Alamy **223 middle** Wildlife GmbH/Alamy **223 bottom** Journal-Courier/Steve Warmowski/The Image Works **224** Archives of the History of American Psychology, The Center for the History of Psychology, The University of Akron **225** Courtesy Dorothy Parthree **226 top row** Hong Xia/Shutterstock; Nirut Jindawong/Shutterstock; Fedor Selivanov/Shutterstock **226 second row** Design Pics Inc./AgeFotostock; Corbis/AgeFotostock; Gerald A. DeBoer/Shutterstock **226 third row** Sabza/Shutterstock; Lydie Gigerichova/Ima/AgeFotostock; Shutterstock **226 fourth row** Matt Jeppson/Shutterstock; ian west/Alamy; Jack Goldfarb/AgeFotostock **226 fifth row** Guenter Fischer/Image/AgeFotostock; Shutterstock; Frank L. Junior/Shutterstock **226 sixth row** GmbH/Shutterstock; Hans Lang/Imagebroker/AgeFotostock; Shutterstock **229 left** Manuscripts & Archives, Yale University **231** MBI/Alamy **236 top** Center for Effective Discipline **237** © Ellen Senisi **238** Hero Images/Corbis **239** Lynn M. Stone/naturepl.com **241** Ronnie Kaufman/Larry Hirshowitz/Getty Images **242 top, all** Albert Bandura, Dept. of Psychology, Stanford University **242 bottom** Geri Engberg/The Image Works **243 text** "Do Violent Games Boost Aggression? Study Adds Fire to Debate," by Rachael Rettner from LiveScience.com, March 24, 2014. Reprinted by permission of EnVeritas Group, Inc. **243 photo** Sean D/Shutterstock **244 top** François Duhamel/© Columbia Pictures/courtesy Everett Collection **244 bottom** Penny Tweedie/Getty Images **245** Nicole S. Young/Getty Images **249** Pete Titmuss/Alamy Stock Photo

CHAPTER 7

pp. 250–51 Adam Hester/Getty Images **252 top** "Jeopardy!" courtesy Jeopardy Productions, Inc. **252 bottom** Angel Chevrestt/New York Post **253** Image Source/Getty Images **255** Tetra Images/Alamy **260** Keith R. Allen/Getty Images/Flickr RF **261 all** Erik Reis/agefotostock **268** Henry Molaison, aged 60, at MIT in 1986. Photograph and copyright: Jenni Ogden. First published in Ogden: *Trouble in Mind: Stories from a Neuropsychologist's Casebook*, OUP, New York, 2012. **270 top** David Turnley/Getty Images **270 bottom** Newscom **272 left** MARKA/Alamy **272 right** Michael Blann/Getty Images **273 top** Steve Prezant/Getty Images **273 bottom** Stephen Morris/Getty Images **275 text** From "Do 'Brain-Training' Programs Work?" by Daniel J. Simons, et al. Summary from psychologicalscience.org, September 30, 2016 © 2016 by the Association for Psychological Science. Reprinted with permission. **275 photo** Association for Psychological Science **276** Wheeler, M.E., Petersen, S.E., & Buckner, R.L. (2000). Memory's echo: vivid remembering reactivates sensory specific cortex. Copyright © *Proceedings of the National Academy of Sciences*, 97, 11125–11129 **279 left** Chris A. Crumley/Alamy **280** © Dart NeuroScience **282** Robert E. Klein/AP **283** Federal Aviation Administration **284 top** AP Photo/Charles Krupa **284 bottom** Spencer Platt/Getty Images **285 top** Joe Raedle/Getty Images **285 bottom both** Elizabeth F. Loftus, et al. *Journal of Experimental Psychology; Human Learning and Memory*. 1978, Vol. 4, No. 1, 19–31 **286 both** Columbus Dispatch **291** 67photo/Alamy Stock Photo

CHAPTER 8

pp. 292–93 Muro/F1 Online/Media Bakery **294 left** Jackie Fultz Martin **294 right** Michele Sibiloni/AFP/Getty Images **297 top** Richard A. Cooke/Corbis/Getty Images **297 bottom** Renee Jones Schneider/Minneapolis Star Tribune/ZUMAPRESS.com/Alamy **299 top** WENN Ltd/Alamy Stock Photo **299 bottom** Geza Farkas/123RF **300 left** akg-images/The Image Works **300 right** Ferenc Szelepcsenyi/Alamy **301** Courtesy Todd Heatherton **302 left** Courtesy of Kendra Keyse/USC **302 center** Solarpix.com **302 right** JSP Studios/Alamy **304 top** Mario Tama/Getty Images **304 middle** Jeffrey Mayer/WireImage/Getty Images **304 bottom** AP Photo/Ivan Sekretarev **305** Larry Downing/Reuters/Newscom **306 top, both** Courtesy Sheena Iyengar **306 bottom** Copyright © 2002 by the American Psychological Association. Adapted with permission. Table 1 from "Maximizing versus satisficing: Happiness is a matter of choice." Schwartz, Barry; Ward, Andrew; Monterosso, John;

Lyubomirsky, Sonja; White, Katherine; Lehman, Darrin R. *Journal of Personality and Social Psychology,* Vol 83(5), Nov 2002, 1178–1197. http://dx.doi.org/10.1037/0022-3514.83.5.1178. No further reproduction or distribution is permitted without written permission from the American Psychological Association. **307** Milles Studio/Shutterstock **310 bottom** 3LH/SuperStock **313 top left** Interfoto/Alamy **313 top center** AP Photo/Manuel Balce Ceneta **313 top right** Jeff Kravitz/FilmMagic/Getty Images **313 bottom left** Mireya Acierto/FilmMagic/Getty Images **313 bottom right** Jason LaVeris/FilmMagic/Getty Images **318 left top** Roberto Westbrook/Getty Images **318 left bottom** Visions of America, LLC/Alamy **319 bottom** Syracuse Newspapers/Caroline Chen/The Image Works **321 top** © 2007 Michelle Trudeau for National Public Radio, Inc. NPR news report titled "Students' View of Intelligence Can Help Grades" by Michelle Trudeau was originally published on npr.org on February 15, 2007, and is used with the permission of NPR. Any unauthorized duplication is strictly prohibited. **321 photo** John Archer/Getty Images **326 bottom** Dan Kitwood/Getty Images **333** Yagi-Studio/Getty Images

CHAPTER 9

pp. 334-35 Getty Images/Blend Images **336** Photo courtesy of Malin Fezehai Malala Fund **337 clockwise from upper left** Cultura Creative/Alamy; Tetra Images/Alamy; Chad Ehlers/Alamy; Jose Luis Pelaez Inc/Getty Images **340 left** Radius Images/Alamy **340 right** 2happy/Alamy **342 top** Blend Images/Alamy Stock Photo **342 bottom** Bruce Forster/Getty Images **346 both** © Ilana Panich-Linsman, All Rights Reserved. **347 top** Saminaleo/Getty Images **347 bottom left** Anyka/Alamy **347 bottom right** Blavarg, Susanna/Getty Images **348 top** Bob Daemmrich/The Image Works **348 bottom** Chor Sokunthea/Reuters/Newscom **349** Alberto Pomares/Getty Images **350** Heather Bragman/Syracuse Newspapers/The Image Works **352 bottom left** Gunnar Pippel/Shutterstock **352 bottom right** Zelig Shaul/Zuma Press **354 left** Peter Casolino/Alamy **354 bottom right** Marmaduke St. John/Alamy **357 top, both** Courtesy of W. W. Norton & Co., Inc. **358 bottom** Christophe Boisvieux/Getty Images **364** Federico Caputo/Alamy Stock Photo **366 both** Paul Ekman Group, LLC **368 left, both** Courtesy of Bob Willingham **368 right top** Danita Delimont/Alamy Stock Photo **367 right middle** Jason Edwards/National Geographic/Getty Images **367 right bottom** Raymond Patrick/Getty Images **368 both** Courtesy of Bob Willingham **369 top** Diego Cervo/123RF **369 bottom** Radius Images/Getty Images **370** Brian H. Thomas/Alamy **371** Courtesy of Dacher Keltner **375** Tyler Olson/123RF

CHAPTER 10

pp. 376-77 Jemma Jones/Alamy **378** AP Photo/Brennan Linsley **380 both** Biophoto Associates/Science Source **383 top** Stu Forster/Getty Images **383 bottom** Keenan/Splash News/Newscom **386** Robin Hammond/NOOR/National Geographic **387 top** ClassicStock.com/SuperStock **387 bottom** Visage/Exactostock **388** Ryan Mcvay/Getty Images **389** Rob Carr/Getty Images **390 top** From Colapinto, John, *As nature made him: The boy who was raised as a girl* (2000), HarperCollins Publishers Inc. **390 bottom** STR/Reuters/Newscom **391 all** From *Warpaint* by Coco Layne **393 top** Pictorial Press Ltd/Alamy Stock Photo **393 bottom** Bill Clark/CQ Roll Call/Newscom **395** Photo courtesy of Lori Duron, Raising My Rainbow **396** Bruce Ackerman/Ocala Star-Banner **397 top** AP Photo/Wilfredo Lee **397 bottom** Everett Collection Inc./Alamy Stock Photo **398 top** Fred R. Conrad/The New York Times/Redux **403** Fred R. Conrad/The New York Times/Redux **404** Jemma Jones/Alamy **405** Michael Desmond/© Showtime Networks/Courtesy Everett Collection **408** Corbis/Getty Images **410 all** Dr. Martin Gruendl, Institute for Psychology, University of Regensburg **411 phone only** The Photo Works **412** Filip Obr/Shutterstock **419** Education & Exploration 3/Alamy Stock Photo

CHAPTER 11

pp. 420-21 Maridav/Shutterstock **422 top** Christine Chew/UPI/Newscom **422 bottom** Steve Granitz/WireImage/Getty Images **423 top** Ana Nance/Redux **426 left** Tim Hill/Food and Drink/SuperStock **427 top** Sam Edwards/Getty Images **427 bottom** nobleIMAGES/Alamy **428 top** Douglas Peebles Photography/Alamy **428 bottom** François Guillot/AFP/Getty Images **430 both** Peter Lawson/Shutterstock **432** Cultura Creative/Alamy **433** Sergio Azenha/Alamy Stock Photo **435 top** Saurer/AgeFotostock **435 middle** Ton Koene/Alamy Stock Photo **435 bottom** Ian Miles-Flashpoint Pictures/Alamy **436 top** Teh Eng Koon/AFP/Getty **436 middle** Travel Ink/Getty Images **437** Lisa Peardon/Getty Images **438 top** Denis Charlet/AFP/Getty Images **438 middle** Image Point Fr/Shutterstock **438 bottom** Doug Martin/Science Source **440 left** AP Photo/Gerald Herbert **440 right** Rubberball/Mike Kemp/Getty Images **443** Norbert Schmidt/AFP/Getty Images **444 right** Marc Romanelli/Alamy **445 top** Janine Wiedel Photolibrary **445 bottom** Purestock/Getty Images **447 top** Compassionate Eye Foundation/Hero Images/Getty Images **447 middle** Jetta Productions/Getty Images **447 bottom** Digital Vision/Getty Images **448 top** Exactostock/Superstock **448 bottom** Wavebreakmedia Ltd UC5/Alamy **449** Corbis **450 top** AP Photo/Ross D. Franklin **450 bottom** AP Photo/Altaf Qadri **452 text** "Sit, Stay, Heal: Study finds therapy dogs help stressed university students," originally published by UBC News, March 12, 2018. Reprinted by permission of the University of British Columbia Media Relations Department. **452 photo** Digital Vision/Getty Images **453 bottom** AFP/Getty Images **455 bottom** Alamy **456** David J. Green-lifestyle themes/Alamy **461** Hero Images/Getty Images

CHAPTER 12

pp. 462-63 Nisian Hughes/Iconica/Getty Images **464 top** AP Photo/Julio Cortez **464 bottom** Blend Images/Alamy **465** Rich Legg/Getty Images **467 top** Ryan Remorz/The Canadian Press/AP Images **467 bottom** David Buchan/Getty Images **468 top, both** Courtesy Keith Pyne, Washington University **469** Ronald Zak/AP **470** Jim Urquhart/Reuters/Newscom **471 top** Glyn Kirk/AFP/Getty Images **471 bottom** Clive Brunskill/Getty Images **472** David S. Holloway/Getty Images **473 top** The Star-Ledger/Aristide Economopoulos/The Image Works **473 middle, both** David Warren/Alamy Stock Photo **473 bottom** Paul Robbins/Alamy **476 bottom** AP Photo/Damian Dovarganes **478 photo only** Drazen Vukelic/Getty Images **479 top left** Gabriel Bouys/AFP/GettyImages **479 top right** David J. Green-work themes/Alamy **479 middle** © Philip G. Zimbardo, PhD **479 bottom** AP **480 top** Joe Robbins/Getty Images **480 bottom** SMI/Newscom **481 photo only** Golden Pixels LLC/Alamy Stock Photo **482 left** Hybrid Images/Getty Images **482 right** Mohamed Omar/EPA **487** Anthony Redpath/Getty Images **488** FEMA/Alamy Stock Photo **489 photo only** The New York Times Photo Archive/Redux **491** AP Photo/Ramon Espinosa **493 top, all** Public Perception, Public Reaction, and the Modal Scientist, *Psychological Science.* © 1990, 1467-9280. David Johnson. Photographs courtesy Judith Hall Langlois, UT Austin. **493 bottom, both** D. I. Perrett, et al. Facial shape and judgments of female attractiveness. *Nature, 368,* 239–242 (17 March 1994); Macmillan Publishers Limited. All rights reserved. **494 top** VStock/Alamy **494 bottom** Asia Images Group Pte Ltd/Alamy **495** Gabe Palmer/Alamy **496** VisitBritain/Ben Selway/Getty Images **501** PeopleImages/iStock/Getty Images

CHAPTER 13

pp. 502-03 Alys Tomlinson/Getty Images **504 top** Andrew Chin/Getty Images **504 middle** Stephen Lam/Reuters/Newscom **504 bottom** Jamie McCarthy/Getty Images **505 top** Josef Lindau/Getty Images **508 text** "Science Finds a Way to Overcome Life's Regrets," by Sarah G. Miller from LiveScience.com, June 30, 2016. Reprinted by permission of EnVeritas Group, Inc. **508 photo** file404/Shutterstock **512 top** Kyodo via AP Images **512 bottom** David R. Frazier Photolibrary, Inc./Alamy **517** Cavan Images/Getty Images **519** Jessica Peterson/Tetra Images/Corbis **520** Imaginechina/Corbis/Getty Images **521 photo only** Masterfile **523 photo only** John Birdsall/The Image Works **523 Table 13.3** Appendix: Items on the Level of Cleanliness Subscale from Ogletree, Shirley M. et al. "College Living: Issues related to housecleaning attitudes." *College Student Journal,* December 2005, 49(4). Reprinted by permission of Project Innovation. **527 left top and right top inset** Camera Press/Mitchell Sams/Redux **527 left bottom and right bottom inset** Brand New Images/Getty Images **529 top** Photodisc/Getty Images **529 middle** Agnieszka Kirinicjanow/Getty Images **529 bottom** Randy Faris/Corbis **530 left and middle** Courtesy Dr. Christine Drea **531 bottom left** Westend61 GmbH/Alamy **531 bottom right** SuperStock **532** GoGo Images Corporation/Alamy **534 top** Wikimedia Commons **534 bottom** Collection of Todd Heatherton. Photo by Sarah Heatherton. **535** Tek Image/Science Source **537 top** Martin Thomas Photography/Alamy **537 bottom** Alamy **543** Rawpixel.com/Shutterstock

CHAPTER 14

pp. 544–45 Vetta/Getty Images **546** Courtesy of Carol Todd **548** Heide Benser/Getty Images **550 text** "Childhood Bullying Can Have Lasting Effects on Mental Health," by Carl Nierenberg from LiveScience.com, December 9, 2015. Reprinted by permission of EnVeritas Group, Inc. **550 photo** SpeedKingz/Shutterstock **552 middle** Courtesy of Richard F. Kaplan **552 bottom** Museo Lazaro Galdiano, Madrid, Spain/Giraudon/The Bridgeman Art Library **555 bottom** Ronald C. Modra/Sports Imagery/Getty Images **559 top** Charles Eshelman/FilmMagic/Getty Images **561 bottom** Dan MacMedan/Contour by Getty Images **563** NIMH National Institute of Mental Health **565** Courtesy of Carol Todd **566 top** Roy Rochlin/Getty Images **567 bottom** Thomas Traill **570 top** Private Collection/Photo © Bonhams, London, UK/The Bridgeman Art Library **570 middle** History and Art Collection/Alamy Stock Photo **570 bottom** Lebrecht Music and Arts Photo Library/Alamy **571 top** Anna Bryukhanova/Getty Images **571 bottom** Mary Evans/Universal Pictures/Dreamworks/Imagine Entertainment/Ronald Grant/Everett Collection **572 bottom, both** Joe McNally/Hulton Archive/Getty Images **576** AP Photo **577** © Universal Studios/Lionsgate Films/Courtesy of Everett Collection **578 top, all** Paul Ekman Group, LLC **578 bottom left** Marsh, A. A., Finger, E. C., Mitchell, D. G., Reid, M. E., Sims, C., et al. (2008). Reduced amygdala response to fearful expressions in children and adolescents with callous-unemotional traits and disruptive behavior disorders. *American Journal of Psychiatry, 165,* 712–720. **578 bottom right** Figure 1 from Marsh, A. A., et al., "Reduced amygdala response to fearful expressions in children and adolescents with callous-unemotional traits and disruptive behavior disorders." Reprinted with permission from *The American Journal of Psychiatry*

165:6, Copyright © 2008, American Psychiatric Association. All Rights Reserved. **580** *Abnormal Psychology,* 4ed, by Seligman, Walker, and Rosenhan. Copyright W. W. Norton & Company, Inc. Used by permission of W. W. Norton & Company, Inc. **583 both** From Osterlin, J., & Dawson, G. (1994). Early recognition of children with autism. A study of first birthday home videotapes. *Journal of Autism and Developmental Disorders, 24,* 247–257. Photographs courtesy Geraldine Dawson. **584** Courtesy of Dr. Ami Klin, (2003) The enactive mind from actions to cognition: Lessons from autism. *Philosophical Transactions of the Royal Society.* **585** Brad Wilson/Getty Images **586 top** Carey Kirkella/Getty Images **586 bottom** Raleigh News & Observer/Getty Images **591** Bill Wagner/Longview Daily News

CHAPTER 15

pp. 592–93 Tom Merton/Getty Images **594** Richard Perry/The New York Times/Redux **595 top** Epics/Getty Images **595 bottom** Stock Montage/Getty Images **597 top** Prisma Bildagentur AG/Alamy **597 bottom** Michael Rougier/Time Life Pictures/Getty Images **598** iStockphoto **600** Ridofranz/iStock/Getty Images **601** Alina Solovyova-Vincent/Getty Images **602 bottom** Will McIntyre/Science Source **604** Horacio Sormani/Science Source **605 top** BSIP/UIG Via Getty Images **605 middle** Alina Solovyova-Vincent/Getty Images **605 bottom** Tim Isbell/MCT/Newscom **607** Lisa F. Young/Alamy **608** Gregg DeGuire/FilmMagic/Getty Images **610 bottom** AP Photo/Bebeto Matthews **612 photo only** Photofusion/UIG via Getty Images **613** Eugene Gologursky/WireImage **615 bottom** Pascal Goetheluck/Scienve Photo Library/Science Source **616** Courtesy of Helen Mayberg M.D. **617** Evan Agostini/Invision/AP **618** Art Directors & TRIP/Alamy **621 top** Peter Yates/The New York Times/Redux **621 bottom, photo only** Zave Smith/Getty Images **622 photo only** ableimages/Alamy **623 top photo** Stockbyte/Getty Images **623 bottom photo** Steve Debenport/Getty Images **627** iStockphoto **629 top photo** DMAC/Alamy **629 bottom photo** Steve Liss/The LIFE Images Collection/Getty Images **635** Steve Debenport/Getty Images

APPENDIX A

p. A3 MediaForMedical/UIG via Getty Images

NAME INDEX

Page numbers in *italics* refer to illustrations.

Blumberg, S. J., 305
Bobowski, N. K., 139
Bocklandt, S., 380
Boden, J. M., 509
Bodenhausen, G. V., 285
Boehmer, A. L. M., 385
Bogaert, A. F., 397, 398, 402, 403
Bogouslavsky, O., 108
Bohlin, G., 143
Bohus, M., 576, 621
Boldrini, M., 80
Bolles, R. C., 239
Bollinger, B., 85
Bollini, A., 572, 573
Boly, M., 92
Bolzenius, K., 348
Bombi, A. S., 236
Bonanno, G. A., 364–65, 450
Bonanno, R. A., 157
Bonbowski, N. K., 348
Bond, D. J., 617
Bonnet, M., 101
Boodoo, G., 317, 319, 323, 327
Booth, A., 161
Bootzin, R. R., 107
Borges, G., 564
Born, J., 106
Bornstein, J., 381
Bornstein, M. H., 236
Bornstein, R. F., 534
Borton, R., 140
Botsis, A. J., 558
Bouchard, C., 380, 381, 427, 528
Bouchard, T. J., Jr., 78, 317, 319, 323, 327
Bourgeat, P., 164
Bouton, M. E., 223
Bowdle, B. F., 488
Bowen, J. D., 164
Bowlby, J., 140
Boykin, A. W., 317, 319, 323, 327
Brackett, M. A., 317
Bradbury, T. N., 494, 496
Bradley, S. J., 394
Bradshaw, C. S., 435
Braidwood, R., 618
Brain, G. R., 264
Bralten, J., 585
Brammer, G. L., 487
Brand, R. J., 446–47
Brandon, T. H., 437
Branningan, A., 486
Branscum, A., 423
Bransford, J. D., 266
Brantley, C., 399
Bratko, D., 527
Braun, K. V., 583
Braunstein, G. D., 409
Breaux, J. G., 409
Breedlove, N. J., 402
Breedlove, S. M., 396, 397, 400, 401, 402
Breiding, M. J., 92
Breitenbecher, D. L., 510
Breland, K., 238

Breland, M., 238
Brennan, L., 422
Brent, D. A., 626
Breslaw, A., 420
Brewer, M. B., 349
Brick, P. D., 437
Brickman, A. M., 318
Brill, K. T., 407
Brinkmann, A. O., 385
Brody, C. L., 437
Brody, D. J., 562, 566
Brody, G. H., 137
Brody, N., 317, 323, 327
Brody, S., 406
Brook, C., 402
Brookmeyer, R., 164
Brooks-Gunn, J., 382
Broutian, T., 435
Brown, A. S., 282, 574
Brown, B., 164
Brown, B. B., 155
Brown, C., 409
Brown, J. D., 511, 512
Brown, L. L., 494
Brown, R., 150
Brown, R. A., 432
Brown, S. W., 119
Brown, T. A., 557
Brown, T. L., 616
Brownell, K. D., 429
Browning, C. R., 414
Brozek, J., 428
Bruggenwirth, H., 385
Brummett, B. H., 447
Brunell, A. B., 509
Bruni, F., 96
Brunoni, A. R., 616
Brunotte, J., 523
Brunstrom, J. M., 345
Bryson, S. E., 261
Buch, A., 409
Büchele, F., 105
Buckley, D., 136
Buckwalter, J. A., 584
Buehlman, R. T., 161
Buhrich, N., 402
Buikema, A., 583
Buisson, O., 406
Buitelaar, J., 76
Bullen, C., 438
Bullis, J. R., 608
Bullmore, E., 346
Bullmore, E. T., 346, 560
Bunge, S. A., 364
Buoli, M., 617
Burg, M. M., 446
Burger, J. M., 486
Burgess, N., 65
Burgess, S., 617
Burkill, S., 92
Burnham, S., 164
Burns, H. J., 286
Burns, T. C., 150
Burstein, M., 623, 624
Burton, K. L., 551
Burton, L. S., 238
Bush, C. P., 509
Bush, E. C., 69
Bushdid, C., 202
Bushman, B. J., 487, 509

Bushnell, M. C., 111
Buss, A. H., 529
Buss, D. M., 410
Buss, K. A., 558
Buster, J. E., 409
Butcher, J. N., 579
Butterworth, M., 392
Buvat, J., 408
Buyken, A. E., 348
Byers-Heinlein, K., 150
Byrne, E. M., 568

Caballero, F. F., 349
Cabello, M., 349
Cacioppo, J. T., 454, 477
Cadenhead, K., 619, 620
Caglar, S., 505
Cahill, S., 612
Cahn, B. R., 113
Cairns, B. D., 154
Cairns, R. B., 154
Califf, R. M., 120
Call, J., 144
Calvini, G., 285
Campbell, A. T., 535
Campbell, J. D., 507, 509
Campbell, K. W., 509
Campbell, P. T., 432
Campbell, W. K., 509, 512
Campeas, R., 612
Camperio-Ciani, A., 401
Canales-Rodríguez, E. J., 576
Canetta, S., 574
Canino, G. J., 559
Canli, T., 526
Cannon, W. B., 339, 357
Cantor, J. M., 402
Cantu, D., 57
Capiluppi, C., 401
Caporael, L. R., 349
Caramaschi, D., 487
Cardeña, E., 579
Carey, B., 621
Carli, L. L., 523
Carlsmith, J. M., 476
Carlson, E., 579
Carlson, E. N., 536
Carlström, E., 401
Carnell, S., 427
Carney, C. E., 108
Carney, R. M., 447
Carpenter, A., 490
Carpenter, L. L., 617
Carpenter, M., 144
Carpenter, W., 571
Carranza-Jasso, R., 223
Carrasco, M., 256
Carrère, S., 161–62
Carrier, B., 111
Carroll, M. D., 424, 425
Carstensen, L. L., 162
Carter, C. S., 409
Carter, R., 435
Carusi, C. P., 242
Carvalho, A. F., 616
Case, B., 624
Case, R., 148
Casey, B. J., 152
Casey, M., 367

Casey, R. J., 493
Cash, B. M., 397
Cashaback, J. G., 245
Casoy, F., 401
Caspi, A., 487, 492, 528, 529, 532
Casson, P., 409
Castellanos, F. X., 586
Castonguay, L. G., 557
Castro-Loli, P., 617
Catala, M. D., 616
Catanese, K. R., 407
Cattell, R. B., 316
Cebrian-Silla, A., 137
Ceci, S. J., 317, 319, 323, 327
Cekic, M., 113
Cepeda, N. J., 255, 259
Cerasoli, C. P., 344
Cesarini, D., 528
Chabas, D., 108
Chabris, C. F., 528
Chaddock, L., 164
Chaimani, A., 614, 616
Chandra, A., 397, 398
Chandrashekar, J., 198
Chang, J., 346
Chang, L. J., 361
Chang, Z., 585
Chant, D. C., 569
Chaplin, T. M., 368
Chapman, B. P., 532
Chapman, S., 438
Charchun, J., 328
Charles, J., 583
Charles, S. T., 162
Charlson, F. J., 546, 564
Charney, D. S., 563
Charuvastra, A., 383, 384
Chase, W. G., 262
Chassin, L., 437
Chatterji, S., 566
Chaturvedi, A. K., 435
Chavez, R. S., 91
Chawarska, K., 582
Check, J. V., 411
Chen, C., 558
Chen, H., 564
Chen, M. Y., 435
Chen, Q., 136
Cheng, H. G., 564
Cherry, E. C., 256
Cherry, F., 486
Chiappa, J. A., 434
Chisholm, D., 546
Chiu, W. T., 546, 557, 559
Choi, I., 466
Chokroverty, S., 101
Choo, P., 453
Chou, S. P., 577
Choudhury, S., 152
Chisler, J. C., 422
Christakis, N. A., 426
Christensen, D. D., 326
Christensen, D. L., 583
Christensen, S. E., 402
Christian, K. M., 80
Christianson, S., 285
Christoff, K., 202
Christopher, F. S., 161

Chronis, A. M., 629
Chronis-Tuscano, A., 630
Chumlea, W. C., 151
Chun, M. M., 255
Chung-Yan, G. A., 470
Cipriani, A., 614
Clark, D., 610
Clark, G. T., 107
Clark, L. A., 524, 553
Clark, R. D., 407
Clark, R. E., 276
Clark-Foos, A., 273
Cleary, P. D., 437
Cleary, S. D., 585
Clore, G. L., 369
Coan, J. A., 161
Coast, J. R., 432
Cochran, B. N., 400
Coe, W. C., 111
Coghill, D., 585
Cogsdill, E. J., 465
Cohen, D., 488
Cohen, G. L., 328
Cohen, S., 443, 444, 454
Cohen-Kettenis, P. T., 394
Coid, J., 577
Colapinto, J., 390
Colcombe, S. J., 432
Colditz, G. A., 382
Coleman, M. R., 92
Coles, E. K., 630
Colligan, R. C., 447
Collins, A., 489
Collins, J., 569
Collins, K. P., 585
Collins, S. A., 121
Colliver, J. D., 577
Colom, F., 617
Comer, J. S., 608
Compton, J. S., 610
Compton, W. M., 120, 577
Comstock, R. D., 92
Comtesse, H., 361
Conger, R., 532
Conn, C., 576
Conneely, K. N., 561
Connelly, A., 270
Conners, C. K., 586
Conron, K. J., 378
Constantine-Ferrando, M. F., 111
Constantino, J. N., 583
Conway, A. R. A., 325, 326
Conway, G. S., 402
Conway, K. P., 577
Conway, L., 378
Cook, G. I., 273
Cook, M., 226
Cooke, B. M., 402
Cooke, S. F., 217
Coolidge, S., 394
Cooper, C. R., 154
Copeland, W. E., 157, 546
Copen, C., 398
Corby, J. C., 111
Coren, S., 106
Corna, F., 401
Coronado, V. G., 92
Cortese, S., 585
Cortez, A., 411

SUBJECT INDEX

Page numbers in *italics* refer to illustrations.

autism spectrum disorder, 582–84, *582, 583, 584*
    case study of, 592–94
    memory and, 326
    shaping and, 231
    symptoms of, 583–84
    treatment of, *624,* 626–28, *627*
automatic processing, 93–94, *94*
autonomic nervous system, *47,* 71, 72–73, *72*
autonomy, shame and doubt vs., *153*
autopilot, 272, 282
availability heuristic, 304–05, *304*
avatars, 464
Avengers: Infinity War (film), 188
avoidant attachment, 142
avoidant personality disorders, *575*
Awkwafina, *467*
axon, 49, 52

babbling, 150
balance, 196
Bale, Christian, *577*
basal ganglia, 42, 64
basic tendencies, 531, *531*
basilar membrane, *190,* 192
Basinger, Kim, *608*
Baumgartner, Felix, *313*
Baxter, Theresa, *119*
Bayer pharmaceutical company, *120*
Beautiful Mind, A (film), *571*
Beck, Aaron, 598, 614
behavior:
    disorganized, 571
    dysfunctional, 621
    eating, 344–48, *345*
    group, 478–81
    monitoring of, 238–39
    motivation and, 336–53, *337*
    neurotransmitters and, 52–58
    nonverbal, 464–65
    thin slices of, 465, *465*
behavioral genetics, 77, 317–18
behaviorism, *15,* 18, *18,* 215, 224, 230
behavior modification, 237, 238–39
behavior therapy, 596, 598–99, *598*
    CBT (cognitive-behavioral therapy), 599, 609, 614–15
    DBT (dialectical behavior therapy), 621–22
bell curve, 322
Benoit, Chris, 92
beta waves, *101,* 102
better-than-average effect, 510, 511
between-groups design, 35
Beyoncé, *5, 491*
Bialik, Mayim, *304*
bicultural identity, 154
Big Five trait theory, 524–25, *524*
Binet, Alfred, 313–14, *313*
Binet-Simon Intelligence Scale, 313–14, 320
binge-eating disorder, *430,* 431
binocular depth cues, 186
binocular disparity, 186, *186*
biological clock, 100, 109
biological predispositions, 237–39, *239*
biological sex, 378–85, *378*
    ambiguity/inconsistency in, 383–85, *383*
    androgen insensitivity syndrome (AIS) and, 385
    congenital adrenal hyperplasia (CAH) and, 384–85
    as continuum, 385, *385*
    endocrine system and, 380

estradiol and, 380–81
five aspects of, *379*
genetics, 379–83
gonads and, 380
hormones and, 379–83, 384–85
intersexuality and, 383–84, *383,* 384–85
Kleinfelter syndrome and, 384
ovaries and, 380, *382*
puberty and, 380–81
semenarche and, 382–83
sex characteristics and, 381–83, *381, 382*
sex chromosomes and, *379,* 380
socialization vs., 389–90, *390*
spermarche and, 382
SRY gene and, 380
support for people who vary in, 419
testes and, 380, *382*
testosterone and, 381
Turner syndrome and, 384
biological therapy, 601–03
biology:
    sexual activity and, 404–09
    sexual orientation and, 399–404, *400*
biology, psychological role of, 44–81
    brain-body communication in, 71–75
    brain structure and, 46–91
    genes and environment in, 76–81
    nervous systems and, 47–58
biopsychosocial model, 423–24, *423,* 551
bipolar disorders, *566*
    artistic genius and, 567–68
    manic episodes, 566–67
    symptoms of, 566, 567, *567*
    treatment of, 567–68, *609,* 617–18
birth defects, 130–36, *133*
birth order, 77
birth weight, intelligence and, *319*
bisexual, 397, *397,* 398, 399
bitter taste, 198–99
blackout, 119
Black Panther (film), 188
blind spot, *178,* 180, *180*
blinking, 261, *261*
blocking, 282
blushing, 371
BMI (body mass index), 424–25, *425*
Bobo doll, observational learning and, 241–42, 244
bodily-kinesthetic intelligence, 316, *316*
body image, *428*
body language, 464–65, *464*
body mass index (BMI), 424–25, *425*
Boko Haram, 336
Booker, Cory, 462, 464, *464,* 465–66, 489
borderline personality disorder, *575,* 576, 621–22, *621*
Boston Marathon, bombing of, *284*
Botox (botulism bacteria), 56, *56*
bottom-up processing, 185
Boyhood (film), 130–31, *130,* 144
Bradshaw, Terry, 86
brain, *20,* 47, *47,* 572–73, *572*
    divisions of, 60–65, *61*
    eating and, 346–47, *346, 347*
    emotions from processes in, 361–63, *361, 362*
    functions of, 56–70, 91
    hemispheres of, 96–99
    memory and, 274–77, *274, 276*
    sexual orientation and, *400,* 403
brain activity:
    and consciousness, *90,* 91–99
    during sleep, 101–03, *101, 103*

brain damage, 68–70, *118,* 270–71
brain development, 137
    electrical stimulation of, 68, *68*
    environmental stimulation and, *137*
brain imaging methods, 60–61, *60*
    see also specific method
brain stem, *61, 103*
"brain-training" programs, 276
Branson, Richard, 48
Breuer, Josef, 596
brightness, 181, *181*
brightness constancy, 189
Broca, Paul, 59
Broca's area, 59, *60,* 66
Brown, Roger, 150
bulimia nervosa, *430,* 431
bullying, 157, *217,* 544–46
    of Amanda Todd, 544, 546, *546*
    long-term mental health and, 550
    prevention of, 157
Bundy, Ted, 576, *576*
    APD and, 576
bystander intervention effect, 489–90, *489, 490*

caffeine, 117, *135*
Calkins, Mary Whiton, 16
Cannon-Bard theory of emotions, *356,* 357, *357*
careers, 159–60
case studies, 30, *30*
category, 296–98, *297*
Cattell, Raymond, 314–16, *315*
causal claims, 33–37
CBT (cognitive-behavioral therapy), 599, 614–15
cell body, 49
cell phone use, 4, *4*
    in classrooms, 255
    and driving, 24, 26–27, 32, 35, 36
Centers for Disease Control and Prevention (CDC), 192, 238, 433, 437, 546
central nervous system, 47–48, *47,* 58, 71
central route, persuasion by, 477, *477*
centration, 146
cerebellum, *61,* 62–63, *62*
cerebral cortex, 63, *64,* 65–70, *66, 174*
cerebral palsy, 134
Champion, Robert, 476
change blindness, 94, *95,* 286, *286*
Chantix, 438
characteristic adaptations, 531
Chastain, Brandi, 92
chess-playing ability, 294, *294*
child development, *see* infant and child development
childhood disorders, 581–86, *582, 583, 584, 585, 586,* 623–30
    attention-deficit/hyperactivity disorder, *582, 585, 586*
    autism spectrum disorder, *582, 583, 584*
    communication disorders, *582*
    intellectual disabilities, *582*
    motor disorders, *582*
    treatment of, 623–30, *624, 625*
childhood memories, 285
chlamydia, 433, 434, *434*
choice:
    maximizing, 306, *306,* 307
    paradox of, 305–06, *306*
    satisficing, 306, 307
choice reaction time, 325
chromosomes, 380, *381*

dopamine, *55, 56–57, 63*, 118, 120, 123, 237–38
  reinforcement and, 237–38
Dorr, Richard, 403, *403*
downward comparisons, 448, 511
Drake, 502, 504, *504*, 513, 533
drawing ability, *314*
dream analysis, 596
dream journals, *104*
dreams, dreaming, 102–05, *104*
drinking, *see* alcohol abuse
drive, drive reduction, 338–40
drugs, psychoactive:
  advertising and, 118, *118, 120*
  altered consciousness and, 116–23, *118*
  see also psychotropic medications
DSM-5, 553–54, *554*, 559, 560, 562, 567, 569, 575, 576
dual coding, 264
dualism, 12–13, 90
Duckworth, Ladda Tammy, *472*
Duncker, Karlo, 311–12
dyslexia, 48

ear:
  infection of, 192, 196
  parts of, 191–92
EAR (electronically activated record), 535
ear buds, 192–93
eardrum, *190*, 191–92
early infantile autism, 582
eating, 344–48, *345*
  brain and, 346–47, *346, 347*
  conditioned response and, 347
  culture and, 348, *348, 349*
  disorders of, 429–31, 430, *430*
  flavor and, 348
  glucose and, 345–46
  healthy, 456
  hormones and, 346
  learning and, 347–48
  motivation and, 344–48, *345*
  obesity and, 426
  preferences and familiarity, 347–48, *347*
Ebbinghaus, Hermann, 280–81
ecosystem goals, 350
ecstasy (MDMA), 121, *121*
ECT (electroconvulsive therapy), 602–03, *602*, 616
EEG (electroencephalograph), 59, *60*, 101–02, *101*
ego, 515–16, *516*
Ego and the Mechanisms of Defense, The (A. Freud), 17
egocentrism, 146–47, *146*
egosystem goals, 350
EI (emotional intelligence), 316–17, *316*
Einstein, Albert, *313*
Ekman, Paul, 366–67
elaboration likelihood model, 477–78, *477*
elaborative rehearsal, 263–64
elderly, 146–65, *159, 164, 165*
electrical stimulation, brain development and, 68
electroconvulsive therapy (ECT), 602–03, *602*, 616
electroencephalograph (EEG), 59, *60*, 101–02, *101*
electronically activated record (EAR), 535
electronic cigarettes, 437–38, *438*
electronic devices, in classrooms, 255
Ellis, Albert, 599

embarrassment, 371, *371*
embryo, 132–33, *132, 133*
Eminem, *313*
emotion, 353–71
  adaptation and, 366–67
  amygdala and, 361–63, *361, 362*
  bodily responses and, 360–61
  body maps of, *360*
  from brain processes, 361–63, *361, 362*
  circumplex map of, 355, *355*
  decision making and, *369, 370, 375*
  expression of, *354*, 366–69, *366, 367, 368*
  moods vs., 354
  motivation and, 336, 365–71, 375
  regulation of, 363–65
  social bonds and, 370–71, *370*
  theories of, 355–58, *356*
  thought and, 369–70
  understanding of, in working with customers and employees, 375
emotional disorders, 551–68
emotional intelligence (EI), *315*, 316–17
emotionality, 529
emotional learning, 362
emotion-focused coping, 448, *448*
emotion label, 358
encoding, 253
endocrine system, 74–75, *75*, 380
endorphins, *55*, 57–58, 114, 616
engaging, escaping vs., 114, 116, *116*
environment:
  addiction and, 123
  intelligence and, 318–19, *318*, 327
  sexual activity and, 409–11
  sexual orientation and, 399–401
environmental stimulation, brain development and, 137
enzyme degradation, 54
epigenetics, 79
epilepsy, 57, 68, 70, 96, 268
episodic memory, 270, *270, 272*
Erikson, Erik, 153, *153*, 159–60
escaping, engaging vs., 114, 116, *116*
estradiol, 380–81
estrogen replacement therapy, 384
estrogens, 74, 380–82
ethical guidelines, 37–38, 225, 284
ethnic identity, 154
etiology, 548–49
Evaluating Psychology in the Real World, 24, 115, 243, 275, 321, 452, 493, 507, 550
Every Student Succeeds Act, 320
evolutionary theory, 16
exams, 449
  anxiety of, 449
  study habits and, 258–59
excitement phase, 405–06, *405*
exemplar model of concepts, *298, 299, 299*
exercise, exercising, 432–32, *432*, 473, 616
exhaustion stage, *442*, 443
exhibitionism, 412
expectancy theory, 520, *520*
experimental groups, 35
experimental methods, 26, 33–37, *33*
experimental psychology, 14
explicit attitude, 474
explicit memory, 269–71, *270, 272*
exposure, 609–10, *610*, 612
exposure and response prevention, 612, *612*
Expression of Emotion in Man and Animals (Darwin), 366

external locus of control, 520
extinction, 222–23, *222*
extraverts, extraversion, 522, 526, *526*
extrinsic motivation, *342*, 343–44
eye, parts of, 177–80
Eysenck, Hans, 522–24, 526

Facebook, *313*, 509, 535
facial expression, *363, 366, 366*, 367–68, *367*, 465
facial feedback hypothesis, 356–57, *357*
facial nerve, 198
fake news, 8, 9
false memories, 285–86
familiar size, 187, *187*
family therapy, *596*, 600, *600*
fantasy, sexual activity and, 410–11
FAS (fetal alcohol syndrome), *135*, 136, *136*
fast fibers, 206
fat shaming, 420–22, *422*, 427
favoritism, 510, *510*
FDA (Federal Drug Administration), 625
fear conditioning, 362, *362*
fear hierarchy, 610, *611*
fear response, 224–25, 610
Federal Drug Administration (FDA), 120, 625
femininity, *see* gender behavior
fetal alcohol syndrome (FAS), *135*, 136, *136*
fetishism, 412
fetus, *132*, 133–34, *133*
FI (fixed interval schedule), *233*, 234
Fifty Shades of Grey (film), 412, *412*
Fifty Shades trilogy (James), 412, *412*
fight-or-flight response, 443–44, *443*
figure and ground, 184, *184*
filter theory, 256
first impressions, 464
first words, 150
Fisher, Carrie, 420, *422*, 427
fitness careers, 461
five-factor theory, 524–25, *524*
fixed interval schedule (FI), *233*, 234
fixed ratio schedule (FR), *233*, 234
flashbulb memories, 284–85
flavor, 196–97
  eating and, 348
Flink, Danielle, 398–99
Flourish (Seligman), 451
flow states, 114
fluid intelligence, 314–15, *315*
fMRI (functional magnetic resonance imaging), *60, 60, 90*
folic acid, 133, *133*
foot-in-the-door compliance strategy, 483, *483*
forebrain, 61, *61*, 63–70, *64*
forgetting, 279, 280–82, *281*
formal operational stage of cognitive development, *145*, 147–48
formal reasoning, 302–03
fovea, *178*, 179
framing, 305, *305*
fraternal birth order effect, 402, *402*
fraternities, 476, *476*
FR (fixed ratio schedule), *233*, 234
free association, 596, *597*
Freeman, Walter, *70*
frequency, 194, *194*
Freud, Anna, *16*, 17, 516
Freud, Sigmund, *15*, 17, *17*, 104, *104*, 341, 514–15, *514, 515*, 516, 517, *517*, 553, 596–97, *597*, 618
Freudian slips, 95, 515
frontal lobes, *61*, 66, *66*, 69, *174*

frontal motor cortex, 91
frotteurism, 412
frustration-aggression hypothesis, 487, *487*
functional fixedness, 311–12, *312*
functionalism, *15*, 16
functional magnetic resonance imaging (fMRI), 60, *60*, 82, *82*
fundamental attribution error, 466
fusiform face area, *66*

GABA (gamma-aminobutyric acid), 55, 57, 119
GAD (generalized anxiety disorder), *556*, 557
Gage, Phineas, 69–70, *70*, 92
Gall, Franz, 59
Galton, Frances, 325
gamma-aminobutyric acid, *see* GABA
ganglion cells, *178*, 179
Gardner, Howard, 316, *316*
GAS (general adaptation syndrome), 442–43, *442*
gate control theory, 206
"gay gene," 401
gayness, 397, 398, *398*
Gazzaniga, Michael, 66–67
gender, 378, *378*, 386–95, *386*
    alcohol use and, 119
    depression and, 566
    dysphoria, 394
    emotional expression and, 369, *369*
    nonconformity, 378
    reassignment, 394
    schizophrenia and, 569
    sex characteristics and, *379*, 381–83, *381*, *382*
gender identity, 376–78, *378*, 390–95, *391*, *392*, *393*
    as androgynous, 393, *393*
    as cisgender, 392–93, 394
    Coco Layne and, *391*
    cognitive development and, 391, *391*, 392
    as continuum, 392–93, *392*
    conversion therapy and, 394
    Coy Mathis and, 376–78, *378*, 385, 386, 393, 394
    David Reimer and, 390, *390*
    discrimination and, 394–95
    gender behavior and, 390–91
    gender dysphoria and, 394
    gender-queer and, 393
    gender reassignment and, 394
    hijra and, 387–88
    Laverne Cox and, 393, *393*
    legal protection and, 394–95
    queer, 399
    situationism and, 391
    support for people who vary in, 395, 419
    as transgender, 393–95, *393*
    variations in, 392–95, 398, 419
    see also sexual orientation
gender noncomformity, 400
gender-queer, 393
gender roles, *354*, 388, *389*
    biology vs. socialization and, 389–90, *390*
    cultural differences and, 389–90
    Malala Yousafzai and, 390
    modeling and, 388
    Mo'ne Davis and, 389, *389*
    operant conditioning and, 389
    socialization and, 388–90, *388*, *390*, *390*
gender schemas, 386–88
    children's toys and, 387, *387*
    individuality of, 387–88

physical aspects and, 387
    stereotypes and, 387, *387*
general adaptation syndrome (GAS), 442–43, *442*
general intelligence theory, 314, *315*
generalized anxiety disorder (GAD), *556*, 557
General Social Survey (GSS), 389, *389*
"Generation Me," 509
Generation Z, 502–04
generativity, stagnation vs., *153*, 160
genes, genetics, 76–79
    addiction and, 123
    biological sex and, 379–83
    intelligence and, 317–19, *318*
    longevity and, *423*
    obesity and, 426–27
    sexual orientation and, *400*, 401
genital stage, 517
genotype, 77
Genovese, Kitty, 489, *489*, 490
German measles (rubella), *135*
germinal period, 132, *132*, *133*
Gestalt theory, *15*, 17–18, *18*, 184, *184*, 309–10
GH (growth hormone), 74–75, 105
ghrelin, 346
Giffords, Gabrielle, *450*
Ginsburg, Ruth Bader, *159*
global workspace model, 91
glucose, 345–46
glutamate, *55*, 57
goals, achieving, 238–39, 308–10
Goldberg, Whoopi, 48
Goleman, Daniel, 317
Gomez, Selena, 502, 504, *504*, 513, 533
gonorrhea, 433, 434, *434*
Goodall, Jane, *28*
Google, 276
Gosling, Sam, 535
grandiose delusions, 570, *570*
grasping reflex, 137–38, *138*
gratitude journal, 350
Greenberg, Brooke, 128, 130, *130*, 138, 140, 149, 151
Greenberg, Carly, 128, *130*
grit, 352–53, *352*
grouping, 184–85, *184*, 297–98
group polarization, 480
groups, study, 35
group therapy, *596*, *597*, 599–600, *623*
groupthink, 480–81
growth hormone (GH), 74–75, 105
G-spot, 406
guilt, 370–71
    initiative vs., *153*
guilt delusions, 570, *570*
gun control, *450*
gustation, 196–202
gustatory cortex, *174*, *197*, 198

habits, 340, *446*, 455–57, *456*
habituation, 197–98, *197*
hair cells, *190*, 192
hair follicle, *204*
hallucinations, 548, 569, 570–71
hallucinogenics, 117, 120–22
hammer, *190*
Hamm, Jon, *613*
happiness, 457
hardiness, 450, *450*
Harlow, Harry, 140–41, *141*
Harrison, George, 285

hazing, 476, *476*
Health and Human Services Department, U.S., 625
health, psychology and, 420–57
    attitudes and, 451–57
    stress and, 439–50
health strategies, 455–57
hearing, 190–96, *191*
    in infants, 139
hearing loss, 163, 192–93
heart disease, 445–46, *446*, *447*
Hebb, Donald, 217
height in field, *187*
hemineglect, 68, *68*
Hemingway, Ernest, 568
Here's the Deal: Don't Touch Me (Mandel), *559*
heroin, 120
herpes (HSV-2), 433–34, *434*
hertz, 194
heterosexuals, 397, 398, *398*
heuristics, 304–05
hijra gender, 387–88
hindbrain, *61*, 62–63, *62*
hippocampus, *61*, 64–65
histrionic personality disorder, 575, *575*
HIV (human immunodeficiency virus), 433, 434, *434*
H.M., *see* Molaison, Henry
Hoffman, Dustin, 326
homeostasis, 339, *339*
homosexuality, 397, 398, *398*
    conversion therapy and, 400–401
    as mental illness, 403–04
homunculus, *see* somatosensory homunculus
hormones, 74–75
    biological sex and, 379–83
    conflicting, 384–85
    eating and, 346
    sexual orientation and, *400*, 401–02
hostile personality, 447, *447*
How Opal Mehta Got Kissed, Got Wild, and Got a Life (Viswanathan), 285
hue, 181–82, *181*
human immunodeficiency virus (HIV), 433, 434, *434*
humanistic approach to personality, *514*, 518–19
humanistic psychology, 18–19, *19*, 338
humanistic therapy, *596*, *597*, *597*
human papillomavirus (HPV), 433, 434, *434*, 435
humor, 311, 364–65
Hurricane Maria, *440*, 488
Hurricane Sandy, 304
hypnic jerk, 102
hypnosis, 110–12, *111*
    theories of, 111–12
hypomania, 567
hypothalamus, *61*, 64, *100*, 346
    sexual activity and, *406*, 407
    sexual orientation and, 403
hypothesis, 25, *25*, 147

I Am Malala (Yousafzai), 334
IAT (Implicit Association Test), 474–75
id, 515–16, *516*
identity, 153–54, *153*
    bicultural, 154
    confusion of role and, *153*, 154
identity delusions, 570
illusory contours, *184*, 185

immune system:
    maternal, 402–03
    stress and, 442–43, 444, *444*
Implicit Association Test (IAT), 474–75
implicit attitude, 474
implicit memory, 271–73, *272*
incentives, 341–42
independent variable, 33–36
individualist cultures, 512–13, *512, 513*
industry, inferiority vs., *153*
infant and child development, 136–51
    inborn reflexes and, 137–38
    language and, 149–50, *149*
    motor skills and, 137–38
    Piaget's theory of, 144–48, *145*
    primary caregivers and, *137*, 140–43
    senses and, 139
    taste and, *199*
infant hydrocephalus, 135
inferiority, industry vs., *153*
informal reasoning, 302–03
informational influence, 482, *482*
informed consent, 38
ingroup/outgroup bias, 469–70, *469*
    minimal group paradigm and, 469
ingroups, 469–70, *469*
    favoritism and, 469
initiative, guilt vs., *153*
inner ear, *190*, 192
insight, 309–10, *309, 310*
insight learning, 240
insomnia, 107–08
institutional review boards (IRBs), 38, *38*
insufficient justification, 476, *476*
insulin, 346
integration phase of neural communication, *51*, 53
integrity, despair vs., *153*, 160
intellectual disabilities, *582*
intelligence, 292–94, 312–29
    birth weight and, *319*
    definition of, 312–13
    differences in, 326–29
    environment and, 318–19
    genetics and, 317–19, *318*
    measurement of, 319–25
    tests of, 313–14, 320
    theories of, 314–17, *315*
intelligence quotient (IQ), 292, *294*, 313–14, 320, *320*, 322, 326–27
intelligence tests, 313–14, 320
interactionists, 537
interference, *279*, 281
internal locus of control, 520
Internet, 276, 502–04, 546
interpersonal intelligence, 316, *316*
interpreter, 98–99, *98*
intersexuality, 383–84, *383*, 384–85
intimacy, isolation vs., *153*, 160
intrapersonal intelligence, 316, *316*
intrinsic motivation, 342–43, *342*
introspection, 14, *14, 15*
introverts, introversion, 522, 526, *526*
intuition, 548
ions, 51
IQ (intelligence quotient), 292, *294*, 313–14, 320, *320*, 322, 326–27
IQ scores, distribution of, 323, *323*
IRBs (institutional review boards), 38, *38*
iris, 177–78
isolation, intimacy vs., *153*, 160

Jackson, Avery, *386*
Jackson, Samuel L., 159, *159*
Jackson, William, *286*
James, E. L., 412
James, William, 15, 16, *16*, 228
James-Lange theory of emotion, 355–57, *356*
    facial feedback hypothesis and, 356–57, *356*
Jamison, Kay Redfield, 567–68, *567*
Jaws (film), 221
Jay, David, 398, *398*
Jay-Z, 5, *491*
Jell-O, 270, 348
Jeopardy! (game show), 250, 252, *252*, 253, 278
jigsaw classroom, 471
"Jim twins," 78–79
Johnson, Dwayne "The Rock," *561*
Johnson, Magic, 48
Johnson, Virginia, 405–07, *405*
Joiner, Thomas, 565
Jones, Mary Cover, 225
Joudrie, Dorothy, 579
journaling, *104, 615*
justification of effort, 476, *476*
just world hypothesis, 466

Kahneman, Daniel, 93, 303, 305
Kanner, Leo, 582
K-complex, *101*
Keenan, Sara Kelly, *383*, 384
Keltner, Dacher, *371*
Kim Jae-beom, 116
Kim Yun-jeong, 116
kinesthetic sense, 204, *204*
Kinsey, Alfred, 405
Klinefelter syndrome, 384
knee-jerk reflex, 72, *72*
Kohlberg, Lawrence, 156, 157
Köhler, Wolfgang, *15*, 17, 309–10, *309*
Korsakoff's syndrome, 119
Kushner, Harold, 455

Lamar, Kendrick, 302
language, development of, 149–50, *149*
Lanza, Adam, *30*
latency stage, 517
latent content, 104
latent learning, 239–40, *240*
laughing club, *453*
law of effect, 229
Lawrence, Jennifer, 420–22
Layne, Coco, *391*
L cones, *182*
L-DOPA, 57
learned helplessness, 564
learning, 10, 12–13, 212–45
    by classical conditioning, 216–17, 218–27, *219, 220, 222, 224*
    computers in classrooms and, 255
    definition of, 215
    eating and, 347–48
    healthy coping and, 456–57
    by operant conditioning, 216–17, 228–40, *229*
    to speak, 150
    types of, 214–17, *216*
    by watching others, 216–17, 241–45
learning disabilities, 48, *582*
Lebanon, 336
left brain hemisphere, 66–67, 96–99, *97*
left-handedness, 69
lens, 178
Leonardo da Vinci, 187

leptin, 346
lesbians, 397, 398
levels of processing model, 264
Levey, Gerald, *78*
LGBTQIA, *404*
libido, 515
life expectancy, U.S., *158*, 159
life satisfaction, 161, 165
light cues, 100
light waves, *178*
limbic system, 63–64, 123
linear perspective, 187, *187*
Linehan, Marsha, 621, *621*
linguistic intelligence, 316, *316*
LinkedIn, 509
Linklater, Richard, 130
listening time, 193
literature review, 25
lithium, 567–68, 617, 622
"Little Albert" case study, 224–25, *224*
lobotomy, 70, *70*, 603, 618
localization of sound, 195, *195*
Locke, John, 215
locus of control, 520, 521
logic, 9, 564
logical thinking, 146–47
longevity, *423*
long-term potentiation (LTP), 217
long-term storage, *257, 258*, 263, *269*, 315
loudness, 193, 194, *194, 195*
Lovato, Demi, 566, *566*
love, companionate vs. passionate, 494, *494*
lowballing, 484
LSD (lysergic acid diethylamide), 120–21
LTP (long-term potentiation), 217
Luna, Audrey, 193
Luper, Paula, *586*

Ma, Yo-Yo, *282*
Mace, John, 403, *403*
Mack, Michelle, 79–81, *79*
Mad Men (TV show), *613*
magnetic resonance imaging (MRI), *276, 572*
maintenance rehearsal, 263
major depressive disorder, 562, *562*
major life stressors, 440, *440*
male-specific antigens, 403
Mandel, Howie, *559*
mania, manic episodes, 566–67
manifest content, 104
mantra, 113
Maria, Hurricane, *440*
marijuana, 121–22, *135*
    medical use of, 122
marketing and advertising, psychology as
    helping you succeed in, 501
Markle, Meghan, *473*
marriage, 160–61, *161*, 454–55
    health and, 454–55, *455*
Marriage Equality Act, 404
Martin, Alexis, 292, *294*, 317
masculinity, *see* gender behavior
Maslow, Abraham, 18, 28, 337–38, 518
masochism, sexual, 412
Masters, William, 405–07, *405*
materialism, 90–91
math ability, *314*
mathematical/logical intelligence, 316, *316*
Mathis, Coy, 376–78, *378*, 385, 386, 393, 394
maturation, 138, *138, 139*
maximizers, 306, 307

McKinnon, Margaret, 283
M cones, *182*
MDMA (ecstasy), 121, *121*
media reports, *9*, *32*
medications for psychological disorders,
    see psychotropic medications
meditation, 112–13, *113*, 115, 622
medulla, *61*, 62, *62*
melatonin, 100
membrane, 51
memory, memories:
    accessing of, 278–87
    acquiring of, 252–56
    autism spectrum disorder and, 326
    brain regions and, 274–77, *274*, *276*
    computer vs. human, 254–55
    emotional events and, 362
    false, 285–86
    intelligence and, 163–64
    long-term storage of, 257, *257*, *258*, 263–78,
        264, *267*
    loss of, 119, 163–64, 268–69, *269*
    research on, 268–70
    retrieval of, *253*, 254–55, 278–87
    sensory storage of, *257*, *258*, 259–61, *260*
    short-term storage of, 257, *257*, *258*, 261–63,
        262
    smell and, 202
memory encoding, 252–56, *253*, *264*, *264*
memory jogs:
    smartphone as, 239, 273
    sticky notes as, 273
memory span, 262
memory tests, 326, *326*
memory traces, 10
menarche, 382
    earlier onset of, 382
menopause, 409
Mensa, 292, *294*, 327
menstruation, 382
    earlier onset of, 382
mental activity, 5–6
    neurotransmitters and, 52–58
mental age, 320, 322
mental health care, abuses of, 603, 618
mental health professionals, finding, 607
mental illness, *see* psychological disorders
mental maps, 296, *296*
mental states, 311
mercury, *135*
mere exposure effect, 473, *473*
methamphetamine (meth), 118, *118*, *119*
method of loci, 280
Methods of Psychology, The, 95, 141, 199, 220,
    301, 359, 402, 444, 485, 530, 577, 616
Michelangelo, 568
midbrain, *61*, 62–63, *62*
middle ear, *190*, 191
Millennials, 502, 504, *504*
Miller, George, *15*, 19, *19*, 262
Miller, Zell, 10
Miller Analogy Test, 323
Milner, Brenda, 270
mind, 5
mind/body problem, 13
mindfulness, *621*, 622
minimal conscious state, *92*, 93
minimal group paradigm, 469
Minnesota Twin Project, 78–79
Mirra, Dave, 92
mirror image, *473*

mirror neurons, 245, *245*
misattribution, 285
    of arousal, 358, *358*
miscarriage, 132, 133
mistrust, trust vs., *153*
mnemonics, 258–59, 280
modeling, 216–17, 242–44, *244*, 598
    cigarette smoking and, *244*
    gender roles and, 388
Molaison, Henry (H.M.), 268–71, *268*, 271, *271*
monocular depth cues, 186, *187*
monozygotic (identical) twins, 77–78
moods, emotion vs., 354
mood stabilizers, 601, *602*, 617–18
moral development, 155–57
moral disengagement, 157
moral reasoning, 155–57
moral treatment, 595
morphemes, 149, *149*
morphine, 120
motion aftereffects, 187–88
motion perception, 187–88
motivation, 336–42
    behavior and, 336–53, *337*
    eating behavior and, 344–48, *345*
    emotion and, 336, 365–71, 375
    understanding of, in working with customers
        and employees, 375
motor cortex, *66*, *67*, 69, *97*, *103*
motor disorders, *582*
motor skills, 138–39
Mount Erebus, *185*
Mozart effect, 9
MRI (magnetic resonance imaging), *276*, *572*
MS, *see* multiple sclerosis
multiple intelligence theory, *315*, 316, *316*
multiple personality disorder, 580
multiple sclerosis (MS), 50, *50*, 52, 76, 92
musical intelligence, 316, *316*
music perception, 192, 193
music therapy, 207
Mutesi, Phiona, 294, *294*, 312
myelin sheath, 52

NAAFA, *see* National Association to Advance
    Fat Acceptance
Nadeau, Maxime, 110
Narcan, 120
narcissism, 509–10, 575, *575*
narcolepsy, 108
    see also sleep, disorders of
nasal passage, *200*
Nash, John Forbes, *571*
National Center for Learning Disabilities, 48
National Geographic, 386
National Highway Traffic Safety
    Administration, 4
National Institute of Drug Abuse, 118, 121
National Institute of Mental Health, *563*
National Institutes of Health, 625
National Research Council, 159, 628
National Sleep Foundation, 109
National Suicide Prevention Lifeline, 565
National Survey on Drug Use and Health, *625*
natural selection, 16
nature/nurture debate, 13, 76–81, 525, 530
need, 337–38
need hierarchy, 338, *338*
need to belong, 123, 155, 348–49, *349*, 350, 565
negative punishment, *232*, 233
negative reinforcement, 232, *232*

negative symptoms, 569
neglect, impact of, *137*, 142–43
Neisser, Ulric, *15*, 19
NEO Personality Inventory, 535
nerve cells, 49–54, *49*
nerve fiber, *196*
nervous system, 46–58, *47*, 72
    disorders of, 46, 50, 57
networks of association, 266–67, *267*
neural communication, 51–54, *51*
neural pruning, 80
neural signals, *174*
neurodevelopmental disorders, 581, *582*
    see also childhood disorders
neurogenesis, 80
neurons, 42–45, *48*, 175
neurotic personality, 524
neurotransmitters, 49, 52–58, *53*, *58*
    behavior and, 52–58
    mental activity and, 52–58
    pain and, 57–58, *58*
neutral stimulus, 219
Newman, Mark, *78*
Newtown, Conn., shooting, *30*
nicotine, 117, *135*
    replacement therapy, 438, *438*
night driving, 163
night vision, 179
NIHL, *see* noise-induced hearing loss
9/11 terrorist attacks, 284
nodes, 266–67
noise-induced hearing loss (NIHL), 192
noisy environment, 193, *217*
non-associative learning, 215–16
Nordal, Katherine, 607
norepinephrine, *55*, 56
normal distribution, 322
normal waking state of consciousness, 90
normative influence, 482, *482*
Norris, James, *595*
Northern Illinois University shooting, 560–61
nurses, psychiatric, *606*

Obama, Barack, 320, 474
obedience, 484–86, *485*
obesity, 346, 424–31, *425*
object constancy, 189, *189*
objectivity, 89
object perception, 183–85, *184*
object permanence, 146
object relations theory, 518
observational learning, 216–17, 241–45, *241*, *244*,
    245, *301*
observational studies, 28–29, *28*
observer bias, *28*, 29
obsessions, 559–60, *559*, 612
obsessive-compulsive disorder (OCD), 559, *559*,
    575–76, *575*
    symptoms of, 559–60
    treatment of, 608, *609*, 612–13, *612*
obstacles, overcoming, 310–12
occipital lobe, *61*, 66–67, *66*, *91*, *174*
occlusion, 187, *187*
OCD, *see* obsessive-compulsive disorder
odorants, *200*, 201
Oedipus complex, 517, *517*
O'Keeffe, Georgia, 568
olfaction, 200–202, *200*
olfactory bulb, *200*, 201–02, *201*
olfactory cortex, *174*, *201*, 202
olfactory epithelium, *200*, 201

olfactory nerve, 201–02, *201*
olfactory receptors, *200*, 201
Oliver, Jamie, 48
Omalu, Bennet, 88
One Flew over the Cuckoo's Nest (Kesey), 602–03
O'Neil, James, 592–94, *594*, 627
O'Neil, John, 594
O'Neil, Miles, *594*
operant, 229, *229*
operant conditioning, 216–17, 228–40, *229*, 389
operant procedures, 622–23, *622*
operational definitions, 34–35
opiates, 117, 120
opponent-process theory, 183, *183*
optic chiasm, *180*
optic nerve, *178*, *179*, 180, *180*
optimal level of arousal, 340–41, *340*
oral personalities, 517–18
oral stage, 517
Organization for Economic Cooperation and Development, 158
organizing concepts, 297–301, *298*
orgasm disorders, *413*
orgasm phase, *405*, 406
Osbourne, Jack, 50, *50*, 52, 76
Osbourne, Ozzy, 50
ossicles, *190*, 192
outer ear, *190*, 191
outgroups, 469–70, *469*
oval window, *190*, 192
ovaries, 380, *382*
overeating, obesity and, 426
overregularization, 150

pain, 57–58, *58*, 205–07, *207*
    gate control theory and, 206
pain receptors, *204*, 206
pain reduction, 112, 120, 206–07
    gate control theory of, 206
panic disorders, *556*, 557–58, 610–11
papillae, *196*, 197–98
Paradox of Choice, The (Schwartz), 307
paranoid personality disorder, 575, *575*
paraphilias, 411–12, *412*
paraphilic disorders, 412, *412*
paraprofessionals, *605*, 606
parasympathetic nervous system, *47*, 72–73, *73*
parenthood, 161–62, *162*
parietal lobe, *61*, 66–67, *66*, *91*, *174*
Parkinson, James, 57
Parkinson's disease, 57, *57*, 63
partial reinforcement, 233
partial-reinforcement extinction effect, 234–35
passionate love, 494, *494*
Pavlov, Ivan, 218–21, *219*, 225–26, 347
pedophilia, 412
Peek, Kim, 326
peer groups, 154–55, *154*
peer review, 8–9
Pemberton, John, 118
Penfield, Wilder, 68, *68*, 203–04
perception, 17, 172–73, *174*, 180, *194*, 200, 205, 211
    stereotypes and, 468, *468*
    see also sensation and perception
performance, 239–40, 244
peripheral nervous system, *47*, 48, 58, 71
peripheral route, persuasion by, 477–78, *477*
persecution delusions, 570, *570*
persistence, *279*, 283, *283*
persistent depressive disorder, 562–63

personal attributions, 466
personality, 504–05
    approaches to, 514–25, *514*
    assessment of, 533–36
    biology and, 525–33, *531*
    careers in understanding of, 543, 591
    hostile personality, 447
    physiology and, 526–27, 530
    relationships and, *491*, 492
    self and, 502–43
    stability of, 522–24, *531*, 532
    type A and B, 446–47
    understanding, 513–39
personality disorders, 574–80, *575*
    antisocial (APD), 575–78, *575*, 576–78
    borderline, *575*, 576
    treatment of, 620–23, *620*
person-centered approach, 518–19, *519*
person/situation debate, 537
persuasion, 476–78
    in advertising, 477, 478, *478*
pet therapy, 452
Pfizer Global Study of Sexual Attitudes and Behaviors, 409
phallic stage, 517
Phelps, Michael, 48, 69, 76, 242
phenotype, 77
pheromones, 403
philosophy, 12
phobias, 224, 556, *557*
    treatment of, 610, *610*
phonemes, 149, *149*
phototherapy, 615, *615*
phrenology, 59
physical bullying, 157, *217*
physical dependence, 122–23, *123*
physical domain, 131
physical punishment, 235–37
physical stimulus, *174*, 175, *178*, *190*, *196*, 200, *204*
Piaget, Jean, 144–48, *145*
pictorial depth cues, 186–87, *187*
"pinched nerve," 49
pineal gland, 100, *100*
Pinel, Philippe, 595
pitch, 194, *194*
Pitt, Brad, 473, *473*
Pittsburgh Steelers, 86
placebos, 612, *612*, 614, 625
place coding, 194–95
placenta, 132
plasticity, 79–81, *79*
plateau phase, *405*, 406
Plato, 12
play therapy, *623*
pleasure principle, 341, 515
pons, *61*, 62, *62*
positive illusions, 511
positive psychology, 18–19, 451–54
positive punishment, *232*, 233
positive reappraisal, 364, *364*, 449
positive reinforcement, 232, *232*, 237–39, 627
positive symptoms, 569
postconventional level, 156
poster sessions, 27
postsynaptic neuron, 53–54
posttraumatic stress disorder (PTSD), 121, 283, *283*, 560–61, *560*, 579
practical intelligence, 316, *316*
preconventional level, 156
prefrontal cortex, *66*, 69–70, *91*, *101*
    emotion and, 563

prejudice, 469, 470, *470*
    modern, 470, *470*
Premack principle, 231, *231*
premature birth, 128, *134*
prenatal development, 132–34, *132–33*
prenatal vitamins, 133
preoperational stage of cognitive development, *145*, 146–47
pressure receptors, 203, *204*
presynaptic neuron, 53
primacy effect, 264–65, *265*
primary appraisals, 447
primary auditory cortex, *66*, 69, *174*, *191*, 192
primary emotions, 354
primary reinforcers, 231
primary sex characteristics, 152, *152*
primary somatosensory cortex, *66*, *67*, 68
primary visual cortex, *66*, 67, *97*, *174*, *179*, 180
Prince, 393, *393*
prism, *181*
proactive interference, 281, *281*
problem-focused coping, 448, *448*
problem solving, 147, *302*, 303, *308*, 314, 621, 622
    techniques of, 308–10, *310*
procedural memory, 272–73, *272*
professional success, 11, 294, 316
prognosis, 619–20, 623, 627–28
projection, *517*
projective measures of personality, 534, *534*
prosocial behavior, 488–89, *488*
prospective memory, 272–73, *273*
prototype model of concepts, 298–99, *298*
proximity:
    relationships and, 491
    vision and, 184, *184*
Prozac, 56
psychiatrists, *605*, 606
psychoactive drugs, *see* drugs, psychoactive
psychoanalysis, 15, 16–17, 596–97, *597*
psychodynamic theory approach to personality, 514–18, *514*, *515*
psychodynamic therapy, 596–97, *596*, *597*
psychographs, 59, *59*
psychological analysis, 18–20
psychological dependence, 122–23, *123*
psychological disorders, 544–86, *547*
    assessment of, 551–54
    causes of, 549–51
    classification of, *554*
    criteria for, 547–49
    gender and, *547*
    impact on lives of, 547–49
    moral treatment of, 595
    treatment of, *609*, 624
    see also specific disorders and therapies
psychological treatment, discredited, 594–95, *595*
psychologists, *21*, 22, *605*, 606
    research methods of, 22–38
psychology:
    contemporary research in, 4, 18–35, *28*
    critical thinking skills and, 6–10
    definition of, 5–6
    philosophical origins of, 12–14
    real-life applications of, 5, 10–13, 48, 115, 157, 214, 238–39, 258–59, 276, 306, 307, 321, 495, 508, 543, 565
    schools of thought in, 14–19, *15*
    as scientific field of study, 13
    subfields of, 20–22, *20*